management

management

Michael A. Hitt
Texas A&M University

J. Stewart Black
University of Michigan

Lyman W. Porter
University of California, Irvine

PEARSON

Prentice
Hall

Upper Saddle River, New Jersey 07458

Library of Congress Cataloging-in-Publication Data

Hitt, Michael A.
    Management/Michael A. Hitt, J. Stewart Black, Lyman W. Porter.—1st ed.
        p. cm.
    Includes bibliographical references and index.
    ISBN 0-13-008847-1
    1. Management   I. Black, Stewart.   II. Porter, Lyman W.   III. Title.
HD31.H5327   2005   2004057334
658—dc22

Acquisition Editor: David Parker
Assistant Editor: Melissa Yu
Editorial Assistant: Richard Gomes
Media Project Manager: Ashley Keim
Marketing Manager: Shannon Moore
Marketing Assistant: Amanda Fischer
Senior Managing Editor (Production): Judy Leale
Production Editor: Cindy Durand
Permissions Supervisor: Charles Morris
Production Manager: Arnold Vila
Buyer: Diane Peirano
Design Manager: Maria Lange
Cover Illustration/Photo: Stone/Getty Images
Illustrator (Interior): ElectraGraphics, Inc.
Photo Researcher: Rachel Lucas
Image Permission Coordinator: Elaine Soares
Manager, Print Production: Christy Mahon
Composition/Full-Service Project Management: GGS Book Services, Atlantic Highlands
Printer/Binder: Donnelley

Credits and acknowledgments borrowed from other sources and reproduced, with permission, in this textbook appear on the appropriate page within text.

Microsoft® and Windows® are registered trademarks of the Microsoft Corporation in the U.S.A. and other countries. Screen shots and icons reprinted with permission from the Microsoft Corporation. This book is not sponsored or endorsed by or affiliated with the Microsoft Corporation.

Pearson Education LTD.
Pearson Education Singapore, Pte. Ltd.
Pearson Education, Canada, Ltd.
Pearson Education–Japan

Pearson Education Australia PTY, Limited
Pearson Education North Asia Ltd
Pearson Educación de Mexico, S.A. de C.V.
Pearson Education Malaysia, Pte. Ltd

10 9 8 7 6 5 4 3 2 1
ISBN 013-185532-8

brief contents

contents

PART ONE
YOU AS A MANAGER   **2**

PART THREE
SETTING DIRECTION   190

PART FOUR
IMPLEMENTING THROUGH PEOPLE 346

Achieve balance.

When we set out to write this text, we were guided by

THREE KEY INFLUENCES

■

Our personal experiences in teaching business students and what we've learned from a great set of colleagues around the world regarding this challenge

■

Our direct involvement with and understanding of the vast wealth of academic research on the topic of management

■

Our experiences working with actual organizations and managers on practical problems

Our goal was to channel these influences and create a text that added value for students and instructors alike. To help achieve this goal, we included the following key features...

balance

key features

1. Strategic Overview

This text is different from most in that it offers a comprehensive and balanced presentation of strategic management and organizational behavior concepts. The reality is that practicing managers need to use both in order to address the current challenges they face and to exploit the future opportunities they identify; it is not an either/or choice. The unique, but interdependent, specialties of three co-authors not only helps to balance the treatment of strategic management and organizational behavior across the chapters, but also to integrate these concepts within chapters. Each chapter begins with a discussion of the strategic importance of the primary concepts within that chapter.

strategic overview

In the minds of many, decision making is the most important managerial activity. Management decisions may involve high-profile issues such as acquiring or selling assets, moving into or out of product segments, leaving or entering markets, or launching national or international ad campaigns. In the case of Shih's strategic decision to withdraw from the U.S. market and divide Acer into two separate businesses, the implications for the organization are significant. For example, leaving the U.S. market enabled competitors to take Acer's abandoned market share, strengthen their positions, and make it more challenging and costly for Acer to reenter later. Obviously, at the time Shih decided to leave the U.S. market, if he could have known that he would later have an opportunity to reenter, he might have never decided to leave. This illustrates one of the key challenges of managerial decision making at any level—making decisions with limited resources. These limited resources could be informational, financial, technical, or human. These constraints and pressures create some of the most powerful challenges in managerial decision making. Consequently, managers need to understand the basic processes of decision making in organizations and the factors that influence them. Several frameworks are available to help explain managerial decision making. Each framework is based on different assumptions about the nature of people at work. So, as an informed manager, you need to understand the models and the assumptions underlying each.

Shih's decision to separate the businesses will require high-level decision to withdraw from the U.S. market caused other managers lower in the organization to make subsequent decisions. As an example, someone had to decide to sell or lease Acer's U.S. facilities. Someone else had to decide how to secure and maintain the facilities until they were sold or leased. Although it is relatively easy to see how the impact of decisions made at the higher levels of an organization can cascade down through the lower ranks, the reverse can also be true. For example, if managers in Acer consistently had not hired engineers with a solid understanding of China, then Shih's decision to focus on China would have been limited in its immediate effectiveness. Managers must incorporate information beyond that immediately associated with the problem or task at hand to ensure that the impact is consistent with and supportive of the direction of the organization overall.

Not all managerial decisions are as visible or as important as those described at Acer. Many managerial decisions involve behind-the-scenes issues such as hiring a new employee or changing a production process. In addition, in many situations you must determine the level of involvement of others (e.g., subordinates, peers) in decisions. When are group decisions superior (or inferior) to individual ones? How much participation is realistic in organizations in which managers still assume responsibility for group actions? For example, Stan Shih had to decide how many and which of his managers to involve. As a new manager, you might have to decide how many people to involve in a new hire decision. In making these choices you need to understand how various factors affect the quality of

2. A Manager's Challenge

We worked hard to ground the management knowledge presented in up-to-date research, while at the same time placing this discussion in the context of practicing managers. To do this, we included examples of managers facing real challenges at the opening of each chapter, in dedicated space several times throughout (called "A Manager's Challenge"), and at the end of each chapter. The managers discussed in these examples represent all managerial levels in different types of organizations (private profit-oriented and public not-for-profit).

diversity
a manager's challenge

Gaining a New Perspective on Decisions at UPS

Managing diverse perspectives for enhanced decision making is a tough balancing act for managers at United Parcel Service (UPS). On the one hand, UPS has built a successful global delivery business by developing standard procedures for nearly all routine decisions, including how drivers should carry their keys when making deliveries. Yet every year, senior managers send 50 middle managers on a program that is designed to add diversity to the "brown" perspective (i.e., typical UPS perspective) so that these middle managers can make better decisions. The program involves managers spending 30 days in communities far from home that have significant poverty and other problems. UPS founder James Casey initiated the Community Internship Program in 1968. Since then, UPS has invested more than $14 million to send 1,100 middle managers through the program, at a cost of $10,000 per participant (plus the manager's regular salary).

Whether managers spend the month cleaning up dilapidated apartments or working with migrant workers, participants say the experience drives home new lessons about diversity. For example, during a month of working with addicts in New York City, division manager Patti Hobbs was impressed by the thoughtful suggestions they offered for keeping teenagers off drugs. Back on the job, she broadened her use of group decision making to involve all staff members in problem-solving discussions rather than only the highest-level managers. "You start to think there's no one person, regardless of position, who has all the answers," she explains. "The answers come from us all."

The program sharpens participants' decision-making skills by taking them out of their comfortable daily work routine. According to Al Demick, UPS's learning and development manager, it "puts people in situations that call on them to use new skills or to use their skills in new ways. Sometimes those are life-and-death situations. People are never quite the same when they come back."

Annette Law, an African American UPS manager from Utah, worked with tenement dwellers in New York City. "I thought I knew

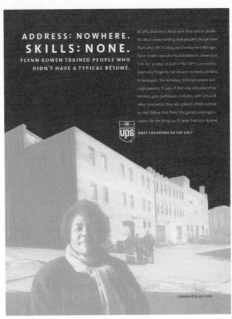

Since 1968, UPS has invested more than $14 million to send 1,100 middle managers like Flynn Bowen to communities that suffer from poverty and other problems. Initiated by UPS founder James Casey, the Community Internship Program is designed to add diversity to the "brown" perspective.

inmates and changed the way he approaches decisions at UPS. "I'm much more sensitive to the fact that we must make decisions on a case-by-case basis," he says. "Things are no longer black and white for me."

Because half of all UPS's new employees are not white, senior managers believe that the program is an important training ground for the mostly white management team.

balance

3. Part-Ending Cases

Even though by necessity we cover specific managerial concepts in separate chapters, the reality for practicing managers is that they often face challenges that are multidimensional in nature. As a consequence, at the end of each part, we take the unique step of providing a concise but integrative case, of no more than six pages, that deals with concepts covered in several or all of the chapters in the part. The cases are written by professionals and designed for use in teaching management concepts. While short vignettes used in the chapters are useful in providing illustrations of specific management concepts, the cases at the end of each part provide students and instructors with the opportunity to explore the integrated nature of many challenges practicing managers face.

PART ONE

integrative case

Clifford Chance—Update

London Business School

By Callum Campbell

Ten years after Geoffrey Howe gazed from the window of his new offices, Clifford Chance had outgrown its Aldersgate headquarters, and the firm had had to retain additional City of London offices. The current managing partner, Peter Cornell, now surveyed a different firm in a very different legal market.

Throughout the 1990s, Clifford Chance continued to add offices to its network (Prague in 1995, Bangkok in 1996, São Paulo in 1998), and to increase the number of staff in its existing offices. By 2002, Clifford Chance had succeeded in becoming the world's largest law firm, by virtue of both its size (3,322 lawyers) and gross revenue ($1,409,032,200). In 1993, 80 percent of the firm's lawyers had been based in its London office. Howe's

outcasts or willing exiles from large mergers, continued to thrive. The most profitable law firms in the world, such as Wachtell Lipton Rosen & Katz, were based almost exclusively in New York. But the number of national firms able to compete for high-end corporate, corporate finance, and banking work was dwindling in step with the expansion of large international networks, like Clifford Chance.

Geoffrey Howe's ambition for his firm in 1993 had taken it to the top of the league tables. But getting there had necessitated a change in strategy. Organic growth could put an office anywhere on the planet, but could not provide critical mass. Nor could it satisfy the firm's aspirations in the key markets of the United States or Germany. On January 1, 2000, Clifford Chance announced the legal industry's most ambitious merger to date, simultaneously joining forces with the 400-lawyer, New York–based law

4. Managerial Perspectives Revisited

We have included another unique feature in this text that reflects the fact that the actual challenges managers face do not come in neat packages. In Chapter 1, we explain a set of four general "Managerial Perspectives" that are relevant to all aspects of management. They are (1) managing in an organizational context, (2) managing through people, (3) managing paradoxes, and (4) managing with an entrepreneurial mindset. We subsequently highlight how these perspectives relate to the chapter content at the end of each chapter in a feature called "Managerial Perspectives Revisited."

managerial perspectives revisited

PERSPECTIVE 1: ORGANIZATIONAL CONTEXT No doubt by this point you see the importance of the organizational context in both individual and group decision making. However, it is worthwhile making the links explicit. For example, as we discussed, time pressures in an organization can significantly affect decision making. On the one hand, the nature of your business may be high velocity and require quick decisions. On the other hand, the culture of your company or just your immediate boss can put pressure on you to make a quick decision when one is not actually needed. Failure to recognize the organizational context could cause you to be late in making a decision in the first situation and unduly early in the second. The cultural diversity of your organization presents both challenges and opportunities. Clearly, when the group and decision making processes ar[...] for more diverse perspectives greater creativity in solving could present challenges in t[...] problems, desire to participa[...] group setting with superiors[...] influence the degree to whic[...] sions. In general, managers w[...] grammed decisions than thos[...] within a given industry the [...] degree to which you face pro[...] ple, in the oil and gas industr[...] to deal primarily with progr[...] push nonprogrammed decisi[...]

PERSPECTIVE 2: THE HU[...] encounter decisions that y[...] a manager it is less likely t[...] mented completely on y[...]

when facing situations in which you believe the benefits of involving others in decision making outweigh any disadvantages, you will have to decide the extent to which you involve others in the formulation and solution phases. For example, as the complexity and ambiguity of the problems you face and the decisions you have to make increase, so does the likelihood that you will need to involve others in decisions. Will you work through people with higher involvement primarily in formulation phase, the solution phase, or both? Clearly, to the extent that you involve others in decision making, the decision formulation and implementation success becomes a function of working effectively with and through others.

PERSPECTIVE 3: MANAGING PARADOXES Managers are likely to encounter paradoxes in decision making. On the one hand, utilizing the rational approach to make and implement decisions can help you avoid common pitfalls of bounded rationality or retrospective decision making. On the other hand, too rigid an adherence to the steps outlined could lead you to fall into the analysis-paralysis trap and miss important timing elements of the decision or ignore valuable and accurate heuristics you have developed over time and with experience or your intuition. You will also have to master the potential paradox that is at the heart of Gresham's law. On the one hand, you cannot ignore or simply delegate away all programmed decisions whether they are urgent or not. At the same time, if you allow them to dominate your time and energy, you will be less likely to address nonprogrammed decisions, which often have a bigger impact on your job performance and overall results for the organization. Diversity presents another element of duality. On the one hand, as a manager you get paid in part for your judgment and ability to make decisions. On the other hand, never checking with others as to how they see a situation or never taking into account the diverse perspectives, experience, and capabilities of those around you can lead you to less creative and effective decisions.

PERSPECTIVE 4: ENTREPRENEURIAL MIND-SET Managers' entrepreneurial mind-set is reflected in the decisions that they make and by the degree of their commitment to those decisions and the processes by which they are made. Overall, an entrepreneurial mind-set in decision making is reflected by being creative and flexible along with a willingness to take some risks. A manager can enrich entrepreneurial activities in the organization by searching for new information and encouraging others to express diverse

5. Helpful Pedagogical Features

The book has a full set of other helpful pedagogical devices in each chapter, including learning objectives, key terms, questions to test comprehension, a set of questions focused on applying the knowledge from the chapter, a short exercise for students to practice their managerial capabilities, and an actual case to be analyzed by students to develop their critical thinking skills.

key terms

bounded rationality (administrative man) model 308
brainstorming 331
cross-functional teams 318
decision making 301
delphi technique 332
devil's advocate 325
dialectical inquiry 331
escalating commitment 326
formulation 302
Gresham's law of planning 312

groupthink 323
heuristic 309
intuitive decision making 311
multiple advocacy 331
nominal group technique 332
nonprogrammed decision 311
opportunity 303
perception 303
perceptual distortion 310
problem 303
programmed decision 311

prospective rationality 328
rational (classical) model 303
retrospective decision (implicit favorite) model 310
satisficing 309
solution 302
standard operating procedure (SOP) 311
structured debate 331
subjectively expected utility (SEU) model 305

test your comprehension

1. What are the two fundamental stages in decision making?
2. What is the basic premise of the rational (classical) model of decision making?
3. How does the rational (classical) model differ from the bounded rationality model?
4. How can information bias negatively affect decision quality?

11. When are SOPs (standard operating procedures) most often used?
12. Describe Gresham's law of planning.
13. Why is analyzing the decision situation a key step in making better decisions?
14. What are the key assets of group decision making?
15. What are the key liabilities?

8. What is an implicit favorite?
9. How does the retrospective decision model work?
10. Describe programmed and nonprogrammed decisions.

When is it appropriate for a manager to be more participative in decision making?
Describe the phenomenon of groupthink. What is its symptoms?
How can we overcome groupthink?
How can managers work to overcome the effects of escalating commitment to past decisions?
20. Compare and contrast the nominal group technique and the delphi technique of decision making.
21. How can cultural values affect decision making?

apply your understanding

1. If your subordinates expect you to be consistent in your decision-making style, but you believe that different decision-making styles (e.g., high involvement of others versus low involvement) are appropriate for specific situations, how can you *change* your decision-making approach but not seem inconsistent to your employees?
2. Think of someone you know personally who is an effective decision maker. What key charac-

teristics would you use to describe this person?
3. What are the strengths and weaknesses of a manager with "good instincts" who seems to make effective decisions but whose approach is more like the retrospective than rational model?
4. Japanese and Korean managers tend to spend considerably more time on and involve more people in the problem formulation stage of decision making than American managers do. What are the pros and cons you see with this?

practice your capabilities

While sitting in your office, you get a call from the plant supervisor that a request has come in from a major customer that would require you to adjust your product line for a custom run of this client's rush order. The plant supervisor has delegated the decision of whether you should stop your current run and meet the customer's request. He needs the decision by tomorrow morning.

vast majority of your midsize customers chose you because of your lower prices. You maintain your profitability with these customers through keeping your costs low. Your principal means of achieving this is through running a high volume of standard products through your product line. Many of your large customers appreciate your low price but are willing to pay a premium for customized service and

resources

As described in the previous pages, this book provides new insights into the world of management and presents those insights in unique ways. The book has been designed specifically to support the instructor teaching the course and to be user-friendly for the students. To this end, the package accompanying this new book includes the following resources:

OneKey Online Courses

OneKey offers the best teaching and learning online resources all in one place. OneKey is all instructors need to plan and administer their course. OneKey is all students need for anytime, anywhere access to online course material. Conveniently organized by textbook chapter, these compiled resources help save time and help students reinforce and apply what they have learned. OneKey for convenience, simplicity, and success. *OneKey is available in three course management platforms: Blackboard, CourseCompass, and WebCT.*

For the student:

■ **Author Q&A Video Interviews**
In this unique resource, we queried faculty from across the country and identified those topics that students find difficult to understand. These brief video clips feature each of our authors speaking in their area of expertise. Some topics include: emotional intelligence, transformational leadership, competitive advantage, and core competencies.

■ **Learning Modules** which include section reviews, learning activities and pre- and post-tests

■ **Student PowerPoints**

■ **Research Navigator**–four exclusive databases of reliable source content to help students understand the research process and complete assignments

Instructor's Resource Center available online, in OneKey  or on CD-ROM

The Instructor's Resource Center, available on CD, at www.prenhall.com, or in your OneKey online course, provides presentation and other classroom resources. Instructors can collect the materials, edit them to create powerful class lectures, and upload them to an online course management system.

Using the Instructor's Resource Center on CD-ROM, instructors can easily create custom presentations. Desired files can be exported to the instructor's hard drive for use in classroom presentations and online courses.

With the Instructor's Resource Center, you will find the following faculty resources:

■ **PowerPoints**
Two PowerPoint packages are available with this text. The first is a fully developed, non-interactive set of instructor's PowerPoints. The second is an enhanced, interactive version of the first with video clips and Web links in each chapter. Both versions contain teaching notes.

(Continued)

■ **TestGen test-generating software**
The printed test bank contains approximately 100 questions per chapter including multiple-choice, true/false, short-answer, and scenario-based questions. Short-answer questions are questions that can be answered in one-to-five sentences. Scenario-based questions are essay type questions developed around a short scenario. (*Print version also available.*)

■ **Instructor's Manual**
This Instructor's Manual offers much more than just the traditional, but limited, chapter outline and answers to the end-of-chapter materials. In addition to these basic items, you will find suggested teaching strategies for 45-, 90-, and 180-minute sessions, chapter coverage suggestions for semester- and quarter-length courses, and modular suggestions for courses focused on general management, strategy, and/or organizational behavior. The coverage for each chapter includes a variety of resources such as exercises, critical-thinking assignments, debate topics, and research assignments. Two appendices contain complete PowerPoint slides and an in-depth Video Guide. (*Print version also available.*)

■ **Test Item File (*Word file*)**

■ **Art files from the text**

Transparencies

A set of color transparencies is available to instructors upon request. The acetates highlight text concepts and supply facts and information to help bring concepts alive in the classroom and enhance the classroom experience. (*In print only.*)

Student Study Guide

This study guide includes a chapter outline, review questions, and study quizzes. Page references to the review questions and quizzes are included.

Video

Video clips highlight management issues at a variety of companies including Patagonia, Ernst & Young, the WNBA, The Golf Network, and more.

Companion Web Site

The text Web site **www.prenhall.com/hitt** features chapter quizzes and student PowerPoints, which are available for review or can be conveniently printed three-to-a-page for in-class note taking.

many thanks

We owe a debt of gratitude to the people at Prentice Hall who worked with us and provided significant support for the development of this book. We thank David Parker, our editor, Shannon Moore, our marketing manager, Amy Ray, Melissa Yu, and Cindy Durand. We also thank Katalin Haynes for her work with us on the current research for the chapters, and Grace McLaughlin for her expert efforts in developing the accompanying Instructor's Manual. Special words of appreciation are due for the following people who reviewed and provided helpful feedback in the development of this book's content:

We would like to extend a very special thanks to this select group of professors who participated in at least three reviews or other developmental activities for this first edition:

James Fletcher
California State University Chico

James Hayton
Utah State University

Alan Heffner
Mary Washington College

Karen Jacobs
LeTourneau University

Coy A. Jones
University of Memphis

Amy Wojciechowski
West Shore Community College

Thank you to the following professors who participated in multiple review activities:

Christopher Alexander
King's College

Joseph Aniello
Francis Marion University

Ralph Braithwaite
University of Hartford

William Burmeister
Elizabethtown College

Art Camburn
Buena Vista University

John Chism
Greenville College

Donal Christian
Brooklyn College

Terry Coalter
Northwest Missouri State University

Brad Cox
Midlands Technical College

Frank DeCaro
Palm Beach Atlantic University

Jennifer Dose
Messiah College

Michael Dutch
University of Houston

Bruce Fischer
Elmhurst College

Isaac Fox
University of Minnesota

Janice Gates
Western Illinois University

Nell Hartley
Robert Morris University

Carol Harvey
Assumption College

Leslie Haugen
University of St. Thomas

Robert Hoell
Georgia Southern University

Jeff Holland
West Virginia University Parkersburg

Craig Hollingshead
Texas A&M University Kingsville

David Hollomon
Victor Valley College

Janet Jones
Trident Technical College

Sal Kukalis
California State University Long Beach

Donna LaGanga
Tunxis Community College

William Laing
Anderson College

Daniel Lybrook
Purdue University

Gregory Moore
Middle Tennessee State University

Cindy Murphy
Southeastern Community College

Ahmet Ozkul
SUNY Oneonta

Hannah Rothstein
Baruch College

David Tansik
University of Arizona

Brian Turner
DeSales University

Anita Vestal
York College

Dennis Williams
Pennsylvania College of Technology

James Woodrow
Vanguard University

Thank you to these professors who participated in early manuscript reviews:

Glenn Boseman
Villanova University

Michael Dutch
University of Houston

Allen Engle
Eastern Kentucky University

Thomas W. Gainey
State University of West Georgia

James Hayton
Utah State University

Robert Hoell
Georgia Southern University

Carol Larson Jones
California State Polytechnic University Pomona

Sal Kukalis
California State University Long Beach

Patricia Lapoint
McMurry University

Juliana Lilly
Sam Houston State University

Lisa McConnell
Oklahoma State University Oklahoma City

Preston Probasco
San Jose State University

Chuck Stubbart
Southern Illinois University Carbondale

Thank you to these professors who participated in the Academy of Management Focus Group 2003:

Michael Dutch
University of Houston

James Hayton
Utah State University

Sal Kukalis
California State University Long Beach

Beverly Little
Western Carolina University

Charlotte Sutton
Auburn University

A special thanks to this large group of professors who helped us clarify and hone the significant pedagogical features of this first edition:

David C. Adams
Manhattanville College

Debbie Adams
Kingswood College

Christopher Alexander
King's College

Allen Amason
University of Georgia

Fred Anderson
Indiana University of Pennsylvania

Thomas Anderson
The Citadel

Sally Andrews
Linn-Benton Community College

Joseph Aniello
Francis Marion University

Bryan Annable
Teikyo Post University

Cathy Arebalo
Rhodes State College

Barry Armandi
SUNY Old Westbury

Frank Arnold
Saint Leo University

Ron Atkins
Salve Regina University

Michael Avery
Northwestern College

Stacy Ball-Elias
Southwest Minnesota State University

Richard Barker
Upper Iowa University

Tope Bello
East Carolina University

John Bennett
Stephens College

Joy Benson
University of Wisconsin

David Bess
University of Hawaii

Stephen Betts
William Patterson University

Dan Bingham
Middle Tennessee State University

Maynard Bledsoe
Meredith College

David Blevins
University of Arkansas Little Rock

Henry Bohleke
San Juan College

Diane Boone
University of Maine

Donald Boyer
Jefferson College

JN Bradley
Central Washington University

Ralph Braithwaite
University of Hartford

Jenell Bramlage
University of Northwestern Ohio

Anne Brophy Chetwynd
Siena College

Jeffrey Bruehl
Bryan College

Beverly Bugay
Tyler Junior College

management by Hitt|Black|Porter

Gary Bumgarner
Mountain Empire Community College

William Burmeister
Elizabethtown College

David Burbidge
California State University Monterey Bay

Helen Burdenski
Notre Dame College

Derek Burnett
Loras College

Gerald Burton
Howard University

John Huonker Burtt
*New Hampshire Community
Technical College Stratham*

Harry Bury
Baldwin Wallace College

Bob Caldwell
University of the Incarnate Word

Art Camburn
Buena Vista University

Doug Campbell
California State University Chico

Dan Caprar
University of Iowa

James Carlson
Manatee Community College

Marilyn Carlson
Clark State Community College

John Carmichael
Union County College

Jane Carswell
Western Piedmont Community College

Joel Champion
Colorado Christian University

Bennett Cherry
California State University San Marcos

Felipe Chia
Harrisburg Area Community College

Jim Chipps
California State University Fresno

John Chism
Greenville College

Hung Chu
West Chester University

Janet Ciccarelli
Herkimer County Community College

Anthony Cioffi
Lorain County Community College

Ann Chirco
Macomb Community College

Donal Christian
Brooklyn College

James Cleveland
Sage College of Albany

Terry Coalter
Northwest Missouri State University

Anne Cohen
University of St. Thomas

Gary Corona
Florida Community College

Brad Cox
Midlands Technical College

Douglas Coyner
San Juan College

Debbie Adams Daly
Appalachian Technical College

Dexter Davis
Alfred State College

Gregory Dean
Warner Pacific College

Thomas Debbink
Tiffin University

Frank DeCaro
Palm Beach Atlantic University

Evelyn Delaney
Daytona Beach Community College

Doc DeLaughter
Flagler College

Emmeline de Pillis
University of Hawaii

Jeanie Diemer
Ivy Tech State College

Nancy DiTomaso
Rutgers University

Glenna Dod
Wesleyan College

Jennifer Dose
Messiah College

Bambi Douma
University of Montana

Sally Dresdow
University of Wisconsin Green Bay

James Dunham
High Point University

Dana Dye
Gulf Coast Community College

Karen Eboch
Bowling Green State University

Eliot Elfner
St. Norbert College

John Elliker
Old Dominion University

Olice Embry
Columbus State University

Diane Enkelmann
Pennsylvania Valley Community College

Alvin Epps
Whatcom Community College

Ann Eubanks
University of Mary Hardin Baylor

Elizabeth Evans
Concordia University Wisconsin

John Evans
Southern New Hampshire University

Dan Eveleth
University of Idaho

Franceen Fallett
Ventura College

Shirley Fedorovich
Embry-Riddle Aeronautical University

Janice Feldbauer
Austin Community College

Bruce Fischer
Elmhurst College

Joseph L. Flack
Washtenaw College

James Fletcher
California State University Chico

Joseph Flowers
Indiana Institute of Technology

Isaac Fox
University of Minnesota

Deborah Francis
Jacksonville State University

Marcelline Fusilier
Northwestern State University of Louisiana

Eugene Garaventa
College of Staten Island

Daniel Geary
University of Richmond

Ashley Geisewite
Southwest Tennessee Community College

James Gelatt
University of Maryland

Robert Gerulat
Empire State College

Jackie Gilbert
Middle Tennessee State University

David Glew
University of North Carolina Wilmington

Bill Godair
College of St. Joseph

Connie Golden
Lakeland Community College

Jorge Gonzalez
Concordia University

Robert Gora
Catawba Valley Community College

Jenifer Greene
Maryville College

Janie Gregg
Mississippi University for Women

Ray Grubbs
Millsaps College

Varina Haney
Aiken Technical College

Roberta Hanson
Metro State College of Denver

Steve Harper
University of North Carolina Wilmington

John Harris II
Malone College

Kimberly Harris
Durham Technical Community College

Michael Harstine
Grace College

Nell Hartley
Robert Morris University

Carol Harvey
Assumption College

Andrew Hawkins
Lake Area Technical Institute

Clair Hayes
Seton Hill University

Mary Ann Hazen
University of Detroit Mercy

Peter Hechler
California State University Los Angeles

Frank Haeg
San Francisco City College

Leslie Haugen
University of St. Thomas

Alan Heffner
Mary Washington College

Jack Heinsius
Modesto Junior College

Harry Hennessey
University of Hawaii at Hilo

James Hess
Ivy Tech State College

James Higgins
Holy Family University

Charles Hill
University of California Berkeley Extension

Tammy Hiller
Bucknell University

Betty Hoge
Limestone College

Corrine Holden
Henry Cogswell College

Jeff Holland
West Virginia University Parkersburg

Craig Hollingshead
Texas A&M University Kingsville

David Hollomon
Victor Valley College

Neal Hooker
Ohio State University

Jeff Hornsby
Ball State University

William Hostetler
Sweet Briar College

Clark Hu
Temple University

Tammy Hunt
University of North Carolina Wilmington

Jo Ann Hunter
Community College of Allegheny County

John Huonker
SUNY Oswego

Dianne Ishida
University of Hawaii Manoa

Lynn Isvik
Upper Iowa University

Mary S. Jackson
East Carolina University

Karen Jacobs
LeTourneau University

Jan Janiszewski
Viterbo University

Amie Janssen
Olney Central College

James Jarrard
University of Dubuque

Coy A. Jones
University of Memphis

Janet Jones
Trident Technical College

John Kachurick
College of Misericordia

Dmitriy Kalyagin
Chabot College

Fred Kitchens
Ball State University

Don Knight
University of Maryland

James Kraai
Indiana Wesleyan University

Donna LaGanga
Tunxis Community College

William Laing
Anderson College

Bernard Lake
Kirkwood Community College

Elsie Larson
University of Maine Machias

Gregg Lattier
Lee College

Gordon Lewis
Carnegie Mellon University

Doyle Lucas
Anderson University

Daniel Lybrook
Purdue University

Chuck Lyons
Hibbing Community College

Ernie Marchi
Curry College

Tish Matuszek
Troy State University

Grace McLaughlin
University of California

David McPhail
Marian College

Gary Melvin
Northern Arizona University

Alan Miller
University of Nevada Las Vegas

Andrew Minko
University of California Berkeley

Gregory Moore
Middle Tennessee State University

Cindy Moss
Appalachian Technical College

Jim Mullen
Elmira College

Colleen Muller
Humboldt State University

Cindy Murphy
Southeastern Community College

Bob Nale
Coastal Carolina University

Chris Neck
Virginia Tech University

Carl Nelson
Polytechnic University

George Nelson
Prairie View A&M University

Inge Nickerson
Barry University

Donatus Okhomina
Alabama State University

David Oliver
Edison College

Elaine Pogoncheff
Lansing Community College

Christopher Press
Emory University

Claudia Rawlins
California State University Chico

Clint Relyea
Arkansas State University

Donald Rickert
St. Louis College of Pharmacy

Charles Rickman
University of Central Oklahoma

Charley Riley
*Tarrant County College
Northwest Campus*

Gary Roberts
Kennesaw State University

Clint Robertson
Wilmington College

Robert Roller
LeTourneau University

Barbara Rosenthal
Miami Dade College

Hannah Rothstein
Baruch College

David Saiia
Ithaca College

Chris Scherpereel
Northern Arizona University

Brenda Sheets
Murray State University

Allen Shub
Northeastern Illinois University

Albert Spencer
Kauai Community College

Carol Steinhaus
Northern Michigan University

Gregory K. Stephens
Texas Christian University

Heidi Stoner
Wilson College

David Tansik
University of Arizona

Assad Tavakoli
Fayetteville State University

Christine Quinn Trank
University of Iowa

Brian Turner
DeSales University

Barry Van Hook
Arizona State University

Carolyn Waits
*Cincinnati State Technical and
Community College*

Gloria Walker
Florida Community College

Denise Ward
East Stroudsburg University

Marcus Wesson
*Troy State University
Phoenix City Campus*

Elizabeth White
Orange County Community College

Ed Wied
Sauk Valley Community College

Anita Vestal
York College

Charlene Williams
Brewton Parker College

Dennis Williams
Pennsylvania College of Technology

Bob Willis
Rogers State University

Frank Winfrey
Lyon College

Amy Wojciechowski
West Shore Community College

James Woodrow
Vanguard University

Dmitry Yarushkin
Grand View College

Elsa Zambrano
Palo Alto College

Thanks to this special group of professors for helping us select a cover:

Janet S. Adams
Kennesaw State University

Thomas Butte
Humboldt State University

Jim Cashman
The University of Alabama

Ken Eastman
Oklahoma State University

Norb Elbert
Eastern Kentucky University

TJ Edwards
Florence-Darlington Technical College

Karen Ford Eickhoff
University of Tennessee Chattanooga

Janice Gates
Western Illinois University

James Hayton
Utah State University

Brian Maruffi
Fordham University

Janet Nichols
Northeastern University

Ahmet Ozkul
SUNY Oneonta

William Pearce
La Roche College

Sonya Premeaux
Nicholls State University

Paula Rechner
California State University Fresno

Susan Roach
Georgia Southern University

Meir Russ
University of Wisconsin Green Bay

Jon Sager
California State University Northridge

Daniel Sherman
University of Alabama Huntsville

Linda Silva
El Paso Community College

Ram Subramanian
Grand Valley State University

Steve Werner
University of Houston

Liesl Wesson
Texas A&M University

Michael Wesson
Texas A&M University

Te Wu
Montclair State University

Thanks to these select professors for reviewing the early design concepts:

Ralph Braithwaite
University of Hartford

Frank DeCaro
Palm Beach Atlantic University

James Fletcher
California State University Chico

Janice Gates
Western Illinois University

Alan Heffner
Mary Washington College

Gary Hensel
McHenry County College

Robert Hoell
Georgia Southern University

David Hollomon
Victor Valley College

Karen Jacobs
LeTourneau University

Coy A. Jones
University of Memphis

Wayne Lane
Florence Darling Technical College

Jane Murtaugh
College of DuPage

Linda Nottingham
Georgia Southern University

Ahmet Ozkul
SUNY Oneonta

Hannah Rothstein
Baruch College

Pat Tadlock
Horry-Georgetown Technical College

Amy Wojciechowski
West Shore Community College

James Woodrow
Vanguard University

Fall 2004 Class Testers:

Ralph Braithwaite
University of Hartford

Hal Gregerson
Brigham Young University

Hannah Rothstein
Baruch College

James Woodrow
Vanguard University

International Reviewers:

 Marilyn Clarke
University of South Australia

 Peter Dixon
University of Tasmania, Australia

 Tan Eng
Ngee Ann Polytechnic, Singapore

 Yeap Peik Foong
Multimedia University, Malaysia

 Drs. Jaap Groot
University of Nijmegen, Netherlands

 Dr. Sreenivasan Jayashree
Multimedia University, Malaysia

 Wan Khairuzzaman
Universiti Teknologi, Malaysia

 Puteri Nor Ashikin Mohammad
University Technology of Mara, Malaysia

 Alan Simon
University of Western Australia

 Keith Thomas
Latrobe University, Australia

 Frank van den Berg
University of Twente Netherlands

 Dianne Waddell
Deakin University, Australia

 Henrik Sorenson
Aarhus University, Denmark

 JJ Coetzee
Unisa Graduate School of Business, South Africa

 Rob Venter
University of the Witwatersrand, South Africa

A special group of Prentice Hall Publishing representatives and managers deserves our thanks for contributing to the development of this first edition:

Phyllis Simon	**Kate Derrick**	**Brent Sheppard**
Jon Axelrod	**Dana Duncan**	**Catherine Traywick**
Katherine Hepburn	**Dave Hill**	**Kelly Bell**
Heather Jackson	**Betsy Nixon**	**Sherry Bartel**
Brett Holmes	**Mary Fernandez**	**Katherine Grassi**
Linda Babat		

We hope that you enjoy reading and learning from this book as much as we enjoyed writing it.

Michael Hitt

Stewart Black

Lyman Porter

management by Hitt|Black|Porter

achieve

author bios

Michael Hitt

Michael Hitt, Ph.D., is a distinguished professor who holds the Joseph Foster Chair in Business Leadership and the C.W. and Dorothy Conn Chair in New Ventures at Texas A&M University. He received his Ph.D. from the University of Colorado.

He has authored, or co-authored, several books and book chapters and numerous articles in such journals as the *Academy of Management Journal, Academy of Management Review, Strategic Management Journal, Journal of Applied Psychology, Organization Science, Organization Studies, Journal of Management Studies,* and *Journal of Management,* among others. His publications include numerous trade and textbooks, including *Strategic Management: Competitiveness and Globalization, 6e* and *Competing for Advantage*.

He has served on the editorial review boards of multiple journals including the *Academy of Management Journal, Academy of Management Executive, Journal of Applied Psychology, Journal of Management, Journal of World Business,* and *Journal of Applied Behavioral Science*. Furthermore, he has served as consulting editor and editor of the *Academy of Management Journal*. He serves on the board of the Strategic Management Society and is a past president of the Academy of Management. He is a fellow in the Academy of Management and a research fellow in the National Entrepreneurship Consortium. He is a member of the *Academy of Management Journal* Hall of Fame.

RESEARCH MADE RELEVANT

Michael Hitt on Strategy

Strategy is often portrayed as the province of top-level managers only. The reality is, a company's strategy is important to the practices and performance of managers at all levels. Our feature, *The Strategic Overview*, grounds the chapter content in the realm of practicing entry-level and mid-level managers. For example, "The Strategic Overview" in **Chapter 10** explains how all managers act as strategic leaders. Strategic leadership is not a function of position or level but rather of focus and behavior. Strategic leaders think and act strategically. They also work closely with other people and build trusting relationships to help implement a strategy. In **Chapter 15**, "The Strategic Overview" stresses the importance of people to the organization (human capital). It emphasizes that firms usually gain an advantage over competitors if they know more than their competitors do, and most of the knowledge that exists in organizations is held by their employees. Another example is shown in **Chapter 3**, which focuses on analyzing and understanding the organization's external environment. First, we contrast operating a subsidiary in Russia with doing so in China. Each country has a unique and different environment. Chinese managers tend to focus more on the long-term but Russian managers make short-term decisions. Forming partnerships with each requires managers to understand the two different environments.

Stewart Black

Stewart Black, Ph.D., is co-founder and president of the Global Leadership Institute. He is also executive director of the Asia Pacific Human Resource Partnership for the University of Michigan and a professor of business administration for the Business School.

Prior to beginning his Ph.D. studies, Dr. Black worked for a Japanese consulting firm where he eventually held the position of managing director. Dr. Black returned to the U.S. and received his Ph.D. from the University of California, Irvine. Dr. Black has held faculty positions at Dartmouth and Thunderbird prior to joining the University of Michigan.

Dr. Black is a leading instructor and scholar in strategic change, globalization, leadership, and international human resource management. His research and consulting focus on the areas of change, global leadership, strategic human resource management, international assignments, and cross-cultural management.

Professor Black is a co-author of numerous books and articles in the area of international human resource management that have appeared in publications such as *Business Week*, *Wall Street Journal*, and *Fortune*, as well as academic publications including the *Academy of Management Review*, *Academy of Management Journal*, and *Journal of Applied Psychology*.

He is a member of the Academy of Management and has served on the executive committee of the international management division. He has served as editor of the *Journal of International Management* and as an editorial board member of the *Academy of Management Journal*.

RESEARCH MADE RELEVANT

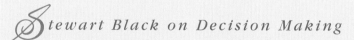

Stewart Black on Decision Making

Today's management students need to understand that decisions made by managers at all levels are critical to a company's performance. A management textbook must offer students many opportunities to develop this important skill. Take a look at our feature, *A Manager's Challenge,* which we developed to meet this important need. In our feature on Global Radio, managers in Europe try to learn from the successes and mistakes of their counterparts in the U.S., who launched a similar satellite-based radio service for motorists. Our feature on managers at several law firms focuses on their need to change their approach from an involved and consensus-oriented one that fit the needs of a small law firm with only a few lawyers, to a more "corporate" or structured model to match the demands of a large firm with over 1,000 lawyers. Both of these managerial challenge features appear in **Chapter 9**.

Lyman Porter

Lyman Porter, Ph.D., is professor emeritus of organization and strategy, in the Graduate School of Management at the University of California, Irvine, and was formerly dean of that school. Prior to joining UCI in 1967, he served on the faculty of the University of California, Berkeley, and was a visiting professor at Yale University.

Currently, he serves as a member on the board of trustees of the American University of Armenia, and was formerly an external examiner for the National University of Singapore.

Dr. Porter is a past president of the Academy of Management. In 1983, he received that organization's "Scholarly Contributions to Management" Award, and in 1994 its "Distinguished Management Educator" award. He also served as president of the Society of Industrial-Organizational Psychology (SIOP), and in 1989 was the recipient of SIOP's "Distinguished Scientific Contributions" Award.

Dr. Porter's major fields of interest are organizational psychology, management, and management education. He is the author, or co-author, of 11 books and over 80 articles in these fields.

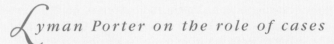

RESEARCH MADE RELEVANT

Lyman Porter on the role of cases

Cases are the cornerstone of bringing management theory and content to life for students. In addition to providing chapter-ending cases that critically bring together key concepts from the chapter, we provide unique part-ending cases that weave together the key learning points from each section in the book. Two chapter-ending cases that we are particularly proud of are "The New Supervisor" from **Chapter 10** and "The Team That Wasn't" from **Chapter 13**. For a great example of our part-ending cases, see **Part Four:** "Ste. Basil Hotel-Moscow: Struggling with Values in a Post-Communist State."

management

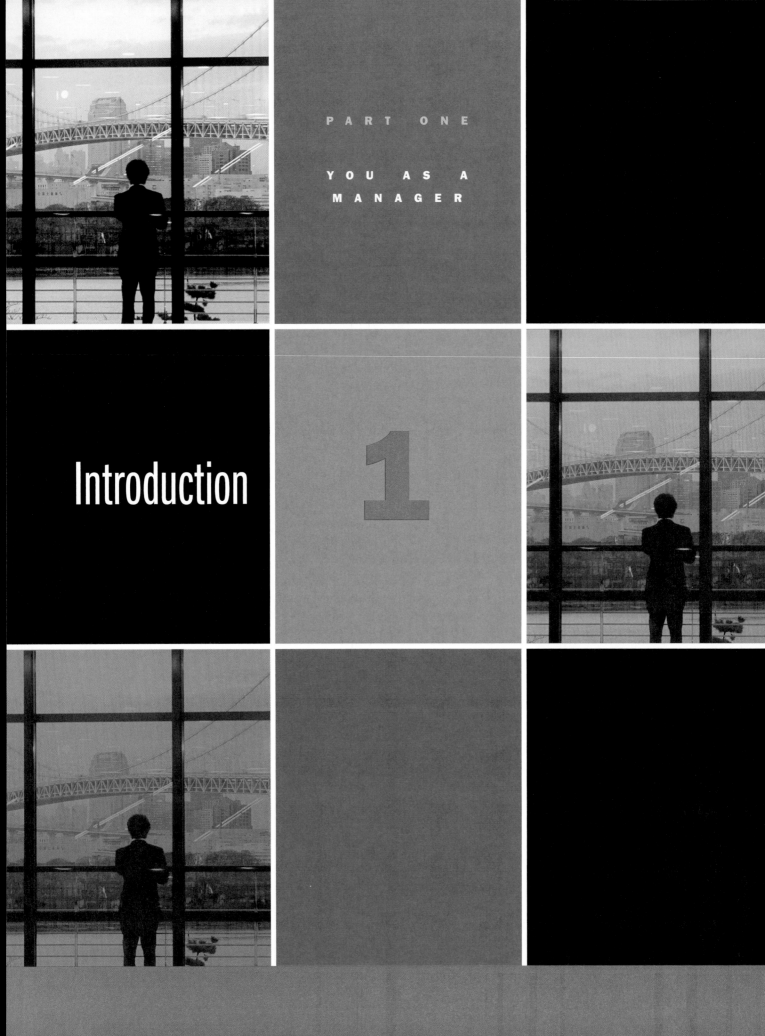

Introduction

1

■

Answer the question: What is management?

■

Explain why management must be understood within the context of organizations and how organizations affect the practice of management.

■

Describe the role of working with and through people in effective management.

■

Explain managerial paradoxes and how dealing with them lies at the core of management.

■

Specify the nature and extent of commitment required for managerial excellence.

■

Define the term "entrepreneurial mindset" and explain its importance for managers.

■

Describe and compare the different elements of managerial work and the different managerial roles.

■

Discuss the skills necessary to be an effective manager.

Managing: Putting It All Together

As chief executive officers of two highly successful and growing firms, Ken Chenault and Meg Whitman confront change, uncertainty, constraints, and the need to make sound decisions on a daily basis. Throughout their careers they've succeeded in meeting these managerial challenges decisively, using skills and insights they continue to hone.

Ken Chenault, chief executive officer of financial services giant American Express, continually looks at life from a variety of angles. As one of his Bowdoin College classmates recalls, "He always impressed us as being prepared. You may not always agree, but he had a handle on five sides of an issue."

That wide-angle view has served Chenault well in his corporate career. Raised in a New York City suburb, he went on from Bowdoin to Harvard Law School, where he sharpened his persuasive and analytical skills. He practiced law for three years in New York City before joining a Boston consulting firm and then returning to New York in 1981 to join American Express's strategic planning group. A couple of years later he accepted a high-risk job heading AmEx's barely profitable merchandise services unit. There, his challenge was to make speedy and decisive changes in the department's lackluster product offerings. Chenault made smart deals with customer-hungry supplier firms like Panasonic, growing the division from $100 million to $700 million in sales in just three years.

Chenault's combination of skills and experience quickly made him a standout manager. In his next job in the charge card division, his challenge was to convince reluctant top management that it was time to update the dull American Express green card or risk losing even greater market share to more daring ventures like the Discover Card. Chenault pointed out the need for change, saying, "[the] success you've enjoyed over time leads you into a rut."

His people skills helped him to be persuasive. Says James Robinson III, then CEO, "Ken would stand up for what he believed in, present his argument effectively—and forcefully when necessary. But it was always done in a professional way rather than in a stubborn way. He wasn't political; he was just someone you listened to."

Eventually, Chenault won the battle to forge a more competitive strategy in the charge card market, and AmEx began the climb back to the top. Under the next AmEx CEO, Harvey Golub, Chenault assumed responsibility for operations that generated over half the company's revenues at the time. One of his first missions, in contrast to the expansions he'd overseen in the past, was a drastic restructuring and cost-cutting effort. Chenault faced the unenviable task of letting 9 percent of the workforce go, and he made the decision to announce the plan himself, in person. The focus, he says, was on the company's survival.

AmEx continued to grow under Chenault's leadership. It now offers the biggest customer rewards program in the world and boasts 100 different types of proprietary cards, along with those issued by its nearly 50 partners worldwide. The number of cardholders has skyrocketed, while Chenault has served as the company's vice chairman, president, and chief operating officer. In 2001, he was named the CEO.

Chenault's management role is partly shaped by the well-established global organization he oversees. In contrast, Meg Whitman is CEO of a different kind of organization—young, brash, and web-based. Ebay, the online auction firm, was founded in 1995. It grew 30 to 40 percent each quarter, by 2000 was serving up to 90 million interactive bidding pages a day, and virtually never closes. Whitman has a goal of reaching $3 billion in annual revenues by 2005, which means achieving a 50 percent annual increase. She is confident that that ambitious target is reachable.

Whitman's confidence has taken her from an education at Princeton and Harvard Universities through management jobs at Procter & Gamble, Walt Disney Co., Stride Rite, FTD Corp. (the flower delivery service), and Hasbro. Approached to head eBay in late 1997, Whitman had never heard of the company and preferred to stay on at the helm of Hasbro's preschool division. But a short time later she was persuaded, and agreed to head what was then a 19-member Internet firm called Auction Web, which existed as a bare-bones, black-and-white web site that resembled the classified ads section of the newspaper.

American Express CEO Ken Chenault is credited with the ability to look at issues from all angles and the diplomacy to persuade others to follow the best path. Chenault has been a highly successful manager. After a short time with a consulting firm, he was named manager of the merchandise services unit in American Express and increased the unit's revenue significantly in just a few years. He is described by colleagues as persuasive, forceful when needed, and yet has good people skills. He was subsequently named CEO, for good reason.

It looked like a risky career move, but Whitman was attracted by the idea that the site had given the Internet a function in people's lives and that it helped them connect, communicate with, and even befriend others around the country. One of the few dot-coms to make a profit from the beginning, eBay had "no substitute in the land-based world," says Whitman. "I just had an overwhelming instinct that this thing was going to be huge." Her instinct was accurate. Industry experts estimate that the online auction market will soon top $4.16 billion in sales.

The pace of change and growth in the online auction industry is hectic, and "the price of inaction is higher than the price of making a mistake," according to Whitman. Decisions that would be spaced over a two- to three-month period at another kind of company occur in a single day at eBay. In one quarter, Whitman made decisions that resulted in the purchase of four different firms ranging from a dealer in collectible autos to the largest online auction house in Europe.

Growth represents more than one kind of challenge for eBay. Many of its mid-level managers are young and creative, and they sometimes resist traditional management discipline and control mechanisms that become increasingly necessary as the company expands. Whitman recalls the resistance that greeted her suggestion, in her early days on the job, that anyone wanting to see her should make an appointment. But in the years since then, she has guided the company from its everyone-does-everything culture to a flexible corporate structure that includes well-defined jobs, formal communication systems, regular management meetings, and layers of experienced managers.

One thing remains secure as the company grows, and that is the "no penalty" philosophy that allows managers to change their minds. Although Whitman credits keeping "focused on our goals" with the company's global growth and expansion, change will certainly remain a part of eBay as it prepares to move beyond the collectibles market to expand and perhaps even dominate in online consumer electronics, books, movies, and music.

It is often said that little is certain but change, so Whitman and Chenault will undoubtedly continue to face tough challenges ahead. Given the management expertise they've developed during their careers and the skills they've demonstrated in applying it to difficult situations, it appears that the confidence their organizations have placed in them is well founded.

Sources: Marjorie Whigman-Desir, "Leadership Has Its Rewards," *Black Enterprise*, September 1999, pp. 72–85; Nelson D. Schwartz, "What is in the Cards for Amex?" *Fortune*, January 22, 2001, pp. 58–70; Kathleen Melymuka, "Internet Intuition," *Computerworld*, January 10, 2000, pp. 48–50; Charles Fishman, "Facetime: Meg Whitman," *Fast Company*, May 2001, pp. 79–92; Karen Bannan, "Sole Survivor," *Sales & Marketing Management*, July 2001, pp. 36–41; http://pages.ebay.com/community/aboutebay/overview/index.html, accessed on September 26, 2001.

Why feature Ken Chenault and Meg Whitman in this opening chapter? The answer is simple: Their careers to date, and especially how they have approached managerial challenges during those careers, illustrate three key themes we emphasize in this chapter and throughout the book: The importance of change, technology, and globalism.

MANAGING EFFECTIVELY IN TODAY'S WORLD: THREE CRITICAL CHALLENGES

Change, technology, and globalism: These are undeniably three of the most important challenges that will have an enormous impact on managers in the near future. Consequently, we will be highlighting them in this and every other chapter for the remainder of the book. We view them as three themes that weave continuously through the different topics that make up this subject called "management."

Change

We begin with this theme because, in our view, it is the most persistent, pervasive, and powerful area of challenge that any manager will have to deal with in any type of organization and in any geographical area of the industrialized world. No matter how new or experienced you are as a manager, you will be confronted with both the need and the opportunity to change. Not making any changes at all is unlikely to be an option. As a Greek philosopher once wrote many centuries ago, "Change alone is unchanging,"[1] and that is still as appropriate a statement today as it was then.

Certainly, in their managerial experiences so far, both Ken Chenault and Meg Whitman have had to cope with, and master, the need to change. Chenault has been involved with change throughout his career—from lawyer, to consultant, to turnaround strategy planner, to CEO. Early in his tenure at American Express, for example, he recognized the need to revamp the firm's lineup of its merchandise services products and took steps to make significant changes. In fact, he has always seemed to be involved in changing either himself or the situation around him.

Likewise, Whitman's career illustrates that she is someone who is definitely not afraid to change. She jumped from staid, well-established organizations to the helm of something completely new and different. Indeed, her breakout success, so far at least, seems to have come as the direct result of her willingness to risk and embrace change. In her current position at eBay, she faces daily changes that occur in the Internet industry. Doing things the same way day after day would be highly unlikely to lead to progress for her or her organization.

Technology

The other two themes that we emphasize throughout the book, technology and globalism, are nearly as important to any manager as is change. No managers in today's world can ignore the impact of technology and the way it affects their jobs and firms. Technology developments, of course, often force managers to make changes—whether they want to or not. One only needs to point to the Internet as a case in point. The Internet has had far-reaching effects on how managers do their jobs.

Another example is the very nature of eBay, which has immersed Meg Whitman in challenges never before faced by any manager—both its numerous opportunities and its potential threats. The playing field for customers, competitors, and one's own organization has changed. As she puts it, "without technology we don't have a company." Similarly, one can hardly imagine a manager at American Express, from Chenault on down, not being affected by technology. Barely more than 50 years ago the world had never even heard of a credit card. Imagine where American Express and its managers would be today if they had ignored this particular form of technology!

Globalism

The third theme, or overarching type of challenge, that managers face is globalism, the increasing international and cross-national nature of everything from politics to business. No longer can managers say that "what happens in the rest of the world does not affect me or my organization." It doesn't matter whether you will ever manage a firm outside of your country of origin or not, although it's becoming increasingly likely that you will. Rather, the point is that global events will almost certainly come from outside *into* your organization. They will affect how you set goals, make decisions, and coordinate and lead the work of other people.

Throughout their careers, both Chenault and Whitman have had to engage in managerial activities that went beyond the borders of one country. The credit card, whether American Express or Visa or Mastercard, is a worldwide phenomenon. The travel services that American Express offers are hardly confined to the 50 American states. Whitman and eBay recognized the global and international implications for competition and performance in the business of online auctions in a very concrete way: by acquiring the largest online auction operation in Europe.

While we have discussed the three themes—change, technology, and globalism—separately, these three managerial challenges are often highly interrelated. Both technological and global developments frequently change the direction of organizations and the way they operate. Thus, the three managerial challenges of change, technology, and globalism form an integrated "iron triangle" of exceptionally strong influences on managers and management (as illustrated in Exhibit 1.1).

exhibit 1.1

Critical Management Challenges for the 21st Century

Managing Strategically to Meet the Challenges

The three major challenges described above combine to create an incredibly complex, dynamic, and competitive landscape in which most managers must operate. To survive and perform well in such an environment managers throughout the organization are required to manage strategically.[2] Clearly, managers at the top of the organization—CEOs like Meg Whitman and Ken Chenault—establish goals and formulate a strategy for the firm to achieve those goals. For the goals to be accomplished, the strategy must also be effectively implemented, which requires managers at all levels of the organization to set and accomplish goals that contribute to the organization's ultimate performance.

The increasing globalization and the enhanced use of technology have contributed to greater changes, emphasizing the importance of knowledge to organizational success.[3] The importance placed on the intellectual capital of the organization requires managers to use their portfolio of resources effectively. Of primary importance are intangible resources like the employees and the firm's reputation. Managers are responsible for building an organization's capabilities and then leveraging them through a strategy designed to give it an advantage over its competitors. They usually do this by creating more value for their customers than competitors.[4]

BMW managers, for example, developed a strategy to use the firm's excellent research and development (R&D) capabilities to design and manufacture several new automobiles, with the goal of increasing U.S. sales by 40 percent by 2008. The top managers at BMW made this decision at a time when other automobile manufacturers were reducing R&D expenditures to control costs. Capitalizing on its strengths and using them strategically to offer consumers more and better auto designs so far has given BMW an advantage over its competitors and contributed to its superior performance.[5]

Managers are responsible for forming the strategies of the major units within the organization as well. Because the strategy has to be implemented by people in the organization, managers must focus heavily on the human factor. As they implement their strategies they will encounter conflicting conditions. Often this means managing multiple situations simultaneously and remaining flexible to adapt to changing conditions. Additionally, achieving an organization's goals requires that managers commit themselves to always being alert to how strategies can be improved and strengthened in advancing the vision that has been established for the organization. Finally, the dynamic competitive landscape entails substantial change. To adapt to this change managers are required to be innovative, entrepreneurial, and to continuously search for new opportunities.

Now we turn to a set of basic questions that will be the focus for the remainder of Chapter 1: (1) What is management? (2) What do managers do? (3) What skills do managers need?

WHAT IS MANAGEMENT?

Before we go any further, it is essential to take time to briefly discuss definitions and terms that will be used throughout this book. So, here is how we will be using the following terms as they relate to the overall focus of this book:

Management: This term has several different uses. The primary meaning for the purposes of this book is as an activity or process. More specifically, we define **management** as the process of assembling and using sets of resources in a goal-directed manner to accomplish tasks in an organizational setting. This definition can in turn be subdivided into its key parts:

management the process of assembling and using sets of resources in a goal-directed manner to accomplish tasks in an organizational setting

1. Management is a *process*: It involves a series of activities and operations, such as planning, deciding, and evaluating.
2. Management involves *assembling and using sets of resources*: It is a process that brings together, and puts into use, a variety of types of resources: human, financial, material, and information.
3. Management involves acting in a *goal-directed* manner to *accomplish tasks*: Thus, it does not represent random activity but rather activity with a purpose and direction. The purpose or direction may be that of the individual, the organization, or, usually, a combination of the two. It includes efforts to complete activities successfully and to achieve particular levels of desired results.
4. Management involves activities carried out in an *organizational setting*: It is a process undertaken in **organizations** by people with different functions intentionally structured and coordinated to achieve common purposes.

organizations interconnected sets of individuals and groups who attempt to accomplish common goals through differentiated functions and intended coordination

Management can also have several other meanings in addition to "a process" or set of activities. The term is sometimes used to designate a particular part of the organization: the set of individuals who carry out management activities. Thus, you may hear the phrase "the management of IBM decided . . . " or "the management of University Hospital developed a new personnel policy . . . ". Often, when the term is used this way, it does not necessarily refer to all members of management, but rather to those who occupy the most powerful positions within this set (top management).

Another similar use of the term is to distinguish a category of people (that is, "management") from those who are members of collective bargaining units ("union" members or, more informally, "labor") or those who are not involved in specific managerial activities, whether or not they are union members ("nonmanagement employees" or "rank-and-file employees"). We frequently use the term *member* to refer to any person (any employee) in an organization without regard to that individual's place in the organization. In this book, we use the term *manager* to refer to anyone who has designated responsibilities for carrying out managerial activities, and *managing* to refer to the process of completing those activities.

Let's now consider the question "What is management?" in a different way: by examining four fundamental *perspectives* of management. These perspectives cut across the entire managerial process. When you begin a journey, it's helpful to have a broad overview of the terrain you are about to travel *before* learning the details of the different parts of the trip. The overview helps integrate the different perspectives and facilitates your understanding of them to provide a meaningful and powerful adventure. And learning about the complexities of management is, we strongly believe, a journey that adds up to a definite adventure!

The broad perspectives presented here and throughout the book are based on information and ideas from a wide variety of sources: our personal experiences and observations as educators, managers, and consultants; research findings from the scholarly literature; extensive study of the subject; and, particularly, hundreds of conversations and interviews with practicing managers over the years. These perspectives represent complementary points of view about management, but they are not mutually exclusive. Rather, each perspective provides a different lens to help you look at the topic and understand its complexities and challenges. These perspectives are presented to provide you with more understanding about what is meant by "management" than you can gain from a single definition. "Management" is too complex a concept to be captured by a definition alone.

In the next few pages, we first state each perspective, followed by typical questions that might be asked about it and our responses to those questions. Thus, the next part of this chapter entails a Q&A approach. The intent of this approach is to encourage you to become more interested in and involved with the material. We hope that it will increase your curiosity about management and stimulate your interest in learning about it.

management occurs in organizations

As you begin the formal study of management, it is important for you to understand that organizations serve as the context for management. And managers, much like the stage, are the constant background for actors in a play. For our purposes in this book, this context can be *any type of organization that employs people*: companies, universities, law firms, hospitals, government agencies, and the like.

LeBron James is a well-known professional basketball player for the Cleveland Cavaliers. LeBron's coach is responsible for managing the team as a whole. The coach formulates the team's strategy and makes adjustments during the game by substituting players, changes offensive and defensive approaches, and gives specific tips to individual players. LeBron, on the other hand, does not manage the team, but he does provide leadership on and off the basketball court. Along with his agent, he also takes an active part in evaluating his endorsements, commercial offers, and other business propositions. Many young people look up to him as a role model. In your opinion, does this make LeBron a manager?

Management Occurs in Organizations; It Does Not Happen in Isolation

Just as water is the necessary environment for fish, or air is for a plane, organizations are the necessary environment for managers to manage. In fact, stated strongly, "management does not exist without organizations."

Q: Can't there be management in nonorganizational settings such as families, political groups, or ad hoc groups?

A: Good question. Managerial activities, such as decision making or communication, can happen in nonorganizational settings such as a family. You can even engage in managerial activities such as planning and goal setting independently, without others being involved. However, these activities in isolation do not constitute management. Management requires integration of all these activities *and* the involvement of other people. This integration only occurs in an organizational context. It is similar to a dialogue taking place only when another person participates in the conversation—otherwise, it's a monologue.

Q: OK, but does the type of organization matter? Does it make a difference whether the organization is small or large, or whether it's for profit or not-for-profit?

A: Certainly, the nuances of effective management change depending on the situation and type of organization. Managing in a small company where you know every employee—such as 80 percent of the businesses in Des Moines, Iowa, that have fewer than 50 employees[6]—is not the same as managing in a large organization like IBM with over 200,000 employees located in more than 100 countries throughout the world. Although in this book we consider organizations of all sizes, the premium placed on good managers tends to increase as size and complexity increase. However, the cost of failing to manage effectively is high in all types and sizes of organizations.

Regardless of the fact that some dimensions of effective management are affected by the size and type of organization, the fundamental substance of management does not change. If the basic essence and nature of management changed dramatically from one organizational type to another, we would need a separate textbook for small organization management, large organization management, private company management, public agency management, and so on. In our view, the essentials of management are critical and universal activities in all organizations.

Each Organization Has Its Own Set of Characteristics That Affect Both Managers and Those with Whom They Interact

While it is critical to understand that management occurs in the context of organizations, all organizations are not the same, even those of similar size or complexity. Each organization has its own "personality" (often referred to as the organization's culture), and its own strengths, weaknesses, problems, and opportunities. These various characteristics affect the organization and all who work within it.

Q: What is it about organizations that creates their particular characteristics, and do they influence effective management?

A: Organizations often bring together a variety of people from different backgrounds—from different ethnicities and cultures (Asian, African American, Arabic, Anglo, Irish, Vietnamese, and so on), different educational levels (high school dropouts, college graduates, and MBAs), different technical backgrounds (engineering, digital arts, and accounting), and different socioeconomic levels (from very poor to very privileged)—who must then work together to achieve common objectives. Thus, developing a degree of shared cooperation becomes essential. This can only be accomplished by gaining

Good managers can make or break all kinds of organizations—large and small, profit and nonprofit. Although the United Nations Children's Fund is a nonprofit organization, its many members worldwide—both volunteer and paid—make it a complex organization to manage. Large, far-flung organizations make a manager's job harder to accomplish. As a result, organizations such as these place a premium on top managers, and they are generally paid well as a result.

acceptance of existing ways of working together, using existing structures and processes, or by developing new structures and processes. These behaviors, structures, and processes over time constitute the personality, or culture, of the organization. Whatever one may think or assume about the personality or culture of, say, a typical unit of General Motors, it is likely to be different from that of Patagonia, the apparel manufacturer headquartered in Ventura, California, where an office message board posts the local surfing conditions. Patagonia's CEO and employees have been known to head to the beach when the surf is up![7] The basic principles of effective management are relevant in all organizations, but the specific characteristics of an organization affect how those principles are applied.

Q: Does this mean that if I am an effective manager in "Organization A," I will automatically be an effective manager in "Organization B"? Or does this mean that because organizations have different personalities, effective management practices can't be transferred from one organization to another?

A: Sound approaches to management do transfer from one organization to another. This does not mean, however, that your behaviors can be identical and still be equally effective in all organizations. For example, if you learn how to read music, you can apply that knowledge from one piece of music to another, but it does not mean that you can play each piece of music the same way. Furthermore, even if the musical score were the same, it does not mean that you would play the piece exactly the same way for different conductors or with different musical groups. But making these adjustments does not change your fundamental understanding of how to read music and your ability to adapt that knowledge to different circumstances. In the same manner, for example, becoming an experienced and competent decision maker is important in all organizations. However, some organizations may encourage participatory decision making, while others are more directive. No matter what the style, it remains important to develop the skills needed to make good decisions.

Effective management is similar in all organizations, but the challenges differ by organization. For example, an effective manager in a large government bureaucracy, such as the Social Security Administration, with its rigid rules, can be quite different from one in a start-up, cutting-edge, high-technology business, such as a new-venture firm, where each experience is new and the rules are developed along the way. Thus, you will need to change how you put management ideas into practice based on the nature of the organization in which you are working, but this fine-tuning does not lessen the importance of acquiring a basic understanding of management. In fact, having that understanding allows you to move more easily from one organization to another and still be effective. This does not mean, however—and we want to emphasize this—that you can ignore the differences from one organization to another; you must adapt the way you manage in each new organization. In fact, one of the quickest ways to become an ineffective manager is to remain rigid in how you carry out your managerial functions!

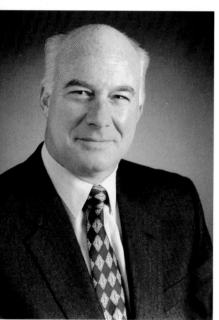

Michael Armstrong had a stellar record as a leader at IBM. When he was subsequently appointed chairman and CEO of AT&T, Wall Street cheered—until the bottom fell out of the telecom stock later on. "[Armstrong] may be a business-school case study of a successful CEO whose skills were not transferable," says Robert Frieden, a professor at Pennsylvania State University.

Managers Must Understand Organizations

Because organizations are the context of management, managers must understand how to operate within them. As we stated earlier, organizations are to management what air is to a plane. Yet, for a plane to fly effectively, a pilot must possess essential knowledge about the characteristics and composition of air, such as how atmospheric density relates to temperature, in order to calculate how much lift it can provide. In the heat of the summer, planes taking off in Phoenix sometimes have to bump passengers when seats are still available on the plane, because as the temperature rises (sometimes reaching 125 degrees Fahrenheit), the air becomes less dense, lift is more difficult, and the weight with which a plane can safely take off declines.

> Q: But what does it really mean to "understand organizations"? I can't possibly know everything about them, so how do I figure out what is more and less important to understand?

A: Just as a pilot does not have to be an astrophysicist or an aeronautical engineer to skillfully fly a plane, you do not need a Ph.D. in organizational science to be an effective manager. However, you do need a solid understanding of some basic features of organizations. Much of what follows in this textbook is designed to provide you with the fundamental knowledge you need in relation to the challenge of managing with skill. Of course, one textbook and one course in management will not provide you with sufficient knowledge. This book, however, will give you the foundation you need to be an effective manager. Without that foundation, you will either learn the hard way from your errors or be an ineffective manager.

Thus, while it is not practical to fully understand all organizations, you need to know how they can affect management practice. The key point is that just as a pilot cannot simply focus on the plane and ignore the conditions of the air, effective managers cannot only focus on management and ignore the organizational context within which it is practiced. Clearly, for example, Ken Chenault knows the difference between what managerial actions are required in the organizational context of credit card processing centers and that of executive boardrooms.

management requires getting things done through people

The act of managing involves an attempt to achieve an objective through the efforts of two, three, ten, a hundred, or even thousands of other people. Somebody acting entirely alone, whether he or she is writing a poem or making a critical investment decision, may be trying to achieve a particular goal, but that person is not managing. Management is, by its very nature, a people-based activity. Managers, no matter how talented, cannot do everything themselves. They need to use the skills and energies of other people, in addition to their own, if they are to be effective. As one high-level executive with a software firm explained:

> *Hard skills, like sales, come easily to me, yet they produce transitory results. Delegating to others, co-creating performance expectations, and trusting people to carry through is not easy. But over the years, I have found that connecting with people one-on-one, and strengthening soft skills, produce meaningful and lasting results.*[8]

The message is clear: If you *don't* want to work with and through other people, then don't become a manager. You won't like the activity, and you are unlikely to be successful.

Managers Must Be Adept at Assessing Other People's Capabilities

A critical managerial skill, and one that can be developed, is that of assessing other people's capabilities. Knowing the capability of an individual or a group of people to complete one or more tasks, as well as judging what level of performance they might be able to reach with additional instruction, training, and motivation, is essential for building an effectively performing unit.

Q: It sounds difficult to be able to evaluate the capabilities of people and to do it accurately. How do you do it?

A: It's not easy and it takes time, effort, and often, experience to develop this kind of managerial skill. However, the important point is that being a manager requires that you do this task well. It's critical to being an effective manager.

Effective Managers Must Be Adept at Matching People's Capabilities with Appropriate Responsibilities

Knowing what a particular individual or particular group is capable of doing is only part of the requirement for successfully getting things done through people. Another equally important requirement is being able to match people with tasks they are best able to perform. In addition to finding the right job for the right person, managers must also ensure that their people have the resources necessary to do the job. Therefore, the manager must be a resource provider (a resource finder and enhancer) as well as a resource coordinator.

Q: That sounds good, but aren't resources always scarce in organizations?

A: Certainly, resources are finite in all organizations. A manager almost always has limited time, equipment, money, and, especially, people. That is why it is vital to use human resources as skillfully as possible—to be able to connect people and tasks effectively. Often, that process involves forming teams, where the whole is greater than the sum of the parts. Knowing the people in your organization and their capabilities is vital, but it also is essential to fully understand the tasks and the jobs to be done. Matching resources and tasks also demands considerable effort to explore whether additional resources are needed. Management is an activity that requires initiative—not passive acceptance of the status quo.

Effective Managers Must Be Adept at Motivating People

The third requirement for successfully getting tasks done through people is motivating them to accomplish the goals. Several years ago Home Depot selected Robert Nardelli as its new CEO because of his managerial accomplishments at his former company, where "he had demonstrated an uncanny ability to develop managerial talent and motivate employees to perform

All jobs require specific skills and capabilities. The job of managers is to match people with the jobs they are best suited to perform. This requires a considerable amount of evaluation of the job and the person applying for it. For example, a cashier's position usually requires the employee learn how to operate the cash register, ensure items are properly priced, and be knowledgeable of the different payment methods available. More importantly, cashiers are frequently the customer's sole contact with the firm. What the customer thinks of him or her is likely to be what the customer thinks of the firm.

exceptionally well."[9] In the current competitive landscape (described earlier in this chapter), formal authority is declining as a useful means for influencing people. Thus, managers must have a good understanding of what people value—what they care about—if they are to be superior motivators.

Q: I don't want to be a psychologist, so how can I understand what each person values and wants out of work?

A: You are not expected to become a psychologist, but it is important that you know some basic approaches to motivate people. In addition, you need to understand how to apply those approaches when it comes to managing specific individuals. That includes not only those who work for you but also your peers and superiors.

Q: But isn't management more than motivating people or getting things done through people?

A: Absolutely. Management is a complex process that requires integration of many different tasks, including planning and organizing what is to be done, along with developing budgets and evaluating outcomes. Motivating and leading people are only two components of this overall process. Nevertheless, unless managers can get things done through people, not much will be accomplished. Managers must multiply the effects of their own efforts by influencing and directing the efforts of other people.

3

management requires simultaneously mastering multiple and potentially conflicting situations

Like most things, if management were easy there wouldn't be such a high premium placed on it. One of the important factors that separates great managers from mediocre managers is the recognition, acceptance, and mastery of managing paradoxes—the ability to cope with forces that pull managers in opposite directions. Great managers do not avoid these tensions but embrace them, harness them, and utilize them.

Q: Are these opposing forces really trade-offs? If so, managers sometimes have to trade off one opposing force for another. Is this correct?

A: Yes, managers at times have to make decisions about trade-offs. Sometimes they do, in fact, have to go with one set of actions to achieve the desired results—for example, expand the investment in the R&D (research and development) area of the company—and in the process, forgo another investment and its potential results. That might mean postponing TV advertising during the Super Bowl for two years. However, great managers do not automatically view competing forces in terms of direct trade-offs; they often recognize that the challenge is to respond to both forces simultaneously in a creative fashion that enables the firm to accomplish both sets of objectives or some portion of them.

Management Is a Complex Process Requiring *Integration*, Yet Managerial Activities Are Often *Fragmented* and Do Not Occur in a Logical, Sequential Fashion

Management requires the integration of a variety of activities, such as planning, decision making, communicating, motivating, appraising, and organizing, yet a manager's day is typically fragmented with interruptions, breaks in sequence, and other distractions. In a sense, a manager is like a "juggler." The manager may need to keep several balls in the air, simultaneously throwing the balls up and catching them. Rarely does the manager take the time to evaluate the competing "ball" and decide to keep one up while somehow suspending the others in mid-air. All of the balls must be continuously juggled or they will be lost.

Likewise, while managers are constantly confronted with rapidly changing activities and discrete bits or chunks of information, it is the responsibility and challenge of the manager to integrate all of them in a meaningful way. As such, the manager must be capable of seeing patterns of important activities and changes in them, inside the organization, and external to it. He or she must then coordinate the resources, people, and activities to achieve the organization's goals.

Q: Although this seems logical, management seems much more simple than you're describing. Isn't the key to simplify management and not make it more complex?

A: Management, as often described by "best-selling" books, may seem simple, and certainly the authors of many of these books would like you to believe that if you just did "X" you would be highly successful. But the reality is that management is complex and requires integration of fragmented actions, information, and resources. Easy solutions may be appealing, but they rarely work. If management were simple, there wouldn't be a new best-seller about it each month. No one would need the new tip of the month.

There may be some value in best-selling management books, but the simple solutions that they offer may work only in a very specific situation; they are unlikely to work in most situations. Solutions that work across a variety of conditions are likely to be more complicated. Effective managers understand that paradoxes—seeming contradictions—lie at the center of their roles and responsibilities and that one of their key challenges is to deal with those paradoxes effectively.

Management Requires *Consistency* and *Flexibility*

Perhaps one of the most important paradoxes is that of simultaneously maintaining consistency and flexibility. Without question, people need some consistency in their organizational lives. Workers could not be expected to perform their jobs well if tasks, or how they were expected to accomplish them, changed each day. Without some consistency, the workplace would be chaotic, and no purposeful organizational objectives could be accomplished. Yet, in the current competitive landscape—with rapidly changing technology, government policies, customer preferences, and competitor capabilities—flexibility, change, and adaptation are essential for survival.

Q: As a manager, how can I be consistent and yet remain flexible at the same time?

A: It is important to understand that as a manager you do not need to make an either/or choice to be consistent all of the time or completely flexible all of the time. For example, your fundamental values and ethical standards need to be fairly stable. People may not agree with your values or ethical standards, but they need to know what they are and that you consistently maintain them. Otherwise, you will appear to be unpredictable and untrustworthy. You also need to exhibit a fair degree of consistency without being overly rigid in your basic approach to dealing with people and problems. People need to perceive that you are open to alternative ideas, but they will have difficulty if you change so often that you seem to be a chameleon.

Managers Must *Reflect* and *Act*

Talk to any manager today, and he or she will tell you that one must rapidly deal with often unexpected situations, decisions, problems, and opportunities. One executive put it this way:

> *The fascinating thing about this job is the incredible variability of it . . . It's a never-ending kaleidoscope. I sometimes compare it to playing tennis with an out-of-control tennis-ball serving machine that just keeps shooting balls at you. You've got to keep moving faster and faster to keep up.*[10]

Quick action is often the difference between first and second place or even last place in the competitive marketplace, as both Starbucks and Amazon.com have demonstrated. Or, as Meg Whitman stated, "In this space [the Internet], the price of inaction is higher than the price of making a mistake."[11] To some extent, then, capabilities like being able to think and make decisions quickly are admirable managerial qualities.

But there is an inherent problem with focusing on the onslaught of daily activities. This problem is similar to running and focusing on the ground only a few feet in front of you. You may notice the stone in the path in time to avoid it, or you may notice a declining or inclining slope in the path and change your pace appropriately. Each individual step you take may be successful, but by focusing on only a few feet in front of you, you may not notice that you are running straight toward a wall or cliff. Take, for example, the case of Charlie Kim, CEO of a Web-based marketing organization. Early in the life of the company he was noted for the blazingly fast "Internet speed" of his decision making, but that began to create problems for his subordinates. Consequently, he has learned to slow down his decision-making process: "It's counterintuitive," he says, "but in order to move faster, you actually need to move slower."[12]

Q: But how can I deal effectively with all the things I need to each day and still have time to reflect?

A: Management is about activity; it is not about philosophy. But managers cannot know if they are headed in the right direction, if their pace is appropriate, or if their current approach is effective, unless they *take* the time to reflect on these things. Because management is about activity, you are unlikely to *find* time to reflect. You are going to have to *make* time. In fact, many of the insights presented in this chapter have come from managers, as we asked them in our interviews to take time to reflect on management. So, while managers must act and often do so quickly, they must also take time to analyze what they are doing, how they are doing it, and, perhaps most importantly, why they are doing it.

Increasingly, Managers Need Global Perspective and Local Understanding of Specific Customers, Governments, Competitors, and Suppliers

International management consultants are fond of saying that in the future there will be two types of CEOs: those who have a global perspective and those who are out of a job. The evidence for the increasing globalization of

3

business is nearly overwhelming, and that is why we make it one of our key themes in this book. It is virtually impossible to read a major magazine or newspaper without finding several stories related to global business in some form—companies entering international markets, competing with foreign competitors, responding to a foreign government's policy change, and so on. This requires a global perspective. However, the paradox is that all business occurs at a local level. The business transactions and the management activities all take place in specific countries with specific employees, government officials, competitors, and suppliers.

Q: But in a practical sense, how do I "think global and act local"?

A: A key is to be able to recognize the drivers behind these competing forces. For many products, it is much cheaper to build one version for the entire world than to have variations for every country. Yet, for many of these products, customers in different countries have different preferences. One compromise is to design the product so it has the widest appeal, recognizing that, as a consequence, it will not appeal to some potential customers. Nevertheless, more sophisticated managers do not trade off global standardization for local appeal or vice versa. Instead, they recognize the inherent challenge in this paradox and seek to standardize aspects of the product that have common appeal and simultaneously customize those features that need to be adapted to local preferences.

For example, McDonald's has a worldwide identity built around the standardization of both its products and its service. The Quarter Pounder and Egg McMuffin are the same product whether you buy them in San Francisco, Singapore, or Moscow. The company also attempts to standardize managerial styles by requiring managers to learn the company's specific approaches to human resource practices, marketing, inventory management, and quality control. However, McDonald's corporate managers must also learn to adjust their financial and marketing approaches to local conditions. Similarly, McDonald's store managers around the world must learn when to add specialized menu

Agreements like the North American Free Trade Agreement (NAFTA) have thrown open doors to customers and firms worldwide. Managers in Miami cannot assume their products will be as appealing in Vancouver or Beijing as they are on their home turf. But they also know that their competitors' products won't be either. In recent years, this has made for a broader playing field with make-or-break competitive consequences.

20

items to suit local tastes—shamrock shakes in Ireland, McRye burgers in Finland, curry potato pies in Hong Kong, and 100 percent kosher beef in Israel.[13] Likewise, Wal-Mart's managers have learned that local conditions often intrude on its stores' customary standardized practices. In Germany, for example, Wal-Mart was forced to raise prices on milk products by the government's cartel office because it had determined that the company was selling them below cost.[14]

You might think of this global/local paradox by comparing it to a view of the landscape from a helicopter. Managers often have to "helicopter up" to a level in order to get a broad perspective of the "forest," or in other words, to obtain a global view. But then they need to come down closer to earth to see the "trees," or the local conditions and marketplace. Managers who can only see what is immediately and directly in front of them risk being ineffective because they can't see "the forest for the trees." At the same time, though, managers who only fly at 20,000 feet also risk being ineffective because they miss the small details and nuances that can influence the success or failure of specific decisions or tasks. Thus, effective management is not a matter of having only a broad global perspective or only a knowledge of the specific local situation; it is a matter of being able to develop *both*.

managers must continuously search for and exploit new opportunities

We previously noted that managers must be committed to continuous learning and to create value for others. However, to survive in the hypercompetitive landscape that exists in the twenty-first century they are required to regularly search for and be open to new opportunities in their current marketplace or to ideas that could create new markets. Entrepreneurship involves identifying new opportunities and exploiting them. Thus, managers must be entrepreneurial.

Q: I thought that entrepreneurs developed new businesses and then managers operated them. Are you saying that managers are entrepreneurs?

A: You are correct about what entrepreneurs do, but entrepreneurship is not exclusive of management, especially in the current environment. Entrepreneurial activity is not limited to new, small firms. Managers in large firms need to be entrepreneurial and create new businesses as well. Developing new businesses requires that the lead person and perhaps others take entrepreneurial actions. Given the amount of change and innovation encountered in most industries and countries, businesses cannot survive without being entrepreneurial.[15]

Q: What is required for a manager to be entrepreneurial and be responsible for all of the other activities explained?

A: Managers must develop an entrepreneurial mind-set. An entrepreneurial mind-set is a way of thinking about businesses that emphasizes actions to take advantage of uncertainty.[16] With an entrepreneurial mind-set, managers can sense opportunities and take actions to exploit them. Uncertainty in the environment tends to level the "playing field" for both large and smaller organizations and for resource-rich and resource-poor ones. Opportunities can be identified by anyone and exploited to achieve a competitive advantage. This is how Microsoft beat its competitors, who were at one time larger and more powerful. Dell achieved a similar result in the personal computer market.

To develop an entrepreneurial mind-set, managers must first be alert and open to investing in opportunities today that may provide benefits in the future. They must be amenable to new ideas and to using them to create value for customers.[17]

Q: So, both large and small firms can be entrepreneurial?

A: Yes. In fact, large and small firms and new and established firms can be entrepreneurial. For reasons described earlier, they not only can be, they must be to survive. Polaroid, once an entrepreneurial company and a market leader in instant photography, no longer exists because it lost its entrepreneurial nature, and market share was winnowed away from it with the development of digital photography technology. As a whole, small and new firms tend to be more entrepreneurial but often lack the ability to sustain this advantage. On the other hand, large, established firms are good at using their size to gain an advantage and in sustaining their strong position as long as new, rival products don't enter the market. However, larger firms have a harder time being entrepreneurial.[18]

An Entrepreneurial Mind-set Requires a Commitment to Constantly Learning New Skills and Acquiring New Knowledge

Management is a complex process. It is not just about strategy, or organizing, or decision making, or leadership. It is about all of these activities and more, but especially, it is about *integrating them*. To integrate activities, managers require multiple skills (as we discuss later in this chapter): technical, interpersonal, and conceptual. These skills can be learned, or at least greatly improved by learning, if there is a commitment by a manager to such learning. Experience alone does not necessarily provide learning, but the desire for and effort to acquire new knowledge from those experiences often produces learning and the development of new capabilities.

Even the best managers with the most experience must stay abreast of the marketplace because conditions can change rapidly. This means not becoming complacent but committing themselves and their staff to continued learning and improvement to meet new challenges and situations.

A: It is dangerous to assume at any point in time that you know all that needs to be known about management. Managers must continuously acquire new knowledge and skills to remain competitive because they constantly confront new situations and challenges. Therefore, a commitment to continuous learning and improvement is vital. Managerial "hubris"—meaning overbearing pride or self-confidence—has been publicly demonstrated in recent years by the failure of prominent companies like Enron and WorldCom. This danger should motivate you to pursue the frontiers of learning and acquire better managerial skills no matter what your level in the organization is.

An Entrepreneurial Mind-set Also Requires a Commitment to Adding Value to Other People's Efforts and to Society

At its best, management is not a selfish activity. It should serve others, both in one's own organization and in society at large. This kind of commitment represents a challenge—a challenge to contribute something that benefits people, whether it be employees, customers, shareholders, or others. Meeting this challenge requires not only a sense of obligation and responsibility but also vision and a burning passion. Otherwise, why be a manager?

WHAT DO MANAGERS DO?

A few years from now, when you are getting started on your career, whether in management or some other endeavor, your parents or friends might ask: "What do you actually *do* in your job?" A manager is a manager, right? Well, as we'll see, it's not quite that simple. Just as we tried to provide some different ways of thinking about "what is management?" we will also do the same with respect to the question, "What do managers do?"

Later in this section (see the next two boxes), two managers describe—in their own words—what they do, what they like most about their jobs, and recent changes they've had to cope with in their jobs. These interviews provide some of the flavor and intensity of actual managerial jobs.

There are also other, analytical ways to look at managerial jobs aside from simply asking managers what they do. Over the years, several systems have been developed to classify (a) managerial functions, (b) the roles in which managers operate, and (c) the characteristics and dimensions of managerial jobs. These typologies can provide you with useful ways to examine the extremely varied nature of managerial jobs and responsibilities. In effect, they provide a road map for thinking about what management is.

Managerial Functions

One way to think about the question "What do managers do?" is to analyze the work of managers according to the different functions or processes they carry out. The first such classification system dates back at least 80 years and has sometimes been criticized for not sufficiently characterizing what managers "really do." However, this system is still, after more than eight decades, widely utilized by management scholars and writers.[19] In fact, as we explain at the end of this chapter, a variation of this traditional typology forms the basis for the general sequencing of the chapters in this book (as well as most other textbooks on the subject of management). The four principal managerial functions that seem most applicable to modern organizations are planning, organizing, directing, and controlling.

Planning Planning involves estimating future conditions and circumstances and, based on these estimations, making decisions about what work is to be done by the manager and all of those for whom she or he is responsible. This function can be thought of as involving three distinct levels or types: *strategic planning*, which addresses strategic actions designed to achieve the organization's long-range goals; *tactical planning*, which translates strategic plans into actions designed to achieve specific and shorter-term goals and objectives; and *operational planning*, which identifies the actions needed to accomplish the goals of particular units of the organization.

planning estimating future conditions and circumstances and making decisions about appropriate courses of action

Organizing To carry out managerial work, resources must be put together systematically, and this function is labeled **organizing**. It involves paying attention to the structure of relationships among positions, and the people occupying them, and linking that structure to the overall strategic direction of the organization. Since the world with which we deal is basically full of uncertainties and ambiguities, the function of organizing is a critical challenge facing managers. At its most basic level, the purpose of this managerial function can be thought of as the attempt to bring order to the organization. Without it, it would be a chaotic environment.

organizing systematically putting resources together

exhibit 1.2
Managerial Functions

directing the process of attempting to influence other people to attain organizational objectives

controlling regulating the work of those for whom a manager is responsible

Directing This function has typically had a number of different labels over the years, including *leading*. The latter term obviously does not have the autocratic connotations associated with the word *directing*. Nevertheless, the core of **directing**, or leading, is the process of attempting to influence other people to attain organizational objectives. It heavily involves motivating those for whom you are responsible, interacting with them effectively in group and team situations, and communicating in ways that are highly supportive of their efforts to accomplish their tasks and achieve organizational goals.

Controlling In contemporary organizations, the word **controlling** is not entirely satisfactory because it implies, as does the word *directing*, that the activity must be carried out in a dictatorial, autocratic fashion. This, of course, is not the case, although in a particular circumstance a manager might act in this manner. The essence of this function is to regulate the work of those for whom a manager is responsible. Regulation can be done in several different ways, including setting standards of performance in advance, monitoring ongoing (real-time) performance, and, especially, assessing a completed performance. The results of such evaluation are fed back into the planning process. Therefore, it is important to consider these four managerial functions as parts of a reciprocal and recurring process, as illustrated in Exhibit 1.2.

Managerial Roles

An alternative approach to describing managerial work was proposed some years ago by a Canadian scholar Henry Mintzberg.[20] He based his classification system on research studies on how managers spend their time at work, and focused on "roles," or what he called "organized sets of behaviors." Although this way of viewing managers' work activities has not replaced the functional approach, it has received a great deal of attention because it provides additional understanding and insights not readily apparent in that more traditional set of categories.

Mintzberg organized his typology of managerial roles into three major categories—interpersonal, informational, and decisional—each of which contains specific roles. Altogether, there are 10 such roles in this system, as shown in Exhibit 1.3 and described in the following sections.

exhibit 1.3
Types of Managerial Roles

Interpersonal Roles:
• Figurehead
• Leader
• Liaison

Managerial Roles

Informational Roles:
• Monitor
• Disseminator
• Spokesperson

Decisional Roles:
• Entrepreneur
• Disturbance Handler
• Resource Allocator
• Negotiator

a week in the managerial life of deb m.

Deb M. is the director of organizational effectiveness for a Canadian oil and gas company.

Question: Describe the type and range of activities you were involved in, as a manager, this past week.

Last week 70 percent of my time was spent in meetings with others. That's a bit high but not totally unusual.

One of the meetings I organized and led. Actually it was a two-day work meeting with HR peers in other parts of the company. We were working on coordinating our HR activities such as recruiting and performance management across the company. We have four separate operating units and each has its own HR department to some extent.

One of the other meetings involved making a presentation to our corporate senior management team regarding our compensation strategy. I was explaining how changes we proposed to make would help us better attract and retain employees with key skills.

I also had a meeting with my boss to review resource needs for my team in order to manage increasing workloads.

I spent several hours interviewing job candidates for a new hire to join my team.

I also conducted an orientation session with a number of our managers to explain our new job evaluation system.

The rest of the time was spent working on several efforts to better integrate and harmonize certain HR practices, such as pay, across the company. This involved both working with my subordinates as well as working on my own.

Question: What do you like best about your job as a manager?

One of the things I like best about my job is that I have the opportunity to influence the decisions and actions that will have a significant impact on the success of the company. Much of our success depends on the people we attract and select into the company and the performance current employees contribute. My job in HR and the work of my subordinates contribute directly to the quality of people we have and how well they perform.

Question: In the past year or so, what is the biggest change you have had to respond to?

We are going through a lot of changes right now. We have changed our strategy and our structure—but most of these changes were planned. The unexpected changes have involved individuals who have either deviated from the agreed-to plan and/or have not shared key pieces of information that would have caused us to plan differently. In the first case, I've had to rely on my interpersonal skills to try and get the person back on track. In the second case, I've had to incorporate the new information and adjust our plans.

Interpersonal Roles Interpersonal roles are composed of three types of behavior and, according to Mintzberg, are derived directly from the manager's formal authority granted by the organization. They are:

1. *The Figurehead Role:* This set of behaviors involves an emphasis on ceremonial activities, such as attending a social function, welcoming a visiting dignitary, or presiding at a farewell reception for a departing employee. A familiar term for this role of representing the organization, borrowed from the military, is "showing the flag." Although one particular occasion where this behavior occurs may not be important in and of itself, the activity across a period of time is a necessary component of a manager's job. If you doubt this, just ask any manager you know! For example, the next time you meet the dean of a business school, ask how often she finds it necessary to participate in figurehead activities—think of commencement ceremonies, for instance—and how important this is for the long-term benefit of the school.

2. *The Leader Role:* This role, in Mintzberg's system, is essentially one of influencing or directing others. It is the set of responsibilities people typically associate with a manager's job, since the organization gives the manager formal authority over the work of other people. To the extent that managers are able to translate this authority into

actual influence, they are exercising what would be called leadership behavior. The leader type of behavior would be demonstrated when, for example, a newly appointed project team leader gathers his handpicked team members together and discusses his vision and goals for the team and his ideas as to how to accomplish them.

3. *The Liaison Role:* This role emphasizes the contacts that a manager has with those outside the formal authority chain of command. These contacts include not only other managers within the organization, but also many individuals outside it—for example, customers, suppliers, government officials, and managers from other organizations. It also emphasizes lateral interactions, as contrasted with vertical interpersonal interactions of a manager, and it highlights the fact that an important part of a manager's job is to serve as a go-between for his or her own unit and other units or groups. The liaison role would apply to the situation where a marketing manager interacts with key customers to learn about their reactions to new product ideas.

Informational Roles This set of roles builds on the interpersonal relationships that a manager establishes, and it underlines the importance of the network of contacts built up and maintained by the manager. The three specific informational roles identified by Mintzberg are the following:

1. *The Monitor Role:* This type of behavior involves extensive information-seeking that managers engage in to keep aware of crucial developments that may affect their unit and their own work. Such monitoring, as previously noted, typically deals with spoken and written information and "soft" as well as "hard" facts. A manager attending an industry conference who spends considerable time in informal lobby and cocktail lounge conversations in order to gather data on current developments in the industry would be an example of this role.

2. *The Disseminator Role:* A manager not only receives information but also sends it. This often includes information that the receiver wants but otherwise has no easy access to without the help of the manager. A supervisor who finds out about reorganization plans affecting his part of the organization and conveys that information to his subordinates would be acting in a disseminator role.

3. *The Spokesperson Role:* A manager is frequently called upon to represent the views of the unit for which he or she is responsible. At lower management levels, this typically involves representing the unit to other individuals or groups within the organization; at higher management levels, this internal spokesperson role could also be supplemented by an external component in which the organization and its activities and concerns often must be represented to the outside world. When the manager of the western region meets with other regional managers and presents the views of his region's sales personnel about how well a proposed new sales incentive plan is likely to work, he is functioning in a spokesperson role.

Decisional Roles The final category of roles in this classification system relates to the decision-making requirements of a manager's job. Four such decisional roles are designated by Mintzberg:

1. *The Entrepreneurial Role:* Managers not only make routine decisions in their jobs but also frequently engage in activities that explore new opportunities or start new projects. Such entrepreneurial behavior within an organization often involves a series of small decisions that permit ongoing assessment about whether to continue or abandon new ventures. This type of role behavior involves some degree of risk, but that risk is often limited or minimized by the sequence of decisions. Suppose, for example, that a lower-level production manager comes up with an idea for a new organizational sales unit that she discusses with her colleagues and then, based on their reactions, modifies it and presents it to upper-level management. Such a man-

ager would be exhibiting entrepreneurial role behavior that goes beyond her routine responsibilities.

2. *The Disturbance Handler Role:* Managers initiate actions of their own, but they must also be able to respond to problems or "disturbances." In this role, a manager often acts as a judge or problem-solver or conflict-settler. The goal of such actions, of course, is to keep small problems or issues from developing into larger ones. If you, as a manager, were to face a situation where your employees could not agree about who would do a particularly unpleasant but necessary group task, and you then stepped in to settle the matter, you would be functioning as a disturbance handler.

3. *The Resource Allocator Role:* Since resources of all types are always limited in organizations, one of the chief responsibilities of managers is to decide how the resources under their authority will be distributed. Such allocation decisions have a direct effect on the performance of a unit and an indirect effect of communicating certain types of information to members of the unit. The manager of front desk services for a large resort hotel who decides how many and which clerks will be assigned to each shift is operating in a resource allocator role.

4. *The Negotiator Role:* This type of managerial behavior refers to the fact that a manager is often called upon to make accommodations with other units or other organizations (depending on the level of the management position). The manager, in this decisional situation, is responsible for knowing what resources can or cannot be committed to particular negotiated solutions. Someone who serves on a negotiating team to set up a new joint venture with an outside company would be functioning in the negotiator role.

If nothing else, the collection of roles described in Mintzberg's analysis of managerial work emphasizes the considerable variety of behaviors required in these types of jobs. In considering these 10 roles, it is essential to keep in mind that the extent to which any particular role is important will vary considerably from one managerial job to another. Obviously, where a job fits within the organization will have a great deal to do with which particular role or roles are emphasized. The front-line supervisor of branch office bank tellers obviously has a different mix of roles from that of the bank's executive vice president. Nevertheless, Mintzberg maintains that the 10 roles form a "gestalt," or whole, and that to understand the total nature of *any* managerial job, *all* of them must be taken into account.

Managerial Job Dimensions

Another extremely useful way to try to gain an understanding of managerial work is to analyze the dimensions of managerial jobs. One particular approach was developed by British researcher Rosemary Stewart.[21] Stewart proposed that any managerial job (and, in fact, any job anywhere in an organization) can be characterized along three dimensions:

- the demands made on it;
- the constraints placed on it; and
- the choices permitted in it.

Looking at managerial jobs in this way not only provides further understanding of what managers do but also permits direct comparisons of different jobs; for example, how the position of "manager of information systems" might compare with that of "financial analyst" or the job of "marketing vice president" versus "plant manager."

a week in the managerial life of greg k.

Greg K. is director of finance and accounting in a large division of a financial services firm.

Question: Describe the type and range of activities you were involved in, as a manager, this past week.

In my managerial job, I have a pretty wide variety of activities that I am involved in—ranging from division project meetings to staff meetings to time to work on my own projects. Here is a brief overview of my activities this past week:

Monday—In the morning I participated in a conference call with various management-level employees to discuss activity at one of our broker/dealers. The remainder of the day was filled with interacting with staff, completing my assignments, and reacting to various inquiries from other departments, divisions, and auditors.

Tuesday—This morning I participated in a bi-weekly status call with our third-party administrator for one of our products. Following the conference call, I met with one of my direct reports (accounting manager) for our weekly staff meeting. We discussed the status of various department projects, staffing issues, upcoming projects, and current events affecting the division. Later that day I met with our accounting coordinator to discuss the status of a pricing project that she was working on.

Wednesday—This was a light day as far as standing meetings; however, I attended a one-hour training class regarding upcoming new product features that we will be offering.

Thursday—Thursdays are typically busy in the mornings due to a biweekly technology meeting that I participate in, and a weekly product meeting that I attend. This typically takes up two to three hours of my morning when both of the meetings occur. This Thursday the head of our department held a monthly staff meeting to discuss general events affecting the department, the division, and the company.

Friday—Today began with a weekly investment meeting in the morning. I represent our division in this meeting that includes other representatives from all divisions of the company. The remainder of the day was spent working on various normal tasks.

Aside from the meetings that I attend throughout the week, the remainder of my work week typically includes other interactions with staff and completion of my other assignments (responsibilities as a "working manager"). I typically interact at least daily (more often than not, multiple times throughout the day) with our department head (VP of finance). We discuss new requests/projects, staffing, status of current projects, etc. I also interact regularly throughout the day with my direct reports (five direct reports) to discuss projects and questions, and provide feedback. I also am responsible for approving all of our sales force travel and expense reports and approving sales support requests that come from our sales force.

Question: What do you like best about your job as a manager?

I think I need to answer this from two angles, one from the perspective of my direct assignments and one from a managerial perspective:

Regarding my direct assignments, the most rewarding part of my job is contributing to a division project that directly impacts the division with findings and recommendations that are communicated to senior management. Feeling part of the division team is very rewarding.

As a manager, I enjoy problem solving and coaching my direct reports regarding issues that they face. My company offers several management development programs, and one that I found especially useful concerned leadership. I try to apply facets of the class to situations that arise in everyday work.

Question: In the past year or so, what is the biggest change you have had to respond to?

From a management perspective, the most challenging change over the past year was terminating two employees (not my direct reports, but I was very involved in the process) and adjusting accordingly on all fronts of the job. I had not previously been involved in a termination, so it was very challenging. The process included performance concerns, HR concerns, reallocating resources within the department to ensure completion of all assignments, and communication to other employees (a very delicate matter).

Demands This dimension of management jobs refers to what the holder of a particular position *must* do. "Demands" are of two types: activities or duties that must be carried out and the standards or levels of minimum performance that must be met. Demands can come from several sources, such as the organization at large, the immediate boss, or the way in which work activities are organized. Typical types of demands would include such behavior as attending required meetings, adhering to schedule deadlines, following certain procedures, and the like. No doubt, for example, Meg Whitman has sales and performance targets to meet in her CEO position at eBay.

Constraints "Constraints" are factors that limit the response of the manager to various demands. One obvious constraint for any manager is the amount of time available for an activity. Other typical constraints include budgets, technology, attitudes of subordinates, and legal regulations. The important point is that any managerial job has a set of constraints, and therefore a key to performing that job effectively is to recognize them and develop a good understanding of how they can be minimized, overcome, or effectively confronted. Ken Chenault, in his past managerial positions at American Express, has had to work within the constraints of deadlines, supplier schedules, customer preferences, and forces in the larger economy he could not control.

Choices This dimension underscores the fact that despite demands and despite constraints, there is always room for some amount of discretionary behavior in any managerial job. Thus, there are a number of activities that a manager *may* carry out but does not have to. "Choices" can involve how work is to be done, what work beyond that absolutely required will be done, who will do particular tasks, and what initiatives not otherwise prohibited will be undertaken from almost infinite possibilities. In her present and past managerial positions, Meg Whitman has faced a multitude of choices about how to make staffing decisions, how to demonstrate leadership, how to respond to changing market conditions affecting Internet use, and the like.

Exhibit 1.4 illustrates these three job dimensions for two different managerial jobs, that of a project team manager in a manufacturing company and a manager of a medium-sized fast-food restaurant. In these examples, though both jobs are definitely managerial in their nature and how their organizations

	Job A: Project Team Manager	Job B: Fast-Food Restaurant Manager
Demands	· Develop new product with strong market appeal · Hold formal weekly progress meeting with boss · Frequent travel to other company sites	· Maintain attractive appearance of restaurant · Keep employee costs as low as possible · Meet standards for speed of service
Constraints	· 12-month deadline for product development · Project budget limit of $1 million · No choice in selecting team members	· Most employees have limited formal education · Few monetary incentives to reward outstanding performance · Federal and state health and safety regulations
Choices	· The organizational structure of the project team · Sequencing of project tasks · Budget allocations	· Selection of employee to promote to supervisor · Scheduling of shifts and assignments · Local advertising promotions

exhibit 1.4

Two Managerial Jobs with Different Demands, Constraints, and Choices

view them, their demands and constraints are quite different. Some of the types of choices permitted, however, are fairly similar. It's the combination of the specifics of these three dimensions that determines what it would be like to be a manager in these or any other positions.

WHAT SKILLS DO MANAGERS NEED?

Like any other human activity, managing involves the exercise of skills, that is, highly developed abilities and competencies. Skills emerge through a combination of aptitude, education, training, and experience. Three types have been identified as critical for managerial tasks, particularly for the leadership component of management: technical, interpersonal, and conceptual (see Exhibit 1.5).

Technical Skills Technical skills involve specialized knowledge about procedures, processes, equipment, and the like and include the related abilities of knowing how and when to use that knowledge. Research shows that these skills are especially important early in managerial careers (see Exhibit 1.6), when the leadership of lower-level employees is often part of the role, and one of the challenges of being a manager is to gain the respect of those being led. In addition, technical skills seem to be a particularly critical factor in many successful entrepreneurial start-ups, such as those involving Steve Jobs and Steve Wozniak at Apple Computer or Bill Gates at Microsoft. Technical skills, whether in an entrepreneurial situation or in a larger organizational setting, are frequently necessary for managing effectively, but usually they are not sufficient. In fact, an overreliance on technical skills may actually lower overall managerial effectiveness. The first Apple computer was designed and built by Jobs and Wozniak, and it was their technical skills that started and expanded the fledgling company. However, as Apple grew, their technical skills became relatively less important because they were able to employ technical specialists. They were not, however, always readily able to exchange those technical skills for other, equally impressive leadership skills. As a result, the company had to search for other managerial talent, with mixed success. After gaining considerable managerial experience in other business endeavors, Jobs did subsequently return to lead Apple—with the assistance of other able managers—in the late 1990s.

Interpersonal Skills Interpersonal skills like sensitivity, persuasiveness, and empathy have been shown to be important at all levels of management, although particularly so at lower and middle levels. A longitudinal study of career advancement carried out at AT&T found evidence that such skills, measured early in careers by psychological assessment methods, were one factor that predicted advancement in managerial ranks 20 years later. However, though lack of these skills has been shown to prematurely limit managerial

exhibit 1.5

Managers' Skills

Technical	**Interpersonal**	**Conceptual**
• Specialized knowledge (including when and how to use the skills)	• Sensitivity • Persuasiveness • Empathy	• Logical reasoning • Judgment • Analytical ability

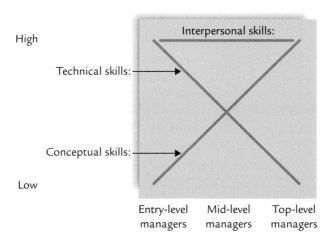

exhibit 1.6

Relative Importance of Managerial Skills at Different Organizational Levels

advancement even when other skills were present, these skills alone are unlikely to guarantee significant managerial achievement. Exhibit 1.7 summarizes the findings of one study that investigated reasons why some fast-rising executives eventually "derailed" or plateaued in their managerial careers even when they appeared to start out with acceptable levels of interpersonal skills. As put compellingly by a pair of management researchers, referring to those who have these skills but who lack other capabilities, "The charming but not

exhibit 1.7

Who Succeeds? Who Doesn't?

Potential managerial leaders share traits early on:	Those who don't quite make it:	Those who succeed:
Bright, with outstanding track records	Have been successful, but generally only in one area or type of job.	Have diverse track records, demonstrated ability in many different situations, and a breadth of knowledge of the business or industry
Have survived stressful situations	Frequently described as moody or volatile. May be able to keep their temper with superiors during crises but are hostile toward peers and subordinates.	Maintain composure in stressful situations, are predictable during crises, are regarded as calm and confident.
Have a few flaws	Cover up problems while trying to fix them. If the problem can't be hidden, they tend to go on the defensive and even blame someone else for it.	Make a few mistakes, but when they do, they admit to them and handle them with poise and grace.
Ambitious and oriented toward problem solving	May attempt to micromanage a position, ignoring future prospects; may staff with the incorrect people or neglect the talents they have; may depend too much on a single mentor, calling their own decision-making ability into question.	While focusing on problem solutions, keep their minds focused on the next position, help develop competent successors, seek advice from many sources.
Good people skills	May be viewed as charming but political or direct but tactless, cold, and arrogant. People don't like to work with them.	Can get along well with different types of people, are outspoken without being offensive, are viewed as direct and diplomatic.

Source: Adapted from M. W. McCall, Jr. and M. M. Lombardo, "Off the Track: Why and How Successful Executives Get Derailed," *Technical Report #21* (Greensboro, NC: Center for Creative Leadership, 1983), pp. 9–11.

brilliant find that the job gets too big and the problems too complex to get by on interpersonal skills [alone]."[22]

Conceptual Skills Often called cognitive ability or cognitive complexity, conceptual skills such as logical reasoning, judgment, and analytical abilities are a relatively strong predictor of managerial effectiveness. These skills are often the major factor that determines who reaches the highest levels of the organization. A clear example of someone who was selected for a CEO job precisely because of his conceptual skills is Jack Welch, the former CEO at General Electric. He was appointed to the top position at GE in 1981 and immediately set out to restructure the organization with the objective of making it more globally competitive. His concept of the company included wiping out its bureaucracy to develop a more flexible organization. At the same time, however, he also championed a new corporate culture, one based on greater empowerment of the employee.

PLAN OF THE BOOK

Now that we have proposed some initial ways to answer the three basic questions of "What is management?" "What do managers do?" and "What skills do managers need?" here in Chapter 1, we want to share with you the overall structure and plan of the remainder of the book. We do this to give you a better understanding for what follows in later chapters. It might even give you some additional insight in answering examination questions that will almost surely come later in the course.

Most books on management, after starting with a set of introductory chapters, group the remaining chapters in clusters around the generally accepted four major functions of management: planning, organizing, directing, and controlling. Our sequence of parts in this book is basically in that order. However, we title the parts in what we consider a more user-friendly and user-useful manner.

The first two chapters (Part 1) are under the heading "You as a Manager." These chapters are intended to provide you with an introduction to the subject of the book (Chapter 1) and to emphasize the critical necessity of managing change (Chapter 2), a central orientation that we think is imperative for anyone aspiring to work in a managerial job.

Part 2 emphasizes the importance of "Assessing the Environment" as a necessary background for considering the various functions of management that are covered later in the book. Chapters 3 and 4 focus on the context for managing in organizations: the outside, or external, environment of management, and the cultural environment. Particularly emphasized in these chapters are the various forces outside and inside the organization that affect how, and how well, a person can carry out managerial responsibilities. Chapter 5 presents the ethical issues that are facing every manager at the start of the new century. Although some books place this chapter toward the end of the book, we purposely place it near the beginning because of the prime importance we attach to this topic.

Part 3 focuses on a manager's role in "Setting Direction." It begins in Chapter 6 by raising issues of broad strategy, followed by Chapter 7, which provides an overview of key elements of organization design and structure consistent with strategic directions. The next two chapters, 8 and 9, address turning strategic direction into action and concrete reality through planning and making decisions.

The fourth part of the book, "Implementing Through People," consists of five chapters dealing with this crucial managerial responsibility. It begins with two chapters devoted to the topic of leadership, an indication of the importance we attach to that subject. The first of these, Chapter 10, discusses some of the basics of leadership and the leadership process. Chapter 11 provides a number of alternative ways to view leadership and concludes with an examination of a number of different contemporary leadership issues. Chapter 12 covers the topic of motivation, and especially the necessity for managers to have a framework for understanding how behavior can be influenced in an organizational context. Chapter 13 turns to the role of groups and teams and how managers can have an impact on improving their processes and performance. In Chapter 14, the topic of communication is explored for its implications in implementing effective leadership in organizations, and Chapter 15 examines the overall issue of managing human resources in the organizational context.

In Part 5, "Monitoring and Renewing," these two necessary managerial activities are addressed from several different perspectives. Chapter 16 reviews some of the basic evaluation and control challenges facing managers. Finally, Chapter 17 returns to the topic of change. Here, and building on some of the issues first discussed in Chapter 2 ("Managing Change"), the emphasis is on managers' proactive role in facilitating organizational renewal and development. That theme, renewal, seems an especially appropriate one on which to conclude the book.

concluding comments

As we conclude this chapter, we want again to reemphasize the recurring themes you will be encountering throughout the remainder of the book: Management involves constant attention to, and an embracement of, change; it cannot be carried out without an understanding of the impacts of technology on managerial functions and processes; and it requires a global as well as a local, or "own country," focus. Technology, globalization, and frequent change combined create a highly complex and challenging environment in which to manage. Managers throughout any organization must manage strategically in order to confront these challenges effectively. An organization's strategy should focus on resources that exploit opportunities for competitive advantage and sustain it.

Also, here at the end of Chapter 1, we want to remind you of the four perspectives we stressed earlier: (1) The Organizational Context: Management takes place in an organizational context; (2) The Human Factor: Management means getting things done through people; (3) Managing Paradoxes: Management involves mastering multiple and potentially conflicting situations simultaneously; and (4) Managerial Entrepreneurial Mind-set: Managers must continuously search for and exploit new opportunities. The challenge for you as a student is to learn more about the implications of these perspectives; that is, to learn more about the subtleties and complexities of the managerial process. This of course requires thought and analysis, but that, really, is only the beginning. Understanding management also requires an ability to synthesize and integrate a diverse array of facts, theories, viewpoints, and examples—in a phrase, as we emphasized earlier, to be able to "put it all together" so that the whole is indeed more than the sum of its parts.

Above all else, however, beyond analysis and synthesis, management requires skill in implementation. This is, perhaps, one of the most difficult skills to develop—how to put into practice the results of analysis and synthesis, and make decisions. If there is one skill that senior managers seem most concerned about among new managers, it is that of implementation.[23] They believe that the typical college graduate in business is much better at analysis than at implementation. Obviously, acquiring experience in managing helps considerably in developing the skill to be able to implement effectively, as both Meg Whitman and Ken Chenault have demonstrated. But experience by itself will not guarantee results. What is also needed is a heightened sensitivity to the importance of developing the skill of implementation. The lack of this skill is analogous to an athletic team formulating a good game plan but then fumbling the ball and dropping passes in the game itself—thus being guilty of "not executing." Therefore, as you read through the remainder of this book, keep to the forefront the message that management is not just about knowing; it is also, and emphatically so, about *doing*.

key terms

controlling 26	management 8	organizing 25
directing 26	organizations 8	planning 25

test your comprehension

1. What is management? Explain the different parts of the formal definition.
2. What is an organization?
3. Does management occur outside of organizations? Why or why not?
4. What creates the "personality" of an organization?
5. If you are an effective manager in one organization, will you automatically be as effective in all other organizations? Why or why not?
6. Identify three people skills important for managers.
7. What is meant by managing paradoxes?
8. Explain how a manager's life is both fragmented and integrated.
9. Why is it important for a manager to be both consistent and flexible?
10. What is the trade-off between reflection and action?
11. Why do managers need to be able to think globally but act locally?
12. Explain the types of commitment required of an effective manager.
13. What is an entrepreneurial mind-set and how does a manager develop and apply it?
14. What are four traditional components (functions) of the overall management process?
15. What is the importance of each of Mintzberg's 10 managerial roles?
16. Describe Stewart's three managerial job dimensions.
17. What are the three major types of skills managers need to develop? Why is each essential to be an effective manager?

apply your understanding

1. Why is it important to examine management from different perspectives? What do you gain from this type of examination? Think of other possible perspectives or metaphors you could use to describe management (e.g., management is a profession; management means "being in charge"). What does your new perspective tell you about management that adds to your understanding?
2. What do you think is the biggest personal reward of being a manager? What is the biggest potential "downside" of being a manager?

3. Think about two different managerial-type jobs you have personally observed (within your family, as a worker, as a customer, etc). Compare them using Stewart's concept of job dimensions. Considering each job's content as analyzed by the three dimensions, which one would you choose? Why?

4. This chapter states that effective managers need technical, interpersonal, and conceptual skills. Do all managers need these in the same mix? In other words, would some managers need more of one than of another? Why? Describe the managerial skills you think you need to develop to be an effective manager, and suggest how this might be done.

Managing Change

2

LEARNING OBJECTIVES

After studying this chapter, you should be able to:

- Explain why personal change is critical to managerial success.
- Describe the general process of change.
- Discuss three common failures of change.
- Describe the general process of enhancing change success.

Leading Change at LSP

Leading Signal Processing (LSP—a disguised name but a real company) produces diagnostic instruments primarily for the health care industry. Over most of its history, its leading-edge products, based on state-of-the-art analog signal technology, were used by scientific and hospital researchers in diagnostic tests and cellular and blood chemical analysis.

After years of success, the CEO noticed digital signal processing emerging as a competing technological platform, though initially it seemed unable to rival LSP's analog technology in performance. He also recognized a shift in customers and end users. In the past, M.D.s and Ph.D.s had performed diagnostics and analyses in research labs and hospitals; now technicians in clinics were increasingly performing these tests. Many of LSP's largest customers were slow to make this transition, but midsize and small customers were quickly changing over to save money. In addition, the market was moving away from separate tests and analyses toward integrated systems and analyses.

While LSP's CEO recognized that these environmental shifts would require changes to retain the company's competitive edge in the marketplace, many of the firm's scientists—analog technology experts—resisted, seeing digital technology as a threat to their jobs. The more the CEO talked about environmental shifts, the harder these scientists worked on customized analog products for customers, especially big customers.

The CEO also realized that the trend toward integrated systems would require LSP's workforce to collaborate using both cross-product and cross-functional teams composed of employees from research, development, marketing, and manufacturing. Such teamwork was rare within LSP.

As competitors brought new digital products to market, LSP's research scientists scoffed at their initially lower reliability and inferior performance. To help his subordinates see the urgent need for change, the R&D manager applied his "80/20 rule," a guideline suggesting that 20 percent of the problem accounted for 80 percent of the solution. He thought he could achieve most of the needed changes if his subordinates recognized the changes in customers and end users—the core 20 percent of the problem. So he hired a new employee who represented the

Medical and biotechnology companies face rapid do-or-die changes. Managers can't just seek to move the organization itself to the forefront. They also have to be prepared to help and persuade the people to personally embrace change. Not doing so can be fatal to the organization.

new users: a clinical technician who held an associate's degree, sported purple hair and a nose ring, had grown up on video games, and preferred intuitive, graphic user interfaces to the complicated text interfaces of LSP's current products. The scientists soon noticed the contrast between the old users and the new— and accepted the need for switching to digital technology and a more user-friendly product for less sophisticated customers.

Implementing the needed changes was even more difficult. Because LSP's scientists had never worked on cross-functional teams, they lacked the communication skills to work with non-scientists, and had poor group decision-making and conflict resolution skills. In addition, the R&D manager had to change his management methods. Instead of holding mainly technical discussions with subordinates, he now had to manage their interpersonal interactions. Thus, what started as a vital business change expanded to require personal changes among LSP's managers as well as changes in how these managers supervised their employees.

strategic overview

Many managers find themselves in situations similar to that of the CEO at LSP, in which they face the development of new digital technology and products. The CEO at LSP had to change the firm's strategy to match its competitors and retain its customers. However, he was slow to do so. He recognized early on that changes in the technology were occurring, but he failed to react, falling victim to some of the forces of failure explained later in this chapter.

LSP's CEO only took action after new digital products were introduced in the marketplace and some of the company's customers, especially small and newer ones, began to switch from the analog-based products to digital-based products. He "failed to see" the potential market for digital products among LSP's customers. He may also have been paralyzed by the uncertainty involved in introducing new technologies and new products based on them.

Even after the CEO recognized the need for change, he could not easily implement it. The researchers and scientists in LSP's R&D unit resisted change efforts. They were relying on more traditional "mental maps." It is likely that the inability to overcome these problems early cost LSP some of its customers. What's worse is that now it may be difficult to win them back. ▪

As a manager you will not only have opportunities to manage change at the organizational level, but you will increasingly have to manage change at a more micro level—managing team change, individual change in subordinates, and personal changes in yourself.[1] These more "micro" aspects of change should receive more attention. Failure to adapt personally, to help other individuals change, or to effectively lead change in a team can all have devastating effects not only for the individuals involved but for the organization overall. After all, how effective would LSP's CEO's effort to transform the company be if the R&D manager was unwilling or unable to change himself or others?

As we highlighted in Chapter 1, the environment for organizations today is one of constant change. Managers must help their organizations stay ahead of or maintain pace with competitors. They must respond effectively to changing societal demographics like the growing number of Hispanic citizens in the United States and rising numbers of women in the workforce. They also must respond to the development of new technologies and global political changes. Because change is so important, and managing it is such a challenge, it's the focus of this entire chapter.

IMPORTANCE OF UNDERSTANDING CHANGE

It's important to recognize that organizational change not only involves revising strategies, structures, or technology; it often requires changes at a more personal level. As the opening case illustrates, changing the strategy and products at LSP requires employees in the R&D area to change their capabilities and requires managers in the marketing department to change their customer knowledge base. Marketing managers need to have significantly more knowledge about new customers and end users. The change in strategy is not possible without individuals in the organization changing. For example, cross-functional teams are necessary to develop the new in-house technology and products to use it. To effectively implement cross-functional teams, the R&D managers must sometimes focus on managing the interpersonal relationships of team members rather than the technical aspects of the project they normally focus on. The managers may have to change how they motivate their subordinates, how they resolve conflicts, or their negotiation style, to support the new strategy. Clearly, change is a fact of organizational life that can affect all aspects of a manager's responsibilities. This is why change is a topic we're going to take on in each chapter. We'll also conclude the book with a chapter on the "macro" aspects of organizational change to bring the discussion full circle.

To help you appreciate this challenge of change and why we emphasize it in this book, let's look at just a few examples of the increasing importance of change in a manager's life and career.

Failure of Change Efforts

The first evidence that change is a subject worthy of extra focus is how often it fails. Obtaining accurate data on the frequency of failure is challenging, but one well-known authority states that between 50 and 70 percent of strategic change efforts fail to meet their objectives.[2]

Nature of Change

The nature of change may give us some insight into why it seems to fail so often and why dealing with it today and in the future is so challenging. Clearly, not all change is equal. Some needed change we can see coming and other change catches us totally by surprise. All other factors being equal, it is easier to deal with predictable change than unpredictable change. With predictable change not only can you see what is coming but you have the opportunity to prepare for the event in advance. For example, if you know the weather is going to change and it is going to snow heavily tomorrow, you can make advance preparations. You can change the worn-out tires on your car, set your alarm earlier to allow for extra driving time, and get back that winter coat that your brother borrowed from you. If you woke up to a totally unpredictable blizzard, your ability to deal effectively with it would be compromised. Exhibit 2.1 shows the results of a recent survey of executives as to how they perceive the predictability of the change they face. As you can see, the vast majority of executives feel that most of the change they face is highly unpredictable.

Some scholars have argued that to the extent that change is increasingly unpredictable, we may have to personally and organizationally change how we deal with it.[3] Instead of having concrete plans for how to respond to anticipated changes, we may have to be more flexible. For example, airline pilots do make flight plans, but they know they may encounter turbulence that will likely alter their flight plans. However, they do not try to specify in advance exactly how they will respond to changing conditions. For example, if they run into unexpected turbulence, they do not specify in advance that they will increase or decrease altitude by a specific amount, but they know that changing altitude is one of the key means they have of dealing with unpredicted changes in their environment.

While it is impossible to plan the details of anticipated change, researchers have found that the planning process for a major change effort can impact employee attitudes, which may ultimately have performance implications. Surveys conducted at two electric power generating plants operating in the challenging and turbulent environment of deregulation show that when employees feel that management is dealing with the change process in a procedurally just manner, trust in management increases.[4]

exhibit 2.1

Predictability of Change

Source: Canadian Conference Board, 2001.

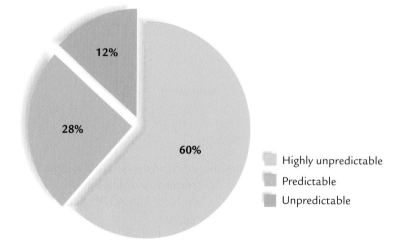

- Highly unpredictable
- Predictable
- Unpredictable

Rate of Change

Another factor that makes change worthy of special focus is the rate of change. Even if most change was unpredictable, if the rate of change was steady or declining, we might be more effective in dealing with it. While objective measures of the rate of change are somewhat hard to come by, the same survey of executives as in Exhibit 2.1 asked about the perceived rate of change. The vast majority of executives felt that the rate of change was increasing (see Exhibit 2.2).

In combination, Exhibits 2.1 and 2.2 offer some intriguing implications. If the rate of change is increasing, then we may benefit by increasing our ability to anticipate change. However, given that much of the change we face is somewhat unpredictable, we may benefit from increasing our ability to respond quickly to changes when we unexpectedly encounter them.[5] Enhancing both these abilities can help us perform better as managers. For example, suppose a new technology allows you to work on an engineering project simultaneously across several time zones with a team of individuals spread out geographically around the world. Further suppose that this in turn helps you respond to changes faster than other managers in your company. This might give you cost savings (e.g., from lower travel costs) and productivity gains (e.g., from faster project completion) that would help you stand out among managers in your company.

Managerial Competency for Leading Change

If we can safely assume that managing change is going to become more important for companies and managers,[6] then it might be instructive to know how good executives believe their managers are at this task. After all, even in the workplace, the rules of supply and demand apply. If the demand for effective leaders of change is high and increasing while the supply is low, then that places a premium price on those who can manage change effectively. That premium price may translate into rewards such as higher pay, more opportunities, or faster rates of promotions for managers who can distinguish themselves at this critical managerial activity.

Exhibit 2.3 suggests that senior executives in this same survey do not see an ample supply of capable leaders of change. Other studies have also

Ability to Manage Change
by Michael Hitt
Q&A
One**Key**
www.prenhall.com/onekey

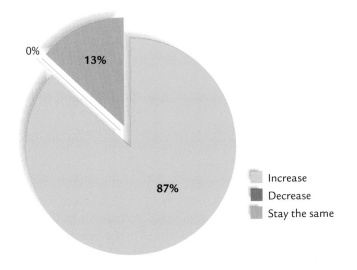

exhibit 2.2
Rate of Change

0%
13%
87%

Increase
Decrease
Stay the same

exhibit 2.3

Prevalence of Change Management Capability

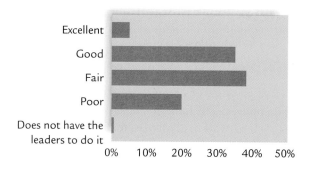

found that change management is consistently regarded as one of the most important capabilities for future leaders and at the same time is one that most managers need to improve.[7] In one study, more than 80 percent of senior executives surveyed and interviewed identified "change management" as one of the most important capabilities for future leaders. Interestingly, in this same study a majority of leaders expressed dissatisfaction with the current level of change management capabilities among even their high-potential managers.[8]

This suggests that the demand for effective managers of change far outstrips supply. This creates a premium for this managerial capability. It also creates a need and justification for special focus on this topic.

FORCES FOR CHANGE

The forces for change can come from almost anywhere. They can come from outside you or your organization and they can come from inside as well. Chapter 3 examines the nature of these forces in great depth. However, even without this in-depth coverage, it is easy to see their general impact on organizations and the people in them.

External Forces

External forces for change are significant for any organization. For example, a new competitor can be a powerful force for change. In fact, Kmart's bankruptcy in 2002 can largely be attributed to its slow response to Wal-Mart. Wal-Mart's early stores were primarily in rural areas and towns. Kmart stores were primarily located in urban areas. As a result, managers at Kmart mostly ignored the competitive threat of Wal-Mart, even when Wal-Mart began to open stores in urban areas. Managers at Kmart just couldn't imagine that a company based in the backwaters of Arkansas (Bentonville) posed a real competitive threat. By the time managers at Kmart tried to change and copy Wal-Mart's everyday low prices, it was too late. Many managers working for retailers in Japan, Germany, France, and other countries paid little attention to Kmart's plight. They failed to learn from Kmart's lack of recognition of the need to change or its slow change in response to Wal-Mart's rise. However, Wal-Mart's globalization and expansion abroad soon got the attention of foreign retailers as the company passed the $250 billion sales mark and became the largest company by revenues on the planet.

Technology can be another important external force for change. As the opening case demonstrated, a fundamental change in technology from analog to digital can require significant change in an organization. Managers at NEC, a large Japanese electronics firm, know this all too well. In the 1990s,

NEC was one of the leading makers of computer displays. Its displays were based on the CRT (cathode ray tube) technology used in television sets. At the time, Lucky Goldstar (now simply LG), a Korean electronics firm, was not a major player in computer displays. With the advent of new flat-screen technology, NEC essentially dropped out of the computer display market and LG rose to be one of the largest suppliers in the world.

Internal Forces

Internal forces for change can come in response to changes in the external environment as well as from change in leadership inside the company. For example, in the opening case, managers within LSP face a variety of changes in strategy, in products, and in working processes as a result of the CEO's view of the changing external environment. It is quite common for changes inside the company to be driven by changes in the company's external environment.

However, this does not need to be the case. Change can be driven by internal factors as well. For example, at Thermo Tech, a small manufacturing firm, a new manager, Tom, was hired. In his previous job and company, Tom had been very successful in getting greater productivity from workers by involving them more in decisions about their work process. Tom's view was that workers know the best way to get their jobs done and the product made, so it only made sense to him to involve them in coming up with new and more productive means of making the product. The supervisors who reported to Tom were of a different mindset and experience. They were used to telling workers how to do their jobs and "supervising" to ensure that they did what they were told. The changes Tom wanted to introduce required supervisors to listen more, ask more questions and provide fewer directives, seek worker input, and praise workers for their contributions. While not all the supervisors believed in the new approach, even those who did were not very skilled at the new required behaviors. Consequently, while they believed the new approach might lead to greater productivity, they were not confident in their ability to effectively implement the new approach immediately.

The key point is that change is a common challenge for most managers. The external environment is constantly changing. New competitors come on the scene; new technology makes old products obsolete or past manufacturing approaches too costly. Shifts in customer preferences can favor one company over another. Change in regulations and laws or in general economic conditions can all require changes inside the company in order for it to survive. The changes that the leadership of the company deem necessary in order to deal with the changes in the external environment ripple through the organization. Managers can find themselves needing to hire new employees with different skills, trying to change the mindset and capabilities of their existing subordinates, and changing their own knowledge and skills. But as we pointed out with the example of Tom, change can come to you even when nothing is changing on the outside. All you may need is a new manager, or for your old manager to get a new idea.

Consider the case of the U.S. Postal Service. While many people think of it as a slow-reacting bureaucracy, managers in the Postal Service have had to deal with and react to a number of changes in the external environment and inside the organization as well. As you read A Manager's Challenge, "Delivering Change at the U.S. Postal Service," ask yourself how well you might have reacted to these changes. How well do you think the managers within the U.S. Postal Service have responded to the needed changes?

a manager's challenge

Change

Delivering Change at the U.S. Postal Service

Imagine being part of the management team of a long-established service business buffeted by fast-moving forces beyond your control. Your facilities have been publicly implicated in the inadvertent spread of anthrax, a deadly biological substance. In addition, your customers are increasingly using newer, faster technologies instead of your slower, more traditional services. You have no idea what to expect as your busiest season approaches. What next?

These are two of the tough issues confronted by managers at the U.S. Postal Service (USPS), the former U.S. government agency that sorts and delivers millions of letters and packages every day. In recent years, managers at all levels within USPS have been challenged by rapidly developing environmental changes. For instance, when anthrax-tainted letters were found in the aftermath of the September 11 terrorist attacks, managers arranged massive decontamination efforts and tightened safety measures. Despite their efforts, the volume of domestic mail plummeted by about half in the following year, and as the economy remained sluggish, Postal Service revenues and profits suffered.

With an eye toward cost-cutting, Postal Service managers turned their attention to planning for the 2002 year-end blizzard of holiday cards and packages. Ordinarily, they paid extra to set up a special shipping and sorting network during December. To save money, they decided to work more closely with FedEx, a competitor in express delivery. The two companies had previously arranged for FedEx planes to carry some Postal Service mail between cities. Now, explained the vice president of the Postal Service's network operations, FedEx was going to carry "much greater volumes during Christmas at the current cost structure, which will be much less [costly] than putting up a dedicated fleet for 10 days."

In 2004, the Postal Service teamed up with United Parcel Service (UPS) to offer a cheaper, no-frills service called "Basic" to the customers of catalogue merchandisers. Shipping merchandise to rural, residential areas is costly for United Parcel Service, but the U.S. Postal Service travels those routes every day. If a customer requests Basic service, UPS picks up the merchandise and routes it to the U.S. Postal Service unit closest to the customer. The Postal Service then makes the final delivery to the customer. Basic service takes a little longer, but it costs customers less.

U.S. Postal Service managers were also concerned about how the Internet was affecting the company's revenues. They recognized that many people appreciated the conven-

Terrorists' anthrax spores, the Internet, and other new technologies have delivered many changes to the U.S. Postal Service in recent years. Ironically, in response to competitive pressures, the USPS teamed up with one of its biggest competitors—FedEx—something that would have been unthinkable back when the USPS was strictly a government organization.

ience of paying bills electronically rather than writing individual checks, inserting them in hand-addressed, stamped envelopes, and sending them by mail. So Postal Service managers decided to forge an alliance with CheckFree, one of the industry's pioneers. Customers pay $6.95 monthly to send up to 20 electronic payments anywhere in the United States. Because the fee is less than the price of buying 20 first-class stamps, the alliance between the Postal Service and CheckFree is expected to attract more customers and bring in more revenue for both companies in the coming years.

Similarly, Postal Service managers responded to the rising popularity of online auction services like eBay by identifying an opportunity to update the traditional cash-on-delivery service. Now a successful bidder can choose to pay for an online auction purchase when the postal carrier delivers it, rather than having to pay by credit card before the item is shipped. In this new twist on an old service, the seller sends the item via Pay at Delivery Priority Mail, requesting delivery confirmation. When the buyer pays and signs for the package, the carrier confirms payment by scanning the package identification. As soon as the confirmation is complete, the seller receives the buyer's payment. This represents yet another change that managers have made to remain competitive and responsive in today's fast-moving environment.

Sources: "New UPS Service Takes on USPS," *Catalog Age*, January 2004, p. 7; Stephen Pizzo, "The Check's Not in the Mail," *Forbes ASAP*, October 7, 2002, p. 14; Kristin S. Krause, "You Don't Have Mail," *Traffic World*, September 23, 2002, pp. 35+.

The key here is to simply recognize that the forces for personal or team change are enormous in number and in power. The practical implication is that personal change will be an inescapable issue for you as a manager. Consequently, at a micro level it is important to have an understanding of (1) the general process of change, (2) the general forces for change failure, and (3) keys for successful change.

PROCESS OF CHANGE

The fact that effective change management seems to be in high demand but short supply suggests that managing change is not an easy process. If it were easy and simple, we would certainly expect many more managers to have mastered it by now. After all, the demand for change management at any level (personal, team, or organizational) is not new. Consider this quote made 500 years ago by Niccolo Machiavelli:[9]

> There is nothing more difficult to carry out, nor more doubtful of success, nor more dangerous to handle than to initiate a new order of things. For the reformer has enemies in all those who profit by the old order, and only luke-warm defenders by all those who could profit by the new order. This luke-warmness arises from the incredulity of mankind who do not truly believe in anything new until they have had actual experience with it.

Thus, while the intensity and rate of change may be greater today than in the past, the basic demand for change management has been around for a very long time. Given that managing change is an important and challenging aspect of life for any manager, it is important to have an understanding of the basic process of change.

One of the most enduring, simple, and yet comprehensive frameworks of the change process was proposed by psychologist Kurt Lewin over 50 years ago.[10] He argued that change, including personal change, went through three distinctive phases: unfreezing, movement, and refreezing.

Phase 1—Unfreezing

As individuals we all develop habits. A habit is a patterned way of doing something that has been successful and therefore reinforced to the point that we exhibit the behavior without really thinking about it. For example, you may have a habit of turning right at a certain intersection in order to go home. This habit may become so strong that you find yourself turning right at that intersection even when you really need to go left in order to go to the grocery store rather than home.

We can think of this general process of forming habits in terms of simple and discrete behaviors, like turning right to go home, or in terms of more complex behavior patterns. For example, when confronted with a conflict, we might develop the pattern of taking steps to fight for our point of view, or we might develop a pattern of trying to avoid the conflict and confrontation.

Similarly, just as we can develop behavioral habits, we can develop cognitive habits or ways of seeing and interpreting events around us. Quite often the cognitive and behavioral patterns are linked. For example, if we form the pattern of viewing conflict as bad, then we might easily form the behavior pattern of trying to avoid conflict when it appears.[11]

In some cases, cognitive and behavioral traits may allow individuals or teams to better adapt to change, and affect performance. In a recent study[12] researchers found that after an unforeseen change in the task environment, teams whose members had higher cognitive abilities were more achievement-oriented and generally more open, and were able to adapt to their new roles better, resulting in higher performance.

Lewin argued that unless we undo or unfreeze these old patterns, it is difficult to change to something new. To better appreciate Lewin's notion, you might think about an ice sculpture. Suppose you wanted to change an ice sculpture of a bird into a fish. You could try to chip away at the old and fashion the new, but it's a difficult process. Instead, what would happen if you unfroze or melted the bird sculpture? You could then use the water to create a new block of ice from which you could carve a fish. Trying to simply carve a fish out of the original bird sculpture is perhaps possible but not very efficient or effective. In other words, from Lewin's perspective, changing to something new requires undoing or **unfreezing** something old. Lewin would probably not agree with the old adage that "you can't teach an old dog new tricks," but would instead argue that an old dog has difficulty unlearning old tricks.

unfreezing undoing old patterns

This was part of the problem for managers at NEC. Since the technology to produce flat panel screens is completely different than that used in CRTs, you have to let go of the old technology in order to get your mind around the new technology. In NEC's case, both senior executives as well as managers in the R&D area resisted letting go of the old. Some of the strongest champions of the new technology were younger scientists, but in a very hierarchical organization such as NEC, they were unable to get older managers to unfreeze their notions about what customers wanted in a computer screen—which was for it to be clear but take up less space.

Phase 2—Movement

Once old tricks are unfrozen, then you are in a position to actually move, to make the needed changes. As a manager, **movement** may involve changing your perceptions, decision making approach, communication style, and so on. Research has demonstrated that one of the biggest determinants of movement is the level of certainty or uncertainty associated with the change.[13] The greater the uncertainty of what will happen, generally the greater the resistance to the change and the less likely that there will be any movement in the desired direction of the change.

movement changing perceptions based on the level of certainty or uncertainty associated with the change

The context in which the decision to change is made can influence managers' perceptions of certainty or uncertainty. For example, in a study comparing a free-market economy (the United States) and a centrally planned economy (the Czech Republic in 1992), national institutional environments were shown to have a strong effect on the perceived level of uncertainty and risk in decision situations.[14]

In general, there is a relationship between the magnitude of the change and the level of uncertainty.[15] For example, the uncertainty of success associated with trying to jump across the Grand Canyon is much greater than that of trying to jump across a one-foot-wide ditch. As a result, you are more likely to try to jump across the ditch than the Grand Canyon. While this may seem obvious, this general principle is of great practical value to you as a manager. It means that as the level of uncertainty associated with a desired change increases so will the likely level of resistance, and therefore, the more you will have to put into planning and preparation in order make the change a success.

We can go back to our opening case to get a concrete example of this. LSP faced several changes that were significant in nature. The magnitude of the changes made the outcome of trying to make the changes somewhat uncertain. Readers with background in engineering or other related sciences will know that the jump from analog signal processing to digital is not a small one. Engineers trained in analog cannot become digital scientists overnight or even over many months. The technologies are significantly different from each other. In addition, the jump from separate diagnostic and testing products to integrated systems is not a small one. Additionally, designing the products so that technicians with two years of college could operate them correctly versus research scientists with Ph.D.s or physicians with medical degrees also represented a major change.

Phase 3—Refreezing

But suppose you see the need for the change and to unfreeze the past; further suppose that you make the initial change. Are you confident that the change will last? What percentage of people who start a new diet or exercise program stick with it? It is less than one in four. Lewin contended that the "pull" of old habits was strong and that simply making the move from the old to the new was not enough to ensure lasting success.[16] This was in part because, whatever it was, the "old" pattern existed in the first place because it was rewarded with success. In other words, most people have the communication patterns, leadership style, decision-making approach, and so on because they worked in the past. In this sense, you can think of old habits and patterns as having a kind of gravity that will pull us back to them unless a greater force is in place to keep us moving forward.

Thus, Lewin talked about "refreezing" after the movement phase. When most people hear the term "refreezing," they usually get images of things frozen solid and unmovable. But Lewin did not mean that the new state should be static with no movement. He did not mean for the term to imply that once change is made there should be no monitoring or adjusting. Instead, the term was designed to reflect the notion that after a change is made forces need to be put in place to keep people and behaviors from giving in to the gravitational pull of the past and reverting back to old patterns.

As a consequence, **refreezing** involves monitoring the change to see if it is producing the anticipated and desired results. To the extent the change is succeeding, the refreezing phase should involve reinforcing the change so that it becomes more established.[17]

refreezing the process of reinforcing change so that it becomes established

One of the changes that needed refreezing for LSP managers was working in cross-functional teams rather than in isolation. Previously, most managers at LSP simply worked with others in their own discipline of R&D, product design, manufacturing, or marketing. The change toward integrated systems that less sophisticated customers could use required employees to work in teams that included members from other disciplines. For example, the teams needed representatives from marketing to provide insights about future customers so that software designers could make the user interface easy for technicians with little education to navigate. Even after employees understood the need for these cross-functional teams and even after they started working in them, they needed continued encouragement and reinforcement to do so. Without this, individuals tended to gravitate back to the areas and people they knew and not work to understand others on the team who came from different disciplines. Cross-functional team managers had to consistently schedule team meetings and praise individuals and groups when they worked on a task together in order to reinforce the new, cross-functional behavior.

For most students and managers, Lewin's model of change makes intuitive sense. It can even make change seem simple. However, we all know that change is not easy. This naturally raises the question "What gets in the way of successful change and how can we overcome these barriers?"

FORCES FOR FAILURE

As we mentioned near the beginning of this chapter, most change initiatives fail. Successful change is uncommon. There are powerful forces that work against change. To help illustrate the forces for failure, we integrate Lewin's model with a more recent framework, which draws on the same principles but illustrates them in a visual way.[18] Exhibit 2.4 illustrates the basics of this framework.

Most change is preceded by something. Usually, it is preceded by success. In other words, people usually have a history of doing the right thing and doing it well. Then something changes in the external or internal environment and the right thing becomes the wrong thing. For example, suppose you had the habit of making decisions on your own without seeking input from subordinates. This pattern worked for you for many years, in part because the decisions you faced as a manager were fairly simple. You had all the knowledge you needed to make the decisions without seeking the input of others. Your individual decision-making approach was right and you were good at it. Then something happened. The nature of your company's customers changed. They now require much more sophisticated products. These new products involve technologies that are new to you. You now need to involve others more in decision making because you don't have all the information or answers on your own. The environment has shifted and what used to be the right thing—individual decision making—is now the wrong thing. However, you are still very good at it.

Starting the change process requires the recognition that what was right for the past is wrong for the future. This is the unfreezing process. If you fail to recognize that the change in customer requirements demands a change in your decision-making approach, the whole change process never even gets started. However, even if you begin to notice that your old approach is not

exhibit 2.4

Change Failure Framework

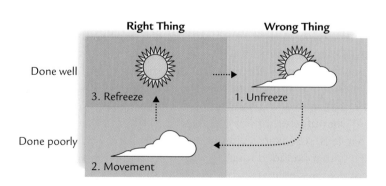

working so well, you also need to recognize not just that individual decision making is now wrong, but that a more participative approach is the new, "right" or required approach.

Unfortunately, even if we accept that the old right thing (e.g., individual decision making) is now the wrong thing, and even if we accept that participative decision making is the new right thing, we do not typically become instantly good at it. As Exhibit 2.4 illustrates, we often have to go from doing the wrong thing well to doing the right thing poorly. For example, if you have made decisions on an individual basis for many years, even if you recognize the need to make decisions in a more participative manner by involving others, you are not likely to be great at it at first. Few of us expect to be proficient instantly at something new, even if we believe that we must make the change. Unless people are confident that they can go from doing the new right thing poorly to doing it well, they fail to move.[19]

As we mentioned, this was part of the reason that the supervisors at Thermo Tech who wanted to adopt Tom's new approach resisted the change at first. They knew that they did not have the skills and abilities and therefore would not instantly be good at getting line workers to offer suggestions for improving productivity. They resisted the change at first because they lacked confidence in their ability to make the change.

Once you start to move toward the new right thing, the gravity of the old starts exerting its force and pulling you back from the change. This is why Tom had to provide extra encouragement to his supervisors at first. Once they became proficient enough, natural positive consequences followed the new behaviors and reinforced or refroze them. Once Tom's supervisors started getting line employees to submit and implement improvement suggestions, and once productivity started improving, the supervisors were motivated to continue in the new behaviors. However, failure often happens during the refreezing phase because, unlike Tom, many managers fail to sufficiently monitor or reinforce the new behaviors. As a result people fail to finish.

Now that we have an overall framework, let's look more specifically at the three failures—failure to see, failure to move, and failure to finish—in order to better understand the dynamics of these change failures, so that we can discuss how to overcome them and effectively manage change in ourselves, in our subordinates, and in teams that we may have to lead.

Unfreezing: The Failure to See

As we mentioned earlier, if people fail to see the need for change, then change cannot get started. So the natural question is "What keeps people from seeing the need to change?"

The Power of Past Mental Maps To answer this question, we must revisit the issue of how we develop certain cognitive or behavioral patterns in the first place. To help with this analysis, we might think of these habitual cognitive patterns as mental maps.[20] Like physical maps, mental maps guide us. We use them to interpret landmarks and decide where we are and how to get to where we want to go. Imagine having a city map that showed a park where there wasn't one, that had a street turning left when it really turned right, or that did not show an intersection where one existed. What would you do with that map? On the other hand, suppose you had a map that was successful at helping you navigate the city, that helped you effectively get where you wanted to go. What would you do with that map? No doubt you would throw

mental map habitual cognitive patterns

out the first and hang on to the second map. Like physical maps, we tend to retain the **mental maps** that have proven successful in the past and throw out those that have not.

For example, suppose you had a cognitive map that led you to believe that conflict was bad, and you followed that map by avoiding conflict when it emerged. You would tend to continue this pattern or hold on to the mental map only if it worked. In other words, if avoiding conflict usually kept you out of uncomfortable confrontations, and if these conflicts you avoided subsequently just disappeared, you would likely hang on to this "conflict avoidance" map. On the other hand, if your attempts to avoid conflicts consistently allowed the conflicts to grow in intensity and later emerge as unavoidable and larger confrontations, you would likely throw out your "conflict avoidance" mental map.

In general, the longer a given mental map has proven itself successful in the past, the harder it will be to give up.[21] In one sense, we can view this as a positive and natural "self-preservation" mechanism. After all, what would happen if we randomly held on to or jettisoned mental maps and their associated patterns of behavior? We would randomly "live and die" as our behaviors did and didn't fit the environment. As conscious creatures, humans tend to have an aversion for random survival. In LSP's case, these old mental maps had been successful for years. Why should the scientists throw them out for "no good reason"?

Overly Simplistic View of the Past and Future   Thus, past success is one of the forces that keeps us from seeing the need for change and even starting the unfreezing process. Even when our past maps begin to falter, past successes simply outnumber and overwhelm the current failures. However, to better understand this phenomenon, we need to dig a little deeper. Part of the reason that current failures do not easily override past success and easily jumpstart the unfreezing process of change is because we often take a somewhat simplistic perspective of the past, present, and future.

As an example, suppose you had a pattern of leading subordinates by telling them exactly what to do, when to do it, and how to do it (what is often referred to in the popular press as "micro management"). Suppose this approach worked for you nine times in a row. On the tenth time, this approach didn't work and you got a bad result. Would you likely change your leadership style when you face your eleventh situation? Based on ten past incidents, it can seem as though you have a 90 percent chance that your directive leadership style will work in the future.

However, this is true only if the future environment or context is the same as the past in which your leadership style worked. For example, your directive leadership style may have worked in the past because the tasks your subordinates faced were simple and well understood by you, or because your subordinates were not very knowledgeable about the tasks. Consequently, you could tell them what to do and they were willing to accept your direction. If the current and future environment involves tasks that are significantly more complex, the complexity may exceed your ability to direct your subordinates' every move. Furthermore, if your subordinates are more capable than they were in the past, they may not need or want your micro management.

Unless you see the difference in the context, you are unlikely to see the need to change your leadership style. In fact, if you do not see the difference in context, it is quite likely that it will take a big disaster or a number of smaller failures before you even begin to question the robustness of your past directive leadership style for the future. After all, one failure in light of nine successes is not very convincing that your style needs to change.

However, five failures in light of nine successes may begin to cause you to question the appropriateness of your directive leadership style for the future. While it is natural for people to wait until the number of failures mounts before they change because they fail to recognize the differences between the past and future context, it can often be quite expensive. Failures are not usually free; they typically have costs (financial, reputational, etc.) associated with them.

Thus, one of the strongest forces for failure to see the need to change is failure to look at and recognize differences between the past and current (as well as future) context. Until we can overcome this force for failure in ourselves and others, it is unlikely that unfreezing will occur and that the change process will even get started.

Maintaining Equilibrium Unfortunately, research and experience have shown that people have an almost automatic or instinctive resistance to unfreezing attempts, and an inherent desire to maintain equilibrium.[22] To better appreciate this, try a simple experiment. Stand face-to-face with a friend. Both of you raise your hands to about chest level with your palms out, facing each other. Now, put the palms of your hands against the palms of your friend. Next, push against your friend's palms to force him or her backward. What happens? Almost instinctively, your friend will push back against you. Normally, he or she will match your pressure so that your hands stay in about the same position and neither person is pushed off balance. In other words, by matching the pressure you exert, the other person keeps the physical position of your hands in equilibrium.

This is often what happens in people. For example, as scientists at LSP were pressured to change, they pushed back with an equal force (i.e., they worked harder on custom analog solutions for big customers) in order to maintain equilibrium.

In summary, there are three key forces that keep the unfreezing part of the change process from even getting started. First, what is to be changed or unfrozen is most likely there for good reason. Whatever the cognitive and associated behavioral pattern, it likely exists because it worked in the past. Second, we often fail to look at and recognize differences in context between the past and present (as well as the future). As a consequence, we typically discount current incidents of failure weight more heavily the past incidents of success. Thus, we fail to recognize the need for change. Third, there seems to be a natural tendency for people to resist pressures to change in order to maintain equilibrium. Consequently, quite often the more pressure that is applied to unfreeze things, the greater the resistance.

Movement: Failure to Move

As we mentioned earlier, even if people see the need for change, they still may not make the desired change. But you might wonder, "Why would people fail to move if they see the need?"

Much of the answer to this question lies in the nature of the desired change. As we mentioned earlier, typically the larger the desired change the greater the associated uncertainty. However, change uncertainty is not a generic phenomenon. It has at least three critical dimensions.[23] Understanding each dimension enables you as a manager to better plan and prepare for the needed steps to achieve the desired movement.

Change Uncertainty The first aspect of change uncertainty is centered in the change itself. As we already mentioned, people's current mental maps and behavior patterns exist because they have proven successful in the past. As the environment changes and what worked before begins to fail, people do question the validity of their past maps and behavior patterns for the future. However, research has found that if all people have is evidence that their old map is wrong but they do not have a clear idea about what new map would be right, they tend to stay with what they know—they tend to keep using the old map even though they are aware that it has faults. In other words, something (even if it is flawed) is better than nothing.

To help illustrate this principle in a more concrete fashion, let's return to the example of leadership style. Suppose you find that your old directive way of leading is just not quite as successful today as it was in the past. Further suppose that you recognize this and see that there is a need for change. What would you do if it were *not* clear to you what new leadership style you should move toward? You might venture off into the unknown and randomly try some new leadership style. You might, but most people don't.

In this we are reminded of the old joke about a man who lost his ring. He searches madly for it and along comes someone who asks, "What did you lose?" "My ring," he replies in a panic. "Where did you lose it?" asks the passerby. "Way over there," the man answers, frantically pointing in a direction away from his current search. "Then why are you looking here?" queries the intended helper. "Because this is where the light is," states the hopeless searcher.

People stay where the light is even when they recognize it is the wrong place. People often keep doing what they do well, even when they recognize that it has become irrelevant, if the new direction that they should go is not clear. Even if they recognize that there is a need to change because things are not working as well as before, if they lack a clear alternative, they quite often intensify their efforts at doing what they know.

Outcome Uncertainty People also fail to move because of uncertainty regarding the outcomes of the change. In other words, people ask themselves the question "Even if I know where I'm going, how clear is it that good things (or bad things) will happen when I get there?" For example, what results will you achieve if you switch from a directive to a coaching leadership style? The less clear the answers are to these sorts of questions, the less likely you are to change.

Requirement Uncertainty The third aspect of change uncertainty has to do with the requirements for the change. In other words, how clear is it that those that have to make the change have what it takes? Do they believe they have the knowledge, skills, tools, and so on, to make the change?

To help illustrate this, imagine that you are the manager of a small group of customer service representatives in a company call center. In the past, the company was focused on trying to serve as many customers as possible. Therefore, in an effort to answer as many calls as possible in a given amount of time, customer service representatives tried to keep the calls short. If they did not have an immediate answer to a customer's question, they passed off (transferred) the customer to the "appropriate" department. Often customers would get passed from one person to another and finally hang up in frustration, never to buy anything from the company again. Now the company executives realize this and instruct managers, such as yourself, to change focus from number of calls to customer satisfaction. You help your people understand what the new objective is (i.e., customer satisfaction). You explain that job performance and therefore job security, pay raises, even bonuses will be based on customer satisfaction and not on the number of calls answered. The threat of job loss and the size of the pay raises and bonuses are all significant. Yet, as you observe your people, they do not seem to be changing. Why? Even if they can see the new destination and even if they value the outcomes of reaching it, they ask themselves, "Do I have what it takes to satisfy customers? Do I have the knowledge I need to answer their questions without having to transfer them to another department? Do I have the communication skills to make my answers clear to customers?" If they do not believe they have what it takes, they are unlikely to make the change, even if they can see that a great reward awaits them if they do change.

Refreezing: Failure to Finish

This final stage of Lewin's change framework is important because he recognized, and research has confirmed, that without reinforcement people will return to past habits and patterns.[24] This is especially true if the results from the change are slow in coming. This is in part why people have difficulty changing their diet or exercise habits. They want the envisioned changes in their fitness or appearance, but when those results are slow in coming, they often return to the old habits.

To better understand the forces that lead to the failure to finish, we have to keep in mind that part of the gravitational pull of past patterns is the past positive consequences they generated. For example, if you had the pattern of sleeping in late and eating cheesecake, it was in part because there were positive consequences for these behaviors. It felt good to sleep in and cheesecake tasted so great. Even if you decide to change and exercise each day and eat more broccoli, if positive consequences of the new behavior are slow in coming, the positive consequences of sleeping in and eating cheesecake become more powerful and pull you back.

The truth is that most significant change does not produce instant, positive consequences. The lack of reinforcement of the new behaviors allows the gravitational forces of the old to pull us back. There are two key reasons why most change efforts do not produce instant, positive consequences.

First, in many cases the change involves something new—new behaviors, new thinking, new skills, and so on. Most people are not instantly good at things they have not done before. Because they are not instantly good, it is only natural that they do not instantly generate good consequences. A customer service representative is unlikely to go instantly from not being able to answer complicated customer queries and having to transfer customers on to someone else to being able to answer all questions and not having to pass off customers. Thus, when they try to answer customer questions without passing the customer on, service reps are likely to *not* do a good job *initially* and may at first actually cause even higher customer *dis*satisfaction. These negative consequences are likely to continue until the service reps get better and reach a certain level of proficiency. Until that point, the negative consequence of customer dissatisfaction plus the positive old and familiar consequence of passing customers on can cause the service rep to give up on the new change and go back to the old way. This leads them to fail to finish. To summarize, the first reason change fails to stick is because the positive consequences that would naturally reinforce the desired change do not happen immediately. They do not happen immediately because the person is not instantly good at the new behavior.

The second reason that change fails to stick is because, even if one persists in the new behavior and incrementally gets better at it, the long process of improvement often makes people feel lost. They don't know where they are in the process and are not sure how much progress they are truly making. When people feel lost, they tend to give up and quit trying to move forward. They fail to finish. After all, what good does it do, they ask themselves, to keep moving when you are not sure that the effort you are expending is doing any good? Anyone who has studied a foreign language can easily appreciate this phenomenon. Often, you study and study and practice and practice, but you are not sure what progress you are really making. Because the progress is small and incremental, it is hard to notice. Without a sense of progress, you give up.

KEYS TO SUCCESSFUL CHANGE

With the overall framework of unfreeze, move, and refreeze and the related common failures of seeing, moving, and finishing, practicing managers want to know how they can overcome the common failures and successfully lead and manage change in themselves and others. That's precisely what the next three sections address.

Overcoming the Failure to See

If people are blind to the need for change, how can you help them see? You can't just say, "See!" If people could see the environmental shifts and therefore the needed changes on their own without your help, they probably would. To better understand why we fail to see the need to change and how we can overcome this failure, we can gain some insights from physical sight. To see physical objects, we need contrast in shape, light, color, and so on.[25] We also see best those objects that are directly in front of us rather than off to the side in our peripheral vision. Even though, in the context of change we are not talking about seeing physical objects, the two factors that help us see physical objects—contrast and confrontation—apply to helping people see the need for change.

contrast a means by which people perceive differences

Contrast   As we mentioned, **contrast** is one of the key means by which the human eye distinguishes different objects. In combination, differences in shape, brightness, and color give us contrast. The letters on this page stand out because of the contrast of black against white. It is such a simple notion that we generally take it for granted. But look at how the contrast lessens as you look from left to right in Exhibit 2.5.

In this simple example, the different levels of contrast are easy to see. In complex personal, team, or organizational settings, there are so many things to look at that people can (and do) selectively focus on elements from the past and present that are similar rather than different. In effect, they can choose to ignore key contrasts and thereby avoid looking at why what worked in the

exhibit 2.5
Declining Contrast

past might not work in the future. This brings us to the second part of the answer to overcoming the failure to see—**confrontation**.

confrontation a means of helping people to perceive contrasts by providing an inescapable experience

Confrontation It is precisely because the organizational and business realities we face are complex that people are able to ignore or literally be blind to the "obvious" differences between the past and present. This is why they do not see the reasons that strategies, structures, cultural values, processes, technologies, and so on must change. The fact that most people do not easily see these contrasts is clear and compelling evidence that they cannot be left on their own to visualize them. Just as we "forced" you to see the contrasts among the balls by putting them front and center on the page, managers often have to confront their people with the key contrasts between the past, present, and future.

Combining Contrast and Confrontation Hewlett-Packard (HP) is a well-known technology company. One of its most important businesses is printers. Printers account for about two-thirds of its profits. However, from 1997 through 1999, HP managers saw their strong position begin to slip away, especially in the low-end range of their product line. Lexmark, a competitor, introduced good-quality printers for under $100 and saw its share of the market double to 14 percent. In response to this change in the environment, the head of the unit, Vyomesh Joshi, determined that HP had to change. It had to build a new line of printers, including a printer for under $49 or $30 cheaper than its least expensive printer at the time. He also challenged his group to go from "concept to shelf" (from idea to putting the printer on retailers' shelves) in three years rather than the normal four.

Most HP managers said they thought building a printer for $49 instead of $79 was impossible. Tom Alexander, a key project manager, knew he needed to "explode their complacency." In a team meeting he created a high-contrast and highly confrontational experience that helped people get past the failure to see. After listening to people say how impossible the task was, Tom grabbed an HP printer, put it on the floor, and stood on it—all 200 pounds of him. In that instant, the people in the room broke through the failure to see barrier and got the message. HP printers did not need to be engineered and constructed as stepping stools. As long as they were, it would be impossible to bring down the cost.

In the end, HP managers delivered a line of 14 inkjet printers and 7 "all-in-one" printers based on just two cost-efficient platforms. The new line came in on time and at the desired cost, including a printer for $49. Following their introduction, HP sold $5.6 billion worth of the new printers (a 12 percent year-over-year increase) at a profit margin of 16.5 percent (a 14 percent increase in profitability). HP took 70 percent of the market share, and much of it came from Lexmark.[26]

Creating High Contrast One of the first keys in creating effective and high contrast is focusing people's attention on key differences. In general, this is often referred to as the 80/20 rule.[27] In general, this "rule" suggests that 80 percent of the desired outcome is provided by 20 percent of the contributing factors. For example, quite often 80 percent of a company's revenues are accounted for by 20 percent of its customers. We also see cases in team sports where 80 percent of the points are provided by 20 percent of the players. While there may be many differences or contrasts that explain 100 percent of the need for change, pointing them all out can often overwhelm or confuse people. This is why it is effective to focus on the core contrasts. At HP, much of a printer's high cost was due to materials and construction that were stronger than needed. Customers needed printers to print, not to stand on. Tom Alexander helped his team see that. The team lowered the new line of printers' cost by changing the design to use less plastic in the case and by using thinner and cheaper plastic. While you can no longer stand on HP printers, you can buy a high-quality one for under $50.

In addition to focusing on the core contrasts, you also want to help people see and remember those key differences. Research has clearly demonstrated that the more you create images in people's minds, the more clearly they can recall the associated messages. There is a reason the old adage says that "a picture is worth a thousand words." Thus, two keys to successfully creating effective contrasts are to first focus on the critical differences and to create images (versus just presenting numbers or words) in people's minds. The image of Tom standing on the old HP printer was worth more in changing people's minds than all the numbers about how Lexmark was taking market share away from them.

Creating Confrontation Clearly pointing out the contrasts between the old and new is a critical first step. However, pointing these contrasts out once is usually not enough. Twice is not enough. To ensure a high level of confrontation, you will likely have to present the contrasts repeatedly, so employees will not view them as "one-time passing parades" which they can simply ignore. Repetition is a powerful means of ensuring high confrontation. However, it is not the only means. An additional means is employing what we might call "inescapable experiences." These experiences need to be of such a nature that they are not easily avoided and that involve as many of the senses—touch, smell, sight, sound, taste—as possible. We know from a wide body of scientific literature that the more senses involved and the deeper their involvement, the higher the impact of the experience and the more that is learned and retained.

A Manager's Challenge on Samsung Electronics illustrates how one executive created a high-contrast and high-confrontation experience for his subordinates in order to bring about needed change. Do you think the same result could have been achieved through a less involved or expensive experience?

To summarize, the steps to creating high contrast and confrontation are as follows:

- Focus on the key differences or contrast—don't "over complicate" the picture.
- Create visual images, or pictures, of the old and new so that the contrast is more than mere words.
- Repeat the messages of the old and new maps over and over and over again.
- Create high-impact, inescapable confrontations.
  - Make sure that the experience involves as many of the senses as possible.
  - Physically ensure that people cannot easily avoid the experience but must take the brunt of it right between the eyes.

Overcoming the Failure to Move

Simplified, some of the most practical and powerful steps in ensuring change success involve overcoming the three sources of uncertainty described earlier in this chapter. Consequently, even after people see that the old way is not working any more and recognize the need for change, they need to see clearly and believe in an alternative to the old way. One of the first means of overcoming the failure to move is to educate people as to what the desired change is. If you want to change from an individual decision-making style, you need

globalization *a manager's challenge*

Changing the International Approach at Samsung

Samsung Electronics is by most accounts *the* leading consumer electronics company in Korea. It has the largest market share and a premiere quality image in Korea. As a consequence, managers in the company became accustomed to premium placement in Korean stores and managed the sales of their products accordingly. Furthermore, managers were used to regular attention and essentially free advertising from Korean newspapers when they launched new products. The company enjoyed high consumer awareness and a good image of the brand in people's minds. When the company expanded operations in the United States, Samsung managers tried to manage their products as they had in Korea. They tried to get premium placement and attention from the media.

To make a long story short, things did not go as expected. The CEO in Korea was convinced that Samsung had to operate differently in the United States than at home, but the message just did not seem to be getting through to his managers. In an effort to change their mental maps, he created an inescapable, high-contrast experience. He put over 50 of the most senior executives on a plane and flew them to the United States. Once there, they went to visit over a dozen stores across the country. The contrasts were stark. Rather than being sold in small shops, as in Korea, Samsung's electronics were being sold in large stores in the United States. And instead of getting prime merchandising space, they were in the bargain bin under the "Clearance Sale" sign, behind market leaders like Sony and even second-tier brands like GE and Philips. Samsung executives could see where their products were displayed, touch the stores, and hear customer comments as they shopped. The brand was king at home but not in the United States. Samsung executives could not escape the repeated and intensive experience there, and the contrast and confrontation had a serious impact on them.

After this experience, the managers at Samsung who were responsible for the United States merchandising approach stopped trying to manage their products as they had in Korea. Instead of trying to sell a premium brand image in the United States, they stressed the value of their

To get its executives to think in more global terms, Samsung sent its executives on a U.S. "shopping spree." The executives were able to see how their products were displayed and sold in America versus Korea, enabling them to see better ways to position the company's products internationally. It was a stark awakening for the executives who weren't used to seeing their products positioned on the back shelves.

products. In other words they stressed the quality and reliability of their products and the great value they provided given the lower price consumers would have to pay compared to a Sony product. In effect, they tried to say, "With Samsung you get nearly the same quality as Sony but for a lot less money." They also abandoned their efforts to work with small shops and instead concentrated on relationships with big stores such as Circuit City, Wal-Mart, and Best Buy.

to not only recognize the need to change, but you have to see the new approach. You may have to get a clear picture of what it looks like to involve others in making decisions. You may have to educate yourself as to how you can effectively involve others in gathering and processing information. Until the new destination is clear, you are likely to stay where you are.

However, simply making the alternative or new destination clear may not be sufficient to get the desired movement or change. Let's return to the example of you as the manager of a team of customer service representatives. You have helped your team see the changes in customer expectations and therefore the need to switch from call processing to customer service. You clearly describe the new destination of customer service. You explain that the objective is to be sure you understand the customer's question and that you answer the question without having to pass the customer on to someone else. Even if people now see the need to change and can clearly envision the new destination, they may fail to move. In addition to helping your people see the new destination, you have to help them see the anticipated benefits of going there. If you want to make a change in their behavior, they must not only have the new behavior clearly in mind, but the anticipated benefits as well. Even after they can picture what good customer service looks like, you have to ensure that they can clearly see the anticipated benefits. You have to help them see how they will benefit if they stop focusing on the number of calls they handle and instead focus on fully answering customers' queries without transferring them from one department to another.

Unfortunately, even if you overcome these first two sources of uncertainty, you are still likely to have to overcome the final one as well, in order to ensure change. As we mentioned earlier in the chapter, the final source of change uncertainty lies in the uncertainty in people's minds about whether they have what it takes to make the change. To overcome this force for failure to move, you have a three-part task. First, you have to know and understand what it takes to execute the change. Citing our previous example, you have to know what knowledge, communication skills, and so on it takes to satisfy customers who call in. Second, you have to assess the level of capabilities possessed by your customer service representatives versus those required. Third and finally, you have to help your subordinates bridge the gap through training, tools, or other resources.[28]

A Manager's Challenge regarding the changes at Oracle helps to illustrate these principles. Oracle is in the midst of a significant change. It will no doubt take some time to see how successful the change will be. However, the significant success of the company and the approach its managers and salespeople have taken in the past makes the current change that much more difficult. In the end, even if salespeople and managers see the need for the change and can clearly envision the new destination, it is not yet clear that adequate training, resources, mentoring, and so on have been put in place to reinforce the desired change.

To summarize, the steps necessary to ensure movement are as follows:

1. Make sure the desired change is clear to those that are expected to achieve it.
2. Make sure those who are required to make the change see and believe in the benefits of the change.
3. Make sure that those needing to make the change have the tools, skills, knowledge, and other resources they need to make the change.
   - Assess the required resources.
   - Assess the gap between required and possessed resources.
   - Bridge the gap.

Overcoming the Failure to Finish

Let's again put you in as manager of the customer service team. Suppose you have been able to get your team to see the need for change and have gotten them moving toward the change. How can you ensure that movement continues and avoid the failure to finish problem? How can you, in Lewin's terms,

a manager's challenge
Change

Managing Change at Oracle

Founder and CEO Larry Ellison has never made any secret of his ambition to drive Oracle to the top as the largest software firm on the planet. Second only to Microsoft in terms of annual revenues from software, California-based Oracle has long been known for its excellent database management software—which dominates the industry—and the tenacity of its aggressive and knowledgeable sales force.

Ellison and his management team saw Internet technology as an opportunity to expand Oracle's product line beyond database management into software for customer relationship management, human resources management, and other applications. This change in strategy thrust the company into heated competition with SAP, Siebel Systems, and other well-established software providers. Meanwhile, IBM and Microsoft (among others) introduced database management software to rival Oracle's market-leading product.

Now, instead of learning about and selling a single, superior product, Oracle's salespeople had to become familiar with a wider range of products and contend with a variety of experienced competitors offering similar products. Although their success was the key to reinvigorating corporate revenues and profits, the salespeople lacked the training and knowledge to match customers with the appropriate specialized software products. The aggressive sales approach that built Oracle into an industry powerhouse—in which salespeople vied to meet demanding quotas—was no longer effective in building long-term relationships with companies that had multiple needs and systems.

Oracle's CEO recognized that change was needed. "We can't possibly have salespeople who are experts in every-thing from our database to our application server," Ellison said. "That's simply impossible." As a result, Kevin Fitzgerald, who manages Oracle's government, education, and health care sales, reorganized his sales personnel so each specialized in certain software products. Similarly, George Roberts, who was in charge of managing North American sales, reorganized the salespeople who sell to major companies so each specialized in particular Oracle products. Management also changed the compensation structure so sales personnel would receive a flat commission and would not be rewarded for overstating a product's capabilities or pushing inappropriate products just to make quota. The goal was to transform Oracle's culture from a highly aggressive one to one that was more customer-oriented. "Culturally, Oracle is doing everything it can to operate differently," stressed Ellison.

Small examples suggest that the organization is moving in the right direction. For instance, the company subsequently released a guide to pricing policies in response to confusion over pricing options. The purpose of the guide is "to let customers make better software purchasing decisions," says Jacqueline Woods, vice president of global licensing and pricing strategy. It later introduced a grid outlining flexible pricing. Now a company can add or subtract Oracle software licenses for its CPUs when its workload changes (for instance, if it needs more processing power at the end of the quarter to close its books). Oracle is also considering an annual software licensing fee to make the pricing even simpler for customers. Small changes such as these indicate that Oracle's managers and salespeople can change, given the right resources, skills, and motivation.

Sources: John S. McCright, "Oracle Keys on SMBs," *Business 2.0*, October 13, 2003, p. 25; Ian Mount, "Out of Control," *Business 2.0*, August 2002, pp. 38+; Monica Roman, "Oracle's Outlook Is Cloudy," *BusinessWeek*, September 30, 2002, p. 48; "Oracle Guide Aims to Clear Up Policies," *eWeek*, August 28, 2002, www.eweek.com.

---

refreeze and ensure that the change lasts? The key lies in addressing the two forces of failure we discussed earlier in this chapter.

As we mentioned, the pull of past patterns and the lack of early, natural positive consequences often causes change not to last. Refreezing is not an instant process because instant expertise in the new behavior is almost never possible. For example, improvement in customer service comes gradually. Early attempts by your customer service reps to answer customer questions and not pass customers on are likely to produce poor results. Customers may even ask to be passed on: "Well, if you can't answer my question, then connect me with someone who can." Initial low proficiency at customer service will produce negative consequences that in general tend to drive out the desired behavior. Consequently, something has to substitute for the early negative consequences and compensate for the likely negative consequences that naturally follow poor proficiency.

For example, suppose one of your customer service reps tries to answer a customer's question but does not do a great job. The customer complains to the service rep: "You don't seem to know very much or have many answers." The service rep might understandably want to revert back to the old pattern and simply pass the customer on to someone else. The old pattern of passing customers on always had the benefit of the sales rep being able to avoid listening to a customer's complaint about not being able to answer the question. In the past, before the customer could really state the complaint, he or she was passed on to somebody else. To compensate for the negative consequences that typically follow early poor proficiency, and to help refreeze the change, you will likely have to do something extra to reinforce the desired behavior. For example, you may have to say, "Jim, I know that call did not go the way you wanted but your effort to answer the customer's question is exactly what we want and what we mean by customer service. I really appreciate your effort." Without positive consequences such as this praise to compensate for the natural negative consequences of low initial proficiency, change toward customer service is hard to maintain.

Once your customer service reps reach a good level of proficiency, they will likely generate their own natural positive consequences. For example, as they gain proficiency and can answer customer questions, they may get unsolicited "thank you's" from customers. At that point, you may be able to modify your motivation approach (which we will cover in depth later in this text). However, until a level of proficiency in the change is achieved that is sufficient to generate positive consequences, you are likely to have to compensate for the natural and negative consequences that come from early poor proficiency.

Many authors and studies of change have addressed the importance of early and consistent positive reinforcement of desired change. In the popular literature on change this theoretically important notion is often referred to as ensuring **early wins**. Whether this or another popular term is used, the concept and the theory behind it are the same. When people engage in change, they need early and consistent reinforcement to overcome the gravitational pull of past patterns and build momentum in moving toward establishing new patterns.[29]

Even if this is successful in getting your customer service reps to not give up on the change, it may not be sufficient to completely refreeze the desired change. The positive consequences you provide through your encouragement are immediate, but what about the pay raise and bonus that your reps are also expecting from this change in customer service? They are not instant. Furthermore, your subordinates may be making progress and slowly getting better at customer service, but it may be difficult for them to determine exactly where they are and how much farther they have to go in order to get the pay raise and bonus they desire.

To the extent that these other rewards are not immediate and to the extent that your customer reps are not sure what progress they are making and may feel lost, they are likely to reduce their efforts or give up on the change. Consequently, it is important to provide feedback on progress so that they gain a sense of movement and progression. This feedback should first and foremost focus on their personal progress. Often, this requires managers to sit down with subordinates in a face-to-face conversation. Managers should point out those areas where subordinates have made progress. As we have stated, the more complicated or long the change, the harder it can be for individuals to have a clear sense of personal progress. However, in cases where the change is not just individual but involves others, people benefit from knowing how the group is pro-

early wins early and consistent positive reinforcement of desired change gressing collectively. For example, at Thermo Tech, Tom gathered productivity data and shared the results with his supervisors and workers to help them see the impact their suggestions were having on results such as output, quality, and cost.

To summarize, the steps to refreezing change effectively are as follows:

1. Create early wins and reinforce desired behavior even when desired outcomes do not emerge because of early lack of proficiency in the new behaviors.

2. Help people see the progress of the change.
   - Inform them of their personal progress.
   - Inform them of the collective progress.

3. Repeat the messages of the old and new maps over and over and over again.

4. Create high-impact, inescapable confrontations.
   - Make sure that the experience involves as many of the senses as possible.
   - Physically ensure that people cannot easily avoid the experience but must take the brunt of it right between the eyes.

managerial perspectives revisited

1   **PERSPECTIVE 1: THE ORGANIZATIONAL CONTEXT**   The context of the particular organization you work in is critical to change. The more changes in the environment outside the organization, the higher the likelihood that changes will occur inside the organization. Clearly, this in turn could require you as a manager to lead changes in your team and to make personal changes as well. The overall responsiveness of your organization is an additional contextual factor of importance. The more responsive the overall organization, in general the higher the demands on you to make changes. As a result, you have to be tuned in to what is going on around your organization, and to the level of responsiveness and expectations of change inside your organization. As we highlighted in the case of the U.S. Postal Service, even if the organization has been slow to change in the past, managers who don't appreciate the greater need for change and the organization's higher responsiveness level would find themselves out of synch with the demands of their job and the expectations of their bosses.

2   **PERSPECTIVE 2: THE HUMAN FACTOR**   Obviously, personal changes that you need to make in your managerial capabilities and approach will be done primarily by you. However, as a manager you can only get team changes made through others. You cannot make the changes for others. If the change is from call processing to customer service, you cannot make the change for your people; they have to implement the change, and until they do, the anticipated organizational benefits will not materialize. While we will highlight change in all the chapters, change has a special relationship with motivation, and we will highlight this in Chapter 12, because, in a sense, implementing change through others involves motivating them to behave differently.

3   **PERSPECTIVE 3: MASTERING PARADOXES**   Because this chapter has focused on change, it is easy to get the impression that when change is needed everything that is old is no good and should be eliminated and replaced by all new and better activities, processes, products, and technologies. It is rarely the case that all the old behaviors or mental maps are no longer good and should be changed. One of the key challenges for managers is to carefully determine what about the "old" ways remains appropriate or effective and what needs to be modified or changed for the future. Mastering the paradox of reinforcing and retaining some current mental maps and behaviors while at the same time unfreezing, changing, and refreezing new mental maps and behaviors is critical to managerial success. This is one of the challenges facing Oracle. On the one hand, they have to change the salespeople's focus on selling one product and being an expert at it to selling a suite of products; on the other hand, they need to preserve their traditional level of drive, motivation, and sense of responsibility.

 PERSPECTIVE 4: ENTREPRENEURIAL MIND-SET   Having and using an entrepreneurial mind-set will facilitate change. In fact, managers who have such a mind-set not only expect but hope for changes to occur in order to take advantage of new opportunities. They constantly search for information and suggest the need for change, and they identify opportunities and exploit them. If, for example, LSP's CEO had possessed an entrepreneurial mindset, he likely would have instituted changes at the *first sign* of digital technology and his company might have been at the forefront of developing and introducing digital products.

Managers having an entrepreneurial mind-set are committed to change and they expect it to be a continuous "way of life" within their organizations. As we have tried to stress in this chapter, patterns of thinking and behaving are established and once established are resistant to change. This was the case at HP. Even though Alexander's standing on an old printer was a key event in getting his team to see the need for change, it took over three years of continuous effort before the desired benefits really showed up in terms of sales and profits. Making change takes serious commitment to continuous learning, yet with an entrepreneurial mindset, such a commitment is much easier. And an organization oriented to continuous change is more likely to be entrepreneurial and remain at the forefront of its industry.

concluding comments

Lewin's theory of change is not only well supported by research but intuitive to both students and practicing managers. We have found the matrix in Exhibit 2.4 a helpful means of capturing the basic elements of change (i.e., unfreeze, movement, refreeze).

As we have stressed, most change is preceded by a history of success. In other words, people usually have a history of doing the right thing and doing it well. Then something changes in the external and/or internal environment and the right thing becomes the wrong thing. Starting the change process begins with recognizing the need to change and unfreezing the past.

Even if you recognize the need for change, change can fail to get going if the new destination is not clear. Unfortunately, even if the target of change is clear, people may still fail to move. They may see the need and even have a clear vision of where they are supposed to go, and still fail to move. They may fail to move because they do not believe that they have what it takes to get there or because they do not believe that the journey and arrival will lead to rewards they value.

For most people going from being competent to incompetent is not an appealing proposition. Consequently, having a clear idea of the change, seeing the benefits of the change, and having the required resources and capabilities to execute the change are required for movement. For most people, movement comes when they can see and believe in a path or a way that will take them from doing the new right thing poorly to doing it well.

Once people start to move toward the new right thing, it is critical to provide early wins to reinforce the desired change. As a manager you will likely have to provide reinforcement until people get to a level of proficiency where they are doing the new right thing and doing it well enough that the expected positive consequences naturally follow. However, as they move, you will also need to help people know how they are progressing individually and collectively in order to continue the refreezing process.

key terms

confrontation   57

contrast   56

early wins   62

mental map   52

movement   48

refreezing   49

unfreezing   48

test your comprehension

1. Why would an increase in the rate of change be important to managers?
2. What is a habit and how does a habit get established?
3. Explain the notion of unfreezing as described by Lewin.
4. Define *refreezing*.
5. How does past success keep people from seeing the need to change?
6. Why do people fail to move or change when there is uncertainty about the required change?
7. How does uncertainty about the outcomes of change affect "movement" or change efforts?
8. If an individual is clear about the nature of the change and its consequences, how does uncertainty about requirements for the change affect movement?
9. What is the "gravitational pull" of past patterns and how does it inhibit refreezing efforts?
10. Why is refreezing an important part of the change process?

11. What role does proficiency at the new behaviors play in refreezing?
12. Why is feedback important in the refreezing process?
13. What role do contrast and confrontation play in unfreezing and overcoming the failure to see the need for change?
14. What is the 80/20 rule and why is it important in the unfreezing process?
15. In addition to a clear target or destination for change, what are the other two factors that are critical to success?
16. Why is it often necessary to provide counterbalancing or compensatory positive consequences early in the refreezing process?
17. What role do natural, positive consequences play in the refreezing process?
18. Why are "early wins" an important aspect of successful refreezing?
19. Why is it important to communicate progress in the refreezing process?

apply your understanding

1. As you think about your own personal history, how difficult has it been for you to make behavioral changes? If you were being interviewed for a job and were asked to describe an incident that demonstrates your ability to change, what would you say?

2. Think about a recent organizational change at school, at work, or someplace else in which you participated. Would you rate it a success or a failure? In either case, based on the concepts in this chapter, what do you see as the strengths and weaknesses of the change effort?

3. If you were to look back on change efforts you led or helped manage, what do you think you did well? In retrospect, what would you do differently and why?

4. As you think about potential change efforts that you may have to manage in the future, what aspects of change management do you think you need to strengthen and why? What aspects do you believe will be strengths that you can leverage?

practice your capabilities

You work as a design engineer in the United States for a Japanese automobile manufacturer. The company has been very successful in the United States; for example, the Carmen is consistently one of the best-selling cars in America. The company has also done well in the SUV (sports utility vehicle) segment. However, in the United States trucks have been gaining market share in terms of the total number of vehicles purchased. Now almost as many trucks are purchased each year as cars. While your company has had a strong reputation with its small trucks, it has no full-size models. This is important because profits and growth are greatest in this segment. You and your bosses have tried to convince the executives in Japan that the company should enter the full-size truck segment. However, it is an expensive move, costing several billion dollars to design, test, and launch a new full-size truck.

The executives in Japan have experience in making only small trucks or large commercial vehicles. The company holds the number-one position in Japan in small trucks and the number-two position in commercial trucks, and it has held these positions for years. Their image of a full-size truck owner in the United States is someone who lives in Nebraska on a farm or someone who lives in Texas and has a gun rack in the back window of his or her truck.

You have tried to convince the executives that regular families, not just ranchers, farmers, and construction workers, buy full-size trucks. Because people use trucks for family transportation, you have tried to convince the senior executive in Tokyo not only to enter the full-size truck segment, but also to produce a four-door model from the outset. Executives in Japan view four-door, full-size trucks as commercial vehicles used by power companies working rural power lines or logging companies hauling crews back and forth between the job site and the nearest town.

You have shown them data that suggest that these perceptions are not correct. The vast majority of full-size trucks never see a dirt road and the majority of four-door trucks from companies such as Ford and GM are purchased with the middle- to highest-end interior options such as leather, wood trim, and CD players. Still, the Japanese executives remain resistant to change.

1. Using some of the concepts from this chapter, what are the key contrasts between the past and the future that the Japanese executives may be failing to see?

2. How can you highlight the key contrasts to help them change their mental maps?

3. What sort of inescapable experience might you be able to use to place the contrasts directly in front of the Japanese executives?

closing case
DEVELOP YOUR CRITICAL THINKING

Changing the Direction of 3M

Managers are proud to work at 3M—and with good cause. 3M has been heralded as one of the great examples of success through change and innovation. Scotch tape and Post-it Notes are just two of its many product innovations. Over the years 3M has thrived by hiring talented scientists and researchers and encouraging them to spend part of every workweek (and some of the company's money) on projects that intrigued them. Small wonder, then, that some managers were concerned when they learned that, for the first time in 3M's 100-year history, an outsider was being brought in as CEO. The new CEO, James McNerney, came from GE, a company known more for its disciplined execution than its freewheeling innovation.

Despite its long-term success, 3M's overhead costs had ballooned and overall growth had slowed by the time McNerney arrived. The company was selling 50,000 industrial and consumer products, but a good number were merely size and color variations of basic items such as pink and not just yellow Post-it Notes. McNerney imposed order by reorganizing the products under six broad categories: health care; specialty materials; industrial products; consumer and office products; electro and communications products; and transportation, graphics, and safety products.

Still, managers were relieved to learn that while McNerney saw the need for changes, he also viewed 3M as a solid company with market-leading products. Rather than make major management changes, McNerney and his team sought ways to lower expenses through selective layoffs, shifting some production overseas, centralizing the purchasing process, cutting the supplier roster, and other cost-cutting measures. In one year, these moves shaved $600 million from 3M's expenses.

McNerney also instituted a systematic process for streamlining internal inefficiencies and improving quality. For example, the company was losing $1 million per year as a result of occasional cracks in its dental ceramics material. Under the new system, specially trained managers investigated and determined that the ceramics were not being correctly cured. Fixing this problem cost relatively little but gave a sizable boost to 3M's bottom line—just one example of effectively applying discipline and direction to a creative company.

Although product development had traditionally been 3M's strength, McNerney believed the company could do a better job of identifying the most promising new items and speeding them to market. In the past, 3M personnel were guided by the rule that "no market, no end product is so small as to be scorned." Sometimes the company would start building a plant for a new product even before the marketing department had finished analyzing the marketplace. Changes were needed to stay competitive in today's pressured business environment. In particular, McNerney wanted 3M employees to have "a more reality-based way of looking at the world."

With about 1,500 products under consideration at any given moment—and a $1 billion research-and-development budget—R&D managers were challenged to change their approach as well. Instead of saying "yes" to most ideas and then letting the marketplace select winners and losers, R&D managers were asked to change and determine early in the development process which ideas had the highest business potential before moving ahead with additional investment. In fact, to facilitate this change, McNerney even considered offering a special award to employees whose ideas were turned down—to publicly demonstrate the importance of understanding when to not move ahead. "I've got to make it culturally okay to say 'no,'" he said. "A 'no' means you can get back to something that has a greater chance of success."

While 3M managers were glad to hear McNerney say, "If I end up killing the entrepreneurial spirit [in 3M], I will have failed," many were nonetheless nervous about the push for accelerated product development, which meant bringing high-potential products to market in half the time. After all, no one predicted much demand for Post-it Notes until after the product was "smuggled" into the market and customers started requesting the product, which was not officially in production. How would middle managers help their subordinates understand the dual notion of "disciplined innovation" and learn to apply it in their areas of expertise?

To send a clear signal about the seriousness of these changes and reward managers who excelled in implementing them, McNerney revamped 3M's performance management and development practices. First, he abolished the company's seniority-based compensation plan in favor of a merit-based structure that offered more pay and promotions to outstanding employees and managers. Next, he established a leadership development school to prepare up-and-coming managers for more responsibility. These changes reinforced a sense of urgency throughout 3M's 70,000-strong workforce and ensured that high-performing managers at all levels would receive financial rewards.

Proposing such changes in a century-old company would have been nearly impossible if the workforce had not been receptive. "I found readiness to change, which quite honestly surprised me," McNerney said. "More people told me to change things than told me not to change things." The CEO has made change more palatable by publicly praising the achievements of 3M's managers and employees. He told *Fortune* magazine: "I think the story here is rejuvenation of a talented group of people rather than replacement of a mediocre group of people. This is a fundamentally strong company. The inventiveness of the people here is in contrast with any other place I've seen."

More changes are ahead. McNerny pushed managers to move 3M into services, an area where the company has little experience, and senior managers now provide more direction on budget allocations to ensure that departments working on higher-potential products receive suffi-cient resources. "I want people to start competing for resources around here again," McNerney commented.

Although he initially shook up 3M, the company has been flying high since McNerney's overhaul. It has posted record earnings and profits, and its share price has steadily climbed.

Questions

1. What patterns did McNerney and his senior managers want to unfreeze within 3M? What patterns did they want to refreeze—and why?

2. If you were a manager at 3M, what kinds of outcomes (such as early wins) would you look for as evidence that the company is embracing change?

3. How would you apply the 80/20 rule fostering change at 3M?

4. Did McNerney and his senior managers try to change too much, too quickly? Should he have accepted the status quo at 3M for a longer time period before implementing his changes? Explain your answer.

Sources: Matthew Miller, "Slimming Down, Bulking Up," *Forbes*, January 12, 2004, p. 175; Jerry Useem, "Jim McNerney Thinks He Can Turn 3M from a Good Company into a Great One—With Help from His Former Employer, General Electric," *Fortune*, August 12, 2002, pp. 127–32; Michael Arndt, "3M: A Lab for Growth?" *BusinessWeek*, January 21, 2002, pp. 50–51; "Q & A with 3M's James McNerney: 'Cash Generation' Is the Aim of the First-Year CEO," *BusinessWeek Online*, January 21, 2002, www.businessweek.com/magazine/content/02_03/b3766086.htm.

integrative case

Clifford Chance—Update

London
Business
School

By Callum Campbell

Ten years after Geoffrey Howe gazed from the window of his new offices, Clifford Chance had outgrown its Aldersgate headquarters, and the firm had had to retain additional City of London offices. The current managing partner, Peter Cornell, now surveyed a different firm in a very different legal market.

Throughout the 1990s, Clifford Chance continued to add offices to its network (Prague in 1995, Bangkok in 1996, São Paulo in 1998), and to increase the number of staff in its existing offices. By 2002, Clifford Chance had succeeded in becoming the world's largest law firm, by virtue of both its size (3,322 lawyers) and gross revenue ($1,409,032,200). In 1993, 80 percent of the firm's lawyers had been based in its London office. Howe's ambition to globalize the firm had been further realized by the fact that 63 percent of the firm's lawyers were now based outside of London.

The last decade had witnessed wholesale change in the legal industry. Where lawyers once assumed they would stay in the same law firm for life, the aggressive and hostile lateral hire of partners, teams, and the merger of whole firms had become the typical strategies in growing a law firm, strategies which were almost unheard of in 1992. In much of Europe and Asia, City of London–origin firms now dominated the landscape. U.S. firms had made fresh inroads into Europe, many striving to blend into the market as "local players." Global brands had yet to entirely usurp other international strategies. The "best-friends" network established by Slaughter and May in the U.K., Hengeler Mueller in Germany, and Bredin Prat in Paris still won covetable mandates, and remained highly profitable. In each European jurisdiction, independent firms, often outcasts or willing exiles from large mergers, continued to thrive. The most profitable law firms in the world, such as Wachtell Lipton Rosen & Katz, were based almost exclusively in New York. But the number of national firms able to compete for high-end corporate, corporate finance, and banking work was dwindling in step with the expansion of large international networks, like Clifford Chance.

Geoffrey Howe's ambition for his firm in 1993 had taken it to the top of the league tables. But getting there had necessitated a change in strategy. Organic growth could put an office anywhere on the planet, but could not provide critical mass. Nor could it satisfy the firm's aspirations in the key markets of the United States or Germany. On January 1, 2000, Clifford Chance announced the legal industry's most ambitious merger to date, simultaneously joining forces with the 400-lawyer, New York–based law firm Rogers & Wells, and the 260-lawyer, Frankfurt-based firm, Pünder, Volhard, Weber & Axster.

Since the fall of the Berlin Wall, Germany had seen an influx of law firms from both the U.S. and the U.K. Prior to 1990, foreign firms were prevented from merging with German firms or establishing a presence in Germany by vigorously upheld Bar Association restrictions. Liberalization of the industry transformed the market. The three largest firms in Germany, Freshfields Bruckhaus Deringer, Linklaters Oppenhoff & Rädler, and Clifford Chance Pünder, were all the result of Anglo-German mergers, and the majority of the top 15 firms in the country were the offspring of mergers with either U.S. or U.K. firms. Clifford Chance's acquisition of Pünder, Volhard was a bold step that brought it an instant presence with a well-respected, if not top-flight, German firm. It was rumored that the courtship had been competitive, as 15 British firms had been in con-

Callum Campbell (EMBA–Global 2003) prepared this update under the direction of Professor Maury Peiperl from public sources. It is designed as a supplement to the case "Clifford Chance: International Expansion" (© 1993, 1994 INSEAD) from *Managing Change: Cases and Concepts* by Maury Peiperl and Todd Jick (Irwin/McGraw-Hill, 2003). ©2003 by London Business School.

tact to discuss possible mergers before the firm decided to throw in its lot with Clifford Chance.

The acquisition of Rogers & Wells was more remarkable. A big merger between a U.S. and a U.K. firm had long been predicted. The first marriage, observers speculated, would precipitate a flurry of engagements. But no one, it seemed, was anxious to go first.

Rogers & Wells traced its history to 1871 when attorney Walter Carter established an office in the New York Life Building to represent insurance companies bankrupted by the Great Chicago Fire of the same year. Prior to the merger, Rogers & Wells had offices in London, Paris, Frankfurt, and Hong Kong. Forty percent of its work was for foreign clients, or U.S. clients abroad. And it had a healthy turnover: gross revenue the year before the merger was $214 million with profits per partner at $760,000.

But Rogers & Wells was perceived to lack a unified firm culture. The managing partner of one New York firm described it in January 2003 as "more a collection of departments, some very good and some less so." At the time of the merger it could boast a top-of-the-line intellectual property practice representing DuPont, among others, and one of the finest antitrust practices, headed by the phenomenally successful Kevin Arquit. Rogers & Wells did not, however, have the resources or critical mass to compete head to head with firms like Clifford Chance on the global stage.

At the same time, Clifford Chance was starting to cash in on its earlier growth strategy. Gross revenue was up to $709 million. Profits per partner were $904,000. But while it had tried hard to build a successful securities practice in New York, it came up against resistance from the established New York players. When the head of that office, Stephen Hood, met Rogers & Wells' managing partner Laurence Cranch at a San Francisco conference, they jointly perceived a mutual interest. The two firms had complementary corporate finance practices; Rogers & Wells' exemplary antitrust practice would fit nicely with Clifford Chance's corporate capability, and other practice areas—regulatory, IP, litigation—could only be improved by expansions. And they already shared clients, including Chase Manhattan, Citigroup, Merrill Lynch, and Morgan Stanley. Stuart Popham, then head of global finance at Clifford Chance, enthused at the time of the merger: "In Rogers & Wells, we found the perfect fit. We were happy to make a commitment." He later said the marriage was "encouraged by our clients."[1]

Leaving aside the cultural challenges to be faced in the merger, a major sticking point remained—the issue of partner remuneration. Clifford Chance was wedded to a lockstep system—partner compensation was accorded by virtue of seniority and seniority alone. Rogers & Wells, by contrast, operated on an "eat-what-you-kill" basis, with partners rewarded according to the revenue they generated for the firm. The disparity between the firms' compensation spreads was also significant. The lowest-earning partners at Rogers & Wells were taking home only $290,000; high earners, $2.3 million—a compensation spread of 1:8. At Clifford Chance, the spread was no more than 1:2.5. Those at the bottom of the lockstep took home £430,000, but maximum compensation was £1.1 million. Once partners got to the top, their remuneration ceased increasing. In the eyes of high-earners at "eat-what-you-kill" firms, the lockstep system was a barrier to just reward. To its proponents, the lockstep system brought a firm and its partners closer together. The two systems represented two quite different paradigms of professional service firm management.

The merger went ahead as planned on January 1, 2000, without the lockstep issue having been resolved. For the first year and a half, partners at the legacy firms continued as they had before. The eventual solution to the remuneration dilemma involved moving Rogers & Wells' partners into the Clifford Chance lockstep system, using a number of criteria, including but not limited to seniority. For several Rogers & Wells partners, that meant a big reduction in take-home pay. But there were high-earning partners that neither firm wanted to lose. Kevin Arquit and Steve Newborn were seen not just as brilliant practitioners within their own sphere, but crucial to bringing work into the corporate department. To keep them in the fold, they would have to be compensated well above the top of the lockstep. And those partners that were taking home less than the lockstep minimum would continue to do so until they moved up.

The jury was still out on the success of the transatlantic merger. The firm was facing charges that it had "de-equitized" the partners of Rogers & Wells. In a memo reported on the front page of the *Financial Times* in October 2001, the firm's U.S. associates explained why Clifford Chance came last in a survey of U.S. law firms, and further charged that the survey "captured neither the breadth nor the depth of associate anger and frustration." And perhaps the most concrete sign that things had not gone according to plan came in December 2002, when Kevin Arquit announced that he would be leaving Clifford Chance for the New York firm Simpson Thacher & Bartlett, a highly-regarded practice, but without Clifford Chance's global reach. Arquit was on record as having said that one of the attractions of Simpson Thacher was its smaller size.

Elsewhere in the network, there had been challenges to the firm's global management. In early summer 2002, three partners and 26 associates left the firm's Italian

Clifford Chance
(from January 1, 2003)

Senior Partner	Stuart Popham	London
Management Committee		
Managing Partner	Peter Cornell	London
London Managing Partner	Peter Charlton	London
Asia Managing Partner	Jim Baird	Hong Kong
U.S. Managing Partner	John Carroll	New York
Continental European Managing Partner	Hans-Josef Schneider	Frankfurt
Finance Director	Chris Merry	London
Executive Partner	Chris Perrin	London
Executive Partner	Phillip Palmer	London
Global Head of Corporate	David Childs	London
Global Head of Litigation	Jim Benedict	New York
Global Head of Finance	Mark Campbell	London
Global Head of Capital Markets	David Dunningham	London
Global Head of Real Estate	Cliff McAuley	London
Global Head of Tax	Douglas French	London

offices in a dispute over the firm's attempts to bring Italian management practices in line with the rest of the firm. And in Bangkok, a former partner was suing the firm for $30 million, accusing Clifford Chance of "imperialism" in its approach to its Asian offices.

An article in the U.K. press entitled "Rule Britannia"[2] argued that the London firms that had globalized were failing to reflect this global footprint in their management structure. The table above shows the results of the 2002 management elections and the extent to which Clifford Chance's strategy continued to be run by London-based lawyers.

Clifford Chance had experienced phenomenal success over the previous ten years. But it was not yet clear that Geoffrey Howe's desire to make the firm truly international had yet been realized. Sixty-three percent of the firm's lawyers now worked outside of the U.K., the second-highest percentage of any of the world's 100 largest law firms. But the London office remained *primus inter pares*—with revenues of £412 million, and a 41 percent profit margin. (The firm's worldwide profit margin was 32 percent.)

In its marketing literature Clifford Chance repeatedly referred to itself as "a truly integrated global law firm." The reality was that while Clifford Chance had made extraordinary progress, the results were still mixed, and it had yet to shed its reputation as a London firm.

exhibit 1

Rank of Law Firms by Number of Lawyers

Top law firms by number of lawyers	No. of lawyers	Countries in which firm has offices	Lawyers outside home country
Clifford Chance (U.K.)	3322	19	63%
Baker & McKenzie (U.S.)	3094	37	83%
Freshfields Bruckhaus Deringer (U.K.)	2430	18	61%
Allen & Overy (U.K.)	2197	20	48%
Linklaters (U.K.)	2000	22	52%
Eversheds (U.K.)	1776	6	4%
Skadden, Arps, Slate, Meagher & Flom (U.S.)	1653	12	10%
Jones, Day, Reavis & Pogue (U.S.)	1565	12	18%
Lovells (U.K.)	1432	15	55%
White & Case (U.S.)	1427	24	60%

Source: American Lawyer *Global 100*, November 2002.

exhibit 2

Rank of Law Firms by Revenues

Rank by revenue	Firm	Gross revenue 2001–2003	Average revenue per lawyer
1	**Clifford Chance**	$1,409,032,200	$424,152
2	Skadden, Arps, Slate, Meagher & Flom	$1,225,000,000	$765,000
3	Freshfields Bruckhaus Deringer	$1,060,716,000	$436,509
4	Baker & McKenzie	$1,000,000,000	$330,000
5	Linklaters	$ 917,376,000	$458,688
6	Allen & Overy	$ 834,238,800	$379,717
7	Jones, Day, Reavis & Pogue	$ 790,000,000	$535,000
8	Latham & Watkins	$ 769,500,000	$660,000
9	Sidley Austin Brown & Wood	$ 715,000,000	$560,000
10	Shearman & Sterling	$ 619,500,000	$595,000

Source: American Lawyer *Global 100*, November 2002.

exhibit 3

Clifford Chance Offices Worldwide

Location	Year of Opening	Partners	Other legal advisers	Trainees
Amsterdam	1973	23	117	3
Bangkok	1996	6	26	0
Barcelona	1993	3	18	14
Beijing	1985	1	10	0
Berlin	1990	11	27	0
Brussels	1968	8	48	1
Budapest	1993	4	18	16
Dubai	1976	3	26	3
Düsseldorf	1990	25	104	0
Frankfurt	1949	74	252	4
Hong Kong	1980	31	112	17
Los Angeles	2002	2	10	0
Luxembourg	1982	5	19	8
London	1987	233	880	208
Madrid	1980	19	52	35
Milan	1993	14	60	25
Moscow	1991	5	31	4
Munich	1996	10	34	0
New York	1871	98	380	3
Padua	1997	1	6	5
Palo Alto	2002	2	5	0
Paris	1962	29	172	23
Prague	1995	2	7	11
Rome	1993	6	21	9
San Diego	2002	2	6	0
San Francisco	2002	14	35	0
Shanghai	1993	2	15	1
Singapore	1981	6	15	4

(continued)

exhibit 3
(continued)

Location	Year of Opening	Partners	Other legal advisers	Trainees
São Paulo	1998	1	11	5
Tokyo	1987	11	38	3
Warsaw	1992	6	13	18
Washington, DC	1949	15	84	0

Personnel Worldwide:

Total number of staff   7,500

Total number of legal advisers (of whom 665 were partners)
   and trainees   3,700

(Approximate figures as at December 31, 2002)

Source: Adapted from www.CliffordChance.com.

Assessing External Environments

3

LEARNING OBJECTIVES

After studying this chapter, you should be able to:

■

Articulate the role of the external environment in management decisions and effectiveness.

■

Explain the five major dimensions of an organization's general environment.

■

Describe the critical forces in the organization's task environment.

■

Describe the key elements of an organization's global environment.

■

Describe the key considerations in conducting effective environmental scanning.

Russia's Black Gold?

Finding oil and gas reserves hiding beneath thousands of feet of dirt and rock is challenge enough for managers in oil and gas companies such as ExxonMobil or British Petroleum. Add to that the challenge of managing operations in locations where political instability, economic turbulence, and social opposition exist—all of which can dramatically affect the organization's performance—and you have a *real* challenge on your hands. This is the case for oil and gas managers looking at opportunities in the former Soviet Union.

As strange as it might sound, many managers of foreign oil companies long for the old days when permission to explore, drill, extract, transport, or sell oil and gas was tightly controlled by the central oil ministry of the former Soviet Union. But after its fall, if managers wanted to drill in Kazakhstan, for example, and ship crude oil to Italy for refining, they had to negotiate separate agreements with Kazakhstan, Russia, and Georgia, depending on the chosen transportation route. There was no guarantee that the government that signed the agreement one particular day would be the one that was in power the next.

As a result, in the 1980s, thousands of wells in Russia lay untapped. The natural pressure pushing the oil to the surface was gone, and the Russians lacked the technology to force the remaining oil out of the ground. Neglect and financial troubles beset Russia throughout the 1990s and reduced production to an all-time low of 6 million barrels per day in 1996.

But in the last five years, a combination of rising world oil prices and increased exports, mostly to Western Europe, have made it more worthwhile than ever to pursue oil and gas production in the former Soviet Union. In 2001 the Russian government proposed changes to the tax code that decreased some of the financing risks that had suppressed investment in oil and gas projects in the past.

Things are so dramatically different, in fact, that today Russia is the world's biggest oil producer. It has more oil and gas reserves than any other country—nearly 350 billion barrels. That's almost 50 billion more than Saudi Arabia. Russian companies, which are now mostly privatized, have invested billions of dollars and raised production by 40 percent since 1998. They've also watched their stock prices soar as a result.

The country's second-largest oil company, Yukos, is led by the richest man in Russia—thirty-something chairman and principal owner Mikhail Khodorkovksy. Instead of drilling expensive new wells, Khodorkovsky adopted Western technology, and partners such as Schlumberger, to get more oil out of Yukos's existing wells by injecting them with water to force the oil out. This lowered its production cost per barrel to a remarkable $1.86, at a time when the global

Changing societal values about pollution and renewable energy sources have caused some consumers to rethink their SUV purchases and switch to hybrid vehicles. One environmental group even ran ad spots asking, "What would Jesus drive?" to provoke thought about the issue. SUVs remain enormously popular, however, leaving automakers to grapple with the dilemma about the extent to which they should pursue the hybrid market.

cost of production was well over $25 per barrel. Khodorkovksy also adopted U.S. accounting methods, hobnobbed with U.S. oil magnates and politicians, and attempted to sell his Yukos shares to British Petroleum, ExxonMobil, or Chevron Texaco—or at least he did until the Kremlin threw him in jail and froze his assets.

The charge against Khodorkovsky was tax evasion, but more likely the Kremlin was wary of the cozy ties he was forming with the West. He loudly opposed a tax hike on oil proposed by Vladimir Putin in 2003, and he sought to build a private oil pipeline to the West. Keep in mind that oil accounts for over half of Russia's exports and has given the financially challenged country newfound clout on the world stage. It's not surprising that Putin objected to foreigners owning controlling interests in the country's most strategic asset.

While the picture in Russia is nonetheless looking brighter than it has in the past, clearly the country's political-legal scenario is still volatile, and other environmental forces continue to pose many risks that managers must confront. Much of the "black gold" lies beneath land that is subject to some of the longest and coldest winters in the world. Add to this free-flowing vodka, workers' living conditions that consist of log cabins and huts without indoor plumbing, and you have an explosive combination. Travelers to the region describe it as similar to the Wild West in the United States back in the 1800s. In Tyumen, things were so wild that many of the elite Black Beret military units that were pulled out of Latvia and Estonia were sent to Tyumen to try to keep order.

How does a manager successfully conduct business in such an environment? Most managers of Western oil companies don't have much choice but to try. Their efforts to expand production in deep waters offshore have largely failed. Chevron Texaco and Royal Dutch/Shell are particularly short on reserves.

Finding the remaining reserves in the rest of the world has become so difficult that most firms are willing to risk the environmental and political turmoil of the former Soviet Union to keep their firms awash in oil—no matter what happens to Khodorkovksy and Yukos.

Sources: "Yukos Told to Work Miracles," *Moscow Times*, January 29, 2004; Janet Guyon, "The Game Goes On," *Fortune* (Europe), November 24, 2003, pp. 70–71; Bill Powell, "Russia Pumps It Up," *Fortune*, May 13, 2002, pp. 85–91; Erik Kreil, "Oil and Gas Joint Ventures in the Former Soviet Union," U.S. Energy Information Agency, accessed at http://www.eia.doe.gov, August 1996; Sebastian Alison, "Russia Sees Second Devaluation as Oil Price Slumps," Reuters Limited, November 23, 1998; A. Konoplyanik, "Special Report—The Russian Oil & Gas Industry: Analysis Raises Questions about Russian Tax Proposal," *Oil & Gas Journal*, August 13, 2001, pp. 54–59; Ian Woollen, "Special Report—The Russian Oil & Gas Industry: Central Asian Gas Crucial to Future Russian Gas Supply," *Oil & Gas Journal*, August 13, 2001, pp. 61–65; Sergei Alexandrovich and Robin Morgan, "Special Report—The Russian Oil & Gas Industry: Russian Service Sector Lagging Behind Country's Emerging Oil Boom," *Oil & Gas Journal*, August 13, 2001, pp. 66–71; "Special Report—The Russian Oil & Gas Industry: Russian Oil Firms Mark Dramatic Turnaround in 1999–2000," *Oil & Gas Journal*, August 13, 2001, p. 67; "Special Report—The Russian Oil & Gas Industry: U.S.–Russian JV Entering Second Decade of Operations," *Oil & Gas Journal*, August 13, 2001, pp. 68–69.

strategic overview

Managers in the oil and gas industry who are thinking about doing business in Russia or other former Soviet Union states should carefully analyze the social, technological, economic, political, and global forces in the external environment. Such an analysis would be a critical first step in strategically deciding whether or not to make an investment in the region. Commonly, a firm that wants to enter high-risk foreign markets like Russia form strategic partnerships with a local firm so that the partner can help guide them through the local political, business, cultural, and other environmental challenges.[1] As noted later in this chapter, however, the institutional and cultural environments often differ across country borders, affecting the strategic decisions made by firms. For example, the institutional environment in Russia has been chaotic as it has tried to move central control of the economy to a more market-based system. Because local governments have been given the authority to make many of the policy decisions once made by the central government, the "rules of the game" change frequently. As a result, Russian managers tend to make short-term decisions. Alternatively, China (discussed later in this chapter) has been making a more evolutionary shift from central government control of the economy to a market-oriented system. With a more stable institutional environment, Chinese managers tend to focus more on making long-term strategic decisions than do Russian managers.[2] Managers desiring to do business in Russia or China would do well to understand each of their institutional environments and carefully select strategic partners knowing their short-term or long-term orientation, because it could affect the amount of commitment they are likely to make. Thus, managers charged with the responsibility of entering these markets should thoroughly scan their environments to help them understand the opportunities and pitfalls.

An analysis of the organization's external environments is critical to developing an effective strategy. Analyzing the general and task environments will provide substantial information enabling managers to identify the opportunities and threats that exist. Managers must develop strategies that take advantage of the opportunities and avoid or overcome the environmental threats.[3] Without a thorough analysis, they are likely to overlook excellent opportunities, leaving them for competitors to exploit. Likewise, they may be unprepared to counter or deal with a major threat, and the organization's performance may suffer as a result. For example, senior executives at Polaroid did not perceive the major threat to their business from the development of digital technology. As a result, its senior executives were forced to declare bankruptcy shortly thereafter.

WHAT DOES THE BUSINESS ENVIRONMENT CONSIST OF?

The **external environment** is a set of forces and conditions outside the organization that potentially can influence its performance. We divide these forces into two related but distinct categories—external task and external general environment. The **task environment** consists of forces that have a high potential for affecting the organization on an immediate basis. The **general environment** consists of forces that typically influence the organization's external

external environment a set of forces and conditions outside the organization that can potentially influence its performance

task environment forces that have a high potential for affecting the organization on an immediate basis

general environment forces that typically influence the organization's external task environment and thus the organization itself

exhibit 3.1
Organization Environment

task environment thus the organization itself. In addition to an external environment, organizations also have internal environments. The organization's **internal environment** consists of key factors and forces inside the organization that affect how the organization operates. Exhibit 3.1 provides a general illustration of these elements. However, for these concepts to be of much relevance to you as a manager, we need to dive into some greater detail. To do this, we will start at the general external environment level and work our way in.

internal environment key factors and forces inside the organization that affect how it operates

GENERAL EXTERNAL ENVIRONMENT

A variety of forces in the general environment can influence an organization's task environment and the organization itself. These forces are typically divided into five major categories: sociocultural, technological, economic, political-legal, and global. Clearly, the strength of impact of a given general external environment varies from industry to industry and firm to firm. As a consequence, it is hard to argue for a particular sequence or order of importance for these general environment forces. The "STEP Global" (i.e., **S**ociocultural, **T**echnological, **E**conomic, **P**olitical-Legal, and **G**lobal) sequence we use simply makes remembering the forces much easier.

Sociocultural Forces

The sociocultural forces of the general external environment consist primarily of the demographics as well as the cultural characteristics of the societies in which an organization operates.

Demographics are essentially the descriptive elements of people in the society, such as average age, birth rate, level of education, literacy rate, and so on. For example, in 1920 the average life expectancy was 53.6 years, and by 2010 it is estimated to be 77 years.[4] As another example of changing demographics, you have no doubt heard about the baby-boom generation, or the 80 million people born in the United States between 1946 and 1964 who now constitute nearly a third of the U.S. population.

But why should you as a manager care about baby boomers or other demographics? It is because demographics can significantly affect both orga-

demographics the descriptive elements of people in society, such as average age, level of education, financial status, and so on

nizational inputs and outcomes. For example, the average level of education and the birth rate in the United States combined can have a significant impact on the supply of workers with a given level of education and training. Specifically, a low birth rate and a modestly increasing level of education could result in a slow-growing or even declining number of technical workers. Clearly, this could have a significant impact on your ability as a manager in a high-tech firm to find the technicians you need to run your business. This is exactly what materialized in the 1990s. Demand for technically knowledgable workers such as software programmers in the United States far outstripped supply. Consequently, for several years the number of visas for foreign workers allowed into the United States by the government was used up before the year was half over. Or consider that people are living longer and that the largest demographic group in U.S. history is about 15 years away from the age at which health problems begin to increase. This could present the health care industry with significant opportunities as well as challenges.

As an international example, consider that Japan's population will actually start declining in 2005. By 2007 the number of people over 65 years of age will have doubled from 10 percent of the population to 20 percent in less than a generation. With one of the world's longest life expectancies (85 for women and 78 for men), fewer workers will be supporting Japan's retirees than at any time in the country's history, and many of Japan's retirees will live so long that they are likely to use up their retirement savings before they die if they retire at age 65.[5] This may present unprecedented opportunities for low-cost senior care centers and may mean that younger workers are faced with higher government taxes to support social security systems for senior citizens.

Although demographics can give us important statistics about our population, societal values are important translators of those numbers into business implications.[6] **Societal values** are commonly shared desired end states. In practical terms, for managers societal values determine the extent to which an organization's products or services have a market. For example, a switch in values from status to functionality moved firms such as Calvin Klein out of the spotlight and L.L. Bean onto the center stage of consumer demand in the early 1990s. This reversed itself in the mid- and late 1990s, as did the fortunes of these two companies. As another example, we can look at the controversy surrounding SUVs (Sports Utility Vehicles) in North America. Throughout the 1990s, SUVs such as the Ford Explorer, Dodge Durango, and Chevy Suburban were the fastest-selling automobiles. However, as concerns about the impact of pollution on global warming increased, people began to create negative sentiment toward SUVs and pressure car companies to make "hybrid" cars. These hybrids would be powered by both conventional combustion engines and electric motors—cars that, instead of 12 miles to the gallon, would get 50 or 60 miles to the gallon. These changing societal values forced managers at these major car companies to weigh the balance between the demands for and against SUVs in deciding what vehicles to produce and in what volumes. In 2004, managers at Toyota decided to introduce the first hybrid SUV. Time will tell if societal values are sufficiently strong for the decision to be successful.

Astute managers need the ability to combine demographics and societal values in order to determine important implications for their organizations.[7] To illustrate this, let's take a look at one demographic fact and one shifting social value. Demographically, the number of 35-to-45-year-olds in the United States peaked in 2000. Without significant changes in the number of immigrants, that

societal values commonly shared desired end states

group will decline in number by 15 percent through the year 2015. Demand for workers in this age group is estimated to grow by 30 percent during this same period. This creates an anticipated labor shortage. Add to this demographic picture a new generation of 35-to-45-year-olds who want a better balance between work and time with their families and you have an interesting situation.[8]

To help bring out the implications of this combination of demographic and societal value facts, imagine that you are a manager trying to recruit an experienced manager from the outside into your firm. There is a labor shortage and the highly qualified person you are trying to recruit does not want to travel as much as the job demands, in order to be home more. What do you do? Every day that the job goes unfilled costs you money because the results from that position are not being produced. The labor shortage means that every person you turn down because of their desire to not travel quite as much as you think the job requires likely lengthens the time the job remains empty and increases the total cost of the vacancy. Failure to understand these external general environment forces could lead to a poor recruiting plan costing the company money. In contrast, if you recognize and understand these demographic and sociocultural forces, you might anticipate the hiring challenge and create an appropriate plan. For example, you might borrow from what several consulting firms have done lately. Many of the most high-profile consulting firms such as Accenture and McKinsey have changed their travel policies. Specifically, many have instituted policies that require consultants to be at client locations on Tuesdays, Wednesdays, and Thursdays, but not Mondays and Fridays. This saves consultants' having to travel on Sundays to get to client locations on Mondays or traveling on Saturdays to get home from working at client locations on Fridays. As this example illustrates, a full understanding of both demographics and values can help you, as a manager, make changes and decisions that can help you increase your effectiveness and your organization's performance.

Technology Forces

Technology is another external environment force that can have brilliant or devastating effects on organizations. A specific technological innovation can spell the birth and growth of one firm and the decline and death of another. For example, the invention of the transistor created firms like Texas Instruments and spelled the death of vacuum tube manufacturers that did not adapt to this technological environment change. While the technological environment can be quite complicated, managers need to keep in touch with two basic aspects of the technology environment—product and process changes.

product technological changes changes that lead to new-product features and capabilities of existing products or to completely new products

Product Technological Changes Product technological changes are those that lead to new product features and capabilities of existing products or to completely new products. As a manager, you need to know what product technology changes are occurring, especially in your industry. For example, managers at Xerox were caught flat-footed when new, small personal copiers from Canon were able to produce the volume and quality of copies at half the price of larger Xerox machines. Palm created a new product category with the invention and successful launch of the Palm Pilot. This had a serious and negative impact on one of the largest makers of paper "day planners" at the time—Franklin Covey. Because firms increasingly win or lose as a function of their technological advantages and disadvantages, as a manager you need to have a broad view and keep in touch with technological advances at home and abroad. For example, in the multibillion-dollar global disposable diaper industry, absorbency technology shifted from "fluff pulp" (a paper-based product) to absorbent chemicals. This technological change was important because the absorbent chemicals could absorb more than fluff pulp and do so while making the diaper thinner. Procter & Gamble, maker of Pampers, almost lost its dominant position in the U.S. marketplace because it didn't keep up with the new absorbency technology that emerged in Japan.[9]

Process Technological Changes   Process technological changes typically relate to alterations in how products are made or how enterprises are managed. For example, a new computer coloring technology brought back animated feature films from a steep decline in the late 1980s and early 1990s because it substantially lowered production costs compared with the old individual frame-by-frame, hand-painted technology.[10] As another example, management information system technology (MIS) such as that used by Wal-Mart (the largest retailer in the world with over $250 billion in annual sales) allows managers to track merchandise on a daily or hourly basis and thereby know which products are selling and which ones are not. This in turn allows them to effectively order merchandise so that they do not run out of hot-selling items (and miss out on the sales revenues) and avoid overstocking poor-selling items (and tie up valuable cash in inventory). Interestingly, this process technology has helped Wal-Mart go from $1 billion in annual sales in 1973 to $1 billion in weekly sales by 1993 and nearly $1 billion a day now.[11] Cisco is another firm for whom technological advances in telecommunications and data transmission have significantly affected the way it operates. For example, in 1995, virtually none of Cisco's revenue came from purchase orders over the Internet. By 2000 over 70 percent of its nearly $20 billion in revenue came over the Internet. Interestingly, a majority of the products Cisco sells are high-speed switches used in transmitting data over the Internet.

Many North American steel manufacturers were driven into bankruptcy because virtually all of the largest firms were slow to adopt an important new process technology—the electric arch furnace. Most large (or what are called integrated) steel companies made steel by starting with raw iron ore and melting and converting it to large steel slabs that were further rolled and refined. Electric arch furnaces allowed so-called "mini-mills" to start with scrap metal, melt it, and make it into steel products. Starting with scrap metal was significantly cheaper than starting with iron ore. While the metal made in mini-mills could not be made into such things as beams for skyscrapers, it could be made into sheet metal for making car exteriors, washing machines, toasters, and so on. Dofasco, Inc., of Hamilton, Canada, was the first, and at the time the only integrated steel company to add this technology to its traditional steel-making processes. However, although the company now enjoys the benefits of the new electric arch furnace technology, it still took it nearly 10 years to adopt the technology after it was introduced.[12]

A Manager's Challenge, "Undoing 230 Years of Success", is a great example of the potential impact of the technological environment and the consequence of failure to adequately recognize or respond to technological changes. It briefly documents the rise and fall of one of the oldest and most revered companies—*Encyclopaedia Britannica*. As you read this example, ask yourself why you think managers at Encyclopedia Britannica were unable to anticipate the two major technological changes that nearly did the company in. Why did managers respond so slowly to the change? What do you think managers at Britannica should do going forward? Should they fight, ignore, or embrace the latest technology?

process technological changes alterations in how products are made or how enterprises are managed

tech nol ogy

a manager's challenge

Undoing 230 Years of Success

In 1768 three Scottish printers invented the most famous reference work in the world—the *Encyclopaedia Britannica*. The first was a three-volume edition. It grew from that to a 30-volume edition that children everywhere depended on when it came time to write a report for school. Encyclopaedia Britannica became the most authoritative and comprehensive encyclopedia in the business.

In 1920, Britannica was acquired by Sears, Roebuck and Company. As a consequence, its headquarters moved from Edinburgh to Chicago. It grew under its new owner and became a household name. In 1941, Britannica was sold to William Benton, who continued to build it and then willed it to the Benton Foundation in the early 1970s. Sales continued to grow in the 1970s and 1980s primarily through a direct–sales force that called on homes everywhere. The baby-boom generation bought these $1,500 to $2,200 sets for their children in record volume, and by 1990, sales reached a peak of $650 million.

What happened over the next 10 short years erased over 200 years of success. During this period, Britannica's sales declined by 80 percent. How did this happen? Managers at Britannica dismissed as irrelevant two technological inventions that proved the undoing of the firm's great history.

The first technology they dismissed was the CD-ROM. Managers at Britannica just didn't think that a CD was as attractive or useful as a set of bound (preferably in leather) books. However, their competitors had different ideas. Companies with inferior products such as Encarta, Grolier, and Compton put their encyclopedias on CDs and sold them not for $1,500 but for $50. Whereas it cost Britannica approximately $250 to produce an encyclopedia set, it cost only $1.50 to manufacture a set on a CD. In many cases, however, customers did not even have to pay the $50 price. Companies such as Microsoft found that they could enhance the appeal of their software by bundling these lesser encyclopedias into their main programs, such as Microsoft Office, free of charge. For a customer, even though the quality of these competitors to Britannica was not nearly as good, the value was better in the minds of many. Why? Customers received lots of information (even if it was less than they would get with Britannica) free. Something for nothing seemed to many customers like a better deal.

As the technological impact of CDs drove Britannica's revenues into a steep dive, executives who at first tried to deny the lasting impact of the technology finally changed

Remember the volumes of encyclopedias that graced the bookcases of homes prior to the Internet age? Undeniably, *Encyclopaedia Britannica* was the most authoritative and comprehensive set of volumes in the business. Technology, however, radically changed the business and the company's future prospects. Slow to adapt, *Encyclopaedia Britannica* almost didn't survive.

their minds and gave in. However, in deciding to put *Encyclopaedia Britannica* on CD, managers encountered two significant problems.

First, they faced the problem of how to sell the product. Their direct-sales channel would not work for the CDs because there was no way to price the product high enough for salespeople to receive the $500 commissions per sale that they were used to getting when they sold bound books. Without a substantial commission, salespeople had little incentive to push the new format. Unfortunately, Britannica did not have other distribution or sales channels for its encyclopedia on CD.

Second, and quite ironically, managers at Britannica discovered that the new technology rendered as a weakness what Britannica's executives had always seen as their greatest strength and differentiator—comprehensiveness. Despite the large storage capacity of CDs, the content of Britannica's encyclopedia could not fit on one CD. However, its "inferior" competitors' encyclopedias fit fine on one CD. Unfortunately for Britannica, customers did not want to hassle with three or four CDs even if there was better content. They wanted to put one CD into their computer, search, and find the information they desired.

With sales declining and problems increasing, Jacob Safra bought Britannica in 1996. Although he put a new management team into place, the nature of competition had changed so dramatically that reviving the business was nearly an impossible task at that point. The company was dealt a near-fatal blow with the next technological change.

That technological change came with the mass-market introduction of the Internet. Post-1997 it was increasingly easy to access a free encyclopedia or gain needed information from an ever-growing list of Web sites and information providers at no cost, as long as you were willing to look at the ads on their sites. Reluctantly, Britannica managers set up their own Web site for reference material and tried to sell their unrivaled volumes of information through a subscription fee of $20. Unfortunately, this proved unattractive to customers when information from other sources was free.

Britannica spotted a glimmer of hope, though, when the Internet ad market collapsed following the burst of the tech bubble in 2001. The company exploited the turmoil by changing its Internet model. Not only must a good search engine find all of the relevant documents; it must put the best 20 or 30 at the top. Britannica does this so Internet users don't have to weed through a lot of material to find the "good stuff." It also gives any subscriber access to its entire site, including the beginnings of all articles, the *Merriam-Webster Collegiate Dictionary*, and articles from many popular and professional magazines. However, it charges a subscription fee to read full articles. Customers don't pay for what they can't find.

To solve its sales commission problem, Britannica set up its first direct-marketing team in 2003. Today, the company's sales are in the $200 million-dollar range—a fraction of what they once were, but the company is surviving. Moreover, all of its products are available on the Internet, CD, and DVD.

Sources: Sarah Balmond, "Encylopedia Britannica Sets Up Direct Team," *Precision Marketing*, May 23, 2003, p. 1; Stephen Ellerin, "Three Publishers' Site Search Solutions," *EContent*, February 2003, pp. 44–48; Philip Evans and Thomas Wurster, *Blown to Bits* (Cambridge, MA: Harvard Business School Press, 2000).

Economic Forces

A wide variety of economic forces in the external environment can also significantly influence organizations. Not all economic forces affect all organizations equally, however. The exact nature of the business and industry determines the specific factors that have the strongest influence on an organization. To better understand these economic forces, we group them into three main categories: current conditions, economic cycles, and structural changes.

Current Economic Conditions Current economic conditions are those that exist in the short term within a country. It is relatively easy for most students to imagine how current economic conditions can have important effects on an organization. For example, the current level of inflation can directly affect how quickly costs rise, which in turn might squeeze profits. The current level of unemployment can directly influence how easy or difficult it is to find the type of labor you need. Current interest rates can determine how expensive it is to borrow money or even how much money your firm can borrow to finance activities and expansions. For example, the economic slowdown in 2000 and 2001 led the Federal Reserve Board to push interest rates down. As a consequence, by 2003 interest rates on home loans reached a 40-year low. Because interest rates were so low, many people decided that it was time to either buy a house or refinance their existing home loan with a lower rate and lower mortgage payment. As a result, home builders and mortgage loan providers saw a significant increase in business.

Economic Cycles But economic activity is not static, and current conditions do not necessarily predict future economic conditions. Economic activity tends to move in cycles. Although it is difficult to predict exactly when an upturn or downturn in economic conditions will occur, understanding that cycles exist and the key factors that move them is critical for managerial activities such as planning. It is also important to understand that specific industry cycles can be more or less pronounced than the general economic cycle of the country. For example, the construction industry tends to have higher peaks and lower valleys than the overall national economy, and the funeral home business tends to have lower peaks and higher valleys than the overall economy (see Exhibit 3.2). If you were not aware of the impact of economic cycles on your particular industry, you might make poor management decisions. For example, if you were unaware of the exaggerated cycles of the construction industry relative to the peaks and valleys of the general economy, you might not plan for enough labor or materials for the upturn in the cycle and might order more materials than necessary or hire too many people during downturns in the cycle.

Structural Changes Perhaps the hardest yet most critical thing to understand about economic conditions is knowing whether changes in the economy are temporary or whether they represent longer-term, structural changes. **Structural changes** are changes that significantly affect the dynamics of economic activity now and into the future. For example, the shift from an agrarian (agricultural) to an industrial economy and then from an industrial to a service economy were all structural changes that took place in the United States. They affected where people worked, what work they did, the education level they needed to do the work, and so on. If structural changes are taking place and you are unaware of them, you can easily make poor managerial decisions. For example, the structural shift to a more knowledge-based work environment will likely change not only the nature of workers but what motivates them. In many service companies such as engineering firms, consulting firms, and law firms, the company's primary assets (its people) walk out the door every day. This is in contrast to industrial companies such as car manufacturers, which have millions of dollars in plant and equipment that stay put even when the workers go home. As a consequence, while a car manufacturer may be able to replace a worker who leaves the assembly line with relative ease and feel only small effects of employee turnover, the same is not true for service companies and for the United States in general, as the structural economic shift from an industrial to an information economy continues. For example, when a star consultant leaves her firm, she takes with her most of her value to the company. Her understanding of client company problems and solutions leaves with her. The phone or fax or other hard assets that stay with the company provide comparatively little value. In fact, in some cases the value is so closely tied to the individual that customers leave the company with an individual's departure and redirect their business to wherever the star consultant goes. Without understanding of this structural economic change, you may miss the importance of employee retention and

structural changes changes that significantly affect the dynamics of economic activity

exhibit 3.2
Overall Economic Cycles and Industry Cycles

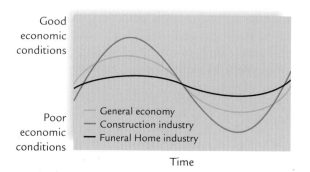

underestimate the role of praising and recognizing the contributions of your star performer in order to keep her at your firm. Or you may not see that allowing this individual to travel to client locations on Mondays (instead of Sundays) in the end saves you money because the change in policy helps you retain rather than lose key performers.

Political and Legal Forces

Political and legal forces can also have dramatic impacts on organizations. Laws frame what organizations can and cannot do. As a consequence, they can create both challenges and opportunities. For example, new pollution laws significantly increased the operating costs of coal-burning power plants. At the same time, these same laws created new business opportunities for firms such as Corning, which developed and sold new filter systems to coal-burning power plants.[13] Tax laws can also have a profound effect on businesses. In the 1970s, tax breaks for oil and gas exploration led to massive activity in states such as Texas. The repeal of those laws pushed many firms, and nearly the state, into bankruptcy.[14]

Perhaps one of the most important political aspects of the external general environment is federal government spending. On the one hand, increases or decreases in government spending can have a significant impact on the overall economy. Total government spending at the local, state, and national levels can account for 20 percent of **gross domestic product** (the total dollar value of final goods and services produced by businesses within a nation's borders). It's a significant amount. If you divide the amount of the total amount the U.S. government purchases by every person in the United States, it comes out to about $6,500 per person. Increases or decreases in total government spending can therefore have a significant impact on overall business activity. For example, following the invasion of Iraq in 2003, the government purchased so much plywood to send to Iraq for boarding up buildings demolished by the war, it created a shortage in the United States. Plywood prices skyrocketed, and that had a serious impact on U.S. home prices.

gross domestic product the total dollar value of final goods and services produced within a nation's borders

However, even if total spending remains unchanged, if spending moves from one area to another, then government spending can still dramatically affect businesses. Consider the nearly threefold increase in military spending during the Reagan presidency. Firms such as General Dynamics profited considerably from this spending. Interestingly, the decrease in military spending during the Clinton administration put many companies, including General Dynamics, out of business or into the arms of another firm.[15] For example, defense spending went from nearly 50 percent of the U.S. federal government budget in the early 1960s to less than 20 percent by the early 1990s. Interestingly, this changed again when George W. Bush followed Clinton into the presidency and increased defense spending again.

More complicated, but perhaps even more important, is whether government spending pushes the deficit up or down. For example, generally, when federal spending pushes the federal deficit up, interest rates also go up. As interest rates go up, money becomes more expensive for firms to borrow, and as a consequence, they typically borrow less. As firms borrow less, they expand their business activities at a slower rate or even contract their overall activity. This can push unemployment up, which in turn pushes consumer spending down. In combination this can create a full-fledged economic downturn. This is essentially what happened in the United States during the recession of 1991. As the George W. Bush administration ran up record-setting deficits after 2001, it has again become a concern. So while the political process governing federal spending and the deficit can be quite complicated, managers cannot afford to ignore their effects.

A Manager's Challenge, "Stormy Seas at Knight-Carver, Inc.," provides a fun illustration of the impact of political changes in the environment combined with economic changes. Knight-Carver was sailing along fine, but when the winds of the external environment changed and the seas got rough, management had to change how they operated the business. As you read this case, which environmental forces do you see as having the strongest impact? Could or should the managers at Knight-Carver have seen these environmental changes coming? How well do you think they responded to the changes?

Global Forces

The Knight-Carver case not only helps illustrate the economic and political-legal forces but the global ones as well. Even though up until the early 1990s the senior management at K-C was not concerned about the global environment, its importance and potential impact existed nonetheless. Management finally woke up to its importance after it was thrust upon them. It was only after economic and political-legal forces prompted customers to look elsewhere for yacht builders that K-C management changed their focus beyond the domestic shores and looked globally for customers and suppliers.

Although all managers should pay attention to the global environment, its importance depends on the organization's size and scope of business. For small organizations, the other general environment forces may be more important and have a much stronger impact. However, for medium-sized and large firms, the global environment can be as important or even more important than any of the other general environment forces we have discussed. This is especially true as the percentage of international sales increases as part of total sales. For example, 70 percent of Coca-Cola's income comes from international sales in over 200 countries; consequently, the global environment is critical to the company's performance. For global firms that operate in multiple countries and try to integrate those operations into an almost borderless enterprise, the line between the other environmental forces and global environments can blur. As an example, for managers at Nokia (with only 3 percent of sales inside Finland) the global economic environment is *the* economic environment that affects them. In addition, in order to succeed, managers at Nokia must focus on sociocultural changes across the world. They must also take into consideration technological changes in wireless communication in Europe, North America, Latin America, Africa, and Asia Pacific. As a consequence, while we separate global as a distinct general environment force, the reality for many companies and managers is that the global environment is intimately intertwined with the other environmental forces.

A Manager's Challenge ("Business in China") helps illustrate the challenge of assessing the global environment and then acting on that assessment. While it may seem thousands of miles away, China has the world's largest population—1.3 billion people, which is about four times the population of

a manager's challenge

Change

Stormy Seas at Knight-Carver, Inc.

In the late 1980s, Dan Carver, the president of a medium-sized yacht-building company, Knight & Carver (K-C), located in peaceful and sunny San Diego, California, was content and happy. His company was doing about $12 million a year in custom yacht building and repair. Carver was about as worried about change as he was about an iceberg floating into San Diego bay from Alaska.

At its peak, the company had 90 employees making and repairing small to medium-sized yachts. Nearly all of its customers were from the West Coast, and all the work was done in a small complex at the San Diego harbor. K-C did most things as well as the next competitor, but when it came to custom interiors, it had superior craftsmanship.

Despite the peaceful atmosphere at K-C, a storm was brewing that would blow the company right into the middle of choppy waters. In 1990, the U.S. government put a 10 percent luxury tax on boats. This instantly added $120,000 to a typical $1.2 million custom yacht. At about the same time, the U.S. economy took a nose dive. The tight economy and the new tax laws caused customers to look for lower-cost alternative boat builders. Suddenly, K-C found that normal customers were having their boats built by Taiwanese, Korean, Indonesian, and Brazilian competitors that management never even knew existed. Senior managers had to change their competitive radar to include these new competitors. To survive these stormy seas, K-C reduced the number of its employees from 90 to about 30. The company also had to change where it looked for customers. Whereas in the past many of its customers came from upscale neighborhoods in southern California such as Rancho Santa Fe, La Jolla, and Newport Beach, sales managers reached out to customers in Japan and Saudi Arabia. Purchasing managers in K-C had to change their orientation as well and started gathering information on suppliers in countries such as Korea.

Ironically, a key boost for this previously domestic company came from the largest *international* boat race in the world, the America's Cup, which came to San Diego in 1994, thanks to San Diego resident and captain of the victorious America3

in 1990, Dennis Conner. The America's Cup and array of international teams from Japan, France, New Zealand, Australia, and elsewhere and spectators from around the world descended on San Diego in the summer of 1994. International racing teams needed space for their boats and leased space from K-C. K-C leveraged these lease payments, used the international connections it established during the race, and took advantage of an improving U.S. economy. These moves helped K-C keep the bank from taking over the business.

But, although the luxury tax was later repealed, the other favorable environmental circumstances were not to be repeated. The America's Cup race next went to Australia and then New Zealand, taking the leasing business with it. The U.S. economy, which roared along through the rest of the 1990s, faltered in 2000 and went into recession in 2001. Spending slowed, particularly on luxury goods like million-dollar yachts.

The last 15 years have been a wild ride, forever changing how K-C executives and employees look at the next 15 years. K-C will likely never again take its eye off foreign competitors or ignore suppliers from throughout the world, any more than it will count on a stable market at home. The company now tracks foreign exchange rates daily, monitors supplier costs around the world, and calls on an international base of customers.

So that K-C's business isn't entirely at the whims of wealthy boat owners, it has expanded its range of activities, boosting its repair business and facilities. The sales of the repair business now contribute a full 70 percent to the company's bottom line. To further diversify its revenue base, K-C took tentative steps into the alternative energy business, building wind turbine blades utilizing its expertise with composite materials like those used to build boats. Managers also changed their sales pitch to customers. In recognition of shifting societal values toward environmental responsibility, instead of stressing only K-C's legendary, high-quality interior craftsmanship, managers now stress its innovation and unblemished environmental record too.

Sources: Joan Raymond, "Enduring Lessons from a Short War," *Inc.*, June 2003; www.knightandcarver.com, accessed on November 23, 2001; Tony Chamberlain, "America's Cup Staying Afloat on a Sea of Cash," *Boston Globe*, September 11, 2001, p. E8.

the United States. Consequently, managers watched China's entry into the WTO (World Trade Organization) in 2001 with keen anticipation. While reading this Managerial Challenge, you might ask yourself what industries would be most affected by China's entry into the WTO. As a manager, can you afford to ignore this issue?

globalization *a manager's challenge*

Business in China

"How to deal with China as a big economic power—that is the largest issue . . . in the first half of the 21st century," according to Japan's former foreign minister, Yukihiko Ikeda. Many managers would agree—not just in Japan but in Taiwan, most of Europe, Canada, Australia, and the United States.

The coming expansion of Chinese industry accompanies monumental changes in its economy and its business infrastructure brought about by its entry into the World Trade Organization in November 2001. The combination of expansion and admission to the world's formal trading system creates an unprecedented opening of what may prove to be the world's largest marketplace for nearly every kind of good and service, from cell phones and tractors to DVDs and blue jeans and the world's largest source of low-cost manufactured goods. For China, "it is a no-going-back, transforming moment," according to Goldman Sachs's CEO, Henry Paulson. Ironically, that economic opportunity also strikes fear into the hearts of many managers.

It is not just fear of investing billions of dollars into China-based enterprises and failing, though that is a very real concern. Many managers, whether bankers, auto manufacturers, or consumer-goods marketers, already know full well the difficulties of finding and choosing the right Chinese business partners, of coping with a protectionist government bureaucracy, of negotiating myriad cultural differences, and of overcoming China's restrictions on building distribution chains and dealer networks. (These rules often leave foreign managers relying on the same distributors their competitors are using inside China.) Add to these risks those that underlie all international trade—language barriers, currency exchange rate fluctuations, changing consumer preferences—and the picture is already daunting.

Many foreign managers, however, also fear that China's own firms, some of which are still state-supported, may reap the largest benefits from its steadily growing consumer demand. Despite a rising standard of living, China is still the world's largest low-wage economy, and it may quickly figure out how to produce many goods more cheaply at home than it is to import them from abroad. For example, Taiwan-based computer maker Acer held the number-one position in China for years. However, over the last few years, domestic maker Legend has substantially increased quality while beating Acer on price. The result is that Legend has replaced Acer in the number one spot within China. As Legend continues to improve quality, it may

Boasting 1.3 billion people, China presents a huge potential market, both in terms of the low-cost labor opportunities it affords and the amount of goods and services that can be sold there. For example, China expects to build 10 million new homes annually through mid-decade—a boom spawned by the liberalization of free trade and market reforms and the country's admission into the World Trade Organization (WTO) in 2001.

take its cost advantage and expand internationally to compete with Acer in Taiwan and around the world.

Chinese managers in firms less successful than Legend recognize that if inefficient domestic firms are forced to reform, thousands of Chinese workers will lose their jobs over the next several years. In the agricultural industry, where small farms are still the norm, employment losses may be particularly severe. Thus, despite the fact that tariffs and distribution barriers are set to drop, these managers may pressure Chinese government officials to resist full-scale foreign competition. The rapid changes in China are taking place within a single generation, and adjustments will be very difficult.

But the market remains very attractive. China is expected to increase its purchases from the United States from $19 billion in 1998 to $44 billion by 2009. Its economy is growing by 8 percent a year, and it took in $66 billion in foreign direct investment in 2000 alone. It is home to 1.3 billion people, of whom about 120 million now have disposal incomes of up to $8,000 a year. For some, like Zhang Xin, who recently earned a computer science degree from one of the country's most prestigious universities and will go to work for a cellular phone network firm in Beijing, it is a land where life is about to change dramatically. For foreign managers, figuring out how to do business in China and deal with competitors coming out of China is a task that keeps them up late at night.

Sources: Bill Powell, "China's Great Step Forward," *Fortune*, September 17, 2001, pp. 128–42; Leslie P. Norton, "WTO Blows Tradewinds Between Taiwan and China," *Barron's Online*, accessed at http://interactive.wsj..com/pages/barrons.htm on November 19, 2001; James Brooke, "Tokyo Fears China May Put an End to 'Made in Japan,'" *New York Times*, November 20, 2001, p. A3.

The Special Nature of the Global Environment

As we already mentioned, for many companies the global environment is not separate from the other general environmental forces. As we noted, when managers at Nokia think about the sociocultural external environment or the technological external environment, they generally have to think about it in a global context. So while for the sake of simplicity we have separated the sociocultural, technological, economic, and political-legal general environment forces from global forces, the reality for many managers is that they are not all that separate. The other reality is that while it is possible and even necessary for many managers to analyze the global environment, as a practical matter they often have to break that analysis down into small pieces. Imagine if you were a manager at Nokia trying to do a global economic analysis across the 100-plus countries in which Nokia operates. As a practical matter this often becomes just too unwieldy. This is why many managers focus their more detailed "global environmental analysis" on one country at a time. This is often called country analysis.[16]

As a manager, how do you assess a country and determine which countries are "good" to do business in and which ones are not? Let's take China, for example. Is it a good country in which to do business? During the early 1980s, China looked like a great place for foreign firms to do business. It had announced an economic liberalization plan and was borrowing billions of dollars to build up its economy and infrastructure. It was a nation rich in natural and human resources. However, China had many millions of people employed in state-owned and inefficient enterprises. These firms were naturally reluctant to see efficient, foreign firms come into the country, fearing that they would produce higher-quality goods at lower prices. Government officials were torn because they saw the need to modernize and yet recognized that they could not have thousands of state-owned firms fail and millions and millions of workers go unemployed. As China's government officials alternately tightened and loosened regulations, many managers saw the country as an economic and political yo-yo.

As the situation in China helps illustrate, most countries have both positive and negative aspects. In the abstract, this means very little. The key to an effective analysis of the country is relating them to a specific industry or organization, and its circumstances. Because industries and businesses operate differently and have different needs, specific policies or government actions pose unequal threats. For example, because KFC can source nearly all of its needed raw materials within China, changes in import duties do not matter. However, Volkswagen must import many components for the cars it builds in China and therefore cares very much about changes in tariffs.

GM expects about 90 percent of its revenue growth over the next 10 years to come from outside the United States because the U.S. car market is saturated and expected to remain relatively flat. Furthermore, it expects a majority of that international growth to come in Asia generally and China specifically. GM's interest is driven largely by the high expected economic growth rate in China (8 to 10 percent compared to 2 to 3.5 percent in the United States), current low car-ownership rates, and rising income levels. GM actually tried doing business in China in 1996 and didn't do well. The average person in China still earns only a few hundred dollars a year, making car ownership a luxury. Nonetheless, the Chinese government urged GM to invest in a $1.5 billion plant there.

Building the factory looks like a smart move. While only 0.1 percent of the Chinese have been able to trade their bicycles in for cars, it's still a huge market worth going after (amounting to over a million cars). Today more cars are sold in China than Germany, and China is now the third-largest auto market in the world, behind the United States and Japan.

That's not to say GM hasn't experienced problems there. Months before it began selling its $7,500 Chevrolet Spark in China, a $6,000 knockoff version was cruising Chinese streets. Even worse, the manufacturer of the pirated version of the car was partially owned by GM's Chinese business partner.[17]

While managers would certainly examine the sociocultural, technological, economic, political, and legal environmental forces when analyzing a foreign country, there are two additional aspects of the external environment that are typically examined in the context of a foreign country, which are not usually part of a "domestic" general external environment analysis. These are the dimensions of the institutional and physical environmental forces. They are often included in analyses of foreign countries primarily because of the vast differences among countries in terms of institutions and physical characteristics.[18]

Institutional Forces The institutional context involves the key organizations in the country. Although the strength and power of institutions can vary from one country to another, they constitute an important consideration in any environmental analysis.[19] Institutions to assess include the government, labor unions, religious institutions, and business institutions. These organizations are important to analyze in a global or foreign country context because they can be (and often are) dramatically different from those "at home."

Physical Forces Physical features such as infrastructure (e.g., roads, telecommunications, air links, etc.), arable land, deepwater harbors, mineral resources, forests, and climate can have a dramatic impact on existing and potential operations in a country and can be substantially different from those at home. For example, China has vast coal resources deep in its interior, but they are not an attractive business opportunity because of the poor rail and road infrastructure in those regions.

PULLING TOGETHER AN ANALYSIS OF THE GENERAL ENVIRONMENT

Even though we have tried to provide a number of examples as we moved through the various elements in the external general environment, it can seem a bit overwhelming. While an analysis of the external general environment is not simple, an integrated example may help to pull all of these concepts together. Let's take Coca-Cola as the example. Exhibit 3.3 provides a brief description of key aspects of the general environment, while Exhibit 3.4 pulls that description into a short summary.

While Exhibits 3.3 and 3.4 are by necessity brief and do not paint a full picture of Coca-Cola's external general environment, you can begin to see how a careful analysis of the general environment can provide useful information to managers in such activities as planning and decision making. For example, the sociocultural information may suggest that managers at Coca-Cola will need to increase their marketing efforts if they are to reach out to ethnic

exhibit 3.3

**Description of the General
Environment of Coca-Cola**

Sociocultural
- Demographics
  Baby boomers drinking less soft drinks as they age.
  U.S. population growth is slowing and much of the growth comes from immigrants who generally drink less soft drinks.
- Values
  Society is increasingly concerned about pollution and recycling.
  Increasing focus on health and the negative aspects of caffeine, carbonation, and sugar.

Technological
- New "canning" technology makes using recycled aluminum easier and cheaper.
- Internet opens up a new means of running promotion contests and activities.

Economic
- Slow economy reduces per-person consumption primarily due to fewer social occasions (parties) at which soft drinks might be served.
- Nearing end of economic downturn and prospects of economic recovery.
- Stricter liability for illness caused by beverage contamination.

Global
- Gradual increase in acceptance of carbonated soft drinks in other countries such as India and China.
- Widely available electricity and increased ability to afford refrigerators in emerging countries and economies.

groups who come from countries and cultures in which drinking soft drinks, especially with carbonation, is not common. The information captured in the global dimension of the general external environment may suggest that managers at Coca-Cola should increase their efforts in emerging foreign markets with large populations such as China.

exhibit 3.4

**The General Environment
of Coca-Cola**

TASK ENVIRONMENT

The task environment is the most immediate external environment within which an organization survives and flourishes and consists of competitors, customers, suppliers, strategic partners, labor, and regulators. Consequently, it typically has the largest influence on the organization, and the fit between the organization and its environment is critical for a manager to understand. Forces in the task environment exert a significant influence on the organization. Because the task environment plays a significant role in the competitive and strategic position of an organization, we will examine certain aspects of these forces in more detail in Chapter 6, when we explore the topic of strategic management.

Porter's Five Forces
by Michael Hitt

Q&A
One**Key**
www.prenhall.com/onekey

Perhaps the most well-known model of analyzing a firm's task environment was developed by Michael Porter, a professor at the Harvard Business School.[20] This framework conceived of the task environment primarily in terms of five environment forces (Porter's Five Forces) that can significantly influence the performance organizations in the same industry (see Exhibit 3.5). These forces are examined to analyze the industry. The original research was designed to explain why some industries were more profitable as a whole than others and why some companies within industries were more profitable than other firms in the same industry. In general, research has supported the validity of this model.[21] Three of the five forces (nature of rivalry, new entrants, and substitutes) primarily have to do with the "competitor" category of the task environment. While these three aspects of Porter's framework are related to this one category, we examine each of them separately to provide you with a reasonable presentation of the five forces framework. The other two forces in the framework—customers and suppliers—relate directly to the second and third aspects of the task environment that we listed at the outset. To these five forces of Porter's framework, we add and will discuss the dimensions of strategic partners, labor, and regulators.

The first aspect of the task environment, according to Porter, is competitors and the nature of competition among them. For example, in analyzing this aspect of the task environment you need to know how big and strong your competitors are relative to you. If you are small and weak relative to your competition, you may choose to stay out of their way and go after business that is less interesting to them. In your analysis of competitors, you also need to know their weaknesses. Those weaknesses may represent opportunities that you can exploit.

Just For Feet took this view; it was a latecomer to the athletic footwear retail business. Competitors such as Foot Locker already had hundreds of retail outlets across the United States when Just For Feet was established. But despite the overall size of Foot Locker, its individual stores were relatively

exhibit 3.5
Profits and Industry Forces

small. To Just For Feet, this represented a weakness and a great opportunity, so it established stores that were three to five times the size of Foot Locker's stores. Just For Feet wanted these stores to be entertainment centers and not just sneaker stores, so its stores offered basketball practice courts, loud music, pro athletes signing autographs, and an endless selection of sneakers. Just For Feet soon became the fastest-growing athletic footwear retailer in the country and one of the 100 fastest-growing companies listed in *Fortune* magazine.[22]

In addition to understanding your competitors, you also need to consider the nature of competition, or rivalry, in your industry. In general, competition can be based on price or on features of your product or service. Simplified, competitors can try to outdo each other by offering the lowest price to customers or by offering the best product or service. The more competition is based on price, generally the lower the profits. This is primarily because it is easier to lower prices than costs. As prices decline faster than costs, profit margins shrink. For example, competition in the airline business has been based on airfare prices since deregulation in 1977. With the stroke of a pen or computer key, airlines can slash prices to try to attract customers. They cannot so easily lower the price of new planes, fuel, or the wages of pilots or flight attendants. Consequently, most U.S. airlines have lost billions from 1980 to the present. The notable exception has been Southwest Airlines. This is primarily because Southwest has had the lowest cost structure of any major airline.[23]

The key for you as a manager is to clearly understand the nature of rivalry in your industry. It is worth noting that in very large industries, such as automobile manufacturing, there are quite often different segments. This is important because the nature of rivalry can differ by segment. For example, in the subcompact segment of the auto industry, competition is largely based on price. However, in the luxury automobile segment, competition is primarily based on quality. Issues of safety, engineering, and handling, not price, dominate the ads for Mercedes, Lexus, BMW, and Infinity. It is only when you have a thorough understanding of this competitive aspect of your industry that you are in a position to combine this information with other data and decide exactly how your company should compete.

New Entrants—Potential New Competitors

The second element of the five forces is the extent to which it is easy or difficult for firms to enter the industry. All other elements being equal, new entrants will increase competition. Unless the size of the entire industry pie is expanding, the greater the number of new entrants, the thinner the slice of pie for each participant. Increased competition (i.e., more entrants) usually leads to lower profit margins because customers have more choices. Unless it is difficult and expensive for customers to switch from one company to another (typically called **switching costs**), companies are forced to pass on greater value to customers when they have more choices. For example, before American Airlines invented the frequent flier program, an airplane seat was an airplane seat. However, with the award of frequent flier miles, airlines increased the switching costs. If you decided to fly on a different airline, you could not take advantage of the upgrades or free flights offered to you by the first airline. Where switching costs are low, the more new entrants, the more choice you have, and the more value each competitor must give you in order to entice you to choose it. This greater value usually comes from lowering profits. For

switching costs the amount of difficulty and expense involved in customers' switching from one company to another

example, if there are five grocery stores within a block of your house, and it costs you very little to go to one store over another, you are likely to go to the store that offers the best deal. As the stores compete for your business, they typically have to lower their profits to offer you a better deal.

The factors that keep new entrants out are termed barriers. **Entry barriers** are the obstacles that make it difficult for firms to get into a business. The bigger the barriers, the harder it is to get into the business. The harder it is to get in, the fewer new entrants. For example, the barriers to entry in the restaurant business are quite low. Even in major cities, you can be in business for less than $100,000. However, if you wanted to break into the semiconductor business, it would cost you $4 to $6 billion just to build a fabrication plant. This doesn't even take into account the cost of designing or marketing your new chip. Generally, the fewer the new entrants, the fewer the total number of players in the industry. This typically means that each player gets a larger slice of the industry pie. It also means that customers likely have fewer choices, and that usually translates into higher profits for the firms already in the industry.

entry barriers obstacles that make it difficult for firms to get into a business

Substitutes

As a task environmental force, **substitutes** focus on the extent to which alternative products or services can substitute for the existing products or services. Substitution is different from competition. Substitution does not involve a choice of one grocery store over another. Rather, it involves opting for another alternative means of satisfying a customer's need. For example, going to a restaurant instead of the grocery store when you are hungry is an example of a substitute. For Greyhound (a bus company) Southwest Airlines became a substitute. When it costs $59 for an hour flight from Irvine, California, to Phoenix, Arizona, on Southwest and it costs $42 for an eight-hour Greyhound bus ride, most people fly rather than take the bus. Generally, the fewer the available substitutes, the greater the profits. For example, if you have no choice in satisfying your hunger except to go to the grocery store for food (i.e., restaurants cannot substitute), grocery stores will make more money. As a manager, this is critical to understand because while competing products are one of the most important defining elements of an industry, you can make poor decisions about strategy, marketing, manufacturing, and so on, if you fail to see potential substitutes. For example, as a manager at Greyhound you can have better buses and drivers than any other bus company in your industry, but if flying becomes a substitute for riding the bus, your company may still be in difficult shape (which is exactly what happened to Greyhound).

substitutes alternative products or services that can substitute for existing products or services

Customers

All managers in organizations have customers to serve. To the extent that there are relatively few customers and these customers are united, they have more power to demand lower prices, customized products or services, attractive financing terms from producers, and so on. The greater the power of customers, the more value they can extract. Unless you can quickly and significantly lower your costs, the more value customers extract, the lower your profits will be. For example, suppose you worked for a diamond mine. To make money, you would need to sell the diamonds you extracted. For nearly 100 years, one company, DeBeers, purchased an estimated 80 to 90 percent of the world's diamonds, in part because it owned many of the largest and richest diamond mines.[24] As a diamond mining company, you are *un*likely to make big profits because DeBeers basically determines the price it will pay for the diamonds it buys from you. Because there are few if any other buyers of your diamonds, you have little choice but to sell your diamonds to DeBeers, and because the company has significant power as a customer, it will pay you a low price. Interestingly, the larger a diamond mine you are, the more this is true. The more diamonds you mine, the less (in relative terms) customers other than DeBeers can take, and as a consequence, the more power DeBeers has over you. But things are changing. It is interesting to note that both governmental pressure to reduce DeBeers's power and several new large diamond discoveries by mining companies not owned by DeBeers has made it much more difficult for it to buy up such a large share of the raw diamond market. As its share of annual raw diamond purchases has declined from 80 percent to 65 percent, so has its power over the market.

Strategic Partners

Strategic partners consist of other organizations that work closely with a firm in the pursuit of mutually beneficial goals.[25] The degree of involvement between or among partners can vary from limited engagement to joint ventures in which participating parties hold equity stakes in the partnership. An example of strategic partnering at the low-involvement end of the spectrum are the airline alliances such as Star Alliance with its main partners United Airlines, Lufthansa, All Nippon Airways, and Air Canada. These strategic partners' "code-sharing" agreements share the codes (flight numbers) of flying routes so that customers can more easily switch between airlines on a given itinerary. These alliances allow passengers to fly on different partner airlines but accumulate frequent flier miles on their main airline. If you were a marketing manager at United Airlines, Star Alliance would be important to understand in deciding how to market the global travel convenience that customers could get by flying on United or one of its strategic alliance partners. However, the existence of this alliance would be important to you as a manager at American Airlines. In fact, it might be so important and influential that it would cause you to create your own alliance among American Airlines, British Airlines, Cathay Pacific, Qantas, and others.

> **strategic partners**
> organizations that work closely with a firm in the pursuit of mutually beneficial goals

These strategic partnerships can become much more involved to the point at which each member of the partnership owns an equity interest in the partnership. Quite often this level of strategic partner involvement manifests itself in joint ventures. For example, KFC and Mitsubishi Real Estate of Japan formed a joint venture for opening up KFC restaurants in Japan. This alliance is not only important to managers within KFC but to managers within McDonald's as well. In the fast-food industry, the right location is critical to success. A manager at McDonald's has to take into consideration KFC's strategic alliance because Mitsubishi Real Estate's long and extensive understanding of the real estate market in Japan makes it more likely that KFC will find and secure ideal locations for new stores. Since the supply of ideal locations is limited, managers at McDonald's have to keep in mind this alliance as they seek out ideal locations for their new restaurants.

Labor

Labor is another important task environment force. Virtually no organization can operate without people. The balance between supply and demand for types of workers significantly affects a firm's performance. For example, if demand exceeds supply, the imbalance can lead to high labor costs. This can be true at the factory floor or executive suite level. Clearly, higher personnel costs could impact a firm's profits unless it can pass these increased costs on to customers. When demand far outstrips supply, you can experience severe labor shortages. You may find that you cannot find the type of workers you need at almost any price. If you are a crew manager of an oil and gas pipeline construction project and you cannot find pipefitters, your business suffers because of either no or slow progress on the pipeline. If you are the manager of a programming group and you just cannot find qualified programmers, your product may get substantially delayed or die because a competitor comes out with its product before you and takes the entire market.

Labor unions are another important dimension in the labor force. While labor unions have declined in the United States over the last several decades, they still are a powerful force in certain industries. For example, nearly 80 percent of the employees in the commercial airline industry are represented by unions. These unions can put powerful pressure on managers to increase wages and offer other desired benefits such as health care or sick days because of the ability of unions to get their members to act in coordination. This is in part why pilots are one of the highest-paid professionals in the United States. A strike by pilots means that planes can't fly because they are not easily replaced. Most airline managers are not pilots, or even if they are, they are not certified to fly the airline's planes. If the planes are not flying, the airlines can't collect revenue but they still have to pay expenses. In just a few short days, a pilot's strike at a company like United Airlines can cost billions of dollars.

Regulators

Regulators consist of both regulatory agencies and interest groups. A regulatory agency is one created by the government to establish and enforce standards and practices, primarily to protect the public's interests. Interest groups are nongovernment organizations (often referred to as NGOs) that are organized to serve the interests of their members. While they have no official regulator or enforcement power, they can exert tremendous influence on organizations.[26]

Regulatory agencies are of special note in an organization's external task environment because of the extent to which they can influence and in some cases dictate organization actions. For example, pharmaceutical companies such as Merck cannot introduce new drugs for sale without the approval of the Food and Drug Administration (FDA). The agency also prescribes the standards that new drugs have to meet and the process of testing and development they must go through to meet those standards. In this context, the regulator determines many of the rules of the competitive game among pharmaceutical companies. The Securities and Exchange Commission (SEC) regulates public companies to ensure proper and full disclosure to protect the investing public. According to the agency, "The primary mission of the U.S. Securities and Exchange Commission (SEC) is to protect investors and maintain the integrity of the securities markets."[27] The bankruptcies of such well-known firms as Enron, WorldCom, Global Crossing, and others, due to improper disclosure of financial information, intensified the role of the SEC, its enforcement of agency regulations, and even led to the resignation of SEC Chairman Harvey Pitt in 2003 because of the view that he was not tough enough in enforcing SEC regulations.

While young managers may not have much experience with regulatory agencies, experienced managers know that agencies such as the SEC, FDA, Federal Trade Commission (FTC), Federal Aviation Agency (FAA), Environ-

"Fur is dead!"—not a slogan furriers long to hear in the face of industry protests launched by nongovernmental organizations such as the Northwest Animal Rights Network (NARN), and, in some cases, taken up by celebrities like game-show host Bob Barker, shown in the photo. Regulatory bodies directly influence firms but organizations such as anti-fur groups can have a huge impact on public opinion—and corporate profits.

mental Protection Agency (EPA), Equal Employment Opportunity Commission (EEOC), and others exert direct and powerful influences on organizations that managers must understand and incorporate into their decisions and actions.

Interest groups such as Greenpeace are often as well recognized by the public as official government agencies. This is primarily because these NGOs have learned that influencing public opinion through the news media can have as much influence on organizations as efforts to lobby lawmakers or organizational executives directly. For example, Greenpeace has refined the art of sending small inflatable boats out to try to block shipments they believe are harmful to the environment. They run the boats dangerously close to the cargo ships creating footage that news stations find hard to resist and that end up being seen by millions of people.[28] Other NGOs of significant power include the National Rifle Association (NRA), National Organization of Women (NOW), the Sierra Club, and Mothers Against Drunk Driving (MADD).

Task Environment Summary

From this introduction and discussion, it should be fairly clear that these task environment forces have a powerful influence on organizations and their performance. Task environments are important, but they do not predetermine success or failure. That is, you can position your organization within a task environment and industry so that your organization performs better than your competitors. We mention this because we do not want to create the impression that if you are in an "unattractive" industry (i.e., one in which the task environment forces are generally aligned to result in lower profits), you are doomed to lower profits. Most airlines have lost money because of the nature of the five forces in that industry; however, as we mentioned, Southwest has made money. In fact, it has made so much money that if you had bought $10,000 of Southwest stock when it was issued about 20 years ago, your stock would now be worth $8.8 million! So clearly, organizations can survive and flourish even in hostile environments. How you can accomplish that is the subject of Chapter 6 on strategic management.

Exhibits 3.6 and 3.7 provide a summary of the task environment for Jet-Blue. JetBlue was started in 2000 and was profitable by 2001. It is famous for

exhibit 3.6

Description of the Task Environment of JetBlue

Competitors
- Rivalry
Primarily based on price which generally hurts performance.
Many established and big players, including profitable ones such as Southwest.
- New Entrants
With $35 million anyone can start an airline; however, the frequency of past failure makes it less likely for new entrants.
- Substitutes
As video conferencing gets better with faster connections, it may substitute for some face-to-face business meetings. It is less likely to substitute for leisure, tourist, or personal visit travel.

Customers
- Business travelers who want convenience.
- Leisure travelers who want low price.

Suppliers
- Airbus supplies all of JetBlue's planes (all are Airbus 320s).
- Many jet fuel suppliers such as ExxonMobil.

Strategic Partners
- Currently not a part of any airline alliance.
- Initial partner with satellite TV provider (it later bought the company).

Labor
- Currently not represented by labor unions.
- Ample supply of pilots and flight attendants due to significant downsizing in other airlines.

Regulators
- FAA dictates many standards and regulations.
- Airport authorities determine access and cost of landing slots and gates at airports.

exhibit 3.7

The Task Environment of JetBlue

its satellite TV available at every seat and at incredibly low prices. To make a profit, it keeps its costs even lower.

THE INTERNAL ENVIRONMENT

Much of this text is about the internal organizational environment, and therefore this section should be considered a very brief introduction. Part of the reason that we introduce the internal organizational environment here is that much of the meaning of external environment can only be found when translated into the organization. In addition, much of what should be done or can be done in response to the external environment is a function of the nature of the organization's internal environment.

Owners

Owners have legal rights to the assets of a company. The owner of a company could be an individual or a collection of shareholders. As an example of a diversified group of people and institutions owning a public company, consider that in 2003, Microsoft had 10 billion shares outstanding.[29] That is enough for each person on the face of the planet to own one share of Microsoft and still leave enough left over for Bill Gates to remain the richest man on earth. The structure and nature of ownership is critical when assessing the relationship between the external and internal environment. For example, if the owner is a single individual, he or she can determine the general objectives of the organization. The owner might determine that maximizing profits is not the ultimate objective and instead place a strong emphasis on giving back to the community. This is the case with the actor Paul Newman. He owns the company Newman's Own, which makes a variety of food products including salad dressings and spaghetti sauces. Since 1982 the company has donated over $150 million to charities, which represents the vast majority of its after tax profits.[30] This would be quite difficult for a public company such as Microsoft, in which the owners include a diversified set of shareholders who in general want a return on their investments rather than the company to give its profits to charitable organizations. This brings up the issue of what are a company's responsibilities to shareholders, communities, and others, which we will examine in depth in Chapter 5, when we examine managerial ethics and corporate social responsibility.

Board of Directors

Companies often have a board of directors or a set of individuals elected by shareholders of the company who represent the interests of the shareholders. As such the board of directors has the responsibility of overseeing the general management of the company but it typically does not run the company. The board can consist of individuals from both inside and outside the company. While boards are not there to run the company, they are not there to simply rubber stamp whatever management wants to do. Boards should understand the nature of the business and its operations, and review major decisions to ensure that the interests of shareholders are being protected. In the past several years, boards have come under greater scrutiny for not being as active or involved as perhaps they should have been.[31] This has primarily been driven by such big corporate bankruptcies as Kmart, Enron, Worldcom, and others where it seems that the problems that caused the downfall of the firms could have and should have been known by board members far in advance of when they finally came out.

Employees

Employees are an additional force in the internal environment. To some extent we can use the two dimensions of the sociocultural external general environment force (i.e., demographics and values) as a means of examining key aspects of employees. In terms of demographics, factors such as age and distribution of age, gender, and ethnic diversity can all be important to managers. For example, in Dofasco (the Canadian steel company mentioned earlier in this chapter) the average age of workers is mid- to late forties. Over the next several years, many of its skilled workers will retire. The importance of labor in its external task environment took on special significance when managers within Dofasco realized that the external labor pool was shrinking just at the time it would need to replace its aging internal workforce. Employee values are also important for managers to consider when trying to understand internal organization environmental forces. In Dofasco's case, employees have a strong value for job security and stability in the tasks they perform. In other words, employees want to know they have a secure job, and they want that job to be largely what it has been in the past. This creates some concern among Dofasco managers when they examine aspects of their general and task environment. In the general environment, economic downturn means that they have to lower their costs to remain profitable. This may require shifting workers from one area of the company to another or even laying some workers off. The shifting steel requirements of customers in its task environment means that Dofasco must be more flexible in the mix of existing products it produces and must be innovative in coming up with new products that meet customer needs. Both of these requirements may require employees to be more flexible in what they do, which is in conflict with the values of many employees. As a consequence, this internal environment force of employee values makes responding to external forces much more challenging.

The U.S. airlines industry has been hard hit by profitability problems in recent years. But JetBlue and other startup airlines have been successful, in part, due to their corporate culture. JetBlue employees, who are not unionized, take on different responsibilities when necessary to keep the company's planes in the air and its costs and fares low. Even the company's CEO, David Neeleman, shown in the photo, helps out where necessary.

Internal and external environmental forces do not necessarily need to be conflicting. They may be complementary. For example, in the case of Jet-Blue, the fact that there was a surplus of pilots in the external labor environment during its start-up and early operations was significant in part because senior managers wanted to have a nonunion employee base. Given that about 80 percent of all employees working for U.S. airlines are represented by unions, an excess supply of pilots (due to the tough economic times from 2000 to 2003) made it easier for JetBlue executives to achieve their internal employee objective.

Culture

Culture is such an important and complex topic that we devote the next chapter (Chapter 4) to the subject. As a consequence, we will be brief here about the nature of culture and its role in the internal environment. As we will elaborate in Chapter 4, the culture of an organization is a learned set of assumptions, values, and beliefs that have proven successful enough to be taught to newcomers. The culture of an organization can have a significant impact on how the external environment is perceived and what are easy or difficult responses to it.

We can see an illustration of the interplay between internal and external environments if we return to the case of JetBlue. For JetBlue an important element of its task environment is price competition. While it is not the only factor, the price of a plane ticket is a significant factor for customers when they decide which carrier to fly. If executives at JetBlue want to attract customers by offering lower prices and at the same time want to make a profit, the company must have significantly lower costs than its competitors. One of the ways to achieve lower costs is by keeping planes in the air longer rather than to have them sitting unused. This is greatly facilitated by having shorter turnaround times at the gate. (JetBlue targets a 30-minute turnaround while the industry average is over an hour.) This requires pilots, flight attendants, baggage handlers, and cleaning crews to all pitch in and help. Having a culture in which all employees want to do what is necessary to turn the planes around quickly also helps achieve the productivity objective, which in turn lowers costs, and ultimately contributes to profits even when JetBlue's prices are low.

As you can see from these examples, a practical application of environmental analysis requires keeping the dual elements of the external and internal environments in mind and relating the two. This is not an easy task and there is no magic formula for doing it well. Part of the trick, however, is having a systematic understanding of both external and internal organizational environments. The first part of this chapter has provided a fairly comprehensive framework for understanding the external general and task environment of organizations as well as the internal environment.

ENVIRONMENTAL SCANNING AND RESPONSE

Given all the elements of the environment that we have covered, it should be clear that effective managers need to scan the environment constantly to monitor changes. This chapter helps that process by pointing out the different critical areas to monitor. Trying to monitor everything would simply be overwhelming. Consequently, the first principle of effective environmental

**Environmental Scanning
by Michael Hitt**

Q&A

www.prenhall.com/onekey

scanning is knowing "what" to scan. Again, the environmental forces we have covered constitute a reasonable framework for the *what* when it comes to environmental scanning.

However, even if you know what to scan, you will still need a plan for how to scan. What do you look for to provide you with information on economic, sociocultural, legal and political, and technological forces? Where do you look for information on competitors, new entrants, substitutes, customers, and suppliers? Business publications such as *Fortune, Business Week, The Economist, Financial Times*, and the *Wall Street Journal* are probably good starting points. However, for industry-specific information, you likely will need to turn to more specialized trade journals.

An important thing to keep in mind concerning public sources of information is that everyone has equal access to them. Consequently, as a manager you have two basic means of gaining advantage. First, you can work at being superior to others in analyzing publicly available information and anticipating how it relates to your job, company, and industry. Second, you can seek advantage by gaining information from nonpublic sources. This may be as simple as asking people you meet in your business (or even personal) travels about developments in any of the areas mentioned in this chapter. For example, an acquaintance may inform you of rising worker unrest in China that could affect your joint venture there long before word shows up in local or, especially, international newspapers. This advance information may help you anticipate and prepare for events rather than just react.

But whether you focus on public or private sources of information, effective scanning has a few basic components (see Exhibit 3.8):

- **Define:** The first step involves determining what type of information you should scan for and where and how you plan to acquire the information.
- **Recognize:** Next you must recognize information as relevant.
- **Analyze:** Once you have recognized information, you need to analyze it and determine its implications.
- **Respond:** Finally, the full force of the information lies in its application to your job, company, or industry. Essentially, in this stage you are answering two key questions: What impact will this information have and how can I respond effectively?

Define

Much of this chapter is devoted to addressing this first issue. The categories of the general external environment forces as well as those for the task environment constitute an effective framework for defining what information you need. As we mentioned, both public and private sources should be utilized in gaining information on all aspects of the external environment.

exhibit 3.8

Environmental Scanning

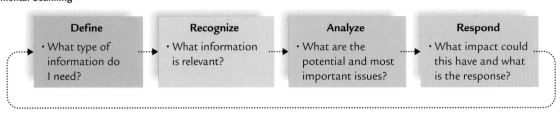

Define	Recognize	Analyze	Respond
• What type of information do I need?	• What information is relevant?	• What are the potential and most important issues?	• What impact could this have and what is the response?

Recognize

Interestingly, in this digital age, information is not hard to come by. In fact, in many cases you are likely to be overloaded with information even if you use the environmental forces framework in this chapter. As a result, you will need to sift through and determine which information is relevant for your situation. This task is facilitated by asking how specific information you gather might relate to your organization. For example, as we mentioned earlier, even if you know that the economy is currently in a down cycle and is expected to recover in the next 12 months, this information may be more important to a housing construction firm than to a funeral home.

Analyze

Effective analysis has at least two separate but related aspects. First, a good environmental analysis needs to look for and examine the interactive effects of different environmental forces. Second, a good analysis needs to explore the specific implications that environmental forces in isolation and especially in combination likely has for your organization. Interactive effects can be of a complementary or even amplifying nature or they can be of a mitigating nature. We will examine both through some examples.

To illustrate the importance of examining mitigating interactive effects between or among different environmental forces, let's assume you were a manager in a residential home construction company. In 2000 the U.S. economy experienced a mild recession and the economy continued in a very slow growth state through 2003. Generally, this would cause people to buy fewer homes (new or used) as they worried about their job security and income. However, at the same time interest rates hit a 40-year low. This made owning a home more affordable. Overall, home purchases and mortgage refinancing hit near record highs. In this case, the low interest rates mitigated and nearly cancelled out the normal effects of a down economic cycle.

Environmental forces can also serve to reinforce or even amplify each other. For example, the declining number of 35-to-45-year-olds in the United States created a talent shortage for many companies starting in about 1998. The rise of technology, especially the Internet, meant that employees could go onto HotJobs.com or Monster.com and find out the general demand for skills and experience such as theirs and what the market rate was for those skills and experience. In combination these two forces meant that employees with valuable and scarce skills were even harder to hold on to. Add to these two forces the political-legal force of few work visas granted to immigrants with highly sought-after skills relative to demand and you have an even more powerful implication if you are a manager charged with attracting and retaining these sorts of in-demand employees.

Respond

How can organizations respond effectively to changing environmental demands? As we explained at the outset, research as well as experience strongly suggest that responding effectively to changes is key to managerial success over time. As a result, it is impossible and impractical to confine our answer to how organizations can respond effectively to environmental changes to just this section. Still, we can frame many of the general responses in the following four categories: direct influence, strategic response, organization agility, and information management.

Direct Influence Managers and organizations are not simply at the mercy of environmental changes; they are not simply passive receptacles that must take whatever the environment dishes out. Managers do and should try to influence the political-legal process when they believe that existing or proposed legal requirements unjustly restrict their activities. For example, in 2001 many U.S. steel companies successfully lobbied the government to impose tariffs on the steel foreign companies were exporting to the United States, claiming these companies were "dumping" steel in the U.S. market (selling it below their cost). But the fact was that the foreign companies were simply able to produce steel at a much lower cost than their U.S. competitors could, and the tariffs were later lifted. However, if foreign steelmakers had, in fact, been dumping products in the United States, then it seems reasonable for managers to try to directly influence this environmental change via political-legal pressure. The fact is, though, pursuing political-legal pressure is a strategy often used by managers to alter their competitive environment for the companies, regardless of whether their allegations hold merit.

Strategic Response But suppose it was found that foreign firms were not dumping their product in the U.S. market. How might U.S. steel firms respond? In this case they might choose among a number of strategic responses. They might form a joint venture with a foreign company overseas in order to take advantage of the lower costs in that locale (such as lower iron ore costs, lower labor rates, and so on). Alternatively, they might merge with another U.S. firm, which is largely what has happened in the United States. The mergers were designed to lower costs by leveraging operations or eliminating duplication. For example, the combined purchasing power of two companies might get them lower costs for raw materials such as iron ore or coal by leveraging their high purchase volumes for pricing discounts. The merged firms might lower costs by eliminating jobs in common support functions such as human resources (HR) because they only need 50 percent more HR staff to support twice the number of employees. We will explore more about strategy and strategic response in Chapter 6.

Organizational Agility To the extent that environmental change is frequent and/or unpredictable, managers might respond by creating a more flexible or agile organization. While we will examine this in great detail in Chapter 7, managers can structure and design organizations for greater (or lesser) flexibility. For example, rules tend to work best when the environment is fairly stable and does not change much. People can follow the rules and because the environment doesn't change much, following the rules is likely to produce results that fit the environment. On the other hand, in environments that change often, rules tend to not work well. They lead to rigidity and inflexibility. In contrast, having people share common values gives them greater flexibility to respond to the changing environment. Because the needs of customers are seen as changing too quickly, managers at Nordstrom stress the customer service value and not rules. They try to help employees value satisfying the customer and to use their own judgment in responding to changing customer needs.

Information Management Exhibit 3.8 illustrates that the process is circular, not just linear. In other words, ultimately your response should feed back into your definition. Information management is a specific response that highlights this feedback loop. For example, if you are a manager in a residential home construction business, you have learned over time and with experience that interest rates are one of the most important forces in the general economic area. As a consequence, you may develop means of capturing all the indicators and estimators of future interest rates. You may further refine this information management system by determining over time which indicators or estimators prove to be the most accurate in forecasting future interest rates. This information management response actually accelerates and enhances your ability to define, recognize, and therefore analyze and respond, or perhaps even anticipate, environmental changes.

Summary of Environmental Scanning and Response

By necessity we have simplified and segmented the discussion of environmental analysis. However, the reality is that one of the greatest challenges you would face as a practicing manager is that the environment does not really come in nice, segmented pieces. Also, quite often a single event can have an impact across multiple segments. An event could affect multiple aspects of your general and task environment.

No one needs to be reminded of what happened on September 11, 2001 (interestingly the date by number is 911, the universal emergency number in the United States). It was the most deadly attack on U.S. soil. The tragedy of the event was almost incomprehensible. Yet, for managers everywhere, the reality of having to deal with it was unrelenting. Even if business was not the most important priority, managers literally around the world had people whose jobs and futures depended in part on their ability to effectively anticipate and deal with the ripple effects of the tragedy; and the ripple effects of this event were potentially massive. If you were in the airline industry, the potential implications were staggering. For example, within 10 days, most major U.S. airlines had announced layoffs of 20 percent of their workforce. Even outside those industries that were most directly affected, managers had to speculate about the business environment impacts. How would the events affect the economy? The United States was already in a significant economic slowdown if not a recession. Would this push the economy over the edge? What would be the likely political reactions and what would their impact be? Would it change government spending? How would the events affect people and their values? There was already an increased desire among workers for a balance between work and family. Would this tilt these sentiments in the direction of family? If so, what would it mean for, say, a recruiting manager? What would be the ripple effects on the economies of other nations? For example, Singapore was already in recession and exports accounted for 160 percent of GDP. Two-thirds of those exports were high tech in nature and the United States was its largest market. Would this throw Singapore into an even deeper recession? What if your company had a factory in Singapore and in China? Unlike Singapore, China's GDP was growing at the time and exports accounted for only 20 percent of GDP. Should you close one of the factories? If so, which one?

As you can see by just this small set of questions the analytical task of environmental analysis for managers in this situation is huge. On the one hand, we presented the task of environmental analysis in an artificially clean and segmented way. As the tragedy of the World Trade Towers illustrates, actual problems do not present themselves in nice, neat packets. On the other hand, imagine trying to analyze the business environment implications without a segmented framework. The task would be overwhelming.

managerial perspectives revisited

1

PERSPECTIVE 1: THE ORGANIZATIONAL CONTEXT   While the external environment is not a deterministic force and inevitably dooms an organization to a predetermined level of performance, it does present important demands, constraints, and opportunities. However, these are not absolutes; they have practical application only in the context of a given organization. For example, an increase in older citizens might create an opportunity for a new pharmaceutical company but present a constraint for a hospital with no room or money for expansion. Consequently, effective managers have to analyze the environment from the perspective of their organization. As we discussed, the ultimate practical value of environmental analysis lies in seeing the implications for your organization and determining the appropriate response. In the absence of the organizational context, external general or task environmental analysis is more an academic exercise than a managerial activity.

2

PERSPECTIVE 2: THE HUMAN FACTOR   Hopefully, this chapter has helped illustrate how complex an assessment of the external environment can be while providing a few concepts and tools to make that easier. What we haven't stressed during the chapter but should stress here at the end is that it is rare for a manager to conduct a formal assessment of the external environment on his or her own. In fact, the more complex the company and the environment, the more likely it is that several people will be involved in the assessment based on their particular specialty or expertise. For example, as a manager, you may need your sales representatives to give you feedback on what their counterparts are doing out in the field. You may need to rely on people in your technology department to keep up with the technological developments of your competitors. You may need people in financial departments to gauge outside forces like interest rates, stock prices, economic outlook, and so on in order to provide you with information to make good decisions about where and how to spend money in the company in response to these environmental forces. It is because of this that we want to highlight here that one of the distinguishing capabilities of a manager relative to external environment assessments is the ability to work with and through others to gather, analyze, integrate, and then act on the assessment.

3

PERSPECTIVE 3: MANAGING PARADOXES   One fundamental challenge of environmental assessments is managing the focus on both the near and long terms. Often, individuals, teams, and companies have to make changes based on assessments of the current external environment. The present cannot be ignored. But the current economic conditions or state of technology as well as other important aspects of the environment are not likely to remain stable. Consequently, to be effective in assessing the environment and then making strategic, planning, and other decisions, as a manager you will need to be able to manage the paradox of simultaneously considering both the present and the future environmental conditions. Another potential paradox associated with effective environmental analysis is that of separating and integrating at the same time. On the one hand, you must segment and divide aspects of the environment to analyze and understand the complexities involved. This is precisely why we have divided the external environment into the general and task categories and have further divided each of these into subcategories. However, an environmental analysis of isolated bits and pieces is incomplete. You must also integrate the results of the separate analyses of the various pieces. Effective environmental analysis is not about doing just one or the other. It is about doing both. As stated in this chapter's introduction, the integration of the analyses should help us identify the environmental opportunities and threats that exist. In addition, even though we use the term "environmental analysis," effective management requires both analysis and action. In fact, the practical relevance of the analysis only comes to life with action—organizational response. The actions should be based on the environmental opportunities and threats identified. As a result, as a manager you will need the ability to both think and do; to both conduct an effective environmental analysis and act and react in ways that help you, your subordinates, and the company deal with the external environment.

 PERSPECTIVE 4: ENTREPRENEURIAL MIND-SET As we noted in Chapter 1, a critical component of an entrepreneurial mind-set is identifying opportunities. Opportunities are most likely to exist in an organization's external environment. Thus, analyzing the external environment is necessary to identify opportunities for the organization to exploit. An organization could identify opportunities afforded by changes in government regulations by analyzing the political-legal environment. For example, Federal Express was started when the airline industry was deregulated.

Analyzing changing demographic trends can also provide opportunities. For instance, the growing Hispanic population in the United States presents many new opportunities for businesses. Assessing the environment can broaden managers' knowledge and understanding and allow them to take advantage of entrepreneurial opportunities like this. It also signifies a commitment to acquire new knowledge and skills. Although new knowledge can be tapped from within an organization, the external environment is an important source. Strategic partnerships can afford access to new knowledge as well.

concluding comments

At this point you can see that while some people might think that the task of external environment analysis is the job of specialized analysts, it is not. It is true that in large organizations entire departments may be dedicated to analyzing the economic or political forces in the environment. Although reports from others inside or outside the company can be valuable, you have to be personally aware of and understand these forces. Without such personal awareness and understanding of critical environmental forces, you might not recognize valuable information even if you had it in your hands. As manager, you must accurately and systematically identify critical factors in the external environment and understand cause-and-effect relationships. Only then will you be able to anticipate, rather than simply react to, external environment challenges.

Certainly, effective analysis of all the various forces within the industry, domestic, and international environments is a big challenge. However, two even larger challenges remain. The first is to begin to see links among the various forces within an environment. For example, it is one thing to do a good analysis of the substitution and customer forces within the industry environment. It is quite another to see that the lack of substitutes and the fragmented nature of customers combine to offer an unprecedented opportunity for growth. Only in drawing the connections can you plan effectively and exploit opportunities for growth.

The second major challenge is seeing the connections between a particular business and its industry, domestic, and international environments. Seeing relationships among them is a quality of a truly gifted manager. If we return to our natural environment analogy, seeing relationships among these environments is like being able to see causes and effects between a plant and its environment. Finding the right conditions to favor growth and survival is as important to business as it is in nature. Organizations thrive or perish according to their fit with their environments.

Meeting the basic challenge of understanding and analyzing individual environmental forces is a significant accomplishment for a manager. Meeting the challenge of seeing relationships among different forces within an environment is exciting. Meeting the challenge of seeing relationships among different environments is a never-ending challenge—one that makes management an exciting and invigorating profession.

key terms

demographics 78	internal environment 77	strategic partners 95
entry barriers 94	process technological changes 81	structural changes 84
external environment 77	product technological	substitutes 94
general environment 77	changes 81	switching costs 93
gross domestic product 85	societal values 79	task environment 77

test your comprehension

1. Define the external environment.
2. What are key differences between the external, general, and task environments?
3. List four examples of important demographics.
4. Why are societal values important to an assessment of the general external environment?
5. What are the key differences between product and process technological changes?
6. Why is an awareness of both critical to an assessment of the technological environment?
7. Why are economic cycles important to consider in addition to current economic conditions?
8. How are structural economic changes different from economic cycles?
9. Why is government spending important to consider when analyzing the legal and political environment?
10. What are the key features of a country's physical environment?
11. Name three key institutions that should be included in an environmental analysis.
12. What are the Porter Five Forces?
13. If the nature of competition or rivalry in an industry is primarily based on price, do profit margins in that industry tend to increase or decrease?
14. What are entry barriers and why do they matter in an analysis of the industry environment?
15. If there are few new entrants to an industry and if entry barriers are large, do profit margins in that industry tend to increase or decrease?
16. What are switching costs?
17. What is the difference between a substitute and a competing product?
18. What are the four steps to effective environmental scanning?
19. Why is there a feedback loop between Response and Define in the environmental scanning and response model?

apply your understanding

1. What key environmental *changes* do you think will increasingly force managers to be proficient at conducting environmental analyses?
2. Are there industries that will be more immune to changes in the global environment and as a consequence will be influenced primarily by their domestic external environment? Name at least two and explain why.
3. What are the most difficult environmental analysis skills to develop? What are some possible means of ensuring that you have these valuable skills?
4. Debate the following statement: Computers and news media have made international environment analysis simpler.
5. Pick a country and go to the library or the Internet to find some information about its resources, government, political and legal systems, and physical infrastructure. What type of business would do well in that country? Why?

practice your capabilities

You are the purchasing manager of a specialty retail company that has just over 20 stores in large shopping malls in California, Colorado, and Utah. These stores specialize in equipment and clothing targeted at "boarders," that is, guys and increasingly girls who surf, skateboard, snowboard, and/or wakeboard. Since U.S. athletes swept the medals in the 2002 Winter Olympics, you have seen an increase both in traffic in your stores and in sales.

The president of the company wants you to come up with an initial analysis and recommendation for the coming year regarding whether the company should anticipate an increase or decrease in sales. Last year sales of equipment declined by 9 percent while sales of clothing dropped by 5 percent. In looking toward the future, you decide to do a quick STEP analysis.

Sociocultural

First you decide you need some information on the demographics of your target customer (i.e., boys and secondarily girls ages 14–24). Is this group growing or shrinking in the three states in which you have stores? Someone mentioned to you that www.governmentguide.com might be a Web site that could help you find this information.

Second, you determine that you also need to try to get a sense of the values of the boarding culture and how strongly they are supported in your target customer population. Many of your current customers talk about the freedom and excellence that boarding represents. The icon of skateboarding is Tony Hawk, so you decide to check out how well his video game is selling. For wakeboards, it's pros like Cathy Williams, Christy Smith, Wayne Mawer, and Dave Briscoe that you need

to check out. For snowboarding, the 2002 Winter Olympics vaulted Chris Klug, Russ Powers, Danny Kass, and J. J. Thomas to the head of the class.

Technology

While you don't feel that technology is affecting your clothing lines that much, you wonder if it might be a factor for equipment. Your top equipment brands are Burton for snowboards, Hawk and Hollywood for skateboards, and Neptune and Connely for wakeboards. So you go to their Web sites to see if any new technological changes are on the horizon.

Economic

You also want to get a sense of what is happening with the economy. Unemployment, inflation, and consumer spending seem like important facts to check out first.

Political-Legal

While no political or legal issues immediately jump to mind as potentially having a big impact on your business, you wonder about insurance laws affecting skateboarding parks or whether helmets or some sort of headgear might be required in the future for snowboarding or wakeboarding. You've seen a few people get rather nasty cuts on their heads when they crashed and the board they were riding hit them, and they required stitches.

1. After gathering information in each of these four areas, which ones seem to point in a positive direction for your business? Which ones seem to point in a negative direction?

2. Currently, your sales are split about 50/50 between equipment and clothing. Does anything in your analysis indicate that this should be changed in the future?

3. What is your overall recommendation? Should purchases move up?

4. On a broader note, should the company think about increasing or decreasing the number of stores it has?

closing case   DEVELOP YOUR CRITICAL THINKING

KB Home Corp.: Its Business Is Building

With over $5 billion in sales, Los Angeles–based KB Home Corp. is the nation's largest home builder. KB has been creating homes for over 45 years and it built more than 25,000 houses in 2002 alone.

How does a company like this manage to survive and grow in an industry that is subject—quite literally—to the winds of change? For instance, weather conditions, from average rainfall to outright disasters such as hurricanes and tornadoes, affect the rate at which homes can be built in a given region. General economic conditions, such as interest rates or unemployment, affect whether people can afford new homes. Demographics can even affect the fortunes of home builders. For example, people tend to purchase their largest and most expensive homes in their mid- to late forties, near the peak of their earnings and when they still have children at home. The majority of the 80-million-strong baby-boom generation were in their forties during the 1990s and into the early part of the twenty-first century. Little wonder that during that period the housing industry set new records for homes built.

Competitors are another important factor that affects home builders. Although KB Home Corp. is the largest builder in the United States (and even builds homes in France), it still faces stiff competition not only from other large builders, such as Lennar and Centex, but from local builders who are successful because they know their suppliers and the customers personally. Bruce Karatz, CEO of KB Home, takes the competition seriously. When KB's land-purchase committee reviews a proposed land deal, one of the important considerations is who the local competitors are.

KB also has to keep an eye on substitutes for single-family homes. To compete with rental units and condominiums, it has a line of less expensive homes and develops neighborhoods with smaller lots to ensure the overall purchase price is competitive while offering the better value of one's own yard and privacy versus sharing a wall, ceiling, or floor with a neighbor in a condominium complex.

KB also has to keep an eye on customers. Managers not only have to keep track of how economic conditions are affecting customers' purchasing power but on their tastes and preferences. For example, KB has significantly modified many of its floor plans by offering larger closets and bedrooms and increasing the number of bathrooms in homes. However, cities and their citizens are increasingly against rapid growth and sprawl of homes and want less density and more open and green space within communities. KB has had to change from being a home builder to being a community and neighborhood designer. This creates a need not only to keep in touch with public sentiment but the potential to try to influence it. Gary Garczynski, president of National Capital Land & Development, put it this way, "Two things people oppose most are growth and density. However, we have to remind the public that houses are where jobs go to spend the night."

Looking forward, KB faces some important challenges in the external environment. As the first home builder listed on the New York Stock Exchange, it has to worry about the up-and-down cycles in its business. Shareholders want steady and growing earnings. One help for KB compared to other builders in this regard has been that it has had a mortgage company for over 40 years. Even if home sales move up and down, the revenue from past purchasers as they pay of their loans is a bit more steady. Also, the entry barriers for new competitors are fairly low. Anyone who can get a contractor's license can start a home building company. Stuart Miller, CEO of Lennar Homes, put it this way, "The history with Wall Street is, they've seen [builder] valuations as a roach motel: Anyone can get in it, but no one ever leaves. That's the perception we are up against."

While KB started in California and builds more homes there than elsewhere, it has expanded into many other states. Because not all states' economies, especially regarding housing, move up and down together, this can help smooth out earnings. However, home building is a local business in many ways and KB managers face the decision of how much more they should expand into other states.

Technology is also an emerging issue. Clearly, e-commerce and the Internet present opportunities for closer links with suppliers and potentially lowering the cost of some supplies. For example, by holding "reverse" auctions, where suppliers bid in real time against each other for KB's business needs, KB's purchasing managers can extract lower prices, enhancing the company's profits. The Internet also presents selling opportunities. Prospective buyers can look at community plans, home floor plans, pictures, and even video tours on the Internet. They can get a free credit report, figure out how much they can afford to spend on their home, and add up its cost—including selected upgrades—without ever leaving home. A mix-and-match design feature even lets potential buyers pick out different home elements like floor plans, carpet, and cabinet colors to see how they will look together. All of this helps pique the interest of buyers.

KB survived the economic downturn in 1991 and faced another in 2001. But record-low mortgage rates in 2002 and 2003 helped boost sales and profits sharply, even though unemployment was up. Also, as housing development restrictions increased, demand outstripped

supply, which raised prices in congested but popular real estate markets in California. Because prices rose faster than KB's costs, it helped profits. The industry was also consolidating. Large home builders were buying up smaller ones to leverage economies of scale such as buying power. In response, small, local companies were emphasizing their community roots and commitments compared to the impersonal and profit-driven "big boys" such as KB These and several other environmental factors had to be considered and analyzed before KB Home managers and executives could effectively move the organization and their people toward the future.

Questions

1. Which do you think are the most important environmental forces for KB Home? Why?
2. Are there environmental forces besides those mentioned that you think KB management needs to focus on?
3. How should KB managers address the issue of aging baby boomers?
4. Based on your analysis of the external environment, what changes do you think managers at KB should make?

Sources: Queena Sook Kim, "Home Reports Rise of 12% in Profit on Still-Solid Sales," *Wall Street Journal*, December 19, 2003, p. A6; Queena Sook Kim, "Home Builders KB, D.R. Horton Post Sharp Gains in Net Income," *Wall Street Journal*, January 17, 2003, p. B3; KB Annual Report 2000; Deborah Prussel, "Henry Cisneros Forms Company to Build Housing in City Centers" *Planning*, September 2000, pp. 25–26. R. E. Blake Evans, "Giants Rule Builder," July/August 2000, pp. 46–48.

Managing Within Cultural Contexts*

4

LEARNING OBJECTIVES

After studying this chapter, you should be able to:

■

Explain why a thorough understanding of culture is important
for all managers.

■

Define *culture*.

■

Explain how culture affects managerial behavior and
practices.

■

Describe the role of fundamental assumptions in corporate,
regional, or national cultures.

■

Map aspects of culture in terms of the extent to which they
are deeply held and widely shared.

■

Describe the key strategies managers can use to create and
change culture.

■

Explain the differences between and describe the
implications of high- and low-context cultures.

GE Medical's Sick Patient in France

Senior executives at General Electric (GE), in an effort to increase its global strategic position in medical technology, bought Companie Générale de Radiologie (CGR), a French company. CGR was owned by the state and manufactured medical equipment, with a specific emphasis on X-ray machines and CAT scanners. When GE acquired CGR, it received $800 million in cash from state-controlled Thomson S.A. in return for GE's RCA consumer electronic business. The acquisition of CGR was viewed as a brilliant strategic move, at the time. Combined with

*Parts of this chapter have been adapted with permission from a chapter written by J. Stewart Black, appearing in J. S. Black, H. Gregersen, M. Mendenhall and L. Stroh (Eds.), *Globalizing People Through International Assignments* (Reading, MA: Addison-Wesley, 1999).

GE's strong position in medical imaging technology in the United States, the acquisition of CGR gave GE an immediate and significant position in Europe. GE executives projected a $25 million profit for the first full year of operations. However, things did not turn out as the strategic planners projected.

One of the first things managers responsible for the integration did was to organize a training seminar for the French managers. They left T-shirts with the slogan "Go for Number One" for each of the participants. Although the French managers wore them, many were not happy about it. One manager stated, "It was like Hitler was back forcing us to wear uniforms. It was humiliating."

Soon after the takeover, GE executives from Medical Systems headquarters in the United States sent American specialists to France to fix CGR's financial control system. Unfortunately, these specialists knew very little about French accounting or financial reporting requirements. Consequently, they tried to impose a system that was inappropriate for French financial reporting requirements and for the way CGR had traditionally kept records. For example, the two systems differed on what was defined as a cost versus an expense. This cultural conflict (and the working out of an agreeable compromise) took several months and resulted in substantial direct and indirect costs.

GE managers then tried to coordinate and integrate CGR into its Milwaukee-based medical-equipment unit in several other ways. For example, because CGR racked up a $25 million loss instead of the projected $25 million profit, an American executive from Milwaukee was sent to France to turn the operations around. Several cost-cutting measures, including massive layoffs and the closing of roughly

When General Electric (GE) purchased Companie Générale de Radiologie (CGR), a French company, to bolster its position in Europe, culture clashes between the two companies were legion. Some GE managers believe that the culture clash sounded a wakeup call to GE not only about its employees abroad but also about foreign consumers and how they differ from their American counterparts.

half of the 12 CGR plants, shocked the French workforce. Additionally, the profit-hungry culture of GE continued to clash with the state-run, noncompetitive history and culture of CGR. As a consequence, many valuable managers and engineers left the French subsidiary.

GE managers' efforts to integrate CGR into the GE culture through English-language motivational posters, flying GE flags, and other morale boosters were met with considerable resistance by the French employees. One union leader commented, "They came in here bragging, 'We are GE, we're the best and we've got the methods.'" Although GE officials estimated that GE-CGR would produce a profit in the second year, it lost another $25 million.

Despite these initial cultural blunders, today GE Medical Systems is one of the strongest competitors in the United States and globally. In fact, some managers believe that the culture clashes experienced in France made everyone aware of the important role that national and organizational cultures play in how people see and react to different events. As a consequence, senior GE Medical Systems managers changed their mental maps to recognize that people do not view the world or management the same everywhere. To facilitate this awareness in others, general cross-cultural training, as well as training specifically in French culture and the business environment, was provided for all Americans transferred to France. With this greater awareness of organizational and national culture, GE Medical Systems executives were able to leverage the knowledge and alternative perspectives of managers in the French acquisition into a powerful and globally competitive enterprise.

Sources: Personal communication, 2002; J. S. Black, H. Gregersen, M. Mendenhall and L. Stroh (Eds.), *Globalizing People Through International Assignments* (Boston: Addison-Wesley, 1999).

strategic overview

As the GE Medical Systems example illustrates, even companies that have strong reputations and many years of experience can run aground on unseen cultural reefs as they navigate in today's complex business waters. Culture is important because it is a significant driver of how people see and interpret events and what actions they take. This is true whether the source of the culture is at the national, organizational, or subgroup level. So understanding what constitutes culture and what makes it so powerful in influencing organizations and their performance is important for all managers.

Many people think culture is something an organization, region, or country has—something you can see, hear, touch, smell, or taste. People who take this view often point to clothing, customs, ceremonies, music, historical landmarks, art, and food as examples of culture. For example, you might notice designated parking places at a company and infer that the culture of the company places high value on status. You might notice that when you exchange business cards with business associates of a given culture they pay very close attention to the title on your card or education qualifications (such as Ph.D.). Based on this observation, you might infer that people from that country place a high value on hierarchy. However, these cultural markers are only the most visible, and in many ways the least powerful, aspects of culture.

Culture can play a major role in organizations, with direct effects on strategic actions chosen by managers and the performance of the strategies selected. For example, most large and many small organizations now sell their goods and services in markets outside their home countries. They also frequently invest in and manage operations in other countries. To sell products in foreign markets and to establish and operate facilities in other countries requires managers to understand the cultures in those countries. Research has shown that most managers who use a strategy of selling their products in foreign markets first market their goods in countries where the cultures are most similar to their domestic environment. It is easier for managers to enter a market where the culture is similar than one which is quite different.[1] They can better understand the similar culture requiring less adaptation to the customers and employees in that culture. For example, organizations in Canada entering into international markets may first market their products in the United States or England. If the organizations are from Quebec, with a strong French influence, they might also market their products in France. As managers gain experience operating in different cultures, they are likely to expand operations to countries where the culture is less similar and thus may operate in many countries. For example, Siemens sells products in 190 different countries, and has established 31 separate Web sites using 38 different languages.[2] To facilitate movement into new international markets, foreign organizations often develop strategic relationships with local organizations. The local business organizations know the culture in those markets and this helps the managers from the foreign company adapt to that culture.[3] Local organizations have contacts with suppliers and government units, but they also can help the managers of their foreign partner learn about and understand the new culture. Developing a better understanding of the culture will help the foreign managers to sell their products in the new market and will also help them to hire and manage the people that they employ in that new market. Thus, as organizations enter more international markets, managers must learn to manage an increasing amount of cultural diversity. That is, they must understand the different cultural values of their customers and employees, respect those differences, and adapt their products and managerial styles to fit the different cultures. An inability to understand and adapt to the local cultures will ultimately produce failure of the international operations. Therefore, success of an international operation hinges on managers understanding cultural differences before they enter foreign markets and adapting their managerial practices thereafter. It also requires that they integrate and use the cultural diversity to their advantage. ■

DEFINITION OF CULTURE

To appreciate the full importance and impact of culture, we need to take a somewhat complex and broad view of it.[4] Although a team of anthropologists identified over 160 different definitions of culture,[5] we define it as follows: **Culture** is a learned set of assumptions, values, and behaviors that have been accepted as successful enough to be passed on to newcomers. This definition gives us a thorough picture of what culture is and how it forms.

As the definition suggests, a culture begins when a group of people face a set of challenges. In an organization, the culture might begin to form when the

culture a learned set of assumptions, values, and behaviors that have been accepted as successful enough to be passed on to newcomers

early members face the initial challenges of starting the organization-securing funding, creating products, distributing products to customers, and so on. Early leaders typically have a set of beliefs that guide their behaviors and choices. For example, a leader might believe that tight supervision of employees is best. To the extent that these early decisions and practices work, they typically are retained. This is why early leaders have a significant impact on the exact nature of the company culture.[6] The assumptions, values, and behaviors that are successful are taught to newcomers. In an organization, these newcomers are new hires. In a national culture, newcomers are essentially children born to the group or immigrants who come into the country. So for the newcomers, the culture is learned, not inherited. Culture is taught to newcomers primarily through symbols and communication, such as stories, speeches, discussions, manuals, novels, poems, art, and so on. Over time, specific assumptions, values, and behaviors come to be shared among the members of the group. However, because circumstances change, what are considered successful responses at one point in time can also evolve and change. As a consequence, culture is adaptive.

With this definition of culture, you can see that the concept potentially can be applied to a group of any size. For example, a large group of people sharing a geographic boundary, such as a country, can have a culture. In fact, many of the studies of culture have used countries as the unit to compare cultural similarities and differences. Within a country, members of the same organization can share an organizational culture. As you might expect, where a smaller group resides within a larger one, such as a company within a country or a work team within a company, research has found that the culture of the smaller group is often influenced by and reflects the culture of the larger group. For example, Japanese companies tend to make decisions by consensus as a reflection of the larger societal cultural value on groups. However, throughout this chapter, whenever we talk about a particular cultural characteristic for a country, region, or company, it is important to keep in mind that there is a distribution of individuals around that characteristic. For example, while Japan as a country tends to have stronger group versus individual orientations, some individuals in Japan are more or less group-oriented than the average. In the same vein, some Japanese companies may have more or less of a consensus decision-making culture compared to the national culture.

MANAGERIAL RELEVANCE OF CULTURE

Before we dive into a deeper understanding of the nature of culture, it may be helpful to first highlight the relevance of culture to you as a manager. Fundamentally, culture is important because it is a strong driver of behavior. As a consequence, an understanding of culture can be helpful to you in understanding why people behave the way they do and in leveraging culture to help accomplish goals as well as achieve the strategic aims of your organization.

Impact of Culture on Behavior

As we mentioned, an understanding of culture is critical because culture can dramatically influence important behaviors. For example, culture can influence how people observe and interpret the business world around them.[7] Even when viewing identical situations, culture can influence whether individuals see those situations as opportunities or threats.[8] Culture can lead to different beliefs about the "right" managerial behavior regarding very specific aspects of management. Consider the research findings presented in Exhibit 4.1

As this exhibit illustrates, at the extremes only 10 percent of Swedish managers believe they should have precise answers to most questions subordinates ask, while 78 percent of Japanese managers think they should. As this specific example illustrates, culture can contribute to preexisting ways of interpreting events, evaluating them, and determining a course of action.[9]

Because culture is not an individual trait but a set of assumptions, values, and beliefs shared by a group, people can and do identify themselves with the culture and the group. To some extent the culture and the group are synonymous in their minds. Research has found that identification with the culture can cause individuals to exert extra effort and make sacrifices to support the culture and the people in it.[10] This means that to the extent your subordinates identify with the culture of your unit or the company, the harder they are likely to work to make it successful. If culture can significantly influence behaviors, which in turn can influence individual, group, or organizational performance, then it is critical to understand what culture is, how it is formed, and how it can be changed or leveraged.

Cultural Diversity in the Workplace

The impact of culture on perception and behavior is perhaps more important now than ever before because of the significant increase in cultural diversity you are likely to encounter as a manager. Globalization is a critical factor in this cultural diversity. Even though cultural diversity has existed among different national, ethnic, regional, and other groups, the globalization of business has increasingly brought that diversity together. As companies globalize and expand operations around the world, they create an increased opportunity and demand for people from different cultures to effectively interact together. One of the key consequences of globalization is that you are much more likely

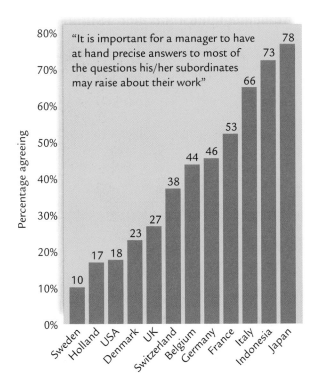

exhibit 4.1

Cultural Differences Among Managers

Source: R. Steers and J. S. Black, *Organization Behavior* (New York: HarperCollins, 1994).

to work with others from a variety of cultural backgrounds. As a result, a thorough understanding of culture—its nature and influence—is a critical component of effective management in these cross-cultural settings.

However, the value of understanding culture is not confined to managers who work in multinational organizations; you do not have to move abroad to encounter cultural diversity. Even if you plan to work in a largely domestic-oriented organization, you will increasingly encounter a culturally diverse workforce and need the ability to understand people with different perspectives and behaviors. To get an idea of the greater cultural diversity you will face, simply consider the following statistics about the United States:[11]

- More than half the American workforce is currently composed of women, minorities, and immigrants.
- In 1970 there were 9.6 million foreign-born workers in the United States; in 2000 there were 28.4 million foreign-born workers—a nearly threefold increase.
- By the year 2015, white males will represent only 15 percent of people entering the workforce.
- The vast majority of all immigrants to the United States now come from Asian or Latin American countries, not from Europe.

These and other statistics point out that as a manager you will encounter an increasingly culturally diverse U.S. workforce. These cultural differences present both challenges and opportunities for managers—challenges that if ignored can have negative consequences for individuals and their organizations, and opportunities that if captured can lead to superior outcomes and organizational competitiveness.

Culture as a Management Tool

Clearly, being an effective manager is not just about understanding others. As we stressed in Chapter 1, managers get paid to accomplish goals with and through other people. Ultimately, as a manager, you need to thoroughly understand culture because it can help accomplish your managerial responsibilities. So how

The United States and its workforce is becoming more diverse, presenting managers with both challenges and opportunities. In the next decade, for example, only an estimated 15 percent of new entrants into the U.S. workforce will be Caucasian males.

does culture do this? Because culture is rooted in assumptions and values, once established, it guides peoples' behaviors without overt or constant supervision. For example, as a newcomer to an organization, once you have learned through the words and actions of others that consensus decision making is the "right" way to make decisions in that company, you make decisions that way even if your supervisor is not watching. As we will discuss later in this chapter, while establishing a specific cultural value is not easy, once it is established it serves as a fairly constant guide to and influence on behavior. An organization's culture can guide what people do and how they do it, without monitoring and directing your subordinates constantly. This is particularly important with the increasingly complex and geographically dispersed organizations we see today. In many cases, managers may not be present to watch over and direct their people every minute. To the extent that culture can guide behavior, it can be a powerful management tool in increasingly geographically dispersed organizations.

For example, we know a jet-fuel sales manager in the Asia Pacific region for ExxonMobil who is based in Singapore. However, he has subordinates residing in Japan, Singapore, and Australia. Among his roughly ten subordinates are five different nationalities. It is impossible for the sales manager to directly and closely monitor the behavior of these subordinates on a daily or even weekly basis. Without a strong commitment to the company's culture regarding superior customer service to guide the sales employees' daily behavior, the sales manager would have little hope of getting the desired results. Instead he or she would be relegated to constantly trying to correct behavior after poor results provided evidence of mistaken actions.[12]

As you can see from this short example, culture can be a powerful means of directing peoples' behavior and accomplishing organizational objectives, such as outperforming competitors. A recent study conducted by the Massachusetts Institute of Technology found that firms with strong culture had better and more reliable financial performance than firms with weaker cultures. Another study of 160 companies over a 10-year period found companies that outperformed their industry peers excelled in what are called the four primary management practices: (1) strategy, (2) execution, (3) culture, and (4) structure.[13] However, as a manager, you have to be careful what you instill as the cultural values. Culture is such a strong force in behavior that the wrong culture can lead otherwise "good people to do bad things." A Manager's Challenge, "Overly Aggressive Culture Derails Enron," helps illustrate this problem. In this example, the culture at Enron stressed the value of achieving growth by any means and at almost any cost. As a consequence, many individuals undertook illegal and unethical actions (a topic we will explore in great detail in Chapter 5) in order to keep the company growing or at least make it appear to be growing. As you read this case,

a manager's challenge

ethics

Overly Aggressive Culture Derails Enron

While growth is the engine that drives shareholder value, pushing the engine too hard can cause things to overheat and then melt down. Enron's leadership did just that—it fostered a hard-charging culture in which some managers cut ethical and legal corners in the unending quest to report ever-higher earnings. Ultimately, the resulting scandal sent Enron into bankruptcy, put thousands of employees out of work, and drove a major accounting firm out of business.

(continued)

Under CEO Kenneth Lay, the Houston-based company shifted from its beginnings in oil and natural gas production to a fast-growth strategy aimed at making Enron the "world's greatest energy company." Lay publicly announced extremely ambitious financial targets and promised the workforce stock options that would become increasingly valuable as the company's stock price went up. The message and value were clear: Results matter more than means— what you accomplish matters more than how you do it. "You've got someone at the top saying that the stock price is the most important thing, which is driven by earnings," one insider said. "Whoever could provide earnings quickly would be promoted." Managers' goals, performance measures, compensation, and career advancement were all geared to reinforcing a culture of growth at any price.

This culture was reinforced by selecting people from the outside who fit the company's core values. Jeffrey Skilling was one of the more visible examples of this. He joined Enron as a rising star with a strong entrepreneurial spirit. Knowing that utility customers wanted to stabilize gas costs while gas producers wanted to charge higher prices over time, the Enron division he headed arranged long-term contracts to sell gas to utilities from a pool of suppliers. Instead of using the traditional accounting method to record revenues when received, however, Skilling insisted that Enron record all the expected revenue at the start of each contract. Thanks to this controversial approach, the company's earnings looked significantly better, and soon Skilling was promoted to president.

Ironically, higher earnings led management to push for more and more deals so Enron could continue to report improved earnings each quarter. Despite some doubts raised by Arthur Andersen, which audited the company's financial statements, senior managers developed elaborate schemes for making earnings look better while making debt look smaller.

Managers fostered a culture that discouraged any internal objections to questionable activities. In fact, says a former Enron executive, "The whole culture at the vice president level and above just became a yes-man culture." Personnel practices reinforced this. For example, risk-management employees who had to sign off on potential Enron deals were, in turn, rated by the managers whose deals they were examining. Thus, risk-management employees had a built-in incentive to endorse the deals because performance ratings had a big impact on compensation and job security. Twice a year, management rated each employee as an "A," "B," or

Can a corporation's culture be too strong? Many believe this was the case at Enron. Enron employees were pushed by top managers such as CEO Ken Lay (shown in the photo at a Senate hearing) and rewarded for delivering bottom line results—even if it meant crossing ethical and legal boundaries. "You do it, it works, and you do it again," commented one former employee of some illicit activities that occurred at the company. "It doesn't take long for the lines to blur between what's legal and what's not."

"C." The "A" employees received much higher bonuses than the "B" employees; the "C" employees got no bonuses at all—and sometimes were forced to leave the company. Small wonder that few were willing to rock the boat. As one employee put it: "Do you stand up and lose your job?"

But losses began to mount within the special corporate entities, and concerns about Enron's accounting pushed the share price lower and lower. Unable to arrange a merger, the company finally filed for bankruptcy in December 2001. Within months, Arthur Andersen lost its license to audit public companies and laid off thousands of workers. Most of Enron's top executives were forced to resign and faced federal charges.

Looking back, experts point to Enron's culture as a major factor in the debacle. Even employees and managers who felt uneasy about the company's activities went along to avoid conflict. "It was easy to get into, 'Well, everybody else is doing it, so maybe it isn't so bad,'" remembers one ex-Enron employee. Another says: "You do it once, it works, and you do it again. It doesn't take long for the lines to blur between what's legal and what's not."

Sources: "Egg on Enron Faces," *BusinessWeek,* January 12, 2004, p. 80; Mitchell Langbert, "The Enron Mob," *Fortune,* December 22, 2003, p. 9; "The Talent Myth," *The New Yorker,* July 22, 2002; Julian E. Barnes, Megan Barnett, Christopher H. Schmitt, and Marianne Lavelle, "How a Titan Came Undone," *U.S. News & World Report,* March 18, 2002, pp. 26+; J. A. Byrne and M. France, "The Environment Was Ripe for Abuse," *BusinessWeek,* February 25, 2002, pp. 118+; Kelly Patricia O'Meara, "Enron Board Accused by U.S. Senate Panel," *Insight,* August 19, 2002, pp. 15–17.

you might ask yourself if you have ever been part of an organization whose culture pressured you to make decisions and behave in ways that you thought were wrong. Also, you might put yourself in the shoes of an employee at Enron and ask yourself, "Would Enron's culture have influenced my decisions and ethics?"

LEVELS OF CULTURE

So far we have talked about culture as though it were a single entity. This is not quite accurate. Culture consists of three distinct but related levels.[14] The structure of these elements is like a tree (see Exhibit 4.2). Some elements are visible. These are often termed **artifacts**, or visible manifestations of a culture such as its art, clothing, food, architecture, and customs. At the beginning of this chapter, we gave the example of designated parking places as a visible manifestation of an organization culture's emphasis on status. The base of the culture, like the trunk of a tree, is its values. **Values** are essentially the enduring beliefs that specific conduct or end states are personally or socially preferred to others. However, what holds the tree up is invisible. Most of the components of culture lie below the surface and are hard to see unless you make an effort to uncover them. These are the **assumptions** of the culture, or the beliefs about fundamental aspects of life.

Cultural Assumptions

Cultural assumptions may seem like a boring or philosophical topic, but understanding them is actually very relevant and practical for managers. Think of cultural assumptions as the soil in which the overall cultural tree grows. The nature of the soil determines many characteristics of the tree. For example, palm trees need sandy, not clay soil. In contrast, an aspen tree won't grow in the sand of the beach. Likewise, certain cultural values and behaviors are only possible with certain underlying cultural assumptions. One of the key implications for managers is that if they understand the fundamental cultural assumptions of a group, they can then begin to understand and even anticipate the values and behaviors of the group. For example, if you know that in the company you just joined hierarchy or status levels between organization levels is important, you can anticipate and not be surprised to find that in meetings junior managers (such as yourself) wait for senior managers to speak before sharing their own opinions.

However, we don't want to create the impression that cultural assumptions are deterministic. Even in the natural world different varieties of trees can grow in the same soil. So it is possible for two groups to share the same assumption about hierarchy and exhibit different behaviors. In one group junior managers only speak after senior managers. In the other group, junior managers never speak in front of senior managers.

Hopefully, you can begin to see that although assumptions may seem to be the most abstract level of culture, they are in fact one of the most practical because values and behaviors grow out of assumptions. If you can understand the underlying assumptions, you can begin to understand the types of values and behaviors they support. Without an understanding of assumptions, you might make a number of mistakes in trying to comprehend, change, or even create a new culture. You might mistakenly try to change the existing culture in ways that are not possible because they conflict with the underlying assumptions. For example, if an Australian manager went to Vietnam, she might attempt to reward individual performance, believing it would improve results. However, while

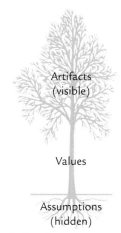

exhibit 4.2
Levels of Culture

artifacts visible manifestations of a culture such as its art, clothing, food, architecture, and customs

values the enduring beliefs that specific conduct or end states are personally or socially preferred to others

assumptions beliefs about fundamental aspects of life

Australia has underlying assumptions about the importance of the individual, Vietnam does not. Its cultural assumptions focus on the importance of the group. In fact, in Vietnam, focusing rewards too much on individual performance might actually deliver worse results because people want to fit into the group and not stand out. Without understanding cultural assumptions, you might not recognize that "to change the fruits, you need to change the roots." But we will save a more in-depth discussion of changing culture for later in this chapter.

Most scholars agree that there is a universal category of assumptions represented in all groups.[15] Exhibit 4.3 summarizes these assumptions and provides examples of the specific forms they might take, as well as their management implications.

Humanity's Relationship to the Environment The first set of assumptions concerns those made about the relationship of humanity to nature. For example, in some groups the cultural assumption is that humans should dominate nature and use it for the wealth and benefit of mankind. In other groups the

exhibit 4.3

Basic Assumptions and Their Management Implications

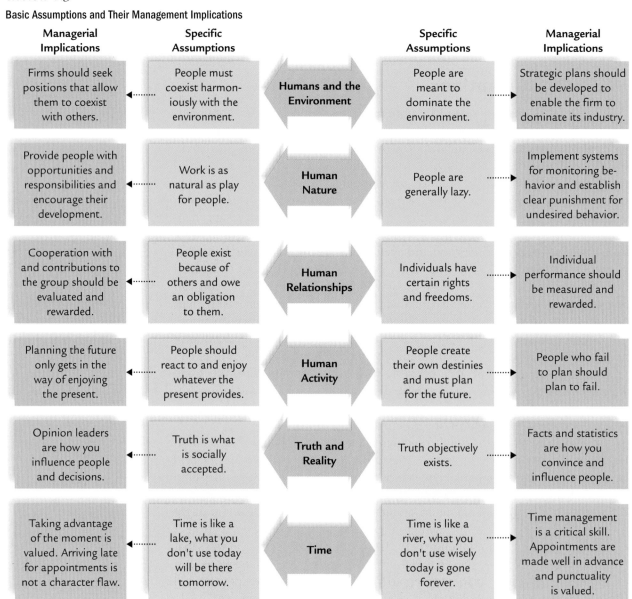

Managerial Implications	Specific Assumptions		Specific Assumptions	Managerial Implications
Firms should seek positions that allow them to coexist with others.	People must coexist harmoniously with the environment.	**Humans and the Environment**	People are meant to dominate the environment.	Strategic plans should be developed to enable the firm to dominate its industry.
Provide people with opportunities and responsibilities and encourage their development.	Work is as natural as play for people.	**Human Nature**	People are generally lazy.	Implement systems for monitoring behavior and establish clear punishment for undesired behavior.
Cooperation with and contributions to the group should be evaluated and rewarded.	People exist because of others and owe an obligation to them.	**Human Relationships**	Individuals have certain rights and freedoms.	Individual performance should be measured and rewarded.
Planning the future only gets in the way of enjoying the present.	People should react to and enjoy whatever the present provides.	**Human Activity**	People create their own destinies and must plan for the future.	People who fail to plan should plan to fail.
Opinion leaders are how you influence people and decisions.	Truth is what is socially accepted.	**Truth and Reality**	Truth objectively exists.	Facts and statistics are how you convince and influence people.
Taking advantage of the moment is valued. Arriving late for appointments is not a character flaw.	Time is like a lake, what you don't use today will be there tomorrow.	**Time**	Time is like a river, what you don't use wisely today is gone forever.	Time management is a critical skill. Appointments are made well in advance and punctuality is valued.

cultural assumption is that humans and nature should coexist harmoniously. The implications of these differing assumptions can be quite significant. At the national level, the cultural assumption that men should dominate nature is prevalent in the United States and can be seen in structures and industry: damming rivers for electricity, mining iron to make steel for automobiles, or logging trees to make homes. However, the implications of this belief may reach beyond these basic activities to strategic planning or management practices in business as well. Consider how most U.S. firms view their business environment and how they strategically approach it. Is the business environment viewed as something that people must accept and with which they must try to harmonize? Or is it viewed as something that must be mastered and dominated if possible? Americans' assumption that the business environment is something to dominate is evident in antitrust laws. Antitrust laws and regulations in the United States are not in place because Americans think they must be submissive to the environment, but simply to counteract marketplace domination by a single firm. For example, the recent difficulties Microsoft has had with the U.S. Justice Department grew out of Microsoft's cultural assumption and determined actions to dominate its environment.[16] Groups that assume humans must subjugate themselves to nature often are characterized by strong notions of fate. As a consequence, the idea of having a strategic planning department is ridiculous because it is not possible for humans to dominate something as powerful as the environment or God's will.

Human Nature Different groups also make different assumptions about the nature of people. Some cultures assume people are fundamentally good, while others assume they are inherently evil. You can see the direct influence of this category of assumptions in different organizations. Douglas McGregor captured this notion well in his classic book, *The Human Side of Enterprise.*[17] McGregor argued that every manager acted on a theory, or set of assumptions, about people. **Theory X managers** assume that the average human being has an inherent dislike for work and will avoid it if possible. Managers accepting this view of people believe that they must be coerced, controlled, directed, and threatened with punishment to get them to strive toward the achievement of organizational objectives. If enough managers in an organization collectively share these assumptions, the organization will have monitoring systems and detailed manuals on exactly what workers' jobs are and exactly how they are to do them. On the other hand, **Theory Y managers** assume that work is as natural as play or rest. Consequently, managers accepting this view of people believe that employees exercise self-direction and self-control to accomplish objectives to which they are committed. Commitment to objectives is a function of the rewards associated with their achievement. Organizations in which Theory Y is the dominant assumption would be more likely to involve workers in decision making or even allow them some autonomy and self-direction in their jobs. Research by Project Globe has confirmed this cultural dimension and demonstrated that it affects how leaders manage organizations.[18] For example, Hewlett-Packard (HP) is known as an organization with a culture based on more Theory Y assumptions about human nature.[19]

Theory X managers assume the average human being has an inherent dislike for work and will avoid it if possible

Theory Y managers assume that work is as natural as play or rest

Human Relationships Assumptions about human relationships really deal with a variety of questions:

- What is the right way for people to deal with each other?
- How much power and authority should one person have over another?
- How much should someone be concerned with him- or herself versus others?

power distance the extent to which people accept power and authority differences among people

**Power Distance
by Stewart Black**

Q&A
One**Key**
www.prenhall.com/onekey

In addressing these and other related questions, Geert Hofstede studied over 100,000 employees within a single firm (IBM) across 40 different countries.[20] He found four dimensions along which individuals in these countries differed in terms of human relationships. One of those four dimensions was the construct of power distance. **Power distance** is the extent to which people accept power and authority differences among people. Power distance is not a measure of the extent to which there are power and status differences in a group. Most organizations and most societies have richer and poorer, more and less powerful members. Power distance is not the existence or nonexistence of status and power differentials in a society but the extent to which any differences are *accepted*. In Hofstede's study, people from the Philippines, Venezuela, and Mexico had the highest levels of acceptance of power differences. In contrast, Austria, Israel, and Denmark had the lowest levels of acceptance.

Even though Americans tend to be at the low end of the power distance continuum, the extent to which this assumption exists can vary across organizations. For example, Southwest Airlines would be at the lower end of the power distance continuum while American Airlines would be at the higher end. The egalitarian attitude in Southwest Airlines seems to stem from its founder and chairman, Herb Kelleher (or "Uncle Herb," as he is known to all Southwest employees). At Southwest, status differentials such as big private offices for upper management, reserved parking places for senior managers, and so on do not exist.[21] These and other symbols of status are much more common and accepted within American Airlines.

A second dimension in Hofstede's study was the extent to which cultures valued individualism or collectivism. **Individualism** can be thought of as the extent to which people base their identities on themselves and are expected to take care of themselves and their immediate families. Hofstede's study found that people from the United States, Australia, and Great Britain had the highest individual orientations. Individuals from these countries tended to have "I" consciousness and exhibited higher emotional independence from organizations or institutions. They tended to emphasize and reward individual achievement and value individual decisions. **Collectivism** can be thought of as the extent to which identity is a function of the group to which an individual belongs (e.g., families, firm members, community members, etc.) and the extent to which group members are expected to look after each other. People from Venezuela, Colombia, and Pakistan had the highest collective orientations. People from these countries tended to have "We" consciousness and exhibited emotional dependence on organizations or institutions to which they belonged. They tended to emphasize group membership and value collective, group decisions.

individualism the extent to which people base their identities on themselves and are expected to take care of themselves and their immediate families

collectivism the extent to which identity is a function of the group to which an individual belongs

Once again, even within a society, the extent to which people within organizations share the assumption that individuals matter more than the group or that the group matters more than the individual can vary. For example, Goldman Sachs has stronger individualistic assumptions than Motorola. At Goldman Sachs, rewards are based primarily on individual performance, while at Motorola rewards are based on individual, group, and overall organization performance.

**Masculine-Feminine
Societies
by Stewart Black**

Q&A
One**Key**
www.prenhall.com/onekey

Human Activity Assumptions about human activity concern issues of what is right for people to do and whether they should be active, passive, or fatalistic in these activities. Hofstede's work also addressed this issue. He argued that there were masculine and feminine societies. **Masculine societies** value activities focused on success, money, and possessions. **Feminine societies** value activities focused on caring for others and enhancing the quality of life.

masculine societies value activities focused on success, money, and possessions

feminine societies value activities focused on caring for others and enhancing the quality of life

Countries such as the United States were at the masculine end of this continuum. In the United States people brag about working 80 hours a week, about having no time for vacations or to watch TV, and about doing several things at the same time on their computers. They believe in phrases such as "people who fail to plan should plan to fail," and "plan the work and work the plan." In other cultures, such emphasis on work is not valued and may even be seen as a waste of time and energy. Other groups hold the cultural assumption that such preoccupation with planning only gets in the way of enjoying the present.

Truth and Reality Different groups also form differing assumptions about the nature of reality and truth and how they are verified or established. The late Harold Geneen, the famous founder of ITT, always talked about "the unshakable facts," or those that would hold up even after intense scrutiny.[22] Truth was assumed to exist and could be discovered through rigorous examination. In other groups, reality is much more subjective and dependent on what people believe it to be. Consequently, opinion leaders or persuasive stories rather than unshakable facts are used to influence people and business decisions.

The famous analogy of the three baseball umpires may serve to illustrate the basic assumptions that people can make about reality and truth. The first umpire stated, "There are balls and there are strikes, and I call them as they are." The second umpire stated, "There are balls and there are strikes, and I call them as I see them." The third umpire stated, "There ain't nothing 'till I call it." Clearly, the nature of the game can change dramatically depending on which umpire is calling the pitch. Have you been in an organization in which the assumption of the first umpire dominated the group? Even if you haven't, you can probably imagine such an organization. In fact, ITT under Mr. Geneen held "first umpire" cultural assumptions about reality and truth.

Hofstede found that cultures differ in the extent to which they need things to be clear or ambiguous. He labeled this **uncertainty avoidance**. Groups high in uncertainty avoidance can be thought of as most comfortable with a first umpire type of culture and least comfortable with a third umpire type of culture. Groups high in uncertainty avoidance create structures and institutions to reduce uncertainty. Groups low in uncertainty avoidance can be thought of as most comfortable with a second or third umpire type of culture and as disliking a first umpire type culture. If you now look back to Exhibit 4.1 you can see that much of the answer to the question lies in how comfortable or uncomfortable one is with uncertainty. Managers from Sweden, the Netherlands, and the United States were most comfortable with uncertainty. Managers from Indonesia and Japan were least comfortable. What is interesting is that although the study in Exhibit 4.1 was based on an entirely different sample, the results are quite similar to what Hofstede found. Countries with high uncertainty avoidance (i.e., they preferred things to be clear) were very much the same countries in which managers thought they should have precise answers to most subordinate questions.

uncertainty avoidance the need for things to be clear rather than ambiguous

Uncertainty Avoidance by Stewart Black
Q&A
One Key
www.prenhall.com/onekey

Time Different groups also form differing assumptions about the nature of time. Is time viewed as a river or a lake? Those who view time as a river generally hold linear assumptions about time. Like a river, time moves on in a linear fashion. What you do not take advantage of today will be gone tomorrow. This assumption creates a great emphasis on time management, being punctual for appointments, keeping appointment books, and so on. The phenomenal success of Franklin Quest (now Franklin Covey) up through the 1990s, a

A company's culture can be the source of strengths, weaknesses, and challenges. What passes for the status quo at Microsoft, such as taking time off to play Frisbee, may be taboo at IBM. The tendency to judge specific values negatively can be especially problematic within a single organization operating in different countries, each with its own set of values. Cultural differences from country-to-country can also pose problems for companies seeking to do business internationally. The European Union and other foreign countries, for example, have tried to sanction Microsoft, viewing some of its practices as anti-competitive.

producer of relatively expensive day planners, is testimony to this orientation in the United States. Until the advent of the electronic day planner, such as the Palm Pilot, Franklin grew at a rate several times that of the general economy. It also enjoyed great success when it expanded into Japan and Korea, two other cultures with linear assumptions about time. In contrast, those who view time as a lake generally hold nonlinear assumptions about time. Like a lake, what you do not dip from the lake today will still be there for you to use tomorrow. This has nearly the opposite effect on management behaviors: being late for an appointment is not seen as a character flaw and setting specific day, hour, and minute schedules is seen as unnecessary.

Hofstede's work also addressed this fundamental assumption. Hofstede found that societies could be segmented based on whether they had a **short-term or long-term orientation**. Short-term-oriented societies tend to view time as a river and focus on immediate results and maximizing time management. Long-term-oriented societies tend to view time as a lake and focus on developing relationships, not expecting immediate results or returns on current efforts.

In spite of its wide acceptance, Hofstede's national culture research has stirred controversy ever since its introduction. Most recently,[23] the underlying assumptions of "culture," as well as the methodology used to collect data and make generalizations, have come under scrutiny. Its critics also claim that Hofstede's study erroneously ignores the effects of organizational and occupational culture. Regardless of the criticism and controversy, Hofstede's dimensions of national culture remain widely used and cited in organizational studies.

All groups confront issues represented by these six categories of cultural assumptions. Different organizations can hold differing assumptions. Different societies can hold different assumptions. Whether you are trying to understand an organization or a country, you must look at the fundamental assumptions first. In general, this involves asking a general set of questions.

short-term or long-term orientation societies that focus on immediate results and those that focus on developing relationships without expecting immediate results

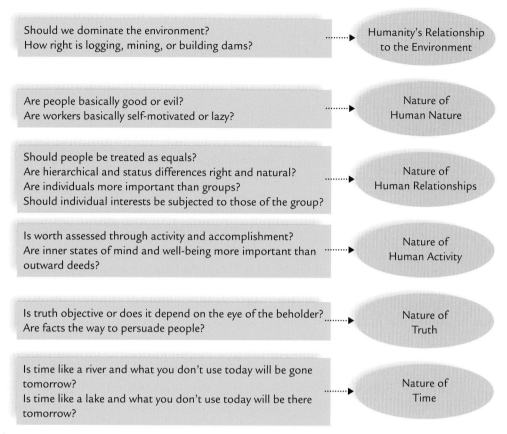

Should we dominate the environment?
How right is logging, mining, or building dams? ·········▶ Humanity's Relationship to the Environment

Are people basically good or evil?
Are workers basically self-motivated or lazy? ·········▶ Nature of Human Nature

Should people be treated as equals?
Are hierarchical and status differences right and natural?
Are individuals more important than groups? ·········▶ Nature of Human Relationships
Should individual interests be subjected to those of the group?

Is worth assessed through activity and accomplishment?
Are inner states of mind and well-being more important than ·········▶ Nature of Human Activity
outward deeds?

Is truth objective or does it depend on the eye of the beholder? ·········▶ Nature of Truth
Are facts the way to persuade people?

Is time like a river and what you don't use today will be gone
tomorrow? ·········▶ Nature of Time
Is time like a lake and what you don't use today will be there
tomorrow?

exhibit 4.4
Questions to Get at Cultural Assumptions

Exhibit 4.4 provides illustrative questions for each of the six categories of cultural assumptions. Given that all groups have formed assumptions relative to these six categories, you could use the questions to begin to understand an organization or national culture new to you.

Cultural Values

Values are typically defined as enduring beliefs that specific conduct or end states of existence are personally and socially preferred by others.[24] Values are like the trunk of a tree, harder to see than the outline of the branches and leaves from far away but critical to the nourishment and stature of the tree. Fundamentally, values guide behavior because they define what is good or ought to be and what is bad and ought not to be.

We can view managerial values as enduring beliefs about specific ways of managing and conducting business that have been deemed successful enough to be passed on. Although some comprehensive frameworks have been proposed for values in general (see Exhibit 4.5 for an early classic), no widely accepted framework for organizing managerial beliefs and values exists.

Because values address what ought or ought not to be, differences in values often lead to clashes and negative judgments about others. For example, American programmers at Microsoft often play "nerf basketball" while trying to solve difficult problems, believing that these types of activities contribute to creative problem solving. In contrast, nerf basketball is not a common sight in the halls of General Motors' programming offices in Detroit.

exhibit 4.5

Classification of Values

Theoretical people	value the discovery of truth. They are empirical, critical, and rational, aiming to order and systematize their knowledge.
Economic people	value what is useful. They are interested in practical affairs, especially those of business, judging things by their usefulness.
Aesthetic people	value beauty and harmony. They are concerned with grace and symmetry, finding fulfillment in artistic experiences.
Social people	value altruistic and philanthropic love. They are kind, sympathetic, and unselfish, valuing other people as ends in themselves.
Religious people	value unity. They seek communication with the cosmos, mystically relating to its wholeness.

Source: G. W. Allport, P. E. Vernon, and Q. Lindzey, *A Study of Values* (Boston: Houghton Mifflin, 1966).

Despite their similar jobs (i.e., writing software code), their differing values lead to not only different behaviors but attributions about those who are not like them. Microsoft's programmers in Washington might look on GM's programmers in Michigan as being boring, dull, and uncreative. GM's programmers might look on Microsoft's programmers as childish or unprofessional.

This tendency to judge different values negatively can be problematic for an organization with operations in multiple countries. For example, programmers in Germany generally do not play nerf basketball to help solve problems. What happens when programmers from Microsoft's German operations have to work on a project with Microsoft's Redmond, Washington, programmers? It could be a serious barrier to productivity if the two sets of Microsoft programmers do not understand each other and consequently do not trust each other.

Because values define what is good or bad, right or wrong, they not only guide behavior but are the source of actions that you can see. In part, this is why archeologists and anthropologists seek out artifacts; they hope to find ones that will help them deduce the values of people who are no longer around to observe. In organizations, this is also why artifacts, such as stories, can provide valuable insights into the organization's culture. For example, what insights into the UPS culture can you glean from the following well-known story?

> *Just before Christmas, a railroad official called a regional UPS manager to inform him that a flatcar carrying two UPS trailers had unfortunately been left on a siding in the middle of Illinois. Most of the packages in these two cars were Christmas presents. Without permission or authorization, the regional manager paid for a high-speed diesel locomotive to fetch the stranded flatcar and haul it to Chicago. The manager then diverted two of UPS's Boeing 727 jets to Chicago to pick up the packages and fly them to their destinations in Florida and Louisiana in time for Christmas. Headquarters wasn't even informed of these extraordinary expenses until weeks after the incident. Once informed, top management applauded the regional manager's decision.[25]*

What does this story tell you about UPS's values concerning customer service? Managerial autonomy? Decision making? Clearly, UPS has a strong value for customer service and for autonomy and empowerment in managerial decision making. By articulating these values and having managers who understand and believe in them, UPS is able to get the desired behaviors and organizational results without having to constantly monitor managers and incur the significant costs of close supervision, such as having many more supervisors.

Because values guide behavior, they are critical for any manager to understand. Not recognizing that values could be different even among employees in the same organization can often lead to unproductive clashes among employees. Later in this chapter, we will talk about sources of cultural diversity within the United States and ways in which you can not only manage employees with diverse values but can use their strengths for greater productivity.

Cultural Artifacts and Behaviors

The visible portions of culture are referred to as artifacts and behaviors. In general, the term "*artifact*" is most often associated with physical discoveries that represent an ancient culture and its values, such as buildings, pottery, clothing, tools, food, and art. Archeologists find artifacts when they dig in the jungles and deserts of the world looking for lost civilizations. In modern organizations, important artifacts include such things as office arrangements (individual offices for all versus open offices with no walls), parking arrangements (reserved spaces for some versus open spaces for all), or clothing. Consider the "uniforms" that managers wear at IBM in New York and Silicon Graphics in California. When you walk in the door at Silicon Graphics, you are more likely to see a manager in Levi's and a polo shirt than in a suit and tie. Although no official dress code policy existed that required all male managers at IBM to wear a white shirt and tie, until the mid-1990s, if you walked into an IBM office, all the men would be wearing a white shirt and tie. A senior IBM executive once commented that several years ago, he decided that since there was no policy, he would go to work in a blue shirt and normal tie. Less than an hour after arriving, he went home to change because he "felt naked without a white shirt on, even though no one said anything."[26]

Artifacts and behaviors are closely linked. For example, while the clothing worn in an organization or even in a country might be a cultural artifact, wearing a certain style of clothing is a behavior. But culture can influence behaviors well beyond what to wear. Culture can influence key managerial behaviors, as Exhibit 4.6 illustrates.

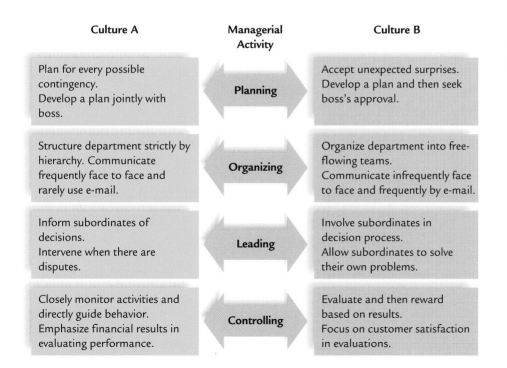

Culture A	Managerial Activity	Culture B
Plan for every possible contingency. Develop a plan jointly with boss.	Planning	Accept unexpected surprises. Develop a plan and then seek boss's approval.
Structure department strictly by hierarchy. Communicate frequently face to face and rarely use e-mail.	Organizing	Organize department into free-flowing teams. Communicate infrequently face to face and frequently by e-mail.
Inform subordinates of decisions. Intervene when there are disputes.	Leading	Involve subordinates in decision process. Allow subordinates to solve their own problems.
Closely monitor activities and directly guide behavior. Emphasize financial results in evaluating performance.	Controlling	Evaluate and then reward based on results. Focus on customer satisfaction in evaluations.

exhibit 4.6

Culture and Managerial Behaviors

CULTURAL DIVERSITY

As a manager, you will encounter greater diversity in organizations in the future. As we mentioned in the beginning of this chapter, diversity comes from two primary sources: (1) increased international activity of organizations and (2) greater diversity in the cultures of employees.

If you include companies, the military, government agencies, and non-profit groups, there are an estimated 2 million U.S. citizens working in other countries.[27] As a consequence, managers in any of these types of organizations need to understand culture in general and specifically the culture of the countries in which they work. With the globalization of business, there is a greater chance that you will have the opportunity to live and work in a foreign country and experience cultural diversity. However, companies are not just sending people out to their foreign operations; they are also bringing employees into their home country operations from their foreign subsidiaries. This aspect of globalization also increases the need for an understanding of culture and how it affects people's perspectives and behaviors. Yet, the impact of globalization on cultural diversity is not restricted to employees of a company. Globalization means that as a manager you are increasingly likely to encounter and work with suppliers and customers with different cultural backgrounds. If that weren't enough, new technology has added an interesting twist to the impact of globalization on cultural diversity. New technology now allows people of different cultures to be brought together without ever leaving home. For example, phone conferencing and videoconferencing capabilities allow people (employees, suppliers, customers, joint-venture partners, etc.) from all around the world to interact. A lack of understanding of culture can make these interactions less effective because when cultural differences manifest themselves, managers misinterpret, misunderstand, and as a consequence mistrust each other.[28] Consider the simple misunderstanding that occurred among managers working for Delphi, the world's largest maker of component parts for cars. While working on a project, the workers from France sent an e-mail in which they "demanded" technical information on a particular component. The employees in Detroit were incensed that their French counterparts would be so rude. However, if you know French, you will recognize that this was all due to a simple misunderstanding. The French word, *demander*, seems like the English word, *demand*, but is best translated as *request*.

Even if you manage in an organization whose primary focus is domestic, supervisors, peers, and subordinates will not be exactly like you. Differences in age, race, ethnicity, gender, physical abilities, and sexual orientation, as well as work background, income, marital status, military experience, religious beliefs, geographic location, parental status, and education, can all influence the assump-

exhibit 4.7

Effects of Cultural Diversity on Productivity

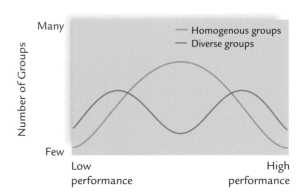

exhibit 4.8
Managing Cultural Diversity for Competitive Advantage

1. **Cost**	As organizations become more diverse, the cost of a poor job in integrating workers will increase.
2. **Resource Acquisition**	Companies with the best reputations for managing diversity will win the competition for the best personnel. As the labor pool shrinks and becomes more diverse, this edge will become increasingly important.
3. **Marketing**	For multinational organizations, the insight and cultural sensitivity that members with roots in other cultures bring should improve marketing efforts.
4. **Creativity**	Diversity of perspectives and less emphasis on conformity to norms of the past should improve creativity.
5. **Problem Solving**	Cultural diversity in decision-making and problem-solving groups potentially produces better decisions through consideration of a wider range of and more thorough critical analysis of issues.
6. **System Flexibility**	Cultural diversity enables the system to be less determinant, less standardized, and therefore more fluid, which will create more flexibility to react to environmental changes.

Source: T. H. Cox and S. Blake, "Managing Cultural Diversity: Implications for Organizational Competitiveness," *Academy of Management Executive* 5, no. 3 (1991), p. 23.

tions, values, and behaviors of people.[29] Within an organization, such diversity can enhance competitiveness or, if ignored or unmanaged, can lower productivity. As illustrated in Exhibit 4.7, culturally homogeneous groups in general produce a normal distribution; that is, most groups with culturally similar members produce average results, with a few groups doing quite well and a small minority doing quite poorly. In contrast, most culturally diverse groups either produce significantly worse or superior results with fewer culturally diverse groups producing results in the middle.[30] The culturally diverse teams that did better than culturally similar teams leveraged diverse perspectives, ideas, and innovations into superior performance. The culturally diverse teams that did worse than culturally similar teams were unable to manage the differences among members effectively. This was in part because members of these groups viewed the differences as liabilities rather than as assets. Exhibit 4.8 provides a summary of the general arguments for viewing cultural diversity as an asset rather than a liability.

STRONG AND WEAK CULTURES

Culture is not simply the total collection of a group of people's assumptions, values, or artifacts. This is because not all of the assumptions, values, or behaviors are equally influential, nor are they equally shared among members of a group. In other words, their strength varies.

To help in understanding this aspect of culture, think of it in terms of mental road maps and traffic signals. The road map, or culture, tells you what the important and valued goals are and what highways or back roads can get you there. However, just as the severity of consequences for assorted traffic violations varies, so too does the severity of consequences for breaching accepted cultural beliefs. With this in mind, think about **strong versus weak cultural values** along two dimensions: (1) the extent to which they are widely shared among group members and (2) the extent to which they are deeply held. This conceptualization is illustrated in Exhibit 4.9.

Strong/Weak Culture by Stewart Black

Q&A
One**Key**
www.prenhall.com/onekey

strong versus weak cultural values the degree to which the cultural values are shared by organization members

exhibit 4.9

Matrix of Cultural Strength

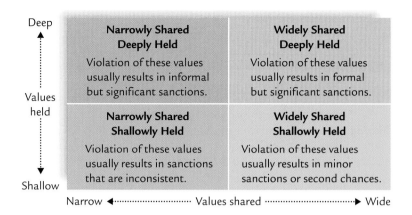

The assumptions, values, or rules of the culture that are widely shared and deeply held are generally those that are accompanied by substantial rewards or punishments. For example, at UPS the value of customer service appears to be widely shared and deeply held. Employees who take steps to satisfy customers even though their actions are not specifically prescribed in a company manual, such as the UPS regional manager who ordered the services of two Boeing 727s, are recognized and rewarded. These rewards and recognition both demonstrate the strength of customer satisfaction as a value in the organization's culture and further strengthen that value.

A Manager's Challenge, "Culture and Motivation at Nordstrom," illustrates this even further. As you will read, the customer service value in Nordstrom's culture is quite strong. It is reinforced with stories, manuals, training, and rewards. Ironically, it was so much a part of its success that when Nordstrom's path to growth changed from opening stores in its "home court" in the Northwest to opening stores in the East and across the country, the company found that the culture was hard to replicate at the same strong level. As a consequence, company results suffered.

What about the case in which the value is deeply held but not widely shared? This is perhaps the best definition of a **subculture**. Organizationwide cultures may not develop because the needed conditions, such as consistent reinforcement or time, are not present. Consequently, subcultures can be as common, or in some cases more common, than an overall corporate culture, and in a study conducted in Brazilian companies, subcultural groups have been shown to have a stronger impact on performance than overall corporate culture.[31] For example, while managers in many departments within the Swedish company Ericsson might be comfortable with uncertainty, those in the accounting department are not, and operate with a much higher expectation of precision. Subcultures can develop within national cultures as well. For example, in the United Kingdom, burping after a meal is considered by some to be a serious violation of proper behavior, but this view is not held strongly by all. Consequently, you are unlikely to be put in jail for burping. However, you might be cut out of particular social circles if you violate that rule. In other cultures, you may offend a host by *not* burping after a meal because it indicates that you were not satisfied with the meal.

In the case of widely shared but not deeply held rules, violations of the rules often carry uniform but rather mild punishments. In many cases, infrequent violation of these rules may carry no punishment at all. We might label this a superficial culture because, while it is widely shared, it does not have deep roots. For example, not interrupting people when they are talking to you is a generally accepted rule of conduct in the United States. However, if one

subculture where values are deeply held but not widely shared

a manager's challenge

Change

Culture and Motivation at Nordstrom

Few retailers have a stronger customer service reputation than Nordstrom. Its sales employees (or "Nordies," as they call themselves) are famous for making extraordinary efforts to satisfy customers. Their inspiration begins when they receive the employee handbook, which says, "Our number one goal is to provide outstanding customer service. Set both your personal and professional goals high. We have great confidence in your ability to achieve them."

For those employees who are unsure just how much confidence that means, it is instructive to read a little further and examine the list of company rules. The first one says:

"Use your good judgment in all situations. There will be no additional rules."

The most famous story of customer service tells of an elderly widow who came to Nordstrom to return tires her husband had bought not long before he died. Nordstrom does not sell tires. Still, the clerk took the tires and gave the woman a full refund.

It is not uncommon for Nordies to drive to another Nordstrom store to retrieve an out-of-stock item for a customer, to drive to a customer's home to make a delivery, to take back merchandise bought at a competitor's store, to call customers to inform them of new merchandise or sales, to write personal thank-you notes for purchases, or to gather items from different parts of the store to assemble a complete outfit. Nordstrom customers don't wait in line. Their salespeople take their credit cards, and return with their receipts and their bagged merchandise.

The company's customer service culture pays dividends not only to the customer but to the sales clerks as well. Average salaries for sales clerks are approximately twice the industry average, and top clerks can earn over $100,000 a year on Nordstrom's bonus structure. They are also given much more authority to adjust a price or do whatever it takes to please the customers than other clerks in the retail clothing industry, who usually must abide by strict rules. Top salespeople also receive special awards, like gift certificates and other perks, as do top customer service representatives.

This organization culture of customer service is reinforced through an incentive system. Nordies are paid a commission of between 6.75 percent and 10 percent on net sales if they exceed the "sales per hour" quota. The sales per hour ratio is simply the net sales an employee makes divided by the number of hours for which the employee is clocked in.

This reward places a premium on repeat customers. For salespeople, it takes time to discover what first-time customers like and don't like, what they need, and what they can afford. Sales clerks already know this about repeat customers; consequently, they can serve repeat customers much more efficiently. As a result, Nordies provide great customer service to turn first-time customers into repeat customers and to keep repeat customers coming back. One clear sign of success is when regular customers insist on working only with a certain sales clerk. This organizational culture contributed significantly to Nordstrom's success from its beginning in 1901 to its stock peak in 1999.

Arguably, the greatest challenge came when Nordstrom's had to change its path to growth. As the Northwest and West Coast started to fill up with Nordstrom stores, the company had to change its strategy and expand to the rest of the United States. Because culture is learned and reinforced daily, it takes experienced and committed employees to transfer the culture to new hires. Nordstrom was successful in transferring its culture to its first store in the East in part because company executives transferred over 100 experienced managers to the one new store. This worked as long as Nordstrom opened just a few new stores a year. But when executives decided to open 20, 30, or 40 new stores a year, as they did from 1999 through 2002, success did not follow. Nordstrom did not have enough experienced managers to move and transfer the culture at the needed strength to so many new stores. The customer service culture got diluted and sales per square foot (a key measure of sale productivity) dropped as did the company's stock price.

Immediately, Bruce Nordstrom and his sons visited stores across the country to talk to employees about what needed changing. The move was in keeping with Nordstrom's longtime philosophy of listening to those closest to their customers (employees). "We weren't as close to the customer as we should have been," said one Nordstrom family member.

Reviving the effort to listen to its customers and staff seems to be working for Nordstrom. For example, in the third quarter of 2003, the company doubled its profits and increased sales by 7 percent, and its stock price began to climb back toward its all-time high. "You can't be Nordstrom if you are focused on the executives. You have to be focused on the customers," seconded industry consultant Betsy Sanders.

Sources: Dan Burrows, "Nordstrom Net Soars 146.8%," *Women's Wear Daily*, November 21, 2003, pp. 2–4; Kathy Mulady, "Back in the Family," *Seattle-Post Intelligence*, June 27, 2001; Len Ellis, "Customer Loyalty," *Executive Excellence*, July 2001, pp. 13–14; http://about.nordstrom.com/aboutus/investor/news/02222001_2000earnings.asp, accessed on November 26, 2001.

occasionally interrupts, it is unlikely that this behavior will be accompanied by any serious punishment.

The importance of conceptualizing cultural values in terms of their strengths is that you then recognize that not all aspects of a culture are created equal. As we will explore shortly, even when we boil culture down to its most fundamental elements, the number of specific assumptions, values, beliefs, rules, behaviors, and customs is nearly infinite. Consequently, trying to learn about all aspects of a new corporate or country culture can be overwhelming. The simplified matrix presented in Exhibit 4.9 provides some mental economy in trying to understand a new culture. This is likely to be of particular relevance to you as you enter a new organization after graduation.

Imagine your first day on the job. There are a million things to learn about the culture of the company and therefore how others might expect you to act. Where should you start? First and foremost, because rewards and punishments are greatest for those aspects of culture that are widely shared and deeply held, these values and rules are worth learning early. While true mastery of a culture may require understanding all aspects of the culture, focusing first on the widely shared and deeply held values can facilitate early learning and adjustment. In a practical sense, learning these values first can keep you from making costly mistakes and damaging your job performance and reputation. As a simple example, in some companies coming late to work or leaving early is no big deal. What you accomplish rather than the hours your work is what is valued. In other companies, the fastest way to get your career derailed is to come in late or be seen rushing out the door at 5:00 P.M.

What if you want to be a force for change and improvement in the company? Where should you start (or not start)? To the extent a specific behavior is widely shared, deeply held, and directly related to one or more of the six fundamental assumptions, the behavior will be difficult to change. It might be called a **core value**. If you fail to recognize that you are trying to change a core value, you are likely to make the common mistake of directing too few resources and effort at the target of change and as a consequence fail. The point here is not that core values should never change but that if they need to change, the resources directed at the change need to match the requirements.[32] For example, after not being selected to succeed Jack Welch at GE, James McNerney took the CEO job at 3M. McNerney instituted a number of changes such as an employee ranking system and a "take no prisoners" approach to inefficiencies that were diametrically opposed to the culture at 3M. Even if the changes are needed, they are so dramatic that many wonder if they can be implemented successfully and how many years the cultural change will take if it is successful.[33]

Understanding the core values of a company can also be important when you are looking for a job. As a newcomer to the organization, you should place a premium on making sure that the organization's core values match yours. You are unlikely to be able to change a company's core values and will not be very happy in an organization with core values that clash with yours.

The simple matrix in Exhibit 4.9 can also be of practical value in international business as well. For example, a business operating in several countries may have to modify its management approach that conflicts with core values of a foreign country. For example, in the United States, most people strongly believe that rewards should be tied to individual behavior and that they should not be distributed equally among members of a group regardless of individual performance. This belief is supported by deep-rooted assumptions concerning individualism. In fact, Jack Welch attributed much of GE's phenomenal success

core value a value that is widely shared and deeply held

to the fact that within the same rank poor performers received no bonus and top performers received bonuses two to three times the size of average performers. Imagine the difficulty a firm from a more collectivist country such as Japan might have in expanding operations to an individualist culture like the United States. In Japan bonuses are based almost entirely on company performance and are not differentiated by individual performance. Everyone at a given rank receives essentially the same bonus, regardless of individual performance. What if Japanese managers tried to implement this type of group or collectivist reward system in the United States? How successful would it be?

CREATING AND CHANGING ORGANIZATION CULTURE

Since organization culture can be a mechanism for guiding employee behavior, it is as important as the company's compensation or performance evaluation systems. In fact, to create and reinforce a particular set of values or corporate culture, alignment between the desired values and other systems in the organization, such as the compensation system, needs to exist. A Manager's Challenge, "One Call; That's All," illustrates how a manager at Federal Express managed the demands for cultural change of technology in its call centers. It also helps illustrate how both performance management and rewards had to be changed in order to change the culture. As you read this case example, what do you see as the role of technology in changing the culture?

Today's organizations face business environments that are more complicated and more dynamic than perhaps at any other point in history. If an organization tried to create specific policies for all possible situations in such a dynamic environment, the resulting manual would be several phone books thick, and consequently of little practical use. Furthermore, by the time it was printed and distributed, the environment probably would have changed enough to make it obsolete. If, on the other hand, employees could be given a set of assumptions and values to use in assessing situations and determining appropriate actions, then the organization could distribute a simple and short booklet on the company's values and let that guide behavior. Because of this, organizational culture, which many managers originally thought was a "fluffy" topic, is now being seen as a strategic issue that can have a significant impact on the firm's bottom line.

For example, in joint ventures, research has found that the similarity or difference between the two organizations forming the joint venture (JV) has a significant impact on the success and performance of the joint venture. The greater the organizational cultural differences between the organizations, the more difficulty the JV has. Also, the more different the managers try to make the JV corporate culture from the original partners, the more difficulty the JV has. Successful ventures, however, need not necessarily create an "even" blend of corporate cultures. A study of 17 Hungarian-Western cooperative ventures shows that most have successfully adopted the values, practices, and systems of the Western partner.[34]

But what can managers do to create effective cultures or to change cultures that are ineffective to match the environment? There are at least five critical strategies for effectively managing organizational culture (see Exhibit 4.10). In fact, you can think of them as spokes on a wheel. When all five are in place, the wheel of an organization's culture is much easier to push to where you want it to go.

tech|nol|ogy

a manager's challenge

One Call; That's All

Federal Express (FedEx) revolutionized the package delivery industry by becoming the first carrier to collect packages from almost anywhere across the globe, deliver them overnight, and track them for customers. Initially, FedEx set up call centers to receive customers' inquiries about the status of their packages. By 1995, it had 16 call centers just within the United States.

In 1998, FedEx saw the Internet as an important new technology that could change its business. Management felt that if customers could check on the status of their packages any time of day or night, without having to be put on hold when call centers were busy, they would be even more satisfied. By 1999 the company had created a Web site where customers could log in and determine the status of their packages.

As customers used the Internet and the Web site to answer basic questions, they increasingly phoned the call centers with more sophisticated questions, along with questions specifically about the Web site. Unfortunately, call center reps had no access to the Web site and were trained in very narrow specialties. Consequently, call center reps would often pass customers along in a series of call transfers to someone they hoped could answer the customers' questions. These transfers calls were often dropped. This frustrated customers. Even when calls were not dropped, customers were still frustrated by what seemed like an endless series of handoffs.

The challenge of changing the technology and its use fell to Laurie Tucker, the manager of all customer service centers. To help senior managers see the basic need for change, she created a short video demonstration for the board. It showed a customer calling in while looking at the Web site, posing a number of questions while the call center rep apologized because he could not see the site. Senior management subsequently gave approval for what became known as "OneCall." The vision of OneCall was that a customer should be able, in one call, to get the desired information and not be passed on to someone else.

The first technical task was to get the call center reps in 16 centers high-speed access to the Internet and to FedEx's Web site. However, this was easier than getting reps to use the technology. Call center reps were initially anxious about the OneCall vision because they had specialized knowledge and wondered how they could possibly answer all questions a customer might ask. Furthermore, most had little or no experience with the company's Web site. Not only would reps need Web access; they would also need training on how to use the company's Web site and how to walk people through the site. In addition, call reps had to be cross-trained in various tasks so customers did not get passed along in a frustrating series of handoffs.

Once call reps were given the technology and the training, Tucker and her team also had to change how performance was measured in order to change the culture from one of specialization to one of full service. Previously, call reps were measured and rewarded on call-time objectives. In other words, the more calls you handled in a day, and, therefore, the shorter you made each call, the better. This contradicted the vision of OneCall. As a consequence, the old call-time measures and rewards had to be dropped. Reps were rewarded with bonuses based on customer satisfaction, which included a variety of dimensions such as efficiency, accuracy, and friendliness.

The results of achieving this level of belief were significant. In fact, within a few short months one of the early centers to undergo the transformation generated $10 million in additional sales from delighted customers. Today, of course, the Internet is used by so many businesses, it may sound strange that a company like FedEx once struggled to use it. The fact is, however, that new technologies are evolving at an ever-quickening pace, so the same sort of learning and adapting process is constantly ongoing.

Source: Angela Greiling Keane, "Relax, It's a FedEx Ad," *Traffic World*, September 15, 2003, p. 33; personal communication, 2002.

Selection

One way to create or change a culture is to select individuals whose assumptions, values, and behaviors already match those that you desire. Disney uses this mechanism with great success in creating a culture of "guest" service in its theme parks. In fact, former president of EuroDisney, Steve Burke, attributes some of that park's early problems (now called Disneyland Paris) to poor

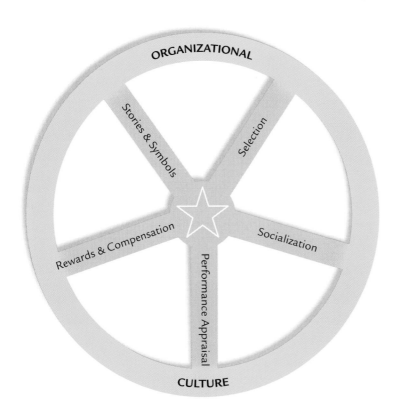

exhibit 4.10
**Strategies to Manage
Organizational Culture**

selection practices and hiring individuals whose attitudes toward friendly customer service were not compatible with Disney's culture. This was also one of the first things Mr. Burke changed upon his arrival in France, and that he felt contributed to the dramatic turnaround of the park.[35]

Socialization

Even if selection is not perfect, congruent cultural values can be introduced and reinforced in new hires through socialization. These efforts might include early orientation, training, and arranged interactions with experienced organi-

To be successful, managers doing business in another country need not only be competent but also informed about the culture in which they are operating. For example, exchanging business cards is a formal ritual in Asia whereas in the United States it's treated very casually.

zational members on a group or individual level. But managers should keep in mind that individuals are not just blank sheets upon which the organization can write whatever cultural scripts it desires. Individuals actively seek out information and try to learn the organization's culture.[36] Consequently, managers should try to facilitate these efforts and monitor them to ensure that individuals are truly coming to a correct understanding of the organization's culture.

Performance Appraisal

Few things signal what the organization values more clearly to newcomers in an organization than what it measures and evaluates. For example, it would do Nordstrom little good to claim that the organization values customer service but then evaluate employees primarily on punctuality. Nordstrom uses "customer praise letters" as well as customer complaints as part of employee evaluation to reinforce its customer service culture.

Rewards and Compensation

Rewards and compensation may be among the most powerful means of signaling what the organization values and reinforcing desired behaviors in newcomers. If we return to the Nordstrom example, it would do the company little good to talk about customer service as a cultural value and then base bonuses on stockroom inventory control. To reinforce the customer service value, Nordstrom bases rewards on sales per hour. The best way to achieve high sales per hour is to work with repeat customers who purchase most of their clothes from you rather than from competing stores. As we explained earlier in this chapter, the best way to get repeat customers who will purchase most of their clothing from you is to serve them better than anyone else. As a manager, it is important to remember that although you may not be able to change the formal reward and compensation system of the organization, you directly control many informal rewards that can significantly affect subordinates (which will be discussed in more detail later in the chapter on motivation). For example, what you praise and recognize people for can significantly influence their values and behaviors.

Stories and Symbols

Organizational culture is also created and reinforced through a variety of symbols. For example, stories can be a powerful means of communicating company values. Earlier, we cited the famous UPS story. Basically, organizational stories tell employees what to do or what not to do. Symbols such as physical layout can also communicate and reinforce specific values of the corporate culture. For example, suppose you were hired by Company X and on your first day at work, as you pulled into the parking lot, you noticed that the first two rows of parking spaces were all reserved and that the spaces closest to the front door were reserved for the most senior executives in the company. What values would you begin to suspect the company held relative to hierarchy or participative decision making? You obviously would want more information before drawing final conclusions, but seemingly small symbols can communicate and reinforce an organization's culture. **Rituals** play a key role in the symbolic communication of an organization's culture. For example, in Japan most major corporations hold a common ritual when their newly hired college graduates join the company. Along with their parents, these new hires gather at a large assembly hall. A representative of the new hires pledges loyalty to the

rituals symbolic communication of an organization's culture

company on their behalf. A representative of all the parents then gives a speech in which he or she commends their children into the company's hands. A senior executive of the company then gives a speech in which he vows on behalf of the company to take care of and continue to nurture these new hires. More effectively than any memo or policy statement, this ritual reinforces the core values of belonging and loyalty.

INTERNATIONAL CONTEXTS AND CULTURES

All of the basics of culture that we have covered thus far apply to cultures at a national or local level. However, just as it is sometimes difficult to generalize about an organizationwide corporate culture, so too is it difficult to generalize about national cultures. Often, important subcultures exist within the boundaries of a nation. Interestingly, Hofstede's study, which has been criticized because it consisted of subjects from within one company, adds important insights precisely *because* all the subjects are members of the same organization. The organization was IBM, which in general is thought to have a rather strong corporate culture. This strong corporate culture might have dampened the differences across national cultures. Yet, in general, Hofstede found greater differences in cultural values between nationalities than within nationalities.

Perhaps one of the most useful concepts for examining and understanding different countries' cultures is cultural context.[37] **Cultural context** is the degree to which a situation influences behavior or perception of appropriateness. In high-context cultures, people pay close attention to the situation and its various elements. Key contextual variables are used to determine appropriate and inappropriate behavior. In low-context cultures, contextual variables have much less impact on the determination of appropriate behaviors. In other words, in low-context cultures, the situation may or may not make a difference in what is considered appropriate behavior, but in high-context cultures, the context makes all the difference. For example, in Japan there are five different words for the pronoun "you." The context determines what form of the pronoun "you" would be appropriate in addressing different people. If you are talking to a customer holding a significantly higher title than yours, who works in a large company such as Matsushita, and is several years older, you would be expected to use the term "otaku" when addressing the customer. If you were talking to a subordinate, several years younger, "kimi" would be the appropriate pronoun. Exhibit 4.11 provides a list of some low- and high-context cultures.

cultural context the degree to which a situation influences behavior or perception of appropriateness

High/Low Context Culture by Stewart Black

Q&A
OneKey
www.prenhall.com/onekey

Low-Context Cultures	High-Context Cultures
American	Vietnamese
Canadian	Chinese
German	Japanese
Swiss	Korean
Scandinavian	Arab
English	Greek

Source: Adapted from E. Hall, *Beyond Culture* (Garden City, N.Y.: Doubleday, 1976); S. Rosen and O. Shenkar, "Clustering Countries on Attitudinal Dimensions: A Review and Synthesis," *Academy of Management Review* 10, no. 3 (1985), p. 449.

exhibit 4.11

Low- and High-Context Cultures

globalization *a manager's challenge*

When in Rome, How Far Should You Go?

U.S. executive Irene Dec was on the spot in Korea. Her lunch hosts were waiting politely for her to begin her meal so everyone else could eat, but she didn't recognize any of the items on her plate. At last she picked up a shrimp-like item and popped it into her mouth.

One of her companions then pointed to the remaining shrimp on Dec's plate and said quietly, "We usually cut that off," indicating the head.

"I had eaten the eyes, the brains—everything," Dec later recalled. As vice president for international investments at Prudential Financial, Dec has learned a great deal in a short time about what women must do to succeed in the global environment. While some U.S. managers fear that a woman abroad would face too many cultural barriers to work effectively in foreign cultures, Dec believes that women are uniquely qualified to succeed. Her experience argues that the ability to build collaborative relationships and develop an understanding of others' behavior are the ingredients that allowed her to work successfully in Korea, Japan, Central America, the United Kingdom, and Scandinavia.

A recent Catalyst survey suggests that Dec may be right. Female respondents who had served in Asia and the Pacific Rim, Europe, and Central and South America felt that gender was not an issue overseas, or that if it was, it was a benefit. However, by practice it seems that many U.S. companies believe the opposite. While women constitute approximately 40 percent of all managers, only 10 percent of U.S. managers sent on overseas assignments are women.

Dec began her overseas travel with a trip to Asia, for which she prepared by reading books and magazines and asking other travelers for their advice. Although a little nervous over the fact that fewer than 5 percent of Japanese technologists are women, she was pleasantly surprised to find that Asians assumed U.S. women were competent or they would not have been sent abroad.

"As soon as they saw I had the knowledge," Dec says, "they immediately respected that. If you have the knowledge, doors are open to you."

Respect for local traditions and customs is second only to competence as a necessary ingredient for success abroad. In Asia, for instance, the exchange of business cards is a formal ritual very different from the casual Western custom of tucking the unread bit of paper into one's pocket. Knowing the importance of such courtesies as receiving the card in both hands, bowing, and reading it carefully helped Dec understand that her own behavior should be somewhat less assertive than it would be at home. She also spent more time listening than she was used to. At meetings, for instance, confrontations were avoided, and it was not unusual for participants to spend up to 25 percent of their time in the meeting simply thinking about what had just been said. If Dec had concerns about anyone's contribution, she understood the need to preserve good relationships and avoid embarrassing others with public confrontations or tough questions. Instead of addressing her concerns at the meeting, therefore, she would deal with them more discreetly on an individual basis.

Meals with co-workers were frequent and offered Dec many opportunities to build relationships in a less formal setting than the office. After her first experience sitting on floor pillows set around a low restaurant table, she learned to wear longer skirts to such gatherings.

Dec's experience and that of the respondents to Catalyst's survey of global businesswomen can be refined down to a few guidelines about working overseas:

1. Learn as much as possible about local and business cultures.
2. Dress conservatively.
3. Be patient.
4. Take cues from those around you.
5. Take advantage of opportunities to socialize.

While all of this advice sounds fine, others in Irene Dec's position wonder about how much they should change and adapt when the local culture is fundamentally different from their own sense of self and from their firm's corporate culture.

Sources: Rajendra Bajpai, Alice Fung, Janet Guyon, Paola Hjelt, Cindy Kano, and Richard Tomlinson, "Family Ties," *Fortune*, October 13, 2003, pp. 113–115; Sully Taylor, Nancy Napier Knox, and Wolfgang Mayrhofer, "Women in Global Business: Introduction," *International Journal of Human Resource Management*, August 2002, pp. 739–742; Kathleen Melymuka, "Global Woman," *Computerworld*, August 6, 2001, pp. 34–35.

With this in mind, consider some of the issues in managing people who come together from high- and low-context cultures. For example, imagine a team composed of one person each from the United States, Australia, Korea, and Japan. The team meets to discuss a global production problem and report to a senior executive from a client company. For the two individuals from low-context cultures (i.e., the United States and Australia), the phrase "Say what you mean and mean what you say" would not only be familiar but would seem right. Consequently, if the senior executive asked if something could be done and the team had already discussed the impossibility of the task, the two team members from the low-context culture would most likely say "no." To say "yes" when you mean "no" would not be right regardless of the fact that a senior executive from a client is in the room. They would likely view someone who would say "yes" when they meant "no" at best with suspicion and at worst as a liar. Yet, for the two team members from high-context cultures, the fact that a senior executive from a client is in the room asking the questions makes all the difference in the appropriate response. For them, in this situation saying "yes" when you mean "no" would be entirely appropriate. To say "no" without consideration of the context would be evidence of someone who is unsophisticated, self-centered, or simply immature. Imagine then the attributions if the American replies that what the client is asking for is not possible while the Korean member of the team says it is. Not only would the client be confused, but imagine the attributions that the American and Australian would make about their Japanese and Korean team members as well as what the Korean and Japanese would think of the other two. Without understanding the influence of culture context, the team trust and effectiveness could break down almost instantly.

From a practical perspective, the key issue is to recognize that neither high-context nor low-context cultures are right or wrong; they are quite different. These differences can influence a number of important managerial behaviors, including communication, negotiation, decision making, and leadership. While we will examine many of these implications in greater detail in subsequent chapters, A Manager's Challenge, "When In Rome, How Far Should You Go?" helps illustrate the concept and some of its implications. It points out that a lack of awareness of this fundamental dimension of cultural differences can lead to misinterpretations, mistaken attributions, mistrust, and ineffectiveness. In contrast, changing yourself and behaviors can create goodwill and more effective working relationships. In reading this case, do you think that trying to change oneself and adapt to a new culture can be taken too far? If you were working in a foreign country which values would be the hardest for you to change?

managerial perspectives revisited

1

PERSPECTIVE 1: THE ORGANIZATIONAL CONTEXT The context of the organization plays a central role in the management of culture. As we've pointed out, a strong culture can be an effective influence on daily behavior even when no one is looking. What the content of that culture should be is largely a function of the organization—what its objectives are, what its history has been, and so on. It is virtually impossible to say that certain cultural values should be the core ones for every organization. At Nordstrom and UPS, customer service is a core value. At 3M innovation is a core value. The context of the organization is especially important when cultural change is needed. How entrenched the old culture is constitutes one of the most important factors to understand when contemplating a cultural change. A cultural value that has existed for a long time and had a history of success can be one of the most difficult elements of an organization to change. This is also true not just for organizations, but for individuals. For example, if you believe in creativity and innovation for the successful management of programmers, and have achieved this through informal "jam sessions" late at night with pizza and rock music, you may have a hard time changing to the more structured approach of programmers in Germany when you are sent there on a special assignment. In this sense, even in the same company, the context of the organizational unit can make all the difference in how even common objectives like innovation are achieved.

PERSPECTIVE 2: THE HUMAN FACTOR Unlike a computer or telephone system, culture only makes a difference with and through people. As a manager, whether you are changing or strengthening a corporate culture, you can only accomplish this by working through people. Part of the challenge is first understanding the different values and beliefs that your employees may have as a function of different family, religious, ethnic, educational, international, or other experiences. If strong organizational cultures are already established then you have to understand where people are today, not just where you want things to be tomorrow. For example, you may want performance to improve but using individual rewards and recognition may not be the best approach if your subordinates have a strong cultural value regarding groups. In the context of working with peers, subordinates, and even bosses who have different cultural backgrounds from your own, the ability and desire to understand their values and beliefs is critical to determining where common ground might be or what changes might be required of them or you in order to work effectively together.

PERSPECTIVE 3: MANAGING PARADOXES Respecting cultural differences while trying to foster cooperation for collective achievement is just one of the many paradoxical challenges related to culture. Clearly, insisting on a common culture without understanding or respecting individual or group differences is unlikely to be effective. At the same time, tolerating differences without ensuring some degree of cooperation when needed is also unlikely to produce desired results. This challenge becomes even more acute when individuals from different nationalities and cultures have to work together within an organization. A common culture can provide unifying direction for cross-cultural teams within a company. However, failure to leverage the cultural diversity of the team members could potentially lead to ineffective team decisions and poor performance. How can you balance the dual objectives of integration while simultaneously tolerating cultural differences? Managers who are uncomfortable with this paradox and don't enjoy working through challenges like this are unlikely to be successful in a business world that is increasingly integrated and diverse.

PERSPECTIVE 4: ENTREPRENEURIAL MIND-SET An important part of an entrepreneurial mind-set is being open to new ideas, opportunities, and perspectives. While this openness is almost always beneficial, it is particularly beneficial in the context of culture. Managers with an entrepreneurial mind-set are more likely to be open to and perceive value in cultural diversity. Diversity in a team setting, for example, should facilitate the development of multiple alternatives and additional opportunities because of the different viewpoints provided by the team's members. An entrepreneurial mind-   set is likely to also help managers be more open to entering new international markets. This in turn has been shown to provide managers with new technological expertise, which aids them in developing and introducing new products.[38]

Similarly, individuals from different cultures have different behavioral patterns and accomplish tasks differently. This creates other learning opportunities for managers. These learning opportunities can transform managers into innovators and entrepreneurs who will lead their organizations to success. However, absorbing this information and putting it to use requires personal reflection and self-examination. Why? Because understanding people who are different from ourselves, culturally or otherwise, can be challenging.[39] Without a good understanding of your own values and beliefs and why you hold them, the likelihood that you'll realize what others have to offer isn't great.

concluding comments

We hope this chapter has demonstrated that what we wear, how we talk, and when we speak are all heavily influenced by cultural assumptions, values, and beliefs. Groups, whether they be a department, a company, or a country, typically develop a shared set of mental road maps and traffic signals to effectively interact with each other. The managerial challenge relating to culture is threefold: understanding, changing, and leveraging culture.

In understanding cultures, you should keep in mind that culture consists of assumptions, values, and behaviors and that these elements of a given culture exist because they have been successful in the past. The six basic areas of assumptions that have been presented can facilitate your ability to understand a new culture. This is not to say that every behavior, custom, or tradition you observe can be traced directly to one of these six categories of assumptions; but many of the fundamental aspects of a culture can be linked to beliefs about humans' relationship to the environment, human nature, human relationships, human activity, truth and morality, or time. The more widely and deeply the assumptions and values are shared, the stronger the cultural value. The stronger a particular cultural value, the greater the rewards or punishments associated with compliance or noncompliance and the more difficult it is to change.

Changing a culture is always a challenge. Behavioral change and compliance can be achieved with enough monitoring and reinforcement. But doing so will extract a heavy cost of time, energy, and money if the new behaviors are not consistent or compatible with widely shared and strongly held values and assumptions. For example, Japanese executives discontinued wearing traditional kimonos and instead changed to wearing Western clothes in the early 1900s. However, Japanese executives did not adopt Western individualistic values and start wearing all sorts of different styles of business attire. You only need spend a few moments in any business district in Japan to see that the modern business attire (dark suit, white shirt, modest tie) is as pervasive as traditional kimonos were. Why? Because, in Japan, people value the group and conforming to it more than individuality. This is a core value, and it has not changed. With this in mind, the challenge in effecting change is to link new desired behaviors to existing values and assumptions. Where this is not possible, old cultural trees—soil, roots, trunk, leaves, and all—must be extracted and replaced with new ones. For most people, this is traumatic, and they usually resist the effort. So to be successful, you must correctly determine not only the behavior, values, and assumptions that fit with the environmental conditions but also the change strategy and the amount of *effort needed* to implement it effectively. In addition, the behaviors of those espousing the new culture must be congruent, or in other words, managers must "walk the talk." Employees are quick to pick up on incongruencies between espoused and actual values and ignore the "talk" and follow the "walk."[40]

The third challenge lies in using cultural diversity effectively. In today's environment, you will encounter individuals—whether customers, competitors, suppliers, subordinates, bosses, or peers—who have a different cultural background from your own. They will have assumptions, values, beliefs, communication styles, management philosophies, and decision-making processes different from yours. Research suggests that if you simply label those differences as good or bad based on your own assumptions and values, you are not likely to be effective in culturally diverse management situations.[41] If, however, you stop and say, "That's interesting; I wonder why it's that way?" you are more likely to be effective in a diverse environment.

key terms

artifacts   121
assumptions   121
collectivism   124
core value   134
cultural context   139
culture   115
feminine societies   124
individualism   124

masculine societies   124
power distance   124
rituals   138
short-term or long-term
   orientation   126
strong versus weak cultural
   values   131

subculture   132
Theory X managers   123
Theory Y managers   123
uncertainty avoidance   125
values   121

test your comprehension

1. List three reasons why it is important for you as a manager to have a solid understanding of culture.
2. Define culture.
3. Describe the three levels of culture.
4. What are the key differences between artifacts and assumptions?
5. Describe the six basic assumptions.
6. Do most companies in the United States hold a dominance or harmony assumption regarding humanity's relationship to the environment?
7. What are the key differences between Theory X and Theory Y managers?

8. Define *power distance* and provide an example of how it affects managerial behavior.
9. Define *individualism–collectivism* and provide an example of how they affect managerial behavior.
10. Would someone from a high uncertainty avoidance culture be more likely to believe managers should or should not have precise answers to questions raised by subordinates about their jobs?
11. Are individuals who believe "time is a river" more or less likely to be late for appointments?
12. Culturally diverse groups often do significantly better or worse than culturally homogeneous groups. What is the key explanation for this?
13. How does the extent to which cultural values are widely shared and/or deeply held affect the strength or weakness of a culture?
14. What is a subculture?
15. What are two practical reasons for identifying the core values in an organization's or country's culture?
16. What strategies can managers use to create or change culture?
17. What are the key differences between high- and low-context cultures? How do they affect managerial behavior?

apply your understanding

1. The stronger an organizational culture, the greater the impact it can have on behavior; however, the stronger the culture, the more difficult it is to *change*. Unfortunately, the environment changes, and values that fit the environment today may be inappropriate tomorrow. What can an organization do to keep the positive aspects of a strong culture and still reduce the risk of becoming extinct by not changing its culture fast enough to accommodate environmental shifts?
2. All organizations have cultures. What are the key cultural aspects of your school? What links are there between key assumptions and values and visible artifacts such as clothing, behaviors, or rituals? Compare your school's culture with that of other schools: How do they differ? How are they the same?
3. If you look forward to working with individuals from a variety of cultural backgrounds, or perhaps even working in foreign countries, what can you do to better prepare yourself for those fixture opportunities?
4. What are the key work values you want in an organization you work for? List at least five. How can you assess the extent to which potential employers have these desired values?

practice your capabilities

John Smith accepted a one-year internship to work in a Japanese company in Tokyo. John had studied some Japanese in college but was not yet proficient. Soon after he arrived in Japan, he received a very thorough orientation to the company, including introductions to all the staff in the department to which he was assigned. His job was primarily to edit and proof English correspondence sent to overseas customers and suppliers.

John quickly settled into his job and felt that he was doing well. Still, he felt that despite his efforts to get to know and be friendly with his colleagues, they always seemed a bit cool and standoffish. Then one night one of the younger workers invited him to dinner with a group. The group consisted of several younger staff, the assistant manager, and the department manager.

Dinner was a light affair at a local restaurant. Everyone seemed very relaxed and joked with each other and with John. While people spoke mostly in Japanese, everyone, including the assistant and department managers, was careful to chat with John.

After dinner the group went to a nearby Karaoke bar where they had drinks and sang songs in English. They loved it when John sang "My Way." By the end of the evening, everyone was laughing and joking nonstop. As John left the group to board his train home, he felt that he had finally broken through and become one of the gang.

The next morning, he couldn't wait to get to work and enjoy this new level of friendship and personal relationships. He smiled and tried to joke with several colleagues soon after arriving at work, but was stunned when they acted as if the previous evening had not even happened. They were all back to their "business" selves, especially the two man-

agers. Was last night just a chance for them to poke fun at him? Was it all a sham? Were they embarrassed to be seen as friendly with John (a foreigner) in front of people from other departments? Were they all just two-faced hypocrites who could not be trusted?

1. What explains the change in behavior toward John?
2. What should John do? Should John confront one of his colleagues at work and ask him or her what is going on? Should he just forget it? Should he try to talk with one of the guys after work? Should he give up on trying to become friends?

closing case
DEVELOP YOUR CRITICAL THINKING

Changing the Culture at General Semiconductor

When Ronald Ostertag took over the management of General Semiconductor, he realized right away that he would have to change the $500 million company's culture if it was to survive. During a presentation he was giving to the board of directors, two of the company's senior managers began to argue publicly, trading embarrassing insults and verbal barbs.

Soon Ostertag had replaced nearly every member of the senior team, but the resulting job insecurity that spread through the ranks pointed out the need to do even further work on shifting the company's culture. "I realized we needed to do something to develop a sense of teamwork," says Ostertag. "We needed to develop a culture of mutual respect that fostered cooperation and innovation."

As if changing the culture was not challenging enough, in the process Ostertag had to contend with the fact that General Semiconductor, an electronics parts manufacturer based in a suburban industrial park in New York, had a workforce spread around the world from North America to Asia, with nearly 6,000 employees speaking five different languages. Only 200 of those workers were employed in the United States.

Ostertag decided on a brainstorming session to bring the new management team together to agree on the company's guiding principles. "Our task," he says in retrospect, "was to put down on paper what our core values

were and then make sure everyone was on the same page." A cohesive mission statement and a list of eight company values, which are called General Semiconductor's "culture points," came out of that meeting and were centered around goals like "quality," "integrity," "good customer service," and "on-time delivery." Soon everyone knew the culture points and even carried them around on small cards. "They knew when they saw me coming, whether it was in the factory in Taiwan or Ireland or here, that I might come up to anyone and ask them to rattle off four or five of those values," says Ostertag. "I didn't mean it as a test, but more to show that that is what everyone here is striving for."

The company's human resources staff helped spread the word throughout the company, with a leadership and problem-solving program developed by the six HR staffers. HR even produced a 135-page information binder full of basic information about the company, its products, its competitors, and its basic financials. Ostertag was confident that such information was empowering, and that it was critical for everyone in the firm to have the same knowledge base from which to work. Two years after the program was implemented, a survey of the management group indicated that 36 of 39 development areas already showed improvement.

Early business results were positive. Market share and revenues were up, and turnover was dramatically down.

Still, it was not enough. Vishay Intertechnology launched a bid to acquire General Semiconductor, believing that even greater improvements could be made and therefore value could be extracted, and ultimately Vishay succeeded in its takeover bid.

Questions

1. What actions do you think had the greatest impact on changing the culture at General Semiconductor?

2. Do you think changing General Semiconductor's culture was critical to its improved performance?

3. What changes would you have made and what actions would you have taken if you had been in Ronald Ostertag's position?

4. What outcomes would you want to measure to determine if your actions were working or not?

Sources: Spencer Chin, "Vishay Finally Gets General Semi," *EBN*, August 6, 2001, p. 1c; Caroline Louise Cole, "Optimas 2001—Global Outlook: Eight Values Bring Unity to a Worldwide Company," *Workforce*, March 2001, p. 44–45.

Ethics and Social Responsibility

5

LEARNING OBJECTIVES

After studying this chapter, you should be able to:

- Describe why an understanding of basic approaches to ethical decision making and corporate social responsibility is important.
- Explain the basic approaches to ethical decision making.
- Identify the different implications of each approach in real-life situations.
- Explain the basic approaches to corporate social responsibility.
- Develop different implications for each approach to corporate social responsibility.

Nicolo Pignatelli and Gulf Italia

Nicolo Pignatelli, president of Gulf Italia (a subsidiary of Gulf Oil), stared at the notice from the Italian government. "How could this be possible?" he thought. The government had given Pignatelli permission to build an oil refinery with a capacity of almost 6 million tons. He had just completed it at a cost of well over $100 million. Now the Italian government was telling him that he could only operate at slightly more than 50 percent capacity (3.9 million tons). On top of that, it was also telling him that not only would he need to get a "production permission" to go from 3.9 to 6.0 million tons in actual production, but then he would need a *separate* "implementation permission" to put into effect the "production permission." Pignatelli didn't know whether to be intimidated or infuriated. Every day that the plant was shut down would cost money. However, even if the refinery were allowed to operate, it needed to operate at or near capacity. If it did not, it would also lose millions because of the high fixed costs.

Pignatelli was understandably upset—he had spent seven long years implementing a strategy to take the company from being one of the small fries in the Italian oil and gasoline industry to one of the major players. When Pignatelli took over, Gulf had crude oil in the Middle East and in southern Italy and gas stations in northern Italy. To this Pignatelli added a retail presence in central and southern Italy by purchasing the 700 gasoline stations from Marathon Oil. This gave Gulf gas stations throughout Italy crude oil to bring into the country. What Gulf lacked was the middle part of the chain—a refinery. Without it, Pignatelli was dependent on competitors for both a refined gasoline supply and wholesale prices. Pignatelli felt that Gulf needed its own refinery to complete the chain from the wellhead to the gas pump.

Building a refinery in Italy proved to be a long and expensive task. Even after receiving permission to build the refinery in northern Italy, local community opposition resulted in five location changes for the company. These changes cost Gulf an additional $16 million. To ensure that the smoke and fumes would not contribute to the city smog, Pignatelli spent extra money on a 450-foot smokestack (twice as tall as normal). Pignatelli also installed a special combustion chamber so that flare towers (used to burn off waste gas) and the loud noise and noxious fumes associated with them weren't necessary. He also added a state-of-the-art water purification system. In fact, Pignatelli demonstrated the quality of the system by personally drinking the waste water. These environmental additions added over $1 million to the project.

To ensure that the refinery was profitable, Pignatelli arranged a joint venture with Mobil Oil. Mobil had many service stations in northern Italy where Gulf's refinery was located, but no refinery of its own. The money Mobil was to invest for its equity share would reduce Gulf's financial burden in building the refinery and cut the shipping costs for Mobil because its stations would be located near the new refinery. However, Mobil had the option of pulling out of the deal if Gulf's refinery could not operate at capacity, because in that case the refined gas would be too expensive for Mobil to buy.

It had taken seven years for the refinery to be approved and built. Over $100 million was on the line. Trying to obtain approval to operate at capacity and a separate authorization to implement that approval might take many more months, if not years. Pignatelli wondered if he was being purposely set up by government officials.

Four options occurred to Pignatelli: (1) play it straight and try to gain government authorization, (2) ask his more influential partners to put pressure on government officials, (3) pay a large sum of money ($1 million deposited to a Swiss bank account) to a "consultant" who had "debottlenecked" problems like this before and who promised Pignatelli that he could fix the situation quickly, or (4) pay money "under the table" directly to government officials to obtain the permissions needed to run the refinery economically.

Pignatelli considered each option. Playing it straight would likely take several months and possibly years before government authorization could be obtained. In the meantime, the refinery would not operate or would operate at such a low capacity that it would lose millions of dollars. Pignatelli was not certain that pressure from his partners would influence government officials. He wondered about the effect of going to the media. Given the current cost of the project, the thousands of jobs that depended on an operating refinery, and time pressures, $1 million seemed like a small price to pay to a consultant to get things debottlenecked. He might be able to gain approval for even less money if he went directly to government officials.

Managers are frequently faced with complex dilemmas requiring them to walk a fine line between doing what's right and doing what's strategic. Doing business in countries where payoffs and bribes to government officials and power brokers is commonplace can be especially tricky—as one CEO who tried to build an oil refinery in Italy discovered.

Source: Personal conversations with Mr. Pignatelli, 1989, 1993.

strategic overview

As the case of Pignatelli illustrates, managers face perplexing ethical and social responsibility issues. Pignatelli seems to be leaning in the direction of hiring a consultant, who might use part of the money for bribes. If Pignatelli does not pay the bribes directly, does this absolve him of responsibility? Bribes are illegal in Italy. Even if bribes are common practice there, does this justify paying them? Does Pignatelli have a responsibility to Italian citizens to build an environmentally friendly refinery above and beyond what is required by law? Is it appropriate for Gulf to spend this extra money and essentially take it away from shareholders? How would you feel if you were a lower-level employee in the company and learned that Pignatelli intended to pay bribes to get things "debottlenecked"? What would your ethical obligations be? Should you ignore the situation or confront Pignatelli? Should you inform your direct boss or go to the media?

Managers in large companies usually act as agents of the owners (as we explain later in this chapter). As such, top executives have an implied obligation to take strategic actions that are in the best interests of the owners or shareholders. If they take actions that help themselves, such as rejecting a takeover offer to keep their jobs, but that may be to the detriment of shareholders, are they acting in an ethical manner? In recent years, numerous executives of top corporations have acted opportunistically, making headlines in the process. Some acted not only unethically but illegally. They harmed both the shareholders and many employees, who lost their jobs when their bosses' misdeeds came to light and the companies went bankrupt.

Both managerial ethics and strategy begin at the top of the organization. For ethical decisions and practices to permeate the firm, top executives must build a culture based on those values. This includes establishing codes of ethics, implementing ethics training for employees, and rewarding ethical behaviors (as discussed later in this chapter). Moreover, it includes behaving in an ethical manner *themselves*.[1]

An ethical organization is especially important when it comes to implementing the strategies developed by top managers. Managers at the top and throughout the organization along with other employees are likely to face many ethical dilemmas throughout the course of doing business. Although the ethical decisions facing Pignatelli seem extreme, most organizations face similar dilemmas on a regular basis.

Managers must also grapple with decisions about how to operate their firms efficiently, yet in a socially responsible manner. To do so, top executives may need to establish standards that exceed the requirements of the law. They must also consider the strategic and ethical impact of their decisions on the organization's stakeholders and employees. And their decisions must be perceived to be fair. (We will discuss the various approaches managers can take to organizational "justice" later in this chapter.) ■

The discussions above coupled with the opening case help to highlight the two key issues of this chapter: managerial ethics and corporate social responsibility. **Managerial ethics** is essentially the study of morality and standards of business conduct. **Corporate social responsibility** is concerned with the obligations that corporations owe to their constituencies such as shareholders, employees, customers, and citizens at large.

managerial ethics the study of morality and standards of business conduct

corporate social responsibility the obligations that corporations owe to their constituencies such as shareholders, employees, customers, and citizens at large

RELEVANCE TO YOU

You may be wondering, "Why should I care about ethics and social responsibility? Aren't these the types of issues philosophers worry about?" To answer this question, you need only pick up recent newspapers or business magazines. Everything from Wall Street trading scandals to accounting frauds at Enron, WorldCom, Tyco, and Global Crossing to environmental pollution cover-ups seems to be in the press daily. For example, Priceline.com lost billions in market value, even before the general market meltdown in 2000, when it was established that the firm had been reporting as revenue the total dollar value of transactions when only a small percentage actually came to

exhibit 5.1

Excellence in Business Ethics
Award Winners

2000 Winners
The Bureau of National Affairs, Inc.
For over a half-century of dedication to employee ownership, despite pressures to sell the company.

Iceland, Inc.
For a precedent-setting move in the United Kingdom toward the sale of all-organic store-brand food, at nonorganic prices.

Whole Foods Market
For a broad-based commitment to customer, stockholder, employee, community, and environmental service.

1999 Winners
St. Luke's (Award for Employee Ownership)
For creating a visionary model of employee ownership, out of the crisis of an unwanted merger.

Equal Exchange (Award for Stakeholder Relations)
For its path-breaking approach to fair trade, defining supplier welfare as part of business success.

Fetzer Vineyards (Award for Environmental Excellence)
For a broad-based approach to environmental sustainability, combined with financial excellence.

1998 Winners
SmithKline Beecham
For its $1 billion commitment to disease eradication.

Wainwright Bank
For dedication to social justice, internally and externally.

S.C. Johnson
For its focus on sustainable community development.

Source: www.business-ethics.com, accessed October 27, 2001.

Priceline.com as revenue for the service it performed. Thus, while a consumer might bid $500 for a flight to Europe and an airline accepted the bid, Priceline.com recorded the full value as sales when only a small fraction was sent to it for brokering the deal in cyberspace. Even its famous spokesperson, William Shatner (Captain James T. Kirk on the series *Star Trek*), said he was surprised by the practice.[2]

Clearly, poor managerial ethics and corporate social responsibility can generate negative publicity, hurt a company's stock price and destroy shareholder value, or make it difficult for the firm to recruit high-quality employees. In contrast, well-managed ethical behavior and corporate social responsibility can have significant, positive consequences for employees, customers, shareholders, and communities. Exhibit 5.1 provides a listing of companies honored for "Excellence in Ethics" by *Business Ethics* magazine. As you read these examples, ask yourself whether you would be more or less likely to work for one of these firms because of its reputation. As a customer, would you be willing to pay a premium price for the product because of the company's reputation?

Fetzer Vineyards, led for 27 years by former CEO Paul Dolan, is among the companies honored for its "Excellence in Ethics" by *Business Ethics* magazine. "We like to think of Fetzer as authentic, innovative, and caring about people and our environment," commented Fetzer's Global Brand Director Tom Meyer. As a consumer, how important are a company's business ethics to you? Would you be willing to pay more for the products produced by such a company?

THE DEVELOPMENT OF INDIVIDUAL ETHICS

At this point in your life, do you think you have a fairly well-established set of ethical beliefs and values? If you do, how did you come by them? What role did family, friends, peers, teachers, religion, job experiences, and life experiences have on the development of your ethical beliefs? To explore this issue, think about a situation in which someone made a different ethical judgment from your own. What if you had been born in a different country, raised by a different family; had attended a different school system, experienced different religious influences; had different friends, and held different jobs? Would you hold the same ethical values you do now? Would you reach identical ethical judgments to those you reach now?

There is little debate that family, friends, peers, teachers, religion, job experiences, and life experiences play a significant role in the development of individual ethical values and judgments. What is debated is which factors play the strongest role because their influence varies from person to person.[3] This debate is unlikely to be resolved soon. Nor is its resolution necessary for our purposes. The primary reason for raising the issue is to realize that in order to understand how others make decisions, you need to understand something about their backgrounds.[4]

Simply labeling ethical judgments that are different from your own as wrong is likely to foster feelings of mistrust (in both directions) and hurt working relationships. The greater the diversity in the workforce, or more specifically among your set of colleagues and subordinates, the greater the need for tolerance and understanding. However, as a manager, tolerance does not mean simply allowing subordinates to come to whatever ethical decisions they individually deem right. Because individual decisions can have consequences for the organization, managers often need to shape and influence the ethical thinking, judgment, and decision making of subordinates.

Consider the following real case that was conveyed to us in a recent conversation. (We have disguised the names at the manager's request.) Imagine you are the marketing manager in a publishing company. Your assistant manager has just recruited a new sales representative, Martha, from a key competitor. Martha worked for your competitor, Dresden, for 11 months after graduating from college. Dresden pays employees a bonus based on performance after the first year of employment. Martha was expecting a $10,000 bonus from Dresden. In discussions with your assistant manager, Martha negotiated for a $10,000 signing bonus if Dresden failed to pay her the performance bonus. Part of the reason your assistant manager agreed to do this is because Martha had been exposed to a number of strategic operations and marketing plans in her first year of employment at Dresden. Given her somewhat junior position in the company, she had not been asked to sign, nor had she signed, a "noncompete" clause that would have prevented her from taking a job with a competitor for a specific time period or disclosing or using the knowledge gained during her time at Dresden. Legally, she was free to take the job with you.

Your assistant manager comes to you and asks if it is okay to try to get Martha to disclose as much as she knows about Dresden's marketing plans. What is your response? Do you think Dresden has an ethical obligation to pay Martha the $10,000 bonus even though she plans to leave only a few days short of completing 12 months of employment? If you were Martha, would you have any ethical misgivings about taking the new job and then relating all you knew about your previous employer's strategic plans? Would Dresden's paying you the end-of-year bonus have any bearing on what you would or would not reveal to your new employer?

UNDERSTANDING BASIC APPROACHES TO ETHICS

So how should you make decisions like these? Are there ethical approaches you can look to for guidance? The answer is that there are some basic approaches. The basic approaches have been around for a long time. This is in part because the challenge of ethical decision making is not a modern one. **Ethical dilemmas**, or the choice between two competing but arguably valid options, are not new and have confronted people throughout history.

In the next section we will describe these basic approaches for two reasons, hopefully without getting mired in the boring details. First, they can be helpful in trying to understand how others approach ethical dilemmas. Second, quite often the lack of a clear approach for making ethical decisions causes **ethical lapses** or decisions that are contrary to an individual's stated beliefs and policies of the company.

In thinking about the first reason, it is important to keep in mind the increasingly diverse workforce and global business environment. Now more than ever before, you are likely to encounter people who use widely different approaches and reach different conclusions about ethical conduct. This is illustrated in a recent study that examined the extent to which salespeople from the United States, Japan, and Korea viewed a set of actions as posing an ethical issue or not. The study found significant difference among these three nationalities.[5] For example, Korean salespeople did not think that

ethical dilemmas having to make a choice between two competing but arguably valid options

ethical lapses decisions that are contrary to an individual's stated beliefs and policies of the company

seeking information from a customer on the price quotation offered by a competitor in order to resubmit a more competitive bid was much of an ethical issue. American and Japanese salespeople saw this as largely unethical behavior. As a concrete example of this view, in most places in the United States a real estate broker cannot tell you how much someone else offered on a house you also want to buy. What do you think? Do you think asking a customer for information on the price submitted by your competitors is ethical or not?

Interestingly, from this same international study, researchers found that Korean salespeople did not think that giving free gifts was as much of an ethical issue, while American salespeople did. General Motors shares this general view and has a policy that restricts the giving of gifts. For example, in a conversation the president of GM's Asia Pacific region mentioned that he could not pay for the golf game of the president of the Philippines when they were discussing a potential new factory in the country. Do you think GM's policy is appropriate or has it gone too far?

Without understanding how or why others come to different conclusions, it is easy to label people holding the "wrong" beliefs as inferior. For example, in a recent study, Chinese and Australian auditors working for the same multinational accounting firms reached different decisions about proper ethical conduct because of different cultural assumptions. Chinese auditors looked to peers while Australian auditors looked to themselves in making ethical decisions. This reference point reflects the cultural group orientation of the Chinese and the individual orientation of Australians.[6] If either set of auditors has simply judged the other to be wrong without a sensitivity to how culture might influence ethical decisions, imagine how difficult it might be for them to work together on a global audit team. In fact, research has shown that ethnocentricity, or the view that your perspective is correct and others are inferior, tends to hurt managerial effectiveness, especially in culturally diverse or international contexts.[7] So, it is important for new managers to be able to examine the basic approaches to ethical decision making and recognize that individuals' backgrounds, including cultural values, influence ethical decisions and behavior.

As we stated, the second reason for examining basic approaches to ethical decision making is to avoid ethical lapses. Ethical lapses are more common than you might think. The pressures emanating from both the external environment and internal company environment often can be overwhelming. This is especially true if managers lack a systematized and explicit framework for thinking through dilemmas. For example, you may believe that because paying bribes is illegal in Italy it is wrong. However, if you were in Pignatelli's situation, the pressures from the external and internal environment would be staggering. You have invested $100 million of your company's money and the company has a strong performance culture. In other words, if you don't perform, you don't have a career. You have invested millions more in buying service stations that won't be profitable if you can't refine your own gasoline because you will have to buy gasoline from other refiners. Not only would an enormous investment be lost but employee layoffs would be huge. The refinery offers many high-skilled and high-paying jobs benefiting individuals and the community. When you put the dilemma in these terms, $1 million in consulting fees seems like a small price to pay. Under pressures like these, can you imagine how it might be possible to make a decision contrary to your stated beliefs?[8]

BASIC APPROACHES
TO ETHICAL DECISION MAKING

Several frameworks, or approaches, to ethical decision making exist. We examine four of the most common: the utilitarian, moral rights, universalism, and justice approaches. An understanding of basic approaches to ethical decision making will help you as a manager to examine your own personal ethics and work more effectively with employees whose ethical perspectives are different.

Utilitarian Approach

utilitarian approach focuses on the consequences of an action

Utilitarian Approach
by Stewart Black
Q&A
OneKey
www.prenhall.com/onekey

The utilitarian approach focuses on consequences of an action. Simplified, using a **utilitarian approach**, results "in the greatest good." Assume you are trying to sell grain to a developing nation and a customs agent demands an extra fee before he will clear your shipment. From a utilitarian perspective, you would try to determine the consequences of the options available to you. For example, you could (1) pay the money, (2) not pay the money and let the grain sit there, or (3) seek intervention from a third party. Which action would result in the greatest good? If there are starving people waiting for the grain, would you argue that the "good" of saving lives outweighs the "bad" of paying an illegal bribe?

Keep in mind when talking about whether an outcome is good or bad that people may see the same outcome differently. In other words, the "goodness" or "badness" of an outcome is often subjective. Factors such as culture, economic circumstances, and religion can all affect those subjective judgments. For example, if you were in Pignatelli's shoes, would you argue that the good of saving 2,000 jobs justified paying off government officials? What if unemployment were high in the region? Would that affect your thinking?

But many situations are not as clear-cut as to whether they constitute an ethical dilemma or just a business decision. How would you handle a situation in which some members of your staff see an impending decision as strictly business with no ethical implications, while others see it as an ethical dilemma?

For an example of this, take a look at A Manager's Challenge, "Changing Horses." In this situation, some members think that a long-term business relationship places certain unwritten obligations on the company to work with a struggling supplier regardless of changes in the business environment. On the other hand, other members of the management team think that the situation is strictly a business-based transaction. They believe that changes in business conditions and performance by the supplier justify changing the relationship. Since the supplier is not meeting its obligations, it's just good business to cut ties with it and move on to a more reliable supplier. On the other hand, if you see this as an ethical dilemma, should you try to influence your co-workers in order to get them to change their opinions? Or, should you change your perspective and simply view it as a business decision like your co-workers do?

Even if you frame the Johannson situation as an ethical dilemma, using the utilitarian approach, what action results in the greatest good and over what time frame? In the short run, continuing to work with Creative Applications will likely hurt your customers as your products do not arrive as fast as you would like. If this persists, it may enable your competitors to move past you and take market share away to the point that you have to reduce your size and

a manager's challenge

Change

Changing Horses

Caren Wheeler was a young purchasing manager in Johannson Wood Products, a 12-year-old company in the Midwest. As the purchasing manager, she was being asked to make a decision about the continued use of a supplier. This represented a big change for Caren. Several other managers in the firm viewed the decision in ethical terms, whereas Caren normally didn't think ethics were relevant unless laws were being broken.

Like many innovative mid-sized firms, Johannson Wood Products had formed strong partnerships with a limited number of suppliers in order to receive supplies on a just-in-time basis and then ship its finished goods in a timely fashion to retail stores. One of those partner suppliers was Creative Applications.

Creative Applications was a small, family-run company that stored and milled Johannson Wood Products' lumber into finished parts. The partnership, negotiated three years ago, had worked well for Creative Applications. Over 60 percent of its revenues were obtained from Johannson Wood Products. In fact, the agreement had come just when Creative Applications was in financial trouble. Although it was not out of the woods yet, the agreement with Johannson Wood Products was critical to Creative Applications' survival.

Recently, however, the partnership had not worked well for Johannson Wood Products. As its sales increased, Creative Applications was having difficulty meeting deadlines. Caren had mentioned this problem to Steve Jackson, Creative Applications' plant manager (and the son of the owner), but no real improvement occurred.

When Caren met with Tom Masters, the president of Johannson Wood Products, and several other managers to discuss the situation, a variety of opinions emerged. Some saw this as an ethical issue and others did not. First the group focused on Steve Jackson's abrasive personality and management style. Many in the meeting felt that he was "a control freak" and could not delegate authority. Consequently, as demand increased, Steve became a bottleneck in Creative Applications' ability to meet delivery deadlines.

One of Johannson Wood Products' managers, who disliked Steve, stated, "I don't think that continuing a relationship with Creative Applications is going to work for us. It's one of those cases where the management capabilities of a small-time operation can't make the transition to a larger producer. We can't afford to keep nursing along a relationship that's not working."

Another manager felt it was unfair to bring personal feelings for or against Steve into the discussion, and replied, "We've always told our vendors that if they were there for us, we'd be there for them. For over two years, Creative Applications really performed for us. Are we going to pull out now that they are facing tough times? Remember eighteen months ago, when we pressured them to lease an expensive piece of milling equipment because of our increased volume? The equipment dealer would only do it on a three-year lease. Creative did it even though it elevated their costs. If we pull the rug out from under them now, that's not fair, and will hurt their chances of survival—we're still 60 percent of their business. Is it ethical to just pull the plug now?"

A third individual interjected, "I propose that we make an offer to either purchase Creative Applications or start our own in-house capability for milling the products. Here is a proposal that details the capital that would be required for either option and the potential savings that could be generated over a three-year period."

"Caren, what do you recommend?" asked Tom Masters. Several different issues raced through her mind. First, she had not really thought about the situation from an ethical point of view, yet clearly some of the team members felt there were ethical issues involved. In her gut, she felt just dropping Creative Applications was the *wrong* thing to do, but she didn't have any formal ethical justification for her feelings. However, even those who thought it was an ethical issue did not really have any formal ethical argument for their conclusions. Caren wondered if she should change her normal approach and take a careful look at the situation from both an ethical and business point of view. Should she try to get the others to change their approach and also consider the ethical issues? Johannson Wood Products was always stressing loyal partnership relationships. Was it ethical to just sever the relationship with Creative Applications? On the other hand, the delays being caused by Creative Applications were beginning to hurt Johannson Wood Products' ability to meet store orders faster than its competition. What was the right thing to do and what was the right approach to take?

Source: Adapted from Doug Wallace, "Changing Horses," *Business Ethics*, November-December, 1994, p. 34.

lay off some employees. On the other hand, demonstrating that you are serious about your promise to work with chosen suppliers could lead to additional commitment from Creative Applications and other suppliers and result in enhanced performance and product deliveries.

Moral Rights Approach

The **moral rights approach** to ethical decisions focuses on an examination of the moral standing of actions independent of their consequences. According to this approach, some things are just "right" or "wrong," independent of consequences. When two courses of action both have moral standing, then the positive and negative consequences of each should determine which course is more ethical. Using this approach, you should choose the action that is in conformance with moral principles and provides positive consequences. From a moral rights approach, if not honoring unwritten commitments to suppliers is simply wrong (i.e., doesn't have moral standing), then cutting off the supplier to make more money is not justified. The managerial challenge here is that the moral standing of most issues is debatable. For example, you might want to say that it is wrong to lie. But is it wrong to make your competitors think you are about to enter one market when you are really about to enter another, in order to give your company the element of surprise? Is it just wrong to say you are not working on a particular new technology when you actually are, in order to influence your competitors not to invest in the new technology and thereby have an advantage when you finally perfect it? Again returning to the case of Johannson Products, how would you handle the situation if one employee believes that honoring unwritten, implicit commitments is just right (i.e., has moral standing) and another employee does not? In many companies both explicit policies as well as corporate values often serve a vital role in defining what is right or wrong when there is no universally accepted determination. If the corporate values of Johannson stress honoring not only legal contracts but implicit promises to suppliers, then should Caren try to get the other managers to change their views and see this as an ethical issue?

Universal Approach

Immanuel Kant, perhaps one of the most famous moral philosophers, articulated the best-known ethical imperative, or **universal approach**. Simplified, Kant's moral imperative was "do unto others as you would have them do unto everyone, including yourself." If you follow this approach, you should choose a course of action that you believe can apply to all people under all situations and that you would want applied to yourself. At the heart of universalism is the issue of rights. For Kant, the basis of all rights stems from freedom and autonomy. Actions that limit the freedom and autonomy of individuals generally lack moral justification. If you were in Pignatelli's situation and took a universal approach to the decision of what to do, it might be difficult to justify paying bribes to government officials either directly or indirectly. To meet the "do unto others as you would have them do unto everyone" criterion, you would have to be willing to let everyone use bribes as a means of getting the ends they desired.

Justice Approach

The **justice approach** focuses on how equitably the costs and benefits of actions are distributed as the principal means of judging ethical behavior.[9] In general, costs and benefits should be equitably distributed, rules should be impartially applied, and those damaged because of inequity or discrimination should be compensated.

Distributive Justice Managers ascribing to **distributive justice** distribute rewards and punishments equitably, based on performance. This does not mean that everyone gets the same or equal rewards or punishments; rather, they receive equitable rewards and punishments as a function of how much they contribute to or detract from the organization's goals. A manager cannot distribute bonuses, promotions, or benefits based on arbitrary characteristics such as age, gender, religion, or race. This is the basic rationale behind the U.S. Civil Rights Act of 1964. Under this law, even if a manager has no intention of discriminating against a particular minority group, if a minority group can demonstrate inequitable results (called *disparate impact*), legal action can be brought against the firm. For example, if 50 percent of a firm's applicants for promotion were women, but 75 percent of those receiving promotions were men, these data could be used to file a claim of discrimination based on the underlying notion of distributive justice.

Justice Approach
by Stewart Black

Q&A
One Key
www.prenhall.com/onekey

distributive justice the equitable distribution of rewards and punishment, based on performance

Procedural Justice Managers ascribing to **procedural justice** make sure that people affected by managerial decisions consent to the decision-making process and that the process is administered impartially.[10] Consent means that people are informed about the process and have the freedom to exit the system if they choose. As with distributive justice, the decision-making process cannot systematically discriminate against people because of arbitrary characteristics such as age, gender, religion, or race. Recent research involving employees across multiple countries consistently suggests that perceived justice is positively related to desired outcomes such as job performance, trust, job satisfaction, and organizational commitment, and is negatively related to outcomes such as turnover and other counterproductive work behavior.[11] Procedural justice is generally studied and interpreted within the context of the organization. However, the findings of a recent study show that factors external to the firm may also have strong effects on counterproductive workplace behavior. In a study contrasting community violence and an organization's procedural justice, violent crime rates in the community where a plant resided predicted workplace aggression in that plant, whereas the plant's procedural justice climate did not.[12]

procedural justice ensuring that those affected by managerial decisions consent to the decision-making process and that the process is administered impartially

Compensatory Justice The main thesis of **compensatory justice** is that if distributive justice and procedural justice fail or are not followed as they should be, then those hurt by the inequitable distribution of rewards should be compensated. This compensation often takes the form of money, but it can take other forms. For example, compensatory justice is at the heart of affirmative action plans. Typically, affirmative action plans ensure that groups that may have been systematically disadvantaged in the past, such as women or minorities, are given every opportunity in the future. For example, special training programs could be instituted for women who were passed over for promotions in the past because they were denied access to certain experiences required for promotion.

compensatory justice if distributive and procedural justice fail, those hurt by the inequitable distribution of rewards are compensated

MORAL INTENSITY
IN ETHICAL DECISION MAKING

As we have pointed out thus far in this chapter, one of the challenges of ethical decision making for a manager is that for many issues and consequences, people do not have identical perspectives. They differ in whether they see a

moral intensity the degree to which people see an issue as an ethical one

magnitude of the consequences the anticipated level of impact of the outcome of a given action

social consensus the extent to which members of a society agree that an act is either good or bad

probability of effect the moral intensity of an issue rises and falls depending on how likely people think the consequences are

situation as involving ethics and in how they would determine their course of action. So the practical question is whether managers can help people come to more common views on the moral intensity of issues.[13] **Moral intensity** is the degree to which people see an issue as an ethical one. This is largely a function of the content of the issue. As a manager you can use this framework both to anticipate the moral intensity of an issue and to diagnose the reasons for differing views about the moral intensity of an issue among people.[14] Moral intensity has six components, as illustrated in Exhibit 5.2: (1) magnitude of the consequences, (2) social consensus, (3) probability of effect, (4) temporal immediacy, (5) proximity, and (6) concentration of effect.[15] In other words, the overall moral intensity of a situation is the result of adding each of these components together.

The **magnitude of the consequences** associated with the outcome of a given action is the level of impact anticipated. This impact is independent of whether the consequences are positive or negative. For example, laying off 100 employees because of a downturn in the economy has less of an impact than if 1,000 employees join the ranks of the unemployed. Many people would judge a 20 percent increase in the price of lawn fertilizer to be of a lower magnitude than 500 people killed or seriously injured because of an explosion in the fertilizer plant caused by poor safety procedures.

Social consensus involves the extent to which members of a society agree that an act is either good or bad. For example, in the United States, there is greater social consensus concerning the wrongness of driving drunk than speeding on the highway.

The third component of moral intensity is **probability of effect**. Even if a particular action could have severe consequences and people agree about the positive or negative nature of that impact, the intensity of the issue rises and falls depending on how likely people think the consequences are. For example, one of the reasons that the advertising of cigarettes has been restricted in many states is because of the increasing evidence of a link between smoking and health problems, including serious ones such as lung cancer. However,

exhibit 5.2

Factors of Moral Intensity

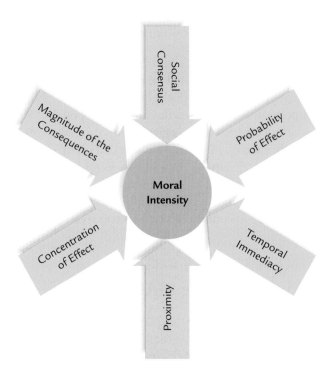

cigarette ads and smoking itself have not been completely outlawed in part because the probability of effect is not 100 percent. The higher the probability of the consequence, the more intense the sense of ethical obligation. Because people are highly likely to be injured if they are in a car accident, the intensity regarding the moral obligation of auto manufacturers to make safer cars is increasing. Options such as side-impact air bags are now available in cars. However, because there is no certainty that you will be in an automobile accident, many of the safety features are not required by law.

Temporal immediacy is the fourth component of moral intensity and is a function of the interval between the time the action occurs and the onset of its consequences. The greater the time interval between the action and its consequences, the less intensity people typically feel toward the issue. For example, even if industrial pollution were certain to lead to global warming and result in catastrophic changes to weather patterns, because the consequences are likely to happen 50 years from now, the moral intensity of industrial pollution is much less than if the effects were to happen next year.

temporal immediacy a function of the interval between the time the action occurs and the onset of its consequences

The fifth component is **proximity**. All other factors being equal, the closer the decision maker feels to those affected by the decision, the more the decision maker will consider the consequences of the action and feel it has ethical implications. Proximity does not just mean physical closeness. Proximity also involves psychological and emotional closeness and identification. Consequently, an affinity between the decision maker and those affected could be a function of many factors, including nationality, cultural background, ethnic similarity, organizational identification, or socioeconomic similarity. For example, if you feel a psychological and emotional affinity for young people in Africa, then decisions about laying off workers by seniority (meaning younger workers will get laid off first) will have greater moral intensity for you even if you live thousands of miles away. Likewise, a decision to close down a poorly performing but slightly profitable factory that could put your parents and neighbors out of work will also likely have greater moral intensity for you than a factory closure in which the affected workers are unknown to you.

proximity the physical, psychological, and emotional closeness the decision maker feels to those affected by the decision

The last component is the **concentration of effect**, or the extent to which consequences are focused on a few individuals or dispersed across many. For example, even though laying off 100 people has a lower magnitude of effect than laying off 1,000 people, laying off 100 people in a town of 5,000 has a greater concentration of effect than laying off 1,000 people in city of 10 million such as Los Angeles.

concentration of effect the extent to which consequences are focused on a few individuals or dispersed across many

The importance of these six facets of moral intensity is twofold. First, as a manager, you can use these facets to anticipate issues that are likely to be seen as significant ethical dilemmas in the workplace.[16] If you can better anticipate issues that are likely to become ethical debates, you have more time to prepare for and may be more effective at handling ethical dilemmas. Second, if you are working with a group that is using the same basic ethical approach and still can't agree on the ethical course of action, you can use these facets to determine the source of the disagreement.[17] The disagreement may stem from different perceptions of the situation on one or more of the moral intensity components. For example, your group, like Caren Wheeler's, may be arguing over the ethics of terminating a relationship with a longtime supplier. In examining the source of the disagreement, you may discover a difference in perception as to the concentration of effect. For example, once it is clear that you represent 60 percent of the supplier's business, others who were discounting this factor may change their opinions. This alone may make it easier to reach a decision.

Nike had to deal with significant negative media coverage regarding its manufacturing of shoes in various countries and the alleged use of child labor in factories it did not own but with which it had contracts (see A Manager's Challenge, "Laboring for Nike Around the World"). Nike executives were both caught off guard by the intensity of the global and domestic public scrutiny and somewhat unprepared to respond at first. If Nike executives had used the moral intensity framework, could they have predicted public reaction? If they could, would the framework have helped them make some anticipatory changes in how they manage their contract manufacturers around the world?

globalization *a manager's challenge*

Laboring for Nike Around the World

Even with celebrities like Michael Jordan and Tiger Woods sporting its apparel, Nike has had trouble shifting the spotlight away from the workers who toil to make its products.

About 450,000 workers, mostly in Asian countries, are employed to produce Nike shoes and clothing. However, none of them are directly employed by Nike. Rather, they are employed by factories that operate as subcontractors to Nike. According to critics, these factory workers are subjected to substandard working conditions, such as exposure to dangerous toxins and carcinogens, poor ventilation and/or air quality, forced overtime, sexual harassment, and corporal punishment and abuse. In addition, critics have argued that these workers do not receive a fair wage and that many are so young their employment violates child labor laws.

Nike claims that the critics are misinformed and cites its efforts to go above and beyond what is legally required in various countries. It has tried to remind people that many workers in places such as Indonesia and China would be without work if they did not contract for shoes and clothes to be manufactured there. These workers gain skills and knowledge that can help them build a better life. Nike notes that as an example of its positive influence, pay for entry-level jobs in Indonesian factories increased 40 percent in just one year. The firm has also increased the age requirements for all factories with footwear manufacturing contracts to 18 years, and for apparel workers to 16 years. These standards exceed those established by the International Labor Organization. The company has also worked with these subcontractor factories to improve indoor air quality and working conditions.

Additionally, Nike has become a founding member of the UN-sponsored Global Compact, a monitoring effort that asks corporations to commit to nine key human rights and environmental standards. These include pledging to protect human rights, upholding the right of workers to

Nike contracts with other companies to manufacture its sporting goods. Frequently these companies outsource the work to factories with low-cost labor in countries abroad, similar to this factory in Ho Chi Minh City, Vietnam. In recent years, numerous human rights organizations have called attention to the terrible conditions workers at these factories endure, casting Nike in a negative light. If Nike executives had used the moral intensity framework outlined in the text, could the company have averted the bad publicity?

unionize, eliminating child labor, and developing environmentally friendly technologies. Nike has also endorsed the principles of the Coalition for Environmentally Responsible Economies (CERES), a 10-point code of environmental conduct that encourages companies to commit to continual improvement in their environmental performance. The CERES principles address issues such as informing the public, reducing risk, restoring the environment, and manufacturing safe products and services.

The company has agreed to apply U.S. safety standards for air quality to its foreign suppliers and says it has converted its use of toxic chemical solvents to water-based products in the assembly of its footwear. Nike employs its own staff of 1,000 labor-practices managers to run a program called SHAPE—Safety, Health, Attitude of Management,

People, Environment. "We are the only company that has people dedicated exclusively to labor-practice enforcement," notes Brad Figel, Nike's lobbyist in Washington.

A 1998 lawsuit alleging the company misled U.S. consumers about conditions in offshore factories was quickly dismissed, but critiques continued. A report released in early 2001 by the nonprofit Global Alliance for Workers and Communities, a group to which Nike has contributed a five-year commitment and a $7.8 million investment, listed findings based on a survey of 4,000 workers at nine Indonesian factories producing Nike products. Nearly 8 percent of workers reported that they had received unwanted sexual comments, nearly 2.5 percent said they had received unwanted sexual touching on the job, and 30 percent said they had been victims of verbal abuse such as yelling or swearing. It is difficult to interpret numbers like these when, for instance, a 1995 U.S. government survey found that 55 percent of women in the U.S. military had experienced workplace sexual harassment. Cultural differences or fear of retaliation may prevent Indonesians from reporting potential abuse. Yet 73 percent were satisfied with their work relationships with direct supervisors, 68 percent with factory management, and 55 percent were happy with company medical clinics. A wide majority also expressed satisfaction with job skills training, family planning services, and recreational facilities.

In any case, Nike called the findings "disturbing" and responded with a remediation plan for 35 Indonesian factories that employ 115,000 people, most of them women whose average age is 23. The plan includes additional independent monitoring as well as specific harassment training, a grievance process and ombudsman program, health and safety policies, and a measure to ensure that all factories are paying the new minimum wage. The company released a similar plan in March 2001 in response to an audit of the Korean-owned Kukdong factory in Atlixco, Mexico, by Verité (a nonprofit labor and trade monitoring organization). This plan includes supporting workers' rights to unionize, formalizing a harassment and abuse policy to include training for all factory workers and managers, instituting confidential grievance procedures, and addressing specific health and safety issues.

In 2003, Nike, Reebok, and a handful of other apparel companies allowed factory condition audits to be posted on the Internet by the Fair Labor Association (FLA), a sweatshop-monitoring group (www.fairlabor.org). Unfortunately, most of the audits indicated conditions for workers abroad hadn't improved much since that organization was first formed in 1997. However, the FLA believes that posting the audits for the public to see will eventually lead to improvements.

Nike still faces several practical challenges when it comes to improving contractors' factories, despite its sizeable investment in money and manpower to do so. For example, while Nike ultimately can withdraw its contracts from noncompliant factories, leverage is stronger with footwear factories, where it is often the only contractor, than at apparel factories, where Nike is usually one of several contractors. In addition, Nike has succeeded financially in large part by keeping costs low primarily through subcontracting to factories in low-wage countries.

If Nike executives were to use the moral intensity framework, how would they assess the positive and negative consequences for workers in these factories? What is the level of social consensus regarding the rightness or wrongness of certain working conditions? How strongly do people feel about employing children, even indirectly through contractors? How likely are the negative consequences of poor working conditions and how quickly might they occur? How close or distant will the public feel to workers thousands of miles away? When there are 450,000 workers, how concentrated will the effects be of the current conditions, and how will Nike's announced changes be perceived by the public?

Sources: Alison Maitland, "Big Brands Come Clean on Sweatshop Labor," *Financial Times*, June 10, 2003; "Kasky Lawsuit Against Nike Dismissed" (February 5, 1999), http://nikebiz.com/media/n_law.shtml, accessed on November 6, 2001; "Nike Joins Global Compact," Associated Press, July 21, 2000; "Nike Releases Remediation Plan for Indonesian Factories," (February 22, 2001), http://nikebiz.com/media/n_gla_3.shtml, accessed on November 6, 2001; Shu Shin Luh, "Report Claims Abuses by Nike Contractors—Sporting Goods Firm Funded Study in Indonesia, Intends to Verify It," *Wall Street Journal*, February 22, 2001, p. A16; Rajiv Chandrasekaran, "Indonesian Workers in Nike Plants List Abuses," *Washington Post*, February 23, 2001, p. E1; Daniel Akst, "Nike in Indonesia, Through a Different Lens," *New York Times*, March 4, 2001; "Nike Releases First Corporate Responsibility Report," *PR Newswire*, October 9, 2001.

MAKING ETHICAL DECISIONS

Increasingly, it seems that individuals and organizations are embracing a philosophy of business ethics perhaps first and best articulated in 1776 by Adam Smith in his classic book, *The Moral Sentiments of Reason*. Smith's basic thesis was that it is in individuals' and organizations' self-interest to make ethical decisions. Still, a significant challenge remains to you as a manager: How can ethical decisions be fostered and encouraged?

The Manager

As we mentioned at the outset, part of the reason for exploring various approaches to ethical decision making is to help you refine your own approach so that when pressures arise, you can make decisions consistent with your ethical framework. To this end, there is perhaps no substitute for taking personal responsibility for ethical decisions. To illustrate this, simply put yourself in Caren Wheeler's position (see A Manager's Challenge, "Changing Horses"). If you were Caren, what might the magnitude of consequences be if Creative Applications is dropped as a supplier? How many jobs might be lost? How likely is this? How soon would it happen? If there is some degree of moral intensity to the situation, what approach would you use to come to a decision? Is it right to drop Creative Applications? Caren is expected not only to provide a recommendation but also a rationale for it. What if you were an executive at Nike? What decision would you make and why?

Even after you have become more comfortable and explicit about how you would resolve ethical dilemmas, the question still remains as to how much you should change your approach to fit in with others or try to change their approach. If you were at Nike, how hard should you work to change the public's perception, persuading them to see the positive benefits workers enjoy? Although it is probably impossible to argue that one of the approaches presented in this chapter is best, applied consistently, each approach does allow a consistent pattern of ethical decision making. This consistency may matter more to those with whom you interact than whether your decisions are always in agreement with theirs.[18] This is in part because your consistency allows others to better understand your approach and trust you than if they perceive your decision making as random and inconsistent.

The Organization

Just as managers try to foster ethical decisions, organizations have a significant impact on ethical decision making. The overall culture of the company can play a significant role. For example, the emphasis on keeping customers happy and income flowing seemed to contribute to a number of rather lax audits by the accounting firm Arthur Andersen (which subsequently went out of business) for companies like Enron and WorldCom. In contrast, firms can also have a positive impact on ethical decision making and behavior. In many firms senior managers take explicit and concrete steps to encourage ethical behavior among their managers. Although there are a variety of ways organizations might accomplish this objective, codes of ethics and whistle-blowing systems are perhaps two of the more visible efforts.

code of ethical conduct a formal settlement that outlines types of behavior that are and are not acceptable

Codes of Ethics Given the ethical dilemmas that managers face and the different approaches for evaluating ethical behavior, many firms have adopted codes of ethics to guide their managers' decision making. A **code of ethical conduct** is typically a formal statement of one to three pages that primarily outlines types of behavior that are and are not acceptable. Exhibit 5.3 reprints the Johnson & Johnson credo, one of the oldest among U.S. corporations. The credo was first adopted in 1945 and has been revised four times to its current version.

An examination of 84 codes of ethics in U.S. firms found three specific clusters of issues addressed in these statements.[19] The first cluster included

exhibit 5.3
Johnson & Johnson Credo

We believe our first responsibility is to the doctors, nurses, and patients, to mothers and all others who use our products and services. In meeting their needs everything we do must be of high quality. We must constantly strive to reduce our costs in order to maintain reasonable prices. Customers' orders must be serviced promptly and accurately. Our suppliers and distributors must have an opportunity to make a fair profit.

We are responsible to our employees: the men and women who work with us throughout the world. Everyone must be considered as an individual. We must respect their dignity and recognize their merit. They must have a sense of security in their jobs. Compensation must be fair and adequate, and working conditions clean, orderly, and safe. Employees must feel free to make suggestions and complaints. There must be equal opportunity for employment, development, and advancement for those qualified. We must provide competent management, and their actions must be just and ethical.

We are responsible to the communities in which we live and work and to the world community as well.

We must be good citizens—support good works and charities and bear our fair share of taxes. We must encourage civic improvements and better health and education.

We must maintain in good order the property we are privileged to use, protecting the environment and natural resources.

Our final responsibility is to our stockholders. Business must make a sound profit. We must experiment with new ideas. Research must be carried on, innovative programs developed, and mistakes paid for. New equipment must be purchased, new facilities provided, and new products launched. Reserves must be created to provide for adverse times.

When we operate according to these principles, the stockholders should realize a fair return.

items that focused on being a good "organization citizen" and was divided into nine subcategories. The second cluster included items that guided employee behavior away from unlawful or improper acts that would harm the organization and was divided into 12 subcategories. The third cluster included items that addressed directives to be good to customers and was divided into three subcategories. Exhibit 5.4 provides a list and description of the clusters and specific categories of issues addressed in these written codes. Most firms did have items in each of the three clusters, though not in all 30 subcategories.

A study of codes of ethics for firms in the United Kingdom, France, and Germany found that a higher percentage of German firms had codes of ethics than British or French firms (see Exhibit 5.5).[20] The greater cultural emphasis on explicit communication in Germany may partially explain this finding. Although only about one-third of the European firms in this study had codes of ethics, approximately 85 percent of U.S. firms have formal codes.

In a separate study, researchers found important differences among firms from what are generally considered more similar than different cultures: U.S., Canadian, and Australian firms.[21] For example, the codes of ethics differed substantially in terms of explicitly commenting on ethics conduct regarding behavior concerning domestic government officials (87 percent of U.S. firms, 59 percent of Canadian, and 24 percent of Australian).

Exhibit 5.6 provides information about the content of the codes of ethics for the firms that in fact had formal codes. Interestingly, while 100 percent of the European firms covered issues of acceptable and unacceptable employee behavior in their codes, only 55 percent of U.S. firms covered these

Cluster 1

"Be a dependable organization citizen."

1. Demonstrate courtesy, respect, honesty, and fairness in relationships with customers, suppliers, competitors, and other employees.
2. Comply with safety, health, and security regulations.
3. Do not use abusive language or actions.
4. Dress in businesslike attire.
5. Possession of firearms on company premises is prohibited.
6. Follow directives from supervisors.
7. Be reliable in attendance and punctuality.
8. Manage personal finances in a manner consistent with employment by a fiduciary institution.

Unclustered items

1. Exhibit standards of personal integrity and professional conduct.
2. Racial, ethnic, religious, or sexual harassment is prohibited.
3. Report questionable, unethical, or illegal activities to your manager.
4. Seek opportunities to participate in community services and political activities.
5. Conserve resources and protect the quality of the environment in areas where the company operates.
6. Members of the corporation are not to recommend attorneys, accountants, insurance agents, stockbrokers, real estate agents, or similar individuals to customers.

Cluster 2

"Don't do anything unlawful or improper that will harm the organization."

1. Maintain confidentiality of customer, employee, and corporate records and information.
2. Avoid outside activities that conflict with or impair the performance of duties.
3. Make decisions objectively without regard to friendship or personal gain.
4. The acceptance of any form of bribe is prohibited.
5. Payment to any person, business, political organization, or public official for unlawful or unauthorized purposes is prohibited.
6. Conduct personal and business dealings in compliance with all relevant laws, regulations, and policies.
7. Comply fully with antitrust laws and trade regulations.
8. Comply fully with accepted accounting rules and controls.
9. Do not provide false or misleading information to the corporation, its auditors, or a government agency.
10. Do not use company property or resources for personal benefit or any other improper purpose.
11. Each employee is personally accountable for company funds over which he or she has control.
12. Staff members should not have any interest in any competitor or supplier of the company unless such interest has been fully disclosed to the company.

Cluster 3

"Be good to our customers."

1. Strive to provide products and services of the highest quality.
2. Perform assigned duties to the best of your ability and in the best interest of the corporation, its shareholders, and its customers.
3. Convey true claims for products.

exhibit 5.4

Categories Found in Corporate Codes of Ethics

Source: Donald Robin, Michael Giallourakis, Fred R. David, and Thomas E. Moritz, "A Different Look at Codes of Ethics." Reprinted from *Business Horizons* (January–February 1989), Table 1, p. 68. Copyright 1989 by Indiana University Kelley School of Business. Used with permission.

issues. By contrast, only 15 percent of the European firms covered issues of political interests (i.e., business/government relations) and 96 percent of U.S. firms covered these issues in their codes.

Research on codes of ethics indicates that organizations believe codes of ethics to be the most effective means of encouraging ethical behavior in their employees.[22] Indeed, if a given firm had a code that covered all 30 categories listed in Exhibit 5.4, employees would have a comprehensive guide for behavior. Unfortunately, the research does not support a strong link between codes of ethics and actual employee behavior. Firms without formal codes seem to have no higher or lower incidents of unethical behavior than those with formal codes.[23] This may be because simply having a formal statement written down is not sufficient. For example, although nearly all of the *Fortune* 500 U.S. firms have codes of ethics, only about one-third have training programs and ethics officers, and only half have distributed formal codes to all their employees.[24]

Successfully Implementing Codes of Ethics Establishing a formal, written code of ethical conduct is an important first step. However, actions speak much louder than words, and employees are unlikely to conform to the formal code unless other actions taken by the organization reinforce the code and communicate that the company is serious about compliance.[25] In some companies positions of ethics officer or ombudsman are being instituted. These individuals are charged with ensuring that the flow of information is rich in both directions. In other words, they have the responsibility of helping information and policies get out to the employees and also to ensure that employees' concerns, observations of misconduct, and the like can flow up and into senior management levels where action to correct things can be taken.

exhibit 5.5

Adoption of Codes of Ethics

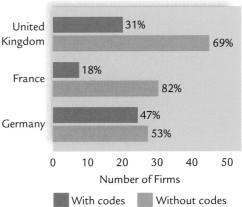

Communication The first step in effectively implementing a code of ethics is communicating it to all employees. For maximum impact, this communication needs to take a variety of forms and be repeated. It is not enough to simply send out a one-time memo. Rather, the code will need to be communicated in memos, company newsletters, videos, and speeches by senior executives repeatedly, over a period of time, if people are to take the content of the message seriously.

Training For the code of ethical conduct to be effective, people will likely need training.[26] For maximum impact, the training needs to be engaging. For example, Motorola developed approximately 80 different short cases. Each case presents a situation requiring a manager to make a decision. Individual participants in the training program were asked to collectively decide what they would do and discuss the ethical aspects of the decision. They then compared their decisions to those of senior executives, including the CEO, and what these executives believe is in keeping with the firm's code of ethics.

exhibit 5.6

Subjects Addressed in Corporate Codes of Ethics

Subjects	UNITED KINGDOM n = 33 Number of Firms	%	FRANCE n = 15 Number of Firms	%	GERMANY n = 30 Number of Firms	%	TOTAL EUROPEAN COUNTRIES Number of Firms	%	UNITED STATES n = 118 Number of Firms	%	SIGNIFICANCE Europe vs. U.S.
Employee conduct	33	100	15	100	30	100	78	100	47	55	SIG
Community and environment	21	64	11	73	19	63	51	85	50	42	NS
Customers	18	39	14	93	20	67	52	87	96	81	SIG
Shareholders	13	39	11	73	18	60	42	64	NA	NA	NA
Suppliers and contractors	7	21	2	13	6	20	15	19	101	86	SIG
Political interests	4	12	3	20	5	17	12	15	113	96	SIG
Innovation and technology	2	6	3	20	18	60	26	33	18	15	SIG

NS = Not significant
NA = No comparable data available
SIG = Significantly different

Lockheed Martin also takes an engaging approach to ethics training with an interesting, innovative twist. In the late 1990s, the company developed a board game based on Scott Adam's "Dilbert" character. The game consisted of 50 ethical dilemmas for which players have to decide among four possible responses. Participants rated this approach much higher in satisfaction than traditional ethics training and seemed to recall the learning points more effectively. Later, when the Dilbert craze wore off, Lockheed Martin used real business ethics problems as a basis for discussion. The company also has an ethics hotline employees can call if they are experiencing a business dilemma.[27]

Although officials at organizations often think that ethics training programs are effective, current research is less conclusive. What we can say based on research is that the greater the psychological and emotional involvement of participants in the training, the greater their retention of the learning points. This may explain why Lockheed Martin's experience with ethics training has been positive.

Reward and Recognition In addition to communicating the code to employees and training them, it is critical to make sure that those who comply are recognized and rewarded. Otherwise, employees will simply view the written code as the "formal rhetoric but not the real deal."

ExxonMobil is a company that recognizes the importance of this principle. It regularly celebrates the story of an individual who has honored the company's code of conduct even when doing so might have cost the company money. For example, one of its drilling teams was setting up to drill for oil in the jungles of a developing country when a government official came by and stated that before they started the drill they needed to pay for an operating permit. However, the official wanted the payment (approximately $10,000) paid to him personally in cash. This was against the firm's code, so the team manager refused to pay. The drilling team and their expensive equipment sat idle for more than a week at a cost of over $1 million. Finally, the government official admitted that all the paperwork and permits were in order and the team was allowed to proceed. ExxonMobil celebrated this incident in its newsletter to reinforce to its employees that the company takes its code of ethical conduct seriously and rewards people who honor it, even if it costs the company money.

whistle-blower an employee who discloses illegal or unethical conduct on the part of others in the organization

Whistle-Blowing A **whistle-blower** is an employee who discloses illegal or unethical conduct on the part of others in the organization. While some firms have implemented programs to encourage whistle-blowing, most have not.[28] As a group, whistle-blowers tend *not* to be disgruntled employees but instead are conscientious, high-performing employees who report illegal or unethical incidents. In general, they report these incidents not for notoriety but because they believe the wrongdoings are so grave that they must be exposed.[29] For example, Randy Robarge, a nuclear power plant supervisor, never intended to be a whistle-blower. To Robarge, raising concerns about the improper storage of radioactive material at ComEd's Zion power plant on Lake Michigan was just part of doing a good job.[30] Research suggests that the more employees know about the internal channels through which they can blow the whistle and the stronger the protection of past whistle-blowers, the more likely they are to initially use those internal rather than external channels such as the media.[31] IBM receives up to 18,000 letters a year from employees making confidential complaints through IBM's "Speak Up" program. Firms such as Hughes Tool Co., General Motors, and Bloomingdale's offer financial rewards to

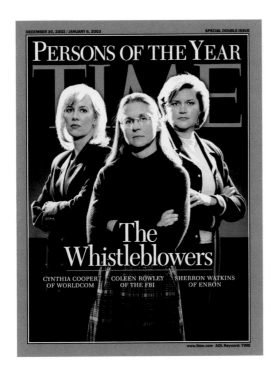

Companies frequently portray whistle-blowers as disgruntled employees, but more often they are conscientious, high-performing employees unable to accept wrongdoing around them. In 2002, *Time* magazine featured three whistle-blowers as its "Persons of the Year." They are (from left to right): Cynthia Cooper, a WorldCom staff auditor, who called attention to a multi-billion-dollar bookkeeping scandal; FBI agent Coleen Rowley, who revealed a 9/11-related scandal; and Sherron Watkins of Enron.

employees who report valid claims.[32] In general, research suggests that the following steps can be effective in encouraging valid whistle-blowing:[33]

- Clearly communicate whistle-blowing procedures to all employees.
- Allow for reporting channels in addition to the chain of command or reporting incidents to one's boss.
- Thoroughly investigate all claims based on a consistent procedure.
- Protect whistle-blowers who make valid claims.
- Provide moderate financial incentives or rewards for valid claims.
- Publicly celebrate employees who make valid claims.

Top Management Example The impact of setting an example is probably no more evident than it is in the case of ethical conduct.[34] Top management both in terms of how they behave personally and how they reward, punish, or ignore the actions of others can severely damage the best intentions and designs of an implementation plan (e.g., communication, training, whistle-blowing, etc.). When it comes to skirting the law or making decisions that when open to public scrutiny fall short, the example of top management is often correlated with the behavior of middle managers. Managers are rarely persuaded by top executives to "do as I say, not as I do." As we pointed out in the previous chapter, leaders at Enron such as Ken Lay and Jeff Skilling set an example of reporting growth at any price. Standard accounting rules were ignored so that higher revenues and profits could be recorded immediately. Once one rule, law, or policy is ignored by senior officers, who is to say that others shouldn't be? This pattern of illegal and unethical conduct was not confined to Enron but was complemented by the behavior of senior partners in the accounting firm that was supposed to monitor and certify Enron's accounting practices—Arthur Andersen. In an effort to retain Enron's auditing business and its more lucrative consulting engagements, leaders at Arthur Andersen ignored Enron's accounting irregularities despite its legal and ethical obligation to report them. In the end, leaders even instructed subordinates to destroy and

"The fish rots from the top of the head." The saying relates to the fact that people in an organization take their cues from the person leading it. Convicted of lying to federal officials about a stock trade, in 2004, homemaking maven Martha Stewart was sentenced to prison. The price of stock in her own company, Martha Stewart Living Omnimedia, plummeted as a result of the scandal: Having once traded for as much as $40 a share, it dropped to under $10 per share, taking a considerable toll on the company and Stewart's net worth.

shred documents (against company policy and legal statutes) in an effort to hide wrongdoing on both sides.

But by following the steps outlined earlier, managers can catch problems before they become national media events and seriously damage the firm's reputation. In addition, new laws in the United States both protect and reward whistle-blowers. Employers cannot discharge, threaten, or otherwise discriminate against employees because they report a suspected violation of the law. Employees who blow the whistle on companies with federal government contracts can actually receive a small portion of the judgment if the company is found guilty. For example, Jane Akre was one of the first to receive such a reward. She was given $425,000 when she blew the whistle on her employer, a TV station that was deliberately distorting the news.[35] However, an award of $52 million to three men who blew the whistle on SmithKline Beecham, a large drug company, really grabbed people's attention.[36]

The Government

The governments of the United States and many other countries have also tried to foster ethical behavior. For example, the U.S. government has enacted a number of laws and regulations designed to achieve this objective. Perhaps the most discussed, given today's global environment, is the Foreign Corrupt Practices Act.

U.S. Foreign Corrupt Practices Act Few issues of ethical behavior have received more attention than questionable payments or bribes. For American managers this issue is at the heart of the **Foreign Corrupt Practices Act (FCPA)**. This act was passed in 1977 primarily in response to the disclosure that U.S. firms were making payments to foreign government officials to win government contracts and receive preferential treatment.

One of the key incidents that sparked the FCPA was the revelation that Lockheed Corporation had made over $12 million in payments to Japanese

Foreign Corrupt Practices Act (FCPA) a law prohibiting employees of U.S. firms from corrupting the actions of foreign officials, politicians, or candidates for office

business executives and government officials in order to sell commercial aircraft in that country. Subsequent discoveries showed that nearly 500 U.S. companies had made similar payments around the world, totaling over $300 million.

Lockheed chairman at the time, Carl Kotchian, argued that the payments represented less than 3 percent of the revenue gained from the sale of aircraft to Japan. Further, these sales had a positive effect on the salaries and job security of Lockheed workers, with beneficial spillover effects for their dependents, the communities, and the shareholders. Mr. Kotchian said that he was "between a rock and a hard spot"; if he made the payments, people might criticize his actions as unethical, and if he did not make the payments, a competitor would. Consequently, the competition would get the contracts, and some Lockheed workers might lose their jobs. Whether you agree with Mr. Kotchian or not, it is instructive to assess which ethical approach he seems to be using. Is it a moral right approach, justice approach, or utilitarian approach?

Until the passage of the FCPA, these dilemmas were purely ethical ones. Upon its passage, many of these ethical decisions became legal decisions because the FCPA made it illegal for employees of U.S. firms to corrupt the actions of foreign officials, politicians, or candidates for office. The act also prohibits employees from making payments to *any* person when they have "reason to know" that the payments might be used to corrupt the behavior of officials. The act also requires that firms take steps to provide "reasonable assurance" that transactions are in compliance with the law and to keep detailed records of them. If Mr. Pignatelli were a U.S. citizen, it would be illegal for him to pay money to a consultant if he had reason to know that some of it might be used for bribes. He could not just claim he had no knowledge of the consultant's actions as a defense. Pignatelli would be bound by law to provide reasonable assurance that no bribes would be paid if the consultant were hired.

The FCPA does not cover payments made to business executives. For American managers, payments made to executives are ethical decisions, not legal ones. The FCPA also does not prohibit payments to low-level government employees to perform in a more timely manner the duties they normally would have performed. These types of payments are typically called *facilitating payments.* For example, a payment of $100 to a customs inspector not to delay the inspection of an imported product would not violate the FCPA because the payment simply facilitates something that the customs inspector would do anyway. However, the payment of $100 to pass a product *without* inspecting it would be a violation of the FCPA because the payment would entice the customs agent to do something he or she is not supposed to do.

Penalties for violation of the FCPA range up to $1 million in fines for the company and $10,000 in fines and up to five years' imprisonment for the responsible individuals. Clearly, a $1 million fine is not a deterrent when deals can be worth $100 million. Rather, the prison terms for individuals are the real teeth in the law.

Clearly, making ethical decisions is not easy. It takes an understanding of various frameworks at the individual level and intervention at the organization and government levels if compliance with particular points of view is to be achieved. While this section has focused on making ethical decisions from the individual point of view, the next section examines the general issues of ethics focusing on the organization. Typically, the issues we cover next are discussed under the general banner of corporate social responsibility.

SOCIAL RESPONSIBILITY

Corporate social responsibility is concerned with the constituencies to which corporations are obligated and the nature and extent of those obligations. As media coverage has increased and organizations such as Greenpeace, the Sierra Club, and the Ralph Nader Group have put more pressure on organizations, they have increasingly come to terms with the amount of resources they should devote to being socially responsible. Consider the following questions that confront managers daily:

- Should a firm implement environmental standards greater than those required by law?
- Should a firm insist on the same high level of safety standards in all its worldwide operations even if the laws of other countries accept lower standards?
- Do all employees, regardless of nationality or employment location, have the same rights?
- Should managerial actions that are illegal or morally unacceptable in one country be allowed in another country in which they are legal or morally acceptable?
- Should managers consider the interests of employees, customers, or general citizens over those of shareholders?

Questions such as these form the substance of social responsibility debates. Both social responsibility and managerial ethics focus on the "oughts" of conducting business. Although several approaches to corporate social responsibility exist, an examination of two fundamental perspectives will help you reflect on how you personally view the issue and how you might effectively interact with others holding differing perspectives.

The Efficiency Perspective

efficiency perspective the concept that a manager's responsibility is to maximize profits for the owners of the business

Perhaps no contemporary person presents the **efficiency perspective** of social responsibility more clearly than the Nobel Prize–winning economist Milton Friedman.[37] Quite simply, according to Friedman, the business of business is business. In other words, a manager's responsibility is to maximize profits for the owners of the business. Adam Smith is perhaps the earliest advocate of this approach. Smith concluded over 200 years ago that the best way to advance the well-being of society is to place resources in the hands of individuals and allow market forces to allocate scarce resources to satisfy society's demands.[38]

Managers as Owners When a manager of a business is also the owner, the self-interests of the owner are best achieved by serving the needs of society. If society demands that a product be made within certain environmental and safety standards, then it is in the best interests of the owner to produce the product to meet those standards. Otherwise, customers will likely purchase the product from competitors. Customers are more likely to purchase from firms that comply with widely shared and deeply held social values, so it makes sense for businesses to incorporate those values into their operations and products. To the extent that the cost of incorporating society's values is less than the price customers are willing to pay, the owner makes a profit.

Critics of the efficiency perspective, however, argue that quite often customers and society in general come to demand safety, environmental protection, and so on only after firms have caused significant visible damage. For example, society might hold strong values about not polluting the water and causing health problems. However, if the consequences of polluting a river are not visible and people are not immediately hurt, social pressure might not emerge to cause the owner to align his actions with societal values until years after the fact.

Managers as Agents In most large organizations today, the manager is not the owner. The corporate form of organization is characterized by the separation of ownership (shareholders) and control (managers). Managers serve as the agents of the organization's owners. Within this context, Friedman argues that managers should "conduct business in accordance with [owners'] desires, which will generally be to make as much money as possible while conforming to the basic rules of society, both those embodied in law and those embodied in ethical custom."[39] From Friedman's perspective, managers have no obligation to act on behalf of society if doing so does not maximize value for the shareholders. For example, packaging products in recycled paper should be undertaken only if doing so maximizes shareholder wealth. Whether such an action satisfies or benefits a small group of activists is irrelevant. Managers have no responsibility to carry out such programs; in fact, they have a responsibility *not* to undertake such action if it is more costly because it does not maximize shareholder wealth. Similarly, charitable donations are not the responsibility of corporations. Instead, managers should maximize the return to shareholders and then shareholders can decide if and to which charities they want to make contributions. Simply put, the profits are not the managers' money, and therefore, they have no right to decide how or if it should be distributed to charitable causes.

From the efficiency perspective, it is impossible for managers to maximize shareholders' wealth and simultaneously attempt to fulfill all of society's needs. It is the responsibility of government to impose taxes and determine expenditures to meet society's needs. If managers pursue actions that benefit society but do not benefit shareholders, then they are exercising political power, not managerial authority.

Concerns with the Efficiency Perspective The efficiency perspective assumes that markets are competitive and that competitive forces move firms toward fulfilling societal needs as expressed by consumer demand. Firms that do not respond to consumer demands in terms of products, price, delivery, safety, environmental impact, or any other dimension important to consumers will, through competition, be forced to change or be put out of business. Unfortunately, however, corrective action often occurs after people are injured.

Arnold Dworkin, the owner of Kaufinan's Bagel and Delicatessen in Skokie, Illinois, learned to pay attention to public safety the hard way. On a Wednesday, calls trickled in to the restaurant from customers complaining of vomiting, nausea, and stomach pains, and by Friday the restaurant had to be closed. Customers were suffering from salmonella bacteria, which was traced to corned beef being cooked at only 90 degrees rather than the 140 degrees required by local health regulations. Although corrective measures were taken, three weeks later another customer was hospitalized with salmonella poisoning. This time the cause was traced to a leaky floorboard above a basement meat-drying table. Kaufman's lost approximately $250,000 in sales and $10,000 in food, and its insurance company paid out more than $750,000 for individual and class-action suits and hospital claims. Interestingly, because Dworkin dealt with the situation in a straightforward manner by disclosing all the information he had to customers and the media, quickly making every repair, and following all the recommended actions suggested by the safety and health board regardless of cost, his business returned to 90 to 95 percent of its original level within two years.[40]

The other major concern with the efficiency perspective is that corporations can impose indirect consequences that may not be completely understood or anticipated. In economic terms, these unintended consequences are called **externalities**. For example, the government of the United Kingdom enticed Nissan with tax and other incentives to build a new automobile plant there. However, the trucks going in and out of the plant created traffic congestion and wear on public roads that were not completely accounted for in the government's proposal. The government had to use tax revenue collected from citizens to repair the roads damaged by Nissan, to which it had given tax incentives (tax breaks). These poor road conditions slowed deliveries to the factory and also created inconveniences for the citizens. However, even when externalities can be anticipated, consumers often cannot correctly factor in or be willing to pay for the costs. For example, the consequences of poor safety controls at a grass fertilizer plant (explosion, fire, toxic fumes, injury, and death) are understood. As a consumer can you correctly assess the costs of a chemical disaster and the increased price you should pay to cover the needed safety expenditures? If the answer is "No," this may cause the plant manager to skip necessary safety practices in order to keep costs low and make a profit. It is not until inadequate safety policies and practices result in a chemical disaster and people are killed or injured that the impact of the externality (i.e., the chemical disaster) is fully appreciated by consumers and therefore appropriately priced in the market.

externalities indirect or unintended consequences imposed on society that may not be understood or anticipated

Social Responsibility Perspective

The social responsibility perspective argues that society grants existence to firms; therefore, firms have responsibilities and obligations to society as a whole, not just shareholders. Thus, while the efficiency perspective states that it is *socially responsible* to maximize the return to the shareholder, the social responsibility perspective states that it is *socially irresponsible* to maximize only shareholder wealth because shareholders are not the only ones responsible for the firm's existence. For instance, creditors of a corporation cannot go beyond the assets of the corporation and seek repayment from the assets of the owners. This protection is termed *limited liability*. This privilege is granted to the corporation by society, not by shareholders.[41] Thus, the existence of the firm is not solely a function of shareholders, and, therefore, the responsibilities of the firm cannot be restricted just to shareholders.

Stakeholders In the social responsibility perspective, managers must consider the legitimate concerns of other stakeholders beyond the shareholders. **Stakeholders** are individuals or groups who have an interest in and are affected by the actions of an organization. They include customers, employees, financiers, suppliers, communities, society at large, and shareholders. Customers have a special place within this set of constituencies because they pay the bills with the revenue they provide.[42] Shareholders are also given special status, but in the stakeholder approach, shareholders are viewed as providers of "risk capital" rather than as sole owners. Consequently, shareholders are entitled to *reasonable* return on the capital they put at risk, but they are not entitled to a *maximum* return because they are not solely responsible for the existence of the firm. To maximize the return to shareholders would take away returns owed to the other stakeholders. Thus, managers must make decisions and take actions that provide a reasonable return to shareholders, balanced against the legitimate concerns of customers, employees, financiers, communities, and society at large. While the evidence is not definitive, there is research to sug-

stakeholders individuals or groups who have an interest in and are affected by the actions of an organization

gest that there is a positive relationship between a stakeholder approach and firm performance.[43]

Concerns with the Social Responsibility Perspective One of the key concerns with the social responsibility perspective is that important terms such as "reasonable returns" and "legitimate concerns" cannot be defined adequately. Given that reasonable returns to shareholders and legitimate concerns of other stakeholders could come into conflict, not knowing exactly what is reasonable or legitimate reduces managers' ability to find the appropriate balance and act in socially responsible ways. This is why from a practical standpoint, even if you believe in the stakeholder framework of corporate social responsibility, making decisions that balance the interests of the different stakeholders is a significant challenge for which there is no magic solution. It is not only possible but quite likely that customers, employees, financiers, communities, and society at large will have conflicting and competing concerns. Consider the case of a manager in a factory that makes corrugated boxes. His customers want sturdy boxes that can be stacked several levels high. Society increasingly seems to want a higher use of recycled paper. However, boxes made of recycled paper either have higher costs for the same strength or lower strength at the same cost compared to boxes made of nonrecycled paper. Shareholders want competitive returns. In such a case, how would you determine the most socially responsible action? If customers tell you that boxes must meet a certain strength requirement regardless of whether they use recycled paper or not, does this outweigh the desires of the other stakeholders? Should you devote more money to researching and developing stronger recycled boxes even though it takes money away from shareholders by increasing costs and reducing profits?

Comparing the Efficiency and Stakeholder Perspectives

The efficiency and social responsibility perspectives differ mainly in terms of the constituencies to whom organizations have responsibilities. The two perspectives differ little in their evaluations of actions that either harm or benefit both shareholders and society (see Exhibit 5.7). Their evaluations differ most markedly when actions help one group and harm the other. Actions that benefit shareholders but harm the other legitimate stakeholders would be viewed as managerially responsible from the efficiency perspective, but

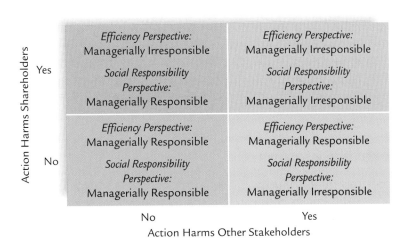

exhibit 5.7
Comparing Efficiency and Social Responsibility Perspectives

socially irresponsible from the social responsibility perspective. Actions that harm shareholders but benefit the other legitimate stakeholders would be viewed as managerially irresponsible from the efficiency perspective, but socially responsible from the social responsibility perspective.

The following quotes illustrate how differently CEOs view the issue of corporate social responsibility.[44]

> *Many factors go into establishing ExxonMobil's credentials as the world's premier petroleum and petrochemical company. One of the most important is operating with meticulous attention to the safety and health of our employees and the communities where we operate, as well as a conscientious regard for the environmental impact of our activities and products.*
>
> —Lee Raymond, CEO and Chairman, ExxonMobil

> *Profits are like breathing. If you can't breathe, you can forget everything else that you're doing because you're not going to be around much longer.*
>
> —Robert E. Mercer, CEO, Goodyear Tire & Rubber, 1983–1988

> *To talk about business altruistically going out and solving the world's problems is nonsense. The role of business is primarily to be successful and profitable, a good employer, and effective in its relationships with all its constituencies, not the least of which are its owners. There are problems that are in the best interest of the health of our economic system and the business that are part of it if they are solved. And there are some social problems that should not be our responsibility other than to support government action by the tax we pay. I do not think that you should look at business as having a primary role in life to solve social problems.*
>
> —Robert H. Malott, CEO, FMC Corporation, 1971–1991

> *I work for the shareholders. I work for the employees. I work for the customers. If I don't make a good profit, I'm not doing a very good job for the owners and for the employees. If I make too much profit, my customers worry. And it's a constant balancing act.*
>
> —Richard E. Heckert, CEO, Du Pont, 1986–1989

> *The only way for a corporation to exist and capitalism to survive is to be part of the whole society. Companies have to be concerned with the owners, the shareholders, the employees, and the customers.*
>
> —David T. Kearns, CEO, Xerox, 1982–1990

> *Corporations can be short-sighted and worry only about our mission, products, and competitive standing. But we do it at our peril. We may need the goodwill of a neighborhood to enlarge a corner store. We may need well-funded institutions of higher learning to turn out the skilled technical employees we require. We may need adequate community health care to curb absenteeism in our plants. Or we may need fair tax treatment for an industry to be able to compete in the world economy. However small or large our enterprise, we cannot isolate our business from society around us.*
>
> —Robert D. Haas, CEO, Levi Strauss

Corporate Responses

As the previous quotes illustrate, how corporations react to the various pressures and constituencies connected to the topic of social responsibility varies widely. These reactions can be simplified and laid out on a continuum that ranges from defensive to proactive, as illustrated in Exhibit 5.8. Although we

exhibit 5.8

Corporate Responses

	Defenders	Accomodaters	Reactors	Anticipators
Belief:	We must fight against efforts to restrict or regulate our activities and profit-making potential.	We will change when legally compelled to do so.	We should respond to significant pressure even if we are not legally required to.	We owe it to society to anticipate and avoid actions with potentionally harmful consequences, even if we are not pressured or legally required to do so.
Focus:	Maximize profits. Find legal loopholes. Fight new restrictions and regulations.	Maximize profits. Abide by the letter of the law. Change when legally compelled to do so.	Protect profits. Abide by the law. React to pressure that could affect business results.	Obtain profits. Abide by the law. Anticipate harmful consequences independent of pressures and laws.

might imagine that firms adopting the efficiency perspective are more likely to be Defenders, Accommodaters, and Reactors, while firms adopting the stakeholder perspective are more likely to be Anticipators, we know of no research that has examined this specific association.

Defenders Companies that might be classified as defenders tend to fight efforts that they see as resulting in greater restriction and regulation of their ability to maximize profits. These firms often operate at the edge of the law and actively seek legal loopholes in conducting their business. Typically, they change only when legally compelled to do so.

Accommodaters These companies are less aggressive in fighting restrictions and regulations but they change only when legally compelled to do so. This type of firm tends to obey the letter of the law but does not make changes that might restrict profits if it is not required to.

Reactors Reactor firms make changes when they feel that pressure from constituencies is sufficient such that nonresponsiveness could have a negative economic impact on the firm. For example, the firm might change to recycled paper for boxes only when the pressure from customers becomes strong enough that nonresponsiveness would lead customers to boycott its products or to simply choose a competitor's products that use recycled paper.

Anticipators Firms in this category tend to believe that they are obligated to a variety of stakeholders—customers, employees, shareholders, general citizens, and so on—not to harm them, independent of laws or pressures that restrict or regulate their actions. Firms in this category not only abide by the law, but they might take action to avoid harming constituencies, even when the constituencies might not be aware of the potential danger. For example, a firm might take steps to protect employees from harmful chemicals within the workplace even before employees suffered negative side effects sufficient for them to demand work environment changes or before safety laws are passed.

The following Manager's Challenge, "Cleaning Up Dirty Little Engines," helps illustrate some of these corporate responses in the face of advancing technology. It focuses on how firms making two-stroke engines for handheld power tools are responding to the emissions and pollution these engines create. As you read, you might ask yourself what the motivation seems to be for

tech nol ogy

a manager's challenge

Cleaning Up Dirty Little Engines

The whine of a two-stroke engine powering a leaf blower, chainsaw, or trimmer, the puff of blue smoke it emits, and the pungent smell of its oil and gas mixture are as common as a warm day in summer. Whether you are walking through a residential neighborhood or driving by the tidy landscape of an office building, you see, hear, and smell this $1.5-billion-a-year industry. There are at least 30 million handheld products in use in the United States. There are $1.5 million blowers, 2.5 million chainsaws, and 5.5 million trimmers sold each year. About two-thirds of the sales are to consumers, and the rest are more heavy-duty products for commercial users. While manufacturers dispute the statistic, the EPA (Environmental Protection Agency) estimates that these blowers, trimmers, and the like contribute 5 percent of the total nonfactory hydrocarbon and NOx (oxides of nitrogen) emissions. (Manufacturers contend the number is closer to 2 to 3 percent.)

Two-stroke engines are so popular because they are extremely reliable, lightweight yet powerful, and fairly inexpensive. However, they are dirty because unlike four-stroke engines, there is not a separate intake and exhaust stroke, and, as a consequence, 30 percent of the gas-oil mix escapes unburned.

In December 1990, the California Air Resources Board (CARB) ordered a Phase I reduction of 30 percent in emissions from handheld engines by 1995 and a Phase II reduction of 80 percent from Phase I levels by 1999. Following CARB's lead, in 1990 the EPA set forth a national regulation requiring a 32 percent Phase I reduction by 1997 and a further 80 percent reduction by 2005. Fred Whyte, president of Stihl, one of the largest manufacturers of two-stroke handheld engines, echoed the sentiments of many manufacturers, "Is this the greatest challenge ever faced by handheld engine manufacturers? No question." Larry Will, vice president of engineering at Echo, stated even more bluntly: "Meeting the regulations is one thing; meeting them and surviving is another."

In fact, companies like Echo, McCulloch, Stihl, and other members of the Portable Power Equipment Manufacturers Association (which has since merged with the Outdoor Power Equipment Institute) enlisted powerful lobbyists to lower and delay the emission reductions. Representatives from the companies argued that the regulations would "virtually eliminate" all two-stroke engines and impose unreasonable cost burdens on consumers. Even if the standards could technically be met, it would cost 15 to 30 percent more. Given how price-sensitive consumers were and given that 70 percent of consumer sales were controlled by "big-box" retailers like Home Depot, Wal-Mart, and Lowe's, no one wanted to be the first company to invest in the new technology and introduce the higher-costing products.

While virtually all the manufacturers were able to meet CARB's standards by 1995 simply by making their engines run cleaner by emitting fewer hydrocarbons in the exhaust, a further 80 percent reduction looked technically impossible. So in the mid-1990s, the manufacturers' association again took up the fight against the regulations.

However, three firms broke ranks—RedMax (a subsidiary of Japan's Komatsu), Tanaka, and Deere & Co. (the $13-billion-a-year farm machinery giant)—and tried to be anticipators. While Deere had originally opposed the California standards, it subsequently lobbied both CARB and the EPA in 1998 to *not* lower standards or delay their implementation. RedMax and Tanaka both created new technology for injecting a shot of pure air between exhaust gases and fuel intake that significantly reduced emissions in two-stroke engines beyond the Phase II CARB standards. Deere had perfected a new technological design it called "compression wave" for its Homelite brand that was similar to RedMax's solution. However, in November 2001, Deere sold its Homelite division to TechTronics Industries of Hong Kong. After a squeeze on price from big-box retailers and higher cost of the new, lower emission engines, Homelite lost $100 million in 21 months.

To meet the CARB standards and deadlines, virtually all of the manufacturers had to buy engines from RedMax and Tanaka. For example, Stihl had to buy 60,000 engines from RedMax. To meet the EPA standards set to take effect nationally in 2005, manufacturers such as Stihl, Echo, and Briggs and Stratton finally launched their own attempts at technological breakthroughs. For example, Stihl has moved from being a defender to an accommodater to, now, a reactor. At the cost of $12 million, Stihl has developed an engine that acts like a four-stroke but is lubricated like a two-stroke and weighs less than 10 percent more. The company shipped its first product incorporating this design in 2002. The result is that these once-dirty little engines have gotten a lot cleaner—about 75 to 90 percent cleaner than they were just five years ago, claims the Outdoor Power Equipment Institute.

Sources: Erwin Chapman, "Handheld Lawn and Garden Products," *Grounds Maintenance*, July 2003, p. 12; Outdoor Power Equipment Institute, *Profile of the Outdoor Power Equipment Industry 2002*; M. Boyle, "Dirty Little Engines Get Cleaner," *Fortune*, May 13, 2002, pp. I146[B-L].

each of the various firms mentioned in exploring new combustion technology. For example, the anticipators: Are they motivated primarily to try to help the environment and reduce air pollution or are they motivated because they believe their competitive position could be enhanced by meeting or beating the proposed regulations with new technology? What would you do if meeting or exceeding environmental or other societal goods potentially hurt your business? For example, what if the technology for exceeding environmental standards for two-stroke engines resulted in engines that were 30 percent more expensive and at the same time weighed 20 percent more? What would you do? What if your market research suggested that commercial users of handheld tools (e.g., trimmers or leaf blowers) were unlikely to pay the premium price or want the extra weight? What would you do? After all, it is one thing for a consumer to deal with the extra weight for an hour or so once a week and it is quite another thing for a small landscaping and yard work company to ask its employees to pack around 20 percent more weight six to eight hours a day, five days a week. What if commercial sales accounted for half of your company's total sales? What would you do?

managerial perspectives revisited

PERSPECTIVE 1: THE ORGANIZATIONAL CONTEXT   When it comes to managerial ethics and corporate social responsibility, the context of the organization is extremely important. While no individual manager will likely win a court case by saying "The devil organization made me do it," it is folly to ignore the tremendous impact that the organization has on individual decisions and behaviors. For example, the company may have a code of ethics, but if its culture is contrary to the code, senior managers should not be surprised when individuals act in ways that go against the code. This is perhaps one of the strongest reasons for a well-established whistler-blower system. Even if the "flow" of the company culture is in one direction, a well-established whistle-blower system can allow conscientious employees to swim against the tide. In addition, managers need to understand the general approach the company takes toward social responsibility. Trying to take an efficiency perspective in a stakeholder-orientated company or vice versa will likely lead to many incidents of frustration. The match between personal ethical and social responsibility orientation and the organization context is critical. For example, applying the tactics of a Defender in an Anticipator organization or vice versa will likely hurt rather than help one's career. While this does not mean that as an individual manager you cannot or should not try to change others around you or the entire organization, it does mean that ignoring the organizational context is naive.

PERSPECTIVE 2: THE HUMAN FACTOR   A manager cannot achieve the desired ethical decisions or approach to social responsibility alone. While personal integrity and ethical decision making is critical for an individual manager, this alone does not satisfy his or her responsibility. Managers are responsible for leading their employees in ways that limit ethic lapses and increase the odds that they behave responsibly. This means, for example, that if your firm does have a code of conduct you have the responsibility of communicating, supporting, and reinforcing the standard with your subordinates. If the firm has a particular orientation toward social responsibility, as a manager you need to help your employees understand what it means and how it applies to the work they do and decisions they make. Only if the managers inculcate the ethical or social responsibility standards of the company in others can it truly have a pervasive impact.

3

PERSPECTIVE 3: MANAGING PARADOXES   Meeting the challenges required to act ethically and in a socially responsible manner will require managing some important paradoxes. On the one hand, as an individual you may have your own personal standards of integrity, ethics, and social responsibility. On the other hand, as a manager you have a responsibility to uphold the standards of your company. What should you do when there is a conflict between the two? Do you have an obligation to correct inappropriate behaviors or blow the whistle on practices that are not in keeping with the company policies or with legal or regulatory standards? The potential paradox between personal and company standards is one of the principal challenges managers face daily regarding ethics and social responsibilities. The other major source of potential paradoxes is between tolerance and compliance. In diverse cultures encountered by firms that operate globally, differences in ethical values and judgments, as well as perspectives on social responsibility, are inevitable. Tolerance and understanding of these differences are important. However, simultaneously, companies are increasingly asking their employees and managers to abide by global standards of conduct and are developing global approaches to social responsibility. As a consequence, managers sometimes face the paradox of balancing tolerance and understanding on the one hand with integrated standards of conduct on the other.

4

PERSPECTIVE 4: ENTREPRENEURIAL MIND-SET   In Chapter 1, we discussed the need for managers to be alert in order to identify and to exploit opportunities. However, some especially lucrative opportunities may present ethical dilemmas. Therefore, managers will need to remain vigilant in balancing their personal standards and the organizational standards with the opportunities to earn large returns. They will need to understand fully how their actions will affect others, especially the organization's stakeholders.

Establishing a values-based culture should help managers remain committed to ethical practices and social responsibilities while simultaneously remaining alert to opportunities and exploiting them. Whatever decisions are ultimately made by the organization shouldn't require a compromise of managers' personal or organizational standards. In fact, emphasizing ethical practices may actually provide the organization with new opportunities because consumers and other stakeholders value such standards. Most people want to work for or do business with ethical and socially responsible organizations versus those that are not.

concluding comments

There is no universal opinion concerning managerial ethics or the social responsibility of corporations. Gray areas remain, and important questions go unanswered regardless of which fundamental perspective you adopt concerning ethical behavior or corporate social responsibility. For example, the efficiency approach argues that managers should seek to maximize shareholders' returns but must do so within the laws and ethical norms of the society. In today's increasingly global environment, a given firm may operate in a variety of societies. What if the norms of one society clash with those of another? Which societal norms should be honored?

A social responsibility approach also operates within equally large gray areas. For example, how can you calculate, let alone incorporate, conflicting needs of constituencies across countries? How can a Korean consumer's needs for low price for paper be balanced against the environmental concerns of Indonesian or Brazilian societies where large forests are being cut to produce paper? How can all of these concerns be balanced against the potential worldwide concern for the depletion of critical oxygen-providing trees?

In addition to the difficulty of determining the relative weight of different constituencies, managers face the challenge of trying to determine the weights of different groups within one category of constituencies across national borders. How are such determinations made? For example, firms may have employees in many countries, and the concerns of these employees will most likely differ. Employees in Japan may want the firm to maximize job security, while employees in England may want the firm to maximize current wages and be willing to trade off future job security. Similarly, German consumers may want firms to have high global environmental standards, and Indonesian consumers may have no such concerns. Which standards should be adopted?

The general debates concerning ethics and social responsibility have raged for generations. The purpose of this chapter has not been to resolve the debate but rather to examine the assumptions and rationales of fundamental perspectives. If there were a magic formula for meeting these challenges, there would likely be little need for bright, capable people (we could just turn the problem over to computer algorithms); nor would there be much excitement in being a manager. We hope this examination enables you to evaluate your own views, so that you will be prepared when situations arise concerning ethics or social responsibility. Perhaps then the pressure of the moment will be less likely to cause you to take actions that you might later regret. Understanding the general frameworks also helps you to better appreciate others who have differing perspectives and, thereby, interact more effectively with them.

key terms

test your comprehension

1. Define *managerial ethics*.
2. What are the key differences between managerial ethics and corporate social responsibility?
3. The utilitarian approach to ethics is often called the "greatest good" approach. What are the key challenges in determining the greatest good?
4. What are the two key elements of the moral rights approach to business ethics?
5. How is the universal approach different from the "golden rule" of do unto others as you would have them do unto you?
6. What are the key elements of distributive, procedural, and compensatory justice and how are the three related to each other?
7. What is moral intensity?
8. What are the six factors that influence moral intensity?
9. How are magnitude of consequences and probability of effect different?
10. Why do more temporally immediate consequences usually generate more moral intensity?
11. What are the two types of proximity that can influence moral intensity?
12. According to Adam Smith, it is in the best interests of managers and organizations to make ethical decisions. What is the basis of his argument?
13. What is a company code of ethical conduct?
14. What are the most common areas addressed in such codes of conduct?
15. Why do companies without codes of ethics seem to be no worse off than companies with codes of ethics in terms of the number of incidents of ethical wrongdoing?
16. What are five powerful means of enhancing the influence of formal codes of conduct on actual employee behavior?
17. What is a whistle-blower?
18. What is the Foreign Corrupt Practices Act?
19. What are the key concerns with the efficiency perspective of social responsibility?
20. Who are the major stakeholders to consider from a social responsibility perspective?

apply your understanding

1. How much would you *change* your ethical values or standards or your view of social responsibility in order to fit into a company? What if you were sent on assignment to another country where the national standards seemed to differ both from the corporate ones and from your personal standards? How much would you change?
2. Which of the basic approaches to ethical decision making most closely matches your approach for dealing with ethical dilemmas?
3. Is it wise for a government to try to legislate ethics through laws such as the FCPA?
4. What is the ethical climate like in your school? What is your school's policy or honor code concerning cheating? What is your ethical responsibility if you see someone cheating?
5. Would you be willing to be a whistle-blower? On what type of issue would you blow the whistle? Inflated overtime submitted on a government contract? Sexual harassment? What organizational and personal factors would you consider?
6. Consider the following scenario: A sales representative from a textbook publisher calls on your professor to try to get him or her to adopt a new textbook. Is it okay for the professor to accept a free lunch from a publisher's sales representative? If it is okay for a professor to accept a free lunch, what about a free game of golf? What about a free set of golf clubs after the game?

practice your capabilities

Your firm has a stated policy that e-mails constitute company correspondence and therefore are subject to screening. Although the policy explanation is included in the thick orientation document that every new employee receives, most employees aren't aware of the policy. Most of those who are aware of it do not believe that their e-mail or other Internet activities are reviewed by the company.

Your boss comes to you with the password to all your subordinates' e-mail accounts and asks you to review them. He has some concern but no hard evidence that one of your subordinates may either be talking with a competitor about coming to work for them or may even be leaking sensitive marketing information to them. He instructs you to not be fooled by what appears in the subject line of the e-mails because anyone with any smarts would not put the real nature of the e-mail there if they were up to something unethical. Therefore, he wants you to read through all their e-mails over the last four weeks and then to monitor them over the next few weeks until the allegation is proven to be true or

groundless. He has transferred a small project from you to ensure that you have the time to complete this review over the next week.

1. What would you do? Would you take the assignment?
2. If so, why? If not, why not?
3. If you didn't want to take the assignment, how could you turn it down without hurting your relationship with your boss or potentially damaging your career?
4. Is it ethical to read e-mail that employees may consider private?
5. Is it ethical not to inform employees of what you are about to do?

closing case

DEVELOP YOUR CRITICAL THINKING

P&G: How Low Can You Go?

You probably know the lengths to which you would go to defend yourself in a life-and-death struggle. How far would you go to defend your firm against its archrival?

The bitter battle between consumer product giants Procter & Gamble (P&G) and Unilever is longstanding, and market conditions over the last several years have raised the stakes even higher. While markets like communications and services have soared, the markets for various consumer products have stagnated, flattened, or even declined. "It's a death struggle to incrementally gain share," said one consumer products consultant of P&G's business environment.

At the same time that investors exert relentless pressure on both P&G and Unilever to raise earnings and increase shareholder value, the two firms have been watching growth slow dramatically for each of the hundreds of brands they control. In laundry detergents, floor care products, household cleaners, makeup, toothpaste, disposable diapers, and hair care products, sales had leveled off in the last few years. P&G in particular had fallen back on bringing out new, improved versions of the same old products. But strategies such as this are not sustainable. "Large companies can die," says Jerry Porras, author and professor at Stanford Business School. "They slowly erode till they get to the point where they're just not great anymore." Was the maker of such long-established brands as Crest, Pampers, Tide, Mr. Clean, Max Factor, and Ivory nearing its end?

Perhaps it was beginning to look that way within P&G, a rule-bound, bureaucratic firm that began as a soap and candle maker in 1837 and rapidly grew into a $37 billion company with 300 brands in 140 countries. After 20 years of 8 percent average annual growth, sales went up just 1 percent in 1997. Figures in 1998 weren't much better, yet the company had promised shareholders it would double sales to $70 billion by 2006. That goal was looking more like 25 years off than the projected six when Durk Jager, a P&G veteran who had been the company's chief operating officer for two years, became its CEO and president early in 1999.

Jager took the reins with a firm hand. "The core business is innovation," he said. "If we innovate well, we will ultimately win . . . You have to do things differently." Being different came hard for P&G, even though it was once an innovator in human resource management. For example, the company still has the oldest known profit-sharing plan in continuous operation, begun almost 100 years ago. P&G was also one of the first companies to introduce disability and death benefit plans in U.S. business. And as early as the 1920s, P&G limited the workday to 8 hours and guaranteed workers 48 weeks of employment per year.

There were internal and external obstacles to the kind of rapid change Jager wanted. Internal forces included an entrenched corporate culture obsessed with controlling information, producing countless drafts of memos, and holding new-product ideas in research and development for years. Jager encouraged employees to scrap "the rules," overhauled the company's reporting lines into seven global business divisions, started an Internet beauty site in San Francisco, acquired the Iams pet-food business and the maker of Pur water filters, launched three big new-product lines, and planned to introduce 15 more. Sales went up, but due to the cost of acquisitions, net income was down slightly after Jager's first year.

External forces were harder to conquer. Investor resistance killed a planned hostile takeover of Warner-Lambert and American Home Products, which would have made P&G the second-largest pharmaceutical company in the world. And then there was the competition.

Pinched as hard as P&G, Unilever pressed ahead for every incremental bit of market share it could wring from its tried-and-true brands. After all, a single percentage point gain in a $6 billion market (like the U.S. market for laundry detergent, for instance) translates into a $60 million gain in revenues. Unilever's Dove brand soap had managed to pull ahead of P&G's Ivory, the former number-one product in the market. Ivory's share stood at 5 percent to Dove's 20. Colgate's does-it-all toothpaste, Total, grabbed 30 percent of the toothpaste market in its first year, leaving P&G's standby, Crest, with only 26 percent.

Earnings did not pick up, and sales grew less than anticipated. Finally, 17 months into Jager's tenure as CEO, operating profits declined for the first time in eight years, and the company's market value dropped by about 50 percent. Jager resigned, to be replaced as chairman by John Pepper, already a former chair and CEO from 1995 to 1999; and by Alan Lafley, another veteran executive, as president and CEO. Pepper and Lafley pledged to return the company's core businesses to a pattern of consistent sales and profit growth. In the consumer products marketplace, however, the battle for market share still raged.

In the summer of 2001, P&G executives hired an outside contractor that, in turn, recruited perhaps a dozen other subcontractors to spy on its competitors in the hair care business, including Unilever. Unilever's brands include Salon Selectives, Suave, Finesse, Thermasilk, Rave, Aqua Net, and Helene Curtis. They compete fiercely with P&G's brands, which include Pantene, Physique, Head & Shoulders, Clairol, and Wella. Such corporate "espionage" by competitive-intelligence firms is neither unknown nor illegal. There is even a professional organization called the Society of Competitive Intelligence Professionals, a kind of trade association for corporate spies, which claims that about $2 billion is spent annually on the activity. And P&G, known for its obsession with the security of its own secrets, has long conducted what it calls competitive analysis. But at some point this particular operation got out of hand. The spies, who operated from a safe house reportedly located in Cincinnati, are alleged to have trespassed at Unilever's hair care headquarters in Chicago, misrepresented themselves to Unilever employees as market analysts, and pored over the contents of Unilever's dumpsters, getting away with about 80 pages of top secret information about its competitor's plans for its brands. These were delivered to P&G and eventually came to the attention of chairman John Pepper. The two companies later settled the complaint.

Questions

1. Assume that P&G's hair care products marketing manager has the Unilever papers on his or her desk. The manager is considering doing nothing with the information, just keeping a lid on the situation and telling those involved to back off. Is this action ethical?

2. Suppose the marketing manager decides that his or her superiors should be told about the raid on Unilever, but they cannot decide whether to suggest sacrificing the contractors to the media to protect P&G, or admitting P&G's wrongdoing and apologizing to Unilever in public. What counsel would you offer, and why? What is the ethical basis for your decision?

3. Can you suggest another alternative to the marketing manager for dealing ethically with the information the company has obtained?

4. P&G is known to conduct rigorous competitive analyses in many of its markets. At what point do you think the gathering of competitive intelligence becomes unethical? Why?

Sources: "Rivals Use Competitive Intelligence," *Holland Sentinel*, September 15, 2003; Katrina Brooker, "Can Procter & Gamble Change Its Culture, Protect Its Market Share, and Find the Next Tide?" *Fortune*, April 26, 1999, pp. 146–152; Katrina Brooker, "Plugging the Leaks at P&G," *Fortune*, February 21, 2000, pp. 44–48; "Procter & Gamble Fires CEO After Only a Year and a Half," *Houston Chronicle*, June 9, 2000, p. 4; Joann S. Lublin and Matt Murray, "CEOs Depart Faster Than Ever as Boards, Investors Lose Patience," *Wall Street Journal*, October 27, 2000, p. B1; Matthew Boyle, "How the Workplace Was Won," *Fortune*, January 8, 2001, pp. 139–146; Katrina Brooker, "A Game of Inches," *Fortune*, February 5, 2001, pp. 98–100; Julian E. Barnes, "P&G Said to Agree to Pay Unilever $10 Million in Spying Case," *New York Times*, September 7, 2001, p. C7; Andy Serwer, "P&G's Cover Operation," *Fortune*, September 17, 2001, pp. 42–44.

integrative case

Xerox—People Problems

By A. Mukund

"Over the years, they've hyped their HR organization, but it ain't a pretty picture."

—*Jim W. Lundy, former Xerox manager,*
in August 2001

Introduction

In August 2000, Paul Allaire, chairman of the leading document management company Xerox, fired the company's CEO Rick Thoman. Commenting on his decision, Allaire said, "We are grateful for Rick's contributions in leading the company through a period of major repositioning. However, both Rick and the board felt it best for the company to move forward with an experienced Xerox team that will lead Xerox people and efficiently execute the strategy." The move attracted a lot of media attention with analysts commenting how Allaire had himself persuaded Thoman to leave a top position at IBM in 1998 and join Xerox.

Thoman, who was second only to IBM head Lou Gerstner, had also been the senior vice president and general manager of IBM's Personal Systems Group, one of IBM's most troubled operating units, which he helped turn around. Prior to this, he had also been the president and CEO of Nabisco International, president and CEO of American Express International, and chairman and co-CEO of American Express Travel Related Services Co.

However, company observers were not very surprised by Allaire's decision, as from the time Thoman had joined Xerox in May 2000, the company had lost around $20 billion in market value. Thoman was reportedly made to resign for his apparent failure to arrest this massive decline. Allaire made Anne M. Mulcahy the president and chief operating officer and reinstated himself as the CEO, though he was past the company's mandatory retirement age for executives.

Although analysts agreed that Thoman had failed to a certain extent at Xerox, they also argued that he seemed to have been made a scapegoat. Allaire's return as the CEO sparked off a round of heated debates regarding Thoman being blamed for the company's troubles, while Allaire himself was being blamed for being party to the deterioration of Xerox's work culture over the decades.

Background Note

The Xerox story goes back to 1938, when Chester Carlson, a patent attorney and part-time inventor, made the first xerographic image in the United States. Carlson struggled for over five years to sell the invention, as many companies did not believe there was a market for it. Finally, in 1944, the Battelle Memorial Institute in Columbus, Ohio, contracted with Carlson to refine his new process, which Carlson called "electrophotography." Three years later, the Haloid Company, maker of photographic paper, approached Battelle and obtained a license to develop and market a copying machine based on Carlson's technology.

Haloid later obtained all rights to Carlson's invention and registered the "Xerox" trademark in 1948. Buoyed by the success of the Xerox copiers, Haloid changed its name to Haloid Xerox Inc., in 1958, and to The Xerox Corporation in 1961. Xerox was listed on the New York Stock Exchange in 1961 and on the Chicago Stock Exchange in 1990. It is also traded on the Boston, Cincinnati, Pacific Coast, Philadelphia, London, and Switzerland exchanges. The strong demand for Xerox's products led the company from strength to strength and revenues soared from $37 million in 1960 to $268 million in 1965.

Throughout the 1960s, Xerox grew by acquiring many companies including University Microfilms, Micro-Systems, Electro-Optical Systems, Basic Systems, and Ginn and Company. In 1962, Fuji Xerox Co., Ltd., was launched as a joint venture of Xerox and Fuji Photo Film. Xerox acquired a majority stake (51.2%) in Rank Xerox in 1969. During the late 1960s and early 1970s, Xerox diversified into information technology business by acquiring Scientific Data Systems (makers of time-sharing and scien-

185

tific computers), Daconics (which made shared logic and word processing systems using minicomputers), and Vesetec (producers of electrostatic printers and plotters).

In 1969, it set up a corporate R&D facility, the Palo Alto Research Center (PARC), to develop in-house technologies. In the 1970s, Xerox focused on introducing new and more efficient models to retain its share of the reprographic market and meet competition from U.S. and Japanese companies. While the company's revenues increased from $698 million in 1966 to $4.4 billion in 1976, profits increased fivefold from $83 million in 1966 to $407 million in 1977.

According to analysts, Xerox management failed in giving a strategic direction to the company as it ignored new entrants (Ricoh, Canon, and Sevin) who were consolidating their positions in the lower-end market and in niche segments. The company's operating costs (and therefore, the prices of its products) were high, and its products were of relatively inferior quality compared to its competitors'. Return on assets soon reduced to less than 8 percent and market share in copiers came down sharply from 86 percent in 1974 to just 17 percent in 1984. Between 1980 and 1984, Xerox's profits decreased from $1.15 billion to $290 million.

In 1982, David T. Kearns took over as the CEO. He discovered that the average cost of Japanese machines was 40 to 50 percent of that of Xerox, which allowed it to undercut Xerox's prices effortlessly. Kearns quickly began emphasizing reduction of manufacturing costs and gave new thrust to the improvement of quality by launching a program that was popularly referred to as "Leadership Through Quality." In addition, he initiated major efforts to develop innovative new copiers and related products. He also worked toward reestablishing the entrepreneurial culture at Xerox. Management layers were cut, greater authority was delegated to lower levels, and employees were allowed to participate in decision making.

In the 1980s, Xerox bought Kurzweil, Datacopy, and Ventura—companies that specialized in optical character recognition, scanning and fax machines, and desktop publishing. It also diversified into financial services, insurance, and investment banking. Allaire succeeded Kearns as the new CEO in 1990 and immediately embarked on a major restructuring program to sharpen Xerox's focus on document processing. In 1992, Xerox entered into various tie-ups with Dell Computer Corporation and Microsoft. In the same year, the company announced a worldwide restructuring program including a 10 percent reduction in the workforce. Over the next few years, the company expanded its global network further by setting up/strengthening facilities and research centers in various parts of the world.

In 1993, Xerox announced a companywide initiative to reduce costs drastically and improve productivity. The company indicated that it would reduce the worldwide workforce by more than 10,000 and close or consolidate a number of operations. This restructuring program achieved pre-tax cost savings of approximately $350 million in 1994, $650 million in 1995, and $770 million in 1996. Xerox reinvested a major portion of these cost savings to streamline business processes and support expansion plans in growth markets. As a result, the company's gross margins improved from 40.7 percent in 1994 to 43.6 percent in 1995.

In 1998, Xerox announced another round of worldwide restructuring, including the elimination of 9,000 jobs through voluntary reduction, early retirement, and layoffs, and the closing and consolidation of various facilities. Xerox announced another worldwide restructuring program to cut costs, improve productivity, and spur growth. The program included cutting costs by $1 billion, sale of $2 to $4 billion worth of assets, and elimination of $5,200 positions worldwide. In the same year, Thoman replaced Allaire as the CEO, though Allaire continued as chairman. Despite these restructuring efforts, poor market conditions resulted in the company reporting a loss of $257 million on revenues of $18.7 billion in 2000.

People Problems—I

In the initial years, Xerox's work culture was reported to be the "envy of the corporate world." The company's chairman, Joseph C. Wilson, and his successor, Kearns, were lauded for forming a positive culture at the company that went on to play a major part in establishing its supremacy in the copier business. A former Xerox HR executive said, "Wilson brought in progressive HR people schooled in HR at outstanding institutions. They helped him build a very people-oriented tradition that became famous for its training, development and sales selection policies."

The strong influence of the HR department on the company's affairs continued when Kearns took over from Wilson. Douglas Reid, who worked as the chief HR executive under Kearns, said, "People came first. There was never any question as senior HR people that people would be treated with respect at all times. We had to make hard decisions, but always treated people fairly and generously. Compensation was designed to be fully competitive. We paid well, attracted quality people, and rewarded people well."

In the 1980s, Xerox faced stiff competition from Canon and Ricoh in the low-end copier business. The company then decided to opt for a total quality movement and cut manufacturing costs. According to analysts, it was the company's strong work culture which helped it fight back effectively as the employees participated wholeheartedly in these programs.

exhibit 1

Xerox—Financial Performance

Year Ended December 31 (in millions, except per-share data)	2000	1999*	1998*
Revenues			
Sales	$10,059	$10,441	$10,668
Service, outsourcing, and rentals	7,718	8,045	7,783
Finance income	924	1,081	1,142
Total Revenues	18,701	19,567	19,593
Costs and Expenses			
Cost of sales	6,197	5,944	5,880
Inventory charges	90	–	113
Cost of service, outsourcing, and rentals	4,813	4,599	4,323
Equipment financing interest	605	547	570
Research and development expenses	1,044	992	1,035
Selling, administrative and general expenses	5,649	5,292	5,343
Restructuring charge and asset impairments	540	–	1,531
Gain on affiliate's sale of stock	(21)	–	–
Purchased in-process research and development	27	–	–
Gain on sale of China operations	(200)	–	–
Other, net	341	285	219
Total Costs and Expenses	19,085	17,659	19,014
Income (Loss) from Continuing Operations before Income Taxes (Benefits)			
Equity Income and Minorities' Interests	(384)	1,908	579
Income taxes (benefits)	(109)	588	145
Income (loss) from Continuing Operations after Income Taxes (Benefits)			
before Equity Income and Minorities' Interests	(275)	1,320	434
Equity in net income of unconsolidated affiliates	61	68	74
Minorities' interests in earnings of subsidiaries	43	49	45
Income (Loss) from Continuing Operations	(257)	1,339	463
Discontinued operations	–	–	(190)
Net Income (Loss)	$ (257)	$ 1,339	$ 273
Basic Earnings (Loss) per Share			
Continuing operations	$ (0.44)	$ 1.96	$ 0.63
Discontinued operations	–	–	(0.29)
Basic Earnings (Loss) per Share	$ (0.44)	$ 1.96	$ 0.34
Diluted Earnings (Loss) per Share			
Continuing operations	$ (0.44)	$ 1.85	$ 0.62
Discontinued operations	–	–	(0.28)
Diluted Earnings (Loss) per Share	$ (0.44)	$ 1.85	$ 0.34

*Financial Statements for 1999 and 1998 were restated as a result of two separate investigations conducted by the Audit Committee of the Board of Directors. These investigations involved previously disclosed issues in our Mexico operations and a review of our accounting policies and procedures and application thereof. As a result of these investigations, it was determined that certain accounting practices and the application thereof misapplied GAAP and certain accounting errors and irregularities were identified. The company corrected these accounting errors and irregularities in its Consolidated Financial Statements.

Source: www.xerox.com.

However, things changed when Allaire replaced Kearns as the CEO in 1990. Reid, who had been an integral part of the company's HR function for almost three decades, decided to leave the organization and was replaced by William F. Buehler, who had hardly two years of HR experience.[1] Employees saw Buehler's appointment as an indication of the fact that HR's role in Xerox's corporate setup was on the decline.

Soon after, many HR executives who were part of Reid's team left the company. According to analysts, they did not want to work under Buehler, who lacked a sufficient HR background. One employee said, "An aura of fear has descended on the HR operations, making it difficult for HR to come forward. Earlier in my career, you would lay your body down on the tracks for certain principles. Today it's not being done for anything big. HR has shifted away from being the ombudsman and voice for the employees to being the implementer of management's policies. The culture that flourished under Reid until 1990—the culture that fostered employee involvement—is disappearing. When I talk to colleagues still there in influential positions, there's a sense of disenfranchisement."

The restructuring moves notwithstanding, the changed work culture at Xerox seemed to have hurt those who mattered the most—the employees. An ex-HR executive at Xerox, Ken Larson, said about the people at Xerox, "They thought they would be there a lifetime; now they have seen their value shrink. They are angry; they feel abandoned. There's a great sense of dissatisfaction with the top leadership. That's pushing the good people out."

The departures were also due to the way employees were being promoted at Xerox after Kearns and Reid left. While the company's policy framework was very clear regarding employee promotion norms, it was reportedly not practiced. Favoritism had become an order of the day—people were promoted on the basis of their relation with the top management. An ex-Xerox executive remarked, "We would gather background and assessment information on all senior managers and sit down with the president and review their potential. The good thing was there was a lot of knowledge shared about the strengths of the executives. But the way people really got promoted was by politicizing with each other. There was always an in-crowd and out-crowd."

Many analysts said that Allaire had decided to treat the HR head position as a "building ground" for preparing promising executives to handle higher positions in the company. This was proved when Buehler was promoted within two years of joining the HR department. Within a short span of time, Xerox began losing its top executives and was reportedly finding it tough to attract new employees as well. Critics of the company's policies said that while in the earlier years, Xerox used to get the best candidates and pay handsome salaries, it was now employing people for the short term and paid only the industry averages.

It was at this point of time that Thoman took control of the company. After joining Xerox, Thoman found severe lapses in the HR control systems of the company. For instance, there were no measures in place to measure per-employee income. In addition, there were a host of problems on the financial management front. Thoman said that he was surprised to realize that the Xerox culture had become all about patronizing the sales force instead of focusing on enhancing customer service.

People Problems—II

Based on his findings, Thoman decided to set things right at Xerox by focusing more strongly on digital equipment rather than the analog ones and by reorgan-izing the sales force to sell digital solutions instead of copying machines in the existing setup. For the first time in Xerox's history, sales personnel had to focus on industry-based targets (such as the automobile industry customers) instead of individual clients. This also meant that their commissions were reduced significantly.

Much to Thoman's chagrin, the reorganization plan met with severe criticism despite the fact that it had been endorsed by a committee of senior executives. Not only were there hassles in the implementation; Thoman found out that certain instructions he had given regarding the plan had not been followed at all. As sales representatives began losing their accounts, they left Xerox and sales staff attrition increased by almost 100 percent. According to analysts, the company failed in training the sales representatives to make the transition from selling photocopiers to offering long-term solutions.

However, there was more bad news in store. Thoman revealed his decision to carry out large-scale layoffs in two installments of 12,000 and 4,500, respectively. The decision was received with unprecedented opposition from various parties concerned. Soon after this, Thoman had to leave Xerox.

Media reports claimed that Thoman's ouster had a lot to do with the fact that Allaire had just not been able to "let go" of the company's control. This was surprising considering the fact that Allaire had invited Thoman to join Xerox, instead of promoting a CEO from within, mainly because he wanted to infuse fresh thoughts into the company. Allaire joined the board after Thoman, which was a typical boardroom move followed in many companies. However, what seemed to have worked to everyone's disadvantage was Allaire's constant interference in Xerox's affairs. For instance, when Thoman wanted to make some changes in the top management, Allaire did not allow him to do so. There were reports that Allaire's "in circle," comprising Mulcahy, Buehler, and others, even threatened to resign if Thoman continued in the company.

Although critics of Thoman's leadership style remarked that he had failed to take into confidence the employees of Xerox for his plans, the debate as to how much he was responsible for the issue continued. Meanwhile, the Mulcahy-Allaire team began working toward putting the company back on track. Mulcahy claimed that her two-decade-long association with Xerox would give her substantial mileage over Thoman.

The Future

Mulcahy's first concern was to put in place "retention programs" to arrest the abnormally high sales force attrition rate. This included increasing their pay and other incentives. Soon, the attrition dropped back to normal

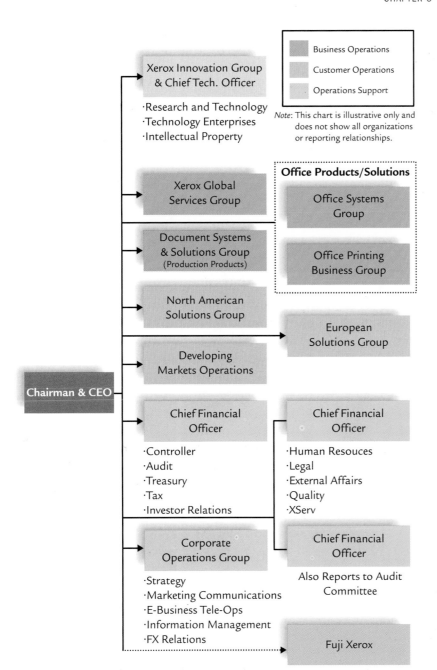

exhibit 2

Xerox—Organizational Structure

Source: www.xerox.com

levels. The company also decided to offer training and education to the personnel via e-learning. Mulcahy and Allaire got in touch personally with thousands of employees to restore their confidence in the company.

However, Xerox continued to face a fall in its profitability, which indicated that the company would have to keep the options of downsizing, consolidating, and cost-cutting open. The company reported a loss of $384 million for the year 2000. By January 2001, its stock had dropped 72 percent over the previous year. The company was reported to be on the brink of bankruptcy; however a $345 million timely credit from GE Capital helped avoid this. Interestingly enough, brushing off any doubts about

the company's future, Mulcahy said, "Paul and I make a great team. We have confidence in each other and support of the board. I have a leadership team that's signed up, is loyal and is participating in the turnaround."

For the fiscal year December 2001, total revenues fell 12 percent to $16.5 billion and net loss rose by 18 percent to $342 million. Company sources attributed this to the global economic meltdown and a higher effective income tax rate. Mulcahy and Allaire indeed seemed to have a tough battle on their hands. According to industry observers, it was all the more important for the duo to pull Xerox out of the various problems it was facing—for this time around, they did not even have Thoman to blame.

Strategic
Management

6

■

Define strategy.

■

Explain the role of environmental analysis in strategy formulation.

■

Explain the strategic planning process.

■

Utilize strategic planning tools, such as the product life cycle model, portfolio matrix, and SWOT analysis.

■

Describe strategy implementation tools such as the Seven S Model.

■

Describe the differences between intended and emergent strategies.

Boeing: Another "Dream" Strategy?

Anyone who thought the 2001 Paris Air Show was going to feature yet another showdown between longtime rivals Boeing and Airbus was in for a surprise. Instead of continuing the head-to-head fight against its growing competitor, Boeing CEO stunned the industry by announcing a major change in strategic direction.

The change came after several months of direct competition with Boeing's sole competitor, Airbus, in the "jumbo" commercial airline market segment. (Jumbo jets carry 400-plus passengers each.) For decades, Boeing had ruled the jumbo segment of the market with its 747. However, in late 1999, Airbus executives announced plans to offer a double-decker, jumbo passenger jet (the A380) that would seat about 550 passengers, surpassing the size and seating capacity of Boeing's 747. At first Boeing executives scoffed at the need for such a plane, hoping to keep Airbus out of the one segment in which Boeing had no competition. However, as Airbus managers racked up orders, Boeing executives had to take the threat seriously. Their first response was to offer a stretch version of the Boeing 747 (747X). After failure to gain even one confirmed order, Boeing management was forced to rethink the firm's competitive position.

Instead of expanding the venerable 747 to compete head-to-head with Airbus, Boeing management decided to launch a smaller, faster passenger jetliner, which they titled the "Sonic Cruiser," and which they anticipated would make its first flight in 2007 or 2008.

"People don't need bigger airplanes," said Alan Mulally, president and CEO of Boeing's $31 billion commercial jet division. "People will pay for speed," he claimed. Although the Sonic Cruiser wouldn't be as fast as the Concorde, it would still surpass the speed of today's passenger jets by about 15 percent, clocking in at just under the speed of sound, and saving about two to five hours per international trip (departing from the United States). Additionally, the Cruiser would consume less fuel than the Concorde, enabling it to fly longer distances and travel nonstop from New York to, say, Jakarta, Indonesia, or from London to Sydney, Australia—farther than any other existing passenger jet. Moreover, with a new and different plane to sell to commercial airlines, Boeing wouldn't have to compete head-to-head with Airbus solely on price.

Airbus, which had been steadily increasing its market share and reducing Boeing's share of the market, analyzed the world market a little differently. Managers at Airbus believed that in the coming years the number of landing gates at major airports would grow much more slowly than the demand to fly to those key destinations. As a result, airlines would find it difficult to increase the number of flights to meet the heightened demand—they would need the A380 to be able to carry more passengers per flight.

European commercial plane manufacturer Airbus keeps throwing a monkey wrench into Seattle-based Boeing's strategic plans. Responding to growing demand by passengers and limited capacity of airport gates, in 1999, Airbus rolled out plans to produce the world's first double-decker passenger airliner, similar to the model shown in the photo. The A380 is designed to carry over 500 passengers and is expected to enter service in 2006. Airbus also claims the A380 is more fuel efficient. Meanwhile, Boeing scrapped plans to build a number of new models, which seemed out of sync with the current needs of commercial airline companies. Boeing finally decided to develop a new mid-sized aircraft designed for speed named the 7E7.

Industry analysts subsequently questioned whether Boeing would be able to develop and implement the Sonic Cruiser or end up killing it for lack of orders, similar to the 747 Stretch. Nonetheless, at the 2001 Paris Air Show, Mulally reassured the public that the Sonic Cruiser would fly. "On a scale of 1 to 10, I am at 11," he said. "That's how sure I am the Sonic Cruiser will go into commercial service."

The analysts had good reason to be skeptical. Indeed, a year after Mulally's announcement at the show, air travel worldwide decreased significantly, and Boeing axed the Sonic Cruiser. The company also began to reevaluate the "need for speed" within the industry. Figuring that financially hard-hit airline companies would rather trim their costs, Boeing reevaluated its strategy once again. Instead of a jet such as the Sonic Cruiser, which would have consumed a lot of fuel, Boeing would produce a mid-sized, fuel-efficient jet called the 7E7 "Dreamliner."

Plans called for the 7E7 to be built entirely of composite materials, making it stronger and lighter than planes made of aluminum and 20 percent more fuel efficient. The problem is that composite materials have never been used to build an entire commercial airliner. Additionally, there is some evidence that when Airbus used composite material on the tail section of one of its airliners, it crashed, in 2001.

Using composite materials would also mean Boeing's production processes would have to change radically, which has traditionally been difficult for the company to do. For example, Boeing production managers were once forced to close two assembly lines for 30 days when they tried to change its manufacturing procedures to cut costs. Airbus executives scoffed at the plans to build the 7E7, calling it a sales representative's "dream" but an engineer's "nightmare."

The cancellation of the Sonic Cruiser and three other planes by Boeing since the early 1990s brings into question the soundness of its strategy development processes. However, without a new and different plane, Boeing sales managers would have to compete directly with Airbus on price, leading to diminished profits and perhaps a price war. Another problem both Boeing and Airbus managers face is the time horizon related to planning and building jumbo jets, which can take up to 10 years. Much can change in 10 years' time, as witnessed by the need for Boeing to change its strategy after the tragedy of 9/11.

Mulally hails these changes as a "fabulous" and nimble response to his firm's customers, but each cancelled project costs Boeing significant amounts in lost investments (and time). It also makes it more difficult for the company to convince its customers that the jet it's currently trying to sell them will actually be built and available. Credibility, in other words, is important to a firm's business strategy too.

Sources: "Daring to Dream," *Airline Business*, January 2004; Stanley Holmes, "Will This Idea Really Fly?" *BusinessWeek*, June 23, 2003, p. 34; Laurence Zuckerman, "Boeing Plays an Aerial Wild Card," *New York Times*, June 17, 2001, pp. BU 3 and BU 11; Stanley Holmes, "Diverging Flight Plans at the Paris Air Show," *BusinessWeek Online*, www.businessweek.com/bwdaily/dnflash/jun2001/nj20010622_159.htm, accessed on August 5, 2001; Stanley Holmes, "Boeing's Sonic Bruiser," *BusinessWeek*, July 2, 2001, pp. 64–68.

strategic overview

For Boeing's senior managers to successfully navigate the future threats and opportunities they face, they must have a strategy for how to compete effectively. Although managers have always needed to devise the means to compete (often referred to as competitive strategies), the dramatic increase of competition within many markets in recent years has enhanced the importance of strategy and the strategic management process. Even though Boeing has only one major competitor, Airbus, its competition has increased. Airbus has become stronger, designed better aircraft, and offered its planes at highly competitive prices. Furthermore, Airbus managers obviously were more effective in analyzing the market because they identified an opportunity in the demand for a larger aircraft and Boeing managers missed or misjudged this opportunity. Because of the failure to effectively analyze the market needs, Boeing management is now experiencing significant problems and trying to find a strategy that works. Thus, Airbus appears to now have a competitive advantage, and Boeing is in danger of losing more of its once dominant market share. Boeing is a prime example of how important it is to use an effective strategic management process; without it, an organization's survival may be threatened, even when a firm has only one major competitor and has enjoyed a strong position in the past.

Another illustration of this increasing competition is provided by the domestic automobile market. As recently as 25 years ago, the largest automobile market in the world, the United States, was dominated by only three major manufacturers: General Motors, Ford, and Chrysler. Chrysler was acquired by DaimlerBenz of Germany and is now DaimlerChrysler. Additionally, the market shares of both GM and Ford have decreased by nearly half in the last several years as foreign competitors, including BMW, Daewoo, Fiat, Honda, Hyundai, Isuzu, Kia, Nissan, Renault, Subaru, Suzuki,

Toyota, and others have captured market share. In fact, in 2003, Toyota passed Ford in car sales in the United States. This provides just one example of how globalization has become a powerful force behind increasing competition. Today competitors from every corner of this world can converge on markets. Communication and transportation technology add to this competitive intensity.

Never has the need been greater to understand how to develop and implement effective strategies. In recent years, major firms such as United Airlines and WorldCom have filed for bankruptcy. Polaroid, once among the top 50 firms in the United States, went out of existence. In 2002, 38,540 firms filed for bankruptcy in the United States. Andrew Grove, former CEO of Intel, observed that only the paranoid firms survive, primarily because they continuously analyze their external environments and competition, but also because they continuously innovate. Managers who help their firms gain a competitive advantage recognize that it is only temporary; they must constantly innovate and stand ready to change their strategy based on their analysis of the competition and other changes in their environments.[1]

While the principles of strategic management are critical for top managers of a company, the principles also are applicable for managers at various levels of the organization. For example, a lower-level manager may be responsible for a single product line in a company with many products. The principles presented in this chapter can be applied to create a strategy for a product line as well as for an entire company. In addition, even though a company's strategy is developed largely by the top executives, it must then be implemented throughout the organization by the other managers and employees. Managers at all levels can do a better job of helping implement a strategy if they understand the strategic management process, how the strategy was developed, and its intended targets.

COMPETITIVE ADVANTAGE

competitive advantage the ability of a firm to win consistently over the long term in a competitive situation

Competitive Advantage by Michael Hitt

Q&A
One**Key**
www.prenhall.com/onekey

Fundamentally, the objective of strategic management is to determine, create, and maintain competitive advantage. So what is competitive advantage? At its essence, the concept of **competitive advantage** is the ability of a firm to win consistently over the long term in a competitive situation.[2] In the case of for-profit organizations, this means consistently gaining greater profits than competitors. If competitive advantage consists of factors that lead to a consistent winning record, what then are these factors?

Competitive advantage is created through the achievement of five qualities: superiority, inimitability, durability, nonsubstitutability, and appropriability.[3] We will explain and examine each of them in just a minute, but before we do it is important to stress that all these qualities are built upon an assumption. The foundational assumption is that the product or service a company provides has perceived value in the eyes of the customer. If what is provided to customers has no value in their eyes, then qualities such as superiority or durability have no practical meaning. While perceived customer value may seem like a totally obvious assumption, very well-known companies with bright managers often spend lots of time and money doing things that customers do not value. For example, Hewlett-Packard (HP) is the market leader in printers. Clearly, managers there must be doing something right, and providing value in the eyes of customers, or customers wouldn't buy their printers. However, HP was spending a lot of time and money on an aspect of its printers that customers did not value. Prior to 2002, virtually all HP printers were strong enough that a 250 pound person could stand on one and use it for a step stool. In fact, HP printers were some of the strongest on the market in this respect. The key question is, "Do customers value this level of sturdiness to the point that they would pay for it?" It will probably not surprise you to learn that HP managers found that the answer was "No." As a consequence, HP redesigned its new line of printers for 2003 with a lower level of sturdiness, lower costs, and lower prices, and it was a huge hit with customers. With the underlying assumption of perceived customer value firmly in mind, let's take a look at each of the five qualities that lead to competitive advantage.

Superiority

The essence of this term and aspect of competitive advantage is straightforward. Are you significantly better than your competitors and if so at what things? For example, Federal Express was one of the first companies to introduce package tracking capability. It created a system for tracking a package all along its route. Thus, it was better than UPS at knowing where a customer's package was. As a student, you no doubt have a comparative advantage at some subjects in school; maybe you are better than most of your classmates at writing or statistics. In the business world, Sony has been able to miniaturize audio and video products (for example, radios, camcorders, and CD players) better than most other electronics firms. Thus, Sony has a superiority advantage at miniaturization of audio and video products. This is sometimes called a comparative advantage because compared to others it is better and has an advantage. It is also sometimes referred to as a distinctive competency because while others may also be good, you are distinctively better.

Inimitability

Superiority alone, however, will not guarantee competitive advantage. In addition, managers must create barriers that make it hard for others to copy their superiority advantages.[4] These barriers can involve a variety of obstacles from tangible ones such as size to more intangible ones such as a company's culture.[5] This general concept is easy to understand if you first apply it to yourself. For example, suppose you are better at statistics than most of your classmates; this gives you a superiority advantage. Further, suppose that your superiority in statistics is a function of having taken several math classes in high school and college. For others to become as good as you are at statistics, they would need to take a similar number of classes. The more classes they have to take, the greater the barrier. You can now take the same idea and apply it to companies.

For example, Disney's theme parks are often cited as having a comparative advantage in friendly employees. While today Disney might be superior to other firms when it comes to friendly employees, one of the key questions is, "Is it easy for other firms to replicate this?" If it is, Disney's superiority advantage will soon disappear. But how easy is it to find and keep employees who can smile for hours on end even while being asked where the nearest restroom is for the ten-thousandth time that day? The harder it is for other firms with theme parks to hire, develop, and keep friendly employees, the longer Disney's comparative advantage will persist.

Durability

This brings us directly to the next aspect of competitive advantage. Some advantages are more durable than others. They might last because they are legally protected. For example, patents can protect an advantage for years. Many scientific patents are 17 to 20 years in length. Advantages such as brand recognition can last a long time and may take years to deteriorate. For example, some argue that for nearly two decades after the death of Walt Disney, the Disney "brand" was largely neglected. It nonetheless endured in the minds of children and their parents.[6]

Nonsubstitutability

You would think that if your firm had a superiority advantage which was hard to imitate and lasted, this would be enough to ensure competitive advantage, but it is not. In addition to these qualities, competitive advantage requires a low possibility of substitution. **Substitution** is concerned with whether or not the customer's need that you fulfill can be met by alternative means. Sometimes students confuse substitution and imitation. It may be easiest to help differentiate the two concepts with a concrete example. Godiva is famous for its chocolates. It has a significant superiority advantage in the taste and smoothness of its chocolate compared to other chocolate makers. Godiva's specialized knowledge makes it difficult for other firms to replicate or imitate the taste and texture of its chocolate. However, if Godiva is to sustain its competitive advantage, customers must find it difficult for a substitute to satisfy the sweet taste and smooth texture that they get when they eat Godiva chocolates. If chocolate lovers find they can satisfy that taste by eating Ben & Jerry's premium ice cream, Godiva's comparative advantage would not sustain its competitive advantage. To illustrate the difference between imitation and substitution even further, let's return to the case of Encyclopaedia Britannica that we examined in Chapter 3. Encyclopaedia Britannica may have the best encyclopedias in the world, and they may be so good that it is very difficult for any direct competitors to copy or imitate them. However, when the Internet made it possible for grade school children to find information for school reports without having to open one of the 30 bound volumes of Encyclopaedia Britannica, the Internet became a substitute. As a consequence, Britannica's

substitution concerned with whether or not the customer's need that you fulfill can be met by alternative means

To sustain a competitive advantage, managers must create barriers that make it difficult for others to copy what their firm does well. The Cheesecake Factory, a company headquartered in California, operates more than 70 restaurants. The centerpiece of the Cheesecake Factory's 200-plus item menu is, of course, its cheesecake, which comes in about 40 varieties. Although patrons frequently ask for recipes, the firm keeps them a trade secret.

comparative advantage at making great bound encyclopedia sets did not help it sustain a competitive advantage in the marketplace.

Appropriability

The final element necessary for competitive advantage is the concept of appropriability. This is a fancy way of asking whether you can actually capture the profits that can be made in the business. For example, even though Nokia had less than 40 percent market share in 1999, it captured roughly 80 percent of the profits made by all mobile phone manufacturers. Scholars, such as Michael Porter of Harvard, talked about this phenomenon in terms of supernormal returns. **Supernormal returns** are the profits that are above the average for a comparable set of firms. These greater-than-average profits are primarily a function of greater-than-average cost-price margins. For example, if the average cost in the industry for a 250 megabyte zip disk is $10 and the average value or price is $15, then the average margin is $5. A supernormal return would be anything above $5 in profit.

supernormal returns the profits that are above the average for a comparable set of firms

At this point it is worth repeating that these elements of competitive advantage are based on the premise of perceived customer value. For example, you may be better at statistics than your classmates and they may face high barriers to become as good as you. This advantage may be durable because you will not soon forget all the great statistical techniques that you have learned. Furthermore, there may be no real substitutes for analyzing data apart from the statistical techniques you have mastered. However, none of this will necessarily translate into a competitive advantage in the job market, unless potential employers value the ability to use statistics. If you are interested in a market research position, then your competencies in statistics could easily translate into a *competitive* advantage in the job market because statistical analysis is a commonly required capability for a market researcher. Similarly, being able to miniaturize audio and video products better than others would lead to few profits for Sony unless the majority of customers wanted smaller radios, camcorders, and CD players.

While in the rest of this chapter we separately examine specific aspects of the strategic management process, including the formulation and implementation of strategy, it all emanates from this one basic objective—competitive advantage. The various tools and frameworks we will review are those that, in both research and practice, have proven helpful to managers in achieving and sustaining competitive advantage.

STRATEGIC MANAGEMENT PROCESS: SETTING DIRECTION

Strategic management is a type of planning process in which managers (1) set the organization's general direction and objectives, (2) formulate a specific strategy, (3) plan and carry out the strategy's implementation, and (4) monitor results and make necessary adjustments. To understand what this means, we need to examine each step in this overall process (see Exhibit 6.1).

Because a strategy is a plan for the future of the company, many of the key elements in the strategic management process are similar to those we will cover later, in the chapter on planning (Chapter 8). Consequently, we will highlight key similarities in the following sections.

Strategic Intent

The first step in the strategic management process is the determination of the firm's strategic intent. **Strategic intent** is not easy to define, but it can be thought of as what the organization ultimately wants to be and do.[7] For

Strategic Intent vs. Strategic Objectives by Michael Hitt

Q&A
One Key
www.prenhall.com/onekey

strategic intent pertains to what an organization ultimately wants to be and do

exhibit 6.1
Strategic Management Process

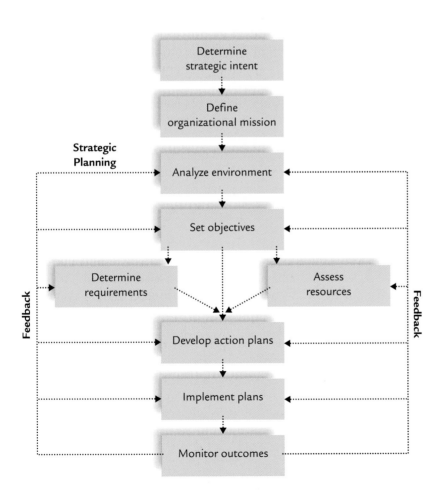

Kellogg's, which boasts over $9 billion in revenue annually, is the number one cereal company in the United States, and the maker of flagship brands such as Frosted Flakes, Rice Krispies, and Froot Loops. Kellogg's strategic intent is to have the company's cereals on every breakfast table in the world. It's a lofty goal, but it gives the company and its employees something for a target.

example, Ford Motor Company's strategic intent is to "be the number one automotive company in the world." British Airways intends to become "The World's Favourite Airline." Xerox Corporation states its strategic intent in equally simple terms: "The World's Document Company." Kellogg's strategic intent is to have "Kellogg's Products on Every Table in the World." As these four examples illustrate, strategic intent captures the general identity, direction, and level of aspirations of the organization. A key point to keep in mind is that while the other specific elements in the strategic planning process constitute the body of a strategic plan, strategic intent is the heart of the plan.[8] As such, one of its key objectives is to inspire.[9] This is why most statements of strategic intent are also statements of "strategic stretch." That is, to live up to the strategic intent, the organization must stretch far beyond where it is today. In practice, an effective statement of strategic intent should paint a general picture of aspiration and engender a strong emotional response in just a few words.

Mission

mission statement articulates the fundamental purpose of the organization and often contains several components

Although statements of strategic intent are typically only a sentence in length, mission statements are usually much longer. A **mission statement** articulates the fundamental purpose of the organization and often contains several components, among them:

- Company philosophy
- Company identity, or self-concept
- Principal products or services
- Customers and markets
- Geographic focus
- Obligations to shareholders
- Commitment to employees[10]

exhibit 6.2
Mission Statement for the
Internal Revenue Service

❧ IRS Mission Statement ❦

The IRS mission is to "provide America's taxpayers
top quality service by helping them
understand and meet their tax responsibilities
and by applying the tax law with
integrity and fairness to all."

An example of a mission statement is provided in Exhibit 6.2. As the example illustrates, while mission statements provide more detail concerning the purpose of the organization, they should support and be consistent with its strategic intent. One of the major differences between statements of strategic intent and mission statements is that mission statements tend to be much more specific in terms of stating objectives or values regarding the various components listed above.

Strategic Objectives

Unless organizational strategic intent and mission are translated into specific performance goals, they are likely to remain statements of good intentions and unrealized achievements. Furthermore, an analysis of the environment is an academic exercise unless the implications find their way into strategic objectives. **Strategic objectives** translate the strategic intent and mission of the firm into concrete and measurable goals. Setting strategic objectives is a critical step in the strategic management process because it facilitates a firm's ability to (1) allocate resources appropriately, (2) reach a shared understanding of priorities, (3) delegate responsibilities, and (4) hold people accountable for results.[11] Specifically, strategic objectives might address any of the following issues:

strategic objectives translate the strategic intent and mission of a firm into concrete and measurable goals

Strategic Intent vs. Strategic Objectives by Michael Hitt
Q&A OneKey
www.prenhall.com/onekey

- Revenue growth
- Profitability
- Customer satisfaction
- Market share
- Financial returns (e.g., return on equity, return on assets)
- Technological leadership
- Cash flow
- Operating efficiency (e.g., costs per unit, expense per employee)

It is important to note that strategic objectives differ from other performance objectives in one fundamental use. Strategic objectives are longer term in nature. They are not yearly objectives or goals. They represent targets for which the company aims over the long term (typically five years or so). Although setting strategic objectives is critical, much of the time managers actually spend on strategic management is taken up in the subsequent steps of the process. These principally involve analyzing the organization's internal environment, formulating a strategy, developing an implementation plan, and monitoring the results.

STRATEGIC MANAGEMENT PROCESS: FORMULATING A STRATEGY

In many ways the essence of competitive strategy is determining how the company is going to compete and achieve its strategic objectives, mission, and ultimate strategic intent. However, this also happens to be one of the most complicated aspects of strategic management and one that has caused scholars and practicing managers alike to write volumes on the topic. Condensing it down to part of a chapter is not an easy task. By necessity, some ideas and concepts can't be included. As a result, we will first present a set of generic strategies for competitive advantage and then discuss several techniques and tools for formulating a firm's generic and specific strategy.

Generic Strategies for Competitive Advantage

The two most-discussed generic strategies are cost leadership and differentiation.[12] To help illustrate each one, let's return to our computer disk example.

cost leadership striving to be the lowest-cost producer of a product or provider of a service and yet charge only slightly less than industry average prices

Cost Leadership Cost leadership simply involves competing by striving to be the lowest-cost producer of a product or provider of a service and yet charge only slightly less than industry average prices. To the extent a firm has lower costs than its competitors (i.e., cost leadership) and can command prices similar to its competitors, it can achieve above-average profits. For a zip disk manufacturer to obtain supernormal returns through cost leadership, it would need to lower its costs below the industry average (from $10 to, say, $7.50) and still be able to charge near the industry average price (i.e., $15). In this case, the firm would make a profit of $7.50 instead of the industry average of $5. It is important to understand that the cost leadership strategy does not necessarily imply price leadership, meaning offering the lowest price. For example, if the cost leader had costs of $7.50 per disk but also charged the lowest price ($12.50), it would earn normal returns (i.e., the industry average of $5).

There are a wide variety of ways to achieve cost leadership. You might do it through technology. If you manufacture computer chips, you might invest in the latest technology to reduce defects and increase your "yield" (percentage of good chips) and thereby reduce your average cost per chip. You might achieve cost leadership through economies of scale. You might increase output through your given factories and thereby reduce your per-unit costs. You might achieve it through economies of scope. Amazon has tried to do this (with better financial results more recently than at first) by trying to push more product through its existing sales channel (i.e., its Web site on the Internet) and distribution network.

A Manager's Challenge, "Leveraging High Tech in the Low-Tech Business of Cement," helps illustrate how a Mexican company, Cemex, has used technology in a traditionally low-tech business to help it achieve its cost leadership position at home, and increasingly, abroad. While reading the case, ask yourself how durable you think the cost advantage is that technology is delivering to Cemex. Can others easily copy Cemex and duplicate its results?

differentiation strategy for making a product or service different from those of competitors

Differentiation Managers pursuing a **differentiation** strategy seek to make their product or service different from those of competitors on dimensions highly and widely valued by customers. If they can do so, they can command a premium price. If managers can also keep costs at approximately the industry average, the premium price allows the firm to earn above-average profits. For a zip disk manufacturer to obtain supernormal returns through differentiation leadership, it would need to keep its costs at approximately the industry

Leveraging High Tech in the Low-Tech Business of Cement

You might not expect managers in a Mexican cement company to have placed cutting-edge technology at the center of their competitive strategy, but that is exactly what managers at Cemex have done. Because cement is basically a commodity, firms often compete on price. Cemex managers are using technology to improve efficiency and lower costs.

Lorenzo Zambrano, grandson of the founder, is the CEO of Cemex, which is based in Monterrey, Mexico, and now over a century old. Zambrano, who spent 18 years working his way through the ranks of Cemex before becoming CEO, has relentlessly sought out ways to use IT to drive down costs and improve efficiency. He has been described as a techno-whiz kid. His favorite "toy" is said to be an IBM Thinkpad. With his Thinkpad, Zambrano checks sales figures any time rather than wait for reports that would come in with data weeks old. Quality control is also automated; sampling machines use lasers to analyze samples and the results are beamed by satellite to the firm's Monterrey headquarters, where these and other results are displayed on-screen. As a consequence, Zambrano can check on the real-time kiln temperatures and quality results on the Cemex network. He can then use e-mail to ask managers why their output or quality might not be up to targets rather than wait for quality problems to show up on the customer's job site. In turn, plant managers can now not only track their units' operations but can compare them with others and exchange ideas and best practices through e-mail with managers throughout the Cemex system. Overall quality is up and staff costs are down because it now takes only a handful of people to run one of Cemex's big cement plants.

However, the benefits of information technology are not restricted to just the cement plants or to senior executives. With communication and information sharing—including information about performance—made easier and faster, employees began to look for ways to create improvements in their own departments. The company's distributed IT systems let managers monitor sales figures, for instance, and at the same time allow lower-level employees access to enough information to create healthy rivalries among different units.

Executives at Cemex have used information technology to improve efficiency and performance. To both reduce costs and use their assets more efficiently and effectively, executives use computers and global positioning system receivers in every cement truck to achieve more efficient routing and more precise delivery times. Previously, any number of things could derail a delivery, including bad weather and traffic. Combining precise information about the trucks' whereabouts with plant output and customer orders, managers are able to calculate more precisely which truck should go where and how to reroute them if necessary. The benefits are enormous when you consider that cement needs to be poured within 90 minutes of being mixed. The new system allows Cemex's logistic managers to accurately direct trucks to be within 20 minutes of their delivery time instead of three hours.

The advanced state of their internal information systems has allowed Cemex executives to expand beyond the borders of Mexico. Because cement is produced and used locally (the average distance between a cement mixing plant and the customer is 60 kilometers), Cemex uses its information technology to significantly improve the efficiency of the companies it buys.

Cemex executives have implemented a strategy of expansion into emerging markets in 14 countries, including Spain, Venezuela, Thailand, Egypt, and Puerto Rico. In 2000, Cemex scored a big coup by buying Southdown, the second-largest cement producer in the United States. It was the first time a Mexican firm had bought a U.S. one. It also made Cemex the third-biggest cement producer in the world.

With each acquisition the company gets better and faster at integrating technical and management methods with those of the parent company. For example, integrating two Spanish acquisitions in 1992 took about 18 months. Armed with laptops and Cemex's information technology system, the integration team reduced that time to under four months in the case of Southdown. This decrease in integration time means real money because the sooner the benefits of Cemex's technology can be put into the acquisition, the sooner the cost savings can be captured. Cemex expects to save about $15 million a year from improved logistics at Southdown, for example. In 2003, the company launched an e-tail site to sell its cement and service its customers online. "We can guarantee our customers that we will deliver our cement in plus or minus 15 minutes," says Francisco Garza, president of North American and worldwide trading operations. "Just like a pizza."

This has helped make Cemex more profitable than either of its two international rivals, Lafarge, based in France, and the Swiss firm Holcim.

Sources: "Cemex Launches E-tail Website, Opens New Customer Service Center," *Caribbean Business*, November 20, 2003, p. 54; Roy Sudip, "Cementing Global Success," *Direct Investor*, March 2003, pp. 12–14; www.cemex.com, accessed July 4, 2002; Julie Watson, "Cemex Buys Puerto Rican Company for Stronger Hold of Caribbean Market," *AP Worldstream*, June 12, 2002; Jenalia Moreno, "Mexican Cement Giant's Deal Laid Solid Foundation for Entering U.S. Market," *Houston Chronicle*, April 10, 2001; "The Cemex Way," *Economist*, June 16, 2001, pp. 75–76.

average, while adding features that would allow it to command a premium price. For example, suppose the firm was able to offer greater memory (1,000 versus 750 megabytes) without substantially increasing the costs of manufacturing the disks, and as a consequence could command a premium price (say $17.50 instead of $15) but keep its prices near the industry average of $10. In this case, the firm would make a profit of $7.50 per disk instead of the industry average of $5. Any number of characteristics might provide the basis for differentiation.

For example, the Sony Viao laptop computer is priced approximately 20 percent higher than comparable laptops by companies such as Toshiba. Yet, it only costs Sony about 5 percent more to make the laptops. Consequently, it earns supernormal returns. Why do people pay the higher price for a Sony laptop? Primarily for three reasons: first, aesthetics. Sony wanted to create an outward design that looked better (cooler in its words) than that of competitors. At least to many who purchase Sony's laptop, they have succeeded. Second, Sony wanted to make its laptops thinner and lighter. Again, at least to an important segment of customers, this is important and they are willing to pay more for less (less weight that is). Third, the Sony brand in general represents electronics that are at the leading edge of style and quality. While this third element has cost Sony literally billions to build over the last 50 years, in one sense it costs the company nothing to add this brand value to its laptops.

The key here is that there are a variety of ways and even layers of differentiation that are possible—style, quality, reliability, speed, fashion, durability, and so on. The key is to add differentiation that customers (or at least an important segment of customers) value at a cost that produces a superior margin. In other words, the cost increase to add the differentiation has to be less than the price premium customers will pay for the differentiation. If it costs you 20 percent more to make your product more reliable and customers will only pay 20 percent more for this differentiation, then it will not generate supernormal profits.

In thinking about ways to differentiate, it is important to keep in mind that this can be done via characteristics directly related to the product or service itself, or might be indirectly related through any of the aspects of the firm's activities. Eveready batteries, for example, might command a premium price because they provide longer-lasting power—a characteristic of the product itself. In contrast, Caterpillar's tractors might command a premium price because Caterpillar can deliver service and spare parts anywhere in the world within 24 hours—a characteristic not of the product but of the firm's related activities.

When customers highly value a variety of product attributes, competing firms can successfully pursue various differentiation strategies at the same time. For example, Apple Computer might try to differentiate its products based on how easy they are to use, while Dell might try to differentiate its products based on how fast and powerful they are. As long as some customers value ease of use more than speed and other customers have the opposite preferences, Apple and Dell might both be successful in their differentiation strategies. If, on the other hand, customers highly and widely value only one attribute for a given product or service, then firms have fewer options for differentiation strategies. The most successful firm will be the one that is the best at the attribute customers value and that can keep costs low relative to competitors. For example, if customers only value computer speed, then the firm that produces the fastest computer will likely earn the highest profits.

strategic scope the scope of a firm's strategy or breadth of focus

Strategic Scope A firm can limit the scope of its strategy (its **strategic scope**), or breadth of focus, by focusing on a specific segment of customers. Although the restriction reduces the total volume and revenue the firm can obtain from a product, it does not necessarily affect its ability to earn supernormal returns. For example, Ferrari differentiates its product based on style and performance and focuses on a very narrow segment of customers (not many people can afford a $250,000 car). A narrow scope strategy also applies to cost leadership. To the extent that the cost leader can provide products or services sufficiently valuable to command prices near the industry average for some targeted segment of customers, it can achieve above-average profits.

To succeed when pursuing a limited scope, or **niche strategy**, there must be significant differences among targeted customers or among geographical segments of customers. A **customer segment** is essentially a group of customers who share similar preferences or place similar value, on product features. For example, in selling cars, clear segments exist. Some people value gas mileage while others value performance. Thus, you can make a high-performance sports car and not really worry about small economy cars taking away your customers. Geographical segments may also exist. First, customers in different locations may prefer different features. If you design and sell suits costing $1,000 or more, you need to know that customers in hot and humid climates prefer cotton fabrics while those in drier and cooler climates prefer wool fabrics. If your firm is particularly strong in wool fabrics, you have a clear geographic segment of customers you can pursue with a differentiation, niche strategy. Second, geographical segments also occur when customers have similar preferences but do not have universal access. The most common reason for this is government intervention. For example, a firm might be able to gain access to customers in France but not in Egypt because of government restrictions, even if the Egyptian customers have preferences similar to those in France for a particular product.

Managers pursuing any one of the four generic strategies (see Exhibit 6.3) must remember that in our fast-changing world, today's competitive advantage may be obsolete tomorrow. Managers who help their firms succeed over the long term make old sources of competitive advantage obsolete before their competitors do. Thus, to have sustainable competitive advantage, managers must continually build temporary competitive advantages, replacing old ones with new ones.

niche strategy a limited scope or breadth of focus

customer segment a group of customers who have similar preferences or place similar value on product features

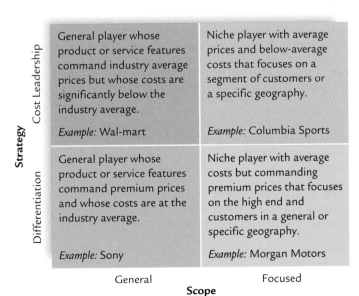

exhibit 6.3
Generic Strategies and Scope

Internal and External Analysis

So how should you determine which of these generic strategies to pursue and what additional specifics should be part of your formulated strategy? This question has been at the center of a raging discussion, debate, and research agenda for the last 30 years. What we can safely say is that a proper determination of a firm's specific strategy requires an analysis of both its external environment and internal capabilities. This view was probably first put forward by Kenneth Andrews in the early 1970s.[13] Since then different concepts and tools have been introduced that have focused more heavily on the external environment or the firm's internal capabilities. However, in the final analysis an assessment of both is necessary as well as a judgment about the correspondence between the two.

Environmental Analysis Because we covered the external general and task environments in Chapter 3, we will not review them in any great detail here. Each one of the forces we covered in Chapter 3 can significantly affect the strategy a firm might develop, as well as whether the firm is likely to succeed or fail.[14] As we discussed in Chapter 3, while both general and task environment forces are important, often forces in the task environment have a more immediate impact on firm performance. Specifically, the forces associated with competitors are of particular importance when thinking about a company's strategy.[15] As a consequence, the forces related to competitors such as the nature of rivalry, new entrants, and substitution covered in Michael Porter's framework are relevant.

In addition, the tool and concept of customer value proposition is important to examine. A **value proposition** is essentially the ratio of what customers get from a firm to how much they pay relative to alternatives from competitors. Clearly, customers can get many things that they value from a particular product or service. If the product is a car, customers get a certain level of performance, reliability, styling, and so on. For that, they have to pay a price. The key question from a strategic management perspective is, "How much of what the customer really wants do I provide and at what price relative to my competitors?" One of the problems identified in the "dot-com bomb," or the implosion of the Internet bubble in 2000, was that many of the companies just did not have a compelling value proposition.[16]

To illustrate, let's simplify things a little. Let's say that you are in the automobile business. Further, let's say that what customers really care about is reliability. Assuming we have objective measures of reliability, such as repair expenses per 10,000 miles driven, we can actually draw the value propositions by plotting differing reliability levels by the price of the car (see Exhibit 6.4). The diagonal line represents essentially equal value. That is, as you move up the line, you get greater reliability, but you pay for it. The customers who really value reliability are willing to pay a higher price for the car. Those who don't value reliability as highly prefer to pay less. But in terms of value, all points along the line are considered equal. From a strategic management perspective, what you care about is your relative position to competitors within a given customer segment. For the sake of illustration, we have divided customers into three segments: low, medium, and high value placed on reliability.

Let's say you produce cars of medium reliability. The attractiveness of the value proposition you present to customers is a function of where you are relative to competitors. In Exhibit 6.4, which company, A, B, or C, represents the best value for the customers? Clearly, it is company C. Company C has a lower price and higher reliability than either companies A or B. Now, of companies A and B, which represents the better value to customers? Actually, their value propositions are quite similar. Company B produces cars with higher

value proposition the ratio of what customers get from a firm to how much they pay relative to alternatives from competitors

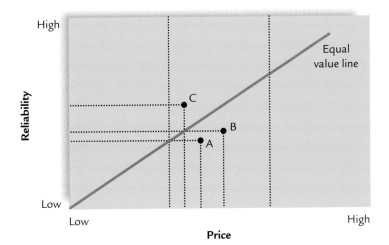

exhibit 6.4
Value Proposition for Three Car Companies

reliability than company A, but customers have to pay a higher price for the increase in quality. If you were company B, competing with companies A and C, where would you need to position yourself in order to offer a more competitive value proposition to your customers? In general, you would have to move up and to the left. In other words, you would have to lower your price and increase your reliability. Specifically, if you matched company C's price and beat it on reliability, you would then offer a superior value proposition, which should enhance your competitive position. You might do this by introducing a new technology that lowered your costs but increased reliability.

The bottom line is that any assessment of the external environment from a strategic management perspective must include an analysis of your competitors and your relative position to them. Although other tools can be used in this process, value proposition has become increasingly widespread because, in the final analysis, it is customers who determine what proposition provides the best value.

Organizational Analysis An analysis of the organization's internal capabilities is equally important to an analysis of its external environment. Of the various tools or frameworks for this purpose, the "value chain" approach proposed by Michael Porter is arguably one of the most cited and widely utilized.[17] The **value chain** is essentially a set of key activities that directly produce or support the production of what a firm ultimately offers to customers. Porter separates the internal components of a firm into five primary activities and four support activities (see Exhibit 6.5). The **primary activities** are those that are directly involved in the creation of a product or service and getting it into the hands of the customer and keeping it there. As the label suggests, **support activities** facilitate the creation of the product or service and its transfer to the customer. Porter stresses that rather than assessing the cost of these activities, managers must assess the value they add to the product or service to truly understand the firm's ability to compete. The absolute value of a product or service is a function of how much customers are willing to pay and how many customers are willing to purchase the product or service. A firm makes a profit if it can produce something whose value exceeds its costs. To determine where value is added in the firm's internal value chains, managers need to understand each of the nine activities in the chain.

Inbound Logistics This component of the value chain consists of activities that are designed to receive, store, and then disseminate various inputs to the products or services. Raw materials, receiving, transportation, inventory, information,

value chain a set of key activities that directly produce or support the production of what a firm ultimately offers to customers

primary activities activities that are directly involved in the creation of a product or service, getting it into the hands of the customer, and keeping it there

support activities activities that facilitate the creation of a product or service and its transfer to the customer

exhibit 6.5

The Value Chain

Source: Adapted from Michael Porter, *Competitive Advantage* (New York: Free Press, 1985).

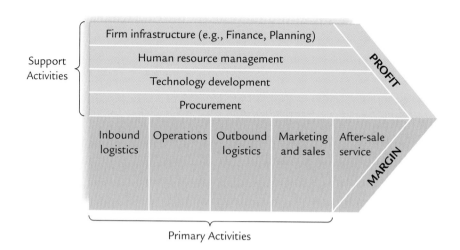

and so on are commonly a part of inbound logistics. In the beer industry, inbound logistics involve getting hops, barley, and malt to various brewing sites.

Operations A wide variety of activities are included within the operations component of the value chain. Activities that transform inputs into the products and services of the firm are at the heart of operations. In addition, activities (such as maintenance) that keep machines in working order would also be included in the operations segment of the value chain. In our beer example, operational issues may involve beer recipes for different products and markets as well as the process of bottling and labeling the products.

Outbound Logistics Simply stated, outbound logistics include activities that get the product or service from the firm to the customers. Our beer factory would need to warehouse the finished product, process the orders, schedule delivery trucks, and distribute its products (either directly or through distributors) to get the product delivered to stores, bars, ballparks, restaurants, and other places where it can be sold.

Marketing and Sales Marketing and sales activities are designed to let customers know about the products and services that are available and entice them to purchase what the firm has to offer. The beer manufacturer would need to advertise, promote its products, sell them, and price them.

Service Service activities are designed to keep the product in the hands of the customer after the purchase and increase the probability of a repeat purchase. Service activities may involve repair, supply of parts, installation, or product adjustment.

Each of these primary activities has associated costs. They enhance the firm's industry position and profitability if a customer is willing to pay more for them than they cost. The importance of the various activities changes depending on customer preferences. For example, in the fashion industry, customers often want the latest styles, colors, and fabrics as soon as possible. This places a premium on both inbound and outbound logistics to ensure that what is produced can be delivered quickly to customers.

In addition to the five primary activities, there are four support activities. As illustrated in Exhibit 6.5, these activities cut across all five of the primary activities; that is, elements of a given support activity facilitate each of the five primary activities.

Procurement The activity of procuring usable and consumable assets is found in each of the primary activities. For example, not only must raw materials used in products be purchased within inbound logistics, but also delivery trucks and scheduling software for the fleet must be purchased so that those materials can arrive for processing. The purchases of machinery and replacement parts are examples of specific procurement activities within operations. Firms often have purchasing departments, but procurement may be handled by various people, from purchasing agents to secretaries.

Technology Development Technology development revolves around expertise and the tools or equipment related to the exercise of that expertise. The technology may be as simple as a pencil for manually recording information or as complicated as a supercomputer and its software. Although technology development is concentrated on product development or process innovation, technology and the means by which it is applied to tasks also has an impact on all five primary activities.

Human Resource Management Given that no activity is completely removed from humans (even automatic processes and equipment are designed and implemented by someone), the process of acquiring, training, evaluating, compensating, and developing human resources is present in all five primary activities. Capable and motivated people can have a profound impact on all activities of a firm, so human resource management is a key support activity. In service firms such as law, consulting, or accounting firms, the quality of the people is what customers purchase. Therefore, this component of the value chain is critical to a service firm's fortune or failure.

Firm Infrastructure Although infrastructure usually brings plant, utilities, and equipment to mind, a firm's infrastructure has less to do with brick and mortar than with functions that support all primary activities. Infrastructure consists of planning, finance, accounting, legal, government relations, and other activities and the information supplied by these functions to the various primary activities. For example, legal information concerning worker safety standards may be needed in operations, and legal information on truth in advertising may be needed in marketing and sales.

Just as each primary activity has associated costs, so do the support activities. Support activities enhance the firm's position and profitability to the extent that they assist primary activities and contribute to final products or services that customers value. Like primary activities, the importance of the support activities also changes depending on customer preferences. Returning to our earlier example of the fashion industry, customers' preferences for the latest styles, colors, and fabrics may increase the importance of planning information in the value chain. Planning information that relates forecasting trends, buying seasons, and purchasing cycles to customer preferences would be valuable. Customer preferences might also increase the importance of technology development in support activity. For example, technology that allows clothes to be dyed after they have been knit into a sweater rather than in the yarn stage would add value. This is exactly what Benneton of Italy has done so that the latest color preferences can be incorporated as late in the manufacturing process as possible. That way there is less time for a mismatch to occur between the changing preferences of customers and the colors delivered by Benneton.

The value chain framework can facilitate your ability to assess what resources you have and how well they are working to deliver value to the customer. One of the benefits of the value chain framework is that it enables you to work through a systematic and reasonably comprehensive analysis without becoming completely overwhelmed. Except for the most simple and small of businesses, it would be easy to miss examining critical aspects of the company.

Leveraging the Value Chain Knowing your firm's value chain is one thing; leveraging for an advantage in the marketplace is quite another. The first step in managing the value chain for greater profits and performance is to determine where in your value chain you have the potential to add the greatest value. If we return to our beer example, let's say that our German customers value a rich-tasting beer and that they are less sensitive to price. If the flavor of beer is largely determined by the quality of the ingredients and that ingredient quality varies widely, we know we need to concentrate on procurement. We must be sure that we have the highest-quality ingredients. Further, let's suppose that being able to identify high-quality ingredients is primarily a function of experienced buyers who can see, smell, and taste quality differences. Now we know that we must be sure that our human resource management systems are superior in terms of recruiting, selecting, and training these ingredient buyers. The power of the value chain model is that it helps us segment business activities and see the important linkages. However, the model per se does not tell us which specific activities add the most value or which linkages among activities are the most important. That all comes from our analysis.

Recent research has suggested that to fully understand a firm's competitive position and advantage, not only do you need to analyze the firm's value chain but how suppliers, distributors, and other business partners fit into a "value net."[18] Because of the increasingly tight connections between firms and suppliers, distributors, and other business partners, the strengths and weaknesses of partners throughout the entire value network affect the competitive position and advantage of a given firm.[19]

Resource-Based Approach The resource-based approach to strategy acknowledges the importance of the external environment but places emphasis on recognizing and then exploiting the internal strengths of the company.[20] A couple of simple analogies may help illustrate this. Suppose you had a group of gifted orchestra musicians. Even if there were lots of customers for jazz music, the resource-based approach would argue against trying to turn these orchestra musicians into jazz musicians. Likewise, it would not make sense to design a passing offense as a strategy in American football if you had a great running back but a quarterback with a terrible throwing arm.

But the resource-based approach to strategy does not assume that you are forever stuck where you are.[21] It does argue, however, that the resources you build or add should deliver competitive advantage. In other words, they should be ones at which you are superior (or can become superior); ones that are hard to copy and durable; ones that cannot be easily substituted; and ones that allow you to capture above-normal profits. Once you have a clear idea of the resources you have, can develop, and have the potential to give you a competitive advantage in the marketplace, then you can begin to formulate a strategic plan as to how to leverage these resources.

You have no doubt noticed that both the core competency and resource approaches share two common elements—value and difficult to imitate. This should not surprise us given that logically, to have an advantage over competitors you must offer customers what they perceive as value, and to sustain that advantage what you offer must be hard for others to duplicate.

Core Competencies While the value chain model helps managers analyze activities and where the firm creates the greatest value, the concept of **core competency** focuses on an interrelated set of activities that can deliver competitive advantage not just in the short-term but into the future. Two scholars, Prahalad and Hammel, argued that competencies that should be considered core would (1) provide access to a wide variety of markets, (2) significantly contribute to perceived customer benefits of the end products or services, and (3) be difficult for competitors to imitate.[22]

As an example, Honda believes that one of its core competencies is the technology behind and the manufacturing of combustion engines. Let's examine this competency in light of these three tests. First, combustion engines have the potential to apply to a wide variety of markets and products. In fact, this has led Honda to produce products that started in motorcycles and now extends to cars, scooters, lawnmowers, snowblowers, and small electricity generators, among other things. Second, the performance of combustion in engines creates results that customers value. For example, better combustion performance can result in significantly better acceleration in cars and motorcycles. Third, combustion technology is hard to imitate. This is partly why Honda moved its engines into various car racing leagues such as Indy and even Formula One.

> **core competency** focuses on an interrelated set of activities that can deliver competitive advantage in the short term and into the future

> **Core Competencies by Michael Hitt**
> **Q&A**
> One**Key**
> www.prenhall.com/onekey

Integrating Internal and External Analyses

Although a variety of tools and techniques can help you integrate your internal and external analyses, in the sections that follow, we review three well-known ones: product life cycle, portfolio, and SWOT analyses.

Product Life Cycle Analysis In considering internal resources or external market conditions, it is important to keep in mind that any snapshot you might take internally or externally needs to be placed in the reality of a moving picture of competition. One of the tools that can help place snapshots in context is the product life cycle analysis. Like people, products go through a life cycle that starts with birth and ends with decline (see Exhibit 6.6). When a product is first born, or developed, it is similar to a baby—it needs constant care and does not produce much. During the birth period, most products provide very little revenue and yet require significant investments of time and money. Revenues during this early stage are provided by "early adopters," or consumers who buy products before they are widely accepted in the marketplace.

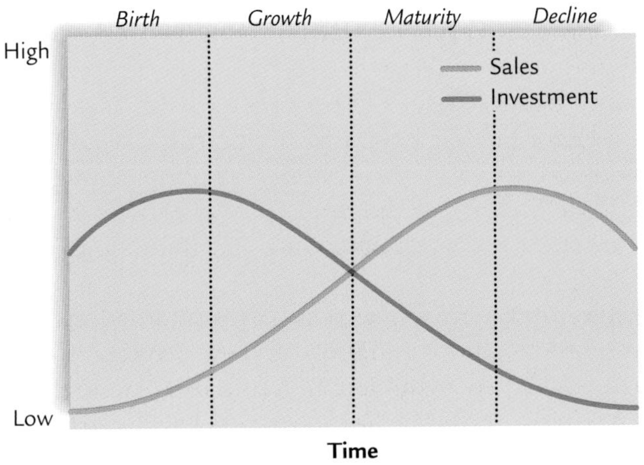

exhibit 6.6
Product Life Cycle

Krispy Kreme doughnuts were first sold in 1937 as part of a family-owned business, which was franchised decades later. In the 1990s, the Krispy Kreme fever gripped the United States. Instead of letting the brand decline as it naturally would in the course of the product life cycle, Krispy Kreme smartly expanded its operations into other countries. The company opened its first store abroad in Toronto in 2001, followed by stores in Mexico, Australia, and the United Kingdom. The Krispy Kreme shown in this photo is located in Harrod's, a London department store. Unfortunately, the low carbohydrate diet craze has recently limited Krispy Kreme's profits. It is not clear if this is a passing fad or if it will have a long-term effect on the success of the doughnut maker.

Often these early adopters can provide valuable information on product or service characteristics that can help broaden product acceptance. This in turn enhances the next stage—growth.

The steepness and height of the life cycle line during the growth period are primarily a function of how quickly and how widely customers accept the product.[23] The degree to which a firm can exploit economies of scale is one of the most important factors that influences the extent of investment needed during the growth stage.[24] The greater the economies of scale, the relatively less investment required during the growth stage. For example, it takes approximately $2 billion to build a new fabrication plant for a microprocessing chip. However, once that initial investment is made, it takes comparatively much less money to produce millions of chips during the growth stage.

The mature stage of the product life cycle occurs when the product or service produces its greatest profits.[25] During this stage, the highest levels of revenues and lowest costs per unit are achieved.

Unless a product is rejuvenated, it typically enters the decline stage because new products or services make it obsolete. The extent to which the new products are "better" (faster, cheaper, more powerful, longer lasting, etc.) is an important factor in how steep the decline curve will be. Switching cost (which we discussed in Chapter 3) is often another powerful factor. The lower the switching costs, the steeper the decline curve. Obviously, significant new product features and low switching costs could combine to produce a steep and dramatic decline.

One of the most attractive aspects of an international marketplace is that, for a given product, firms can seek out new markets to start the product life cycle all over again (see Exhibit 6.7). A firm can extend the life of a product by taking it international. The key to success for this strategy is managers' abilities to correctly identify countries whose sociocultural, technological, eco-

exhibit 6.7
International Product Life Cycles

nomic, and political conditions match the product and to identify any modifications that could be accomplished economically and would enhance its acceptance in a particular country.[26]

A Manager's Challenge ("Flashback, Flash Forward: The Long-Lived VW Beetle") discusses a product—the original VW Beetle—that was kept alive for half a century by the international marketplace. In fact, in this example not only did the international markets keep the VW Beetle alive, but they kept it alive long enough that it was reborn as the new Beetle. While there are clear and intended similarities between the look of the old and new Beetles, everything else (engine, steering, brakes, suspension) is virtually brand new. You might even ask yourself if this rebirth would have been possible without the extended life that international markets gave the product.

In summary, product life cycle analysis helps you examine the product and how it matches its environment to estimate the likely shape of its life cycle curve. Having an idea of a product's life cycle—the steepness of the curve and how long each stage will last—can significantly enhance your ability to plan properly for increases or decreases in equipment purchases, workforce size, advertising, or distribution.

Portfolio Analysis In many ways, portfolio analysis is an extension of product life cycle concepts. It starts with the assumption that a firm has multiple products and that those products are at different stages of their life cycles. Portfolio analysis has two basic parts. The first is focused on determining where various products currently are in their life cycles. Based on this analysis, the second part is focused on creating corporate strategic plans for where the firm ought to place its investments.

One of the earliest portfolio analysis techniques was the BCG matrix, developed by the Boston Consulting Group. This tool requires managers to assess the market attractiveness of a particular product or business and the attractiveness of its current position in the market, primarily in terms of market share (see Exhibit 6.8).

Products or strategic business units (SBUs are units that are considered strategically important and typically have profit and loss accountability) that have relatively low market share in unattractive markets are classified as **dogs**. These products are often in the decline stage of their life cycle. If a way cannot be found to teach the old dog a new trick, the product or business is often sold or shut down. For example, 5-and-1/4-inch diskettes and drives were made in the millions and made millions in profits during the 1980s, but they were dog products in the 1990s.

dogs products or SBUs that have relatively low market share in unattractive markets

globalization *a manager's challenge*

Flashback, Flash Forward: The Long-Lived VW Beetle

Peace, Flower Power, and Disney's Herbie the Love Bug were all components of the 1960s. The fading of these things from the social scene in the 1970s may have been of little consequence to many, but the decline of consumer interest in the Beetle posed a significant problem for Volkswagen. Back in the 1960s, when the Volkswagen Beetle was introduced, it was one of the best-selling cars of the times. It had an odd but endearing shape. It got good gas mileage and was fairly reliable. When it broke down, it was easy to fix. Unfortunately for VW, Japanese manufacturers offered a better value proposition. For nearly the same price, consumers could purchase significantly more reliable cars. These cars caught consumers' eyes but blindsided Volkswagen.

Because the United States was the biggest market for the car, VW could have simply accepted the market loss and killed the Beetle. Instead, management looked at the life cycle of the car and other markets. After assessing its options, Volkswagen selected Brazil as the next market for the Beetle. Brazil was chosen for several reasons. First, it was a developing country with an automobile market clamoring for affordable but reliable cars. Second, Brazil's roads were not in very good condition, and the four-wheel independent suspension of the Beetle was ideal for rough roads. (This was one of the reasons the Beetle was a car of choice for off-road races like those shown in Disney's "Love Bug" movies.)

Because the Beetle was well matched to market conditions in Brazil, it achieved a popularity there nearly as strong as it had enjoyed in the United States 15 years earlier. Volkswagen produced the Beetle in Brazil until the mid-1980s.

When the car's popularity declined in Brazil and production ceased, Volkswagen moved its production to Mexico. Customers there had been purchasing "bugs" since 1964. Producing them in Mexico allowed Volkswagen to capture more of the Mexican market by avoiding import duties and other restrictions.

Surprisingly, Volkswagen reopened production in Brazil in 1993, with hopes of again marketing the Beetle in the United States. However, here Volkswagen may have tried to squeeze too much from a product that was in the declining stages of its life cycle. The reintroduction of the Beetle in the United States did not approach the peak of its first appearance. Convinced there was still interest in the original concept in the United States and other countries, VW undertook a thorough research program to find out how people of all ages, income levels, and lifestyles felt about the car. Based on the results, the company totally redesigned the Beetle. It changed the styling, suspension, and engine, and even moved the trunk from the front to the back.

The reintroduction of the car in the late 1990s was a huge success, boosting VW sales dramatically over its 1985 levels. Back orders were common, and discounts were nowhere to be found. In fact, demand was so strong that some dealers were able to sell Beetles above the suggested list price. The redesigned car rolled away with several coveted awards, including North American Car of the Year, *Motor Trend*'s Import Car of the Year, and *Money Magazine*'s Best Car of the Year, and it was the only car in its class to achieve a five-star safety rating. In early 2002, Volkswagen unveiled a new Beetle Turbo S, the most powerful and sports-equipped "bug" ever available in the United States.

Volkswagen's successful reintroduction of the Beetle depended on its' correctly reading the product's life cycle relative to the countries in which it was sold and making the right changes to attract a new segment of the marketplace. But all good things must come to an end, or so the saying goes. In 2003, because of falling demand, Volkswagen ended production of the original Beetle in Mexico. The company's remarkable ability to extend the product's life cycle, however, has allowed the brand to outlive most other car models by decades. Alas, the original Beetle is finally dead. But its offspring lives on.

Sources: Keith Crain, "Say Goodbye to an Old Friend," *Automotive News*, July 14, 2003, p. 12; Volkswagen press releases, April 4, 2001 and January 4, 2002; David Kelly, *Getting the Bugs Out* (New York: John Wiley & Sons, 2001); Jerry Dubrowski, "VW Unveils New Beetle," Cable News Network online, January 5, 1998; Casey Wian, "Beetle Mania Spreads," Cable News Network online, May 5, 1998; Gregory L. White, "U.S. Car Sales Jumped by 6% in September," *Wall Street Journal*, October 6, 1998, pp. A3, A8; "Volkswagen U.S. September Sales Best Since 1985," *Reuters Limited*, October 2, 1998.

question marks products or SBUs that have relatively low market share in attractive markets

Products or SBUs that have relatively low market share in attractive markets are classified as **question marks**. Managers need to find a way to increase their share of the market, be satisfied with a relatively small share, or get out. You may wonder, "If we're in an attractive market, why would we exit?" The answer is typically found in the internal organizational analysis. For

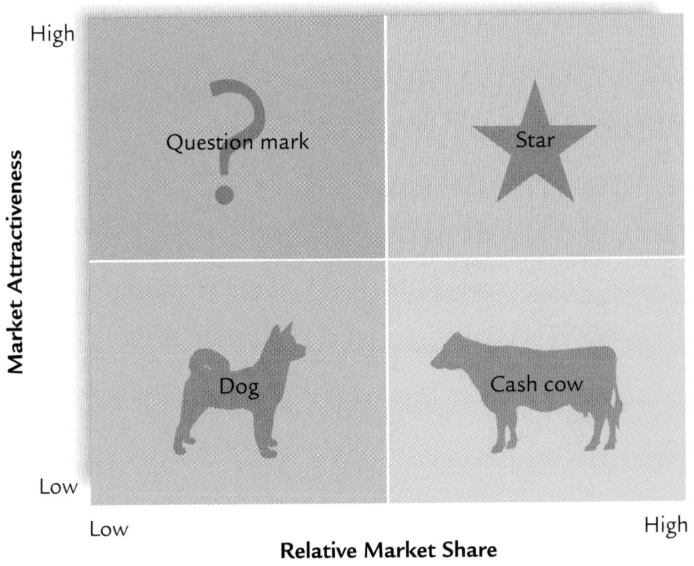

exhibit 6.8
BCG Matrix

example, you would choose to exit an attractive market because you simply do not have the capabilities or resources to be successful, including such things as technology or capital to invest. In the early 1990s, CDs and CD-ROM drives looked like hot markets, but they required different technology and manufacturing capabilities than 5-and-1/4-inch diskettes or disk drives. As a consequence, only a few leading companies, such as Sony, were able to readily make a successful transition to the new products.

Products or SBUs that have relatively high market share in markets with unattractive futures are classified as **cash cows**. In this case, managers need to feed the cow enough to keep it alive but milk it for all it is worth. Cash cow products or businesses are typically at the maturity stage of their life cycle. Often, the excess cash that is generated is used to fund investments in question marks or promising new products. For example, 3-and-1/2-inch diskettes and disk drives were considered cash cow products for the mid- and late 1990s and the money was used to fund new products such as read/write CD drives and disks.

Stars are products that have relatively high market share in markets with attractive futures. Typically, stars are in the birth or growth stages of their life cycle. As we discussed in the section on product life cycles, the birth and growth stages usually require the highest investments of time and money. While CDs and CD-ROM drives might have been considered question marks for Sony in the early 1990s, they were considered star products later in the decade. However, the introduction of the MP3 player soon followed. Today, some experts predict that in only five years' time, CDs will become as scarce as vinyl records.

The basic idea behind portfolio analysis is to make sure that the corporation is diversified and does not have too many dogs, does not spend too much time on question marks, and has enough cash cows to fund the future stars. The exact products or businesses that constitute a balanced portfolio change over time. Some stars may mature and become cash cows or even decline and become dogs.

The same basic idea of analyzing market attractiveness and your firm's capabilities and strengths can also be used to construct an international portfolio analysis and plan (see Exhibit 6.9). In constructing a matrix such as in the

cash cows products or SBUs that have relatively high market share in markets with unattractive futures

stars products that have relatively high market share in markets with attractive futures

exhibit 6.9
International Matrix

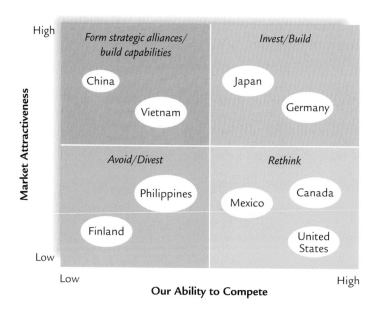

exhibit, you essentially assess the attractiveness of different countries and your ability to compete in those markets. In this context, dogs are markets that are unattractive, for which you have a low ability to compete successfully. For example, in Exhibit 6.9, Finland and the Philippines are dog markets for our hypothetical company. The strategic planning and management implication here is to avoid dog markets and, if you are in one of these markets, to get out.

Markets that are unattractive but in which you have strong competitive capabilities require some rethinking (United States, Mexico, and Canada in Exhibit 6.9). You need to ask questions such as, "Do those markets have segments that could be attractive? Can we introduce new products that leverage our current strengths?" If nothing can be done to make the market more attractive, the company should milk its current products while preparing to exit the market.

If particular markets are attractive (China and Vietnam in Exhibit 6.9), but you have low competitive capabilities, you have two basic options. First, you can form strategic alliances with partners who have capabilities you lack and who can benefit from those you have. Second, you can take the time and money to build the capabilities you need to compete in the market. For example, China might represent a very attractive market for your new beverage product, but you lack managers who understand the Chinese distribution system. You can take on a partner who has this understanding, or you can train or hire managers with this understanding.

Finally, you should invest and build in markets that are attractive and in which you can be competitive (Japan and Germany in Exhibit 6.9). These "star" markets can provide significant revenues in the future.

In summary, most **portfolio analysis** techniques are designed to assist you in assessing the attractiveness of a market (within a country or across countries) and your current or potential competitive position in that market. Thus, these techniques bring together many of the insights gained from the external and internal analyses discussed in the previous sections.

SWOT Analysis This approach to competitive analysis requires managers to consider their firm's strengths and weaknesses as well as any opportunities and threats for its continued operation. **SWOT analysis** stands for strengths,

portfolio analysis techniques designed to assist managers in assessing the attractiveness of a market

SWOT analysis requires managers to consider their firm's **S**trengths, **W**eaknesses, **O**pportunities, and **T**hreats for its continued operation

weaknesses, opportunities, and threats. SWOT analysis is more a basic framework than a specific strategic planning tool.[27] In conducting a SWOT analysis, you first evaluate your firm's strengths. Next, you evaluate your firm's weaknesses. In doing so the frameworks of core competencies and resource analysis can be of great help. Alternatively, you might utilize the value chain framework previously discussed to work through an analysis of your firm's strengths and weaknesses. For example, what parts of the value chain do you do well? Sourcing? Marketing? What do you perform poorly? Customer service? Public relations?

Once you have considered your firm's internal environment, SWOT analysis requires you to then move to the external environment. First, you ask, "What are the opportunities facing our firm?" Insights gained from a product life cycle analysis or portfolio analysis can help address this part of the SWOT analysis. For example, what products or businesses are about to enter the growth stage? What countries have conditions conducive to growth of particular products or businesses? Also, insights gained from using the five-forces framework discussed in Chapter 3 can help identify not only potential opportunities but threats as well within your industry. For example, new products that could become substitutes for your products or new entrants into your markets could constitute serious threats.

The important insights of a SWOT analysis come only after you examine the matches and mismatches between the organization's strengths and weaknesses and the environment's opportunities and threats. For example, Wal-Mart (the largest retail organization in the world, with over $250 billion in sales) currently has many international opportunities.[28] Wal-Mart's strengths include the ability to get large volumes of products to customers at low prices. However, as a result of its strong focus on the U.S. market, very few Wal-Mart managers have experience or knowledge of foreign markets. Fortunately for Wal-Mart, few competitors can capture immediately these international opportunities; however Wal-Mart must be careful not to wait too long in pursuing international expansion opportunities because Carrefour, a French discount

Wal-Mart is the world's biggest retailer with over $250 billion in sales annually—more than the GDP of some countries—giving the company considerable strength in the SWOT paradigm. However, the Arkansas-based powerhouse faced serious threats from retailers abroad who were more familiar with the local competitive landscape when it tried to expand internationally. To counter that weakness, Wal-Mart formed partnerships with foreign retailers and also acquired established foreign retail chains.

retailer, is also expanding internationally. This very simple SWOT analysis may explain why Wal-Mart has responded to international opportunities, but not at a frantic pace. In 2003 Wal-Mart had more than 3,200 stores in the United States, over 625 in Mexico, over 200 in Canada, roughly 100 in Germany, 20 in Puerto Rico, 15 in Brazil, 11 in Argentina, and 31 in China across its main store brands (primarily Wal-Mart, Sam's Club). Wal-Mart knows that if an opportunity to make money exists in these foreign markets, a competitor will seek them out. To effectively respond, Wal-Mart has utilized partners with knowledge of specific international markets, developed managers within Wal-Mart, hired people who can help it expand internationally, and simply bought existing operations in various countries such as Germany, where it bought 21 Wertkauf stores.

STRATEGIC MANAGEMENT PROCESS: STRATEGY IMPLEMENTATION

Once a strategy has been formulated, it must be effectively implemented for desired results to materialize. Some evidence indicates that an average strategy superbly implemented is better than a great strategy poorly implemented.[29] Consequently, strategy implementation is at least as important as strategy formulation. Consider the case of Kathy Freeman at Ashland Consulting (in A Manager's Challenge, "Changing Strategy at Ashland Consulting"). It can be a great strategy to decide to switch from doing lots of small projects for many clients to doing more involved projects for fewer clients. After all, there is a learning curve consultants have to follow regarding a client—its industry, competitors, products, value chain, internal resources, and so on. The further up that curve you go, the higher the mountain a competing consultancy has to climb. To the extent that these greater insights into the client allow you to give better advice, the more value you will provide to the client. Thus, we have some basic ingredients for competitive advantage. However, if key managers such as Kathy Freeman cannot change their behavior and translate that strategy into action and get it effectively implemented, in practical terms the strategy is no more valuable than the paper it is printed on. At the same time, this translation has personal implications. Freeman must change aspects of herself as well as her team if she is to be successful. What do you see as the key changes for implementing the new strategy successfully?

Seven S's

Perhaps the most widely used strategy implementation framework is that developed by one of the largest and best-known strategy consulting firms— McKinsey Consulting. About 20 years ago, McKinsey discovered that when many of its clients implemented strategic plans that it recommended, things actually got worse for the clients. McKinsey realized that having clients do worse when they follow your advice is not the way to build a successful consulting firm. What emerged from McKinsey's efforts to unravel this mystery was the Seven S framework (see Exhibit 6.10).

Essentially, McKinsey discovered that the reason clients were doing worse when they implemented the new strategies was because the strategies were being implemented within old structures, shared values, systems, skills,

Change

Changing Strategy at Ashland Consulting

Kathy Freeman could hardly believe it had been only five years since she graduated from a state university in California with her B.S. in business and joined Ashland Consulting, a small firm specializing in strategic consulting. During those five years, she had advanced from research associate to associate consultant to consulting team leader. As team leader, Freeman was now responsible for a team of four people specializing in strategic market entry projects, and she reported directly to one of the five senior partners.

Recently, Freeman and all the other employees in the firm had participated in a two-day company retreat. During those two days, the senior partners had outlined the new strategic vision and plan for the company. In the past, the firm had focused on clients in the Bay Area near San Francisco and the states of Oregon and Washington. Additionally, the firm had somewhat specialized in consulting for firms interested in expanding into Asian markets and helping Asian firms, especially Japanese firms, set up subsidiaries in the western United States. The senior partners believed that the firm needed to broaden its geographical scope beyond the West Coast and Asia and expand its offerings beyond new-market entry.

In the past, the firm's revenues came primarily from doing many small projects for a variety of clients. The new vision called for doing more involved projects and doing more projects for fewer clients. Essentially, the rationale was that Ashland could add more value, and therefore be harder for competitors to dislodge, if it focused on fewer clients and developed much deeper relationships with them. This involved a shift from short-term project focus to long-term relationship development and management, as well as a shift from specialized projects (i.e., market entry) to more general strategic consulting.

Freeman saw three major challenges related to this change in strategy. First, she would have to translate these general, new strategic directions into concrete goals and activities for her team. Second, she would need to help her team members identify their strengths and weaknesses relative to the requirements of the new strategy and help them with a development plan. Third, if she was to do these first two tasks well, she would also need to change and adapt herself. Freeman's background gave her specialized skills and knowledge in market entry, particularly in Japan. She had lived and worked in Japan and spoke the language. This set of skills had served her well under the old strategy. However, if she did not change, they might become liabilities or at least limitations under the new strategy.

To help translate the general strategy into concrete goals and actions, Freeman held a one-hour meeting with her team members. During the meeting she briefly restated what the old strategy had been and what the new strategy was, as well as the underlying rationale for it. She then asked her team to discuss what implications they saw for themselves as a result of the new strategy. Quickly, several team members mentioned that they would need to broaden their base of competencies from market entry to such areas as joint ventures, alliances, restructuring, and so on.

After the team meeting, Freeman reviewed the team's past clients to look for repeat customers or other indications of potential for deeper client relationships. She identified three firms out of the 15 or so that her team had worked with over the last 24 months.

She next called a meeting with the team to get their ideas about how they might develop deeper relationships with these repeat clients. One of the most promising ideas was to make some unsolicited bids on projects. Several team members had heard of projects the clients were undertaking in the near future on which Ashland might bid.

After this meeting, Freeman realized that she would need to undertake significant changes in how she managed her team's performance plans as well as her own. It was clear that for the team to succeed in forming stronger relationships with fewer clients across a broader area of strategic consulting, both she and her team members would need to change and develop new competencies. None of this development was currently present in any of her team members' or her own personal performance goals. This needed to change and be corrected.

Still, it would not be possible for her or any of her team members to be equally good at all the required competencies, at least not for a while. Her next big managerial task would be to crystallize her thoughts about what each team member should add to his or her skill set and set her own development priorities. The challenge would be to find the right set at the intersection of what development areas represented individual interests and strengths and what would serve the strategy and client best. For example, in her own case, Freeman was great at receiving RFPs (Request for Proposal) from clients and then responding. She was not good at probing for potential consulting opportunities. This was a needed skill if she was to get more work with fewer, focused clients. However, by personality, Freeman enjoyed the more defined and concrete aspects of responding to RFPs compared to the more ambiguous activity of general relationship building and probing for opportunities. Still, she could see that she would need to change if she was to manage herself and her team to success under the new strategy.

exhibit 6.10

Seven S Model

Source: Richard Pascale, *Managing on the Edge* (New York: Simon & Schuster, 1990).

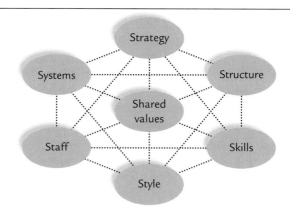

1. **Strategy**—Plan or course of action leading to the allocation of firm's resources to reach identified goals.

2. **Structure**—The ways people and tasks relate to each other. The basic grouping of reporting relationships and activities. The way separate entities of an organization are linked.

3. **Shared Values**—The significant meanings or guiding concepts that give purpose and meaning to the organization.

4. **Systems**—Formal processes and procedures, including management control systems, performance measurement and reward systems, and planning and budgeting systems, and the ways people relate to them.

5. **Skills**—Organizational competencies, including the abilities of individuals as well as management practices, technological abilities, and other capabilities that reside in the organization.

6. **Style**—The leadership style of management and the overall operating style of the organization. A reflection of the norms people act upon and how they work and interact with each other, vendors, and customers.

7. **Staff**—Recruitment, selection, development, socialization, and advancement of people in the organization.

styles, and staff. These old aspects of the organization were inconsistent with the new strategy. Like a body that rejects an incompatible new organ, the old aspects of the organization worked against, overwhelmed, and in practical terms rejected the new strategy.

The Seven S McKinsey framework asserts that while each S is important, it is the congruence and fit among them that is critical. For example, IBM has a strategy of leveraging solutions developed for one client, such as Bank of Tokyo-Mitsubishi, for other clients in the same industry, such as Citibank. This strategy requires significant sharing of information across organizational units. First, to be successful, a structure must facilitate full and timely information exchange. Second, success also requires organizational members who trust each other and who value sharing information. Third, compensation systems must reward people on more than their personal results because the positive effects of their information sharing could easily show up in another unit or even another country. Fourth, effective information sharing also requires data gathering, analysis, and dissemination skills. People are not necessarily gifted in all these activities. Fifth, there are key positions where information is generated and transferred. Staff with the highest information skills must be placed in these critical positions. Finally, the leadership style of senior managers must be consistent with the other aspects of the model. This simplified but true example helps illustrate that the key to successful strategy implementation is having an internal organization that is consistent with and supportive of the strategy.

STRATEGIC MANAGEMENT PROCESS: STRATEGY EVALUATION

The final step in the strategic management process is evaluation. Just as evaluation and feedback can improve individual performance, so can they enhance organizational performance. When a small number of managers are responsible for the organization's strategic, tactical, or operational objectives, their individual performance evaluations can often provide a rough indication of how the organization is doing. If the individual's personal objectives are tied directly to operational objectives and they are all meeting or exceeding their goals, the organization as a whole is likely meeting its operational objectives. Most organizations carry out annual or even quarterly organizational performance evaluations. Typically, the strategic results are given to the more senior executives, and the operational results are disseminated principally to lower-level managers. Like individual feedback, organizational performance evaluation is used to reinforce efforts that have contributed to desired results and to correct those that have not.

STRATEGY AS PATTERN

To this point in this chapter we have presented strategic management from the dominant view that it is and should be a rational, conscious plan of action. This perspective is not universally shared, not even in Western firms. As pointed out earlier, many cultures believe that humans do not control their destiny and that strategic management is a vanity born of not knowing one's place in the universe. But even if we do accept the perspective of using planning and strategy as rational, conscious, and purposeful action, we often may not act on that belief. Scholars such as Henry Mintzberg have argued that strategies often emerge from patterned behavior rather than from planned and intended actions.[30]

According to Mintzberg, observers often assume that the actions an organization took were planned and intended. Also, journalists often impute a strategy to a corporation based on observed patterns of actions, whether the managers who took those actions had those purposes in mind or not. Mintzberg argues that often the pattern results from a string of actions rather than intentions and explicit plans. That is, certain actions were reinforced by positive consequences, and they were repeated and expanded only as long as positive consequences continued. In turn, these patterns were interpreted by observers as intended. Sometimes even organizational members later interpret these patterns as though they were intended from the outset. Thus, even in firms with managers who believe in planning and strategic management, strategy may come from actions that had positive consequences rather than intentions. Floris A. Maljers, former chairman of the board of Unilever, echoes the view of strategy as pattern:

> *Unilever is often described as one of the foremost transnational companies. Yet our organization of diverse operations around the world is not the outcome of a conscious effort . . . the company has evolved mainly through a Darwinian system of retaining what was useful and rejecting what no longer worked—in other words, through actual practice as a business responding to the marketplace.[31]*

Mintzberg points out that we need to recognize the existence of both *deliberate* strategies and *emergent* strategies. The importance of this distinction is that deliberate strategies focus our attention on analyzing key factors in the domestic and international environment and trying to plan for the future. In contrast, emergent strategies focus our attention on the consequences of past and present actions. An awareness of both influences allows us to focus on the past, present, *and* future and incorporate our own judgments and the environment when we assess what works or doesn't work in the competitive marketplace.

managerial perspectives revisited

PERSPECTIVE 1: THE ORGANIZATIONAL CONTEXT While an assessment of the external environment is critical to any formulation of strategy, effective strategy cannot be formulated without consideration of the organization. External environments are influential but they are not deterministic. In other words, environments are not the sole determinant of successful strategies. From a resource-based or even a core competency approach to strategy, appropriate strategy is derived in part from the advantages within the organization. For example, Disney theme parks would be crazy to ignore the culture of customer service it has built up over the years as it competes with companies such as Six Flags. At the same time, great customer service without an emphasis on its characters such as Mickey Mouse or Winnie the Pooh would likely not draw as many people to its theme parks. Its characters constitute a very important internal resource. However, even "fit" approaches to strategy call for a careful consideration of the requirements and resources of the organization. This is in part why Six Flags has created a relationship with Warner Brothers to license its characters (Bugs Bunny and others) for use in its parks. In addition to attracting teenagers to its well-known thrill rides, Six Flags wants to use the Warner Brothers cartoon characters to attract younger kids and their parents. However, while virtually all kids know that Mickey Mouse is a Disney character, few automatically associate Bugs Bunny with Six Flags.

PERSPECTIVE 2: THE HUMAN FACTOR While it is possible for a strategy to be formulated by a single individual or a small group, it is not possible for it to be implemented except with and through others. British Airlines' senior executive team can decide that the company's new strategy will focus on superior customer service but until gate agents, flight attendants, reservation agents, and others actually change their behavior and provide superior service to customers, the strategy has little impact on the financial performance of the company. This is why strategy implementation through others is one of the most critical activities of managers. Sometimes those not involved in the formulation of the strategy fail to recognize the critical role they play in its actual success by implementing it effectively through their subordinates. Imagine Ashland Consulting's success at changing its strategy if lower-level managers such as Kathy Freeman are not able to see what the strategy means for her and her team and if she cannot get her team to change their focus and behavior.

PERSPECTIVE 3: MANAGING PARADOXES One concern in formulating strategies that presents a potential paradox to managers is the tension of being committed to a strategy over the long term versus being responsive to changes in the organization's environment. If management changed strategies too frequently, it is likely that employees (as well as customers, suppliers, and shareholders) would have difficulty achieving a coordinated action. Furthermore, no strategy would be fully realized. It typically takes some time for a strategy to be communicated and implemented by the organization's employees. It takes time for a strategy to have an effect in the market. As we pointed out with the example of British Airlines, quite often the financial impact of the strategy is not realized until most of the employees change their behavior to fit with the strategy. On the other hand, aspects of the environment do change. In fact, the current competitive environment for many organizations is highly dynamic. New technologies emerge, new competitors arise, laws and regulations change, and so on. If a strategy becomes too rigid or if management keeps a given strategy too long when the environment is changing rapidly, that inflexibility can threaten the very survival of a company. For example, many believe that Lucent's sticking with digital technology and delayed reaction to photonic technology was a major reason the firm suffered financially from 2000 to 2003 and lost 80 percent of its market value. Polaroid changed too slowly to use the digital technology in photography and eventually lost the market for its products to new competitors.

4

PERSPECTIVE 4: ENTREPRENEURIAL MIND-SET   One reason that firms do not change their strategies as needed is because they are not entrepreneurial. That is, they are not continuously searching for new opportunities in the market. Thus, their managers lack an entrepreneurial mind-set. Gary Hamel, former scholar and now a prominent strategy consultant, argues that the firms likely to win in the current competitive landscape are bold and innovative in all areas of their business.[32] To respond to this need, others have argued that organizations can engage in strategic entrepreneurship. That is, they simultaneously search for new opportunities (entrepreneurial) and take actions to gain and sustain competitive advantages (strategic).[33] Strategic entrepreneurship is important for managers and employees. They need to be committed to innovation as a means of gaining or maintaining a competitive advantage. Managers can only master this and other balancing acts if they are committed to developing the required conceptual and practical skills. For many managers the ambiguity associated with entrepreneurial opportunities and the competitive actions in the market necessary to gain a competitive advantage requires additional commitment to become more tolerant of ambiguity. In fact, this ability has been identified in several studies of effective leaders who must both formulate and implement strategies effectively.[34] Perhaps the greatest commitment is that which is required to implement and follow through on a strategic change. Yet, a commitment to strategic change is a part of an entrepreneurial mind-set.

concluding comments

Because strategic management is a process of determining where the organization wants to go and how it will successfully compete, it is a critical managerial function. The logic that senior managers must understand the strategic management process is self-evident. Yet it is equally important for entry-level managers to understand the process. Entry-level managers may not be involved in strategy formulation for the entire company, but they must implement the strategy for it to succeed. Furthermore, entry-level managers need to know what the corporate-, business-, or operational-level strategies are in order to make decisions that support overall strategic objectives. Managers make many daily decisions, and those decisions can have a complementary or conflicting impact on the overall direction and performance of the organization. So, it is important that they make informed decisions; it is too costly to monitor all managers to determine whether their decisions and actions are consistent with the overall strategy. Rather, they can be more effective and efficient when they are guided by a clear understanding of strategic management process in general and the strategy of the company in particular. In addition, part of the value you bring to an organization is a function of what it needs as dictated by its strategy. Initially, you need to be able to understand a firm's strategy in order to assess if and how and where you can add value. However, even if there is a good match at the outset, no strategy lasts forever. To understand what changes you personally may have to make or help others make, you need to be able to understand strategy in general, your firm's strategy in particular, and be able to translate those general elements into concrete implications. This is why strategy and strategic management are not the exclusive property of only senior executives but are relevant and vital for all managers.

key terms

cash cows   213
competitive advantage   194
core competency   209
cost leadership   200
customer segment   203
differentiation   200
dogs   211
mission statement   198

niche strategy   203
portfolio analysis   214
primary activities   205
question marks   212
stars   213
strategic intent   197
strategic objectives   199
strategic scope   202

substitution   195
supernormal returns   196
support activities   205
SWOT analysis   214
value chain   205
value proposition   204

test your comprehension

1. What is competitive advantage?
2. What are the five required elements for competitive advantage?
3. What is the difference between the competitive threats of imitation and substitution?
4. What is the purpose of strategic intent?
5. Name five elements that are typically included in a mission statement.
6. Define value proposition.
7. What is a customer segment?
8. What is the purpose of strategic objectives?
9. How can a firm's value chain be used to conduct an organizational analysis?
10. What is the difference between primary activities in the value chain and support activities?
11. What is a niche strategy?
12. What are the three tests of an effective core competency?

13. What are the similarities between core competency and resource-based approaches to strategy?
14. What are the typical stages in a product's life cycle and how can this be used in strategic planning?
15. What is the difference between a dog and a question mark in the BCG portfolio analysis model?
16. What is the typical relationship between cash cows and question marks in the BCG portfolio analysis model?
17. How can a portfolio analysis be used in developing global strategies?
18. What does SWOT stand for?
19. What is the difference between the generic strategies of cost leadership and differentiation?
20. What are the elements of the Seven S model?
21. What is the key principle behind the Seven S model?

apply your understanding

1. Effectively *changing* strategies is often one of the most difficult tasks of management. Why do you think this is the case?

2. How does the articulation of strategic intent affect the strategic planning and management process? Could organizations be just as effective without clear statements of strategic intent?

3. What would a SWOT analysis of your university look like? What are your school's key strengths and weaknesses? What are the major threats in the external environment? What are the opportunities? Make a list of all you can think of.

4. Looking at your life, to what degree do you have an intended versus emergent strategy? Are the classes you're now taking and planning to take in the future more a function of intended steps or of positive and negative consequences encountered as you took classes over time?

5. With this assessment in mind, what do you see as the positive and negative aspects of intended and emergent strategies for individuals or for organizations?

practicing your capabilities

You are one of the senior managers in a small company that provides software and computer training to the employees of larger companies. Your firm has not really had a concrete strategy (let alone a statement of strategic intent or a mission statement). The company started when a group of friends who did freelance training met and decided to pool their company contacts and hire some additional help to meet the demand which currently exceeded their collective productivity. The company is now three years old and has a total of 35 employees—most of whom are trainers.

The management team meets to discuss the firm's future and strategy. You suggest that the team conduct a simple SWOT analysis to inform the discussions. The following is the collective group's assessment:

Strengths

- The management team has done a good job of hiring people who have both solid technical capabilities and good skills at teaching others.
- There is a good pool of technical talent from the local university.
- There are strong relationships with a few of the larger companies in the area.

Weaknesses

- There has been some inconsistent pricing of training for clients based on case-by-case negotiations and relationships. Some contracts have high margins and some have low margins.

- Employees have no idea what the value proposition being sold to customers is.
- You do not have a strategy for current or future business.

Opportunities

- Demand seems to be reasonably strong and growing.
- There is potential for expanding geographically as some current customers have offices in other cities and have inquired about providing training in those locations but do not want to pay the travel and lodging costs of your local trainers to go to these other sites.

Threats

- Some of the large "temp" companies (i.e., firms that provide temporary, contract employees to other firms, such as Manpower or Kelly) who do a lot of training of their temps are beginning to market their training capabilities to their clients. The prices being quoted by these firms is about 15 percent higher than your prices. Customers are somewhat price-sensitive.
- The type of training you provide is hard to differentiate. The real difference is not in the content of the training (e.g., everyone covers the same topics when teaching people how to use MS Powerpoint) but in how well trainers do the job and how much the students enjoy the experience and remember what they learned.

1. Based on this general assessment, what is your assessment of the firm's customer value proposition and recommendations for the future?

2. What should the firm's strategy be? Should it try to expand geographically?

3. What additional internal or external assessment is needed for you to make a solid strategy recommendation? Of these additional assessments, what are the top two priorities and why?

closing case
DEVELOPING YOUR CRITICAL THINKING

Blockbuster Fast Forwards for Growth

After years of successful growth, Blockbuster, the world's largest video rental chain, is gearing up for change amid a potential sell-off by its parent company, Viacom. Video and DVD rental sales have begun to flatten, and new technology, including digital movies on demand, threatens Blockbuster's original core business. To ensure growth, it needs a new strategy.

David P. Cook, a young entrepreneur, created the first Blockbuster video rental store. To capitalize on customer dissatisfaction with mom-and-pop video rental stores, which offered a limited selection of titles, short hours, and minimal customer service, Cook created the now-familiar video superstore, the large, brightly lit Blockbuster stores. He created an environment where customers could browse through thousands of titles in film genres ranging from classic to foreign to musical, western, drama, and animated.

The Blockbuster concept was an instant hit, and when the original managers cashed out in 1987, investor Wayne Huizenga took over the business. Blockbuster's growth exploded under his energetic leadership; the number of stores increased rapidly over the next 10 years, and the chain was soon the largest in the United States and the world.

Several different strategies contributed to making the company the nation's largest video rental chain. First, both mom-and-pop shops and large chains, such as the 200-store Erol's chain, were bought and converted into Blockbuster stores; and new stores were built. The underlying rationale for these massive acquisitions was that Blockbuster really did not have a proprietary business; it could protect its market share only by being the first and the biggest, making it more difficult for others to imitate its successful formula. Blockbuster later purchased Mr. Movies, a 68-store chain in Minnesota and Iowa, as part of a plan to enter small towns and rural areas.

Blockbuster also pursued an aggressive franchising plan, signing up impressive financiers for its franchises, such as George W. Baker, a former executive of Kentucky Fried Chicken, and the Zale family, which had made its fortune in the nation's largest jewelry business. By the time the company had 2,000 stores, half of them were franchised, and multiunit franchises continue to grow.

Blockbuster's next expansion strategy was to capture promising international markets, particularly in industrialized nations where VCR ownership was highest. The first regions Blockbuster entered were Canada, Western Europe, and Japan. The number of Blockbuster stores around the world now stands at about 8,700.

Although movie rentals represented Blockbuster's original core business, Huizenga found it necessary to diversify as early as 1993 when the videocassette rental market first began to go soft. Several factors led to this trend. First, the market for VCRs in the United States began to mature as penetration of U.S. homes hit its peak. Second, the retail market for videotape sales started to pick up, and discount stores sold videos at prices low enough that people began to purchase rather than rent their movies. Blockbuster was slow to enter the video sales market. Third, competition from other chains such as Hollywood Video cut into Blockbuster's market share. Finally, Blockbuster also needed to diversify because technology like pay-per-view was bringing consumers new ways to enjoy movies. Additionally, the market for video games was growing rapidly and represented an entertainment substitute for movie rentals.

The morphing of the entertainment industry didn't stop there, though. Soon afterward, Blockbuster saw an increase in competition from satellite TV and digital-on-demand technology. Products such as TiVo and Replay TV make recording and watching your own choice of movies at home a much more attractive option for consumers. Firms like Netflix, already one of the 10 busiest e-commerce sites, also created strong competition. At Netflix or one of about 20 similar Web sites, consumers can select the movies they want to rent with the click of a computer mouse. Netflix mails the first DVD out, usually the same day, and includes a prepaid return envelope. When the customer returns the first film, the second one is mailed.

Netflix doesn't charge late fees either, just a monthly subscriber fee. For a flat fee of $20 customers can check out as many movies as they want. To counter Netflix, Blockbuster started its own movie mail-out service, and a flat-fee subscription service like Netflix has, only for in-store rentals

Another element of Blockbuster's diversification strategy was a store-within-a-store test with RadioShack Corp., in which 130 Blockbuster outlets in four test markets operated ministores carrying an array of electronic products ranging from cellular phones to DVD players. According to Blockbuster's CEO John Antioco, the experiment, which ran for a year before the two companies agreed to dismantle it, suggested that while the tested model wasn't perfect, Blockbuster customers wanted "an assortment of products that are much more closely aligned with our core business and includes more name brands." The company plans to continue its relationship with RadioShack and to try to find a way to offer the right mix of consumer electronics in its stores.

They say the curse of man is that he forgets. Unfortunately, instead of learning from its early experience with videotape, Blockbuster was also slow to begin selling DVDs in its stores. Wal-Mart and other retailers had already captured a significant part of the market. When Blockbuster did finally start selling DVDs, reportedly, its CFO wouldn't allow them to be sold for a price any lower than retail, unlike Wal-Mart, which was selling them at a discount. Not to be outdone, Blockbuster reached out for yet another strategy—one that allowed customers to trade in previously viewed and played games and DVDs for any type of store credit—something Wal-Mart didn't do.

Viacom's announcement, near the end of 2003, that it would consider selling Blockbuster to raise money created another strategic bump in the road for the company. Was Viacom dumping Blockbuster because it was worried it might not be able to stay on top of the entertainment heap? Would the once-mighty Blockbuster go the way of the mom-and-pop rental stores it had put out of business years earlier?

Questions

1. How aggressively should Blockbuster move into selling video game players, games, and accessories versus its past focus on rentals? Why do you think it was slow to enter the DVD sales market?

2. Has the Blockbuster concept lost its novelty in the U.S. market? Can a subscription strategy help revive it?

3. Should Blockbuster push harder into international markets, where digital-on-demand technology is not yet available?

4. In what other ways can Blockbuster try to redefine its core business and pursue other options in entertainment or home electronics? Or do you believe such a strategy would fragment the business?

Sources: Paul Sweeting, "Fewer Rentals Leave Big Hole in Hollywood," *Video Business,* January 12, 2004, p. 7; Enrique Rivero, "Blockbuster Is the Latest Victim of Wall Street Alarmists," *Video Store,* December 21, 2003, p. 9; Richard Sandomir, "Wayne Huizenga's Growth Complex," *New York Times Magazine,* June 9, 1991, pp. S22–26; Sally Goll Beatty, "Viacom's Blockbuster Rethinks Strategy," *Wall Street Journal,* November 20, 1995, p. A1; Chris Taylor, "The Movie Is in the Mail," *Time Canada,* March 18, 2002, p. 40; David Koenig, "Blockbuster to Test Subscriptions," *AP Online,* April 25, 2002; Doug Desjardins, "Blockbuster Scores with Games, DVDs," *DSN Retailing Today,* May 6, 2002, p. 5; "Blockbuster Embarks on Mission to Become Gamers' Most Comprehensive Rental and Retail Resource," Blockbuster press release, May 13, 2002; Sam Diaz, "Digital Video Recorders Challenge Television-Advertisement Makers," *San Jose Mercury News,* June 13, 2002; www.blockbuster.com, accessed on June 20, 2002.

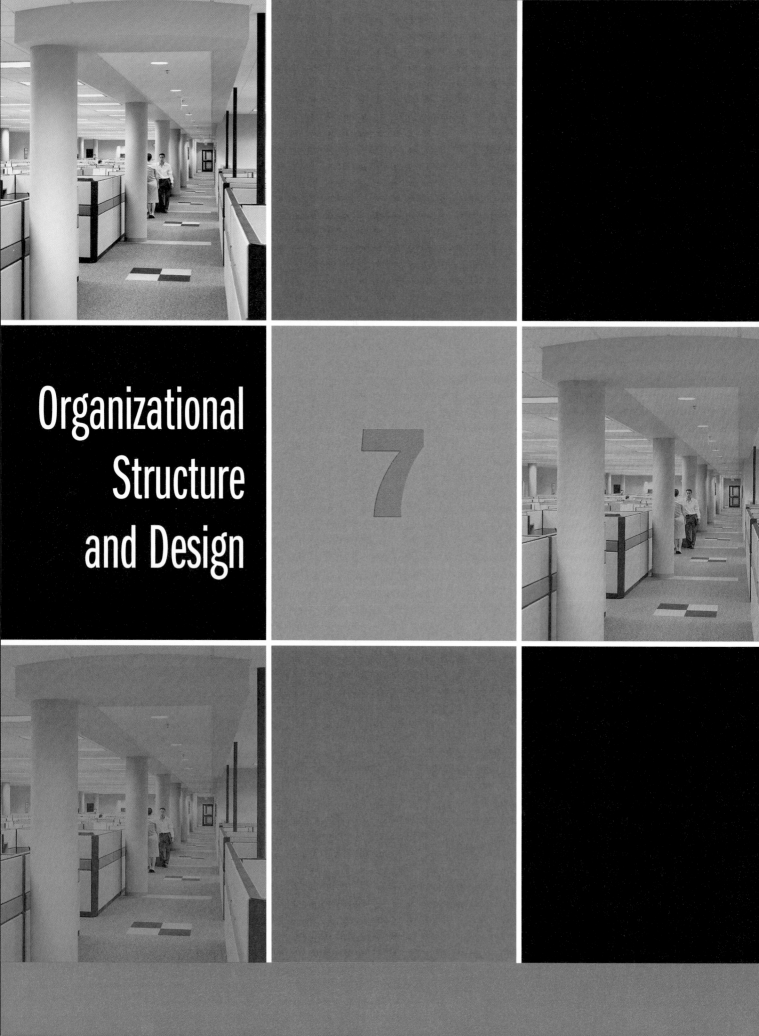

Organizational Structure and Design

7

■

Explain the concepts of organizational structure and design.

■

Explain the concepts of differentiation and integration and their role in organizational structure and design.

■

Describe mechanisms used to achieve differentiation and integration and balance these two structural dimensions.

■

Identify the various structures used by organizations and describe their strengths and weaknesses.

■

List the environmental factors that influence organizational structure.

■

Determine the appropriate organizational structure for a firm given a set of internal and external factors.

Becton Dickinson Restructuring in Europe

In 1996 we witnessed the dawn of the European Union, and in 2002 one of the most visible signs of the actual integration was implemented—the elimination of member country currencies and the mass introduction of the euro. This unification and reshaping of Europe caused many executives to reexamine how they operated and the appropriateness of their companies' structures in the region. Becton Dickinson, a diversified health care products multinational corporation, was one of the firms that needed to rethink the organizational structure it used in its European operations.

Becton Dickinson (BD), a nearly $5 billion firm, originally focused on the domestic U.S. market. However, the integration of Europe caused executives to turn their attention increasingly to Europe. For much of its history, BD was organized primarily by product and divided its products into three major areas. Its Medical Systems unit consisted of product groups such as anesthesia, infusion therapy, hypodermic, intravenous catheter, and operating room products. Its Bioscience unit included product groups such as labware, cell biology, immunology, and cellular analysis. Its Clinical Laboratory Solutions unit included product groups such as diagnostic systems, vacutainer systems, and health care consulting. A division president was in charge in each of these product divisions. Throughout much of its history, the heads of these product divisions focused mostly on selling products in the United States. In addition, a separate division president (international division) was responsible for all product sales outside the United States.

For many years, Becton Dickinson's international division was organized by geography, not by product as in the United States. Its operations in Europe were organized by country. For example, Becton Dickinson France carried all the firm's products; the country manager of the French division was then responsible for sales and profits across all BD's product lines within France. The same was true for Germany, the United Kingdom, and so on. This organizational structure worked quite well, because for many years, countries in Europe had quite different standards and regulations concerning most of the products BD made and sold. However, the formation of the European Union and its monetary integration reduced the different product standards and made it easier to do business throughout the region—some executives speculated that it would be like the "united states of Europe."

The European Union held the promise that Becton Dickinson could make a product, such as insulin

New Jersey based Becton Dickinson and Company (BD), which has over 25,000 employees in more than 50 countries, is one of the top sellers of syringes in the world. BD also sells a variety of other medical supplies, devices, laboratory equipment, and diagnostic products, including Ace brand bandages. For years, the company was organized by product line in the United States. Foreign divisions were organized by country. When the European Union was formed, BD had to rethink its structure. Should it reorganize its EU division by product line like in the United States?

syringes, to one standard and sell it across all member nations. This would dramatically increase the efficiency of BD's operation in Europe, reduce the per-unit cost, and potentially increase profits. However, with this opportunity came an interesting challenge: How should the company structure its operations in Europe?

One obvious solution was to organize in Europe the same way as in the United States—by products. In this case, within the International Division it would form a European Hypodermic Products Group, a European Diabetic Care Products Group, and so on. However, no one could say how long it would be before customers in one country, such as France, would view products and take actions similar to customers in another country, such as Germany. Certainly, the language in which they conducted business would not quickly unify.

Another alternative was to organize the entire company by global product. That is, instead of having an international division, each product division would have worldwide responsibility. Consequently, if this structure were adopted, the global head of a product such as Diabetic Care would have responsibility for product sales across the world, including Europe. However, even if all member countries in the European Union adopted similar standards, would those standards be the same as other large markets such as the United States and Japan?

The future structure of the company was further complicated by the nature of some of its most important customers, many of which were hospitals. Hospitals were somewhat different from other customers because they bought products across all of BD's product categories. In other words, one hospital might buy products from the hypodermic, diabetic care, intravenous catheter, and operating room, specimen collection, cellular analysis, and tissue culture labware product groups. A product structure in Europe might involve having 10 different sales representatives from 10 different product groups call on each hospital. Would the customer prefer to have one representative of all of BD's products make the sales call instead of dealing with 10 different sales representatives from the same company?

Becton Dickinson's U.S.-based competitors were increasingly entering overseas markets, and foreign competitors were also setting up operations in the United States. The U.S. health care crisis and the sub-

stantial publicity about rising health care costs were exerting downward pressures on prices. All these pressures meant that BD could not afford to implement the wrong structure. Was it prepared to use a global structure? Would a country structure in Europe be better? Choosing the right organizational structure might make the difference between success and failure in the changing and increasingly competitive environment facing Becton Dickinson.

Sources: Cinda Becker, "BD Makes IT Moves," *Modern Healthcare*, November 24, 2003, p. 45; *2001 Annual Report*, BD.com, accessed on March 3, 2002.

strategic overview

As the case of Becton Dickinson illustrates, today's complex environment presents a variety of questions about how firms should be structured to survive and prosper. A firm's structure can determine the success or failure of its strategy and its overall performance. The European Union changed the competitive landscape for BD and its competitors. As a result, BD managers had to carefully reevaluate the structure of their organization to determine if the current one would continue to work or a new one would be needed for the company to compete.

As we have discussed in previous chapters, the firm's strategy must be carefully implemented for it to be successful. *How* the strategy gets implemented is largely a question of how managers organize the firm's activities; in other words, what they determine to be the firm's structure.[1] For example, in the United States, Becton Dickinson division presidents were responsible for the sales and profits of the products under their control. BD then had an international division for organizing its activities abroad. In its international division, the heads of each of the geographic units (i.e., country managers) were responsible for the sales of all BD products in their assigned countries. This way, both the firm's products and international strategies were implemented.

Another issue related to Becton Dickinson was how much authority each manager of the product divisions and each country manager in Europe had to develop their own strategies differently from those in the rest of the firm. As we will see, the centralization or decentralization of a firm's structure also affects

the implementation of its overall strategy and the strategy of its divisions. Sometimes a firm's structure affects the very strategy it should choose.[2]

An increasingly common structure used by organizations today is a network structure (which we discuss in more detail later in this chapter). For example, when a firm decides to outsource its manufacturing operations as Nike and many other athletic shoe makers do, it must establish a network structure allowing it to maintain close contact with the firms to which it is outsourcing the work. The company also might need to maintain close relationships with a number of suppliers to ensure the quality and timely supply of goods. Because organizations often have many alliances, a network structure becomes important for implementing this type of cooperative strategy.[3]

Even if you are several years away from having the responsibility of actually redesigning or restructuring an organization, it is important to understand the fundamentals of organizational design and structure so that you are better prepared to help implement structures to make them effective. There are usually multiple structural options. You must understand common organizational structures and the general advantages and disadvantages of each. This includes the principles linking particular structures, organizational strategy, and the external environment and the key factors that determine a good fit among these elements. Finally, as a manager, you must be able to apply this knowledge in planning and implementing appropriate organizational structures.

PRINCIPLES OF ORGANIZATIONAL STRUCTURE

organizational structure the sum of the ways an organization divides its labor into distinct tasks and then coordinates them

organizational design the process of assessing the organization's strategy and environmental demands and then determining the appropriate organizational structures

organizational charts illustrate relationships among units and lines of authority among supervisors and subordinates

Organizational structure can be defined as the sum of the ways an organization divides its labor into distinct tasks and then coordinates them.[4] **Organizational design** is the process of assessing the organization's strategy and environmental demands and then determining the appropriate organizational structure. Often, organizational structure is talked about in terms of organizational charts. **Organizational charts** illustrate relationships among units and lines of authority among supervisors and subordinates through the use of labeled boxes and connecting lines. For example, Exhibit 7.1 shows the organizational chart of Suncor Energy.

While organizational charts represent important aspects of an organization's structure, they do not equal organizational structure. Just as the structure of someone's physical anatomy is more complex than what is visible, so too is an organization's structure more complex than what can be depicted in a chart. Understanding of the principles of organizational structure and design is the key to interpreting correctly the organizational charts that you can see, while not losing sight of an organization's structural aspects, which are not so visible but are just as important.

This journey starts with the fundamental dynamic of organization structure and design—the simultaneous separation and pulling together of people and activities.[5] On the one hand, all but the smallest of organizations have to separate people and tasks. In organizations of even moderate size, it is not effective for everyone in the organization to do the same thing. At the same time, it is also not effective for any given individual to try to do everything. Some *differentiation* or separation and specialization is required to get tasks accomplished, even in a small organization of just a dozen people. On the other hand, if these separate people and tasks are not pulled together, they can veer off in different directions without contributing to the ultimate needs of the customers or objectives of the organization. Consequently, some *integration* or coordinating and bringing together of people and tasks is also necessary. Balancing this pushing of people and tasks apart and pulling them together is the basic challenge of organizational structure and design. Fundamentally, the "right" structure or the right balance of differentiation and integration is a function of the demands in the environment and the organization's strategy.

To get at this basic challenge of organizational structure and design, we first examine some of the core elements of organizing and then look at some of the most common organizational structures. With these basics in place, we then explore the challenge of designing structures that can fit the changing demands of the environment and the organization's strategy.

exhibit 7.1

Suncor Energy Organizational Structure

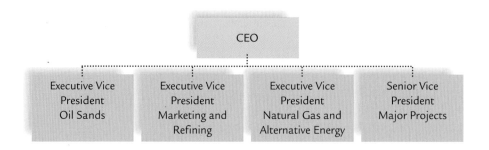

Differentiation

To understand the organizing process, one of the first elements we need to examine further is differentiation. **Differentiation** is the extent to which tasks are divided into subtasks and performed by individuals with specialized skills.[6] The main benefit of differentiation is greater specialization of knowledge and skills. For example, because of the complexity of building a commercial jetliner, Boeing has engineers who specialize in designing wings and others who design airplane doors. Even among those who design airplane doors, some focus primarily on designing the door hinges, while others focus on designing the locking mechanisms that keep the doors sealed at 35,000 feet. This differentiation by what employees do is typically referred to as **task differentiation**.

The nature of differentiation is not limited just to the tasks people perform, but can also involve employees' thoughts. This is called **cognitive differentiation** and is the extent to which people in different units within the organization think about different things and the extent to which people think about similar things differently.[7] For example, accountants typically think about assets and liabilities, while marketing managers think about brand image and market share. However, these two groups might also think about the same thing differently. Accountants might think about organizational performance in terms of financial results, while marketers might think about organizational performance in terms of customer satisfaction.

So why is this important? It is important because while differentiation does bring greater specialization, it often makes pulling all this specialized capability together to deliver a product or service to the customer a challenge. Suppose both design engineers and manufacturing personnel at Boeing need to work together to make a newly designed 777 door operate properly. Greater separation and specialization make this coordination harder because designers may think about door performance in terms of design sophistication while manufacturing managers may think about door performance in terms of the ease of making and installing the door on the plane. If Boeing ends up with a door that is well designed but difficult and expensive to install, it may suffer any number of undesirable consequences. It may end up with an expensive door that takes away from profits because it is costly to install. Or it may end up with a door that doesn't operate easily or properly because of mismatches between design and assembly.

Integration

In contrast to differentiation, **integration** is the extent to which various parts of the organization cooperate and interact with each other.[8] The key benefit of integration is the coordinated movement of different people and activities toward a desired organizational objective. As a consequence, one of the driving forces of integration is interdependence. **Interdependence** is essentially the degree to which one unit, or one person, depends on another to accomplish a required task.

There are three types of interdependence.[9] *Pooled interdependence* occurs when various groups are largely independent in their functions but collectively contribute to a common output. For example, two product groups at BD might send products to the same hospital to meet the customer's overall needs. *Sequential interdependence* exists when the outputs of one group become the inputs of another group. For example, at Boeing

differentiation the extent to which tasks are divided into subtasks and performed by individuals with specialized skills

task differentiation differentiation by what employees do

cognitive differentiation the extent to which people in different units within an organization think about different things or about similar things differently

integration the extent to which various parts of an organization cooperate and interact with each other

interdependence the degree to which one unit or one person depends on another to accomplish a task

the raw materials of aluminum provided by the purchasing department become the inputs of the pressing department. That department then shapes the aluminum sheets for doors and its outputs become the inputs of the door assembly department. *Reciprocal interdependence* exists when two or more groups depend on one another for inputs. For example, at Boeing the new-product development department relies on the marketing research department for ideas to investigate, and marketing research relies on new-product development for new products to test on customers. In principle, the greater the interdependence, the greater the need for cooperation, and thus integration.

A Manager's Challenge, "Restructuring for Growth," illustrates how a new structure and set of interdependencies can create required changes for individual managers. Kevin Nabholtz at Suncor Energy discovered that the new structure for the company put him in a new organizational unit that required managing levels of interdependency that previously had been absent in the organization, and with which he personally had little experience. Thus, the change in company structure resulted not only in a change in structure for the unit in which he worked, but also what it required of him as a manager to work effectively within the new structure. How big a change does this seem to you? What do you see as the most important changes required of Kevin Nabholtz as a result of the organizational structure change?

Another factor that can influence the need for integration is uncertainty. **Uncertainty** for a firm refers to the extent to which future input, throughput, and output factors cannot be forecast accurately. The more difficult it is to accurately forecast these factors, the greater uncertainty the firm faces. The greater the uncertainty, the greater the need for integration and coordination because as events unfold, individuals and organizational units have to coordinate in real time their responses to the events.

Integration and coordination can be achieved through a variety of mechanisms.[10] The appropriateness of each mechanism is related to the level and type of interdependence and the extent of uncertainty in the environment.

uncertainty the extent to which future input, throughput, and output factors cannot be forecast accurately

Rules Rules essentially establish "if-then" guidelines for behavior and consequence. For example, the rule may be, if you are going to miss class, then you must notify the professor in advance. In a sense, rules are the standard operating procedures (SOP) for the organization. In general, the more task independence, the more useful rules are as an integration mechanism. In contrast, the more task interdependence and uncertainty, the less useful rules are as an integration mechanism. For example, suppose you work as a manager in the promotion department of a record company. Concert cancellations due to weather, travel problems for the band, or any number of other unpredictable factors would likely make coordination and integration through the use of rules not very effective. Rules might work well in the accounting department of your record company where the environment and requirements are standard and stable but would likely be less effective in the changing environment of the promotion department.

Goals As task uncertainty and interdependence increase, the probability that preset rules can effectively coordinate tasks declines. Consequently, goals become a more effective coordination mechanism. Instead of specifying what individuals should do, goals specify what outcomes individuals should achieve. Effective goals define quantitative outcomes and often require high levels of effort to achieve. Specifying the outcomes, but not the process,

a manager's challenge

Change

Restructuring for Growth

I n January 2002, Suncor Energy instituted a new organizational structure that had profound implications for Kevin Nabholz. The new structure called for the creation of a unit, called Major Projects, that would take many engineering and construction activities that had previously been contracted to outside providers and bring them "in-house."

Suncor Energy is an integrated energy company; however, unlike most oil companies, Suncor does not drill for oil, it mines oil. It mines tar sand in northern Alberta, and extracts the oil from the sands through heat and pressure. It then sells the crude oil to others or refines it internally into products such as gasoline, and sells it through its retail division, Sunoco.

Over the past five years, Suncor had been involved in expanding its oil sands operations. In fact, it has spent nearly $1 billion each year and plans to spend that much on new engineering and construction each year over the next 10 years. Suncor executives felt that this level of engineering and construction justified having "in-house" expertise, so they created an organizational unit with the responsibility for managing these projected construction projects.

Kevin Nabholz was put in charge of the new unit, which now had reciprocal interdependence with other business units. For example, the oil sands unit could determine that it needed a new vacuum tower (a construction project in excess of $100 million). That need would become the input for Nabholz at Major Projects. He would supervise all the engineering and construction (including any use of outside contractors) and then the output from his unit (the new vacuum tower) would become the input for the oil sands unit.

For Nabholz this represented a significant change in the skills required to be successful. Whereas in the past most business units were fairly autonomous and supervised their own construction projects by contracting with outside firms, now working closely with these internal business units would be key to success. If effective coordination of projects' requests, approval, construction, and handover for operation was not achieved, all the desired efficiencies and cost savings of creating this new organizational unit would likely be lost. In addition, whereas before engineering and construction activities were largely contracted out to out-

Suncor Energy, Inc., based in Calgary, doesn't drill for oil. It extracts oil from sand using heat and pressure, producing light crude oil, diesel fuel, and custom blends—a process it pioneered in 1967. In recent years, the company has been expanding rapidly, spending about $1 billion annually on new construction projects. To handle the expansion the company formed a special unit called Major Projects, headed by manager Kevin Nabholz. Nabholz is shown inspecting one of Suncor's oil sand tanks near Fort McMurray in northern Alberta.

side firms, now Nabholz would directly supervise employees within Suncor to do much of the project design, estimation, engineering, and supervision of outside contract construction companies and workers.

While some could view the organizational structure change as small, it represented a whole host of required changes and adjustments for Kevin Nabholz as the new manager of the unit. Specifically, whereas before there was very little interdependence regarding engineering and construction among the units, now there was a significant level. Nabholz's success would depend in part on his making the necessary changes and adjustments in his thinking and leadership to ensure that these higher levels of interdependence were well managed and coordinated in the new organizational structure.

Source: Speech given by Kevin Nabholz, March 14, 2002, Calgary, Canada.

maximizes individuals' flexibility in how they get things done, yet facilitates integration by ensuring that people are working toward the same end. For example, university professors encounter students with a wide variety of needs and situations. Rather than provide professors with set rules, the university typically sets goals in terms of student proficiency. The goals, in terms of learning, ensure that professors are working toward the same end but have the flexibility to respond to specific needs and situations.

Values In cases of high task uncertainty and interdependence, values become an important coordinating mechanism. Values specify what is fundamentally important, such as customer satisfaction, but unlike goals, they do not specify quantitative outcomes. Values are a better integrating mechanism over goals when there is high uncertainty and high interdependence. Shared values ease coordination under these conditions, because they specify what is important while maintaining flexibility concerning exactly what or how things are accomplished.

Exhibit 7.2 helps illustrate the level of appropriateness of rules, goals, and values in conditions of low to high levels of uncertainty. The exhibit also helps illustrate an important practical matter—overlap. As a matter of practice, it is impossible to specify the line where rules stop being effective and goals start or where goals stop being effective and values start. Consequently, as a manager you need to understand the principal relationship of rules, goals, and values with different levels of uncertainty. At the same time you will also need to use your judgment. You will have to judge how much of a combination of, say, rules and goals might be appropriate, and exactly when the uncertainty level gets high enough that as a coordination mechanism rules are largely not helpful to you.

Formalization

formalization the official and defined structures and systems in decision making, communication, and control in an organization

One way to balance both differentiating (separating) and integrating people and activities is through formalization. **Formalization** can be thought of in terms of the official and defined structures and systems in decision making, communication, and control in the organization. These mechanisms can explicitly define where and how people and activities are separated as well as how they are brought together. While all organizations have to manage differentiation and integration, they vary substantially in how much formalization they use to accomplish this.

exhibit 7.2

Appropriateness of Rules, Goals, Values

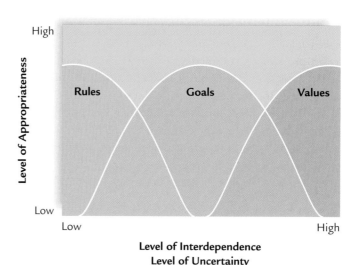

One of the common means of formalization is official designation of what we typically call **line of authority**. Line of authority essentially specifies who reports to whom. It is often called line of authority because in organizational charts a line is typically drawn between subordinates and their boss. If you are part of an organization that strictly adheres to line of authority, consistently bypassing the lines to get things done could get you labeled as a rebel or as disrespectful. On the other hand, only looking to your boss in an organization that mostly ignores lines of authority might result in people perceiving you as lacking initiative or motivation.

More formal organizations also tend to stress **unity of command**. This is simply the notion that an employee should have one and only one boss. If you were working in a highly formal organization with a strong orientation to unity of command, you would only have one boss who would evaluate your new idea and who could direct your work. This does not mean that your boss would necessarily have the authority to approve your new-product idea but only that you would not report to two different bosses.

Additionally, more formal systems tend to specify span of control. **Span of control** refers to the number of employees reporting to a given supervisor. More formal organizations tend to have narrow rather than wide spans of control. The logic for this is fairly obvious. Normally, the fewer people you have to supervise, the more closely you can watch and control them. However, several factors can influence the effectiveness of span of control. First, the nature of the task is an important factor. All other things being equal, the more routine subordinates' tasks, the wider the effective span of control can be. In other words, for you as a manager you can effectively supervise more subordinates if they have predictable and routine tasks. Another factor influencing effective span of control is subordinates' capabilities. Generally, the greater the subordinates' capabilities, the less close supervision they require and the greater can be the effective span of control. Also, your own managerial capabilities influence effective span of control. The greater your managerial capabilities, the wider the span of control you can handle effectively. Putting these three factors together, you can see that if your subordinates were highly skilled and you were a highly capable manager, you could have an effective wide span of control even with subordinates who had nonroutine jobs. Exhibit 7.3 provides a brief summary of key factors that influence effective span of control.[11]

Consistent patterns of span of control can affect the overall "shape" of the organization. Narrow span of control throughout the entire organization tends to result in a rather **tall organization structure**, or one that has multiple layers or is high in terms of vertical differentiation. Wide span of control throughout the organization will generally lead to a more **flat organization structure**. Given similar number of employees, a flat organization will have fewer layers in its hierarchy than a tall organization. Exhibit 7.4 shows examples of tall and flat organizational structures, as well as span of control.

The appropriateness of a tall or flat organization is largely affected by the external environment. Tall and formal organizations tend to be slower at making decisions and responding to changes in the business environment. As a result, tall organizations tend to be best suited to stable external environments. Because many organizational environments have become more dynamic, managers often respond by trying to "flatten" their organizational structures—often removing whole levels of hierarchy and people in the process, which is often called downsizing. They do this so that information does not have to travel as far (say from the bottom to the top) for decisions to be made and as a consequence they can make and implement them faster.[12]

line of authority specifies who reports to whom

unity of command the notion that an employee should have one and only one boss

span of control the number of employees reporting to a given supervisor

tall organization structure one that has multiple layers or is high in terms of vertical differentiation

flat organization structure has fewer layers in its hierarchy than a tall organization

exhibit 7.3

Factors That Influence the Span of Control

- *Job complexity*—Jobs that are complicated require more managerial input and involvement and thus the span of control tends to be narrower.
- *Job similarity*—If one manages a group of employees performing similar jobs, the span of control can be considerably wider than if the jobs of subordinates are substantially different.
- *Geographic proximity of supervised employees*—Because employees who work in one location are more easily supervised than employees in dispersed locations, physical proximity to employees tends to allow a wider span of control.
- *Amount of coordination*—A narrower span of control is advisable in firms where management expends much time coordinating tasks performed by subordinates.
- *Abilities of employees*—Supervisors who manage employees who are more knowledgeable and capable can have a wider span of control than supervisors managing less knowledgeable and capable employees. The greater the abilities of employees, the less managerial inputs are required and thus a wider span of control is possible.
- *Degree of employee empowerment*—Because employees who are trusted and empowered to make decisions need less supervision than employees with less autonomy and decision-making discretion, supervisors who empower their employees can have a wider span of control.
- *Ability of management*—More capable managers can manage more employees than less competent managers. The abilities of managers to educate employees and effectively respond to their questions lessen the need for a narrow span of control.
- *Technology*—Communication technology, such as mobile phones, fax, e-mail, workshare software, can allow managers to effectively supervise employees who are not geographically proximate, have complex and different jobs, and require significant coordination.

exhibit 7.4

Tall and Flat Organization Structures

Tall Organization Structure

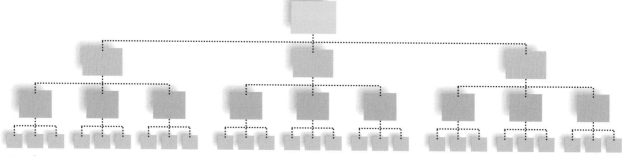

4 Levels
Span of Control = 3
Total Employees = 40

Flat Organization Structure

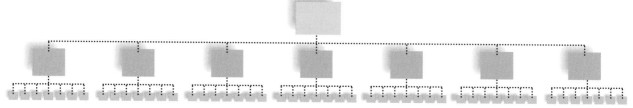

3 Levels
Span of Control = 7
Total Employees = 57

It is important to note some of the managerial challenges that this general movement to flat structures creates. As environmental uncertainty increases for many organizations, managers push toward flatter structures so that information can flow faster and decisions can be made more quickly. However, the environmental uncertainty also tends to result in more non-routine tasks than routine tasks. This tends to push toward narrow spans of control, which in turn pushes toward taller, not the desired flatter, organizations. So what is the managerial implication and challenge of all this? Flatter organizations and wider spans of control with more nonroutine tasks are only possible if subordinates and managers have higher capabilities. This creates a premium for you as a manager to develop the ability to help your subordinates increase their capabilities and to increase your own managerial competencies.

Today and in the future, technology is arguably one of the most powerful factors influencing effective span of control and helping companies to be flatter. For example, the following Manager's Challenge ("Reach Out and Touch Someone") describes how technology has enabled a human resource manager to retain his previous span of control despite having subordinates physically spread throughout Asia doing nonroutine work. Do you think the manager could have retained his previous span of control and effectiveness without technology? Does it seem to you that technology will increasingly allow bosses to have subordinates reside great distances away and still remain productive?

In summary, formalization mechanisms such as span of control, line of authority, and chain of command work to both separate and integrate people and activities. They do so in an explicit and official way. For example, your line of authority specifies who your boss is and separates you and your tasks from others who have a different boss. At the same time, the line of authority integrates the other people who report to the same boss that you do.

Informalization

While virtually all organizations have some degree of formalization, even the most formal organizations also have some degree of informalization. The **informal organization** consists of the unofficial but influential means of communication, decision making, and control that are part of the habitual way things get done in the organization. Informal structures for decision making, communication, and control are often not represented in organizational charts, yet they pervade the day-to-day functioning of many organizations. For example, formally you may have only one boss to run your new-product idea by, but informally you may need to chat with a manager in another area to get her opinion on the feasibility of manufacturing the product. Just as the degree of formalization can vary from company to company, so too can the degree of informalization. But it can also vary not just from one company to another but from one country to another. For example, one study compared U.S. and Japanese firms and found that the Japanese relied much more on informalization.[13] In Japanese companies much of the decision making, communication, and control were accomplished through informal, face-to-face meetings between people who did not have formal reporting relationships. This process is referred to as *nemawasi*. In Japanese organizations, *nemawasi* takes the form of informal conversations in which incremental decisions are made so that by the time an official meeting is held to make the formal decision, the decision has already been made informally.

informal organization the unofficial but influential means of communication, decision making, and control that are part of the habitual way things get done in an organization

tech|nol|ogy

a manager's challenge

Reach Out and Touch Someone

Ed is the Asia Region Human Resource Manager for DuPont. Just a few short years ago, he and his staff all resided in Singapore—the regional headquarters for the company. Ed had a span of control of about eight people. He had subordinates with specialized responsibilities for training, compensation, recruiting, executive development and succession planning, benefits and pensions, performance management, and organizational development. Each area of specialization had to be coordinated in order to support the overall strategy and operations of the company in the region as well as the more specific activities of the various business units within specific countries. Ed's subordinates were for the most part experienced and well-trained professionals. Ed himself was an experienced HR executive.

However, as competition grew in the region and costs became an increasingly important factor in the firm's profitability, senior management looked for ways to both save money and increase the effectiveness of support units such as HR. One of the factors that added expense was the firm's practice of bringing into the regional headquarters those specialists who were the best at what they did, regardless of their nationality. Unfortunately, this meant that many had to be paid extra for relocating from their home country to Singapore. For example, Ed was originally from Australia. In addition, while the company had business activities in virtually every country in Asia, the investments in some countries were greater than in others. For example, significant investment was being put into China. The implication for HR was that its support was needed to different degrees in different countries. Because of the company's recent and large investment in China, businesses in that country needed training support at a level several times that of other countries.

Executives wanted to lower costs and increase effectiveness. They lowered costs by placing employees in their home countries where possible. This avoided the extra fees

employees were paid for working outside their home countries. They also located HR activities where they were needed most to increase effectiveness. For example, training was located in China where it was needed most. However, Ed relocated back to Australia. He was married and had two boys approaching their teenage years, and therefore was happy to do this. However, the change would mean he would have subordinates not next door to his office but scattered all around the region—a region where it is a 10-hour flight from Sydney to Tokyo.

In addition to Ed's managerial capabilities and the competency of his subordinates, technology played a key role in keeping his span of control about the same, despite a significant increase in physical distance between him and his subordinates. Ed instituted a biweekly staff meeting via conference calls. In many cases, his staff would join via mobile phone as they called in from hotels, airports, and factories around the region. E-mail also served as a significant means of keeping in touch and sharing documents. Even though it was hard to catch people in their offices because of so much travel, they could all access their e-mail each day or several times a day to keep in touch and stay coordinated. On projects that needed input from several subordinates, Ed used software that enabled everyone to log onto the company's internal system and see the same document at the same time and make and see edits, changes, additions, and so on in real time.

While staying coordinated in such a large region was a challenge, Ed did not think it would have been possible to maintain his previous span of control and be effective were it not for all the technology to which he had access. He also felt that in addition to saving money by not relocating so many people, many of his staff (including himself) were much more motivated and happy to be living in their home country because of various family and personal considerations. Thus, technology not only facilitated effective span of control but also increased satisfaction.

Source: Personal communication, 2002, 2003.

Centralization and Decentralization

centralized organizations restrict decision making to fewer individuals, usually at the top of the organization

In addition to the extent to which the organization's structure is formal or informal, the extent to which it is centralized or decentralized is also important. Centralization and decentralization refer to the level at which decisions are made at the top of the organization or at lower levels. **Centralized organiza-**

tions tend to restrict decision making to fewer individuals, usually at the top of the organization. In contrast, **decentralized organizations** tend to push decision-making authority down to the lowest possible level. For instance, European multinational organizations tend to be decentralized and allow units in different countries to make decisions according to local conditions. Often this enables them to adapt to host government demands and different consumer preferences.[14] For many years, Philips, a large multinational electronics firm headquartered in the Netherlands, was viewed as one of the premiere examples of a decentralized international organization. Philips operated in over 60 countries around the world. Many of the larger-country units enjoyed considerable freedom and autonomy. For example, even though the V2000 videocassette recorder (the first VCR) was developed at the company's headquarters, the North American division of Philips refused to purchase and sell the product in the United States and Canada. Instead, North American Philips purchased a VCR made by a Japanese rival and resold it in the United States and Canada under the brand name of Philips.

Japanese firms, on the other hand, exhibit a stronger degree of centralization and tend *not* to delegate decisions as frequently as either European or American firms.[15] Most Japanese multinational firms operate like centralized hubs into which information flows, and from which decisions are announced to foreign subsidiaries. In fact, Japanese firms have encountered increasing complaints from host nationals in local subsidiaries about a "bamboo ceiling." This term refers to the exclusion of host nationals from strategic decision making because nearly all key positions in the subsidiary are occupied by Japanese expatriates sent by headquarters to ensure more centralized control.[16]

Often, students feel that formalization and centralization are essentially the same thing, and that informalization and decentralization are also synonyms. This is not the case (see Exhibit 7.5). You can have a very formal organization that is highly centralized, but you can also have a formal organization that is fairly decentralized. For example, as we illustrated above, Philips is a fairly decentralized company in that decisions are pushed down into the organization. At the same time, Philips is also relatively formalized. Lines of authority, chain of command, official policies, and so on are prevalent. In contrast, the U.S. military is both formal and centralized. On the other hand, you can have a highly informal organization that is decentralized or highly centralized. For

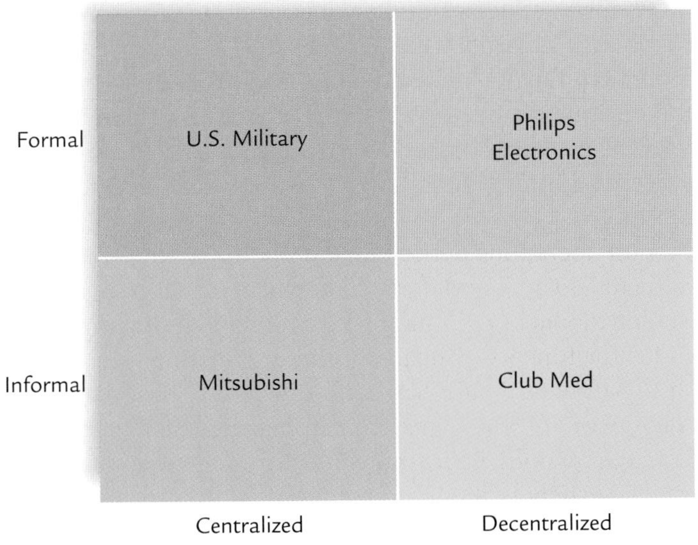

decentralized organizations tend to push decision-making authority down to the lowest level possible

exhibit 7.5

Combinations of Formal/Informal and Centralized/Decentralized

example, the research we just cited on Japanese firms suggests that on average they are relatively centralized but at the same time function through a high degree of informalization. Likewise, it is quite common for family-owned businesses to be both centralized and informal. That is, the owner makes most of the decisions but informal connections, communication, and control, rather than the formal structure or rules, dictate how things get done. In contrast, Club Med is fairly decentralized and informal. Each general manager of a resort is fairly free to make decisions that meet the needs of his or her unique market. Coordination is achieved through a vast array of informal relationships built up among general managers and with corporate managers.

Some research suggests the more intense the firm's information needs, the more formal and centralized its IT (information technology) structure becomes.[17] JCPenney executive VP and CIO (Chief Information Officer), Steve Raish, followed this trend in restructuring the 100-plus-year-old company, which previously had taken pride in its decentralized structure. Raish was appointed to the position in early 2001 and has been trying to centralize IT decision making and control since that time. To some extent his efforts represent a continued migration of IT centralization at JCPenney. Other IT projects undertaken at the company include scanning at the point of sale and the central recording and storage of the data collected, as well as the centralized buying of merchandise.[18]

COMMON ORGANIZATIONAL STRUCTURES

Now that we have examined the core elements of organizing, we can explore some of the most common organizational structures. Although a variety of structures exist, six structures represent the most common forms. We examine each of these basic structures, although variations can be obtained by combining more than one form. In reality, most organizations do *not* have pure forms but have hybrids. Once we have reviewed these basic organizational structures and briefly examined their general strengths and weaknesses, we can then move to a more detailed discussion of the conditions that determine which type of structure you as a manager would want to adopt.

Functional Structure

Perhaps the simplest structure is the functional structure (Exhibit 7.6). The functional structure organizes the firm around traditional functional areas such as accounting, finance, marketing, operations, and so on. This structure is one of the most common organizational structures in part because it separates the specialized knowledge of each functional area through horizontal differentiation and can direct that knowledge toward the firm's key products or services.

Firms with operations outside their domestic borders might also adopt a functional structure. The key difference between a purely domestic organization and a multinational organization with a functional structure is the scope of responsibilities for functional heads in the multinational firm. In a multinational, each department would have worldwide responsibilities. Thus, while each subsidiary would have a local human resource manager, the top human resource manager would be responsible for directing worldwide human resource activities such as hiring, training, appraising, or rewarding employ-

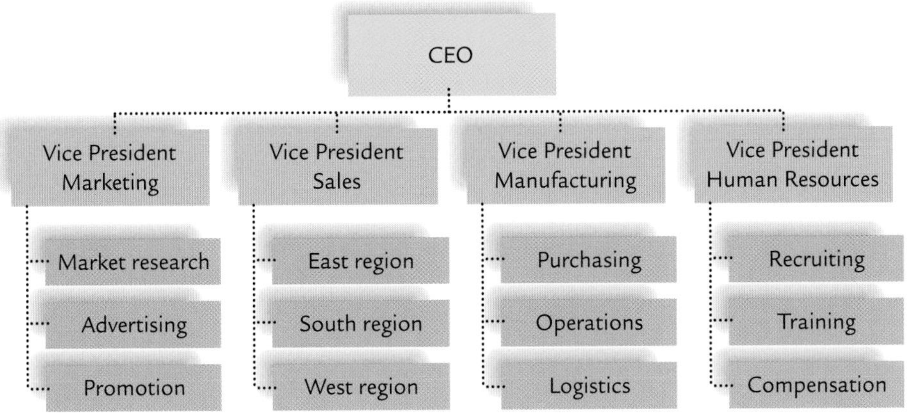

exhibit 7.6
Functional Structure

ees. This structure is most common when the technology and products of the firm are similar throughout the world.

The major advantages of this structure include the following:

- Well suited to small to medium-sized firms with limited product diversification.
- Facilitates specialization of functional knowledge.
- Reduces duplication of functional resources.
- Facilitates coordination within functional areas.

A global functional structure can also reduce headquarters–subsidiary conflicts because operations throughout the world are integrated into their functional areas, and functional department executives are charged with global responsibility. This, in turn, enhances the overall international orientation of managers. For example, the higher a marketing manager rises in the marketing department, the more that manager needs to think about and understand the firm's global marketing issues.

The primary weaknesses of this structure include the following:

1. Often creates problems of coordination across functional groups.
2. Creates restricted view of overall organizational goals.
3. Can limit attention paid to customers as functional groups focus on their specific areas.
4. Can lead to slower organization response to market changes.
5. Often burdens chief executives with decisions that involve multiple functions.

In an international setting, a functional structure has disadvantages when the firm has a wide variety of products and these products have different environmental demands, such as different government restrictions or standards, customer preferences, or performance qualities. This weakness is exacerbated when different functional departments experience different demands by geographical area. For example, if the accounting practices are similar between the United Kingdom and France but the advertising approaches differ, this will tend to exaggerate coordination difficulties between the accounting and marketing departments.

Product Structure

In a product structure, the firm is organized around specific products or related sets of products (Exhibit 7.7). (While we use the term "product," it also applies to services.) Typically, each product group contains all the traditional functional

exhibit 7.7

Product Structure

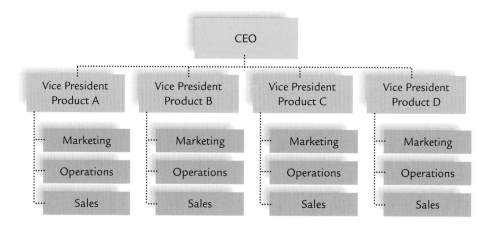

profit center unit or product line
in which the related expenses are
deducted from the revenue generated

departments such as finance, marketing, operations, human resource management, and so on. Each product is generally treated as a **profit center**. That is, the related expenses are subtracted from the revenues generated by the sales of that product. Most commonly, the heads of the product or services groups are located in the headquarters of the company. However, this is not necessarily the case. For example, the headquarters for Honeywell's commercial and residential control product group is in Minnesota, while the headquarters for its commercial flight instruments product group is in Arizona.

The principal advantages of a product structure include the following:

1. Individuals in different functional areas within the product group focus more on the products and customers.
2. Performance of the product (i.e., profit and loss) is typically easier to evaluate.
3. There is usually greater product responsiveness to market changes.
4. It often reduces the burden of the top executive in making operating decisions compared to the functional structure.

The major disadvantages of the product structure include:

1. Duplication and lack of economies of scale for functional areas (for example, IT, finance, human resources, and so on).
2. Can create problems for customers who purchase products across multiple product groups.
3. There can be more conflicts between product group objectives and overall corporate objectives.
4. There is an increased likelihood of conflict between product groups and greater difficulty coordinating across product groups.

Multinational firms also use global product structures. This typically happens when customer needs for a given product are more or less the same the world over. After Becton Dickinson adopted a global product structure, the head of the Biosciences unit became responsible for global strategy formulation and implementation for those products.

Division Structure

The division structure can be viewed as an extension of a product structure. Exhibit 7.8 provides a partial organizational chart of the division structure of Becton Dickinson described at the outset of this chapter. Divisions typically consist of multiple products within a generally related area, though specific products

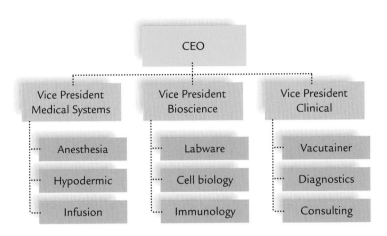

exhibit 7.8

Division Structure

may not necessarily be closely related. At GE, there are over 11 different business units, organized to produce a diversified portfolio of products including financial services, transportation, energy, insurance, medical systems, and even entertainment products following the company's purchase of NBC. Within each unit, there are very broad arrays of product groups and specific products. For example, the Medical Systems Division within GE consists of 12 different product groups like cardiology, radiology, emergency room equipment, and products related to orthopedics and sports medicine. Within each of these groups are literally dozens and dozens of specific products. Clearly, it takes a significant size and diversity of products before a division structure is appropriate. Typically, in a division structure, all functional activities are placed within each division.

Common strengths of a division structure include:

1. Organizing various product families within a division can reduce functional duplication and enhance economies of scale for functional activities.
2. To the extent that product families within a division serve common customers, customer focus can increase.
3. Cross-product coordination within the division is eased.
4. Cross-regional coordination within product families and within the division is often eased.

Associated disadvantages include the following:

1. Typically only appropriate for diversified, large companies with significant numbers of specific products and product families.
2. Can inhibit cross-division coordination.
3. Can create coordination difficulties between division objectives and corporate objectives.

Like domestic firms, multinational firms can and do use this structure. In this case, each division is charged with worldwide responsibility. Because division structures are generally extensions of product structure, they have many of the same advantages and disadvantages. For large, diversified multinational firms, the division structure is one of the more common structures.

Customer Structure

As the name implies, customer structures are organized around categories of customers (Exhibit 7.9). Typically, this structure is used when different categories of customers have separate but broad needs. For example,

exhibit 7.9

Customer Structure

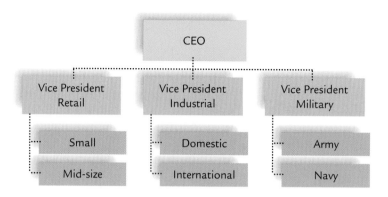

industrial customers might purchase a different set of products than retail customers.

The primary strengths of this organizational form include the following:

1. Facilitates in-depth understanding of specific customers.
2. Increases responsiveness to changes in customer preferences and needs as well as responsiveness to moves by competitors to better serve customers.

The primary weaknesses of this organizational form include the following:

1. Typically leads to duplication of functional resources in each of the customer units.
2. Often creates difficulty in coordinating between customer units and corporate objectives.
3. Can fail to leverage technology or other strengths in one unit across other units.

Many multinational firms find this organizational form difficult to implement because of differences among customers across regions and countries. For example, even though IBM initially had a consulting unit focused on government customers, it found that trying to organize the unit on a global basis yielded more disadvantages than advantages. This was because different governments had different needs and different ways of selecting computing solution providers. Thus, while government customers in the United States were significantly different in their needs from other IBM customers, the advantage gained by focusing on this customer segment proved not to be the case across the rest of the world.

Geographic/Regional Structure

Firms can structure themselves around various geographical areas or regions (Exhibit 7.10). Within this structure, regional executives are generally responsible for all functional activities and products in their regions. The Western Regional Vice President might be responsible for all key business activities for the states of Washington, Oregon, California, Nevada, Montana, Utah, Idaho, Wyoming, Colorado, Arizona, and New Mexico. The individual regions are often treated as profit centers. In other words, each region's profitability is measured against the revenues it generates and the expenses it incurs.

The major advantages of a geographic or regional structure include:

1. Typically leads to in-depth understanding of the market, customers, governments, and competitors within a given geographical area.
2. Usually fosters a strong sense of accountability for performance in the regional managers.

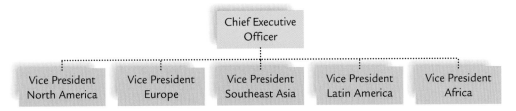

Strengths:
- Facilitates local responsiveness
- Develops in-depth knowledge of specific regions/countries
- Creates accountability by region
- Facilitates cross-functional coordination within regions

Weaknesses:
- Often creates cross-regional coordination difficulties
- Can inhibit ability to capture global scale economies
- Duplicates resources and functions across regions

exhibit 7.10

Geographical/Regional Structure

3. Increases responsiveness to unique changes in the unique market, government regulations, economic conditions, etc. for the geography.

The major disadvantages of a geographic or regional structure include:

1. Often inhibits coordination and communication between regions.
2. Can increase conflict and coordination difficulties between regions and corporate office.
3. Normally leads to duplication of functional resources across the regions.
4. Separating production facilities across multiple regions can inhibit economies of scale.
5. Can foster competitive behavior among the regions, which is particularly frustrating for customers who have operations across multiple regions.

A number of multinational firms employ geographic/regional structures. This is primarily because customers' demands, government regulations, competitive conditions, availability of suppliers, and other factors vary significantly from one region of the world to another. The size or scope of the region is typically a function of the volume of business. For example, in consumer products companies, the Middle East and Africa are often included in the European region because the volume of sales in these areas is too small to justify separate regions (EMEA—Europe, Middle East, and Africa). On the other hand, for most oil and gas companies with a geographic structure, the Middle East is a separate region on its own.

Matrix Structure

A matrix structure consists of two organization structures superimposed on each other (Exhibit 7.11). As a consequence, there are dual reporting relationships. That is, one person essentially reports to two bosses. These two structures can be a combination of the general forms already discussed. For example, the matrix structure might consist of product divisions intersecting with functional departments or geographical regions intersecting with product divisions. This is essentially the structure that Procter & Gamble had for many years. The two overlapping structures are based on the two dominant aspects of an organization's environment.

exhibit 7.11

Matrix Structure

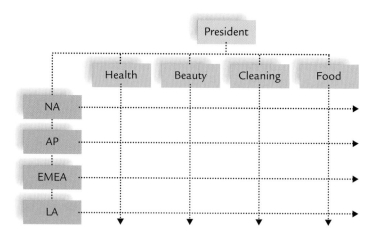

The major strengths of a matrix structure include:

1. Typically facilitates information flow throughout the organization.
2. Can enhance decision quality because before key decisions are made, the organization considers the two intersecting perspectives.
3. Is best suited to a changing and complicated business environment.
4. Can facilitate the flexible use of human resources.

The major disadvantages of a matrix structure include:

1. Often increases complexity of performance evaluations because people often have two bosses.
2. Can inhibit the organization's ability to respond to changing conditions quickly.
3. Can diffuse accountability.
4. Often leads to conflicts as the differing perspectives and objectives of the intersecting units come together.

In multinational companies matrix organization structures come and go with some frequency. They come into play quite often because while economies of scale for global product, division, or even customer structures are compelling, often regional differences relative to governments, culture, languages, and economies are also strong. This is precisely what has been behind P&G's product and regional matrix. In multinational companies, matrix structures go out because they are difficult to manage. ABB, a large industrial company based in Switzerland, for many years had a division/regional matrix. However, in the late 1990s senior executives determined that the conflicts and difficulties of managing the matrix outweighed the benefits and they changed to a global division structure.

Mixed Organizational Structures

As we mentioned earlier, although there are pure forms, any combination of the basic organizational structures is possible. The typical objective of a mixed or a hybrid organizational structure is to gain the advantages of one structure and reduce its disadvantages by incorporating the strengths of different structures. Because many of these hybrid structures are reflected in contemporary organizational forms, we will explore this issue in more depth in the next section; however, Exhibit 7.12 provides an example of a hybrid functional, product, customer structure.

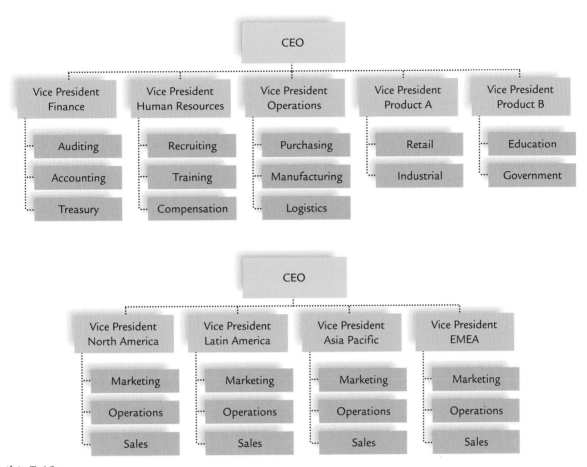

exhibit 7.12
Hybrid Structure

NETWORK ORGANIZATIONAL STRUCTURES

There are a wide variety of contemporary organizational structures. Many of them do not have common labels or names. This is in part because many of them have their essence not in organizational charts but in the configuration of organizational units and activities. Consequently, one logical way of addressing these forms is by utilizing a concept you were introduced to in the previous chapter—that is, the value chain. Much of what managers are doing in contemporary structures is reconfiguring the firm's value chain in an effort to gain cost savings and specialization benefits, and improve integration and coordination.

While it might be slightly oversimplified, often these contemporary structures are referred to as **network structures**. However, even if we adopt this term, it is too generic to reflect the variety of structures. At a minimum we should not think of one generic network structure. Rather, we should think of a "Low Networked" to "High Networked" continuum. At the low "networked" end would be structures in which the quantity and magnitude of externally networked activities is limited. That is, a firm would own and execute most of its primary and support value chain activities and network with outside organizations for only a limited number of more minor value chain activities. At the high "networked" end of the spectrum would be structures in which the quantity and magnitude of externally networked activities is nearly unlimited. At the high end of the continuum, the number of externally networked value chain activities would exceed those owned and executed internally.

network structures formal or informal relationships among units or organizations (e.g., along the firm's value chain)

exhibit 7.13

Outsourced Structure

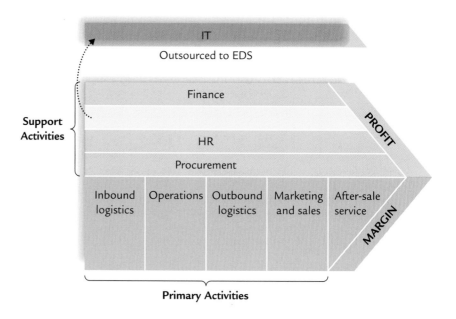

outsourcing the practice of taking a significant activity within the organization and contracting it out to an independent party

To illustrate this, let's start at the low end of the continuum. One of the simplest ways of taking a value chain activity and networking with an external organization is to outsource that activity. **Outsourcing** is the practice of taking a significant activity within the organization and contracting that activity out to an independent party. For example, Xerox has a multibillion-dollar contract with EDS to perform virtually all of Xerox's IT functions. In fact, a major portion of EDS's revenues comes from performing virtually all the IT functions for a variety of customers (see Exhibit 7.13).

As we mentioned in Chapter 4, Nike outsources or contracts out essentially all of its shoe manufacturing, or what is essentially the operations segment of the primary activities in its value chain. It is networked or connected to its many contract manufacturers. In fact, it is so tightly connected that it can design a shoe at its Beaverton, Oregon, headquarters, send the blueprints via satellite to one of its contractors, and receive back by FedEx a prototype shoe from a contract factory all within a week. It is important to note that, increasingly, activities that executives once believed could only be done internally such as IT, human resource administration, design, manufacturing, sales, and customer support, are being outsourced today. Technology has made it possible to network activities together and retain reliability as well as lower costs.

At the high end of the continuum, a firm would have more value chain activities networked to external organizations than owned and executed internally. To illustrate this, suppose that you were better than anyone else at clothing design. Suppose further that in creating your company, you formulated a strategy in which you wanted to compete by having superior design, world-class raw materials, and close relationships with retailers. Based on this strategy, you might want to own and control only a few elements of the entire value chain. For example, in today's environment, you could design an organization in which you performed design, procurement, and sales, but virtually nothing else. You could network with a company such as Ryder to perform all of your inbound logistics. You could network with various contractors in Asia to manufacture your designs. You could network with UPS to perform all of your outbound logistics. You could network with Avaya (a spinoff of Lucent

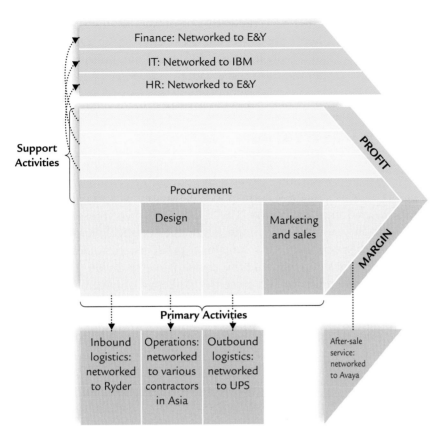

exhibit 7.14
Network Structure

Technologies) to handle all your customer service. You could network with IBM to run all of your Internet and IT functions. You could network with Ernst & Young to run your HR, finance, and tax functions. You could then focus your energies on elements of the value chain (design, procurement, and sales) that you believed would give you a strategic advantage (see Exhibit 7.14).

Using value chain as a tool for understanding contemporary organizational forms, you can see that the potential configurations of value chains in terms of what a company internally owns and controls and what it networks with others to provide are almost infinite. Today you can network to have subelements of any value chain activity performed by others or you can network entire pieces of the overall value chain. For example, National Semiconductor Corp. (NSC) realized substantial savings within its global supply chain by outsourcing its logistics activities. The company, which reported $1.6 billion in sales in 2003, distributes semiconductor chips and related products to thousands of customers worldwide. As volumes grew and demands for faster delivery increased, NSC decided it needed the expertise of a provider to handle distribution and value-added inventory functions most effectively. It outsourced its inventory and distribution activities to Federal Express.[19]

Like the more traditional structures, network structures have both advantages and disadvantages. One of the most compelling theoretical advantages was argued to be that networking would allow managers to focus on core competencies or the activities that yield competitive advantage. By concentrating on core activities, managers could do them better. To some extent this is true. However, the "noncore" activities that are networked cannot simply be contracted out and forgotten. The reality is that it takes time, attention, energy, and skill to manage these relationships with external organizations. Even if Xerox determines that IT functions are not core and outsources them to EDS, if EDS does not deliver what Xerox needs, then Xerox's performance suffers. Simplified, network structures can give you greater focus and specialization on specific value chain activities but they also come with the challenge of coordinating and integrating the organizations that are performing the networked activities.

Summary Observations

As you look back through this section of the chapter and different structures, you may notice an interesting pattern. In general, the advantages and disadvantages of various structures correspond reasonably well to either gaining or losing specialization or integration. This is because when you separate parts of the organization you tend to gain the advantages of specialization. What you get in terms of specialization by functions, products, customers, regions, or value chain activities depends on how you separate or divide units. However, when you separate units, you enhance the challenge of integrating their activities. Many of the basic elements of organizing that we discussed at the outset of this chapter are utilized in part to facilitate more effective integration. For example, rules, objectives, and values can all be utilized in any of the common structures to facilitate greater integration and coordination.

Many of the more modern and popular concepts regarding organizational structure are designed to help companies maintain the advantages of specialization and overcome or at least reduce the integration and coordination difficulties that naturally occur. For example, GE's former CEO, Jack Welch, made the term **boundaryless organization** popular. The notion was that the barriers to effective integration that hierarchy, function, geography, and so on cause would be overcome by teams of people who were empowered to work across boundaries. However, as modern as this term may sound, it really represents a tool that has been used in organizations for a long time. Teams and committees composed of members from different areas of the company have been around for decades as a means of overcoming integration challenges. Likewise, modern terms such as "quality blackbelts" (i.e., internal experts on quality) or "best practice champions" are contemporary reincarnations of the longtime practice of designating liaisons. **Liaisons** are individuals who are designated to act as a bridge or connection between or among different areas such as quality, manufacturing process, and so on.

In the end, one of the fundamental dynamics that all managers must understand about organizing is that both specialization (differentiation) and integration are needed. Specialized activities have to be performed but they must come together in a way that offers competitive value to a customer. Each of the basic structures delivers advantages and disadvantages regarding both differentiation and integration. Regardless of the modern buzzwords or legacy lexicon, most managers face a dual challenge. On the one hand, they want to capture the desired advantages of a given structure. However, every structure has its natural disadvantages. As a result, managers also have to use formal or informal mechanisms to reduce or eliminate these natural disadvantages.

boundaryless organization
barriers to effective integration are overcome by people empowered to work across boundaries

Boundaryless Organization by Michael Hitt

www.prenhall.com/onekey

liaisons individuals designated to act as a bridge or connection between different areas of a company

DESIGNING ORGANIZATIONS

Fundamentally, in designing organizations managers face the challenge of capturing both specialization and integration advantages while minimizing the often mirror-image disadvantages. This begs the question "How should they decide to actually structure an organization?" As we have already alluded to, the two main determinants of this decision are the external environment and the strategy of the company. Now we want to go into this in greater detail.

External Environment

As we mentioned earlier, a key factor in determining the match between the environment and organizational structure is environmental uncertainty.[20] While we offered a somewhat simpler description of environmental uncertainty earlier in this chapter, now we want to expand on that description. We do this with two related but separate constructs: the extent to which the environment is (a) complex and (b) dynamic.

Environmental Complexity Let's examine the first element of environmental uncertainty—complexity. Simplified, environmental complexity is fundamentally about the breadth and depth of differences and similarities. Complex environments have greater breadth and depth of differences than simple environments. While differences and similarities could be assessed potentially in terms of thousands of dimensions, there are several core categories. These core categories include products, customers, technology, competitors, suppliers, and geography.

The complexity relative to products can vary widely from firm to firm. For example, a Bic pen is made up of approximately seven parts. Each part is produced with relatively low technology, and the assembly of the parts into the final product also involves relatively low technology. At the other end of the continuum, when Boeing puts together a 747 jumbo jet, it has a huge breadth of over 1 million parts it must assemble. The depths of these components range from a simple metal bolt to a panel composed of rare composite materials. Thus, Boeing has in absolute terms, and certainly relative to Bic pen, a complex product environment.

Customers constitute another important category when assessing environmental complexity. For example, McDonald's serves hamburgers to millions of customers each day but the differences among these customers is relatively small compared to their overall size. In contrast, Toyota serves millions of customers each year but their needs are different enough that key aspects of Toyota cars, such as the suspension systems and emissions, are very different from one region of the world to another.

Technology constitutes another important category when assessing environmental complexity. Technology complexity includes both the diversity of technology required and the level of its sophistication. For example, Lucent utilizes analog, digital, and photonic technologies in its products. The technology involved in both the manufacturing of its photonic switches for transmission of data along fiber optic lines and in the actual products themselves is of a depth that many people with Ph.D.'s in physics have a hard time understanding it all.

Competitors also constitute an important category of environmental complexity. The greater the number and diversity of competitors, the more complex the firm's environment. For example, in terms of commercial aircraft, while Boeing has a fairly complex product environment, it has a much more simple competitor environment. For all intents and purposes, its only other competitor is Airbus. This does not mean that competing against Airbus is easy but only that its competitor environment is more simple than that of a company like GAP that has literally thousands of clothing manufacturers and labels competing for the same customers.

Suppliers are an additional category of environmental complexity. The greater the number and diversity of suppliers, the more complex the firm's environment. For example, again if we return to Boeing, despite its having a more simple competitor environment, it has a complex supplier environment. While Boeing does most of the designs of commercial aircraft it produces, it utilizes literally hundreds of suppliers, some making such large components as the entire tail section.

The final category, geographic complexity, is included not because it is separate from the previous categories but because it tends to have a significant impact on all the categories above. This is principally because the more geographic regions covered, the greater the probability of differences across the other categories. For example, the greater the number of countries in which a firm operates, the greater the probability of dissimilarities between the countries (their governments, laws, customer preferences, language, etc.). These differences can in turn increase the breadth and depth of differences relative to products, customers, technology, competitors, and suppliers. Consequently, the greater the geographic scope, the greater the complexity.

Environmental Dynamism

The second element to evaluate the overall uncertainty of the environment is the extent to which the environment is static or dynamic.[21] Static environments may have few or many factors, but these factors tend to remain stable over time. For example, the manufacturing technology for pens as well as the component parts has changed little in the last 30 years. In contrast, factors in dynamic environments change rapidly. For example, advancements in areas such as composite materials and electronics have changed significantly for commercial aircraft over the last 30 years. The fashion industry operates in an even more dynamic external environment. Benetton faces an environment in which colors, fabric, and styles change not just year to year but season to season.

Firms facing dynamic environments often describe them as "white water" environments in reference to the challenges of navigating a raft down the ever-changing rapids of a river. The rapidly changing external environment typically requires quick internal organization changes. You will likely recall that in Chapter 2 we discussed how the changing internal and external environment requires both personal changes and leading change in others. While we have emphasized the importance of change in each chapter, we will discuss at length, in Chapter 17, why organizational change is difficult, and systematic methods for enhancing success.

By combining the dimensions of simple–complex and static–dynamic, we can create a four-cell matrix that provides a broad backdrop against which organizational design structures can be placed (see Exhibit 7.15). In general, the more complex and dynamic the environment, the more the organizational structure needs to coordinate different groups' efforts and the greater the speed with which this coordination needs to take place. This means that the more complex and dynamic the firm's environment, the more the structure will need to make use of mechanisms that facilitate coordination and integration such as values, teams, and liaisons.

Organization Strategy

The second major element that managers must consider in designing their organization's structure is the company's strategy.[22] Unfortunately, there are no simple rules that we can use to say, "If your company's strategy is X then

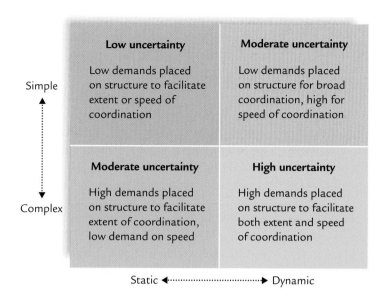

exhibit 7.15

Matrix of Organizational
Uncertainty

you should adopt structure Y." However, there are a few principles that can help you understand the relationship between strategy and structure.

The first principle of relating structure to strategy is that the structure should complement and leverage the strategy. But how can we determine if a given structure complements or leverages the strategy? In reality, this is a hard question to answer because there is no "one way" of formulating strategy. However, we can gain important insights into this principle by examining one of the most common strategy formulation approaches. As we discussed in the previous chapter on strategy, one of the common means of formulating strategy is to determine the company's core competencies or resources that produce value for customers, are hard to imitate, and are scarce. By focusing on these identified competencies or resources, we can more easily evaluate the fit or misfit of a proposed structure with the strategy.

A Manager's Challenge, "Restructuring Citicorp Credit Card," provides an effective illustration of how a company changed its structure to fit with its strategy of low cost and brand identity. What role do you think changes in the European Union played in Citicorp restructuring its organization and reconfiguring its value chain? What role do you see transportation as well as telecommunication technology playing in Citicorp Credit Card's new structure?

Moving from Domestic to International Structures

Up to this point, we have mentioned the basic organization structures in terms of both a domestic and international context. Now we want to take a more focused look at organization structure in an international context. Very few firms begin as international organizations. Most start in one country and for a period of time focus on the customers within that country. Although international organizations would be easier to understand if they evolved steadily and systematically, they do not do so. However, there is a general relationship between the nature of the firm and its structure. This relationship was first proposed over 30 years ago[23] and has generally been supported,[24] including recently.[25] Simplified, the theory and findings are represented in Exhibit 7.16.

The first dimension of the matrix is the extent of foreign sales. For example, 97 percent of Nokia's sales are made outside of its home country in Finland. The second dimension of the matrix is extent of product diversification. Product

globalization *a manager's challenge*

Restructuring Citicorp Credit Card

In the 1990s, Citicorp Credit Card executives faced the significant challenge of how to restructure their organization to complement the company's strategy. Their strategy called for emphasizing the Citicorp brand and leveraging their global size to capture economies of scale and reduce costs.

As one of the largest banks in the world, Citicorp had global brand recognition. In general people associated good customer service and stability with the brand. Citicorp executives in the credit card business felt that they could leverage their brand to differentiate their products. Credit card customers valued good customer service and wanted a stable company behind their card. It had taken Citicorp decades to build up its brand recognition and reputation. Few competitors would be able to imitate it.

However, the credit card business is one of very thin margins. Since the price of credit cards (that is the interest charged to customers) is transparent and widely publicized, competing on price by offering lower and lower interest rates is not an attractive way for Citicorp to make money. Controlling costs is really the key to increasing profit margins.

To determine how to leverage the company's brand name and control costs, Citibank executives examined their value chain. They described their value chain in simple terms. First, they marketed their branded credit card to customers. Then they had to manufacture the "blanks." Blanks are simply the plastic cards without the individual's information printed on it (name, number, expiration date, etc.) or encoded on the magnetic strip. After the blanks were manufactured, they were then "printed." Individual information was printed and encoded onto the card. Once printed, the cards were mailed to the respective customers. The customers then used their cards to make purchases and those transactions were processed. Finally, the customers were billed, money collected, and customer questions answered.

Prior to the restructuring, Citicorp Credit Card had what would best be called a geographic structure. That is, all the elements of the value chain were replicated in every major country. While this allowed each country to focus on its customers and respond rapidly to unique competitive situations, it often resulted in different levels of customer service, which hurt the global brand image. The duplicated activities increased costs.

Given its strategy, how should Citicorp Credit Card restructure itself? One of the first things it did was centralize marketing and brand management. This helped the company standardize and make consistent the company logo, colors, and customer service standards. To capture economies of scale, all manufacturing of blanks for the United States, Canada, and Europe was relocated to the United States. For the United States and Canada, these blanks were then printed in the United States. For all of Europe, the blanks were shipped to the Netherlands and printed there. Once printed, all cards for Europe were mailed from the Netherlands. Again to capture economies of scale, virtually all transactions for all of Europe, Canada, and the United States were processed in the United States. Because of different languages and currencies, customer service was kept in each country. However, now that there is a common currency throughout Europe, regional customer service centers are being established operated by multilingual customer service agents.

This modern structure defies simple classification. Some activities, such as brand management, are centralized, while others, such as customer service, are much more decentralized. Yet, the structure complements the strategy. By centralizing brand management, Citicorp has ensured that customers continue to see a consistent image of a stable and customer service–oriented company. By consolidating manufacturing of blanks as well as the printing and mailing of cards, Citicorp significantly lowered the cost per unit. This was especially true for processing transactions. The low cost of sending data internationally allowed Citicorp to consolidate its technicians, as well as hardware and software.

The full result of the restructuring will not be known for years, but the preliminary results are positive. Although executives will not disclose specific results, they report that revenues are up and costs are down substantially. In combination, profits have also increased significantly.

Source: Personal communication, 2003.

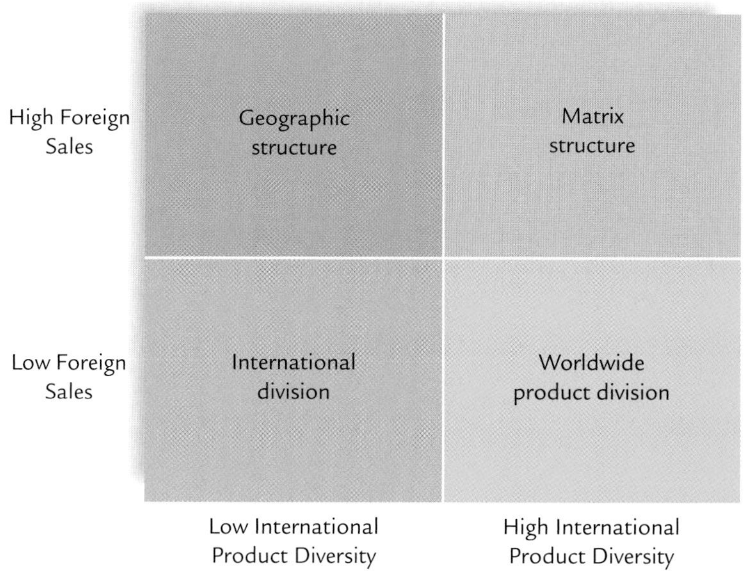

exhibit 7.16

**International Strategy
and Structure**

	Low International Product Diversity	High International Product Diversity
High Foreign Sales	Geographic structure	Matrix structure
Low Foreign Sales	International division	Worldwide product division

diversification is the extent to which the firm has many different products across many different segments and even industries. For example, Nokia sells primarily mobile phones and network equipment for mobile phone systems. This represents fairly low product diversification. In contrast, GE has many different products across such diversified industries as jet engines, lighting, medical equipment, television and broadcasting, plastics, and power plants.

Low foreign sales and low product diversification generally lead to the formation of an international division to look after international sales. Because there is not that much in foreign sales to look after and because the products are relatively similar, it works to put all the international sales of all products under one roof—the international division. This is what BD had for many years. Most of its products were medical in nature and foreign sales were only a small fraction of total sales.

Low product diversification but high foreign sales usually leads to a geographic structure. This was the case with Nokia until recently. It was divided into five major geographical regions—Europe, Middle East and Africa (EMEA), North America, Latin America, and Asia Pacific.

Low foreign sales but high product diversification typically leads to global product divisions. In the case with low foreign sales and low product diversification, it made sense to put all foreign sales under one roof. However, when you have low foreign sales but high product diversification, it makes the most sense to put the foreign sales under the roof of each product.

High foreign sales and high product diversification typically lead to a matrix structure. This was the case for ABB. Like GE, ABB is a large industrial company with a very diversified set of products from train locomotives to power transmission. Because the products are different, it needed to separate them by product. However, because international sales are a large percentage of overall sales, the company also had a geographic structure. In combination, this formed a product–geography matrix structure.

Thus, while there are some associations between strategy and structure in international firms, there is not a clear sequence in development. At best, it seems that the development of international organizations can be divided into two basic states: initial international structures and advanced international structures. Although most international organizations do not jump directly into advanced international structures, there is no consistent sequence companies follow. Rather, the advanced global structures are determined more by the nature of the size of the organization's international sales, product diversity, size of foreign R&D, and foreign manufacturing.[26]

Domestic Organization with an Export Department As firms venture out from their domestic market to foreign ones, they usually begin with a limited number of products. Typically, the products to be sold in foreign markets are designed and produced in the domestic market. Consequently, the primary international task is exporting the products to foreign markets. At this stage, most firms simply add an export department to their existing structure to handle the specialized tasks, such as international shipping and customs regulations.

Domestic Organization with an International Division Once the volume of exports exceeds the capabilities of a few specialists, firms commonly establish an international division. International divisions typically are responsible for all functional activities relative to international markets. The international division often has its own small department for accounting, finance, marketing, and sales. However, production activities are not usually part of the international division. Products are produced within the normal domestic organizational structure and then modified or simply turned over as is to the international division. Consequently, the products that tend to be pushed into the international division are those that have broad appeal and for which there are relatively fewer customer differences across countries.

Adding an international division has a number of advantages. First, it is an efficient means of dealing with the international market when a firm has limited experience. The focus on international activities and issues within the division can foster a strong professional identity and career path among its members. It also allows for specialization and training in international activities, which can be valuable later when the firm moves more heavily into the international marketplace and needs individuals with global capabilities. The focus on international markets, competitors, and environments can also facilitate the development of a more effective global strategy. Further, because the top officer of the international division often reports to the CEO (or similar senior executive), international issues often receive high-level corporate consideration and support with this structure.

One major weakness of an international division is its dependence on other divisions for products and support. Because domestic sales of a particular product often make up the largest percentage of the product's overall sales, low priority may be given to international sales. Other parts of the firm that supply products and services to the international division may be unwilling to make modifications that cost them time and money, even if the changes would facilitate greater international sales.

Advanced Global Structures As international sales as a percentage of overall sales increase and as the organization expands into a larger number of countries, it becomes increasingly difficult to maximize the benefits of an international division and minimize the weaknesses. When the organization outgrows its initial international structure, it can choose from among six advanced global structures. As mentioned, there is no particular sequence from one structure to another. These six advanced global structures correspond to the basic functional, geographic/regional, product, division, customer, and matrix structures already discussed, except that they have global rather than domestic scope and reach.

Organizing to Think Globally and Act Locally

Given the increasingly international environment in which organizations compete, it is important to examine one other factor that managers must consider when designing organizational structures, that is, globalization or localization demands.[27] **Globalization** is the tendency to integrate activities on a coordinated, worldwide basis. Firms are pushed in the direction of globalization when benefits gained from worldwide volume, efficiencies, or economies of scale are significant. These benefits could include economies of scale for production, greater leverage of high-cost distribution networks, and greater leverage of expensive research and development activities. In a variety of industries, the minimally efficient production scale is beyond what could be supported in a single market. If we return to our example of Boeing, the break-even point for a new commercial aircraft is approximately 300 planes, with each plane costing in excess of $100 million. This requires total sales of $30 billion. In order to get an acceptable return on its investment, Boeing has no choice but to try to develop planes that will have global appeal because the U.S. market alone is not big enough. The high level of research and development and scale economies such as these push toward globalization and to centralization of activities such as product development and manufacturing.

By contrast, differences among countries and customer preferences are two key factors that push toward localization. **Localization** is the tendency to differentiate activities country by country. Firms are pushed in the direction of localization when benefits from location-specific differentiation and adaptation are significant and factors such as economies of scale are small. Procter & Gamble recently faced the pressures of localization for a laundry detergent it developed. Although P&G wanted to develop one detergent, Visor, for all of Europe and capture the efficiencies of a single development, manufacturing, and marketing effort, it found significant differences between countries. These differences pushed P&G from globalization toward localization. For example, it found that Germans prefer front-loading washers, while French prefer top-loading washers. This created a problem. The detergent did not get distributed as well among the clothes when poured into a front-loading washer. As P&G discovered, it is not easy to get an entire nation to change from front-loading to top-loading washers. As this example points out, the greater the differences between countries and the more significant these differences are for a product or service, the greater the need for localization.

Forces can simultaneously push toward globalization and localization, requiring firms to be globally integrated and locally responsive. In the case of P&G, the manufacturing process pushed for integration because making detergent is basically continuous; that is, like many chemical products, the final product is delivered after a long process of mixing various chemicals in different states and at different temperatures until you get the desired chemical reactions for the final product. This means that the process cannot be stopped at discrete points and finished elsewhere, nor is it economical to alter the process to create different detergents. Both these factors push toward globalization, or the concentration of manufacturing activities without much modification for local market conditions. On the other hand, the significant differences in laundry machines between Germany and France pushed toward localization.

globalization the tendency to integrate activities on a coordinated, worldwide basis

localization the tendency to differentiate activities country by country

In the case of P&G, it solved the problem by developing a plastic ball into which detergent could be poured and that then could be thrown in with the clothes in a front-loading machine. The plastic ball was designed to dispense the detergent gradually though small holes as the ball bounced around in the clothes while they were being washed.

In general, firms heavily involved in international business face strong pressures for both integration and differentiation. They need specialists for marketing to Germans, dealing with French government officials, and complying with U.S. accounting rules. However, they also face greater needs for integration. These increased integration needs can be met in a variety of ways.

Direct Contact Often, direct contact is an important means of integration by sharing information. One of the largest firms in the world, Matsushita, has an interesting way of accomplishing this. Because research and development is vitally important in the consumer electronics industry, Matsushita has a large central research and development lab. To make sure that managers know what is going on in the lab and to ensure that lab scientists know what the market's emerging needs are, Matsushita holds an annual, internal trade show. Senior managers throughout Matsushita's worldwide operations gather and examine research results and potential new products. Managers also feed back information about market differences, customer preferences, and competitor positioning to research and development scientists. The result is a massive sharing of information that has helped keep Matsushita ahead of competitors.

Liaison Liaison roles are designed to enhance the links, and therefore information flows, between two or more groups, be they teams, departments, divisions, or subsidiaries. Part of Matsushita's success in the videocassette recorder (VCR) market was due to a purposeful liaison. The vice president in charge of Matsushita's U.S. subsidiary was also a member of the senior management committee of the parent company in Japan and spent about a third of his time in Japan. This facilitated the link between headquarters and the United States, which was the most important consumer market for VCRs. In addition, the general manager of the U.S. subsidiary's video department had previously worked for many years in the video product division of the production and domestic marketing organization in Japan. This created a strong link between the product division in Japan and the U.S. subsidiary. Also, the assistant product manager in the U.S. subsidiary had spent five years in the central VCR manufacturing plant in Japan. Through these three individuals, Matsushita succeeded in ensuring that vital links at the corporate, product, and factory levels were established between Japan and the United States.

Teams When integration needs arise across a wide set of functional areas, teams can be an effective integration mechanism. Philips is an example of a firm that utilizes teams as an integrative mechanism. This may stem from the fact that the firm was founded by two brothers, one an engineer and the other a salesman, who worked together in charting Philips' early strategic course. Whatever the origin, Philips has long had an office of the president, as opposed to a single CEO. The office of the president is composed of a technical, commercial, and financial executive. Furthermore, for each product, there is a team of junior managers from commercial and technical functions. These teams integrate various perspectives and information around a single product to ensure that interfunctional differences are resolved early and that necessary design, manufacturing, and marketing issues are integrated from the outset in an effort to increase the success of the product.

Motorola is one of many multinational corporations with manufacturing facilities like the one shown in Tianjin, a port city in north China near Beijing. To compete, Motorola has demonstrated its commitment to the Chinese economy—especially because local rivals are usually government-owned and are tightly allied with local officials. With 10,000 employees in the country, however, Motorola contends it is as "Chinese" as any of its competitors.

SIGNS OF POOR STRUCTURE–ENVIRONMENT FIT

Structure-Environment Fit
by Michael Hitt

Q&A
OneKey
www.prenhall.com/onekey

Even if the organization's structure matches the environment at one point in time, it may not be appropriate forever. Environments change and so should organizational structures. Inappropriate organizational structures block needed information sharing, focus attention away from information that needs to be gathered, and, consequently, hurt decision quality, organizational prosperity, and perhaps even survival. With the wrong structure, managers increasingly make bad decisions, in part because they lack needed information. In the absence of timely, relevant information, effective decisions concerning what products to produce, what quality standards to set, or how to reduce costs, how to advertise, or how to position products against competitors decline. Because inappropriate organizational design and structures can severely inhibit organizational effectiveness, what are some of the key warning signs that a mismatch exists?

One of the first warning signs is decision makers' inability to anticipate problems. If problems caused by competitors, governments, customers, suppliers, and so on consistently arise without advance notice, this is a warning sign that the organizational structure is inhibiting environmental scanning, data gathering, or information dissemination. If the organization is not designed or structured to correct this problem, decision makers will have to react to rather than anticipate the environment and will be placed at a competitive disadvantage to other organizations.

Another key warning sign is an increase in conflict that prevents effective implementation. This sign, in particular, can indicate that the limits of a functional structure are being stretched and that information exchange mechanisms, such as cross-functional teams, liaisons, or other lateral relations, are needed.

There may also be signs at the individual level. When the number of individuals who do not know what is expected of them or who receive conflicting expectations increases, this is an early warning sign that the organizational structure is not appropriate for the environment.

Recognizing these warning signs allows managers to step back and analyze the external environment and the company's strategy. What has changed in the external environment? Are the changes pushing for a flatter structure? Do they require greater specialization regarding customers, products, regions? How does the structure need to change to meet the changing demands of the environment? Is the company's strategy still appropriate? If it is, how can the organizational structure and value chain be reconfigured to better meet the needs of the strategy? To answer these and related questions, managers must have a clear and deep understanding of the principles of organizational structure and design.

managerial perspectives revisited

1   **PERSPECTIVE 1: THE ORGANIZATIONAL CONTEXT**   The term "organizational structure" makes it clear that when it comes to structure, it is impossible to do so independently of the organizational context. First and foremost, you need to consider the organizational context of strategy. The structure needs to fit the strategy. If the strategy is one of speed to market and innovation, then a structure with many layers and strong unit boundaries is inappropriate. For example, Nike needs to get new shoe models to market as fast as possible, so it has a very flat structure. You also have to consider the nature of the organization—its culture and strengths and weaknesses. For example, if the new strategy is one of speed to market and the old organization structure fostered slow, formal, and deliberate decision making, then simply putting in place a new structure on top of old behaviors will not necessarily work. Even if the new structure is the right one for the strategy, its effective implementation has to be considered and planned for in the context of the overall organization.

2   **PERSPECTIVE 2: THE HUMAN FACTOR**   One of the most consistent mistakes made in structuring organizations is to assume that if you change the "boxes and lines"—that is, the organizational chart—that desired new behaviors, flows of information, and so on will automatically follow. They do not. Making an existing or especially new structure work effectively can only happen by working with and through others. In many cases, to meet the objectives of the structure may require new skills and capabilities of people. If you don't work with your employees to help them acquire the skills and capabilities they need, all the organizational structure and design brilliance in the world will make the new organization chart only as valuable as the paper it's printed on. As we discussed previously, Suncor created an entirely new unit with its Major Projects group. However, if manager Kevin Nabholz is unable to help his subordinates learn how to interact effectively with the other units in the company, then the projects his group is supposed to design and build are likely to come in late, over budget, or with the wrong operating performance levels.

3   **PERSPECTIVE 3: MANAGING PARADOXES**   Developing an organizational structure that is integrated yet allows differentiation is a potential paradox managers face. Because of the complexity of the competitive marketplace, very few organizations can afford to choose one over the other. Yet, differentiation makes integration difficult to achieve, and vice versa. Nonetheless, managers must find an appropriate balance between the two types of structures, that matches the strategy adopted by the organization. In Suncor's case, by separating the team working on major projects—differentiating it, in other words—the company was able to bring the specialized engineering and construction talents of many different people to each project. On the other hand, if the coordination between the team working on the projects and the business units that ultimately operate the finished equipment is ineffective, the benefits of this specialization are lost. This is also true in the international context. Most firms face pressures both for global integration and local differentiation. For example, even though Boeing operates in a global environment, the company must master the challenge of thinking globally but acting locally. It gains economies of scale by keeping the basic structure of the 747 the same regardless of where the customer is located or where the plane will be used. On the other hand, the sales process is different for customers in different countries, and planes may require minor adaptations. For example, the labels and signs on the various components within the plane, like its exits, restrooms, and instrument panel, might need to be translated into a different language, depending on the primary country in which the plane will be flown. Boeing's organizational structure must enable it to handle both.

4 PERSPECTIVE 4: ENTREPRENEURIAL MIND-SET In Chapter 1, we explained the importance of an entrepreneurial mind-set to innovation and the ultimate survival and success of an organization. The organization's structure can have a major effect on the development and implementation of an entrepreneurial mind-set. For example, too much formalization may hinder the flexibility needed to be entrepreneurial and innovative. The overcentralization of authority may lead to the same outcome. But a highly differentiated structure along with strong integration can produce more entrepreneurial activity and innovation. As an example, the geographic differentiation of Becton Dickinson in Europe exposed the entire firm to many different local and often unique ideas and ways of operating. If the organization of the company is both strong and integrated, these ideas can be communicated to other units and used by them to create more and better products and services. Likewise, a network structure allows the organization to participate in a number of alliances with external partners. Managers can garner knowledge from these partnerships to enhance their own innovations. For example, Dell makes use of its strategic alliances and knowledge it gains from its partnerships to stay on top of the innovation constantly occurring in its industry.[28]

A commitment not only to the proper design but to the effective implementation of an organization's structure is critical to success. However, changes in structure can occasionally be interpreted by some as threats to power and status of individuals in the organization. As we discussed in Chapter 2, perceived threats to the core elements of a person's sense of self are often the most vociferously resisted. Consequently, a commitment to follow through with reorganization efforts is important, given the potential effect it can have on an organization's entrepreneurial activity, ability to innovate, and overall competitiveness.

concluding comments

Organizational structures can be thought of as information networks or circuits on a circuit board. The structure influences who talks to whom about what and how often, what information moves through the organization, and at what speed. As business and society move from the industrial age to the information age, appropriate organizational structures will be increasingly critical to a firm's success in the marketplace. Likewise, your understanding of and skills at designing effective structures become increasingly critical to your career success. You must be able to quickly and accurately analyze the complexity and dynamism of the internal and external environments.

As Citicorp illustrates, the structure has to fit the environment and the organization's objectives. Citicorp's emphasis on brand and costs placed an emphasis on a structure that would centralize brand management and capture economies of scale in other activities.

In addition, to have a successful managerial career, you need to understand the sometimes opposing forces of globalization and localization. Successful organizational structures may require you to find solutions that meet both needs simultaneously, or to organize various functional activities at different points along the continuum from centralized global activities to decentralized local activities.

In general, designing organizational structure can be one of the more complex activities of management. Its critical role in organizational competitiveness virtually guarantees that managers who understand and are skilled at organizational design will be those who are increasingly given more responsible positions.

key terms

boundaryless organization 250
centralized organizations 238
cognitive differentiation 231
decentralized organizations 238
differentiation 231
flat organization structure 235
formalization 234
globalization 257
informal organization 237

integration 231
interdependence 231
liaisons 250
line of authority 235
localization 257
network structures 248
organizational charts 230
organizational design 230
organizational structure 230

outsourcing 248
profit center 242
span of control 235
tall organization structure 235
task differentiation 231
uncertainty 232
unity of command 235

test your comprehension

1. Define organizational structure. How does it differ from organizational design?
2. What is the main purpose of organizational charts?
3. What is *task differentiation*, and what is its role in organizational design?
4. Why is cognitive differentiation important in organizational design?
5. What are the three major types of interdependence among organizational units?
6. In an organization with a relative high level of certainty and low to moderate level of interdependence among business units, would you recommend rules, goals, or values as the principal means for facilitating integration?

7. In an organization with a relative low level of certainty and high level of interdependence among business units, would you recommend rules, goals, or values as the principal means for facilitating integration?
8. How is line of authority different from chain of command?
9. How does span of control typically relate to tall and flat organization structures?
10. What are the key pros and cons for both centralization and decentralization in organizational structure?
11. What are the key advantages and disadvantages of the functional structure?
12. Why is a matrix structure one of the most difficult to manage effectively?

13. What are the most common advantages and disadvantages of network structures?
14. What are the critical elements of an organization's internal and external environments that a manager should assess in considering a new organizational structure?
15. What are the four basic elements that influence the uncertainty of an organization's external environment?
16. What role does information play in the context of organizational uncertainty?
17. What is the principal role of direct contact, liaisons, and teams in organizational design?
18. How does moving from a purely domestic to an international organization affect organizational structure?
19. What are some of the key warning signs of a poor structure–environment fit?

apply your understanding

1. Universities are typically organized by departments or colleges such as business, biology, engineering, political science, and so on. Is this an appropriate structure? What aspects of the environment support this structure? Are there any aspects of the internal or external environment that currently or in the near future push for *changes* in university structures?
2. Organizational design skills are critical to career success, but total organizational design or redesign typically is not put in the hands of newly hired managers. Why then is it important for you to understand early in your career the structure and the specific differentiation and integration mechanisms of the organization you work in?
3. What would be the likely influence of a collectivist culture (refer back to Chapter 4) on the formal or informal aspects of an organization's structure? What would you expect the influence to be of a strong hierarchical cultural value on line of authority or chain of command in a company's structure?

practicing your capabilities

A friend calls to ask for your advice. She is being offered the position of brand manager for a new sports drink in a large food and beverage company. Everything about the new position (and pay) sounds great to your friend; however, she's been asked how she wants to structure her unit. Specifically, she has been asked how many people she would be comfortable having to report to her. Based on her following description, what span of control would you advise her to take on in her new position?

Most new managers at this level have about four to six subordinates. Your friend indicates that she could have as few as three and as many as thirteen, depending on what she requests and her rationale for the request. Prior to this promotion, your friend has been working on a brand team for three years and acting as the informal team leader for the last 14 months. She was told that part of the reason she was given the promotion is because of how well she seemed to manage her team (three others who were all doing primarily market research work).

The new sports drink has been on the market for six months and has enjoyed a successful launch in the United States and Asia. Continued expansion in Europe and Latin America is expected. Your friend e-mailed you a brief profile of the 13 potential subordinates.

Market Researcher: Three different people are currently working on marketing research related to the product. Much of their work was done prior to the launch and now they focus on customer satisfaction and competitive response. Two of the people work in the United States (one on the East Coast and one on the West Coast) and the other works in Japan.

Statistician: There are two statisticians. One currently is based in the corporate headquarters on the East Coast and the other is based in the European regional headquarters in London. Both do essentially the same job of analyzing data and looking for statistical relationships between customer characteristics, product characteristics, marketing/promotion activities, and buying patterns.

Advertising Specialist: There are three advertising specialists. One deals primarily with print media; one focuses on broadcast media (principally radio and TV); the third specializes in "alternative advertising" that includes everything from promotional contests to the Internet. The print ad and broadcast staff are based in the company's East Cost office, while the alternative advertising person telecommutes from his home in San Diego. The company's nearest West Coast office is in Los Angeles.

Administrative Assistant: There is one administrative assistant, who works for the brand manager that launched the sports drink. This individual acts as secretary, organizer, and general assistant to the brand manager.

Marketing Specialist: There are four marketing specialists. Each one resides in a different region (i.e., United States, Asia, Europe, and Latin America). They are primarily responsible for creating the marketing strategy for their regions. Given that the product has not really launched yet in Europe and Latin America, the two individuals in those regions are currently working on other products and task forces.

Based on this information, your friend presses you for advice.

1. How many total subordinates should she go for? What should be her span of control?
2. If not all 13, which specific subordinates should she ask to have and why?
3. Even while attempting to give your friend some tentative advice on the first two questions, are there other issues you would want to understand or are there questions you would like to ask your friend before providing a more definitive recommendation? If you could only ask three questions, what would be your top priority questions and why?

closing case DEVELOPING YOUR CRITICAL THINKING

Restructuring the Organizational Restructure at Kimberly-Clark

In 2003, Kimberly-Clark, the maker of paper products including Kleenex, Huggies, and Depends, announced it was creating a radical new structure to shore up underperforming parts of its business by restructuring its products into three categories. The categories were "grow," "sustain," and "fix"—somewhat unconventional categories. They weren't devised based on product type, cutomers, or geographic locations in which they sold, but instead on the perceived strength of the products themselves.

Background

Kimberly, Clark and Company was established in 1872 by four young businessmen, John A. Kimberly, Havilah Babcock, Charles B. Clark, and Frank C. Shattuck. Based in Neenah, Wisconsin, the company initially manufactured paper, but over the years it began to branch out, broadening into the personal hygiene consumer products area to compete with companies like Procter & Gamble.

In 1978, Kimberly-Clark introduced what would become its top seller: Huggies disposable diapers. Huggies were an instant hit and soon became the nation's number-one brand. In the next two decades, Kimberly-Clark introduced Depends for adults, training pants for toddlers, and merged with Scott Paper, a leading maker of toilet paper and paper towels. Today, the merged company sells its products in over 150 countries around the world. In about 80 of those countries, it holds the number-one or number-two spot in the marketplace.

Restructuring Problems

Like many corporate mergers, the merger between Kimberly-Clark and Scott Paper in 1995 didn't roll out smoothly. Most of Scott's senior management team left after the merger, and Kimberly-Clark fell behind integrating the two companies. The following year, operating income and sales dropped.

Although senior management finally worked through the integration challenges of the merged companies by the late 1990's, the dawn of the twenty-first century brought new challenges. Chief among these was the lack of growth in developed countries for Kimberly-Clark due to product saturation. If the company were to continue to grow, it had to look to new markets. This was complicated by the fact that it was losing market share to its fiercest rival. P&G introduced a high-end line of Pampers in 2002 that was grabbing market share from Huggies. Given the tough competition in disposable diapers, Kimberly-Clark tried to diversify by going into the related product category of disposable baby-wipes used when changing diapers. These growth plans were upset when Johnson & Johnson, the prominent maker of baby shampoo, launched its own line of baby-wipes.

It was in the context of these competitive dynamics that senior management announced the radical reorganization plan in 2003. In the "grow" category (brands and sectors growing the fastest) would be products like training pants, household towels and wipes, and Kleenex. In the "sustain" category (brands generating solid returns) would be U.S. infant care products and other facial tissues lines. In the "fix" category would be products related to European personal care as well as the U.S. professional washroom business. The sales of these products were relatively flat and although they accounted for about 20 percent of sales, they brought in just 10 percent of profits.

Senior managers argued that this reorganization would help increase the company's speed to market, streamline its decision making when it came to allocating capital, and deliver cost reduction on a sustainable basis. However, while making the reorganization announcement, Kimberly-Clark also announced it would revise its sales forecasts downward from 6 to 8 percent annually to 3 to 5 percent. Predictably, shareholders did not like this, and Kimberly-Clark's stock price closed down for the day.

When Kimberly-Clark rolled out its finalized organizational structure plans in early 2004, the reorganization had been reorganized. Rather than organize products by the "grow, sustain, fix" categories, management announced that it would organize around personal care, washroom products, and emerging markets. Specifically, management planned to combine the company's North American and European personal care groups under one organizational unit. The same would happen for products related to the washroom business. In addition, management would create an "emerging markets" business unit to maximize growth of all its products in Asia, Latin America, and Eastern Europe.

Questions

1. Why do you think Kimberly-Clark considered restructuring its corporation based on "grow, sustain, and fix" categories?
2. How well do you think such a structure might work? What do you perceive would be its advantages and disadvantages?
3. Why do you think Kimberly-Clark reorganized its business structure in 2004 when it finalized its restructuring plans?

Sources: Jack Neff, "K-C Huggies Plans Baby Wipe, Wash Line," *Advertising Age*, December 8, 2003, pp. 49–50; Sam Solley, "Kimberly-Clark Rejigs to 'Repair' Weak Brands," *Marketing (UK)*, July 31, 2003, p. 3; "Kimberly-Clark Earnings Fall in 2Q," *Associated Press*, July 24, 2003; Stephanie Anderson Forest and Heidi Dawly, "Pulp Fiction at Kimberly-Clark," *BusinessWeek*, February 23, 1998.

Planning

8

LEARNING OBJECTIVES

After studying this chapter, you should be able to:

■

Define planning and explain its purpose.

■

Differentiate between strategic, operational, and tactical plans.

■

Explain the planning process.

■

Identify key contingency factors in planning.

■

Explain budgeting as a planning tool.

■

Describe an MBO planning system.

■

Describe effective goals.

Procter & Gamble in Eastern Europe

P rocter & Gamble (P&G), the marketer of Tide detergent, Crest, Swiffer Sweepers, Vidal Sassoon hair care products, and hundreds of other well-known consumer brands, relies heavily on its international markets to sustain long-term growth. Currently, P&G markets almost 300 products to more than five billion consumers in 140 countries, and the company has over 100 manufacturing plants around the world.

A significant portion of P&G's sales are in Western Europe. So it was only natural that P&G corporate and regional executives had a significant interest in the opening of Eastern Europe in 1989, as the Berlin Wall fell. P&G subsequently entered specific

Eastern European countries, which had been deprived of quality Western material goods. However, rather than enter rapidly and make mistakes, the regional executives formulated a specific plan for doing so. The steps to this plan included: (1) analyzing the environment, (2) setting objectives and strategies, (3) determining resources, and (4) monitoring outcomes.

1. Analyzing the Environment

Given the instability of the Eastern European countries, P&G executives in Europe took their time to analyze the environment before expanding. In February 1990, company executives from both corporate headquarters and regional operations took a tour of major markets to assess strengths and weaknesses among the countries, including Hungary, the Czech Republic, and Russia. Executives returned with notes and impressions on both the risks and benefits involved in those markets.

Risks

- Poor infrastructure
- Unstable governments and tense political atmosphere

Benefits

- 400 million consumers
- Highly educated and inexpensive workforce
- Movement to a free market system

Based on the environmental assessment, the company decided to focus first on Poland, the Czech Republic, and Hungary and to enter Russia later, and to do so very cautiously.

2. Setting Objectives and Strategies

P&G executives' next step was to set objectives for its expansion into Eastern Europe. In addition to long- and short-term financial objectives, they had several strategic objectives. Two important objectives were

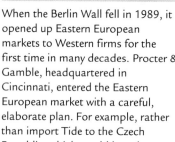

When the Berlin Wall fell in 1989, it opened up Eastern European markets to Western firms for the first time in many decades. Procter & Gamble, headquartered in Cincinnati, entered the Eastern European market with a careful, elaborate plan. For example, rather than import Tide to the Czech Republic, which would have been too costly, P&G engineers worked with a Czech plant to produce and manufacture Tide there.

(1) to achieve the lowest cost and best quality sourcing and (2) to achieve superior distribution.

To provide low-cost, high-quality products, executives determined that they would eventually need regional production capacity, because the high cost of importing goods into the region would make them less affordable to consumers. However, the executives wanted to begin operations quickly without too much risk. So the option of building plants in the beginning was rejected.

The next option was to acquire local manufacturers, although this carried some risk. For example, how could an Eastern European plant manufacture with the same efficiency and high quality as a Western plant? Nonetheless, the strategy was less risky than building the plants from scratch. One such acquisition occurred in the Czech Republic, where P&G found a company called Rakona. P&G engineers worked with Czech employees at the Rakona plant to conduct test runs of Ariel detergent—the equivalent of Tide detergent in Western Europe. After only a few weeks, the detergent produced in the Czech plant was identical to that produced in Western Europe.

To achieve the highest market share, P&G executives decided that they had to expand rapidly. But they found that distribution channels in Eastern Europe were very poorly developed. In the United States, a case of detergent can be delivered to almost any location within 24 hours. However, they found that even under favorable circumstances in Russia, it could take three weeks for a case of detergent to be transferred from the Moscow area across Siberia to Vladivostok on the eastern shore.

3. Determining Resources

Once objectives and strategies were set, P&G executives determined what resources were needed. The executives figured that the most critical resource was human—the employees who would build the business in Eastern Europe. Both experienced P&G managers from other parts of the world—including the headquarters in Cincinnati—and local men and women would be needed. And, these employees would need both technical and managerial skills to succeed.

4. Monitoring Outcomes

During the implementation of its plan, P&G executives were careful to monitor the outcomes, both financial and strategic, in each of the countries they entered. The results have reflected an overall success story in Eastern Europe. After four years of operation, annual sales rose to $500 million, making the company the largest consumer goods firm in the entire region. Twenty-five brands served the markets, and most were among the top two or three in their product categories. The business also became profitable within the first four years, although it had taken eight years to turn a profit in Western Europe.

In recent years, P&G has heightened its marketing strategy by pooling the purchasing of information on its brands from sixteen different European companies to help it determine trends. The company's executives remain optimistic about their long-term business in Eastern Europe. Because of its careful, thorough planning, the company expects to net high returns over the long term.

Sources: "P&G Overhauls Euro Data Strategy," *Precision Marketing*, October 31, 2003, p. 1; Personal communication with John Pepper, 2001; P&G 2001 *Annual Report*; John Pepper, "Leading the Change in Eastern Europe," *Business Quarterly*, Autumn 1995, pp. 26–33.

strategic overview

The opening case clearly illustrates the importance of a manager's ability to formulate and implement effective plans. Although planning has been an important managerial activity for some time, it is perhaps more important and perplexing now than ever before. On the one hand, the increase in competition means that if an organization, business unit, or individual manager fails to plan and as a consequence drifts off course or loses momentum, competitors are likely to overtake it. On the other hand, the speed of change and rapid flow of information increasingly require plans that are flexible and dynamic. In today's world, a rigid plan can be as fatal as no plan at all. As important as competition and the rate of change are, both must be viewed within the context of globalization for a manager to be successful today and in the future. Increasingly, as a manager you must not only be aware of local competitors, but also those in other parts of the world. In addition, you must recognize that because information flows throughout the world nearly instantaneously, it can create the need for rapid and dramatic changes in your plans.

Effective planning at all organizational levels can have a significant impact on the firm's performance. Without effective planning, P&G might have failed in its efforts to enter and compete successfully in the Eastern European markets. But, the company's activities in these markets turned out to be highly effective, in part because managers had a plan and regularly reevaluated and changed it. Managers need to continuously analyze and understand their external markets, and adjust their plans accordingly. Today, the instantaneous availability of information, rapid changes in economies, markets, and the political environments of countries that firms do business with impact planning continuously. Managers need to be prepared to adapt to changes that occur rapidly, no matter what their plans are—or were.

This requires managers to accurately analyze their internal resources. Managers at P&G, for example, determined that people were the most important component of the plan to enter and succeed in the Eastern European markets. Their conclusion is borne out by current research. In fact, some current research suggests that an organization's human capital is absolutely critical to the successful implementation of a firm's strategic plans.[1]

An analysis of the organization's internal resources and external environment helps a manager determine the company's strengths, like the organization's core competencies, along with its weaknesses and how they might affect its future plans.[2] This analysis can also identify the other resources managers will need to implement their plans and ultimately achieve their goals. ▪

AN OVERVIEW OF PLANNING

objectives the end states or targets that company managers aim for

plans the means by which managers hope to hit the desired targets

planning a decision-making process that focuses on the future of an organization and how it will achieve its goals

Few activities are more basic to management than deciding where the company is going and how it is going to get there. Organizational **objectives** are the end states or targets that managers aim for, while **plans** are the means by which managers hope to hit the desired targets. **Planning**, then, is essentially a decision-making process that focuses on the future of the organization and how it will achieve its goals. From this perspective, setting organizational objectives has to precede the development of organizational plans. Without objectives or targets, plans make very little sense. Objectives help set direction, focus effort, guide behaviors, and evaluate progress.[3] Interestingly, managers sometimes spend so much time formulating objectives that they neglect to develop detailed plans that will enable them to achieve their goals. This is akin to making a commitment to graduate from college without any idea about what classes to take or when certain classes need to be taken. It is easy to see why organizational results are significantly influenced not just by objectives but also by the plans for hitting the targets. We now explore the types of plans that exist, the basic planning process, and the methods for implementing plans effectively.

Types of Plans

Strategic/Tactical/ Operational Plans by Michael Hitt

Q&A

OneKey

www.prenhall.com/onekey

Today, few organizations of any size offer just one product or service. As a consequence, they cannot develop a single plan to cover all organizational activities. For example, you may recall from Chapter 7 that Becton Dickinson has businesses ranging from hypodermic needles to surgical equipment. To understand the planning process for complex organizations, we need to differentiate among three types of plans[4] (see Exhibit 8.1).

exhibit 8.1

Types of Plans: Key Differences

	Strategic Plans	**Tactical Plans**	**Operational Plans**
Time Horizon	Typically 3–5 years	Often focused on 1–2 years in the future	Usually focused on the next 12 months or less.
Scope	Broadest; originating with a focus on the entire organization	Rarely broader than a strategic business unit	Narrowest; usually centered on departments or smaller units of the organization
Complexity	The most complex and general, because of the different industries and business potentially covered	Somewhat complex but more specific, because of the more limited domain of application	The least complex, because they usually focus on small, homogenous units
Impact	Have the potential to dramatically impact, both positively and negatively, the fortunes and survival of the organization	Can affect specific businesses but generally not the fortunes or survivability of the entire organization	Impact is usually restricted to specific department or organization unit
Interdependence	High interdependence; must take into account the resources and capabilities of the entire organization and its external environments	Moderate interdependence; must take into account the resources and capabilities of several units within a business	Low interdependence; the plan may be linked to higher-level tactical and strategic plans but is less interdependent with them

Strategic Plans Strategic plans focus on the broad future of the organization and incorporate both external environmental demands and internal resources into the actions managers need to take to achieve the long-term goals of the organization. There is some evidence that the rigorous use of strategic plans is associated with superior financial performance.[5] As we examined in the previous chapter, strategic plans cover the major aspects of the organization including its products, services, finances, technology, and human resources. Although the concept of "long term" has no precise definition, most strategic plans focus on how to achieve goals one to five years into the future. For example, after the passage of NAFTA (North American Free Trade Agreement), the Mexican state of Sonora, which borders Arizona, had a strategic plan to revitalize its economy. In evaluating the state's strengths and weaknesses, government officials decided that the most effective way to revitalize its economy was to take advantage of its beautiful beaches and to encourage tourism.

strategic plans focus on the broad future of the organization and incorporate both external environmental demands and internal resources into managers' actions

Tactical Plans Tactical plans translate strategic plans into specific goals for specific parts of the organization. Consequently, they tend to have somewhat shorter time frames and to be narrower in scope. Instead of focusing on the entire corporation, tactical plans typically affect a single business within an organization. While tactical plans should complement the overall strategic plan, they are often somewhat independent of other tactical plans. For example, the tactical plans of the transportation department for Sonora called for improving the roads leading from the border with Arizona to the beach resorts. The tactical plans of the commerce department called for making special low-interest loans available to companies that would build western-styled quality hotels in the targeted region. While the tactical plans of the transportation and commerce departments were different, both served to support the overall strategic plan of Sonora. A Manager's Challenge, "The Bellagio: Using Technology for Effective Tactical Plan Execution," provides an interesting example of how one company used technology to enhance the execution of an important tactical plan—the hiring of nearly 10,000 workers in five instead of the normal nine to twelve months for a new hotel. As you read this, imagine yourself facing the planning challenge of hiring 10,000 workers in less than half the normal time and still having to ensure that the right people with the right capabilities and characteristics are selected.

tactical plans translate strategic plans into specific goals for specific parts of the organization

Operational Plans Operational plans translate tactical plans into specific goals and actions for small units of the organization and focus on the near term. The near term is typically 12 months or less. These plans are the least complex of the three and rarely have a direct impact beyond the department or unit for which the plan was developed. For example, in the case of the Mexican state of Sonora, the purchasing section within the department of transportation created an operational plan that called for the purchase of several new road graders and a new steamroller to facilitate the expansion of the main highway from a two-lane to a four-lane highway.

operational plans translate tactical plans into specific goals and actions for small units of the organization and focus on the near term

As summarized in Exhibit 8.1, strategic, tactical, and operational plans differ from each other on five important dimensions: time horizon, scope, complexity, impact, and interdependence.[6] While these differences matter, the three types of plans should be aligned and integrated with each other. Unfortunately, this type of alignment and integration occurs in only one-third of companies.[7] In addition to types of plans, for a more complete understanding, we need to examine planning at different levels in the organization.

tech|nol|ogy   *a manager's challenge*

Bellagio: Using Technology for Effective Tactical Plan Execution

When Mirage Resorts decided to build the Bellagio, one of Las Vegas' most luxurious hotels, it was no small feat. The blueprints called for 3,000 rooms, a large gallery to hold a fine-art collection, a glass-domed conservatory, a theater equipped to hold Cirque du Soleil's new water show, an eight-acre replica of Italy's Lake Como—along with the most upscale designer shops and gourmet restaurants. The cost of this, before Bellagio's doors even opened, would run about $1.6 billion. In addition, Mirage had to find a way to recruit nearly 10,000 workers to staff the hotel. Clearly, the company needed a tactical plan to accomplish this.

As construction got underway, Mirage Resorts' human resource executives began the hiring process. Because of the number of jobs that needed to be filled—by the right people— HR executives at the Mirage had to come up with a plan for receiving and sorting through the anticipated tens of thousands of applications. Even after extracting the best candidates from the applications, managers still had to interview thousands of candidates and to make employment offers.

As part of their plan, executives budgeted $1 million for a computer software system that would screen as many as 75,000 job candidates. The plan was to complete this screening in three months and to eliminate those who were not suitable and extract those who might be. To recruit the initial applicants, executives planned to run large ads in newspapers announcing that they were hiring employees for the new hotel. The plan called for a toll-free number that applicants would call to make an appointment to fill out an application (not for an interview).

Once the applicants were on file in the computer system and the software program had culled out the inappropriate applicants, the plan called for interviews of an estimated 25,000 to 30,000 candidates at a rate of 700 interviews per day! To do this, executives estimated that they would need to hire and specially train 180 interviewers. In other words, the plan called for hiring people to hire people. The results of the interviews would be entered into a database for later reference.

The plan called for some low-tech screening mechanisms as well. For example, if a candidate showed up to the interview late without notifying someone, he or she would be dropped from the process. Then Vice President Arte Nathan explained it this way: "If people didn't show up for their appointments, we figured they'd be no-shows at work, too."

The hiring plan also anticipated the need to conduct as many as 20,000 background checks on candidates that suc-

Opening the Bellagio hotel-casino in 1998 required its owner, Mirage Resorts, Inc., to hire a whopping 10,000 employees in only five months' time. The task included screening 75,000 applicants and conducting as many as 700 interviews a day to find the best candidates. Similar to building the hotel, it was no small undertaking. Careful and systematic planning, however, made the hiring process a success.

cessfully made it through the interviews. This would need to be done in short order—within just a month or two—and so the plan was to contract with a professional firm to conduct these background checks on behalf of Mirage Resorts.

This was the plan. So how well did things go? Overall, the plan was well constructed and executed. Instead of the normal nine months it had taken the company to staff a new hotel in the past, this plan resulted in the attracting, screening, and hiring of 10,000 employees in only five months. Arte Nathan also claimed that the process saved the company not only time but direct costs on items such as paper, temporary help, and file space to the tune of $600,000. Bellagio opened on time and with the right employees trained and in place, in part because of the effective tactical plan for hiring.

Sources: "Bellagio," *Meetings & Conventions*, November 2003, p. 4; E. P. Gunn, "How Mirage Resorts Sifted 75,000 Applications to Hire 9,600 in 24 Weeks," *Fortune*, October 12, 1998, p. 195; J. Gurzinksi, "A Raft of Preparation at Bellagio," *Las Vegas Review Journal*, September 30, 1998.

Organizational Levels

In addition to plans that address strategic, tactical, and operational issues of the organization, managers at different levels of the company face different planning challenges. Exhibit 8.2 provides a graphical representation of the three primary levels of a corporation. Managers at each level attempt to address somewhat different questions.

Corporate Level Most corporations of even moderate size have a corporate headquarters. However, complex and large organizations, such as Brunswick with $3.4 billion in annual sales, often divide the various businesses of the company into large groups. For Brunswick, these groups include marine and recreation. The heads of these groups are typically part of the group of senior executives at the corporate headquarters. Executives at the corporate level in large firms would include both those in the headquarters and those heading up the large corporate groups such as finance, human resources, legal, and so on. These corporate-level executives would primarily focus on questions such as the following:

- What industries should we get into or out of?
- What markets should the firm be in? For example, is it time to move aggressively into China? If so, what businesses should move first?
- In which businesses should the corporation invest money?

In the case of Brunswick, if coordination across the marine and recreation groups or across businesses within the groups is beneficial, it is the responsibility of corporate-level managers to recognize and capture those opportunities.

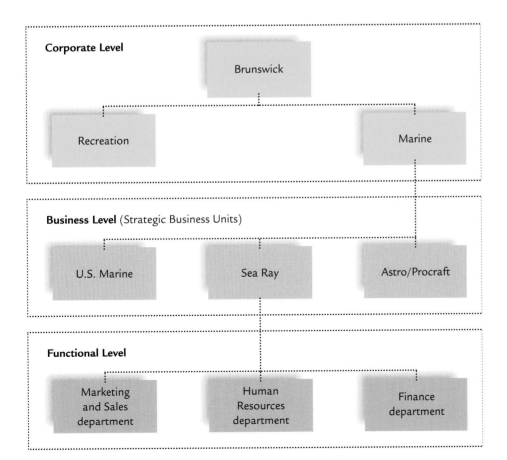

exhibit 8.2
Organizational Levels

Business Level The next level is sometimes referred to as the SBU, or strategic business unit level. At this level managers focus on determining how they are going to compete effectively in the market. For example, within the marine area that includes businesses such as Sea Ray boats and Mercury engines, managers attempt to address questions such as the following:

- Who are our direct competitors?
- What are their strengths and weaknesses?
- What are our strengths and weaknesses?
- What do customers value in the products or services we offer?
- What advantages do we have over competitors?

In Chapter 6 we examined some of the tools business-level managers can use to answer these questions. However, the questions help you see that the planning questions that SBU-level managers face are more focused on how to compete effectively in the business of today than on what businesses to be in tomorrow. If coordination across different departments (finance, marketing, product development, and so on) or units within the SBU is needed, SBU-level managers are responsible for recognizing and capturing those opportunities.

Functional Level At the functional level, managers focus on how they can facilitate the achievement of the competitive plan of the business. These managers are often heads of departments such as finance, marketing, human resources, or product development. Depending on the SBU's structure, functional managers may include managers responsible for the business within a specific geographic region or managers who are responsible for a specific product like Sea Ray boats. Generally, these functional managers attempt to address questions such as the following:

- What activities does my unit need to perform well in order to meet customer expectations?
- What information about competitors does my unit need in order to help the business compete effectively?
- What are our unit's strengths and weaknesses?

The main focus of functional managers' planning activities is on how they can support the SBU plan. Functional-level managers are responsible for recognizing and capturing the opportunity, if coordination between individuals within a unit is needed or beneficial.

Interaction Between Plan Types and Levels

Strategic plans typically get developed at the corporate level. In fact, strategic planning is arguably the key planning responsibility of corporate managers. Corporate managers, however, tend not to get involved in developing tactical or operational plans. SBU-level managers may be involved in developing strategic plans for their business units and are usually involved in developing tactical plans for their business. However, SBU-level managers typically do not get involved in developing operational plans. In contrast, functional-level managers are not often involved in developing either strategic or tactical plans. Instead, their planning responsibilities tend to focus on the development of operational plans. Exhibit 8.3 illustrates the general pattern of planning responsibility by organizational level. Keep in mind, however, that the specific pattern in any given organization could be different. For example, the size of the

Types of Plans

Strategic plans

Tactical plans

Operational plans

Organizational Levels

Corporate level

Business level

Functional level

exhibit 8.3

Interaction Between Plans and Levels

organization could affect the pattern. In small organizations, corporate managers might be involved in developing strategic, tactical, *and* operational plans.

THE PLANNING PROCESS

The planning process has seven key elements: environmental analysis, objectives, requirements, resources, actions, implementation, and outcomes (see Exhibit 8.4). In this section, we will examine each of these elements and their role in the overall planning process.

Analyzing the Environment

The first element of the planning process is an assessment of the environment. Managers who formulate or implement plans in the absence of any assessment of the environment may very well fall short of producing the desired results. In contrast, managers who carefully scan the environment and incorporate the information gathered into the planning process can enjoy greater success in the outcomes of the plans they formulate and implement.[8]

Forecasts   One of the principal tools managers use in assessing the environment is a forecast. Forecasts are or can be made about virtually every critical element in the environment that managers believe could affect the organiza-

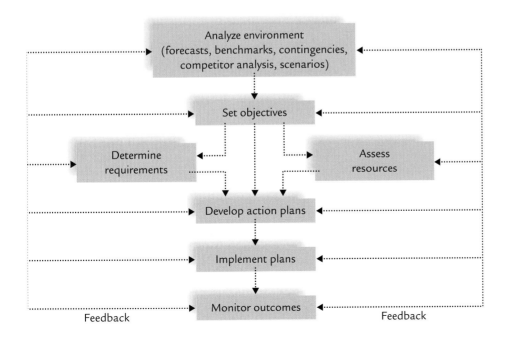

exhibit 8.4

Planning Process

tion or their area of responsibility.[9] For example, if you were in the residential construction business, interest rate forecasts would be important to you. Generally, as interest rates go up and borrowing money becomes more expensive, fewer people purchase new homes. Those that still purchase new homes necessarily have to purchase less expensive homes than they could if interest rates were lower. Planning for the number of houses to build in the coming year would, as a consequence, be influenced by the interest rate forecast. We saw this issue in Chapter 3 with KB Homes.

Interestingly, there is a cascading effect of forecasts. For example, if you forecast that you will build only 1,000 homes instead of 1,500 homes over the next year because interest rates are expected to rise from 6 percent to 7 percent, then you might also forecast a decline in revenues. This may lead the purchasing manager to plan for smaller purchases of lumber and may lead the human resource manager to plan for a smaller number of construction workers. The key point for managers is that it's vital to know what the key forecasts are in the company and to keep track of any changes so that any cascading effects can be recognized earlier rather than later.

Environmental Uncertainty Obviously, forecasting accurately is a tough business. Things frequently change and don't work out the way we anticipate.[10] In Chapter 3, we talked about the key external general and task environmental forces that can change things. In 1988, no one was predicting the fall of the Berlin Wall in 1989. In early 2000, no one was predicting the worst two years of stock market performance that followed in 2002. The key issue for managers and their planning activities is that the greater the environmental

Minnesota Mining & Manufacturing (3M) was founded in 1902 by a lawyer, a doctor, two railroad executives, and a meat market owner hoping to get rich by mining a superhard material called corundum, used to make grinding wheels. But the soft rock 3M was mining turned out to be an inferior abrasive for wheel grinding, so the company began producing sandpaper instead. Unfortunately, it wasn't a very good product because the humidity in Minnesota kept the paper from drying properly. The company's first breakthrough product, Wetordry sandpaper—developed in response to the humidity problem—didn't come out until 1921.

uncertainty, the more flexible their plans need to be. In some cases, managers may even develop **contingency plans**. Contingency plans typically identify key factors that could affect the desired results and specify what different actions will be taken if changes in key events occur.[11]

For example, suppose you were a manager at KB. Clearly, forecasts of future interest rates would be important to you. The forecast might call for interest rates to remain unchanged for the next year. But can you trust the forecast? Rather than just rely on the forecast, you might be better off to develop contingency plans. For instance, what if interest rates go up one point? It is likely that people will buy fewer houses or less expensive houses. Your contingency plan might be to offer reduced financing charges if customers include certain upgrades in their homes such as granite countertops. You could perhaps afford to offer buyers this incentive because your profits from the upgrades might be greater than the costs of the finance subsidies. By having this contingency plan in place in advance of the change in interest rates, you can be more prepared to respond.

A Manager's Challenge, "Changing Well-Laid Plans at EMC," provides a great illustration of how dramatically plans may have to change when reality turns out to be different from forecasts. In this case, the forecast of the future was based on such a successful past that few people anticipated how dramatically and quickly things could change. This past success made the future seem deceptively certain, and so EMC did not have contingency plans to fall back on when it became clear that reality would not match forecasts. Why do you think EMC failed to have any contingency plans? Do you think it would have fared better if it had had some contingency plans?

Benchmarking A more recent and popular means of assessing the environment is benchmarking. **Benchmarking** is the investigation of the best results among competitors and noncompetitors and the practices that lead to those results.[12] In terms of results, managers might assess competitors that have the highest revenue-to-employee ratio as a means of assessing productivity. Managers would then compare their own revenue-to-employee ratio to get an idea of where they stood relative to competitors. As part of this assessment, they would also investigate the practices that appeared to contribute to high revenue-to-employee ratios. For example, they might find that the firms with the highest ratio tend to have fewer levels of managers because they push decision-making authority down in the organization and have a strong focus on participative management and employee involvement.

These same types of assessments might also be made of noncompetitors. The inclusion of noncompetitors has potential pitfalls and benefits that are different from benchmarking competitors. Clearly, noncompetitors can have underlying business factors that make appropriate comparisons difficult. For example, a telemarketing company that sells relatively inexpensive items over the phone will have a much lower revenue-to-employee ratio than a maker of supercomputers. The telemarketing firm has a relatively labor-intensive business, while the maker of supercomputers has a technology-intensive business. These same problems of comparison and relevance can be present when examining the best practices of noncompetitors. The inventory practices of a service firm may be difficult to apply directly to a manufacturing firm. However, by looking outside one's set of competitors, totally new and significantly better ways of doing things can be found.

Consider the case of Outback Steakhouse. Even though the steel industry was totally different from the franchise restaurant industry, Outback

contingency plans identify key factors that could affect the desired results and specify what actions will be taken if key events change

benchmarking the investigation of the best results among competitors and noncompetitors and the practices that lead to those results

a manager's challenge

Change

Changing Well-Laid Plans at EMC

If you were a shareholder of the telecommunications corporation EMC during the 1990s, and you sold your shares near the end of that decade, you would likely be retired (and not reading this text). During that period, EMC returned a staggering 84,000 percent to shareholders! By the end of 2000, the company controlled 71 percent of the upper-end of the data storage market. Seventy percent of its $8.9 billion in revenues and 92 percent of its $2.3 billion in operating profits were derived from sales of its storage hardware.

But then the bubble burst. Telecom companies and dotcoms that had spent nearly $2 billion on EMC products in 2000 spent virtually nothing in 2001 as they struggled for survival. In addition, other key customers froze their IT budgets. As a consequence, EMC saw its revenues plunge. If that weren't enough, IBM and Hitachi launched products and a price war aimed at EMC's most lucrative segment of products. In 2001, EMC tried to maintain prices but could not. It saw its market share drop from 71 percent to 57 percent and watched in horror as its gross margins dropped by 25 percentage points to 32 percent, as it lowered its prices to compete with IBM and Hitachi, but could not lower its costs as fast.

HR managers had staffing plans and compensation plans, sales managers had sales plans, R&D managers had research plans for 2001 that were based on a growth trajectory and forecast mirroring results in 2000 and years prior. Suddenly, all of those plans had to change—and not just for one year. The troubles of 2001 did not just mark a bad year but revealed a turning point for EMC.

Prior to 2001, data storage was a mission-critical function of virtually all firms of moderate or larger sizes. Customer information, financial data, inventory, sales, purchasing, and personnel data all needed to be stored, duplicated, and protected. In addition, IBM, Hitachi, and EMC had their own proprietary systems. In other words, an IBM system could not talk to or work with a Hitachi or EMC system or vice versa. In fact, once a customer selected a storage system, it was, in a sense, held hostage to it, because it was just too expensive to subsequently switch to another system.

Joe Tucci, EMC's new CEO in 2001, announced a bold change in strategy that would change EMC's future. Tucci was going to split EMC into two companies. The first would continue to make "the best storage hardware in the world." The second would focus on software and services with the ultimate objective of creating software that could manage storage requirements regardless of the hardware (IBM, Hitachi, or EMC). In fact, Tucci wanted 50 percent of revenues to come from software and services by 2004.

This had a profound impact on managers throughout the company. For example, HR managers not only had to scrap their hiring and recruiting plans, but they had to develop plans to downsize (terminate) 19,000 people. In addition, they had to revise future recruiting plans to focus on software engineers and others who could help develop the new integrative software that would be needed to achieve Tucci's revenue target of 50 percent.

Sales managers of the new software group had to implement new motivation and incentive plans. EMC hardware products traditionally had cost its customers millions of dollars. Consequently, commissions were very significant to its sales force. In addition, because the products of its three main rivals were incompatible, motivating sales people to "kill" the competition was the norm. In the new software sales unit, EMC's products would cost only thousands of dollars—not millions. Furthermore, the salespeople found themselves in the awkward position of telling their customers that whatever storage hardware they now chose (IBM, Hitachi, or EMC) didn't matter. Yet these same salespeople had previously spent years telling them that no hardware could match EMC's.

Some of EMC's R&D managers had to completely shift their plans, as well. Whereas in the past they had simply been concerned with developing technologies to enhance the speed, reliability, and performance of EMC's proprietary products, now they would need to focus on competing products and develop technologies and software language that would not only work with those products but enhance their features, too.

And what does Tucci say about all of EMC's prior plans to which it ultimately laid waste? "Companies that are afraid to disrupt themselves almost 100 percent of the time end up being disrupted [by competitors]. I'm doing what our competitors never thought we had the intestinal fortitude to do."

Sources: Amit Asaravala, "EMC Is Resolute," *Intelligent Enterprise*, December 10, 2003, p. 8; EMC *Annual Report*, 2001; Daniel Roth, "Can EMC Restore Its Glory?" *Fortune*, July 22, 2002, pp. 107–10.

Benchmarking—examining the best practices of one's competitors—can work across industries, too. Outback Steakhouse, an international restaurant chain, borrowed an idea utilized by steel mills to motivate its managers, which includes a profit-sharing plan. Outback Steakhouses are managed by a three-person team: a managing partner, manager, and kitchen manager. Because the restaurants are open only for dinner, managers and employees are also able to enjoy a better work–life balance, making Outback an attractive employer.

Steakhouse found a motivational practice used by several "mini-mills" in the steel industry that it incorporated with great success. Like any franchise restaurant, Outback makes money as its restaurants make money. The person who makes or breaks a restaurant is the local restaurant manager. In particular, the manager must hire the right people and motivate them effectively to ensure good food and service for the customers. The key for Outback is how to motivate its restaurant managers. The "best practice" that Outback adopted was giving the restaurant managers some ownership in the restaurants they managed. That way if a restaurant made money, so did the manager. The manager felt more like an owner and less like an employee. The adoption of this best practice has had a positive effect on the success of Outback Steakhouse. Thus, even though benchmarking noncompetitors requires some judgment as to what is relevant or appropriate, it can also lead to ideas and practices that put you ahead of the competition.

Benchmarking can be a useful activity even for young managers. For example, suppose you were a sales manager with five salespeople reporting to you. You might want to benchmark outcomes such as revenue-per-salesperson as well as processes such as goal setting. How were other sales mangers setting goals with their subordinates? The key principle in benchmarking is constant curiosity about what others are accomplishing and how they are doing it.

Setting Objectives

The second element in the planning process is the setting of objectives or desired outcomes. As we mentioned at the beginning of this chapter, it is difficult to establish or implement specific actions without an idea of where those steps are intended to go or what they are expected to achieve.

Priorities and Multiple Objectives One of the first challenges for managers as they set objectives is to determine priorities.[13] Not all objectives are of equal importance or value. Furthermore, some objectives might be important now and less important later. Without a clear understanding of which objectives are most important and temporal priorities, employees may be working at odds with each other or create unnecessary conflicts.[14]

Consider your own university. Most universities have multiple and sometimes conflicting objectives. For example, on the one hand, students feel they pay tuition in order to learn leading-edge content from the best professors the school has to offer. Universities cannot ignore the expectations of this important set of its constituents. At the same time, in order to generate leading-edge knowledge, universities must hire top researchers and fund their research. Without a clear idea of the university's priorities, department heads may find it difficult to determine how best to plan the allocation of the department budget. How much of the budget should go toward activities that help develop the teaching skills of the faculty? How much should go toward funding research?

Similar potential conflicts might exist for a sales manager weighing the objectives of increasing market share and profitability. In many instances, market share can be gained by lowering prices, but this usually hurts profits. The salespeople who work for the manager would have a difficult time knowing exactly where and how to focus their efforts unless she makes her priorities clear. Are they to sacrifice a sale in order to protect profit margins? Should they offer a small discount to get the sale? At what point would the discount be considered too big to be acceptable? These are the kinds of practical questions that have to be addressed in setting multiple objectives.

There can also be temporal priorities among objectives.[15] For example, suppose you are launching a new product in an established market with well-positioned competitors. You might decide that your current objective is to gain market share and thereby establish a presence in the market. You tell your salespeople to go after 10 percent market share and to offer discounts of up to 20 percent when needed to get the sale. However, once your product is established at, say, a 10 percent market share, you want your salespeople to focus on profitability objectives over increased market share. Without a clear understanding of this sequence in priorities, your salespeople would not be as able to help you achieve your overall objectives. If there are sequences to objectives, spelling them out in advance can help subordinates better understand what is expected of them.

Measuring Objectives Once you've made your organization's objectives clear, how are you going to measure them? For example, you might determine that financial performance is the number-one objective. However, financial performance can be measured in a variety of ways.[16] It can be measured in terms of profits relative to sales or profits relative to assets. For example, recall that Nordstrom measured clerks' performance in terms of sales per hour. This is in contrast to many other retailers that simply measure net sales. Why does this small difference matter? If your salespeople are measured on net sales, they will likely be motivated to work the greatest number of hours they can. In contrast, Nordstrom's sales-per-hour objective causes clerks to focus on "sales efficiency" or selling the most in every hour they work, not necessarily on working more hours. As we mentioned before, the best way to improve sales per hour is to sell to repeat customers, because as soon as they walk in the door you know the types of things they like, what their budget is, and so on. Specific measures matter. Even slight differences such as net sales versus sales per hour can have important influences on behavior.[17]

As another illustration of the importance of measures, consider the case of Onvance. The company installed TVs in convenience stores that aired constant segments on local sports and weather, interspersed with copious bursts of 10- to 30-second commercials for products in the stores. The commercials sent products flying off the shelves, but the operation ultimately went bust. One problem was that managers measured performance based on total stores and brands it handled, not profits.

Determining Requirements

The third element in the planning process is the determination of requirements. Managers essentially address the question "What will it take in order to get from here to there?" The "there" is essentially the objectives discussed in the previous section. The "here" requires an assessment or knowledge of where things are today.

To begin the process of determining what is required to get from here to there, you first need to understand the key drivers for the journey. For example, let's suppose you are in the athletic shoe manufacturing business, and your objective is to increase your market share from 10 percent to 15 percent. What is it that drives market share? To drive market share you determine you need to do two things. First, you determine that you need a new line of products at the top end where you currently have none. Second, you determine that superior shoe cushion is a key driver of market share for mid-priced running shoes. You discover that running shoe customers make their purchases based on how well a shoe absorbs ground impact. Currently, your cushion technology is not superior. Consequently, it will take new material to improve the shock absorbency of your shoes.

Assessing Resources

The fourth element in the planning process is an assessment of the required resources and the resources available to you. While this element is closely tied to the identification of requirements, the two are not the same. The easiest way to differentiate the two may be to think of requirements as what is needed to achieve the objectives, and resources as how much is available.

Resources Required Let's return to our athletic shoe example and the key requirement of a new line of products at the top end of the market. Relative to this key requirement, the first critical question is, "What resources are needed to produce a new high-end product?" Let's suppose you determine that it will take three top product-design engineers two months and a budget of $100,000 to produce a prototype. Further, you determine that it will take new equipment at a cost of $500,000 to manufacture the new high-end shoes. Finally, you determine that it will take an advertising and promotion budget of $2 million to effectively launch the new line. These, of course, do not address all the resources required to design, produce, and sell the new high-end product line, but they do illustrate the financial, human, equipment, and technology resources that might be required.

A Manager's Challenge, "Planning to Enter a New Country," helps illustrate the difficulty of assessing required resources when the task is new to the planners. While planning is often presented as a logical and straightforward managerial function, that presentation can be deceptive. When facing new situations, you often "don't know what you don't know" and therefore have difficulty determining what is required, even if you know what you want to do.

Resources Available Knowing what resources are required leads naturally to the next assessment: What resources are available? Clearly, for a plan to be effective it must not only be well formulated but it must be feasible to implement.[18] If the resources required significantly exceed those available,

globalization *a manager's challenge*

Planning to Enter a New Country

Greg is the business development manager in a mid-sized consulting and training firm based in southern California. The firm specializes in the identification and training of individuals suited for international assignments. The firm was started several years ago based on the research of two professors who identified certain characteristics that were associated with success when individuals were sent from their home country to a foreign country on assignment. Typically, these assignments are three or so years in length.

The firm had developed a survey instrument that assessed individuals on the dimensions shown to enhance international assignment success. Essentially, individuals would complete a paper-and-pencil test. Greg's firm would compute the scores and generate a report, highlighting the strengths and weaknesses of the individual relative to an international assignment.

While much of the original research was based on samples of U.S. managers being sent to various countries around the world, over the last several years, Greg's firm had done further research looking at the validity of the instrument with samples of managers from various other countries. The research had included managers from Korea being sent abroad, managers from Japan being sent overseas, as well as managers from various European countries. The results suggested that the same dimensions that were associated with success for Americans going overseas were valid for managers of other nationalities being sent abroad.

The executive team had identified Japan as a market in which they could expand their testing and training business. Japan sent more of its managers on international assignments than nearly all the other Asian countries combined. Furthermore, Japanese companies had a history of providing training, especially language training, to managers sent overseas on assignments. However, Japanese companies had virtually no history of using tests to either identify high-potential international assignment candidates or to give candidates insights about their strengths and weaknesses.

Greg's challenge was to plan the firm's entry into the Japanese market. Should it create an office on its own, create a joint venture with an existing Japanese company, or simply license its products for resale in Japan to a company there? The senior executives determined that they did not want to share the anticipated profits with a joint venture partner or a licensee. They determined that they would enter the Japan market through direct investment.

Now Greg had to determine what it would take to enter the market. However, he did not speak Japanese and had not lived in the country before. He had heard many stories of famous (and much bigger) companies that had tried to enter the Japanese market and failed. Greg found that many of the legal questions about what it would take to set up an office in Japan could be answered. But what would it take in terms of the number and types of salespeople to sell the company's instrument and training in Japan? How long would it take? Greg had learned from others experienced with doing business in the country that Japanese firms were often hesitant to use a product their peers did not use, like the testing instrument Greg's firm had developed. However, the fact that virtually no other competitors had an assessment instrument in Japan was what made the market look so promising. How could Greg spell out what was required to enter and succeed in the market when he personally did not have expertise there? Greg couldn't determine if the firm had the money or other resources for the entry plan to succeed until he knew what was required, and yet he was not confident he knew or could fully determine what those requirements were.

Source: Personal conversation. Names have been disguised at the company's request.

either new resources need to be acquired or the plan must be changed. Changing the plan may require going back and changing the objective. In assessing resources available, managers must ask themselves questions such as the following:

- Do we have the needed human talent to meet the requirements?
- Even if we have the needed talent, is it available? Can we take people off what they are currently working on in order to put them on the new project?
- If we don't have the necessary talent, can we develop or acquire it within the needed time frame?

- Do we have the financial resources available? Can we get additional funding from the debt or equity markets?
- Do we have the required technology or can we gain access to it at a cost-effective price?

While these are certainly not the only questions managers would need to ask, they provide a reflection of the types of questions that would need to be addressed in order to determine if there is a gap between the resources required and those available. If there is a gap, managers must determine if it can be bridged or if the objectives and key requirements need to be changed to fit the available resources. For example, when a division of EDS changed its strategy to focus on selling solutions to product development problems and not just computer-aided-design (CAD) products, it found that it needed new salespeople with different skills. Before, when they sold CAD products, salespeople from EDS usually talked to middle-level executives in the engineering and product design areas. In trying to sell more integrated solutions, EDS salespeople needed to talk with more senior executives. In the end, EDS managers both trained some of their best existing salespeople and recruited new salespeople as well.

Developing Action Plans

The fifth element in the planning process is the development of specific action plans. The action plans are essentially the marching orders that everyone uses to accomplish the established objectives.

Sequence and Timing A key element of an effective action plan is the sequence and timing of the specific steps or actions that must be taken.[19] One of the common tools used to graphically display the sequence and timing of the specific actions is a Gantt Chart (see Exhibit 8.5). Time is typically on the horizontal axis and the tasks to be done are on the vertical axis. The chart shows when actions are to be started and how long they are expected to take for completion. It shows which actions are first, second, or last in the process and whether a preceding action must be completed before a subsequent one can be started or whether there is expected overlap in the timing of specific actions.

In addition to the planned sequence and timing, the actual progress can be charted as well. This allows managers to better assess their progress against

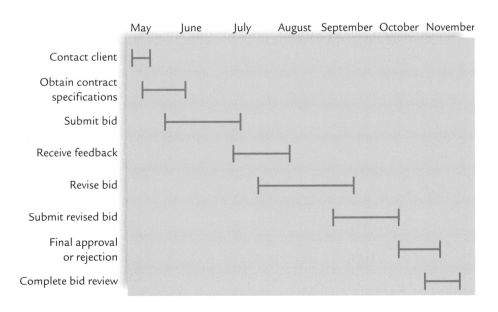

exhibit 8.5
Gantt Chart

the plan and potentially make adjustments. Today, sophisticated computer programs can assist managers in formulating and implementing plans involving literally hundreds of raw materials and components that must be brought together in the right amounts and sequences for the cost-effective production of finished goods.[20]

Accountability   The second key aspect of effective action plans is a specification of who is accountable for which specific actions. Knowing who is responsible for what can facilitate coordination when more than one person will be executing various actions in the overall plan.[21] Accountability also increases the likelihood that the steps are taken when they should be and done as well as they need to be. Let's go back to our shoe example. You personally take responsibility for hiring the three product design engineers. You assign one of your subordinates the task of securing space for the designers within the next month. You decide to outsource the manufacturing and assign another subordinate the task of finding reliable contract manufacturers within the next 10 weeks. Finally, you assign another of your subordinates to work with the marketing group to begin generating possible ideas for the promotion and advertising for the launch.

Implementing Plans

Once the action plan has been created, it then needs to be implemented. The quality of the plan implementation can determine the actual results as much as the quality of the plan itself. However, much of the success of the implementation can be assured by doing the previous steps in the planning process well. Plans often fail in the implementation stage because of inadequate assessment of resources required and available. Again let's return to our shoe example. Your subordinate is successful in finding a contract manufacturer with a great reputation. In fact, the company has made shoes for Nike in the past. In checking with Nike, you found that it gave the manufacturer a good endorsement. You discover, however, that for your shoes the company will need new sewing machines. The workers will need training in order to properly operate the new machines. However, because of the company's poor communication with its workers, the workers mistakenly think the new machines will require fewer workers. As a consequence, they resist the new training for fear they will eventually lose their jobs. Their resistance delays the production of the new shoes, and a critical window of opportunity in the marketplace is lost.

This illustrates in a simple way why plan implementation can be as critical and sometimes more critical than the overall plan objectives. However, no matter how carefully you work out the implementation plan, you will still need to monitor and adjust your implementation efforts because unanticipated events almost always happen.

Monitoring the Implementation   Even if the previous steps in the planning process are done well, there is no guarantee that the plan will be successfully implemented. This is why it is essential for you to monitor the implementation of the plan. In particular, you need to monitor three critical factors.

First, you need to monitor the progress of the plan and its implementation. Are those responsible for taking specific actions well aware of their responsibilities and the timing of their expected actions? Are they adequately motivated and prepared to implement their portion of the plan? Are the necessary actions being taken at the right time? Are they being done at the desired or necessary level of quality? These are the types of questions that you as a manager need to ask in order to monitor the progress of the implementation. This is why quite often, plans have "milestones" or specific objectives that mark progress along the total journey. For example, you might have a milestone of producing a prototype of your high-end shoe by week nine of your schedule. This way as week nine approaches, you have a specific means of determining if things are going according to plan or not.

Second, as a manager you need to monitor the level of support that the plan receives as it is being implemented.[22] You cannot assume that just because a plan is in place, people will support it. You have to constantly assess whether you are providing the required support for the plan's effective implementation. This support might take the form of encouragement, money, or coaching. Few plans of any complexity or duration can be effectively implemented without continuous support. Are the other key supporters providing the encouragement needed? One of your key responsibilities as a manager is to monitor and ensure that the required support is there. For example, in putting your high-end shoe launch plan into effect you may want to monitor the level of support from those in the marketing department. The marketing department may need to do a number of things in advance of the launch of the new shoe. They may need to talk with reporters working for magazines such as *Runner's World* to start creating some "buzz" about the new shoe; they might need to talk with large retailers such as Foot Locker to get them excited about not only ordering the shoe but placing it near the front of their stores in a special display. You cannot afford to have this great shoe coming off the factory line with nowhere to go because of poor support from marketing.

Third, as a manager you need to monitor the level of resistance. While we will address managing change in a later chapter, it is important to point out here that many plans and their implementation involve change. To the extent that they do, you should anticipate and monitor resistance to the plan's implementation. We discussed many of the fundamental reasons for resistance to change in Chapter 2. Still, it deserves a bit of space here because resistance has been the cause of the death of many plans. As we discussed in Chapter 2, one of the general causes of resistance is when people have to do new things and anticipate doing them poorly at first. You can use this principle to help you identify possible sources of resistance.

For example, you might expect the marketing department to be thrilled to have a high-end shoe to promote. However, there are several new activities that will be required of the marketing people that they may not be good at initially. Specifically, the launch of your new shoe requires the marketing people to try to get some endorsements or at least use of the shoes by famous runners. Unfortunately, they have never dealt with celebrities. They don't know how to make contact with celebrity runners or how to pitch them on using your shoe. Because people in the department aren't familiar with the process, they may shy away from it—they may even say they are making progress even though they are not really putting much effort into it. Why are they resisting contacting celebrity runners? Even if they see that it is the right thing to do, they resist because they fear failure at first. You may need to provide extra encouragement or even hire a special consultant to help you make the connections and contacts with the celebrity runners.

Real-Time Adjustment Because we live in a dynamic environment, any plan whose formulation and implementation lasts more than a few days or weeks is likely to need to be adjusted. As the environment changes, what was originally a perfectly acceptable objective may become unrealistic or too easily achieved, and therefore, may need to be changed. Likewise, what were perfectly reasonable timeframes and required resources at one point may become unreasonable because of sociocultural, technological, economic, or political–legal changes.

This realization has at least two implications. First, it may suggest that as a manager working in a dynamic and changing environment, you need to plan the way a fire department does. A fire department cannot anticipate exactly where or even when fires are likely to break out. Its plans are built upon certain principles of fighting fires and around general categories of fires. If you are a manager in a phone company, one of the key principles is redundancy. If a catastrophic event happens and knocks out your equipment, you have to have backup because if original equipment is somehow damaged or destroyed, you can't get new equipment put in as replacement fast enough. This lesson was reinforced for AT&T after the 9/11 attacks in New York City. Now it has 200 semi-trailers of backup equipment ready to roll at a moment's notice. Second, as a manager you need to help your employees recognize and accept the need to adapt plans in real time. You may also need to foster capabilities that enable them to adapt effectively. These capabilities might include skills like good environmental scanning and quick requirement and resource assessment abilities. The key point to remember is that in today's dynamic environment, a fixed and rigid plan may be as dangerous as no plan at all.

Monitoring Outcomes

The final element in the planning process involves monitoring outcomes. If the objectives have been well defined from the outset of the planning process, there should be little question as to what outcomes are to be monitored or how they are to be measured. If the plan was expected to result in increased financial performance and it was to be measured in terms of increased sales, then the outcome should be easy to gauge.

However, most plans also produce unanticipated consequences.[23] The plan and its implementation may produce negative or positive unanticipated consequences. Both can be valuable sources of learning. To help illustrate this, let's return once again to our athletic shoe case. Let's suppose that through implementing the plan, you discover it takes more advertising money than anticipated to launch your new high-end line of shoes. You find that customers have an image of your firm as a middle-range shoe maker and have difficulty at first believing that you could produce a line of athletic shoes with the technology, quality, and "sizzle" of other makers that are already in the high end of the market. On the unexpected positive side, you also discover that a stitching machine that you bought for your high-end shoes produced a straighter and stronger stitch at a lower price than the machines you were using for your low-end shoes. Using the new machines on both your low-end and high-end shoes will lower your costs, and yet allow you to promote higher quality. This may help you compete with other makers at the lower end of the market who produce lower-quality shoes.

The example above illustrates that managers should capture as much knowledge as they possibly can when monitoring outcomes. There also needs to be a feedback loop so that what they've learned can be used to modify and improve other aspects of the planning process.

PLANNING TOOLS

Managers use a variety of planning tools. For example, earlier in this chapter we referred to Gantt Charts as one of the tools managers can use to facilitate the timing and sequencing of actions. In this section we discuss a tool that is widely used: budgets.

Budgets

Budgets are used to quantify and allocate resources to specific activities. In most organizations, budgets are proposed and set on an annual basis. Budgets might address a variety of issues. For example a **capital expenditure budget** specifies the amount of money that is planned to be spent on specific items that have long-term use and require significant amounts of money to acquire. These items might include things such as equipment, land, or buildings.

Another common budget is an expense budget. An **expense budget** typically includes all the primary activities on which the unit or organization plans to spend money and the amount that is allocated for each item for the upcoming year. Virtually all profit and nonprofit organizations of a moderate or larger size have expense budgets, both for planning and for control purposes.

Most organizations have a two-phased process relative to budgets. The first consists of managers looking ahead and planning their needs. They then put together a budget specifying things like expected capital expenditures or expenses. This **proposed budget** provides a plan of how much money is needed and is submitted to a superior or budget review committee. Once the proposed budget is submitted, it gets reviewed, often in the context of other proposed budgets. An **approved budget** specifies what the manager is actually authorized to spend money on and how much.

Almost regardless of the type of budget, two main approaches to the budgeting process can be taken. The first approach is typically called the **incremental budgeting approach**.[24] In this approach, managers use the approved budget of the previous year and then present arguments for why the upcoming budget should be more or less. This may include particular increases or decreases. Incremental budgeting is efficient because managers do not need to spend significant time justifying the allocation of money toward the same sorts of purchases each year. The principal negative consequence of incremental budgeting is that it can result in "budget momentum." In other words, items that have been given money in the past may be allocated money in the future merely because they have been allocated money in the past. Consider the true case of a small town in North Carolina. Every year, sometime near Christmas, all of the parking meters on the main street are turned off; people park free. Most of the city residents think that this is just the city's way of giving folks a nice Christmas gift. Actually, it is the City Council's way of maintaining its budget level given the incremental approach the mayor takes to budgeting. The council figures out any surplus still on hand toward the end of the year and computes how many days of free parking downtown will be needed to eat up the surplus. It then allocates that many days of free parking to maintain the same level of funding for the next year. As in this case, incremental budgeting can create a "use it or lose it" mindset, which can in turn lead to the inefficient use of valuable resources.

The **zero-based budgeting approach** assumes that all allocations of funds must be justified from zero each year.[25] In other words, the fact that your

---

budgets used to quantify and allocate resources to specific activities

capital expenditure budget specifies the amount of money to be spent on specific items that have long-term use and require significant amounts

expense budget includes all primary activities on which a unit or organization plans to spend money and the amount allocated for the upcoming year

proposed budget provides a plan for how much money is needed, and is submitted to a superior or budget review committee

approved budget specifies what the manager is actually authorized to spend money on and how much

incremental budgeting approach where managers use the approved budget of the previous year and then present arguments for why the upcoming budget should be more or less

zero-based budgeting approach assumes that all allocations of funds must be justified from zero each year

department was given $100,000 for computer equipment purchases last year does not provide any justification per se for it receiving money for computers this year. Zero-based budgeting requires starting from a base of zero funds and then justifying the resources being requested for each activity. The benefit of this approach to budgeting is that items that cannot be justified on their own current merits (regardless of their past merits and allocated budgets) will not get money. This then leaves the money available for items or activities that can be justified. In general, this can lead to an overall more effective allocation of the organization's financial resources. However, zero-based budgeting takes time because each item must be justified each year. Some items that need money allocated to them may cost more in time and energy trying to justify their proposed funding than they are worth.

In either approach, budgets are typically used as planning tools by managers to determine priorities, required resources, and keys to implementation. In particular, because money is usually a scarce resource in most organizations—there is almost never as much money available as there are requests for it—allocating money among various activities almost forces a discussion of the relative priority among activities. This is true at all three organization levels. For example, department managers are likely to find they have more demand for money than they have money to allocate. Similarly, corporate officers are likely to find departments and business units requesting more money than the organization has. This leads to a determination of which units and their related activities are of highest priority and should receive budget approval.

In this sense, budgets can be an effective means of integrating and quantifying many aspects of the corporate-, business-, and functional-level plans. While the budgeting process per se does not guarantee that managers will make good decisions about the integration and coordination process nor that they will make good decisions about priorities, it does raise the likelihood of these key items being discussed and determined.

GOAL SETTING

Goal setting is a specific planning process for managing performance. Normally, we think of it at the individual level, though all of the principles are applicable to setting goals for teams, units, and overall organizations. It is important to examine goals. The research suggests that effective goals can have a significant and positive impact on performance. Much of the research about effective goal setting can be captured in an easy-to-remember and practical acronym—SMART. "Smart" goals have five key characteristics.

Specific As we mentioned relative to organizational objectives in the planning process, goals for firms, units, subordinates, or for oneself should be specific. For example, you may have received feedback from different people or just sensed that "you need to improve your communication skills." Improvement in this area may in fact yield significant benefits; however, as stated, it is too vague. To be effective, it must be much more specific. Suppose you decide that "communication skills" is too broad and you narrow the scope and make your goal specifically to improve your listening skills. Is this now a good goal? Is it specific enough? The answer is "no." You need to assess what it is you do or don't do that makes you a less-than-effective listener. Perhaps you often interrupt people when they're speaking because you think you know what they are going to say. You determine that your goal is to not interrupt people and wait for them to finish before saying what you have to say. Is this a good goal? Is it specific? While this alone may not make you a great listener, it is a good goal in terms of being specific, and the research strongly suggests that you are more likely to make progress toward a specific goal than a vague goal.

Measured One way to determine that a goal you have set is specific enough is by whether you think you could measure progress and improvement as well as the ultimate result. Could you measure the number of times you interrupted versus the times you listened and waited for others to finish what they had to say? Clearly, you could. Could you measure others' perception of whether you were interrupting or listening and waiting for them to say what they had to say? Clearly, you could. But having a goal that is measurable is only part of the battle. In addition, you need to actually measure progress toward the goal. Goal setting is most effective when progress toward the goal is measured and measured often. So how often is often? The research does not provide an absolute answer. What we do know is that once a year is not often enough. In fact, twice a year does not seem to be often enough. Beyond that, it seems that the frequency of measurement needs to be related to the nature of the activities associated with the goal. For example, if you talk with people dozens of times per day and therefore have the opportunity to hit (or miss) your goal of not interrupting many times per day, then assessing your progress once a month is too infrequent. Daily self-measurement may be appropriate. However, from a practical perspective, you would be unwise to ask others every day how you are doing on listening and not interrupting. This you may want to do weekly or monthly.

Agreed Even if a goal is specific and measurable, if those involved in its achievement do not agree to it, it is unlikely to be met. For organizational goals, this means that a substantial portion of employees must agree to the goal. For unit goals, those in the unit must agree and accept the goal. For subordinate goals, the individual subordinate must accept the goal. (You will recall that this was a specific aspect of MBO.) Personal goals must be accepted and committed to. Returning to our original example, suppose you lay out the specific goal of not interrupting people and measure progress but do not really accept the goal. (Maybe you don't think interrupting is a bad thing and in fact you believe it saves time in conversations.) In this case, the goal is unlikely to be effective. Obviously, the reverse is true if you accept or are committed to the goal.

Here there is a very practical implication for managers. Because managers are in a position of power , subordinates often say what they believe the manager wants to hear—even when it is not what the subordinates really think. For example, if you say, "Tom, I think this is a challenging but doable goal for you. Don't you?" how is Tom going to reply? A verbal agreement from a subordinate without any real commitment behind the words will likely not result in the goal being achieved. As a consequence, when it comes to the "agreed" part of SMART goals, it is important to listen carefully and invite subordinates to candidly express their commitment to or resistance regarding specific goals. Again, the fundamental objective of this part of SMART goal setting is not superficial agreement but deep commitment.

Realistic Now you have a specific, measured, and agreed to goal. Will it be effective? Not if it is unrealistic—or if it is too easy. Goals that are too easy are not effective and goals that are too difficult are also not effective. To understand why, let's look at each case in turn. First, goals that are too easy are not effective for two reasons. On the one hand, they are not effective because they

William Heinecke (shown), an American-born Thai citizen who founded The Pizza Company restaurant chain, competed against Pizza Hut in Thailand and won. Within six months of its start in 2001, The Pizza Company had captured about 70 percent of the market in Thailand. Part of Heinecke's success included relying on local knowledge and a fired-up staff. He is a proponent of employees being given stock options, because it helps them think like owners. The next pizza battle he plans to launch is in the Middle East.

do not inspire motivation. In general, people are not motivated to try to achieve things that they perceive as being too easy. Often, they wait until the last minute to put any effort into achieving the goal, believing that a little effort at the last minute will enable them to hit the target. On the other hand, easy goals are not effective because they do not deliver substantial results. First, even if they are achieved, easy goals by their nature do not have a big impact on results—organizational, unit, subordinate, or personal. Ironically, because easy goals are seen as easy, the low motivation they inspire often results in the goals being missed. Goals that are too difficult are also not effective. If a goal is seen as impossible or just highly unlikely to be achieved, people are not motivated to try to hit the target. After all, why waste precious time and energy trying to hit an unachievable target? Thus, effective goals must be challenging but achievable or realistic.

To make this concrete, let's return again to a personal goal of not interrupting others and listening to what they have to say. Assuming you have dozens of opportunities each day to hit or miss this target, is it realistic to set a goal of not interrupting 100 percent of the time, especially at first? If it is a challenging but realistic goal, that is fine. But if you see it as unrealistic, it will not be effective. Perhaps the realistic goal is to not interrupt more than 50 percent of the time during the first week.

Time Bound Even specific, measured, agreed, and realistic goals need to be time bound to be effective. In other words, goals need a specific time span within which they are to be achieved. For goals that will take a substantial time to achieve, say, a year or more, shorter time intervals are needed. For example, suppose you think that the right level of listening and not interrupting is 80 percent. In other words, you think that in eight out of ten conversations you should not interrupt but should instead listen and wait until the person has said what he or she has to say. Furthermore, you think that it will take you three months to achieve this goal. The three months becomes the general time boundary within which you plan to achieve the goal. However, as we suggested at the end of the section on making the goal realistic, you may have other time frames that become intermediate milestones for your ultimate goal. You may set a time frame of one week for going from 10 percent listening (90 percent interrupting) to 50 percent listening and not interrupting. You may then set a time frame of one month to get to a level of 70 percent listening and not interrupting.

MBO

Management By Objectives (MBO) is a specific type of goal-setting process, similar to SMART. Research suggests that MBO systems are most effective if top management demonstrates clear support for and involvement in the system.[26] Most of the general characteristics just described are critical to a successful MBO process. Exhibit 8.6 provides a graphic illustration of how MBO works. First, specific goals are set. The achievement of these goals should translate into results that support the organization's strategic, tactical, and operational plans and objectives. Goals need to be difficult but achievable. As you would expect, when accomplished, difficult but achievable goals have a positive impact on performance.[27] Participation by subordinates in setting their goals tends to lead to difficult but achievable goals. In addition, the goals need to be accepted by subordinates. Goal acceptance has a positive impact on both motivation to perform and actual performance.[28] Participation by subordinates in the goal-setting process increases goal acceptance.[29] MBO goals need specific time frames, and periodic review and evaluation are necessary. Based on these reviews, subordinate performance improves according to the quality of feedback given to subordinates.[30] Individuals need to know if what they are doing is on or off target so that they can retain or adjust their behaviors. Also, feedback can affect the goal-setting process. Specific feedback may indicate that the original goals were too easy, too difficult, or just not directed at appropriate targets.

exhibit 8.6
The Process of MBO

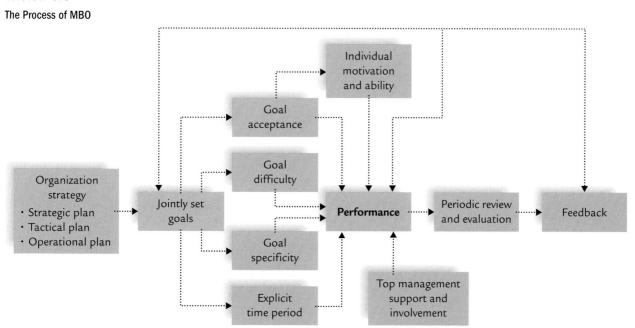

managerial perspectives revisited

PERSPECTIVE 1: THE ORGANIZATIONAL CONTEXT   Given that we ended this chapter by focusing on goals and used personal goals to illustrate the key concepts, the relevance of the organizational context for goal setting in particular and the planning process in general may not be completely obvious. However, organizational context is critical. Clearly, you could set personal goals and plan your work and projects independent of the organizational context. However, this would likely result in suboptimal personal career and organizational results. At a personal level, we are likely to make greater contributions and gain greater recognition for future advancement if our personal goals are aligned with the strategy and direction of the organization. For example, suppose your company had a low-cost strategy and productivity gains were central to lowering costs in your area of responsibility. How bright would your career prospects be if you were weak at productivity analysis but failed to ever set any improvement goals in that area? The same general principle applies to goals for subordinates, units, and the overall organization. One of the important organizational contexts that we should always consider when setting goals is the strategy of the organization. In addition, the plans that we put in place should consider not only the direction of the company but its culture as well. As we mentioned earlier in this chapter, the details of a plan for change would be different in an organization with a culture that resists change compared to one that embraces it. Thus, many of the details of effective plans have to account for both the direction of the organization and its nature.

PERSPECTIVE 2: THE HUMAN FACTOR   Goals and plans for organizations, whether the plans are strategic, tactical, or operational, require input from others and their coordinated efforts to accomplish. In fact, a common mistake of those charged with formulating plans for projects or new-product launches is that they do not think carefully enough about the role that others play in the implementation of the plan. The more complex the plan, the more likely that its successful implementation and achievement will depend on multiple people. Managers need to not only develop plans but manage others in the implementation of the plans. This fact is highlighted in the opening case, where P&G determined that the most important resources for successful entry into Eastern European markets were the people, employees, and managers who would ultimately implement its strategy abroad.

PERSPECTIVE 3: MANAGING PARADOXES   It should be clear by this point that planning has inherent potential paradoxes. On the one hand, failure to achieve desired results is often a function of not having a thoughtful and detailed plan. As the saying goes, "those who fail to plan, plan to fail." On the other hand, in a dynamic world of change where new competitors appear frequently, innovative technology is developed and used unexpectedly, and customer preferences evolve rapidly, managers cannot afford to rigidly maintain even well-developed plans; they must be prepared to modify, adapt, or even discard thoroughly developed plans. The need to develop thorough plans and be completely committed to their implementation, yet simultaneously flexible if they need to be changed later, presents something of a paradox to managers. Sometimes the challenge of dealing with change tempts managers to not develop thorough plans in the first place. They might reason that some of their efforts will be wasted if the situation were to change. This is faulty reasoning. The environment will always be undergoing changes. The key to responding to these changes is first detecting them. A thorough plan may be one of the best means of detecting signs that the environment is changing and different from what was expected. A thorough plan can serve as an "image projector." When the environment does not reflect back what you have projected, the more detailed the projection, the more specific the discrepancies that can be detected, and the more refined your adjustments and changes to the plan can be.

4   **PERSPECTIVE 4: ENTREPRENEURIAL MIND-SET**   As discussed in the introduction to this chapter, the strategic planning process helps to identify opportunities. If managers have an entrepreneurial mind-set, they will be better able to identify these opportunities when analyzing the environment their companies are attempting to do business in, and they will be more likely to formulate a strategy to exploit these opportunities. The required commitment comes primarily in a disciplined approach to plan formulation and an energetic implementation. Sometimes when you have put so much effort into formulating the plan, you can feel as though the implementation will go well with little further effort. But while poor planning quite often guarantees poor implementation, thorough planning does not guarantee effective implementation. To be effective, managers have to be committed to implement it and even to possibly change it as needed. For example, at EMC, even though managers have spent considerable time formulating their plan to focus on software, due to the history of the company, even its existing customers may resist the new plan. It will take considerable commitment to overcome the natural obstacles, implement the planned actions, and then achieve the goals desired. Yet, it is important to emphasize that too much commitment to a particular plan without regard for changes in the environment can be detrimental. An entrepreneurial mind-set is needed to make plans and implement them, and yet remain flexible and open to environmental opportunities as things change. The planning process itself provides the overall needed discipline for an organization to excel, while an entrepreneurial mind-set helps maintain the necessary flexibility.

concluding comments

Planning requires a determination of where the organization wants to go and how it is going to get there. This process includes an assessment of the organization's external and internal environment. Early in their careers, managers typically are more involved in operational plans. Consequently, some organizations or individuals might be tempted to ask why young managers should understand all aspects of the planning process.

The basic answer to this question is twofold. First, lower-level managers are more motivated to implement their specific responsibilities if they know the larger plan. Second, lower-level managers face thousands of specific decisions daily. They cannot make these specific decisions in a way that works toward the organization's overall objectives if they do not understand those objectives. This process would be like facing a series of choices of turning left or right and of slowing down or speeding up, without knowing your ultimate destination.

In an ever-globalizing environment, managers are simultaneously faced with three critical planning challenges. First, they must try to learn from the past. Many things that went right or wrong in the past may be helpful in guiding action and shaping plans for the future. Second, managers must keep their ears and eyes closely focused on signals in the current environment—signals from competitors, customers, governments, and so on. The rate of change in the current environment is so fast that too little attention to the present could forfeit the future. Finally, managers must think about and plan for the future. It is the incorporation of three different time perspectives (past, present, and future) that makes planning one of the most challenging managerial activities.

key terms

approved budget   287
benchmarking   277
budgets   287
capital expenditure budget   287
contingency plans   277
expense budget   287

incremental budgeting
   approach   287
objectives   270
operational plans   271
planning   270
plans   270

proposed budget   287
strategic plans   271
tactical plans   271
zero-based budgeting
   approach   287

test your comprehension

1. What are the key functions of setting objectives?
2. Define strategic plans.
3. Provide an example of a tactical plan.
4. What are the key elements of operational plans?
5. What are the key differences between strategic, tactical, and operational plans?
6. What impact does organizational level have on managerial planning activities?
7. What are the key issues that managers at the corporate level focus on relative to planning?
8. What type of plans do people at the business level primarily undertake?
9. What are the seven elements in the planning process?
10. Why is forecasting critical to the planning process?
11. Under what conditions are contingency plans most beneficial?
12. What is benchmarking and what role does it play in planning?
13. Why is determining the priority of objectives important?
14. In what ways does measuring objectives influence plan implementation and plan changes?
15. What is the difference between defining requirements and assessing resources in the planning process?
16. How can a Gantt Chart facilitate the sequence and timing issues in planning?

17. How can budgeting be used as a planning tool?
18. Describe the two basic approaches to budgeting.
19. What are the strengths and weaknesses of incremental and zero-based budgeting?
20. What is the role of MBO in strategy formulation and implementation?
21. What are the five key elements in effective goal setting?

apply your understanding

1. In your university, professors likely have objectives regarding teaching, research, and service to the university. From your perspective what are the relative priorities of these three objectives? If you could, how would you *change* the priorities and why?
2. Think of an action plan in which you were recently involved. Which elements of the planning process were done well? Which ones were done poorly? What was the impact of these strengths and weaknesses on the outcome?
3. As you look at your own experience and capabilities, where are your strengths and weaknesses relative to the seven elements of the planning process? What is your plan of action for strengthening your planning capabilities?
4. Think about the last goal you set for yourself. How SMART was it?

practice your capabilities

Two months ago you were made manager of a group of six gate agents for a regional airline. One of your subordinates comes to you for advice. The previous manager gave him some rather low marks on his performance evaluation. He wants to make some improvements but feels that he cannot do everything at once. Below are the previous manager's comments about the employee.

Punctuality: Joe is usually on time and rarely misses work without prior notification. However, he never shows up early or stays late to help out during busy times.

Customer Service: In general, Joe does not seem to be a happy person. He is never rude to customers but he does not seem to make them happy either. When problems arise, such as delayed flights, Joe gives customers information and answers their questions in a very matter-of-fact manner. He rarely shows any empathy, and a customer has never complimented him for his service when I have been around.

Check-in Knowledge: Joe has a good understanding of check-in processes. He knows who can get upgrades and what is required. He understands seat assignment policies and executes them with great consistency. However, he fails to notice in advance those customers who have too many bags or whose bags are too large, which simply creates delays and customer frustrations when they have to check bags as they are about to board the plane.

Security Procedures: While this is an area that is new to everyone and something that changes monthly, Joe seems relatively up-to-date. Soon, airport security personnel will conduct all the "at gate screenings," so this aspect will diminish in importance in the future.

The regional carrier you are employed by has a new strategy that emphasizes customer service. In addition, it is trying to reduce delays and improve its on-time performance.

1. What area(s) would you recommend that Joe try to improve? Why?
2. Create one to three SMART goals and have Joe (a classmate) do the same. Compare the goals. How similar are they? Which goals need to be reevaluated or changed? Assuming that your assessment of Joe is similar to that of his previous boss and that Joe is typical of the other five subordinates you have, what objectives would you set for your team and what plan would you lay out for achieving them? Even if you don't have all the information you need from the brief description above, what questions would you ask and what information would you need to develop a thorough plan?

closing case DEVELOPING YOUR CRITICAL THINKING

Planning a New Program Launch at LDC

"Pam" (a disguised name but a real person) was director of training at a large, mid-western training company—Leadership Development Center (LDC). As such, one of her responsibilities was to plan the launch of new training programs. LDC had a reputation for excellent programs targeted at mid-level managers. However, the top executives at LDC felt that the company needed more training for senior executives who were the bosses of these mid-level managers. LDC executives felt that if senior executives personally experienced the quality of LDC training, they would be more likely to recommend and approve training requests for their mid-level managers.

For the new Senior Executive Leadership Program, Pam discussed with her boss and her peers what the program objective ought to be. Some thought the program should be a "loss leader," or in other words, that it should lose money but pay for itself by generating more participants for LDC's mid-level managerial programs. Others thought that the new program should break even financially. Everyone agreed, however, that the program should be of a sufficient quality that participants would have a very favorable impression of LDC. As a result, they would be more likely to encourage their employees to attend LDC programs and approve their requests to do so.

Pam determined that the program's success would be measured in three ways. First, the number of participants in the first program would be measured. Pam calculated that it would take about 18 participants for the program to break even financially. Second, she would survey all participants regarding their satisfaction with the program, its content, materials, facilities, administration, and instructors. Finally, LDC would track the number of mid-level managers from the companies of those attending the senior executive program to see if there was an increased participation level.

In launching the program, Pam looked at the past marketing costs of other new programs. Past new launches had cost about $30,000 in brochure and mailing expenses. She figured that an extra $5,000 ought to be enough to launch the new senior executive program.

The current budget did not anticipate the launch of the senior executive program, but another program in marketing had been cancelled, and so there was $20,000 still in the budget for that program, which Pam thought she could spend on the new senior executive program. In addition, she thought she could access $15,000 from the general contingency budget of $30,000.

One of the first things she would need to do would be to talk to various possible instructors and select a "faculty director." This person would design the specific content of the program and coordinate the other instructors and their content. Once the faculty director was chosen, the program would need to be designed, and from the design, a brochure would need to be created. She estimated that the program design would take three weeks and that the design of the brochures would take an additional two weeks. Printing the brochures would take four days, and assembling them for mailing would take another three days. Delivery of the mailed brochures would take about a week. Normally, LDC allowed about 12 weeks between the time people received brochures and when their program applications were due. In general, program applications were due (along with the program fees) three weeks before the start of the program. Two weeks before the program start, all the materials (handouts, notebooks, etc.) would need to be assembled.

Pam had two people who would assist in the implementation of the plan, and report directly to her. Tammy would be responsible for contacting the brochure design firm and the printing company and seeing to it that the brochure was ready on time. In addition, she would secure the mailing list and arrange for an outside contractor to stuff the envelopes with brochures for mailing. Dan would be responsible for venue details. LDC had its own training facilities and had contracts with several nearby hotels for lodging arrangements. Dan would also be responsible for the assembly of all the materials, which meant getting handouts and other materials from the instructors on time.

As the plan was put into action, everything seemed to go fine. A faculty member was selected to be the faculty director, and the program design and content were ready in two rather than the anticipated three weeks. The outside design firm quickly produced a brochure that with a few modifications was ready for mailing. Tammy obtained several mailing lists that had the names of senior executives in medium to large companies. The mailing went out about five days early.

Inquiries regarding the program were 100 percent higher than other new programs that LDC had launched in the past. However, as time wore on, the ratio of inquiries to registrations was not good. Typically, one in every ten people who contact LDC for further information regarding a particular program ended up registering for it. However, with eight weeks to go before the program's start, the inquiry to registration ratio was 100 to 1 (not 10 to 1). With only four weeks to go before the start of the program, only ten participants had signed up. Pam was in a panic as to what to do.

Questions

1. What adjustments would you make at this point? Would you cancel the program or run it at a loss?

2. Draw out a Gantt Chart of the sequence and timing of key activities. What insights does this give you regarding the plan and its implementation?

3. What do you think went wrong? What do you see as the strengths and weaknesses of the planning process?

4. LDC seemed to follow a planning process that had worked well for its mid-level managerial programs. Are there differences between senior executives and mid-level managers that might explain why the plan did not work out as anticipated? Could these differences have been anticipated? Should they have been?

Individual and Group Decision Making*

9

■

Explain the traditional model of decision making.

■

Recognize and account for the limits of rationality in the decision process.

■

Describe the role of risk and uncertainty in decision making.

■

List the conditions when decisions are best made individually and when they are best made collectively.

■

Name the steps to facilitate group participation in decision making.

■

Describe the barriers to effective decision making and ways to overcome them.

Changing the Course at Acer

D ifficult times often require leaders to make bold decisions. This is exactly what Stan Shih, founder of Acer, a Taiwan-based computer company, did when he and his senior team made the decision to leave the world's largest computer market—the United States. They also made another strategic decision: Split the company in two and spin off the division that makes Acer-brand PCs from the division that makes computers and related products under contract for other companies such as IBM and Sony.

Stan Shih founded Acer in the 1970s, primarily building computers for other companies. Subsequently, he and his top management team also succeeded, for a time, in building the Acer brand name and selling its own PCs in Taiwan and around

*Portions of this chapter have been adapted from *Organizational Behavior*, 5th edition, by Richard M. Steers and J. Stewart Black with permission from the authors and the publisher.

the world. However, during the late 1990s, as companies such as Dell built cheaper yet more powerful PCs, Acer lost share in the U.S. market. Part of the problem was that customers in more developed markets were less eager to buy computers from a little-known Asian company with a "Made in China" label because in the past it had connoted low quality.

Three reasons drove Acer's decision to spin off branded manufacturing operations from contract manufacturing operations in 2000. First, some computer companies were increasingly hesitant to hire Acer to make their computers because they feared disclosing information to a potential competitor. Separating the brand-name side from the contract-manufacturing side reassured industrial customers that sensitive data would not be shared internally and that innovations from IBM or Sony would not show up on Acer computers. Second, the contract manufacturing unit makes only a limited range of computer products for sale under the brand names of other companies. Focusing on fewer products and fewer industrial customers would help lower costs and increase profits for the manufacturing side of the business. And, third, Shih and his managers saw pushing the Acer brand separately from contract manufacturing as a way to build a foundation for selling technology services in Asia—a potentially huge and lucrative market.

As a result, for two years the company focused on selling its Acer brand-name PCs in China, a more familiar and faster-growing market much closer to its headquarters. "China and Taiwan share not just the same language and culture, but a lot of our Taiwanese suppliers are already there [in China],"

Companies are learning that the door to globalization swings both ways. After losing U.S. market share on its brand-name computers, Taiwan-based computer manufacturer Acer decided it would exit the U.S. sales market. Instead, Acer focused on selling its PCs and technology services closer to home in China and Asia—a more familiar and faster-growing market located near its headquarters.

observed J. T. Wang, Acer's president. The company scored a competitive coup by becoming the first to sell a handheld computer with a Chinese-language operating system. It also introduced one of the first tablet PCs, which was a smart idea considering that in many Asian countries, including China, their written language does not easily lend itself to use with a traditional keyboard.

In the fast-paced PC market, however, the game is always changing. Shih, who had been at Acer's helm for nearly three decades, knew Acer's decision to leave the U.S. market was not written in stone. Three years after deciding to leave the U.S. market, he decided to return. However, this time instead of trying to compete in the PC segment with Dell, he focused on a new niche. Acer invested heavily in research and development in order to figure out how to make it easy to integrate innovative new PCs with consumers' other household electronics products, like their televisions, phones, and office-related equipment. Among the new products it unveiled were the Aspire PC, e-Tablet, E 2GO, and E Radio.

Management's decision to focus on a particular consumer need was finally rewarded with a top-10 brand. Management subsequently set an ambitious goal—increase U.S. sales by sixfold by the end of 2006—a formidable challenge considering the stiff competition it faces from IBM, Hewlett-Packard, and Dell (the market leader).

So far the decisions seem to be working. Acer managers have returned the company to profitability on razor-thin margins—one of the few PC companies to do so.

Sources: Steve Burke, "Acer's Full House," *Computer Reseller News*, December 15, 2003, p. 92; Mark Riehl, "Acer Saddles Up Multimedia Powerhouse," *eChannel Daily News*, December 12, 2003; "Ace of Acer," *New Straits Times*, December 4, 2003; John G. Spooner, "Acer Offers a Wide-Screen Notebook," *CNET News.com*, November 17, 2003; Bill Powell, "The Legend of Legend," *Fortune International*, September 16, 2002, pp. 34+; Bruce Einhorn, "A Proud Papa Called Acer," *Business Week*, September 9, 2002, pp. 24+; Charles S. Lee, "Acer's Last Stand?" *Fortune*, June 10, 2002, pp. 50+; Chris Hall, "Acer Breaks New Ground," *Electronic Business Asia*, February 2002, pp. 24+.

strategic overview

In the minds of many, decision making is the most important managerial activity. Management decisions may involve high-profile issues such as acquiring or selling assets, moving into or out of product segments, leaving or entering markets, or launching national or international ad campaigns. In the case of Shih's strategic decision to withdraw from the U.S. market and divide Acer into two separate businesses, the implications for the organization are significant. For example, leaving the U.S. market enabled competitors to take Acer's abandoned market share, strengthen their positions, and make it more challenging and costly for Acer to reenter later. Obviously, at the time Shih decided to leave the U.S. market, if he could have known that he would later have an opportunity to reenter, he might have never decided to leave. This illustrates one of the key challenges of managerial decision making at any level—making decisions with limited resources. These limited resources could be informational, financial, technical, or human. These constraints and pressures create some of the most powerful challenges in managerial decision making. Consequently, managers need to understand the basic processes of decision making in organizations and the factors that influence them. Several frameworks are available to help explain managerial decision making. Each framework is based on different assumptions about the nature of people at work. So, as an informed manager, you need to understand the models and the assumptions underlying each.

Shih's decision to separate the businesses will require high-level managers below the CEO to make additional decisions to redesign the organization, appoint new managers in the newly created businesses, allocate resources to the separate businesses, and establish goals for each business, among others. In fact, these decisions are necessary to implement Shih's strategic decision. Clearly, Shih's decision to withdraw from the U.S. market caused other managers lower in the organization to make subsequent decisions. As an example, someone had to decide to sell or lease Acer's U.S. facilities. Someone else had to decide how to secure and maintain the facilities until they were sold or leased. Although it is relatively easy to see how the impact of decisions made at the higher levels of an organization can cascade down through the lower ranks, the reverse can also be true. For example, if managers in Acer had not consistently hired engineers with a solid understanding of China, then Shih's decision to focus on China would have been limited in its immediate effectiveness. Managers must incorporate information beyond that immediately associated with the problem or task at hand to ensure that the impact is consistent with and supportive of the direction of the organization overall.

Not all managerial decisions are as visible or as important as those described at Acer. Many managerial decisions involve behind-the-scenes issues such as hiring a new employee or changing a production process. In addition, in many situations you must determine the level of involvement of others (e.g., subordinates, peers) in decisions. When are group decisions superior (or inferior) to individual ones? How much participation is realistic in organizations in which managers still assume responsibility for group actions? For example, Stan Shih had to decide how many and which of his managers to involve. As a new manager, you might have to decide how many people to involve in a new hire decision. In making these choices you need to understand how various factors affect the quality of your decisions. Finally, what approaches can managers use to improve decisions in organizations? A knowledge of effective decision making can help you as a manager to make the most efficient use of your limited time and resources. ■

DECISION-MAKING CONCEPTS

A characteristic of effective leaders and effective work groups is their ability to make decisions that are appropriate, timely, and acceptable. If organizational effectiveness is defined as the ability to secure and use resources in the pursuit of organizational goals, then the decision-making processes that determine how these resources are acquired and used is a key building block. For our purposes here, we define **decision making** as a process of specifying the nature of a particular problem or opportunity and selecting among available alternatives how to solve a problem or capture an opportunity. In this sense decision making has two aspects: the act and the process. The act of decision making involves choosing between alternatives. The process of decision making involves several steps that can be divided into two distinct categories. The first,

decision making a process of specifying the nature of a particular problem or opportunity and selecting among available alternatives to solve a problem or capture an opportunity

formulation a process involving identifying a problem or opportunity, acquiring information, developing desired performance expectations, and diagnosing the causes and relationships among factors affecting the problem or opportunity

solution a process involving generating alternatives, selecting the preferred solution, and implementing the decided course of action

exhibit 9.1

Classical Decision-Making Model

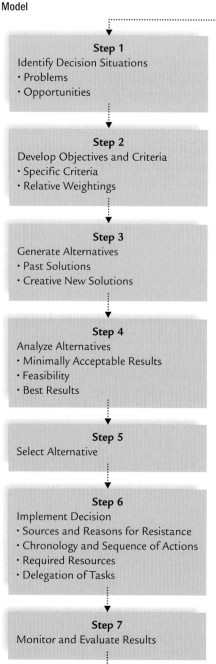

Step 1
Identify Decision Situations
• Problems
• Opportunities

Step 2
Develop Objectives and Criteria
• Specific Criteria
• Relative Weightings

Step 3
Generate Alternatives
• Past Solutions
• Creative New Solutions

Step 4
Analyze Alternatives
• Minimally Acceptable Results
• Feasibility
• Best Results

Step 5
Select Alternative

Step 6
Implement Decision
• Sources and Reasons for Resistance
• Chronology and Sequence of Actions
• Required Resources
• Delegation of Tasks

Step 7
Monitor and Evaluate Results

formulation, involves identifying a problem or opportunity, acquiring information, developing desired performance expectations, and diagnosing the causes and relationships among factors affecting the problem or opportunity. The **solution** phase involves generating alternatives, selecting the preferred solution, and implementing the decided course of action. Following the implementation of the solution, the manager monitors the situation to determine the extent to which the decision was successful.

INDIVIDUAL DECISION MAKING

It is no easy task to outline or diagram the details of the decision-making process. Research has been mixed about how individuals and groups make decisions.[1] Even so, at least three attempts to describe the decision-making process are worth noting. These three models are (1) the rational/classic model; (2) the administrative, or bounded rationality, model; and (3) the retrospective decision-making model. Each model is useful for understanding the nature of decision processes in organizations. While reading these models, pay special attention to the assumptions that each makes about the nature of decision makers; also note the differences in focus.

The Rational/Classical Model

The **rational model** (also known as the **classical model**) represents the earliest attempt to model decision processes.[2] It is viewed by some as the classical approach to understanding decision processes. This approach involves seven basic steps (see Exhibit 9.1).

Step 1: Identifying Decision Situations   In the classical model, the decision maker begins by recognizing that a decision-making situation exists, that is, that problems or opportunities exist. A **problem** exists when a manager detects a gap between existing and desired performance. This is the situation we commonly associate with decision making and it is the reason that decision making and problem solving often are talked about interchangeably. For example, you may find that your subordinates just have more work than they can get done. As a consequence, you may decide to hire an additional worker.

Although as a manager you will confront lots of problems and have to decide how to solve them, you will also encounter opportunities. An **opportunity** exists when a manager detects a chance to achieve a more desirable state than the current one. For example, for managers in Brunswick this happened when they decided to buy Baja Boats. At the time of the purchase, Brunswick with its SeaRay, Bayliner, Procraft, and other brands was already the number-one recreational boat builder in North America. Buying Baja Boats represented an opportunity to expand into a market niche that executives thought would grow in the future and in which they did not have a significant presence at the time.

The Role of Perception. Whether you view a situation as a problem or as an opportunity is to some extent a function of your **perception** or way you see a situation based on your experiences, personality, and current needs. For example, managers facing the same business situation often have different interpretations of the situation. Some see it as an opportunity, whereas others may see the situation as a threat.[3] With that in mind, you may find it useful to check how others see the situation rather than simply acting as if your perception of the situation is the right one.

A Manager's Challenge illustrates how United Parcel Service (UPS) tries to give managers experiences that will broaden and diversify their knowledge base. The example illustrates how changes in experience base and emphasis on diversity affect not only managers' perceptions but also the decisions they make. Do you think having similar experiences would influence your perception of future problems? As a consequence, do you think you might change the way you make decisions?

Step 2: Developing Objectives and Criteria Once you have identified the decision-making situation, the next step is to determine the criteria for selecting alternatives. These criteria essentially represent what is important in the outcome. For example, before you can decide which job applicant to hire, you need to determine the important characteristics or outcomes needed. If you need the new hire to be effective at sales, then good interpersonal skills might be a criterion. However, it is rare that a single criterion will be sufficient to guide the decision-making process, in part because one factor rarely produces all the desired results. For example, good interpersonal skills alone will not likely lead to great sales results; superior motivation and knowledge of the selling process are also needed. When several criteria are involved, it is often necessary to weight the various criteria. For example, you might decide that a new hire's sales ability depends on four things: interpersonal skills, motivation, product knowledge, and understanding of the selling process. However, the impact of these factors may not be equal. As a manager, then, you might assign a weight to each criterion: for example, motivation, 30 percent; interpersonal skills, 25 percent; understanding of the selling process, 25 percent; product knowledge, 20 percent.

Step 3: Generating Alternatives Once the objectives and criteria are established, the next step is to generate alternatives that achieve the desired result. How can a particular problem be solved or a given opportunity captured? Most of us consider first the alternatives that we have encountered or used in the past. If a current situation is similar to the past, past solutions can be effective. However, situations change and to the extent that the current situation is dissimilar to the past or if past solutions have not succeeded, we must generate new alternatives. However, creative alternatives may be needed even when the current situation is familiar and past solutions have worked for at least two reasons. First, even though a particular solution was effective in the past in what may seem to be a similar situation, no two situations are identical and subtle differences may reduce a past solution's effectiveness today. Second, even if the past solution could succeed today, alternative solutions might be even more successful. For example, a sales manager at EDS needed to hire a new salesperson. In the past product knowledge and industry experience seemed to be the keys to success. However, although many of the current products were similar to those in the past, increasingly customers wanted salespeople to help integrate the different products into a "seamless solution." Success in this case required trust, which placed a greater premium on interpersonal skills than on

rational model (classical model) a seven-step model of decision making that represents the earliest attempt to model decision processes

problem a gap between existing and desired performance

opportunity a chance to achieve a more desirable state than the current one

perception a way one sees a situation based on experiences, personality, and current needs

diversity
a manager's challenge

Gaining a New Perspective on Decisions at UPS

Managing diverse perspectives for enhanced decision making is a tough balancing act for managers at United Parcel Service (UPS). On the one hand, UPS has built a successful global delivery business by developing standard procedures for nearly all routine decisions, including how drivers should carry their keys when making deliveries. Yet every year, senior managers send 50 middle managers on a program that is designed to add diversity to the "brown" perspective (i.e., typical UPS perspective) so that these middle managers can make better decisions. The program involves managers spending 30 days in communities far from home that have significant poverty and other problems. UPS founder James Casey initiated the Community Internship Program in 1968. Since then, UPS has invested more than $14 million to send 1,100 middle managers through the program, at a cost of $10,000 per participant (plus the manager's regular salary).

Whether managers spend the month cleaning up dilapidated apartments or working with migrant workers, participants say the experience drives home new lessons about diversity. For example, during a month of working with addicts in New York City, division manager Patti Hobbs was impressed by the thoughtful suggestions they offered for keeping teenagers off drugs. Back on the job, she broadened her use of group decision making to involve all staff members in problem-solving discussions rather than only the highest-level managers. "You start to think there's no one person, regardless of position, who has all the answers," she explains. "The answers come from us all."

The program sharpens participants' decision-making skills by taking them out of their comfortable daily work routine. According to Al Demick, UPS's learning and development manager, it "puts people in situations that call on them to use new skills or to use their skills in new ways. Sometimes those are life-and-death situations. People are never quite the same when they come back."

Annette Law, an African American UPS manager from Utah, worked with tenement dwellers in New York City. "I thought I knew all about diversity," she observes. "But what I saw were people just like me, only their opportunities and choices were different."

Michael Lockard, a finance and accounting manager, helped inmates in a Chicago prison prepare for release by sharpening their interviewing and job-search skills. The experience shattered Lockard's preconceived notions about

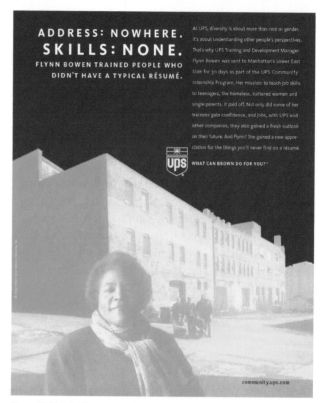

Since 1968, UPS has invested more than $14 million to send 1,100 middle managers like Flynn Bowen to communities that suffer from poverty and other problems. Initiated by UPS founder James Casey, the Community Internship Program is designed to add diversity to the "brown" perspective.

inmates and changed the way he approaches decisions at UPS. "I'm much more sensitive to the fact that we must make decisions on a case-by-case basis," he says. "Things are no longer black and white for me."

Because half of all UPS's new employees are not white, senior managers believe that the program is an important training ground for the mostly white management team. "We've got 330,000 U.S. employees," says the program coordinator. "There are all kinds of personalities and all kinds of diversity. We need managers who can manage those individuals." Although executives cannot point to a financial return on this investment, feedback from participants indicates that they not only bring a new perspective to work decisions, but also they are inspired to volunteer in their home communities. "We will never really know how many lives we have touched," sums up a recent participant.

Sources: Karen Pelkey, "Resident Participates in Company's Community Internship Program," *Farmington Valley Post*, July 24, 2003; Jennifer J. Salopek, "Just Like Me: UPS's Unique Intern Program Transforms the Perspectives of Leaders," *T&D*, October 2002, pp. 52+; Louis Lavelle, "For UPS Managers, a School of Hard Knocks," *Business Week*, July 22, 2002, pp. 58–59.

technical or product knowledge. As a consequence, the sales manager had to not only generate different alternative candidates (i.e., people with stronger interpersonal skills rather than product and technical knowledge) but he also had to use different means of generating these alternative candidates. He had to place ads in newspapers and trade magazines outside the computer industry.

Step 4: Analyzing Alternatives The fourth step in the process involves analyzing the alternatives generated. To begin, you need to determine which alternatives would produce minimally acceptable results. Any alternatives that are unlikely to at least achieve the minimally acceptable outcome can be eliminated. Next, you need to examine the feasibility of the remaining alternatives. Returning to our hiring example, you may have found three candidates for your sales position who would likely produce minimally acceptable sales results. But one candidate's salary needs exceed your budget; therefore, that person is not feasible. Once infeasible alternatives are eliminated, the next step is to determine which of the remaining alternatives would produce the most satisfactory outcome. Typically, the criteria and weights produced in step two are applied at this point. For example, of the two remaining candidates for the sales position, Jane and Martha, you might rate both people on each of the four criteria (see Exhibit 9.2).

As you can see, even though Jane scored lower than Martha on both sales and product knowledge, Jane is the better candidate. Her higher overall score is a function of scoring higher on the most important criteria (i.e., motivation and interpersonal skills).

Step 5: Selecting Alternatives Selecting an alternative flows naturally out of your analysis. The classical model argues that managers will choose the alternative that maximizes the desired outcome. This idea has often been expressed by the term **subjectively expected utility (SEU) model**. This model asserts that managers choose the alternative that they subjectively believe maximizes the desired outcome. The two key components of this model are the expected outcome produced by a given alternative and the probability that the alternative can be implemented. In our hiring example, Jane would seem to be the candidate who will produce the greater sales because she received the higher total score on the criteria believed to lead to sales success. The SEU model suggests that before you select Jane, you will assess the probability that if Jane is offered the job, she will come to work for you. If Jane is the better

subjectively expected utility (SEU) model a model of decision making that asserts that managers choose the alternative that they subjectively believe maximizes the desired outcome.

Candidate	Criteria	Rating*	×	Weight	=	Score
Martha	Motivation	8	×	.30	=	2.40
	Interpersonal	6	×	.25	=	1.50
	Sales knowledge	7	×	.25	=	1.75
	Product knowledge	6	×	.20	=	1.20
				Total Score	=	6.85
Candidate	Criteria	Rating	×	Weight	=	Score
Jane	Motivation	9	×	.30	=	2.70
	Interpersonal	8	×	.25	=	2.00
	Sales knowledge	6	×	.25	=	1.50
	Product knowledge	5	×	.20	=	1.00
				Total Score	=	7.20

*1 = Low; 10 = high

exhibit 9.2

Applying Criteria in Analyzing Alternatives

candidate but won't work for you, then she really isn't the better candidate; Martha is.

Step 6: Implementing the Decision In the classical model of decision making, effective decision implementation has four components. First, you assess sources and reasons for potential resistance to the decision. For example, Joe, a district sales manager in your company, might resist the decision to hire Jane because Martha is his personal friend, and Joe told Martha he could help get her the sales job. Second, you determine the chronology and sequence of actions designed to overcome resistance to the decision and ensure that the decision is effectively implemented. For example, you know that Joe believes sales process and product knowledge are the most important things in hiring a new salesperson. You also know that Martha was rated higher on these criteria than Jane. Consequently, you might decide to first explain to Joe that in making your decision, you weighted motivation and interpersonal skills much higher than sales process or product knowledge and explain that company and independent studies support this weighting. Furthermore, you might assign Jane to a district sales manager other than Joe to ensure that she gets a good start with the company. You might also decide to place her in a month-long training program to better familiarize her with your products and send her to a one-week course on "The Selling Process" when it is next offered. Setting the chronology and sequence of actions leads naturally into the third step: an assessment of the resources required to implement the decision effectively. For example, you know it will cost you $4,500 for the sales training course for Jane. Moreover, you need to determine whether you could delegate implementation steps to others (such as scheduling Jane for "The Selling Process" program) and can ensure that those individuals understand and are held accountable for those steps and outcomes.

Step 7: Monitoring and Evaluating Results The final step in the classical model involves monitoring and evaluating the results. To do this, you must gather information and compare results to the objectives and standards you set at the beginning. This is trickier than it may seem. First, you must gather the right information or the evaluation will be distorted at best and meaningless at worst. For example, in the case of hiring Jane, gathering information only on the number of sick days she has taken is unlikely to help you evaluate her early job performance. You might think it is silly that anyone would gather information on sick days taken when sales are what is important, but it is not uncommon for information that is easy to collect to obscure what is important. Often, the most important information is the hardest to gather. For example, gathering information on the number of sales calls Jane makes is much easier than gathering information on the attitude she presented to the customer during those sales calls. Yet, the latter may be more important than the former in closing the sale. In addition, the longer the lead time between actions and results, the more important appropriate performance indicators are, even if they are not easy to gather or evaluate. The key point here is the importance of monitoring and evaluating results in order to detect problems with the original decision and its implementation so that corrective actions can be taken. If the appropriate information is not gathered, the purpose of this final step is defeated.

A Manager's Challenge provides a look at two manager/owners of travel agencies and how they weighed their options and decided not to let new technology put them out of business. In the end they also decided to use the technology to enhance their business. As you read A Manager's Challenge, ask

tech nol ogy

a manager's challenge

Travel Agencies Find New Technological Paths to Profits

When Delta Air Lines stopped paying commissions to travel agencies for selling tickets on U.S. routes, the decision came as no surprise to Rita Baron and Barbara Hansen. Baron owns Baron Travel in Atlanta, Georgia; Hansen and her son own Sunflower Travel in Wichita, Kansas. Both owners had to make critical decisions about whether to toss in the towel or use technology to stay in the travel agency game.

A decade ago, travel agents earned at least a 10 percent commission on any airline tickets they sold, and they enjoyed close relationships with airline sales representatives. Starting in 1994, however, many U.S. airlines cut costs by capping commission levels. At the same time, new software technology allowed people to surf the Internet in pursuit of airfare bargains and in this way bypass travel agents. By 2001, the airlines were paying travel agencies just $20 for selling any ticket (regardless of value) on a domestic flight. By 2002, nearly every U.S. airline had entirely eliminated commissions on domestic flights as a way to boost profitability.

Caught in the ongoing financial squeeze of lower revenues from airlines, more than 6,000 travel agencies went out of business. Both Baron Travel and Sunflower Travel decided to pass the loss of revenue from disappearing commissions on to customers via service fees in the range of $40 per ticket. In implementing this decision, Barbara Hansen recognized she had to prove her worth to customers. Thus, she uses her extensive industry contacts to search for the lowest possible fares. Now, says Hansen, "we can often beat the fares customers see on the Web." She has taken on the technology of the Web with old-fashioned person-to-person networking.

To stay in business, Hansen knew she would have to set Sunflower Travel apart from its local and online competitors. Because of her personal interest in the South Pacific, she decided to focus on selling specialized tours to Australia and New Zealand. Once she developed a relationship with an established tour company operating in those countries, she then decided to use the technology that nearly put her out of business to her advantage. She decided to use the Internet to promote her tours. For instance, she linked her site with the New Zealand Tourist Office Web site and offered online wine retailers special Australian food and wine tours.

In this case, the new technology of the Internet and a change in commission policy by airlines presented both Hansen and Baron with a problem. Interestingly, each solved essentially the same problem with a different solution.

Sources: Tess Pearson, "Why Use a Travel Agent?" *Travel Agent*, September 29, 2003, p. 20; Nancy Fonti, "Atlanta Travel Agency Experiences Many Industry Changes," *Atlanta Journal-Constitution*, May 17, 2002, www.ajc.com; Paulette Thomas, "Case Study: Travel Agency Meets Technology's Threat," *Wall Street Journal*, May 21, 2002, p. B4.

---

yourself if you see the situation as a problem or an opportunity. What do you think of each manager's solution?

To many, the classical model makes considerable sense. However, it is important to understand the assumptions on which it is built:

- Problems are clear.
- Objectives are clear.
- People agree on criteria and weights.
- All alternatives are known.
- All consequences can be anticipated.
- Decision makers are rational:
  - They are not biased in recognizing problems.
  - They can process all relevant information.
  - They appropriately incorporate immediate and future consequences into decision making.
  - They search for the alternative that maximizes the desired result.

The potential weaknesses of the classical model are easily exposed if you recall your own decision about what university to attend. How clear was the problem or your objectives? Did everyone (you, your parents, your friends, etc.) agree on the criteria and weights for evaluating alternative schools? Did you know or even consider all the possible alternative universities? Could you fully anticipate the consequences associated with attending each school? Were you completely unbiased in your definition of the problem or the opportunity of which school to attend, and did you objectively review all the relevant information? Did you appropriately emphasize short-term and long-term consequences? Did you search for alternatives until you found the one that maximized your desired outcome? If you answered no to some of these questions, you're not alone. A large body of research has shown that people are not as rational as the classical model assumes.[4] In fact, we can identify a series of factors that inhibit people's ability to accurately identify and analyze problems, as shown in Exhibit 9.3.

Thus, whereas the rational, or classical, model shows how decisions *should* be made (i.e., it works as a prescriptive model), it falls somewhat short concerning how decisions are *actually* made (i.e., as a descriptive model).

The Bounded Rationality Model

An alternative model, one not bound by the preceding assumptions, has been presented by Herbert Simon.[5] This model is called the **bounded rationality model** (or the **administrative man model**). As the name implies, this model does

bounded rationality model (administrative man model) a model that assumes that people usually settle for acceptable rather than maximum options because the decisions they confront typically demand greater information-processing capabilities than they possess

exhibit 9.3

Factors That Inhibit Accurate Problem Identification and Analysis

Factor	Description	Illustration
Information Bias	A reluctance to give or receive negative information.	You are favoring Jane as the candidate and dismiss information about a performance problem she had at her last job.
Uncertainty Absorption	A tendency for information to lose its uncertainty as it is passed along.	It is not clear how well Martha did in her previous job, but by the time the feedback gets to you, she is described as a poor performer.
Selective Perception	A tendency to ignore or avoid certain information, especially ambiguous information.	Jane may have several employment alternatives and may even be considering going back to school, but you ignore all this in making her the offer.
Stereotyping	Deciding about an alternative on the basis of characteristics ascribed by others.	Jane graduated from a private high school and went to a highly rated college on a partial scholarship, so you figure she must be a great hire.
Cognitive Complexity	Limits on the amount of information people can process at one time.	You initially have 200 applicants for the position but decide to eliminate anyone with less than three years sales experience.
Stress	Reduction of people's ability to cope with informational demands.	Your company's market share is slipping because you don't have enough salespeople in the field, so you feel you just can't look at every bit of information on every candidate.

not assume complete individual rationality in the decision process. Instead, it assumes that people, although they may seek the best solution, usually settle for much less, because the decisions they confront typically demand greater information-processing capabilities than they possess. They seek a kind of bounded or limited rationality in decisions.

The concept of bounded rationality attempts to describe decision processes in terms of three mechanisms. First, in the rational model, it is argued that people identify all possible solutions and then select the best alternative. Simon and other scholars have argued that this is not what people actually do. Instead, people examine possible solutions to a problem one at a time. If the first solution fails to work or is evaluated as unworkable, it is discarded and another solution is considered. When an acceptable (though not necessarily the best) solution is found, people stop searching for new alternatives. Thus, if the first alternative is workable, the search-and-analysis effort is likely to stop.

Second, rather than using explicit criteria and weights to evaluate alternatives, the bounded rationality model argues that people use heuristics. A **heuristic** is a rule that guides the search for alternatives into areas that have a high probability for yielding success. Thus, instead of looking everywhere for possible candidates for the new sales position, you might use a heuristic that says the best people for the job you have open are those already doing the job. Consequently, you might try to hire someone away from your competitor. This could also help you make the decision more rapidly. This is why we often see the same companies coming back to certain universities—because in the past graduates from those schools have performed well for the company.

The third mechanism is the concept of satisficing (not to be confused with "satisfying"). **Satisficing** is selection of a minimally acceptable solution rather than pushing farther for an alternative that produces the best results. Whereas the rational model focuses on the decision maker as an optimizer, this model sees him or her as a satisficer. As explained by March and Simon:

> *An alternative is optimal if (1) there exists a set of criteria that permits all alternatives to be compared and (2) the alternative in question is preferred, by these criteria, to all other alternatives. An alternative is satisfactory if (1) there exists a set of criteria that describes minimally satisfactory alternatives, and (2) the alternative in question meets or exceeds all these criteria. . . . Finding that optimal alternative is a radically different problem from finding a satisfactory alternative. . . . To optimize requires processing several orders of magnitude more complex than those required to satisfice.*[6]

On the basis of these assumptions about decision makers, it is possible to outline the decision process from the standpoint of the bounded rationality model:

1. Set the goal to be pursued, or define the problem to be solved.
2. Establish an appropriate level of performance, or criterion level (i.e., knowing when a solution is acceptable, even if it is not perfect).
3. Employ heuristics to narrow the solution to a *single* promising alternative.
4. If no feasible alternative is identified, lower the aspiration level and begin the search for a new alternative solution (repeat steps 2 and 3).
5. After identifying a feasible alternative, evaluate it to determine its acceptability.
6. If the individual alternative is unacceptable, initiate a search for a new alternative solution (repeat steps 3–5).

heuristic a rule that guides the search for alternatives into areas that have a high probability for yielding success

satisficing the tendency for decision makers to accept the first alternative that meets their minimally acceptable requirements rather than pushing them further for an alternative that produces the best results

Maximizing Satisficing by Stewart Black

Q&A
OneKey
www.prenhall.com/onekey

7. If the identified alternative is acceptable, implement the solution.
8. Following implementation, evaluate the ease with which the goal was (or was not) attained and raise or lower the level of performance accordingly on future decisions.

This decision process is quite different from the rational model. In it we do not seek the best solution; instead, we look for a solution that is *acceptable*. The search behavior is sequential, involving evaluation of one solution at a time. Finally, in contrast to the prescriptive rational model, the bounded rationality model is descriptive; that is, it describes how decision makers actually identify solutions to organizational problems.

The Retrospective Decision Model

A third model focuses on how decision makers attempt to rationalize their choices after they are made. It has been variously referred to as the **retrospective decision model**,[7] or the **implicit favorite model**.[8]

One of the most noted contributors to this perspective was MIT professor Peter Soelberg. As Soelberg observed the job choice processes of graduating business students, he noticed that, in many cases, the students identified implicit favorites (that is, the alternative they wanted) very early in the recruiting and choice process. For example, one student might identify a manufacturer in Arizona as a favorite. However, students continued their search for additional alternatives and quickly selected the best alternate (or second) candidate, known as the "confirmation candidate." For example, the student might select a high-tech firm in California as his alternate firm. Next, the students would attempt to develop decision rules that demonstrated unequivocally that the implicit favorite was superior to the confirmation candidate. They did so by **perceptual distortion** of information—that is, highlighting the positive features of the implicit favorite over the alternative. For example, the student might leave out vacation time as a criterion because his favorite firm in Arizona has a very poor vacation policy compared with the alternative firm in California. However, the student might heavily weight a criterion of housing costs because they are cheaper in Arizona, the student's favored choice. Finally, after deriving a decision rule that clearly favored the implicit favorite, the student announced the decision and accepted the job in Arizona.

Ironically, Soelberg noted, the implicit favorite was typically superior to the confirmation candidate on only one or two dimensions. Even so, decision makers generally characterized their decision rules as being multidimensional. For example, in the case of the two firms in Arizona and California, the jobs offered were quite similar, and the salary, travel, benefits, and promotion prospects were also nearly identical. Yet the student would claim that the Arizona firm was superior on several counts.

The entire process is designed to justify, through the guise of scientific rigor, a decision that has already been made intuitively. By this means, the individual becomes convinced that he or she is acting rationally and making a logical, reasoned decision on an important topic. Consider how many times you have made a decision in a similar way when looking for clothes, cars, stereo systems, and so on. You start with an item that catches your eye and then spend considerable time convincing yourself and your friends that this is the "best" choice. If your implicit favorite is the cheapest among the competition, you emphasize price; if it is not, you emphasize quality or styling. Ultimately, you end up buying the item you favored, feeling comfortable that you made the right choice. Here, however, we do not want to create the

retrospective decision model (implicit favorite model) a decision-making model that focuses on how decision makers attempt to rationalize their choices after they are made

perceptual distortion highlighting the positive features of the implicit favorite over the alternative

impression that **intuitive decision making**, or the primarily subconscious process of identifying a decision and selecting a preferred alternative, is bad or wrong. Although some firms often base their decision-making practices on rational analyses,[9] some research has found that not only are intuitive decisions often faster in many situations but also the outcome is as good or better than a methodical, rational approach.[10]

Types of Decisions

So which decision process do you think best describes how you make decisions? Are you a rational decision maker, a bounded rational decision maker, or a retrospective decision maker? Perhaps you are all three at different times. Maybe it varies by the type of decision.[11] Most decisions can be divided into two basic types: programmed or nonprogrammed. A **programmed decision** is a standard response to a simple or routine problem. The nature of the problem is well defined and clearly understood by the decision maker, as is the array of possible solutions. Examples of programmed decisions can be seen in college admission decisions, reimbursement for managers' travel expenses, and promotion decisions with many unionized personnel. In all these decisions, specific criteria can be identified (e.g., grade-point average and test scores for college admission, per-diem allowances for expense account reimbursements, or seniority for union promotions). The programmed decision process is characterized by high levels of certainty for both the problem formulation and the problem solution phases, and rules and procedures typically spell out exactly how to respond.

On the other hand, **nonprogrammed decisions** occur in response to problems that are either poorly defined or novel. For example, should a university president with limited funds expand the size of the business school to meet growing student demand, or should she expand the university's science facilities to bring in more federal research contracts? No alternative is clearly correct, and past decisions are of little help; instead, the decision maker must weigh the alternatives and their consequences carefully to make a unique decision—a nonprogrammed decision.

In most organizations, a significant relationship exists between the programmed and nonprogrammed decisions and organizational hierarchy. As shown in Exhibit 9.4, for example, top managers usually face nonprogrammed decisions, as in the case of the university president. On the other hand, college deans or department heads as well as faculty or students seldom get to make such decisions. Furthermore, lower-level managers (such as first-line supervisors) typically encounter mostly programmed, or routine, decisions. Their options and resources, as well as risks, are usually far less than those of top managers. And, as we might expect, middle managers fall somewhere in between.

One final point should be made here concerning the relationship between programmed and nonprogrammed decisions. Programmed decisions are usually made through structured, bureaucratic techniques. For example, **standard operating procedures (SOP)** are often used for programmed decisions. SOPs specify exactly what should be done—the sequence of steps and exactly how each step should be performed. In contrast, nonprogrammed decisions must be made by managers using available information and their own judgment, often under considerable time pressure. The ambiguity of the prob-

intuitive decision making the primarily subconscious process of identifying a decision and selecting a preferred alternative

programmed decision a standard response to a simple or routine problem

nonprogrammed decision a decision about a problem that is either poorly defined or novel

standard operating procedure (SOP) established procedure for action used for programmed decisions that specifies exactly what should be done

exhibit 9.4
Decision-Maker Level and Type of Decision

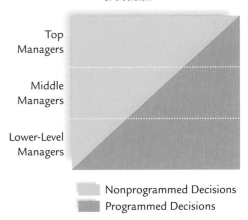

Nonprogrammed Decisions
Programmed Decisions

exhibit 9.5

Gresham's Law and Making Decisions

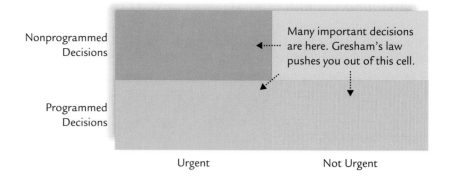

Gresham's law of planning
the tendency for managers to let programmed activities overshadow nonprogrammed activities

lem in part contributes to the uncertainty of the outcome. The uncertainty of the outcome of nonprogrammed decisions leads to an interesting and important consequence. It is the tendency for managers to let programmed activities over-shadow nonprogrammed activities. This tendency is called **Gresham's law of planning**.[12] Thus, if a manager has a series of decisions to make, he or she will tend to make those that are routine and repetitive before focusing on those that are unique and require considerable thought. When asked why they do this, many managers reply that they wish to clear their desks so they can concentrate on the really serious problems. Unfortunately, the reality is that managers often don't actually get to the more difficult and perhaps more important decisions. They may just run out of time or continue to occupy their time with the pro-grammed decisions (and their more certain outcomes) than with the nonpro-grammed decisions (and their less certain outcomes).

The implications of Gresham's law for managerial decision making are clear. As a manager you must make needed decisions in a timely fashion. As a consequence, you may want to check yourself periodically to see where you are spending your "decision-making time" to see if you are falling prey to Gresham's law of planning. The matrix in Exhibit 9.5 may help you with this assessment.

Influences on Effective Decision Making

From a practical perspective, perhaps the most important question for man-agers to ask is "What influences effective decision making?" Quite simply, practicing managers want to make good decisions. Consequently, it is helpful to briefly examine the major factors that hurt decision quality and then exam-ine what we can do to enhance individual decision quality. At least three gen-eral factors influence decision quality (see Exhibit 9.6).[13]

exhibit 9.6

Influences on the Decision Process

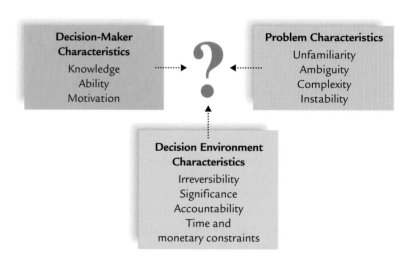

First, there are the characteristics of the decision maker. Earlier in the chapter we discussed that we may not be as rational as we like to believe. We can have implicit preferences for alternatives and simply construct rationales for those implicit biases to make it seem as though we are being rational and objective. We can have limitations to our information-processing capabilities and, as a consequence, limit the alternatives we examine. If our motivation is not sufficient, we can easily satisfice and simply accept the first workable solution rather than push to find the best of several workable solutions. If we lack familiarity with the problem or have insufficient knowledge, we can make less than ideal decisions. If we have too much familiarity with the problem, we can be too quick to select solutions that have worked in the past. In the process we might not consider sufficiently what might be different about the past and current situations that might make past solutions inappropriate for the present problem.

Second, the nature of the problem or opportunity itself can influence decision quality. The greater the ambiguity of the problem, the harder it is to be certain of the "right" decision. Also, as we have already discussed, we may shy away from ambiguous problems and, as a consequence, the neglect of the needed decision can result in less than ideal outcomes. The complexity of the problem can also affect the outcome. The more complex the problem is, the more challenging both the decision and its effective implementation are likely to be. The extent to which the problem is stable or volatile can also influence decision effectiveness. Clearly, the more volatile the problem, the greater the chance that the problem will change and, as a consequence, the selected solution won't match the problem.

Third, the decision is influenced by the environment in which the decision is made. Time constraints or any relevant resource constraints (e.g., people, money, equipment, etc.) can influence the decision's effectiveness. For example, the more time pressure you are under, the greater the chance that you might "miss" something or become vulnerable to any or all of the bounded rationality limitations we already discussed. If the decision is irreversible and you make the "wrong" decision, you obviously lack the opportunity to modify the decision and correct the results. The importance of the decision can create its own pressures, which in turn can influence the effectiveness of the decision.

Making Better Decisions

If all of these major factors can influence the effectiveness of decisions, what can you do as a manager to avoid these pitfalls and enhance the probability of making a "good" decision?

Analyze the Situation First, recognizing the pitfalls is a key factor to success. For example, if you are unaware of Gresham's law, you have little opportunity to assess whether or not you are falling victim to it, and without this awareness, it is almost impossible to deliberately get yourself out of this particular pit if you've fallen into it. As simple as this first step may seem, it is vital. Consequently, one of the first steps to better individual decision making is better decision situation assessment. Exhibit 9.7 provides a simple set of questions related to the three categories of factors diagrammed in Exhibit 9.6 that you can ask yourself in order to have a clearer picture of the situation and the potential pitfalls.

Scan the Environment As we discussed, nonprogrammed decisions typically are more ambiguous than routine decisions. As a consequence, there is a greater risk that your decision could be wrong and carry important, negative

Decision-Maker Characteristics
1. Do you have an implicit favorite solution?
2. Do you have a tendency to satisfice and go with the first workable solution?
3. Do you feel overwhelmed by the amount of information you are having to process?
4. Do you feel a lack of knowledge about the problem?
5. Are you particularly unfamiliar or familiar with the problem?

Problem Characteristics
1. Does the problem seem quite ambiguous?
2. Is the problem substantially complex?
3. Does the problem seem stable or volatile?

Decision Environment Characteristics
1. Are you under significant time pressures to make the decision?
2. Do you face substantial resource limitations (e.g., people, money, equipment, etc.) relative to the problem and its solution?
3. Is the decision irreversible?
4. Are the problem and your decision of substantial importance?

consequences for yourself and others. For example, as the university president, if you make the wrong decision about the direction the organization should take, it could be costly, both financially and politically. In fact, your job may depend on making the right decision. On one hand, if you expand the science facility, you still have no guarantee that the added faculty will bring in more contracts and grants; besides, by doing so, you may be denying admission to a large number of qualified business students. You may also alienate the business faculty and companies that recruit those graduates. On the other hand, building the business programs could alienate the science students and faculty, may allow a rival university to get ahead, and may prompt many of your best scientists to go elsewhere. As a result, the more complex, ambiguous, and volatile the problem, the more environmental scanning you may want to do prior to making the decision. For example, as the university president you would want to seek as much useful information as you could from outside the organization. In doing so you may discover that a rival school is about to expand its own science complex and wants to hire away your best scientists. On one hand, you may wish to defend what you have, especially if you view the business school as less important to your institution's goals. On the other hand, if your state's governor and legislature have made it clear that they want more business education, you may have to factor this into your decision as well. Environmental scanning may help you gain useful information that can lead to a higher-quality decision.

Think Through the Process As we stated earlier in the chapter, even though the rational approach may not always be descriptive of many decision-making processes, you can and most often should use it to guide your decision making.

Be Creative Especially if you discover in doing an analysis of the decision-making situation that you have an "implicit favorite" solution or if you are very familiar with the situation but the current situation differs in respect to past situations, being creative can be an important key to making effective decisions. This is also true if the problem is complex or unfamiliar. For example, your problem is how to make a raw egg stand up without assistance and without losing any of the substance inside the egg for 10 seconds on the surface of your desk. In other words, you can't prop it up against something, or use glue, extract the yolk and egg white, and so on. Get creative. Try spinning it. Try balancing it. What works? There is a way to do it.

Know the Right Timing Clearly, you have to be aware of the timeliness of your decisions. Many decisions involve problems or opportunities that have time constraints. For example, deciding to enter a race after it's half over will not generally work out well. At the same time, deciding to run the race before any of the other competitors or spectators show up may not work out well either. Decisions can be made too early or too late. Making a decision sooner than needed can prevent you from creating a full set of alternatives or from examining them thoroughly. Making a decision too late can leave you with a great set of alternatives and a comprehensive analysis and no beneficial results. In popular management literature, this last tendency is often referred to as "analysis paralysis" or the failure to move and make a decision because you are stuck in the process of analyzing the situation, objectives, alternatives, and so on. To avoid poor timing, ask yourself and others when a decision is needed and why. Make sure the timing of the decision is clear and makes sense.

Increase Your Knowledge If you are clear about the needed timing of the decision, you can help yourself avoid the pitfall of analysis paralysis and still increase your knowledge to make a better decision. The old standby foundation questions that you may have been taught in grammar school are perhaps the best guide for adding relevant knowledge for better decisions: who, what, where, why, and how.

Be Flexible Thankfully, most decisions are not irreversible. As we will explore more fully later in this chapter, much of the sense of irreversibility of decisions comes from the decision maker's desire to seem consistent rather than from the nature of the decision itself. For example, once you jump out of an airplane and start falling, the nature of the decision is irreversible, so you better have a parachute. Consequently, as the rational model of decision making argues, it is important to monitor the outcomes closely and be prepared to modify or even completely change your decision if it seems that the desired outcomes will not materialize.

A Manager's Challenge on Global Radio provides one example of a group of managers who are trying to ensure that they are making good decisions in the face of considerable uncertainty. In deciding to launch a satellite radio broadcasting company, they first scanned the environment carefully to both learn from the actions of others (their successes and mistakes) and the nature of the market for this service. In addition, they are trying to be creative in coming up with solutions to the problems they face relative to their overall decision to launch the business. In general they remain committed to the business but flexible in their decisions about how to structure specific aspects. In reading A Manager's Challenge, what is your impression of the managers? Have they scanned the environment well enough? Do you think their decision to go ahead is a good one?

GROUP DECISION MAKING

The three models described at the beginning of the chapter attempt to explain certain aspects of individual decision making. However, those models can also illuminate aspects of group decision making. Many of the basic processes

globalization _a manager's challenge_

Deciding to Put European Radio into Orbit

Will European listeners on the go tune into satellite radio? Managers at Global Radio, based in Luxembourg, are planning for a resounding "yes" as they prepare to introduce a pan-European satellite broadcasting system in 2006. Along the way, the managers must make a number of key decisions, despite considerable uncertainty about the level of demand, programming content, competition, and financial backing.

Fortunately, Global Radio's managers are learning from the experiences of their U.S. counterparts, XM Satellite Radio Holdings and Sirius Satellite Radio. Both use satellites to beam 100 mostly commercial-free channels of sports, music, news, children's shows, and entertainment programs to subscribers who pay from $100 to $350 to buy special car-radio receivers and an additional $10 (XM) or $13 (Sirius) monthly fee. Managers at XM and Sirius have committed billions of dollars in the expectation that truck drivers, commuters, and others who drive for long periods will pay for clear, continuous reception of specialized radio programming anywhere in the country. So far, however, the U.S. ride has been bumpy because of slow growth in the number of subscribers and new competition from digital radio technology, which makes ordinary radio signals sound much better without any monthly fee.

Watching how U.S. companies cope has helped Global Radio's managers become more knowledgeable about the nature and complexity of the decisions they face. For example, managers at Sirius and XM had little success selling add-on gadgets that equip existing car radios to receive satellite radio signals, so they finally struck deals with major car manufacturers such as Ford, Chrysler, and Honda to install satellite-ready receivers as an option in new cars. Because of this, managers at Global Radio decided that partnering with European car manufacturers earlier in the development process would help its product designers create smaller, more cost-effective in-dash receivers suitable for factory installation.

In addition, Global Radio's managers realize that although the European market has many similarities to the U.S. market, there are many critical differences as well. The total number of new cars sold in Europe and the United States is about the same, yet the population of Europe is approximately double that of the United States and income levels are generally lower in Europe. Digging still deeper, the managers found distinct preferences within specific European regions for radio programming based on different languages, sports activities, popular music, and news. As a result, Global Radio decided to look beyond in-car subscriptions to find ways of boosting at-home demand among certain European audiences. Managers also decided to extensively test its subscription service and analyze feedback from car manufacturers, distributors, and customers before introducing it across the continent.

Finally, the management of Global Radio has to contend with a hazy competitive outlook and significant financial uncertainty. Specifically, managers are concerned about raising sufficient money to build and launch three satellites for full radio coverage throughout Europe. Would potential investors be discouraged by the slow growth of U.S. satellite radio and the unpredictability of the global economy? Only time will tell whether investors, car manufacturers, and—ultimately—listeners are on Global Radio's wavelength.

Sources: Adapted from Stephen A. Blum, "Global Radio Learns from U.S. Satellite Radio Missteps," *Interspace*, September 11, 2002; "FCC Approves Digital Radio," *Dow Jones Newswires*, October 10, 2002, www.wsj.com; Brian Werth, "Companies Push Satellite Radio While Public Interest Lags," *Herald-Times* (Bloomington, IN), September 10, 2002, www.hoosiertimes.com.

remain the same. For instance, using the rational model, we can observe that both individuals and groups identify objectives. Both individuals and groups may also attempt to identify all possible outcomes before selecting one and, more than likely, both will fail in that attempt. Both individuals and groups are often observed engaging in satisficing behavior or using heuristics in the decision process. And both individuals and groups develop implicit favorites and attempt to justify those favorites by procedures that appear to others to be rationalization. Many of the dynamics and process of groups that relate to decision making as well as other group activities are covered extensively in Chapter 13.

Impact of Groups on Decision Making

What makes group decision making different from individual decision making is the social interaction in the process, which complicates the dynamics. In some situations, group decision making can be an asset, but at other times it can be a liability. The trick for you as a manager is to discover when and how to invite group participation in decisions. Some assets and liabilities of group decision making are shown in Exhibit 9.8. Going one step further, let us look at what we know about the impact of groups in the decision process itself, especially relative to nonprogrammed decisions:

- In *establishing objectives*, groups are typically superior to individuals in that they bring greater cumulative knowledge to problems.
- In *identifying alternatives*, individual efforts ensure that different and perhaps unique solutions are identified from various functional areas that later can be considered by the group.
- In *evaluating alternatives*, group judgment is often superior to individual judgment, because it involves a wider range of viewpoints.
- In *choosing alternatives*, involving group members often leads to greater acceptance of the final outcome.
- In *implementing the choice*, individual responsibility is generally superior to group responsibility. Whether decisions are made individually or collectively, individuals perform better in carrying out the decision than groups do.[14]

From the list in Exhibit 9.8, you can see that you cannot conclude that either individual or group decision making is superior. Rather, the situations and the individuals involved should guide the choice of decision technique.

One question about the effects of group participation remains to be asked: Why does it seem to work in many instances? A partial answer to this question has been offered by Ebert and Mitchell.[15] First, they suggest that participation clarifies more fully what is expected. Second, participation increases the likelihood that employees will work for rewards and outcomes they value. Third, it heightens the effects of social influence on behavior. That is, peers will monitor and exert pressure on each other to conform to expected performance levels. Finally, it enlarges the amount of control employees have over their work activities. In many cases, participation in decision making can be useful in both organizational goal attainment and personal need satisfaction.[16]

Assets +
- Groups can accumulate more knowledge and facts.
- Groups have a broader perspective and consider more alternatives.
- Individuals who participate in group decisions are more satisfied with the decision and are more likely to support it.
- Group decision processes serve an important communication function, as well as a useful political function.

Liabilities −
- Groups often work more slowly than individuals.
- Group decisions involve considerable compromise that may lead to less than optimal decisions.
- Groups are often dominated by one individual or a small clique, thereby negating many of the virtues of group processes.
- Overreliance on group decision making can inhibit management's ability to act quickly and decisively when necessary.

exhibit 9.8

Assets and Liabilities of Group Decision Making

Because participation helps involve employees and increases satisfaction and interaction, it has been an important part of quality improvement efforts. For example, team-based efforts to improve products and processes have always worked best when they included significant participation in decision making.

CONTINGENCY MODEL OF PARTICIPATIVE DECISION MAKING

A central issue facing managers is the extent to which they should allow employees in the work group to participate in decisions affecting their jobs. For example, as work situations, time pressures, and even subordinate capabilities change, does the level of participation in decisions need to change? The short answer is "yes." Although many advocates of participation emphasize both case examples and even scientific research showing how participation led to improved decision quality, increased commitment of members to decision outcomes, and increased satisfaction resulting from involvement, participative decision making is not a panacea. A careful review of the research suggests that it is not appropriate for every situation.[17] If participative decision making is not appropriate for all situations, how can you as a manager determine when it will and won't be effective and, therefore, when you should change your decision-making style or approach from one of making the decision on your own to one of involving others in a participative process?

Participative Decision Makers

To determine some of the variables that make up good participative decisions, researchers have explored the characteristics of the decision makers. Essentially, researchers have asked the question, "When participative decision making is effective, what do the people involved look like?" First and foremost, research suggests that those participating in the decision-making process must have sufficient knowledge about the content of the decision. Companies such as Ford, Federal Express, Procter & Gamble, and Boeing have put together **cross-functional teams** (consisting of members from marketing, finance, operations, human resources, etc.) for new product launches because each member has unique knowledge that adds value to the overall product launch decision. In contrast, asking people to become involved in decisions that are completely outside their area of expertise does not lead to either better-quality decisions or more commitment to the decisions and their implementation.

In addition to content knowledge, members also need to have a general desire to participate. Not everyone wants to become involved in decisions. The desire to participate results from the individuals' believing that (1) they have relevant content knowledge, (2) their participation will help bring about change, (3) the resulting change will produce outcomes they value or prefer, and (4) participation is valued by the organization and fits with its goals and objectives. When General Motors first started encouraging more employee involvement in decisions, workers resisted the effort because they did not believe it was "for real." This belief was based on the fact that involvement had not been a part of the company's history; in the past, decisions were made by managers and implemented by employees. As a consequence, it took sustained support from top management before workers believed participation was legitimate.

cross-functional teams
employees from different departments, such as finance, marketing, operations, and human resources, who work together in problem solving

Participative Decision-Making Process

Like individual decision making, participative decision making involves related, yet separate, processes. Using the classical model of decision making, a participative group moves through the same seven steps, but involvement of group members can vary in each of those steps. Low involvement allows members to communicate their opinions about the problem, alternatives, and solution but not to influence the final determination. High involvement allows members not only to communicate their opinions but also to make final determinations. Thus, degree of involvement could range from high to low on each of the seven elements of the classical decision model. Exhibit 9.9 provides a sample in which a particular group has high involvement in the front end of classical decision making but low involvement on the back end.

Because involvement can vary for each step of the classical decision-making model, a question naturally arises whether any one configuration is better. One study directly examined this question.[18] This study found that high involvement in generating alternatives, planning implementation, and evaluating results was significantly related to higher levels of satisfaction and work group performance. The authors argued that involvement in generating alternatives was important because solutions almost always came from alternatives generated. They found that involvement in planning the implementation was important because the outcome was affected more by the way a solution was implemented than by the solution itself. Finally, they noted that involvement in evaluating results was important because feedback is critical to beginning the decision cycle again.

One of the interesting implications from this line of study is that group members also need to understand group processes for participative decision making to be effective. That is, skill in analysis, communication, and handling conflicts can be as important as knowledge and the desire to participate. For example, one of the critical capabilities in identifying problems is environmental scanning. Not everyone is skilled at scanning the environment and recognizing problems or opportunities; yet, it is hard to begin participative decision making without members who can recognize problems and opportunities. For generating alternatives, a critical capability is creativity. For selecting a solution, a critical process capability is managing conflict—it is unlikely that a group can agree on a preferred solution without some conflict. As a consequence, managing that disagreement effectively is a critical process skill. In this sense, much of what is covered in Chapter 13 on groups and teams and their effectiveness applies to effective group decisions.

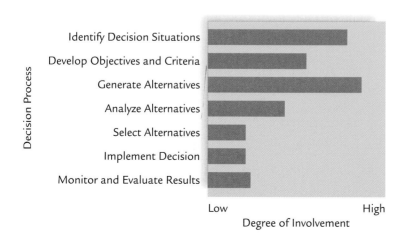

exhibit 9.9

Sample Configuration of Degree of Involvement and Decision Process

exhibit 9.10

Contingency Factors for Effective Participative Decision Making

1. Do potential group members have sufficient content knowledge?
2. Do potential members have sufficient process knowledge?
3. Do members have a desire to participate?
4. Do members believe that their participation will result in changes?
5. Do members positively value the expected outcomes?
6. Do members see participation as legitimate and congruent with other aspects of the organization?
7. If the answer to any of the above questions is no, is it possible to change the conditions?

Source: N. Margulies and J. Stewart Black, "Perspectives on the Implementation of Participative Approaches," *Human Resource Management 26*, no. 3 (1987), pp. 385–412.

Exhibit 9.10 provides a summary of the questions a manager should ask in determining whether participative decision making is likely to be effective.

On the basis of a long-term research project, Victor Vroom and his colleagues Phillip Yetton and Arthur Jago also developed a theory of participation in decision making that has clear managerial implications.[19] It is possible to categorize this model as either a model of leadership or a model of decision making. The model not only considers how managers should behave in decision-making situations but also prescribes correct leader behavior regarding the degree of participation. Given its orientation toward leadership behavior, we cover this theory in depth in Chapter 14.

A Manager's Challenge illustrates one situation in which the move from more involvement in decision making to less involvement seems to be effective. Clearly, when too many people are involved in decisions and when those decisions involve areas of specialization in which the participating members lack expertise, lower levels of participation are more appropriate than higher levels. This is exactly the situation in many law firms that have experienced significant growth. What is your assessment of the situation and the managers' response? Does the changing situation seem to justify less participation in decisions?

DECISION SPEED AND QUALITY

Have you ever heard of Gavilan Computer? If you own a laptop computer, by all rights you should have, but odds are you haven't. In the early 1980s, Gavilan Computer was at the forefront of computer technology and had a virtual monopoly on the developing—and lucrative—laptop computer market. By 1984, however, Gavilan had filed for bankruptcy. Despite a $31 million stake from venture capitalists, the company experienced long delays and indecision that cost the company its early technological and market advantage. Competitors entered the market niche, and Gavilan failed to exploit its advantage. As one executive observed, "We missed the window."[20] What happened to Gavilan has occurred with alarming frequency in many corporations—especially those involved in high-technology industries—as the indecisive fall by the wayside.

In a series of studies of decision making in industries characterized by frequent change and turbulence—so-called high-velocity environments—researchers Kathleen Eisenhardt and L. J. Bourgeois attempted to determine what separates successful decision makers and managers from unsuccessful

a manager's challenge

Change

Law Firms Change Decision-Making Style

Traditionally, all the partners in a law firm participated as a group in making decisions, individually or in committees. This system built consensus and commitment and brought diverse backgrounds and opinions to the deliberations. Over time, however, as law firms have merged or added partners, the custom of participative decision making has led to bottlenecks and complications when questions about finance, technology, or other specialized topics appear on the agenda. Not only do the partners need more time to come to agreement on such issues, but also their decisions are not necessarily better as a result of group participation.

Today law firms face more competition than ever before and feel more pressure to retain and serve corporate clients by keeping up with the faster pace of business. To operate more efficiently and more effectively in such an environment, some large law firms are changing the way they make internal decisions.

For example, Piper Marbury Rudnick & Wolfe is a law firm with 950 attorneys located in offices across the United States. The 300 lawyers at its largest office, located in Chicago, recently changed to a more centralized method of decision making. Instead of bringing all the partners together to vote and then manage the outcome of each decision, the chairperson relies on professional managers who specialize in particular areas of expertise, including marketing, information technology, human resources, and finance. "We realized that because of our size, we had to adopt a corporate model," states the chairperson, Lee I. Miller. "It streamlines our decision making. We are able to react quickly, decisively."

However, partners accustomed to participative decision making may not easily accept the idea of delegating decisions to professional managers without group input. "At times it's a bitter pill," says a partner at the law firm Stellato & Schwartz. "When you ascend to the position of partner, it's based upon your ability to show loyalty, longevity, and business acumen. Inherent in those qualities is a desire to lead. But sometimes that desire has to be set aside for the good of the team." For their part, the managers who make decisions on behalf of law firms must constantly and carefully evaluate how the outcome of each major decision is likely to affect the firm and its partners, even when dealing with support functions such as human resources and finance.

Consider the situation at Wildman Harrold Allen & Dixon, an Illinois law firm where John Holthaus is executive director. As an accountant who holds an M.B.A. degree, Holthaus has the technical and managerial background to make the myriad day-to-day decisions that keep the law firm operating smoothly. One way Holthaus proved his worth was by renegotiating the firm's lease to save on rental expenses. "I view my job as that of a hospital administrator who takes care of all the details so the doctors can take care of their patients," he explains. "I'm trying to make it easier for the attorneys to focus on serving their clients." Knowing that Holthaus understands the law firm's objectives and takes care of the tiniest details, the partners have come to rely on him rather than getting bogged down in endless group meetings to make decisions.

Source: Adapted from John T. Slania, "More Firms Mind Their Business: Corporate Model Helps Streamline Decision Making," *Crain's Chicago Business,* January 28, 2002, p. SR10.

---

ones.[21] In high-velocity industries (e.g., microelectronics, medical technology, genetic engineering), high-quality, rapid decision making by executives and their companies is closely related to good corporate performance. In these industries, mistakes are costly; information is often ambiguous, obsolete, or simply incorrect; and recovery from missed opportunities is extremely difficult. In view of the importance of speed for organizational innovation, performance, and survival, how do successful decision makers make high-quality, rapid decisions? And how are those decisions implemented rapidly?

Eisenhardt and Bourgeois found that five factors influenced a manager's ability to make fast decisions in high-velocity environments (see Exhibit 9.11). These five characteristics are moderated by three mediating processes that determine the manager's and group's ability to deal with the quantity and quality of information:

In the early 1980s Gavilan Computer was at the forefront of computer technology. By 1984, Gavilan had filed for bankruptcy.

1. **Accelerated cognitive processing.** The decision maker must be able to process and analyze great amounts of information quickly and efficiently. Some people—and some groups—can simply process information faster and better than others. Obviously, the faster a manager can process what is presented, the quicker the decision can be made.

2. **Smooth group processes.** To be effective, the manager must work with a group that has smooth, harmonious relations. This is not to say that everyone always agrees. Quite the contrary—members of effective groups often disagree. However, it is the way they disagree and resolve their disagreements that counts. Fast decisions are aided by group members who share a common vision and who are mutually supportive and cohesive.

3. **Confidence to act.** Finally, fast decision-making groups must not be afraid to act. As we already noted, some people are reluctant to make decisions in the face of

exhibit 9.11

Factors of Fast Decision Making

1. *Real-time information.* Fast decision makers must have access to and be able to process real-time information—that is, information that describes what is happening right now, not yesterday.
2. *Multiple simultaneous alternatives.* Decision makers examine several possible alternative courses of action simultaneously, not sequentially (e.g., "Let's look at alternatives X, Y, and Z altogether and see how each looks."). This adds complexity and richness to the analysis and reduces the time involved in information processing.
3. *Two-tiered advice process.* Fast decision makers make use of a two-tiered advisory system, whereby all team members are allowed input but greater weight is given to the more experienced coworkers.
4. *Consensus with qualification.* Fast decision makers attempt to gain widespread consensus on the decision as it is being made, not after it is made.
5. *Decision integration.* Fast decision makers integrate tactical planning and issues of implementation within the decision process itself (e.g., "If we are going to do X, how might we do it?").

uncertainty, and they tend to wait until they can reduce the uncertainty. They may fall victim to analysis paralysis. Unfortunately, in high-velocity environments, this uncertainty is never eliminated. Thus, to be effective, fast decision makers must be willing to choose when the appropriate time comes even in the face of uncertainty.

Remember that this research is focused on high-velocity environments, not all organizational environments. That is, in businesses that are characterized by relative stability (e.g., the funeral home industry), rapid decisions may prove disastrous. Because stability allows time for more complete data collection and processing, managers in stable environments have less need for immediate action. Thus, as a manager of a team, you need to assess the time factors that characterize your industry. Then you will be able to make decisions appropriate for your industry.

PROBLEMS IN GROUP DECISION MAKING

At least two problems can negatively affect decision effectiveness in group decision making: groupthink and escalating commitment to a course of action.

Groupthink

Increased attention has been focused in recent years on a phenomenon known as **groupthink**. This phenomenon, first discussed by Irving Janis, refers to a mode of thinking in which pursuit of agreement among members becomes so dominant that it overrides a realistic appraisal of alternative courses of action.[22] The concept emerged from Janis's studies of high-level policy decisions by government leaders. These included decisions by the U.S. government about Vietnam, the Bay of Pigs, and the Korean War. In analyzing the decision process leading up to each action, Janis found indications pointing to the development of group norms that improved morale at the expense of critical thinking. A model of this process is shown in Exhibit 9.12.

Symptoms of Groupthink In studies of both government and business leaders, Janis identified eight primary symptoms of groupthink. The first is the *illusion of invulnerability.* Group members often reassure themselves about

groupthink a mode of thinking in which pursuit of agreement among members becomes so dominant that it overrides a realistic appraisal of alternative courses of action

**Groupthink
by Stewart Black**

Q&A
OneKey
www.prenhall.com/onekey

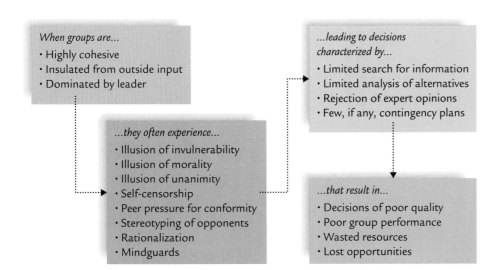

exhibit 9.12

The Groupthink Process

Source: Adapted from Gregory Moorhead, "Groupthink: Hypothesis in Need of Testing," *Group and Organization Studies 7,* no. 4, December 1982, pp. 429–44. Copyright © 1982 by Sage Publications, Inc. Reprinted by permission of Sage Publications, Inc.

obvious dangers, becoming overly optimistic and, thus, willing to take extraordinary risks. Members fail to respond to clear warning signals. For instance, in the disastrous Bay of Pigs invasion of Cuba in the 1960s, the United States operated on the false assumption that it could keep its invasion of Cuba a secret. Even after news of the plan had leaked out, government leaders remained convinced of their ability to keep it a secret.

Victims of groupthink also tend to collectively *rationalize* and discount warning signs and other negative feedback that could lead to reconsideration of the course of action. For example, Motorola discounted the new competitive potential of Nokia in the early 1990s. After all

- Nokia had a 100-year history in the forest products industry, making products such as rubber boots for fishermen, not high-tech mobile phones.
- Europe would not likely adopt a unified digital standard because the various countries had never demonstrated any real ability to coordinate and cooperate.
- Even if they did, the markets of these countries (Germany, France, or Italy) paled in comparison to the size of the U.S. mobile phone market.
- Finland (the home of Nokia) had fewer people than Chicago during the day.

We all know what happened. In 1990 Nokia was not even listed in the top 100 recognized brands. By 2002 Nokia was number six—ahead of Intel and right behind GE. Motorola's 35 percent global market share of mobile phones was cut in half while Nokia's global share went from virtually nothing to 40 percent at its peak. Today Nokia is the number-one cell phone maker in the world.

Next, group members often believe in the inherent morality of the group. Because of this *illusion of morality*, they ignore the ethical or moral consequences of their decisions. Leading tobacco companies continue to run advertisements about free choice about smoking, completely ignoring the medical evidence of the hazards involved.

Stereotyping the enemy is another symptom of groupthink. In-group members often stereotype leaders of opposition groups in harsh terms that rule out negotiation on differences of opinion. Often they also place tremendous pressure to conform on members who temporarily express doubts about

Organizational dynamics such as groupthink can lead companies to discount competitive threats. When the Finnish company Nokia—which had traditionally manufactured forest industry products, including rubber boots—entered the U.S. mobile phone market in the 1990s, competitors like Motorola didn't take it seriously.

the group's shared illusions or who raise questions about the validity of the arguments supporting the group decisions.

Moreover, group members often use *self-censorship* to avoid deviations from group consensus. They often minimize to themselves the seriousness of their doubts. Partly because of self-censorship, the *illusion of unanimity* forms. Members assume that individuals who remain silent agree with the spoken opinions of others and falsely conclude that everyone holds the same opinion.

Finally, victims of groupthink often appoint themselves as *mindguards* to protect the leader and other members of the group from adverse information that could cause conflict over the correctness of a course of action. The mindguard may tell the dissident that he or she is being disruptive or nonsupportive or may simply isolate the dissident from other group members. For many years, FBI agents in the Washington headquarters who expressed views contrary to the party line found themselves transferred to less desirable locations.

Consequences of Groupthink Groupthink can have several adverse consequences for the quality of decision making. First, groups plagued by groupthink often limit their search for possible solutions to one or two alternatives rather than all possible alternatives. Second, such groups frequently fail to reexamine their chosen action after new information or events suggest a change in course. Third, group members spend little time considering nonobvious advantages to alternative courses of action. Fourth, such groups often make little or no attempt to seek experts' advice either inside or outside their own organization. Fifth, members show interest in facts that support their preferred alternative and either ignore or disregard facts that fail to support it. Finally, groups often ignore possible roadblocks to their choice and, as a result, fail to develop contingency plans. This last consequence is similar to retrospective decision making—the decision is made and then data are selected that support the decision. Because the decision is reinforced by peers, unwillingness to reexamine and change directions is even more powerful in groups than in individuals.

Overcoming Groupthink Because a groupthink mentality poses such serious consequences for organizations, we must consider how to minimize its effects. Janis suggests several strategies. To begin, group leaders can reduce groupthink by encouraging each member to evaluate proposals critically. Also, leaders can ensure that the group considers a range of alternatives by not stating their own positions and instead promoting open inquiry.

Other strategies for preventing groupthink involve getting more suggestions for viable solutions. This can be done by assigning the same problem to two independent groups. Or before the group reaches a decision, members can seek advice from other groups in the organization. Another technique is to invite experts outside the group to challenge members' views at group meetings.

Groupthink may also be prevented with strategies directed at the group members themselves. For example, for each group meeting, a member can be appointed to serve as a **devil's advocate**, a person whose role is to challenge the majority position.[23] Also, after reaching preliminary consensus, the group can schedule a second-chance meeting. This allows group members an opportunity to express doubts and rethink the issue.

If groups are aware of the problems of groupthink, they can use the steps discussed to minimize the likelihood of falling victim to this problem.

devil's advocate a group member whose role is to challenge the majority position

exhibit 9.13

Guidelines for Overcoming
Groupthink

For the company
- Establish several independent groups to examine the same problem.
- Train managers in groupthink prevention techniques.

For the leader
- Assign everyone the role of critical evaluator.
- Use outside experts to challenge the group.
- Assign a devil's advocate role to one member of the group.
- Try to be impartial and refrain from stating your own views.

For group members
- Try to retain your objectivity and be a critical thinker.
- Discuss group deliberations with a trusted outsider and report back to the group.

For the deliberation process
- At times, break the group into subgroups to discuss the problem.
- Take time to study what other companies or groups have done in similar situations.
- Schedule second-chance meetings to provide an opportunity to rethink the issues before making a final decision.

These steps, summarized in Exhibit 9.13, offer advice for leaders, organizations, individuals, and the process itself.

Escalating Commitment to a Decision

escalating commitment the tendency to exhibit greater levels of commitment to a decision as time passes and investments are made in the decision, even after significant evidence emerges indicating that the original decision was incorrect

Whereas groupthink helps to explain how policy-making groups put blinders on and stifle dissenting opinions when making major decisions, the concept of **escalating commitment** to decisions offers an explanation of why decision makers adhere to a course of action after they know it is incorrect (i.e., why managers "throw good money after bad"). To understand the problem of escalating commitment, consider the following true examples:

- At an early stage of U.S. involvement in the Vietnam War, Undersecretary of State George Ball wrote the following in a memo to President Johnson:

  The decision you face now is crucial. Once large numbers of U.S. troops are committed to direct combat, they will begin to take heavy casualties in a war they are ill equipped to fight in a noncooperative if not downright hostile countryside. Once we suffer large casualties, we will have started a well-nigh irreversible process. Our involvement will be so great that we cannot without national humiliation stop short of achieving our complete objectives. Of the two possibilities, I think humiliation would be more likely than the achievement of our objectives—even after we have paid terrible costs.

- A company overestimated its capability to build an airplane brake that met certain technical specifications at a given cost. Because it won the government contract, the company was forced to invest greater and greater effort to meet the contract terms. As a result of increasing pressure to meet specifications and deadlines, records and tests of the brake were misrepresented to government officials. Corporate careers and company credibility were increasingly staked on the airbrake contract, although many in the firm knew the brake would not work effectively. At the conclusion of the construction period, the government test pilot flew the plane; it skidded off the runway and narrowly missed injuring the pilot.

- An individual purchased a stock at $50 a share, but the price dropped to $20. Still convinced about the merit of the stock, he bought more shares at the lower price.

Soon the price declined further, and the individual was again faced with the decision to buy more, hold what he already had, or sell out entirely.[24]

How do we account for such commitment by individuals and groups to obvious mistakes? At least three explanations are possible. First, we can point to individual limitations in information processing. People may be limited in both their desire and ability to handle all the information for complex decisions. As a result, errors in judgment may occur. For example, the company in which our stock investor purchased shares may have significant operations in countries in which negative changes in exchange rates are occurring or in which government regulations have changed. Our investor simply may not be able to completely comprehend these issues and how they are hurting the company's performance and subsequent stock price. A second approach is to explain decision errors as a breakdown in rationality because of group dynamics. For example, our stock investor may have received the tip from a trusted friend or he could be the friend of the company's CEO and, therefore, have a strong emotional commitment. Although both explanations may help us understand the error, Staw suggests that they do not go far enough. "A salient feature . . . is that a series of decisions is associated with a course of action rather than an isolated choice."[25]

To help explain such behavior, Staw turned to the social psychological literature on forced compliance. In studies of forced compliance, individuals are typically made to perform an unpleasant or dissatisfying act (e.g., eating grasshoppers) with no external rewards. In general, after they comply, individuals bias their own attitudes to justify their previous behavior (e.g., eating grasshoppers is not a bad thing because they are high in protein). This biasing of attitudes is most likely to occur when the individuals feel personally responsible for the negative consequences and when the consequences are difficult to undo.

On the basis of these findings, Staw and his colleagues carried out a series of experiments to find out how willing people would be to continue to commit valued resources to a course of action after it was clear that the original decision had been wrong. They found that decision makers actually allocated more money to company divisions that were showing poor results than to those that were showing good results. Also, decision makers allocated more money to a division when they had been responsible for the original decision to back the division. In short, decision makers were most likely to spend money on projects that had negative consequences when they were responsible.

To find out why, Staw suggested a model of escalating commitment (Exhibit 9.14). This abbreviated model shows that four basic elements determine commitment to an action. First, people are likely to remain committed to a course of action (even when it is clearly incorrect) because of a need to justify previous decisions. When people feel responsible for negative consequences and a need to demonstrate their own competence, they will often stick to a decision to turn it around or "pull a victory out of defeat." This is a form of retrospective rationality; the individual or members of the group seek explanations so that their previous decisions appear rational. For example, banks that loaned billions of dollars to Asian countries in the late 1980s and early 1990s continued to loan more money even after it was clear that the governments would have great difficulty repaying the loans. They continued these loans in

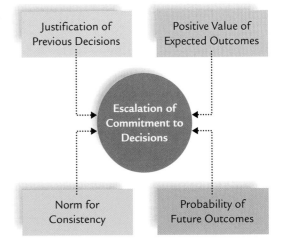

exhibit 9.14

Contributing Factors to Escalation of Commitment to Decisions

part to support their original decision. If they didn't continue the loans, they might be forced to recognize that their original decision was a mistake. This dynamic is not limited to headline decisions.[26] It can affect our continued commitment to personal decisions as well. For example, sometimes as individuals we stick with a boyfriend or girlfriend long after it is clear to us that it is not a good match to avoid admitting that the original decision was a mistake.

In addition, commitment to a previous decision is influenced by a norm for consistency. That is, managers who are consistent in their actions are often considered better leaders than those who flip-flop from one course of action to another. For instance, in a Gallup poll on former President Clinton's popularity, respondents who were dissatisfied with his performance described him as "inconsistent."

prospective rationality a belief that future courses of action are rational and correct

Finally, two additional factors—the perceived probability and value of future outcomes—jointly influence what is called prospective rationality. **Prospective rationality** is simply a belief that future courses of action are rational and correct. When people think they can turn a situation around or that "prosperity is just around the corner," and when the goal is highly prized, they exhibit strong commitment to a continued course of action, influenced in part by the feeling that it is the proper thing to do.

Overcoming Escalation of Commitment   Because escalation of commitment can lead to serious and negative consequences for organizations, we must consider how to minimize its effects.

1. First, as a manager, you should stress in your own mind and to others (superiors, peers, and subordinates) that investments made in the past are sunk costs—that is, they cannot be recovered. All finance theory argues that sunk cost should be ignored in making future decisions, and only future costs and future anticipated benefits should be considered.

2. Second, you must create an atmosphere in which consistency does not dominate. This requires stressing the changing aspects of the competitive, social, cultural, and commercial environment surrounding a business and focusing on the importance of matching current decisions to current and expected future environments rather than to past decisions.

3. Third, you can encourage each member to evaluate the prospects of future outcomes and their expected positive value critically. You can invite experts from outside the group to challenge members' future expectations.

4. As with groupthink, a member can be appointed to serve as a devil's advocate to challenge the majority position.

In summary, when we consider effective decision-making processes in organizations, we must ward off the threats of groupthink and escalating commitments. Each can subvert even the most carefully considered decisions.

CULTURAL DIMENSIONS OF DECISION MAKING

To this point we have talked about decision making as though it applied the world over. Although we still have much to learn about decision making in different countries and cultures, we can identify several factors that affect decisions. Many stem from the cultural differences we examined in Chapter 4.

One of the factors affecting decision making is the extent to which a culture adopts an individualist or collectivist orientation. For example, in exploring a contingency framework for participative decision making, we cited research suggesting that participation was not effective in all situations and that it should be used when it matches specific elements of a situation. However, it is worth noting that most researchers of participative decision making have come from individualistic cultures such as the United States, Canada, and the United Kingdom. In countries such as Japan, Indonesia, and Korea, managers and employees have a much stronger collectivist orientation. As a consequence, involving others in decision making may not simply be a function of contingency factors but participative decision making may simply be viewed as the "right" thing to do. In collectivist cultures, even when an individual decision maker believes he or she has all the relevant knowledge, a strong collectivist value often leads to the inclusion of others in the decision-making process.

These cultural clashes can often be seen when individuals from opposite orientations must work together. For example, when managers from more individualistic cultures are assigned to work in more collectivist cultures, they quite frequently experience difficulties because they tend to make too many individual decisions and not include others.[27]

Basic values concerning hierarchy can also influence decision making across countries.[28] As discussed in Chapter 4, managers in countries such as Malaysia, India, and Thailand have a higher acceptance of hierarchical differences between people (high power distance, in Hofstede's terms), whereas managers in countries such as Israel, Australia, and Denmark do not. Power distance can significantly affect the problem-analysis stage of decision making, especially when it involves group decisions. In low-power-distance cultures, group members tend to openly and directly disagree with each other in discussing the merits or risks of a given alternative. In high-power-distance cultures, such open discussions are less acceptable when individuals of differing ranks are involved. For example, in Thailand, if a lower-ranked individual had a significant difference of opinion with his or her superior, directly raising this during a group meeting would not be acceptable. Rather, the individual would try to find a time, perhaps after work, when she could present her opinion privately to the superior.

On the surface, one might expect organizations in cultures that have high levels of power distance to suffer from problems of groupthink because employees are less willing to voice their concerns or make critical comments, especially when superiors are present. Interestingly, many of these cultures have developed business practices to counterbalance this potential problem. For example, in Japan, managers use a technique called *nemawashi*. This term is borrowed from gardening and refers to the process of gradually snipping the roots of a tree or bush that is to be transplanted to reduce the shock to the plant. In business, *nemawashi* translates into many private or semiprivate meetings in which true opinions are shared before a major decision-making meeting. This allows differences of opinion to be stated while protecting respected hierarchical status. In addition, meeting after work at a bar or restaurant also allows for more direct discussions and disagreements. Both of these practices serve to counteract groupthink fostered by high power distance.

In addition, the extent to which cultures differ in their tolerance of risk can affect decision making. In countries with a relatively low tolerance of uncertainty and risk, such as Japan and Germany, nonprogrammed decisions are avoided as much as possible by using standard operating procedures. For example, the operating manual at BMW for how to work through an engineering problem is thick and detailed. Even though the specific engineering problems may vary, BMW executives have tried to make the decisions as programmed as possible. In contrast, managers in countries with relatively high tolerance of uncertainty and risk, such as Australia and the United States, tend to seek out nonprogrammed decisions and to give senior management more responsibility

Australian and U.S. companies like Nordstrom are likely to turn to nonprogrammed decision making and give their employees more decision-making latitude.

for nonprogrammed decisions. For example, the employee manual at Nordstrom simply states, "Nordstrom Rules: Rule #1: Use your good judgment in all situations. There will be no additional rules. Please feel free to ask your department manager, store manager, or division general manager any question at any time."

In addition to cultural values and the way they can affect the decision-making process, social and even corporate cultural values can affect nearly every aspect of decision making. For example, what is seen as a problem, what is viewed as an acceptable or desirable outcome, what criteria are used in assessing various alternatives, how an alternative is chosen (e.g., by the highest-ranking member, majority votes, consensus, etc.), or who is involved in planning the implementation can all be influenced by the underlying organizational or national culture. However, knowing the basic building blocks of decision making helps you ask the right questions and discover important differences in decision making when you work with people from other cultures.

STRATEGIES FOR IMPROVING DECISION MAKING

Now that we have focused on the problems and processes involved in decision making and have examined several decision models, differences between individual and group decisions, participation in decision making, constraints on effective decision making, and cultural influences, we can consider additional ways of improving the decision-making process. At the beginning of the chapter, we mentioned that decisions can be divided into two phases: problem formulation and problem solution. Strategies to improve decision making can also be divided into the same two categories.[29]

Improving Problem Formulation

Problem formulation focuses on identifying the causes for unsatisfactory behavior and finding new opportunities and challenges. This process is often inhibited by the failure of group members to look beyond the familiar.

Structured Debate (Problem Formulation)	Creativity Stimulants (Problem Solution)
Devil's advocate	Brainstorming
Multiple advocacy	Nominal group technique
Dialectical inquiry	Delphi technique

exhibit 9.15
Techniques for Improving Decision Making

Groupthink and escalating commitment often limit critical analysis or comprehensive searches for information and solutions. As a result, improvement in problem formulation may require the use of structured debate. **Structured debate** is a process to improve problem formulation through the use of a devil's advocate, multiple advocacy, and dialectical inquiry (see Exhibit 9.15).

structured debate a process to improve problem formulation that includes the processes of devil's advocate, multiple advocacy, and dialectical inquiry

Devil's Advocate As discussed earlier, a devil's advocate is a group member whose role is to disagree with the group. For example, if you asked a group of American automobile company executives why their sales are down, they might blame Japanese imports. In this case, a devil's advocate would argue that the problem lies not with the Japanese, but with the Americans themselves and their poor product quality. Through this process, the group is forced to justify its position and, as a consequence, develop a more precise and accurate picture of the problem and its underlying causes.

Multiple Advocacy **Multiple advocacy** is like the devil's advocate approach, except that more than one opposing view is presented. Each group involved in a decision is assigned the responsibility of representing the opinions of its constituents. Thus, if a university is concerned with enhancing racial and cultural diversity on campus, it might establish a commission including African Americans, Hispanics, Asians, women's groups, and so forth. The resulting dialogue should lead to the identification of a useful agenda for discussion.

multiple advocacy a process to improve decision making by assigning several group members to represent the opinions of various constituencies that might have an interest in the decision

Dialectical Inquiry **Dialectical inquiry** occurs when a group or individual is assigned the role of questioning the underlying assumptions of problem formulation. It begins by identifying the prevailing view of the problem and its associated assumptions. Next, an individual is asked to develop an alternative problem that is credible but has different assumptions. By doing so, the accuracy of the original assumptions is examined and possibly altered. As a result, group members are forced to "think outside the box" and look at new ways to analyze a problem. These efforts are particularly helpful in overcoming groupthink and escalating commitment, because they question the underlying assumptions of group behavior.

dialectical inquiry a process to improve decision making by assigning a group member (or members) the role of questioning the underlying assumptions associated with the formulation of the problem

Improving Problem Solution

Problem solution involves development and evaluation of alternative courses of action and selection and implementation of the preferred alternatives. To improve this process, group members must be as thorough and creative as possible. Stimulation of creativity expands the search for and analysis of possible alternatives. Three such mechanisms are useful.

Brainstorming **Brainstorming** is a process of generating many creative solutions without evaluating their merit. It is a frequently used mechanism to provide the maximum number of ideas in a short period of time. A group comes together, is given a specific problem, and is told to propose any ideas that

brainstorming a process of generating many creative solutions without evaluating their merit

come to mind to solve the problem. In such sessions—at least at the early stages—criticism is minimized so as not to inhibit expression. Once all the ideas are on the table, the group considers the positive and negative aspects of each proposal. Through a process of continual refinement, the best possible solution under the circumstances should emerge.

nominal group technique
a process of having group members record their proposed solutions, summarize all proposed solutions, and independently rank solutions until a clearly favored solution emerges

Nominal Group Technique The **nominal group technique**, typically referred to as NGT, consists of four phases in group decision making.[30] First, individual members meet as a group, but they begin by sitting silently and independently generating their ideas on a problem in writing. This silent period is followed by a round-robin procedure in which each group member presents an idea to the group. No discussion of the idea is allowed at this time. The ideas are summarized and recorded (perhaps on a blackboard). After all individuals have presented their ideas, each idea is discussed to clarify and evaluate it. Finally, group members conclude the meeting by silently and independently ranking the various ideas or solutions to the problem. The final decision is determined by the pooled outcome of the members' votes on the issue.

The NGT allows the group to meet formally, but it does not allow members much discussion; hence, the term *nominal* group technique. A chief advantage of this procedure is that everyone independently considers the problem without influence from other group members. As we found, this influence represents one of the chief obstacles to open-minded discussion and decision making.

delphi technique a decision-making technique that never allows decision participants to meet face-to-face but identifies a problem and offers solutions using a questionnaire

Delphi Technique In contrast to NGT, the **delphi technique** never allows decision participants to meet face-to-face. Instead, a problem is identified, and members are asked through a series of carefully designed questionnaires to provide potential solutions. These questionnaires are completed independently. Results of the first questionnaire are then circulated to all group members (who are still physically separated). After viewing the feedback, members are again asked their opinions (to see if the opinions of others on the first questionnaire caused them to change their own minds). This process may continue through several iterations until group members' opinions begin to show consensus.

The decision-making process includes a variety of problems. Individuals and groups have various biases and personal goals that may lead to suboptimal decisions. Moreover, groups often censor themselves. Even so, techniques such as those discussed here aim to minimize many of these problems by insulating individual participants from the undue influence of others. This allows individuals greater freedom of expression, and the group receives far less filtered or slanted information with which to make its decision. Thus, although not perfect, these techniques can give managers mechanisms to improve both the quality and the timeliness of decisions made in organizations.

The Role of Technology

Much has been made in recent years about the role of technology in decision making at the individual and group level.[31] For routine but complex tasks such as scheduling aircraft, raw materials, and material and component flow through a factory, computers and software vastly increase decision makers' capabilities. These tools can process amounts of information that would be overwhelming for an individual and at a speed that would be impossible for a human being. For example, despite all the problems and huge losses for commercial airlines in the United States during the 1990s, JetBlue became a successful start-up in 1998 and made money when other airlines were losing billions. Part of its success was due to the liberal use of new technology. By putting laptops and software in the hands of pilots, the company did away with the dozens and dozens of people typically required to make decisions about flight paths, scheduling, fuel intake, and so on.[32]

There is also a wide variety of technologies for helping groups communicate and make decisions without having to get together face-to-face. Technology that allows group members in different locations to view a common document at the same time and make real-time changes is increasingly being used by design teams in industries such as automobile manufacturing. The "virtual" aspects are argued to save considerable travel costs and the real time aspects are argued to increase group decision effectiveness. Given how new the technology is, it is difficult to say with confidence whether all the anticipated and hyped benefits are real. One review of recent studies comparing decision making in face-to-face versus computer-mediated communication groups found that computer-mediated communication leads to decreases in group effectiveness, increases in time required to complete tasks, and decreases in member satisfaction compared to face-to-face groups.[33] The study concluded with cautions about the unbridled rush by organizations to adopt computer-mediated communication as a medium for group decision making.

managerial perspectives revisited

PERSPECTIVE 1: ORGANIZATIONAL CONTEXT   No doubt by this point you see the importance of the organizational context in both individual and group decision making. However, it is worthwhile making the links explicit. For example, as we discussed, time pressures in an organization can significantly affect decision making. On the one hand, the nature of your business may be high velocity and require quick decisions. On the other hand, the culture of your company or just your immediate boss can put pressure on you to make a quick decision when one is not actually needed. Failure to recognize the organizational context could cause you to be late in making a decision in the first situation and unduly early in the second. The cultural diversity of your organization presents both challenges and opportunities. Clearly, when the group and decision-making processes are managed well, cultural diversity can be leveraged for more diverse perspectives regarding the problem or opportunity as well as greater creativity in solving the problem. At the same time, cultural diversity could present challenges in terms of different levels of comfort with ambiguous problems, desire to participate, or how to confront differences of opinion in a group setting with superiors present. The nature of the organization can also influence the degree to which you face programmed and nonprogrammed decisions. In general, managers working in a railroad company likely face more programmed decisions than those working in the fashion industry. However, even within a given industry the culture of the specific company can influence the degree to which you face programmed or nonprogrammed decisions. For example, in the oil and gas industry, ExxonMobil tends to allow lower-level managers to deal primarily with programmed decisions, whereas El Paso Energy tends to push nonprogrammed decisions lower in its organization.

2

PERSPECTIVE 2: THE HUMAN FACTOR   Even as a manager, you may encounter decisions that you can and should make individually. However, as a manager it is less likely that these individually made decisions can be implemented completely on your own without the involvement of others. Even when facing situations in which you believe the benefits of involving others in decision making outweigh any disadvantages, you will have to decide the extent to which you involve others in the formulation and solution phases. For example, as the complexity and ambiguity of the problems you face and the decisions you have to make increase, so does the likelihood that you will need to involve others in decisions. Will you work through people with higher involvement primarily in formulation phase, the solution phase, or both? Clearly, to the extent that you involve others in decision making, the decision formulation and implementation success becomes a function of working effectively with and through others.

3

PERSPECTIVE 3: MANAGING PARADOXES   Managers are likely to encounter paradoxes in decision making. On the one hand, utilizing the rational approach to make and implement decisions can help you avoid common pitfalls of bounded rationality or retrospective decision making. On the other hand, too rigid an adherence to the steps outlined could lead you to fall into the analysis-paralysis trap and miss important timing elements of the decision, or ignore valuable and accurate heuristics you have developed over time and with experience, or your intuition. You will also have to master the potential paradox that is at the heart of Gresham's law. On the one hand, you cannot ignore or simply delegate away all programmed decisions whether they are urgent or not. At the same time, if you allow them to dominate your time and energy, you will be less likely to address nonprogrammed decisions, which often have a bigger impact on your job performance and overall results for the organization. Diversity presents another element of duality. On the one hand, as a manager you get paid in part for your judgment and ability to make decisions. On the other hand, never checking with others as to how they see a situation or never taking into account the diverse perspectives, experience, and capabilities of those around you can lead you to less creative and effective decisions.

4

PERSPECTIVE 4: ENTREPRENEURIAL MIND-SET   Managers' entrepreneurial mind-set is reflected in the decisions that they make and by the degree of their commitment to those decisions and the processes by which they are made. Overall, an entrepreneurial mind-set in decision making is reflected by being creative and flexible along with a willingness to take some risks. A manager can enrich entrepreneurial activities in the organization by searching for new information and encouraging others to express diverse viewpoints. Although escalation of commitment to a prior decision and groupthink (if a group participates in the decision) do not reflect an entrepreneurial mind-set, the devil's advocate approach, brainstorming, delphi technique, and the nominal group technique can be used by managers to facilitate a more entrepreneurial approach to decision making. Using such approaches displays managers' commitment to be innovative and to be entrepreneurial in continuously searching for new opportunities when they make important decisions.

concluding comments

Decision making is a critical part of any managers' life. You could construe much of what a manager does as decision making. Motivation could be viewed as a decision regarding how to motivate a subordinate. Strategic management could be viewed as deciding what strategy to pursue. Communication could be viewed as a decision about what to say and how to say it. However central decision making may be to managing, to say that it is everything seems to us a bit much.

Still, as a manager you will make many decisions—large and small. As a consequence, you need a reasonably comprehensive but usable framework for guiding your decisions. We have suggested that thinking about decision making in terms of formation and implementation can fit this need. In formulation, it is important to remember that we often select solutions that meet our minimum objectives rather than spending extra time and energy trying to find the solution that maximizes their objectives. However, to appear rational, we often construct objectives and criteria after the fact to justify the decision we have already made. Groups can add a social dynamic to this tendency and make group members feel even more comfortable that they have been rational than individuals might feel alone. After all, if everyone else feels like it's a good decision, it must be. Managed properly, groups can also be an antidote to many of the limitations we described. Consequently, depending on how well the group dynamics are managed, group decision making can render decisions and results that are significantly better or worse than individuals might achieve on their own.

Thus, making a group decision or involving others in decision making is not a panacea to the common pitfalls. The decision of how much to involve others is a function of several factors including the knowledge and motivation of potential participants in the decision, the nature of the problem and decision, the environment in which the problem exists, and the speed with which the decision needs to be made.

Understanding these basics provides a foundation for awareness of how cultural values can influence decision making. This in turn better enables you as a manager to make effective decisions in an increasingly global and culturally diverse environment.

key terms

bounded rationality (administrative man) model   308
brainstorming   331
cross-functional teams   318
decision making   301
delphi technique   332
devil's advocate   325
dialectical inquiry   331
escalating commitment   326
formulation   302
Gresham's law of planning   312

groupthink   323
heuristic   309
intuitive decision making   311
multiple advocacy   331
nominal group technique   332
nonprogrammed decision   311
opportunity   303
perception   303
perceptual distortion   310
problem   303
programmed decision   311

prospective rationality   328
rational (classical) model   303
retrospective decision (implicit favorite) model   310
satisficing   309
solution   302
standard operating procedure (SOP)   311
structured debate   331
subjectively expected utility (SEU) model   305

test your comprehension

1. What are the two fundamental stages in decision making?
2. What is the basic premise of the rational (classical) model of decision making?
3. How does the rational (classical) model differ from the bounded rationality model?
4. How can information bias negatively affect decision quality?
5. How can selective perception influence decision formulation?
6. What are the key advantages to understanding the bounded rationality model of decision making?
7. What is satisficing? How does it differ from satisfying?
8. What is an implicit favorite?
9. How does the retrospective decision model work?
10. Describe programmed and nonprogrammed decisions.
11. When are SOPs (standard operating procedures) most often used?
12. Describe Gresham's law of planning.
13. Why is analyzing the decision situation a key step in making better decisions?
14. What are the key assets of group decision making?
15. What are the key liabilities?
16. When is it appropriate for a manager to be more participative in decision making?
17. Describe the phenomenon of groupthink. What are its symptoms?
18. How can we overcome groupthink?
19. How can managers work to overcome the effects of escalating commitment to past decisions?
20. Compare and contrast the nominal group technique and the delphi technique of decision making.
21. How can cultural values affect decision making?

apply your understanding

1. If your subordinates expect you to be consistent in your decision-making style, but you believe that different decision-making styles (e.g., high involvement of others versus low involvement) are appropriate for specific situations, how can you *change* your decision-making approach but not seem inconsistent to your employees?
2. Think of someone you know personally who is an effective decision maker. What key characteristics would you use to describe this person?
3. What are the strengths and weaknesses of a manager with "good instincts" who seems to make effective decisions but whose approach is more like the retrospective than rational model?
4. Japanese and Korean managers tend to spend considerably more time on and involve more people in the problem formulation stage of decision making than American managers do. What are the pros and cons you see with this?

practice your capabilities

While sitting in your office, you get a call from the plant supervisor that a request has come in from a major customer that would require you to adjust your product line for a custom run of this client's rush order. The plant supervisor has delegated the decision of whether you should stop your current run and meet the customer's request. He needs the decision by tomorrow morning.

Your line is in the middle of an extended standard run that will produce product for five of your midsized customers. Your company competes in part by offering both low cost and service. The vast majority of your midsize customers chose you because of your lower prices. You maintain your profitability with these customers through keeping your costs low. Your principal means of achieving this is through running a high volume of standard products through your product line. Many of your large customers appreciate your low price but are willing to pay a premium for customized service and alterations to the products that come off your line.

If you stop the line to make the changes in equipment needed to run the custom order, you will incur both costs and delays to your current standard run. You are about two-thirds of the way through your standard run. It will take approximately three hours to change over to the custom run and two days to run it.

You have made this particular changeover before but not in the last six months. You know the basics of the changeover but the person most knowledgeable about the details regarding the exact changes in the equipment is out sick today. She left you a voice mail message that she expects to be back to work tomorrow.

In general your team is fairly experienced and does not require close supervision, with the excep-

tion of two new members to your team of nine product line operators. They are generally willing to be involved in decisions but are also happy just to "do their jobs."

1. Should you make this decision on your own or should you involve the group?
2. Would you stop the current run and change over for the custom run? Why or why not?
3. If you insist that it's impossible to decide, what information must you have in order to make the decision?

closing case

DEVELOP YOUR CRITICAL THINKING

Schwab Trades Security for Uncertainty Online

When a company decides to completely transform the way it does business, the decision is far from automatic. Executives at the venerable investment firm Charles Schwab have faced this challenge twice in a few short years.

Schwab started out as a discount retail brokerage company. For years it touted three standards for itself: Give no advice to customers, make no cold calls, and pay no commissions to brokers. Instead, Schwab targeted savvy customers who did their own analysis of stocks and didn't rely on recommendations from analysts. For these do-it-yourself customers, Schwab offered an attractive value proposition—they could make stock trades through Schwab for lower fees than they could through big brokerage firms like Merrill Lynch and PaineWebber. In order to charge the lower fees, Schwab kept its costs low by not having an expensive research department. Consequently, Schwab wasn't able to provide the reports and analyses of companies that "full-service" brokerages did. However, for the "independent" customer Schwab had decided to target, the strategy of lower trading fees for fewer reports was an attractive trade-off.

After years of success, Schwab faced its first major decision—the decision to commit to low-cost Internet trading. With no exposure to the Internet but seeing that the change in technology provided its customers with a quick and low-cost way to trade, Schwab made the decision in the late 1990s to venture into the world of Web-based stock trading. The company reached its first-year goal of 25,000 Web accounts within two weeks. "We were totally unprepared," says a senior manager of the firm.

Schwab's online assets ballooned to $81 million, yet there were snags.

Possibly because the online brokerage unit had not yet been integrated with the rest of the investment units, regular phone and branch representatives could not help online customers. As a consequence, if you were an online customer you could trade for a lower price than a regular Schwab customer but you could not get the same service. The result was that Schwab forced its customers to choose between service and price, a situation many found unattractive. The only way to solve the problem—and take advantage of what looked like an enormous opportunity—was to make a total commitment to Internet trading.

The decision was far from easy, especially because it meant accepting a huge drop in revenues from higher commissions customers paid for phone and branch-based transactions. But as CEO Charles Schwab himself said, "We really have no choice. It's just a question of when." Within a few months, the revamped trading service was ready. As predicted, both revenues and stock prices dropped dramatically at first, and customer complaints about the difficulty of using the Web site made it clear what investors really want: fast, accurate information they can understand and easily use. Schwab got help in two ways—by going to outside sources such as Credit Suisse and First Boston for research information to distribute to customers, and by hiring a Web design firm to revamp its site. Product innovation and a daring marketing decision paid off handsomely for several years.

Then the stock market plummeted and the U.S. economy went into a recession. By the end of June 2001, overall revenue for the firm was down 38 percent and profits were gone. Two months later, Schwab cut nearly 25 percent of its staff and took a $225 million restructuring charge. Eventually, senior managers had to decide to cut as much as 40 percent of its employees.

In the aftermath of the burst stock market bubble, executives faced a new decision. They needed to restore profitability and show that they could create revenues and build assets once again. They also needed to ensure that employees didn't begin leaving in large numbers. Executives knew that part of the firm's recovery would need to come from cost cutting. But they did not believe that cutting costs alone would revive the firm. Schwab's revenues were directly tied to trading volume of its customers and volume was down dramatically with the stock market slump. With no idea how long the stock market slump would continue, executives had to decide where they could get additional revenues.

The decision executives faced was whether they should add to discount online trading a much more traditional service—financial advice—something it had not done in 28 years. Executives also had to decide how to differentiate Schwab's service from other full-service brokerages if it were to succeed. What would Schwab's new niche be? Inevitably, many Schwab executives and employees who didn't buy into the new approach ended up quitting or retiring early from the firm.

Nonetheless, Charles Schwab and David Pottruck, co-CEO, decided to offer financial services in part because most of the company's customers were baby boomers facing retirement in a few years, and financial planning was becoming increasingly important to them. Many of these customers were worried by the market's dramatic downturn and didn't want to "go it alone" anymore when it came to investing their money. Some executives were concerned that if Schwab didn't offer financial advice to its customers, they would go elsewhere for it. The company would then be left with the low-fee business of executing transactions while its competitors would earn handsome fees for the recommendations they were giving to Schwab's customers.

Schwab and Pottruck ultimately decided the way they would differentiate the company would be to capitalize on "conflicts of interest." In many firms, financial advisers get paid commissions on the transactions they can get customers to execute. These commissions can create incentives to recommend stocks, funds, insurance, and so on that pay the highest commissions rather than are in the best interests of the customers. This creates a potential conflict of interest. In addition, most full-service brokerages also have investment banking relationships with the companies they cover. As a consequence, there is often an incentive to give favorable reviews and ratings of these companies to ensure continued and very lucrative investment banking relationships. Schwab got a big boost when Goldman Sachs and other traditional firms were investigated and fined millions of dollars for releasing positive public recommendations of firms that their own analysts privately thought the stock was not worth owning.

Executives at Schwab thought that it would be possible with sophisticated technology and noncommissioned financial advisers to offer a stock-recommendation program that would be personalized, easy-to-use, and free of conflicts of interest. Instead of paying $20 million a year to hire analysts, it made a one-time $20 million bet on Web technology—to develop Schwab Equity Ratings. Schwab Equity Ratings is a computerized rating system that offers buy and sell recommendations for 3,000 stocks based on 24 criteria, including company fundamentals, price–earnings ratios, and historical stock movements. Each stock is rated on a A–F scale—just like a report card.

The software automatically checks client portfolios, compares them with a computer-generated list of stocks recommended for each client's risk profile, and sends the results to the client. Schwab claims the software is just as efficient as its human counterparts. One year after rolling it out, Schwab pointed to the fact that companies rated an "A" were down by about just 6 percent (in a bear market) whereas companies it had rated an "F" were down far more—nearly 31 percent. Schwab also ran a controversial ad showing a brokerage manager at a competing firm shouting to fellow brokers: "Let's put some lipstick on the pig!"—apparently in an effort to pump up a stock with lousy fundamentals.

Even so, Schwab faced a number of challenges implementing its new strategy. For one, the company makes most of its money off of trades. Weren't the automatic Equity Ratings e-mails sent to customers tantamount to a stockbroker calling to make a trade? Did the e-mails encourage investors to make more trades than they otherwise would have?

The decision to offer financial services also had the potential to create conflict with Schwab's network of independent financial advisers. These people don't work for Schwab but work closely with the company to help customers set up accounts and execute recommendations. By offering investment advice directly and hiring employees to do so, wasn't Schwab competing with them? Independent agents and these advisers generate about 30 percent of the new money that comes into Schwab.

Finally, in an effort to court "big money" instead of just earning $36 per trade, Schwab purchased U.S. Trust, a company that manages the money of millionaires. Schwab also started charging smaller investors fees if their accounts were under $50,000.

Results have been encouraging. Schwab is now managing more money than ever before for investors. The company's revenues are also up—generally, revenues are climbing from what they were in 2000. But net income is lower and Schwab's stock price is a fraction of what it was before the bubble burst. However, that's true for many companies besides Schwab.

Questions

1. Do you think Schwab's decisions in recent years have been smart considering the company's long history to the contrary? What are the risks inherent in offering the new service? How can Schwab managers balance these risks as they move into this area?

2. How should Schwab decide what to do about the potential for channel conflict?

3. When the stock market improved in 2003, do you feel Schwab was well positioned to take advantage of it?

Sources: Amy Feldman, "Schwab's Changing Face," *Money,* October 2003; Niamh Ring, "Schwab Makes Its Play in Independent Research," *American Banker,* November 20, 2003; Fara Warner, "Taking Stock at Schwab," *Fast Company,* June 2003; "Downsizing May Cost Schwab $50 Million in Half," *American Banker,* August 14, 2003; Erick Schonfield, "Schwab Puts It All Online," *Fortune,* December 7, 1998, pp. 94–100; www.schwab.com, accessed December 4, 1998 and February 17, 2002; Fred Vogelstein, "Can Schwab Gets Its Mojo Back?" *Fortune,* September 17, 2001, pp. 93–98.

integrative case

Paragon Information Systems

IVEY

Richard Ivey School of Business
The University of Western Ontario

Keith Collins, president and chief executive officer of Paragon Information Systems of St. John's, Newfoundland, faced a crisis. On July 19, 1996, four days after his appointment, two vice-presidents resigned to start a new company in direct competition. They recruited away the entire sales force, members of the technical section and support staff. Paragon was reduced from 50 to 36 people by the end of August. Collins needed to respond.

Newtel Enterprises Limited— Corporate Structure[1]

Paragon was a wholly-owned subsidiary of NewTel Enterprises Limited (NEL), which was itself 55.6 per cent owned by BCE Inc. (BCE). NEL was a Newfoundland-based company whose principal operations in the telecommunications and information technology industries were conducted by Paragon and four other subsidiaries:

- NewTel Communications Inc. (formerly Newfoundland Telephone Company Limited), a wholly-owned subsidiary, provided telecommunications and information handling services throughout Newfoundland and Labrador and operated nationally and internationally as a member of Stentor. NewTel Communications was subject to regulation by the Canadian Radio-television and Telecommunications Commission (CRTC).

- NewTel Mobility Limited, a wholly-owned subsidiary, was a provider of wireless communications including cellular telephone, paging and two-way radio in Newfoundland and Labrador.

- NewTel Information Solutions Limited, an 80 per cent owned subsidiary, was an information technology integrator with expertise in mainframe systems development and data centre operations, local area network installation, microcomputer systems development and support, wide area network management and information technology planning. Minority owners included Andersen Consulting at 10 per cent and Bell Sygma Inc. at 10 per cent.

- NewTech Instruments Limited, a wholly-owned subsidiary, was a full service contract manufacturer of electronic, electromechanical and cable assemblies for the telecommunications, marine and defence industries in a global market.

Paragon Information Systems Inc., a wholly-owned subsidiary, was an information technology firm focusing on systems integration, application development and computer networking in the Newfoundland and Labra-

exhibit 1

Consolidated Four-Year Review:
Newtel Enterprises Limited
(in thousands of dollars, except
per share amounts)

	1997	1996	1995	1994
Income Statement Items				
Operating revenues	$ 331,425	324,229	315,401	296,685
Operating expenses	$ 240,175	241,695	238,867	211,810
Extraordinary item	$ (85,480)	–	–	–
Net income (loss)	$ (49,069)	30,550	25,458	32,826
Financial Ratios				
Earnings (loss) per average common share	$ (2.72)	1.70	1.42	1.92
Book value per common share	$ 14.16	18.22	17.88	17.76
Rate of return on average common equity (%)	10.93	9.43	7.97	11.02
Debt to total capital (%)	52.1	45.5	48.0	48.0
Other Statistics				
Capital expenditures	$ 67,016	61,745	83,693	84,484
Salaries and wages	$ 84,749	82,630	86,540	80,574
Number of employees	1,945	1,951	2,004	2,128
Average common shares outstanding (000)	18,018	18,006	17,886	17,138

Source: NewTel Enterprises Limited, op. cit.

dor market. Through its newcomm division, the company provided Internet access, Web site development and support to the business market.

The NEL mission statement was

To provide sustained and consistent growth in shareholder value, through primary focus on telecommunications and related businesses in Atlantic Canada. Essential to our success will be exploitation of emerging competitive opportunities, responsive customer service and an effective, action-oriented management team.

Exhibit 1 provides consolidated financial highlights for NEL. Exhibit 2 provides a breakdown of the contributions to revenues and net income by subsidiary.

exhibit 2

Four-Year Review of Subsidiary
Operating Revenues and Net
Income

	1997	1996	1995	1994
Operating Revenues				
NewTel Communications	$264,847	$269,433	$263,964	$263,727
NewTel Information Solutions	45,743	40,321	38,340	5,327
NewTel Mobility	20,023	15,556	13,037	9,414
Paragon Information Systems	14,816	12,315	14,860	11,871
NewTech Instruments	11,253	9,820	8,245	6,943
Consolidated Eliminations	(25,257)	(23,216)	(23,045)	(1,911)
Total Consolidated	$331,425	$324,229	$315,401	$296,685
Net Income				
NewTel Communications	$ 31,912	$ 28,226	$ 25,002	$ 32,068
NewTel Information Solutions	3,696	2,080	1,100	–
NewTel Mobility	3,024	2,053	1,509	–
Paragon Information Systems	511	(207)	242	–
NewTech Instruments	776	495	404	–
Consolidated Eliminations	(3,508)	(2,097)	(2,799)	–
Total	36,411	30,550	25,458	–
Extraordinary item	(85,480)	–	–	–
Total consolidated net income (loss)	$(49,069)	$ 30,550	$ 25,458	$ 32,826

Note: All 1995 figures and only the 1994 Total Consolidated Revenues and Total Consolidated Net Income (loss) figures have been adjusted to conform to the NEL 1996 Annual Report presentation.

Source: NewTel Enterprises Limited, op. cit.

Paragon Corporate History

Three entrepreneurs founded Paragon in 1988. The company provided information technology (IT) systems integration, software development, and computer networking products and services to business customers throughout Newfoundland and Labrador, with a main focus on hardware. Total employee count was 50. A second NEL subsidiary, NewTel Information Solutions (NIS), focused more on the services side of the IT business. The latter company was formed by the purchase and privatization of the IT services department of the government of Newfoundland and the subsequent acquisition and consolidation of the IT assets of NewTel Communications. Total employee count was about 250.

In mid-1995, the president of Paragon, one of the three founding executives of the company, was transferred to NIS as the vice-president of marketing. NEL installed a new president at Paragon. However, by the spring of 1996, Paragon's board was dissatisfied with the performance of both the new president and the company. The chairman of Paragon's board—to whom Keith Collins reported at NewTel Communications—approached Collins, advised him that the president of Paragon was about to be removed, and asked if he would take on the job. Collins agreed and subsequently took over as president and chief executive officer on the morning of Monday July 15, 1996.

Cultural Differences

A long-term NEL employee, Collins's background was in telecommunications, not in IT. Aware that switching industries could be difficult, he relished the change and challenge involved. He was also aware that the working relationship between Paragon and the parent company NEL had always been fairly uneasy. Differences stemmed from the backgrounds of the two companies. Paragon had been a relatively freewheeling entrepreneurial venture under its founding owners. The acquisition by NEL mandated a tighter level of governance, and Paragon became accountable for operating within budgets and for meeting performance targets. Thus, relations between parent and subsidiary were strained at both the leadership and operating levels.

The Crisis Situation

On Friday July 19, 1996, the vice-president of marketing at NIS and two vice-presidents of Paragon, all three of them the founding executives of Paragon, tendered their resignations. They advised Collins that they intended to found a new company in the IT systems space to compete with Paragon. It became apparent to Collins that this move had

been under consideration for some time and that his appointment as president had triggered the action, particularly given that he was new to the IT systems business.

The owners of the new company acted quickly to recruit former employees by playing on the past tenuous relationship between Paragon and NEL and by projecting that Paragon would not survive. By the end of August, Paragon experienced a significant drain on its human resource base, shrinking from 50 to 36 employees. In addition to the loss of management expertise, the entire sales force departed along with important technical and support staff. A similar message was played to Paragon's suppliers and clients to undermine its presence in the marketplace. By the end of August 1996, the company found itself in difficult circumstances. A substantial part of Paragon's corporate knowledge resided with the new competitor, and conjecture about the future of Paragon was rampant.

Initial Reaction and Perspective

Faced with the initial onslaught, Collins first reaction was, "Why me"? Very quickly however, he was able to place things in perspective. He had been sent in because the existing processes, strategy and team were not producing the required level of financial performance. The remaining employees were willing to stick with Paragon through the crisis and thus were more open to the fundamental changes required. The disadvantage of the situation was that expertise had been lost from Paragon, leaving it in a weakened condition. This issue was amplified by the fact that the former Paragon management had set up a competitor in Paragon's market space. The advantages of the situation were that the people responsible for Paragon's prior performance were gone, thus making change easier to enact, and Paragon had an established parent company and board of directors to provide support. The board was in fact extremely supportive, having a "whatever you believe you need" attitude, and it assured Collins that there was no intent to close the company down. The need to refocus and restructure the company had always existed. The crisis situation was the catalyst that provided the opportunity.

Reducing Uncertainty

The first major task Collins faced was to reassure employees, suppliers and clients that he had not been sent in to close down Paragon, that the company was in rebuilding mode and would survive and prosper into the future. He met with employees either individually or in small groups, assured them that the company was rebuilding, and solicited their input and advice as to how they could move the company forward. He advised them that he had the backing of the board and the parent company NEL, and they need not be concerned about their employment status.

The same message was conveyed at meetings with clients, i.e., no matter what they had heard from the new entrant to the marketplace or any other players, Paragon was rebuilding. Collins asked for their patience for a few weeks while he rebuilt, and he confirmed that Paragon would honor any previous commitments. On the one hand, clients were willing to cooperate to the extent that they provided copies of proposals and contracts they had entered into with Paragon, given that some of these had disappeared from Paragon's own files. On the other hand, clients were happy that in the future there would be more competition in the marketplace.

Collins flew to meet with Paragon's suppliers and technology partners who had also been advised by the new company that Paragon would be closing down. The suppliers appreciated the fact that Collins made the effort to meet with them and to reassure them that Paragon was both staying in business and intending to grow its business into the future. Thus, knowing that he had support at the corporate level, Collins was able to reassure major stakeholders that the company would remain in business.

The Rebuilding Process

To rebuild the company, Collins needed a new senior management team. Of the previous team, only the controller, the vice-president of software development and the latter's most senior report remained. Collins had two leadership sources: to use people in the organization who had previously been overlooked, and to hire from the outside. He found that the former were well able to rise to most of the challenges presented to them. However, for a job such as the vice-president of sales and marketing, he had to go outside and was able to find a candidate willing to undertake the rebuilding of the department.

Throughout the reshaping process, the underlying strategy was to become more client-focused. However, no attempt was made to immediately restructure the company. The rebuilding process had the impact of stopping the flow of resignations by the end of September. During the rebuilding, it became apparent that Paragon had previously been managed like a personal fiefdom. The "in" employees were favored by previous management and received preferential compensation packages when compared to other equally

skilled employees doing the same work at the same level. Thus, Collins and his new team adjusted compensation levels, increasing the overall level of compensation in the company fairly substantially. In some cases salaries increased from 15 per cent to 25 per cent. Full support was received from the board of directors. The impact was increased stability in the employee group.

Moving Forward

At the end of September, the management team started to look at a new business strategy for the future. They used a SWOT analysis to review company capabilities, opportunities in the marketplace, and which existing activities to continue and abandon. Strategic objectives were set in the areas of marketing, finance, organizational functioning, innovation and abandonment. They found that the company's past strategy focused on the hardware market, yielding margins of eight per cent to 10 per cent. They determined that, going forward, they should concentrate on adding value by providing services around applications. Typical margins in this area were between 35 per cent to 50 per cent. The Internet was gaining momentum at the time, yet the company had no Internet strategy. This presented a substantial opportunity. After two months of activity, the strategic plan and the necessary structure to support it were presented to the board for approval. Immediately thereafter, they were presented to the entire employee body. Management's aim throughout was to "foster an environment in which employees understand their role and value to the organization and are engaged in the strategic process."[2]

The strategic plan and new organizational structure reinforced the gains already made in stabilizing the employee group. By January of 1997, the beneficial impact on corporate culture became evident in the form of a strong sense of participation and ownership throughout the company. On a regular basis, management presented business and financial information to employees at general meetings. An open culture was reinforced. The people who had stayed, and those who had joined, all felt they had endured a difficult set of circumstances, and now they saw a way to improve the company in the future. The following tenet from Paragon's Strategic Direction Statement emphasized the company's approach to its employees: "We will invest in our company so that people will be proud to work here. They will feel supported, recognized and rewarded for their contribution to our shared success."[3] See Exhibits 3, 4, 5 and 6 for an encapsulation of Paragon's new approach.

exhibit 3

Excerpts from Paragon's 1997
Organizational Functioning
Objectives

1. Foster a performance-oriented culture at Paragon that recognizes and supports the contribution of each employee.
2. Implement a new performance-based compensation plan for all groups.
3. Implement a corporate Team Award to recognize and reward the shared success of Paragon's employee group.
4. Establish the optimal organization structure to support Paragon's business objectives.
5. Introduce a new performance management system to provide the framework for individual performance measurement and employee development.

Source: Paragon Information Systems, op. cit.

exhibit 4

Excerpts from Paragon's
Communications Approach

1. Two-way: telling *and* listening.
2. Presented 1997 strategic plan to all staff.
3. Involved managers and cross-section of employees in developing 1998 plan.
4. Regular work group meetings.
5. Regular company information sessions.
6. Monthly reports on financials, sales, etc.
7. Monthly president's information update.
8. Relaxed, 'open door' management style.
9. Regular informal 'team builders.'

Source: Paragon Information Systems, op. cit.

exhibit 5

Excerpts from Paragon's
Compensation Approach

1. Annual study of IT market compensation.
2. Set 'target compensation' for each job, consisting of 'fixed' and 'variable' pay.
3. 'Fixed' pay is base salary expressed in a multi-year scale (e.g., four years to top).
4. Progression up the scale is based on technical certification, demonstrated competence and experience.
5. 'Variable' pay is a per cent of base salary, tied to achieving Paragon's financial and customer service objectives.
6. Sales compensation plan is tied primarily to sales team performance.
7. 'Target compensation' levels are reviewed annually.

Source: Paragon Information Systems, op. cit.

exhibit 6

Excerpts from Paragon:
Learning from the Process

1. A clear business strategy is an essential element to build employee enthusiasm and commitment to corporate goals.
2. Informed, equipped and committed employees can be a company's greatest assets, and are worth investing in.
3. Fostering a culture in which employees feel engaged in the growth process may be a company's strongest contribution to its own success.
4. Compensation is a means to an end, *not* an end in itself.
5. It's impressive what a group of people can accomplish when they don't care who gets the credit.

Source: Paragon Information Systems, op. cit.

Impact on Performance

The new strategy was implemented in 1997. Training was recognized as a priority and investment in this area tripled. Although productivity improvement was neither a stated 1997 objective nor a focus area, financial performance more than doubled that of any previous year in Paragon's history. Revenues were up 17 per cent and expenses were down six per cent over 1996. The company continued to grow in 1998. Markets expanded beyond the province to the Atlantic region and new technology partners were added. By the end of 1998, the company had 80 employees. The company's portfolio of capabilities expanded to include IT consulting, systems integration, Tier 1 computer systems, computer networking, software development and integration, business Internet/electronic commerce, and world-class technology partners.

Notes

1. NewTel Enterprises Limited 1996 Annual Report, supplemented as necessary by the reports for years 1994, 1995, 1997 and 1998.

2. Paragon Information Systems presentation to the Newfoundland and Labrador Employers' Council Fall Conference: November 13, 1997.

3. Paragon, op. cit.

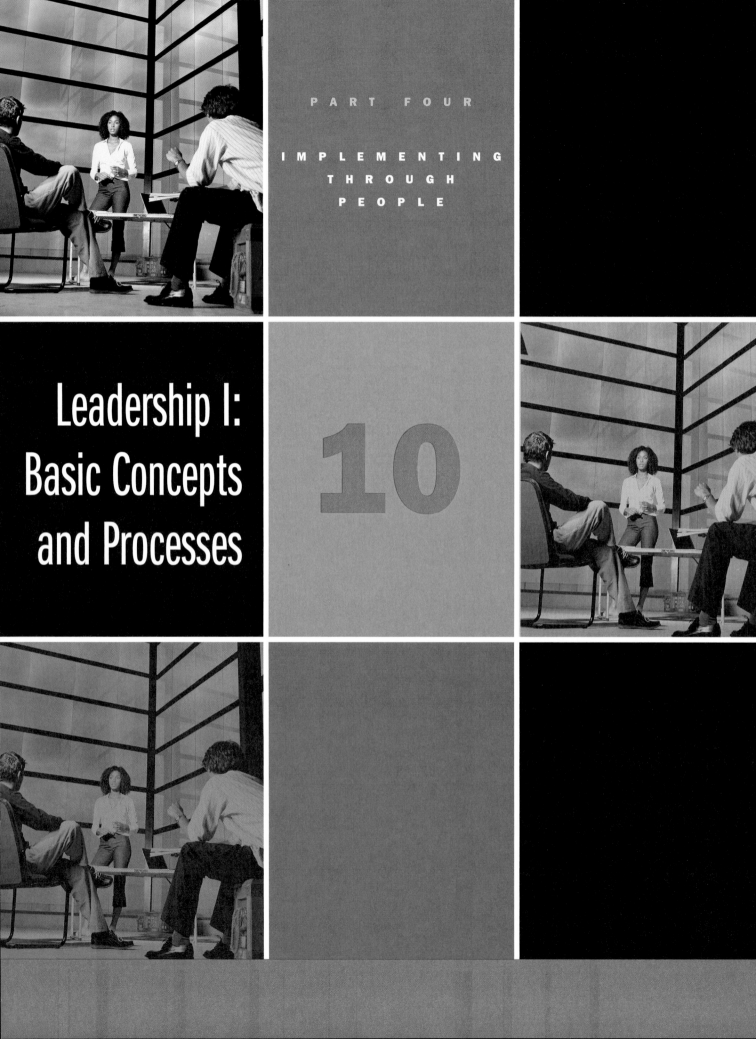

Leadership I: Basic Concepts and Processes

10

LEARNING OBJECTIVES

After studying this chapter, you should be able to:

- Describe the fundamental nature of leadership as part of the managerial role.
- Identify the different types and sources of power available to a leader
- Analyze the issues involved in the use of power.
- Explain the current view of the importance of leadership traits and skills.
- Discuss the utility of the two major categories of leader behavior.
- Analyze the importance and nature of the leader–follower relationship.
- Describe how different situations affect the leadership process.

Abraham Lincoln: Leadership Model for Yesterday and Today

Mount Rushmore doesn't contain any carved figures of CEOs. But it does contain carvings of four leaders: George Washington, Thomas Jefferson, Theodore Roosevelt, and Abraham Lincoln. Many Americans like to perpetuate the image of Abraham Lincoln as a country boy who read his way to a law degree—and, ultimately, the presidency—without formal training. It makes people feel as though anything is possible if they try hard enough. It makes each citizen feel as if he or she has the potential to be a leader.

Abraham Lincoln was, indeed, a country lawyer before becoming a politician. He was successful at his profession, and thus fairly well off financially. He was also a consummate leader. His success—as a lawyer and as a president—largely depended on his ability to use power wisely and to communicate honestly with the people he wanted to influence. As president of the United States, Lincoln held a substantial amount of power; he had the capacity to exert influence on people and policies. But power alone did not make Lincoln a leader; rather, his skill at delegating authority by allowing others to make decisions about details, his quest for knowledge about public opinion, his ability to communicate his thoughts clearly and concisely, his willingness to compromise, and his famous honesty all contributed to his success as a leader. For instance, Lincoln had the power (and the desire) to abolish slavery, but he understood that nearly half the nation depended on the practice socially and economically. So he proceeded with small policy changes, each intended to convince the American public that the abolition of slavery was the only way to end the devastating Civil War and ultimately save the United States.

Mount Rushmore doesn't contain any carved figures of CEOs. But it does contain carvings of four leaders: George Washington, Thomas Jefferson, Theodore Roosevelt, and Abraham Lincoln. Each man possessed significant leadership skills and qualities that a nation needed during his time. Today, millions of visitors come to see Mount Rushmore and gain inspiration from these four great leaders.

Lincoln also had charisma—in other words, he was able to inspire people to think and act as he did. Part of his charisma was his ability to speak the language of ordinary people. His speeches and public papers were filled with wit, puns, and colorful but clear arguments and calls for action. His sense of humor saved him from some sticky situations and showed the American public that he was human. His legendary honesty not only served him well in office during one of the most difficult stages of American history, but it is probably the single characteristic most often attributed to Lincoln nearly 150 years after his presidency.

What might today's CEOs and managers learn from Lincoln's leadership style? First, honesty and integrity may be the strongest and most enduring qualities of any leader. Second, listening carefully to others, even when they are offering criticism, can provide valuable information. Third, a willingness to compromise may benefit the organization. When analyzed this way, Lincoln's success seems attainable by any person aspiring to become a managerial leader.

Source: David Herbert Donald, "Leadership Lessons from Abraham Lincoln," *Bottom Line*, February 15, 1996, pp. 13–14.

strategic overview

In the past decade, the concept of strategic leadership has emerged. Originally, the term was used to refer to people who were members of top management.[1] However, others have argued recently that "strategic leadership" is not a function of position level but rather of focus and behavior. In other words, strategic leadership can be exhibited at any level in the organization, and, moreover, for an organization to perform well, effective leaders are actually critical at all of the organization's levels.

Basically, strategic leadership involves thinking and acting strategically while working with others to create a viable future for the organization.[2] To act strategically in a leadership role, managers or leaders have to anticipate events (analyze the external environment), envision the organization's future (analyze the internal resources and develop a vision for the organization or some unit within it), and remain flexible in order to adapt to conditions as they change.

Leaders have to exert their power at times but use it effectively, in order to implement the organization's strategies while simultaneously managing and motivating people to do their tasks well, remain committed to the organization, and work to see that the strategic vision is realized. While acting strategically, leaders should also exhibit integrity and build good working relationships (based on trust and equitable treatment) with their followers. Trusting relationships between leaders and their followers is sometimes called "internal social capital." Leaders can use social capital to their strategic advantage (e.g., using human capital to help implement the organization's strategy).[3] In the process of building relationships with followers and implementing the organization's strategy, a leader likely will need to call on technical, interpersonal, and conceptual skills. Additionally, a leader will need to use social and emotional intelligence capabilities and be self-confident in order to think and act strategically in an effective manner. Similar to the situations confronting Abraham Lincoln, strategic leadership is highly important to organizations, but also challenging to provide.

However, although acts of leadership in an organization can be widespread and commonplace, often they are not. The central issue, then, both for organizations and for individual managers, is to turn leadership potential into reality. The very fact that so many articles and books have been, and continue to be, written on the topic of leadership is a good indication that this challenge is not being met well by either the typical organization or the practicing manager.

Leadership is an undeniably critical part of the overall managerial process. It is at the very center and heart of that part of managing that deals with "Implementing Through People" (the title of this part of the book). Without leadership, organizational performance would be minimal. Indeed, it would be difficult if not impossible to talk about the accomplishments of twenty-first-century organizations of all types—whether in business, government, education, or other settings—without referring to the role that leadership played in those successes. So it is a given that leadership is important to organizations, and, of course, to society at large. What is not so clear is how to increase its presence and effectiveness. That is the managerial challenge.

Leadership is, above all, a process of influence, as the opening story about Abraham Lincoln illustrates. As such, leadership can occur *potentially anywhere* in an organization. Leadership is not a set of behaviors limited to the chief executive officer, the executive vice president, the director of manufacturing, the regional marketing manager, or, for that matter, a sports team's coach or its captain. It is a process that can be exhibited by almost anyone, at almost any time, and in almost any circumstance.

In this chapter we will first confront an age-old question, "What is leadership?" and then explore how answers help us understand the relationship between leadership and its close cousins, influence and power. This provides a background for analyzing the nature of the leadership/influence process: the traits and characteristics of people who are most likely to become leaders; the types of behaviors that leaders typically exhibit; the role and influence of followers, including the leader–follower relationship; and the situational circumstances most likely to affect the success of leadership attempts.

WHAT IS LEADERSHIP?

While studying this chapter, it is important to keep in mind that although leadership is a familiar everyday term, it nevertheless is far more complex than we might assume. For that reason, it is an especially interesting and intriguing subject. It is also a topic that is easy to oversimplify and therefore one that often leads to conclusions that are incorrect, misleading, or unjustified. In fact, we could say, "It's not what we don't know about leadership that is the problem; it's what we know that isn't so."

Let us take a look at how organizational scientists have defined the term "leadership." Unfortunately, there is no clear consensus because, as one prominent scholar observed some years ago, "There are almost as many definitions of leadership as there are persons who have attempted to define the concept."[4] Consistent with most definitions, however, we define **organizational leadership** as an interpersonal process involving attempts to influence other people in attaining some goal. This definition, therefore, emphasizes leadership as a social influence process.

While there is general agreement that leadership is an influence process, there is less agreement on (a) whether the definition must refer only to influence used by those occupying designated leadership positions ("manager," "president," "chairperson," "coach," etc.), (b) whether the influence must be exercised deliberately and for the specific attainment of the group's or organization's goals, and (c) whether compliance of others must be voluntary. Our view on each of these issues follows.

Acts of leadership behavior *can be exhibited by anyone* in an organization and are not limited only to those holding designated leadership positions. In particular, this means that leadership should not be thought of as occurring only, or even mostly, at the top of the organization—in positions like those held by Ken Chenault at American Express and Meg Whitman at eBay (refer back to Chapter 1). Thus, leadership behavior is not confined just to the CEOs (Chief Executive Officers) of organizations. Leadership can also be seen in the actions of the first-line supervisor who inspires her subordinates to implement safety procedures to avoid production downtime. Leadership is demonstrated by the group member who champions his team's new product and convinces others of its potential. Leadership is shown by the human resources manager who makes sure—without being ordered to—that those in the HR division treat all applicants for positions with the company respectfully and equitably. Leadership is exhibited by workers who set an example for their co-workers by continually seeking ways to improve processes and working conditions.

Ordinarily, however, positions that are labeled managerial or supervisory have more opportunities to exert leadership. Also, leadership behavior is expected more frequently from supervisors and managers than from people in other types of roles. Such expectations often profoundly affect the behavior of both those who hold such positions and those around them. In other words, expectations count! For instance, in a company such as pharmaceutical giant Johnson & Johnson, which prides itself on its dedication to ethics in management, subordinates expect their managers to demonstrate such standards—to lead by example. A manager who does not abide by the ethical principles of

organizational leadership
an interpersonal process involving attempts to influence other people in attaining some goal

Former New York City mayor Rudolph Giuliani (pictured on the left) is widely regarded as having exhibited critical leadership ability in the aftermath of the 9/11 attacks. The leadership exhibited by New York City's firefighters, police, and other personnel, however, greatly contributed to Guliani's ability to handle the crisis.

the company, or who is even perceived as not adhering to them, may lose first the trust of his subordinates, and then the ability to be an effective leader.[5]

People act as leaders for many reasons, and their efforts are not necessarily aimed solely at the attainment of a group's or organization's goals. Sometimes, leaders' motives can be directed at multiple objectives, including their own as well as, or instead of, the organization's. Motives are seldom pure, but we assume explicitly that effective organizational leadership requires organizationally relevant, goal-directed behavior, regardless of any other personal objectives.

Use of coercion to gain compliance ("do this or you will be fired" threats) is not typically considered leadership. However, the dividing line between what is and is not coercion is often very difficult to determine. Whether others' responses must be purely voluntary for leadership to occur is not an easy question to answer. When other people comply with someone's attempts at leadership, the reasons may be many and the degree of willingness can range from grudging to enthusiastic. The safest generalization is this: The greater the degree of purely voluntary actions by followers toward the leader's intended direction, the more effective the leadership.

The preceding discussion raises a further key issue: What is **effective leadership**? Put most simply, it is influence that assists a group or an organization to meet its goals and objectives and perform successfully. This implies that effective leadership is enabling behavior—that is, it is behavior that helps other people accomplish more than if there had been no such leadership.[6] Obviously, there are many examples from the past—Joan of Arc and Abraham Lincoln—and the present—Colin Powell[7] and the former mayor of New York City during the 9/11 attacks, Rudy Giuliani—just to name a few, who could be mentioned in this regard. By their actions they have added a leadership ingredient to the sum of the efforts of many people and thereby helped them to achieve together more than they would have otherwise.

effective leadership influence that assists a group or an organization to meet its goals and objectives and perform successfully

Again, effective leadership augments and assists by unlocking the potential that resides in a collection of people.

LEADERSHIP AND POWER

power the capacity or ability to influence

It is virtually impossible to consider leadership as a type of social influence without also taking into account the idea of power. **Power** is typically thought of as the capacity or ability to influence. Thus, the greater a person's power, the greater the potential for influencing others. Power can be used "to change the course of events, to overcome resistance, and to get people to do things that they would not otherwise do."[8] However, the fact that a leader, or anyone else, has power does not guarantee that he or she will use it—or use it well. Possession and use are two different matters.

Whether a leader will use power depends on many factors. One principal reason it is not used is the anticipation of possible undesirable consequences from its use. The use of power is often believed to generate negative reactions. As has been said, "For many people, power is a 'four-letter' word."[9] The famous but somewhat exaggerated statement of this view of power was made more than a century ago in Britain, when Lord Acton wrote to Bishop Mandell Creighton that "power tends to corrupt [and] absolute power corrupts absolutely."[10]

It is not too difficult to think of an organization where power has been used inappropriately by a would-be leader. This was illustrated several years ago when a chief executive officer of a consumer products manufacturer was removed from office, even though he had presided over a major turnaround bringing the company out of bankruptcy. The reason he was dismissed was because of the way he used his power to intimidate subordinates. On occasion, he even threw objects at them when he was angry. His actions so severely damaged morale at the company that the board of directors had no other option but to find a new CEO.[11]

It would be misleading, however, to regard power only from the perspective of the damage it can do. In many circumstances, a leader's skillful use of power can produce positive outcomes. In fact, frequently the problem in organizations is not that leaders use too much power but rather that they fail to use the power available to them.[12] This was noted by two behavioral scientists who have studied leadership extensively, when they said: "These days power is conspicuous by its absence. Powerlessness in the face of crisis. Powerlessness in the face of complexity . . ."[13]

Types and Sources of Power

position power power based on an organizational structure

personal power power based on a person's individual characteristics

Power, however it is used, does not arise spontaneously or mysteriously; it comes from specific and identifiable sources. The two major types of power, based on their sources, are position powers and personal powers.[14] **Position power** is based on a manager's rank in an organizational structure and is given to the manager by superiors. **Personal power** is based on a person's individual characteristics.

Clearly, someone who wants to be a leader could have large amounts of both types of power, which should facilitate the exercise of influence. On the other hand, a would-be leader might be low on both, in which case the task of leading obviously would be made more difficult. For instance, a lower-level manager who lacks initiative in developing new products or programs and who is a poor communicator, with little tact, would find it difficult to inspire subordinates to put out extra effort to make changes and reach new goals. This manager lacks personal power and would be unlikely to gain a promotion—thus also failing to increase his position power. In many situations, though, a potential leader who is low on one type of power—for example, occupying a relatively junior-level position—can compensate for that by having very strong personal leadership characteristics that are recognized by other people regardless of the person's formal status in the organization.

To better understand the nature of power in organizations, it is helpful to think about several subtypes of position power and personal power (Exhibit 10.1).[15]

Position Powers A person's position in an organization provides a base for the exercise of this type of power. Specifically, the major kinds of power that are attached to a position include legitimate power, reward power, and coercive power.

Legitimate Power. **Legitimate power** is a type of position power granted to a person, say a manager, by the organization. It is sometimes called **formal authority.** In the work setting, such power is intended to give a manager a designated right to expect compliance by his or her employees. Both parties, in effect, agree in advance that requests by the manager are appropriate and within reason, and both parties agree that the subordinates are obligated to respond to those requests.

In today's organizations, with increasing levels of education of the workforce and changing societal norms about what is "legitimate" authority, the effectiveness of this type of power has distinct limits. Often, subordinates will disagree about the scope of a manager's authority; that is, they question the boundaries of what are "appropriate requests." For example, many managers used to expect their secretaries or assistants to make personal appointments for them and perform other non-work-related services. Today, the relationship between a manager and her assistants has changed, and these types of requests are generally not considered legitimate.

The precise scope of legitimate authority in today's complex organizations is frequently ambiguous, and the resulting agreement between manager and subordinate can typically be more implicit than explicit, leaving room for potential conflict. In addition, the extent of a manager's formal authority is bounded by subordinates' perceptions of that person's credentials. If the basis of a person's selection for a managerial position is questioned, the leverage of legitimate power is somewhat reduced. For example, take a medium-sized firm where the CEO decides to appoint a close relative who has little knowledge of the business to an executive-level position that in the past has been filled by employees who have worked their way up through the ranks. In this

legitimate power (formal authority) a type of position power granted to a person by the organization

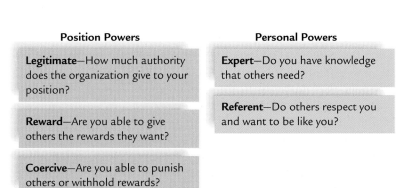

Position Powers	Personal Powers
Legitimate—How much authority does the organization give to your position?	**Expert**—Do you have knowledge that others need?
Reward—Are you able to give others the rewards they want?	**Referent**—Do others respect you and want to be like you?
Coercive—Are you able to punish others or withhold rewards?	

exhibit 10.1
Types of Power

case, subordinates may not acknowledge that the relative has a right to the formal power that would normally be associated with the position, and thus they might not respond to requests rapidly and enthusiastically. This would probably be especially the case in many Western work situations, but perhaps not as much so in Asian cultures, where family connections are viewed as more appropriate for determining who should occupy high-level positions. In essence, though, in most organizational settings, formal authority represents power, but it definitely is not unlimited power.

A Manager's Challenge, "Getting Schooled in Technology," describes how one person in a leadership role used his legitimate power, based on his position as superintendent of a school system, to make major changes in the use of technology in his organization. He also supplemented that kind of power with expert power (discussed later) brought in from outside the organization.

Reward Power. One of the strongest sources of position power for any manager is **reward power**, that is, the authority to give out rewards, especially differing amounts of highly valued rewards to different people. In any hierarchy, this power can have significant effects on others' behavior because it involves dispensing relatively scarce, but desired, resources. Only a few people, at most, can receive plum assignments; only one or two subordinates usually can be given the largest yearly performance bonus; only one person can be awarded the promotion. Because the use of reward power can have such potentially important consequences, a manager needs to be very alert to how his administration of rewards is being perceived. Aside from their direct impact, rewards also have a signaling effect. They let subordinates know, for example, where they stand with the boss.

However, the use of rewards also can have possible negative effects. Their use can sometimes decrease the motivation of those who do not receive them or receive what they regard to be insufficient amounts. Consequently, managers need to use reward power carefully and skillfully.

Coercive Power. **Coercive power** is the power to administer punishments, either by withholding something that is desired, such as a raise, or by giving out something that is not desired, such as a letter of reprimand. In typical organizations, such power is used sparingly these days, at least directly and overtly; but it is sometimes used indirectly in the form of implied threats. A manager, for instance, can let it be known that noncompliance with her requests will result in assignment to the least desired projects or committees. A manager in charge of assigning shift work could subtly influence subordinates by assigning those who do not agree with his policies to a series of inconvenient split shifts.

A major problem with the use of coercive power is that it can cause recipients to avoid being detected by disguising their objectionable behavior, rather than motivate them to perform in the desired manner. Furthermore, the use of coercion can generate retaliation. Threatening employees with reduced hours or a pay cut if they don't take on more duties or accept a less-than-generous incentive plan might result in work slowdowns, increased numbers of faulty parts, or complaints to government regulators. Any of these actions would obviously be counterproductive.

It should also be noted that although people with higher-level positions have greater ability to apply coercive power, its use is not confined to managers and supervisors. Potentially, anyone has coercive power. For example, a lower-level employee can harm someone higher by withholding valuable information or making a situation more difficult than it might otherwise be.

reward power a type of position power based on a person's authority to give out rewards

coercive power a type of position power based on a person's authority to administer punishments, either by withholding something that is desired or by giving out something that is not desired

tech|nol|ogy

a manager's challenge

Getting Schooled in Technology

When Dr. Timothy Jenney became superintendent of the Virginia Beach City Public Schools, he had to contend with a school district that was well behind the technology curve as well as critics who were concerned about applying business principles in an educational setting. In this top management position, he had the power to make decisions about allocating the district's multimillion-dollar budget to cover school salaries, training, books and materials, and other expenses. According to the organization chart, Jenney officially reported to the school board. In reality, however, his decisions and actions would be scrutinized and dissected by many more people, including elected officials, parents of the district's 76,000 students, and local businesses who hired the district's graduates.

Early in his tenure, Jenney determined that upgrading the district's technology would be one of his top priorities. He therefore designated $7.5 million for technological equipment, training, and programs, despite the fact that when he took over, the district was $12 million in red. This decision sparked considerable attention and debate, not just because of the amount spent, but also because any unspent money would have reverted to the control of city officials. The superintendent responded by explaining his reasoning using factual evidence from an outside expert's comparison of the district's existing technology with current industry standards. "That was exactly the right thing to do," Jenney remembers. "The study bought credibility and buy-in from the board and the community."

Jenney's technology initiatives included providing computer labs and technology specialists for all 85 schools; offering district-wide distance learning courses; building a state-of-the-art staff development center; establishing a high-tech workforce training center for students; and developing a Web site to communicate the district's goals, activities, and accomplishments. To accomplish this agenda, he had to overcome what he calls "institutional inertia"—the staff's tendency to maintain the status quo. Jenney therefore offered a $300 reward to each employee who could show that he or she was computer literate. This saved thousands of dollars in training costs while giving staff members a tangible incentive to adopt the new technology.

The superintendent also believed his school district would benefit from the skills and knowledge of staff members recruited from the business world for key positions such as chief financial officer, chief information officer, and assistant superintendent. In addition, he worked with subordinates to prepare a long-range strategic plan, which was later posted on the school district's Web site along with information for students, parents, staff members, and families considering a move to Virginia Beach.

In late 2002, the district opened a 137,000-square-foot, $22.5 million facility called the Advanced Technology Center—perhaps the district's crowning achievement. The Advanced Technology Center is a special high school offering tech-oriented training in programs like digital design, computer-aided drafting, and Internet security. Competition to get into the school is fierce—almost like applying for a job—and the prospects for graduates, bright: It is highly unlikely these students will be flipping burgers when they graduate.

Jenney knows that some in the community remain unsure about his businesslike approach to education. "They think we're comparing children to widgets, but we're not," he says. "Dealing with children is a different kind of business—the product is teaching and learning."

Sources: Michelle Mizal-Archer, "Star Techies," *Virginia Beach Beacon*, February 20, 2003, p. 10; Susan McLester, "Grand Plans and Bold Moves," *Technology and Learning*, June 2002, pp. 6+; "Virginia Beach: Ahead of the Curve," *Technology and Learning*, June 2002, pp. 6+; Virginia Beach City Public Schools Web site.

This use of coercive power by subordinates may be subtle, but in some cases it may actually be quite effective for that reason.

Personal Powers Personal powers are attached to a person and thus stay with that individual regardless of the position or the organization. For those who want to be leaders, personal powers are especially valuable because they do not depend directly or only on the actions of others or of the organization. The two major types are expert power and referent power.

expert power a type of personal power based on specialized knowledge not readily available to many people

Expert Power. **Expert power** is based on specialized knowledge not readily available to many people. It is precisely because many people do not have a particular kind of knowledge that makes expertise a potential source of power. The potential is translated into actual power when other people depend on, or need advice from, those who have that expertise. The best example of expert power in everyday life is the physician–patient relationship. Most people follow their doctors' directives not because of any formal position power but because of the potential negative consequences of ignoring their expertise. Given the increased percentage of knowledge workers (i.e., those who have some special expertise) and the increased use of sophisticated knowledge in many types of contemporary organizations, it is becoming imperative for most managers to have some type of expertise. Having expertise may not necessarily set a manager apart from her subordinates, but not having it may greatly diminish the effectiveness of various forms of position power.

Expert power is not confined to higher organizational levels. Some of the most specialized, and yet most needed, knowledge in an organization can be possessed by lower-level employees.[16] One only needs to observe a boss trying to find a particular document in a file to appreciate the expert power that an administrative assistant often has in certain situations; or to watch the high-level executive waiting impatiently while the technician makes repairs on the computer or fax machine. These examples illustrate the fact that dependencies create an opportunity for expertise to become power, whatever the position a person holds. Several years ago, Jack Welch, then CEO of General Electric, used this principle deliberately by introducing the idea of "mentoring up" into the organization. He started by requesting that several hundred of his worldwide executives reach down in the ranks and pick younger, "Webified" subordinates to teach them the intricacies of the Net. Based on this experience, the upper-level executives indicated that they had become more receptive to receiving inputs from those in lower-power positions.[17]

referent power a type of personal power gained when people are attracted to, or identify with, that person; this power is gained because people "refer" to that person

Referent Power. When people are attracted to, or identify with, someone, that person acquires what is called **referent power**. This power is gained because other people "refer" to that person. They want to please that person or in some way receive acceptance. Referent power often can be recognized by its subtle occurrences. A subordinate, for example, may begin using gestures similar to those of his superior or even imitating certain aspects of his speech patterns. More importantly, the subordinate may find his opinions on important work issues becoming similar to those of his boss.

For anyone in a leadership position in a work setting, being able to generate referent power is clearly a great asset. It is a cost-free way to influence other people. Referent power makes it possible to lead by example rather than by giving orders. A manager can use her referent power to change work habits, for example. If she comes in early, stays late, takes shorter breaks, and finishes her work rather than putting it off until the next day, her subordinates may model themselves on her behavior and change their own work habits as well.

A problem with referent power, however, is that it is not obvious how such power can be deliberately and easily developed. There is no formula for how to increase your referent power, and making attempts to get others to like or admire you can frequently cause the opposite reaction. Certain personal attributes, such as honesty and integrity, obviously help. Also, experience and a demonstrated record of success certainly help. The basic lesson seems to be that the referent power of a potential leader is built up over time by consistent actions and behavior that cause others to develop admiration.

A Manager's Challenge, "Lighting the Way at Amazon.com," describes someone who can employ both types of personal power: expert and referent. He has demonstrated expertise and is using that kind of power to make major organizational changes. He is also likely to take advantage of the opportunity to use and build his referent power.

a manager's challenge

Change

Lighting the Way at Amazon.com

Thomas J. Szkutak is using his background in light bulbs and plastics to help the online retailer Amazon.com light the way to lower costs and brighter profits. Before joining Amazon.com as chief financial officer, he held the same position at GE Lighting, a Cleveland-based division of General Electric that makes a wide variety of lighting instruments for home and commercial use. Earlier in his career he was part of the management team for the GE Plastics business in Europe, Africa, India, and the Middle East. Jeff Bezos, Amazon's CEO, wanted Szkutak to help his company identify and implement changes that would "continue to drive down costs so that we can even further lower prices for customers."

How did Szkutak apply the personal powers and management skills he honed in lighting manufacturing and plastics production to his current role as CFO of a cutting-edge, Internet-based retailer? It didn't hurt that his résumé included GE. GE is a recognized leader in corporate finance training. Every year, 350 college recruits—the best and the brightest of the bunch—go through its prized, two-year Financial Management Program in Ossining, New York, which was begun in 1919. These "star" graduates walk out of the course with the confidence that people will listen to them. Szkutak is no different.

Moreover, although GE Lighting employs 33,000 around the world and Amazon employs some 8,000 or so, the two companies face some similar challenges. Both are battling for global market share against formidable competitors and selling products to price-sensitive customers. Yet there are differences, as well—bottom-line differences. Whereas GE Lighting is a mature business that ekes out a relatively small profit margin of 10 percent year after year,

Amazon is spending heavily to spur future growth and profits. Lower, Wal-Mart-like prices are helping the e-retailer attract consumers interested in buying products other than just books, which has contributed steadily to continued growth and higher profitability for the company. "Lowering prices will go on for years and years, and that's just how we're going to do business," Bezos says.

So, why did Bezos choose Szkutak—whose management background is so concentrated in old-line manufacturing companies—for a key leadership position in a fast-paced online business like Amazon? It was precisely because of Szkutak's reputation for cost-cutting at GE, where he and his managers constantly searched for creative ways to contain costs. Since cost-cutting is one of Amazon's major priorities on the path to better profitability, Bezos believed the former GE executive would bring considerable expert power to his duties as CFO at Amazon. Szkutak also can wield referent power because GE's managers and finance executives are admired around the world and he was a senior executive with the company for 20 years.

So has the bet paid off? Yes: 2003 marked Amazon's first full year in the black. Since hiring Szuktak, Amazon has dramatically streamlined its network of product distribution centers, one of its largest and most criticized expenses. Despite a rise in sales, the company has still managed to cut order fulfillment expenses significantly, thanks to better inventory software and smarter storage. It also has honed its order "sorting" process, allowing it to ship roughly one-third more inventory with the same number of people.

"They have made incredible progress in operations," said one industry research director.

Sources: Mary E. Behr, "If at First You Don't Succeed," *CIO Insight*, November 2003, p. 51; Rob Hoff, "Amazon & Co. Still Floating in Froth," *BusinessWeek Online*, October 23, 2003; Lotte Chow, "All in the Grooming," *CFO Asia*, October 17, 2003; adapted from Gene G. Marcial, "Amazon Turns a Page," *BusinessWeek*, October 14, 2002, p. 172; "New CFO at Amazon.com," *Publishers Weekly*, September 9, 2002, p. 12; "Career Journal: Who's News," *Wall Street Journal*, September 3, 2002, p. B10; Monica Soto, "Amazon.com Hires GE Executive as Chief Financial Officer," *Seattle Times*, August 31, 2002.

Using Power

There are at least four key issues for managers to think about in relation to the use of power (as shown in Exhibit 10.2):

- How much power should be used in a given situation?
- Which types of power should be used?
- How can power be put to use?
- Should power be shared?

How Much Power to Use? The answer to this question seems to be: Use enough to achieve objectives but avoid using excessive power. Using too little power in organizational settings can lead to inaction, and this is especially the case when change is needed but strong resistance exists or is anticipated. Often, managers seem reluctant to wield power because of anticipated opposition. Yet, the use of power is sometimes the only way to accomplish significant change. "Managing with power means understanding that to get things done, you need power—more power than those whose opposition you must overcome."[18]

Using too much power, though, also can be a problem. When more power is used than is necessary, people's behavior may change, but resentments and reactions often are self-defeating to the power-user in the long run. In many organizational situations, people have a sense of what is an appropriate amount of power. If that sense is violated, a manager may actually undermine his power for the future. Excessive use of power in work organizations, like excessive use of police force in civil disturbances, can result in potentially severe negative reactions.

Which Types of Power to Use? Answers to this question depend on characteristics of the situation and circumstances: what has happened before, what type of change is needed, what amount of resistance is expected, where opposition is located, and the like. Each type of power, whether a position power or personal power, has particular impacts. Some types of power, especially referent and expertise, have relatively low costs. That is, their use generates little direct opposition. Thus, they would seem to be the powers to use whenever possible. The problem, however, is that they may not be strong enough to have an impact. If a manager has very little referent power, then trying to use that method is not likely to accomplish much. Similarly, if the expertise of the manager is not perceived as high, regardless of the actual degree of expertise, then subordinates are unlikely to be motivated to change. In such cases, the use of a form of position power, such as formal authority or reward power,

exhibit 10.2

Four Key Issues in Using Power

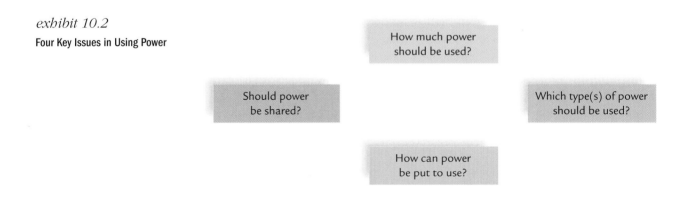

might be necessary. However, the risks of creating negative reactions are increased, thereby lessening the effects of such power.

How Can Power Be Put to Use? Power, in its various forms, provides the basis for influence. However, power must be converted into actual manager/leader behaviors. The skillful use of different types of power is a type of expertise that can be developed. This means that the total amount of power available to you as a manager is not a fixed quantity but rather can be expanded or contracted over time.

To put power to use involves **influence tactics**, that is, specific behaviors used to affect the behavior and attitudes of other people. A number of such tactics have been studied,[19] and a representative sample of them is shown in Exhibit 10.3. Obviously, different types of power match up with some tactics more than others. For example, a high degree of expertise would support the use of rational persuasion. Someone possessing a great deal of referent power could more effectively use inspirational appeals than could someone with less referent power. A leader with little position power would have trouble using legitimating tactics.

The other major factor affecting the use of specific influence tactics is the circumstances of the situation, particularly in regard to the targets. Thus, if the target of influence is a person higher up in the organization structure, pressure would likely be an inappropriate and ineffective tactic. Likewise, exchange might work very well with a peer but perhaps be unnecessary in a typical situation involving subordinates. On the other hand, rational persuasion could be a potentially useful tactic in a wide variety of situations, whether with superiors, peers, or subordinates.

influence tactics specific behaviors used to affect the behavior and attitudes of other people

Emotional Intelligence by Lyman Porter

Q&A

One**Key**

www.prenhall.com/onekey

---

exhibit 10.3

Types of Influence Tactics

Rational Persuasion: The agent uses logical arguments and factual evidence to show a proposal or request is feasible and relevant for attaining important task objectives.

Apprising: The agent explains how carrying out a request or supporting a proposal will benefit the target personally or help advance the target person's career.

Inspirational Appeals: The agent makes an appeal to values and ideals or seeks to arouse the target person's emotions to gain commitment for a request or proposal.

Consultation: The agent encourages the target to suggest improvements in a proposal or to help plan an activity or change for which the target person's support and assistance are desired.

Exchange: The agent offers an incentive, suggests an exchange of favors, or indicates willingness to reciprocate at a later time if the target will do what the agent requests.

Collaboration: The agent offers to provide relevant resources and assistance if the target will carry out a request or approve a proposed change.

Personal Appeals: The agent asks the target to carry out a request or support a proposal out of friendship, or asks for a personal favor before saying what it is.

Ingratiation: The agent uses praise and flattery before or during an influence attempt or expresses confidence in the target's ability to carry out a difficult request.

Legitimating Tactics: The agent seeks to establish the legitimacy of a request or to verify authority to make it by referring to rules, formal policies, or official documents.

Pressure: The agent uses demands, threats, frequent checking, or persistent reminders to influence the target person.

Coalition Tactics: The agent seeks the aid of others to persuade the target to do something or uses the support of others as a reason for the target to agree.

Source: G. Yukl, *Leadership in Organizations* (Upper Saddle River, NJ: Prentice Hall, 2002), p. 160.

empowerment sharing of power with others

Should Power Be Shared? In recent years, the concept of empowerment has become prominent in management literature.[20] In its broadest sense, **empowerment** simply means the sharing of power with others, where those with high amounts of power increase the power of those with less. In organizational terms, this means that those higher in the formal structure provide more power, especially with regard to decision making, to those lower in the structure. This, of course, can be done organizationwide, but it also can be done by the individual manager/leader. A company that strongly embraces empowerment is Novo Nordisk, a Danish pharmaceuticals company, with sales of over $3.5 billion per year. The manager of one of its clinical units, for example, describes the organization as "a debating and arguing culture"; however, he also points out that once a decision has been made, "externally, we show extreme loyalty to the company . . . grumbling after the fact isn't tolerated here."[21]

For empowerment to take place, managers cannot simply declare that those below them have more power. They must provide the necessary means, such as, for example, delegating more formal authority to make specified decisions, offering increased training opportunities to develop expertise and self-confidence, providing more resources and access to information to be able to implement effective decisions, and avoiding the sudden withdrawal of shared power at the first sign of trouble. Subordinates must be allowed to learn to use their increased power. Those who advocate empowerment suggest that it is a key leadership practice for helping organizations to achieve high performance and, especially, to cope successfully with major changes and transitions.[22] Empowerment also has the possible advantages of facilitating organizational commitment, learning, and innovation. While the benefits of these kinds of employee attitudes and behaviors seem obvious, leaders engaging in empowering actions will need to consider carefully how much power to share and how to enable others to share that power. Empowerment is a potentially effective leadership approach, but it is not by itself the answer to all organizational performance issues.

In 1963, Mary Kay Ash founded Mary Kay Cosmetics—famous for the pink Cadillacs the company's sales representatives drive. Ash's goal was to empower women to succeed financially and personally—an uncommon endeavor in the early 1960s. She encouraged employees to prioritize their lives according to a simple but empowering motto: God first, family second, career third. The company's manager-directors, Jean Wilson (front), Jo Shuler, Betty Lucido, June Chisman, and Vicki Crank (rear) continue to adhere to that motto today.

LEADERS AND THE LEADERSHIP PROCESS

We now turn from how leadership is related to power and how the hierarchical structure of organizations influences the uses of different kinds of power, to examining leadership as a process. This process has three fundamental elements in organizations: leaders, followers, and situations. Even though the role of leader typically gets most of the attention, all three factors must be considered to gain a comprehensive understanding of how the process unfolds. As shown in Exhibit 10.4, what has been termed the "locus of leadership" is the intersection of these three variables: where and when the leader with a particular set of characteristics and behaviors interacts with a specific set of followers in a situation with certain identifiable characteristics.[23] Each element influences and is influenced by the other two variables, and a change in any one will alter how the other two factors interact.

The impact of each of these three variables on the basic leadership process will be discussed in more detail in the sections that follow. We begin with the leader: specifically, leaders' traits, skills, and behaviors.

exhibit 10.4

Locus of Leadership: Intersection of the Basic Components of the Leadership Process

Leaders' Traits

One critical component of what leaders in managerial roles bring to the work setting is their **traits**, that is, the relatively enduring characteristics of a person. The scientific study of the role of leaders' traits has had a somewhat roller-coaster history: At the beginning of the twentieth century, the "great man"—note that it was not the "great person"—view of leadership was in vogue. That is, leaders, almost always thought of as only men in that era, were assumed to have inherited combinations of traits that distinguished them from followers. The notion, then, was that those destined to be leaders were "born," not made. As years passed, however, this theory faded away because of the difficulties of proving that traits were, in fact, inherited. Instead, the focus shifted in the 1920s and 1930s to a search for specific traits or characteristics—such as verbal skills, physical size, dominance, self-esteem—that would unambiguously separate leaders from nonleaders.

The current view is that although specific traits do not invariably determine leadership effectiveness, they can increase its likelihood.[24] As shown in Exhibit 10.5, among the traits that research has indicated are most apt to predict effective leadership are drive, motivation to lead, honesty/integrity, self-confidence, and emotional maturity.[25]

traits relatively enduring characteristics of a person

- *Drive:* A high level of energy, effort, and persistence in the pursuit of objectives.
- *Motivation to lead:* A strong desire to influence others, to "be in charge." Such a person is comfortable with the use of power in relating to other people.[26]
- *Honesty/Integrity:* Trustworthiness. Someone with this trait is a person whose word can be relied on consistently and who is highly likely to do what he or she says.[27]
- *Self-Confidence:* A strong belief in one's own capabilities.[28] People with this trait set high expectations for themselves and others,[29] and they tend to be optimistic rather than pessimistic about overcoming obstacles and achieving objectives. Obviously, in contrast to honesty/integrity, this is a trait that in the extreme can be

exhibit 10.5

Leaders' Traits

Source: Adapted from S. A. Kirkpatrick and E. A. Locke, "Leadership: Do Traits Matter?" *Academy of Management Executive* 5, no. 2 (1991), pp. 48–60.

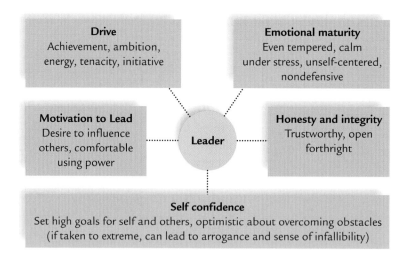

a negative. It can result in a sense of infallibility and in an attitude of arrogance that can alienate potential followers. In other words, too much self-confidence can lead to what has been called "the shadow side of success."[30] That is, too much success in leadership, paradoxically, can produce the seeds of later leadership problems. No matter how much confidence managers have in themselves, their staffs, and their employees, nothing substitutes for preparation. The manager who relies on self-confidence at the expense of planning is setting the scene for potential disaster.

■ *Emotional Maturity:* Remaining even-tempered and calm in the face of stress and pressure. Persons with maturity tend to be accurate in self-awareness about their own strengths and weaknesses; moreover, they are less likely to be self-centered and to be unduly defensive in the face of criticism.[31]

Most of the research on traits has involved only, or mostly, men. The extent to which the findings would generalize to both genders remains a subject for further research. Also, it is important to reemphasize that traits, such as those listed, do not guarantee that a person will become a leader or will necessarily lead effectively. Very few people possess every critical trait at an exceptionally high level. However, if a person has one or more of these relatively enduring characteristics, the probabilities for successful leadership are increased. Traits provide potential, but other factors such as skills, attitudes, experience, and opportunities determine whether the potential will be realized.

Finally, most of the research on the relationship of personal traits to the effectiveness of leaders has not considered the impact of culture. It has focused primarily on Western, mostly American, work environments. Whether traits can universally predict successful leadership is still an open question (see the discussion of the GLOBE research project in the next chapter). It may be that in at least some cultures, other or different traits would be equally or more influential. In fact, the very notion that particular personal qualities or leadership traits are critical to successful influence is open to question in many non-Western cultures, such as those in Southeast Asia. In countries such as Korea or Malaysia, for example, a person often is in a leadership position by virtue of ownership or family position, and others show respect for that reason rather than because of certain personality features.[32]

Leaders' Skills and Competencies

In Chapter 1 we discussed three types of skills that are important for anyone in a managerial position: technical skills, interpersonal skills, and conceptual skills. As we pointed out in that chapter, early in a managerial career the first two categories of skills—technical and interpersonal—loom especially large in determining whether someone will advance to higher organizational levels. As a person moves up in the organization, the relative importance of technical skills decreases, the importance of interpersonal skills continues to remain strong, and the importance of conceptual skills becomes increasingly critical. Since, as we have emphasized, leadership is a major element in the overall process of management, it should be clear that all three of these types of skills are vital to the leadership function. This is particularly so because leadership involves attempts to influence other people in desired directions. The greater a person's technical, interpersonal, and conceptual skills, the more likely that person will be able to exert significant amounts of influence.

In the last 15 years or so, two other sets of skills or competencies have become increasingly prominent in research relating to influence processes: "emotional intelligence" and "social intelligence." The first of these, **emotional intelligence**, has probably received the most attention to date,[33] one of its chief proponents even going so far to say it "is the sine qua non [indispensable ingredient] of leadership."[34] The essence of emotional intelligence, as the name implies, involves an awareness of others' feelings and a sensitivity to one's own emotions and the ability to control them.

As shown in Exhibit 10.6, [35] emotional intelligence has been conceived by one of its adherents as having five key components: self-awareness, self-regulation, motivation, empathy, and social skill. Three features of emotional intelligence seem particularly important for a manager to consider: (1) it is distinct from IQ or cognitive intelligence; (2) although in part determined genetically, it probably can be learned or improved by training, coaching, practice, and—especially—effort; and (3) it seems obviously relevant to performing effectively as a leader in an organizational setting.

An illustration of two managers who had contrasting levels of emotional intelligence occurred several years ago at a news division of BBC, the British media organization. A decision had been made to close a particular unit, one that employed some 200 journalists. The executive who announced the decision to the employees exhibited self-centered behavior in addition to delivering the message in a brusque, uncaring manner. It created such a negative reaction that it appeared that the executive might have to call in company security. The next day, a different executive spoke with the same set of employees in a calm and understanding manner

emotional intelligence
involves an awareness of others' feelings; and a sensitivity to one's own emotions and the ability to control them

**Influence Tactics
by Lyman Porter**

Q&A
One**Key**
www.prenhall.com/onekey

Emotional Intelligence	Social Intelligence
· Self-Awareness	· Social Perceptiveness
· Self-Regulation	· Behavioral Flexibility
· Motivation	· "Savvy"
· Empathy	
· Social Skill	

exhibit 10.6

Components of Emotional and Social Intelligence

and with a high degree of empathy for their situation. He was actually cheered.[36]

Although social intelligence shares some similarities with emotional intelligence, the two competencies also differ to an extent. Whereas major components of emotional intelligence involve self-awareness and self-regulation, **social intelligence** is more focused outward on being able to "read" other people and their intentions. (See Exhibit 10.6.) Social perceptiveness thus is a principal ingredient. However, so also is what has been called "behavioral flexibility" or the ability and motivation to modify one's own behavior in response to what is perceived socially. Thus, like emotional intelligence, social intelligence puts a premium on being able to monitor one's own behavior and adjust that behavior according to assessment of the social context and circumstances. Again, as with emotional intelligence, social intelligence is both desirable and important for leadership and something that a person can work on and presumably improve. A person who is socially intelligent is someone who has considerable tacit knowledge—knowledge that is not always directly made explicit—or, to use a more everyday term, savvy.

Leaders' Behaviors

For leadership to occur, traits and skills must be transformed into behavior. Thus, considerable research has focused on leaders' behaviors and their impact on subordinates and followers. As far back as the 1950s, researchers zeroed in on two fundamental types of leader behaviors: those involving assistance in the direct performance of the task, and those involving the interpersonal relationships necessary to support task performance. These two types have been called by different names over the years, but probably the easiest terms to remember are "task behaviors" and "people behaviors." Examples of these behaviors are shown in Exhibit 10.7.

Task Behaviors The key aspects of **task behaviors**, also termed "initiating structure" behaviors, center on specifying and identifying the roles and tasks of the leaders themselves and their subordinates. Such behaviors involve planning assignments, scheduling work, setting standards of performance, and devising the procedures to carry out the tasks.

People Behaviors This dimension of leader behaviors has also been termed "consideration" or "relationship oriented." Essentially, **people behaviors** include being friendly and supportive, showing trust and confidence in subordinates,

social intelligence the ability to "read" other people and their intentions and adjust one's own behavior in response

task behaviors behaviors that specify and identify the roles and tasks of leaders and their subordinates, such as planning, scheduling, setting standards, and devising procedures

people behaviors behaviors that focus on interaction, such as being friendly and supportive, showing trust and confidence, being concerned about others, and supplying recognition

exhibit 10.7
Leaders' Behaviors

Task Behaviors (Initiating Structure)	People Behaviors (Consideration)
· Specifies roles and tasks	· Is friendly
· Plans assignments	· Is supportive
· Schedules work	· Shows trust and confidence in subordinates
· Sets performance standards	· Shows concern for subordinates' welfare
· Develops procedures	· Gives recognition to subordinates for their accomplishments

being concerned about their welfare, and supplying recognition for their accomplishments.

Because of the consistency with which these two dimensions of leader behavior have been identified in a wide variety of research studies over the years, you might expect that the most effective leaders would rate high on both dimensions—that is, be both strongly task oriented and strongly people oriented.[37] This has not been conclusively demonstrated, although it has been found that leaders who score highest on people behaviors tend to have the most satisfied subordinates.

Relevant to the issue of the types of leader behaviors is the question of whether female leaders demonstrate different patterns of leader behaviors from those displayed by males. Some research has been said to show that women are more likely than men to exhibit high levels of people skills and that consequently men and women have different leadership styles. However, this issue has been surrounded by considerable controversy. To date, there is insufficient evidence to draw decisive conclusions.[38] What seems clear is that the *individual* differences among women and among men are probably far more important than any relatively small overall average difference between the two gender groups.

Considering all of the research that has been carried out on leader behaviors across the past five decades, the principal message for those in managerial positions would seem to be this: Effective leaders need to focus on *both* structuring the work (task behaviors) *and* supporting and developing good interpersonal relationships with and among subordinates (people behaviors). Looking at leadership in this way is a very useful method for you to use to self-assess your own leadership behavior: "How am I doing on task behaviors *and* how am I doing on people behaviors?"

A Manager's Challenge, "GM Manager Proves Leadership Knows No Boundaries," provides a good example of someone whose task and people behaviors in her leadership role have resulted in major achievements by her organization. This manager's exposure to ideas gained from interactions with firms outside of her own country facilitated the development of her skills in using both types of leader behaviors.

FOLLOWERS AND THE LEADERSHIP PROCESS

We now turn our attention to the second key component of the leadership process: those who *receive* the leadership and influence, namely, followers or subordinates. The amount of research on followers has been considerably less than that on leaders. This is understandable, given the historical emphasis in Western societies on the role of leaders, but it represents a somewhat distorted and probably misleading picture of the complete process.

Followers provide significant opportunities for, and sometimes constraints on, successful leadership.[39] The U.S. Military Academy at West Point recognizes this point by utilizing cadets' first year to instruct them in the basics of followership. As a former West Point instructor stated: "[New] cadets don't know how to lead soldiers well. They don't know how to motivate or train or reward or discipline effectively." Consequently, the first year is used to teach them to be good followers and in so doing to demonstrate to them what makes an effective leader.[40]

globalization *a manager's challenge*

GM Manager Proves Leadership Knows No Boundaries

Facing intense competition from highly efficient international rivals such as Honda and Toyota, managers at General Motors are constantly searching for ways to boost the quality of GM's cars, trucks, and sports utility vehicles while slashing costs.

Consider the situation at GM's gigantic metal stamping plant in Marion, Indiana, in the late 1990s. The plant was designed in the 1950s to maximize the output of fenders, doors, and other auto body parts. As the decades passed, the plant's workforce had to make do with outdated machinery and processes. Crews spent hours changing over equipment to produce different parts while unneeded machines stood idle. Worse, among the millions of metal parts produced by the plant, thousands were found to be defective. Finally, in a bid to boost market share by improving quality and productivity, GM's executives reorganized the division and began modernizing the individual factories.

After the modernization had been underway for several years, GM's head of manufacturing—who had managed the Indiana factory years before—brought in metal-shop veteran Cathy Clegg as Marion's manager. Clegg began her GM career as an engineer at a Cadillac plant, then progressed through management positions at various U.S. and Canadian GM plants. In one of her assignments, she gained additional opportunities to observe procedures developed in other countries by working with Toyota managers in a joint venture (JV) factory in California. By the time Clegg took over at Marion, she had had experience managing cutting-edge facilities and had absorbed ideas from the world's best car makers.

Putting her international exposure and experience to work, Clegg became a familiar sight on the plant floor as she established strong connections with the plant's 200 managers and supervisors and got to know its 1,400 hourly workers. She made a point of meeting frequently with engineers and diemakers to discuss quality improvement measures and equipment efficiency. Employees had been dispirited by earlier layoffs, but as Clegg and her managers mapped out further improvements, she helped others to see that the program was actually protecting the plant's future and creating new jobs.

Managers need both task skills and people skills. Cathy Clegg (second from left), a General Motors manager, learned new, cutting-edge task skills at plants GM operated in conjunction with Toyota. Clegg then "imported" these skills to GM's Marion, Indiana, metal stamping plant, which she managed for a time. This know-how, coupled with Clegg's people skills, led to her subsequent promotion to the top position at one of GM's full-assembly line plants.

Within a year, the highly developed relationship between Clegg, her management subordinates, and the workforce at large was showing results. The Marion plant achieved significantly faster output at a much lower cost than in any previous year. Moreover, the number of defective parts had plummeted.

In 2003, Clegg was promoted to run GM's full assembly-line plant in Fort Wayne, Indiana. "Historically speaking it has been rare for women to lead major automotive plants," says a GM spokesperson about Clegg's promotion. "Cutthroat competition requires GM to appoint the best person for a particular job, regardless of gender, race, or religion."

As was the case at the Marion plant, Clegg knows she will have to build credibility and rapport with the Fort Wayne employees to inspire all of them to pull in the same direction. She doesn't make much of the fact that she's a woman, either. At the end of the day, it's her performance that will count, she says.

Sources: Urvaksh Karkaria, "Breaking the Manager Mold," *The Journal Gazette*, December 14, 2003; Ted Evanoff, "Manager Heads Up Revitalization of GM's Marion Plant," *Indianapolis Star*, March 24, 2002, p. E3; Ted Evanoff, "Stamp of Quality," *Indianapolis Star*, March 24, 2002, pp. E1, E3.

What Followers Bring to the Process

Followers, of course, have characteristics similar to leaders: personality traits, past experiences, beliefs and attitudes, and skills and abilities. What may be different, though, are the amounts and nature of these characteristics in relation to the leader's. In fact, rarely would they be exactly the same. Also, in a work setting, followers typically have lower position power than the leader. However, in increasingly flatter and less hierarchical contemporary work organizations, the difference is not likely to be as great as in the past. The difference in power is also being decreased by the greater access to information by subordinates due to Internet technology. Such a decrease in the difference between followers' and leaders' formal authority is changing the very nature of the leadership process in today's organizations and presenting new challenges to would-be leaders. In contemporary organizations leaders cannot assume that they possess more expertise and knowledge than those in a follower position.

Not to be overlooked, moreover, is the fact that almost every leader is also a follower of someone else in the organization. Thus, most people in organizations have to learn how to become good followers as well as good leaders. As a knowledgeable observer has pointed out: "Organizations stand or fall partly on the basis of how well their leaders lead, but partly also on the basis of how well their followers follow."[41]

A classic example of someone who turned a subordinate or follower's role into a future top executive role was a former president of the United States, Dwight Eisenhower. His army career progressed slowly following his graduation from West Point and, in fact, it took him some 26 years to be promoted to the rank of colonel just before World War II began in 1939. By 1943, however, he had been advanced over 360 more-senior officers to be made a four-star general and named Supreme Commander of Allied Forces in Europe. The fact that he had served as an outstanding subordinate for his superiors, Generals Douglas MacArthur and George C. Marshall, as well as being a leader of those who reported to him, was more than a minor factor in his ascendancy to a top executive position.[42] Learning how to be effective in a follower role can be a significant ingredient in becoming an effective leader, but this is not the same thing as saying that all followers can or will become good leaders.

Effects of Followers' Behavior

Leaders influence followers, but the reverse is also true: Leaders act, followers respond, and leaders react to those responses. Especially important in these evolving interactions are the followers' perceptions of the leaders—that is, the followers' views of a leader's characteristics and the reasons for the leader's behavior. It appears that followers often check their perceptions against the traits they think leaders *should* possess and the behaviors they *should* display.[43] In effect, followers seem to develop what have been called "implicit leadership theories," and they tend to judge a leader's actions against particular standards or expectations they have in mind.[44] When expectations aren't met, followers may blame leaders for a group's or organization's failures; likewise, when expectations are met, leaders typically get the credit.

Some theorists argue that leaders in organizations, just like certain stars of athletic teams, frequently get excessive—and sometimes undeserved—credit or blame for outcomes they may not have affected quite so decisively.[45] It seems that until recently, at least, no story concerning Microsoft, for example, could be written without mentioning Bill Gates. Rightly or wrongly, he became the icon of the company. Articles commending or criticizing some new software product of the company seemed to place all of the praise or blame squarely on the leader at the top: Bill Gates. It is likely, however, that others in his organization should have received a relatively greater share of the attention.

The Leader–Follower Relationship

As we have discussed, in organizational work settings leaders and followers engage in reciprocal relationships: The behavior of each affects the behavior of the other. In cases where a leader has direct contact with a group of followers, such as in a work unit, two-person leader–follower relationships are built between a supervisor and each subordinate. Research shows that these relationships may vary considerably in scope and content from one leader–follower pair to another.[46] That is, how Susan as the leader (supervisor) relates to John as a follower (subordinate) in carrying out the work of the unit may be quite different from how Susan as leader relates to Sam as a follower.

This line of research has led to the development of a conceptual approach to leadership that focuses on leader–follower relationships: **leader–member exchange (LMX) theory**.[47] Based on this theory, an increasing body of research appears to suggest that the quality of such two-person relationships can strongly influence the effort and behavior of subordinates.[48]

LMX theory focuses on the types of relationships that are developed between leader and follower rather than on only the behavior of the leader or of the follower. As described in the theory, the leader's central task is to work with followers on building strong, mutually respectful, and satisfying relationships. However, the degree to which such relationships develop depends as much on the behavior and performance of the follower as on the actions of the leader.[49] Also, developing such deep relationships is not always easy, and one of the major issues for the leader is that this approach can be time-consuming. In fact, as shown in Exhibit 10.8, in later versions of the LMX theory the leader–member relationship is viewed as taking time to develop across different stages—for example, from that of a "stranger" interaction, to an "acquaintance" relationship and, ultimately, to a "mature partnership."[50]

leader–member exchange (LMX) theory a relationship-based approach to leadership that focuses on the importance of strong, mutually respectful, and satisfying relationships between leaders and followers

exhibit 10.8

Development of Leader-Member Relationships over Time

Source: Adapted from G. B. Graen and M. Uhl-Bien, "Relationship-Based Approach to Leadership: Development of Leader-Member Exchange (LMX) Theory of Leadership over 25 Years: Applying a Multi-level Multi-domain Perspective," *Leadership Quarterly* 6, no. 2, Special Issue: "Leadership," (1995), pp. 219–47.

Relationship Characteristic	Relationship Stage		
	Stranger	**Acquaintance**	**Maturity**
Relationship-building phase	Role-finding	Role-making	Role implementation
Quality of leader-member exchange	Low	Medium	High
Amounts of reciprocal influence	None	Limited	Almost unlimited
Focus of interest	Self	⋯⋯▶	Team

Time

LMX theorists stress, of course, that not all leader–follower relationships develop into the partnership phase, and some may not even get to the acquaintance stage. However, if the mature relationship phase can be reached, each party can exercise sizable influence over the other for the benefit of both themselves and the organization. What is significant about the LMX approach is that it places particular emphasis on how individualized leader–follower relationships develop and on the potentially important consequences that can flow from high-quality relationships.

SITUATIONS AND THE LEADERSHIP PROCESS

The third key element in the analysis of the leadership process is the situation surrounding the process. In addition to followers, the two most important categories of situational variables are the tasks to be performed and the organizational context.

Tasks

The nature of the work to be performed provides a critical component of the situation facing leaders. Change the task, and the leadership process is highly likely to be changed. Research evidence across many studies indicates that several of the most important dimensions of tasks that affect the leadership process include whether they are relatively structured or unstructured and whether they involve high or low levels of worker discretion.[51] For example, a manager of a group of newly trained but relatively inexperienced tax preparers at a firm such as H&R Block would probably need to use a fairly high degree of task-oriented leadership to be sure that precise guidelines were being followed in analyzing clients' often complex returns. Alternatively, a project leader in charge of reviewing the work of a group of highly educated scientists doing advanced research in a pharmaceutical company such as Merck would probably be more concerned with ensuring a continuous flow of new scientific information and securing additional funding for the group even when it appears they are not producing immediately useful results. This manager might use a more person-oriented, less directive form of leadership with the research staff.

Organizational Context

The term "organizational context" in this instance means both the immediate work group (those who come in direct face-to-face contact with a leader) and the larger organization (composed of all individuals and groups who do not usually have frequent direct personal contact with a leader). A number of features of the organizational context can affect the leadership process. Of particular importance is the fundamental culture of the organization, that is, its history, traditions, and norms. Someone who has come out of a large and comparatively slow-moving company probably would find that the style of leadership he used effectively there is not equally effective in a fast-changing, start-up entrepreneurial firm. The reverse, of course, would be equally true. A leadership style consistent with the fun, informal culture at Ben & Jerry's Ice Cream would not necessarily work at a larger and more traditional firm in, say, the banking industry. These may be extreme cases, but they illustrate that an organization's culture is highly likely to determine what forms of leadership will succeed. In addition to culture, other important parts of the organizational context affecting leadership include its structure (Chapter 7), its human resource policies (Chapter 15), and its pattern of controls (Chapter 16).

This completes our consideration of the basic concepts and processes of leadership. In the next chapter we review various perspectives or models of leadership and a number of issues that arise in relation to how managerial leadership is demonstrated in organizational contexts.

managerial perspectives revisited

1

PERSPECTIVE 1: THE ORGANIZATIONAL CONTEXT As we have just discussed, the organizational context provides a significant situational element in determining the success or failure of a manager's leadership efforts. Those efforts, as we also have emphasized, can take place not only at the top of the organization, but virtually anywhere within it. For any given manager, however, the organization provides a major resource to support leadership: It provides position power. How managers choose to use that particular source of power will have a lot to do with how effective they will be. A particular aspect of the organizational context that impacts a manager's leadership attempts is the culture of the organization. Culture has the potential to either facilitate or hinder those leadership efforts, and a manager needs to understand the nature of that culture to be effective.

2

PERSPECTIVE 2: THE HUMAN FACTOR Abraham Lincoln is generally acknowledged as a great leader. But, even he, like any leader, could not have accomplished very much of consequence without being able to work through other people. Lincoln could not do everything by himself, which he recognized, but he was masterful in his ability to influence other people. As we have stressed in this chapter, leadership is a social influence process, and Lincoln knew how to excel at this at a very high level of competence. Leadership is also a process of "enabling" the behavior of other people. Thus, effective leadership helps others to accomplish more than they would have without the leader's influence. Above all, therefore, leadership is a people-intensive and a people-assisting process.

3

PERSPECTIVE 3: MANAGING PARADOXES The process of managerial leadership involves dealing with a number of potential paradoxes. One of the most important is the ever-present danger of using too much or too little power. Striking that balance is a challenge for every leader in any type of organization. Leaders are expected to exert power, but have to be careful not to use it when unnecessary. They also have to decide how much power to share with followers and subordinates and how much to retain. On the surface, it would seem best to increase subordinate empowerment in many situations. With some types of tasks or decisions, however, especially those requiring fast action, managers need to retain their authority and responsibility. Also, not all followers may be up to the challenge of being empowered because of lack of knowledge, skills, or motivation. An additional decision faced by leaders is the relative emphasis to place on task-oriented versus people-oriented behaviors. An over-focus on one or the other is likely to lead to major problems.

 PERSPECTIVE 4. ENTREPRENEURIAL MIND-SET   Recently, some experts have argued that to be entrepreneurial and strategic at the same time, managers need not only an entrepreneurial mind-set but that they also need to exhibit leadership to establish such an entrepreneurial culture within their organizations.[52] Leaders must exhibit an entrepreneurial mind-set for followers to do the same. Additionally, leaders play an important role in helping their followers to develop an entrepreneurial mind-set and to foster the conditions and incentives for them to use it. For example, leaders can reward risk-taking actions on the part of their subordinates, thereby encouraging their creativity. Finally, leaders face the challenge of how the entrepreneurial skills they foster in their subordinates should ultimately be used.

concluding comments

Every manager should also want to be a leader, and an effective leader at that. Every manager has the potential to *become* a more effective leader. But, for most people, becoming an effective leader is not an easy or quick task. Most of us, unfortunately, are not endowed with brilliant leadership qualities. Therefore, we don't necessarily begin a managerial job or career with an extremely high degree of referent power. Rather, a managerial position provides us with a certain amount of position power, and we also probably have acquired at least some degree of expertise. From that point on, it is a matter of gaining additional expertise and building our own referent power based on our actions and the example we set. It's also a matter of learning how to diagnose situations where leadership is called for and how to get the most out of whatever resources we have available. Not easy, but doable.

To make accurate diagnoses of leadership situations requires reasonable insight into, and an accurate assessment of, several key elements: our own personal strengths, the attitudes and capabilities of those we are trying to lead, the nature of the jobs to be done, and the organizational environment. In other words, leadership is not just action. It involves good planning, good observation, and, especially, good thinking. Knowing what to look for is half the battle of knowing what to do in a leadership context.

Finally, it is important to keep in mind that effective leadership, despite attempts to oversimplify it, is a fairly complex topic. There are plenty of leadership dilemmas and paradoxes that make decisions difficult. For example: Act quickly and decisively, but take time to involve others and gain their commitment; use power, but don't overuse it; be consistent, but be flexible; be task oriented, but don't forget to be people oriented; and, like nuclear disarmament negotiators, "trust, but verify." Those who can master these contradictory pulls and tugs by looking at the big picture will be the ones who are more likely to become effective leaders in the long run.

Even in the short run, though, remember that leadership can be exercised almost anytime and anywhere in the organization by almost anyone, regardless of position or depth of experience. It can be exercised, that is, if you *want* to do so. In other words, intent counts for a lot in leadership and its effects.

key terms

coercive power   354
effective leadership   351
emotional intelligence   363
empowerment   360
expert power   356
influence tactics   359
leader–member exchange (LMX)
   theory   368

legitimate power (formal
   authority)   353
organizational leadership   350
people behaviors   364
personal power   352
position power   352
power   352
referent power   356

reward power   354
social intelligence   364
task behaviors   364
traits   361

test your comprehension

1. What is leadership? Why is it characterized as a social influence process?
2. Who can be expected to exhibit leadership in an organization?
3. What is *effective* leadership?
4. What is power?
5. Differentiate between *position power* and *personal power.*
6. What are the three types of position power?
7. Is the use of coercion to change behaviors an accepted method of leadership?
8. What kind of power are subordinates most likely to have? Why?
9. What is referent power, and how can it be developed?
10. What are four key issues managers need to consider when using power?
11. What are influence tactics? How are they related to power?

12. What is empowerment? Is it always a good idea?
13. What is the "locus of leadership"?
14. What are the three key variables in the leadership process in organizations?
15. According to current views of leadership, what traits are most likely to predict effective leadership?
16. What is emotional intelligence, and how does it differ from social intelligence?
17. Compare the two major categories of leader behavior.
18. Why is it important to consider the characteristics of followers?
19. Explain why LMX theory is considered a relationship-based rather than a leader-based approach.
20. How do the two major categories of situational variables affect the leadership process?

apply your understanding

1. Think of a specific leader in your work situation, in a friendship group, on a sports team, or in the news. What types of power does he or she appear to use? How does he or she use these different types of power? Would you consider this person to be an effective leader? Why or why not?

2. Do you think people are born leaders? Are there specific traits that can be seen early in a person's life or career that identify that person as a leader? Can someone without these specific traits go on to become a leader?
3. Think of a leader you have had at work, school, or some other situation. How did your actions as a follower help or hinder that leader's effectiveness? What kind of a relationship did you have with the leader? Did it differ from the relationships the leader had with other members of the group? If there were different relationships, did this situation contribute to the group's effectiveness? Did it seem fair to you?
4. Using a specific situation, analyze the contributions of the leader, the followers, and the effectiveness of the leader.

practice your capabilities

Ted Willis has been hired as the new supervisor for the parts department of an automobile dealership. On his first day his manager, Linda Dunn, tells him, "You have a tough assignment. In the group you supervise there is an active troublemaker who has managed to keep from getting fired because he is the only employee who knows the inventory system. Three other employees follow his lead in consistently finding things to complain about, and the other four employees stay out of trouble by doing only what they are told." Linda handed the personnel files for the department employees to Ted. "The most important thing," Linda continued, "is that you change the sloppy way work is being done in the department and improve the accuracy in filling parts orders."

After hesitating a moment, Ted asked, "What *was* the former supervisor like?" "Well," replied Linda, "He had semi-retired on the job and let the employees do what they wanted. He was not concerned about accuracy in filling orders or maintaining the inventory. As I said before, it is a tough assignment, especially since all your employees have been with the dealership for more than five years, and most are friends with the owner."

Ted smiled, "I guess I have my work cut out for me."

1. How would you define the leadership problems in this situation?
2. What situational factors should Ted take into account before deciding on what leadership actions to take?
3. Identify the sources and amounts of power available to Ted and his new work group. How could they affect Ted's ability to lead this group?

closing case   DEVELOP YOUR CRITICAL THINKING

The New Supervisor

Grace Reed had been working at the County Medical Society Answering Service for 18 months when she received a promotion to shift supervisor. Grace was quite excited. She had worked very hard to develop the technical skills for answering calls and the interpersonal skills for communicating with patients and their doctors. Also, she had demonstrated her desire for the promotion by volunteering for overtime and holiday work. Finally, she had been promoted. However, now she faced problems she had not anticipated. How would she be able to convince her friends to take her seriously in her new role as their boss? How was she going to maintain her friendships and still maintain the discipline needed in this workplace?

The Medical Society's physicians were extremely disappointed in the level of dedication and care shown by the former county answering services, which handled not only physicians but business and private accounts as well. They decided to start their own answering service. Their operators would handle only medical calls, would be better trained to recognize urgent and emergency calls, would receive better benefits, and would be paid at a higher rate than the competing answering services. The doctors believed that by structuring the enterprise in this way, they could attract and retain the best possible workers. They would also have the largest available worker pool from which to choose and would not have to worry about being able to find replacement operators. They hired a professional manager to oversee the day-to-day operations, and each shift had a supervisor whose responsibilities included routine scheduling of workers; recognition of and planning for especially heavy days and shifts; handling complaints from doctors, hospitals, pharmacies, or patients concerning the handling of their calls; learning how to operate new equipment and subsequently training their operators in its use; and maintaining the high level of service required by the physicians. These duties were in addition to working her or his own eight-hour shift.

Grace was the fourth operator hired by the organization, and the first operator promoted from within the ranks to be supervisor. When she was first hired, she was lucky to train with a very experienced, competent operator. She modeled her own skills on those of her trainer and worked diligently to handle the most calls with the fewest mistakes and even fewer complaints. Where the other operators handled only 60 to 70 individual incoming lines, Grace routinely handled 100 to 120 lines, including some of those with the highest volumes of calls. She not only cleared her own calls but frequently assisted other operators in clearing their backlogged messages. When extremely difficult calls came in, such as suicide calls or nuisance calls from patients to whom even the doctors did not want to talk, it was often Grace who was asked to handle them. She rapidly developed excellent relationships with all of "her" doctors, their staffs, and even their families. During her first year, she was named operator of the month five times. In her second year, she worked with the existing supervisors to learn how to schedule the workers and received advanced training in the other office operations and procedures beyond answering calls.

Although the work was extremely fast paced and required concentration, there was always time for talking with the other operators, joking, and having fun. Strong friendships grew among the operators, who frequently socialized after hours and on their days off. There was a strong feeling of family in the office. The high levels of training and pay led to extremely low turnover rates. There were always waiting lists of applicants for the positions. If an operator wished to leave, he or she had no problem finding work at hospitals or for the phone company. Morale was generally high due to the respect the operators felt they received from "their" doctors for the high-quality work they performed, the higher levels of

pay and benefits they received in comparison with operators at other organizations, and the high degree of friendship among operators.

Her friends at the answering service threw Grace a party when she received her promotion. Everyone who wasn't working attended. Everyone was happy for her and sincerely wished her well. They all knew now that you could be promoted from the ranks! Grace was anxious to assume her new responsibilities and even try some new procedures she had been devising.

Within a month, Grace wasn't nearly as happy with her promotion as she had thought she would be. Her friends, who were now her subordinates as well, didn't seem to pay attention to her suggestions concerning their job performance. They ignored her instructions and frequently treated them as a joke. She worked many hours planning schedules only to have the operators switch shifts, leave early, or arrive late, saying they were sure she wouldn't mind because she understood all of their personal complications with their romantic relationships. She was their friend after all; of course, they knew she would cut them some slack. And her best friends seemed to be some of the worst offenders.

Grace soon realized that her new position was missing one thing—authority to go with her new responsibilities. She had no authority to sanction any of her subordinates: She couldn't dock their pay, make them work overtime, or cut back on their hours. She couldn't shorten their lunch breaks or eliminate their coffee breaks. Any such sanctions could only come from the overall company manager. If she tried to insist that a new procedure be used or that scheduled hours be worked and the operator balked, she had no recourse. If she complained to the manager, she would be viewed as unable to do her job. She couldn't complain to her friends, because they were part of the problem. She tried acting very authoritarian and harshly insisting on the new methods. She was met with hostility, and her friends stopped talking to her. One day she had had enough and berated a group of her friends about how they gave her no respect, they were uncooperative, and they weren't doing their jobs, and she was fed up with it. After all, she didn't ask them to do anything she wasn't willing or able to do herself. Morale was plummeting (hers as well as the other operators') and productivity was falling. Grace felt like a failure at the job she had worked so hard to get, and, even beyond that, she felt she was losing her friends.

Grace knew that something was going to have to change. She needed to try something new, to somehow regain the respect of her subordinates and find a new way to inspire improved performance and efficiency and restore morale. And she had to accomplish all this while maintaining her friendships with the other operators.

Questions

1. Which traits, skills, and behaviors associated with successful leaders does Grace possess? Are there characteristics she could enhance to improve her leadership ability?

2. Why did Grace have problems making changes and maintaining discipline when she first was promoted to a position that required leadership?

Source: Personal communication to the authors.

3. Analyze Grace's leadership situation in terms of her sources of power: Are there types of power she couldn't or shouldn't use? What types of power could she draw on, and how could she use those types to greatest effect?

4. Are there substitutes for leadership present in this situation? What neutralizers must Grace overcome to be an effective leader?

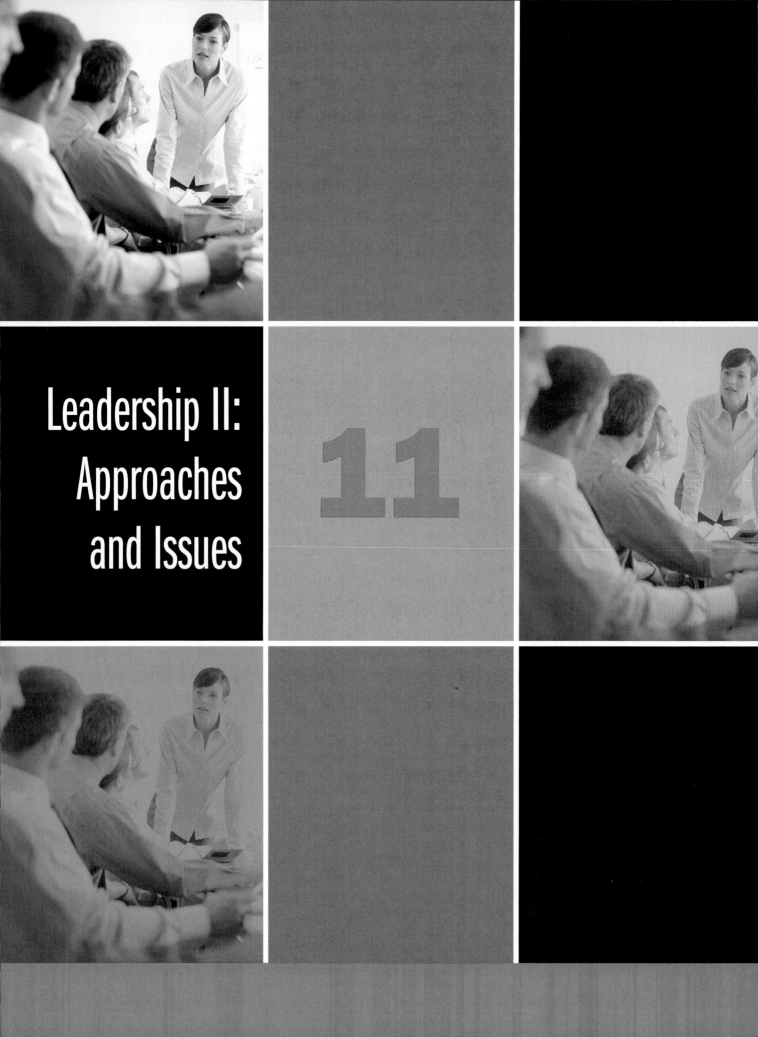

Leadership II: Approaches and Issues

11

■

Compare and contrast the various approaches to,
and theories of, leadership.

■

Describe the similarities and differences between leadership
and management.

■

Differentiate between charismatic, transformational,
and transactional leaders.

■

Discuss e-leadership.

■

Analyze the effects of culture on theories of leadership.

■

Explain the ways in which an individual can improve her/his
own leadership capabilities.

Dealing with Disaster

When terrorists attacked New York's World Trade Center on September 11, 2001, managers of companies located in the buildings faced an unexpected and devastating disaster. Even though many had contingency plans, they never anticipated the massive scope and life-threatening danger of this attack.

Both Marsh Inc., the world's largest insurance broker, and Martin Progressive, a fast-growing technology consulting firm, had offices in the twin towers. Marsh's CEO was not there when the attack occurred, but Martin Progressive's cofounder and 19 colleagues were on the 77th floor of the north tower when the first jet hit. Despite differences in organizational size, managers of both companies demonstrated leadership in handling the disaster's far-reaching repercussions.

Of the nearly 2,000 Marsh employees and managers working in the WTC, 315 lost their lives. CEO John Sinnott and his managers placed the highest priority on responding to employees' needs. First they established an emergency call center where employee volunteers worked the phones to locate missing colleagues and field families' inquiries. They also reserved hotel rooms where families of missing employees could wait for news. The CEO, senior managers, and human resources personnel met with the families twice daily to provide updates, answer questions, and offer comfort.

Almost immediately, Sinnott realized that many of Marsh's 36,000 employees worldwide would be upset. "Early after the attacks, we also had to think about the people who had made it out of the building or people who knew colleagues who were missing," Sinnott says. "They were traumatized." Therefore, he brought in professionals to counsel surviving employees and victims' families. Less than three weeks after the attacks, he also arranged to televise a nondenominational memorial service held in Manhattan so thousands of employees around the world could participate.

Meanwhile, other Marsh managers focused on getting the business back on track as quickly as possible. When the twin towers fell, the company lost 600,000 square feet of office space and vital computer capacity. Managers scrambled to relocate the displaced employees to company offices throughout the area. They also worked with partner companies to quickly restore the technology and data fueling Marsh's customer service systems.

Looking back, Sinnott stresses that Marsh's contingency plans "really did not contemplate the magnitude of this sort of event." Yet, because the corporate culture places a high value on people, managers and employees could make value-driven decisions when disaster struck. "There's not one person who can take credit for this," the CEO notes. "The entire firm had to pull together." He adds that highly visible leadership—

Managers at companies such as Marsh, Inc., and Martin Progressive, located in the World Trade Center, were accustomed to shepherding their companies in and out of trouble prior to 9/11. Following 9/11, however, they found their employees wanted a completely different kind of leadership from them. For many of these managers, the event required a level of leadership they have never before imagined.

evidenced by the senior managers' remaining in constant communication with employees and their families, for example—was a major factor in getting Marsh through the difficult weeks following the attack.

Like Marsh's managers, John Kneeley of Martin Progressive responded to the attack by putting people first. After his office windows shattered, Kneeley calmed his employees as a coworker stuffed two briefcases with financial records and other vital data. He then led everyone downstairs to safety and phoned his Chicago office, which was serving as a communications center because others were calling in to report or receive news.

Kneeley knew his firm's survival depended in large part on his leadership at that moment: "There are going to be 40 people who are looking to see how I respond to this." He told his employees, "Let's start making lists: Who was up in the building, who should have been up in the building, and people we shouldn't need to worry about." Yet Kneeley also realized that many small companies in the WTC had gone out of business following a 1993 terrorist bombing. "They failed for reasons of not reacting quickly enough, not having a contingency plan," he says. Knowing this, he kept reassuring employees that Martin Progressive would survive.

However, Kneeley soon learned that his employees were more concerned about the effect on people's lives than about their employer's survival. "My response at first was very mechanical, 'the company's coming back together,' before I realized [employees] didn't really care," he says. "I think I was ill-informed in terms of what people were looking to me for. People were looking for the humanitarian part." As a result, in the hectic days that followed, he made time for long conversations with coworkers who were shocked by the attack but relieved and thankful that no Martin Progressive employees had been hurt.

Sources: Adapted from Joseph B. Treaster, "Marsh & McLennan Is Maintaining a Policy of Silence," *New York Times*, September 10, 2002, p. C6; "Executive Perspective: John Sinnott, Chairman & CEO, Marsh Inc.," *Risk Management*, September 2002, pp. 20+; Thomas S. Mulligan, Jeff Leeds, and Lisa Girion, "After the Attack: The Victims; For CEOs, a Test Like No Other," *Los Angeles Times*, September 21, 2001, pp. A1+.

strategic overview

In the introduction to the previous chapter on leadership, we explained the strategic importance of leadership in the organization. Leaders at all levels who think and act strategically lead to higher-performing organizations. Two of the most important resources that they manage are human capital and social capital.[1] The opening case in this chapter clearly shows the critical nature of leaders managing the human relationships. While the events of 9/11 affected the strategies of both Marsh Inc., and Martin Progressive, leaders in both of these firms had to focus on the human concerns with sensitivity to the interpersonal relationships. Not only were these humane actions, they were a necessity. These human concerns had to be managed before other issues related to the business operations or changes in the firm's strategy or its implementation could be made a priority.

As explained in the introduction to Chapter 10, strategic leadership entails developing a vision and empowering others to achieve it. To do so often requires that changes in the organization be made to implement the strategy chosen. As a result, some leaders attempt to use a transformational leadership style (to be discussed in detail later in this chapter) to make the changes needed. In many ways, the leaders at Marsh Inc., and Martin Progressive displayed characteristics of transformational leaders by being sensitive to people's needs and open to learning. The situation was unique—one they had never faced before. Thus, they had to learn how to respond and prioritize what needed to be done. As noted later in this chapter, leaders also have to integrate features of a transactional style as well. Since most leaders are also managers, they are responsible for distributing rewards to their employees. Employees expect to be rewarded for their work, and leaders must decide who and how each is rewarded.

Today, leaders who operate in a purely domestic environment often are impacted by global competition and an environment that challenges them to deal with issues related to the diversity of cultures. In fact, leaders typically may have team members located in multiple countries and/or with a diversity of cultural values. As such, they must be sensitive to the cultural differences in the leadership style they display. Some authors argue that while cultural diversity presents both challenges and opportunities for leaders, adaptation to the characteristics of other cultures may be necessary to be globally competitive. For example, in China and other Asian countries, social relationships form the basis for the conduct of business. In a sense, these relationships are a form of social capital. On the other hand, leaders of firms from Western countries, where independence is a prominent cultural characteristic, may be at a disadvantage in building the successful alliances necessary to be competitive in some international markets. They may need to develop a new set of cultural values in order to build and sustain trusting relationships that will enable their firms to compete more effectively in these markets.[2] ■

The events of September 11, 2001, were dramatic and unprecedented. But they also served to highlight the critical necessity for managers to be able to engage in leadership. Leadership, in fact, is central to management and crucial to organizations. Additionally, leadership is a complex subject. For all of these reasons, we devote two chapters to the topic to ensure thorough coverage of critical leadership issues facing managers. The academic research literature is replete with a multitude of studies of leadership, resulting in a number of approaches or "theories of leadership" that provide different ways to think about the topic. Additionally, because of the "romance of leadership"[3] on the part of both managers and the general public, scholars and consultants continue to provide a substantial amount of advice about how to be an effective leader. In this chapter we try to highlight important leadership approaches and eliminate some of the "noise" from contradictory research findings, various supposedly informed opinions and "how-to" prescriptions.

In the previous chapter, we examined some of the fundamentals about leadership: its definition; the connections of influence and power to the leadership process; and the interrelated and interactive roles of leaders, followers, and the situation in determining the success of any leadership efforts. Those discussions provide the basis for taking a deeper look at leadership in this chapter. Since leadership is a more complicated process than the popular media would sometimes have us believe, we begin by viewing the process through different lenses or models, emphasizing the point that there is more than one useful way to analyze the process. Later, we consider some of the current issues that are prominent in both the academic and popular press with the intent of providing a richer picture of how leadership is being enacted in organizations here at the beginning of the twenty-first century. Finally, we take into account all that we have covered in both the previous and the present chapters to provide some guidelines to consider for capitalizing on your own leadership opportunities in organizational settings.

DIFFERENT APPROACHES TO UNDERSTANDING LEADERSHIP

The leader. The followers. The situation. Each is essential for telling the story of leadership. But it is the *interactions* of the three variables that determine the outcomes of the leadership process in particular circumstances. Common sense, as well as theories of leadership, would tell us that no specific approach to leadership, regardless of the characteristics of the leader, the followers, and the situation, will work equally well all the time. Thus, since the 1960s or so, a number of different conceptual approaches to leadership have been developed. Each of these has focused on describing combinations of key variables necessary for leadership effectiveness. Several of the most prominent approaches, usually identified by the names of their major proponents, are:

- Blake and Mouton's "Managerial Grid"
- Hersey and Blanchard's Situational Leadership model
- Fiedler's Leadership Contingency Theory
- House's Path-Goal Theory
- Vroom and Yetton's Normative Decision Model
- Substitutes for Leadership

As you read about each of these different ways of looking at and thinking about leadership, focus on the particular parts of the leader/follower/situation combination that are being emphasized. The relative emphases that the different approaches put on each of these three components of the leadership process are summarized in Exhibit 11.1. None of these theories or approaches has "the" correct way of viewing leadership, but each provides an interesting and helpful window for making sense of leadership complexity.

Blake and Mouton's "Managerial Grid"

This approach, developed by psychologists Blake and Mouton, was one of the earliest to grow out of research on the topic of leadership.[4] Blake and Mouton, using findings from a number of studies, proposed that leaders should view their role as consisting of two primary dimensions: a focus on the tasks to be accomplished and a focus on the people performing them. The term "**Managerial Grid**" was used because it was proposed that these two dimensions could be thought as going from low (a score of 1) to high (a score of 9). Thus, a graph could be constructed, as shown in Exhibit 11.2, with the x axis

managerial grid a method for measuring the degree to which managers are task oriented and people oriented

exhibit 11.1

Leadership Perspectives:
Relative Emphasis on Leader,
Follower, and Situation

Perspective	EMPHASIS ON:		
	Leader	Follower	Situation
Blake and Mouton: Managerial Grid	XX		
Hersey and Blanchard: Situational Leadership Model	X	XX	
Fiedler: Contingency Leadership Model	XX		XX
House: Path-Goal Theory	XX	XX	XX
Vroom/Yetton: Normative Decision Model	XX	X	XX
Substitutes for Leadership		XX	

X = Strong Emphasis
XX = Very Strong Emphasis

being the degree to which a manager was task oriented, and the y axis the degree to which a manager was people oriented. Using this system, managers could be rated on each dimension (by themselves or by others, such as subordinates), and their position plotted on the graph (for example: 3 on the x or task-oriented axis, and 7 on the y or people-oriented axis).

The central theme of the Blake and Mouton approach was that the best managers would be those highest on both dimensions—a high-high leader—or, in terms of the grid, a 9,9. Those who were high on task orientation but low on people concern (9,1), or vice versa (1,9), were viewed as obviously lacking in one or the other of the two critical skills needed for leadership success. Those who were in the middle on both dimensions (5,5) were regarded as

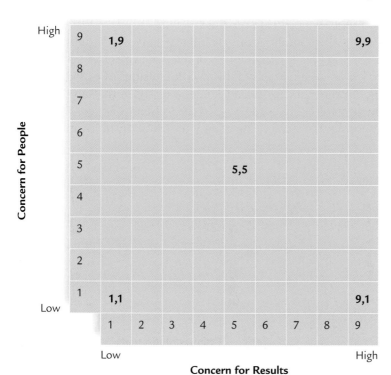

exhibit 11.2

**Blake and Mouton:
The Leadership Grid**

Source: Adapted from R. R. Blake and A. A. McCanse, *Leadership Dilemma— Grid Solutions* (formerly *The Managerial Grid* by R. R. Blake and J. S. Mouton) (Houston: Gulf Publishing Company, 1991), p. 29.

average or mediocre leaders, neither highly successful nor definite failures. Note that this approach to leadership puts heavy emphasis on the leader, and gives relatively little attention to the attributes of the followers and, especially, the characteristics of the situation. A high-high leader (or anyone rated close to 9 on both dimensions) was thought to be the best kind of leader, irrespective of who the followers are and what kinds of situations or contexts confront the leader. The "managerial grid" approach could thus be thought of as a "universal" leadership theory—that is, one that says that there is one absolute best type of leader—one who is high on both a task orientation and a people orientation—under *all* conditions. This approach, developed in the 1960s, was, at least to some extent, anchored in the available scholarly research evidence of the time, and had a simplicity that was highly appealing to practicing managers. It helped to highlight two dimensions of leader behavior that are clearly important. On the other hand, it clearly ignores many important situational variables that affect both how leaders behave and how successful they are. Research has not confirmed that one type of leadership style, whether the so-called high-high style or any other style, is universally appropriate and effective.

Hersey and Blanchard's Situational Leadership Model

situational leadership model a model that states that different types of appropriate leadership are "contingent" on some other variable, in this case "the situation"

The **situational leadership model** is one of the earlier contingency approaches to leadership.[5] It thus is a model that states that different types of appropriate leadership are "contingent" on—or depend on—some other variable, in this case "the situation." Although labeled a "situational" approach, the model focuses primarily on a single aspect of the situation: the followers—specifically, on their "readiness" to engage in learning new tasks. Subordinates' readiness, as used in this approach, consists of two parts: their ability (in relation to a specific task), and their willingness to undertake the new task. The behavior of leaders is also considered to consist of two factors: supportiveness and directiveness. Supportiveness is similar to high people orientation, and directiveness is similar to high task orientation. The model advocates that certain combinations of these two types of leader behaviors are best or most appropriate for a given set of subordinate readiness levels.

The specific details of this model are shown in Exhibit 11.3. As can be seen, combining low and high levels of the two aspects of subordinates' readiness, and low and high levels of the two dimensions of possible leader behavior, results in different proposed leadership styles that are presumed to be most effective for each of the four sets of circumstances. Thus, for tasks in which subordinates are low on ability and low on motivation to undertake

exhibit 11.3

Hersey and Blanchard: Situational Leadership Model

Source: Adapted from P. Hersey, K. H. Blanchard, and D. E. Johnson, *Management of Organizational Behavior: Leading Human Resources,* 8th ed. (Upper Saddle River, NJ: Prentice Hall, 2001).

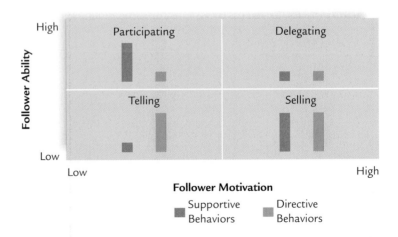

them, leaders should, according to the model, exhibit relatively low support-iveness but high directiveness. That is, leaders should firmly set goals, provide explicit directions and deadlines, and monitor performance closely. The appropriate leadership style for this combination of circumstances is given the informal label "telling" by Hersey and Blanchard.

When subordinates have low ability for the tasks but high initial moti-vation to perform them, then leaders should exhibit both strong supportive-ness and strong directiveness. Thus, leaders should be highly encouraging, but at the same time should take charge in defining objectives and explaining methods for performing the tasks. This combination of leader behavior is given the label "selling."

For the third set of subordinates' readiness characteristics—high ability but low motivation—leaders need to utilize subordinates' ideas and sugges-tions as much as possible in order to strengthen their interest in the task and to obtain their commitment; yet they need not be highly directive since the subordinates' capabilities for performing the tasks are already high. The style most appropriate for these conditions: "participating."

The final combination of followers' characteristics, high ability and high willingness to perform, is the appropriate setting, according to the model, for both low supportiveness and low directiveness on the part of the leader. In other words, for this situation, the leader can rely on a high degree of delega-tion and expect followers to perform well on their own with a minimum of leader involvement. Thus, the recommended style: "delegating."

There is much about the Hersey and Blanchard Situational Leadership Model that is intuitively appealing. First, as with the Blake and Mouton Managerial Grid approach, it is a relatively simple and straightforward model. Second, the summarizing leadership style labels ("telling," etc.) are under-standable and easy to remember. Third, like the Managerial Grid approach, the model uses research findings to emphasize two important types of leadership behaviors, people-oriented ("supportiveness") and task-oriented ("directive-ness"), that form the four categories of leadership styles.

Despite these positive features of the model, there are some fairly obvious problems with its implementation. Subordinate readiness levels, for example, typically do not come in simple high and low combinations. Often, subordinates will be around the middle on both ability and motivation or willingness, rather than definitely high or definitely low on one or both. Also, the model requires leaders to make an accurate assessment of the two subordinate readiness char-acteristics, and this is not always easy to do—especially in the case of trying to gauge their "willingness" to perform particular tasks. Probably the most critical deficiency in the Hersey and Blanchard model is that it considers only subordi-nate readiness as a feature of the task and organizational environment. It essen-tially ignores other possible major features of the context such as the amount and type of interaction with other individuals or units in the organization, the culture of the group or organization, the history of past events, and the like. Subordinate or follower readiness is important for any leader to consider, but by itself does not determine how leaders should behave nor the success of their efforts.

Fiedler's Leadership Contingency Theory

This theory, also developed several decades ago, grew out of a program of Fiedler's research that centered on leaders' attitudes toward their co-workers. Specifically, leaders were asked to rate, on a series of scales (e.g., "pleasant–unpleasant," "supportive–hostile," "open–guarded"), the person from their

LPC (least preferred co-worker) theory a contingency theory of leadership that identifies the types of situations in which task-oriented or person-oriented leaders would be most effective

present or past work experience with whom they could work least well. This person was termed by Fiedler their "**least preferred coworker**" **(LPC)**.[6] Thus, leaders who rated this person relatively harshly received low LPC scores, whereas leaders who rated their least preferred coworker relatively favorably received high LPC scores. Basically, a leader's LPC score was interpreted to indicate the degree to which a leader was especially task oriented (low LPC score) or person oriented (high LPC score).

Fiedler's theory was that leadership effectiveness would be contingent on the type of leader (low or high LPC) *and* the relative degree of favorability of the situation for the leader. According to the theory, a favorable situation for the leader exists when three conditions are present:

- when relations with subordinates are good
- when the task is highly structured
- when the leader has considerable position power

An unfavorable situation would be when these conditions are the opposite. For example, a vice president of finance who has been assigned the task of preparing the company's annual report, who will be able to work with the same team that produced last year's report, and who also is regarded as excellent by top management would be in a highly favorable situation. In contrast, the leadership situation would be less favorable for a senior manager asked to develop a new product in conjunction with a subordinate who had hoped to be promoted into the position now held by the new manager. The theory predicts, as shown in Exhibit 11.4, that *low* LPC leaders, that is, those most task-oriented, are most effective in highly favorable *or* highly unfavorable situations, such as that encountered by the VP of finance in our example. On the other hand, high LPC (high relationship-oriented) leaders will do best in moderately favorable or moderately unfavorable situations. The reasoning, according to the theory, is that task-oriented leaders do not need to be especially sensitive to interpersonal relations in very favorable situations, and in very unfavorable situations a strong task orientation by the leader is the only approach that will work. Conversely, when situations are neither especially favorable nor unfavorable, the theory presumes that leaders more attuned to other people's feelings will do best.

exhibit 11.4
LPC Theory

SITUATION

Favorable (for leader)	Unfavorable (for leader)
Good subordinate relationships	Poor subordinate relationships
Highly structured task	Unstructured task
Leader with high amount of position power	Leader lacks position power

LEADERS

Low LPC Perspective	High LPC Perspective
Rates least preferred coworker harshly	Rates least preferred coworker favorably
Task oriented	Person oriented
Most effective when situation is either highly favorable or highly unfavorable	Most effective when situation is neither highly favorable nor highly unfavorable

Fiedler's theory has been the object of considerable research over the years. Reviews of this research indicate some support for it, but various details of the theory have been criticized.[7] Probably its chief value is that when it was originated in the 1960s, it highlighted the importance of the nature of the situations leaders face, and it suggested how those situational conditions could make it harder or easier for leaders of particular types to be effective. The theory therefore has a very important implication: It is more difficult for leaders to change their styles than it is for the situation to be changed (or to match leaders with particular types of situations). It also clearly is a contingency theory and not a universal approach in which one type of leadership should work best in all situations.

House's Path–Goal Theory

House and his associates in the 1970s proposed what was termed a **path–goal theory of leadership**.[8] Essentially, this perspective emphasized that the leader's job was to increase subordinate satisfaction and effort by "increasing personal payoffs to subordinates for work-goal attainment and making the path to these payoffs easier to travel by clarifying it, reducing roadblocks and pitfalls, and increasing the opportunities for personal satisfaction en route."[9]

The path–goal analysis of the factors involved in leadership effectiveness draws heavily from expectancy theories of motivation (to be discussed in the next chapter). Thus, it assumes that the leader's role is to influence subordinates' estimated probabilities for being able to convert their efforts into performance that leads to desired rewards. Also, much like several of the other leadership approaches, path–goal theory emphasizes two basic types of leader behavior: supportive leadership (people oriented) and directive leadership (task oriented). In addition, as with LPC and other contingency theories, path–goal theory assumes that a particular leadership approach will work better in some task situations than in others. As illustrated in Exhibit 11.5, if tasks

path–goal theory of leadership a contingency theory of leadership that focuses on the leader's role in increasing subordinate satisfaction and effort by increasing personal payoffs for goal attainment and making the path to these payoffs easier

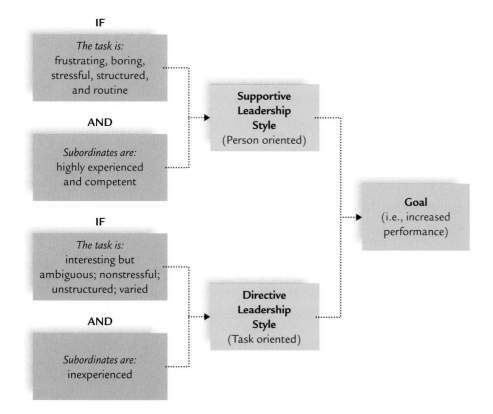

exhibit 11.5

Path–Goal Theory

Source: Adapted from R. J. House, "A Path-Goal Theory of Leader Effectiveness," *Administrative Science Quarterly* 16, no. 5 (1971), pp. 321–39.

are frustrating, boring, or highly stressful, supportive leadership behavior is assumed to help increase subordinate enjoyment and reduce anxiety, thereby raising effort and satisfaction. If tasks are intrinsically enjoyable and interesting, it is assumed that supportive, people-oriented leadership will have little net effect.

Directive, task-oriented leadership behavior, according to the theory, becomes especially important when tasks are varied and unstructured *and* when subordinates are inexperienced. Such directive behavior is assumed to reduce ambiguities in the situation and to clarify the paths to successful task performance. On the other hand (see Exhibit 11.5), if subordinates are highly experienced and competent *and* tasks are relatively structured, directive leadership behavior will be superfluous and possibly even resented. In this respect, path–goal theory has similarities to Hersey and Blanchard's Situational Leadership Model.

As with Fiedler's LPC contingency theory, the main contribution of House's path–goal theory has been to provide additional insights into the interactions among leader behavior, task characteristics, and follower competencies; and to identify which interactions are most likely to result in more productive and satisfying outcomes. It differs from Fiedler's theory in that House assumes leaders can modify their styles to suit the situation rather than having to have the situation changed to fit the leader. The path–goal theory's primary value is in helping potential leaders to think systematically about what types of behavior on their part might work best in what types of situations.

Vroom and Yetton's Normative Decision Model

normative decision model
a contingency model that prescribes standards to determine the extent to which subordinates should be allowed to participate in decision making

Strictly speaking, Vroom and Yetton's **normative decision model** is not a model of leadership.[10] However, it addresses a major issue faced by leaders: the extent to which subordinates should participate in decision making. It is also a contingency model in that it is designed to help leaders determine how much and what type of subordinate participation to use in particular situations. The model is not simply analytical; it also *prescribes* when to use participation as a result of that analysis. Thus, it is called a "normative" model because it provides standards or rules for making such decisions.

The model focuses on two key variables that determine the effectiveness of decisions when measured by group performance: quality and acceptance. Decision quality refers to the merit or degree of excellence of the course of action that is chosen. The quality of a decision becomes more crucial as the consequences of that decision become more important and when considerable variability exists among alternatives. Examples would be when important goals are being set or when major procedural changes are to be made. Decisions about relatively trivial matters such as where to place a piece of office equipment would not require significant decision quality.

Decision acceptance refers to the amount of subordinate commitment to implementing the chosen alternative. Acceptance is especially important when high levels of subordinate effort and motivation are needed to execute decisions after they are made. If a decision can be implemented directly by the leader without involving followers, for example, then it would not matter a great deal whether decision acceptance was high.

The Vroom and Yetton model proposes that leaders have five basic decision-making procedures available, as shown in Exhibit 11.6. These procedures range from highly autocratic (termed AI in the model), where the manager makes the decision or solves the problem alone, to highly participative

exhibit 11.6
Normative Decision-making
Model: Decision-making Styles

Decision Style[a]	Definition
AI	Leader makes the decision alone.
AII	Leader asks for information from team members but makes the decision alone. Team members may or may not be informed what the situation is.
CI	Leader shares situation with each team member and asks for information and evaluation. Team members do not meet as a team, and the leader alone makes the decision.
CII	Leader and team members meet as a team to discuss the situation, but the leader makes the decision.
G	Leader and team members meet as a team to discuss the situation, and the team makes the decision.

[a]A = autocratic   C = consultative   G = group

Sources: V. H. Vroom and P. W. Yetton, *Leadership and Decision-Making* (Pittsburgh, PA: University of Pittsburgh Press, 1973); V. H. Vroom and A. G. Jago, *The New Leadership: Managing Participation in Organizations* (Englewood Cliffs, NJ: Prentice Hall, 1988).

(termed G), where the group itself makes the decision. In determining which procedure to use in given situations, a manager could train herself to ask a series of yes–no questions, in a decision-tree style of inquiry, as shown in Exhibit 11.7. As can be seen, the decision tree involves eight components of a situation—the amount of information possessed by the manager and the subordinates, the likelihood that subordinates will accept an autocratic decision, and so forth. By answering this series of questions about the situation, a leader should be able to choose a procedure that will result in effective decisions.

This model (and later versions of it) has been found to have a fairly high level of validity in predicting successful decisions, and it has been used extensively in management development programs.[11] However, as previously noted, although it is a contingency model that is relevant to leadership, it only deals with a portion of total leadership behavior: the extent of participation in group decision making.

Substitutes for Leadership

One other important contingency approach needs to be considered. It is not a leadership theory as such, but it raises significant issues for managers to consider—namely, in some circumstances, there can be **substitutes for leadership**.[12] That is, a greater use of leadership behaviors is not always the only, or even the best, solution for some managerial problems. In certain work settings, other approaches can at least partially substitute for the need for leadership or can sometimes overcome poor leadership. Examples of some possible substitutes for leadership are shown in Exhibit 11.8.

Extensive training and experience, for example, can lessen the need for leadership direction in such fast-paced and complex jobs as air traffic controller or police emergency work. The decision speed required in these job situations often would not allow time for intervention by a leader, so prior training substitutes for such influence. Furthermore, in many technical and professional jobs, high levels of formal education reduce the need for close supervision. It is safe to assume that an attorney or scientist or computer programmer working for a company will probably not need the same amount of supervision, and certainly not the same type, as an employee with few skills

substitutes for leadership
alternative approaches that can at least partially substitute for the need for leadership or can sometimes overcome poor leadership

exhibit 11.7

Normative Decision-making Model for Leaders' Use of Participation: Decision-Tree Questions

Source: Adapted and reprinted from *Leadership and Decision-making* by Victor H. Vroom and Phillip W. Yetton, by permission of the University of Pittsburgh Press. © 1973 by University of Pittsburgh Press.

Decision Method

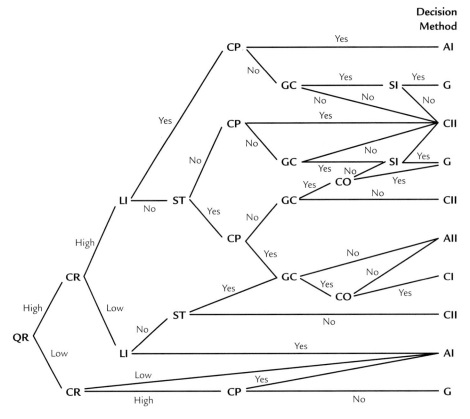

State the Problem

QR How important is the quality of this decision?

CR How important is subordinate commitment to the decision?

LI Do you have sufficient information to make a high-quality decision?

ST Is the problem well structured?

CP If you were to make the decision by yourself, is it reasonably certain that your subordinates would be committed to it?

GC Do subordinates share the organization goals to be attained in solving this problem?

CO Is conflict among subordinates over preferred solutions likely?

SI Do subordinates have sufficient information to make a high-quality decision?

exhibit 11.8

Examples of Possible Substitutes for Leadership

Source: Adapted from S. Kerr and J. M. Jermier, "Substitutes for Leadership: Their Meaning and Measurement," *Organizational Behavior and Human Performance* 22, no. 3 (1978), pp. 375–403.

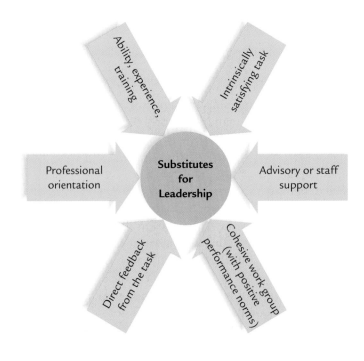

working in a relatively new position. Too much attempted leadership of such professionals would probably hinder, rather than facilitate, their performance. Similarly, workers in jobs that supply considerable amounts of intrinsic satisfaction, such as those involving the development of an exciting new product or service, would be unlikely to need leaders to increase their motivation. These examples point to the conclusion that the amount and type of leadership required can vary considerably from situation to situation. Too much attempted leadership, or too much of a particular leadership approach, sometimes can be as dangerous for the organization—and for the would-be leader—as not enough leadership.

In addition to substitutes for leadership, there are also "**neutralizers of leadership**," that is, aspects of the organization or work situation that can defeat the best efforts of leaders. Examples would be inflexible organization procedures that do not give leaders sufficient freedom of choice, or an organizational compensation policy that does not allow them to appropriately reward exceptional performance. Thus, neutralizers, like substitutes, emphasize the importance of situational contingencies and how they can impact the effectiveness of leadership. In the case of neutralizers, however, that impact is often dysfunctional.

neutralizers of leadership
aspects of the organization or work situation that can defeat the best efforts of leaders

CONTEMPORARY LEADERSHIP ISSUES

In recent years, scholars in the field of leadership have raised several issues that have become increasingly important for management practice. These issues include: the similarities and differences between leading and managing; charismatic leadership; transformational leadership; e-age (electronic-age) leadership; and leadership across different national cultures. Each raises interesting implications for the leadership function of managing.

Leading and Managing: The Same or Different?

Leading and managing are two activities that take place in all organizations, and the two terms often are used interchangeably. The processes appear to be similar in many respects. The question is: Do they completely overlap, or are they distinctly different? The answer depends on how the two terms are defined, especially "managing."

The case for viewing leadership as different from management has been made in recent years by several prominent behavioral science scholars.[13] It focuses on the role of leaders in creating vision for organizations or units, promoting major changes in goals and procedures, setting and communicating new directions, and inspiring subordinates. This set of activities is then contrasted with more mundane, task-oriented "managerial" functions such as dealing with interpersonal conflict, planning and organizing, and, in general, implementing goals set by others (the leaders).

When leading and managing are defined in these ways, then, of course, they are different. However, if managing is considered from a broader perspective, as it is throughout this book, then the two activities do not differ as much as might appear on the surface. That is, managing *ought* to involve most of the kinds of activities that are included in the leader's role. Removing such "leading" activities from managing makes an artificial distinction between the two and relegates managing to a routine, almost trivial activity—which it is not. A Manager's Challenge, "New Wal-Mart Pharmacy Manager Offers Prescription for Change," describes someone who is simultaneously a manager *and* a leader.

a manager's challenge

Change

New Wal-Mart Pharmacy Manager Offers Prescription for Change

After nearly 10 years with Wal-Mart, Kimberly Brade landed her first management position. As head of the pharmacy department at the chain's Supercenter store in North Richland Hills, Texas, she was responsible for a team of employees who fill prescriptions and provide advice to thousands of customers every week. Wal-Mart began putting pharmacies into its stores in 1978. Almost 10 percent of the world's largest retailer's sales are generated by its pharmacies. Managing and staffing these pharmacies can be challenging because many are open seven days a week and, in some cases, operate nearly 24 hours a day. Wal-Mart's managers have responded by offering a variety of schedules that allow pharmacists to balance their work and personal lives. In addition, management invites hundreds of pharmacy students to intern at Wal-Mart stores during the year so they can gain a more realistic view of the job's requirements and activities.

Brade started working for Wal-Mart when she was just 16 years old. Seeking a job with some connection to medicine, she became a part-time pharmacy clerk in one of the chain's local stores while in high school. The experience convinced her to enroll in a pharmacy program at college, even as she continued to work for Wal-Mart. Before graduating with her pharmaceutical degree, she joined the retailer's 10-week internship program. After graduation, she was assigned to manage the chain's North Richland Hills pharmacy.

In Brade's view, an effective manager needs the same qualities as an effective pharmacist: good listening skills, empathy, and the ability to offer appropriate advice. Managing a high-volume pharmacy inside a huge Wal-Mart store is difficult because the store must compete with small, locally owned pharmacies. "For a company this size, customer service is key," she said. Brade was careful to give her staff the scheduling and supervisory support they needed to give customers some personal attention—and she expected her staff to give her the support she needed to properly dispense medicines and respond to customers' drug-related questions.

Still, Brade tried to do even more for her customers than was just required. Pharmacists, she observed, "can offer a lot more to the health care system than they are now, with only a little change in the way the community pharmacy operates." Wal-Mart, for example, now sponsors in-store diabetes and blood pressure screening and has begun supporting women's health and children's fitness programs. Some stores offer free vaccines to children.

Brade sees opportunities like this to set the direction for this type of grassroots change. She worked with her staff to better educate customers about their medical conditions and effectively coordinate their prescriptions with their treatments. "Working at retail, you are still in health care and you can do a lot to help people. Dealing with the customers is the part I enjoy the most," she said.

Sources: Mike Troy, "Wal-Mart Still Bullish on Supercenter Growth," *Drug Store News*, October 20, 2003, pp. 1–3; "In-Store Experience Helps Decide Direction," *Chain Drug Review*, July 22, 2002, pp. 68+; "Wal-Mart Earns Place Among Top Rx Providers," *Chain Drug Review*, August 5, 2002, p. 38.

The relation of leading to managing can be illustrated by use of a Venn diagram, similar to those encountered in mathematics classes. Such diagrams consist of circles that are completely independent of each other, circles that overlap one another completely, or circles that partially overlap. Imagine all the leaders from one organization in one circle and all the managers from that same organization in another. The two circles are likely to be partially, but not totally, separate (as shown in Exhibit 11.9). A person can be a leader, and a person can be a manager; but many people, such as Kimberly Brade, are *both* leaders and managers. Leadership is a very important component of management, but management involves more than just leadership. Thus, although not all leaders are managers, and not all managers are leaders, modern organizations need most of their managers to engage in leadership behavior such as fostering innovation and creativity, finding better ways to achieve or exceed goals, and inspiring

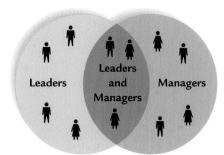

exhibit 11.9

The Overlapping Roles of Leaders and Managers

other people. Consequently, in this chapter and in this book, we view organizational leadership as a process that should be included as a significant part of the managerial role, but it is definitely not the total role.

Charismatic Leadership

As mentioned in the previous chapter, when we were reviewing types of personal power, charisma is an especially strong form of referent power. The term "charisma" has a theological origin and comes from the Greek word for "gift." It literally means "divinely conferred gift." Its relevance for organizational settings was first highlighted in the early decades of the twentieth century by sociologist Max Weber.[14] He described the **charismatic leader** as someone who has influence over others based on inspirational qualities of the individual rather than on that person's formal power or position. Thus, followers or subordinates are assumed to identify with that person because of those exceptional qualities. Many people, of course, would like to think they are endowed with charisma, but only relatively few people have these special powers. If they were common, they wouldn't be exceptional.

The term "charisma" has been used particularly in the political sphere to describe those who are especially influential with large numbers of people. Examples include historical figures such as Mahatma Gandhi, Nelson Mandela, Winston Churchill, Mother Teresa, Martin Luther King Jr., and John F. Kennedy. In the business world, such people as Lee Iacocca, Sam Walton, and Richard Branson come to mind.

It is only in the last couple of decades that the concept of charisma has been used explicitly in scholarly examinations of organizational leadership.[15] One of the first such analyses focused on the specific traits and behaviors of charismatic leaders, such as

- Strong needs for power
- High levels of self-confidence
- Strong beliefs in their own ideas[16]

charismatic leadership
leadership by someone who has influence over others based on individual inspirational qualities rather than formal power

From her humble beginnings in rural Mississippi, Oprah Winfrey (shown with Laura Bush) has become one of the most charismatic leaders of our time. In 1998, *Time* Magazine named her one of the 100 most influential people of the twentieth century. As the chairman of Harpo, Inc., she manages employees as she does audiences—with emotion and intimacy.

In terms of their behaviors, charismatic leaders, more than other types of leaders, are especially likely to:

- Model desired behavior
- Communicate high expectations for followers' performance
- Be concerned with, and try to influence, the impressions of others
- Emphasize ideals, values, and lofty goals

The last two points above are exemplified by the views of a business executive often described as charismatic: Herb Kelleher, founder of Southwest Airlines. He would always tell new employees: "I want you to be able to tell them [the employees' children] that being connected to Southwest Airlines ennobled and enriched your life—it made you bigger and stronger than you ever could have been alone."[17]

Another analysis of leadership from a charismatic perspective focuses on particular types of leaders' behaviors that seem to enhance effects on followers.[18] These include:

- Emphasizing a vision for the organization that represents a major, but achievable, change
- Taking innovative or unorthodox types of actions to achieve goals
- Demonstrating self-sacrifices on behalf of the organization

This perspective highlights the idea that anything leaders can do to create follower dissatisfaction with the status quo, to articulate compelling visions, and to offer innovative solutions, will increase followers' feelings of collective identity with their leaders and the probability of charisma being attributed to those leaders.[19]

Based on the several scholarly analyses just discussed, Exhibit 11.10 presents a summary set of attributes of charismatic leaders.

Since charisma is a type of "special power" possessed by relatively few people, can a typical manager or leader try to increase his or her charisma? It is clear that people cannot create this type of power simply by assuming they have it, or by asking for it or demanding it. It must be generated or conferred in some fashion. Although few managers have the personality traits to easily or spontaneously produce the levels of charisma that certain renowned business and political leaders have achieved, people in leadership positions can increase the chances that their subordinates will be motivated to follow them and work with and for them. The kinds of behavior, summarized in Exhibit 11.10, are ones that can be developed.

One final point should be raised about charisma: its potential downside. A highly charismatic and, indeed, overpowering leader does not always suit the requirements of the situation. Take, for example, the case of Christos Cotsakos, former CEO of online brokerage company E*TRADE. Widely viewed as charismatic, Cotsakos, among his other traits, moved extremely fast. He modeled that behavior for his subordinates, even going so far as to sponsor a day of Formula One racing for his top aides. (He spent his "spare time" working on his Ph.D. in economics at the University of London.) He also was not shy about espousing company values and setting high goals: "At E*TRADE, we're an attacker, we're predatory . . . "; "(Our culture) is all about getting people excited about how they can make a difference as a person and as a team . . . "; "(We have) a lust for being different . . . ."[20] Cotsakos was leader of E*TRADE during the heights of the dot-com boom. When circumstances changed and the external environment became more competitively complex for dot-com

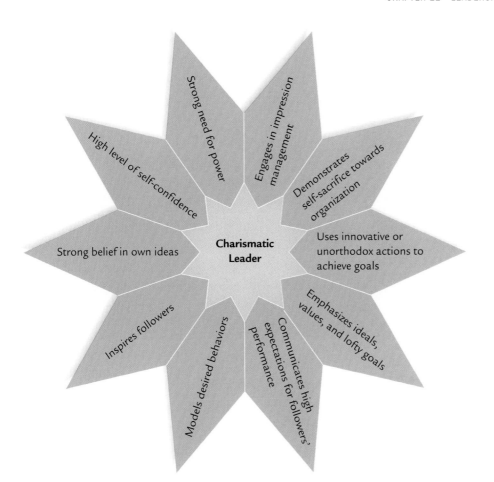

exhibit 11.10
Attributes of the Charismatic Leader

Charismatic Leader

- Strong need for power
- Engages in impression management
- Demonstrates self-sacrifice towards organization
- Uses innovative or unorthodox actions to achieve goals
- Emphasizes ideals, values, and lofty goals
- Communicates high expectations for followers' performance
- Models desired behaviors
- Inspires followers
- Strong belief in own ideas
- High level of self-confidence

firms, the company's directors released him as CEO and turned to someone with an apparently different style to guide the organization.

It should also be obvious that charisma can be used for harmful ends as well as good. Society and the world at large are only too familiar with how an apparently extreme level of charisma may be used by certain "leaders"—such as, for example, Adolf Hitler in Nazi Germany before and during World War II, and the cult figure Jim Jones of Jonestown mass suicide fame—with disastrous consequences. Charisma represents special power, but that does not guarantee that it will always be used for worthy goals.

Transformational Leadership

In the past couple of decades, an approach that is quite similar in many ways to charismatic leadership has been even more studied, and indeed often advocated, by scholars who write about leadership.[21] That concept is **transformational leadership**. Both ways of looking at leadership involve the notion of being able to motivate followers to make major changes or to achieve at very high levels. Thus, the original concept of transformational leadership, authored by political scientist James M. Burns, was that it was a process in which "leaders and followers raise one another to higher levels of morality and motivation."[22] Later refinements of this approach—by social scientists specifically addressing organizational contexts—emphasized that leaders are transformational even if they don't necessarily appeal to "higher levels of morality and motivation," as long as they motivate followers to ignore their own self-interests and work for the larger good of the organization.[23] Put another way,

Transformational Leadership by Lyman Porter

Q&A

One**Key**

www.prenhall.com/onekey

transformational leadership leadership that motivates followers to ignore self-interests and work for the larger good of the organization to achieve significant accomplishments; emphasis is on articulating a vision that will convince subordinates to make major changes

Three decades ago, an Austrian body-builder and aspiring actor with Republican leanings would have been a rather unlikely choice for the governorship of California. Overcoming many obstacles, Arnold Schwarzenegger nonetheless convinced voters he was the best person for the job in 2003. "I came here with absolutely nothing, and California has given me absolutely everything," said Schwarzenegger. He exhibits what many people would regard as classic traits of leadership, including a high need for power and a high level of confidence.

attributions of charisma are strongly based on leaders' personal traits and characteristics, but attributions of transformational qualities are largely based on what leaders do as well as what they say.

Transformational leaders, like charismatic leaders, inspire their followers. However, this is done not only through followers' identification with the leader, as in the case of charismatic leadership, but also through the empowerment and coaching of followers. It is in this latter respect that the concept of transformational leadership differs from charismatic leadership. With transformational leadership, followers are not required to be highly dependent on their leaders. Also, whereas instances of charismatic leadership are rare, transformational leadership behavior is assumed to be potentially possible almost anywhere throughout the organization.[24]

Those who advocate greater transformational leadership in organizations typically contrast it with so-called **transactional leadership**,[25] as shown in Exhibit 11.11. The latter is regarded as leadership that is more passive and that emphasizes the exchange of rewards or other benefits for compliance by followers. Transformational leadership is seen as an approach that underscores the importance of leaders' appeals to followers' organizational or "common good" interests, whereas transactional leadership is seen as focusing more on leaders' reliance on followers' pursuit of self-interests to motivate their performance. In many respects, however, this distinction is artificial, since individuals often act for both their own interests *and* organizational interests.

transactional leadership

leadership that focuses on motivating followers' self-interests by exchanging rewards for their compliance; emphasis is on having subordinates implement procedures correctly and make needed, but relatively routine, changes

exhibit 11.11

Transformational Versus Transactional Leadership

	Transformational Leadership	Transactional Leadership
Leader gains subordinates' compliance by:	Inspiring, empowering, and coaching followers	Exchange of rewards and benefits
Appeals focus on:	Organizational and "common good" interests	Self-interest
Type of planned change:	Major organizational change	Routine changes

Another distinction drawn between transformational and transactional leadership by some experts is that the former involves motivating subordinates to make major changes, while the latter involves the implementation of routine changes and procedures. Again, this distinction is not always clear-cut in many organizational situations. A Manager's Challenge, "Hyundai's U-Turn in the U.S. Market," describes a leader who clearly is transformational but who also exhibits elements of transactional leadership.

In any event, a transformational perspective does focus on motivating people to make highly significant, or even unusual, achievements and accomplishments. Several studies have explored how transformational leaders influence their followers to achieve such exceptional results. One study of 12 CEOs, for example, found that transformational leaders (a) recognized the

globalization *a manager's challenge*

Hyundai's U-Turn in the U.S. Market

For more than a decade after South Korean automaker Hyundai entered the lucrative U.S. market, senior managers faced several major challenges. First, they had to enlarge the dealer network so more car buyers could shop for Hyundai vehicles in local showrooms. Second, they needed to reassure skeptical buyers about the quality of their vehicles. That was a difficult job considering the fact that Hyundai and its products like the Yugo had even become the butt of jokes by late-night comedians. The automaker even had trouble recruiting an American executive to jump-start its Hyundai Motor America company. As a last resort, it turned to its corporate lawyer, Finbarr O'Neill, a likable Irishman. When O'Neill was named acting chief operating officer of HMA, annual U.S. sales were stalled below 100,000, and the U.S. division had been without a CEO for several months.

O'Neill immediately called a meeting to ask Hyundai's 50 U.S. dealers for suggestions. O'Neill and the dealers brainstormed through pages and pages of ideas. One of the dealers later observed, "[O'Neill] said, 'I can't work on all of these at once, so let's pick the top 10 and that's where I'll start.' That was Hyundai's defining moment. It's when we got leadership."

Soon afterward, O'Neill was appointed CEO and embarked on a daring plan to transform a market laggard into a market leader. He was aware that Hyundai had made significant strides in improving quality, despite lingering doubts among U.S. buyers. He proposed offering an unusually generous warranty—a 10-year/100,000-mile coverage on engines and transmissions—to prove that the Korean-built cars were actually reliable.

Backed by a high-profile advertising campaign, the warranty offer sparked renewed interest among dealers and buyers alike. As sales picked up, more dealers signed on. Within a few years, O'Neill had almost 600 U.S. dealers selling Sonata cars, Santa Fe SUVs, and other Hyundai models.

Even the smallest details were important to O'Neill, especially when it came to dealers. Crisscrossing the country, he dropped in on two showrooms every week to discuss his plans, ask questions, and gather feedback. "Profitable dealers do more for brands and make guys like me look a lot smarter," he said. "I've got to know if there's anything Hyundai does that's standing in the way of them selling cars."

Sales soared a remarkable 400 percent under O'Neill's leadership, and put Hyundai on track to reaching its goal of selling 1 million cars a year by 2010. The warranty plan was effective in attracting public attention, but "if the product itself didn't fulfill the expectations, we wouldn't have had the success we have had," O'Neill said.

Despite his achievements, O'Neill and much of his management team departed Hyundai in 2003. Some Hyundai insiders reportedly said there was jealousy in Hyundai's corporate ranks over the turnaround success O'Neill and some of his colleagues in the American unit were enjoying. That, they say, helped lead to the fallout and O'Neill's departure. Even for the best of leaders, heading up a major geographical component of a multinational company can be tricky business.

Sources: Mark Rechtin, "Hyundai to Extend Warranty Through '08," *Automotive News,* October 6, 2003, p. 3; Mark Rechtin, "Hyundai Hit by Senior Exodus," *Automotive News,* September 8, 2003, p. 21; Keith Naughton, "Kicking Hyundai into High Gear," *Newsweek,* January 6, 2003, p. 73; "For Hyundai CEO, Hubris Is Danger No. 1," *Automotive News,* May 6, 2002, p. 35; Fara Warner, "Finbarr O'Neill Is Not a Car Guy," *Fast Company,* November 2002, pp. 84+.

need for major changes, (b) helped subordinates prepare for and accept such changes, and, especially, (c) were particularly skillful in persuading subordinates to accept a new way of doing things. That is, they communicated a new vision within the organization. The study indicated that transformational leaders

- Viewed themselves as agents of change
- Were thoughtful risk-takers
- Were sensitive to people's needs
- Stated a set of core values to rally around
- Were flexible and open to learning
- Had good analytical skills
- Had considerable confidence in their vision for the organization[26]

Another study of 90 leaders in both the corporate world and the public sector came to similar conclusions:

> [Transformational leaders] paid attention to what was going on, they determined what parts of events at hand would be important for the future of the organization, they set a new direction, and they concentrated the attention of everyone in the organization on (that new future). This was . . . as true for orchestra conductors, army generals, football coaches, and school superintendents as for corporate leaders.[27]

It is clear from these studies that transformational leadership (a) can occur in widely varying circumstances, (b) emphasizes a particular focus on a vision and how to implement it, and (c) requires considerable perseverance and dedication by the leader. Exhibit 11.12 summarizes a set of guidelines for those who aspire to transform their organizations, or their parts of organizations.[28]

E-age Leadership

A new issue that has emerged within the last few years is whether leadership that is required in the e-age is fundamentally different from the non–e-leadership of earlier decades.[29] The answer so far seems to be "no." "**E-leadership**"—a term sometimes found in recent publications—involves heavy reliance on the use of information technology to supplement more traditional leadership methods. Leaders in the e-era who know how to use the technology effectively can apply it, for example, to stimulate innovation; to open up communication channels and gain increased input and participation; and to evaluate and control opera-

e-leadership involves heavy reliance on the use of information technology to supplement more traditional leadership methods

exhibit 11.12
Guidelines for Transformational Leadership

Those Who Want to Be Transformational Leaders Should:
Develop a clear and appealing vision
Develop a strategy for attaining the vision
Articulate and promote the vision
Act confident and optimistic
Express confidence in followers
Use early success in small steps to build confidence
Celebrate successes
Use dramatic, symbolic actions to emphasize key values
Lead by example

Source: Adapted from G. Yuki, *Leadership in Organizations*, 3rd ed. (Upper Saddle River, NJ: Prentice Hall, 1994).

Entrepreneur Jeff Bezos, the founder of Amazon.com, is the quintessential e-leader, having reinvented an old business model for a wired world. Bezos' original plan to sell books on the Web eventually transformed Amazon into a virtual marketplace, where all kinds of products are sold. Leadership, says Bezos, "applies in the 'big,' when you're talking about somebody like the president of the United States. It also applies in the 'small,' when you are a leader inside your own family and teaching your kids right from wrong. That requires tremendous leadership."

tions on a real-time basis. If there is any difference, then, between so-called e-leaders and non–e-leaders, it is that the former know how to maximize the use of information technology to strengthen their leadership efforts.

One company that recognizes the importance of using Internet technology in building leaders' skills is Ford Motor Company.[30] In the company's "Leadership for the New Economy" training program, participants begin preparing for the program by working collaboratively in virtual spaces or "e-rooms" well in advance of the first in-class session. Later, program participants engage in an online auction where they bid on the opportunity to meet individually with various outside experts who could help them on assigned projects. The company also maintains a Web site focused solely on leadership that anyone, anywhere in the organization, can visit and learn about best leadership practices and also obtain access to various materials on the topic. In effect, employees throughout the organization are "rewarded" for using the Internet by being able to develop their own e-leadership abilities.

A Manager's Challenge, "Bringing Leadership Training Online at eBay," describes how another company is emphasizing e-leadership for its managers.

Leadership Across Different National Cultures

A final issue with respect to leadership, power, and influence is this: Does leadership differ fundamentally across national cultures, or do the similarities outweigh the differences? The answer is that nobody knows for sure, although researchers are attempting to find answers.[31]

As some observers point out: "*Leadership* is a fairly modern concept. It did not appear in English-language usage until the first half of the 19th century and has been primarily the concern of Anglo-Saxon influenced countries. Prior to that, and in other countries, the notion of *headship* has been more prominent, as in the head of state, chief, or other *ruling* [italics added] position."[32] Or, as another scholar put it, "The universality of leadership [as a part of the managerial role] does not . . . imply a similarity of leadership style throughout the world."[33]

Experts on Southeast Asia, for example, point out two essential cultural features that affect leadership situations and the use of power and influence in that area of the world: requirements for order and compliance and requirements

tech|nol|ogy   *a manager's challenge*

Bringing Leadership Training Online at eBay

With over 60 million registered users across the globe and annual revenues topping $1 billion, eBay dominates the online auction market. The company, which was founded in 1985, has demonstrated rapid earnings growth. In one particular year, for example, earnings jumped up an amazing 172 percent. And since eBay carries no inventory itself, profit margins for the company are a tidy 80 percent-plus.

However, most of eBay's employees are far younger than the average employee in the U.S. workforce, and many are under the age of 25. When CEO Meg Whitman came to eBay in 1998, some 80 percent of these younger employees had no previous management experience. To keep up with growth, the most promising customer support representatives had been quickly promoted into management positions within only minimal leadership training. So when a companywide survey revealed strong employee interest in formal leadership training, eBay's managers began planning a program for these customer service managers and other employees from its U.S. locations.

Training employees located in far-flung areas presented a challenge for eBay's management team. They decided to bring all the participants to eBay's Salt Lake City facility for initial assessment and an introductory seminar, and then create a separate program for managers based elsewhere. After assessing each participant's current leadership skills, the trainers delivered presentations on basic leadership principles such as influencing others. Senior managers attended these presentations to demonstrate their commitment. "There was a lot of discussion in the sessions about the importance of good leadership to eBay's strategy," remembers a consultant who worked with eBay's trainers.

The Salt Lake City participants continued their training by attending monthly classroom sessions on various topics over the course of the next year. Rather than have the other participants travel to Salt Lake City for monthly classes, the eBay trainers created a Web-based training course for participants to access from their own locations. When they were in Salt Lake City for the introductory seminar, these "remote students" received training in how to learn from a self-study online course. Back at their home locations, they studied leadership modules online at their own pace and had access to special chat rooms where they could exchange ideas online with other participants. After working through each module, the participants wrote a script explaining how they would role-play a situation to apply the skills they had just learned. Then they e-mailed their scripts to an eBay trainer who reviewed them and helped all remote students further practice their skills in an online group practice session.

Was the online training as effective as the in-person training? Definitely, according to the participants and their managers. Sixty percent of the in-person students and 67 percent of the online students reported that the learning experience was enhanced by having the opportunity to share experiences with each other. Moreover, 74 percent of the in-person students and 67 percent of the online students reported acquiring the ability to more effectively listen and provide feedback to employees. Most important, 86 percent of the in-person students and 78 percent of the online students stated that their new leadership skills were having a positive effect on the job. "With the entire management team attending these sessions, we are in a much better position than before, not only in terms of productivity, but also on the customer service level," summarizes Jeff Anderson, eBay's human resources director. The training of its younger employees has also undoubtedly contributed to eBay's long-term success. Whereas many other dot-coms have failed, eBay's profits and stock price look sounder than a lot of more "senior" companies.

Sources: "Meg Whitman on eBay's Self-Regulations," *BusinessWeek Online*, August 18, 2003; Rob Hoff and Peter Burrows, "Meet eBay's Auctioneer-in-Chief," *BusinessWeek Online*, p. N; adapted from "EBay Tackles Its Customer Support Training Challenge," *Institute of Management and Administration Report on Customer Relationship Management*, June 2002, pp. 1+; Melanie Wells, "D-Day for EBay," *Forbes*, July 22, 2002, pp. 68+; Miguel Helft, "What Makes EBay Unstoppable?" *Industry Standard*, August 6, 2001, pp. 32+.

for harmony.[34] The first of these cultural "requirements" involves traditional values that support the acceptance of hierarchies, conformity, and deference to authority. The necessity for the cultural value of harmony involves not only obligations of the subordinate to the superior but also obligations of the superior to respect the subordinate and care for his or her welfare. Clearly, this is a quite different leadership style than is found in most Western societies. In most Asian cultures, for example, this style can be summarized in the word

Li Yifei is MTV China's general manager. Smart, confident, and female, Li Yifei has had to take a different approach to dealing with male business people in that country. "Particularly as a woman in China, you have to be a little bit softer, and humble," she says. Due in part to the traditional values of the Chinese, for example, MTV China only airs for a few hours a day.

paternalism, where a leader is regarded as the provider "father" who will take care of the subordinate in return for responsible behavior and performance. This style is also often found in Central and South American countries where there is a strong emphasis on collective as opposed to individual values.[35]

Despite such differences related to cultural norms and traditions, some similarities in leadership practices—such as greater use of subordinate participation—are beginning to appear with increasing regularity around the world because of the spread of industrialization.[36] Thus, forces for differences in leadership and influence practices due to culture are combating forces for similarities due to industrialization and the increasing levels of education associated with it. Results from the most recent and comprehensive large-scale investigation of attributes of effective leadership across more than 60 different national cultures appear consistent with this conclusion.[37] As Exhibit 11.13 shows, according to the data collected for this study, certain leader attributes, such as "trustworthy" and "decisive," are viewed as positive across all cultures. Likewise, certain other attributes, such as "dictatorial" and "asocial," are universally viewed as negative. The reactions to other leader attributes, however,

paternalism where a leader is regarded as the provider "father" who will take care of the subordinate in return for responsible behavior and performance

Examples of leader attributes universally viewed as *positive*	Examples of leader attributes universally viewed as *negative*	Examples of leader attributes viewed as *positive* or *negative* depending on the culture
+	–	+/–
+ Trustworthy	– Noncooperative	+/– Ambitious
+ Encouraging	– Irritable	+/– Individualistic
+ Honest	– Dictatorial	+/– Cunning
+ Decisive	– Ruthless	+/– Cautious
+ Communicative	– Egocentric	+/– Class Conscious
+ Dependable	– Asocial	+/– Evasive

Source: R. J. House, "Cultural Influences on Leadership and Organizations: Project GLOBE," in W. Mobley (ed.), *Advances in Global Leadership*, vol. 1 (Stamford, CT: JAI Press, 1998).

exhibit 11.13
The Effect of Culture on Attitudes Toward Leaders' Attributes

such as "cautious" and "ambitious," are highly contingent on the particular culture and its values. These characteristics, therefore, are viewed positively in some cultures but distinctly negatively in other cultures.

Because of expanding industrialization, the need for effective leadership has become a worldwide phenomenon. Precisely *how* that need is being met in specific organizations and in specific countries, however, still appears to be influenced by cultural circumstances and traditions. Nevertheless, the picture of particular leadership styles and practices around the world at the beginning of the twenty-first century may change dramatically during the next few decades. It already is in some places, as exemplified by Li Yifei, head of Viacom's China MTV.[38] Li is trying to lead a youth-oriented organization while, at the same time, she deals with the mostly older male-entrenched regulatory bureaucracy of China. She is normally confident, brash, and up front, but when interacting with the authorities she modifies her style somewhat. A century ago, or even a decade ago, it would have been unlikely that her natural leadership style would have been tolerated, let alone accepted in that kind of setting.

IMPROVING YOUR OWN LEADERSHIP CAPABILITIES

With so many approaches available to analyze leadership, and so many different issues relating to the topic, it is sometimes easy to lose sight of the leadership forest because of all of the trees of theories, findings, and opinions. However, they actually have more in common than might be apparent at first glance. Therefore, it is possible to take away something useful from each of them—and to take advantage of all of them when considered together—to develop your own leadership capabilities. That is the subject of this section.

We want to stress that we are talking about improving your leadership capabilities for managing within organizational settings. This discussion assumes that you now, or sometime in the not-so-distant future, will very likely be in a position to exert leadership of a group or unit somewhere inside an organization—in short, the discussion assumes a realistic scenario.

To provide an integrated approach—which is diagrammed in Exhibit 11.14—we will use the framework of the basic elements of the leadership process that we have emphasized throughout these last two chapters: leader, follower, and situation. Furthermore, we focus on two categories of capabilities that anyone in a leadership role can develop and improve: to be able to assess and to be able to act.

exhibit 11.14

Improving Your Leadership Capabilities

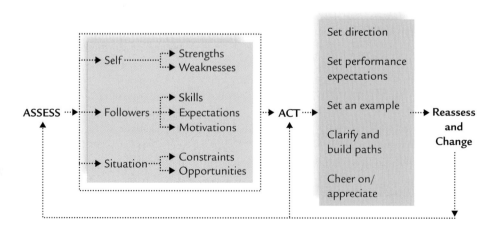

Assess

Assess, then act. Assess what? For one, your own current capabilities for performing as a leader. Second, the abilities, expertise, motivation, and attitudes of others, the potential followers. And, third, the constraints and opportunities presented by the situation.

Your Own Leadership Capabilities (Think back to the discussion of "Leaders' Traits, Skills, and Behaviors" in Chapter 10.) As good a starting place as any for making an assessment is that of your own capabilities and characteristics in relation to the leadership role you are assuming. Know thyself first! is a simple but useful slogan to remember. We are not talking about some sort of deep, moody introspection. Rather, we are suggesting a realistic estimate of your own strengths, limitations, and characteristics that you bring to this kind of opportunity. What are your greatest personal attributes that would help you in this situation? For example, how would you rate the amount of: your relevant experience; your technical expertise; your oral presentation skills; your ability to persuade and influence other people; your level of motivation and drive to be successful in this kind of position? What are your tendencies that would be a factor in your leadership role? Are you more likely to be focused on tasks or on people? Is your leadership style, at least initially, more likely to be directive or supportive? As a test of how realistic you are being in making this kind of self-assessment, you might ask yourself a brutally candid question: Would others who know me well definitely agree with my self-appraisal?

Others' (Followers') Capabilities (Think about the discussion of such leadership approaches as the Hersey/Blanchard Situational Leadership Model and the Vroom/Yetton Normative Decision Model.) The second important area of assessment involves taking stock of the capabilities of those whom you will be leading. What is the range and average level of their relevant skills and expertise? In answering this question, be sure to evaluate not only their current levels but also to what extent those levels of experience and skills can be expanded and developed by training or other methods you could facilitate. What kinds of expectations, especially for you as a leader, do your potential followers bring to the situation? Are those expectations appropriate and realistic, and, if not, can they be modified? What are the motivation levels of those whom you are going to lead? If high, what will be the problems in maintaining those levels and how can you take advantage of them? If generally low, how can you go about raising them? One example would be by achieving some early success for the group that inspires confidence in you as a leader and elevates their motivation to continue performing at that level.

Situational Constraints and Opportunities (Consider Fiedler's Leadership Contingency Model and Substitutes for Leadership.) What is the nature of the situation you will be encountering as you assume a leadership position? Will it likely continue to be that way over time? Is the situational environment for your group or unit relatively stable, or is it, as is highly probable, changing fairly rapidly? What kinds of task challenges are facing your group, and are they relatively easy and uncomplicated or are they difficult and complex? This is an area of assessment in which it is easy for a leader to make overly optimistic evaluations and to underestimate the degree of task(s) difficulty. What are the time frames facing you and your unit? Are hard-and-fast deadlines part of the picture, or is the period for achieving particular results more ambiguous and less certain? Would using substitutes for some aspects of your direct leadership cause more problems than they would fix? Or, is this a kind of situation where you can use such substitutes in a way that will allow you to concentrate your own efforts and energies in more targeted and productive directions? What is the nature of the organizational environment, including its culture and its broad goals and objectives, that affects you and your unit? There obviously are many aspects and features of the environment that potentially could be assessed by you as a leader, which puts a premium on being both selective and perceptive.

Act

No one who wants to be effective in a leadership role can simply sit around and excessively and endlessly assess what resources are available, what conditions exist, and what seems to need to be done. As a leader you must act and not just assess! But what kind of actions? Obviously, no general guidelines can cover all eventualities and all conditions. However, here is where several of the leadership approaches discussed earlier in this chapter—such as path–goal theory and transformational leadership—can be helpful in suggesting the types of actions that are likely to be essential in almost any leadership situation.

Set a Direction The findings from research on leadership provide overwhelming support for the importance of a leader making sure that a direction is set for a unit or group—making clear the goals and objectives for it. *How* this is done, whether with a high degree of follower participation or not, is a separate issue. However, no matter how much input you receive from others and what weight is given to that input, you need to articulate your own view of what the direction should be. This is consistent with the emphasis on "vision" in the research on transformational leadership, or what one former president of the United States somewhat dismissively labeled "the vision thing." It is also consistent with most people's ideas about what a good leader should do. People working in an organizational unit want to know where the leader thinks that unit should be headed, even if they may disagree with that direction. They also want to know how the unit's efforts fit in with the larger organization's fundamental strategy and goals. It is up to you to take steps to provide this crucial information.

Set Performance Expectations Related to the above action of setting a direction, a leader also needs to be clear about performance expectations for the group or unit. Again, whether potential followers see these expectations as too high, too low, or about right, they want to know what you, as the leader, think they should be. Thus, if you are in a leadership position you need to be clear and explicit about your standards and consequences of meeting or not meeting them. This is fulfilling another expectation that many people hold concerning what an effective leader should do.

Set an Example A leader, by her or his own behavior, needs to demonstrate the qualities and level of performance that are expected of others. Nothing discourages followers faster than a leader saying one thing and then behaving in a manner wholly inconsistent with stated standards of performance. People learn very rapidly to pay attention to your actual leadership behavior rather than just your words, especially if the two are inconsistent. To use a popular but relevant phrase, you need to "walk your talk."

Clarify and Build Paths As specifically emphasized by path–goal leadership theory, it is important for leaders to indicate the ways in which their units can reach their goals. You, of course, are not the only resource for clarifying paths, as others in the group may have more expertise and knowledge about the best paths than you do. However, in your leadership role you often may have more resources than others in the unit to draw on to make sure that the collective wisdom about best paths is widespread within the group and about how those paths can be used in the most effective way. Thus, you need to consider how you can capitalize on your personal and position powers to make the paths toward goal accomplishment as smooth, direct, and accessible as possible.

Cheer On and Appreciate As some leadership scholars have pointed out, the era of the single "heroic" leader at the top is rapidly disappearing.[39] In this day and age of dynamic, fast-moving, and often highly complex organizations, no leader, no matter where located within the organization, can get the job done alone. When you find yourself in a leadership position, you will need the commitment, support, involvement, and ideas of others. To obtain these key resources, you will need to provide encouragement and support and, especially, appreciation for their efforts. In short, you will need to cheer them on and recognize their accomplishments. Then, your own leadership efforts have a good chance of being multiplied!

Reassess and Change

The circumstances a leader faces are never completely static. Developments and events are constantly occurring. Therefore, you cannot just assess the situation and your followers' capabilities once, say, at the beginning when you assume a leadership role, and expect everything to remain the same. You must reassess more or less continually. Or, to use a phrase prominent in the literature on leadership, you must constantly keep "scanning the environment" to both anticipate and decide on changes that may be needed. Not only changes by the followers, but particularly changes by you. Is your relative emphasis on tasks versus people still the right mix? Is your style, or typical way of working with other people, being effective or do you need to alter it in some way? Is the direction you and your group set previously still the best direction, and are the paths that seemed to work well in the past to achieve those objectives still the best ones to use with the changed conditions facing your unit? In short, you must be able to change and—which may be harder—you must be willing to change!

managerial perspectives revisited

PERSPECTIVE 1: THE ORGANIZATIONAL CONTEXT Some of the specific issues relating to leadership are directly affected by the organizational context. Take, for example, the challenge of so-called e-leadership. The issue is not whether the e-environment for leadership is here to stay. Rather, the issue is how an organization's specific policies and practices can help or hinder managers' use of e-technology to enhance their leadership efforts. Another leadership issue that is directly impacted by the organizational context is managers' attempts to exercise transformational leadership. Think about it: How many transformational leaders can exist within the same organization? How does a higher-level (in the organization) transformational leader affect the efforts of someone lower in the hierarchy who wants to be his or her own transformational leader? These are just some of the knotty leadership issues involved when the organizational context is taken into account as a significant variable. This is especially so when one considers that leadership potentially can take place anywhere in the organization.

PERSPECTIVE 2: THE HUMAN FACTOR The opening story to this chapter, about the efforts of two organizational leaders following the catastrophic events of September 11, 2001, demonstrates the critical importance of the people aspects of leadership. If nothing else, the accounts

of the post–9/11 activities of organizational leaders underscored what we emphasized in Chapter 10: "Leadership is a people-intensive process." Furthermore, almost all of the perspectives and models of leadership that we analyzed in this chapter emphasized the "people" responsibilities of leaders. "Leadership" and "working through people" are inseparable. Any manager who also wants to be a leader has to work through people. There is no other way.

 PERSPECTIVE 3: MANAGING PARADOXES At the end of Chapter 10, we mentioned some of the potential paradoxes faced by leaders: for example, "act quickly and decisively, but take time to involve others . . ."; "use power, but don't overuse it"; and "be consistent, [but] also be flexible." In addition, as noted in this chapter, there are other apparent paradoxes that pervade the leadership literature. Two of the more important are: Managing and leading are two distinctly different activities; and, transformational approaches and transactional approaches are mutually exclusive. Both of these statements are often presented as either-or choices. In fact, they are not. Managers can be leaders and vice versa. Furthermore, leaders often use a style that reflects both transformational and transactional characteristics; they do so because both are necessary to be effective.

It should be clear, then, that all-or-nothing approaches to thinking about leadership are seldom helpful in dealing with real-world leadership problems and choices in courses of action.

PERSPECTIVE 4: ENTREPRENEURIAL MIND-SET The last part of this chapter talked about "improving your own capabilities." Because of its importance to effective management and its potential effect on others through the leadership style displayed, we recommend developing an entrepreneurial mind-set and the capabilities to use it in practice. This is certainly one of the chief commitments required to be an effective leader: namely, it is possible to improve as a leader, but you also have to want to do so. An entrepreneurial mind-set means that leaders are committed to being innovative. They continuously search for opportunities and encourage their employees to be creative. Leaders can facilitate the creative efforts of their employees by fostering an entrepreneurial culture within their organizations. Such a culture results in a set of shared values regarding innovation and enhances the commitment of everyone in the organization to entrepreneurial achievement.[40]

concluding comments

Here in Chapter 11 we have presented a number of potentially useful perspectives on the leadership process that have come from the behavioral and organizational science literature. The important point is to consider how each of them can help you increase your understanding of different aspects of an admittedly complex, and sometimes even baffling, process. No single theory itself provides a foolproof formula for guaranteeing success as a leader. However, the conceptual models and ideas in this chapter can serve to stimulate your thinking about the process of leadership and how you can develop your own distinctive approach to this critical managerial function.

In the latter part of this chapter we discussed some ideas for improving your own leadership strengths. We particularly tried to emphasize that in assessing (a) the capabilities of yourself as a potential leader, (b) those of others you might lead, and (c) the constraints and opportunities provided by the situation, the perspectives and models from the earlier part of the chapter could apply directly to this assessment process. But, as we also stressed, to lead one must not only assess but act—and then assess again, act again, and so on. Leadership is a managerial process, but it is a flow and not just a set of discrete actions.

Throughout these last two chapters we have covered a considerable number of topics relating to leadership in organizations, starting in Chapter 10 with the basics of power and influence, and the roles of the leader, the followers, and the situation. We continued here in this chapter by reviewing major approaches and models of leadership, discussing some of the most important current issues relating to leadership, and finally, providing guidelines for improving your own leadership capabilities. That's a lot about one topic! The challenge is how to put together and, in a sense, to integrate all of this information. There is no easy way to do this. One good way, however, is to think about specific leadership situations you have observed, or perhaps have directly been a part of, and then try to use different parts of the material covered in these two chapters to analyze what happened and why it happened. Can you now understand something about leaders and the leadership process that you didn't grasp before? If so, you may be better prepared for the next time you are involved in a leadership opportunity.

key terms

charismatic leadership   391
e-leadership   396
LPC (least preferred coworker)
 theory   384
Managerial Grid   380

neutralizers of leadership   389
normative decision model   386
paternalism   399
path–goal theory of leadership
 385

situational leadership model   382
substitutes for leadership   387
transactional leadership   394
transformational leadership   393

test your comprehension

1. Why are there so many different approaches to leadership? Do they have anything in common?
2. What are the two dimensions of behavior in Blake and Mouton's Management Grid?
3. What is the best type of leader according to Blake and Mouton's theory?
4. Why could one consider the Managerial Grid to be a "universal" leadership theory?
5. Describe the four types of behavior identified in Hersey and Blanchard's Situational Leadership model. What are the components of each?
6. What are the major criticisms of the Hersey and Blanchard Situational Leadership model?
7. What did Fiedler mean by one's "least preferred co-worker"? What is the major principle involved in Fiedler's theory?
8. According to House's path–goal theory, what is the main responsibility of a leader?
9. According to path–goal theory, when should a leader use supportive leadership? Directive leadership?
10. Why is Vroom and Yetton's Normative Decision Model included in a chapter on leadership and not just in a chapter on decision making?

11. What are the key variables and the basic decision-making procedures included in the Vroom and Yetton Normative Decision Model?
12. What is meant by a substitute for leadership? Give an example.
13. Are leadership and management the same? Why or why not?
14. What is a charismatic leader? What are some of the specific traits of such a leader?
15. What is the "downside" of charismatic leadership?
16. What is the difference between a transformational and a transactional leader? Is one necessarily better than the other? How does each bring about change?
17. What is e-age leadership? Is it different from traditional leadership? Why or why not?
18. Is leadership the same in different cultures? If not, are there any elements that appear to be similar in different cultures?
19. Are leadership styles across the globe becoming more similar or more different? Why?
20. In order to change your leadership capabilities, which elements must you assess, and which elements require action?

apply your understanding

1. Which of the many approaches to leadership do you think is the best? Defend your reasoning.
2. How would you characterize yourself—as a transformational, transactional, or charismatic leader? Which would you rather be? Can you change your style?
3. Adolf Hitler, Joseph Stalin, Jim Jones, Kenneth Lay (Enron), Bernard Ebbers (WorldCom)—all were "leaders." Were they effective leaders? Why or why not?
4. (A) Select the country in which you have spent the majority of your time up to now. Is the type of leadership in that country/culture changing? What is the basis/evidence for your answer? (B) Select a large and influential country (in terms of the world's economy) other than the country you named in (A). Is the type of leadership in your (A) country becoming more or less similar to the type of leadership in (B) country/culture? Explain your reasoning.

practice your capabilities

A Type of Direction

Scott Davis is the manager of a plant that manufactures camping equipment. The employees are highly trained and experienced in their jobs, and their performance has been excellent. Mr. Davis recently promoted Will Taylor to be supervisor of the department that manufactures sleeping bags. Will has worked in the plant for the past 12 years and has the best production record in the department.

After a month of Will's supervision, his employees in the sleeping bag department requested a meeting with Mr. Davis. They stated that Will was making it impossible for them to achieve their production goals. They characterized Will as a dictator and a perfectionist.

Comments by the employees included: "Will is rejecting finished sleeping bags that meet quality cri-

teria for perfection." "The only way to do the job is his way." "The job of supervisor has made him a dictator." "He tells you that the job must be done exactly the way he would have done it." "If he keeps up his loud orders, we will need to get earplugs."

1. What are the possible problems with Will Taylor's leadership style?
2. Would Will be more effective if he changed his style of leadership? If yes, how should he change it? If no, what should he change? Use the theories in this chapter to justify your response.
3. What should Scott Davis do after the meeting with the employees?

Source: Adapted from J. P. Howell and D. L. Costley, *Understanding Behaviors for Effective Leadership* (Upper Saddle River, NJ: Prentice Hall, 2001).

closing case

DEVELOP YOUR CRITICAL THINKING

Ethics on the Line at Baxter International

Harry M. Jansen Kraemer Jr., the CEO of Baxter International, an Illinois-based medical supply company, has become something of a legend for some of his unorthodox views on management. For one, Kraemer believes employees should try to balance their personal lives with work. He personally never gets to the office before 8:00 A.M., and he's rarely there after 6:00 P.M. Evenings are reserved for spending time with his family, doing what families do—homework, exercising, or reading.

During Kraemer's tenure at Baxter, gross margins have been excellent and profits have increased strongly.

By comparison, most industry rivals have experienced flat or slower-growing revenues. In the midst of this ongoing rosy scenario, however, certain unexpected problems at a company that had been recently acquired put Kraemer's leadership to the test in a highly public way.

The trouble started when four elderly patients who had received dialysis treatment for kidney ailments at a Madrid hospital died within a few days of each other. The deaths were followed by over 40 others worldwide. Spanish health authorities investigating the incidents discovered that the blood filters used by both facilities were from a single batch made by Althin Medical, the company that Baxter had recently taken over. As a precaution, Baxter moved quickly to recall that batch of filters and began investigating what went wrong. It ordered internal reviews and hired an independent expert to analyze all available data.

Further, the president of Baxter's renal division recalled all of the Althin dialysis filters that had been sold to customers worldwide and blocked distributors from shipping any filters still in stock. It also assigned deputy general counsel Marla Persky to head a 27-member task force to study the catastrophe. Persky convened experts from manufacturing, toxicology, clinical affairs, and other company areas via conference call twice a day for a month to scrutinize every aspect of the product and its use.

After countless tests and analyses, an engineer in Sweden observed a few tiny bubbles at one end of the filter—bubbles that should not have been present. Digging deeper, the task force learned that the bubbles were residue from a special liquid injected to identify leaks in the filters. Even though the nontoxic liquid was routinely removed after the leak tests, clearly a miniscule amount remained in some filters. The task force's theory was that when this liquid was warmed by a dialysis patient's blood, it turned into a gas and provoked a deadly pulmonary embolism. As soon as this theory was confirmed by careful testing, Persky informed her boss, who immediately called Kraemer to explain the situation. The CEO told his subordinate: "Let's make sure we do the right thing." It was a phrase Kraemer had used often over the years, and every Baxter manager understood what it meant.

Kraemer and his managers could have found ways to downplay the incidents, evade responsibility, or deflect blame. If they had simply shut down the filter division without fanfare, few people outside the industry would have paid any attention. They might have said that Althin's previous owners and managers shared some responsibility, because the division had been under Baxter's control for only a short time. Or they might have implicated the manufacturer of the liquid used in testing the filters. Moreover, they could have argued that without the opportunity to test the filters used by the patients who died, Baxter's experts would be unable to determine the precise cause of the problem.

Other top managers might have been tempted to sidestep the issue. Not Kraemer. After consulting with his executive team, he confronted the situation head-on by quickly releasing an expression of sympathy to the families of the patients. "We have a responsibility to make public our findings immediately and take swift action, even though confirmatory studies remain underway," his statement added. Although his experts could not determine whether the filters had definitely caused the 50-plus deaths to which they were linked, Kraemer ordered Althin's two factories closed. He also set aside a multimillion dollar pool for settlements with the patients' families, who reportedly received about $290,000 each.

Next, Kraemer and the head of the renal division met with U.S. Food and Drug Administration officials to explain the results of Baxter's tests and discuss what they planned to do. He met with government officials in Spain and elsewhere to share information about the filter situation and personally apologize. Going further, Baxter managers alerted competitors to what had been learned, in case any other factories used a similar process to identify leaks in their filters.

In all, the company spent more than $150 million to cover the cost of shutting down Althin and paying out settlements. Sales in other divisions continued so strong that the company was still able to achieve its overall financial goals. However, in light of the filter-related deaths, Kraemer told his board's compensation committee to cut his yearly performance bonus by 40 percent and to cut the bonuses of his top managers by 20 percent.

Kraemer describes his approach to leadership as "a delicate blend of self-confidence and humility." At the same time, he and his management team clearly understand the importance of "doing the right thing." "I've got 48,000 employees, most of whom care about the environment, or they are parents," he states. "I'm representing them."

Questions

1. Using the leadership theories and perspectives presented in this chapter, analyze Kraemer's leadership in having Baxter "do the right thing."
2. What elements, if any, of charismatic, transformational, and transactional leadership behavior did Kraemer display? Explain your answer.
3. How did his followers' capabilities affect the leadership shown by Kraemer?
4. Compare Kraemer's leadership with that of other corporate leaders whose actions have been highly publicized, such as those at Enron, WorldCom, and Adelphia. Do you think there were major situational circumstances that caused Kraemer's actions to differ, apparently, from those of the leaders at the other companies?

Sources: Harry Kraemer, "Keeping It Simple," *Health Forum Journal*, Summer 2003, pp. 15–21; Bruce Japsen, "Baxter International Makes Settlements in Dialysis Filter-Related Deaths," *Chicago Tribune*, August 24, 2002; Keith H. Hammonds, "Harry Kraemer's Moment of Truth," *Fast Company*, November 2002, pp. 93+; Michael Arndt, "How Does Harry Do It?" *BusinessWeek*, July 22, 2002, pp. 66+; Harry Jansen, "Baxter's Harry Kraemer: 'I Don't Golf,'" *BusinessWeek Online*, April 1, 2002

Motivation

12

LEARNING OBJECTIVES

After studying this chapter, you should be able to:

■

Analyze the motivational forces present in a specific situation.

■

Differentiate between the various content and process theories of motivation and indicate how each can be helpful in analyzing a given motivational situation.

■

Explain how job enrichment can influence an employee's motivation.

■

Compare and contrast the various approaches to reinforcement and describe their relative advantages and disadvantages for use by managers.

■

State how goal setting can affect motivation.

■

Name the major types of social influence on employees' motivation and explain how each type can impact motivation.

■

Describe how values and attitudes toward work can influence motivation.

Motivation Works Stitch by Stitch

Angel Lorenzo is a shift supervisor at Grupo M, a high-quality clothing factory that is also the Dominican Republic's largest private employer, with 12,000 employees working in 22 factories. Like most Grupo M employees, Lorenzo sees his job, overseeing 14 teams of machine operators who assemble thousands of pairs of pants every day, as part of a greater whole. "My job is to let them [the machine operators] know that they are the most important people in this factory. If they don't do their jobs well, we lose clients—and nobody prospers. But if we strive to follow the mission and the rules of the company, prosperity follows for everyone."

How does Grupo M foster the dedication among employees that has helped it grow 10 to 20 percent a year, selling approximately $200 million worth of clothing to companies like Polo, Hanes, Levi Strauss, Liz Claiborne, and Tommy Hilfiger?

Fernando Capellan, the company's founder and president, offers his workers many different kinds of incentives. Some would be considered progressive almost anywhere in the industrialized world; in traditionally agricultural Dominican Republic, they are remarkable. Free medical, dental, and vision and subsidized child care help workers meet their health and family needs, relieving basic concerns so they can better focus on the job. Free English classes offer employees rewarding opportunities for learning and self-improvement. Company sports leagues (including free equipment and uniforms) for employees and their children help to provide a sense of belonging and organizational culture.

Grupo M, a factory in the Dominican Republic, produces high-quality clothing for American labels like Polo, Liz Claiborne, and Tommy Hilfiger. Grupo M is the Dominican Republic's largest manufacturer. It pays its employees twice that nation's minimum wage (about $63 U.S. per week). Employees are provided with free medical, dental, and vision; subsidized child care; and free English classes.

Capellan recognizes that there are job skills to be learned as well. His company offers a six-month job-skills training program for all new sewing machine operators that gives them the confidence to work more independently. The program also focuses on self-improvement through courses in basic writing skills, as well as on personal health and safety and community awareness. Grupo M has won a number of awards for its labor and corporate citizenship practices. It even shared—with such global giants as IBM and Pfizer—a corporate conscience award for empowering its employees. The award was presented by the Council on Economic Priorities, a U.S. nonprofit watchdog group.

Several years ago a group of young Grupo M employees in their twenties and early thirties was sent to Israel and China to acquire needed background and skills in working with knits and other tex-

tiles. The new unit they established on their return to the Dominican Republic is thriving now, and its share of the company's revenues continues to grow. "For us to be sent abroad for such a period of time, and then to be given the responsibility to help lead such an important effort, would be unheard of at other companies," according to Angela Ogando, a member of the group. "This is a company that believes in investing in its young people. It believes in its workers and what we can do."

That confidence in his workforce is certainly Capellan's watchword. "We have proven that you don't have to run a factory like a sweatshop in order to be profitable and to grow," Capellan said. "In fact, we believe that we have been able to innovate, to expand, and to do what we have done because of the way that we treat our people. Everything that we give to our workers gets returned to us in terms of efficiency, quality, loyalty, and innovation. It's just smart business."

Just how smart is easy to see by a look at the numbers. Grupo M pays its operators nearly twice the country's minimum wage (roughly $63 U.S. a week). Apparel makers in Nicaragua and China, among other countries, pay much less. So Grupo M's garments cost its customers about 9 cents per minute of labor, compared to 7 or even 5 cents in other countries. Yet the quality of its goods is so much higher, thanks to its motivated workforce, that Grupo M is "absolutely competitive," according to Bob Zane, senior vice president for manufacturing and sourcing at Liz Claiborne. The company also enjoys extremely low turnover among its nonseasonal staff. "While its production costs may be greater," said Elliot Schrage, with the Council on Foreign Relations, "its productivity also improves sufficiently enough to maintain its competitive edge."

Grupo M is going to need that edge more than ever in the coming years. An expiring quota system designed to protect U.S. textile workers will end soon, which means the company will see more competition from foreign firms that pay their workers less. To compete, Grupo recently opened a factory in a newly established free-trade zone, just across Dominican Republic's border in Haiti.

As Grupo M attempts to stay competitive, the level of motivation of its employees in their jobs will be

critical. What they do at work, and what happens to them at work, is all important: "My work is my life," says shift supervisor Angel Lorenzo. "It's the reason that I can support my children and have a home, so I take it very seriously."

Sources: Nancy San Martin, "Two Nations Mend Relations, One Plant at a Time," *Miami Herald*, November 3, 2003; William Armbruster, "Curtain Call," *Journal of Commerce*, February 10, 2003, pp. 12–15; Charles Arthur, "Haiti's Not-So-Free Zones," *Multinational Monitor*, June 2002, pp. 6+; Cheryl Dahle, "The New Fabric of Success," *Fast Company*, June 2001, pp. 252+.

strategic overview

Acritical issue shown by the opening vignette is the strategic value of motivating employees. The employees working for Grupo M receive higher wages and greater benefits than the employees of many of their competitors. Thus, the company's labor costs are higher than its direct competitors. Yet external analysts argue that the firm maintains its competitive advantage for several reasons, all related to the highly motivated employees. The employees produce higher quality products than do their competitors' employees, are more productive, and have lower turnover (that is, fewer employees leave the firm for other jobs). Higher productivity means that they turn out more products for the time worked. So, even though they are paid more, they produce more, which reduces the overall cost per product. Angel Lorenzo, the manager who supervises 14 teams of machine operators, clearly sees the connection between his employees' motivation and the company's performance. He stated that if his employees do not do their jobs well, the company will lose clients (e.g., because of lower-quality goods). Therefore, motivating his employees to perform effectively is of considerable strategic importance.

As the Grupo M example illustrates, organizations and managers who can successfully motivate their employees are

rewarded with high performance. However, that is not so easy to accomplish. If it were, every employee would be an outstanding performer. One major obstacle is that conditions beyond a company's or a manager's control can affect employee motivation. Furthermore, these conditions keep changing. The state of the economy, for instance, constantly fluctuates, and this can influence the motivation level of many employees. Also, family and other personal circumstances that arise from outside the organization come into the work situation and affect attitudes about staying or leaving and a willingness to put in extra effort on the job. Understanding these and other forces that impinge on motivation has been a continuing challenge for managers ever since the beginning of the industrial age. However, what we hope to demonstrate in this chapter is that regardless of factors not directly under one's control, the motivation of other people potentially can be influenced by anyone in a managerial position. In other words, managers have many opportunities to affect the motivation of those who work with and for them—especially if they understand some of the basic principles that are involved in the motivational process. If you as a manager want to be able to demonstrate leadership, then you need to develop your capabilities to motivate those around you.

From a motivational perspective, the views and actions of Fernando Capellan at Grupo M raise some interesting issues. Perhaps the most important one is: Will his approaches to motivating the people who work for him be successful in a wide variety of other organizations and settings? Does the fact that Grupo M is located in the small, developing country of Dominican Republic limit how applicable those approaches are to locations and circumstances that are quite different? Would they work as well in a large manufacturing firm situated in the industrial East Coast of the United States? In a rural area of China? In a Wall Street securities firm? In an advertising firm in London? Does the fact that Capellan is owner and founder and chief executive make a difference? Would his motivational methods and attitudes achieve the same results if he were a lower-level shift supervisor such as Angel Lorenzo is? These are just some of the intriguing questions raised by this opening vignette.

WHAT IS MOTIVATION?

motivation set of forces that energize, direct, and sustain behavior

When we use the term "motivation," regardless of the setting, what does it mean? **Motivation** can be thought of as the set of forces that energize, direct, and sustain behavior. These forces can come from the person, the so-called "push" of internal forces, or they can come from the environment that surrounds the person, the so-called "pull" of external forces. It is therefore essential for managers to recognize the importance of both sets of factors—a major type of duality—when they are analyzing motivational causes of behavior.

It is important to stress at the outset that an overemphasis on one set of forces to the exclusion of the other can lead to a faulty diagnosis and to actions that do not solve motivational problems. For example, a manager might assume that her subordinate's level of sales calls is low because he is lazy, when in fact appropriate incentives have not been provided that tap his needs or interests. The manager would be assuming the cause to be lack of an internal push force, whereas a more accurate diagnosis in this case would focus on inadequate pull forces. This kind of misreading of motivation, which is easy to do, could lead to the loss of a potentially valuable employee. Likewise, an assumption that a clerical worker is doing an especially good job in order to please his supervisor would be putting weight on external or pull forces to explain his motivation, while perhaps not giving enough credit to internal push forces. This worker might be a person who is highly motivated no matter what kind of supervision or direction he receives. In both of these examples, a broader view of motivational factors should lead to more valid and useful assessments.

Throughout this chapter, different types of motivational forces will be examined, with particular emphasis on what psychologists and other behavioral scientists have had to say about the content and process of motivation. First, though, we begin with a framework to analyze the sources of motivational forces in the work situation. Following that, several major behavioral theories of motivation are examined. In later sections of the chapter, attention is focused on how reinforcement systems and the social environment of work can affect the strength and direction of motivation.

SOURCES OF MOTIVATION

As shown in Exhibit 12.1, there are three basic categories of variables that determine motivation in the work setting:

- Characteristics of the individual
- Characteristics of the job
- Characteristics of the work situation

The first category, the individual's characteristics, is the source of the internal, or push, forces of motivation, that is, what the employee *brings to* the work setting. The individual's contributions to motivational forces con-

exhibit 12.1

Key Variables That Influence
Motivation

INTERNAL (PUSH FORCES)		EXTERNAL (PULL FORCES)
Characteristics of THE INDIVIDUAL (examples)	**Characteristics of THE JOB (examples)**	**Characteristics of THE WORK SITUATION (examples)**
Needs	Feedback	Immediate Social Environment
· For security	· Amount	· Supervisor(s)
· For self-esteem	· Timing	· Workgroup members
· For achievement		· Subordinates
· For power	Work load	
Attitudes	Tasks	Organizational Actions
· About self	· Variety	· Rewards & compensation
· About job	· Scope	· Availability of training
· About supervisor		· Pressure for high levels of output
· About organization	Discretion	
	· How job is performed	
Goals		
· Task completion		
· Performance level		
· Career advancement		

sist of three major subsets of variables: (a) needs—such as the need for security, self-esteem, achievement, or power; (b) attitudes—toward self, a job, a supervisor, or the organization; and (c) goals—such as task completion, accomplishment of a certain level of performance, and career advancement.

The second and third categories of basic causal variables refer to the external, or pull, forces of motivation. Characteristics of the job focus on what the person *does* in the work setting. These include how much direct (without the intervention of anyone else) feedback the person receives by performing tasks, the workload, the variety and scope of the tasks that make up the job, and the degree of discretion the person is allowed in meeting the requirements of the job.

The other external category, work situation characteristics, refers to what *happens to* the individual. This category has two sets of variables: the immediate social environment composed of the supervisor(s), members of the workgroup, and subordinates; and various types of organizational actions, such as, for example, reward and compensation practices, the availability of training and development, and the amount of pressure applied to achieve high levels of output.

Taken together, the three major categories of variables—individual, job, and work situation—can serve as a useful framework for analyzing the sources of motivation, whether in Bangkok, Lima, or Chicago. Focusing on them also forms a good basis for considering the major theories of motivation relevant to managing in organizational settings. These theories are presented next. In addition, it is important to remember that the specifics of any of these sources can change at any time, which in turn can affect an individual's or group's motivation. Therefore, the alert manager watches for such possible changes and reevaluates, if necessary, his or her approach to motivation.

MOTIVATION THEORIES APPLICABLE TO WORK SITUATIONS

Several theories of motivation are particularly relevant for work settings. Each of these theories highlights one or more of the variables just discussed (and displayed in Exhibit 12.1). Each theory also provides managers with useful perspectives for understanding motivational challenges and problems and ways to deal with them.

Before examining the basic features of these motivational theories, however, it is important to note that almost all were developed by American behavioral scientists. Thus, an obvious question is: Do these theories apply only in the context of American culture and society, or are they also useful in analyzing motivation in other societies and cultures?[1] Unfortunately, the answer is not clear. Based on the available evidence, the best answer is that some of the theories do have relevance beyond the American context, but others may have fewer worldwide applications. However, these theories should not be automatically rejected because they originated in a particular cultural context, nor should they be routinely accepted as always applying equally well across different cultures. Their usefulness to the manager resides in providing possible ways of looking at motivational problems and issues, whatever the context.

Psychologists who have studied the topic typically have categorized motivation theories into two types: content theories and process theories, as shown in Exhibit 12.2. The two types together provide us with a deeper understanding of motivation.

Content Theories

content theories motivation theories that focus on what needs a person is trying to satisfy and on what features of the work environment seem to satisfy those needs

Content theories focus on what needs a person is trying to satisfy and on what features of the work environment seem to satisfy those needs. Such theories try to explain motivation by identifying both (a) internal factors, that is, particular needs, and (b) external factors, particular job and work situation characteristics, that are presumed to cause behavior. Two content theories, need hierarchy and acquired needs, are concerned with identifying internal factors, and one, the two-factor theory, is concerned with identifying external factors.

Need Hierarchy Theories The most prominent need hierarchy theory was developed a half century ago by psychologist Abraham Maslow.[2] His theory has had a certain appeal to managers, probably because it is easy to remember and contains five types of needs that are arranged in a hierarchy of strength and influence.

exhibit 12.2

Motivation Theories

	Content Theories	Process Theories
Focus	· Personal needs that workers attempt to satisfy · Features in the work environment that satisfy a worker's needs	· How different variables can combine to influence the amount of effort put forth by employees
Theories	· Maslow's Need Hierarchy · McClelland's Acquired Needs Theory · Herzberg's Two-Factor Theory	· Equity Theory · Expectancy Theory

The five needs in Maslow's hierarchy (starting with the most essential or prepotent) are:

- Physiological: Needs for the most basic essentials of life, such as air, water, food, shelter, and so on.
- Security (safety): The needs to feel safe and secure and not to be threatened by circumstances in the surrounding environment that might jeopardize continued existence.
- Social (belongingness): The needs to be loved, to interact and relate to other people, and to be accepted by them.
- Esteem: The needs for a sense of one's own worth and competence and for recognition of that worth from other people.
- Self-actualization: The needs to be personally fulfilled, to feel a sense of achievement and accomplishment, and especially, to develop one's own unique capabilities and talents to the highest possible level.

An example of a manager operating in a very intensive information technology environment who attempts to give attention to virtually all of these needs in his interactions and dealings with his employees, and who is strongly supported by his company in doing so, is provided in A Manager's Challenge, "An Information Systems Manager's Approach to Meeting Employees' Needs."

The essence of **Maslow's need hierarchy** theory is that an individual is motivated to satisfy the most basic or potent needs first (such as physiological needs) and then, if those are satisfied, move to the next level. The actions of Grupo M, as described in our opening story, illustrate an organization that strives to make sure that its employees' basic needs are satisfied. According to the theory, when those needs have been fulfilled, individuals will be more likely to concentrate their efforts on satisfying higher-level needs. However, if these persons' basic physiological and security needs should become threatened, they would then be likely to revert to focusing on those lower-order needs. They would decrease their efforts to satisfy social, esteem, and achievement needs until or unless the threat has passed.

Maslow's need hierarchy
theory that states people fulfill basic needs, such as physiological and safety needs, before making efforts to satisfy other needs, such as social and belongingness, esteem, and self-actualization

SAS Institute, one of the world's leading software developers, knows it's no better than the talent of the programmers who work for it. When the company's employees leave the building for the evening, CEO Jim Goodnight knows that it's his job to motivate them to come back the next day. Toward that end, SAS offers its employees a plethora of benefits unheard of at most companies—onsite day care, extensive healthcare facilities, an art museum, assistants to help employees with their day-to-day personal matters, and even live entertainment in the company's lunchroom.

tech|nol|ogy

a manager's challenge

An Information Systems Manager's Approach to Meeting Employees' Needs

Is attention to employees' needs just as important in technology-intensive work environments as it is in low-tech work situations? One manager of a technology-oriented organizational unit apparently thinks so.

He is John Loranger, vice president of information systems for the famous catalog and Internet retailer, Lands' End of Dodgeville, WI. Loranger puts a strong emphasis on developing good relationships with the employees in his division. "I'm absolutely nothing without the 250 people here," he says. He views getting to know his staff and creating a work environment they want to stay in as "my other 40-hour-a-week job." His commitment shows. With 50 percent of new hires coming from referrals made by current employees and turnover well under 10 percent, the division's staff is remarkably stable.

Loranger honors employees' social needs by making it a point to meet every new hire and ask, "How have we treated you? How's your family adjusting to the move?" He instills the same people orientation in the managers who work for him and says of the manager's job: "You need to listen. Make sure that if there's something going on in [an employee's] life—they've had a death in the family, they're going through a divorce—if their performance slacks off a bit, you've got to give them a little flexibility. When they get through it, they're going to work extra hard because they know you were there for them when they needed you to be."

Lands' End avoids what Loranger calls "hokey retention incentives," such as giving away expensive cars and trips, but it does meet esteem needs by giving spot bonuses like a $50 dinner or gift certificate for performance above and beyond the norm. It also hosts frequent special events to bring employees together outside their work environment. "People work better together when they know each other on a nonwork basis," says Loranger. One recent event featured a performance by Garrison Keillor, for example.

Self-actualization needs are also heeded. Weekly one-on-one meetings between employees and their managers offer opportunities for career development and performance feedback. Lands' End fosters the idea that employees who want to grow by moving to other parts of the company can only strengthen the firm through their increased understanding of the way its different units work. The human resources representative for Loranger's department also holds random feedback sessions with employees to keep up to date with how well things are going and whether people are satisfied with their environment. And Loranger himself has regular lunches with his staff. As he puts it, "If you try every day to maintain a great working environment, treat people right and compensate them fairly, I believe that retention will take care of itself. This philosophy has always worked for Lands' End."

The question is, however, how well will Loranger's philosophy work at Sears, which purchased Lands' End in 2002? Before being acquired by Sears, Lands' End earned record profits. So far, Sears is being careful not to rock the boat of the Wisconsin retailer—one of the last successful, direct-only apparel companies—particularly Lands' Ends' very successful Web site, information technology systems, and, especially, its loyal and passionate workforce. "The trick will be to take advantage of Sears' size without losing the culture and nimbleness that got Lands' End where it is in the first place," says Erik Kinikin, vice president of Giga Information Group, a technology advising firm.

Sources: Debby Stankevich, "Lands' End to Boost Other Sears Apparel," *Retail Merchandiser*, November 2003, p. 6; Carole Sloan, "Sears Grows Home with Lands' End" (cover story), *Home Textiles Today*, March 17, 2003, pp. 1–2; Joanne Derbort, "Can He Prevent Indigestion?" *Baseline*, December 2002, p. 24; Melissa Solomon, "Staff Relationships: Your Other Full-Time Job," *Computerworld*, November 6, 2000, p. 54.

A good example of this theory occurred a few years ago at a plant of Ahlstrom Fakop, a Polish subdivision of Finnish paper and power equipment manufacturer A. Ahlstrom. Managers at the plant were having trouble motivating employees in the formerly state-owned enterprise. Offering incentive pay had not worked. Only when managers let employees know that no one would be laid off if sales targets were reached did employee morale pick up. Many of the employees were more concerned with keeping their job than with their pay level as their country moved from a state-controlled to a market economy.[3]

An even more extreme example of this principle occurred in the 1990s in the Los Angeles area. Young Thai nationals were working in garment workshops under conditions that approached slavery. For example, they were not allowed to leave the building in which they lived and worked (for up to 18 hours per day) for months and even, in some cases, years.[4] Need hierarchy theory clearly would have predicted that the workers would not have been concerned with satisfying higher-order needs like belonging, esteem, and self-actualization when their most basic needs—physiological and safety—were not being met.

The key to understanding a person's motivation, then, from a need hierarchy perspective, is to identify that person's most basic need that is not yet satisfied. For the Thai garment workers in Los Angeles, that level would be the most basic: physiological needs. Once a need has been satisfied, it ceases to be a motivator unless its fulfillment is threatened again. But, if it is threatened, that more basic need becomes the focus of attention, as in the Polish manufacturing plant example.

Many questions can be raised about need hierarchy theory. For example, do the needs occur in the same hierarchical order across all cultures and countries? Probably not. The theory was developed in an American context, and there is no convincing evidence that the hierarchy is universal, either from country to country or from one person to the next. As one knowledgeable scholar has argued, based on extensive research findings from a number of countries:

> *Maslow's hierarchy puts self-actualization (achievement) plus esteem above social needs, above security needs. This . . . is a description of a value system, the value system of the U.S. middle class to which the author belonged. I suggest that . . . for (some) countries [such as Greece and Mexico], security needs should rank at the top; for (other) countries [such as Denmark and Sweden] . . . social needs should rank at the top; and (for still other) countries [such as Portugal and Chile], both security and social needs should rank at the top.[5]*

Not only does the hierarchy of needs probably not have the same order across different cultures, it almost assuredly is not ordered the same from one individual to another. Furthermore, different individuals have quite different thresholds for satisfaction of a given need before they try to satisfy the next level. For example, someone who as a child grew up in a family whose financial resources were extremely scarce may go to inordinate lengths to assure current financial security as an adult even though the person is quite well off. Such individual differences in both the order of needs and the threshold for satisfying them clearly adds complexity for managers who attempt to base actions on the theory.

Although Maslow's need hierarchy theory is relevant to work situations, it was not developed specifically for that purpose and therefore it has been difficult for researchers to determine its validity or usefulness in predicting behavior in organizational settings. Probably the greatest value of the theory is that it provides a way of thinking about motivation that highlights the issue of psychological needs, and the differing strength of those needs, that a person could be trying to satisfy at work.

A somewhat more simplified variation of need hierarchy theory was published subsequent to Maslow by behavioral scientist Clay Alderfer. His alternative version, labeled ERG theory for Existence-Relatedness-Growth, collapsed Maslow's five levels into three and provided a more straightforward way of thinking about need hierarchies. (Exhibit 12.3 provides a graphic comparison of the two classifications of needs.) Although sharing many similarities with Maslow's original theory, ERG theory differs in some respects.[6]

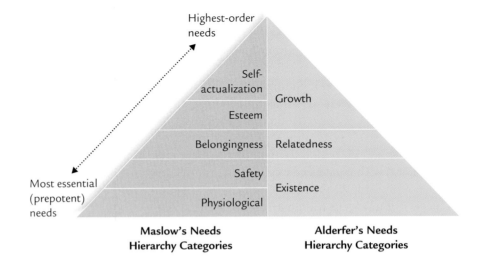

exhibit 12.3

Maslow's and Alderfer's Needs Hierarchies Categories

For example, it presumes that different levels of needs can be active at the same time and thus a lower level does not have to be completely or even mostly satisfied before higher-level needs can emerge. Also, Alderfer's version suggests that even though a lower-level need has already been satisfied, a person may revert to focusing on that level if he or she is frustrated in trying to satisfy a higher level. Thus, an employee blocked in trying to gain opportunities for increased personal growth because she keeps getting assigned routine tasks may concentrate instead on socializing at work and gain even more satisfaction (than before) of relatedness needs. ERG theory presents an interesting alternative to Maslow's earlier, more complicated version, but the key point is that both theories focus on individuals' attempts to satisfy particular types of needs and on how that can affect the amount and direction of motivation.

From the standpoint of individual managers in an organization, there is probably relatively little they can do personally to affect employees' satisfaction of basic physiological needs, unless, of course, they are both the owner and chief executive, as is the case with Fernando Capellan at Grupo M. Many managers frequently do, however, have an opportunity to help ensure that employees' safety needs are not threatened and, within the limits of company policy and economic conditions, that security needs are met as much as possible.

With regard to satisfaction of employees' higher-order needs, managers can use their imagination and creativity to play a much more prominent and influential role. Many managerial actions can help employees obtain satisfaction of social, esteem, and even self-actualization needs. For example, at Branch-Smith, Inc., in Fort Worth, Texas, managers encourage their employees to "report" on fellow employees. As part of a program called "Caught in the Act," they ask employees to write a short note of praise when they see another employee performing exceptionally well. These write-ups are then posted on the employee bulletin board and also reproduced in the company newsletter.[7] In this example, satisfaction of the needs of both parties is probably increased: self-actualization needs of the initiator for the "selfless" act of taking the time and trouble to write up the deeds of another employee, and esteem needs of the recipient through public recognition.

In recent years a number of companies have provided their employees with an innovative opportunity to satisfy self-actualization needs at the same time that they help other individuals, for instance by sponsoring a day where employees can work with a volunteer organization such as Habitat for

Since 1976, Habitat for Humanity has built more than 50,000 houses for families throughout the United States, and another 100,000+ houses in communities around the world. Many managers encourage their employees to volunteer for Habitat for Humanity—in some instances, to build homes for their own coworkers. In the future, Habitat houses are expected to shelter 1 million people.

Humanity to build homes for disadvantaged families. This type of program allows employees to make a difference in their communities as well as build camaraderie and increase their feelings of self-worth.

Acquired Needs Theory Another content theory that is centered on needs was developed by an American psychologist, David McClelland.[8] This **acquired needs theory** focuses on learned needs that become "enduring predispositions" of individuals, almost like personality traits, and that can be stimulated or activated by appropriate cues in the environment. McClelland considered three of these needs to be especially important (and hence his theory is sometimes referred to as the "three-need theory"): affiliation, power, and achievement. However, most of the attention other researchers have given to the theory of acquired needs has concentrated on the need for achievement.

acquired needs theory
motivation theory that focuses on learned needs that become enduring predispositions for affiliation, power, and achievement

In McClelland's theory, a person who has a high need for achievement is someone who habitually strives for success or attainment of goals in task situations (though not necessarily in other types of settings). The research data collected by McClelland and his associates indicate that high need achievement individuals prefer to

- work on tasks of moderate difficulty
- take moderate risks
- take personal responsibility for their actions
- receive specific and concrete feedback on their performance

In other words, high need achievers want challenges, but realistic challenges, not impossible ones. Especially important from a managerial perspective, McClelland's theory suggests that the need for achievement can be increased by "appropriate" training, that is, by showing people how to recognize and respond to relevant achievement cues. As might be assumed, this feature of the theory has proved to be quite controversial, since many experts doubt the extent to which permanent changes in need for achievement can be brought about by such training.

Is a need for achievement a universal motive? Is it, for example, as prevalent in Brazil as in the United States, or in India as much as in Germany? A study that was carried out across 20 countries appeared to show that achievement, along with power, can be considered a universal motive.[9] Although countries with quite different cultures—for example, very different attitudes toward individuality and collectivism—were included, the study indicated that a high-achieving type of person could be found in each country or culture. The findings suggest that the percentage of high-achieving people varies considerably from country to country, but the critical point is that there are definitely people of this type in every culture that has been studied: "It seems that the primary goal of achievers everywhere is to attain recognition for themselves."[10]

Interestingly, research findings show that there were fairly large changes in the level of achievement motivation in both Japan and the United States in the first several decades after World War II.[11] There was a definite overall decrease in achievement motivation in Japan between the 1970s and the beginning of the 1990s, especially in younger generations. This could be due, in part, to the increase in overall prosperity in Japan during that particular time span. On the other hand, younger people in the United States showed higher levels of achievement motivation at the beginning of the 1990s than their counterparts did in the late 1960s and early 1970s, perhaps reflecting the decreasing levels of economic security that occurred in the United States over that time span. Taken together, these findings seem to reinforce the conclusion that achievement motivation can be influenced by strong forces in the larger societal environment, such as changing cultural attitudes toward work and changing economic conditions. Research from the mid-1990s, incidentally, appeared to indicate that achievement motivation remained somewhat lower in Japan than in the United States, but that could change again with future societal changes in the two different countries.[12]

two-factor theory motivation theory that focuses on the presumed different effects of intrinsic job factors (motivation) and extrinsic situational factors (hygiene factors)

Two-Factor Theory In the early 1960s, Frederick Herzberg, an American psychologist, proposed a motivation theory that came to be called the "two-factor theory."[13] The **two-factor theory** focused on the distinction between factors that can increase job satisfaction ("motivators") versus those that can prevent dissatisfaction but cannot increase satisfaction ("hygiene factors"). As shown in Exhibit 12.4, motivators are "intrinsic" factors directly related to the *doing*

exhibit 12.4

Herzberg's Two-Factor Theory: Motivators and Hygiene Factors

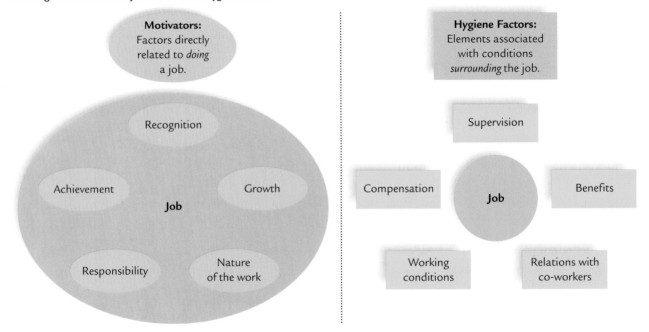

of a job, such as the nature of the work itself, responsibility, personal growth, and the sense of achievement and recognition directly received by performing the work. The other factors, "hygiene" factors, are "extrinsic" to directly performing the job. They, instead, are associated with conditions *surrounding* the job. Included in this set are supervision, relations with coworkers, working conditions, and company policies and practices related to benefits and compensation.

Within the past few years, General Electric Company has given some attention to this distinction between the two types of factors with respect to the motivation of sales personnel. Unlike other areas of the company, such as finance and manufacturing, where there traditionally has been a high level of satisfaction, sales managers tended to have more complaints—about too much paperwork, too many lateral transfers, and too little time to talk directly with their customers. GE executives started by giving attention to hygiene factors, such as cutting down on paperwork and bureaucratic red tape for the sales managers. Then they turned to motivator factors: They instituted new training programs and, in particular, gave the sales managers total responsibility for individual clients rather than having a different manager deal with each product line.[14]

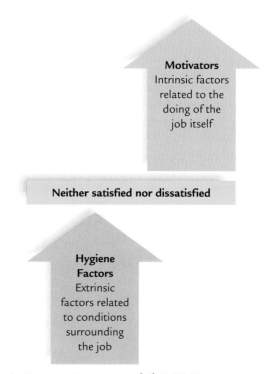

exhibit 12.5

Herzberg's Two-Factor Theory: Differential Effects of Hygiene Factors and Motivators

As shown in Exhibit 12.5, the two-factor theory predicts that "motivator" factors actively increase satisfaction, while hygiene factors only decrease dissatisfaction to a state of "neither satisfied nor dissatisfied."

The theory proved an immediate hit with practicing managers when it was first proposed some years ago, because it contains a relatively simple message: If you want to motivate employees, focus on improving how the job is structured—what they *do*—so that they obtain positive job satisfaction. Simply taking care of the hygiene factors can prevent dissatisfaction but will have no effect on positive motivation.

Although intuitively appealing, the two-factor theory has been criticized by many scholars as being overly simplistic. For one thing, research has shown that satisfaction and motivation are not the same thing. Reacting positively to something, such as being pleased with doing a more challenging set of tasks, does not necessarily mean that you will have increased motivation or a stronger desire to perform the job better. Therefore, although changing the nature of the work can often lead to an increase in intrinsic satisfaction, it does not necessarily follow that motivation to perform is increased. Critics thus contend that the theory blurs the distinction between satisfaction and motivation. Also, subsequent research has shown that it is not possible to distinguish clearly between variables that only increase satisfaction and those that only decrease dissatisfaction.

Implications for Job Design Despite these and other criticisms, however, the widespread attention given to the two-factor theory has had one very important consequence in the years after it was proposed: an increased emphasis on the design of jobs; that is, on the combinations of specific tasks put together to form particular jobs.[15] If nothing else, the two-factor theory was responsible for influencing both organizational scholars and employers to consider the issue of how the content of jobs affects the motivation to perform those jobs. It highlighted the question of whether it is possible to provide increased opportunities for employees to experience greater feelings of responsibility,

job enrichment increasing the complexity of a job to provide greater responsibility, accomplishment, and achievement

job characteristics model approach that focuses on the motivational attributes of jobs through emphasizing three sets of variables: core job characteristics, critical psychological states, and outcomes

accomplishment, and achievement, as, for example, described above in the changes made in GE sales managers' jobs. The general approach to designing jobs that tries to provide such opportunities is called **job enrichment**.

One of the most comprehensive approaches to the design of enriched jobs with high potential for increased motivation has been labeled the "job characteristics model."[16] Developed by two organizational scientists, J. Richard Hackman and Greg Oldham, the **job characteristics model** emphasizes three components (as shown in Exhibit 12.6):

- Core job characteristics, such as skill variety and task significance
- Critical psychological states, such as experienced meaningfulness of work and experienced responsibility for outcomes of the work
- Expected outcomes, such as high internal work motivation and high work effectiveness

The Hackman-Oldham model also includes factors (called "moderators") such as individual differences in growth need strength that are presumed to affect the likelihood that enriched jobs will lead to the desired outcomes, although this aspect of the model has not received consistent validation in research studies.[17] Clearly, though, not every employee wants more responsibility, autonomy, and the like—but many do. The message for managers from this model is that if they can create or adjust jobs to include more of the "core characteristics" (see Exhibit 12.7), they may be able to increase the motivation and satisfaction of many of the employees who work in those jobs. Indeed, a useful way for managers, who often have highly

exhibit 12.6

Job Characteristics Model

Source: Adapted from J. R. Hackman and G. R. Oldham, *Work Redesign* (Reading, MA: Addison-Wesley, 1980).

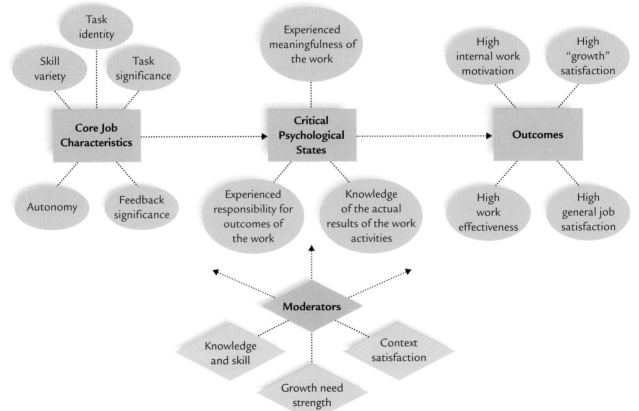

exhibit 12.7

Core Job Characteristics in Job Characteristics Model

Core Job Characteristics	Definition	Example
Skill variety	The degree to which a job requires a variety of different activities in carrying out the work, involving the use of a number of different skills and talents of the person.	The aerospace engineer must be able to create blueprints, calculate tolerances, provide leadership to the work group, and give presentations to upper management.
Task identity	The degree to which a job requires completion of a "whole" and identifiable piece of work, that is, doing a job from beginning to end with a visible outcome.	The event manager handles all the plans for the annual executive retreat, attends the retreat, and receives information on its success from the participants.
Task significance	The degree to which a job has a substantial impact on the lives of other people, whether those people are in the immediate organization or in the world at large.	The finance manager devises a new benefits plan to improve health coverage for all employees.
Autonomy	The degree to which a job provides substantial freedom, independence, and discretion to the individual in scheduling the work and in determining the procedures to be used in carrying it out.	R&D scientists are linked via the company intranet, allowing them to post their ideas, ask questions, and propose solutions at any hour of the day, whether at the office, at home, or on the road.
Feedback from job	The degree to which carrying out the work activities required by the job provides the individual with direct and clear information about the effectiveness of his or her performance.	The lathe operator knows he is cutting his pieces correctly, as very few are rejected by the workers in the next production area.

Source: Adapted from J. Richard Hackman and Greg R. Oldham, *Work Redesign* (Reading, MA: Addison-Wesley, 1980).

enriched jobs themselves, to think about enriching the jobs of their subordinates is to make those jobs more like their own!

A model example of job enrichment in action was provided by the Kern River Asset Team, located in Bakersfield, California. The organization was responsible for producing approximately 21,000 barrels of crude oil per day for Chevron Oil, prior to the company merging with Texaco in 2001. Several years ago, the Kern River Team restructured its operation into self-managing work teams, with each team responsible not only for the specific part of the oil extraction process they were previously responsible for, but also for many tasks formerly handled by managers. For example, the oil and water separation team members no longer just operated the machinery to separate the two components; they also handled the planning and prioritizing of their set of tasks, choosing how to combine specific tasks into efficient work routines. They also identified and implemented opportunities for process improvements, decided on measurement criteria, and flowcharted their progress. The new setup was far more motivating for team members compared to their former situation where they merely separated oil and water day after day.[18]

Process Theories

Process theories of work motivation deal with the way different variables combine to influence the amount of effort people put forth. In other words, while content theories address the issue of *which* variables affect motivation, process theories focus on the issue of *how* variables affect it. The four most prominent

process theories motivation theories that deal with the way different variables combine to influence the amount of effort people put forth

process types of theories are equity theory, expectancy theory, social cognitive theory, and goal-setting theory.

Equity Theory Developed in the early 1960s by psychologist Stacy Adams, **equity theory** proposes that individuals will compare their circumstances with those of others and that such comparisons may motivate certain kinds of behavior.[19] As one observer has pointed out, a particularly vivid example involves professional athletes:

> *(Such) athletes often make the news by demanding that their contracts be torn up before their terms expire. The reason for this apparent lack of respect for contract law usually involves feelings by these athletes that the previously agreed on rates of pay are [now], by some standard [of comparison], not fair.[20]*

Equity theory, as shown in Exhibit 12.8, assumes that people know what kind of effort and skills they put into their jobs and what kinds of outcomes (salary, promotions, etc.) they receive from their employer. The theory also assumes that individuals are likely to compare (a) their *ratios* of inputs to outcomes to (b) the *ratios* of other relevant people such as colleagues or acquaintances (in or outside their organization). Such comparisons determine whether the individual feels equitably treated. The most important assumption—as in the example of the professional athletes just cited—is that if the comparisons result in feelings of inequity in favor of the other persons, the individual making the observation will be motivated to try to take steps to reduce such feelings. (It should also be pointed out that comparisons can result in feelings of inequity that favor the observer. In that case, the individual could take steps, such as increasing one's own inputs, to reduce the perceived inequity. However, the commonsense assumption is that this kind of situation—where the other comparison person's ratio of outcome to inputs is perceived as being worse than one's own—will occur relatively infrequently.)

equity theory motivation theory that focuses on individuals' comparisons of their circumstances with those of others and how such comparisons may motivate certain kinds of behavior

exhibit 12.8
Equity Theory

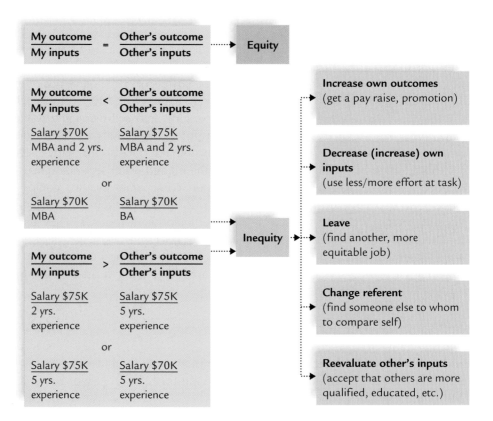

Equity theory states that individuals have a number of ways to reduce their feelings that others are "doing better" than they are. One way is to increase their own outcomes, such as getting a salary increase or obtaining a promotion. Another response might be to decrease their inputs; for example, they might try to put less effort into the task and still receive the same level of outcomes, if possible. A third action might be to leave their current situation so that they can obtain a new outcome/input ratio.

If people do not think they are being rewarded equitably—that is, do not believe they are obtaining "distributive justice"[21] (in social scientists' terminology)—they have other ways of dealing with the situation. They might simply change the object of their comparison—that is, they might decide to compare themselves to different people; for example, neighbors instead of work colleagues, whom they think have ratios more similar to their own. This involves no change of behavior but only a change in the way of looking at a situation. Likewise, people might reevaluate the inputs and outcomes of those with whom they are comparing themselves, as in "she has more skills than I thought she did" or "his job isn't as good as I thought it was."

Except in limited experimental situations, equity theory has not been very successful in predicting *which* method of dealing with inequity a person will use in a given situation. However, the chief value of this theory is that it highlights the importance of perceived equity and the role of comparisons to others' circumstances in affecting motivation. In effect, equity theory emphasizes the social nature of motivation.

Expectancy Theory Psychologist Victor Vroom (previously mentioned in Chapter 11) formulated a motivation theory applicable to work settings that is based on people's expectations.[22] Although details of the theory can get complicated, the basics are easy to understand and are diagrammed in Exhibit 12.9. **Expectancy theory** focuses on the thought processes people use when they face particular choices among alternatives, particularly alternative courses of action. With reference to the work situation, the theory (in simplified form) proposes that individuals have two kinds of beliefs that can affect the amount of effort they will choose to put forth. One such belief (typically referred to as an "expectancy"), effort (E) to performance (P), symbolized as (E → P), is the probability that a certain amount of effort will lead to a certain level of performance: "If I try to do this, will I succeed?" The other belief (often called an "instrumentality" belief), performance to outcome (O), symbolized as (P → O), is the probability that a particular level of performance will lead to (will be instrumental in obtaining) particular "outcomes" or consequences: "If I succeed, will I get praise from the boss?" The third key variable in the theory is

expectancy theory motivation theory that focuses on the thought processes people use when they face particular choices among alternatives, especially alternative courses of action

Expectancy Theory by Lymon Porter

Q&A

One Key

www.prenhall.com/onekey

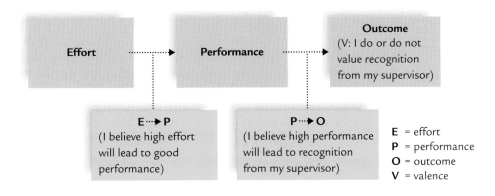

exhibit 12.9

Components of Expectancy Theory

E = effort
P = performance
O = outcome
V = valence

the valence (V), or anticipated value a person attaches to an outcome: "How much will I like praise from the boss if I get it?"

Expectancy theory states that the three key variables interact in a multiplicative, not additive, manner to determine the choice of the amount of effort needed to perform a particular task:

$$\text{Effort} = (E \rightarrow P) \times (P \rightarrow O) \times V$$

Since, according to the theory, these three variables are multiplied to determine level of effort, a low value of any one of the three would lead to the prediction that motivation would be very low. For example, even if a sales representative strongly believes that a certain level of performance (like meeting a sales quota) will lead to a very desirable reward (like positive recognition from her supervisor), her motivation will be low if she does not also have a strong expectation that effort will lead to that level of performance. To restate: Both expectancies and the anticipated value of the outcome must be high for a person to be highly motivated.

A number of implications for managerial practice flow from this theory. For each of the theory's three key variables, managers can take steps to increase employee motivation. The E $\rightarrow$ P expectancy can be modified by a variety of methods. If a person believes he doesn't have the skills needed to reach a certain level of performance, such self-perceptions can be changed. His manager can encourage him to get additional training and further practice, and by appropriately guiding and counseling him, build his confidence (thereby influencing his E $\rightarrow$ P expectancy). Employees who believe they are capable of performing well will be more motivated to achieve their goals.

Additionally, by consistently recognizing accomplishments, managers can increase employees' perceptions of the probability of obtaining a desired outcome if they have performed well (thereby influencing the P $\rightarrow$ O expectancy). How many times, however, do employees perform at a level strongly desired by the organization only to find that, from their perspective, the organization ignores or does not sufficiently recognize their accomplishment? If this happens continually, their level of motivation is certain to decrease.

On the other hand, the reverse is true: If difficult but desired levels of performance are reached and the supervisor or organization recognizes it in an explicit way, future levels of motivation can be increased. Employees are more motivated to perform well when they have a very strong expectation that they will be rewarded. This is the situation at software firm Metiom, Inc. Each year the 30 top software solutions sales representatives gain membership in an elite company group called "Inner Circle" and are rewarded with exceptional perquisites for themselves and their families. All members in the organization know that they have an opportunity to join the Inner Circle and gain its benefits if they perform exceptionally well.[23]

The following points sum up, from an expectancy theory perspective, the key ways that you as a manager can potentially influence employees' motivation:

- Identify rewards that are valued
- Strengthen subordinates' beliefs that their efforts will lead to valued rewards
- Clarify subordinates' understanding of exactly where they should direct their efforts
- Make sure that the desired rewards under your control are given directly following particular levels of performance

■ Provide levels and amounts of rewards that are consistent with a realistic level of expected rewards

One final issue relating to expectancy theory should be noted: Its application can be affected by cultural circumstances. For instance, in certain countries in the Middle East—where there is a strong emphasis on fate— attempts to change effort → performance (E → P) expectancies might not succeed. Likewise, attempts to single out an individual for public praise in a collectivistic culture, such as in many Asian or Latin American countries, would not likely have as positive an effect on that person's performance as it might in Germany or Australia, where individualism is a stronger characteristic. An approach that considers how individuals calculate the potential personal benefits in pursuing one course of action over another seems more relevant to most Western cultures than to cultures that place less emphasis on personal gain.

Although the psychological processes described in expectancy theory are not necessarily culturally bound, since they can occur anywhere, the frequency with which they occur probably is. For any culture, however, the key point is that expectancy theory is probably most useful in understanding and predicting levels of motivation that involve deliberate choices in the amount of effort to be put forth, rather than routine behavior that is largely determined by habit.

Social Cognitive Theory A process theory closely related to expectancy theory, and one that has received considerable recent attention among organizational scholars, is **social cognitive theory (SCT)**, developed by social psychologist Albert Bandura. For our purposes, we will concentrate on one key component of SCT: **Self-efficacy**. The concept of self-efficacy can be defined as "an individual's . . . confidence about his or her abilities to mobilize motivation, cognitive resources, and courses of action needed to successfully execute a specific task within a given context."[24] In other words, self-efficacy is the extent of a person's confidence that he or she can accomplish a given task in a specific situation. Such beliefs have three dimensions: magnitude (how difficult a task can be accomplished), strength (certainty of accomplishment), and generality (extent to which similar but not identical tasks can be accomplished). Research to date appears to show conclusively that when individuals have high self-efficacy beliefs, their work-related performance is better.[25]

From a managerial perspective, you should be asking this question: How can somebody's self-efficacy beliefs be increased? As shown in Exhibit 12.10, social cognitive theory proposes four major determinants:

■ *Enactive Mastery Experience:* Succeeding on a similar prior task *and* attributing that success to one's own capabilities rather than to luck or circumstances: for example, "I have the skill that it takes to succeed on this task," rather than, say, "I was lucky," or "I only did what was expected."

■ *Vicarious Learning/Modeling:* Knowledge gained by observing or learning how others successfully perform a task and then modeling one's own behavior in a similar manner.

■ *Verbal Persuasion:* Statements from others that convince a person that he or she can successfully perform the task. For instance, "As your manager, I have full confidence that you have the ability to perform this task quite successfully."

social cognitive theory (SCT) a theory that focuses on how individuals think about, or "cognitively process," information obtained from their social environment

self-efficacy an individual's confidence about his or her abilities to mobilize motivation, cognitive resources, and courses of action needed to successfully execute a specific task within a given context

exhibit 12.10

Social Cognitive Theory: Methods to Increase an Individual's Feelings of Self-efficacy

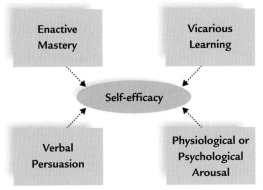

■ *Physiological and Psychological Arousal:* Potential energizing forces that can increase self-efficacy beliefs if the focus is directed to the task. For example, generating expressions of enthusiasm from colleagues can raise the arousal level of an individual. However, if such heightened arousal is focused on one's self—as is often the case, for example, when one is giving a speech—rather than on the task, it can be distracting and thus detrimental to self-efficacy and subsequent performance.

It should be clear from the above that if you are a manager there are several different ways to influence positively the self-efficacy of those who work with and for you. You can create opportunities for them to exhibit enactive mastery by taking on and succeeding in difficult tasks that they may have been initially reluctant to try to do. You yourself can model successful behavior for them, or you can arrange working conditions so that they can learn from those employees most experienced and competent at the task. You can, of course, attempt to convince them that they should be able to do a task successfully, but this is not always easy to do. And, of course, you can try to increase their energy level by inspiring them or directing their emotions toward specific task accomplishment. An essential point to keep in mind is that these various approaches to increasing others' self-efficacy are not mutually exclusive. One or more of them can be used together. Findings from research provide convincing evidence that you can motivate others to improve their performance. And, as A Manager's Challenge, "Sales Potential All Bottled Up," illustrates, increasing a person's self-efficacy is something that is probably applicable in many different types of cultures.

Goal Setting A somewhat different type of process theory that has attracted considerable research attention in recent years is **goal-setting theory**.[26] The notion of goal, a desired end state, highlights the importance of intentions. "Goal setting theory assumes that human action is directed by conscious goals and intentions."[27] Therefore, if managers can influence goals and intentions, they can directly affect performance. The level at which goals are set is a potentially powerful determinant of motivation, and obtaining a person's commitment to particular goals is crucial.[28]

The findings from goal-setting research point to two basic conclusions:

■ More challenging (higher or harder) goals, if accepted, result in higher levels of effort than easier goals.
■ Specific goals result in higher levels of effort than vague goals.[29]

Paula Hankins, manager of a Pier I Imports store in Nashville, Tennessee, used specific goals to motivate her employees to increase their sales during the holiday season. She decided to post the sales numbers from the previous season and the sales goal for the current season where everyone could see them. In this way, Hankins thought the sales personnel would be motivated to improve. She was gratified when the first day's sales level showed a 40 percent increase over the same day a year before, which was even higher than the 36 percent increase she had set as a goal.[30]

Despite consistent findings supporting a goal-setting approach in a number of well-controlled experiments, one dimension of goal setting has produced inconsistent and often contradictory results. This is the issue of whether goals that are set through a process of participation (by those who will be asked to meet them) result in higher performance than goals that are arbitrarily assigned by someone else such as a supervisor.

goal-setting theory assumes that human action is directed by conscious goals and intentions

globalization *a manager's challenge*

Sales Potential All Bottled Up

Mark Johnson (a real person whose name we have changed) was in a panic. He was meeting with the Asia Pacific Regional president in less than two weeks, and he would have to explain to him why sales were down 15 percent and profits were down 40 percent in the last six months since Johnson arrived.

Johnson was the managing director of a joint venture (JV) between Pepsi and a formerly state-owned enterprise that made and bottled carbonated cola and noncarbonated fruit beverages in Vietnam. The JV was established to bottle and distribute Pepsi beverages initially in southern Vietnam and eventually throughout the entire country. To everyone's delight, the JV did well during the first couple of years of operation. During that time, the JV management focused on the existing customers of the Vietnamese partner who were other state-owned enterprises. Johnson was sent to the JV in its third year of operation in large part to add a consumer-focused marketing and distribution strategy to the initial institutional base of customers.

Soon after his arrival, sales and profits began to decline. When Johnson asked his sales manager, marketing manager, and individual salesmen why sales and profits were declining, they simply shrugged their shoulders or blamed the rainy season. Johnson was totally frustrated. The sales targets for consumer sales were clear. The commissions that salesmen would receive if they hit their sales targets were very lucrative by Vietnamese standards. With unemployment at 12 percent, Johnson could not understand how salesmen would not be motivated by the reward system.

In a bit of desperation, Johnson went with one of the salesmen on some sales calls. What he discovered amazed him. First, even though his Vietnamese was not good, he could tell that the salesman was not comfortable with cold calls (calling on a new customer for the first time). Second, it was clear that the distribution and retail industries in Vietnam were significantly more fragmented than in the United States. Therefore, to achieve a particular volume of sales, a salesman in Vietnam might have to make 10 times as many sales calls. Johnson also discovered that most of the roads outside the main cities of Vietnam were dirt; during the rainy season they became almost impassible for the motorcycles and bicycles that were the primary means of delivering products to retailers.

While the salesmen acknowledged the performance expectations and lucrative rewards they would receive for meeting their targets, they were not motivated to try very hard. Why? Because they did not believe they had what it took to be successful. In particular, their past experience in dealing with long-established institutional customers gave them an understanding of managing existing customer relationships and taking orders, but not of making cold calls to small distributors and retailers. Although not the only issue, one of the ways to motivate the salesmen was to provide them with the information, training, and skills they needed—for example, procedures for making cold calls and how to become more efficient in consumer distribution activities. This increased their beliefs that they could hit their sales targets with these new customers and, consequently, obtain the promised rewards.

Source: Personal communications to author (JSB), 1998–2003.

There is some research that suggests that cultural factors may be particularly influential in determining whether participation is effective in the goal-setting process.[31] A study jointly conducted on American and Israeli university students showed that lack of participation had a much more serious negative effect on the Israeli students than on the American students. The authors of this study interpreted the findings as consistent with cultural differences between the two countries. "The results lead to the conclusion that the difference between Israelis and Americans is not their attitude toward participation but their reaction to assigned goals."[32] This research suggests that participation in goal setting will be more effective in countries and cultures where expectations of collective decision making exist, including decisions about goals. When such cultural expectations (or norms) are weaker, as in the United States, participation in goal setting may have much less effect. Overall, however, the basic conclusion across accumulated research findings from many studies is that setting goals has consistently positive effects on performance, no matter how those goals are set.

THE ROLE OF REINFORCEMENTS
AND CONSEQUENCES

Actions that occur before behavior takes place, such as setting goals, are considered antecedents to performance. Such antecedent actions can influence behavior, especially by clarifying expectations. However, events that happen to the individual *after* behavior—the consequences of performance—also can have a powerful effect on determining future motivation by reinforcing tendencies to continue or discontinue that behavior.[33] Consequences can be positive, neutral, or negative and can vary from insignificant to overwhelming. The deliberate application of them, however, provides a manager with a potentially powerful set of tools to influence performance. That is, they are powerful tools *if* the consequences are applied appropriately. As will be clear from the discussion that follows, this is not always easy to do.

Reinforcement Approaches

Analysis of the different reinforcement approaches focuses on whether particular behaviors will likely be repeated or lessened. The two principal approaches that can be used to increase the probability of behavior desired by the manager or organization are positive and negative reinforcements.

positive reinforcements

desirable consequences that, by being given or applied, increase the likelihood of behavior being repeated in the future

Positive Reinforcements Positive reinforcements are desirable consequences, often referred to as "rewards," that, by being given or applied, increase the likelihood of behavior being repeated in the future. In many instances, the use of positive reinforcements, such as a manager praising an employee for good performance, strengthens the likelihood of that behavior in the future, especially if such praise is not seen by the subordinate as routine or insincere. However, positive consequences also can inadvertently reinforce behavior that is not wanted.[34] For example, an employee may take a shortcut at considerable risk to the organization to achieve an important performance goal. The employee's manager congratulates the person for reaching the goal so quickly but does not realize that the risky behavior is also being reinforced. Other examples of managers' unintended reinforcement of the "wrong" behavior when trying to make changes that are intended to have positive results are described in A Manager's Challenge, "Can Motivation Go Wrong?" It should be fairly obvious that managers need to be more alert to the range of the potential effects of their actions on subordinates' motivation and future behavior.

One of the foremost experts on the use of rewards and reinforcements, Steven Kerr, suggests that for positive reinforcements (rewards) to be effective in motivating behavior in organizational settings, they should have the following attributes:

- *Equitable:* The size of rewards should be roughly related to the quality and/or quantity of past job-related performance.
- *Efficient:* Rewards must have some capacity for affecting future performance; for example, by making clear that a particular level of future performance will lead to a desired reward.
- *Available (capable of being given):* Managers and organizations should not talk about or offer rewards that are not readily available or are available in such small amounts that they are viewed by recipients as not really rewarding at all. As Kerr states: "Organizations with miniscule salary increase pools spend hundreds of management hours rating, ranking, and grading employees, only to waste time, raise

a manager's challenge

Change

Can Motivation Go Wrong?

The head of a public relations firm gave her staff the task of producing a report on their company's history to celebrate its tenth anniversary. The staff members, who always procrastinated, underestimated the time the project would require and were in danger of falling behind. The deadline could not be put off, however, so the head of the firm allowed them to drop all their other work and even hired temps to help them.

After a chaotic race to the finish line, the project was done, and the head of the company gave the staff a bonus to reward them for their hard work. What lesson did they probably learn about the effects of their procrastinating?

This real example demonstrates how easy it is for managers to mistakenly reinforce the wrong behavior with the best intentions when making changes. The head of the public relations firm gave her staff several reasons to continue an undesirable behavior—she lightened their workload, hired extra people to help them, and even gave them a cash bonus at the end. Nearly all the consequences of their poor time management were actually positive!

An insurance company trying to make a change in order to crack down on the number of overpayments sent to policyholders by mistake at the same time discouraged its employees from doing the research needed to clarify the amounts that were really due. It maintained strict standards that required a certain percentage of claims to be settled within 48 hours, so

new hires soon became aware of the norm: "When in doubt, pay it out."

To make matters worse, the company gave 5 percent raises to outstanding workers, 4 percent raises to above average workers, and 3 percent to all others even if their work was negligent and irresponsible. In fact, what the company seemed to reward the most was attendance. Those who had three or more separate instances of absence or lateness in any six-month period received no raise at all. So, while workers were highly motivated to show up to gain the 3 percent, they were not well enough rewarded for the quality of what they produced while they were there. Few workers chose to exert themselves enough to win the extra 1 or 2 percent above the minimum.

These examples illustrate that motivation can "go wrong" when managers fail to clarify goals and desired behaviors, especially when trying to make changes. The leaders of organizations need to take the long-term view of results and maintain a "big picture" view of the goals of the total organization. Asking a few key questions can be revealing, too. For instance: Is innovation and risk-taking desired even though rewards go to those who use tried-and-true methods and don't make any mistakes? Are employees' communication skills highly valued, but recognition and praise given only for technical achievements? Is employee empowerment strongly endorsed and advocated in spite of the fact that the organization retains rigid controls over all aspects of its operations and resources?

Sources: Curtis Sittenfeld, "Great Job! Here's a Seat Belt!," *Fast Company*, January 2004, p. 29; Judith L. Komaki, "Reinforcement Theory at Work: Enhancing and Explaining What Employees Do," in Porter, Steers, and Bigley, *Motivation and Work Behavior*, 7th ed. (New York: McGraw-Hill, 2003); Steven Kerr, "On the Folly of Rewarding A, While Hoping for B," *Academy of Management Executive*, February 1995, pp. 7–16.

expectations, and ultimately produce such pitiful increases that everybody is disappointed and embarrassed."

- *Not exclusive:* The possibility of obtaining rewards should not be limited to only a small percentage of employees. The more people that are "ineligible" or excluded from the possibility of obtaining rewards, the less likely a given reward will have a widespread effect.

- *Visible:* To be effective in having more than a very limited impact on the motivation of a number of people, rewards should be visible not only to recipients but also to others who possibly could obtain them in the future.

- *Reversible:* This attribute of effective rewards does not, of course, refer to a reward that can be taken away once given. Rather, it refers to rewards that can be denied or not given in the future, if circumstances warrant. The classic example in modern business organizations is the bonus. Unlike an annual pay raise, a bonus can clearly be a one-time-only reward. It also is a type of reward that can be given again in the future. That feature provides managers with a great deal of flexibility.[35]

Negative Reinforcements The *removal* of undesirable (i.e., negative) consequences, that is, consequences that a person performing an act does not want, can increase the likelihood of that behavior being repeated in the future. The removal of such undesirable consequences is called a **negative reinforcement**, just as the addition of desirable consequences is called a positive reinforcement. In both cases, they are reinforcing if they cause behavior to be maintained or increased. For example, a salesperson working in a sales territory with very difficult and demanding customers finds that, by putting in extra effort, the unpleasant experiences he has been encountering are reduced when he is transferred to a different territory. If he believes the transfer or promotion was a result of his hard work, the removal of the undesirable consequences (the difficult territory with difficult customers) has reinforced the likelihood that he will try hard to please his customers in his new territory. In this instance, both the company and the salesperson benefited from the negative reinforcement.

negative reinforcements undesirable consequences that, by being removed or avoided, increase the likelihood of a behavior being repeated in the future

Negative reinforcements, however, can also work against the best interests of the organization. For example, if a supervisor finds that giving a particular subordinate an "average" rating results in avoiding unpleasant confrontations with that subordinate that have occurred in the past—when the subordinate was given well-deserved "below-average" ratings—the supervisor's current action is negatively reinforced. However, the subordinate will probably continue with subpar performance, and the organization also will be deprived of accurate information on the subordinate that may be crucial in future promotion decisions.

Both of these reinforcement mechanisms—positive reinforcements and negative reinforcements—maintain or increase particular types of behavior and performance. Thus, they provide managers with potentially potent ways to increase desired behavior. However, if care is not taken, their use instead can lead to continuation or increases in behavior that is not wanted.

In contrast to these two reinforcement mechanisms for maintaining or enhancing particular behaviors, two other methods involving consequences, discussed next, are methods to *decrease* the probability of particular behaviors.

Punishments Punishments are undesirable consequences that are given following behavior in order to decrease the likelihood it will be repeated. In some organizations, punishments are seen as an effective way to prevent behavior that is not wanted. In many other organizations, however, punishments are discouraged, often because their use is seen as either inappropriate or ineffective. Also, they can have inadvertent effects of increasing behavior that is not wanted. For example, an undesired effect of a deliberately applied punishment occurs when a penalty is applied for excessive absenteeism, yet the behavior that is reinforced is not better attendance but more sophisticated excuses for being absent. This example illustrates that in organizations it is typically quite difficult to make sure that punishments have only the effects intended and no other effects.

punishments undesirable consequences that are applied to decrease the likelihood of behavior being repeated in the future

There are many examples of unintended punishment, with possible undesirable consequences. These include giving added pressure and responsibilities to someone who has shown that she can handle stress, or giving additional committee assignments to the person who has shown that he is exceptionally responsible in meeting commitments. Unless a manager is highly alert, unintended punishments happen more often than might be expected.

Extinction Another approach used to decrease behaviors is to avoid providing any positive consequences as the result of that behavior. This process is referred to as **extinction**. It is a well-demonstrated research finding, and a fact of everyday work life, that behaviors that do not lead to positive reinforcements tend not to be repeated, or at least not repeated as much. Managers can use the principle of extinction to their advantage by deliberately not reinforcing employee behavior that they consider undesirable. For example, managers might refrain from reacting positively to a joke that may be of questionable taste.

extinction the absence of positive consequences for behavior, lessening the likelihood of that behavior in the future

The principle of extinction, also, however, poses two challenges for managers. One is the inadvertent lack of attention to rewarding behavior that should be reinforced. A typical example of this often occurs in manufacturing organizations with respect to safety behavior. Frequently, safe work behavior is simply taken for granted by supervisors and is not explicitly reinforced. As a result, because safe behavior usually requires extra time and effort, employees gradually lose motivation to take these extra steps, and eventually an accident occurs. Another common example of unintentional application of the principle of extinction occurs when an employee puts in extra effort on a key project but receives little or no recognition or acknowledgment from the boss. In this type of case, the motivation to behave similarly the next time would not likely be strengthened, not only for the individual involved but also, and even more importantly, for other employees who observe these situations and their outcomes.

The second potential hazard of either the deliberate or unintended use of extinction is that it can leave the interpretation of important situations in the hands of employees rather than under the control of the manager. Explicit reinforcements or punishments provide the recipients with clear, or at least clearer, information regarding what their managers find desirable or undesirable behavior and performance.

The effects of each of these approaches to the use of reinforcements are summarized in Exhibit 12.11.

Planned Programs of Positive Reinforcement

Organizations often institute programs to apply systematically the principles of reinforcement theory (often called "behavior modification" or "applied behavior analysis" programs). These programs involve four basic steps:

exhibit 12.11
Reinforcement Approaches and Their Effects

Reinforcement Approach	Managerial Action	Effect	Example
Positive reinforcement	Provide desirable consequence	**Increase probability** of behavior being repeated	Highway construction supervisor receives bonus for each day a project is completed ahead of schedule.
Negative reinforcement	Remove undesirable consequence	**Increase probability** of behavior being repeated	Management stops raising output quotas each time workers exceed them.
Punishment	Provide undesirable consequence	**Decrease probability** of behavior being repeated	Habitually tardy crew member is fined the equivalent of one hour's pay each day he is late to work.
Extinction	Removable desirable consequence	**Decrease probability** of behavior being repeated	Group member stops making unsolicited suggestions when team leader no longer mentions them in group meetings.

1. Specify desired performance precisely. (Example: "Lower and keep the accident rate below 1 percent.")
2. Measure desired behaviors. (Example: "Monitor safety actions A, B, C.")
3. Provide frequent positive consequences for specified behaviors. (Example: "Give semiannual monetary rewards for performing a procedure safely 100 percent of the time.")
4. Evaluate the effectiveness of the program. (Example: "Were accidents kept below 1 percent over the previous six-month period?") Then make progress public knowledge.[36]

Programs of this type have been effective in a wide variety of work settings and in parts of the world as diverse as the Middle East, Europe, and the United States.[37] It is important to point out, however, that the effectiveness of the basic principles of reinforcement does not depend on formal company programs for their application. Any person in a managerial position can utilize these principles. They will be likely to have their greatest effect on the third of the three elements that make up the definition of motivation—the persistence of behavior.

SOCIAL INFLUENCES ON MOTIVATION

Although the point is sometimes overlooked, understanding motivation involves more than simply analyzing individual behavior. If our concern is about behavior in organizational work settings, it is crucial to recognize—as emphasized in Exhibit 12.1 at the beginning of this chapter—the powerful influence of the social context, particularly the individual's immediate workgroup as well as supervisors and subordinates.

Influence of the Immediate Workgroup

The immediate workgroup affects many aspects of a person's behavior, but one of the strongest effects is on motivation. This is particularly true for organizations operating in cultures and countries that have strong collectivistic tendencies and traditions, such as those in Asia and Latin America.[38] In such cultures, the individual is likely to be heavily influenced by the **in-group**, the group to which the person belongs, but less influenced by others who are not members of the in-group. Although stronger and more prevalent in collectivistic cultures than in some others, group influences on individuals' motivation can occur in almost any culture or organization, given appropriate circumstances.

in-group group to which a person belongs

What are those circumstances? Primarily, they involve (1) the existence of a group in which an individual is a member, the in-group, and especially (2) the strong desire of the person to be part of that group and to receive that group's approval. When this situation exists, the level of effort or motivation a person exerts almost certainly will be affected by the group's influence.

The direction of social influence on motivation will likely depend on the group's norms—the group's expected standards of behavior for its individual members. When those norms support the organization's goals, the influence will be to increase levels of motivation. When the norms oppose the organization's objectives, the influence will be to decrease levels of motivation to perform. And, as originally demonstrated in a study many years ago, the more cohesive a group is, the more it can affect performance motivation in either direction—up or down.[39] (Group norms will be discussed in detail in Chapter 13.)

A person's workgroup can affect motivational aspects of his or her work behavior other than just levels of performance. For example, a study of teenage workers in fast-food restaurants demonstrated that when an employee decided to leave the organization, it increased (not decreased) the desire of close friends to continue working at the restaurant. Although such a result might seem unexpected, the researchers explained the finding by hypothesizing that the friends who remained working at the restaurant had to reexamine ("justify") their reasons for staying, which resulted in a stronger determination to do so.[40] Thus, the social influence of the workgroup friends in this study clearly affected motivation of at least one type of behavior: staying with the organization.

Recently, Amway Company has directly acknowledged the influence of the workgroup on motivation by completely changing its traditional door-to-door sales approach in China. Stores with workgroups have replaced the individual-based sales network. The pay for each member of the group is directly tied to the performance of every other member, thereby motivating each to contribute to the overall store effort. Also, Amway has supported this workgroup approach by providing leadership training that emphasizes the focus on the group's impact on each person's motivation.[41]

Influence of Supervisors and Subordinates

Supervisors and subordinates, not just workgroup peers, are also part of the immediate social environment that can influence motivation. The impact of supervisors or leaders on the motivation of their employees is linked to their control of powerful rewards and potential major punishments, as we discussed earlier. However, it is important to emphasize that the motivational impact of someone in a supervisory position is not the same for all subordinates. In other words, although the person next highest in the organization typically has a strong effect on the motivation of those he or she supervises, that effect is often uneven. The same supervisor can be a source of increased motivation for some employees and a source of dampened motivation for others.[42] Much depends on the one-on-one interpersonal relationships that are developed over time in each supervisor–subordinate pair.

Subordinate employees themselves are not without influence on the motivation of their superiors, especially through their ability to punish behavior by subtly withholding rewards. Although subordinates typically do not have the same amount of reward leverage over their superiors, as is the reverse case, they are not powerless.[43] For example, they could withhold some expertise that only they have (and that the supervisor may not have) when not pleased with an action of the supervisor. A systems analyst, unhappy with the assignment she has been given, could resist pointing out some key technical details to her boss. Although such subordinate behavior is unlikely to be overt, it can affect the supervisor's motivation to act in the future in ways that produce these kinds of reactions.

Influence of the Organization's Culture

Not to be overlooked is the impact that the culture of the larger organizational context (beyond the workgroup) can have on employees' motivation. As one management scholar emphasized, "From a management perspective, [corporate] culture in the form of shared expectations may be thought of as a social control system."[44] This influence on motivation is exercised primarily through norms, in this case the organization's expected patterns of appropriate and acceptable behavior. Just as with a peer group, the more that an individual desires to remain part of an organization, the more he or she will be influenced by that organization's culture. The organization can be considered simply a larger type of group, with its culture often having a less direct influence on motivation than the immediate workgroup, but an influence nonetheless. Organizations that have gone through mergers or acquisitions know only too well that the imposition of unfamiliar cultural features and norms can have potentially devastating effects on the motivation of the members of the "new" entity.[45]

INFLUENCE OF VALUES AND ATTITUDES TOWARD WORK

No analysis of motivation in the work setting can be complete without consideration of the influence of an individual's values and fundamental attitudes toward work. Such values and attitudes are especially sensitive to cultural differences within a country or across countries. Managing in a global context requires attention to these differences if one is to understand work motivation beyond the cultures of a person's own group or country.

Values

Chapter 4 has already provided a general discussion of culture and cultural values. With that as a backdrop, we can look at the role of those values as they specifically affect motivation. As a reminder, values are enduring beliefs that a specific mode of conduct or end state of existence is preferable.[46] As this definition implies, values can be "end state," as in the case of "equality" or "liberty," or they can be "instrumental" and influence means to ends, such as the values of being cooperative, supportive, or competitive. Both kinds of values affect motivation levels because they influence what members of a particular culture consider crucially important. That in turn can influence goals and intentions. Values also affect what kinds of behaviors individuals will find rewarding and satisfying.[47] A Manager's Challenge, "A Great Management Job?" describes how one organization, National Student Partnerships, is relying heavily on the values of its employees to motivate their willingness to join and stay with an enterprise paying a relatively modest salary.

As might be expected, different cultures put different weight on particular values. Exhibit 12.12 shows how one set of scholars summarizes core value differences among three cultures from diverse parts of the world: American, Japanese, and Arabic.[48] Obviously, the valence (desirability) of different rewards would be quite different across these three cultures. Thus, from an expectancy theory framework of motivation, for example, managers supervising employees from these three cultures would need to consider the types of rewards to offer in return for high levels of performance.

To illustrate the role of cultural values in influencing the motivation of particular behaviors, it is instructive to focus on the dimension of "individualism-collectivism" that was first discussed in Chapter 4. As you recall, individualism is the subordination of a group's goals to a person's own goals, whereas collectivism is the subordination of personal goals to the goals of a group

ethics

a manager's challenge

A Great Management Job

How would you recruit someone for a great management job in a major U.S. city? The position you need to fill, Regional Director of a growing national organization, requires a bachelor's degree but little experience; it offers full health care benefits; it is busy, rewarding, and challenging; and best of all, the organization exists for just one purpose—to help others. On the other hand, the top salary you can offer is severely limited.

In fact, quite a few people are happy to work for National Student Partnerships (NSP), and for other organizations whose goals or mission satisfy employees' intrinsic needs. NSP employees' dedication to helping needy people find jobs in their local communities is what keeps alive the dream that inspired Brian Kreiter to start NSP in 1999, with fellow Yale student Kirsten Lodal. The company now has a small full-time staff, including several regional directors, a development director, a communications director, a chief operating officer, an executive director, and hundreds of unpaid student volunteers who provide the one-on-one services NSP offers in its 14 chapters nationwide.

Relying on outside financial backing to help pay its modest managerial salaries, NSP demonstrates how nonfinancial rewards can motivate those whose needs for achievement, affiliation, or self-actualization outweigh their desire for material reward, even if only temporarily. NSP, which recruits volunteers at campuses across the country, is well aware of the tension many students experience between their high ideals and their professional goals. "For the future social worker," said an NSP program coordinator, "this is an incredible hands-on experience working with people in the community. For the people who could care less about welfare but want to go to Salomon Smith Barney, we put them in charge of finances."

Peter Groves was on his way to a job interview at a Big Five accounting firm when Kreiter, a close friend, offered him the job at the fledgling operation, at half the salary Groves expected from the corporate world. It's not that NSP isn't goal oriented; it simply has values somewhat different from those of the corporate mainstream. "We resemble other modern-day companies in that we are very concerned with our bottom line," said Kreiter, who is unpaid. "Our bottom line just happens to be improving our community and giving others a hand."

That struck a chord, not just with Groves but with the many others who have accepted the challenge of helping to build a nonprofit organization from the ground up. "The idea of working my way up the ladder and paying my dues is just really unattractive," said Groves. "The only thing really missing is the chance for any of us to make a lot of money. But if you're going to work 10 hours a day, you might as well find a job you can throw your heart around."

Sources: Robert Scott Banaszak, "Letters," *Washington Monthly,* May 2003, pp. 2–3; Vanessa Blum, "Rookies with Heart," *Fast Company,* December 1999; Laura Meckler, "Students Work to Get People off Welfare," *Detroit News,* September 24, 1999, p. A8.

(which frequently is an extended family but may also be a workgroup).[49] An interesting line of research dealing with this dimension of culture as it affects motivation was carried out with Asian and American college students. The research project compared the preferences of the two sets of subjects for allocating rewards to members of work groups: according to "equality" (every member gets an equal share of the rewards) or according to "equity" (mem-

Equity vs. Equality
by Stewart Black

Q&A
OneKey
www.prenhall.com/onekey

exhibit 12.12

Differences in Core Values among Three Cultures

	American	Japanese	Arabic
Core Values	Competition	Group harmony	Reputation
	Risk-Taking	Belonging	Family Security
	Material Possessions		Religious Belief
	Freedom		Social Recognition

Source: Reproduced by permission. Adapted from table 3.3 from *Multicultural Management 2000* by Farid Elashmawi and Philip R. Harris, Ph.D. Copyright © 1998, Gulf Publishing Company, Houston, Texas, 800-231-6275. All rights reserved.

bers are rewarded in proportion to their individual contributions). The findings showed that although both Asian and American college students generally preferred equity as the basis for rewards, students from Hong Kong and Korean backgrounds tended to put relatively more emphasis on equality than did the Americans. This is in line with the basic hypothesis that those who are raised in a culture that values collectivism will be influenced by this value when put into a work situation. They will be more likely than those raised in an individualistic culture to consider the needs of everyone in their group, even if this means deviating somewhat from the generally preferred equity reward allocation. The research also showed that while Asian student subjects have a greater tendency to use equality as an allocation basis for rewards to in-group members, they did not necessarily extend this tendency to members of out-groups. Thus, Asian students were apparently distinguishing clearly between those two types of groups.[50]

Attitudes Toward Work

Understanding how different groups or cultures view the meaning of work, that is, how much the activity of working is valued, helps us to gain additional insight into motivational differences across cultures. The famous sociologist Max Weber was one of the first to describe how the meaning attached to work has affected motivation in industrial societies. His contention was that in so-called "Christian countries" of his era (late nineteenth and early twentieth centuries), Protestant religious values emphasized and supported hard work and the accumulation of wealth. This idea led him to coin the well-known phrase "the Protestant work ethic."[51] According to Weber, many people in the United States and in northern European countries were assumed to be guided by such an ethic, whether or not they were literally "Protestants."

A body of scholarly research carried out in the last decades of the twentieth century on the meaning of work focused especially on **work centrality**, defined as "the degree of general importance that working has in the life of an individual at a point in time."[52] To measure work centrality, researchers asked working adult respondents to rate the importance of work to them and also to compare its importance to other major life roles such as leisure, family, and religion. The resulting overall score for four countries, on an index from low to high, is shown in Exhibit 12.13. It can be seen that for these particular cultures, work was relatively more important and more central in life experiences in Japan than it was in the other three countries including the United States.[53]

Not all features of the work environment are valued equivalently by different groups of employees. A recent research study,[54] for example, sheds some light on this issue. The study was carried out on a sample of some 4,500 "knowledge workers and managers"—arguably a segment of employees that will be one of the most important to organizations in the future—from 10 large, technology-intensive companies (including those in aerospace, software, and pharmaceutical industries) that have major operations in North America, Europe, and Asia. Survey data were collected from this sample and analyzed by age, gender, and geographical region of the respondents. The focus was on what aspects of the work situation are seen as most important. The findings demonstrate that there are differences by age, gender, and region. Factors such as "career advancement" and "professional career development" were rated more important by

work centrality the degree of general importance that working has in the life of an individual at a point in time

exhibit 12.13

Work Centrality: Country Differences

Source: Adapted from I. Harpaz and H. Fu, "Work Centrality in Germany, Israel, Japan, and the United States," *Cross-Cultural Research* 31, no. 3 (1997), pp. 171–200.

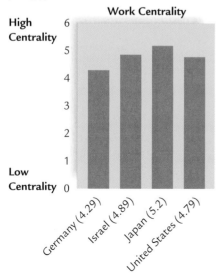

younger versus older employees. Women, at early stages of their careers, put more emphasis on job security and less on financial rewards, compared to men. At later stages, women put more importance on career advancement and professional development than did men in the sample. The major difference by region involved "international opportunities" (for career advancement), seen as more important by Asians and Europeans, compared to Americans.

What are the motivational and managerial implications of such research findings that examine the meaning and importance of work, and different features of work, in different cultures and groups? First, they show that since work does not generate the same relative degree of importance among employees, compared with other significant areas of their lives, managers face different motivational challenges relating to different sets of employees or in different cultural contexts. Second, since the meaning of work appears to vary among different categories of employees and in different countries, the findings indicate that specific incentives—such as pay raises, time off, or opportunities for career advancement—will not have the same motivational effect in all situations and with all people. The message is that managers cannot assume that everyone else will value work, and different elements of work, in the same way that they themselves do. A sensitivity to these differences, therefore, can be highly useful in addressing motivational issues and problems.

managerial perspectives revisited

1

PERSPECTIVE 1: THE ORGANIZATIONAL CONTEXT   The organization is a major source of influences on motivation. Its culture, its policies, its routines, its formal compensation and reward systems, and its other relatively enduring and continuing characteristics all contribute to affecting the efforts of its members to perform well. If you find yourself in a managerial role, it will be important to gain an understanding of these influences and how they impact your own efforts to motivate other people. Often, many features of the organization cannot be easily or, certainly, quickly changed, so it is up to you, as a manager, to determine how to make those organizational characteristics support your motivational initiatives; in other words, how to make the organizational context into a positive motivational force.

2

PERSPECTIVE 2: THE HUMAN FACTOR   For any manager, motivation is inherently a *people* process. Of course, as a manager you would be concerned about your own individual level of motivation, but your effectiveness as a managerial leader will depend on your ability to motivate other people. No matter how highly motivated you are yourself, if you can't motivate others you won't be successful. Thus, it is critical that you have some understanding of how you are affecting the motivation of others, and what steps you can take to maintain or increase that motivation. A good place to start is to consider how you can increase others' sense of their own self-efficacy for the tasks that make up their jobs, and then, how you can generate social influences in the work situation that will reinforce the results of higher levels of self-efficacy.

3

PERSPECTIVE 3: MANAGING PARADOXES   The process of motivation is filled with paradoxes. For example: Should you attempt to increase the "push" forces of motivation, or instead concentrate more on the "pull" forces? Should reinforcements be provided, or withheld, if performance is good but not superior? Should the focus be entirely on strengthening the intrinsic job-related factors of motivation, or do the extrinsic factors surrounding the job also deserve attention? Should some of your time be spent on trying to understand individual differences in response to different incentives, or is it better simply to assume that—within limits—most people respond more or less the same to, say, the opportunity for promotion? Likewise, are cultural differences among a set of subordinates to be given major attention or should motivational efforts be better spent elsewhere?

4

PERSPECTIVE 4: ENTREPRENEURIAL MIND-SET   An entrepreneurial mind-set can affect employee motivation in several ways. First, a manager using an entrepreneurial mind-set searches for new opportunities to motivate her employees, and she is willing to try new motivational techniques. Fernando Capellan, founder of Grupo M (discussed in the opening of this chapter), used an entrepreneurial mind-set to establish programs that provided free medical, dental, and vision and subsidized child care to all employees—benefits unheard of in the Dominican Republic, where the firm is located. Second, if a manager wants her employees to be innovative and develop more effective ways of doing their jobs or providing service to the firm's customers, she must create an entrepreneurial culture. Additionally, her employees must be motivated to be innovative. As such, managers should reward innovative behaviors in ways that satisfy employees' needs.

Certainly, motivating others in an effective manner can be challenging. Motivating those you are attempting to lead is difficult because so many variables and forces are involved that determine motivation. Managers must be committed to evaluating their employees and the environment in which they work to understand what will motivate them and what won't. Combining this commitment with an entrepreneurial culture can be a powerful motivational force.

concluding comments

Motivation is a topic that interests employers, practicing managers, and organizational scholars alike. For companies and other employers, having a highly motivated workforce is often viewed as essential for guaranteeing high levels of organizational success. Having talented employees is not enough if that talent is not coupled with motivation. For managers, a good understanding of the topic provides potentially great leverage in positively influencing the work behavior and performance of those who work with and for them. For organizational theorists and researchers, the topic represents a major scientific challenge to gain insight and knowledge, especially knowledge that can be transformed into better-performing organizations.

As we emphasized early in this chapter (Exhibit 12.1), thinking about motivation in terms of the three variables—individual, job, and work context—that together determine levels of motivation provides an essential framework for understanding motivational issues and problems. Knowing what the individual brings to the work situation (the internal "push" forces), what the individual does in the situation (part of the external "pull" forces), and what happens to the individual (the other part of the "pull" forces) provides basic clues for making accurate motivational diagnoses.

Armed with this framework, it is possible to make practical use of the several behavioral theories concerning motivation. For the manager, the theories, both those that relate to what motivates people (the content theories) and those that relate to how people become motivated (the process theories), are not ends in themselves. Rather, they should be seen as means or aids to gaining a deeper understanding. They provide multiple ways of gaining insight into the combined effects of a fairly complex set of forces.

Being able to analyze and examine the roles of goals, reinforcements, and values and attitudes provides an additional dimension for those who have to put motivation into practice. Knowing how goals can be used effectively, how the use of various types of reinforcements can create quite different effects, and how the values and attitudes that people bring with them to the work situation (and which are also further developed at work) can shape their responses to motivational initiatives, provides additional managerial insights.

Finally, and particularly important, is the necessity for managers of today's multicultural and often multinational workforces not to have a self-centered and ethnocentric view of how to motivate other people. We are all prisoners, to some extent, of the narrow focus of our own particular cultural, ethnic, and socioeconomic backgrounds. But this can get us into more trouble in managing motivation than anything else. It is crucial, therefore, in attempting to become effective motivators, not to assume that everyone else is like us and will react the same way that we would.

key terms

acquired needs theory 419	job characteristics model 422	punishments 432
content theories 414	job enrichment 422	self-efficacy 427
equity theory 424	Maslow's need hierarchy 415	social cognitive theory (SCT) 427
expectancy theory 425	motivation 412	two-factor theory 420
extinction 433	negative reinforcements 432	work centrality 438
goal-setting theory 428	positive reinforcements 430	
in-group 434	process theories 423	

test your comprehension

1. What is motivation?
2. What is meant by "push" forces? "pull" forces? Give examples of each.
3. What are three major characteristics that determine motivation in organizations? What are some of the variables within each?
4. What is the difference between a content theory and a process theory of motivation?
5. What are the levels in Maslow's need hierarchy? What determines when a person is likely to move from one level to the next?
6. What are some of the characteristics of an individual with a high need for achievement?
7. Can the need for achievement be considered a universal motive?
8. Explain the difference between "motivator" and "hygiene" factors in Herzberg's theory. What effects are these factors presumed to have on an individual's motivation?
9. How can managers affect motivation by changing job content?
10. What are the components of the job characteristics model?
11. According to equity theory, what might happen if a worker thought he or she was putting in more effort than a coworker, yet the

coworker received a higher salary or larger bonus?

12. What is the basic equation that represents expectancy theory? Explain in words what each variable means.

13. According to expectancy theory, what can a manager do to increase an employee's motivation?

14. What is an example of how cultural differences can impact expectancy theory?

15. What is self-efficacy? What are the ways in which it can be increased?

16. What kinds of goals increase motivation? Is it important for managers to help workers set goals?

17. How are antecedents related to consequences and reinforcement?

18. What attributes do positive reinforcements need to have to motivate behavior?

19. What is the difference between a negative reinforcement and a punishment? Give an example of each.

20. What are the major social influences on work motivation? Give an example of each.

21. Does the effect of values on motivation differ among cultures?

22. What is work centrality? Why is it important for managers to understand this concept when attempting to improve motivation?

apply your understanding

1. You have taken a job as production manager in the electronics plant your company has just bought in Hungary. Your subordinates will be local workers, and your primary goal is to increase their productivity through increasing their motivation. Which motivational theories would you use? Are there any you think would not apply? Why?

2. Is the use of positive reinforcement always the best approach to motivational problems? When might other types of "consequences" be more appropriate?

3. Examine some of your own goals. How did you set them? Were they effective in motivating your performance? If you analyze them in terms of goal-setting theory, how would you change the way you set them in the future?

4. Both equity and expectancy theory suggest that individuals make conscious, reasoned choices concerning their performance. When would a person be most likely to do this? Have you ever seriously analyzed a work situation in the ways suggested by these theories and then changed your behavior as a result?

5. Which motivational forces are stronger: push or pull? Or are they equal? How might their relative strength change with different circumstances? Why?

practice your capabilities

For 28 years, Jim Preston had been a leading salesman at Atlas Electrical Supply Co. He had constantly qualified for the company's monthly incentive bonuses. Jim was very proud of those bonuses, which not only reflected his high value to the company but also allowed him to provide a higher-than-average standard of living for his family. Some months ago, Atlas was bought out by Carey and Co., and Sarah Powell was assigned as the new supervisor for the salesforce. Although the same incentive system was still in place, Jim had not qualified for a bonus since the buyout and did not even show the same company spirit as before. Sarah, quite worried about Jim's change in attitude and productivity, talked informally with both Jim and his coworkers.

Sarah learned that Jim resented being supervised by a woman, especially one younger than his daughter. She also learned that he was upset with many of the other salesmen, mostly younger than he, because of their attempt to unionize the office staff. Finally, she discovered that Jim was still receiving and acting on directives from his former boss who had been moved to another part of the company.

Sarah called Jim in for a meeting at which he first stated that he was never told explicitly who his new supervisor was and then blew up at her, yelling, "All of you new brass are the same—always trying to squeeze more out of the little guy. You think you know everything about selling? I was selling electrical parts and supplies before you or any of the other new Carey supervisors were old enough to know what they are. Now you're telling me how to do my job. Why don't you get off my back? It's my business if I don't earn any bonuses!"

Upon reflection, Sarah decided to try to motivate Jim by adding to the product lines he sold, giving him a larger district, and moving him upstairs to a slightly larger office. Jim, however, didn't respond and seemed focused only on his upcoming retirement. Frustrated, Sarah asked if he would like to take early retirement. When Jim declined the offer, Sarah recommended to her boss that they give Jim a

"golden handshake." After all, nothing else seemed to be working.

1. Using the theories presented in this chapter, analyze Jim's behavior and Sarah's lack of success at motivating him.
2. If you were Sarah and your boss declined the suggestion to fire Jim, what would you do next to try to motivate Jim?

Source: Adapted from C. C. Pinder, *Work Motivation: Theory, Issues, and Applications* (Glenview, IL: Scott, Foresman and Company, 1984). Reprinted with permission of Scott, Foresman and Company.

closing case

Motivating Leo Henkelman

Despite his bearlike stature, Leo Henkelman was invisible to his employer. To Sandstrom Products, he was nothing more than a strong-backed laborer, a paint mixer who attended to the mill for over a decade. The plant was full of such employees, who came to work each day, did their jobs, complained about the college-educated lab technicians, and collected their paychecks. The money was good and the work was steady, but still Henkelman could not help thinking, "This ain't living." Things would have to change, not only at work but in his personal life.

Henkelman's first job out of high school had been in the slaughterhouse where his father was the foreman. Five days a week, on a shift that began at 3:00 A.M., his task was to stand in the production line and hammer purple USDA stamps onto the sides of every carcass of beef that passed by. The work was extremely boring, but the pay was decent. He might have stayed at the job longer had he not had a fight with another employee who landed in the hospital. It was his father who fired him.

After a short stint in construction, Henkelman landed a job at Sandstrom Products, a $5.5 million maker of paints, coating, and lubricants. He started as a paint runner, the bottom job at the plant, and spent his days putting paint into cans and putting the cans into boxes. After a year, he was promoted to mill operator and began mixing paints in a blender, following the formulas supplied by the labs. Henkelman's work environment was the plant floor—dark, noisy, and reeking of strong fumes. Adjacent to the plant was the lab, filled with college-educated professionals who wore white shirts and carried business cards. In his work, Henkelman was forced to interact with the lab, particularly

if a formula did not work. Time after time, he would suggest solutions to the problem, and the lab basically rejected his ideas. Extremely frustrated, Henkelman realized that the company was not interested in his brain but in his brawn.

To solve the problems with paint mixing, Henkelman learned to rely less on the formulas supplied by the labs and more on his own experience. Although the mill operators helped each other, the lab mandated that they were to follow the formulas or else. Henkelman admitted that "we did a lot of things under the cover of 'Don't tell nobody that we did this, but we're gonna check this out to see whether it works, because we don't believe the guys in the lab.'" The ongoing feud between the blue-collar plant and the white-collar lab was not only costly and inefficient to the company, but demeaning to all parties involved. As the product quality suffered, customers began to drop off, and Sandstrom saw its profits eroding.

Finding little at work to challenge him, Henkelman sought solace in spending time with friends at bars after work. On many days, he would show up for work with a hangover, only to turn around and return home sick. On other days, he drove around with friends and lost track of time, forgetting to show up for work at all. Once, he was arrested and lost his driver's license. Realizing that he needed to straighten out his life, Henkelman sought help and slowly began to change his life. Then he underwent back surgery, which caused him to miss three months of work, and his wife threw him out of the house. For a while he lived on the edge of despair, wondering if his life would ever change.

In the meantime, Sandstrom's future was severely threatened. For the past five years, the company's net income had been negative. Jim Sandstrom and Rick Hartsock, the company's top executives, knew that they had to make radical changes. Employees were not solving problems as they should, and morale at work was at a record low. Ironically, Rick Hartsock realized that to save the company from failure, he would have to hand the reins to the employees to solve their own problems. It was then that the company decided to experiment with a motivation technique it called "open-book management."

Like many of his colleagues, Leo Henkelman was skeptical. "Just another fad," he thought. What did appeal to him, however, was the focus on results and not on process. Under open-book management, the top brass would provide the objectives and allow employees to figure out how to achieve them through creative problem solving, teamwork, and individual initiative. Hungry for the trust and respect that were offered to him, Henkelman signed up for three teams right away: plant equipment, process control, and merit pay.

The first task for the plant equipment team was a proposal to buy a new $18,000 forklift. The old forklift was over 20 years old and, according to its driver, unreliable and unsafe. The team completed a cost and productivity analysis and presented it to the corporate heads. But management argued that, while it was not a bad idea to buy a new forklift, funds were limited and could be used for something more worthwhile. Henkelman could not help but feel let down and began to feel skeptical again. Same old story, he thought. However, a few days later, Henkelman and his team were surprised to learn that the forklift expenditure was approved. Spirits boosted, Henkelman said, "It gave me the idea that we can make a difference. It made me feel that we weren't doing all this work for nothing."

As Sandstrom transformed into a company managed by its employees, Henkelman saw the barriers to information begin to fade away. Where the lab had always ruled over the technical manuals, Henkelman and the other plant workers were now allowed to consult them if they wanted to resolve an issue. He eventually even received a password that gave him access to the formulas on the computer, an event unheard of in prior times. No longer paralyzed in a specific job role, he could update the formulas so the process flowed more smoothly. His attitude began to change in his work.

Henkelman's life began to turn around at the same time. He stopped drinking and got an apartment, where he lived alone. With so much spare time, he went into the office and explored the computer, teaching himself about the business. He filled his empty hours, but more importantly, he filled himself with knowledge, with confidence, and with hope. As a virtual new "owner" in the company, he thought it was his duty to understand every aspect of the business. In the old days, he had only learned what he needed to know to do his narrow job well. Now he wanted to understand the entire process, to help grow the business.

Henkelman and the members of the merit pay team took on the challenge of redesigning an entirely new compensation system. Plant managers had previously used a mixture of seniority and favoritism to compensate their employees, and the subordinates had always been unhappy about this. The workers believed that pay should more closely reflect performance: how useful a worker was on the job, how much a worker knew, and how well tasks were done. These beliefs were not altogether contradictory to that of management; both wanted a highly skilled and effective workforce.

The first proposal drawn by the team offered plant workers incentives to cross-train in their jobs. However, when management and the team fully analyzed the numbers, they both concluded that the proposal was unrealistic. Rather than dismiss the issue, however, management asked for a proposal that made fiscal sense to almost everyone. Deep in the middle of the analysis, Henkelman came to the realization that he was beginning to think like an owner, not like an hourly employee. The new proposal found a way to pay for the added costs of training but at the expense of some paychecks. Some members of the team quit, but Henkelman was determined to stick it out. After months of hard work—meeting formally, debating with coworkers, striking a balance between paying incentives and maintaining equality among workers—the team came up with an innovative compensation system, which was eventually adopted by the company.

This was a critical turnaround in Henkelman's career. Despite the demands that management made on the team's process, Henkelman felt needed and alive for the first time in his working career. He noted, "Because of that I felt and still feel today that I have control of my destiny."

His attitude completely overhauled, Henkelman sought other responsibilities within the company to tap into his strengths. Taking a major promotion, Henkelman was put in charge of scheduling production and even became plant manager for a while. What he found is that neither job suited him. Always a doer, he found it difficult to delegate tasks to others. In a few months, a technician job opened in the lab. Generally, technicians had college degrees in chemistry, and Henkelman had not even taken chemistry in high school. But Bob Sireno, the lab's technical director, wanted Henkelman for the job. He eventually got it.

Henkelman put away his blue-collar shirt and moved to the lab. He would still do what he had always done—make paint—but instead of following orders, he would guide the process from the beginning to the end. His new job allowed him to work with customers, to develop new formulas, and to use his hands-on experience to solve problems where other, less-experienced chemists had failed. Bob Sireno admitted that in a year's time Henkelman had developed skills that had taken college graduates five years to develop. When a complex problem appeared, it was Henkelman who was chosen to solve the problem—shirt sleeves rolled up and mind determined to make it work.

With a new identity and a new attitude about work, Henkelman remains a valuable team member to Sandstrom Products. Instead of dreading the feuding and the tedium of mixing paint, he now looks forward to each new day, wondering what challenges he will overcome.

Questions

1. Using Maslow's hierarchy of needs, identify the basic needs that Leo Henkelman was attempting to fulfill. How did these needs manifest themselves? How were these needs eventually satisfied?

2. Assess the variables that affected Leo Henkelman's motivation—characteristics of the individual, of the job, and of the work situation.

3. Using the job characteristic model (Exhibit 12.6), analyze Leo Henkelman's motivation: (a) as a worker on the plant floor prior to the introduction of "open-book management"; and (b) as a technician in the laboratory.

4. The company's open-book management approach was designed to get all employees to focus on helping the business make money. What do you think of "open-book management" as a tool for motivating employees? In what kind of organizational circumstances would it work best? In what kind of circumstances might it be ineffective?

Source: Republished with permission of *Inc.* magazine, Goldhirsh Group, Inc., 38 Commercial Wharf, Boston, MA 02110. "Before and After," David Whitford, June 1995. Reproduced by permission of the publisher via Copyright Clearance Center, Inc.

Groups and Teams

13

LEARNING OBJECTIVES

After studying this chapter, you should be able to:

- Describe the similarities and differences between groups and teams.
- Identify and compare different types of groups.
- Name the factors that influence group formation and development.
- Analyze the various structural and behavioral characteristics of groups.
- Identify the advantages and disadvantages of self-managing, cross-functional, global, and virtual workgroups and teams.
- Explain the differences in the various types of team competencies.
- Distinguish between the two major types of group conflict, and discuss their causes and consequences.
- Explain how managers can help their workgroups develop into high-performing teams.

And May the Best Team Win

Around-the-world yacht race may not seem to have much in common with corporate management, but for Doug Webb, CFO of a major information technology firm called Logica, the "exercise of human interaction against the sea" was a perfect metaphor for solid teamwork.

"I am sending this via e-mail on the eve of Leg Five," he wrote of the 2000–2001 BT Global Challenge race, "a 6,020-mile crossing of the Southern Ocean from Sydney,

Australia, to Cape Town, South Africa." Webb's crew had finished Leg Four in fourth place, up from ninth and only four minutes shy of first place. "That leg," Webb said, "showed a team working together more closely than it had at any time." The group had already weathered a collision with a fishing boat and a serious medical emergency that required evacuation of one of the crew. According to Webb, these obstacles actually helped to develop the team's cohesion.

How did these 13 amateur sailors, randomly assigned to one of 12 identical, 72-foot yachts, manage to form close enough bonds to succeed through 10 months of being forced into close quarters, tense competition, and stormy seas?

The first success factor was preparation. After developing diverse teams including students, detectives, a ballet dancer, software engineers, marketing executives, and so on, race organizers brought crews together nine months before the race to spend three days getting to know one another and learning how to communicate. Listening skills and the ability to give and receive feedback were stressed, as well as conflict management strategies. Other training sessions were conducted over the weeks that followed.

Webb, who served as helmsman for Team Logica, recalls that one of his crew's earliest decisions was that all members would have different roles on board but an equal voice in decision making, though the skipper clearly had to make the most critical choices. Just as many different people in a successful firm

In 2000–2001, Logica, an info-tech firm, put teamwork to the test. Sporting a crew of over a dozen diverse employees from all walks of life, "Team Logica" set sail on a multi-month race around the world. Called the BT Global Challenge, the contest is dubbed "the world's toughest yacht race." In terms of fostering teamwork, the trip was a success—despite the fact that Team Logica came in fourth.

bring their perspectives to the CEO's vision, onboard the yacht, "a much broader base of expertise can be tapped, and ultimately better decisions are made."

The second factor was uncovering the key to making the diverse team members cohesive after the race was underway. Each person on Team Logica had different skills and had a different reason for being there. Some came to win, others came for the experience. By maintaining a relaxed atmosphere that included playing music on the deck loudspeakers, Webb's team managed to satisfy everyone's goals by making the rigors of going fast and trying to win into an enjoyable experience.

Some conflict could not be avoided. Skill differences caused some role shifting to occur during the race. With coaching, some members grew into their roles, while others were moved to tasks where they could perform better. Even Webb was replaced as watch leader, a transition he admits was for the best. There were occasional failures, but blame was never placed on individuals.

Communication was crucial to building trust, a key ingredient in a team whose members could literally be depending on one another for survival. Questions about responsibility surfaced after the accident with the fishing boat, for example, but uninhibited discussions among the crew soon restored confidence. Team Logica later successfully weathered 77-knot winds and 35-foot waves in an unexpected storm.

In the final leg of their 30,000-mile adventure, the group became cohesive and worked effectively as a team to achieve a satisfying fourth-place finish.

Sources: Doug Webb, "Rhyme of the Ancient Manager," *Forbes*, September 10, 2001, pp. 76–77; Helen Riley, "A Sea Change for the Better," *Supply Management*, November 15, 2001, pp. 28–30; Sherrill Tapsell, "Racy Business," *New Zealand Management*, February 2001, p. 14.

strategic overview

Because so many complex tasks and objectives are beyond the capabilities of a single person, groups and teams, rather than individual employees, form the fundamental building blocks of twenty-first-century organizations. For example, strategic decisions are generally more effective when made by a team of executives (often called a top management team) than by an individual. That is because most strategic decisions are highly complex, as we learned in Chapter 6. Also, research has shown that these teams make higher-quality strategic decisions if they have diverse functional backgrounds.[1] Diverse teams bring different sets of knowledge, skills, and attitudes to the decision-making process. They also consider a broader range of information and have access to more resources that can help them make more effective decisions. These decisions often lead to stronger competitive actions than decisions made by more homogeneous top management teams.[2] Yet, more diverse teams frequently experience greater conflict (as we explain in this chapter) and therefore may take more time to make decisions. Thus, the quality of the resulting decisions has to be balanced with the need for making a rapid decision such as one in response to a substantial new and pressing threat in the environment by a major competitor.[3] If these problems of conflict can be overcome, a diverse top management team can also help to implement a complex, strategic action by explaining and championing it to different groups within the firm and to separate and distinct constituencies external to the organization (like suppliers, unions, and shareholders). The same sort of diversity can work for other teams within the organization, particularly cross-functional teams.

Groups engage in a diverse set of activities, ranging, for example, from developing new products, to designing automobiles, to constructing budgets, to formulating strategic plans. Even those people who are inclined to be independent entrepreneurs eventually face this reality test: If an organization is not based on high-performance groups and teams, it likely will not be able to compete effectively in the current or future competitive landscape. Therefore, it is absolutely crucial that anyone aspiring to a career in management be able to meet two fundamental challenges: how to be an effective *member in* a group or team, and how to be an effective *leader of* a group or team. This was well stated recently by eBay CEO Meg Whitman, featured in earlier chapters, who said: "We hire people who aren't focused on me, me, me. One of the first questions I ask when I interview people is: 'What are the most effective teams you've been on, and how did those teams work?' "[4]

The adventures of Team Logica might seem far removed from the daily challenges faced by managers in today's work organizations, but they are not. In the flatter and leaner organizations of the early twenty-first century—with their increased emphasis on speed and flexibility—the importance of being able to manage and operate effectively in groups and teams is even greater than it has been in the past.

Organizations of all types and sizes, whether in business, government, health care, or other settings, are much more likely to use groups and teams now than even a few years ago.[5] This represents a major change in the way organizations function. Consequently, it requires a change in the mind-set of both managers and their subordinates. People need to change their attitudes toward group work and emphasize teamwork rather than individual work. Of course, there will always be a place for the brilliant employee working alone who produces a remarkable innovation or creative achievement. Also, not all individuals or cultures adapt equally well to a group-oriented organizational environment.[6] Nevertheless, because they are operating in global markets, organizations now depend more and more on highly networked and interconnected relationships involving groups and teams. Managing such networked relationships requires strong collaborative skills and the ability to work successfully with, and in, groups and teams. These skills are

TEAMS demonstrate enhanced:
- Coordinated interaction
- Personal responsibility for group outcomes
- Individual identification with group

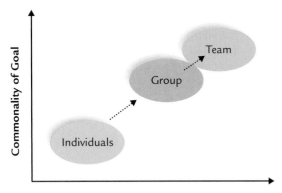

exhibit 13.1

Individuals-to-Group-to-Team Continuum

Source: Adapted from M. E. Kossler and K. Kanaga, *Do You Really Need a Team* (Greensboro, NC: Center for Creative Leadership, 2001).

group a set of people, limited in number (usually from 3 to 20), who have some degree of mutual interaction and shared objectives

team a type of group that has additional characteristics: a high degree of interdependent, coordinated interaction and a strong sense of members' personal responsibility for achieving specified group outcomes

necessary to build social capital within an organization and with groups and organizations outside the organization as well. With such skills, managers are in a much better position to be able to lead and gain the acceptance and commitment of others to the important strategic changes common in today's organizations.

It is important to differentiate between groups and teams. They are the same under some circumstances and "not" the same under other circumstances. A **group** is typically defined as a set of people, limited in number (usually from 3 to 20 or so), who have some degree of interaction and shared objectives. A **team**, on the other hand, is a type or form of group. In effect, a team has additional characteristics beyond a "mere" group: a higher degree of coordinated interaction and, especially, a stronger sense of members' personal responsibility for achieving specified group outcomes.[7] Also, groups that become teams typically have created a high level of members' identification with the group. In other words, it matters to members that they are a part of the unit. A useful way to think about the relation between groups and teams is to view it as a continuum, as illustrated in Exhibit 13.1. Individuals are put into—or put themselves into—a group. The group may or may not go on to become a team.

The distinguishing features of teams are aptly illustrated, of course, in the opening example about the yacht race team. The Logica crew was a group but, in addition, it eventually transformed into a team. Put simply, all teams are groups, but not all groups are, or become, teams.[8] In the yacht race case, however, the group did indeed quickly evolve into a true team, as evidenced by what we learned from the description. Just as in the case of the sponsors of that yacht crew, a major objective in most of today's organizations is to have workgroups develop and evolve quickly so that they behave more like teams. Although hardly anyone would disagree with this as a goal, the organizational and managerial challenge is to make this actually happen. Such desired results usually cannot be guaranteed without considerable effort, and this is a central issue we return to later.

This chapter begins by briefly identifying the various types of groups that operate in organizational settings. Then we discuss how groups are formed and developed and what some of their most important characteristics are, such as their structure, norms, and degree of cohesiveness. This is followed by an analysis of a critical issue common to many groups, namely, conflict. The chapter concludes with a consideration of the challenges involved in improving group effectiveness.

BASIC TYPES OF GROUPS

Most people who work in organizations are part of at least one group, and often of several different groups. These groups can be of different types, and one major distinction among them is simply whether they are "formal," that is, established by the organization, or "informal," established by particular individuals without direct involvement by the formal organization. Examples of the basic types of groups to which almost all organization members could belong are illustrated in Exhibit 13.2 and described here.

exhibit 13.2

Types of Groups

Type of Group	Features	Examples
Command (Supervisory)	One supervisor with a number of subordinates Relatively enduring Membership changes relatively slowly	Clerical units Manufacturing assembly units Local sales managers reporting to a regional sales manager
Project/Task Force	Temporary Specific limited purpose Group members are aware of temporary nature of group	Product design teams Management information systems teams to develop upgraded computer systems Term project groups in university classes
Committee	Either permanent or ad hoc Meet only periodically Members have different permanent jobs and/or supervisors Membership typically does not represent an employee's highest commitment	Budget committees Safety committees Promotion review committees
Formal	Command (supervisory) Project/Task force Committee	
Informal	Group not originated by the organization Voluntary membership Obvious differences and boundaries between members and nonmembers	Group of employees who lunch together on Fridays Van pool group The "water cooler group"

Formal Groups

Within and across almost any kind of organization there are typically three fundamental types of formal groups: command (supervisory), project/task forces, and committees.

Command (Supervisory) Groups A **command (supervisory) group** consists of a supervisor or manager and all those who report to that person; for example, those who report to a particular production supervisor or to a sales manager in a department. Such groups are usually considered to be the basic work units of an organization. Depending on the nature of the tasks assigned to each person, however, the amount of interaction among members may vary considerably from one command group to another. For example, in a clothing manufacturing plant, a group of workers may be assigned to work on a particular style of jeans. They all work to construct the same garment, but because one is sewing the pocket to the leg while another is putting in zippers and yet another is topstitching the waistband, there is very little opportunity for interaction. Contrast this with a marketing team for a toy company, where the members meet frequently to discuss new products, schedule advertising campaigns, and decide on special promotional activities.

Command groups are usually considered relatively enduring, rather than temporary. Also, membership in these groups changes relatively slowly. These factors together affect the nature and quality of the interpersonal interaction among group members. The fact that you know that you will be interacting repeatedly with the same people for an indefinite length of time can have a powerful effect on your relationships with those other members.

command (supervisory) group a group whose members consist of a supervisor or manager and all those who report to that person

project/task force a
temporary group put together by an
organization for a particular purpose

Project/Task Forces A **project/task force** is a group put together by an organization for a particular purpose; for example, to design a new product or to work on a particular problem (e.g., how to develop a more rapid and effective response system for customer complaints) that cuts across different organizational units. The Speed Team at IBM, described in A Manager's Challenge, "If You Blinked, You Missed It," is a perfect example of a project team, operating in a technology-rich environment, put together to achieve very specific objectives in the absolute minimum amount of time.

tech|nol|ogy
a manager's challenge

If You Blinked, You Missed It

Managers in all kinds of organizations, large and small, are rediscovering the many uses of teams. Teams, or groups of people with coordinated goals who share the responsibility for achieving their ends, can get work done quickly and effectively. They can offer innovative solutions, help others throughout the organization accept and adjust to change, and forge unofficial links and ties that smooth the way for achievements beyond their assigned tasks. Teams can even be formed just to break the rules.

At IBM, the information technology (IT) unit is staggeringly large—100,000 people worldwide. Most teams consist of about 3 to 15 people, but this enormous unit carries a big responsibility—to produce successful software projects for IBM to market to its corporate and consumer markets. To help coordinate the efforts of a unit this size, Steve Ward, IBM's former chief information officer, used to meet regularly with a 200-member leadership council, still an unwieldy group. But at one November council meeting, Ward decided that speedy action had to become IT's top priority in the months to come, or IBM might be beaten to market by the eager dot-com start-ups that were already nipping at its heels.

"One of the things that frustrates me most," he said, "is the length of time between the 'aha' moment and the moment when you actually start changing the organization's direction, getting it to where it needs to be." Ward wasted no time changing direction in this case. The following morning he formed a 21-member ad hoc cadre called the Speed Team and gave them their assignment. It was straightforward: Get the 100,000 members of the IT unit working faster, focusing on Web-based applications.

The team got right to work. "I think that we will have failed if the Speed Team is still together three years from now," Jane Harper, the team's co-leader initially said. (In fact, it accomplished its goal in about seven months.) "Our plan, when we started this, was to come together, look at

To compete with multiple rapid startups, IBM, led by CEO Sam Palmisano, needed a way to speed up the development process in the company's mammoth IT unit, which has over 100,000 employees. In 2000, IBM developed a project/task force called the Speed Team, described as "a passionate posse of employees hell-bent on improving internal velocity and efficiency." After knocking down numerous "speed bumps" on the road to rapid product development, the 21-member team disbanded roughly a year later.

what works, look at why projects get bogged down, create some great recommendations about how to achieve speed, get executive buy-in, and try to make those recommendations part of the fabric of the business."

Speed Team members fanned out across the IT unit and started looking for and dislodging what they called "speed bumps," barriers to speed. One of the team's first realizations was the fact that time is a tangible resource, just like money or people. Given that, the team focused on two kinds of initiatives for change. "Quick hits" could be accomplished almost immediately and included creating "speed ratings" for performance reviews and getting all IT leaders to better articulate their priorities on the basis of time. Some longer-term projects, those that needed up to 90 days to be accomplished, included coordinating the finance department more closely with IT priorities so funding for new projects wasn't cut when it was time for launch and establishing how little time it should take for new applications to roll out.

Along the way, the Speed Team had time to pick up a few lessons about teams that passed directly into the company's culture. For example, for a team to act swiftly requires a mix of skills, experience, and tenure at the company. Teams also need ultra-clear goals and priorities. According to Ward, "You need to say, 'Our goal is to sell $2 billion a month on the Web,' and then work with our team to achieve that goal." Not surprisingly, teams also thrive on fast communications links, such as instant messaging, teleconferencing, and video-

conferencing. Because information was quickly shared, streamlined communication helped the Speed Team members to work and follow up more effectively, minimize administrative delays, and deal more efficiently with processes that couldn't be eliminated. Going by the spirit of the process rather than the letter of it sometimes helped, too; according to Harper, strict business processes yield high-quality work, but "if you're a smart cook, you don't have to measure every teaspoon of salt; you just take a few pinches."

Ray Blair, Harper's co-leader, wrote the Speed Team's epitaph. "Our evidence of success is that our changes have been adopted by the organization. People have begun to think about the need for speed in their work. We're no longer necessary. Our job was to be catalysts, and catalysts can't linger around."

Even though many dot-coms went bust and IBM's business environment has changed since the Speed Team disbanded, that hasn't changed the "need" for speed. "Five years ago we thought speed was important," Harper said recently. "One year ago we knew speed was important. Now speed is survival."

Source: Anni Layne, "Report from the Past—Jane Harper," *Fast Company*, January 2001; Scott Kirsner, "Faster Company," *Fast Company*, May 2000, pp. 162ff.

As the IBM Speed Team example illustrates, project teams and task forces differ from command groups in that they are intended to be temporary. Their members know that the group will likely cease to exist once the project or task is completed. This not only changes members' perceptions and their interactions with one another, but it also changes their relationship to the appointed leader of the project or task force group. Because of the nature and importance of the goals and objectives set for them, though, task forces constitute some of the most critical group-like activities within, and even across, organizations, and they often involve virtual (non-face-to-face) group situations. Illustrations of typical task forces include the following, for example:

- The *Sacramento Bee*, a highly regarded northern California newspaper, put together a task force to investigate workplace injuries as part of its major review of operations. The task force developed several recommendations concerning configurations of equipment, training, and work-station safety and health. These recommendations resulted in a drop in injury-related costs from $2.2 million to $490,000 within four years.[9]

- Bell South created a task force with members from Security and Information Technology in order to assess the vulnerability of the company's computer systems. They uncovered 30,000 points of access to its systems, evaluated the level of risk involved, and suggested solutions for each problem.[10]

- When quality control numbers stopped improving, Revlon set up a Corporate Quality Control Task Force. The members of the task force were charged with discovering which factors were having a major impact on quality, developing plans to correct the problems, and assigning specific quality control responsibilities to various departments.[11]

- Duke Power, Bell South, Carolina Power and Light, and 32 independent telephone companies formed a joint task force to develop a $500 million regional personal communication services network.[12]

committee a group that is either permanent or temporary (ad hoc) whose members meet only occasionally and otherwise report to different permanent supervisors in an organization's structure

Committees **Committees** can be either permanent or temporary (ad hoc) in terms of the length of their existence. Typically, the most important feature of committees in organizations is that their members meet only occasionally and otherwise report to different permanent supervisors in the organization's structure (Exhibit 13.3). Thus, interaction is episodic, and for most members this is not the formal organizational group to which they have the highest degree of commitment. For instance, a budget committee may meet several times during a company's fiscal year, with the members likely coming from each of the major departments or divisions. The primary jobs of the budget committee members, however, are in their own organizational work units, not serving together on the budget committee. Nevertheless, such a committee's decisions may have critically important implications not only for its members, but also for the larger organization.

formal group a group that is designated, created, and sanctioned by the organization to carry out its basic work and to fulfill its overall mission

The preceding types of groups are all examples of **formal groups**; that is, groups that are designated, created, and sanctioned by an organization to carry out its basic work and to fulfill its overall mission. However, in many respects informal groups are just as, and sometimes more, important for a manager to pay attention to, and understand, than formal groups.

Informal Groups

informal group a group whose members interact voluntarily

An **informal group** is one whose members choose to interact voluntarily, not by organizational mandate. A typical example is friendship groups. Although there is no formal joining process, these groups often have fairly obvious boundaries between members and nonmembers. At any given time, people think they know (perhaps incorrectly from the point of view of others in the group) whether they are a member of a certain group or not. Just observing who eats lunch with whom, or who talks especially frequently to whom, for instance, is often a clear signal of a friendship group's boundaries. Such informal groups can be fairly temporary, but more typically they last for considerable periods of time.

Most important for a manager is the fact that friendship and other informal groups can significantly affect the attitudes and performance of their members in relation to organizational tasks and objectives. A set of employees who were originally strangers, for example, might develop into an informal group after carpooling together over a period of time. If the conversations within this group focus on negative reactions to new organizational policies, then the group could become a source of opposition to those policies. However, informal groups often can provide considerable assistance to managers in dealing with organizational challenges. The key for the manager is whether the group's norms (see discussion later in this chapter) or standards of behavior can be influenced in the direction of support of organizational and workgroup goals. To do this requires an ability to recognize the existence and membership of important informal groups, to gain an understanding of what the group's current norms are, and to be able to identify where the leadership is

exhibit 13.3

Examples of Committees Present in Many Organizations

· Governance	· Compensation	· Oversight
· Executive	· Finance	· Audit
· Steering	· Safety	· Ethics
· Disaster planning	· Long-range planning	· Public relations

within the group. If these steps are taken, then the potential exists for informal groups to become positive forces. Research has shown, in fact, that while "friendship groups do socialize more . . . they also spend more time discussing the task, are more committed and more cooperative [with each other]."[13]

CHARACTERISTICS OF GROUPS AND TEAMS

All groups have certain characteristics or features that affect the degree and types of influence they have on their members and their level of collective performance. Some of these are structural, while others relate to basic features of groups, such as their norms and the degree of cohesion among their members. For all of these characteristics, it is important for leaders and managers to understand their likely effects. Particularly, managers need to be on the lookout for how changes, from both inside and outside the organization, can alter one or more characteristics which in turn can have profound impacts on group functioning and performance.

Structural Characteristics

Just as organizations have structure (as discussed in Chapter 7), so do groups, albeit on a smaller scale. Four of the most essential structural features of groups are size, composition, differentiated roles, and differentiated status.

Size As one review of research on groups stated, "Current literature yields a consistent guideline [for determining the best size for a group]: [use] the smallest number of people who can do the task."[14] Similarly, another review of studies carried out in the United States found that member satisfaction decreased as groups got larger, and leaders' behaviors toward members became more task-oriented and less people-oriented.[15] Likewise, a large-scale study of command group size in 58 offices of a U.S. federal agency found that organizational productivity per employee decreased with increasing size.[16]

What is an optimal group size? Of course, there is no single answer to this question, since it would vary based on the types of tasks facing the group. However, research shows that with increasing group size the sense of personal responsibility for a group's output or performance tends to decrease. The phenomenon of reduced effort per person in larger-sized groups has been labeled **social loafing**.[17] Individuals in larger groups apparently are more likely than those in smaller groups to assume that other members will "carry the load." In large groups, also, individual members' specific contributions are less easily identified, and this appears to be a major factor in encouraging such "loafing."[18]

social loafing the phenomenon of reduced effort per person in large groups

There are, however, some approaches that can be used to counter the social loafing tendency. For example, it is possible to structure group tasks to encourage full participation by group members. A key lies in how readily an individual's contribution to the final result can be identified. One experiment using college swim team members found originally that the athletes swam faster in individual time trials than they did at the same distance and with the same stroke during relays. In the normal situation, only the team time was announced at the end of the race, and the times of individual swimmers were not available. When the relay race was structured so that each individual's time was announced aloud at the end of his or her lap, the individuals actually swam faster during the relay than in the individual heats.

Results such as these suggest that managers may be able to encourage higher individual levels of effort on group projects by building in some form of acknowledgment of the contributions made by each member of the group to the final outcome of the project.[19]

Interestingly, additional research seems to indicate that social loafing in groups is less likely to occur in collectivistic cultures (see Chapter 4), such as Asian countries, than in more individualistic cultures such as the United States or Australia, because of the much stronger group orientation in collectivistic cultures.[20]

process costs increasing costs of coordination as group size increases

The other major reason why group performance per person may decrease as group size increases is simply the increasing costs of coordination, the so-called **process costs**. As groups become larger, the number of person-to-person relationships increases significantly, and coordination becomes more cumbersome. Also, larger size brings additional opportunities for interpersonal conflicts between individuals and among subgroups within the group.

All of the disadvantages of large group size must be weighed, of course, against the potential advantages of having a more extensive pool of talent, skills, and expertise to boost performance and take on additional problem-solving tasks.[21] Having too few people in a group, especially when tasks are many and complex, defeats the whole purpose of putting together people in the first place. In determining the best size for formal work groups, managers need to consider the probable losses due to process costs in relation to the likely gains due to larger integrated efforts.

Another managerial challenge relating to group size is that it is not always constant; it can change, sometimes dramatically. The effects are illustrated in the story of a relatively small company called Next Jump, Inc. It started out as a tiny venture organized by a group of friends. Those friends hired their friends. A "family tree" was even posted, showing the relationships among all of the employees. In just three months the company grew from 30 to 105 employees. As it grew, Charlie Kim, the CEO, tried to maintain the family feeling in the firm. Unfortunately, the idea of one large "team," with all members focused on the same goals, all working cohesively together, didn't work as the company got larger. Meetings fell apart and confusion and conflict increased. People started quitting. The "family tree" was taken down. Charlie Kim, in his managerial role, was experiencing the effects that a different size group can have on its members and on its management.[22]

Composition Groups may be composed of individuals who are very similar or very dissimilar. If the former is the case, we describe the group as *homogeneous*. If the latter is the case, the composition would be regarded as *heterogeneous*, or diverse. Most groups these days have some degree of diversity, and many have a great deal. As Exhibit 13.4 shows, there can be different types of diversity within groups, including variations in observable and perhaps more surface characteristics such as race/ethnicity, gender, and age; and variations in underlying and less immediately obvious attributes such as values, skills, knowledge and information, and length of time (tenure) in the group and in the organization.[23]

Some managers deliberately take advantage of diversity in dealing with groups. For example, Jerry Hirshberg, the former president of Nissan Design who helped turn Southern California into a global center of automobile design, purposely combined employees with radically different professional and/or cultural backgrounds into teams. Hirschberg believed that the natural

Types of Diversity	Potential Consequences
Observable Attributes	**Affective Consequences**
· Race	· Satisfaction
· Ethnicity	· Identification with the group
· Gender	· Conflict within the group
· Age	
Underlying Attributes	**Cognitive Consequences**
· Values	· Innovation
· Skills	· Amount and quality of new ideas
· Knowledge and Information	
· Tenure	**Communication-Related Consequences**
	· Decreased frequency within group
	· Increased frequency outside of group

Source: Adapted from Frances L. Milliken and Luis L. Martins, "Searching for Common Threads: Understanding the Multiple Effects of Diversity in Organizational Groups," *Academy of Management Review* 21, no. 2 (1996), pp. 402–23.

conflict in these diverse teams results in "moments of friction and collision [that lead to] opportunities for breakthroughs."[24]

The key managerial question, of course, is: Does a greater amount of diversity within groups more often help or hinder such outcomes as effective group functioning and performance? Research to date shows that there is no simple answer to this question.[25] Instead, as shown in Exhibit 13.4, we need to look at the effects of group diversity on more specific and immediate consequences, such as

- Members' reactions (so-called "affective consequences"), including satisfaction, identification with the group, and conflict within the group;
- The output of members' thinking (cognitive consequences), including the amount of new ideas or innovations emerging from the group; and
- Communication effectiveness, both inside and outside the group.

Research to date on these kinds of consequences is only suggestive and not conclusive, especially given the fact that, as noted above, there are different kinds of diversity.[26] However, research findings tend to show that increased diversity potentially:

- Has somewhat negative effects on members' reactions and interactions with each other;
- Has somewhat positive effects on increasing the quality of the outputs of members' thinking together as a group, presumably because a wider range of opinions and ideas are discussed; and
- Leads to decreased frequency of communication within a group but more communication with those outside a group.

In short, the challenge for you as a manager is to maximize the significant benefits that are possible from having group diversity—and to try to minimize potential disadvantages by anticipating what some of those might be and directly addressing them. One way that seems especially promising in this regard is to give extra attention to developing strong group norms of cooperation; that is, to emphasize the objective of each member viewing and valuing the importance of cooperation within the group.[27] Also, research evidence suggests that it is early in a group's existence that diversity based on members' differences in values and attitudes is most likely to cause difficulties. Therefore, to gain the potential advantages that diversity offers, groups and their leaders need to realize that they should try to work through those initial differences and turn them into advantages rather than obstacles. The encouraging finding is that it appears that the longer a group works together, the more likely it is to find ways to do just that—to succeed in overcoming those initial differences in values and attitudes.[28] Whatever else can be said, though, one thing seems absolutely certain: The use of increasingly diverse work teams, especially—but not only—multinational groups, is becoming commonplace.[29] Therefore, the diversity challenges for managers are growing, not lessening.

Differentiated Roles In groups of any size, different members perform different roles; that is, they occupy different positions with sets of expected behavior attached to those positions. This is most vividly illustrated in certain athletic teams, where players have specialized roles when the team is on offense and different roles on defense. Roles in work groups are not always as clear-cut and can range from being fairly general, such as performing analytical duties, to being highly specialized with specific task assignments, such as monitoring particular pieces of equipment. More and more, however, organizations are attempting to loosen rigid role boundaries in groups in order to gain greater flexibility in meeting unexpected competitive and environmental challenges. The spirit of this change is illustrated in the following quote from the leader of the Electronic Media Team at the U.S. Information Agency: Referring to the new roles of team members, he said, "in the old days, people had very specific job descriptions, and they rarely ventured outside of them." The challenge of teams is to get people and teams moving "outside the box" (that is, to think more creatively about how to fulfill their roles).[30]

One obvious type of role that is assigned or emerges in almost all groups is that of leader. In the past, the leadership role in workgroups has tended to be specialized and concentrated in one person, the supervisor. However, the clear trend in today's highly competitive organizations is to attempt to spread the leadership functions of structuring tasks and lending

French chef Alain Ducasse (left) is shown cooking with his aides in the kitchen of his Monaco restaurant, Le Louis XV. Each member of Ducasse's cooking staff has his own role on the team, with the overriding goal being the creation of the ultimate meal. The team evidently works well together. In 2003, *Guide Rouge*—the French food lover's "bible"—awarded Le Louis XV its three-star rating.

personal support and encouragement as widely as possible among the group's members. This is especially so in so-called self-managing teams, but it also is becoming more common even in typical command-type groups.[31] For example, at a plant of Texas Instruments, the role of team leader is rotated among group members rather than assigned permanently to any one individual.[32] The principle involved is that if responsibility for leadership functions is more broadly shared and accepted, the group will be able to respond faster and more effectively to rapidly changing pressures and circumstances.

Two particular issues that groups face with respect to role—and that you yourself have probably faced in your own group experiences—are role ambiguity and role conflict. **Role ambiguity** refers to a situation in which the expected behaviors for a group member are not clearly defined, which can increase the stress level for that person. **Role conflict** emerges when a member has to fulfill two or more contrasting sets of expectations, such as taking time to be friendly with customers versus meeting a certain quota of customers to be served during a work period. One manager who has faced role conflict is Lina Echeverria, Core Technology Director of Glass Ceramics at Corning. Her effectiveness is evaluated on two primary criteria: (1) keeping the research scientists happy, which involves relatively hands-off leadership and letting them work when, how, and on what they want; and (2) keeping the company happy, which involves being a hands-on directive leader, holding down costs, and making sure the research scientists are productive.[33] In such a situation, a manager has to make choices that are often very difficult.

Differentiated Status Not only do members have different roles in groups, they also often have different levels of status or rank. **Status** is the standing or prestige that a person has in a group, and it can be based on a number of factors such as perceived leadership abilities, seniority, or special skills, among others.

Research has shown that status differences can strongly influence interactions within the group.[34] For example, higher-status members tend to receive more communications than do lower-status members, and lower-status members tend to defer to higher-status members when groups are making decisions.[35] Such effects might be especially strong, of course, in high-power-distance cultures, such as those in South America and Asia. However, in cultures with low or medium power distance, effective communication and decision making are likely to be inhibited in groups if status differences and their effects are too extreme. Relevant information would be less likely to be widely shared and thus not be given sufficient attention.

Behavioral Characteristics

There are two chief features of groups and teams that involve behavioral-type characteristics: namely, the norms that develop in groups and the degree to which groups are cohesive.

Norms

Norms, as we indicated in our earlier discussion of informal groups, are a group's shared standards that guide the behavior of its individual members. For example, when members of a group behave similarly toward supervisors or outsiders, such as stopping nontask conversations when they enter the room, they are demonstrating the effect of group norms. It would be very

Role Ambiguity by Lyman Porter
Q&A Key
www.prenhall.com/onekey

role ambiguity a situation in which the expected behaviors for a group member are not clearly defined

role conflict a situation in which a member of a group faces two or more contrasting sets of expectations

status the standing or prestige that a person has in a group, which can be based on a number of factors such as perceived leadership abilities, seniority, or special skills

norms a group's shared standards that guide the behavior of its individual members difficult, if not impossible, for groups to function if they did not have norms.[36] Each person's behavior would be too unpredictable for coordinated action to take place. Norms also help to reduce ambiguity; thus, they provide members with cues and useful guidelines about how to behave. Such normative information is particularly important for new members of a group who need to learn what is going on in the work situation as rapidly as possible.

Characteristics of Group Norms An understanding of norms and their significance can be gained by reviewing several of their main features:

- Norms are usually established for the more important issues of concern to the group; for example, rates of minimally acceptable output or performance.
- Norms do not necessarily apply to all members of the group; some apply only to certain members (like the leader), usually based on the status or particular role of those members. For example, it may be acceptable for a senior member of a group, but not for a junior member, to arrive late for meetings.
- Norms vary in the degree of their acceptance by group members; some norms are accepted and endorsed by virtually all members, others by only a majority. For instance, norms regarding how to deal with work problems might be accepted by everyone, but norms regarding desirable attire might be endorsed by only certain members.
- Norms vary in how much deviation members are permitted in following them; in other words, some norms are very loose and permit a great deal of leeway in behavior, while other norms, especially those regarding key group issues, are much more restrictive on members' behavior.[37] For example, a member of a group who talks to outsiders about the group's internal problems might receive severe censure from fellow group members, whereas someone who talks louder than normal during meetings might be tolerated (up to a degree, at least) by group colleagues.

Development of Group Norms Norms do not suddenly and magically appear in groups. They seldom, if ever, develop in a purely spontaneous way. Rather, they arise out of interaction among group members. An example of a typical norm development process is shown in Exhibit 13.5. Key factors that often have a major influence on the process include the following:[38]

- *Early behaviors:* Typically, initial behaviors, especially in newly formed groups, establish standards for subsequent behavior. In committees, for example, the first few meetings help establish norms about how candid, or how indirect, discussion of sensitive issues is likely to be. Such quickly established norms are often difficult to reshape or change later.
- *Imported behaviors:* Members of a group often bring with them standards of behavior that were prominent in their former groups. "When in doubt, stay with the familiar" seems to be the (sometimes incorrect) watchword of many people in organizations. When a high-status member imports a norm, as in the case of those with acknowledged expertise or high power, the prominence of that norm is likely to be strong. A new chief executive officer (CEO), for example, may believe in a norm of communication "only through channels" regarding suggestions and input from members of the organization, even though this may run counter to the previous norm of openness and the "door is open at any time" fostered by the former CEO. However, because the new CEO has high status, few are likely to challenge this imported norm.
- *Critical events:* A sudden challenge to the group, such as criticism from another group, can create specific and vivid responses that form the basis for how members should be expected to respond in the future. A time of crisis makes people

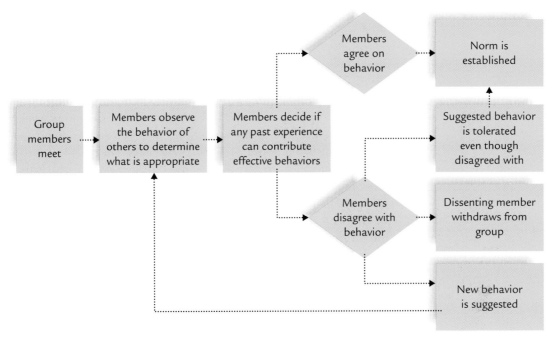

exhibit 13.5

Example of the Development of Group Norms

Source: Kenneth Bettenhausen and J. Keith Murnighan, "The Emergence of Norms in Competitive Decision Making Groups," *Administrative Science Quarterly*, 30 (1985), pp. 350–72.

particularly alert to cues in their environment and thus tends to reinforce norms that emerge from that period. In a corporation that has announced layoffs, for example, new norms regarding the overt display of diligent work habits may emerge.

- *Explicitly stated standards:* Not to be overlooked is the fact that leaders or high-status members of a group may simply assert that "this is how we will do it around here!" Newly appointed supervisors and athletic coaches, for example, frequently use this approach with their groups or teams.

Effects of Group Norms Since norms are, essentially, accepted standards, their primary effect is to shape or influence the behavior of individual members of a group. Thus, norms can be thought of as constraining or reducing the variability of actions and attitudes across a set of group members. That is, the existence of strong norms tends to narrow individual differences in behavior and beliefs. This results in a certain degree of **conformity**, or close adherence to the group's norms by the individual members.

conformity close adherence to the group's norms by the individual members

Whether such conformity is "good" or "bad" depends on the perspective of the viewer. If the norms support a manager's goals for a group—say, for example, that everyone should look for opportunities to make creative suggestions to improve the group's effectiveness—then the manager would regard conformity as very helpful. A few years ago, a large, national transit company reorganized around cross-functional groups following a decade of financial and labor problems; about half (42 percent) of the groups were successful and about half (48 percent) were unsuccessful. The groups deemed successful had developed stronger norms of open communication and leadership, and they behaved more like teams.[39]

If norms conflict with the objectives a manager is trying to achieve, then greater conformity would be regarded as negative. The obvious implication for you as manager is that you should be as concerned about the content or direction of group norms as about the amount of conformity to them.

From the point of view of an individual member of a group, norms can sometimes be too constraining. In that case, the individual may deviate from the group's expected attitudes and behavior. Such divergent actions or expressed views are potentially troubling to others in the group because they can threaten the group's solidarity and, perhaps in extreme cases, even its existence. Therefore, the group sometimes imposes sanctions on the deviant in an attempt to bring about greater conformity. The classic case in certain Western work situations, particularly at the hourly worker level, is the individual who works faster or slower than the group thinks he or she should. Such persons, sometimes labeled "rate busters" or "slackers," are often subjected to ridicule or ostracism to persuade or force them to work at a rate more in line with the group's norms for production effort.

Cohesion

cohesion the degree to which members are motivated to remain in the group

Another major property of groups is their amount of **cohesion**, "the degree to which members are motivated to remain in a group," to *want* to stay in it.[40] Group cohesion is usually considered to have many advantages and to be highly desirable if it can be developed.[41] Indeed, when managers and organizations attempt to turn groups into teams, they are, in effect, trying to generate stronger group cohesion. However, as will be discussed later, high levels of group cohesion may not always result in positive outcomes.[42]

Development of Group Cohesion There are no sure-fire ways for you as a manager to build strong cohesion in groups which you lead or in which you are a member. However, the available research suggests three factors that can be potentially important in developing greater group cohesion:

- Strengthening interpersonal attraction among group members;
- Generating a record of high performance and past success of the group; and
- Fostering competition with other groups.[43]

The most consistently important of these factors appears to be the first, namely, whether members of the group think they have something in common with other members and tend to like being with them; that is, whether they feel like they belong to a true team. The evidence for the other two factors in bringing about cohesion is not as clear-cut, but both past group success and current or anticipated conflict with other groups seem to unite groups and increase their cohesion, especially if strong interpersonal attraction among members is already present. Obviously, a group whose members don't especially like being with each other may disintegrate when faced with competition from external groups, rather than develop greater cohesion, which again places a premium on developing interpersonal bonds.

Effects of Group Cohesion Increased cohesiveness of groups can have a number of potential advantages.[44] Chief among these is an increase in the quantity and quality of group interaction.[45] A second potential advantage of greater group cohesion is that the group has stronger influence on each member to conform to the group's standards or norms. Assuming—and this is a critical assumption—that those norms are positive from the manager's perspective, then this is a significant advantage. A third possible advantage is that cohesive groups appear to be more effective in achieving goals that group members accept, although research on this point is not totally consistent. A final possible advantage of higher group cohesion is that members tend to have greater satisfaction with the group.

As positive as these potential advantages might seem, high group cohesion sometimes can be a mixed blessing from a manager's point of view (see Exhibit 13.6). First, if the group has norms that do not support the organization's goals, then greater cohesion is definitely a minus. Individuals may be more influenced in the "wrong" direction—as when, for example, a group of workers tolerates sexual harassment—than if there is little cohesion. Another possible disadvantage of strong group cohesion is that deviance from group norms may not be handled effectively. Highly cohesive groups are more likely to reject any deviance, even if it represents creative ideas that could ultimately be useful to the group. Related to this is the danger that groupthink[46] (previously discussed in Chapter 9) may be accentuated in highly cohesive groups. Dissenting viewpoints, as expressed in the phrase "devil's advocate," often can be quite useful to a group in causing it to critically test its opinion or decisions.

Still another potential disadvantage of high within-group cohesion, but one that is frequently overlooked, is that between-group cooperation may be adversely affected. Most organizations have many work groups; some have hundreds or more. The challenge, for higher-level managers, is to have these groups and teams work together and interact smoothly and reliably. So, it is a concern if higher within-group cohesion hinders intergroup cooperation. For example, in developing and marketing a new product, problems may develop among the production, marketing, and sales departments. If the production group is highly cohesive and has a norm of never allowing outsiders to know they have problems, they may be reluctant to notify other units that a key piece of equipment is not functioning correctly. Without this information, the marketing department might generate unrealistic expectations for the release date, and the sales teams then would promise higher numbers of the product to customers than would actually be available.

This example illustrates that the active promotion of strong within-group (team) cohesion by managers could decrease rather than increase overall functioning of the larger organization because of the potential for increased fragmentation. This situation is sometimes encountered in highly decentralized organizations, where employees show extremely strong loyalty to their own unit, for example, marketing, but considerably less concern for the welfare of other units, say, production, and the need to coordinate with them. Thus, in this case, intraunit cohesion may gain greater autonomy for the unit, but it can hinder the achievement of integrated organizationwide objectives.

Positive effects	Negative effects
• Increased quality and quantity of group interactions	• Counterproductive norms may be emphasized
• Strengthened adherence to group norms	• Useful or creative ideas may be ignored if they deviate from established norms or values
• Increased effectiveness in achieving group goals	• Increased probability of developing groupthink
• Augmented individual satisfaction with group membership	• Potential decrease in intergroup cooperation

exhibit 13.6

Effects of High Levels of Group Cohesion

FORMATION AND DEVELOPMENT OF GROUPS AND TEAMS

Groups in organizations form for many reasons and in many ways. Most often, of course, the company or organization deliberately puts groups together to serve stated organizational purposes. Informal groups, however, are another matter. They form more or less spontaneously on the basis of actions by their members and to serve those members' self-interests, which may or may not coincide with those of the organization.

Influences on the Formation of Groups and Teams

The most important factors influencing the formation of groups in organizations are the goals of the organization, the opportunities for interaction and sharing mutual knowledge, and the psychological needs of potential group members.

Organizational Goals The goals and purposes of the larger organization directly affect the nature of its formal groups. The organization creates new groups, whether command, task forces, or committees, based on its judgment that needs are not being met adequately by existing groups. New groups may arise because of organizational growth, changes in the products or services the organization offers, or simply perceptions by key managers that greater efficiency and effectiveness can be gained by adding to, altering, or combining existing groups. See A Manager's Challenge, "Are Teams Worth It?" that shows how a major company created a team-based structure when faced with the necessity to make major changes, and how well that structure worked out.

A key issue for organizations and managers when new groups are formed is whether they will be given adequate resources to accomplish their specific goals.[47] The leader of a team that developed the data storage system for a major product at Honeywell Defense Avionics stated, "My most important task . . . was to help this team feel as if they owned the project by getting them whatever information, financial or otherwise, they needed."[48]

If you are a member of a new group put together by the organization, you are likely to have a number of questions, such as

- Why am I, rather than someone else, in the group?
- What are the real reasons why the group was put together?
- What are my new responsibilities going to be?
- Are the stated objectives for the group realistic and are they the actual goals that will be measured?

Such questions naturally occur to anyone who becomes part of a new group, but they don't always get asked directly or openly. Managers who form groups must therefore anticipate questions such as these, whether or not they are raised explicitly, and must be prepared to provide necessary information and explanations. If you become responsible for putting together a new organizational group, you need to recognize that, as discussed earlier, the formation of a new group does not necessarily mean that a new team has been created. You may have the hope that your new group will develop into a team with a strong sense of shared responsibility for the group's performance and output, but cohesiveness and cooperation are not something that you can decree. Managers cannot simply declare new groups to be "teams" and expect that they will operate that way. Team development depends on managerial skills and follow-up actions to elicit true teamwork in more than name only.[49]

a manager's challenge

Change

Are Teams Worth It?

How do teams affect performance when a company is confronted with a major change? One of the best-documented recent tests was conducted by Bell Atlantic, which provided telephone service to the mid-Atlantic states (before merging with GTE to become Verizon). Bell Atlantic derived its corporate value from three areas: employee productivity, service quality, and employee satisfaction. All these contributed to the performance of the company's 45 consumer call centers, where about 6,000 sales consultants served the firm's residential customers.

The company decided to convert the call centers to a team structure to help support its corporate goals of shareholder value, customer satisfaction, and employee commitment. The conversion took about two years—and was about half completed at the time of the study.

The sales consultants' jobs were unchanged by the conversion to a team structure. But in the centers where teaming had begun, a committee of employees and an assistant manager helped to identify and communicate team needs. Teams were seated together in work areas from which high dividing walls had been removed, and training was provided in team processes, cooperative communication, and problem-solving skills. Teams also met weekly to discuss results and solve problems, and a special feedback system was developed to acknowledge members' efforts and share best practices with their colleagues.

The evaluation project looked at two call centers that had implemented the team organization, and a third which had not. Together the three employed about 140 people. Data for the comparison came from observations and feedback from Bell Atlantic managers and sales consultants. Fifteen months of productivity measures plus service quality data and two employee surveys also measured perceptions about how well the new teams were working.

According to the productivity data, the sales consultants who worked in teams outperformed the others in three of the company's four productivity measures. They generated an average of $21,000 more per year in sales revenue than their nonteamed peers—representing a potential total revenue gain of $127 million per year.

Teams also scored slightly higher on 13 service quality criteria such as job knowledge, courtesy, and accuracy. Even larger gains were logged in employee satisfaction. The number of employee suggestions increased, participation in meetings went up, and employees became more active in identifying and solving problems. Given these positive results, Bell Atlantic chose to proceed with converting the remaining call centers.

Clearly, employees enthusiastically accepted the joint decision making, cooperative problem solving, and cross-training aspects of teaming. Other factors that helped the team concept succeed were the existence of team champions; thorough assessment of support systems such as communication, performance measurement and feedback, and continuous improvement; and a high-level plan of action that covered pre- and post-team implementation and plenty of training.

Source: Alison Overholt, "Wireless in San Diego," *Fast Company*, January 2004, p. 84; Priscilla S. Wisner and Hollace A. Feist, "Does Teaming Pay Off?" *Strategic Finance*, February 2001, pp. 58–64.

Opportunities for Interaction and Sharing Mutual Knowledge In the formation of groups and their possible development into teams, physical proximity is obviously a helpful factor. When people have the opportunity to work together closely, it can facilitate learning about similarities of interests and experiences. These similarities can provide a basis for the development of friendships that can assist the work of the group.

However, in this age of electronic communication, groups are often highly dispersed geographically and cannot use the advantage of close physical proximity. In such circumstances, it becomes even more critical to increase opportunities for interaction, even if that is only via electronic messages. In other words, in dispersed "virtual" groups, it is essential to take steps to develop mutual knowledge—to find "common ground"—among members.[50] These could include such actions as attempting if at all possible to have at least one initial face-to-face meeting, arranging possible visits by one or more team members to other members' local sites, encouraging members to share information about their particular work context (time constraints, other task demands, local customs, etc.), and, especially, to take extra efforts to make sure that members has access to all relevant information.[51]

Psychological Factors There are many personal reasons that motivate organizational members to form closer relationships in groups, especially basic human needs for security, social support, self-esteem, and status. By belonging to groups, even virtual ones, employees are often able to fulfill needs that may not be well satisfied by the work itself. Thus, the feeling of belonging to a group at work can be highly rewarding for many individuals. It can be, in effect, a significant way for individuals to achieve a distinct social identity that is meaningful both for themselves and for others who interact with them.[52]

Stages of Group Development

Whether groups are formed by the organization or by voluntary actions of individuals, they tend to move through distinct or identifiable developmental stages as they mature.[53] One popular early statement on this issue utilizes an easy-to-remember set of terms for such stages: "forming" (getting acquainted), "storming" (expressing differences of opinion), "norming" (building consensus on basic issues), and "performing" (carrying out cooperative group actions).[54] Although this model has considerable appeal as a way to think about phases of group development across time, it does not apply universally to all groups. As one set of management scholars has noted, "It seems unlikely that a single sequence can describe the development of all kinds of teams [groups]."[55]

Despite this fact, several identifiable stages do show up with some regularity in organizational contexts (Exhibit 13.7).

Formation If you are forming a new group, you will face some unique challenges. One kind of challenge is presented when potential team members are not used to a group-oriented approach to work. If they have been comfortable in working within a prevailing individual-based organizational culture, they are obviously facing a significant change. In dealing with this kind of challenge, it will be particularly useful to keep in mind Lewin's model of change—unfreezing-change-refreezing—that was discussed extensively in Chapter 2.

Another kind of challenge in the formation stages is that the group's members will have lots of questions, whether they ask them openly or not. For example, they will want to know who is in the group and why they are there, who is leading the group, and where each person is "coming from" in terms of his or her existing attitudes and viewpoints. Nearly all new groups go through this "getting to know you" stage. ExxonMobil faced this situation when it formed two new teams—one in Finland and one in Texas—to design and build a new deep-draft caisson vehicle. Each team was made up of company engineers, outside contractors, and vendors. In order to succeed, each team had to forge strong bonds among its members immediately. The teams did many things to build team camaraderie quickly, including having t-shirts made up with a logo each team designed, and drafting their own mission statements, charters, and project plans.[56]

exhibit 13.7

Stages of Group Development

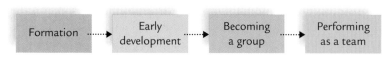

Formation ┈┈▶ Early development ┈┈▶ Becoming a group ┈┈▶ Performing as a team

┈┈▶ Indicates progression

Early Development Following a group's formation and initial interactions, an early development stage settles in that may last for some time, depending on the nature of the group and its tasks. In this stage, members learn what is expected of them, what is acceptable behavior, and how well they relate to each other. Typically, members cautiously exchange, and sometimes jealously guard, information. If you are the group's leader it is an important time for learning about how opinions within the group overlap or differ on key matters. Often, conflicts over group goals or the means to reach them may emerge in this stage. An analogy to adolescence in human development might be apt for helping you understand this stage of group development.

Becoming a Group In this stage, at least a minimum amount of consensus about group issues begins to appear, as well as a degree of individual identity with the group and its goals. How much cohesion and group identity will actually emerge will vary widely from group to group at this stage. A critical factor will be how well the group is meeting each member's needs and how well members think the group is being led. In this stage particularly, if you are in a leadership role you can have considerable impact on the group's development and help it to become a true team.

Performing as a Team In this stage, a group is able to perform like a team and take actions as a coherent entity and not just as a set of loosely affiliated individuals. Internally, this means that the group is able to influence members' attitudes and behavior on matters of importance to the group, and externally it means that others in, or outside, the organization are being affected by its actions. Several years ago, for example, Sterling Winthrop Pharmaceuticals Research Division, a one-time subsidiary of Eastman Kodak Company that was located in Pennsylvania, constructed a one-million-square-foot complex. Construction was finished early, on budget, and with an exceptional safety record. The company credits that feat to the development of an intense team

Few people gave Olympic gold medal winners Jill Bakken and Vonetta Flowers much of a chance in the Olympics' first-ever, women's bobsled event in 2002. Bakken and Flowers weren't even expected to be the best U.S. team. Flowers had ended up on the bobsled team somewhat haphazardly after having failed to make the Olympic track team. "A lot of people saw us as the 'other' team," she said. "We came here to prove those people wrong." She is the first black athlete ever to win a gold medal in the Winter Olympics.

identity. That identity was tied to shared beliefs in cooperation, commitment, and the individual value of each team member.[57]

Each of the preceding four stages can be illustrated by the following story of a project group that was put together in a large consumer products company:

- *Formation:* During a reengineering effort at this company, eight managers from various functions were asked to work together to take on the project of analyzing the company's effectiveness in a number of areas and making performance-enhancing recommendations. In the early group meetings, most people were uncomfortable and unsure. Some were quiet, offering no input and waiting for others to move the meetings along. Some bonded in immediate alliances, and yet others jumped right in and began trying to perform the team's tasks.

- *Early Development:* Soon the group members began to understand the scope of their task. They began to understand who among them really had influence, and who the leaders were. Some work was accomplished, and while the members' relationships and confidence improved, overall the group's performance was very low.

- *Becoming a Group:* Next, the group began to focus on encouraging group, rather than individual, behavior. They began listening to each other and assessing suggestions in terms of the group's goals rather than as a display of each individual member's goals. They found ways to resolve conflicts and established standards of group conduct.

- *Performing as a Group:* The group now regarded themselves as a team. The next hurdle was learning that they did not always have to agree with each other—that they could disagree and still accomplish their task. They began evaluating all parts of suggestions, coping with divergent opinions and creatively managing their conflicts. Their effectiveness and performance steadily continued to improve.

- *Outcome:* Over the 15 weeks of the team's existence, they analyzed the order taking, product scheduling, sales reporting, and pricing processes in their company. They identified and recommended several cost reduction and process improvement plans, with their recommendations resulting in savings of $2.5 million to their company.[58]

Returning to the general issue of stages in group development, whether a team's actions across these stages are continuously effective or not is another matter. Events internal or external to the group could still cause it to revert to an earlier stage of development, where it might need to re-form and attempt to become a "performing group" all over again. However, if a group has no specified ending point, that is, an "adjourning" phase, there is no inherent reason why the performing stage cannot last indefinitely. To keep a group or team in this stage continually is a clear managerial and leadership challenge.

EXAMPLES OF PROMINENT GROUPS AND TEAMS IN TODAY'S ORGANIZATIONS

Now that we have examined some of the basic characteristics of groups and teams and how they form and develop, we are ready to look at some examples of particular kinds of groups and teams that are becoming increasingly prominent in today's organizations (see Exhibit 13.8). Not every organization will have each of these groups, but where they do exist they present some special managerial challenges.

Type	Potential Advantages	Potential Disadvantages
Self-Managing	More team-like behavior	Not all employees want to manage themselves
Cross-Functional/ New Product	Increased creativity Dispersed knowledge Speed to market	Increased group conflict
Global	Increased creativity from diversity of backgrounds	Paralysis Inaction Failure
Virtual	Increased speed of communication Decreased costs	Increased misinterpretation Lack of trust Difficult to manage

exhibit 13.8
Prominent Groups and Teams in Today's Organizations

Self-Managing Workgroups (Teams)

A relatively recent, but increasingly important, variant of a command work-group is the **self-managing**, or so-called autonomous, group—a workgroup that has no formally appointed supervisor. These groups are similar to command groups in that the members coordinate their organizational work as if they all reported to the same formally appointed supervisor. However, the group manages itself on behalf of the organization's objectives, and its members usually appoint their own informal team leaders.[59] The group is made up of a number of members with diverse skills that can be applied to the group's task. It generally is responsible for decisions concerning how to accomplish the work—which members will perform which tasks and in which order. They also frequently do jobs traditionally associated with supervision, such as conducting team meetings and solving productivity problems. A major reason that some organizations—Xerox, Procter & Gamble, and General Motors, among many others—put together such self-managing units is to develop more team-like group behavior compared with that of the more traditional command group. When the New York Regional Office of the Department of Veterans Affairs reorganized a few years ago, for example, it abandoned its historically rigid hierarchical structure, opting instead to organize the workforce into 16 12-member, self-directed workgroups in which each member has multiple functions. The workgroups do not report to a manager as such, but instead they are assigned to a "coach," usually someone who has previously been a supervisor.[60]

The idea of group self-management, however good it appears in principle, may not appeal to all employees who might be affected. Furthermore, it cannot be assumed to fit into all types of cultures.[61] Therefore, managers and organizations who want to establish such groups need to consider potential pitfalls and resistance as well as the possible advantages.

Cross-Functional New Products (Services) Groups

Groups that draw their membership from distinctly different types of units within an organization, such as R&D and marketing, have been around for many years. However, their number and importance have increased markedly in recent years. A primary objective for such groups or teams is to bring to bear

self-managing (autonomous) workgroup a group that has no formally appointed supervisor but is similar to command groups in that the members coordinate their organizational work as *if* they all reported to the same formally appointed supervisor; members usually appoint their own informal team leader

on the task as much creativity and dispersed knowledge as possible. A good example of a cross-functional team operating in a very basic industry is one put together by Golden West Bakery plant in Greater Manchester, England. The plant makes buns for McDonald's hamburgers. A cross-functional team composed of members from both production and maintenance was put together with the dual goals of improving productivity and reducing waste. The team managed a complete overhaul of both the maintenance and production processes that was so successful that the company decided to restructure to take greater advantage of an increased use of teams of all types.[62]

Other major objectives of cross-functional teams, especially in high-technology firms, are to speed the products to market while at the same time controlling or minimizing costs. This sounds good, but the reality is often that the outcomes are less favorable than expected because of the inherent potential for increased conflicts in groups composed of members with widely varying initial perspectives.[63] To deal with this basic issue, research results suggest approaches (indicated below) that managers can use to try to increase the following attributes of effective cross-functional groups:[64]

- Members' feelings of "ownership" ("at-stakeness") of the group's decisions; approach: Work to see that each member believes that he or she has the opportunity to influence the group's decision making.[65]
- Transparency or openness regarding members' motivations, expectations, and personal agendas; approach: Try to make sure that such differences brought into the group are freely discussed and shared.
- "Mindfulness" or, essentially, reaching high-quality decisions; approach: Ensure that all divergent points of view are explicitly recognized and examined.
- High levels of synergy mutual cooperation ("synergy"); approach: Facilitate the building of as much trust as possible within the group, so that no one feels that someone else will try to take advantage of them.

Global Teams

Another type of group that is becoming increasingly prominent, especially in larger organizations, is the multinational group (almost always referred to as a "multinational team"). It is usually a highly diverse group, whether representing one or several functional areas, because members are often from very different cultural backgrounds. For reasons that we have already discussed, diverse teams potentially offer major advantages for organizations. However, reality is not always quite so rosy. All too frequently, the efforts of such groups end up in paralysis, inaction, or even outright failure.

One set of researchers divides up multinational teams into three general types: the destroyers, the equalizers, and the creators.[66] "Destroyers" are groups that turn out to be utter disasters; they channel their members' efforts and attention into unproductive conflicts and interpersonal attacks. For example, one member of a European destroyer team described the team environment candidly: "Those Brits on our team are too serious; the Germans are so stuck-up about engineering that they don't think anyone else has a brain; and the French couldn't care less about production quotas." "Equalizer" types of teams are those that think they are doing well and have little apparent conflict, yet seem unable to produce any result other than one of mediocrity. Essentially, equalizers are underperforming teams that fail to take advantage of their cross-national diversity. "Creator" teams are those that directly accept and build on their differences and use them to enhance their creativity.

Virtual Teams

As mentioned earlier in this chapter, organizations are increasingly establishing "**virtual teams**" or groups composed of individuals who do not work together in close physical proximity. Members of virtual teams are often geographically dispersed, cross-organizationally or cross-nationally. As their names imply, such groups rarely, if ever, meet in person and instead conduct most or all of their business via electronic communication. Such virtual teams are utilized, for example, by GTech, a company that manufactures lottery equipment. It reorganized its Information Technology Department into virtual teams based on standardization of procedures and a skills database which allow the department to assign the appropriate personnel to each problem no matter where they are located. This move resulted in a savings of $3 million in 2001, or about 35 percent per desktop system. In 2003, GTech was also selected as one of the 100 best IT companies to work for, according to *Computerworld* magazine.[67]

virtual team a group composed of individuals who do not work together in close physical proximity

Increased speed of communication and decreased costs in meeting together are obvious advantages of such groups. Nevertheless, as can be imagined, virtual teams also have their own associated set of potential problems. First, communication, though fast and sometimes nearly instantaneous, can be incomplete and easily subject to misinterpretation by the receiver. Second, trust among group members may be very difficult to develop because of the absence of the typical getting-to-know-you socialization process that occurs with nonvirtual groups that meet face-to-face. Third, managerial supervision may be more difficult than in a typical group. Issues that can crop up in any group, such as role ambiguity and social loafing, for example, may be intensified in virtual groups.

BUILDING AND MANAGING GROUPS AND TEAMS

Throughout this chapter in various places we have mentioned some of the steps that you as a manager can take to increase the quality of group functioning and the satisfaction of group members. Here in this section we focus on three issues that are particularly critical in building and managing groups and turning them into true teams: developing team competencies, dealing with team conflicts, and improving group effectiveness.

Developing Team Competencies

As we have emphasized throughout this chapter, working with, and in, a group is different from simply doing your own individual job well. It is the interaction with other people, whether face-to-face or by electronic and other indirect means, that makes the difference. Therefore, to be able to perform effectively in a group, it is important that you develop competencies in teamwork. To be a competent team member is not necessarily the same thing as being a competent individual performer. A very useful way to think about what is required from you in a team situation is to consider three basic areas of teamwork competencies: **k**nowledge, **s**kills, and **a**ttitudes (KSAs).[68] Specific examples of team competencies in these three areas are shown in Exhibit 13.9.

Knowledge (K) in the group context refers to the necessary understanding of facts, concepts, relations, and underlying relevant information

exhibit 13.9

Examples of Specific Team
Competencies in Three Areas

Knowledge	Skills	Attitudes
· Knowledge of team mission, objectives, norms	· Adaptability and flexibility	· Team orientation
· Task sequencing	· Mutual performance monitoring and feedback, self-correction	· Shared vision
· Team role interaction patterns	· Coordination and task integration	· Team cohesion
· Understanding team work skills	· Communication	· Mutual trust
· Teammate characteristics	· Decision making and problem solving	· Importance of teamwork

Sources: Adapted from J. A. Cannon-Bowers and E. Salas, "A Framework for Developing Team Performance Measures in Training," in M. T. Brannick, E. Salas, and C. Prince (eds.), *Team Performance Assessment and Measurement: Theory, Methods, and Applications* (Mahwah, NJ: Lawrence Erlbaum Associates, 1997), p. 47.

necessary to perform team tasks. As shown in Exhibit 13.9, examples of the kinds of specific knowledge that are especially useful in team situations include knowledge about the team's mission and goals, the sequencing of tasks faced by the team, fellow team members' roles and responsibilities, and teammate characteristics.

Skills (S) (as noted in Chapter 10) refer to highly developed behavioral and cognitive capabilities that are necessary to carry out team tasks and meet team goals. These include (as shown in Exhibit 13.9) such competencies as adaptability and flexibility in relation to accomplishing team tasks; being able to monitor one's own and fellow team members' performance; communication; being able to accept and give criticisms; and being able to assume leadership responsibilities within the group.

Attitudes (A) involve relatively stable feelings and beliefs about something. In other words, our attitudes, generally speaking, indicate how we view important parts of our environment. In a group-work situation, these important attitudes would include (see Exhibit 13.9) those toward the concepts of teams and teamwork, the need for team cohesion, assessment of a team's capabilities, and the level and importance of trust within a group.[69]

A helpful way to analyze required team competencies in the areas of knowledge, skills, and attitudes was developed a few years ago by a group of organizational psychologists[70] and is displayed in Exhibit 13.10. This system of analysis categorizes the types of team competencies needed, using two variables: (1) Whether a needed competency is specific to a given task, or applies to all kinds of tasks; and (2) whether a needed competency is specific to a given team, or applies to all kinds of teams. The resulting categorization scheme organized along these two dimensions can be summarized in a 2 × 2 table, as shown in Exhibit 13.10.

By far, the most important type of competency in this classification system for you as a potential manager is represented in the bottom right of Exhibit 13.10: "transportable team competencies." **Transportable competencies** are those that can be utilized in *any* situation. They are helpful for anyone who works with a variety of teams and with teams that face a wide variety of tasks. Therefore, transportable KSAs are the most essential group competencies for any manager or team member to develop. A knowledge of what is

transportable competencies competencies that can be utilized in any situation

Relation to Task

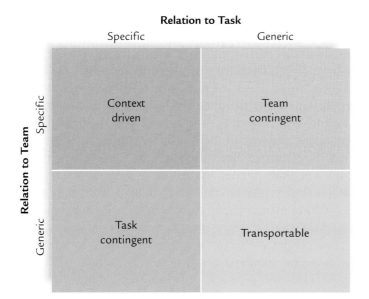

exhibit 13.10

Types of Team Competencies

Source: Adapted from J. A. Cannon-Bowers, S. I. Tannenbaum, E. Salas, and C. E. Volpe, "Defining Competencies and Establishing Team Training Requirements," in R. A. Guzzo, E. Salas and Associates (eds.), *Team Effectiveness and Decision Making in Organizations* (San Francisco: Jossey-Bass Publishers, 1995), p. 339.

required to work together in teams of any type is crucial and highly transferable. Interpersonal, communication, and team-building capabilities are the hallmark of transportable team skill competencies. An especially important attitude would be an appreciation for the value and usefulness of teamwork. In short, it is clearly worth your time and effort to acquire and improve team competencies that are portable.

In the upper-right corner of Exhibit 13.10 are **team-contingent competencies**—competencies that are specific to the particular team, but applicable to tasks that vary. Many typical command (supervisor-led) groups would be examples of teams that need these types of competencies. Such groups require a high level of team-member knowledge of each other—each member needs to know what each other member's skill and expertise is. Members also need to have a clear understanding of how their group coordinates with the larger organization. In these kinds of group circumstances, the composition of the group's membership is particularly important. This can be seen when there is a change in that composition (addition or loss of a member) that usually reduces the team's effectiveness until a new member can be brought up to speed. Skills needed in this team-dependent category include skills that apply to a wide variety of tasks, such as leadership, communication, and conflict resolution skills. Also, since the composition of the team is so crucial, the perception of strong team cohesion would be an important attitude.

In the upper-left corner of Exhibit 13.10 are "**context-driven**" competencies. As the category name implies, the particular circumstances—relating to both task and team—in which the group is performing are crucial to the competencies that are needed. They are competencies that would be specific to both the unique nature of the particular tasks and the particular composition of teams. The task-specific/team-specific kinds of knowledge needed would, for example, include a shared understanding of the different parts of the specific overall task, information about other team members' habits and tendencies, and an understanding of the team's norms. The kinds of teams that would benefit from such context-driven competencies would include surgery teams, military combat teams, and sports teams. An example from the sports world illustrates the need for both task-specific *and* team-specific knowledge. Many professional leagues in sports such as basketball and baseball have mid-season

team-contingent competencies competencies that are specific to the particular team, but applicable to tasks that vary

context-driven competencies competencies that are specific to both the unique nature of the particular tasks and the particular composition of the team

all-star games, where the best individual players from each team (or, at least from most teams) in one part of the league come together to play the best players from the other part. Thus, all of the players are experts at their own tasks. They have high task-specific knowledge and skills. However, they lack the high level of team-specific knowledge they have regarding their own teams. The consequence of this situation is that the performance of players on all-star teams typically turns out to be lower than the performance of those same players when playing on their own regular teams. The problem is the relative lack of team-specific knowledge.

Examples of skills needed in this category would include the ability to reallocate duties among members under changing circumstances, and the ability to develop common understanding of overall task requirements. In the area of attitudes, a task-specific/team-specific type of competency would be the development of a collective sense of team strengths and weaknesses.

task-contingent competencies competencies that are needed in teams that perform a specific and recurring set of tasks but have varying sets of members

Task-contingent competencies (lower-left corner of Exhibit 13.10) are needed in teams that perform a specific and recurring set of tasks but have varying sets of members. In the knowledge area, team members in this category of teams would need expertise regarding the specific task characteristics they would encounter on a regular basis. Skills needed would be those that are highly related to the particular set of tasks involved. An attitude that would be helpful in this kind of situation would be a positive view of working as part of a team, regardless of who the other team members are. Examples of teams that need these kinds of competencies among their members would be many aircraft crews, firefighting teams, and the like. For this task-driven set of conditions, it doesn't matter who is on the team on a given day, just that members are competent in performing their particular tasks. Members of the team have to trust the other members to do their jobs, *even if* they have never met each other before. As long as the pilot knows how to take off and land, and the navigator knows how to navigate, the team is okay.

Dealing with Team Conflict

When people work together in groups, there is always the potential for conflict within the group. Disagreement or opposition between or among group members can occur for a number of reasons and can have a variety of consequences. Although the effects of group conflict, such as a marked decrease in cohesion within the group, often can be negative, that is not always so. In fact, some types of conflict, particularly task or substantive conflict (discussed next), can have positive effects. For instance, a senior executive at Keane, an information technology firm based in Boston, views it this way: "We can agree our way into horrendous decisions. But when people are allowed to express their opinions, no matter how disagreeable, magic can occur. More ideas are put on the table, which can lead to more discovery, which can lead to quantum leaps in improvement and innovation. . . . When marketing and engineering disagree violently about something, you've got a wonderful opportunity to figure out how to make improvements by meeting both [of their] objectives."[71]

The important point to remember is that conflict among members within groups is fairly common, and it is not always something to be avoided. In fact, the absence of any conflict at all can be a sign that the group is not openly generating a variety of viewpoints and potential approaches for solving problems and making good decisions.

Types of Group Conflict   Researchers have generally distinguished two basic types of group conflict: task conflict and relationship conflict. **Task conflict** is conflict that focuses on differences in ideas and courses of action in addressing the issues facing a group. It is also sometimes called cognitive (thinking)[72] or substantive conflict.[73] Research indicates that at least some amount of task conflict often can be beneficial to the group,[74] especially for less routine and more complex tasks.[75]

The other major type of conflict that can occur in groups, relationship conflict, is usually found to be almost always dysfunctional. **Relationship conflict** focuses on interpersonal differences and is sometimes called affective or emotional conflict.[76] It is usually a negative type of conflict for groups because it distracts focus from tasks and ideas.[77] It discourages rather than encourages consideration of multiple points of view and the open discussion of ideas and solutions.

Causes of Group Conflict   There are many potential causes of group conflict, but they can usually be linked to one of the two types of conflict.

The causes of task conflict, for example, include:

- Ambiguities regarding the task;
- Differences in goals, objectives, and perspectives (e.g., stemming from differences in functional backgrounds[78] among group members;
- Scarcity (actual or perceived) of resources to accomplish group goals.

Possible causes of relationship conflict are:

- Dissimilarities in the composition of the membership of the group, including demographic diversity (in age, ethnic/cultural background, gender, etc.) and status/power differences;[79]
- Differences in interpersonal styles of individual members;
- Differences in values.[80]

Several of the potential causes of group conflict can occur together; for example, when a very diverse group that includes several people with distinctive interpersonal styles or quite different values encounters a highly ambiguous task. When there are such multiple causes, finding ways to deal with the conflict becomes even more difficult, of course.

Managing Group Conflict   If you are put in the position of leading a group, what can you do to help your group deal with conflict? Probably the most important managerial guideline for dealing with group conflict is to try to increase the ratio of substantive to relationship conflict.[81] This would mean, for example, strongly encouraging a culture of openness to express differences of opinion about task methods and objectives, and also being especially receptive to novel or creative approaches to coping with task requirements.[82] In this way, maximum amounts of relevant information can be brought to bear on the issues faced by the group,[83] and unintended groupthink tendencies can be minimized. In addition, you should help to clarify and reduce task ambiguities and try to get the group to focus on larger goals beyond individual member interests—goals, in other words, that emphasize the common interests of all the group members. Also, there is evidence to suggest that active attempts that are taken to avoid relationship conflicts may be the best way to eliminate or at least reduce their harmful effects on group members' satisfaction and performance.[84]

task (substantive) conflict conflict that focuses on differences in ideas and courses of action in addressing the issues facing a group

relationship (affective) conflict interpersonal differences among group members

Demographic differences, differences in interpersonal styles, and differences in values can lend a group strength. However, the same differences can also become the source of intragroup conflict. Managers should actively emphasize the common interests of members and discourage personal conflicts between them.

intragroup conflict differences that occur within groups

intergroup conflict differences that occur between groups

Most of what we have been talking about so far applies to conflict *within* groups (**intragroup conflict**). In organizational settings, of course, conflict *between* or among groups—**intergroup conflict**—can also occur frequently. Strategies for managing intragroup conflict apply equally well to intergroup conflict. Therefore, managers should look for opportunities to reduce unnecessary relational conflicts in those intergroup interaction situations and increase the focus on substantive differences. Also, emphasizing larger, more organizationwide goals can help increase cooperation and thus performance.[85] So, for example, if sales and production can concentrate on the issue of improving customer satisfaction—to elevate it to the highest priority—then their differences on how many variations of a product to make and market can be minimized or resolved. As with intragroup conflict, the potential exists for positive effects from intergroup conflict.

Improving Group and Team Effectiveness

Teams and groups are not static parts of organizations. They come into existence, go out of existence, and change over time. Additionally, and most important, their effectiveness and performance can be changed and improved. As a leader of a group, however, this is not necessarily easy to do. There is no magic formula to bring this about. Nevertheless, there are some useful approaches to consider that have the potential for helping to improve a group's performance in organizational settings.[86]

Assessing the Effectiveness of Groups What exactly do we mean by group effectiveness? What distinguishes highly effective groups from less effective groups? A survey of 61 U.S. companies revealed that about two-thirds used objective, quantifiable criteria to measure group effectiveness; these included measures of production output, quality improvements, cost reductions, and turnaround times. A number of the companies also used more subjective criteria including member participation, cooperation, and involvement.[87]

How can we tell when a group is performing especially well? Analyses of research findings by one of the foremost experts on group effectiveness, Richard Hackman, suggest three major indicators (Exhibit 13.11):[88]

1. Whether the group's outputs—products, services, or decisions—are valued by those who receive or use them. Are a committee's recommendations implemented? Does a product development group's creation ever get put into production? Is upper management satisfied with the performance of a customer service unit?

2. Whether the group's capacity for further cooperation among its members is maintained or increased. In early 1994, Walt Disney, Inc., had one of the most talented, experienced, and stable management teams in the movie industry, but its capacity for continued effective interaction was severely tested. The president of Disney, Frank Wells, was killed in a helicopter crash; the production chief, Jeffrey Katzenberg, left in a well-publicized rift when he was passed over for the president's job; and the CEO, Michael Eisner, underwent quadruple bypass surgery.[89] Despite this series of disastrous events, the top group directing the fortunes of Disney at that time was able to maintain the capacity for ongoing cooperation and teamwork in the years that immediately followed.

3. Whether members gain satisfaction and a sense of growth and well-being from being part of the group. A group or team is unlikely to be regarded by outsiders as effective if its own members do not seem satisfied and are not experiencing feelings of accomplishment by being part of the group.

Most observers would probably say that the first of these criteria of effectiveness—acceptance of the group's outputs by others—is the most important one in organizational settings. However, if neither of the other two indicators can be achieved by a group, it is highly unlikely that it will be able over time to produce valued output. Thus, all three are important components of group effectiveness and need attention from anyone who wants to improve groups. A Manager's Challenge, "Two Teams: Two Different Results," provides a vivid example of two groups where there was no difficulty in assessing their effectiveness. Although operating in the same external cultural environment and with certain other similarities, the groups went in opposite directions in building effectiveness.

Ingredients Necessary for Group Effectiveness For a group to perform effectively, it must be able to do three things especially well:

1. Exert enough effort to accomplish its tasks at acceptable levels of quantity and quality;

2. Obtain sufficient knowledge and skills to carry out its work;

3. Use appropriate strategies to apply its effort, knowledge, and skills effectively.[90]

· Any product or service they develop is highly desired and valued by customers.

· Increased cooperation among members is encouraged and achieved.

· Group membership increases individual members' feelings of satisfaction, personal growth, and overall well-being.

Source: J. R. Hackman (ed.), *Groups That Work (and Those That Don't): Creating Conditions for Effective Teamwork* (San Francisco: Jossey-Bass, 1990).

exhibit 13.11

Characteristics of Highly Effective Groups

globalization *a manager's challenge*

Two Teams: Two Different Results

The country of Israel was the setting for a study of two teams that ended up with quite different effectiveness results. The two teams—both operating in the public sector—had the same timetable, budget, and project scope, but were established to complete two very different tasks in the late 1990s. One project was an immediate success; the other languished throughout months of bickering by team members. What made the difference?

The Center for Business Promotion (CBP) was an arm of Israel's Ministry of Trade and Commerce. It was staffed by a small team of seven or eight professional members with one or two secretaries and a pair of student interns. Its charter was to attract foreign investors and tourists to Jerusalem, a vibrant but impoverished city, through the creation of accurate and accessible databases available through special Web sites. With economic renewal via tourism a top priority in the mayor's office, the CBP team went right to work on the Web site project as an informal workgroup, despite having responsibilities for many other diplomatic, media, and economic duties.

Its first step was to jettison the Ministry's outdated sources and send the two interns out to collect fresh data by scanning newspapers and attending venture capital and professional conferences looking for likely entrants in the data bank. The team also carefully avoided Ministry interference, hired a consultant to help them find contractors to build and update the Web site, and within six months delivered to foreign investors diskettes of current data about Israeli companies that were later replaced by the Internet site.

Meanwhile, the city of Jerusalem put together an Internet Committee to build a similar site for attracting foreign tourists. The site was to offer easy access to a valuable data bank of hotels, restaurants, and attractions and allow the option to make reservations online. Team members spent an unproductive year arguing over who would own the Web site, and in the meantime they had to hire an outside company to actually construct the site.

Although the outside company had many ties to the municipal government and its key computer systems, it failed over and over to develop online information systems for residents of Jerusalem and made several costly mistakes. A year after the Internet Committee was formed, work on the site had not even begun. With pressure mounting to complete the project, and to integrate the Web site with government tourist offices, a second Internet Committee was formed. Turf battles broke out as committee members tried to use the project to benefit their own departments, ranging from engineering to culture to treasury.

Months later, after a reorganization of the committee into two separate units and the creation of a second proposal, the city of Jerusalem finally had an Internet site, though its content had little to do with the original purpose.

Sources: Alon Peled, "Outsourcing and Political Power: Bureaucrats, Consultants, Vendors and Public Information Technology," *Public Personnel Management,* Winter 2001, 20 pp.; Alon Peled, "Creating Winning Information Technology Project Teams in the Public Sector," *Team Performance Management,* 2000, pp. 6–14.

These three bases for achieving high levels of group effectiveness sound simple, but they are major challenges for leaders of groups. To assure that these components are actually in place consistently, managers need to address several issues:

Develop Appropriate Group Structures To be effective, groups need clearly defined tasks and objectives that can motivate their members. Groups also need to be sized appropriately to their tasks, and they need a membership with a sufficient mix of skills and expertise. This means that if a group leader has the option of choosing the members, those selection choices will often make a large difference in how well a group performs initially and what its capacity is to improve.

Develop Appropriate Support from the Organization[91] Groups operating within companies and organizations need support from their surrounding environment such as rewards for effective collaboration among members,[92] education and technical training for performing critical group tasks,[93] relief from other duties, and access to necessary information. For example, a few years ago, managers in the U.S. Information Agency (USIA) found that after a reorganization of the agency into self-managing teams, their major problems centered around a lack of administrative support.[94]

Obtain Appropriate Coaching and Consultation Assistance In the day-to-day world of work, most groups need outside help (whether from inside or outside the larger organization) to reduce potential conflicts, increase coordination in dealing with problems within the group, and provide strategies for approaching the group's tasks. Increased collaboration is an important objective,[95] and the message here is that it is often the case that a group should not try to go it alone. It should not hesitate to seek assistance from wherever seems most appropriate—especially assistance that can be relatively objective and "with no axes to grind."

Exhibit 13.12 provides a summary of the preceding points and shows how the manager's attention to the group's structure, support from the organizational context, and relevant coaching and consultation can help increase each of the three ingredients necessary for group effectiveness: high levels of effort, sufficient knowledge and skills, and appropriate strategies for applying effort and skills. The points presented and summarized in the exhibit do not provide a cookbook for group or team success. Rather, they are useful guidelines for managers and organizations to consider in approaching *their* task of helping groups to improve performance for themselves and for those who rely on the outputs of their work. Likewise, Exhibit 13.13, based on extensive research,[96] provides a helpful checklist for those who assume leadership positions in groups and teams to measure how well they are fulfilling that role in their groups. If team members concur that their leader is in fact doing a good job in these various areas of the role, then it is likely that the group (and not just the leader) will perform well.

exhibit 13.12

Enhancing Group Effectiveness

		POINTS OF LEVERAGE	
Necessary Processes	**Group Structure**	**Organizational Context**	**Coaching and Consultation**
Apply ample effort	Motivational structure of group task	Organizational reward system	Remedying coordination problems and building group commitment
Acquire sufficient knowledge and skill	Group composition	Organizational education/ training system	Remedying inappropriate "weighting" of member inputs and fostering cross-training
Develop task-appropriate performance strategies	Group norms that regulate member behavior and foster scanning and planning	Organizational information system	Remedying implementation problems and fostering creativity in strategy development

Source: Adapted from J. R. Hackman (ed.), *Groups That Work (and Those That Don't): Creating Conditions for Effective Teamwork* (San Francisco: Jossey-Bass, 1990), p. 13.

exhibit 13.13

A Checklist for Leaders of Groups

How well do you:
- ❑ Encourage members to learn from each other?
- ❑ Recognize and praise members for their contributions?
- ❑ Keep key people outside the [group] informed about its accomplishments?
- ❑ Promptly inform members about major developments that [may] affect them?
- ❑ Give [group] members authority to make [at least some] important decisions?
- ❑ Openly accept and respond to feedback from [group] members?
- ❑ Review the [group's] performance at the end of major tasks?
- ❑ Offer specific and concrete suggestions for how members can improve?
- ❑ Understand what motivates members to work hard?

Source: Adapted from G. L. Hallam, "Seven Common Beliefs about Teams: Are They True?" *Leadership in Action* 17, no. 3 (1997), pp. 1–4.

managerial perspectives revisited

1 **PERSPECTIVE 1: THE ORGANIZATIONAL CONTEXT**   Organizations are increasing their reliance on groups and teams, compared to years past. It also seems irrefutable that any given group or team is strongly affected by the organizational context that surrounds it. Thus, as a manager or leader of a group you will have to look both inward toward the group and its members and outward toward that organizational environment if you are to be effective. In a way, the larger organization can be considered as a sort of group of groups. It will be up to you to gain an understanding of the resources and constraints that are provided by those "other groups" and how that knowledge can assist you in developing a high-performing *team.*

2 **PERSPECTIVE 2: THE HUMAN FACTOR**   The building blocks of groups and teams are, of course, its people. Managers need to find ways to meld the talents of individual persons into a coherent and functioning unit. This means that you will need insight into how to assign individual members to the particular tasks and jobs that make up the group's work, and then, especially, how to encourage their maximum efforts to cooperate and coordinate with each other. It also means that it will be a challenge to stimulate each person's creativity in contributing to the overall set of group tasks without at the same time triggering unacceptable levels of relationship conflict among team members.

3 **PERSPECTIVE 3: MANAGING PARADOXES**   Managers frequently find themselves simultaneously being both members of groups and leading their own groups. This requires nimbly shifting roles, and often doing so quickly. However, at times, these roles may create a paradox for the manager. He or she may have to deal with other paradoxes related to groups as well. For example, diverse groups tend to make better decisions but are more difficult to manage and are likely to experience greater conflict than more homogeneous groups. Too much diversity can result in excessive conflict, and too much homogeneity can lead to insufficient innovation and creative problem solving.

PERSPECTIVE 4: ENTREPRENEURIAL MIND-SET Individuals may have entrepreneurial mind-sets but as we have explained in previous chapters, this mind-set can apply, too, to an organization or groups and teams within an organization. This is important because research has shown that teams can be more creative than individuals due to the different ideas and shared knowledge of the individuals that comprise it. Of course, individuals are unlikely to bring their ideas to the table unless creativity and innovation are encouraged. Thus, having an entrepreneurial mind-set within the organization is needed to motivate groups and teams to innovate too.[97] Today, a number of large corporations have R&D teams to develop and design new products. Commonly, these teams are cross-functional with design engineers, scientists, manufacturing engineers, and marketing specialists all working to develop the same product. Each member brings his or her valuable knowledge and skill sets to the process. Not only can teams be more creative, if managed appropriately; they can also develop better-quality products with the features consumers want. However, the innovation process must begin with the organization making a commitment to having an entrepreneurial mind-set and encouraging groups and teams to do likewise.

concluding comments

Groups are becoming increasingly vital parts of contemporary organizations operating in a world of accelerated change and competition. Consequently, if you aspire to become an effective manager or executive in an organization, you will need to be able to (1) understand different types of groups and how they function and (2) know how to lead them effectively. These are fundamental challenges, but they can be met.

Many people who carry out their own individual work exceedingly well, and who interact very comfortably in one-to-one relationships, often run into difficulties when called on to manage group activity. Groups multiply the number of interpersonal relationships involved, which in turn creates a level of complexity that needs to be assessed and mastered.

To be able to manage groups successfully is a skill that can be learned. It requires deliberate effort to be perceptive and to notice many subtle nuances as well as the more obvious aspects of interpersonal relationships occurring inside groups. Are certain norms forming, and if so, what are the directions of these norms? Is a group developing cohesion, and does it lend support to the organization's larger goals or only to the narrow self-interests of the immediate group? Is there conflict within the group, and is it focused on better problem solving or only on potentially destructive personal relationships? Attention to these and similar issues will provide a solid base for leading productive groups.

Successful management of groups also requires constant awareness of how the conditions surrounding groups are changing and how that evolving context will affect what groups do and how they perform. Two of those major changes occurring in the environment in which groups operate are the rapidly increasing use of technology to facilitate interactions among group members, and the expanding global activities of many organizations. Both of these trends carry with them the potential for many positive improvements. However, they also can present particular challenges to leaders of groups to be able to utilize technology effectively and to take advantage of global opportunities. These and other features of the organizational context outside of a group are nearly as important as the interactions that take place inside it in determining how effectively it performs.

Finally, as we noted early in this chapter, there is strong pressure in many of today's organizations for managers to develop their groups so that they become real "teams," with all that that term implies. Groups that turn into teams have the potential to vastly magnify the productivity and quality of a set of individuals, as demonstrated in the case of Team Logica at the beginning of this chapter. But true teamwork must be created and nurtured by skillful managing.

key terms

cohesion   462
command (supervisory)
  group   451
committee   454
conformity   461
context-driven competencies   473
formal group   454
group   450
informal group   454
intergroup conflict   476

intragroup conflict   476
norms   459
process costs   456
project/task force   453
relationship (affective)
  conflict   475
role ambiguity   459
role conflict   459
self-managing (autonomous)
  workgroup   469

social loafing   455
status   459
task (substantive) conflict   475
task-contingent
  competencies   474
team   450
team-contingent
  competencies   473
transportable competencies   472
virtual team   471

test your comprehension

1. What are the similarities and differences between a group and a team?
2. What are the major types of groups found in organizations? Give examples of each.
3. What is the fundamental difference between a formal and an informal group?
4. How do organizational goals affect the formation of groups?
5. What are some of the concerns of new group members?
6. How is proximity related to the formation of informal groups?
7. What personal needs may be satisfied by group membership?
8. What are the four stages of group formation? What are the important features of each?
9. What are the structural characteristics of groups? Why is each important?
10. Is there an optimum group size? Why or why not?
11. What is "social loafing"? Can managers do anything to minimize or eliminate it?
12. To what extent is social loafing likely to be equally prevalent in all cultures?

13. How do heterogeneous groups differ from homogeneous ones?
14. What are some of the types of diversity found within groups? What effects can diversity have on group members and on group functioning?
15. Provide examples of role conflict and role ambiguity that illustrate the difference between the two terms.
16. Why are norms important to groups?
17. What are some of the key factors that often have major influences on the development of norms?
18. Is it always good to have a high level of conformity within a group?
19. Can managers affect the level of conformity within a group? Why or why not?
20. What is meant by group cohesion? How does it develop? Are high levels of group cohesion always desirable?
21. How does a self-managing (autonomous) workgroup differ from a typical command group?
22. What are the advantages and disadvantages of virtual teams?

23. Why is there an increased usage of cross-functional workgroups in organizations today? How can managers increase the effectiveness of these groups?
24. What are KSAs, and how are they related to team competencies?
25. What are the causes of the two basic types of group conflict?
26. Can managers eliminate group conflict? Should they try?
27. What are three major indicators that can be used to identify high-performance groups?
28. What kinds of issues must managers address when attempting to improve group effectiveness?

apply your understanding

1. As a manager, would you rather work with highly diversified teams or with more homogeneous teams? Why? Which types would be best for which types of situations?
2. Think about a group in which you have been involved at work, at school, or perhaps while playing a sport. What were the structural characteristics of the group? What were some of its norms? Would you characterize it as a group or as a team? Why?
3. Some students groan and complain when told they must participate in a group project. Why do you think this is? What is it about group work that irritates some students *so* much?

After reading this chapter, can *you* think of ways to structure and lead a group to gain these individuals' cooperation and motivation?

4. As a manager, if your workgroup is demonstrating considerable intragroup conflict, what would you do?
5. Which type of team—self-managing, cross-functional, global, or virtual—do you think is the most difficult to manage, and why?
6. How would you characterize your own level of group competency? What do you think are the most important KSAs relevant to groups and teams that you should master next?

practice your capabilities

It is 3:00 P.M. on the afternoon before your team project is due in your management class. You are about to meet with your team to put the finishing touches on your paper. Each member had originally agreed to provide two pages of material on disk, with a hard copy for editing. As your group members arrive for the meeting you find out that some don't have even one page prepared and that almost all are handwritten. You realize there is a lot to do if this paper is going to be in shape to turn in tomorrow. The parts must be integrated, typed, proofread, edited, polished, and exhibits must be made.

There are six of you on the team. The varsity athlete has been grateful when meetings have been postponed or cancelled to accommodate practice. Unfortunately, today she must attend a mandatory practice from 4:00 to 9:00 P.M. The international student has good oral but poor written English, would like to help, and has strong ideas. However, this student always feels resented by

you. The two of you just don't get along. The fraternity president was aware that tonight's formal dance would provide a conflict for this meeting. However, he had spent a lot of time polishing and editing part of the paper and provided hard and disk copies of it. Another member has just gotten the lead in the school play and has absolutely no interest anymore in this class project. Frustrated by past missed deadlines, willing to settle for a so-so paper, and unwilling to miss tonight's rehearsal, the actor has provided a handwritten rough draft. The last member has airline reservations for 4:30 this afternoon, just finished scribbling down some ideas, doesn't care who writes the paper, so long as it gets done, and is willing to lend the team a laptop computer.

As the team leader, you wonder how things could possibly have gone so wrong and what you are going to do now, keeping in mind that this group is going to have to work together again next week to develop a presentation to give to the class.

1. What type(s) of conflict exist in this group? How have they affected its productivity?

2. Keeping in mind issues discussed in this chapter, what would you, as team leader, do now?

Source: Adapted from S. B. Wolff and J. W. Wohlberg, *OB in Action: Cases and Exercises*, 6th ed. (Boston: Houghton Mifflin, 2001), pp. 205–6.

closing case

DEVELOP YOUR CRITICAL THINKING

The Team That Wasn't

The last thing Eric Holt had expected to miss about New York City was its sunrises. Seeing one usually meant he had pulled another all-nighter at the consulting firm where, as a vice president, he had managed three teams of manufacturing specialists. But as he stood on the balcony of his new apartment in the small Indiana city that was now his home, Eric suddenly felt a pang of nostalgia for the way the dawn plays off the skyscrapers of Manhattan. In the next moment, though, he let out a sardonic laugh. The dawn light was not what he missed about New York, he realized. What he missed was the feeling of accomplishment that usually accompanied those sunrises.

An all-nighter in New York had meant hours of intense work with a cadre of committed, enthusiastic colleagues. Give and take. Humor. Progress. Here, so far anyway, that was unthinkable. As the director of strategy at FireArt, Inc., a regional glass manufacturer, Eric spent all his time trying to get his new team to make it through a meeting without the tension level becoming unbearable. Six of the top-level managers involved seemed determined to turn the company around, but the seventh seemed equally determined to sabotage the process. Forget camaraderie. There had been three meetings so far, and Eric hadn't even been able to get everyone on the same side of an issue.

Eric stepped inside his apartment and checked the clock: Only three more hours before he had to watch as Randy Louderback, FireArt's charismatic director of sales and marketing, either dominated the group's discussion or withdrew entirely, tapping his pen on the table to indicate his boredom. Sometimes he withheld information vital to the group's debate; other times he coolly denigrated people's comments. Still, Eric realized, Randy held the group in such thrall because of his dynamic personality, his almost legendary past, and his close relationship with FireArt's CEO that he could not be ignored. And at least once during each meeting, he offered an insight about the industry or the company that was so perceptive that Eric knew he *shouldn't* be ignored.

As he prepared to leave for the office, Eric felt the familiar frustration that had started building during the team's first meeting a month earlier. It was then that Randy had first insinuated, with what sounded like a joke, that he wasn't cut out to be a team player. "Leaders lead, followers . . . please pipe down!" had been his exact words, although he had smiled winningly as he spoke, and the rest of the group had laughed heartily in response. No one in the group was laughing now, though, least of all Eric.

FireArt, Inc., was in trouble—not deep trouble, but enough for its CEO, Jack Derry, to make strategic repositioning Eric's top and only task. The company, a family-owned maker of wine goblets, beer steins, ashtrays, and other glass novelties, had succeeded for nearly 80 years as a high-quality, high-price producer, catering to hundreds of midwestern clients. It traditionally did big business every football season, selling commemorative knickknacks to the fans of teams such as the Fighting Irish, the Wolverines, and the Golden Gophers. In the spring there was always a rush of demand for senior prom items—champagne goblets emblazoned with a school's name or beer mugs with a school's crest, for example. Fraternities and sororities were steady customers. Year after year, FireArt showed respectable increases at the top and bottom lines, posting $86 million in earnings three years before Eric arrived.

In the last 18 months, though, sales and earnings had flattened. Jack, a grandnephew of the company's founder, thought he knew what was happening. Until recently, large national glass companies had been able to make money only through mass production. Now, however, thanks to new technologies in the glassmaking industry, those companies could execute short runs profitably. They had begun to enter FireArt's niche, Jack had told Eric, and, with their superior resources, it was just a matter of time before they would own it.

"You have one responsibility as FireArt's new director of strategy," Jack had said to Eric on his first day. "That's to put together a team of our top people, one person from each division, and have a comprehensive plan for the company's strategic realignment up, running, and winning within six months."

Eric had immediately compiled a list of the senior managers from human resources, manufacturing, finance, distribution, design, and marketing, and had set a date for the first meeting. Then, drawing on his years as a consultant who had worked almost solely in team environments, Eric had carefully prepared a structure and guidelines for the group's discussions, disagreements, and decisions, which he planned to propose to the members for their input before they began working together.

Successful groups are part art, part science, Eric knew, but he also believed that with every member's full commitment, a team proved the adage that the whole is greater than the sum of its parts. Knowing that managers at FireArt were unaccustomed to the team process, however, Eric imagined he might get some resistance from one or two members.

For one, he had been worried about Ray LaPierre of manufacturing. Ray was a giant of a man who had run the furnaces for some 35 years, following in his father's footsteps. Although he was a former high school football star who was known among workers in the factory for his hearty laugh and his love of practical jokes, Ray usually didn't say much around FireArt's executives, citing his lack of higher education as the reason. Eric had thought the team atmosphere might intimidate him.

Eric had also anticipated a bit of a fight from Maureen Turner of the design division, who was known to complain that FireArt didn't appreciate its six artists. Eric had expected that Maureen might have a chip on her shoulder about collaborating with people who didn't understand the design process.

Ironically, both those fears had proved groundless, but another, more difficult problem had arisen. The wild card had turned out to be Randy. Eric had met Randy once before the team started its work and had found him to be enormously intelligent, energetic, and good-humored. What's more, Jack Derry had confirmed his impressions, telling him that Randy "had the best mind" at FireArt. It was also from Jack that Eric had first learned of Randy's hardscrabble yet inspirational personal history.

Poor as a child, he had worked as a security guard and short-order cook to put himself through the state college, from which he graduated with top honors. Soon after, he started his own advertising and market research firm in Indianapolis, and within the decade, he had built it into a company employing 50 people to service some of the region's most prestigious accounts. His success brought with it a measure of fame: articles in the local media, invitations to the statehouse, even an honorary degree from an Indiana business college. But in the late 1980s, Randy's firm suffered the same fate as many other advertising shops, and he was forced to declare bankruptcy. FireArt considered it a coup when it landed him as director of marketing, since he had let it be known that he was offered at least two dozen other jobs. "Randy is the future of this company," Jack Derry had told Eric. "If he can't help you, no one can. I look forward to hearing what a team with his kind of horsepower can come up with to steer us away from the mess we're in."

Those words echoed in Eric's mind as he sat, with increasing anxiety, through the team's first and second meetings. Although Eric had planned an agenda for each meeting and tried to keep the discussions on track, Randy always seemed to find a way to disrupt the process. Time and time again, he shot down other people's ideas, or he simply didn't pay attention. He also answered most questions put to him with maddening vagueness. "I'll have my assistant look into it when he gets a moment," he replied, when one team member asked him to list FireArt's five largest customers. "Some days you eat the bear, and other days the bear eats you," he joked another time, when asked why sales to fraternities had recently nose-dived.

Randy's negativism, however, was countered by occasional comments so insightful that they stopped the conversation cold or turned it around entirely—comments that demonstrated extraordinary knowledge about competitors or glass technology or customers' buying patterns. The help wouldn't last, though; Randy would quickly revert to his role as team renegade.

The third meeting, last week, had ended in chaos. Ray LaPierre, Maureen Turner, and the distribution director, Carl Simmons, had each planned to present cost-cutting proposals, and at first it looked as though they were making good progress.

Ray opened the meeting, proposing a plan for FireArt to cut throughput time by 3 percent and raw-materials costs by 2 percent, thereby positioning the company to compete better on price. It was obvious from his detailed presentation that he had put a lot of thought into his comments, and it was evident that he was fighting a certain amount of nervousness as he made them.

"I know I don't have the book smarts of most of you in this room," he had begun, "but here goes anyway." During his presentation, Ray stopped several times to answer questions from the team, and as he went on, his nervousness transformed into his usual ebullience. "That wasn't so bad!" he laughed to himself as he sat down at the end, flashing a grin at Eric. "Maybe we can turn this old ship around."

Maureen Turner had followed Ray. While not disagreeing with him—she praised his comments, in fact—

she argued that FireArt also needed to invest in new artists, pitching its competitive advantage in better design and wider variety. Unlike Ray, Maureen had made this case to FireArt's top executives many times, only to be rebuffed, and some of her frustration seeped through as she explained her reasoning yet again. At one point, her voice almost broke as she described how hard she had worked in her first 10 years at FireArt, hoping that someone in management would recognize the creativity of her designs. "But no one did," she recalled with a sad shake of her head. "That's why when I was made director of the department, I made sure all the artists were respected for what they are—artists, not worker ants. There's a difference, you know." However, just as with Ray LaPierre, Maureen's comments lost their defensiveness as the group members, with the exception of Randy, who remained impassive, greeted her words with nods of encouragement.

By the time Carl Simmons of distribution started to speak, the mood in the room was approaching buoyant. Carl, a quiet and meticulous man, jumped from his seat and practically paced the room as he described his ideas. FireArt, he said, should play to its strength as a service-oriented company and restructure its trucking system to increase the speed of delivery. He described how a similar strategy had been adopted with excellent results at his last job at a ceramics plant. Carl had joined FireArt just six months earlier. It was when Carl began to describe those results in detail that Randy brought the meeting to an unpleasant halt by letting out a loud groan. "Let's just do *everything*, why don't we, including redesign the kitchen sink!" he cried with mock enthusiasm. That remark sent Carl back quickly to his seat, where he half-heartedly summed up his comments. A few minutes later, he excused himself, saying he had another meeting. Soon the others made excuses to leave, too, and the room became empty.

No wonder Eric was apprehensive about the fourth meeting. He was therefore surprised when he entered the room and found the whole group, save Randy, already assembled.

Ten minutes passed in awkward small talk, and looking from face to face, Eric could see his own frustration reflected. He also detected an edge of panic—just what he had hoped to avoid. He decided he had to raise the topic of Randy's attitude openly, but just as he started, Randy ambled into the room, smiling. "Sorry, folks," he said lightly, holding up a cup of coffee as if it were explanation enough for his tardiness.

"Randy, I'm glad you're here," Eric began, "because I think today we should begin by talking about the group itself . . ."

Randy cut Eric off with a small, sarcastic laugh. "Uh— I knew this was going to happen," he said.

Before Eric could answer, Ray LaPierre stood up and walked over to Randy, bending over to look him in the eye.

"You just don't care, do you?" he began, his voice so angry it startled everyone in the room.

Everyone except Randy. "Quite the contrary—I care very much," he answered breezily. "I just don't believe this is how change should be made. A brilliant idea never came out of a team. Brilliant ideas come from brilliant individuals, who then inspire others in the organization to implement them."

"That's a lot of bull," Ray shot back. "You just want all the credit for the success, and you don't want to share it with anyone."

"That's absurd," Randy laughed again. "I'm not trying to impress anyone here at FireArt. I don't need to. I want this company to succeed as much as you do, but I believe, and I believe passionately, that groups are useless. Consensus means mediocrity. I'm sorry, but it does."

"But you haven't even *tried* to reach consensus with us," Maureen interjected. "It's as if you don't care what we all have to say. We can't work alone for a solution—we need to understand each other. Don't you see that?"

The room was silent as Randy shrugged his shoulders noncommittally. He stared at the table, a blank expression on his face.

It was Eric who broke the silence. "Randy, this is a team. You are part of it," he said, trying to catch Randy's eye without success. "Perhaps we should start again . . ."

Randy stopped him by holding up his cup, as if making a toast. "Okay, look, I'll behave from now on," he said. The words held promise, but he was smirking as he spoke them—something no one at the table missed. Eric took a deep breath before he answered; as much as he wanted and needed Randy Louderback's help, he was suddenly struck by the thought that perhaps Randy's personality and his past experiences simply made it impossible for him to participate in the delicate process of ego surrender that any kind of teamwork requires.

"Listen, everyone, I know this is a challenge," Eric began, but he was cut short by Randy's pencil-tapping on the table. A moment later, Ray LaPierre was standing again.

"Forget it. This is never going to work. It's just a waste of time for all of us," he said, more resigned than gruff. "We're all in this together, or there's no point." He headed for the door, and before Eric could stop him, two others were at his heels.

Questions

1. In what stage of development is FireArt's strategy team? What characteristics of the team point to this stage of development?
2. Do you believe Eric Holt is an effective team leader? Why or why not? What could he do to improve the effectiveness of the team?
3. What is the underlying attitude behind Randy Louderback's behavior? Why may he be trying to undermine the success of the team?
4. Categorize the type of conflict this group is experiencing. (That is, is it related to a task or to personality?) How could the conflict be resolved? Do you think Eric can change the behavior of group members?

Communication
and
Negotiation

14

LEARNING OBJECTIVES

After studying this chapter, you should be able to:

■

Explain why communication is vital for effective management.

■

Describe the basic process of communication.

■

Explain how culture can influence communication.

■

Identify key barriers to effective communication.

■

Describe approaches to overcoming communication barriers.

■

Describe the basic process of negotiation.

A Communication Collision

t was a car lover's dream. Two brothers, Jack and John Goudy, left their desk jobs to open their own auto repair shop. At first, just the two brothers did brake jobs and replaced exhaust systems. Then, as business grew, they hired a few workers and moved to a larger shop. Within a decade, Two J's Auto Repair was cranking in sales of half a million dollars per year, but then those sales reached a plateau and gradually began to decline. So John, who was in charge of sales and accounting, searched for a new way to improve business. He found it by using technology. John began integrating cutting-edge technology into the shop operations. But he had to convince his workers, including Jack (who spent more time in the shop than in the office), that his strategy for rebuilding Two J's would be successful.

John convened a staff meeting to communicate his new strategy to the employees. Armed with graphs and charts, he talked about profit sharing, employee involvement, and state-of-the-art technology. "From today on, we're a completely different business," he predicted. He did not know how prophetic that statement would prove to be. John's audience did not share his enthusiasm; in fact, they did not understand his message at all because they had received no previous training in the areas of finance, human resources, or the use of technology. They didn't understand the vocabulary he used or the ideas he was presenting. "It was a sea of blank faces with an occasional mutter here and there," John recalls. Thus, the flow of miscommunication at Two J's began.

John purchased a new computer-information system, which reduced the amount of paper communication generated by the office. But employees eventually discovered that the original estimates and the final invoices did not match each other, which caused them to believe that he was withholding work hours—and pay. He installed a closed-circuit TV in the shop so that, when customers phoned to inquire about the status of their repairs, he could glance quickly at the monitor and answer them. Unfortunately, shop workers believed that John had installed the TV as a surveillance tool to monitor them, and they resented what they perceived to be a lack of trust.

Although John had provided his employees with an elaborate explanation of the profit-sharing plan (which they did not understand), they were skeptical of it because of mixed messages he sent: John often groaned about poor profits but would suddenly arrive at work driving a new sports car. Sensing declining morale, John started to hold daily "release meetings,"

When Jack and John Goudy left their desk jobs to open their auto repair shop, it seemed like a car lover's dream. But poor communication between the two and their staff members turned the one-time dream into a nightmare. Fortunately, they realized their "failure to communicate" and were able to improve the situation.

designed to let employees voice their frustrations and concerns. But even these backfired. "John talked about working together like a football team," says one employee. But the meetings quickly dissolved into lectures. "John talked, we listened." Another employee observes, "It was clear John didn't care much about what we thought. He was too excited about his big ideas."

Jack, meanwhile, tried to serve as a go-between for John and the workers. "John wasn't working in the shop anymore," he explains. "Unfortunately, he dismissed their ideas when they offered suggestions." Eventually, even Jack and John could be heard fighting in the office. "They routinely got into yelling matches, one threatening to walk out on the other," says one veteran Two J's worker.

Finally, despite John's efforts to attract new customers and provide better, faster repairs through technology, workers began to leave the shop for jobs with other companies. At first, he did not understand what had gone so wrong; he had not realized how grueling running his own business could be. He also knew that he was not a strong communicator. "Every day there were questions," he comments. "After a while, they just ground me down." When the company hit rock bottom, John started to get the message. He began to recognize the importance of communication—not only with customers, but with his own workers—and proceeded to make small changes. "Now [when I attend staff meetings], I bring a yellow pad, scribble, and listen."

This chapter is about the importance of communication—whether it takes place via yellow pad or computer—throughout an organization.

Source: Elizabeth Conlin, "Company Profile: Collision Course," *Inc.* 14, no. 13 (December 1992), pp. 132–42.

strategic overview

Effective communication is crucial for managers in formulating a successful strategy and implementing it. Strategy formulation requires a substantial amount of communication. To identify a potentially successful strategy, managers must analyze their external environment, such as their competitors, their markets, industry forces, and government regulations. This first requires them to absorb and evaluate a large amount of information communicated to them before taking action based on it. Taking action to support the strategy then means communicating the relevant information to others in the organization, convincing them of your strategy, and explaining what they have to do to implement it.

In the opening case example, John's strategy for Two J's Auto Repair was to use technology to give customers better service by making faster repairs and providing them with more information about the repairs in progress. However, his strategy failed because of overall poor communication. First he developed the strategy alone, which means he may not have gathered and evaluated enough information from his employees. Second, the implementation of the strategy was unsuccessful because he communicated it poorly, to them and his brother.

For example, Two J's employees did not understand the reason why the new technology was being implemented, and John didn't listen effectively to them. Besides needing better listening and receiving skills, it appeared there were interpersonal barriers between him and his employees that he needed to overcome before any new strategy could be successfully implemented. Without doing these three things—gathering adequate amounts of information, including information from his employees; properly listening and communicating his goals to them; and using good communication skills to foster better interpersonal relations, the strategy John designed for Two J's predictably failed. ■

Most of us take communication for granted because we do it every day. Communicating effectively, however, is not easy.[1] Accurate and persuasive communication within and between organizations, person to person, person to group, or group to group, is frequently, and sometimes unexpectedly, difficult, as the opening case example demonstrates. Receivers often do not have a complete understanding of what senders mean. But the heart of **communication** is exactly that: the process of transferring information, meaning, and understanding from sender to receiver. And carrying out that process convincingly and proficiently is an absolute essential for a manager to exercise leadership. In fact, leadership is unlikely to be successful in the absence of excellent communication skills. The first step for a manager to become an outstanding leader, therefore, is to become an outstanding communicator.

In this chapter, we start with an overview of the basic communication process, followed by an examination of the modes and media of communication. These topics provide a background for the next section on the organizational context of the communication process as it affects managers. Although the organization can facilitate managerial communication, it also can be one of the key sources of barriers to communication—interpersonal, organizational, and cultural—which are discussed in the following section. This section in turn is followed by one that, appropriately, highlights some of the steps that managers can take to reduce or overcome these barriers.

The final parts of this chapter focus on one particular area of communication that is especially critical for managers—negotiation. In those sections, we discuss the impact of cultural influences on negotiation strategies

communication the process of transferring information, meaning, and understanding from sender to receiver

and on the negotiation process itself. Throughout this chapter we need to keep in mind a basic perspective: Although communication is a universal human activity, successful communication is not habitual. It requires motivation, skill, and knowledge.

BASIC MODEL OF COMMUNICATION

How do people communicate? How do they send and receive messages? What factors can disrupt communication? Let's look first at the basic model of the communication process (Exhibit 14.1).[2]

All communication involves four actions and five components. The four actions are encoding, sending, receiving, and decoding. The five components are sender, message, medium, noise, and receiver. The actions and components combine to transfer meaning from the sender to the receiver. The sender originates the message by **encoding** it, that is, by constructing the message. The message is the content of the communication. The sender then transmits the message through a **medium**. A medium is the method or means of transmission, not the message itself. Examples of media are spoken words, video, written memos, faxes, and e-mail messages. The receiver acquires, or receives, the message by hearing it, reading it, or having it appear on a fax or computer. The receiver then begins **decoding** the message, that is, interpreting it. Sometimes distractions interfere with the message; these interferences are called **noise**. Noise contributes to misinterpretations of the original message, and it is only through feedback, or verification of the original message, that communication problems may be located and corrected.

The basic model of communication is fundamental and universal; that is, it occurs whenever communication takes place, regardless of the culture or organization. However, while the basic acts and components of the communication process are the same everywhere, how the acts are carried out and the nature of the components are deeply influenced by cultural, organizational, and even personal contexts.[3] Who can send messages to whom, what kinds and what volumes of messages are sent, by what medium are messages transmitted, what sort of interference or noise is likely to occur, and what cues are available for decoding are just some of the many examples of the types of communication issues that can vary from manager to manager, from organization to organization, and from country to country.

encoding the act of constructing a message

medium the mode or form of transmission of a message

decoding the act of interpreting a message

noise potential interference with the transmission or decoding of a message

exhibit 14.1

Basic Communication Model

Sender
1. Encodes message
2. Chooses a medium (channel)
3. Sends the message

Noise: Can interfere at any point

Receiver
1. Receives message
2. Decodes message
3. May send feedback for clarification

MODES OF COMMUNICATION

Communication can occur in either a verbal mode or a nonverbal mode, as shown in Exhibit 14.2. Each mode has particular characteristics and issues that an effective manager must understand.

Verbal Communication

Most of us think of spoken words when we think of verbal communication. The key, however, is not that the words are spoken but that words—language—are used to convey meaning. Consequently, when we talk about verbal communication, we mean *both* oral and written communication.

Oral Communication The spoken word has the potential advantages of being vivid, stimulating, and commanding attention. In most organizational situations, it is difficult for receivers—the listeners—to ignore either the speaker or the words spoken. Just think about the last time someone spoke to you directly. Even if you weren't interested in what the person had to say, wouldn't it have been difficult to simply ignore the person, turn, and walk away?

Also, oral communication is exceptionally flexible for both the sender and receiver. While you are speaking, you may try to make a point a certain way, but along the way change your words in order for the listener to understand you. Because oral communication is generally interactive, it can be quite responsive and adaptive to circumstances. However, this mode of communication has the major disadvantages of being transitory (unless recorded) and subject to considerable misinterpretation. Even when individuals use the same language, the subtle nuances of the spoken word may be missed or incorrect meaning attached to them. Oral communication between those whose first languages differ, as in many management situations today, simply multiplies the chances of intended meaning going awry.

exhibit 14.2
Modes of Communication

	VERBAL MODE (LANGUAGE USED TO CONVEY MEANING)		NONVERBAL MODE
	Oral	**Written**	
Examples	· Conversation · Speeches · Telephone calls · Videoconferences	· Letters · Memos · Reports · E-mail · Fax	· Dress · Speech intonation · Gestures · Facial expressions
Advantages	· Vivid · Stimulating · Commands attention · Difficult to ignore · Flexible · Adaptive	· Decreased misinterpretation · Precise	· Effectiveness of communication increases with congruence to oral presentation · Can emphasize meaning
Disadvantages	· Transitory · Subject to misinterpretation	· Precision loss in translation · Inflexible · Easier to ignore	· Meanings of nonverbal communication not universal

Written Communication When messages are put in writing, as in letters, memos, electronic mail, and the like, the opportunity for misunderstanding the words of the sender are decreased. The receiver may still misinterpret the intended message, of course, but there is no uncertainty about exactly what words the sender has used. In that sense, written communication has precision. However, not everyone writes well, and so greater precision does not necessarily lead to greater understanding. This is further complicated when the words need translation from one language to another. For example, Americans often write when requesting action "at your earliest convenience," meaning that the request is somewhat urgent, but Europeans frequently interpret it to mean they can respond whenever they want. Or consider how Northwest Airlines' slogan "Give Wings to Your Heart" was translated into Chinese: "Tie Feathers to Your Blood Pump." Because the writer/sender does not know immediately how well or poorly the message is getting across, written communication has the disadvantage of not being very flexible. In addition, it is often not as vivid or compelling as oral communication. Although you might find it difficult to ignore someone speaking to you, it would probably be much easier to ignore a letter you received.

Nonverbal Communication

In direct interpersonal communication, nonverbal actions and behaviors often constitute significant messages. A whole range of actions, or lack of them, has the potential for communicating. The way you dress, speak words, use gestures, handle utensils, exhibit facial expressions, and set the physical distance to the receiver are just some of the many forms of nonverbal communication.

As a manager, keep in mind that when verbal and nonverbal messages are contradictory, receivers often may give more weight to the nonverbal signals than to the words used. For example, you may say to employees, "I have an open-door policy. Come and talk to me whenever you need to." However, if you never seem to be able to find the time to see them or rarely look up from your work when employees enter, they will soon come to believe the nonverbal message, "I'm busy," rather than the verbal message, "I encourage you to talk with me."

Of course, when nonverbal messages are consistent with the spoken message, the odds of effective communication taking place are increased. For example, suppose that in addition to saying you had an open-door policy you looked up when employees entered, made eye contact with them, smiled, and turned away from your computer and the report on which you were working. In combination, what sort of message do you think you would be sending?

The problem for managers in many of today's organizations where they work with employees from different cultural backgrounds and often work across international borders is that there are no universal meanings to the various nonverbal actions. For example, the traditional "OK" sign in the United States is a gesture for money in Japan and is a rather rude gesture in Brazil. You might think that just toning down your nonverbal gestures would be a good way to avoid inadvertent wrong messages. Such an effort would be fine in Finland, but someone in Italy or Greece might infer from your subdued nonverbal cues that you are uninterested in the discussion. Because there is no simple answer, you should learn about the nonverbal cues and gestures of countries and cultures with which you deal the most.

MEDIA OF COMMUNICATION

The means of communication, or, in other words, *how* or by what methods, information is transmitted from sender to receiver, are typically referred to as communication media (or, in the singular, medium). In organizations, there basically are a limited number of types of media that can be used. These range from the very personal and direct face-to-face interaction to the very impersonal and indirect posted notice or bulletin board that is a frequent characteristic of organizational settings. In between are telephone conversations, electronic messages, letters, memos, and reports.

It is obvious that these different media have different sets of characteristics, such as the following:

- personal–impersonal nature
- speed in sending and receiving
- availability of multiple cues to assist receivers in acquiring accurate meaning from the messages
- opportunity to receive immediate and continuing feedback from the receiver

The term that has been used to summarize the nature of these characteristics of different media is called "**media richness**."[4] Different media are classified as rich or lean based on their "capacity to facilitate shared meaning."[5] (See Exhibit 14.3.) Thus, interpersonal, face-to-face interactions, for example, would be regarded as rich because they provide several types of information and multiple ways to obtain mutual understanding between sender and receiver, whereas a general e-mail message sent to a number of receivers would be regarded as leaner because it lacks some of the features listed above. The general principle here is that the more ambiguous the message to be communicated and the more complex the issue, the richer should be the medium of communication.

The concept of media richness has important implications for managers when they communicate. It serves to emphasize that different media have different capabilities for conveying message meaning, and that managers therefore should be sensitive to matching message with medium. Using face-to-face meetings to convey simple, straightforward information, such as the time of a meeting next week, would be an unnecessary waste of a rich medium. That is, it would involve too much time and effort of both sender and receivers to obtain shared meaning of a relatively unambiguous message. On the other hand, using a memo, for example, rather than a face-to-face meeting, would probably be a poor choice for settling a serious disagreement with subordinates. The medium

media richness different media are classified as rich or lean based on their capacity to facilitate shared meaning

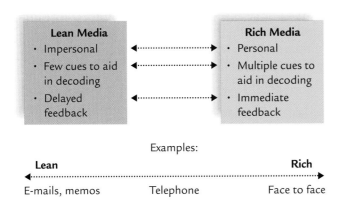

exhibit 14.3
Factors Contributing to Media Richness

Hundreds of dispatchers at Burlington Northern Santa Fe Railway's Network Operations Center in Fort Worth, Texas, communicate constantly via the company's wireless network with locomotive crews across the country operating trains like this one. The dispatchers serve a function similar to that of air traffic controllers. Clear communication between the dispatchers and crews is imperative to prevent rail accidents.

would be too lean to enable the manager to resolve a complicated, highly ambiguous matter.

Often, of course, time pressures and distance may make it relatively costly for a manager to use a richer rather than a leaner medium. That is why, in recent years, technological advances in such communication media as instant electronic messaging (see A Manager's Challenge, "Staying Connected Through Instant Messaging") or videoconferencing often provide acceptable trade-offs—in managing this type of duality—between an ideally rich, face-to-face medium for resolving complex issues, on the one hand, and an ideally low-cost written memo (whether sent via e-mail or otherwise), on the other hand.[6] The key point, if you are a manager, is to choose a medium that best suits the degree of potential ambiguity in the message, consistent with the constraints of circumstances and the resources of you and your organization. The choice of an appropriate medium should not be left to chance.

THE ORGANIZATIONAL CONTEXT OF COMMUNICATION

Managers do not deal with communication in the abstract. Rather, they deal with it within an organizational context. The structure and processes of organizations powerfully shape the nature and effectiveness of communication that takes place within and between them.[7] Organizations, whether businesses, hospitals, or government agencies, have a set of defining characteristics, all of which affect communication in one way or another.[8] Thus, organizations

- Are composed of individuals and groups
- Are oriented toward goals
- Have differentiated functions
- Have intended coordination
- Have continuity through time

tech nol ogy

a manager's challenge

Staying Connected Through Instant Messaging

Sitting in the Nevada headquarters of YellowPages.com, senior vice president Dennis Warren notices an incoming message pop up on his computer screen and types "OTP. SB." In Chicago, the local sales representative who sent the note sees the letters flash on his monitor and understands that Warren is "on the phone" and to "stand by" for a response. Warren is one of a growing number of managers using instant messaging (IM) technology to stay in touch with colleagues and subordinates located in the same office or even thousands of miles away. Sales representatives who need immediate answers to clinch a deal simply bring up the IM software and send the boss a brief, to-the-point question that automatically appears in a box on his screen. In turn, Warren types a terse response to suggest a particular strategy or approve a special discount. No trading telephone messages, no waiting for answers to e-mail messages, no small talk—just instant communication to keep the business running smoothly and productively.

Although IM lacks the richness of face-to-face communication, it is speedy, convenient, and inexpensive. Users can tell at a glance whether a particular person is online and available to receive a message. If necessary, they can type messages and exchange files with a dozen or more people at one time, essentially convening online meetings. Clearly, IM, with its live interaction and support for mobile employees, is helping companies keep their workforces connected at a fraction of the cost of phone calls and letters.

For example, sales managers at Pacific International Marketing in California, which handles vegetables and other fresh produce, used to have to call 35 salespeople in 5 cities every time market prices changed on any item. The company's phone bill was enormous, and managers spent a good deal of time on the phone. These days, managers simply send out an IM alert whenever a price changes, saving both time and money. Executives in the home office of Jennifer Convertibles, a bedding and furniture retailer, use IM technology to communicate with 200 store managers around the United States. By replacing voice-mail with IM, the company did away with 7,000 phone calls per week and slashed its annual communication costs by at least $50,000.

Despite the benefits, not everyone is a fan of IM communication. Why? Because IM, by-and-large, has come into corporate America through the back door. Many employees

According to the research firm IDC, approximately 76 million employees worldwide sent instant messages in the workplace in 2003—more than half are using free IM software, such as Yahoo or AOL, downloaded off the Web. Because IM messages bypass servers, viruses and the transmission of the firm's proprietary information are more difficult to guard against.

download free IM software from sites like Yahoo! and AOL onto company computers without permission from top managers, who tend to view it as a new tool for goofing off and chatting with one's friends.

Even when IM is used for legitimate managerial business purposes, some managers say they have difficulty staying focused on tasks such as writing reports when IM messages suddenly appear on the computer screen. Others feel pressure to stay close to their computers, even late into the evening, in case colleagues in other time zones have questions or need decisions. Moreover, free downloadable IM software creates security holes because the messages and files being shared never pass through a server. That means they can't be scanned for viruses, nor can they be monitored by management or archived.

Nonetheless, IM is coming into its own in the business workplace as software developers devise industrial-strength versions with security and auditing features. For example, the Federal Emergency Management Agency (FEMA) uses IM to coordinate its emergency relief workers in the field following a hurricane, flood, or other disaster.

The fact is that any technology—even the telephone—can be a distraction if improperly monitored, explains one FEMA director. The trick for managers is to figure out how to capitalize on IM's advantages while minimizing its pitfalls.

Sources: Drew Robb, "Instant Messaging: A Portal to Online Threats?" *Government Procurement*, December 2003, pp. 10–13; Matthew Sarrell, "Corporate IM," *PC Magazine*, November 11, 2003, p. 132; Yudhijit Bhattacharjee, "A Swarm of Little Notes," *Time*, September 16, 2002, pp. A4+; Anne Stuart, "IM Is Here. RU Ready 2 Try It?" *Inc.*, July 1, 2002, pp. 76–81.

Organizations of any size, regardless of country, are not simply a random set of individuals who by chance come together for a brief period with no purpose. The fact that they have goal orientations, structures, and coordination greatly influences the nature and amount of communication that takes place. This influence can be analyzed in terms of directions, channels, and patterns of communication.

Directions of Communication Within Organizations

Because organizations of any degree of complexity have both differentiated functions and more than one level of positions with more or less responsibility, the directions of communication within them can be classified according to the level for which they are intended:

downward communication

messages sent from higher organizational levels to lower levels

upward communication

messages sent from lower organizational levels to higher levels

lateral communication

messages sent across essentially equivalent levels of an organization

- **Downward communication** is sent from higher organizational levels to lower levels; for example, from the organization's top executives to its employees, or from supervisors to subordinates.

- **Upward communication** is sent from lower organizational levels to higher levels; for example, from nonmanagement employees to their supervisors, or from a manager to her boss.

- **Lateral communication** is sent across essentially equivalent levels of an organization; for example, from one clerical assistant to another, from the manager of Product A to the manager of Product B, or from the marketing department to the engineering design department.

The contents of communications within organizations usually vary according to the direction of the communication activity. As shown in Exhibit 14.4, downward communication typically involves such matters as goals, objectives, directions, decisions, and feedback. Upward communication commonly focuses on information, suggestions, questions, problems, and requests for clarification. Lateral communication is oriented toward exchanges of information—both formal and informal—that assist or affect coordination and joint problem solving.

While the subject matter of communication in a particular direction tends to be fairly similar in most medium to large organizations, the culture of the organization (or the culture of the country in which the organization resides) can affect the process. For example, in an organization in which authority and hierarchy are stressed, upward communication might be more formal than in an organization with a more egalitarian culture. As a simple illustration, in a strongly hierarchical organization, a conversation might start with the subordinate

exhibit 14.4

Directions of Communication within Organizations

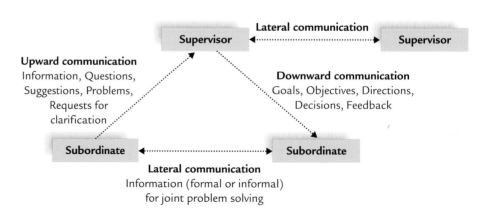

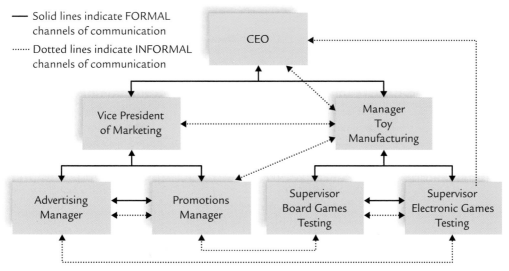

addressing a superior several levels above as Mr. or Ms. Jones. In many countries, such as Korea, the conversation might start by addressing the superior by his or her title, such as Director Park. In organizations with less emphasis on hierarchy, the conversation might start by addressing the superior by his or her first name. Likewise, organizational or country culture can influence the frequency and flavor of upward communications. For example, in organizations with strong hierarchical values, upward communication tends to be less frequent.

In summary, organizational communications flow upward, downward, and laterally. The direction of the communication has a significant impact on the type of communication that is likely to take place. In addition, however, the culture of the organization and the region or country in which the organization is located can further determine the exact form that communication will have and even the frequency of each direction of communication.

Channels of Communication Within Organizations

Organizational channels, or routes of communication, consist of two fundamental types: formal and informal. Both types are essential for organizational functioning, and neither type can easily substitute for the other.

Formal communication channels are those that are authorized, planned, and regulated by the organization and that are directly connected to its official structure. Thus, the organization's designated structure indicates the normal paths for downward, upward, and lateral formal communication. Formal communication channels (shown in Exhibit 14.5) are like highlighted roads on a road map. They specify organizational members who are responsible for tasks and communicating information to levels above and below them and back and forth to adjacent units. Also, formal channels indicate the persons or positions to whom work-related messages should be sent. Formal channels can be modified, and thus they have some flexibility, but they can seldom be disregarded.

Informal communication channels are communication routes that are not prespecified by the organization but that develop through typical interpersonal activities of people at work. Channels can come into existence and change or disappear rapidly, depending on circumstances. However, they may also

formal communication channels routes that are authorized, planned and regulated by the organization and that are directly connected to its official structure

informal communication channels routes that are not prespecified by the organization but that develop through typical and customary activities of people at work

exhibit 14.5
Formal and Informal Channels of Communication in Organizations

endure in many work situations, especially where individuals have been working together over a period of time. If a specific pattern becomes well established, it would ordinarily be called a "network" (to be discussed later).

Several important features of informal communication channels should be noted:

- They tend to operate more often in the lateral than in the vertical direction compared to formal channels (see Exhibit 14.6) because they are not designated by the organization and its top officials.

- Second, information flowing through informal channels often moves extremely fast, principally because senders are highly motivated to pass information on. The so-called grapevine is a classic example of rapid transmission of messages through informal channels.[9] In recent years, the communication capabilities of the Internet have facilitated the emergence of large-scale, word-of-mouth networks. Some researchers propose that these mechanisms are poised to have a significant impact on informal information flow in organizations.[10]

- A third feature is that informal channels carry work-related as well as nonwork information. The fact that channels are informal does not mean that only gossip and other messages unrelated to jobs and tasks are carried by them. In fact, crucial work-related information is frequently communicated in this way. Of course, some of the messages passed through informal channels may contain inaccuracies or be negative, and thus seen by some managers as a source of problems. However—and this is important to emphasize—few organizations could exist for very long if they had to rely only on formal communication channels!

Patterns of Organizational Communication

communication networks

identifiable patterns of communication within and between organizations, whether using formal or informal channels

Identifiable patterns of communication that occur with some regularity within and between organizations, whether using formal or informal channels, are typically called **communication networks**. Put another way, communication networks are stable systems of interconnections. Thus, networks involve consistent linkages between particular sets of senders and receivers. For example, as shown in Exhibit 14.7, a middle-level divisional marketing manager in Los Angeles might have a particular network that involves her boss in New York, three key managers in other departments in the New York headquarters, her seven subordinates located in major western cities, and two outside vendors of market research data. Another network for the same manager might involve two lower-level managers in other units in the Los Angeles office and their for-

exhibit 14.6

Characteristics of Formal and Informal Communication Channels

Formal Communication Channels	**Informal Communication Channels**
· Authorized, planned, and regulated by the organization	· Develop through interpersonal activities of organization members
· Reflect the organization's formal structure	· Not specified by the organization
· Define who has responsibility for information dissemination and indicate the proper recipients of work-related information	· May be short-lived or long-lasting
	· Are more often lateral than vertical
	· Information flow can be very fast
· May be modified by the organization	· Used for both work-related and nonwork information
· Minor to severe consequences for ignoring them	

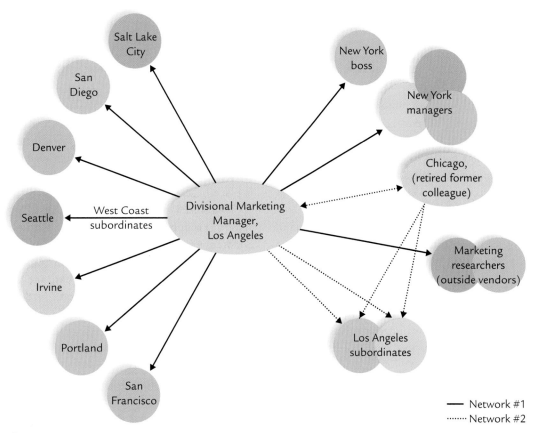

exhibit 14.7

Examples of Two Organizational Communication Networks

mer colleague and old friend who is now a sales supervisor in Chicago and who has access to inside information on how well new marketing approaches are working in that region.

An example of a larger, more organizationwide network would be the Coca-Cola Company's worldwide pattern of communication relationships between its headquarters in Atlanta and its bottlers and distributors. Of course, networks can also be formed across organizations as well as within. This is what often happens when sets of managers from two companies— such as BASF South East Asia and Shell Eastern Petroleum Ltd., for example—have to work together on issues that arise in an international joint venture, in this case the Ellba Eastern Plant at Seraya on Jurong Island, Singapore.[11] A particular challenge in building an effective network for a project that was to last for a number of months and which involved a number of participants from different organizations is illustrated in A Manager's Challenge, "Communication Is Secret Weapon for Change." The challenge here was to change the way communication had been carried out in the past—and thus to develop more effective networking processes—on this type of large, complex project that has many sources of senders and receivers.

The importance of communication networks to managers is that they can provide significant and regular sources of information, both of the formal and informal type, that might otherwise take a much longer time to obtain if the various links had to be set up from scratch each time some new topic or problem came up. Also, when managers are members of established networks,

a manager's challenge

Change

Communication Is Secret Weapon for Change

Imagine the complications of managing communication among the workforces of several competitors who must work on the same government project. Increasingly, after intensive bidding battles to win contracts for complex systems of equipment, managers at major manufacturing firms must face this situation when they have to collaborate with the very competitors they have just defeated.

Consider what happened when BAE Systems, one of Europe's largest aerospace and defense companies, won a multimillion-dollar contract. As a condition of being designated the prime contractor by the U.K. Ministry of Defense to design a very large and sophisticated new product, BAE was required to work with a number of companies in order to finish on schedule and within budget. "With products as complex as [this one], the days of single-source suppliers are over," and "we had to become more collaborative," said Ian Haddleton, BAE's integrated systems solutions manager. As many as 1,000 people from BAE and other firms were going to participate in the months-long redesign project. Therefore, in preparation, management decided to foster closer collaboration by making major changes in the company's approach to communication in carrying out such a complicated endeavor.

To start, BAE managers "agreed on a set of values with our customer that is now the guideline and principle for anyone working on the project," Haddleton explained. Based on these values, all project participants would be able to determine what information was important and with whom it should be shared. As an example, employees of BAE and other collaborating companies agreed to air concerns early in the project so they could be adequately analyzed and addressed before key design decisions were locked in place.

Next, BAE managers set up a Web-based data exchange system to support collaborative communication among the hundreds of project participants. "With a project of this size and the number of companies involved, it's always difficult to know who is responsible for what, and whom to ask when needing advice or information," Haddleton noted. The data exchange system stored the latest information about each participant's role and responsibility. It also allowed participants to upload project-related data (such as proposed design specifications) so that others could post comments, questions, and suggested changes for all to review. And because the system was Web-based, BAE could control access and not have to ask other companies to replace their proprietary communication systems.

Changing their approach to communication helped BAE's managers become more effective in keeping the product's design on course month after month. "Now, more than ever before, it's much easier for us to function as an extended team," summarized Haddleton. "The way we work today is certainly an improvement over the way things used to be done."

Sources: Stephen Windsor-Lewis, "Communicating to Avert Industrial Action at BAE Systems," *Strategic Communication Management*, December 2003–January 2004, pp. 18–22; "Product Development's Secret Weapon: Communication," *Design News*, June 17, 2002, pp. S1+; "BAE Systems Strengthens AMS After MBDA Missile Merger," *Defense Daily*, May 1, 2001; Frances Tusa, "The Rise of European EW," *Journal of Electronic Defense*, June 2001, pp. 54+.

---

it can make it easier for them to influence the other people or groups involved in the networks. Consequently, for both of these reasons, managers need to pay particular attention to what networks they can and want to be a part of, and to the composition of those networks. It is no accident that the term **networking** has come to signify a process that has the potential for gaining advantages for a manager (or anyone for that matter) by having one or more sets of individuals or groups with which one can interact easily and regularly, and with whom one can communicate a sense of confidence and trust.

In traditional Western organizations, it has always been relatively easy for males in management positions to establish various networks with other males (thus providing the basis for the phrase "old boys' network"). However, at least until very recently, it has been much harder for women and members of underrepresented ethnic groups to establish similar helpful networks in their organizations. Research suggests, in fact, that organizational networks

networking a process of developing regular patterns of communication with particular individuals or groups to send and receive information

involving individuals from these groups are different in terms of both composition and relationships from the traditional networks composed primarily of white males.[12] It does not make such networks any less important or useful to managers from these groups, but it does serve to emphasize that network patterns of communication in organizations can vary based on a number of different situational circumstances, including the age, gender, and ethnicity of the individuals involved.

BARRIERS TO COMMUNICATION

Although the organizational context provides numerous opportunities for effective and productive communication, it likewise can present many barriers that interfere with the communication process. Such barriers can arise from several different sources, including interpersonal, organizational, and cultural (see Exhibit 14.8).

Interpersonal Barriers

Obstacles to interpersonal communication can occur with either the sender or the receiver. The burden is simultaneously on both the sender and the receiver to ensure accurate communication. It is, however, the sender's obligation to choose the language and words—to encode the message—carefully to carry the greatest precision of meaning. Precision is especially important if the sender is trying to persuade the receiver to do something in a language or communication style different from what the receiver prefers. For example, if you are trying to convince your boss to authorize a new project and you use an informal style and choice of words, your boss may not be receptive if she

Level	Origin of Barrier	Affects Communication Between:
Interpersonal	· Selective perception · Frame of reference · Individual differences · Emotion · Language · Nonverbal cues	· Individuals or groups
Organizational	· Hierarchical (barriers resulting from formal structure) · Functional (barriers resulting from differences between functional departments)	· Individuals and/or groups within an organization · Individuals and/or groups in different organizations
Cultural	· Language · High/low-context culture · Stereotyping · Ethnocentrism · Cultural distance	· Individuals or groups in different organizations with different national cultures · Individuals or groups from different organizational cultures · Individuals or groups from diverse cultural backgrounds within an organization

exhibit 14.8

Barriers to Communication

selective perception the process of screening out some parts of an intended message because they contradict our beliefs or desires

Selective Perception by Lyman Porter

www.prenhall.com/onekey

frames of reference existing sets of attitudes that provide quick ways of interpreting complex messages

prefers a more formal approach. You will probably need to adjust your style for the communication to be effective.

The receiver, of course, is often the source of communication breakdowns. For example, the receiver might have a **selective perception** problem.[13] That is, the receiver may unintentionally screen out some parts of the intended message because they contradict his beliefs or desires. For example, you might stress the increased productivity that would result from a proposed project, but your boss is focusing on the estimated cost of the project. Although selective perception is a natural human tendency, it hinders accurate communication, especially when sensitive or highly important topics are being discussed. Another way to state this point is that individuals tend to adopt **frames of reference**, or simplified ways of interpreting messages, that help them make sense of complex communications, but these shortcuts may prevent the intended message from being received.[14]

Individual differences between senders and receivers in terms of such basic characteristics as their age, gender, ethnicity, or level of education sometimes can be the source of communication barriers. In general, it would be reasonable to assume that the fewer the differences between the two parties on these kinds of attributes, the lower the communication barriers. Even where these kinds of differences exist, however, such as a difference in gender between sender and receiver, the research evidence tends not to find consistently serious impediments to effective communication related to that characteristic.[15] It is more a matter of a manager being very alert to the *possibility* that individual differences in sender and receiver characteristics could impose a significant obstacle to good communication in a specific instance, rather than assuming it will never be a barrier or, conversely, will always be a barrier.

Emotions can be another barrier.[16] How the receiver feels at the time can influence what gets heard or how it gets interpreted. You certainly have had the experience of feeling that someone was "touchy" or overly sensitive when responding to your message. As a consequence, comments that normally would be taken as mere statements get interpreted as criticisms.

Language can also be a barrier. Even for people who speak the same language, a given word or set of words can mean different things to different people.[17] For example, saying "That's a bad haircut" to a 50-year-old means something completely different than if it was said to a 15-year-old. The 50-year-old will likely interpret the words to mean that the barber did a poor job. The 15-year-old will likely take the statement to mean he looks "cool."

Nonverbal cues can also be barriers to effective communication in two basic ways. First, people can send nonverbal signals without being aware of them, and therefore create unintentional consequences.[18] For example, you might make minimal eye contact with your boss while trying to convince her to approve your proposed project, and yet be unaware that you are doing so. Your boss might think the project has merit but interprets your low level of eye contact as an indication that you are hiding something. Your boss could then reject a project that she might otherwise have authorized. Second, as we have already touched on, nonverbal cues can mean different things to different people.[19] A weak handshake might indicate politeness in Indonesia but communicate lack of confidence in Texas.

Organizational Barriers

Just as interpersonal barriers can limit communication, so can organizational barriers. Such barriers can interfere with communication between individuals or groups within the same organization, between individuals or groups from two different organizations, or between entire organizations. The basis of these barriers lies within the hierarchical structure of organizations. All organizations of any complexity have specialized functions and more than one level of authority. This specialization creates a situation that is ripe for communication difficulties. For example, one person might come from marketing and the other from research and development. The person in marketing might think nothing of exaggerating while the person from research and development always understates her points. Consequently, the marketer might see the R&D scientist as unimaginative and boring, while the scientist might view the marketer as superficial and careless. In addition, the two parties might come from different levels in the organization. The differences between responsibility and level of authority could cause a senior executive to expect an explanation of the broad impacts of a proposed project on the entire organization, and a junior technical expert to focus on the detailed schedule of the project.

Cultural Barriers

Communication and culture are tightly intertwined. Culture cannot exist without communication, and human communication only occurs within a cultural context. Since the act of communicating is so closely connected to the surrounding environment, culture can ease or hinder it. Thus, similarity in cultures between senders and receivers facilitates successful communication—the intended meaning has a higher probability of getting transferred. Differences in culture hinder the process. The greater the cultural differences between sender and receiver, the greater the expected difficulty in communicating. Therefore, other things being equal, it should be easier, for example, for an American manager to communicate with an Australian subordinate than with a Greek subordinate.

Organizational cultures can also differ. The industry of an organization, for example, can influence its internal culture, as we pointed out in Chapter 4. Therefore, it is more likely that an executive at Warner Brothers could communicate successfully with an executive at Disney than with an executive at Exxon. It is not that extreme cultural differences prevent good communication; rather, the possibilities for breakdowns in communication increase in proportion to the degree of differences in the background and customs of the two parties.

The extent to which a sender and receiver differ in a high-context or low-context communication style also significantly influences the effectiveness of the communication. As we discussed in Chapter 4, individuals in high-context cultures tend to pay great attention to the situational factors surrounding the communication process and as a consequence substantially alter what they say and how they say it based on the context.[20] (See Exhibit 14.9.) Individuals in low-context cultures tend to pay less attention to the context and so make fewer and smaller adjustments from situation to situation.[21] Although the greatest differences in high- and low-context cultures occur across countries, there are also such differences across organizations. For example, Japan is a high-context culture that has three distinct levels of language that a speaker uses, depending on his or her status compared with that of the listener. Thus, there are actually five different words for "you" that are used, depending on relative rank and status. However, even within Japan, communication is much more high context in Mitsubishi Heavy Industries than in Nintendo.

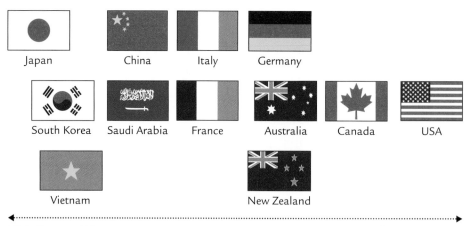

High-Context Cultures
- More and greater adjustments in messages
- Rank of receiver will probably affect message and medium
- Nonverbal communication cues may be very important
- Medium may be as important as message

Low-Context Cultures
- Fewer and smaller adjustments in messages
- Rank of receiver may or may not affect message or medium
- Nonverbal communication cues not as important
- Message is more important than medium

exhibit 14.9

Communication Differences in High- and Low-Context Cultures

Source: www.crwflags.com/fotw/flags.

What is most problematic when individuals from high- and low-context cultures communicate is that each often forms negative interpretations about the other's communication approach. Individuals from low-context cultures tend to interpret the wide swings in words and style indicative of people from high-context cultures as evidence of insincerity, hypocrisy, and even instability. These interpretations make trust difficult and at the extreme can make effective communication impossible. On the other hand, individuals from high-context cultures view the lack of change in communication style of individuals from low-context cultures as evidence of immaturity, selfishness, or lack of sophistication.

In Japanese culture, managers are taught that to communicate effectively, you should "say what you mean, and mean what you say."[22] Vague directives and instructions are seen as a sign of poor communication skills. The assumption, therefore, is that the burden of proof for effective communication is on the speaker. In contrast, in cultures such as those in Arabic countries and in Latin America, the assumption is that both the speaker and the listener share the burden for communicating effectively. In cultures in which speaker and listener share communication responsibilities, chances of unpleasant encounters and direct confrontations and disagreements tend to decrease.

Probably the greatest single cultural barrier that can affect communication across different departmental, organizational, regional, or national cultures is ethnocentrism.[23] **Ethnocentrism** is the belief in the superiority of one's own group and the related tendency to view others in terms of the values of one's own group. Ethnocentrism leads individuals to divide their interpersonal worlds into in-groups and out-groups. As we discussed in Chapter 13, in-groups are groups of people with whom you identify and about whom you care.[24] Members of the in-group tend to be trusted, listened to, and have

Ethnocentrism by Lyman Porter

Q&A
OneKey
www.prenhall.com/onekey

ethnocentrism the belief in the superiority and importance of one's own group

information shared with them. Members of out-groups tend to be viewed with skepticism, if not suspicion, and are not given full information. This type of behavior exists in organizations as well as in interpersonal interactions. When British European Airways merged with British Overseas Airways Corporation some years ago to form British Airways, the ethnocentric orientation of each side almost led to the bankruptcy of the merged unit, which lost nearly $1 billion before the communication barriers were overcome.

Another cross-cultural barrier to communication closely related to ethnocentrism is **stereotyping**, the tendency to oversimplify and generalize about groups of people. The more firmly held the stereotype by a communicator, the harder it is to overcome preconceived expectations and focus on the specifics of the message that is being sent or received. Stereotyping occurs both within and between cultures and thus it affects communication in virtually all organizational settings. For example, suppose you are a technical service manager in a software company and the president has a definite stereotype of people in your position. Generally, the president sees technical service managers as focused on details and unable to see the big picture. With a strong stereotype of this sort, the president may not recognize that you understand and are considering the competitive implications (not just the technical ones) of a new software tool.

stereotyping the tendency to oversimplify and generalize about groups of people

A third major cultural barrier to communication can be labeled **cultural distance**.[25] This concept refers to the overall difference between two cultures' basic characteristics such as language, level of economic development, and entrenched traditions and customs. Cultural distance was illustrated by a study that gathered 21 senior executives from major corporations in Japan, the United States, Brazil, the United Kingdom, and India for a five-week period of cultural explorations. The executives attended lectures and seminars, built rafts and climbed cliffs together, and even traveled in fact-finding teams to the countries represented. Nevertheless, observers reported that communication remained a problem the entire five weeks.[26] Although much of the difficulty came from obvious language differences, a more subtle difficulty came from cultural differences. Many of the Japanese managers, attempting to fit in, adopted American nicknames, but they actually hated being called by them. The Americans couldn't understand why the Japanese were so quiet, not realizing that they felt that it was unwise to speak first at a meeting. The more senior the Japanese executive, the more he listens, and the executives on this trip were quite senior. Similarly, a development project undertaken by Alcan Aluminum Ltd., of Canada and the Chinese National Nonferrous Corporation brought together managers from both firms to learn more about each other's culture. Even though a set of managers from China spent a whole year in Canada studying North American business methods, effective communication remained an elusive goal throughout the period for both sides.[27] Such examples emphasize that the degree of cultural distance between organizational employees from different nationalities represents a potentially very difficult communication barrier to overcome. The severity of the problem should not be underestimated.

cultural distance the overall difference between two cultures' basic characteristics such as language, level of economic development, and traditions and customs

IMPROVING COMMUNICATION

The various barriers discussed in the preceding section can interfere with effective communication, but there are ways to deal with—or overcome—them, and improve your communication capabilities. How important is it for

Cross-cultural communication problems can stem from language differences, but more subtle problems occur because of cultural differences and biases such as *stereotyping* (the tendency to oversimplify and generalize about groups of people) and *ethnocentrism* (the belief that one's own culture, or group, is superior).

you to have a commitment to developing good communication skills? Consider this: "In the *Wall Street Journal*/Harris Interactive survey, recruiters rated [business] school graduates on a variety of attributes—and then rated the attributes in terms of how important they are in a job candidate. Topping the list of 24 attributes are communication and interpersonal skills."[28] As the *Wall Street Journal* article went on to say: "Interpersonal communication . . . skills are what corporate recruiters crave most but find most elusive in MBA graduates."

Given the obvious importance of this topic, in the remainder of this section we discuss some of the most essential approaches that are necessary for you to consider in improving your communication abilities as a manager in organizations.

Improving Listening Skills

When the subject is improving communication skills, most people first think of improving their speaking or writing skills. However, contrary to popular belief, probably the single best thing you can do to enhance your communication skills is to focus on improving your receiving rather than sending skills.

Be More Open-minded Stereotyping, enthnocentricity, rigid frames of reference, and selective listening can all become barriers to comprehending the intended message of a sender, so one of the first things to do to enhance listening skills is to spend time developing a greater awareness of your personal tendencies in the direction of any of these problems. Once you have a better awareness of these tendencies, you can monitor and control them during conversations. Part of the reason for direct and conscious attention to this area is that most people speak at about 120 words per minute and yet can listen at about a rate of 1,000 words per minute.[29] This creates the opportunity for our minds to wander or make judgments about what we are hearing. These tendencies can distort what is heard and how it is interpreted.

Develop Empathy Once personal tendencies have been examined, the next step is developing empathy. **Empathy** is identifying with and understanding the other person's feelings, situation, and motives. To some extent, this requires thinking about the situation of other people. What are their feelings relative to the topic at hand? What are their motivations? Why are they talking about what they are? These and other questions can help you enhance your understanding of the personal context of the message being sent.

empathy the ability to put yourself in someone else's place and to understand his or her feelings, situation, and motives

Listen Actively The next step to improving communication is to take actions to ensure that you—the receiver—hear and understand what the sender is trying to communicate. In conversations, making eye contact is a good way to help speakers feel comfortable and convinced that you are sincerely interested in understanding what they have to say. It is important to focus on the content of the message being sent regardless of the style of its delivery. Even if people are not choosing the best words or they are making grammatical errors, they may have something quite valuable to communicate. Focusing on style over substance can cause the value of the message to be missed. To make sure you understand what is being said, ask clarifying questions. Also, even when you think you have understood the message, it is a good idea to paraphrase, that is, restate what you think the message is. This can be put in the form of a question or statement. For example, you could ask, "So are you saying that . . . ?" Or you can put it more directly by saying something such as, "What I understand you to be saying is . . . ".

Observe Nonverbal Cues As we discussed earlier in this chapter, nonverbal cues are critical to effective communication.[30] Listening more open-mindedly and actively to the words is only part of the task. You also need to concentrate on observing nonverbal cues. In cross-cultural settings, this means that you need to remember that a nonverbal cue or gesture can have different meanings in different cultures. There is little substitute for learning about the nonverbal cues and gestures of the culture of those with whom you will be interacting.

Improving Sending Skills

There are many situations in which you will be the sender of a message. Effective communication can be enhanced by developing better sending skills.

Simplify Language One of the first things a sender can do to enhance communication is to simplify the language in the message. Clearly, what is simple will vary, depending on the audience. Simplifying may involve eliminating jargon that might not be familiar to all members of the audience. It may also involve choosing more succinct and active words and shorter sentences. Perhaps the best clue for spotting complicated and passive language is excessive use of prepositions. The more prepositions in a sentence, the higher the likelihood that the language could be simplified and the message could be stated more directly.

Organize Writing Executives consistently complain about the poor writing skills of new managers.[31] Their complaints lie not in spelling or grammar mistakes, though clearly these should be eliminated, but in the lack of logical thought processes. As a manager, you are likely to write more reports and memos than you may want, and the effectiveness of those written communications will have an important impact on your career. Consequently, developing good writing skills is vital to being an effective manager. Nothing substitutes for practice.

Understand Audience Perhaps the single best thing a sender can do to enhance the effectiveness of communications is to understand the audience.[32] For example, consider the following questions, which come from the material we have covered thus far in this chapter:

- What is the direction of the communication (up, lateral, or down), and does the receiver have any expectations concerning this type of communication?
- Is the communication formal or informal, and how should it be structured to have the intended impact on the receiver?
- Are there expectations from the receiver about the explicitness or implicitness of the message you want to send?
- Does the receiver have any biases for or against certain modes of communication (e.g., for or against e-mail, face-to-face conversations, and so on)?

If you do not understand the person or persons to whom you are sending a message, it is almost impossible to answer these questions. Knowing your audience (i.e., the receiver or receivers) is critical to improving your sending skills. Knowledge of the audience is particularly important in cross-cultural settings, and Exhibit 14.10 lists some ways to improve cross-cultural communication.

Organization-Level Improvements in Communication

Organizations can take steps to change their policies and methods for how and when managers should communicate. Unfortunately, guidelines for this more structural approach are not as well developed as those for individual managers. A study of research and development laboratories within 14 large multinational firms, however, provides some suggestions.[33] The study produced strong evidence for the importance of **gatekeepers**, or so-called "boundary-spanning" individuals who are at the communication interface between separate organizations or between units within an organization. Large companies especially need to be able to structure the activities of gatekeepers to maximize their usefulness to the communication process and to make sure that the most critical information is both sent and received. Findings from the study

gatekeepers individuals who are at the communication interface between separate organizations or between different units within an organization

exhibit 14.10

Tips on Being a More Effective Cross-Cultural Communicator

1. Study general principles that apply to all types of intercultural communication.
2. Learn about the fundamental characteristics of the other cultures with which you will be working.
3. For high-context cultures, learn as many details in advance about the target organization(s) and their specific individual representatives.
4. For high-context cultures, use at least a few words or phrases in the listener's language.
5. For high-context cultures, be especially careful about body language and tone of voice.
6. For low-context cultures, organize written communications so that the major points are immediately and directly stated.
7. Study and respect communicators' preference for greater degrees of formality, especially compared with the typical American approach of casual informality.

indicated that communication could be improved by implementing rules and procedures that increased formal communication, replacing some face-to-face communication with electronic communication, developing particular communication networks, and even creating a centralized office to manage communication activities.

COMMUNICATION AND NEGOTIATION

In the last sections of this chapter, we focus on one particular type of communication that is especially crucial for a manager, namely, negotiation. **Negotiation** can be thought of as the process of conferring to arrive at an agreement between two or more parties, each with their own interests and preferences. The purpose of negotiation is to see whether the parties can arrive at an agreement that serves their mutual interests. Since reaching an agreement inherently involves communication, negotiation and communication are inseparably linked. Thus, the negotiation process can be considered a special part of the general communication process.

negotiation the process of conferring to arrive at an agreement between different parties, each with their own interests and preferences

The Importance of Negotiation to Managers

Today's managers often find themselves in the role of negotiator. This can occur in different types of situations. One type is during the ongoing, day-to-day activities of the manager's organizational unit, where there is a need to negotiate a settlement or resolution of some kind of disagreement. This could be a disagreement between the manager and his own boss, between the manager and another manager from a different unit, or between the manager and one or more of his subordinates. Disagreements could also occur between subordinates or between entire departments. Typically, in these kinds of circumstances the manager would function as an individual negotiator.

The other basic type of negotiation situation in which managers could find themselves would be where they are part of a formally appointed negotiating team representing their unit or organization in discussions with representatives from another unit or organization. In either kind of negotiating situation, managers are taking on the role of facilitator—attempting to ensure that all parties can agree on a common course of action. Also, regardless of the specific features of the situation, the principles of effective approaches to negotiation can help settle any kind of disagreements that a manager might encounter—inside or outside an organization.

Achieving More Effective Negotiations

Managers have available several potentially helpful approaches to increasing their chances of achieving successful negotiation outcomes. (See Exhibit 14.11.) One especially useful principle to keep in mind when serving as a

Less effective	More effective
• Positions	• Interests
• People Involved	• Problem/Issue
• Maintaining/Increasing Competition (Win/Lose Focus)	• Decreasing/Lessening Competition (Collaborative Focus)

exhibit 14.11
Improving Effectiveness of Negotiations

negotiator is to focus on the parties' *interests*, not their positions.[34] Each side to a dispute has interests, whether or not they enter into negotiations with fixed positions. **Interests** are a party's concerns and desires—what they want, in other words. **Positions**, on the other hand, are a party's stance regarding those interests. Thus, an interest, for example, would be the desire by a subordinate to receive a specific challenging new assignment. A position, in this example, would be a statement by the subordinate that "I am the one who should receive this new sales territory because . . . ". It is easier to get agreement on interests rather than positions because: (a) for a given interest there are probably several possible positions that could satisfy it; and (b) behind two opposed positions, there are likely to be at least some interests of the two parties that are shared rather than in direct conflict.[35] Thus, if such mutually compatible interests can be identified, the chances of reaching an acceptable conclusion to the negotiations are increased. In the example above, even though the boss is not able to give the desired new sales territory to this particular subordinate, a common interest may be identified—such as the desire of both parties to see that the subordinate's good performance in the past is rewarded with some other kind of challenging new assignment in the future—even though it can't be this particular assignment now.

A second, sound principle for negotiations (again, see Exhibit 14.11) is to focus on the problem or issue, rather than on the people involved, as we discussed in the section on conflict in Chapter 13 ("Groups and Teams"). The key point here is that a negotiator should endeavor to concentrate on the substance of the disagreement rather than on who is doing the disagreeing or what they are like as people. This principle is well summarized in the advice to negotiators to "be hard on the problem, soft on the people."[36]

Another helpful principle for managers who are involved in negotiations (Exhibit 14.11) is to try to lessen the competition between the two parties (an "I win, you lose" situation) by establishing an atmosphere of collaboration (a "we all win" situation). **Collaboration** is an attempt to get both parties to attack a problem and solve it together, rather than have one party defeat the other, as in a win–lose athletic contest. Thus, both parties should be encouraged to develop creative solutions that increase the total amount of resources available to be shared or divided by the two parties.

Finally, if managers find that negotiations are extremely complex and the parties seem emotionally invested in the outcome, they can often request intervention by a neutral third party. Sometimes disinterested managers within the organization may be asked to serve in this role. The third-party negotiator can serve the role of judge, mediator, or devil's advocate. In the role of a judge, the manager handles negotiations and decides on the best possible course of action, which the parties then agree to follow. In mediation, the manager controls the negotiation process, but someone else makes the final decision based on the arguments presented—possibly a senior executive in the organization. As we have discussed in other chapters, a devil's advocate asks questions that may oppose the positions of both parties. The attempt here is for all parties to think about positions that they may not originally have considered.

Key Factors in Cross-National Negotiations

As noted earlier, as a manager you may find yourself a member of negotiating teams. With the greater frequency of international assignments, this may particularly be the case when working in situations that require negotiations across national borders. Because of the advances in transportation and com-

---

negotiation "interests" a party's or parties' concerns and desires—in other words, what they want

negotiation "positions" a party's or parties' stance regarding their interests

collaboration part of negotiation in which parties work together to attack and solve a problem

munication technologies, along with expanding capital flows worldwide, organizations are engaging in ever-larger amounts of foreign trade and international business partnerships. Together, all of this activity increases the importance of your being able to negotiate successfully in cross-national circumstances as well as in your own organization or country.

Analysis has shown that there are three principal variables that determine the outcome of negotiations in general, and especially in these kinds of cross-national situations: the people involved, the situation, and the process itself.[37] Research from an array of internationally oriented studies also indicates that each of these variables is strongly influenced by cultural differences.[38]

People Although there are some cultural differences in preferred negotiator characteristics, there seem to be some traits and abilities that are fairly universal for the task of negotiation. They include good listening skills, strong orientation toward people, and high self-esteem, among others.[39] In addition, ability to be influential in the home organization appears to be a commonly preferred personal attribute.

Opinions about the qualities of effective negotiators do vary in different countries, however. Exhibit 14.12 lists the qualities that managers from the United States and three other countries think are important for effective negotiators. As the exhibit indicates, the opinions about these qualities vary considerably by culture. For example, U.S., Japanese, Chinese (Taiwan), and Brazilian managers differ in the importance they attach to "ability to win respect and confidence." It is rated much higher in the two Asian cultures than in the other two cultures. For American and Brazilian managers, planning skills and judgment and intelligence are rated as more highly desired negotiator characteristics than they were in the two Asian cultures. But there are also differences even between the two Asian cultures. The Japanese placed highest importance on "dedication to the job," whereas "persistence and determination" ranked number one with the Taiwanese.

Situations of Negotiations The second major variable affecting negotiation outcomes is the set of situational circumstances. Probably the most important are the location of the negotiations, the physical arrangements, the emphasis on speed and time, and the composition of the negotiating teams.

exhibit 14.12

Important Characteristics Needed by Negotiators in Four Countries

U.S. Managers	Japanese Managers	Chinese Managers (Taiwan)	Brazilian Managers
1. Preparation and planning skill[a]	1. Dedication to job	1. Persistence and determination	1. Preparation and planning skill
2. Thinking under pressure	2. Ability to perceive and exploit power	2. Ability to win respect and confidence	2. Thinking under pressure
3. Judgment and intelligence	3. Ability to win respect and confidence	3. Preparation and planning skill	3. Judgment and intelligence
4. Verbal expressiveness	4. Integrity	4. Product knowledge	4. Verbal expresssiveness
5. Product knowledge	5. Listening skill	5. Interesting	5. Product knowledge
6. Ability to perceive and exploit power	6. Broad perspective	6. Judgment and intelligence	6. Ability to perceive and exploit power
7. Integrity	7. Verbal expressiveness		7. Competitiveness

[a]*Note:* Characteristics are listed in order of importance.

Source: J. L. Graham and Y. Sano, *Smart Bargaining: Doing Business with the Japanese,* 2nd ed. (New York: Harper Business, 1988).

Location. Typically, there is a strong tendency to want to negotiate on your own turf or at neutral sites, especially for critical negotiations. The so-called "home court advantage" seems to be universal; everyone feels more comfortable and confident, and has greater access to information and resources, when negotiating at home. For international negotiations, negotiations conducted in a manager's own offices or even in his or her home country can be a psychological advantage.

Characteristics of locations, however, can vary by culture. For example, in the United States almost all negotiations occur in a formal setting, such as an office or conference room. In contrast, in Japan and Mexico, where relationship building is crucial, major parts of the process are likely to occur in an informal or nonwork setting, such as a restaurant or golf course. In Korea, the final contract produced from the negotiations is likely to be signed in a formal and public setting rather than in someone's office.

Physical Arrangements. The usual American approach to setting up a room for negotiations is to place the parties on opposite sides of a table, facing each other, which has the obvious effect of emphasizing competing interests. Other arrangements are possible, including seating the parties at right angles or along the same side "facing the problem" or at a round table where all are part of the total problem-solving effort.[40]

Emphasis on Speed and Time. Americans typically avoid wasting time. They want to "get right to the point" or "get down to business." Other cultures differ from that viewpoint. In Mexico or China, for example, the norm is to invest considerable time in relationship building and other activities not directly related to the central negotiation process. Consequently, in such cultures, speed is sacrificed, and the effectiveness and efficiency of subsequent negotiations often hinge on how well relationships have been developed.

Composition of the Negotiating Teams. The composition and size of teams representing the parties can also influence negotiations. For example, the more people involved at the negotiation table, the more preparation that needs to be done to ensure that the team presents a united front. The composition of the team in terms of decision-making authority is also important. If individuals at the table have authority to make binding decisions, the negotiations are generally more efficient than if they do not.

Team composition can vary significantly by culture. In countries that are sensitive to status differences and ranks (for example, Singapore, India, Venezuela, Japan), having similar status, position, age, and authority between the negotiating teams is much more important than in other countries (like New Zealand, Canada, United States). The size of negotiating teams also can differ markedly by culture. In the United States, where go-it-alone heroes are admired, team size is ordinarily much smaller than in more collectivist-oriented cultures such as those of Taiwan, China, and Japan. The resulting mismatch in size can communicate unintended messages. Taiwanese, for example, might interpret a single negotiator or a small team as a sign that the other party does not consider the negotiations to be important. Similarly, Americans might interpret the presence of a large team from a Taiwanese firm as an attempt to intimidate them with numbers.

The Negotiation Process The third, and probably most crucial, variable determining the outcome of negotiations is the negotiating process itself. The five common stages in this process, which are basically the same across all cultures,[41] are described below and shown in Exhibit 14.13. They are also illustrated in A Manager's Challenge, "American–Japanese Negotiations," which explores the five stages as they apply to two particular cultures—Japan and the United States.

exhibit 14.13

The Five Stages in the Negotiating Process

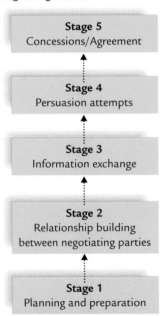

Stage 5
Concessions/Agreement

↑

Stage 4
Persuasion attempts

↑

Stage 3
Information exchange

↑

Stage 2
Relationship building between negotiating parties

↑

Stage 1
Planning and preparation

globalization *a manager's challenge*

American–Japanese Negotiations

The United States is Japan's largest trading partner. Japan is the United States' second-largest trading partner after Canada. Given the critical economic (as well as political and military) relationship between the two countries, opportunities for negotiations occur frequently. Unfortunately, the two countries differ substantially in their approaches to negotiations.

If you think of negotiations as a dance, then Americans and Japanese are moving to quite different music and, as a consequence, toes get stepped on during the process. Based on the five fundamental processes of negotiation, we can map the importance each culture places on each stage and how much time each tends to spend at each stage. As the diagram illustrates, the differences in patterns make for an awkward dance.

Both Americans and Japanese value and spend time on preparation, but Japanese spend slightly more time. However, they differ dramatically at Stage 2. While Americans place relatively little value on, and do not spend much time on, developing relationships, Japanese are just the opposite. Japanese also spend more time on, and more highly value, the exchange of information.

Both cultures place significant value on persuasion and on the conclusion of negotiations. However, the two critical timing differences are that by the time Americans want to be well into the persuasion stage (Stage 4), the Japanese are just wanting to end the relationship-building stage (Stage 2). As the diagram also demonstrates, Japanese tend to take more time overall for negotiations.

At the conclusion of negotiations, when negotiating with each other, Americans typically rely on long and extremely detailed contracts that explicitly spell out the obligations of each party and the penalties for noncompliance. In Japan, on the other hand, written agreements are often quite short and only describe the general intentions and obligations of the two parties. The last paragraph of such agreements in Japan may simply state that if disagreements arise, both parties will try to resolve them in good faith.

Unless adjustments are made on one side or the other, or by both parties, even though the two cultures share the same basic sequence of negotiation stages, misunderstandings can easily develop from the difference in importance attached to each stage and how long each stage typically lasts.

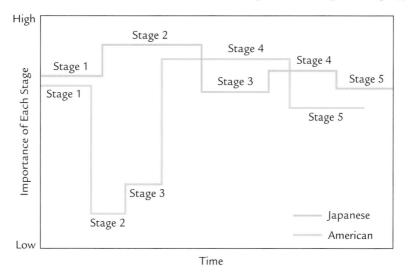

Stage 1: Planning and Preparation. This stage involves laying the foundations through advance planning and analysis prior to any face-to-face interactions. At this stage, individuals or teams conduct background research, gather relevant information, and plan their strategy and tactics. In addition, preliminary decisions are made about what the objectives will be and what can and cannot be conceded during the course of the negotiations.

Stage 2: Relationship Building between Negotiating Parties. This stage is commonly referred to as "nontask time," in which each side attempts to establish comfortable working relationships with the other side. As we pointed out earlier,

Americans are inclined to make this stage briefer and believe such activities are relatively unimportant. On the other hand, negotiators from some other cultures such as Latin America, the Middle East, and Asia believe exactly the opposite. Research suggests three types of behaviors during this stage: developing trust, developing personal rapport, and establishing long-term association.[42]

Stage 3: Information Exchange.   In this stage, each party attempts to learn about the needs and demands of its counterparts. Managers from the United States often attempt to hurry through these activities with an attitude of "you tell me what you want, and I will tell you what I want."[43] In contrast, managers from Asian cultures take a much more indirect, more drawn out, and more thorough approach to acquiring and exchanging information. Arabic and Latin American managers appear to follow a similar approach, except that the latter are even more leisurely in their use of time at this stage.[44]

Stage 4: Persuasion Attempts.   This stage focuses on attempts to modify the position of the other party and to influence that side to accept the negotiator's desired set of exchanges (for example, an exchange of a certain price for a certain quantity or quality of goods or services). American managers usually treat this as the most important stage, with assertive and straightforward efforts to obtain a desired conclusion. Such persuasion can sometimes involve the use of warnings or threats to try to force the other party to agree.[45] Managers from Arabic countries tend to show tactics similar to those of Americans at the persuasion stage, but they are less inclined to hurry. Negotiators from Asian cultures take a slow, careful approach but do not tend to use direct assertiveness in persuasion until later in the negotiations. As reported in one research study, "when not sure of the offer, they frequently resort to the tactics of 'pretending to lack authority' or 'deliberately delaying [a] counter offer'."[46] Managers from Latin American cultures tend to use a mixture of approaches during this stage by showing a moderate degree of assertiveness but also a willingness to use the tactic of "calculated delay" when this seems advisable.[47]

Stage 5: Concessions/Agreement.   At this final point, if reasonable progress has been made, compromises and concessions are made that permit each party to take away something of value. Since American managers tend to begin the negotiation process with positions fairly close to what they will finally accept, they do not have much leeway for concessions.[48] Managers from Arabic and Latin American countries seem to open negotiations from more extreme positions, which permit them to offer concessions late in the process. Managers from Asian countries often employ "normative appeals" (such as "it's your obligation") to try to get the other party to offer concessions.[49]

managerial perspectives revisited

1   PERSPECTIVE 1: THE ORGANIZATIONAL CONTEXT   Almost all types and forms of managerial communication are affected by the organizational context. The structure and characteristics of organizations can facilitate or impede effective communication. The policies and procedures of the organization likewise can help or hinder a manager's attempts to send and receive information and meaning to and from different sources. Particularly affected by the organizational context is the direction of communication. The meaning of transmitted information varies considerably depending on whether it is being sent or received upward, downward, or laterally. The organizational context also presents major challenges and opportunities to build powerful communication networks.

2   **PERSPECTIVE 2: THE HUMAN FACTOR**   The very phrase "interpersonal communication" suggests the centrality of the people aspects of communication. As we discussed earlier in this chapter, among the chief barriers to successful communication are the interpersonal ones. Managers who can gain insight into this kind of potential barrier and how such processes as "selective perception" and "frames of reference" can affect communication will increase their chances of becoming more effective communicators. We also observed in the latter part of the chapter how certain characteristics of people help determine the likelihood of constructive outcomes of negotiations in cross-cultural circumstances.

3   **PERSPECTIVE 3: MANAGING PARADOXES**   Communication can be a source of paradoxes to be managed. For example, a manager has to be alert to how both verbal and nonverbal modes of communicating affect potential receivers. A verbal message may convey one meaning, but a nonverbal message may convey another. Oral and written communication can also present paradoxes. Managers often attempt to reinforce their intended messages by sending them by both modes of communication, but this does not guarantee successful communication. In other words, being effective at communicating in one mode is not the same thing as being effective in the other. If they are ineffective at one or both, their messages can be misperceived, causing more confusion rather than more collaboration among their employees. Therefore, it is critical for most managers to hone both forms. In the area of negotiations, another paradox to be managed is the necessity to pay attention to the differences between "interests" and "positions."

4   **PERSPECTIVE 4: ENTREPRENEURIAL MIND-SET**   As we have said, a key component of being entrepreneurial is identifying opportunities. To identify opportunities, managers have to gather substantial amounts of information and analyze them. They must remain alert to unique trends and changes in markets and customer needs. Gathering this information requires managers to communicate with many people and engage in active listening. Furthermore, exploiting opportunities requires them to communicate their ideas and strategies effectively to others in the organization.

The other relevant observation that can be made here is that this is an area (as with leadership in general) where people can develop and definitely improve their skills if they have sufficient desire to do so. Those with an entrepreneurial mind-set are more likely to try. The same is true for becoming a more skilled negotiator: A commitment to improving can result in positive benefits.

concluding comments

As emphasized at the beginning of this chapter, being a good communicator, and knowing how the communication process works, is essential for becoming an effective manager and leader. In fact, most experienced managers will tell you that communication skills are vital to career success, and a variety of studies emphatically support this claim. Of course, the first step is to understand the nuances of the basic communication process. But that is only a starting point. Although the process seems simple enough, the major challenge is to be able to implement that process successfully on a regular and consistent basis. That, in turn, requires applying your knowledge about the nature of organizations and some of the other key functions of managing (such as planning, organizing, and leading) that have already been discussed in previous chapters.

If good communication were easy, then everyone would be able to do it well most of the time. However, in any organizational context, there are always barriers and obstacles that interfere with effective communication. It is critically important, therefore, to be very aware of these potential obstructions in order to be able to take steps to overcome and deal with them. Communication is an excellent example of a management activity where there is a great cost to naiveté and inexperience and a great benefit to be gained by awareness and analytical insight. Very few people are naturally superb communicators, but there is ample opportunity to become a much better communicator if you focus on developing that awareness and insight.

It also will be especially helpful in your management career if you can add some understanding of the process of negotiation to your repertoire of communication skills. As we noted in this chapter, negotiation is a particular type or form of communication—because of the up-front recognition and acknowledgment of different interests and preferences as the starting point for the process. Various factors, such as cultural differences, can increase the difficulty and complexity of the process. Again, however, like communication in general, being able to become a better negotiator is a capability that can be honed. Gaining negotiation experience is especially helpful, particularly if that experience is followed by careful analysis and attention to what was learned from the process.

key terms

collaboration   512
communication   491
communication networks   500
cultural distance   507
decoding   492
downward communication   498
empathy   509
encoding   492
ethnocentrism   506

formal communication
    channels   499
frames of reference   504
gatekeepers   510
informal communication
    channels   499
lateral communication   498
media richness   495
medium   492

negotiating "interests"   512
negotiating "positions"   512
negotiation   511
networking   502
noise   492
selective perception   504
stereotyping   507
upward communication   498

test your comprehension

1. What is communication?
2. What are the parts of the communication model?
3. What is noise? How does it affect the communication process?
4. Why is oral communication usually more compelling than written communication?
5. Which mode of communication is the most flexible? The least flexible? Why?
6. Why is it important for nonverbal cues to be

consistent with verbal cues? What happens if they are not congruent?
7. What is meant by "media richness"?
8. What are some of the characteristics of media that you should consider when deciding which one to use for a given message?
9. What are the typical differences in content of upward, downward, and lateral communication within organizations?

10. What are the differences between formal and informal communication channels? When would you use each?

11. What is a communication network?

12. Why is networking important?

13. What are the three types of barriers to effective communication?

14. How are selective perception and frames of reference related?

15. In what way can emotions become a barrier to effective communication?

16. What are the principal differences between high-context and low-context cultures relative to communication?

17. What is ethnocentrism, and how does it impair effective communication?

18. What is cultural distance?

19. What are the two basic methods for improving your communication ability?

20. Discuss the four ways to improve your listening skills.

21. What are some of the methods used to improve your sending skills?

22. What can organizations do to improve communication within them?

23. In negotiation, what is the difference between an "interest" and a "position"?

24. What are four helpful principles for effective negotiation?

25. What are the key factors in cross-national negotiations?

26. Describe each of the five stages of negotiations and how they can contribute to the overall outcome.

apply your understanding

1. Despite the considerable emphasis that most companies and other types of organizations put on communication, why do you think that many employees feel there is inadequate communication with and from their managers?

2. Assume that you are now working in the first, truly management position in your career. What is likely to be the most important communication issue/problem you will face in the first few months in that position?

3. Will the probable continued increase in electronic communication within and between organizations be likely to increase or decrease the communication issues/problems faced by the typical manager? Explain the reasoning behind your answer.

4. How can a knowledge of the basics of negotiation assist managers in doing their day-to-day activities, especially in regard to exercising leadership and influence? Can you provide examples?

practice your capabilities

When Chris Barnes was promoted to manager in the production department at Telmark Plastics, sales had been increasing for three years, and productivity and morale in the department were high. Lately, however, orders have been slowing. Some days there haven't been enough orders to keep all of the workers busy. And it isn't just in Chris's department. An economic downturn has sent the entire company into a tailspin. The CEO has instructed all managers to find ways to cut costs by 22 percent immediately.

Feeling very pressured and too busy to talk to any of the workers right away to get their opinions, on Tuesday, Chris sent the following short memo to the production department employees:

"TO: Production Workers:
I have been instructed to cut costs by 22 per-
cent. This means we will need to make some

tough decisions. We will have a meeting to
discuss alternatives on Friday afternoon at
5:00 P.M.

Through the rest of the week, Chris noticed clusters of workers having intense conversations that stopped whenever he approached. Productivity was slipping. There was more absenteeism than normal. Every member of the department appeared angry, depressed, and worried.

On Friday afternoon, as soon as Chris entered the meeting room the yelling started. The entire evening shift seemed to think they would probably all be laid off. The day shift had somehow come to the conclusion that they were going to have to take significant pay cuts or maybe be replaced by less expensive workers. Chris finally managed to calm everybody down and told them that the meeting wasn't to announce layoffs or pay cuts, but to discuss any other ways they could think of to cut costs. Didn't they read the memo?

Chris had expected everyone to show up with creative ideas on how to cut costs, not expectations of being laid off! What had gone wrong?

1. Comment on Chris's choice of media for (a) the announcement and (b) the meeting. Would you have made the same choices?
2. Identify any barriers to communication in this situation. How could they have been reduced?
3. If you were Chris, what would you do following the meeting to improve the communication between yourself and your workers?

closing case

How One Company Tackled a Major Communication Problem

Since 1946, when Paul Iams founded The Iams Company in Dayton, Ohio, to raise the nutritional level of packaged pet food, the product category has grown into a $7 billion business. Procter & Gamble saw so much profit potential in pet food that it bought Iams in 1999. Today, the company's 2,500 employees produce premium dry and canned foods for dogs and cats at 11 facilities in the United States and the Netherlands, although the main office is still located in Dayton. Iams-branded dog and cat food products are sold through supermarkets, drug stores, pet stores, feed outlets, and other retail locations. A second Iams brand, Eukanuba, is sold only through veterinary offices.

In 1982, Clay Mathile, an Iams employee since 1970, bought the company from the founder. Within three years, Iams—still a private company—was ringing up $50 million in annual sales with a 200-person workforce. Then human resources managers decided to conduct the company's first survey of employee attitudes. The employees reported generally positive attitudes. However, management was troubled by the unexpectedly strong response to a question asking whether employees agreed with the statement: "We do not get enough information about how well our work group and company are doing."

Digging deeper into the survey results, Mathile and his managers realized that Iams employees were asking for more frequent and more detailed communication regarding both their particular facility's performance and the company's performance overall. Even though Iams was not publicly held, employees were paid bonuses based on sales and profits and were therefore keenly interested in following the company's progress. As a result, Mathile and his team began thinking about a formal process to share key information more often with employees, supervisors, and plant managers, addressing these internal audiences as if they owned company stock. Just as important, the process had to allow information to flow upward as well

When the Dayton, Ohio, pet food company, Iams, conducted its first employee survey, employees indicated they weren't receiving enough information about how the company was doing. Since that time, Iams has made a point to communicate more effectively with its staff. Among other things, the company shuts down its factories and offices for a few hours each quarter to brief employees about the company's current financial situation and its future plans. Iams's attempts to communicate better also included training "VP of Canine Communication" Kersee to greet visitors at the company's corporate headquarters.

as downward so managers could take the pulse of the organization and, at the most basic level, determine whether the employee audience understood the messages.

Taking a cue from the quarterly reports that public companies issue to stockholders, senior managers began traveling to meet with groups of employees every three months. Each Iams factory or office shuts down for a few hours during the quarter so that the employees and supervisors can hear top managers talk about the company's current financial situation as well as safety accomplishments and future plans. In addition, senior managers make a point of welcoming new employees and explaining Iams's mission and strategy. Then, each facility's top managers discuss local goals and results and acknowledge promotions and other achievements. Finally, a manager from headquarters reports on developments in one department, such as new employee benefits or upcoming product introductions.

At the end of each meeting, senior managers and local facility managers stand in front of the room and field audience questions. Over the years, employees have asked about a wide range of topics such as the impact of Iams's overseas expansion on its U.S. facilities and even individual problems with health care benefits. If none of the managers can answer a particular question, one takes responsibility for researching the issue, responding to the questioner, and posting the answer for the entire facility.

"It is a two-way street," says John Meyer, who helped implement the meeting process when he was senior vice president at Iams. "The leadership looks for feedback and ideas from every level of the company and employees are kept well-informed, focused on company goals, and motivated to follow through." Employees find out every quarter whether their facility and the entire company is on track toward the year's goals, rather than being surprised when they receive their year-end bonus checks. They also appreciate being praised for their accomplishments and having an open forum where they can interact directly with top local and corporate managers, instead of filtering comments and questions through an intermediary such as the human resources staff.

This tradition of quarterly meetings has continued under the leadership of Jeff Ansell, who became president after Procter & Gamble acquired Iams. These days, senior managers fan out to visit 11 facilities worldwide every three months. Managers in certain departments also use technology to share information with a far-flung employee base. For instance, managers used to bring the North American sales force together for twice-yearly new-product briefings.

In between, they scheduled telephone conference calls as needed to discuss upcoming product introductions.

With the advent of videoconferencing technology, however, sales managers can now see and talk with the entire sales team at any time. Displaying new products and prototypes, transmitting detailed product data, and facilitating group discussions is easier and cheaper than ever before, because participants simply gather in the nearest company conference room to prepare for a divisionwide sales meeting. Moreover, with online chats, e-mail, and other Web-based tools, managers can assess what the sales force needs to know and reinforce key data when necessary. "[Online] functions such as surveys and quizzes drive the information home," comments Scott George, who manages enterprise systems for Iams.

Taking communication a step further, Iams management has appointed Kersee, a golden retriever, as vice president of canine communication. She samples company products and greets employees and visitors in the Dayton headquarters. Once Kersee's formal instruction was completed, her trainer even sent Iams's employees a list of the 30-odd commands the dog knows. All this communication seems to be paying off: Iams has increased its annual revenues to more than $1 billion, with higher sales to come as Procter & Gamble pushes for more market share in the next decade.

Questions

1. What effects, if any, is Iams's emphasis on quarterly meetings of employees with senior-level managers likely to have on the quality and extent of day-to-day communication between lower-level managers and their immediate subordinates? How will it help or hinder that communication?

2. How has the richness of the media used by Iams managers changed over the years? How do you think these changes have affected senders and receivers?

3. Do the communication benefits of holding companywide quarterly meetings outweigh the costs of halting operations so employees can attend and having executives travel in person to different locations for the meetings? Explain the basis for your answer.

4. Analyze the communication network structure at Iams. Who is involved? At what levels(s)? In what ways?

5. Does this case suggest any linkages between the type and extent of managerial communication, on the one hand, and employees' trust in management and their motivation to perform?

Sources: Jack Neff, "P&G Claims Iams Is Top Dog in Pet Food," *Advertising Age*, March 10, 2003, pp. 4–5; John Meyer, "Strategic Communication Enhances Organizational Performance," *Human Resource Planning*, June 2002, pp. 7+; Jack Neff, "It's a Dog-Eat-Dog World," *Food Processing*, June 2001, pp. 49+; Elisabeth Goodridge, "Users Tap Collaborative Functions of E-Learning Apps," *InformationWeek*, December 10, 2001, p. 34.

Managing Human Resources

15

■

Explain how the management of human resources is both a role for the human resource management department and all managers.

■

Describe the key means by which companies find job candidates.

■

Explain how companies select job candidates.

■

Highlight the keys to effective socialization and training.

■

Describe the common methods of managing performance.

■

Discuss the various compensation and reward systems commonly used.

■

Explain how various laws affect core HR activities.

Brunswick's Global Human Resource Challenge

"The world is bigger than a bowling ball." This is the message that senior executives were trying to communicate to Brunswick's 21,000 employees. Brunswick, a U.S.-based, $3.7 billion firm, is a leader in the recreation market. In addition to its traditional and well-known lines of bowling and billiard products, it is also the world's largest manufacturer of recreational boats, including Hatteras Yachts, SeaRay, Bayliner, Maxim, Baja, Princecraft, and Trophy boats, and it holds a dominant position in the health and fitness sector with its Life Fitness and Hammer Strength products. Brunswick dominates the U.S. market in all its major product lines, but only 18 percent of its revenues are generated outside the United

States. To continue to grow, it must expand into global markets. According to one senior executive, "We are number one in the United States in virtually every product line we have. We need to expand our activities into the global marketplace."

When asked what was the biggest constraint to the implementation of this strategy, an executive replied, "People. At the moment we do not have the human resources necessary to implement our globalization strategy." The company faces many challenges as it tries to expand internationally. For example, Brunswick wants to expand into Brazil. Although Brazil has thousands of lakes and rivers potentially waiting for people to enjoy them by boat, it also has laws that restrict the importation of boats costing more than $3,500. The obvious solution is to manufacture boats in Brazil. However, this solution is not as easy to implement as it seems. A variety of human resource challenges first must be resolved.

One of the first challenges Brunswick faces is determining if there is an actual market for recreational boats in Brazil. This seems like a market research challenge, but for many firms like Brunswick, it is more fundamentally a human resource challenge. The critical human resource issue is: Does Brunswick have

Brunswick has long been a dominant player in the sporting goods market in the United States. The company's international sales, however, are much smaller. Growth will require expanding internationally—a huge challenge for Brunswick's human resource personnel, who will need to staff the new divisions. To some extent, Brunswick has met the cross-cultural challenge by making strategic acquisitions. In 2001, it acquired Sealine International, a leading boat builder in Europe, and Princecraft, Canada's leading builder of aluminum fishing, deck, and pontoon boats.

the people capable of assessing the recreational boat market in Brazil?

Even if Brunswick can assess the Brazilian market and even if that assessment is positive, it still faces several human resource challenges. Who should it select to manage the Brazilian operation? Does Brunswick have anyone with the necessary skills to succeed in the job? He or she must understand how to socialize and train new employees to ensure that they perform their jobs effectively.

Can the firm identify and select the skilled people it needs in the Brazilian labor market in sufficient numbers and at a wage that will enable them to manufacture boats cost-effectively? If not, the potential for Brunswick boats in Brazil cannot be realized. Will Brunswick's traditional means of evaluating and managing performance work in Brazil? Besides competitive wages, how will the company motivate and compensate employees? What benefits will it need to provide to attract and retain quality employees?

Brunswick's strategy may be excellent, but without adequate answers to these human resource management questions, it will never be effectively implemented and translated into successful results.

Source: Personal communication with Brunswick senior management, 1999, 2000, 2001, 2002.

strategic overview

Historically, many organizations have promoted the idea that people are their most important asset. Unfortunately, their actions didn't support their claims. For example, when the economy enters a recession and organizations encounter reduced demand for their goods and services, they cut costs by laying off employees. Yet recently, organizations have begun to reassess the importance of their employees. One of the reasons for this change is the realization that employees generally possess the knowledge that enables the firm to compete effectively in the marketplace. In fact, much of the knowledge in a firm is held by its employees. As such the employees become critical assets. The firm's employees are also its most unique resource and cannot be easily imitated by competitors. Firms that have greater knowledge about technology, customers, manufacturing processes, and the products and services consumers want can therefore win competitive battles. But it is predicated on the ability of the organization to learn, innovate, and change its processes.[1] To do these things effectively requires human talent.[2]

As a result, human resource management has evolved in recent years, particularly the strategic aspects of it.[3] In this chapter, we underscore the importance of this link. As the opening case on Brunswick suggests, organizations must have adequate *amounts* of human capital to implement a strategy of any value. However, the company must also have *quality* human capital, especially among its managers. As such, the company's human resources efforts should be aimed at identifying and selecting employees who have the knowledge, skills, and capabilities the organization needs to compete; and fostering and retaining those employees with good compensation and reward systems.

In general, human resource management (HRM) typically encompasses the activities of acquiring, maintaining, and developing the organization's people—its human resources. The traditional view of these activities focuses on planning for staffing needs, recruiting and selecting of employees, orienting and training staff, appraising their performance, providing compensation and benefits, and managing their career movement and development. From this perspective HRM involves both the activities of the human resource department and its specialized staff as well as all managers. While the HR department

likely sets policies and practices for hiring people, for example, managers are quite often involved in selecting employees because, of course, once hired, the new employees are going to go to work for them. Similarly, while the HR department may set up the exact performance appraisal forms and processes, managers are the ones who actually assess employee performance. Thus, while it is important for you to understand the role of a company's human resource department, it is even more important for you as a future manager to understand your role in managing human resources. How can you manage your human resources effectively? In general, you need the following capabilities:

- You need the ability to *recruit* and *select* the right people.
- You need the ability to effectively *socialize* and *train* people in your unit.
- You need the ability to effectively *evaluate* their performance.
- You need the ability to determine *reward* systems that will motivate high performance.
- You need to know what additional experience or education your subordinates need to *develop* to advance in their careers.

One of the most enlightening studies on the importance of effective human resource management and career success looked at cases of career derailment. The study found that the number-one reason for managerial career derailment, or, in other words, the number-one reason why managers who got *on* but then at some point were *bumped off* the upwardly mobile career track, was their inability to successfully carry out the activities associated with effective human resource management.[4] Consequently, managers who gain a competitive advantage at human resource management activities place themselves squarely in a superior position for upward movement and greater opportunities and responsibilities. While the bulk of this chapter focuses on the key elements of effective human resource management, the actual practices in HR are particularly affected by laws and regulations. Managers need to be familiar with these laws and regulations and how they affect different HR activities. Consequently, a summary of them appears at the end of the chapter.

Brunswick's dilemma illustrates two key issues: (1) firms' ability to survive and prosper in the future is increasingly a function of the human resources they have and (2) as a manager, your career success or failure depends on how well you manage human resources. We can all think of firms whose success seems tied to products, technology, or strategy, but not people. Where would Apple be without the Macintosh, iMac, or iPod? Would Sprint be an important competitor in long distance without fiber optics? Clearly, these and other "golden eggs" seem to lie at the heart of certain firms' fortunes. True, but the real key to any golden egg is the goose that laid it. Such valuable resources do not just materialize. Without bright, capable, and motivated people, Apple would not have developed the Macintosh or iMac. Without people who recognized the growing need for data transmission and the superiority of fiber optics for transmitting digital data, Sprint would not have seized the advantage in this arena. In short, people invent and utilize technology; people gather, analyze, and disseminate information; people formulate and implement strategy. Thus, Brunswick's dependence on people for its future success is not unique or even uncommon. Both the quality of a firm's strategy and the success of its implementation depend on getting the right people and maximizing their performance and potential.

THE STRATEGIC ROLE OF HUMAN RESOURCE MANAGEMENT

As we discussed in the chapter on strategic management, competitive advantage comes through creating and leveraging products that provide value to customers but are hard for competitors to imitate. For example, Southwest Airlines has been one of the few airlines to consistently deliver profits since deregulation in the late 1970s in the United States. Why? Is it unique planes? No. Southwest only operates Boeing 737s, but anyone can buy these planes from Boeing. Is Southwest's secret to competitive advantage its reservation system? No. In fact, until the Internet made it easy for many people to go online to make reservations, Southwest was not part of the major reservation systems that most travel agents used in booking flights. This actually put Southwest at a competitive disadvantage because travel agents would have to call Southwest, rather than look on their computer screens as they could do for United, American, Delta, and other airlines, in order to find out prices and availability, and book a reservation. So what has accounted for Southwest's competitive success? By their own account, Southwest's executives believe it is their people and the way they manage their human resources that has been and continues to be the key to their success.

HR and Strategy Formulation

While the traditional view of HR as a function has not involved strategy formulation, it is a perspective that is changing.[5] Increasingly, executives are looking at their people and their present and future capabilities to determine what the company's competitive strategy ought to be.[6] As one executive put it, "In football, if you have a quarterback with a great arm, does it make sense to design an offense built upon the run?" Recall from our discussion of competitive advantage in the strategic management chapter that competitive advantage comes largely from creating value for customers through resources that are hard for competitors to copy. The capabilities employees possess are often hard for competitors to copy. To the extent that these capabilities also create value for customers, they become a source of competitive advantage and can therefore play a role in what the company's competitive strategy ought to be.

HR and Strategy Implementation

Clearly, not every strategy is or should be driven by a firm's human resources. However, it is hard to think of a strategy that can be effectively implemented without the proper management of its human resources. For example, earlier in this text we introduced Nordstrom's and how it competed in part through superior service. This superior service comes largely from Nordstrom employees, not technology, the physical structure of the stores, or other resources in the company. If Nordstrom managers do not select employees who have a natural orientation to customer service, if it does not train them in specific techniques and practices of customer service, if it does not compensate and reward them for superior customer service, then the superior customer service that is a core element of the company's strategy will fail to materialize. Consequently, both executives in charge of the HR function and managers throughout an organization need to manage the human resources in a way that supports and helps implement the strategy.[7]

Exhibit 15.1 incorporates these various perspectives into a strategic framework of human resource management (HRM). As the figure illustrates, specific human resource activities (planning, job analysis, recruiting, selecting, socialization and training, job design, performance appraisal, compensation, and development) exist within the context of the firm's strategy and environment. The fit of these human resource activities with the strategy and environment leads to competitive advantage for the organization and for the individual manager.[8]

exhibit 15.1

General Framework of HRM

HUMAN RESOURCE MANAGEMENT ACTIVITIES THAT GET THE RIGHT PEOPLE

To this point, we have explored the link between competitive advantage and human resource management and have also briefly examined the importance of the fit between HRM practices and the firm's strategy. We now outline the key HRM activities listed in Exhibit 15.1.

Simplified, there are two main HRM goals: (1) getting the right people and (2) maximizing their performance and potential. Although there are a number of activities related to these two general categories, all managers need to get the right people into the right place at the right time and then help them maximize their performance and future potential. For example, a brilliantly creative person might be right for a firm that competes through product innovation such as 3M but the wrong employee for an organization that competes via cost leadership and low fares such as America West Airlines.

Getting the right people cannot be accomplished without understanding and aligning HRM activities with the corporate strategy. Although it is necessary to discuss each of these activities separately, you should not forget that they are related and that success or failure in one activity can significantly influence the success or failure of another. For example, Disney's ability to select "cast members" (employees) with a happy disposition to work in its theme parks enhances the effectiveness of the "friendly service" training they receive. These two activities combined help keep millions of guests pouring through the gates into the parks each year.

Planning

Human resource planning activity is concerned with assessing the future human resource needs (demand), determining the availability of the type of people needed (supply), and creating plans for how to meet the need (fulfillment). At the organizational level, HR planning is sometimes a shared responsibility among HR specialists and executives in other functional areas like accounting, finance, marketing, and operations.

Forecasting Demand   The key objective is to determine how many and what type of employees the firm needs at a point in the future, say, one or five years hence, considering the firm's strategy and the general business and economic environment. For example, many Japanese electronics firms estimated in the mid-1990s that the product segments of music and games would increase at double-digit rates for 20 years. Much of the assembly work of putting together the various components of the music- and game-playing machines would require relative low-skilled and low-cost labor.

Assessing Supply   At the time, much of what these firms produced for export to other countries was assembled in Japan. As they looked at the future labor supply in Japan, two key facts emerged. First, based on demographic trends, it was clear that the population of Japan in the age range of 19 to 35 (the most common age of assembly workers) was going to shrink. Second, based on economic growth expectations, many of these companies forecast that labor costs were going to increase significantly. Thus, many of the managers in electronics firms in Japan determined that the demand for low-cost and low-skilled labor for product assembly would outstrip the supply of these types of workers in Japan.

Formulating Fulfillment Plans   The firms analyzed that demand would outstrip supply by approximately 2 to 3 million people by the turn of the century. To address this shortfall, many of these senior executives and government officials examined the possibility of allowing immigrants into Japan to fill the labor shortage and lower the labor costs. However, this approach generally lacked political and popular support. As a consequence, many executives of these electronic firms decided to automate some aspects of component manufacturing and also examined the automation of final assembly. However, while some components could be manufactured cost-effectively through automation, automating final assembly looked to be too costly. As a consequence, most of the executives in these firms decided to aggressively move final assembly operations offshore to countries with a good supply of semi-skilled and low-cost labor such as China, Vietnam, and Indonesia.

Even though the human resource management department might be specially charged with looking at HR planning, individual managers must also be skilled planners as well. As a manager you will want to be able to determine the number and types of employees you will need in your units, assess the supply in the marketplace, and develop a plan to get the right people. Just as with the organization, as a manager, you cannot distinguish between a "right" and "wrong" employee without thoughtful consideration of your firm's strategy. For example, after his first departure from Apple, Steven Jobs started a company called NeXT to compete in the high-end computer and work station market. Within just a few years, Jobs decided to shift the firm's strategic orientation from hardware to software. For managers in product development, this meant that they needed more programmers than engineers and that they initially needed fewer employees overall. Because the market for software programmers was tight, NeXT managers focused their efforts on attracting dissatisfied programmers at other companies and highlighted the exciting things that they were doing at NeXT.

To fulfill your employment needs, you may need to consider the use of *part-time or temporary* employees. This can give you the flexibility to meet significant but temporary increased demand for employees. It allows you to reduce your workforce more easily if demand falls as well as to try out employees before hiring them permanently if demand remains strong.

You may decide to *outsource* specific workforce demands.[9] For example, many companies now outsource their call center jobs involving customer service or telemarketing to other companies such as Convergys Communication. In a sense, this offloads the fluctuations in demand for call center representatives to another company that specializes in these tasks and has concentrated capabilities in hiring and training people for these jobs.

Job Analysis

Job analysis is a critical but often overlooked human resource activity. **Job analysis** is concerned primarily with determining the scope and depth of jobs and the requisite skills, abilities, and knowledge that people need to perform their jobs successfully.

job analysis determination of the scope and depth of jobs and the requisite skills, abilities, and knowledge that people need to perform their jobs successfully.

For example, when Motorola decided to shift its strategic orientation away from simply filling customer orders to world-class quality, managers analyzed the nature of factory jobs under the new strategy. They discovered that factory jobs required employees who could read at the ninth grade level and who had a basic understanding of simple statistics such as means and standard deviations. This analysis provided valuable information that Motorola incorporated into its HR planning process. Unfortunately for Motorola, many of its current employees at the time were underqualified. Managers had to decide whether to try to train the existing employees and get them to the level required or whether to let them go and replace them with more capable employees who could handle the new quality control systems and procedures.[10] In the end, Motorola did both but focused heavily on training existing employees.

The data and insights that come from a job analysis are typically used to create a *job description*, or a list of duties and capabilities required for the job. Typically, this leads to a *job specification*, or a statement that describes the skills, experience, and education that a candidate should have to perform the job.

Recruiting

Recruiting is primarily concerned with determining what the desired candidate pool consists of and attracting those candidates to specific positions within the organization. As with the other activities we have already discussed, the desired pool of candidates cannot be determined without considering the firm's strategy. Whom you want is a function of whom you need. Whether you can get the type of person you want is a different story. Can you offer them what they want? Can your competitor offer them more?

Let's consider the first question. The key to knowing whether you can offer people what they want is to find out what they do want. Consider the case of UPS in Germany. When UPS expanded into Germany, managers had a difficult time selecting good drivers because they simply were not attracting high-quality applicants. Several factors contributed to this, most notably the fact that the brown UPS uniforms were the same color as those of the Nazi youth group during World War II. UPS was not offering what high-quality prospective drivers wanted and was, in fact, offering something (brown uniforms) they did not want.

The second question is not simply a matter of whether you can offer candidates more money than your competitors. People are not motivated only by money. Rather, it is important to consider the work environment, the nature of the work, the flexibility of the benefits, and the opportunity for advancement as factors that could attract candidates to your organization.

Once you have assessed these two questions, a variety of approaches can be used to generate job candidates. Each one has its strengths and weaknesses and, as a consequence, should be used as the situation dictates. Some companies try to persuade firms and their managers to go "high-tech" to select their candidates. These companies use tools like skills tests, psychological tests, and even artificial intelligence to make candidate selection faster, cheaper, and better. After reading A Manager's Challenge, "Guru's Gamble on a High-Tech System," what do you think? Would you be inclined to use such a service?

job posting an internal recruiting method whereby a job, its pay, level, description, and qualifications are posted or announced to all current employees.

Job Posting **Job posting** is a popular internal recruiting method whereby a job, its pay, level, description, and qualifications are posted or announced to all current employees. Increasingly, posting is done electronically through e-mail. Job postings help ensure that all qualified employees have an opportunity to apply for a particular job. Job posting can also help current employees have a better idea of the types of jobs available and the qualifications needed to be successful in those jobs. This can allow them to plan their careers. On the negative side, job postings can generate unqualified applicants who need to receive explanations about why they were unqualified and did not get the job. Without adequate explanation, they are likely to wonder whether the job was really "open" when it was posted. If employees begin to doubt the process of posting jobs, it can generate skepticism and limit candidates and therefore also the posting's effectiveness.

Advertisements Advertisements in general or specialized publications can also be an effective means of generating job candidates. National business newspapers such as the *Wall Street Journal* cast a wide net. Professional magazines such as *HRMagazine* cast a very specialized net. Regional or local publications, such as your city newspaper, focus on the local labor pool. Increasingly, the Internet is being used as a source of advertising job openings. As use of the Internet matures, it is likely to develop regional and industrial segments that will facilitate a more targeted advertising of jobs.[11] The major downside of advertisements is the time and expense of screening out and rejecting unqualified candidates.

Employment Agencies Employment agencies can also be effective in generating job candidates in some fields. The agency's effectiveness is largely a function of how well it understands your organization and the requirements of the specific job. Agencies tend to be expensive and usually not cost-effective

tech|nol|ogy

a manager's challenge

Guru's Gamble on a High-Tech Selection System

How can managers seeking to fill an open position determine which candidate represents the best match with their company's needs and work style? Former Guru.com founder Ray Marcy thought he had a high-tech answer to this perennial human resource management challenge. Marcy realized that managers who post job openings often receive hundreds of responses. Then they have to spend hours (perhaps even days) wading through each applicant's credentials to narrow the field and select the most qualified candidates.

Marcy proposed a radically different approach to the selection process. He believed that Guru could use artificial intelligence (AI) software to sift through candidates for open positions and identify a handful of highly qualified finalists from which client companies could select. As a result, managers seeking to hire a new employee would invest far less time in the selection process—but wind up with a far better match between the candidate, the job, and the company.

To implement this approach at Guru, Marcy hired an industrial psychologist to develop psychological tests that would show what companies were actually seeking in job candidates. In addition, he hired an AI expert to create the technology that would electronically evaluate candidates for posted jobs. Despite this high-tech emphasis, Marcy also recognized the importance of maintaining human contact during the selection process.

If you were a manager posting an open job on the Web site, a Guru "talent agent" would immediately call to learn more about the position's requirements and the company's work style. The agent would ask you if you are seeking to hire someone who is independent, accommodating, risk-taking, creative, or has other work-style traits. Next, the talent agent uses the AI system to identify qualified candidates from among those in Guru's database and other job-search databases. Using Guru's online system, these candidates complete a work-style assessment test so the talent agent can compare their styles with the styles desired by the hiring manager. Finally, the talent agent sends the hiring manager information on the three candidates whose background and work styles most closely match what you are seeking. The entire process, from the time you submit an open position

As a manager, would you be inclined to use skills tests, psychological tests, and even artificial intelligence to ferret out the best job applicant? If so, how much would you be willing to pay to screen each candidate? What is the value of this approach for selecting the best employees?

to the time you receive a listing of matching candidates, takes 48 hours or less.

Guru's fee for screening and recommending candidates was $7,500, about one-third of the cost of using a traditional search firm to fill an open position. However, some techno-savvy companies have built their own internal systems to help their managers select candidates for open positions, and other online job sites have similar tools.

Moreover, before Guru could fully capitalize on the artificial intelligence screening system, the marketplace changed dramatically. Tech firms laid off thousands of workers following a crash in the economy's tech sector, and employers found themselves less willing to pay high fees to hire them. The result was that assessment didn't end up becoming the mainstay of Guru.com's business—hiring freelance activity did. Nonetheless, many placement firms do use these elaborate screening methods.

Source: Sarah Fister Gale, "Putting Job Candidates to the Test," *Workforce Management, 2003 Vender Directory*, vol. 82, issue 11, p. 90; Stephanie Clifford, "Guru's Gamble," *Business 2.0,* July 2002, pp. 92–93.

for low-level and low-paying jobs. In contrast, most openings at the senior management level use executive search firms as part of their recruiting efforts. As their fee for finding an acceptable candidate, these firms typically charge at least one-third of the successful candidate's first-year compensation.

Employee Referrals Managers may find current employees a great source for job candidates. Current employees with tenure in the organization understand the organization, its culture, and often the particular job that needs to be filled. They usually know something about an applicant as well: work history, educational background, skills and abilities, personal characteristics, and so on. Given that their recommendation puts their own reputation on the line to some degree, current employees tend to recommend individuals whom they believe will do well. Their personal relationship with the recommended candidate allows employees not to just sell the company on the individual but to sell the individual on the company. In general, research suggests that current employee referrals is one of the most effective recruiting methods. Employee referrals are less effective when the firm is looking for a different type of employee than it currently has. Current employees tend to recommend people like themselves. So a company pushing into international activities or new technology may find its employees don't know people in these new areas to then refer.

School Placement Centers School placement centers are also a popular source of job candidates. Placement center offices can range from those found in high schools, technical schools, and junior colleges to universities and advanced degree programs. If given adequate time and clear job specifications and requirements, school placement centers can do much of the prescreening, filtering out unqualified candidates. This can save the firm significant time and money in the recruiting process. Schools are increasingly using video conferencing capabilities to set up "virtual" interviews and online job fairs. Technology helps firms broaden the field, allowing them to reach places to which they may not be able to travel physically. The weakness of school placement centers is that they often deal with so many companies and students that they might not know enough about either to conduct ideal screening.

Internet Companies are discovering that the Internet is a powerful recruiting tool. Most major companies use their corporate Web sites to list jobs and attract candidates. In addition to using their own sites to attract candidates, companies are increasingly using sites such as Monster.com. Monster.com now has over 20 million résumés in its data base and is the number-one online job search site. Careerbuilder.com and Yahoo's Hotjobs.com are two other sites where companies frequently post ads.

Selecting

Successful selection is a function of effective planning, analyzing, and recruiting, as well as applying appropriate selection techniques.[12] Even if you get the right set of candidates before you, you need to be able to determine which one is best for the job. For example, international banks such as Bank of America or Citibank have no trouble attracting people to overseas positions, because international experience is important in the increasingly global banking industry. However, managers selected for overseas assignments sometimes fail and have to return home early at a cost of about $150,000 per employee. The early returns not only cost the company but also hurt employees' careers.

These failures are partly a function of poor specification of the characteristics that predicted success in an overseas assignment and limited use of effective selection techniques.[13]

One of the key points to keep in mind relative to any selection technique is that if legally challenged, the organization must be able to demonstrate that the selection technique is valid. A **valid selection technique** is one that can differentiate between those who would be more successful in the job and those who would be less successful. For example, educational background is often used in selecting new hires because knowledge typically has a proven relationship with job performance. That is, it is hard to perform well in a job for which you do not have the requisite education and knowledge. There are a variety of selection techniques; each has its own strengths and weaknesses.

Interviews The most widely used selection technique is the interview. In most cases, the interview is unstructured. An **unstructured interview** is one in which interviewers have a general idea of the types of questions they might ask but do not have a standard set. As a consequence, interviewers might ask different candidates different questions. With different questions and responses, comparing candidates can be like comparing apples and oranges. Not surprisingly, a major weakness of unstructured interviews is that they tend to have low levels of validity.[14] In contrast, **structured interviews**, in which interviewers ask a standard set of questions of all candidates about qualifications and capabilities related to job performance, can be quite valid. Validity can be further enhanced by carefully recording interviewee responses on a standardized form and taking approximately the same time in each interview. Exhibit 15.2 provides tips for interviewers and Exhibit 15.3 provides tips for interviewees.[15]

Work Sampling There are a variety of techniques that could be classified as work sampling. Essentially, all these techniques attempt to simulate or exactly duplicate the job the person would be doing if hired. The underlying rationale is straightforward: If you perform poorly or well in the work sample, you would likely perform similarly in the real job. In general, the main strength of work sampling techniques is that they make a reasonably accurate prediction

Valid Selection Techniques
by Stewart Black

Q&A
One**Key**
www.prenhall.com/onekey

valid selection technique a screening process that differentiates those who would be successful in a job from those who would not

unstructured interview one in which interviewers have a general idea of the questions they might ask but do not have a standard set

structured interview one in which interviewers ask a standard set of questions of all candidates about qualifications and capabilities related to job performance

1. Plan the interview by reviewing the candidate and the job specifications.
2. Establish rapport with a friendly greeting and start the interview with a nonjob question.
3. Follow structured set of questions.
4. Avoid questions that require or solicit a simple *yes* or *no* response.
5. Try not to telegraph, or give cues for, the desired answer.
6. Make sure the candidate has plenty of time to answer—do not monopolize the conversation.
7. Listen carefully and paraphrase key candidate answers to be sure you understand what they meant to say.
8. Ask for specific, not general, examples of the candidate's experience and accomplishments.
9. Leave time at the end of the interview to answer questions from the candidate.
10. At the close make sure the candidate knows what the next steps are and approximate timing.
11. After the candidate leaves, review your notes and highlight important points while they are fresh in your mind.

exhibit 15.2
Tips for Interviewers

exhibit 15.3

Tips for Interviewees

- Prepare for the interview by researching the company through articles and its own Web site.
- Smile and provide a warm greeting and firm handshake if the interviewer extends his or her hand.
- Make sure that your overall appearance (hair style, clothing, makeup, and so on) match the nature of the business and culture of the company.
- Watch your nonverbal behavior to ensure that you maintain good eye contact and convey enthusiasm without being overly expressive with your hands or other body movements.
- Try to solicit the interviewer's needs early in the interview.
- Early in the interview be sure to get a complete picture of the job through questions such as, "Can you tell about what has led people to succeed in this job in the past?"
- Explicitly relate yourself and capabilities to the interviewer's needs through statements such as, "You mentioned that one of the keys to this position is the ability to motivate others. In my experience at XYZ. . . ."
- Take your time before answering; you do not need to begin talking the instant the interviewer asks a question.
- Conclude the interview by thanking the person for the opportunity and expressing your interest in the company and the position.

of how an individual will do in a job. The main drawback is that they tend to be time- and cost-intensive. Research supports the validity of work sampling techniques.

assessment centers a work sampling technique in which candidates perform a number of exercises, each one designed to capture one or more key aspects of the job

Assessment Centers **Assessment centers** utilize work sampling techniques. Typically, candidates are required to go through a number of exercises, and each exercise is designed to capture one or more key aspects of the job. For example, a supervisor's job might require good prioritization skills. The assessment center might have an "in-basket" exercise to assess this skill. The exercise consists of an in-basket filled with letters, memos, and reports that the candidate must read and then prioritize. The individual's ability to recognize and respond to high-priority items comes out during the exercise. In general, research supports assessment centers as an effective selection method for new hires as well as for individuals moving up in a firm.[16]

work simulation situations in which job candidates perform work they would do if hired or work that closely simulates the tasks they would perform

Work Simulation **Work simulation** techniques typically involve situations in which job candidates perform work that they would do if hired or work that closely simulates the tasks they would perform. For example, when Nissan set up its new assembly plant in Tennessee, it required potential line workers to assemble flashlights to assess manual dexterity, a key requirement for assembly line workers. At Motorola, technical writing job candidates are given a piece of equipment, shown how to use it, given time to practice using it, and then are required to write a technical description of the equipment and operation manual. This gives Motorola a clear idea of those who can write technical material well.

Written Tests Written tests are also widely used. This is due in part to the fact that the tests can be administered cost-effectively to a large number of job candidates. Cognitive ability and intelligence tests measure an individual's general cognitive complexity and intellectual ability. Although the validity of these tests has been mixed, they do seem to be acceptable predictors for supervisory and management jobs. Personality tests are more controversial. While they can be reasonably good predictors of people's ability to work well with other particular personalities, they have not been good overall predictors of job performance.[17] Integrity tests are a more recent development. These tests try to assess the general level of a person's honesty. In general, they seem to be of debatable validity.[18] Written tests have the advantage of being inexpensive to administer, but the results are more valid regarding general performance and success than for success in a specific job.

Background and Reference Checks Background checks attempt to verify factual information that applicants provide. Between 10 and 15 percent of applicants either lie about or exaggerate factual information. As a consequence, checking to make sure applicants graduated with the degrees they claim, from the schools they cite, and held the jobs with the responsibilities they describe can be quite valuable. The objective of reference checks is to get candid evaluations from those who have worked with the job candidate. However, recent legal judgments against past employers who made negative statements about previous employees have led employers to provide only factual information, such as title, years employed, and so on. Consequently, reference checks are declining in value.

Physical Examinations Companies that require physical examinations as part of the selecting process typically do so because the job has high physical demands. In addition to helping them select physically qualified candidates, physical exams also protect firms. First, the physical exam information may help firms reduce insurance claims. Second, it may help protect the firm from lawsuits by identifying high-risk applicants, such as someone who might experience a heart attack from the physical strains of the job. However, given recent legislation in the United States, managers must be careful to ensure that the physical requirements being screened in the examination are in fact related to job performance and are not sources for discrimination.[19] For example, Burlington Northern Santa Fe Railway required its employees to take a medical examination as a method to evaluate a range of employee injury claims. In March 2000, BNSF included in these medical exams a genetic factor only for employees claiming work-related carpal tunnel syndrome. In 2001 a court ordered the company to stop testing employees because the test had nothing to do with an employee's current degree of carpal tunnel syndrome. On the other hand, physical examinations can be used for screening out people who are inappropriate for the physical demands of the job. Drug testing is another screening mechanism companies use to ensure that employees' judgment and capabilities are not impaired while on the job.

HUMAN RESOURCE MANAGEMENT ACTIVITIES THAT MAXIMIZE PERFORMANCE

Once the right people are in the right positions, the organization needs to ensure that they are performing well. What constitutes maximum performance and potential is largely a function of the organization's strategy. For example, 3M chooses to compete on new-product innovation and strives to have the majority of its revenue come from products that are less than five years old. It, therefore, needs employees who can think of and test new ideas. For 3M, maximum performance and potential are largely defined in terms of employee innovations. Based on this, 3M undertakes a variety of activities to maximize employees' creativity. Five specific categories of activities can significantly influence employee performance and potential.

Socialization and Training

Just as early life experiences can shape the general character, personality, and behavior of people, so too can early training and socialization experiences shape important aspects of employees' performance.[20] For example, early training and socialization affects (1) the probability that new hires will stay with the firm, (2) the extent to which they will perform well, and (3) the degree to which they will develop to their full potential.[21]

Managers can use a variety of training methods to enhance the performance and potential of employees. We cover several here. Although early career training is important, in today's changing environment, training and learning are likely to become career-long.

Orientation One of the first opportunities for an organization to shape the expectations and behavior of new employees is during orientation programs.[22] Typically, these programs provide a broad overview of the industry, the company and its business activities, its key competitors, and general information about working in the company (such as key policies, pay procedures, and fringe benefits). Work unit orientation sessions are typically more narrow and are generally designed to help the new employee get up to speed on the new job, co-workers, work unit policies and procedures, and expectations. To maximize the effectiveness of orientation programs, managers should consider the following recommendations:[23]

- Keep paperwork to a minimum to avoid information overload. Do include paperwork that must be completed immediately.
- Include an informal meeting with the individual's immediate supervisor.
- Alternate heavy information, such as that related to benefits and insurance, with lighter live or video presentations from corporate officers.
- Provide a glossary of terms unique to the organization.
- Match each new employee with a "buddy" (that is an experienced worker) based more on personality compatibility than similarity of jobs.

On-the-Job Training Techniques On-the-job training (OJT) is the most widely used training technique in organizations. As Exhibit 15.4 illustrates, there are a wide variety of techniques that a manager can use to train employees. Over your career, you will likely be exposed to most, if not all, of these approaches.

Off-the-job Training Techniques Off-the-job training can also be used with positive effect. The most common off-the-job training approach is the classroom-based program. The program may be only an hour, or it may be several weeks in length. It may be conducted by in-house experts (employees of the company) or by outside experts from industry or education fields, such as a university professor. The program may involve lectures, case studies, discussions, videos, or simulations. Individual-based programs are also increasingly popular. Formal correspondence courses are sometimes used when employees have different learning speeds and motivations but the learning objectives are clear. Computer-assisted programs are also used when employees have different learning speeds and motivations. Current technology now allows for text, graphics, and a variety of visual displays as well as interaction. Many programs now adjust content and difficulty level in real time based on how well the individual is doing.

exhibit 15.4

On-the-job Training Techniques

1. *Expanded Responsibilities.* This training technique expands the job duties, assignments, and responsibilities of an individual.
2. *Job Rotation.* Also called *cross-training*, this practice moves individuals to various types of jobs within the organization at the same level or next-immediate-higher level for periods of time from an hour or two to as long as a year.
3. *Staff Development Meetings.* Meetings are usually held offsite to discuss facts of each individual's job and to develop ideas for improving job performance.
4. *"Assistant to" Positions.* Promising employees serve as staff assistants to higher-skill-level jobs for a specified period of time (often one to three months) to become more familiar with the higher-skilled positions in the organization.
5. *Problem-Solving Conferences.* Conferences are held to solve a specific problem being experienced by a group or the organization as a whole. It involves brainstorming and other creative means to come up with solutions to the basic problems.
6. *Mentoring.* A guide or knowledgeable person higher up in the organization helps a new employee "learn the ropes" of the organization and provides other advice.
7. *Special Assignments.* Special tasks or responsibilities are given to an individual for a specified period of time. The assignment may be writing up a report, investigating the feasibility for a new project, process, service, or product, preparing a newsletter, or evaluating a company policy or procedure.
8. *Company Trainers.* Special programs can cover such topics as safety, new personnel procedures, new product or services, affirmative action, and technical programs.
9. *Outside Consultants.* Recognized experts are brought to the company to conduct training on such topics as goal setting, communications, assessment techniques, safety, and other current topics of importance. They often supplement training done by company trainers.
10. *Consultant Advisory Reviews.* Experts in specialized fields meet with various managers and employee groups to investigate and help solve particular problems. The emphasis is on problem solving rather than training.
11. *Reading Matter.* A formal program is created to circulate books, journals, selected articles, new business material, and so on to selected employees. An effective program also includes periodic scheduled meetings to discuss the material.
12. *Apprenticeship.* Training is provided through working under a journeyman or master in a craft. The apprentice works alongside a person skilled in the craft and is taught by that person. Apprenticeship programs also often include some classroom work.

Source: Adapted from W. P. Anthony, D. L. Perrewé, and K. M. Kacmar, *Strategic Human Resource Management* (Fort Worth, TX: Harcourt Brace Jovanovich, 1993).

Training Objectives Orientation and training programs can have a variety of objectives. However, at a fundamental level, these programs are intended to address employee technical, interpersonal, or conceptual abilities. Technical skills can range from being able to read and perform simple math to being able to program a supercomputer. As mentioned earlier, when Motorola made a strategic commitment to quality, it discovered that over a third of its employees could not read, write, or do math at a level that the new quality control program required. This discovery led to a massive technical training effort.

Because very few employees work in isolation, improved interpersonal abilities are the target of a wide variety of training programs. Programs might address skills such as effective listening, conflict resolution, negotiation, and coaching. In a recent study, executives cited poor interpersonal skills as one of the biggest problems in new college or M.B.A. graduates.[24]

The final category is conceptual abilities. This category includes a variety of skills and abilities, such as problem solving, decision making, planning, and organizing. A given training program might be designed to address just one of these categories, two, or all four.

Regardless of the category the program is designed to target, most successful programs provide participants with several things:

- An understanding of what is and is not the correct behavior.
- A clear knowledge of why certain behaviors are correct or incorrect.
- Sufficient opportunities to practice the desired behaviors.
- Feedback on performance with further opportunities to practice and improve.

An important part of well-designed training is an evaluation of its effectiveness.[25] Perhaps the simplest means of assessing training is what is often called the "smile index," or the satisfaction of participants with the training. This is quite often gathered just after the training is finished via a questionnaire. Clearly, it is unlikely that any training participants do not like will be retained by them and have a positive impact on their knowledge or behaviors. However, the fact that participants enjoyed the training or thought it was useful does not guarantee that it will have the intended impact. A more rigorous assessment of training would involve a pre-training and post-training assessment. For example, if the training were primarily intended to convey knowledge, then a "pre and post" assessment design would involve assessing the knowledge level of participants before the training and at some point afterward. These basics would also apply to an assessment of the skills they learned. In addition, if the training is intended to improve job performance, such as quality, you might assess the impact of the training by comparing important metrics, such as defects per 1,000, before and after the training. While a reduction in defects might tell you if the training had the intended effect, it does not tell you if the training was cost-effective. Determining this is much more complicated. In general you have to assess both the direct (such as the cost of trainers) and indirect costs (such as the productivity lost due to workers being in the training instead of on the job). You then have to compare these costs to the benefits, such as the savings from fewer returns due to higher quality. However, one key challenge is determining the period over which to add up the benefits. For example, if higher quality is saving you $100 per day in returns, should you estimate the total value of these savings over a week, a month, a year, or several years? Your answer dramatically influences the total benefit quantification and therefore the final determination of whether the training costs are exceeded by the benefits, and if so by how much.

Job Design

job design the structuring or restructuring of key job components

Job design is focused on the structuring or restructuring of key job components. A job design typically includes the responsibilities. Thus, while job analysis focuses on what the components of a job are, job design is the process of determining which components ought to be put together and how they should be arranged to enhance performance.[26] For example, does an assembly-line worker work in isolation and repetitively attach a given part to a product, or does he work in a team with others building an entire unit? Dell is one company that has assembly-line workers work in teams that assemble entire computer units. In some texts, job design would be much earlier in the sequence than we have placed it. In general, for a brand new job that has never been filled before, job design does take place early in the sequence. Also, traditionally jobs were designed and then appropriate people were selected to fit into the jobs. The reality of today's dynamic environment has changed that approach. In some cases, it is possible and appropriate to design jobs and then try to match people to them, but in other cases, jobs might need to be designed or redesigned to fit the available people. There are also situations that require a combination of both fitting the person to the job and fitting the job to the person. For example, **job sharing** involves two people working part-time in the same job. Effective job sharing requires two individuals who can coordinate well and have similar capabilities. It has become popular with working mothers who are faced with balancing family and economic/professional demands. Increasingly, technology is allowing managers to design and redesign jobs in ways not possible before. For example, JetBlue, a relatively new airline and one of the most profitable, saved money by having its reservation agents work from home instead of putting money into large call centers.

During the early and mid-1990s, reengineering became a popular concept regarding the design or redesign of work. **Reengineering** is the fundamental rethinking and radical redesign of business processes to achieve dramatic improvements in critical, contemporary measures of performance, such as cost, quality, service, or speed.[27] Computer and information technology today have allowed organizations to design more enriched, satisfying, and productive jobs. Increasingly, organizations are looking at ways to give employees more flexibility in the way their work is accomplished. Technology is one way to provide that flexibility. Maximizing subordinates' performance and your unit's performance is your goal as a manager regarding effective job design.

job sharing situation in which two people share the same job by each working part-time

reengineering fundamental rethinking and radical redesign of business processes to achieve dramatic improvements in critical, contemporary measures of performance, such as cost, quality, service, or speed

Performance Appraisal

Before organizations or managers can encourage or correct the actions of employees, they must know how the employees are doing. Performance appraisal is concerned with (1) establishing performance objectives and standards, (2) measuring performance against those standards, and (3) providing feedback to employees concerning that measurement and evaluation.[28] As we stated before, the objectives of the job and the standards against which performance is measured must be driven by the strategy of the firm. When Motorola decided that it would compete on quality, it set "six sigma" as its standard. A six-sigma quality standard allows for only 3.4 defects per 1 million opportunities. For Motorola, this had wide-ranging implications from the factory floor to the corporate kitchen. On the floor, this meant that only 3.4 products per million could have a defect. For the kitchen, it meant that only 3.4 muffins for every million baked could be burnt. While six sigma was not immediately achievable for Motorola, the strategic intent did have a significant impact on the standard against which employees' performance was evaluated.

For most managers, performance appraisal is perhaps the most important, yet most difficult, human resource activity. This difficulty is not only because of the complexity of evaluating past performance and setting future performance targets, but because performance appraisals involve communicating to employees how they are doing relative to established targets. Often employees are not quite measuring up to established standards and require feedback for corrective action; however, few people like to give or receive negative feedback. Still, without this feedback, neither individuals nor organizations can maximize performance. As a consequence, all managers need to understand the key factors that drive effective performance appraisal systems and be skilled at implementing them.

exhibit 15.5
Graphic Rating Scale

Employee name:			Dept.		
	Excellent	Good	Average	Fair	Poor
1. Quality of work	☐	☐	☐	☐	☐
2. Quantity of work	☐	☐	☐	☐	☐
3. Cooperation	☐	☐	☐	☐	☐
4. Dependability	☐	☐	☐	☐	☐
5. Initiative	☐	☐	☐	☐	☐
6. Job knowledge	☐	☐	☐	☐	☐
7. Attitude	☐	☐	☐	☐	☐

Graphic Rating Scales Perhaps the most popular method of providing performance feedback is through graphic rating scales (see Exhibit 15.5 for an example). A graphic rating scale typically lists a set of qualities on which the employee is evaluated. The level of performance on each of these items is then rated in terms of a graduated scale. The scale typically ranges from 1 to 5. The degree of specificity concerning the definition of each point on the scale can range from one-word descriptors (e.g., 1 = poor) to complete sentences (e.g., 1 = Does not meet the minimum standards).

The popularity of graphic ratings is due to two main factors. First, they are relatively quick and easy for managers to complete. Given that most managers have many employees whom they must evaluate and that managers typically are not rewarded for writing up high-quality evaluations, they have a natural incentive to complete the evaluations as quickly as possible. Second, because the evaluation items and the rating scale are common across employees, it is easy to quantify the results and compare employees' performance ratings.

However, there are two key limitations that as a manager you should keep in mind relative to graphic rating scales. First, the characteristics being evaluated may not be clearly defined; thus they are left to individual interpretation. Consequently, one manager might focus her interpretation of "interpersonal skills" on conflict resolution abilities, while another manager might focus his interpretation on listening skills. Given the two different interpretations, it is difficult to compare the employees evaluated by the two different managers. Furthermore, the two different managers might have different interpretations of the rating scale. One manager might only allow the top 5 percent of employees to receive a high rating of "5 = excellent." Another manager might interpret a "5" as applicable to the top 20 percent of employees. Once again, the different interpretations would make comparing employees rated by different managers difficult.[29] This incomparability is important because over 85 percent of firms use performance appraisals to determine merit increases, bonuses, and promotions.

Behaviorally Anchored Rating Scales Behaviorally anchored rating scales (BARS) are designed to keep many of the advantages of the graphic rating scales and reduce the disadvantages. The general design of BARS is similar to graphic rating scales in that managers rate employee characteristics using a quantitative scale. However, the characteristics are specified in greater detail

Behaviorally Anchored Rating Scales by Stewart Black

www.prenhall.com/onekey

behaviorally anchored rating scales (BARS) a performance appraisal system in which the rater places detailed employee characteristics on a rating scale

and described in terms of behaviors rather than abstract qualities. Likewise, the scales are much more tied to descriptions of specific behaviors rather than ambiguous terms (see Exhibit 15.6 for an example). The greater specificity and link to behaviors reduces, but does not eliminate, the potential for noncomparability of ratings across different raters.[30] However, some potential for manager bias remains.[31]

360-Degree Feedback The primary rationale behind 360-degree feedback appraisal systems is that an individual's performance should be viewed from multiple perspectives.[32] Most **360-degree feedback** systems involve collecting appraisal evaluations from an individual's boss, peers, and subordinates. In some companies, evaluations are also collected from suppliers and customers,

360-degree feedback

performance appraisal system in which information is gathered from supervisors, co-workers, subordinates, and sometimes suppliers and customers

exhibit 15.6

Behaviorally Anchored Rating Scale

Source: Table from *Strategic Human Resource Management* by William P. Anthony, Pamela L. Perrewé, and K. Michele Kacmar, p. 456. Copyright © 1993 by Harcourt Brace & Company, reproduced by permission of the publisher.

Position:		
Job dimensions:		
Plans work and organizes time carefully so as to maximize resources and meet commitments.	9	
	8	Even though this associate has a report due on another project, he or she would be well prepared for the assigned discussion on your project.
	7	This associate would keep a calendar or schedule on which deadlines and activities are carefully noted, and which would be consulted before making new commitments.
	6	As program chief, this associate would mange arrangements for enlisting resources for a special project reasonably well, but would probably omit one or two details that would have to be handled by improvisation.
Plans and organizes time and effort primarily for large segments of a task. Usually meets commitments, but may overlook what are considered secondary details.	5	This associate would meet a deadline in handing in a report, but the report might be below usual standard if other deadlines occur on the same day the report is due.
	4	This associate's evaluations are likely not to reflect abilities because of overcommitments in other activities.
	3	This associate would plan more by enthusiasm than by timetable and frequently have to work late the night before an assignment is due, although it would be completed on time.
	2	This associate would often be late for meetings, although others in similar circumstances do not seem to find it difficult to be on time.
Appears to do little planning. May perform effectively, despite what seems to be a disorganized approach, by concerted effort, although deadlines may be missed.	1	This associate never makes a deadline, even with sufficient notice.

depending on the nature of interaction the employee has with these constituencies. The positive aspect of 360-degree feedback is that because data are gathered from multiple sources, employees are encouraged to focus on all key constituencies. This reduces the tendency, for example, to simply cozy up to the boss and work poorly with peers or subordinates. The major drawback is the time and energy it takes to collect, process, and effectively feed the data back to the individual. In addition, a recent study shows that 360-degree feedback might not have the validity attributed to it. Lowest-performing employees sometimes give themselves the highest ratings. These individuals were relatively easy to spot because their supervisor ratings were significantly lower. However, a problem occurs for "modest" employees, or employees who underrate themselves. This research suggests that more modest feedback recipients might be underrated by their supervisors. The study also found that peers often overestimated the performance of poor performers.[33] Estimates are that between 1995 and 2005, the percentage of U.S. companies using some form of 360-degree evaluation doubled from 25 percent to 50 percent.[34]

Effective Performance Feedback Regardless of the system of evaluating employee performance, the results of the evaluation need to be fed back effectively to employees to make a positive difference in their performance. First, if expectations concerning unacceptable, acceptable, or superior performance were not clear to the employee prior to the appraisal, negative assessments will not likely influence motivation or performance. Consequently, performance expectations must be clear and acceptable to the employee from the beginning. Second, if the employee believes that, as the manager, you are biased in your observations, your assessment will not have the effect you desire. This is why recording both positive and negative **critical incidents** is important. This simply involves the recording of important, specific incidents in which the employee's behavior and performance were above or below expectations. This record then allows you to avoid remembering only the most recent events and also facilitates your ability to talk about specifics in the appraisal interview.[35] This brings us to a brief list of recommendations for an effective performance appraisal interview:

critical incidents recording of specific incidents in which the employee's behavior and performance were above or below expectations

1. Review key work objectives, goals, or standards against which the employee's performance is measured.
2. Summarize employee's overall performance by reviewing specific positive and negative incidents.
3. Discuss causes of weak performance and listen carefully to the employee's explanation.
4. Discuss alternative means of improving future performance and encourage employee input.
5. Establish an agreed approach, timetable, and review process for future improvement.
6. Establish key objectives, timetables, and standards for the upcoming performance period.
7. Leave the meeting on an encouraging and positive note.

These may seem like simple steps, but they can go a long way to improving the effectiveness of one of the most difficult yet important human resource challenges you face as a manager. However, if they have not been part of your experience, implementing them can be a challenge, as the management team at Nissan discovered. As A Manager's Challenge, "Nissan Imports Effective HRM Techniques," reveals, while importing HR practices (especially around performance management) can help the company, they can be a challenge for both senior managers to get implemented and for middle managers to adopt and utilize.

globalization *a manager's challenge*

Nissan Imports Effective HRM Techniques

Carlos Ghosn and his management team have brought Japan-based Nissan Motors back from the brink of near-bankruptcy in large part by importing effective human resource management techniques. Born in Brazil, raised in Lebanon, and educated as an engineer in France, Ghosn speaks five languages and has worked all over the world. After French automaker Renault bought 44 percent of Nissan in 1999, top management brought him in as Nissan's CEO.

He and the 17 Renault managers who joined him at Nissan faced the difficult challenge of turning around a company hobbled by inefficient HR traditions. These traditions included focusing mainly on hiring new college graduates to replenish the management ranks, promoting managers based on seniority, compensating managers based on position, and *not* requiring managers to provide performance appraisals of or feedback to their subordinates. Ghosn and his managers drew on French and U.S. management practices to help Nissan turn around.

When he became CEO, Ghosn quickly established a series of cross-functional teams to examine company processes and recommend reforms. Instead of following the tradition of selecting team members based on their length of tenure, Ghosn and his managers chose members based on their enthusiasm for change. The teams' proposals became part of a multi-pronged plan to boost operating margin, reduce costs, and cut debt. In implementing this plan, Ghosn broke with Japanese HR tradition to reach deeper into the ranks, involving middle managers who previously would have had no say in such matters.

This and other HR changes were initially seen as radical for a Japanese company. For example, Ghosn and Kuniyuki Watanabe, the senior vice president for human resources, instituted a new system of merit-based reviews, promotions, and pay. Watanabe was familiar with these techniques from his days with Nissan's U.S. operations. "Giving your personal appraisal directly to the individual is not a job Japanese [managers] are used to doing, and I hated it [at first]," he remembers. "But it was great training for me. I'm fine with it now." However, many Japanese managers without this exposure were not so fine with it. For most managers it involved a radical change from implicit and informal goal setting and performance feedback to a more explicit and formal approach.

On top of this, Nissan changed to a more Western model of rewarding, promoting, and developing managers based on performance rather than seniority. "We're moving to a system where it doesn't matter if you've been in the company 10 years or 40 years," Watanabe adds. "If you contribute, there will be opportunity and reward." This means middle managers have to make tough judgments about performance and potential and communicate their decisions and rationale.

The changes seemed to make a positive, if painful, difference. Nissan's operating profit improved and its costs and debt dramatically fell. Another indicator of Ghosn's success: Leading Japanese corporations are following his lead and importing more effective HR practices to improve performance.

Sources: David Welch, "How Nissan Laps Detroit," *BusinessWeek*, December 23, 2003, pp. 58–60; Benjamin Fulford, "Gambatte!" *Forbes*, July 22, 2002, pp. 72+; Andy Raskin, "Voulez-Vous Completely Overhaul This Big, Slow Company and Start Making Some Cars People Actually Want Avec Moi?" *Business 2.0*, January 2002, pp. 61–67; and Chester Dawson, "Ghosn's Way," *BusinessWeek*, May 20, 2002, pp. 27+.

Compensation

Although rewards and compensation can be instrumental in getting the right people, their primary function is retaining and maximizing the performance of employees once they have entered the organization. Rewards by their nature are designed to encourage desired behaviors. As already discussed, desired behaviors must be linked to the firm's strategy. Thus, reward systems also must be linked to the firm's strategy.

Unfortunately, employees are often rewarded for doing one thing and yet expected to do another. For example, as Motorola began to shift from simply shipping products to producing world-class quality products, employees continued to be rewarded for timely shipments (with quality levels well below six sigma). Furthermore, employees were punished if shipments were late, even if quality levels of the late shipments approached six sigma. Because rewards were not aligned with the firm's new strategy, results of the six-sigma effort at Motorola were less than what senior executives expected. As another example, most stockbrokers at retail brokerage firms are rewarded with bonuses based on the volume of transactions they complete. This leads many brokers to "churn" individual investors' accounts. That is, brokers buy and sell shares in order to generate commissions even though the investment objectives of the investors did not justify such frequent transactions. As a consequence of this churning and the associated fees charged to customers, investors often take their accounts to competing brokerage firms. In the end, the reward structures encourage churning, but churning ultimately hurts firm revenue and broker commissions because customers defect.

pay structure a range of pay for a particular position or classification of positions

broadband systems pay structures in which the range of pay is large and covers a wide variety of jobs

Pay Most firms establish a pay structure based on the level in the company and type of position. A **pay structure** establishes a range of pay for a particular position or classification of positions. Traditionally, pay structures have been hierarchical and segmented. Most companies are now moving to **broadband systems** in which the range of pay is large and covers a wide variety of jobs.[36] Exhibit 15.7 provides a graphic illustration of a traditional pay structure and a more modern broadband system. The major advantage to a broadband system is the greater flexibility it gives organizations to match pay to individual value and changing labor market conditions.

exhibit 15.7

Traditional and Contemporary Pay Structures

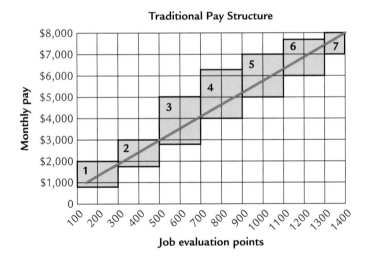

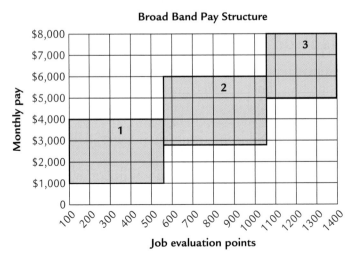

Another important pay trend is the movement away from an individual's total compensation package being primarily composed of salary and toward a greater portion of compensation being at risk.[37] **At-risk compensation** is simply pay that varies depending on specified conditions. These conditions might include the general profitability of the company; hitting particular budget, revenue, or cost savings targets for a unit; or meeting specific individual performance targets. Increasingly, companies are placing a higher portion of total compensation "at risk." This is primarily because if total compensation is made up of salary and if salaries are raised at a level comparable to inflation, inflation and subsequent salary increases can add significantly to company costs. On the other hand, if a higher percentage of compensation is tied to performance, higher compensation costs only occur with higher performance. Consequently, **incentive plans**, or approaches that tie some compensation to performance, are increasingly being spread throughout the organization, whereas traditionally they were reserved for only the most senior managers.

Benefits Traditional benefit plans include items such as medical, dental, and life insurance. In the past, companies used to compete for employees and retain them in part through offering attractive benefit plans. However, as companies added more and more features to the plans to make them attractive to a broader base of employees with differing needs, companies found themselves paying 20 to 40 percent of salary in benefits. To reduce the soaring benefit costs and still meet differing employee needs, companies began to offer **cafeteria-style plans**, in which employees had a set number of "benefit dollars" that they could use to purchase the specific benefits that fit their particular needs.

Rewards and Motivation Although much of the responsibility for reward and compensation systems is placed on the human resource department, effective rewards are more than the dollars paid out in salaries and bonuses or the dollars tied up in health care and other benefits. And though individual managers can influence pay increases and the like, they also have the greatest control over equally powerful rewards such as recognition and praise. Consequently, it is important for you to understand the broad range of rewards and how they influence the performance of your employees.

Career Systems and Development

One of the most powerful motivators for people to join organizations and to perform is the opportunity to grow and develop.[38] Career and employee development systems are designed to respond to that particular motivation and to ensure that the human capabilities needed in the organization are being developed. The **career paths** (i.e., a set and sequence of positions and experiences) organizations want employees to have to prepare for certain responsibilities is largely a function of the firm's strategy. For example, Sony is simultaneously trying to capture global efficiencies and respond to local market conditions. Sony tries to capture economic efficiencies by manufacturing nearly all of its small, handheld video cameras for markets throughout the world at a single factory in Japan. Yet, it also tries to sell these cameras in a way that appeals to the different local tastes across the globe. Consequently, Sony places a high premium on international experience for career paths that lead to the top of the organization. Sony also competes on integrated team design. That is, individuals from various functional areas such as market

at-risk compensation pay that varies depending on specified conditions, including the profitability of the company; hitting particular budget, revenue, or cost savings targets for a unit; or meeting specified individual performance targets

incentive plans systems that tie some compensation to performance

cafeteria-style plans benefit plans in which employees have a set number of "benefit dollars" that they can use to purchase benefits that fit their particular needs

career paths sets and sequences of positions and experiences

research, engineering, sales, and finance work together at the outset of a new product development. Therefore, Sony places a premium on employees' working in several functional areas over the course of their careers, or what is referred to as **cross-functional job rotation**.[39]

cross-functional job rotation opportunities for employees to work in different functional areas and gain additional expertise

While responsibility for organizational career and development systems is often that of the human resource function, individual managers are those most knowledgeable about the development needs of specific employees and are often those to whom individual employees go in search of career guidance. In addition, managers develop reputations as being effective or ineffective at employee development, and these reputations influence the quality of subordinates managers attract, which in turn affects the performance of their units. Thus, while some may view employee career pathing and development as an activity for which the HR department is responsible, it is actually a critical activity at which all managers must be skilled.

Promotion Employees can and should expand and improve their capabilities in their jobs, and development need not involve promotion. However, for a large percentage of an organization's employees, job development is the means to gain promotion to positions of greater responsibility and pay. In large companies promotions often involve relocations as well. For example, many employees within IBM say that the initials stand for "I've Been Moved" because of the frequent association of promotions with geographic relocations. With an increasing percentage of couples who both work, these relocations, especially international relocations, can be challenging.[40] These **dual-career couples**, or couples in which both partners work full-time in professional, managerial, or administrative jobs, frequently do not want to be separated, and yet finding a job for the other partner, especially in a foreign country, can be a serious obstacle to an individual's accepting a promotion and transfer. Furthermore, work visa restrictions may prevent employment of the spouse in a foreign country even if a transfer or interim job can be located. To cope with this challenge, companies are expanding their spouse relocation assistance programs and are also forming informal associations so employees interested in relocating can exchange information about transfers and job opportunities in order to help each other out.[41]

dual-career couples couples in which both partners work full-time in professional, managerial, or administrative jobs

Termination Despite your best efforts to recruit, hire, train, compensate, and manage the performance of your employees, you may find that you have to terminate or fire an employee. Firing for cause usually involves the termination of an employee for criminal behavior such as theft of company property, or violation of company policies such as sharing confidential information with its competitors. Most companies have detailed and written policies about the criteria for "cause terminations" and the steps that a manager must follow to fire an employee who meets these conditions. An employee can also be fired *for failure to perform*. Again, most companies have detailed policies about what must be done first before an employee can be fired for poor performance. Often these policies involve the following:

1. Informing the employee of the performance standards.
2. Formally and specifically documenting incidents of poor performance.
3. Informing the employee of these performance failures, reiterating the standards, and setting time frames and actions for performance improvement.
4. Formally informing the employee of the consequences of failure to meet the standards and time frame established for performance improvement.

If the employee's performance does not improve sufficiently subsequent to taking these measures, many companies require his or her manager to work with a specialist in the HR department to actually fire the employee.

Layoffs Layoffs involve the termination of groups of employees because of economic or business reasons and are not a function of the employees' performance per se. Research has demonstrated that companies suffer in their ability to attract and retain good employees in the future if they do not conduct layoffs in a *reasonable* manner. Clearly, "reasonable" is open to interpretation, but practices that seem to be perceived as reasonable include outplacement aids such as résumé writing assistance, career counseling, office space access, secretarial help, and job-hunting assistance. Often these activities are outsourced to companies that specialize in helping laid-off workers find employment.

Labor Relations

Labor relations come into play when employees are represented by formal unions who represent them for collective bargaining of their wages, benefits, and other terms of their employment. Some industries such as the airlines have a large proportion of employees represented by unions. For example, in the airline industry not only are some of the lower-paid employees, such as baggage handlers, represented by unions, but highly paid employees, such as pilots, are also represented by unions. While the percentage of employees represented by unions in the United States has declined over the last 50 years,[42] effective labor relations remain critical for many companies and managers. Managers must find a balance between meeting the needs of the unionized employees on such core issues as compensation, benefits, and job security, and meeting the needs of the business including controlling costs, remaining flexible to respond to a changing environment, and sustaining a reputation that allows the company to attract and retain needed employees now and in the future.

LAWS AND REGULATIONS AFFECTING HRM

Perhaps more than any other area of management, laws and regulations affect human resource management. For example, a group of flight attendants for Delta Airlines filed suit because Delta had weight limits for flight attendants. The suit claimed discrimination because while the weight limits were applied to all flight attendants, both male and female, there were no similar standards applied to pilots. Delta first argued that the weight limits were legal because certain size limitations were necessary for flight attendants to perform their jobs in the limited space on planes. Despite this argument, Delta later dropped the weight requirements for all flight attendants.[43]

Exhibit 15.8 provides a summary of the laws enacted in the United States that have had a significant impact on human resource practices and policies. The basic intent of most of this legislation has been to ensure that equal opportunity is provided for both job applicants and current employees. Because the laws were intended to correct past inequalities, many organizations have voluntarily implemented or been pressured by employees and other constituencies to implement **affirmative action programs** to ensure that organizational changes are made. These programs may involve such things as

affirmative action programs hiring and training programs intended to correct past inequalities for certain categories of people based on gender, race and ethnicity, age, or religion

exhibit 15.8

Major U.S. Federal Laws and Regulations Related to Human Resource Management

Act	Requirements	Covers	Enforcement Agency
Thirteenth Amendment	Abolished slavery	All individuals	Court system
Fourteenth Amendment	Provides equal protection for all citizens and requires due process in state action	State actions (e.g., decisions of governmental organizations)	Court system
Civil Rights Acts of 1866 and 1871 (as amended)	Grant all citizens the right to make, perform, modify, and terminate contracts and enjoy all benefits, terms, and conditions of the contractual relationship	All individuals	Court system
Equal Pay Act of 1963	Requires that men and women performing equal jobs receive equal pay	Employers engaged in interstate commerce	EEOC
Title VII of CRA	Forbids discrimination based on race, color, religion, sex, or national origin	Employers with 15 or more employees working 20 or more weeks per year; labor unions; employment agencies	EEOC
Age Discrimination in Employment Act of 1967	Prohibits discrimination in employment against individuals 40 years of age or older	Employers with 15 or more employees working 20 or more weeks per year; labor unions; employment agencies; federal government	EEOC
Rehabilitation Act of 1973	Requires affirmative action in the employment of individuals with disabilities	Government agencies; federal contractors and subcontractors with contracts greater than $2,500	OFCCP
Americans with Disabilities Act of 1990	Prohibits discrimination against individuals with disabilities	Employers with more than 15 employees	EEOC
Executive Order 11246	Requires affirmative action in hiring women and minorities	Federal contractors and subcontractors with contracts greater than $10,000	OFCCP
Civil Rights Act of 1991	Prohibits discrimination (same as Title VII)	Same as Title VII, plus applies Section 1981 to employment discrimination cases	EEOC
Family and Medical Leave Act of 1993	Requires employers to provide 12 weeks of unpaid leave for family and medical emergencies	Employers with more than 50 employees	Department of Labor

Source: Raymond A. Noe, John R. Hollenbeck, Barry Gerhart, and Patrick M. Wright, *Human Resource Management: Gaining a Competitive Advantage* (Burr Ridge, Ill.: Richard D. Irwin, 1997), p. 107. Copyright 1997. Reproduced with permission of The McGraw-Hill Companies.

taking extra effort to inform minority candidates about job opportunities, providing special training programs for disadvantaged candidates, or paying special attention to the racial or gender mix of employees who are promoted.

As business globalizes, laws in the United States have begun to have implications outside its formal borders. For example, the Civil Rights Act of 1991 was passed requiring U.S. firms to abide by the same nondiscrimination laws relative to their U.S. personnel overseas as their U.S. employees residing in the United States.[44] One of the specific implications of this law is that unless a particular host country prohibits women from occupying managerial positions, a U.S. firm cannot discriminate against a woman candidate being sent overseas on assignment even if the norms and values of the host country would make it difficult for a women to be effective. At the time the law was passed, only 3 percent of U.S. **expatriate employees**—employees sent overseas on temporary assignments for three to five years—were women, and 41 percent of all U.S. managers were female. This suggests that there may have been some gender bias in the selection of U.S. expatriate managers in the past. Add to this the fact that increasingly, U.S. firms are *requiring* an international assignment as part of a person's development for top management positions. Given that only 3 percent of those receiving this opportunity were women, U.S. firms may find that they face a severe **glass ceiling** problem and lawsuits because of gender discrimination against women relative to international assignments. A "glass ceiling" is an invisible barrier that prevents women from being promoted to the highest executive ranks.

Countries to which managers might be sent for development opportunities only complicate the situation. For example, since Japan is the United States' second-largest trading partner, U.S. firms are likely to send employees to operations in Japan. However, in Japan, less than 1 percent of all managers are women. This may suggest that in a traditionally male-dominated society, female expatriate managers from the United States might have difficulty being successful. Yet, the Civil Rights Act of 1991 mandates that the gender of a U.S. candidate cannot be a factor in the selection decision. It is interesting to note that despite initial inclinations to think that women expatriates would have a more difficult time in Japan than male expatriates, research actually suggests that women do just as well as men in Japan.[45]

Keep in mind that the intent of most of the legislation and regulation in the United States is designed to provide equal opportunity. This, however, does not prevent organizations from using certain criteria that you might think of as discriminatory, if it can be demonstrated that the criteria are **bona fide**

expatriate employees employees sent overseas on temporary assignments of three to five years

glass ceiling an invisible barrier that prevents women from promotion to the highest executive ranks

IKEA was chosen by *Working Mother* magazine as the best company for working moms in 2003. Forty-seven percent of IKEA's highest paid employees are female, and turnover among them is very low, relative to the rest of the industry. The company also allows job sharing and flextime, and part-time employees working at least 20 hours a week receive full benefits. When the son of salesperson Cindy Clark was diagnosed with leukemia two years ago, the company allowed Clark (shown in the photo) to take six months off.

bona fide occupational qualifications (BFOQ)

qualifications that have a direct and material impact on job performance and outcomes

occupational qualifications (BFOQ), or qualifications that have a direct and material impact on job performance and outcomes.[46] For example, you might think that not hiring male employees who have a mustache or beard (or requiring them to shave them before being hired) would constitute discrimination. However, Disney has such a policy for its theme park workers and has prevailed when taken to court. Disney was able to retain the policy despite legal challenges because the company was able to demonstrate statistically that customers reacted better to and were more satisfied with clean-shaven park employees than those with beards and mustaches. In Disney's case, being clean shaven is a BFOQ.

Sexual Harassment

Over the last 10 years, sexual harassment has become a major workforce issue, especially given the significant financial penalties that can be assessed to organizations that allow it to occur. Sexual harassment takes two basic forms. The first is sometimes termed *quid pro quo* and involves requests or implied suggestions that sexual relations are required in exchange for continued employment or benefits such as promotion. The second form involves actions that create a "hostile environment." A hostile environment can be created through jokes, touching, comments, pictures, and other means of communicating unwanted sexual innuendo. Sexual harassment suits have increased dramatically over the last several years. As a consequence of the judgments (which are often several hundred thousand dollars), companies are increasingly offering training programs to try to help managers understand the law and avoid such incidents.

Workforce Diversity

Effective management of workforce diversity is a growing management challenge. Historically, diversity in the United States was defined in terms of differences along traditional racial categories. Today, most organizations think of workforce diversity in terms of a wide range of factors, including age, gender, race, religion, cultural background, education, and mental and physical disabilities. Hispanic women in the U.S. workforce increased 71 percent between 1990 and 2000, Asian women increased 65 percent, and African American women 29 percent. African American men increased 22 percent, while white males increased only 8 (see Exhibit 15.9). The diversity of backgrounds raises a variety of human resource management questions. For example, with the

exhibit 15.9

Increasing Diversity of U.S. Workforce

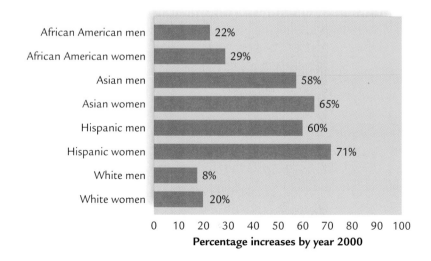

Cisco is a leader in recruiting disabled employees. The San Jose, Calif.-based company, a maker of Internet routers, recruits the employees through various disability organizations, including regional groups like Project Hired, TransAccess, Sensory Access, and national groups such as the National Disability Business Council. These employees are often among their most loyal and hard working.

need to reach out to such a diverse group of potential employees, what types of recruiting efforts will be effective and avoid unintended discrimination? How can the diverse backgrounds, perspectives, and talents of employees be effectively managed?

Managing Workforce Diversity While there are ethical arguments for why organizations should embrace diversity, efforts to effectively manage workforce diversity typically are justified in terms of business reasons. These reasons include the following:

- Need to attract enough capable workers to meet turnover and growth demands of the business.
- Enhanced creativity and innovation when solving problems.
- Knowledge and understanding of the diverse marketplace and customers.

The experience of most organizations, however, is that these advantages are hard to obtain. Just as multiple perspectives, values, and ways of thinking can bring new insights and creativity to a problem, they can also create a significant management challenge. Diverse workgroups often encounter the following problems:

- Communication problems and misunderstandings.
- Mistrust.
- Conflict and incompatible approaches to resolving the conflict.
- Lower group cohesiveness and greater subgroup formation based on elements of diversity such as language, race, or gender.

Given the potential benefits and the significant challenges of effectively managing workforce diversity, we review some general guidelines for you as a manager to follow:

- *Know yourself.* How much exposure have you had to people with ethnic, racial, religious, educational, or cultural backgrounds different from your own? How tolerant and understanding of the differences have you been? How comfortable were you? How curious were you?

- *Prepare yourself and your employees.* How skilled are you and your employees at listening, conflict resolution, negotiation, and communication?
- *Provide support.* To what extent are there support groups for employees with minority backgrounds to keep them from feeling unappreciated and wanting to leave the organization? To what extent do minority employees have mentors who can help them understand and become an effective part of the organization?
- *Guide behavior.* To what extent do you monitor the behavior of your subordinates and peers? How consistent are you in providing positive reinforcement of behaviors that foster tolerance of and effective use of diversity? To what extent do you privately provide negative feedback to individuals who display intolerance or other problem behaviors?

From both a domestic and international perspective, workforce diversity is only going to increase. One of the ways you can distinguish yourself from others and add value to your organization is through your understanding of the ability to work effectively with subordinates, peers, customers, and suppliers with diverse backgrounds. A Manager's Challenge, "Marriott Provides a Step Up," profiles one company in which senior managers have changed how they help middle managers successfully meet the diversity challenge. As you read the box, you might ask yourself which HR practices you would find most helpful to you if you were a manager in the Marriott company.

Globalization

Globalization also poses a significant challenge to human resource management. Many argue that the world is getting smaller. However, from a human resource perspective, the world is getting larger! If you look at the history of almost any multinational corporation (MNC), at its beginning the firm operated in one or a very limited number of countries. As it grew, it expanded into more and more countries. Telecommunication and transportation technologies in particular have facilitated this expansion. Now companies such as Philips and Citicorp operate in over 70 countries around the world. For them, that translates into employees speaking over 40 different languages, dealing with 70 different governments, interacting with 10 different major religions, and coping with hundreds of different customs, holidays, and traditions. As companies expand into new countries and cultures, the world for them gets larger and more complicated.

Most firms cannot simply avoid expanding overseas. Consider where the workers will be in the future compared with where they are now. Exhibit 15.10 indicates that most of the future workers will be in developing countries. Given that most of the large MNCs are headquartered in developed countries and most of the workers in the future will be in developing countries, continued expansion abroad seems inevitable.

As firms expand outside their home countries, they will confront a variety of HRM challenges. For example, do the selection techniques that work in one country also work in another? Can one performance appraisal form be applied in all operations around the globe? Must reward systems be adapted and changed from one country to the next? If they must be adapted, how can a firm avoid the risk of employees perceiving these differences as inequitable? What must a firm do to ensure that it provides development opportunities for employees in all its operations? For example, recently a Korean multinational firm was seeking to fill its top global marketing position.

a manager's challenge

Change

Marriott Provides a Step Up

For managers at Marriott International, maintaining a core of workers to handle entry-level jobs and provide excellent service is critical to supporting its competitive position and continued growth. Moreover, nearly one-third of Marriott's managers started in hourly-wage positions, another reason why this group is vital to the company's success. However, given the changing composition and nature of the entry-level workforce, Marriott managers have come to recognize that compensation alone will not attract, motivate, or help retain the workers they need. Managing a diverse workforce who speak some 30 languages can be a real human resource challenge.

To learn more about the changes in its workforce, Marriott managers conducted a study and learned that about one-quarter of the workers had literacy problems. In response, Marriott initiated an on-site English as a Second Language (ESL) program during work hours. The business reason? Workers who speak English can better serve U.S. hotel guests.

However, managers were still busy offering advice about family conflicts and child-care solutions and sometimes lending money to employees for urgent bills. Instead of dealing with customers, some managers were spending too much time doing social work. As a result, Marriott managers changed their approach to human resource management. They added programs such as the Associate Resource Line, a confidential service that counsels employees across a broad spectrum of personal matters. They also started up social services referrals and child-care referrals to attract and motivate hourly workers—and keep turnover lower than that of competitors.

Following government changes to welfare programs, Marriott management instituted Pathways to Independence to help welfare recipients become productive workers. Participants learn business skills like work punctuality as well as life skills like money management. For a $5,500-per-person investment (half funded by government subsidies), more than 3,000 former welfare recipients now work for Marriott—a new labor pool that, importantly, has a below-average turnover rate.

Critics say Marriott's managers are too paternalistic. But success stories show how these alternative approaches

More than 30 languages are spoken among Marriot's 135,000 employees. The hotel chain has been honored for its work–life practices by many organizations, including *Diversity, Inc., Working Mother,* and *Latina Style* magazines and by the NAACP. In an industry where the hourly employee turnover rate is 80 to 90 percent, Marriot's 35 percent turnover rate is exceptionally low.

have added value. For example, Thong Lee, a bartender in the Seattle Marriott, learned English through the hotel's classes and used his company stock and pay to buy rental properties. And he remembers when his boss shut down the hotel laundry for a day so the staff could attend his mother's funeral. The result? A loyal employee.

By responding to the changing composition and needs of the entry-level workforce, managers help sustain Marriott's competitive position and its reputation for exceptional service. The company's continued growth has delivered even more opportunities for employee personal and professional growth, which managers highlight to attract and retain employees. In fact, *Fortune* regularly places Marriott among the best 100 U.S. companies to work for—an accomplishment that further enhances managers' ability to recruit and retain good employees.

Sources: Adapted from Alynda Wheat, "The Anatomy of a Great Workplace," *Fortune,* February 4, 2002, pp. 75+; Jonathan Hickman, "America's 50 Best Companies for Minorities," *Fortune,* July 8, 2002, pp. 110+; "America's 50 Best Companies For Minorities," *Fortune,* July 9, 2001, pp. 122+; Joanne Gordon, "The New Paternalism," *Forbes,* November 2, 1998; "Best Companies for Asians, Blacks, and Hispanics," *Fortune,* August 2, 1998.

exhibit 15.10

Where the Workers Are

Source: U.S. Department of Labor, 1997.

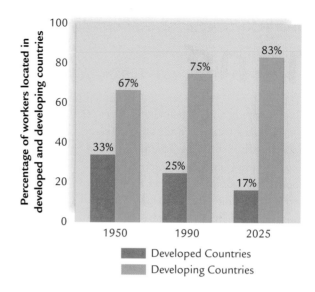

Must the best possible person for this job be Korean? How does any global firm ensure that it finds and develops the best possible talent wherever in its worldwide operations that talent might be located? When a firm needs to send employees outside their native countries as a means of developing their international skills and abilities, how does it effectively select these individuals? How should these employees be trained prior to their international assignments? How can these individuals be effectively evaluated when factors such as real changes in exchange rates, government price controls, and other external factors significantly influence bottom-line results of overseas operations? These are just a sampling of the questions and human resource management challenges raised by today's increasingly global environment.

managerial perspectives revisited

1 PERSPECTIVE 1: THE ORGANIZATIONAL CONTEXT The organizational context is extremely important when it comes to human resource management. In many ways the appropriate HR practices are a function of the organization. Change the context of the organization—its strategy, culture, or industry—and you are likely to need to change the characteristics or capabilities needed in the employees you want to recruit, how you orient them, what training they need, and how you manage their performance or structure their compensation. For example, the HR policies and practices at Marriott provide considerable help and support to managers who are trying to manage effectively their increasingly diverse workforce.

2 PERSPECTIVE 2: THE HUMAN FACTOR From one perspective, human resource management is all about working through others; it is about achieving results by attracting, selecting, training, appraising, compensating, and developing others. Because human resource management also typically involves the policies and practices of the company through the human resource department, as a manager, effective HRM will likely also involve working with and through people in your HR department. Again, Marriott is a great example of this. While the HR department set key policies and practices that helped managers work effectively with a diverse workforce, those policies would likely not be sufficient to attract and especially retain quality employees unless Marriott's supervisors and managers were skilled at HR activities such as managing employee performance.

 PERSPECTIVE 3: MANAGING PARADOXES   Meeting the HRM challenge creates some important potential paradoxes. On the one hand, individual managers have their own personal views on the effective management of human resources. On the other hand, as managers in an organization, they have to work with, support, and uphold the policies and practices of the company. At times there may be a conflict between the two. In such cases, do managers have an obligation to try to correct company practices that are not in keeping with what their values are or what they believe—or that may be inappropriate or even illegal? This dynamic tension between personal and company standards is one of the principal paradoxes managers face when it comes to managing and motivating the firm's people.

 PERSPECTIVE 4: ENTREPRENEURIAL MIND-SET   The entrepreneurial mind-set is reflected in the behavior and actions of a firm's employees. Southwest Airlines employees hold and display an entrepreneurial mind-set. The company is known for being entrepreneurial, primarily because of the innovative, creative, and strategic actions individual employees use to provide good customer service. Southwest Airlines is able to achieve these outcomes because of its unique culture and the high-quality employees it is able to attract—and because the Southwest managers seek out these behaviors in employees and reward them. To maintain the company's competitive edge, its managers are committed to constantly improving its human resource management capabilities.

Most firms have dedicated HR departments, and managers can fall into one of two traps: When companies have effective HR policies and practices, managers can fall into the trap of relegating HR to the HR department. While the HR department is designed to support and facilitate the effective management of human resources in the company, it's no substitute for individual managers' taking the initiative to engage in key HR activities.

concluding comments

In this chapter, we presented human resource management as a set of activities performed by all managers rather than a set of functions locked within a human resource department. A company's human resources are its most fundamental source of competitive advantage. In addition, individual managers can create competitive advantages for themselves in their careers through superior management of human resources. In particular, managers who can match their management of human resources with the strategy of the organization may find themselves in a superior position relative to their peers.

As a manager, it is unlikely that you will want to leave activities such as recruitment, selection, training, or development of your employees entirely to the human resource department. While human resource departments in most companies play a formal role in all the activities we have covered in this chapter, if you want to get the right people and maximize their performance, you will need to be involved in and skilled at these activities as well.

Relegating HR activities to a specific department is an old school of thought and not reflective of today's environment. As business continues to push toward being knowledge based, the effective management of intelligent employees becomes increasingly important. As an executive of an engineering service firm said to us, "I watch the company's assets walk out the door at the close of business each day." From that perspective, effective human resource management becomes a central job of every manager.

key terms

affirmative action programs 547	career paths 545	job posting 530
assessment centers 534	critical incidents 542	job sharing 539
at-risk compensation 545	cross-functional job rotation 546	pay structure 544
behaviorally anchored rating scales (BARS) 540	dual-career couples 546	reengineering 539
bona fide occupational qualifications (BFOQ) 550	expatriate employees 549	structured interview 533
	glass ceiling 549	360-degree feedback 541
broadband systems 544	incentive plans 545	unstructured interview 533
cafeteria-style plans 545	job analysis 529	valid selection technique 533
	job design 538	work simulation 534

test your comprehension

1. What are the key human resource activities at which a manager must be skilled?
2. Why is it important to keep the firm's strategy in mind when engaged in HR activities such as selection?
3. What are two advantages of part-time or temporary employees in meeting a firm's workforce needs?
4. What are the principal aspects of job analysis?
5. How can job posting help a firm with its internal management of human resources?
6. Describe five effective means of recruiting new employees.
7. What does it mean for a selection technique to be valid?
8. What is the primary difference between structured and unstructured interviews and what effect does this difference have?
9. What is the basic rationale for work sampling as a selection method?
10. Identify three written tests used in selection and describe their validity.
11. Why are reference checks of little use in selection?
12. List the five things that can be done to make orientation programs more effective.
13. Define *reengineering* and explain its use in organizations.
14. What are the key differences between graphic rating scales and behaviorally anchored rating scales?
15. List seven steps that can be taken to make performance appraisal sessions more effective.
16. Why are organizations moving away from traditional pay structures to more broadband pay structures?
17. What is a cafeteria-style benefit plan?
18. What does it mean to fire someone for cause?
19. What is the purpose of affirmative action programs?
20. What is a BFOQ?
21. What is the difference between quid pro quo and a hostile environment in cases of sexual harassment?
22. Describe three things you can do to improve your capability to manage greater diversity in the workforce.

apply your understanding

1. What do you think will change most dramatically in the future in terms of what it will take to attract young people to companies?
2. Think about the best and worst bosses you've ever had. To what extent did human resource management skills differentiate the two? In particular, which skills?

3. As you look forward to a future management position, what HRM strengths and weaknesses do you feel you have?
4. If you look at your university, what HR activities does it perform well? What are needed improvements?

5. What do you think will be the most challenging HR activities in the future?

You are captain of a firefighting squad consisting of two trucks and 12 firefighters. You have two females in your squad. As firefighters your squad is on duty for 24 hours and then off duty for 24 hours at a time. When on duty you all live together in the firehouse where you eat, sleep, train, relax, and hang out together. Some days are so intense with calls that you do not have time for anything else. Other days by comparison are quite slow.

The effectiveness of your team is a function of skill and trust. The techniques of suppressing a fire or evacuating people from a burning building may be lost on the average person, but the depth of these required skills are vital. A significant amount of trust is also required to be effective. For example, if you were injured in a burning building, you would want to know that your team members would be able to get you out.

In most firehouses, including yours, the addition of women has happened only recently. All women firefighters have to pass the same physical and skill tests given to the men. However, firehouses have traditionally had a strong flavor of male-oriented conversation, humor, and activities such as lifting weights as a means of helping the team bond.

One of your newest female recruits has come to you complaining of a sexually hostile work environment. She complained that the jokes she over-hears are full of offensive humor and that several of the guys have offensive pictures inside their lockers. Because the firehouse is an older one, there are not separate locker rooms or showers. Although separate shower times have been scheduled, the recruit also complained that some of the guys had "accidentally" walked in when she was showering because they "forgot" the schedule.

The other female member of the squad, who has been in the unit for nearly a year, disagrees with the description of the environment as sexually hostile, but would not really go into any details or specifics.

1. What actions would you take?
2. Suppose, in talking individually with the guys in the squad, some say that they can see that a couple of the younger, single guys might be a bit "macho" in their conversations among themselves. What would you do if these younger guys report that they feel the new female recruit is simply eavesdropping on private conversations?
3. How would the fact that the new female recruit seems to be as physically strong and more skilled than two of the younger "macho" guys in the squad affect your actions? What would you do differently if she were not a good performer?

closing case

Alliant Energizes Diversity Training

As the U.S. workforce grows older and more diverse in composition, managers face new challenges in attracting, retaining, and managing skilled workers at all organizational levels. Thanks to demographic changes, immigration patterns, and cultural shifts, the labor pool contains more ethnic groups, more older workers, and more women than ever before. Some companies have reluctantly accepted this diversity, while others—such as Alliant Energy—have embraced it wholeheartedly.

Alliant provides electrical power and natural gas to customers in Wisconsin, Iowa, and Illinois; it also operates power plants in Mexico, Brazil, China, Australia, and New Zealand. As senior managers take Alliant deeper into the international marketplace, seeking to double overseas business within five years, their dedication to diversity has become a key corporate goal. "Diversity throughout Alliant Energy is a business issue," says Errol B. Davis Jr., the president and CEO. "Diversity—in both our workforce and customer base—will help give us a competitive advantage. By creating a more cohesive, competitive workforce, we will be able to reach new markets more effectively."

Alliant's managers define diversity as differences in gender, race, age, physical and mental abilities, lifestyles, cultures, education, ideas, and background. They expect all employees to appreciate and seek out the different perspectives that come from diversity and be intolerant of behaviors that conflict with their mission of nurturing a diverse workforce. Their first step in the process of embracing diversity was to create a Diversity Steering Team consisting of 15 employees representing every level of the organization, with a mix of genders, races, and ages.

Using a companywide survey, the team set out to gauge employees' perceptions of diversity issues such as affirmative action, job satisfaction, interpersonal relationships, and work attitudes. After analyzing the results, team members concluded that employees were confused about Alliant's definition of diversity and management's expectations regarding diversity. In response, they recommended that all employees receive diversity awareness training to better understand the range of perspectives within a diverse workforce, and the benefits of diversity.

To communicate senior management's commitment to diversity, a vice president or department manager introduced each eight-hour workshop. Then a facilitator took over to explain the benefits of diversity, state Alliant's expectations, and discuss behaviors that are consistent or inconsistent with diversity. The highlight of the workshops, however, came when employees participated in two exercises designed to help them think through the issues. In the first exercise, each employee was asked to identify specific actions he or she would take to support diversity. In the second, employees worked in groups to create a list of diversity ground rules. For example, one group created the rule that "all offensive jokes and language should be eliminated from the workplace." Another group created a rule they initially worded as "respect the ideas of others" and later revised to "accept, understand, respect, and celebrate our differences." This active participation helped employees carry the momentum back to their own work areas.

After two years, all 2,500 employees had completed the diversity training. Alliant's management received generally positive feedback from employees; most employees seemed to believe that the training helped them to support diversity in their own work groups. The Diversity Steering Team then carried its diversity mission to outside suppliers and contractors who represent the company. This ensured that all behaviors would be consistent with Alliant's diversity expectations.

To continue supporting diversity throughout the organization, top management recently created an internal Diversity Council. This group is charged with recommending and driving the implementation of new policies and programs to promote diversity values. Alliant's executives have also initiated new programs to attract and retain a more diverse workforce. The purpose is to encourage ethnic diversity and bring women into nontraditional positions within the organization.

The steps that Alliant's managers have taken to promote diversity are innovative in two ways. First, rather than make the human resource department solely responsible for diversity, senior managers have demonstrated their active support and involvement. Second, the diverse composition of the Steering Team and Diversity Council helped these groups address diversity on a larger scale. Now every department and unit of Alliant supports diversity, and the company's long-term commitment to diversity will allow every employee to make valuable contributions to global growth and higher profits in the coming years.

Questions

1. If you were a manager in Alliant, what might be different or have to change about how you manage human resources in terms of recruiting, hiring, training, performance appraisal, compensation, or development?

2. Why is Alliant so committed to diversity of its human resources? How will this benefit the company?

3. Do you believe the company is forcing the issue of diversity? Is it necessary to make diversity training mandatory for all employees? Explain your answer.

4. Independent surveys suggest that companies cannot easily quantify the effects of diversity. How would you suggest that Alliant measure the effects of a diverse workforce? If a company ignored workforce diversity, how might it be affected?

Sources: "Brazil Sends Alliant Nuts," *Power Economics*, November 2002, p. 31; "Alliant Surges into Brazil, China, Australia," *Business Journal* (Milwaukee), June 8, 2001, http://milwaukee.bizjournals.com/milwaukee/stories/2001/06/01/focus3.html; "Alliant Energy Corp.," *Business Record* (Des Moines), June 11, 2001, pp. 18+; Nancy Mueller, "Wisconsin Power & Light's Model Diversity Program," *Training and Development*, March 1996, pp. 57–61; and Alliant Web site (www.alliantenergy.com).

integrative case

Ste. Basil Hotel–Moscow: Struggling with Values in a Post-Communist State

By Charles A. Rarick, Barry University
©2003, CA Rarick, Barry University, Miami, Florida, USA.

Abstract

This case profiles the difficulties experienced by an American expatriate operating a luxury hotel in Russia. The American general manager is confronted with problems of employee motivation, poor customer service, corruption, and the possible loss of the hotel to its Russian partner.

It was a typical October day in Moscow as Greg Hill looked out the window of his office in the Ste. Basil Hotel. As he saw the snow begin to fall he realized that it was going to be a very long, cold winter in Russia and he longed for the sunshine and warmth of his previous assignment in Miami Beach. While the move to Moscow had been a difficult experience, he and his wife had adjusted reasonably well, and Greg believed that the move would position him for advancement in his American company. He felt that the hardship of living in Russia would be offset by advancement opportunity but he was now very concerned about his future. A deeply religious man, Greg began to pray for a solution to his problems.

The Ste. Basil Hotel in Moscow is a four-star hotel located in Red Square. The idea for a luxury hotel was conceived by Louis Cunningham, CEO of LCC Properties. LCC owned a number of luxurious hotel properties in the United States, Canada, South America, and Japan. Cunningham developed the idea for a luxury hotel after a visit to Russia in 1994 in which he and his wife toured the former communist state. Cunningham noticed that the quality of hotels in the country was poor, most being old Soviet style in appearance and operations. Cunningham knew that a number of American and European businesspeople were traveling to Russia, and that an opportunity existed for a hotel that matched the level of quality found in the West. On subsequent visits, Cunningham spotted an abandoned construction site near St. Basil Cathedral and decided that it would be a prime location for a luxury hotel. The site was owned by the Russian government, which agreed to provide the site if LCC would invest the necessary $50 million to develop it into a four-star property. The Russian government also insisted that LCC create a partnership with the state-owned airline that would take 51 percent of the operation. Although Cunningham didn't like the idea of minority interest in the project, he was excited about the location, and even more excited about the prospect of being a pioneering capitalist in a former communist country.

With the fall of the Soviet Union in 1991, Western businesses began to take an interest in the former communist state. The reform movement begun by Mikhail Gorbachev would eventually result in the collapse of the Soviet Union, and the satellite states would gain their independence. The early reform movement of *glasnost*, or "openness," resulted in the lifting of censorship, the release of dissidents, and greater tolerance for religious freedom. Glasnost was followed by *perestroika* or "restructuring," in which the economy was decentralized and privatized. Military spending was cut and free elections were held. As the former communist superpower turned toward capitalism, Western businesses looked for opportunities.

A Luxury Hotel in Moscow

Louis Cunningham was one of those seeking this new opportunity. Although Cunningham was extremely excited about the project and had a particular interest in seeing a capitalist spirit come to Russia, he was forced to delegate most of the responsibilities for the new venture, due to the failing health of his wife. The new hotel was named the Ste. Basil because of its proximity to St.

Basil Cathedral. Cunningham chose the abbreviation "Ste." because he thought it would "add class" and provide the luxury image the hotel sought to project. Cunningham selected Greg Hill to be the general manager of the new hotel and to oversee completion of the construction of the facility. Greg Hill was a 47-year-old general manager of a luxury hotel in Miami Beach, Florida. He had worked for LCC since graduating from a small college in the Midwest with a degree in hospitality administration. Hill and his wife, who were raised in St. Louis, Missouri, had moved a number of times as Greg gained increasingly responsible positions with LCC. With their two children away at college, the Hills felt that moving abroad would be less difficult than it had been when the children were younger. They did enjoy living in Miami and hoped to retire to south Florida at a later date. The opportunity to build and manage a new hotel in a former communist country was an offer that Greg felt he could not turn down. He believed that success in this project could move him into the ranks of upper management at LCC. Mrs. Hill was a teacher in Miami and enjoyed other cultures. She looked forward to living in a foreign country, and in fact often felt that moving to Miami was like living in a different country. The Hills were friendly people, and although not considered worldly, they were open to new experiences and adjusted to new situations well.

The move to Moscow and the completion of the hotel's construction provided many unforeseen difficulties, but the Russian partners were helpful in overcoming most obstacles. Greg Hill developed the Ste. Basil into a fine hotel. It stood out in great contrast to the poorly equipped and managed hotels which were remnants of the Soviet era. The Ste. Basil provided its guests with an outstanding restaurant and café, an indoor pool, an exercise facility, a dry cleaning service, satellite television, modem/data portals, conference rooms, currency exchange, a gift shop, and concierge services. The rooms were clean, modern, and spacious. The hotel catered to foreign businesspeople from the United States and Europe and was one of the highest priced hotels in Moscow. Room rates ranged from $215 to $450US per night. Conference facilities could also be rented and the hotel provided a catering service to conference participants. With increasing business between Russia and the West it was believed that the Ste. Basil would be the obvious choice among business travelers.

Recruitment of Employees

The Ste. Basil would have to fill all positions, with the exception of general manager, with local labor. Since Greg Hill was the only American expatriate, he felt that he should be actively involved in the recruitment and selection process. With the help of his Russian partners, Hill placed an advertisement in the *Moscow Times* for all hotel positions. The advertisement was in English since it had been decided that all employees should be proficient in the English language. Response to the advertisement was overwhelming. Thousands of people arrived to apply for the positions. Many of the people who sought employment at the Ste. Basil were educated beyond job requirements. The Ste. Basil received applications from scientists, attorneys, doctors, professors, writers, as well as recent university graduates. Greg was told that the applicants could make much more money working for an American company than continuing in their present professions.

Greg was assisted in applicant screening by his assistant general manager. Victor Popov was appointed by the Russian partners to act not only as the assistant general manager, but also to help Greg with his assimilation and understanding of Russian culture. Victor had at one time been employed in the airline industry as an engineer. He held degrees in engineering, including a master's degree in radio engineering from the St. Petersburg Electrotechnical University. Victor's great-grandfather had been a pioneer in the development of radio and the family name was well respected in Russia. Victor spoke fluent English and German, in addition to his native Russian. His hotel experience was limited to a short assignment in an East German hotel, and it was never clear to Greg what his responsibilities were in that assignment. Greg and Victor went through each application and began eliminating individuals who were clearly not qualified. Anyone who had previous hotel experience was eliminated from further consideration. It was thought that these employees had acquired bad habits working for state-owned hotels and it would be very difficult to retrain them. The only exceptions would be for critical positions such as chef, which required previous experience. Victor strongly suggested that older applicants (over 35 years of age) should also not be selected. Greg was not sure about this request, but he deferred to Victor's judgment. Greg, however, refused to follow Victor's advice and eliminate all female applicants with small children. Greg did eliminate anyone who had an advanced degree such as an attorney, scientist, or physician, feeling that such a person would become quickly dissatisfied with the position.

After the initial screening, applicants were invited for an interview. This proved difficult since many of the applicants did not have a telephone and could not be reached except by mail. Greg decided to eliminate those candidates since the applicant pool was more than sufficient. When word got out that the hotel was interviewing, some of the applicants without telephones walked in and requested interviews. Victor granted some of these applicants interview appointments. The interviewing and selection process took two weeks and included structured and unstructured questions, questions asking applicants to provide their recommendations to hypothetical problems they might experience on the job, a written test of English ability, and a short intelligence test (in English). For the most part Greg was discouraged by the responses of the applicants, especially the responses to the unstructured and situational questions. Many of the applicants provided very short answers or were unable to answer at all. These applicants were eliminated from further consideration. In the end, however, Greg and Victor were able to assemble a workforce which both felt would be satisfactory.

Orientation and Training

A mandatory three-day orientation session was conducted for all employees. The orientation program provided employees with information on LCC Enterprises such as its history and mission; basic training on the importance of customer service; grooming; manners; and company policy. After the three-day orientation program, specific job training was provided. Greg was assisted at this point by a team of six expatriates from LCC who were brought in for the short-term training assignment.

Greg had expected that the employees would be very motivated to learn their jobs since their compensation was considerably more than most had previously received in their careers in Russia, and working at a luxury American hotel provided a degree of status. He was disappointed by the responses to the training program. Many of the new employees seemed more interested in asking about compensation, benefits, and how the hotel would benefit them, than specific questions concerning their responsibilities. Greg noticed some of the employees dozing off during the orientation program. In addition, Greg was discouraged by the reactions he received from some of the employees to a gift the hotel gave on the first day of orientation. The hotel provided, as a welcoming gift to each employee, a large basket of toiletries wrapped with a large red ribbon. Some of the employees wanted two or three of the baskets and some asked for money instead. Although this disappointed Greg, many employees appeared grateful for the opportunity to work and seemed motivated to do a good job. Greg was pleased that with the exception of two people, all employees were able to successfully complete their job-specific training. With the employees selected and trained, the Ste. Basil Hotel was ready to begin welcoming guests.

A Slow Start

During the first few weeks of operation Greg spent most of his time with external relations. He was busy dealing with suppliers, government officials, and travel industry representatives. Greg delegated much of the day-to-day operations to Victor, who would consult with him if a problem arose which he could not handle. Occupancy was very low, as expected, yet the restaurant and café did a brisk business from the start. The low level of occupancy was somewhat beneficial in that it allowed the staff time to continue to learn their duties on-the-job. The American trainers had returned home, and with Greg busy with other matters, Victor made decisions and answered questions from the staff.

Although Greg did not have much contact with many of the employees during this time he did notice that in general the employees did not seem to present the warm, hospitable atmosphere that the hotel sought. The employees infrequently smiled and often seemed to be in a bad mood. Greg mentioned this point to Victor who told him that it was "the Russian nature," but that he would ask the employees to try harder. Greg decided that while he was too busy to intervene, he would try to "catch someone doing it right" and reward him or her with positive reinforcement. On several occasions when he found an employee smiling or presenting the proper attitude he would give them an "O.K." sign (thumb and forefinger closed in a circle) as a show of approval. Much to his surprise this provoked a negative reaction in the employees. Greg was also surprised by the frequent use of the Russian word "nyet"; in fact, it seemed to Greg that the "no" word was almost an automatic response to any request.

Trouble with Victor

As time went on, Greg was able to devote more of his attention to internal operations. He was beginning to become concerned about Victor's approach with employees. While Victor was a handsome and confident man, and appeared to be well liked by the hotel's customers, his approach to employee relations was unattractive. In one particular case a desk clerk was fired in a loud outburst in front of several guests. It was particularly troubling in that the clerk, Svetlana, was a favorite of Greg's. Svetlana was a divorced mother of two young girls who had been struggling to provide the sole support for her family after her husband left. Svetlana was a devout member of the Russian Orthodox Church and Greg considered her to be an honest, conscientious, and faithful employee. Victor informed Greg that he had terminated her for excessive time off. Victor explained that

Svetlana had asked for two days off to care for one of her children who was sick and she did not return to work for a week. Victor explained that he had assumed that she had quit, and so he was surprised to see her behind the front desk working. Her attitude was poor, according to Victor, and she insulted him, so he lost his temper and fired her in front of all parties present. As Greg probed further he was told by Victor that there is an old Russian proverb—"A dog is wiser than a woman. It never barks at its master." It was clear to Greg that Victor had a low opinion of women and that he was engaging in behavior which was inconsistent with LCC company policy. Greg informed Victor that he was going to contact Svetlana and hear her side of the story.

With some difficulty, Greg was finally able to contact Svetlana and he asked her to come in to the hotel to discuss the matter. Svetlana told Greg that she did request two days off but that her other child had also become ill and she needed to care for her too. She was fearful to let Victor know that she would not be able to come in for the additional days. Greg was sympathetic and told her that he would reinstate her. When Victor was told of Greg's decision he just shook his head and said "nyekulturny" and walked away. Greg was not sure what this meant but he was sure it wasn't favorable. Greg decided that all decisions concerning employee discipline would first have to be approved by him and he issued a memo stating the policy. Victor took the memo very seriously and proceeded to consult Greg on all personnel matters. He did seem genuine in his actions (although Greg was not completely sure of this) but the constant requests for Greg's approval became a nuisance.

Additional difficulties continued to arise with Victor. It concerned Greg that Victor began spending a lot of time in the hotel restaurant with a small group of Russian men. They didn't appear to ever eat a meal, they only smoked and drank vodka and gave disapproving stares at anyone who came near them. The group appeared to Greg to be a bit rough and not the type of clientele that the hotel sought to attract. After a few weeks Greg decided that it was time to investigate. He began by checking into the amount of money the group was spending in the restaurant and was he shocked to discover that Victor was providing the drinks free of charge to the group. When questioned about this, Victor replied that these men were important to the success of the hotel and that the money for their drinks was money well spent. Greg was confused by the response and continued to ask about the men. Victor finally stated in a firm tone—"Trust me General Manager, I know what I am doing." Greg felt that he had better let the issue go for now but that he should keep an eye on the situation.

Attempt at Improvement in Customer Service

With the issues concerning Victor still in his mind, Greg decided that he must begin to address the issue of customer service, and he would probably need to do it without Victor's assistance. Although business was beginning to increase, customer feedback indicated that many guests felt that the hotel staff was not on par with what was expected from a four-star hotel. Guests commented that the staff was "unhelpful," "uncaring," "cold," and "went out of their way to avoid work." These frequent comments were an embarrassment to Greg and LCC properties, so he decided that he should ask for help from the corporate staff to bring the hotel up to standard.

With the arrival of two customer service trainers from the United States an ambitious training program was instituted. Every employee, including supervisory staff, would be required to complete 20 hours of additional training. The trainers repeated the initial training in guest relations which the employees had experienced when they were first hired, and additional training was conducted in handling problem guests and seeking continuous improvement in customer relations. An incentive program was designed by the trainers where each guest would be given a card on which they could recommend an employee for recognition for their good service. At the end of each week the hotel would reward the employee who had accumulated the most recommendations with a certificate for a free meal for two in the hotel restaurant. In addition, the employee would have his or her picture placed at the front desk with the caption "Employee of the Week." In the next few weeks it did appear that customer service was improving; however, Greg worried that the improvement might be short-lived and that the Ste. Basil would not be able to match the level of service found in other LCC properties. He had heard that some of the employees resented the competitive nature of the incentive.

A Visit by the Krysha

During the following months business improved at the Ste. Basil. As Greg was in his office reviewing the hotel's revenues and expenses for the past six months, a smile grew on his face. While there were still some problems with customer service, employee punctuality, and employees showing initiative, Greg felt that LCC would be pleased with the operating results of the hotel. The hotel continued to show strong gains in occupancy. The restaurant and café were doing well, but the conference facilities were still underutilized, in Greg's opinion.

Greg's thoughts were interrupted by a knock on the door. Victor entered and asked if he could speak with him for a moment about a "very important matter." Greg welcomed Victor in and was surprised to see that he was not alone. Behind him were four men that Greg had seen previously in the hotel's restaurant with Victor. Greg introduced himself and the men remained silent. Victor seemed very uncomfortable as he explained that the men had requested that the hotel hire them for their services. Greg was not sure what Victor meant, but he was developing an uneasy feeling that something was wrong. Victor explained that the men were needed for "security purposes." Greg realized that Victor did not mean to imply that they were asking for security guard positions and so he asked that the men please step outside the office for a moment. As they did, Victor began to explain that these men were members of the Russian mafia and that they wanted protection money. Victor explained that it was quite common in Russia to pay for such a service, but Greg was adamant in his refusal to pay. Greg berated Victor for even bringing the men into his office and questioned why he was meeting with them in the hotel restaurant. Victor stated that he was protecting Greg and the hotel from problems, and that Greg should consider the fact that an American was recently murdered in Moscow by the Russian mafia. Greg told Victor to leave the office and to inform the men that the Ste. Basil did not need their services.

The Russian Cold

As Victor left the office, Greg's telephone rang. It was Dmitry Puzankov, attorney for the Russian partners. Dmitry explained to Greg that the partners wanted to meet with him to discuss some contract matters. When pressed for an explanation, Dmitry explained that the partners wanted to negotiate the profit distribution of the agreement and some "other changes" including their request that Victor be made "Executive General Manager." Upon ending the conversation with Dmitry, Greg telephoned down to the front desk as he wanted to meet with Svetlana and he knew that she was scheduled to be working. Greg had come to rely on Svetlana for advice on Russian culture. He was informed that Svetlana had not reported to work due to illness of one of her children. As Greg watched the snow fall upon the Moscow streets below he wondered about the security of his present position, the personal safety of himself and his wife, and his future with LCC properties. It seemed to Greg that the temperature of his office had suddenly dropped as a cold chill ran throughout his body.

Notes

1. Crane, R. (2000). *European Business Culture*. Harlow, England: Financial Times/Prentice Hall.
2. Fader, K. (1998). *Russia*. San Diego, CA: Lucent Books.
3. Gesteland, R. (1999). *Cross-Cultural Business Behavior*. Copenhagen: Copenhagen Business School Press.
4. Mitchell, C. (1998). *Passport Russia*. San Rafael, CA: World Trade Press.
5. Morrison, T., W. Conaway, and G. Borden. (1994). *Kiss, Bow, or Shake Hands*. Holbrook, MA: Adams Media.
6. Munro, R. (2002). "Moscow's Top Hotels Greet the Good Times." *The Moscow Times*, May 21.
7. Newman, P. (1997). "Economic Terrorism in a Moscow Hotel." *Macleans*, October 27.
8. Sears, W. and A. Tamulionyte-Lentz. (2001). *Succeeding in Central and Eastern Europe*. Woburn, MA: Butterworth-Heinemann.
9. Smith, B. (1994). *The Collapse of the Soviet Union*. San Diego, CA: Lucent Press. Torchinsky, O. (1997). *Cultures of the World: Russia*. New York: Marshall Cavendish.

Control

16

■

Discuss the effects of too much or too little control
in an organization.

■

Describe the four basic elements of the control process
and the issues involved in each.

■

Differentiate between the different levels of control
and compare their implications for managers.

■

Explain the concept of standards and why they
are so important in organizations.

■

Compare bureaucratic and clan controls.

■

Identify the important qualities required for information
to be useful in the control process.

How Much Control Is Enough?

Can a single individual topple an entire multinational corporation? The answer is, surprisingly, yes. The lack of control at Barings' investment bank sank the 233-year-old British bank and rocked the financial world. In early 1995, a 28-year-old trader caused one of the most spectacular collapses in modern financial history. When the dust finally settled, Barings had suffered trading losses in excess of $1 billion. Ironically, just two years earlier, Peter Baring, the company's CEO, had stated in a speech, "[Financial] derivatives need to be well controlled and understood, but we believe we do that well here."

Baring Brothers was one of the oldest and most prestigious banks in Great Britain, a bank to the House of Windsor. In 1803, one of the Baring ancestors had financed the Louisiana Purchase for the United States. Barings' money had also helped to keep

British armies in the field during the Napoleonic Wars. The Baring family had run the firm for 233 years, and Peter Baring was carrying on the tradition.

In 1992, Barings sent Nick Leeson to assume a post as the chief trader of Baring Futures in Singapore. Leeson traded futures contracts on the Nikkei 225, Japan's version of the Dow Jones index. His job was to exploit the small differences in the buying and selling of these contracts, otherwise known as arbitrage. The trading of futures was considered a relatively safe bet because they generally only resulted in small profits or losses at one time. But Leeson became more sophisticated in his trading knowledge, and he became more "bullish" (that is, he took greater risks).

On January 17, 1995, a massive earthquake devastated Kobe, Japan, and the Nikkei responded with uncertainty. Later that month, the Nikkei plunged more than 1,000 points. For Barings and for Leeson, this natural disaster turned into a financial disaster. The traders in the Far East panicked, Leeson in particular.

Leeson made huge investments betting on the rebound of the Nikkei. While traders at other investment banks cut their losses, Leeson proceeded to put Barings' money into billions of dollars' worth of

Workers are shown exiting the Barings Bank Building in London, after it was purchased by Dutch financial group ING for only 1£. Barings had been one of the oldest and most prestigious banks in Great Britain before employee Nick Leeson bankrupted it by speculating in the Nikkei 225 (Japan's version of the Dow Jones index).

futures contracts that would only make money if the Nikkei rose. Traders in Tokyo and Singapore watched, but they figured that the bets that Barings was making were offset by hedges in other areas. However, this turned out not to be the case. For every percentage point that the Nikkei slipped, Barings lost tens of millions of dollars. Eventually, the losses exceeded Barings' net worth.

Whether senior management really knew what was going on in Singapore is not clear. Someone at the London headquarters knew—because Leeson had made the investments with borrowed funds, a common practice. As Leeson's bets lost, Barings in London funneled $900 million to Singapore to offset the losses. By late February, the Nikkei had not bounced back, and Leeson and his wife skipped town.

Barings went bankrupt on February 26. As British regulators took control of the bank, Interpol, the international intelligence agency, sent out an alert to all governments in neighboring countries to find Leeson. A few days after the bank's collapse, the "rogue trader" walked into the arms of police at Germany's Frankfurt airport.

How could such a large, prestigious bank like Barings be so naive to the public activities of a single trader?

Sources: Pavia Dwyer, "Descent into the Abyss," *BusinessWeek*, July 1, 1996, pp. 28–29; Stephen D. Kaye, "Ripples from a Fallen Bank," *U.S. News & World Report*, March 13, 1995, pp. 68–72; Bill Powell, Daniel Pedersen, and Michael Elliott, "Busted!" *Newsweek*, March 13, 1995, pp. 36–43.

strategic overview

As shown in the opening case example of Barings, control is a critically important component of management activities in organizations, and it can play an important role in how an organization's strategy is developed and implemented and in the evaluation of its success. Oftentimes, control is exercised based on the financial outcomes of a strategy, such as an organization's profits. However, another means of control is sometimes used; it is focused on the type of strategy selected and the manner in which it is implemented. While controls focused on strategy (as opposed to financial outcomes) are difficult to develop and apply, they are crucial to ensuring that the organization remains innovative. Financial controls often focus on achieving short-term results such as meeting the firm's profit goals for a quarter or a year. But when the focus is on strategy, managers must look toward longer-term results, such as investing in the development of innovative new products. In fact, the types of controls implemented can affect the formulation of future strategies. Research has shown that when managers use controls focused on strategy, they are better able to focus on the long term and develop more effective organizational strategies.[1]

The type of control can also affect both the formulation and implementation of strategies by managers. Bureaucratic controls tend to focus on controlling behavior in organizations with rules and regulations. Universities often employ bureaucratic controls because of the large number of students, faculty, and employees whose behavior they must oversee. However, these controls are frequently tight and may constrain the types of strategies that can be pursued. For this reason, universities often make major changes only very slowly. Alternatively, controls based on the organization's culture (called "clan controls," and explained later in this chapter) better ensure that the strategies chosen fit well with the values of the organization. For example, Southwest Airlines has a unique culture and utilizes it to select new employees who share the organization's values. This same culture, or clan control, governs the behavior of managers and employees who then have the same vision for the organization. Because all of the employees understand Southwest's culture and "buy into it," managers are better able

to develop effective strategies that match the firm's values and implement them.

Regardless of the types of controls used, managers shouldn't feel so controlled or constrained that they can't respond to environmental changes such as challenges from competitors and the prospect of innovative products being introduced to the market. Many organizations now employ the Balanced Scorecard approach (explained later in this chapter) to ensure that managers are able to balance controls and needed flexibility to continue to learn, innovate, and change.

Probably the most critical part of that challenge, for individual managers as well as for organizations, is where to draw the line between too much control and too little control. Most of us can think of examples from our own work or other group experiences where we have encountered the downside of excessive control by individuals or supervisors or the organization itself through its rules and regulations. At the extreme, overcontrol conjures up images of "Big Brother," where you cannot make a move without first obtaining permission from someone higher up in the organizational structure.[2] More typically, too much control can result in resentment and squelched motivation.

At the other extreme, too little control, as illustrated in the opening example, can expose an organization and its managers to very costly risks. In milder forms, undercontrol contributes to sloppy operations and failure to utilize resources efficiently and effectively. Errors or mistakes can increase, and the organization may not know where or when problems are occurring and, particularly, how to fix them. In severe cases, the potential consequences can be catastrophic for the organization, as they were for Barings.

Exercising control, then, presents not only major challenges for managers but also difficult dilemmas. The issue gets further complicated by the fact that, as we will discuss later, there are different types of control. A certain type of control may be quite effective in one situation but very ineffective or even damaging in different circumstances. The bottom line is that managers, no matter where they are in an organization or at what level, will have to deal with fundamental questions of control.

Managerial control problems occur in sophisticated organizations and in all countries. The example in the opening paragraphs makes this abundantly clear. If a major multinational corporation such as Barings can have difficulties with control, so can smaller organizations with fewer resources and less sophisticated systems. Likewise, if these kinds of problems can develop within a firm headquartered in the United Kingdom and doing business across the globe, they can occur in any location or culture where managerial activity takes place. Exercising effective control is a universal and exceedingly important managerial challenge.

To explore the issue of control, we first look at the role that control plays in organizations and the way it relates to other managerial functions such as strategy and planning. Next, the four basic elements of the control process—establishing standards, measuring performance, comparing performance against standards, and evaluating results (and, if necessary, taking action)—are reviewed. Following this is a discussion of the different levels of control (strategic, tactical, and operational) and the various forms of control. This chapter concludes with an examination of factors that can influence the effectiveness of controls, such as their focus, amount, and the cost of implementing them. How consideration of these factors leads to crucial managerial choices is also explored.

THE CONTROL FUNCTION IN MANAGEMENT

On the face of it, the word "control" sounds negative. It can mean restraints, constraints, or checks. This clearly connotes restricted freedom of action—an idea that many people, especially in some cultures, may find troublesome. Certainly, within the context of organizations, **control** involves regulation of activities and behaviors (see Exhibit 16.1). To control, in an organizational setting, means to adjust or bring conformity to specifications or objectives. In this sense, then, the control responsibilities of managers are bound to restrict someone's freedom. A manager cannot control without restricting. However, whether this is good or bad for the individual or group that is being controlled, for the manager who determines the amount and type of control, or for the organization at large depends on the consequences of the control and whose perspectives are being considered.

Some amount of control in organizations is unavoidable. The very essence of organizations is that individuals give up total independence so that common goals and objectives may be accomplished. As one organizational scholar put it, "The coordination and order created out of the diverse interests and potentially diverse behaviors of members is largely a function of control."[3]

control regulation of activities and behaviors within organizations; adjustment or conformity to specifications or objectives

exhibit 16.1

The Control Function in Management

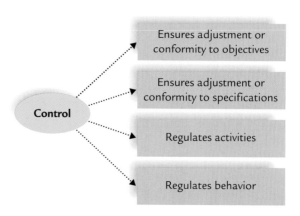

Thus, control is a fundamental characteristic of organized activity. Managers should always keep in mind, however, that control is a means for achieving a goal and is not the goal itself (as well exemplified in A Manager's Challenge, "Steak Right").

The managerial function of control comes at the end of a chain of the other major functions of planning, organizing, and leading. (Indeed, that is why a chapter on control is almost always found toward the end of most management textbooks.) If those prior functions are carried out well, generating positive responses to controls will be much easier. Conversely, if major problems exist in planning, organizing, and leading, almost no amount of attention

a manager's challenge

Change

Steak Right

For fine restaurants, cooking is an art, not a science. The reputation of the food at these restaurants is usually a function of the chef's creativity. So the ideas of standardization and tight control are generally alien to upscale restaurants.

This is not the case with Morton's Restaurant Group, a company that operates more than 65 expensive steak houses and runs many aspects of them with McDonald's-type precision. Morton's CEO, Allen J. Bernstein, firmly believes that tight controls have been the key to his firm's financial success. By the late 1990s, the company had quadrupled the number of its restaurants and increased net income as well.

Then, the external environment changed. An economic slump—coupled with businesses spending less on travel and entertainment—hurt Morton's revenues and profits. In addition, the expansion of high-end steak restaurants such as Ruth's Chris Steak House and Smith & Wollensky had intensified the competitive environment in many markets where Morton's operated. Despite these external pressures to make significant changes that would reduce costs, Morton's kept its customers loyal and attracted new fans by refusing to compromise its strict controls on food preparation and presentation.

The controls start with the "bible." This phone-book-thick illustrated binder prescribes, ingredient by ingredient, the preparation of the 500 items coming from the kitchen. The binder exactly specifies everything from the sauces to a medium-rare porterhouse steak. The presentation of the food is also not open to individual interpretation. Color photographs line the wall of every Morton kitchen. Evaluation of presentation then becomes a relatively easy

matter. Either the dish to be served looks like the photograph, or it doesn't.

The push for control is so stringent that each restaurant has a food and beverage controller who spends 12 hours a day tracking the movement of every item. Even the potatoes must meet rigorous standards. "I weigh every potato," says Andrew Moger, a food and beverage controller in the Manhattan Morton's. "They have to be at least a pound apiece."

The adherence to portion regulation and presentation is coupled with an effective cost control and inventory-tracking system. Morton's is said to be able to track a single lost steak, which is no small matter with such valuable inventory.

The result is a consistent atmosphere and a dependable menu that brings loyal customers back again and again. "I like knowing what to expect," says one regular customer who brings clients to Morton's for business entertaining. "You never worry about the food or service. When business is involved, you can't trust things to chance."

Morton's consistency through tough times paid off when a mad-cow disease scare hit the industry early in 2004. The company's sales didn't suffer, and its revenues actually climbed. Its consistency produced by the highly developed control system has also made it a desirable tenant in the buildings in which it rents space.

"Landlords want to use us as an anchor," explains Bernstein. "We're in demand because developers can get other tenants if we're there. Of course, they want their new Morton's to be like the old ones in every way." And—regardless of changes in the external business environment or increased competitive pressures—the steak house intends to be just that.

Sources: Carol Hymowitz, "Managers Are Starting to Loosen Budgets as Optimism Grows," *Wall Street Journal*, January 6, 2004, p. B1; Rod Smith, "Castle Harlan Completes Acquisition of Morton's," *Feedstuffs*, August 12, 2002, p. 6; G. Collins, "A Big Mac Strategy at Porterhouse Prices," *New York Times*, August 13, 1996, pp. C1, C4.

exhibit 16.2

Control's Feedback Loop

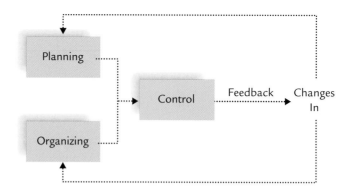

to control is likely to work very well. In this sense, effective control is a managerial function that depends heavily on the other functions that precede it. When these preceding functions work well, control tends to work well. When they don't, control can become a major headache for a manager.

Control can also be thought of as a "causal" variable because the results of control efforts can inform and improve the planning process of the organization. Control is thus part of a feedback loop into planning and organizing (see Exhibit 16.2) that can help managers adapt to changing circumstances and conditions. When either the internal or external organizational environment changes, good control systems let managers know if the current ways of operating are still meeting the organization's objectives. For example, a decade or so ago, certain sales agents within Prudential Insurance Company tried to increase their revenues and their personal bonuses based on larger sales through "churning." The churning involved persuading customers who had long-standing policies with built-up cash value to take out new, bigger policies on the promise that these new policies would not cost them more. Customers were not told that the cash values of their old policies were being used to pay the higher costs of the new policies. So while the customers were not laying out any more cash in monthly premiums than they did before, the new policies were, indeed, costing them. An external audit at one point warned senior management of excessively high turnover among "mature policies." Unfortunately for Prudential, however, while this control provided an early warning signal, managers did not do enough to investigate, and the company was hit by a raft of lawsuits.[4]

THE BASIC CONTROL PROCESS

The basic elements of the control process in an organizational setting are simple and straightforward (see Exhibit 16.3):

1. Establish standards.
2. Measure performance.
3. Compare performance against standards.
4. Evaluate results (of the comparison) and, if necessary, take action.

Each of these basic components involves important managerial attention and decisions.

Establish Standards

Specification of what management expects is absolutely critical at each step of the control process. This starts at the top of the organization and, ideally, should eventually involve every level of employee. First and foremost, those at

exhibit 16.3

The Basic Elements in the Control Process

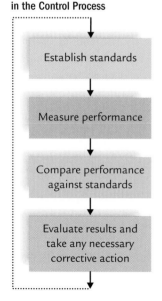

If anyone knows how to put on the "ritz," it's the Ritz-Carlton's 25,000 employees located at its 57 hotels worldwide. Each Ritz employee gets over 100 hours of customer service training annually. A daily "SQI" (Service Quality Indicator) in every hotel is displayed on TV screens for hotel personnel to see. The SQI monitors production and guest service processes up to the minute so service problems are apparent and can be immediately remedied.

the highest levels should be able to articulate a vision and formulate broad strategic goals for the organization. For instance, the motto of Dart Transit Company, a long-haul company that for 70 years has operated with a network of independent truckers, is "to exceed the expectations of our customers."[5] From this example, it is easy to see how particular **standards**, or targets of performance, might be developed. Without a strategic vision and goals for the overall organization, managers in various parts of the organization find it difficult to develop meaningful and agreed-upon performance yardsticks.

standards targets of performance

The establishment of standards—wherever they exist throughout the organization—requires as much specificity as possible. The reason for this is that measuring performance against standards cannot readily be accomplished if the standards are vague. A standard of "efficiently respond to customer complaints," for example, does not provide usable guidelines for determining whether the standard has been met. A standard of "responds, on average, to three customer complaints per hour" would permit an objective measurement of performance.

However, for some aspects of performance, especially in higher-level and more complex jobs such as those in research laboratories, it is often not possible nor even desirable to set up easily quantified standards (such as number of discoveries per year). In these kinds of positions, the most important elements of performance may be the most difficult to measure, such as the probable long-term impact of a given discovery. Moreover, as in the example in the preceding paragraph, the *quality* of response to customer complaints may be more important than the *rate* of response. However, quality is often more difficult to measure. As shown in Exhibit 16.4, the more abstract the standard, the greater the possibility of confusion in measuring performance, and the greater the problem of gaining the acceptance of those measurements by members whose performance is being assessed.

Other issues also can arise in the establishment of standards (see Exhibit 16.5). One revolves around the decision regarding who should set the standards. In general, research has shown that in setting standards, participation by those who will be affected is beneficial in two respects.[6] First, because they have had

exhibit 16.4

The Effect of Specificity of Standards on Performance Measurement

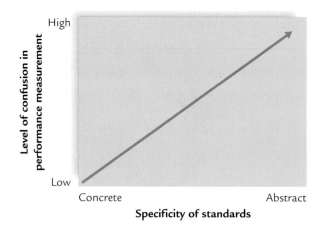

exhibit 16.5

Issues in Establishing Standards

some opportunity to influence the standards being set, those affected are more likely to be committed to meeting them. Second, involving those who have to meet the standards often results in a useful exchange of information and expertise that, in turn, results in more appropriate standards. At Siemens AG's top-notch medical solutions plant in Forchheim, Germany, for example, managers are striving to achieve a cost-savings goal of 10 percent per year, while at the same time improving quality manufacturing performance. To do so, they have involved all of the workgroups in the control process, and each group meets weekly with their manager to examine the past week's performance and set goals for the following week. Initial results are impressive: a shortening of delivery time by 90 percent (from 22 weeks to 2 weeks) and substantial improvements in reliability.[7]

Another issue is the degree of difficulty of the standards themselves. As we saw in the chapter on motivation, the research on goal setting points to the conclusion that difficult but achievable goals seem to result in the highest levels of performance.[8] Similar views have been expressed regarding goals in the budgetary process. Thus, "the ideal budget is one that is challenging but attainable."[9] Achievable budget standards are regarded as desirable because they reduce the motivation to manipulate data or to focus only on short-term actions at the expense of long-term objectives. Achievable budgets also have the potential for increasing morale and generating a "winning atmosphere."[10] This assumes, as noted, that the budgetary targets are not only attainable, but also reasonably difficult. Here, again, where to draw the line between goals that are too challenging and those that are not challenging enough is itself another duality type of managerial challenge. An interesting side note on the topic of budgets is that some companies have rejected the use of budgets, and the wrangling over what the data indicate. In the absence of budgets, they use alternative financial and nonfinancial goals and measures. Companies that have rejected budgets require employees to measure themselves against the performance of competitors and against internal peer groups. Since employees do not know whether they have succeeded until they can look back on the results of a given period, they must make sure that they beat the competition. A key feature of many companies that have rejected budgets is the use of rolling forecasts, which are created every few months and typically cover five to eight quarters.[11]

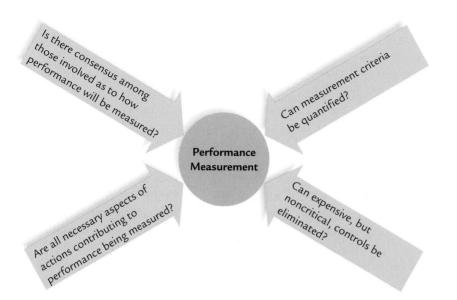

exhibit 16.6

Issues in the Measurement of Performance

Measure Performance

The second step in the basic control process is the measurement of performance, the actions of people and equipment that the organization wants to monitor (see Exhibit 16.6). Some years ago, the Bank of America faced a crisis. Both its stock price and earnings per share had been dropping precipitously for several years, and one year the bank suffered a loss of half a billion dollars. This situation was blamed on, among other factors, "runaway operating expenses, sloppy credit monitoring, [and] loose controls."[12] The CEO at the time resigned, and a former CEO, Tom Clausen, was brought back to rescue the company. He immediately impressed upon the employees the importance of measuring and controlling costs. He provided data showing that the bank spent $.70 to obtain $1 of business. He set a goal of reducing those costs, and within a year he managed to lower the figure to $.63 and get the bank on the road to recovery.[13] If specific and concrete standards have been set, as in this example, measurement is facilitated, and there is more likely to be agreement on how performance is to be measured.

When readily quantifiable criteria do not exist, however, it becomes especially important to obtain as much consensus as possible about the way in which performance is to be assessed. To use an analogy, when true/false or multiple choice tests are used in a class, the score a student receives is seldom contested (even though the quality of the questions often is). On the other hand, the score given to the answers on a test composed of essay questions is frequently disputed between student and teacher. The more the instructor and the class members can agree in advance about the qualities of good answers and on how the essay questions will be graded, the more likely the measurement process will be accepted. This occurs even though that process is clearly subjective. Similarly, in work situations, gaining up-front commitment to the performance measurement methods will reduce later complaints about what those measurements showed and what they mean to individuals and to the organization.

Since performance in many jobs involves multiple activities, it is important for measurement to be comprehensive. If only some aspects of performance are measured, results can be misleading; they can skew the data that are used for the next two steps in the control process, especially the taking of action to change performance. Companies such as Kodak, Motorola, Rolls Royce, and General Electric utilize a comprehensive control technology called "stage-gate" throughout the life of a project. Each project is divided into several stages with "gates" between them. Collectively, the gates act as comprehensive quality control checks that have to be passed before the gate will open, allowing the project to move on to the next stage. This allows management, at each gate, to review the progress of the project and decide whether it merits continued funding.[14] A potential danger, of course, is that promising new products might be killed too soon by overeager, stage-gate keepers.

Finally, even though measurement should be comprehensive, not everything that possibly could be measured should be measured. Measurement has a cost, and the usefulness of the information obtained may not justify the costs. The issue here is one of criticality, that is, what is measured should be highly relevant to the goals of the organization. Activities that are necessary but that do not provide relevant indicators of progress toward goals do not justify the expense to measure them. What is easy to measure may not be what is most important to control (as we also noted in Chapter 15).

Compare Performance Against Standards

Comparing performance results against previously set standards is the third step in the control process. Just as performance measurement is strongly influenced by the standards, so are comparisons affected by the kinds of measurements available. If key measurements have not already been built into the system, it is usually not possible to go back and reconstruct them for purposes of comparison. Sometimes managers realize too late that appropriate comparisons cannot be made.

When several dimensions of performance have been measured, this step in the process can involve multiple comparisons. If those comparisons all point in the same direction, interpretation is relatively straightforward. However, the picture of performance that emerges from a set of comparisons may be inconsistent or contradictory. That is, some comparisons may show good adherence to standards and targets, and others may reveal problems. So managers need to know how to interpret the patterns of comparisons and to draw appropriate conclusions. A single negative comparison may outweigh a number of positive comparisons, or vice versa.

For example, after a major restructuring, Safeway found that its sales per grocery store had nearly tripled and its sales per employee had also risen by 70 percent. Overall profits were up, but customer satisfaction scores were down. What were managers to make of this? In Safeway's case, sales per store and per employee as well as overall profits were up because it had sold off or closed its least profitable stores (many of which were operating at a loss). All of this might paint a very positive picture. However, the fact that customer satisfaction was down was potentially a bad sign. Grocery stores make money through volume. Therefore, if dissatisfied customers were to start spending less at Safeway and more at competitors, the positive results could deteriorate rapidly. Consequently, placing too much emphasis on per-store sales compared with customer satisfaction would be a control mistake.

In this third control step, managers need to compare expected performance with actual performance. These comparisons often involve both subjective estimates as well as objective ones. However, even if the comparison involves only objective, quantitative numbers, judgment is still needed. For example, suppose Safeway's customer satisfaction numbers were down from

Razor-thin profit margins in the grocery business make inventory and ordering mistakes costly. Wegman's Food Markets, Inc., an upscale supermarket chain based in New York, is attempting to mitigate those mistakes by encouraging its suppliers to use UCCnet. UCCnet is essentially an online catalog. Wegman's already shares data via UCCnet with more than 100 of its suppliers and hopes to access the rest soon. The company believes the system can save millions of dollars annually for the entire industry.

5.5 to 5.2. Anyone can compute that customer satisfaction had declined by 0.3 points. However, the key question is, "Is this drop significant?" The answer to this question requires managerial judgment.

Evaluate Results and Take Action

The fourth step, evaluate results and take action, is arguably the most difficult managerial task in the entire control process. The results that emerge from the performance comparisons may or may not require action. Managers need to consider whether any single comparison or a pattern of comparisons requires action to be taken. If actual performance deviates from expected performance, how much of a difference is required before something is done about that difference? That question has no single answer. It requires evaluation of the importance and magnitude of the deviation.

An analogy illustrates what is involved in this type of judgment. In industrialized countries, the directors of the national banking system—the Board of Governors of the Federal Reserve System, in the case of the United States—periodically receive the most current data about the national economy; for example, the unemployment rate, the consumer price index, the index of consumer confidence, the rate of new starts in home building, and the like. These data are compared against predetermined benchmarks, and then a decision must be made about whether to take action (for example, to increase interest rates). The problem for the board, as for any manager in an organization, is to determine which data are most important and how much of a change is significant. However, the issue is even more complicated. Managers must determine whether a slight change in the same direction for all of the indicators is more or less important than a major change in just one indicator. As any macroeconomist would testify regarding the national economy, this type of judgment is not easy.

The other basic judgment that must be made in this fourth step is what action to take if the pattern and size of deviations from expected performance are determined to be significant. Managers need knowledge about the causes of the deviation as well as about the potential actions that are possible.

Clearly, the evaluation and action step of control requires managers to have strong diagnostic skills as well as a certain level of expertise. Sometimes, the causes of a problem may be easily recognized, but the decisions about which actions to take to correct them may be extremely difficult. Conversely, the most effective actions may be well known, if only the causes could be clearly identified.

If a manager discovers major negative differences between performance and standards, some type of action is clearly needed because failure to act can lead to more severe problems in the future. However, if the deviations are major but positive, the necessity for action is usually much less (see Exhibit 16.7). Such positive differences, though, may in fact provide valuable insights about unexpected opportunities that should be pursued. For example, a major maker of baby food discovered stronger-than-expected sales of its new line of toddler foods in Florida. Further investigation revealed that the increased sales were not due to a higher-than-expected number of toddlers; rather, they were due to older customers with teeth problems who bought the product because it was easier to chew. This led to a whole new line of packaged foods targeted at this particular consumer segment.

To help maintain positive performance, employees who are doing better than expected can be given increased recognition and rewards to reinforce their excellent performance. Likewise, sales that exceed their forecast may mean that production should be increased or the product line should be extended. Costs that are below target may suggest an efficient practice that could be duplicated for other employees to follow, to reduce the costs even further. In short, it is as important to evaluate surprises on the upside as it is on the downside.

One other issue is involved in determining what action managers should take in the case of significant deviations from standards (whether in the positive or negative direction). This is the judgment about whether the standards are correct and the performance is the problem, or whether the performance is appropriate but the standards are too difficult or too easy. That is why a broken-line feedback arrow is shown from "Evaluate Results" to "Establish Standards" in Exhibit 16.3, indicating that the standards may need to be adjusted. Over time, standards are sometimes modified as experience is gained and the feasibility of existing standards is better understood. If a great deal of effort and care has been used in setting the standards and participation in setting them was broad, then

exhibit 16.7

Outcomes of Performance Measurement

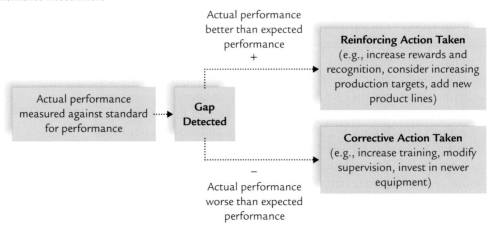

the issue is probably likely to be one of performance. If, though, the standards have been set hastily or without appropriate input from the relevant parties, then performance may not be the problem. This kind of issue points out once again the tight interconnection of the four basic steps of the control process.

SCOPE OF CONTROL IN THE ORGANIZATION

Even though the four steps of the control process are similar wherever they occur in organizations, the scope of what is being controlled can vary widely. This, in turn, affects how the steps are actually put into use. A bank provides a simple illustration. The bank manager may need to assess whether she has an adequate level of deposits relative to outstanding loans. The scope is quite broad because the outcome of this assessment could affect the entire organization. If the ratio is too low, the bank may need to reduce its level of lending or try to get more deposits. On the other hand, the manager may also need to evaluate the ratio of human bank tellers to automatic teller machines at each branch. In this case, the scope is much narrower because the issue only involves a small part of the bank's total set of activities. In the former instance we would label the scope as "strategic," and in the latter instance it would be regarded as an "operational" control issue. These represent two of the three major categories of control scope. The third, and intermediate level between strategic and operational, is a category typically called "tactical." (Refer back to Chapter 8, "Planning," for a discussion of the three categories of "strategic," "tactical," and "operational.")

In the remainder of this section, we look at the issues involved in each of these three types of control classified by the breadth of their scope. However, it is useful to remember that no hard-and-fast boundaries separate the three types (see Exhibit 16.8). The differences between strategic and tactical control issues often are blurred, and likewise, it is not always clear whether a control issue should be considered tactical or operational. Nevertheless, the three categories help remind managers where they should focus their attention.

Strategic Control

As discussed in Chapter 6, strategy refers to the direction for the organization as a whole. It is linked to the mission of the organization and to the basic plans for achieving that mission. Thus, **strategic control** is focused on how the organization as a whole fits its external environment and meets its long-range objectives and goals. Strategic control systems, where they exist, are designed to determine how well those types of objectives and goals are being met.

A particular challenge in formulating strategic controls is the fact that strategic goals are broad and, especially, long term. This means that such goals

Strategic, Tactical, and Operational Control Systems by Michael Hitt

Q&A
One**Key**
www.prenhall.com/onekey

strategic control assessment and regulation of how the organization as a whole fits its external environment and meets its long-range objectives and goals

exhibit 16.8
Types and Scope of Control

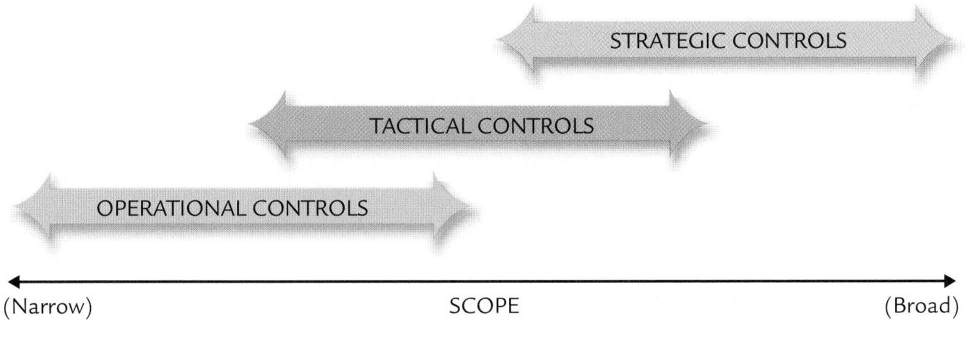

STRATEGIC CONTROLS

TACTICAL CONTROLS

OPERATIONAL CONTROLS

(Narrow)   SCOPE   (Broad)

typically are more abstract than goals for particular units. Consequently, setting strategic standards and measuring strategic performance can be especially challenging. For this reason, research has shown that only a relatively small number of firms in both Europe and the United States have yet set what could be termed strategic control systems.[15] The numbers will undoubtedly increase in the future, but important obstacles interfere with establishing such systems.

A significant factor that affects whether strategic control systems can be set up, and whether they will be effective, is the unpredictability of the external environments in which many organizations operate and from which they obtain resources. This also makes it difficult to develop standards and measures that are relevant for more than short periods of time. In fact, it is particularly difficult for firms to develop useful criteria for assessing the long-term performance of individual managers.[16]

Environmental conditions for large companies affect how much leeway each division or unit is given in determining its own competitive strategies for dealing with its particular markets.[17] The issue is essentially one of how much strategic control systems should be centralized versus decentralized, and how much variation should be allowed by unit. Such a decision involves not only matters of strategy but also of organization structure (Chapter 7).

Sometimes, in fact, because of changes in the external environment, companies find they have to reverse course on their overall strategic approach to controls. Thus, McDonald's has restructured its U.S. operations to reinstate controls it had abandoned in the mid-1990s. Why? Because it was suffering a decreased earnings trend. To deal with this, it is controlling not only its ingredients but also the experience customers have in its restaurants. It has gone back to more inspections of every store and the use of mystery shoppers. It is also making more use of extensive customer surveys.[18]

Research indicates, however, that "the efficiencies of managing through centralized control may be greater . . . when the operating environments of divisions in multidivisional organizations are relatively stable and predictable" (see Exhibit 16.9).[19] When there is more uncertainty in the environment, centralized control becomes less efficient. In other words, in relatively turbulent environments, it is difficult for centralized strategic control systems to keep up with events, and, consequently, more responsibility for control must be delegated to major units. When the environment is changing rapidly, as it is for many companies these days, too much reliance on organizationwide strategic goals and standards of performance that are set too far in advance can interfere with the needed speed and flexibility of the various operating units to respond effectively to the environment, especially in complex organizations with many types of units.[20]

exhibit 16.9

Degree of Centralization of Control in Relation to Environmental Stability

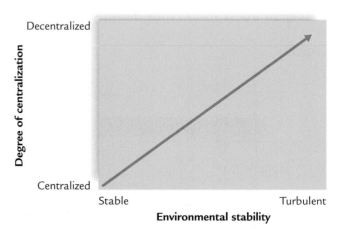

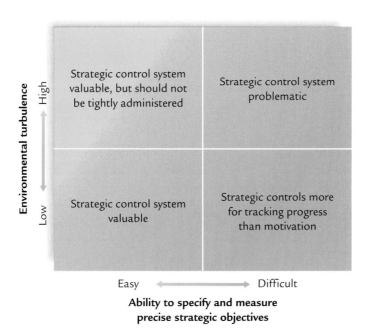

exhibit 16.10

Approaches to Strategic Control

Source: M. Goold and John J. Quinn, "The Paradox of Strategic Controls," *Strategic Management Journal* 11, no. 1 (1990), pp. 43–57 (p. 55).

As shown in Exhibit 16.10, both the degree to which it is possible to measure precisely how well performance conforms with strategic goals and the degree of turbulence or uncertainty in the environment can affect the value of having strategic control systems.[21] They are most likely to be useful when measurement is easy and operating environments are relatively calm, as in the case of the cement industry, for example. Although this industry basically follows the ups and downs of the construction industry, the factors that significantly affect these movements are relatively well known. For instance, changes in interest rates have a significant impact on building booms and busts. As rates go down and money is cheaper to borrow, construction increases. As rates go up and money becomes more expensive to borrow, construction decreases. Thus, for a concrete firm, strategic controls such as being number one in sales in a region can be relatively useful.

Conversely, strategic controls are probably least useful when exact measurement is difficult and the environment is fluctuating rapidly. As recently as five years ago, putting up a Web site for a company involved contracting with a vendor that specialized in the unique and various languages used on the Internet. Companies providing such services have seen their world change dramatically. New languages and tools have emerged so that almost anyone with a little skill and knowledge can create a professional-looking Web site. In such a turbulent environment, strategic goals do not last long. Therefore, strategic controls are of more limited value in these types of organizations.

Strategic control is especially challenging in international organizations, as A Manager's Challenge, "Global Expansion Sends Interpublic Spinning Out of Control," illustrates. Even with advances in communication and transportation technology, Sydney is still a long way from Paris, so to speak. Consequently, strategic control across a worldwide organization that crosses cultural, economic, social, political, and religious borders and is 16 time zones away is significantly more difficult than for a purely domestic organization.

globalization *a manager's challenge*

Global Expansion Sends Interpublic Spinning Out of Control

The Interpublic Group of Companies owns some of the advertising world's best-known agencies, including McCann-Erickson, Lowe & Partners, and Foote, Cone & Belding. To become a global marketing powerhouse, Interpublic, in the mid-1990s, began acquiring a variety of sports-related businesses such as British raceways and a German soccer team. However, it turns out that Interpublic's managers have had difficulty digesting these acquisitions and keeping them under control.

The expansion into sports marketing had been spearheaded by Sir Frank Lowe, founder of the Lowe advertising agency purchased by Interpublic in 1990. Lowe and his managers saw a bright future for selling global sports television rights and managing athletes' endorsement careers. They envisioned making sponsorship deals with General Motors and other major Interpublic clients. Over the course of three years, they created a new division, Octagon Motor Sports, and stocked it with sports agencies, racing schools, raceways, and even a go-cart track.

Lowe and his managers at Octagon had to oversee planning, marketing, budgeting, personnel, and every other aspect of sports businesses spread across thousands of miles. For instance, they negotiated long-running contracts for partner companies to sell tickets and racing merchandise. However, these contracts allowed Octagon little say in how they handled them. Octagon's managers also contracted with clients to provide them certain sports marketing services. In some cases, however, they agreed to deliver the same services to competitors in the same industry—agreements they could not realistically fulfill. Moreover, disorganized parking facilities and massive traffic jams plagued Octagon-owned Silverstone, the raceway where the British Grand Prix car race has long been held. The problems were so severe that the International Automobile Federation warned it might not hold future Grand Prix events at the site.

After Octagon's problems came to light, Lowe admitted he knew little about operating such businesses. "I thought, right, I've run a tennis tournament, maybe I know something about sports marketing. Boy, was I wrong." Although the managers were experienced in controlling advertising activities, they lacked experience in sports marketing. They didn't know what to control or how to control it. According to a high-ranking racing official, "Octagon's management was the problem. They weren't up to the task."

Octagon was overhauled when John J. Dooner Jr. became Interpublic's CEO in 2001. Many high-level Octagon managers were replaced, untenable contracts were settled, unprofitable business units were sold, and the company renamed Brands Hatch Circuits. Still, within one year, the racing company's financial performance swung from a profit of $11.5 million to a loss of more than $57 million. Dooner recognized that sports marketing is based on "a different economic model" than advertising: "The service industry is flexible because our assets are intellectual capital and people," he says. "But when you own a team or sports venue, the flexibility of upsizing and downsizing quickly isn't there."

But, the CEO can be fired quickly. Accounting irregularities subsequently forced Interpublic to restate its earnings, not once but twice. However, even those misstatements couldn't improve the earnings. So in 2003, Dooner was demoted and replaced with Interpublic vice president David Bell, who sold off more racetrack parcels and instituted additional cost cutting and staff reductions to prevent the company from spinning out of control. "We're digging out from a deep pit," Bell said. The company hopes the "pit" will be only a brief "stop" on the way back to profitability.

Sources: "Interpublic Cutting Ties to Racing Business," *Wall Street Journal,* January 6, 2004, p. B2; "Stuart Elliot in America," *Campaign* (UK), March 7, 2003, p. 21; Vanessa O'Connell and Erin White, "Off-Target Marketing: For Interpublic, Going Beyond Ads Proves Wrong Turn," *Wall Street Journal,* October 21, 2002, pp. A1, A9; Suzanne Kapner, "Ad Company Makes Bad Bet on Auto Races," *New York Times,* October 19, 2002, pp. B1, B4; Gerry Khermouch, "The Shock Waves Rocking Interpublic," *BusinessWeek,* December 2, 2002, p. 54.

Tactical Control

tactical control assessment and regulation of the day-to-day functions of the organization and its major units in the implementation of its strategy

Tactical control focuses on the implementation of strategy. Thus, this level covers the fundamental control arrangements of the organization, those with which its members have to live day to day. Tactical control forms the heart and, one might say, the soul of an organization's total set of controls. Four of the most important types of tactical control systems are financial controls, budgets, the supervisory structure, and human resource policies and procedures.

	Tactical Controls	Strategic Controls

exhibit 16.11

Characteristics of Strategic and Tactical Controls

Time Frame

Limited   Long, unspecific

Objective

Controls relate to specific, functional areas

Controls relate to organization as a whole

Types of Comparisons

Comparisons made within organization

Comparisons made to other organizations

Focus

Implementation of strategy

Determination of overall organizational strategy

The first two types of control, financial and budgetary, contain elements of both strategic and tactical control systems. To the extent they focus on the entire organization, they tend to be more toward the strategic end of the continuum (see Exhibit 16.11), and the more they focus on specific units within an overall organization, they tend to be toward the tactical end. We have chosen to discuss them in this section since they most often focus on organizational units, but keep in mind that they, especially financial controls, can also be used as well for some strategic control considerations.

Financial Controls Financial controls include several important quantitative ratios involving key financial statistics. Although such financial data are always generated at the organizationwide level as well as at the organizational-unit level, they are especially useful at the unit level as a form of tactical control.

The data used for the most important financial controls involve a basic cost-benefit analysis. For example, ratios relevant to the **profitability** of a given unit are constructed from revenue data (benefit) in relation to given amounts of investment (cost). The ratio is called **ROI** (**return on investment**, or alternatively, **ROE, return on equity**) and compares the amount of net profit before taxes (the numerator of the ratio) to the total amount of assets invested (the denominator). Thus, a unit that has a profit of $500,000 for a given year from invested assets of $10 million would have an ROI of 0.05 for that year. If another unit generated that same amount of profit on invested assets of only $5 million, its ROI would be 0.10 and would thus be considered to have had superior financial performance—it generated equal benefit for less cost.

Other financial ratios that are commonly used to assess unit performance include, in addition to profitability ratios, those related to **liquidity** (current assets in relation to current liabilities), which provides an indication of how well the unit can meet its short-term cash requirements; **leverage** (total debt to total assets), which provides an indication of ability to meet long-term financial obligations; and **efficiency** or **activity** (for example, the amount of sales in a given period relative to the cost of inventory used to generate those sales), measuring how efficiently assets are utilized.

profitability ratio of cost to benefit

ROI (return on investment) measure of profitability obtained by dividing net income by the total amount of assets invested

ROE (return on equity) alternative term for ROI

liquidity measure of how well a unit can meet its short-term cash requirements

leverage ratio of total debt to total assets

efficiency (activity) ratio of amount of sales to total cost of inventory

exhibit 16.12

Examples of Company Financial Ratios

Ratio	Formula	Company			
		The GAP, Inc. 2001		The Limited, Inc. 2001	
		In $ millions		In $ millions	
PROFIT					
Return on Investment	Net Profit before taxes / Total Assets	241 / 7,591	0.03	904 / 4,719	0.19
LIQUIDITY					
Current Ratio	Current Assets / Current Liabilities	3,044 / 2,056	1.4	2,682 / 1,319	2.0
LEVERAGE					
Debt to Asset	Total Debt / Total Assets	2,525 / 7,591	0.33	1,975 / 4,719	0.42
ACTIVITY					
Inventory Turnover	Sales / Inventory	13,847 / 1,677	8.3	9,363 / 966	9.7

Examples of these four types of ratios for two organizations in the retail industry for the year 2001 are shown in Exhibit 16.12. It can be seen from the exhibit that The GAP had a lower ROI than The Limited that year, somewhat less liquidity, a slightly more favorable leverage ratio, and a slightly less efficient use of inventory. Thus, if these had been two units within the same larger organization, one would say that for this year The Limited unit was doing better overall insofar as financial performance was concerned.

The important point here, regarding the various financial ratios, is not the detailed steps that need to be taken to calculate the ratios. Rather, it is that when the ratios are calculated, they can be used to compare one organization, or one unit, to another. Thus, it is the comparative nature of the ratios that provides managers with information needed to take action during control. The numbers used to calculate a ratio, such as inventory turnover, for example, will show whether the ratio is relatively unfavorable, and if so, an examination of the two components used in the ratio will also indicate whether the problem seems to be in the amount of sales (too low) or in the amount of inventory (too high) or both. In other words, financial ratios can provide a very useful diagnostic tool for managers to determine where to take control action to improve situations.

Another financial measure is sometimes used for control purposes in business organizations. That measure is called the **break-even point (B-E P)**. Essentially, a B-E P analysis is a quantitative formula used to determine what volume of some product or service must be sold before a firm's fixed and variable costs are covered by the next sale. That is, the break-even point is where the selling price of a unit of a product (or service) minus its variable costs exceeds the fixed costs for that unit. Clearly, the lower the fixed costs, the fewer the units of goods or services that need to be sold for a break-even point to be reached. Likewise, the lower the variable costs, the higher the profit per unit and therefore the fewer the units that need to be sold to reach that point. Break-even analysis, then, provides a way for managers to gauge whether new products or services have a potential to turn a profit. Managers can therefore exercise control *before* new ventures are

break-even point (B-E P)

amount of a product that must be sold to cover a firm's fixed and variable costs

undertaken. Even more important, for ongoing operations, a break-even point analysis focuses managers' attention on reducing or controlling the two categories of costs—fixed and variable—to take the pressure off the need to sell larger volumes.

An example of where a break-even point analysis can illustrate comparisons between two organizations, or business units, is provided by the airline industry. Many of the larger airlines have set up separate subsidiary airlines to handle short-haul commuter routes, for example, American Eagle, a part of American Airlines. These commuter airlines can operate on relatively small volumes of passenger traffic because their costs—like lower wage bases for their pilots—produce lower break-even points. Similarly, certain independent airlines—if they are especially efficient—can charge very low fares on many of their routes and still make a profit. Southwest Airlines, which uses a flexible point-to-point route system instead of the hub-and-spoke system of most other airlines, and avoided the cost of meals by serving only snacks long before other airlines did, is a good example.[22]

Although a B-E P analysis can provide extremely useful information for managers for control purposes, such an analysis also has limitations. Looking strictly at the numbers of a B-E P analysis may discourage certain decisions that could ultimately result in very profitable activities that do not initially appear to be profitable. Also, it is not always easy to allocate costs between fixed and variable categories, and it is sometimes difficult to project costs accurately, especially variable costs. Like other financial controls, a B-E P analysis can be an aid to exercising effective control, but it is not by itself a guarantee of wise decisions. What it does do, however, is highlight the potential advantages to be gained by controlling specific types of costs.

Budgetary Controls Budgets are used in almost every organization (as we discussed in Chapter 8 on "Planning"), and, like financial controls, can sometimes be considered elements of a strategic system. **Budgetary controls**, however, are more usefully viewed as a significant tactical control because they focus on how well strategies are being implemented. In contrast to purely strategic control, budgetary controls

budgetary control a type of tactical control based on responsibility for meeting financial targets and evaluating how well those targets have been met.

- Typically cover a relatively limited time frame (usually 12-month or 3-month periods).
- Focus exclusively on one type of objective (financial).
- Usually cannot be used to compare a total organization's progress relative to its competitors.[23]

Anyone occupying a managerial position is controlled by budgets and uses budgets to control others. A budget is a commitment to a forecast to make an agreed-upon outcome happen.[24] Thus, it is more than a forecast, which is simply a prediction. A budget is designed to influence behavior so that forecasts or plans for expenditures and (where relevant) revenues can be achieved. It "controls" by assigning responsibility for meeting financial targets and for evaluating how well those targets have been met. It would be difficult indeed to maintain an organization if none of its members were held accountable for limits on expenditures.

When using budgets as a form of control, managers face several important issues, as shown in Exhibit 16.13. One is the question of whether to use a fixed budget for a specific period, usually 12 months, and stick with those numbers, or to revise it midway during the period based on changes in operating conditions. Ace Hardware, for example, now uses a rolling planning and budg-

exhibit 16.13

Issues in Budgetary Control

Issue	Questions
Rolling budgets and revision	Should the budget period be for 12 months followed by another 12-month budget a year later, or should a calendar quarter be added each time a new calendar quarter begins?
	Should the budget remain fixed for the budget period or should it be revised periodically during the period?
Fixed or flexible budgets	Should performance be evaluated against the original budget or against a budget that incorporates the actual activity level of the business?
Bonuses based on budgets	Should incentive compensation, if any, be based on actual versus budgeted performance, or on actual performance against some other standard?
Evaluation criteria	Should the budget used to evaluate performance include only those items over which the evaluated manager has control, or should it include all unit costs and revenues appropriate to the managerial unit?
Tightness of the budget	What degree of "stretch" should there be in the budget?

Source: Adapted from N. C. Churchill, "Budget Choices: Planning vs. Control," *Harvard Business Review* 62, no. 4 (1984), pp. 150–64 (p. 151).

etary process. With the old annual-type of process, the conditions on which Ace's budget were based were frequently out of date by the time the budget was finalized. In the middle of a recent year, however, the company's sales were within 5 percent of the expected amount and closely tracked the budget. "We haven't had sales so close to budget at this point in the year in five years," said the company's manager of financial planning and analysis.[25] A rolling budgetary process with relatively frequent revisions has the advantage of being more current and therefore more accurate; however, it also can take more managerial time and effort.

Another budget issue is whether compensation bonuses should be based on the achievement of budgetary targets. This sounds good, but it has the great disadvantage of encouraging budget game-playing, because the person being evaluated has an incentive to provide high-cost and low-revenue estimates. This way, by creating "budgetary slack" with relatively easy targets, the person has a higher probability of hitting the targets and earning a bonus. Thus, managers who supervise the preparation of budgets need to be alert to how a bonus system of this type can distort estimates and thus undermine control. Managers also need to make sure that they don't inadvertently create a short-term focus on the part of subordinates attempting to meet budgetary targets at the expense of achievement of more important, longer-term organizational goals.26

A third budgetary control issue involves the question of whether those responsible for meeting specified targets should be evaluated only on expenditures and revenues over which they have direct control, or whether they should be evaluated on a final "net" figure based on all costs and revenues for a given unit. The former results in a more direct link between managerial behavior and budgetary responsibility, but the latter is the ultimate "bottom line," especially for publicly held corporations. For example, as a manager of a sales unit, you might have strong control over the revenues that your unit generates and the money spent on travel expenses. When these travel expenses are subtracted from sales, your unit might look very good. However, if your unit also uses marketing and promotion materials to get these sales, they may need to be factored into the overall assessment. Otherwise, you may overspend on marketing and promotion activities.

The final, and perhaps most important, managerial control issue regarding budgets is how tight or loose to make them. Should a budget require those charged with meeting it to make an extra "stretch"? As we have said before, research indicates that the best performance results from goals that are challenging but achievable. Since budgets represent goals, this conclusion seems highly relevant to the issue of budgetary control.

Supervisory Structure Controls The basic **supervisory structure** of an organization is probably the most widespread tactical control system that a typical organizational member encounters. The amount and form of such control varies considerably from organization to organization, but almost always exists in some form. In organizations of any size, there is always someone or some group to which an employee or manager reports. (Recall the discussion of Span of Control in Chapter 7, "Organization Structure and Design.") Even in the most collegial and least bureaucratic types of work organizations, such as research laboratories and nonprofit enterprises, some sort of reporting structure almost always regulates the activities of each member. However, such supervisory control structures, like other controls, can fail.

This was demonstrated several years ago at the Ohio Division of the American Cancer Society. Up until then, the organization had enjoyed a great deal of success. However, in 2000 the Board of Directors announced that its chief administrative officer had embezzled $7.5 million over a period of approximately three years. This had occurred even though a new CEO had checked all security arrangements when he started a few years before. The administrative officer had used a variety of schemes to steal the funds, such as billing for imaginary services, charging personal home repairs and expenditures to the organization, and transferring money to secret accounts in Europe. The board and top management were shocked to find out that all of their controls had failed in this instance. The administrative officer had never received a background check (which would have revealed previous problems), was the only person authorized to sign large-amount checks with only one signature, and, especially, had received no direct supervision of his day-to-day activities.[27]

Human Resource Controls **Human resource policies and procedures** are a fourth major type of tactical control that affects everyone working in an organization. We have discussed these in detail in Chapter 15, but what is important to stress about them here is that they provide a number of different opportunities for control (see Exhibit 16.14):

- Selection procedures can specify the range of abilities that will be brought into the organization.
- Training can improve skills and elevate performance to meet standards.
- Appraisal and evaluation methods can reinforce desired behavior and discourage undesirable levels of performance.
- Compensation can be used to motivate employees and increase their efforts in particular directions.

supervisory structure a type of tactical control based on reporting levels in an organization

human resource policies and procedures a type of tactical control based on the organization's overall approach to utilizing its human resources

exhibit 16.14

Opportunities for Control in the Human Resource Function

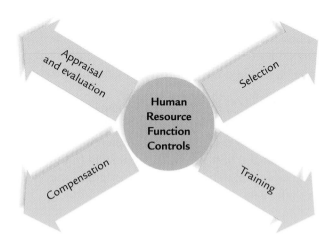

An example of using human resource procedures to reinforce desired behavior occurred when Standard Life of Scotland, one of the largest insurance companies in Europe, changed its performance evaluation and reward systems to a "contribution management system." The new system focused on the importance (not just the number) of an employee's accomplishments, the effort to develop the competencies to accomplish critical tasks, and the employee's contribution to customer satisfaction and the overall performance of the business. The change in approach required employees to be highly involved in goal setting, training plans, and rewards determinations. As a result of these changes in HR procedures, the company has gone from being one of the lowest-ranked on performance and customer satisfaction to one of the highest within the United Kingdom. It was also voted Company of the Year five years running in its industry.[28]

Because the effects of human resource policies and procedures are so extensive, they are very powerful means of control. When used with skill and deftness, they are a significant aid to the achievement of organizational objectives, as in the above Standard Life of Scotland example. When used ineptly, and with heavy-handedness, however, they can hinder organizational progress.

Contrasting Approaches to Using Tactical Controls   The ways in which tactical control systems are implemented say a great deal about an organization—what it is like to work there and how effective the control is. These control systems characterize an organization and are a critical part of its identity. For these reasons, it is important to specify and discuss the two fundamental approaches to tactical control: (a) imposed, or bureaucratic, control and (b) elicited, or commitment or clan, control (see Exhibit 16.15).[29] Most organizations use a combination of these two approaches but also tend to emphasize one over the other.

bureaucratic control an approach to tactical control that stresses adherence to rules and regulations and is imposed by others

Bureaucratic control stresses adherence to rules and regulations and a formal, impersonal administration of control systems. Thus, for instance, ExxonMobil has a thick operating manual for refinery managers. It specifies everything from which types of capital budget requests need which type of approval to equipment maintenance schedules. This approach highlights rational planning and orderliness. It heavily emphasizes detecting deviance from standards. But its foremost feature, in a control sense, is that control is *imposed* on the person, group, or activity. From an employee's perspective, "others" do the controlling.

commitment (clan) control an approach to tactical control that emphasizes consensus and shared responsibility for meeting goals

Commitment, or clan, control stresses obtaining consensus on what goals should be pursued and then developing a shared sense of responsibility for achieving those goals. It is called a "clan" approach to control because of the

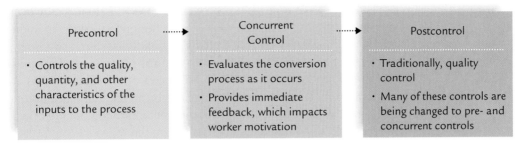

exhibit 16.16
Operational Controls

relating it to the three basic elements involved in any type of service or goods production: inputs, transformation, and outputs (Exhibit 16.16).[31] These three elements can be related to the location of control in the production process: before transformation occurs, or **precontrol**; during transformation, or **concurrent control**; and after transformation takes place, or **postcontrol**.

Precontrol of Operations This form of operational control focuses on the quality, quantity, and characteristics of the inputs into the production process—for example, the purity of steel, the grade of beef, the number of passengers, the age of patients, the test scores of entering students, the aptitudes of job applicants. Such precontrol is illustrated by a specification that the rail transport organization, Conrail, set up for its suppliers of communication products. It began requiring telecommunication suppliers to guarantee that the parts they provide would continue to work even if struck by lightning. As a result, Conrail was able to cut the number of communication failures resulting in train delays from 300 to 3 per month on a major route.[32]

The more stringent the control over the quality of inputs, the less need for control at the later two stages. The higher the quality of army recruits, for example, the easier it is to train them to be competent soldiers. However, there is a cost involved in exacting precontrol standards. Higher-quality inputs typically cost more, and the effort to ensure that the quality is high also increases costs. Nevertheless, those costs in many cases may be well justified by what is saved in the later control steps and by the positive evaluation of the eventual goods and services. In other words, customers may be willing to pay more for better products and services.

Concurrent Control of Operations Concurrent control involves real-time assessment of the quality of the transformation process, that is, evaluation of the conversion of inputs to outputs while it is happening. For example, eVineyard, an Internet wine retailer, created its business plan based on having a virtual, concurrent control of inventory. Because of the regulatory complexities of distributing liquor industry products for interstate sales, wine has to be passed through a local wholesaler and retailer before it gets shipped to the consumer. eVineyard set up local retail "shops" next door to local wholesalers, and paid cash for daily shipments. "We don't buy wine until we have an order, so we don't have inventory cost," explained one of the company's marketing managers. In fact, the eVinyard took possession of bottles just long enough to package and ship them to buyers. This type of concurrent control enabled the company to hold down its costs and prices and survive the dot-com crash as well as take over competitors wine.com and wineshopper.com.[33]

Other typical examples of concurrent control are the monitoring of a customer service representative's performance while handling a telephone inquiry

precontrol a type of operational control that focuses on the quality, quantity, and characteristics of the inputs into the production process

concurrent control a type of operational control that evaluates the conversion of inputs to outputs while it is happening

postcontrol a type of operational control that checks quality *after* production of goods or services outputs

or the inspection of fruit while a batch is proceeding along a conveyer belt to the canning machinery. This type of control is designed to provide immediate feedback so that operations can be changed rapidly to decrease errors or increase quality. To have effective concurrent control procedures, however, managers must give considerable attention in advance to how such systems are designed and implemented. Also, managers need to be aware that this kind of control can have strong impacts on the motivation of those carrying out the operations, since the feedback is so immediate and often very direct.

Postcontrol of Operations Postcontrol was the traditional form of control in manufacturing—checking quality *after* a product (TV sets, shoes, furniture, etc.) was produced. Thus, companies typically have had quality control inspectors or whole departments that checked the rate of defective products and then decided what to do if those rates were too high. For example, Toyota inspects each car coming off the assembly line on a basic list of criteria. It also randomly inspects cars based on a significantly longer and more detailed list of quality criteria. In recent years, quality control at many companies has been greatly diminished in favor of pre- and concurrent controls. The adage has been: "*Build* quality into the product, rather than inspect quality into the product."[34] Also, the more contemporary approach to operational control has been to shift control responsibilities to operations personnel and away from separate evaluators at the end of the process.

FACTORS IN CONTROL EFFECTIVENESS

Regardless of good intentions, control systems in organizations may break down completely, as illustrated at the opening of this chapter, or they may not work very well. There can be many reasons for this, but alert managers can take the initiative to reduce these possibilities. The effectiveness of control is very much under the control of managers. Again, there are no automatic prescriptions or rules of thumb for managing the control process well. Instead, managers can use certain potential sources of influence to increase the probabilities of success. In this section, we look at some of the key factors that determine the effectiveness of controls (see Exhibit 16.17).

exhibit 16.17

Key Factors in Determining the Effectiveness of Controls

Key Factor	Concerns
Focus of control	· What will be controlled? · Where should controls be located in the organizational structure? · Who is responsible for which controls?
Amount of control	· Is there a balance between over- and undercontrol?
Quality of information collected by the controls	· Is the information useful? · Is the information accurate? · Is the information timely? · Is the information objective?
Flexibility of controls	· Are the controls able to respond to varying conditions?
Favorable cost–benefit ratio	· Is the information being gathered worth the cost of gathering it?
Source of control	· Is control imposed by others? · Is control decided by those who are affected?

Focus of Control

The decision of where to focus control in an organization involves critical choices based on what actions and outcomes should receive the greatest attention. The guiding principle for focusing control is that it should be closely linked to the strategic goals and, particularly, the planning process of the organization. For example, in Chapter 4, we talked about Nordstrom's strategic focus on customer service. As a consequence, while the company would probably not be wise to ignore inventory controls, the focus would need to be on how to maintain a high level of customer satisfaction.

To be most effective, planning should be part of the control process, and control should be part of the planning process. Priorities should be set to select what is to be intensely monitored and controlled and what is to be given less attention. As software firms have found out, for example, little is to be gained from requiring star programmers to come to work on a precise schedule, given that the real objective is to produce innovative software. It is worth considerable control effort in that kind of organization, however, to make sure that the software that is written is as absolutely error-free as possible. Conversely, it is extremely important for restaurants to have their serving personnel be on time so that service is given promptly, whereas an occasional small mistake in taking a customer's order could be tolerated.

One approach to determining the focus of control that has become popular in the last decade or so is the so-called "**balanced scorecard**." Essentially, the advocates of this approach argue that historically—since the early years of the twentieth century—there has been an overfocus on financial measurements such as ratios and budgetary control procedures and a corresponding neglect of other important areas of measurement of a company's performance.[35] To remedy this, the developers of the balanced scorecard approach proposed an integrated and "balanced" set of measures for four critical areas ("perspectives" as they called them):[36]

Balanced Scorecard by Michael Hitt

Q&A

OneKey

www.prenhall.com/onekey

balanced scorecard an integrated and "balanced" set of measures for four critical areas or perspectives: financial, customers, internal business, and innovation and learning

- The (traditional) financial perspective: How do shareholders perceive the company?
- The customer perspective: How do customers perceive the company?
- The internal business perspective: How well is the company doing in excelling in internal business operations and procedures?
- The innovation and learning perspective: How well is the company doing at innovating, improving, and creating value?

It is also argued by the originators of this approach that the financial perspective primarily pays attention to the past, while the other three categories are much more future oriented. In effect, a presumed advantage of the balanced scorecard is that it requires managers to link measures of organizational success more closely to strategic objectives and to assess whether success in one area may be coming at the expense of poor performance in another area(s). It is intended, therefore, to bring greater focus and concentration on a total set of the most important areas of evaluation and control.

Many companies appear to have adopted some form of the balanced scorecard approach, with one estimate being that 40 to 60 percent of large U.S. firms were using it by 2000.[37] Such companies as Mobil Oil (now ExxonMobil) and Cigna Insurance, for example, credit the use of the balanced scorecard with helping to improve their corporate performance.

As might be expected, however, some issues have been raised about the details of the balanced scorecard approach. One is whether these are the "correct" and only four major areas to measure. A missing area, for example, is how employees perceive the organization and whether it is doing a good job of attracting and retaining talent. Another issue concerns whether each and every organization needs balance across all four areas or whether it should concentrate on only one or two of the areas or some other sort of mix.[38] Still another issue—which is common to any system or overall approach to control measurement—concerns the degree of difficulty in designing and implementing the types of measures called for in this comprehensive approach.[39] Regardless of these issues, however, it is clear that the balanced scorecard has introduced a fresh and needed approach to focusing control on more than just financial numbers.

Focus of control refers not only to what is to be controlled but also to where control should be located in the organizational structure. This means paying careful attention to which people or positions in the structure have responsibility for different types and areas of control and how broad or narrow is their scope of responsibility. Control responsibility that is too diffuse can lead to omissions, and responsibility that is too concentrated can result in bottlenecks and decision delays. For example, if too many different people are assigned responsibility for quality control of a complex set of equipment, each may assume that one of the others has taken care of a particular problem, and, as a consequence, some aspect of control gets left undone. On the other hand, if only one person is charged with inspecting all the pieces of equipment, that person may get overloaded, with the result that some critical detail gets inadvertently overlooked. Either way, effective control could be compromised.

Amount of Control

As we discussed at the beginning of this chapter, one of the greatest control challenges for any organization or manager is to determine the appropriate amount of control. The consequences of these choices can mean the difference between the life and death of an organization, as illustrated by A Manager's Challenge, "Control: Too Much or Too Little?"

Effective control involves finding a balance between overcontrol and undercontrol. Often, less-experienced managers tend to apply more control than is necessary in their eagerness to demonstrate that they are "in charge." This in turn can produce unintended resentment and resistance. Thus, new managers need to be aware of this tendency and moderate it.

If this were not a big enough challenge by itself, it is compounded in multinational corporations. In those organizations, perceptions of what is too much oversight can vary considerably from one country and culture to another. For example, tight monitoring of a manager's time and movements is more accepted in countries such as Thailand; however, managers in Australia are likely to react quite strongly and negatively to tight monitoring.

When managers have more experience, they have a better basis for gauging the minimum levels of control that will get the job done without incurring unjustified risks. Even seasoned managers often find it difficult to judge correctly the degree of control required, and problems of undercontrol can crop up where least expected. No predetermined "right" amounts of control apply to all work situations. The best guideline for a manager to follow is to view the amount of control as something that, within limits, can be adjusted. Additionally, the undesirable consequences of excessive control and the dangers of too little control need to be made part of careful assessments of per-

tech nol ogy

a manager's challenge

Control: Too Much or Too Little?

Controls that are too tight can keep an organization from functioning at its best. But controls that seem too tight for some organizations may be just right for others. Consider the case of C.R. England, a long-haul refrigerated trucking company based in Salt Lake City. The very nature of the business itself, which requires shipping quickly from one destination to another to maintain freshness, dictates the necessity of tight controls. England's managers needed to find the most efficient way to transport customers' products across the country without making their employees feel like prisoners.

"We want to run this place like the cockpit of a jetliner, where you have hundreds of different instruments before you at all times and know exactly where you are," explains Stephen Glines, vice president for technology. Thus, England relies on strict centralized control maintained by a computerized system and a satellite communications network that tracks hundreds of operations, from truck arrivals to invoice accuracy. Every worker is graded weekly on performance, based on computerized data such as the number of minutes needed to wash a truck or process a bill. "I don't think anyone likes to be this closely monitored," Glines says. "But most people start using the information as a learning tool." That may be why England's tight controls are so successful: Employees actually view the controls as positive, not negative. Since England instituted these controls, annual turnover—in an industry where 100 percent turnover is the average—has dropped 25 percent. "We're working to retain the drivers we have rather than spend almost $8,000 per driver to hire new ones," said CEO Dan England. And the company, more profitable than ever, has gained a competitive edge.

On the other hand, just as a loose pair of shoes can make its wearer stumble, so can loose controls cause an organization to slip and fall. When Banc One and First Chicago NBD merged, managers from both banks fought for months over who would run what and who would get more funding in the new organization (renamed Bank One Corporation). Even the computers couldn't communicate with each other. Meanwhile, without strong centralized control, managers in each region were applying different credit requirements for loans. When top management made revenue growth the main goal, the workforce moved quickly to expand lending without clearly assessing whether the loans would return long-term profits or not.

Then Jamie Dimon was named CEO virtually the day the stock market bubble burst. Dimon, who made it his business to know everything about Bank One, soon discovered that many of the loans the bank had extended in good economic times would be far less profitable in an economic downturn. "You don't run a business hoping you don't have a recession," the CEO said later. Bank One had so many problem loans that Dimon set aside $2.2 billion to cover potential losses and instituted national credit guidelines and rigorous controls for analyzing the profitability of each loan. He slashed expenses by 17 percent, dumped unprofitable loans, and transformed a crazy-quilt of deposit systems into one efficient platform. And, despite the objections of managers who said the two banks' computer systems could not be connected, the CEO insisted on making that a priority. "Unless the computers talk to each other, you can't do acquisitions. You can't build a great bank." In three years' time, Bank One went from a $511 million loss to a $3.5 million gain, making it an attractive merger partner for J.P. Morgan in 2004.

Sources: Shawn Tully and Julie Schlooser, "The Dealmaker and the Dynamo," *Fortune*, February 9, 2004, pp. 76–82; Allan Sloan, "The Kid Stays in the Picture," *Newsweek*, January 26, 2004, p. 42; "Carrier Panel Assesses Industry Position," *Refrigerated Transporter*, September 2003, p. 38; "Dan England," *Utah Business*, January 2001, pp. 28+; "Measure It to Manage It," *Fortune*, February 6, 1995, pp. 78+; Shawn Tully, "The Jamie Dimon Show," *Fortune*, July 22, 2002, pp. 88–96.

formance requirements and not inadvertently or casually overlooked. As we have already mentioned, involving those who will be directly influenced by the control measures in setting the amount of control increases the chances that an appropriate level of control is set from the outset. Furthermore, if adjustments need to be made, this initial involvement will likely reduce the resistance to needed changes.

Quality of Information

Effective control requires knowledge based on data; that is, it requires good information. Four characteristics that determine the quality of information are usefulness, accuracy, timeliness, and objectivity.

Usefulness Not all data collected for control purposes are equally useful in managerial operations and decisions. Sometimes data that were once useful continue to be collected, even though the original purposes for obtaining that information have disappeared. Such a situation was discovered several years ago in a division of the Borg-Warner Corporation. Because of major changes in the operating environment at an automotive transmission unit, the company decided to find out which accounting reports, if any, were actually helpful to managers. Did the information contained in the reports actually assist managers to do their jobs better? The answer was a resounding "no." Investigation indicated the accounting department thought it was gathering data that two separate groups could use: corporate managers and plant managers. Yet, it turned out that the information being disseminated was of assistance only to the first group. As a result, the accounting department worked with operations managers in the plants to develop control reports that would help them do their particular jobs more effectively.[40]

Accuracy Data or numbers that are inaccurate or misleading not only fail to provide a good basis for control steps but also breed cynicism among those whose performance is being measured. Since control actions, especially those designed to change behavior that does not meet agreed-upon standards, can have such powerful effects, it is vital that substantial effort be put into obtaining data that are absolutely valid. Otherwise, no information is better than inaccurate information.

Timeliness Even accurate data, if they arrive too late, are not useful. This is true for any organizational actions, but especially so for purposes of control. In the fast-paced world of global business, data that are out of date are of virtually no use. For effective control, information must arrive on time to those who can take action and make any required changes. In everyday life, for example, information that reaches truck drivers 10 minutes after the wrong route has been taken is not very useful. Effective control systems require speed.

Objectivity Objectivity, especially as it relates to control, can be a two-edged sword. Almost everyone would agree that objective facts are better than subjective, and possibly biased, opinions. However, for some kinds of performances, objective data may not be possible to obtain or even may be misleading. In diving competition, for example, objective measurement of the exact height that a diver jumps off a springboard may be much less important than the subjective opinion of an experienced judge about the form of the dive. Similarly, in organizations, some of the most easily measured activities, and therefore the most easily controlled, may be relatively insignificant for the achievement of major, strategic goals. All other factors being equal, objective information would be preferred, but in many situations those other factors may not be equal, and thoughtful judgments rather than unimportant "facts" may provide the best basis for action decisions.

For example, in a customer service call center, it is relatively easy to gather objective data on the length of time a customer service agent spends on the phone with each caller. However, comparing the number of callers served by each agent may not tell you the most important thing—how well each customer was served. In fact, if the number of calls answered becomes the key performance measure, customer service agents may begin to provide poor service in order to get customers off the phone quickly and move on to the next customer, thereby maximizing the number of calls they take in a day. In this case, it is clear that the objective data (the number of calls taken) may not be the most important data (that is, how well the customer is served). Measuring customer service effectively may require having a supervisor randomly listen in on service calls or going to the cost and effort of trying to measure customer satisfaction by polling customers who have called in to the service center.

Flexibility

For control to be effective, its procedures must respond to changing conditions. Organizations and managers become accustomed to control procedures that are already in place. It is a human tendency to stay the course when things appear to be going well. But that tendency can defeat effective control. Well-designed control systems should be able to account for changing circumstances and adjust accordingly. Rigidity of control systems usually is not a feature to be prized. Flexibility is.[41]

Favorable Cost–Benefit Ratio

The designs of some control systems look good on paper, but they prove to be impractical or costly to use. To be effective, the benefits of controls must outweigh both the direct financial costs and the indirect costs of inconvenience and awkwardness in implementation. Elaborate, complicated control systems immediately raise the issue of whether they will be worth the expense involved. Sometimes, the simplest systems are nearly as effective. Consider again our customer service call center example. While objective customer satisfaction data may be preferable to subjective supervisor evaluations, the cost of obtaining satisfaction ratings directly from customers may be significantly more and not provide much better information than well-trained supervisors.

Of course, some situations may call for intricate controls because of the extremely high costs that would occur from unacceptable performance. Organizations that must carry out certain activities associated with high levels of hazard—such as nuclear power plants, military weapons units, and federal air traffic control agencies—need to invest heavily in control systems that ensure an exceedingly high degree of reliability. Consequently, they have to make costly investments—in, for example, continual training, backup staffing, and very expensive equipment—to control operations and reduce the possibility of a catastrophic accident to absolute minimum levels.[42] In such cases, high control costs are obviously justified.

Sources

The source of control often affects the willingness of organization members to work cooperatively with the system. As we discussed earlier, in recent years many organizations have changed from bureaucratic control to control that relies more on members' monitoring their own or their team's performance. Thus, the source of control is shifted, and the change may increase positive reactions because employees have more trust in a process over which they have some influence.

Similarly, controls that provide information from equipment or instruments often seem less resented and more fair than controls involving what can be viewed as the sometimes arbitrary actions of supervisors. This principle was illustrated at UNUM Insurance Company several years ago when it installed an elaborate information system (involving more than a $30,000 investment in hardware and software per employee) to help improve the performance of the company's information systems professionals by measuring the amount of work to be done, identifying errors as they occur, and assisting in correcting those errors. The affected employees accepted the errors identified by the new system more readily than they had from supervisors because the system had no personal "axe to grind."[43] For any type of control, the source has a great deal to do with the acceptability of the system. Acceptability, in turn, affects how well control systems work in practice and not just in theory.

managerial perspectives revisited

PERSPECTIVE 1: THE ORGANIZATIONAL CONTEXT Organizations could not function as organizations without control. It's as simple as that. It is not a question of whether to have control or not have control. Instead, the basic issues involve how much and what type. Early in the chapter we emphasized that control as an organizational and managerial process is closely connected to other major organizational processes, such as planning, organizing, and leading. Control is affected by these processes, but in turn control also affects them. Thus, control is integral to an organization's entire set of activities.

PERSPECTIVE 2: THE HUMAN FACTOR Within any organization setting, for the process of control to work effectively, it needs the cooperation of the people who are affected by it. Many aspects of controls, as we pointed out, are impersonal in nature, as when instruments provide information on whether some product or process is within quality boundaries. However, it ultimately is up to people at some level, or several levels, to take action based on that information. If the people affected by managerial control activities are working to defeat and impede control, eventually the quality and quantity of organizational performance are affected. On the other hand, if they are supportive, performance can be enhanced. Often the reactions of the people affected by control are a good barometer of whether the organization is heading in the right direction in its other activities.

PERSPECTIVE 3: MANAGING PARADOXES Two major potential paradoxes for managers to consider with respect to the topic of control are: (1) To make sure that they and their associates view control as a "means" and not as an "end." Sometimes managers get so obsessed with the necessity and importance of control that they send the unintended message that it is in fact *the* objective, rather than simply being a way to assist in meeting organizational goals; (2) to determine where the most appropriate balance is between overcontrol and undercontrol. Either condition, if not detected and modified, can lead to unfortunate consequences.

PERSPECTIVE 4: ENTREPRENEURIAL MIND-SET   If managers adopt an entrepreneurial mind-set, they are more likely to develop balanced controls—controls that meet both the firm's financial and strategic objectives. These managers understand the importance of adhering to financial budgets and constraints, but they aren't blinded to entrepreneurial opportunities that may exist and require money to develop. Morever, the *types* of control used depend on a manager's entrepreneurial mind-set. On the one hand, a strong managerial emphasis on financial control has been found to produce less innovation. On the other hand, a managerial emphasis on strategic control tends to facilitate innovation within an organization.[44] Why? Financial controls tend to cause managers to focus on short-term gains rather than long-term opportunities.

In addition, the use of clan control versus bureaucratic control by a manager is likely to help him or her take a long-term perspective and be more innovative—especially when these values are inculcated within the organization's culture. When this occurs, members of the organization, or firm, are highly committed and share a strong set of mutually agreed-on values. Such a commitment may be easier to obtain in a smaller organization, but many larger organizations can nonetheless benefit from clan control because they have more committed members whose efforts they can mobilize than do their competitors of similar size and complexity.

concluding comments

Control is a crucial, albeit many times difficult and sometimes even unpleasant, managerial function. As we have emphasized repeatedly throughout this chapter, the challenge for managers is to make wise decisions about how much, and where, control needs to be used, and then how to apply that control. Control is essential, but many a manager and even many an organization have run into severe difficulties because the control process has not been well handled.

Knowing the basic elements of the control process is a helpful start in gaining perspective about how to exercise appropriate control. Understanding some of the pitfalls and obstacles that can interfere at each of these steps provides a basis for avoiding unnecessary "rookie" mistakes. Not many managers would have the aspiration to be a great "controller," but likewise, most would not like to be known as excessively naive about the need for control. Keeping in mind the factors that influence control effectiveness—such as the focus, amount, and degree of flexibility—is a way to reduce the chances of unintended control blunders and improve the probabilities of success.

Clearly, control is a matter of both science and art. On the one hand, there are a variety of quantitative measures available to assess individual, group, and organizational performance. Particular areas, such as finance and operations, tend to use many quantitative control measures because they deal with things that are easy to count (money, products, defects). However, the fact that something can be easily measured doesn't mean it should be. Likewise, the fact that something is hard to measure doesn't mean it should not be. The key to managerial success relative to control is making good judgments and *then* good measurements. Without good judgment concerning what, how, and when to measure something, the measurements are of little value. Control can add real value to an organization, but that outcome is not guaranteed unless managers with judgment make it happen.

key terms

balanced scorecard   591
break-even point (B-E P)   582
budgetary control   583
bureaucratic control   586
commitment (clan) control   586
concurrent control   589
control   568
efficiency (activity)   581

human resource policies and
   procedures   585
leverage   581
liquidity   581
operational control   588
precontrol   589
postcontrol   589
profitability   581

ROE (return on equity)   581
ROI (return on investment)   581
standards   571
strategic control   577
supervisory structure   585
tactical control   580

test your comprehension

1. What is meant by "control" in organizations?
2. How is the control function linked to other managerial functions?
3. What is meant when control is described as a "causal variable," as well as being a dependent variable?
4. What are the four elements of the control process?
5. Who is responsible for setting standards?
6. What are standards and how are they used in organizations?
7. What are the key issues managers must consider when establishing standards?
8. When measuring performance, can nonquantifiable data be helpful? How?
9. What is the limiting factor in comparing performance against standards?
10. Which is the most difficult managerial task in the control process? Why?
11. What happens when a gap is detected between expected performance and actual performance?
12. What is the difference between "reinforcing action" and "corrective action"? When would you use each?
13. Compare strategic, tactical, and operational control. Why are the boundaries between each not always clear?

14. When are strategic controls more useful? Less useful?
15. What is the relationship of the external organizational environment to the development of strategic controls?
16. Contrast budgetary control with strategic control.
17. What is the main focus of tactical control?
18. List and discuss four types of tactical controls.
19. Describe four managerial control issues involving budgets.
20. What is the fundamental difference between bureaucratic control and commitment (clan) control?
21. Define operational control.
22. What is the relationship between pre-, concurrent, and postcontrols of operations? Which type is best?
23. What are the seven factors of control effectiveness?
24. What are the advantages and the problems involved in using a balanced scorecard approach?
25. What factors determine the usefulness of information to the control process?

apply your understanding

1. Do you think it is possible for an international firm to have a common control system even for a single activity, such as manufacturing, when it has plants in countries such as India, Australia, Japan, the United States, and Germany? Explain your answer.

2. If you were the manager of your university's control system for exams, would you tighten or loosen the amount of control? For what signals would you look to determine whether your adjustments were appropriate?
3. In general, do you think that people respond to control systems or that control systems respond to people? In other words, will people generally conform to the tightness or looseness of a control system, or should the tightness or looseness of the control system depend on the nature of the people involved?
4. If you were a worker and management wanted to tighten controls over your job, what would they need to do to get you to go along with the tighter controls?

practice your capabilities

Charlie had begun her career at one of Krom's department stores as a sales clerk during high school. She loved it there. Krom's stocked cutting-edge fashions, with stock changing as rapidly as the customers' styles. It was a high-energy, fast-changing environment in which to work. An internship during college helped her gain her first entry-level management job in the chain after graduation. Promotions had been steady, and two months ago Charlie began her new job as assistant store manager. If she performed well in this position, the next step would be to manage her own store. She had decided that she would impress upper management by controlling costs and improving the efficiency of the store. Her predecessor in the assistant manager position—who had received a promotion—had been, in her opinion, far too easygoing. He had allowed the sales and stock personnel to perform their jobs more-or-less as they saw fit, within broad limits. When Charlie took over as the new assistant manager, however, she decided: "I'll tighten things up."

Charlie's first action was to make a thorough review of the company rules and procedures for stock and sales personnel. For three weeks, she made daily inspections of the stock rooms to make sure all of the boxes were stacked properly and neatly, and that all boxes that were opened were immediately unpacked and the merchandise put away. She noted every example of incorrect storage. On the sales floor, she inspected every garment display, sometimes even rearranging them. She watched each move the sales clerks made, and once or twice noted the specific amount of time spent in conversation between employees and compared it to the time they spent with customers. She timed lunches and rest breaks and reviewed everyone's time cards. After three weeks of review and inspections, she called a meeting for Monday morning, before customers arrived, to announce the changes she would be making.

"I really want our store to shine! We need to impress top management with our efficiency and level of sales. Remember, there are bonuses available for increases in sales above the company average, for cost containment in the stock rooms, and even for low absenteeism and tardiness. So, from now on, this store is going to run like clockwork. There will be no more skirting the rules. We will be working according to the letter of the law. I am issuing a copy of the company policy manual to each of you along with the rules you will be following in implementing these policies. I have several ideas on how we can improve the operation of this store and help us all qualify for those bonuses." Charlie then went on to tell the store personnel about all of the new forms she was having printed that would detail each task with signature lines where each employee would sign off whenever he or she finished a specific task. Arrival, departure, and break times would be much more closely monitored than before. Additionally, sales personnel would constantly be walking the sales floor looking for customers in order to increase sales. There should be very little time for idle conversation. There were so many new rules to explain that the meeting took over two hours. Charlie ended the meeting by saying: "Let's have the best, most efficient, store in the chain! I know you can do it."

1. How do you think the store personnel are going to respond to Charlie's new rules and regulations, in light of the fact that they should have increased opportunities to earn bonuses? Why?
2. Using the concepts in this chapter, analyze the types of control that Charlie is using.

closing case

Ford Slams the Brakes on Costs

Top managers at Ford Motor Co. had good reason to wonder whether Ford would live to celebrate its centennial in 2003. The company had overcome tough times during the 1940s, when Henry Ford II brought it back from the financial brink. Starting in the 1970s, Ford and its domestic rivals began feeling the pressure from foreign automakers with highly efficient designs, streamlined production methods, and better quality controls.

By the time William Clay Ford Jr. (nephew of Henry Ford II and great-grandson of the founder) became CEO in 2001, costs at the number-two U.S. carmaker had spun out of control and quality concerns were mounting.

The new CEO was keenly aware of how far the company had fallen in just a few years. Consider that in 1999, Ford reported record profits topping $7 billion. In 1996, it was even poised to unseat number one, General Motors. Yet by 2001, under former CEO Jacques Nasser, the company was losing $5.5 billion. Nearly all its $15 billion cash hoard had been spent acquiring Volvo's car operations and the Land Rover business plus starting several fruitless e-commerce initiatives. Meanwhile, price-sensitive and quality-conscious customers were choosing foreign-made cars and trucks instead. This trend drove Ford's overall U.S. market share below 22 percent.

Furthermore, Ford's costs were considerably higher than those of GM and other automakers, which severely damaged its profit situation. In the late 1990s, the company was earning an average of nearly $2,000 on every vehicle sold in North America. But costs kept creeping up, in part because car designers and engineers were not held to strict standards for the price of parts or for costly production changes to make the new models. For example, purchasing managers were instructed to buy 126 different fuel caps and 150 different radios for installation in the vehicles rolling off Ford's assembly lines. Such seemingly small inefficiencies repeated over and over added up to a major cost disadvantage within a few years: Soon the company was losing nearly $200 per vehicle sold.

Trouble was also brewing in the company's credit division. Ford Credit's managers wanted to fuel vehicle sales, so they set looser guidelines that allowed more customers to qualify for low-interest and no-interest loans—including a higher number of customers with below-average creditworthiness. As the economy faltered, more borrowers fell behind on their repayments, and Ford repossessed more vehicles than planned. Losses at the credit unit ended up contributing to even higher losses for Ford overall in 2001.

On becoming CEO, Bill Ford's top priority was reasserting control from the top down at Ford. He changed senior managers at Ford Credit, appointed the former CEO of Ford Europe to oversee international purchasing, named a new chief operating officer, and brought back Ford's retired chief financial officer to tighten the reins on corporate finance. This new management team helped Ford develop a comprehensive plan to slash costs by $4.5 billion and more in the years to come. The plan called for laying off 35,000 workers to drastically reduce payroll costs, axing four vehicle models to simplify the manufacturing process, closing factories to boost efficiency, and standardizing vehicle parts to reduce the number of different parts purchased. Additionally, the plan called for fine-tuning production to raise quality levels and lower recall and warranty claim costs, imposing higher creditworthiness thresholds to reduce credit losses, and revamping both rebates and low-interest-rate loans to improve profitability. After one of a dozen inside efficiency teams found out most personnel were getting their news online, Ford even canceled company-paid magazine and newspaper subscriptions. "We're still trying to put the brakes on a freight train," commented the CEO, whose personal sacrifice included downsizing to a smaller corporate jet. "We've got to stop it before we can turn it around."

Supporting the turnaround, Ford management pushed to speed up new-product development and vehicle introductions to generate more cash more quickly and—just as important—to generate excitement among dealers and customers. Although the company was relying heavily on budgets, schedules, and other formal methods to enforce the controls, the CEO personally visited numerous Ford plants and offices to pump up workforce commitment. "I'm asking you to work hard," he told employees. "Keep the big picture in mind. Think about what really matters. Do that and nothing else."

However, some parts of Ford had difficulty adjusting to the new controls. Managers in the luxury car division, for instance, could not meet a speedy launch schedule for a new Jaguar aluminum-chassis model; without the new model, the division fell short of its revenue and profit goals. In addition, managers working on a new Mustang model tried to get Bill Ford to approve a development plan that failed to meet the company's profit goals. Although they assured the CEO that they soon would resolve the profit-sapping issues, Bill Ford refused to authorize any plan that did not explicitly meet the goals. Similarly, he sent engineers trying to improve the fuel economy of Ford's SUVs back to the drawing board until they could produce a plan to meet the target of boosting fuel efficiency by 25 percent within three years. In all these cases, rather than second-guess Ford managers, the CEO set clear limits and asked specific questions to steer his subordinates in the right direction.

Still, the new controls were already having an effect in other key areas. By concentrating on producing fewer vehicles of better quality, Ford's manufacturing units helped lower warranty claims and recall fewer vehicles. And higher quality gained the company higher marks in customer surveys. Working with their counterparts in purchasing and engineering to standardize parts and arrange better deals with global suppliers, production managers also squeezed $240 from the cost of every vehicle produced. In all, Ford managers have made enough cuts to lower costs by $6 billion so far.

Bill Ford is also committed to setting and meeting standards that affect the environment, such as achieving higher fuel efficiency and designing more hybrid vehicles like the Toyota Prius, whose sales are beginning to take off. Setting and meeting standards to achieve these goals and all the other goals needed to support a turnaround will be neither fast nor easy. "What keeps me up at night is that we're not moving fast enough," the CEO says. "Yes, we are making progress, but are we making it fast enough?" Ford knows that the company's future depends on how well he and his managers continue putting the brakes on costs while hitting the accelerator on quality and sales.

Questions

1. Discuss Bill Ford's actions using the steps of the basic control process as a model. Did he follow this process? What did he do in each step? Did he leave out any important steps? What is left to do?

2. Can Ford's turnaround plan be characterized as tactical or strategic controls, and why? How are the actions and decisions of lower-level managers likely to be influenced by the plan?

3. How does the amount of control used by Ford's credit managers affect control and performance in other areas of the parent company?

4. Thinking in terms of focus of control and amount of control, what caused the problems at Ford in the first place? Is Ford's management proceeding appropriately in their attempts to improve the situation? Why or why not?

Sources: Jean Halliday, "Pedal to the Metal," *Advertising Age*, November 17, 2003, p. 4; Amy Wilson and Brad Wernle, "Ford Share Slides Toward 75-Year Low," *Automotive News*, October 6, 2003, p. 8; Betsy Morris, "Can Ford Save Ford?" *Fortune*, November 18, 2002, pp. 52+; Scott Miller, "Ford Speeds Cost Cutting," *Wall Street Journal*, September 23, 2002; Danny Hakim, "A New-Model Ford on a Risky Track," *New York Times*, September 29, 2002, sec. 3, pp. 1, 12; Kathleen Kerwin, "Bill Ford's Long, Hard Road," *BusinessWeek*, October 7, 2002, pp. 88–92.

Organizational Development and Transformation

17

■

Identify the internal and external forces for change
in an organization.

■

Discuss the technological, cultural, strategic, structural,
and systems dimensions of change.

■

Analyze the process managers should use in evaluating
the need for change.

■

Describe the process of organizational change.

■

Diagnose the causes of resistance to change and discuss
possible approaches to dealing with such resistance.

■

Describe three approaches to planned comprehensive
organizational change and compare their similarities
and differences.

The Softer Side of Microsoft

When a company is earning $10 billion in annual operating income, why make changes? Microsoft has enjoyed more than 25 years of success as a global leader in computer software. "We've done well," admits CEO Steve Ballmer. Still, he says, "there's an opportunity to really be amazing—to be amazing as a business, to be amazing in the positive impact that we have on society. But we have to do some things a little bit differently to be as amazing as we hope we can be."

There are many forces, both outside and inside the organization, to prompt changes at Microsoft: The external forces include competitive challenges from rivals such as Oracle, reputational challenges in the aftermath of its battles with the U.S. Justice Department and the Securities and Exchange Commission, and economic challenges resulting from the worldwide slump in PC sales that has dampened demand for the company's computer-related products and slowed sales and profit growth.

Internally, the company faces the challenges that come with a change in top management, given that Steve Ballmer replaced legendary company founder Bill Gates as CEO. Ballmer and Gates had jointly made every key decision, an arrangement that was beginning to slow the firm's ability to deal with fast-moving environmental developments. Also, company personnel were accustomed to competing fiercely with each other as well as with rival companies. This aggressive behavior had alienated many distributors and industry partners. Additionally, it had fueled internal conflicts between Microsoft departments that spilled over to adversely affect relations with customers.

Bill Gates's Microsoft has long been renowned for its reputation as being "cut-throat" and highly competitive. In recent years Gates and CEO Steve Ballmer (left) have tried to "soften" the company's image by encouraging more collaboration and cooperation among its employees. Do you think a kinder, gentler Microsoft will emerge?

Microsoft's leaders recognized that the company could not be as successful in the future as it had been in the past without making significant, proactive changes to address these external and internal issues. The changes made focused on multiple areas—the company's strategy, structure, and culture.

The changes started with a new mission statement: "To enable people and business throughout the world to realize their full potential." Accordingly, Microsoft began expanding the scope of its strategy beyond just technology. The new strategy focuses on improving customer, supplier, and competitive relationships through an emphasis on corporate values. Part of that endeavor included making Microsoft a great place to work so as to attract the most talented professionals in the industry. "We wanted to become the IT employer of choice—particularly with the dot-com boom," says Steve Harvey, Microsoft's director of people, profits, and culture. "Five years ago we were probably one of the unexciting places to work." Throughout Microsoft's campuses, flat-screen televisions play news and music, keeping employees abreast of what's going on in the world. X-box consoles allow employees to unwind while experiencing

one of the company's products. WiFi connections allow employees to work at home while staying connected to Microsoft's intranet wirelessly. Today, 89 percent of the company's employees say they love working at Microsoft. And, of course, happy Microsoft employees are more likely to be able to make customers happy, too.

Culturally, the changes were also intended to create a different level of interpersonal relationships. Departments are now encouraged to collaborate rather than compete with one another. Coordination meetings were held to support this collaboration in order to boost quality and better satisfy customers and partners while avoiding internal competition. Employees were asked to evaluate their leaders, and these evaluations are part of a new procedure for identifying and developing leadership talent within the organization. Microsoft also encouraged all employees to think more broadly about how their actions and decisions affect relations with those outside the company. The new cultural focus is on respectfulness and accountability, and these qualities are now being specifically evaluated as a part of each employee's performance review. "We're going to work even harder on these positive relationships, whether that means an investment of time, an investment of energy, or being honest and open and respectful," Ballmer says.

Structurally, in 2002, Microsoft reorganized into strategic business units (SBUs). Each SBU leader is responsible for his or her unit's profit and loss, and they are given access to financial information and tools for setting goals and monitoring their unit's performance. They are also allowed to make decisions that were formerly reserved for top management. This decentralization of decision making coupled with the real-time financial information empower managers to make their own decisions on product development, and enable the organization to respond more rapidly to changes in the external environment. Microsoft also instituted a new measurement figure—revenue per employee. This directly links the performance of each employee to the performance of the company as a whole. The firm constantly reviews the data to assess areas for growth and expansion and to reevaluate the overall structure of the company.

The changes are not without risk, however. Although speed is desirable in the fast-paced technology industry, too much emphasis on deadlines could restrain innovation. And, the company risks the possibility that customers, partners, and regulators will see the changes as only cosmetic. However, CEO Ballmer believes that not making the changes would result in much greater risk, which is why he continues to push for profound changes throughout the organization.

Sources: Paula Rooney and Barbara Darrow, "Microsoft Under Pressure," *Computer Reseller News*, February 2, 2004, p. 6; Simon Kent, "Inside the Best Place to Work in Britain," *Personnel Today*, July 8, 2003; Steve Bodow, "Microsofter," *New York Times Magazine*, November 24, 2002, pp. 72–75; "CRN Interview: Steve Ballmer, Microsoft," *Computer Reseller News*, July 8, 2002, pp. 20+; Jay Greene, "Ballmer's Microsoft," *BusinessWeek*, June 17, 2002, pp. 66+.

strategic overview

A major driver of organizational change is the external environment in which the organization exists. Changes in many of these external forces mean that managers must alter their organizations' strategies. For example, when competitors implement a successful strategic action, such as introducing a popular new product to the market, the organization may have to respond to protect its share of the market. The development of new technologies, the introduction of new industry regulations, and changes in the demographic composition of society will also frequently result in the need for new strategies to respond to the opportunities or threats these environmental changes pose.[1]

Moreover, to be effective, new strategies must be implemented successfully, as we have described in previous chapters. Implementation may require changes in other organizational characteristics, such as its culture, as the Microsoft example showed. Southwest Airlines is another example. Many airlines have tried to imitate the strategy of Southwest Airlines, hoping to duplicate its success. During the period of 1994–2003, Southwest earned a total profit of approximately $3.6 billion. This amount was three times the earnings of the airline company with the second-highest profits. Many other airlines experienced major losses during this 10-year period. Although some of these airlines have managed to imitate Southwest's low-cost strategy, few have been able to duplicate the way in which it *implements* its strategy. For example, Southwest has a unique culture and reportedly some of the best human capital in the industry.[2] Other airlines would need to make drastic changes in their corporate cultures to duplicate the organizational culture at Southwest. As a result, Southwest Airlines continues to lead the industry.

Organizations never stay the same because the world around them never stays the same. From ancient times forward, all organizations have had to build the capacity to change into their structures.[3] Making changes and managing that process have been essential to the vitality of all organizations throughout time and especially today. However, as the opening story of Microsoft's efforts to make significant changes demonstrates, managing the change process is no easy task. While the need to change is often obvious, making successful changes presents formidable managerial challenges. As Steve Ballmer and most managers discover, sooner or later, there are fundamental issues of change that need to be confronted. For example:

- How much change is enough?
- How fast should change take place?
- How should the need for continual changes be balanced against the need for a minimum level of stability and continuity?
- Who should be the major players in change processes, and what should their roles be?
- Who, exactly, is likely to benefit and who could be harmed by particular changes?

How these and other similar questions are answered will determine the fate of attempted changes in any organization, including Microsoft.

Throughout this book, we have emphasized understanding *change* as a major theme because it is so critical to managerial success. In fact, we devoted the second chapter to this topic. Here, in the concluding chapter of the book, we return to that critical topic. Chapter 2 highlighted the importance of change and provided a general framework for managing change. In this final chapter we focus specifically on bringing about change in organizational settings, and we address specific means and methods used in changing the overall organization as well as units within it. The present chapter builds on Chapter 2, but it also presumes a basic knowledge of the other topics covered in this book. This knowledge will be helpful in analyzing the significant issues involved in organizational development and transformation.

Organizational contexts, because of their complexity, provide many opportunities as well as many challenges for making changes. Some of these changes are very unplanned and reactive, often involving unpleasant consequences for those who work in organizations. A sudden layoff of a large number of employees to reduce expenses quickly is one familiar example, such as Lufthansa's decision to cut 4,000 jobs in its catering division, and Boeing's layoff of some 17,000 employees in 2002, both due to the worldwide slump in air travel following the events of September 11, 2001.[4] Other changes, like those at Microsoft, involve more planning and often have the intent of transforming the entire organization or at least major parts of it so that sudden, drastic changes, like major reductions in personnel, will not be necessary. When a change is planned, comprehensive, and apt to modify important characteristics of the organization, the terms "organizational development" or "organizational transformation" are applicable. (We also discuss a special use of the term "organizational development" later in this chapter.)

The first parts of this chapter examine general issues and principles relating to organizational development and transformation. We first review why organizations change—focusing on the forces that can cause changes. Particular attention is given to analyzing internal and external forces of change, and on recognizing and diagnosing those forces as they affect the need for change. Specific areas of the focus of changes are considered next: technology, shared values and culture, strategy, structure, systems, and staff. These sections in turn provide a background for an examination of managerial choices regarding the preparation, implementation, and evaluation of the change process.

The chapter concludes with an analysis of three major, typically organizationwide, approaches to planned change frequently used in contemporary organizations. These include the Organizational Development (OD) approach, Process Redesign (also known as Reengineering), and the development of the Learning Organization. We will look at how these approaches are used, and at their relative strengths and weaknesses.

FORCES FOR CHANGE

The causes of organizational change originate from both external and internal forces, and a manager must be alert to all of them (see Exhibit 17.1). Sometimes those causes arise almost totally from factors outside the organization, such as economic or business conditions, technological developments, demographic shifts, and the like. At other times, the forces are mostly from inside

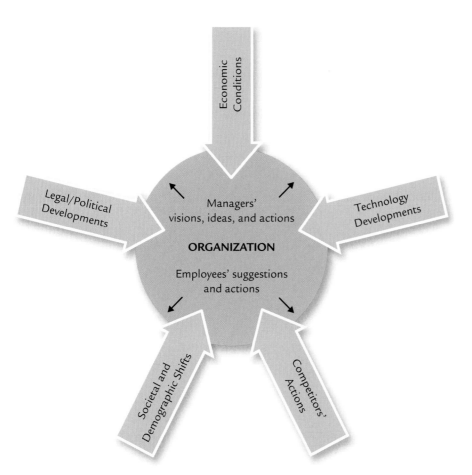

exhibit 17.1
Forces for Change

the organization. Internal forces include such factors as managerial decisions to make changes and employee pressures for urgent changes. Often, of course, the total set of causes of change represent a combination of both external and internal reasons.

Forces Outside the Organization

A whole host of forces outside the organization, as discussed earlier in Chapter 3 on the external environment, can bring about changes inside it. Here we mention again several of the most important.

Economic Conditions Obvious forces for change affecting business organizations are developments in the economic environment. If the economy is weak, then many companies are likely to reduce their workforces or at least limit hiring, prune low-profit product lines, and the like. Thus, DuPont Textiles and Interiors (a subsidiary of DuPont), in 2002, laid off 10 percent of its workforce and shut down two plants because of a worldwide economic downturn. The company stated that "We must act quickly and decisively to match our resources with current market realities."[5]

Conversely, if the economy is vibrant and expanding, many firms consider adding new services or products, creating new units or divisions, increasing their geographic areas of operations, and undertaking similar growth changes. Thus, in response to a healthy economy and increasing demand for its motorcycles, Harley-Davidson spent some $800 million between 1995 and 1999 to open two new manufacturing plants.[6]

Analogous to these business-world examples, many nonbusiness organizations, especially governmental agencies, contract or expand in relation to economic conditions because their budgets are directly impacted by those forces. In recent years, for example, the various projects planned by the National Aeronautics and Space Administration (NASA) have been put on slower timetables because of severe budget cuts.[7]

Competitors' Actions Regardless of the state of the economy, most businesses and many other organizations are likely to be extremely sensitive to moves made by their direct competitors, especially those in response to changes in the market or customers' preferences. The actions of other significant players in the immediate environment often can trigger changes inside a given organization, even when that organization would prefer not to make any changes at that time. For example, in response to competitors' moves, Mellon Bank has decided to get out of the traditional, slow-moving and low-yield retail banking business and is now concentrating on managing mutual funds and performing settlement services, which are more high-growth and high-fee businesses. Mellon later expanded into Europe when the U.S. money management market appeared to be oversupplied.[8] Actions by competitors in the deregulated Mexican insurance market led Metropolitan Life to acquire major Mexican subsidiaries (Asegurado Hidalgo and Seguros Genesis) in order not to be shut out of that market.[9]

Technology Developments Changes in technology developed outside an organization frequently require it to respond, whether it wants to or not. Technological advances offer both opportunity and threat to organizations, but if they are major breakthroughs and relate directly to an organization's core activities, managers have little choice but to make corresponding changes. (A Manager's Challenge, "Can High-Tech Solutions Save EDS?" illustrates how EDS had no choice but to change because of technology developments.) Several years ago, for example, the technological advancements provided by the Internet persuaded a traditional face-to-face personnel recruiting company to make major changes in how it does business, to the extent that it not only changed its corporate name from "Romac Industries" to "kforce.com," but it also became an innovator in its non-high-tech industry by using the Internet to allow job applicants to post short, streaming video commercials for themselves.[10]

Legal/Political Developments When governments make new laws or courts issue new interpretations of those laws, managers need to respond, even when the solutions or types of changes that should be made are not obvious. In the United States, the passage of Title IX of the 1964 Civil Rights Law required universities to provide equal resources and opportunities to male and female students (in relation to their proportions in the student body). Directors of intercollegiate athletics at U.S. universities eventually realized that this would have major implications for their area of activities. Because of tight budgets, however, these particular managers (the athletic directors) found it difficult to add enough women's sports to equalize the proportion of men to women athletes. Nevertheless, some managers handled this situation much better than others and made the changes more quickly and with less conflict within their organizations. Clearly, however, the external force of law in this instance caused changes that were unlikely to have come about for any other reason. Also, in this example, the political climate added a force to the legal enactment that hastened the need to make these changes.

tech|nol|ogy

a manager's challenge

Can High-Tech Solutions Save EDS?

What happens when an industry leader is outpaced by more innovative, nimble newcomers? That was the situation facing EDS, a pioneer in the information systems business. Founded in 1962, EDS steadily expanded until it was serving 9,000 corporate and government customers in 42 countries. By the late 1990s, EDS was ringing up $19 billion in annual sales. With such success, management saw no reason to make changes—even as IBM and other rivals raced ahead with new technology for the Internet age.

EDS's culture of independence meant that its 48 business units rarely shared information or technology. On occasion, one division would invest time and money developing a system—only to learn, part way through, that another division already had such a system in place. Tellingly, EDS's management could not send e-mail directly to all 140,000 employees, because the company used a patchwork of 16 e-mail systems! Sales results became available only after the finance department closed the books at the end of each quarter—which meant that management had to wait weeks to examine the month-by-month figures. Once EDS gained a reputation for lagging technology, sales growth slowed. Even some customers that signed with EDS were reluctant to be publicly linked to such a stodgy company. "When Scott McNealy of Sun Microsystems first had us do a piece of a contract for him, he wouldn't let us publicize the deal, because he thought we were too 'old economy,'" remembers one EDS executive. "Sun was cool. We were the knuckle draggers."

When Dick Brown was appointed CEO of EDS in 1999, he began visiting corporate customers to hear firsthand about their needs. On one such visit, he met with Janet Wejman, the senior vice president of Continental Airlines, for which EDS managed vital accounting, payroll, and reservation systems. "Systems were crashing, deliveries were failing, projects were late," Wejman told Brown. The CEO promised changes very soon. Within two weeks, he had a new account team working more closely with the airline's personnel to correct the problems.

EDS then leveraged its technical expertise by creating a Web-based service called Dashboard in response to its annual customer satisfaction survey. Dashboard showed at a glance how well EDS was meeting the needs of Continental and every major customer—for all of EDS's global managers to see. A green circle indicates that things are going smoothly. A red light signals an urgent problem—and other managers frequently pitch in to help, a significant break with the past. "At the old EDS, the culture was, 'Fix the problem yourself. And while you're fixing it, make sure you're signing new business,'" says one manager. The new Dashboard system has been so effective that EDS has begun selling it to its customers.

New technology supported by changes in structure and culture helped EDS successfully sign 111 percent more business in 1999 than it had just one year before. Unfortunately, the impressive turnaround was not to last. Eager for growth, Brown pushed executives to win news-making "megadeals," requiring heavy up-front investment by EDS but yielding poor earnings. The company then had a disastrous 2002, losing $24 billion in market value. After shocking investors by missing earnings estimates by a whopping 80 percent that year, Brown resigned, amid allegations of accounting problems and conflicts of interest by top EDS executives.

In 2003, Michael H. Jordan, who had resurrected Westinghouse in the 1990s, took over as CEO of EDS. Jordan hoped to cut internal costs by applying EDS's technological wizardry to the company itself, like replacing its 137 billing systems with just one system and consolidating its data centers. He also wanted to reorganize the salesforce around specific industries so salespeople could provide more relevant technological expertise to their customers—something IBM had already done.

The situation at EDS was so grim, however, that some wondered if the once-mighty market leader would survive. But so far the "second" turnaround seems to be working. Early in 2004, EDS had numerous new corporate contracts in the pipeline, and its stock was trading at a 52-week high. It appeared the corporation, founded over 40 years ago by Ross Perot, would live to fight another day.

Sources: Steven Land, "EDS CEO Says His IT Beats IBM," *VARBusiness*, February 23, 2004, p. 18; Andrew Park, "EDS: What Went Wrong," *BusinessWeek*, April 7, 2003, p. 60; W. A. Lee, "EDS Lands Major Tech Outsourcing Pact from B. of A.," *American Banker*, December 13, 2002, p. 14; Marie Lingblom, "EDS Dashboard to Aid Customers," *Computer Reseller News*, December 9, 2002, p. 126; Bill Breen, "How EDS Got Its Groove Back," *Fast Company*, November 2001, pp. 106–10.

Nonsmoking restaurants are evidence of new societal values, leading many business owners to fear for their profits in the face of legal bans on smoking in public places. However, in a survey conducted by Zagat, the prominent restaurant guide publisher, approximately three-quarters of 18,000 respondents in New York, Los Angeles, and San Francisco supported restaurant smoking bans. Previous surveys by Zagat have shown that patrons list smoking as a top area of improvement for restaurants.

Societal and Demographic Shifts Other types of external forces for change can take longer to develop and be more subtle and difficult to detect, such as changing societal attitudes toward various products, services, and practices. Many employers around the United States, as well as many restaurants and bars, for example, recently have had to change their practices regarding letting employees and customers smoke in indoor settings. In response to both tighter legal restrictions and changing levels of customer tolerance to smoking in confined areas, these organizations have had to pay attention to an area of employee/customer behavior they had long ignored.[11]

Shifting demographic patterns, such as the aging of populations in the United States and Japan in recent years, are another type of slow-moving external force. For example, within the last few years, the U.S. Bureau of the Census has projected that between 2010 and 2020, the number of people in the United States over age 60 will jump by over 30 percent, while almost all other age groups will stay roughly the same in numbers.[12] Such alterations in the age makeup of society will, for example, challenge retailing and other consumer-oriented firms to change product mixes and take new approaches to sales and marketing. These kinds of demographic shifts do not take place overnight, of course, but they can exert a powerful force nevertheless.

Forces Inside the Organization

As with external factors, many potential forces inside the organization can cause change to take place. Two of the most important are (1) managerial decisions and (2) employee preferences and pressures.

Managerial Decisions Managers at any level of an organization operate under certain constraints that limit their freedom of action. However, in many instances they have considerable authority to make changes in their particular parts of the enterprise. Generally, of course, even in this age of flatter organizational structures, the higher up that managers are in an organization, the more leeway and the more power they have to institute change. Managers are often reluctant, though, to use their power for this purpose. Indeed, as pointed out in Chapter 10, some authorities would argue that managers tend to *underutilize* their power to make changes, rather than use too much power.[13] The risk, obviously, is that an attempted change will be unsuccessful, and the manager may end up with less power than before. Therefore, as will be discussed in the next section, one of the most critical leadership issues facing you as a manager is accurately evaluating the need for change. When managers do make decisions to change, though, those decisions can affect the status quo in major ways.

Employee Preferences and Suggestions Managerial decisions are not the only source of change inside organizations. Lower-level employees often are an excellent source of innovative suggestions for change. For example, a few years ago the Children's Hospital and Health Care Center in San Diego, California, decided that because of continuing communication problems between management and staff, and associated low morale and severe job dissatisfaction, it needed more input from employees. It proceeded to institute monthly meetings where each supervisor was required to report ideas and suggestions from a set of employees not reporting to them. As a result of these suggestions, changes were made throughout the organization that have led to higher levels of job satisfaction and improved manager–employee communication.[14] The challenge for managers in obtaining employee preferences and suggestions, of course, is to sort out the creative proposals and hunches that have potential for increased performance and improved work climate from those that would be ineffective or unworkable if implemented.

In extreme instances, of course, employees may exert overt pressure for changes. In September 2002, for example, in response to employees' objections to the introduction of new cargo-handling technologies, employers proceeded to lock out dock workers in the Los Angeles area, which basically stopped traffic into the Port of Los Angeles for several weeks and caused losses approaching $2 billion.[15]

Managers need to distinguish employee pressures that address legitimate needs for change from pressures that attempt to obstruct or intimidate. Making such judgments wisely and responding appropriately are essential managerial skills, as discussed in the next section. Regardless of the extent to which managers have that skill, however, employees can be a stimulus for change that frequently cannot, and should not, be ignored.

FOCUS OF ORGANIZATIONAL CHANGES

When managers decide that change is needed, or when they realize that they have no choice but to make changes, one of the first issues they face is: What do I change? To help us answer that question it is useful to refer back to Chapter 6 ("Strategic Management") and the discussion of the McKinsey "7S" model of strategy implementation. Here, we will highlight five of those Ss that are particularly relevant for this section on the "focus of organizational changes." In addition, however, we will also include a non-S sixth focus, "technology." Any

a manager's challenge
Change

Fixing Up Home Depot

Many founders step aside once their companies are established to let more experienced managers assume leadership. Rarely, however, is an outsider brought in as CEO of a major company after the founder leaves. Yet when the cofounders and directors of home improvement retailer Home Depot wanted to remake the company from the top down, they recruited Bob Nardelli from General Electric to replace cofounder Arthur Blank as CEO. In turn, Nardelli has recruited executives from General Electric, Yahoo!, and other companies to fill the top slots in human resources, marketing, and other functions. "This is a business that has to reach outside of itself," he says. "It's easier for me to come in and change some things because I don't have the institutionalized point of view." Can outsiders effect the kinds of changes needed for Home Depot to reach Nardelli's ambitious goal of nearly doubling worldwide sales to $100 billion within five years?

One key challenge at Home Depot is to kindle cultural change in a company steeped in "do it yourself" initiative. When the chain was expanding rapidly, the cofounders encouraged buyers and store managers to make decisions on their own. After two decades, however, fierce competition and tight economic times slowed sales growth. By the time Nardelli took over as CEO, the company had posted four consecutive quarters of declining store sales. The entrepreneurial culture became a liability as buyers and store managers continued to place orders and stockpile costly inventory without central guidelines or coordination. (In fact, store managers did not have e-mail to communicate with each other or with headquarters before Nardelli joined.)

To keep costs in check, the CEO wanted to make profit-enhancing efficiency a hallmark of Home Depot's culture. He and his managers consolidated buying from nine regional buying offices to one. That step alone squeezed more competitive prices out of vendors, bolstering profits.

Nardelli and his managers also challenged the chain's legendary but often-abused refund policy, which allowed anybody to return anything for cash at any time. After investigating the costs and sharing the results with store managers, they changed the policy to offer store credit rather than a cash refund for items returned without a receipt—a change that saves at least $10 million per year.

Home Depot's strategy and technology have also been renovated. The company opened special outlets to serve contractors, who buy much more than the average do-it-yourselfer. It started soliciting business from corporations that buy lumber and other construction materials in volume, and offered home repair and maintenance services to "do-it-for-me" people. To streamline inventory management and ordering, stores received high-tech carts equipped with wireless handheld bar-code scanners and order entry tablets. As a result, instead of assigning 20 employees to check stock and manually write up orders, each store needs only four employees to scan the shelves and submit orders.

Nardelli's efforts, however, initially came on like a buzz saw to Home Depot's employees. Many of the company's regional managers quit, and its 300,000 employees were challenged to adapt. One analyst expressed concern that Home Depot was changing too much, too fast. To which the CEO responded: "The rate of internal change must be greater than the rate of external change, or we will fall behind." Other industry analysts were very critical of the changes.

Just when it seemed Nardelli wouldn't survive the attacks, the results rolled in. Home Depot's profits soared 28 percent, and its cash reserves rose to $5 million, compared to a negative $8 million when he had taken over. Naysayers were quieted.

"There is an infinite capacity to improve what you do. Innovation and technology have never let me down," says Nardelli. "We have totally transformed how these stores are run."

Sources: "The Fixer-Upper," *Institutional Investor-International Edition*, January 2004, pp. 14–15; "From Clicks to Bricks," *Brandweek*, October 28, 2002, p. 9; Patricia Sellers, "Something to Prove," *Fortune*, June 24, 2002, pp. 88+; Patricia Sellers, "Exit the Builder, Enter the Repairman: Home Depot's Arthur Blank Is Out," *Fortune*, March 19, 2001, pp. 86+; Sandra Bolan, "Home Depot's Mobile Redux," *Computing Canada*, February 15, 2002, p. 19.

change will almost certainly involve at least one of these areas of focus, and most changes will involve several. (See Exhibit 17.2.) A Manager's Challenge, "Fixing Up Home Depot," is a good example of change that involves multiple focus areas of change. Especially complex and comprehensive changes—"transformational changes"—will involve all six.

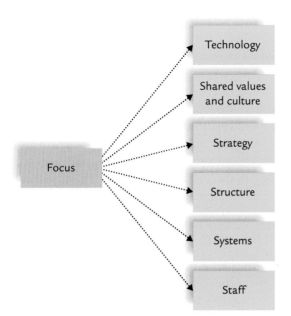

exhibit 17.2
Focus of Organizational Changes

Technology

For many organizations, the most obvious and most frequent object of change is technology (see Exhibit 17.3). This has always been the case in manufacturing and capital-intensive companies, where replacing and upgrading equipment and technology have been the keys to organizational survival and an ability to keep ahead of the competition. In recent years, however, virtually all types of firms, government agencies, and nonbusiness organizations have been giving increasing attention to improving and expanding their information technology.[16] For example, Emerson (formerly Emerson Electronics) began using a new Internet program, Emerson Express, to consolidate its smaller shipments into full-truck shipments for a savings of approximately $11 million a year. To implement this technology-driven change, each of the company's 50-plus autonomous divisions sends information concerning upcoming shipments to a central location where diverse shipments can be consolidated.[17]

exhibit 17.3
Some Specific Examples of Focus of Change

Focus	Examples
Technology	· Update computer systems · Use holography in product design
Shared Values and Culture	· Implement diversity awareness program · Institute participatory decision making throughout organization
Strategy	· Change from niche market to general market focus · Change focus from individual customer to large corporate customer
Structure	· Change from a geographic to a customer structure · Implement an international division
Systems	· Replace batch with continuous flow manufacturing · Change from last in/first out to first in/first out inventory valuation
Staff	· Encourage cooperation through cross-training program · Increase number and availability of training workshops for lower-level employees

Thus, for almost any organization at the beginning of the twenty-first century, from the corner dry cleaner to the largest multinational, making changes in technology becomes a prime and nearly continual focal point. The critical issues for managers, however, involve the significant and often unexpected spillover effects of changes in technology on other areas such as structure, systems, and staff. New equipment, for example, can result in entirely different patterns of work relationships among employees, and that, in turn, can create considerable confusion. Such effects, if they are major or last a long time, can dilute or even cancel the positive effects of the improvements. A focus on technology is, therefore, a frequent starting point of changes, but it is not necessarily a good indicator of where major problems may occur.

Shared Values and Culture

The shared values and culture of the organization, as discussed in Chapter 4, are a second potential focus for change in organizations (see Exhibit 17.3). In its way, changing an organization's culture can be as potent in its consequences as making major changes in technology systems. In fact, if it were easy to make changes in the culture of an organization, managers likely would try to do so more often. Despite such powerful potential, however, the embedded traditions and accepted ways of doing things that constitute an organization's culture can be extremely difficult to change successfully. For example, when China Development Industrial Bank bought Grand Cathay brokerage of Taiwan, over 100 of Grand Cathay's key employees left within the first year as a result of the new culture that had been imposed. As one departing employee put it, "Grand Cathay had a very democratic culture. When policies were made, we were always invited to give feedback. Our opinions mattered. But the new management has a very autocratic style."[18]

A key to changing an organization's culture is to start by trying to change its values, since what is valued is the underlying essence of the culture. One company that did make a successful change in its basic culture and values was the Barnes and Noble bookstore chain. Its owner, Leonard Riggio, decided to redefine the individual bookstores as social meeting places rather than just places to buy books. Thus, the cultural milieu of the stores was changed at the

Barnes & Noble is not only a place to buy books but also a place where customers can eat, read, and socialize with other people. The firm has developed its stores in a way to encourage people to linger and enjoy their time in a Barnes & Noble Stores.

beginning of the 1990s by changing the physical layout and appearance of the stores. Small nooks for sitting, reading, talking, and browsing were created, and in some locations coffee bars were installed. The core value of selling books was converted to one of selling entertainment and social interaction.[19]

Substituting new shared values for old values is hardly a simple process, though. The assertion of new values in a mission statement is easy. Getting them accepted and, as social scientists would say, "institutionalized," so that they become part of the basic fabric of the organization, is exceedingly difficult. Changing a culture, by whatever means, may take a long time and not achieve necessary changes quickly enough. More likely than not, it is easier and less costly for managers to attempt to change other factors, such as strategy or structure. Nevertheless, culture does represent a significant, if difficult, target for fundamental changes.

Strategy

Because an organization's overall strategy, along with its basic mission statement and espoused values, provides major directions for its activities, it can serve as another potent focus of managerial change efforts (see Exhibit 17.3).[20] In contrast to its culture, an organization's strategy or set of strategies may be less difficult for managers to change. Top management typically is more in control of determining strategy than the other characteristics of the organization and, in fact, is expected to do so. Thus, by announcing strategic changes, which may occur after extensive consultation with managers throughout the organization, managers at the highest levels can strongly influence change.[21] Of course, whether strategic changes are then implemented effectively is another matter entirely.

Asserting changes in strategy is vastly different from actually bringing about such changes. For example, a few years ago, Honda sought to convert itself from "a local company in Japan, with a global viewpoint, into a global company with a local viewpoint." Its new strategy was to be as flexible as a small local company while developing and using all of the strengths of a large, global company. To support this new strategy, the organization developed such systems as a global product supply network, a new flexible manufacturing system, and a global standard layout. Today Honda sets the benchmark in the area of flexible manufacturing; its major North American production facilities can assemble nearly any vehicle it sells.[22]

Structure

Changing the structural makeup of organizations is sometimes one of the most valuable tools managers have to create other desired changes, like improved productivity or more creative problem solving (see Exhibit 17.3). Many structural changes, such as reorganizing on a product basis rather than a geographic one or consolidating major divisions, can be made at the macro, or total organization, level. Nokia, which has offices on multiple continents, had formerly been organized on a geographic basis, but recently reorganized by product. Now each division operates with its own strategy and profit and loss responsibility.[23]

Other structural changes can be made at the intermediate level, involving such actions as combining or dividing departments or changing locations and reporting relationships within or among units. Still other structural changes can be made at very micro levels, such as forming new project groups or altering the composition of particular jobs or positions. The Mayo Clinic, for example, several years ago formed a group of 13 examining physicians and 17 staff members into a new unit called its Executive Health Program, to specialize in conducting annual physical examinations on over 2,500 executives.[24]

As with changes in strategy, changes in structure are not especially difficult to pull off initially, but making them work to generate the desired effects can be particularly challenging for managers. Research shows that almost no other events in organizations can create as much political maneuvering as potential, or rumored, reorganization changes.[25] The ambiguity of the effects of such changes, coupled with their potential importance for the jobs of those who may be directly affected, causes high levels of anxiety and frequent political activity.

Systems

Another major object of change can be the systems of formal processes or procedures used in, and by, an organization (see Exhibit 17.3). Such changes involve attention to the sequence and manner in which work activities and operations are carried out. For example, Intel has changed its procedure for opening new plants. In order to avoid problems with small differences from one plant to another, its new procedural system for opening new plants is to "copy exactly," even, for example, down to the color of the workers' gloves.[26]

Changes in processes and procedures often come about because of prior changes in technology or structure. In this sense, modifications of the way work is performed, whether by individuals or groups, can be considered residual changes. The purchase of new equipment, for instance, would be a primary change, and the adoption of new procedures because of this equipment would be the secondary change. Recent advances in biotechnology, for example, have allowed pharmaceutical firm Merck to dramatically change its systems for developing new drugs. Current methods have been replaced by a new, "molecular profiling" process.[27]

Staff

Finally, people—both individuals and groups—can be the focus of major changes (see Exhibit 17.3). Essentially, changes that focus on people involve one or more of four elements:

- Who the people are.
- What their attitudes and expectations are.
- How they interact interpersonally.
- How they are trained or developed.

In the first instance, change can be brought about by adding, subtracting, or interchanging people. Bringing in a new supervisor or transferring a difficult employee from one unit to another are examples of change focusing on the selection and placement of people.

The second element, attitudes and expectations, often can be an important focus because people act on the basis of them, and they sometimes can be modified without excessive effort or cost by the manager. Providing people with new information or a new way to look at problems, issues, or events has the potential—but no certainty—of creating significant change in their behavior.[28]

Attempts to alter the way staff relate to each other—such as by being more cooperative with, and more supportive of, each other—represent a third people-oriented change focus.

The fourth and often most lasting people-change approach involves direct enhancement of their knowledge, skills, and abilities—typically through education, training, and personal development activities. Such change can improve the performance of individuals, groups, and even larger units, regardless of any other changes a manager might initiate.

As with other types of changes, however, efforts to change people can be costly. Managers need to weigh the costs of managerial time and effort, and frequently significant budgetary expenditures, against potential benefits such as a more capable workforce, increased creativity and innovation, better morale, and, perhaps, decreased turnover.

EVALUATING THE NEED FOR CHANGE

Is change always necessary? To answer that question, you should undertake two critical steps. One is to recognize the possible need for change and to correctly assess the strength of that need. The other is to accurately diagnose the problems and issues that the change or changes should address. Misjudgments at either step can lead to severe problems, if not outright disaster.[29] Jumping in to make changes before taking *both* these steps is a recipe for almost certain failure.

Recognizing and Assessing the Need for Change

As we have stressed earlier, making changes is definitely not a cost-free activity (see Exhibit 17.4). This puts a premium on not making changes where the costs will outweigh the potential benefits. It also means that it is crucial to make an accurate assessment of the strength of forces behind the need for change.

Proactive Recognition Effective managers, no matter where they are in the organization's structure, are those who can recognize needs for change at the earliest possible time. This is because they should have systems and methods in place to monitor the environment in which they and their units operate, and these systems should be capable of detecting clues that may not yet have become obvious warning signs.[30]

This kind of planned, proactive assessment of the need for change is intended to provide advance notice so that changes can be made sooner, with better planning and potentially with less cost. Methods can range, for instance, from elaborate and sophisticated information systems to more mundane activities such as trend-spotting of anomalies in sales reports and

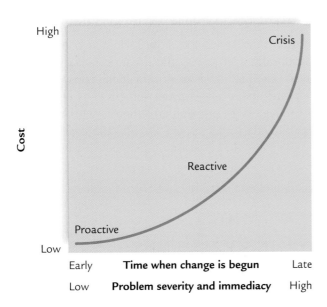

exhibit 17.4
Relative Cost of Change

actively seeking out the views of clients, customers, and employees. Starbucks, the coffee house giant, is demonstrating proactive assessment by studying various ways to retain its current customers and attract the next generation of young coffee drinkers. It has even gone so far, in its consumer assessment methods—as to hypnotize a group of 20+-year-olds to try to find out what they *really* think about Starbucks. Among the early results of such assessment is the company's establishment of Starbucks Express, which allows customers to e-mail their orders to the stores they patronize, which then will have their coffee waiting for them in personalized cups when they arrive.[31]

Reactive Recognition Not *all* needs for change can be identified in advance, regardless of how much proactive recognition is attempted. Invariably, some developments in the internal or external environment will take place so quickly, or reach critical mass so unexpectedly, that managers must *react* to them rather than *plan for* them in advance. In such instances, the forces for change become too large to ignore, and the issue becomes one of how and when to react rather than whether or not to react.[32] This kind of situation has faced AOL, the major player in Internet access, in the early years of the '00 decade. Its core business was faced with a slowdown in subscriber growth, declines in advertising revenue, and questions about its accounting practices. In reaction, AOL has initiated several changes, including trying to move from a marketing to a service culture and taking greater advantage of exclusive content programming drawn from its Time Warner affiliates.[33]

Diagnosing Problems

The recognition that change needs to take place is only a starting point. Much like a physician identifying the source of a symptom in a patient, the next step is to make an accurate diagnosis of what is causing the problem or issue so that changes can be made to deal with it effectively. Initiating changes that do not improve the underlying causes is sometimes worse than making no changes at all. Thus, managers need to avoid premature conclusions about causes. Instead, they should obtain information from a variety of sources, if possible; compare those sets of information to uncover consistent patterns or trends; and, especially, attempt to determine what are the most likely causes. The end result of a comprehensive analysis of this type should be an accurate, valid diagnosis of what, and who, needs to change.

This type of diagnosis was carried out by the First National Bank of Chicago several years ago when the bank decided that its process costs were too high and turnaround times too slow in its small business loans department. Before instituting a change, officials attended a roundtable discussion on small business lending sponsored by a local consulting firm, conducted surveys with its customers about proposed process changes, and obtained information on practices at competitors. What was learned from this process was that the bank needed to work with small businesses more in the manner that it worked with individual consumers, rather than in the way it interacted with large businesses.[34]

THE CHANGE PROCESS

So far in this chapter, we have focused on the background and context of change in organizations: the forces for change, the types of change possible, and, especially, managers' roles in understanding, assessing, and evaluating

exhibit 17.5
The Change Process

```
Planning          Implementation          Evaluation
and                                        of
preparation                                outcomes
        ↖              ↗
        Dealing with
        resistance to
        change
```

the need for change. Now we turn to the change process itself: planning and preparing for it, implementing it, dealing with resistance to it, and evaluating its outcomes (see Exhibit 17.5).

Planning and Preparation for Change

Once a manager or a group of managers has been convinced that change is necessary (refer back to Chapter 2 and the discussion about helping people see the need for change) and that an accurate diagnosis has been made of the causes requiring change, preparation for the changes can begin. As shown in Exhibit 17.6, such planning calls for attention to several important issues.

Timing Managers are often tempted to initiate something quickly, especially if the need for change seems exceptionally strong. Whether rapid implementation is a good idea or not represents a difficult judgment call. Acting too quickly can lead to changes that are not well planned and that often fail because they lack sufficient support. On the other hand, waiting too long to make necessary changes can also be a recipe for failure. In the summer of 1997, Gilbert Amelio, then CEO of Apple Computer, was ousted by the company's board of directors precisely because, according to knowledgeable observers in the industry—and "many of Apple's own employees"—he did not move "quickly enough to help return the company to profitability" and failed to "act with a sense of urgency."[35] It is clear that the timing of changes can be critical to their success.

Building Support One of the best guarantees for successful implementation is to build support for change in advance. Developing this foundation requires especially careful consideration of who will be affected by the changes and how they will likely react. This means that managers need to have a clear

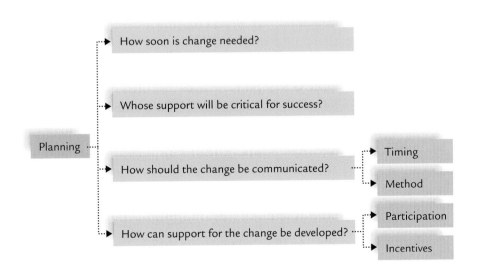

exhibit 17.6
Planning Choices for Change

understanding of the situation and circumstances in which the changes will take place if they are to increase the probability of success. It also means that this kind of analysis, in turn, must be followed with support-building activities by the manager. Several of these are discussed here.

Communication A key step in building support for major changes is to communicate about them in advance to those who will be affected. Cooperation is likely to be enhanced the more that people understand (a) the reasons for the changes and, especially, (b) the ways in which those changes are likely to impact them. In the early 1990s, General Electric's Fanuc Automation North America plant in Charlottesville, Virginia, changed from a directive, "do as I say, no questions asked" form of management to a team-based structure. The success of such a major change was credited to management's commitment to open communication. Top management explained the proposed change to all employees; required hours of training in problem solving, goal setting, and conflict management; and set up scheduled meetings both with individual groups and with the entire workforce.[36] If, in contrast to this example, the reasons for the changes and their anticipated effects cannot be clearly communicated, that may signal that the changes have not been sufficiently planned, and they may not have a high enough probability of success. Seldom do changes fail because of too much communication, but they are likely to encounter difficulty when too little information is provided.

Particularly important in using communication to build support for proposed changes is to provide a compelling rationale for those changes. Those to be affected need to know the specific objectives of the changes and how those relate to the larger goals and values of the unit or total organization. For example, Mark Speer, Director of Management and Organizational Development at Miller Brewing Company, emphasizes that: "One of the foundations of changing an organization is having people really understand the business, where they add value to it and how they impact the bottom line." To put this principle into practice, he has initiated a Business Literacy Program, which is designed to teach employees all there is to know about beer, from the molecular level on up.[37]

It is also important in communication to focus special attention on those who are likely to be influential in shaping the attitudes of their colleagues. In other words, extra effort spent on communication with opinion leaders can be a good investment. During the reorganization of Cookson Group, the multibillion-dollar parent corporation of a group of international manufacturing companies, the headquarters treasury unit was given the job of reviewing and revising funding and capital investment policies and practices at each company. The unit found that the key to success was to meet with senior management in each company before starting the review to convince them of the benefits to be gained by centralizing capital investment procedures.[38]

Participation During the planning stage, obtaining the participation of those to be affected by changes can help build later support for those changes. Plans can often be improved and commitment gained through such participation. In addition, participation can build trust because those initiating the changes, in effect, are allowing themselves to be influenced about how and when to make the changes. An example of effective use of participation is Toyota's efforts to involve a wide set of employees from different areas—engineering, logistics, sales, and manufacturing—in deciding how to change the way the Corolla model is made. The change suggestions involved not only design, but also such other issues as cost-cutting and quality enhancements.[39]

Of course, the use of participation is not cost free. It takes time and effort on the part of both managers and employees and may not be feasible if speed is essential or if it is not easy to arrange for effective participation. Also, participation may backfire if participants' suggestions and requests diverge widely from managers' goals. Furthermore, if those asked to participate sense that their input is not really wanted and that a manager is only "going through the motions," this can quickly lead to a feeling of being "manipulated." In such cases, participation has eroded rather than built support for change. Nevertheless, participation should at least be considered as a viable approach. The real issue is whether the failure to use participation makes change more difficult to implement than using participation. The answer is often "yes."

Incentives One other factor that can help build support for change is to emphasize incentives for those who will be affected. Simply communicating how the change itself will directly affect them in a positive way can often increase support. Examples are the installation of new equipment to make work easier, or reorganization to provide clearer direction, or additional training to add to an employee's repertoire of skills. At other times, providing incentives may involve conferring benefits directly to those affected. This could include, for example, either nonmonetary incentives such as more desirable working conditions, or the use of some form of monetary incentives such as increased compensation for increased responsibilities. Of course, in some circumstances, providing explicit incentives is often not practical. However, in certain instances, offering something tangible in return for support of changes that may cause extensive adaptation and even stress on the part of those affected may be appropriate and may directly encourage stronger support.

Managers should consider some important cautions, however, when weighing the possibility of using incentives to generate support for change. One is that providing incentives to those likely to be most affected may make them feel they are being "bought off." Thus, the use of incentives for change, especially monetary incentives, can potentially boomerang by increasing skepticism and cynicism of managers' motives and thus increase, rather than decrease, resistance to the changes. Furthermore, offering explicit incentives one time for a change may increase the probability that those affected will expect incentives any time a new change is made in the future. Therefore, introducing incentives as a way of building support for change is not something that should be done lightly and without consideration of possible serious, though unintended, side effects.

Implementation Choices

Where planning for change leaves off and implementation of change begins is often difficult to specify because the process is, or should be, more or less continuous. Regardless of where that boundary is, however, implementing change involves several critical choices for managers (see Exhibit 17.7). Three of the most important are discussed here.

Choice of Focus Earlier in this chapter, we identified six types, or focuses, of change: technology, shared values and culture, strategy, structure, systems, and staff. To initiate the change process, one or more of these focuses need to be selected. The choice depends in large part on the objectives to be accomplished, which in turn are linked to the problems identified in the assessment of the need to change. If the major problem is outdated equipment, then, obviously, changing the technology will be the focus of choice. However, if the problem is one of sluggish growth in sales compared with competitors, then the choice of focus is not so self-evident. It could be that the organization is not sufficiently market oriented, which could indicate a need for change in the cul-

exhibit 17.7

Implementation Choices

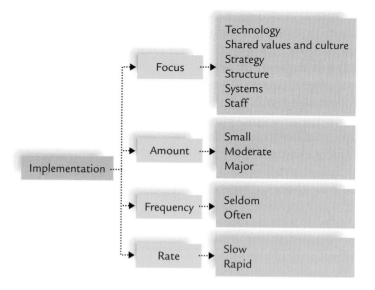

ture of the organization. That is exactly what took place in the 1980s with the famous breakup of AT&T. The seven newly created "Baby Bells" were suddenly thrust into an unregulated environment, and employees had to get used to marketing their companies' services rather than relying on their former monopolistic advantage to gain customer business. The managers of these new organizations needed to make substantial changes in their traditional ways of doing business, that is, the culture that had been entrenched for years and years.[40]

Changing organizational cultures also was exactly the area of focus that was required in a quite different setting when enterprises in former Eastern European countries such as Poland and Hungary were required to shift from operating in socialist-run economies to being effective in market-based economies. During the early 1990s in Budapest, Hungary, the U.S. telephone company Ameritech found two major cultural problems in attempting to oversee the privatization of MATAV, Hungary's telephone company: (1) convincing workers and managers that customer satisfaction is important to organizational effectiveness and (2) encouraging initiative in employees.[41] No simple changes such as replacing managers or buying new equipment would suffice to bring about the magnitude of change that was required in this case.

Often, the problems uncovered in the assessments of the need to change require attention to several simultaneous areas of focus, such as a new strategic direction for the organization *and* a major modification of its culture and structure that more closely fits the new strategy.

Choice of Amount Even after managers have decided what approaches to take and have started to implement those choices, they must also confront another, but related, set of issues: How much change should take place? That is, how comprehensive should the change be, and what parts of the unit or the whole organization should be affected? These questions have no easy answers.

When change is too little, the benefits are not likely to outweigh the costs involved. For example, 3M Corporation tried for several years to fix its magnetic data storage business problems through minor cost-cutting changes. After 10 years of escalating losses, it finally divested itself of this part of the company.[42] Even modest changes can take a great amount of effort and cause disruptions that are almost as great as if the change were much more sizable. Thus, managers must decide whether implementing minimal changes is worth these costs, or whether they should simply wait until the problems are large enough to justify the substantial investments that will be required. The argument in favor of making minimal changes, however, is that even though the immediate cost–benefit ratio may not be favorable, changes postponed until later will be much more expensive; therefore, the longer-term benefits can easily prove the worth of making small changes early. The old adage of "pay me now, or pay me later" comes to mind here.

Changes can be too massive as well as too small. Although managers may be tempted to make big changes once they decide to make changes, they often overlook the potential costs. Of course, very large changes are sometimes what is called for, especially when major changes are occurring in the unit's or organization's environment. Major magnitude changes also can have the positive side effect of "galvanizing the troops" so that organization members support the changes as not only necessary but also as inspiring their best efforts. However, as we will discuss later, any change can cause resistance, and big changes can cause immense resistance. Thus, too great a change, in effect, can create more chaos and more problems than were there initially. When this happens, no change at all would have been better than the change that was made.

The lesson for managers is that great care must be taken in deciding how much change should be implemented.[43] Potential problems exist in making changes so small that they either don't justify the costs or they produce minimal effects. Similarly, there can be other kinds of dangers in making changes that are too large. In particular instances, however, one of these extremes may in fact be the best alternative. The general guideline, therefore, is that the amount of change should fit the severity of the problems, and this should be determined by sound analysis of the strength of the need for change. A Manager's Challenge, "Ownership Changes Prompt Internal Changes at Avaya Ireland," illustrates a company that, as a result of fierce international competition, made a choice to implement large, major changes that resulted in a significant award for the quality of its products.

Choice of Frequency Another aspect of change that needs to be considered is the frequency of changes. In these times of competitive pressures and relative turbulence in many organizational environments, change must be implemented much more often than in the past. In some sense, change is a more or less constant condition. However, if specific changes, especially those of at least moderate size, are made continually, organization members can get mentally and physically exhausted. Imagine, for example, that you are a member of a sales department in a large, geographically dispersed company. First, management decides that sales data should be centralized and installs a new data information system linking all the regions. Next, management reorganizes the structure of the department by geographic region rather than by type of product. Next, management institutes a team structure linking sales with marketing and research and development personnel for new projects. Each of these changes, by itself, may improve customer satisfaction and employee performance. However, if they all occur within a short space of time, you might not have time to adjust to any one change before finding yourself in the midst of a new change. Therefore, the frequency of changes must be considered along with their size to gauge the effects on those who will have to respond.

Choice of Rate Just as the amount and frequency of change represent important choices in making changes, so does the rate of change. If the pace of change is too slow, conditions that created the need for it in the first place may again shift significantly so that the wrong problems are being dealt with by the end of the entire change process. Also, change that is too slow can frustrate

globalization *a manager's challenge*

Ownership Changes Prompt Internal Changes at Avaya Ireland

Avaya Ireland (AI) has been challenged to change throughout most of its history. The company was founded in 1961 as Telectron to make telephone networking equipment for businesses in Ireland. During the early 1980s, it was purchased by AT&T; during the mid-1990s, it was spun off by AT&T as part of Lucent Technologies; and in 2000, it was spun off by Lucent as part of Avaya, Inc. Each of these ownership changes forced AI's management to reevaluate the company's people, strategy, structure, and processes in the context of global competition.

While AI was part of AT&T, for example, technology began evolving away from the current product line, a recession dampened sales, and costs crept higher. Entrenched in an insular structure organized by function, managers focused on their own areas rather than paying close attention to the external environment and tackling companywide strategies. AI's executives had no consistent process for setting objectives, developing plans, and communicating with staff. Worse, they had no mechanism for recording and responding to customer complaints or measuring customer satisfaction.

Under Telectron's management, the workforce had not feared for their jobs. But AT&T operated internationally and had to contain costs to stay competitive. When AT&T laid off workers to cut costs, morale plummeted. An internal survey conducted shortly afterward revealed that, compared with AT&T's workforce in Europe, Africa, and the Middle East, the workforce in Ireland was significantly less satisfied with the corporation's values, leadership, working relationships, and empowerment. At the same time, AI's managers were acutely aware that AT&T's management could adjust to difficult conditions in one country or unit by shifting operations to another. Thus, AI was unlikely to survive within AT&T without making profound changes to become more responsive and market oriented.

AI's management started by planning to revamp the structure for more flexibility, collaboration, and empowerment. Experts helped management train employees in teamwork and team leadership principles in preparation for a transition away from a functional hierarchy to a team structure. Next, they set up an off-premises meeting so representatives of each department could take a fresh look at the company's situation away from the pressures of the daily work routine. This meeting identified four problem areas:

(1) lack of teamwork, (2) inadequate training, (3) poor communication, and (4) insufficiently defined roles for managers and employees. Rather than address only these areas, AI's top management decided to strive for a higher level of excellence by challenging the company to win the European Foundation for Quality Management Award.

To do this, they defined targets for product development and seven other internal processes keyed to the award's standards. Then they assigned cross-functional teams to assess AI's capabilities and determine what changes in skills, attitudes, and actions would be needed to hit those targets and qualify for the award. The teams returned with numerous ideas that management implemented, such as analyzing and eliminating outdated products and wasteful procedures. AI's executives also created a Customer Solutions Centre to impress customers with the company's technical strength and encourage interaction with customers. Finally, they established a process for aligning individual and team goals with the company's strategic objectives so the workforce would understand where the organization was headed, how it would get there, how performance would be measured, and what was in it for them.

These decade-long changes transformed AI from a company fighting for survival in Ireland to a world-class winner of the European quality award, a singular accomplishment because some of the best companies in Europe vie for this honor. In winning, AI also proved how implementing changes beyond the obvious fixes can propel a company to new heights. Moreover, in internal surveys, AI's employees say they are more customer focused and concerned about quality and innovation. Among those innovations is VOIP, or "voice-over-the Internet-protocol," which can slash corporate phone bills. Demand for VOIP is expanding exponentially, and Avaya's leading switchboard product integrates the new technology without a company having to replace its entire system, including its phones.

Today Avaya Inc.'s future is looking brighter than ever, and its financial viability is coming across loud and clear. In just one year, for example, its stock price soared an astounding 400 percent—not bad for a firm once considered to be just an old telephone-equipment company fighting to survive.

Sources: Pablo Galarza, Stephen Gandel, and Lisa Gibbs, "Best Investments," *Money*, January 2004, p. 64; Phil Hochmuth, "Avaya Looks to Reinvent Itself," *Network World*, November 11, 2002, pp. 25+; Graham Dwyer and Ciaran Doyle, "Award-Winning Results from Implementing Strategic Change at Avaya Ireland," *Journal of Organizational Excellence*, Winter 2002, pp. 29–41.

many people who want to see at least some early and tangible results in return for their efforts. For instance, suppose a company spent several months putting together new work teams and training employees in decision-making techniques, group processes, conflict resolution techniques, and use of computerized performance tracking. Then, however, suppose it delayed installing the new equipment and software. Employees would likely be frustrated by not being able to put their new knowledge and skills to immediate use.

Change that is too rapid can also cause major problems. Whether the change is primarily technological, structural, procedural, or some other focus, people need to adapt to the rate. Rates that are excessively fast can exceed the typical person's ability to cope and increase resentment and resistance. It has even been suggested that in situations of rapid change, the work experience may be so stressful and so damaging to a person's self-identity as to trigger violent behavior.[44]

Of course, managers sometimes deliberately and appropriately make rapid changes. One obvious case is when the forces for change are so overwhelming that swift change is essential. Furthermore, managers sometimes institute a fast rate of change precisely to determine who can keep up and who cannot. In such circumstances, a rapid rate may be a viable change tactic—if the manager has carefully considered what is to be accomplished and what the potential negative consequences or costs might be. In many other cases, however, managers have not adequately assessed the possible costs and benefits and may have simply implemented an abrupt change because of their eagerness to see results quickly.

As with choices about the amount of change, managers often face clear options about the rate of change they can choose. However, there is one major difference. When dealing with the rate of change, managers can make midcourse corrections more easily than they can when it comes to the amount of change. (It is very difficult, for example, to suddenly convert a large change into a small change.) If the initial pace has started slowly, managers can increase it if this appears desirable. Likewise, a change that has started out rapidly can be slowed, allowing for adaptation to catch up with events. Thus, just as the rate of speed of a car can be increased or decreased depending on road conditions, so can the rate of change in organizational settings. Of course, just as in a car, if the rate is changed too often or too drastically, it can be very uncomfortable for those required to adapt. This in turn can reduce confidence in the person responsible for the changes.

Resistance to Change

Those who lead organizations tend to be favorably disposed toward change. They see, from their perspective, the necessity for it and believe it is best for the organization. Consequently, although almost any change carries with it the seeds of resistance, managers are often surprised and frequently disappointed by resistance. They should not be. Some degree of resistance may be inevitable in organizational changes, and in some cases resistance may actually be positive in that it highlights important issues that may need more careful consideration.[45]

In this section we examine some of the reasons for resistance and some general approaches for dealing with it.

Reasons for Resistance The basic reason people resist change can be summed up in an old saying (slightly restated) that is applicable to many organizational circumstances: "The devil people know is preferred to the devil they don't know." Change embodies potential risks and threats for those affected.

They think they know how to size up those risks and threats in their present situation, but they are uncertain what they will be in the changed situation. Thus, the "known" present will be preferred to the "unknown" future, and therefore change is likely to be resisted. Within this overall context, some more specific reasons for resisting change can be identified.

Inertia. People in organizations get comfortable with their present ways of doing things. Even if they perceive no increase in risks, people simply find it easier to do things the way they always have rather than to operate or behave differently. Ingrained and overlearned habits die hard.

Mistrust. Even if those proposing change emphasize positive future consequences, people often doubt that they will actually occur. Such skepticism is especially magnified if change occurs in an existing climate of mistrust or if previous change efforts have failed.

An example is clearly illustrated in a change effort at the World Bank. In 1997, the top management of the World Bank attempted to make a major change in the organization's structure and procedures to model it more as a consulting firm and to reduce perceived overstaffing. To accomplish this, existing managers had to apply for the newly reduced number of management jobs. Selection committees then made up short lists of those qualified for each job, and top managers made the final decisions. This change effort resulted in near panic among the bank's managers because of memories of a similar change effort undertaken by the World Bank in 1987. At that time, top management similarly required all employees to resign, and then had managers choose whomever they wanted to work for them. This resulted in perceived cronyism, loss of morale, and continued inefficiency. The 1997 change revived memories of the debacle of 10 years earlier.[46] In such a situation, any supposed positive advantages of a change are likely to be highly discounted by those affected.

Lack of Information. A third contributing factor to resistance to change can be a lack of adequate information about both the need for the change and what its effects are likely to be. Even a seemingly small change such as a minor reorganization of a specific unit can produce opposition, often of a subtle nature, simply because basic information is not provided.

Lack of Capabilities. As we saw illustrated in A Manager's Challenge "Sales Potential All Bottled Up," back in Chapter 12 ("Motivation"), a sometimes powerful cause of resistance to change is the perceived lack of capabilities on the part of those who will be expected to implement the change. If people feel threatened by changes they think will require skills and abilities they do not presently have, then resistance is almost guaranteed.

Anticipated Consequences. Another reason for resistance can be straightforward assessments of expected gains and losses by those affected; in other words, employees determine what is best for protection of their self-interests. Those affected by the change may consider possible loss of status or influence, which may be ignored or underestimated by the managers who are instigating the change. Calculations of whether a change is "good" and should be supported, or is "bad" and should be resisted can be quite different from the viewpoint of those initiating the change and those who receive it. The two sides' self-interests, often defined by each party as "better for the organization," may be diametrically opposed.[47]

Dealing with Resistance to Change Resistance to change typically involves more than one of the preceding factors. As a result, from a manager's perspective, there is probably no "quick fix" to reduce or eliminate resistance.

However, this does not mean that resistance cannot be minimized. Therefore, having a framework for analyzing the resistance can be helpful. Some ways to analyze, and deal with, resistance are discussed next.

Force Field Analysis. One very useful way of looking at the problem of resistance is what is called a "**force field analysis**," as first proposed some years ago by psychologist Kurt Lewin. This analysis, as depicted in Exhibit 17.8, uses the concept of *equilibrium*, a condition that occurs when the forces for change, the "driving forces," are roughly balanced by forces opposing change, the "restraining forces." Such a condition results in a relatively steady state that is disrupted only when the driving forces for innovation become stronger than the restraining forces for inertia (the two forces that some have called the "in" forces[48]). If we apply this analysis to typical organizational changes, we see that managers basically have two choices: Add more force for change, such as putting more pressure on subordinates to conform to new procedures; or reduce the resistance forces, such as convincing informal leaders that they will benefit from the change. The basic problem with increasing the driving forces is that this often results in increasing the opposing forces. Therefore, Lewin's analysis suggests that weakening restraints may be the more effective way to bring about change. (This is similar to the old Aesop fable about the contrasting strategies of the wind and the sun who compete to get persons to take off their coats. The sun won.)

What are some ways to reduce resistance to change? Several approaches are the same as those discussed in the section on "Planning and Preparation for Change," since it is in the planning stages that potential resistance can first be anticipated and steps taken to address it. However, not all forms of resistance can be foreseen or dealt with in advance, so various other approaches are also

force field analysis uses the concept of equilibrium, a condition that occurs when the forces for change, the "driving forces," are balanced by forces opposing change, the "restraining forces," and results in a relatively steady state.

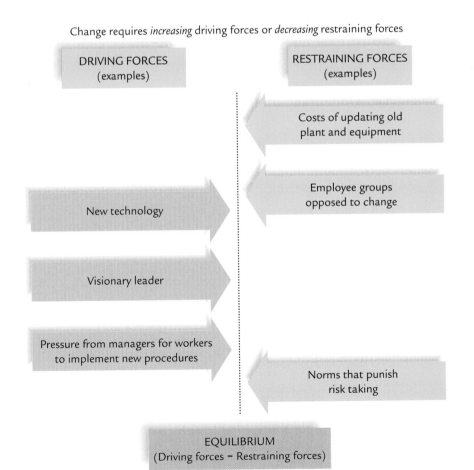

exhibit 17.8
Force Field Analysis

exhibit 17.9

Possible Methods for Dealing with Resistance to Change

Approach	Commonly Used In Situations—	Advantages	Disadvantages
Negotiation and Agreement (e.g., use formal or informal processes to gain advanced agreement to change before implementation)	In which someone or some group will clearly lose out in a change, and in which that group has consider-able power to resist	Sometimes major resistance can be reduced or avoided	Can be expensive in many cases if it alerts other groups to want to negotiate too
Participation and Involvement (e.g., involve affected employees in planning the change)	In which the initiators do not have all the informa-tion they need to design the change, and in which others have considerable power to resist	People who participate are more likely to be commit-ted to implementing change, and any relevant information they have will be integrated into the change plan	Can be both time-consuming and awkward if participants design an inappropriate change
Communication and Education (e.g., provide increased information to employees concerning the short- and long-term effects of the change)	In which there is a lack of information or inaccurate information and analysis	Once persuaded, people will often help with the implementation of the change	Can be very time-consuming if many people are involved
Facilitation and Support (e.g., offer seminars in stress management, personal development, anger resolution, etc.)	In which people are resisting because of problems in adjusting to the changes	No other approach works as well with problems of adapting to changes	Can be expensive, and still fail
Explicit and Implicit Coercion (e.g., use position power to order change)	In which speed is essential, and the change initiators possess considerable power	It is speedy and can overcome many kinds of resistance	Can be risky if it leaves people angry at the initiators and lowers trust in them

Source: Adapted and reprinted by permission of *Harvard Business Review.* An exhibit from "Methods for Dealing with Resistance to Change" by John P. Kotter and Leonard A. Schlesinger (March/April 1979), p. 111. Copyright 1979 by the President and Fellows of Harvard College; all rights reserved.

needed in this stage. A set of such approaches, with their associated advantages and disadvantages, is shown in Exhibit 17.9. Particularly important in this exhibit is the column showing the circumstances in which a particular approach is most likely to be effective. The message here is that not all approaches will work in all situations, and a manager must be selective in choosing when and where to use a particular method. Several factors are especially critical in making these choices, such as:

- Timing of use of approach.
- Cost in managers' and employees' time.
- Cost in financial and other resources.
- Degree of risk involved.
- Importance of the issues involved.

Participation. Participation may be very effective in defusing some resistance, or even identifying valid reasons why the change might not work, but it can be a costly use of everyone's time and can be risky for managers because the outcomes are hard to predict. For example, in a setting in which past change efforts have failed or have hurt employees (for example, through lay-offs), asking for people's participation may not seem legitimate.

Communication. Communication can be relatively inexpensive, but if it comes too late, it may not have much effect. For example, communicating and emphasizing to employees that a firm's profits have dropped sharply, after layoffs have already been announced, may seem like an after-the-fact attempt to justify the layoff action and may only result in increased levels of mistrust and resistance in the future.

Facilitation. Facilitation and support would probably be welcomed by those who might not want to go along with the changes, but the costs can be sub-stantial, especially if outside consultants are used.

Coercion. Coercion, such as threatening transfers or denying future promotions, is risky and not designed to lessen resistance, but it may overcome resistance in the short term. For this to work, management must have the power to follow through with threats, and the threats must be of sufficient magnitude to motivate compliance on the part of employees. In extreme situations managers may have no other choice, but if this option is chosen, they need to recognize that it will likely increase mistrust and resistance to change efforts in the future.

A final point to be made about dealing with resistance to change is that managers should recognize that the amount and nature of resistance may be very useful diagnostic tools to gauge whether the change is appropriate and will actually bring about desired results if implemented. To put this another way, managers need to *listen* to resistance and determine whether they have accurately assessed the need for change and the process of implementation. The fact that resistance arises certainly does not mean that the proposed change must be abandoned or postponed. On the other hand, it may be a very important signal that managers ignore at their peril, as illustrated in the fol-lowing example of an actual situation.

The owner of a small tire store bought three major new power tools for his tire replacement mechanics. The owner believed that the power tools would improve the performance and satisfaction of his employees—less time and less muscle power would be required. However, within one month, all three tools were out of commission: One had been left in the trunk of a customer's car, one had been run over by a truck, and one had been dropped from a hoist. When the owner probed the reasons for the losses, he found that they were not purely acci-dental. The employees, who had worked together for over 12 years, could not talk to each other over the noise of the power tools, and they had always enjoyed the camaraderie on the job. Without the opportunity to explain their opposition to the change, they became dissatisfied with their new working conditions and, in effect, sabotaged the new tools.[49] Had the owner appreciated why the employ-ees might resist, he could have considered other, perhaps superior, alternatives.

Evaluation of Change Outcomes

Once change has been carried out, whether throughout the entire organization or within one unit, managers need to evaluate the outcomes. If the effects of changes are not appraised in some manner, managers have no way of know-ing whether additional changes are needed and also whether the particular approaches implemented should be used again in similar circumstances. To carry out the evaluation process, three basic steps are required: data collection,

exhibit 17.10

Evaluating Change Outcomes

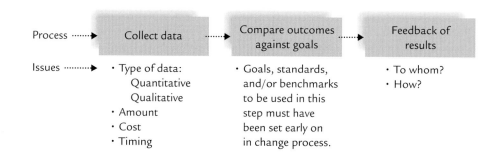

Process ┈┈▶	Collect data	Compare outcomes against goals	Feedback of results

Issues ┈┈▶	• Type of data:
	    Quantitative
	    Qualitative
	• Amount
	• Cost
	• Timing
		• Goals, standards, and/or benchmarks to be used in this step must have been set early on in change process.	• To whom?
			• How?

comparison of results against goals, and feedback of results to those affected by the changes. (See Exhibit 17.10.)

Data Collection   The data that can be collected to evaluate the outcomes of change essentially come in two forms: objective (quantitative) data and subjective (attitude) data. Both types can be useful to the manager who has implemented change, and often it will be necessary to tap several sources of each type. For example, after introducing major new information technology, a manager could evaluate by measuring changes in output per employee, speed of response to customers, accuracy in reports, attitudes of employee users within the organization, and attitudes of clients who deal with employees using the new technology.

It is important to keep in mind that the collection of different sets of data (such as these) to measure change outcomes may well require significant costs. Therefore, not every type of data that could be collected should be collected. As with other organizational actions, the benefits should be weighed against the costs. The point, though, is that significant sources of data should not be overlooked, and the more types of data that can be collected, the more likely the analysis of the effects will be informative. Also, in most cases, data should be collected at periodic intervals to measure the lasting power of the change. A recent survey showed that two-thirds of companies are using some form of scorecard software to measure everything from financial progress to customer satisfaction. These scorecards can be customized to reflect only the measures the company wishes to track. Then, by targeting the distribution of this kind of data, a company can ensure, for example, that managers from marketing, finance, and research and development are all discussing the same measures in meetings.[50]

Comparison of Outcomes Against Goals   Collection of data is only a first step in evaluating outcomes. The crucial next step is the comparison of those outcomes against the goals and various benchmarks or standards set in advance of the change. Without those goals and standards, interpretation of the data will be almost meaningless. To know that sales increased by 3 percent is interesting but lacks meaning unless it can be compared with some explicit objective, such as a 5 percent increase. Likewise, to know that employees' job satisfaction after the change averages 3.5 on a 5-point scale doesn't tell a manager much unless that can be measured against a goal of "at least 3.0." In other words, absolute results are not as informative as relative results. Goals and benchmarks that have been specified in advance of change efforts provide the basis for making meaningful relative comparisons.

Feedback of Results   A final step in evaluating change outcomes is communication of the findings to those who are involved with or affected by the change. Managers seldom, if ever, neglect to provide this information to interested superiors. However, when it comes to subordinates, this step is frequently overlooked or seen as desirable but not mandatory. This may be short-sighted. Failure to provide feedback can leave subordinates and other employees with a sense of frustration, and they may even question a manager's motives for not supplying it. It also can produce an element of distrust, making it even harder to carry out successful changes in the future.

Managers can provide feedback to both superiors and subordinates in a variety of ways, including written reports, direct oral reports and briefings, discussions with small groups, and the like. No one method is more effective than others. The key point is that in nearly all cases, some feedback about the effects of changes is better than no communication at all.

SPECIFIC APPROACHES TO PLANNED CHANGE

Throughout the earlier parts of this chapter, we have presented general issues and principles relating to organizational change and renewal. Here, in this final section, we look at three specific, usually organizationwide, approaches to planned change. The first is *organizational development*, which is an approach with a strong behavioral and people orientation. The second is the more engineering-based approach called *process redesign* (or *reengineering*). The final part of this section describes what is almost more a particular framework or perspective than a change approach as such, namely, *organizational learning*.

The Organizational Development (OD) Approach to Change

The essence of an **organizational development (OD)** approach to change is its emphasis on planned, strategic, long-range efforts focusing on people and their interrelationships in organizations.[51] While "organizational development" may seem like a general term that could be applied to almost any aspect of the topic of organizational change, as we noted at the beginning of this chapter, it in fact refers to a specific approach to bringing change to organizations. It grew out of behavioral science research aimed at improving the communication and quality of interactions among individuals in groups. Researchers put together groups of individuals in sessions away from the workplace in what were termed basic skill training groups, or, as they came to be called for short, **T-groups**.[52] The T-group orientation over time broadened into a focus on interpersonal relationships throughout the larger organization, and hence the attention to *organizational*, not just group, development.

Values and Assumptions The early formulation of what eventually evolved into the OD approach placed particular importance on certain values and assumptions, and they have remained at the heart of this approach to change to this day.[53] One set of these values related to the people in organizations: First and foremost is the assumption that "people are the cornerstone of success in any organizational endeavor."[54] A second value or assumption is that most people desire opportunities for personal growth and enhancement of their capabilities. Another basic value belief about people that underlies this approach to change is that their emotions are as important as their rational thoughts. Therefore, the open expression of these emotions can be critical in facilitating real change.

The fundamental assumption about organizations in the OD approach is that they are systems composed of interdependent parts, and, thus, a change in any one part can have major effects on other parts.[55] Another assumption is that the way organizations are designed and structured will influence the interpersonal

Organizational Development by Michael Hitt

Q&A OneKey
www.prenhall.com/onekey

organizational development (OD) approach to organizational change that has a strong behavioral and people orientation, emphasizing planned, strategic, long-range efforts focusing on people and their interrelationships in organizations

T-groups groups of individuals participating in organizational development sessions away from the workplace; also called basic skills training groups

relationships among the people within them. In other words, the behavior of people in organizational settings is at least partly caused by the conditions they encounter there—and these conditions can be changed.

Basic Approach to the Process of Change The basic OD approach to organizational change was described in Chapter 2, involving the three fundamental steps of: unfreezing, movement (changing), and refreezing.[56] Thus, in an OD approach to change, the initial challenge is to critically examine existing behavioral patterns by getting people not to take them for granted but to question them and look at their effects.

In the traditional OD approach, both the first and second steps—unfreezing and movement—will benefit from the use of **change agents**, individuals specifically responsible for managing change efforts.[57] These people can be either internal change agents, that is, from inside the organization—often from the human resource area—or they can be external change agents from outside the organization. In either case, the OD change agent is someone who is not a member of the particular groups or units directly involved. Frequently, this person is a consultant, someone with presumed expertise in helping groups see the need for change and in making changes.

The changes themselves are achieved by the use of one or more **interventions**, that is, "sets of structured activities," or action steps, designed to improve the organization.[58] Some of these interventions, such as fact finding, begin in the unfreezing stage, and others, such as team building and coaching/counseling, take place in the changing stage. Several of the more common types of interventions are shown in Exhibit 17.11.

change agents individuals who are responsible for implementing change efforts; they can be either internal or external to the organization

interventions sets of structured activities or action steps designed to improve organizations

exhibit 17.11

Types of OD Interventions

Intervention	Objective	Examples
Diagnostic Activities	To determine the current state of the organization or the parameters of a problem	Interviews Questionnaires Surveys Meetings
Individual Enhancement Activities	To improve understanding of and relationships with others in the organization	Sensitivity training (T-groups) Behavior modeling Life and career planning
Team Building	To improve team operation, abilities, cohesiveness	Diagnostic meetings Role analysis Responsibility charting
Intergroup Activities	To improve cooperation between groups	Intergroup team building
Technostructural or Structural Activities	To find solutions to problems through the application of technological and structural changes	Job enrichment Management by objective New technology introduction
Process Consultation	To disseminate information concerning the future diagnosis and management of human processes in organizations including communication, leadership, problem solving and decision making, and intra- and intergroup relationships	Agenda setting Feedback and observation Coaching and counseling Structural change suggestions

Source: Adapted from Wendell L. French and Cecil H. Bell Jr., *Organization Development: Behavioral Science Interventions for Organizational Improvement*, 5th ed. (Upper Saddle River, NJ: Prentice Hall, 1995), p. 165.

The priority in the second change stage is on exploring new forms of behavior and relationships. Particularly important at this point is an emphasis on behavioral processes, such as leader–group relations, decision making, intergroup cooperation, and the like. This **behavioral process orientation** is a key distinguishing feature of the OD approach to organizational change.

Merely engaging in new and different ways of behaving, relating, and interacting is not enough, of course, for changes to have lasting effects. This is the reason for the third stage, refreezing. As we saw in Chapter 2, the intent of this third stage was to make sure that the changes "stick" and that behavior and relationships don't easily return to their former—less effective—states. However, since the time of the original formulation of the three-stage change process many years ago, the goal of refreezing has been broadened into the objective of **organizational renewal**. The idea behind organizational renewal recognizes that in a fast-changing, competitive world, new habits and patterns rapidly become outdated themselves and may need to be replaced after relatively short periods of time. Therefore, the emphasis has shifted from simply locking changes into place and instead to developing a capacity for renewal, a goal that incorporates flexibility and the ability to change more or less continually.

In recent years, the OD approach to change, which formerly was almost a rigid set of procedures that required specific behavioral science expertise in the form of an experienced change agent, has evolved into a more general approach that places more emphasis on the direct use of line managers as potential change agents. Also, many of its intervention methods, such as team building, have become day-to-day, mainstream organizational activities. The OD legacy survives in various forms in many organizations today, but other comprehensive approaches to organizational change have attracted increasing attention from many managers in the last decade or so. Two of these are process redesign and organizational learning.

Process Redesign (Reengineering)

Process redesign, also often called simply "**reengineering**," involves a fundamental redesign of business processes to achieve (intended) dramatic improvements.[59] Technology, especially information technology, of course, usually plays a central role in such reengineering efforts. However, the human and managerial issues related to process redesign are also extremely crucial to its success in organizations. (See Exhibit 17.12.)

This approach to comprehensive organizational change first appeared in the late 1980s, and seemed to peak in popularity in the mid-1990s.[60] In one form or another it is still in use today, although clearly less so than a decade ago. The approach is based on two key principles: Many companies have business processes for meeting customer needs that are inefficient and outdated,

behavioral process orientation key distinguishing feature of the OD approach to organizational change that focuses on new forms of behavior and new relationships

organizational renewal a concept of organizational change that proposes a goal of flexibility and capability for continual change

process redesign (reengineering) involves a fundamental redesign of business processes to achieve dramatic improvements

Objectives	Coverage	Potential Drawbacks
· Reduce Costs	· Breadth	· Requires high level of persistence and involvement of top management
· Shorten Cycle Times	· Depth	· Effort may be greater than results
· Improve Quality		· High chaos factor
		· High levels of resistance

exhibit 17.12
Issues in Process Redesign

and many organizations have structures that involve more people than are necessary for efficient operations. The objectives are to reduce costs, shorten cycle times, and improve quality.[61] For example, one of the earlier applications of this approach was some years ago at IBM, where the credit approval process was shortened from two weeks to two hours with no increase in staff.

Those process redesign efforts that appeared to achieve the most success had both breadth and depth.[62] Breadth of reengineering means change in terms of the redesign of a set of processes across a complete business unit rather than a change in a single, limited process. Depth of reengineering means change in a related set of core organizational elements such as roles and responsibilities, structure, incentives, shared values, and the like, rather than any one or two of these elements.

Adequate breadth and depth by themselves, however, are not enough for process redesign to succeed. Implementation has turned out to be exceedingly difficult. A major commitment must come from the top of the organization, that is, from key executives (of the overall organization or its major units) who can supply the necessary resources to implement these activities and who can take the time to demonstrate personal involvement in the entire redesign process. Like any comprehensive change approach, for reengineering to be successful, enormous energy, planning, coordinated effort, persistence, and attention to detail are required. Without substantial backing, it is likely to fail.

Even under the best of circumstances, however, reengineering does not always produce effective change, and this has caused some disillusionment after the early enthusiasm for it.[63] For one thing, the amount of effort required has not always seemed commensurate with the results obtained. One European commercial bank, for example, saw its reengineering effort yield only a 5 percent cost reduction rather than the anticipated 23 percent reduction.[64] Because of less-than-expected effects, some managers and organizations simply decide not to continue with reengineering projects.

A second reason that some managers have become disenchanted with process reengineering, regardless of any positive benefits such as increased efficiency, is that it can cause more or less constant disorder and considerable resistance, or, as some managers have called it, "mass chaos."[65]

As the history of companies' attempts to implement process redesign illustrates, it is an approach to organizational renewal that is not exactly embraced by many of those who have to take part in it. In fact, one of the co-authors (Hammer) of the book that was most influential in popularizing this approach has stated that the people aspects of reengineering were not always given enough attention. "I was insufficiently appreciative of the human dimension. I've learned that's critical."[66] Nevertheless, despite its problems, at least some CEOs and other corporate leaders appear to remain positive about the potential of this comprehensive approach to change.

Organizational Learning

organizational learning
exhibited by an organization that is skilled at creating, acquiring, and transferring knowledge, and at modifying its behavior to reflect new knowledge and insights

Although the concept has been around for some time, it is only relatively recently that **organizational learning** has become a major focus in approaches to organizational change and renewal.[67] To date there is limited evidence regarding its impact on overall corporate performance, but the evidence that is available appears to support a positive relationship between firms' use of the organizational learning concept and their financial performance.[68]

By way of definition, an organization that is good at this process is said to be "skilled at creating, acquiring, and transferring knowledge, and at modifying its behavior to reflect new knowledge and insights."[69] Such an organization, in fact, would be called a *learning organization*. The central idea is that organizations that emphasize this perspective are (1) attempting to change and improve continuously, not just periodically, and, especially, (2) basing these improvements on a foundation of new knowledge they have acquired.

Several factors have been shown to facilitate learning by organizations:

- Existing and well-developed central, core competencies of current personnel.
- An organizational culture that supports continuous improvement.
- The availability of organizational capabilities (such as managerial expertise) to be able to implement the necessary changes.[70]

Clearly, managers and organizations cannot simply decide, or declare, that learning should take place. The elements listed above need to be in place as a starting point if organizational learning is going to lead to any real benefits. Then, a number of activities need to take place to implement fully an ongoing learning process in organizations. Five of the more important are explained here.[71]

Systematic, Organized, and Consistent Approach to Problem Solving A learning process in organizations requires the continual collection of factual data, rather than reliance on assumptions or guesswork, to aid problem solving and decision making.

Experimentation to Obtain New Knowledge Learning organizations do not simply solve current problems. They experiment with new methods and procedures to expand their knowledge and gain fresh insights. They engage in a steady series of small experiments to keep acquiring new knowledge consistently and to help employees become accustomed to change. For example, such major manufacturing companies as Corning, Allegheny Ludlum, and TXI Chaparral Steel constantly try new methods and processes to see whether they can improve their productivity. As they become experienced with learning and experimenting, they become less resistant to change in general. Also, however, learning organizations invest in bolder, one-of-a-kind experiments such as substantial demonstration or pilot projects.

Drawing Lessons from Past Experiences Enterprises with strong learning cultures pay particular attention to lessons from both past failures and past successes. They exemplify the old maxim: "It is not having had the experience that is important; it's what you learn from the experience that's important." To do this requires managers and the organization to draw conclusions and not leave such learning to hit-or-miss chance. Because of problems with the development of its 737 and 747 planes, Boeing initiated a three-year project to compare the development of these planes to the earlier, more reliable 707 and 727 planes. This project resulted in a booklet of "lessons learned," which was then used in the development and manufacture of the 757 and 767.

Learning from the Best Practices and Ideas of Others Organizations and their managers that are strongly committed to learning are also humble in a certain respect. They do not assume that they already know how to do everything better than other organizations, whether they are competitors, enterprises outside their own industry or sphere of operations, or customers. They consistently spend resources to scan their environments to gain information and knowledge from a variety of external sources. One increasingly common form of this is **benchmarking**, where the best practices of competitors are identified, analyzed, and compared against one's own practices. Thus, for example, the world's leading petroleum producers use reports from Environmental Information Services

benchmarking identification, analysis, and comparison of the best practices of competitors against an organization's own practices

exhibit 17.13

Top Ten Business Processes
Being Benchmarked

Rank	Business Processes Being Benchmarked
1.	Customer Service / Satisfaction
2.	Information Systems / Technology
3.	Employee Development / Training
4.	Process Improvement / Management
5.	Call Centers / Help Desks
6.	Performance Measurement / Improvement
7.	Employee Recruiting / Staffing
8.	Manufacturing / Assembly
9.	Human Resources
10.	Project Management

Source: http://www.benchnet.com, accessed December 18, 2002.

to benchmark against their competitors in terms of compliance with, and involvement in, environmental issues.[72] Exhibit 17.13 shows the top-10 business processes that are being benchmarked by a large number of companies, and Exhibit 17.14 shows which major organizations in the United States are currently most active in their use of the benchmarking approach.[73]

Other ways of generating this kind of learning include putting together **focus groups** of customers that spend time in small groups for intense discussions of the positive and negative features of products or services. The objective in using these and similar methods is to gain knowledge that would be difficult, if not impossible, to get only from people and available data inside the organization. In other words, learning organizations work hard at not being parochial and insular.

Transferring and Sharing Knowledge Another core activity of an organizational learning approach is to make sure that the new knowledge that is gained is actually disseminated widely throughout relevant units of the organization. This requires that managers be alert to both the need for information sharing and ways to do it. The latter would include such activities as distributing reports, developing demonstration projects, initiating training and education programs, and rotating or transferring those with the knowledge. General Motors, for example, developed a series of specialized tours of its NUMMI plant in Fremont, California, to introduce new workers to the distinctive procedures being used there. Tours were developed not only for hourly employees but

focus groups small groups involved in intense discussions of the positive and negative features of products or services

exhibit 17.14

Major U.S. Organizations
Utilizing Benchmarking

Rank	Organization
1.	Bank of America
2.	TRW
3.	American Express
4.	Xerox
5.	U.S. Army
6.	Dana
7.	U.S. Department of Veterans Affairs
8.	Eastman Kodak
9.	Social Security Administration
10.	Internal Revenue Service

Source: http://www.benchnet.com, accessed December 18, 2002.

also for upper and middle managers, with each tour concentrating on issues most relevant to the targeted group. It also offers numerous on-site training courses that are open to all employees.[74] These activities, which are not cost free, are provided as part of an ongoing pursuit of continuous improvement.

As an approach to change, an organizational learning perspective has much to offer. It emphasizes paying constant attention to the possible need for changes, and it embodies the goal of renewal—of pushing organizations to continually reinvent themselves through the purposeful and persistent acquisition of new knowledge. The implementation of active organizational learning directly confronts the fundamental issue stated at the beginning of this chapter: Since environments never stay the same, successful organizations can never stay the same. One of the best ways to both keep up with changing environments and keep ahead of them is for managers to focus intently on instilling a learning culture in their areas of responsibility.

managerial perspectives revisited

1 **PERSPECTIVE 1: THE ORGANIZATIONAL CONTEXT** As a manager, being able to change oneself (as we discussed in Chapter 2) is important and necessary. As a manager, being able to change an organization (or a part of it) is important and necessary—and very difficult. If it is hard to change oneself, it is even harder to change other people! Nevertheless, in the organizational environments of today and the foreseeable future, the need for organizations to keep changing and renewing will always be present. However, the ease or difficulty of carrying out changes and renewal will be strongly affected by the particular conditions—structure and culture—existing in an organization. Here, again, organizational context will be crucial in determining the success or failure of managers' efforts to bring about these changes.

2 **PERSPECTIVE 2: THE HUMAN FACTOR** People can be either the great facilitators or the great roadblocks of change. Since people in organizations will be the ultimate implementers of any change, no change will succeed without eventually, even if not at first, getting people to support it. People, as a variable in the process, are more than just responders or recipients of change, however. They also potentially can be a great source of ideas about what changes need to be made, about how changes should be carried out, and whether or not changes are working the way they were intended.

3 **PERSPECTIVE 3: MANAGING PARADOXES** Potential paradoxes lie at the heart of many organizational changes, and transformations. For example, managers must weigh change versus stability. Making major changes is difficult because people resist changes, especially major ones. Moreover, while changes may be needed quickly, rapid change can produce organizational chaos if implemented incorrectly. Take, for example, the rapid changes in Russia's economic system in the late 1980s. The changes appeared to be a move in the right direction, but the Russian government didn't have the necessary infrastructure to support and implement many of them. Of course, the changes in Russia were massive. Smaller-scale changes within companies trying to transform their organizations (like United Airlines after it declared bankruptcy) can, nonetheless, be a major undertaking.

Managers are constantly confronted with potential paradoxes like this when deciding on the kinds of changes to make and their timing and implementation. Those managers who have the greatest understanding of the trade-offs facing them—pros and cons—will have the best chances of achieving success and renewing their units or organizations.

 PERSPECTIVE 4: ENTREPRENEURIAL MIND-SET   In organizations where managers have adopted an entrepreneurial mind-set and diffused it throughout the organization, changes are easier to implement. An entrepreneurial mind-set makes the organization and the people in it more flexible. On the other hand, many organizations have to make major changes because they have not been entrepreneurial and therefore have lost their competitive advantage to other, more entrepreneurial organizations. These organizations, for example, may need to develop and introduce new products in the market in order to compete with organizations that have outpaced them. However, in developing substantially new products, organizations may require a change in their culture to encourage more creativity and risk-taking by their employees. In other words, these firms will need to develop an entrepreneurial mind-set, which itself can be difficult to do. Consequently, unless managers who are responsible for particular organizational development and transformation initiatives are themselves committed to the changes—and demonstrate their commitment to them—employees aren't likely to follow. Above all, managers need to be committed to the goal of constant organizational renewal and improvement. Commitment to the status quo is the antithesis of managing effectively in organizations. Adopting an entrepreneurial mind-set will help managers make this type of commitment.

concluding comments

Clearly, change in organizations is often necessary—but hardly ever easy. What may seem like an obvious need for change from the point of view of the person in charge, the manager, may not seem that way at all to those who have to adapt and carry out the change. People resist change for a variety of reasons, many of them valid. In general, if people do not *feel* or *believe* in the need for change, they are likely, at best, to be apathetic supporters of change and, at worst, to be active resisters. Therefore, creating a shared feeling of the need for change and a belief in its necessity is one of the first and most critical steps in achieving successful change.

As we have discussed in this chapter, producing effective change requires an analysis of the likely sources and reasons for resistance and a consideration of the most effective possible approaches for overcoming that resistance. Once people are "unfrozen," they need a new "state" to move toward. In other words, as a manager, you will need to persuade people not only that the place where they are currently is untenable, but also that the place where you want them to go is better. In addition, they will need from you a clear sense of *how* they are going to get from where they are now to the new place you want them to go.

Simplified, change is about helping people you manage answer three basic questions: (1) What's wrong with just staying put? (2) Where do we want to go instead? (3) How are we going to get there? Without convincing answers to these essential questions, most people are unlikely to change. The stimulating thing about managing change, however, is that no two situations are identical, nor are the people who are involved in, or affected by, the change.

In the final analysis, organizations and managers need to view the condition of "things as they are" with extreme skepticism. Like the principle in physics that says "nature abhors a vacuum," the status quo in organizations should be regarded almost as anathema. It is fraught with dangers, many of which are subtle and hard to recognize. Consequently, managers need to be ever alert against becoming prisoners of their own success and just sticking with what has worked in the past. Being able to make meaningful changes that lead to organizational renewal in a way that adds value is one of the premier managerial challenges of our times.

key terms

behavioral process orientation 632	interventions 632	process redesign (reengineering) 633
benchmarking 635	organizational development (OD) 631	T -groups 631
change agents 631		
focus groups 635	organizational learning 634	
force field analysis 626	organizational renewal 632	

test your comprehension

1. List the forces that act from outside an organization to bring about change within it.
2. What are an organization's internal forces for change?
3. What components within an organization can be changed? (Hint: This chapter discusses six of them.)
4. What is the key to changing an organization's culture?
5. Is it more difficult to change an organization's strategy or its culture? Why?
6. What elements are involved in attempting people-focused change in an organization?
7. What is meant by proactive and reactive change?
8. What are the four major steps in the change process?
9. What are some of the considerations managers face when planning change?
10. Why is it important to involve in the planning process those who will ultimately be affected by a change?
11. List the drawbacks to using incentives to gain cooperation during a change.
12. Why is it important to be careful in choosing the amount and rate of change? What are the benefits and drawbacks involved in large- and small-scale change? In rapid or slow change?
13. Why do employees resist change?
14. What are some of the ways managers can overcome employees' resistance to change?
15. What is meant by force field analysis?
16. In evaluating the outcome of planned change, what types of data are used?
17. What are the three steps in evaluating the outcome of a planned change?
18. What is the emphasis of the OD approach to change?
19. What are the key steps in the OD approach to change?
20. What is a change agent? Where do they come from?
21. What is the difference between the breadth and the depth of reengineering?
22. Describe a "learning organization."
23. How can you tell when you are encountering a learning organization?

apply your understanding

1. Think of the last organizational change that affected you. Maybe your university, for example, recently changed some policy on major curriculum requirements or something similar. Were you a supporter of or resister to the change? What mistakes did the organization make? What could it have done differently to facilitate the change?

2. The exact outcomes of change programs are often not evaluated. Why do you think this is the case?

3. Changes in strategy are generally not effective without changes in other aspects of the organization. Why do you think this is the case?

4. Crisis change is more common but more costly than anticipatory change. What do you think the keys are to effective anticipatory change?

5. How easy, or difficult, is it to convert a traditional organization to a learning organization?

practice your capabilities

Two years ago, GenCom gave its Production Review Committee responsibility for developing and implementing procedures to improve manufacturing productivity. Jerry, the manager of the engineering department, is the co-chair of the committee along with Gene, the production manager. They and the three other committee members have joint responsibility for deciding on any major changes intended to improve productivity. This month's regular meeting of the production review committee had already started when Gene hurried in. "Have you seen these production figures? Have you? They are incredible—just look at the increase in productivity in this department!" Jerry was surprised at Gene's enthusiasm, and said, "Wait a minute, slow down. Just what are you talking about that has you so excited?" At this, Gene realized the other members of the committee hadn't yet seen the new report and quickly handed copies of it around. He then took a deep breath and started explaining.

"Several months ago, I ran into Kim, the manager of extract processing, and said that I was somewhat disappointed by the latest productivity figures and wished someone could figure out a way to improve them. I didn't think about that statement until just this morning when Kim walked into my office and handed me this report. It seems she has had her team working on the problem for the last four months. They collected information on productivity levels at other similar companies and carefully studied the procedures of the most successful. They worked with several of the ideas in their group, testing the ideas separately and in combination and with new additions until they found a method that seemed to work. Wow! I'll say it seems to work. Just look at those figures. I think we ought to immediately implement their idea in all of the production units. Just think of the profit improvements that would result from across-the-board performance improvements matching these."

Jerry and the other members of the committee were pleased with the report and decided to accept Gene's recommendation for a companywide application of the new procedures developed by Kim's team. They had all been anxious to find a new initiative that would really work, since their last two change attempts had been unsuccessful. In fact, both previous initiatives had been scrapped rather quickly. The first one had not worked because the plant didn't have the right type of equipment and infrastructure to support it. The second had failed because of high levels of resistance from employees. However, after discussion, the committee members were convinced that this new approach would definitely work, and they decided to implement it throughout all relevant units. After all, it had worked out exceedingly well in Kim's department.

1. Analyze the forces for, and focus of, change in this situation.

2. What problems might you anticipate with the committee's decision to implement Kim's procedures companywide? How would you try to deal with those possible problems?

closing case

Telefonica Calls for Change

The pace of change within the global telecommunications industry has quickened as more countries eliminate monopolies and encourage competition through deregulation and privatization. Spain cleared the way for competition starting in 1998, allowing British Telecommunications and other rivals to challenge Telefonica, which formerly held a monopoly position as the nation's largest telephone company. By then, Telefonica was ready to compete in a deregulated market. Ten years earlier, its top managers had anticipated deregulation and planned a comprehensive program of change to prepare itself for the new environment. Since deregulation, Telefonica has continued to change by expanding into other countries and other offerings beyond traditional dial-up phone service.

Prior to deregulation, Telefonica was a slow-moving, government-owned bureaucracy with more than 100,000 employees who were virtually guaranteed lifelong employment. Prices were high, and customers with questions or problems could contact the company only during a five-hour daily window. The wait for a new phone line could go on for weeks. And when customers lost service, the outages lasted 150 minutes on average.

Looking ahead, however, Telefonica's managers realized that competition and emerging technological developments would give customers new choices and new power. They realized that the company risked losing its market leadership position if changes were not made. Therefore, they decided on a new mission: to become the "favorite provider of telecommunications, voice, data, sound, and image services" to current and potential customers. The new mission pointed the way toward a more customer-oriented future for Telefonica.

At this point, management looked toward one division as a model for change throughout the organization. The Alicante unit in Eastern Spain, with a workforce of more than 1,200, was one of the company's most profitable and fastest growing. Eyeing the opportunity for additional growth in Alicante, Telefonica's top management decided to invest heavily in new equipment and networks there. Yet new technology alone would not boost revenues without customer service improvements that could only occur by making structure, culture, strategy, process, and people changes.

Alicante's managers decided to get rid of the existing bureaucratic controls and the hierarchical rigidity that facil-itated downward communication while preventing communication between departments. They also recognized the need to make customer service a priority for middle managers, front-line managers, and employees, which required a cultural shift from a monopoly mind-set to a competitive mind-set. Moreover, they wanted the entire staff to have the training and motivation to participate in problem solving and improvements to support the new goals and mission. Finally, they wanted to change employee attitudes by rein-stilling a sense of pride in working for Telefonica. Yet, change could not be so rapid that it would alienate the staff nor so slow that it would have little effect on performance.

In consultation with middle management, Alicante's senior managers drafted a plan outlining the basic processes, technologies, training, and communications that would be needed to achieve specific annual goals for service improvements. They gathered broad-based support by circulating this document among lower-level managers and employees for comments and suggestions. Nearly all of these changes were incorporated into the plan, which was submitted to headquarters for review in the context of the overall corporate strategy. After the plan was communicated to all employees of Telefonica, the Alicante division began implementation.

First, senior and middle managers formed teams to study the division's current practices, identify tasks that did not deliver customer value, and design new processes and procedures in line to achieve the service goals. Second, they set up a training program to educate the entire staff about the goals, the new practices, and the standards to be used in measuring progress. Third, as milestones were achieved, management put together a best-practices manual to document and share the most effective procedures within the corporation.

Once this plan was underway, the next step for Alicante's top managers was to design an educational program to build the management skills, teamwork capabilities, and commitment of middle managers. In designing this program, they asked middle managers to describe the factors that might cause Telefonica to succeed or fail in a competitive environment. They also asked middle managers about their self-image as leaders and the characteristics that Telefonica managers would need to help fulfill the company's goals and mission. The middle managers identified advanced technology, new services, and responsiveness to customer needs as main factors in making

Telefonica more customer oriented in a competitive market. They noted that failure could occur as a result of poor planning, lack of workforce commitment, excessive hierarchical levels, and inability to adapt to market realities.

Further, the managers felt under intense pressure from senior managers as well as from the need to follow rules and achieve results. They believed they were bearing the burden of moving the company forward yet lacked sufficient connections with each other; and they did not have an opportunity to effectively plan because they were constantly solving unexpected problems. According to the middle managers, the ideal Telefonica manager would be strongly committed to the firm, be open to change, be a team player, be ready to listen, be an inspiration to others, and be willing and able to delegate to others. Alicante's senior managers asked the managers what skills and knowledge they needed to become an ideal manager. The managers responded by asking for training in goal setting, teamwork, organizational skills, problem solving, motivation, and communication.

Not only did the managers receive training in these six areas; Alicante's executives invited them to participate in drawing up a year-long development plan to spread what they called the "new management style" through better communication, training, employee empowerment, and processes. For example, the unit began issuing a monthly newsletter to reinforce customer-oriented goals and values. It also distributed a quarterly report to educate all employees about new services available for customers, and publicly recognized employees and managers who proactively came up with creative solutions to problems. At the end of the year, all managers were surveyed to assess their progress in changing their management style. The response showed that 75 percent were satisfied with the results; 92 percent said that top management had provided the support needed for managers to make the change.

Alicante's progress prompted Telefonica to extend this change process throughout the company as it made the transition to a deregulated, private company (with a small ownership stake retained by the Spanish government). Soon the internal changes prompted external changes appreciated by customers. Telefonica reduced rates, offered 24-hour customer service, installed new phone lines within 24 hours, and cut the length of service outages by 20 percent. It also moved aggressively into South American markets and added new technologies and services such as Internet access and wireless communication. To reward performance, management offered stock options to the entire workforce.

Within a few years, however, hypercompetitive conditions caused the company to stop expanding its expensive wireless operations across Europe and sell assets in the wake of a multibillion-dollar loss. Although Telefonica had reduced its rates, some services were more expensive than comparable services offered by other European telecommunication firms. Services like 12P, a broadband intranet package from competitor Jazztel, are cheaper than Telefonica's. And more rivals are challenging in Spain and other markets, competing ruthlessly on price.

Nonetheless, Telefonica still holds about three-quarters of the Spanish market. "The market is not big enough to support more than two or three major players, and we will see business failures, mergers, and acquisition in the next years," said one analyst. To remain a player at the forefront, Telefonica must continue to evolve in order to give customers what they want.

Questions

1. Analyze the process that Telefonica's management used to create change within the company.
2. What factors reduced the amount of resistance to this change by managers and employees?
3. Once the change was successful in Alicante, what problems might management have faced in instituting this change throughout Telefonica at large?
4. Would you consider Telefonica a learning organization? Explain your answer.
5. Could other highly bureaucratic companies change their cultures and processes as radically as Telefonica, or were there particular circumstances here that would limit this kind of change to this specific organization?

Sources: Julian Bright, "The Rain in Spain Falls Mainly on New Entrants," *Total Telecom Magazine*, October 2003, pp. 16–18; "Spain: Phone Company to Sell Shares," *New York Times*, September 3, 2002, p. C8; Suzanne Kapner, "Telecom Giants Retrench in Europe," *New York Times*, July 26, 2002, p. W1; Enrique Claver, Jose L. Gasco, Juan Llopis, and Reyes Gonzalez, "The Strategic Process of a Cultural Change to Implement Total Quality Management: A Case Study," *Total Quality Management*, July 2001, pp. 469+; Stephen Baker, "Takeover Escape Artist," *BusinessWeek*, April 10, 2000, pp. 20+; Enrique Claver, Jose L. Gasco, Juan Llopis, and Enrique A. Lopez, "Analysis of a Cultural Change in a Spanish Telecommunications Firm," *Business Process Management Journal* 6, no. 4 (2000): pp. 342+; Peter Heywood, "Spain's PTT Shapes Up," *Data Communications*, August 1998, p. 36.

HR Restructuring—The Coca-Cola & Dabur Way

By A. Mukund

"We had grown but we hadn't structured our growth."

—*Dabur sources in 1998.*

"Three major strands have emerged in Coke's mistakes. It never managed its infrastructure, it never managed its crate of 10 brands, and it never managed its people."

—*Businessworld in 2000.*

The Leader Humbled

It all began with Coca-Cola India's (Coca-Cola) realization that something was surely amiss. Four CEOs within seven years, arch-rival Pepsi surging ahead, heavy employee exodus, and negative media reports indicated that the leader had gone wrong big time. The problems eventually led to Coca-Cola reporting a huge loss of US$52 million in 1999, attributed largely to the heavy investments in India and Japan. Coca-Cola had spent Rs 1500 crore for acquiring bottlers, who were paid Rs 8 per case as against the normal Rs 3 (1 crore = 10 million). The losses were also attributed to management extravagance such as accommodations in farmhouses for executives and foreign trips for bottlers.

Following the loss, Coca-Cola had to write off its assets in India worth US$405 million in 2000. Apart from the mounting losses, the write-off was necessitated by Coca-Cola's overestimation of volumes in the Indian market. This assumption was based on the expected reduction in excise duties, which did not happen, which fur-

ther delayed the company's break-even targets by some more years.

Changes were required to be put in place soon. With a renewed focus and energy, Coca-Cola took various measures to come out of the mess it had landed itself in.

The Sleeping Giant Awakes

In 1998, the 114-year-old ayurvedic and pharmaceutical products major Dabur found itself at the crossroads. In fiscal 1998, 75 percent of Dabur's turnover had come from fast-moving consumer goods (FMCGs). Buoyed by this, the Burman family (promoters and owners of a majority stake in Dabur) formulated a new vision in 1999 with an aim to make Dabur India's best FMCG company by 2004. In the same year, Dabur revealed plans to increase the group turnover to Rs 20 billion by the year 2003–2004.

To achieve the goal, Dabur benchmarked itself against other FMCG majors, such as Nestlé, Colgate-Palmolive, and P&G. Dabur found itself significantly lacking in some critical areas. While Dabur's price-to-earnings (P/E) ratio[1] was less than 24, for most of the others it was more than 40. The net working capital of Dabur was a whopping Rs 2.2 billion whereas it was less than half of this figure for the others. There were other indicators of an inherently inefficient organization, including Dabur's operating profit margins of 12 percent as compared to Colgate's 16 percent and P&G's 18 percent. Even the return on net worth was around 24 percent for Dabur as against HLL's 52 percent and Colgate's 34 percent.

The Burmans realized that major changes were needed on all organizational fronts. However, media reports questioned the company's capability to shake off its family-oriented work culture.

Restructuring the Mess the Coca-Cola Way

In 1999, following the merger of Coca-Cola's four bottling operations (Hindustan Coca-Cola Bottling North West, Hindustan Coca-Cola Bottling South West, Bharat Coca-Cola North East, and Bharat Coca-Cola South East), human resources issues gained significance at the company. Two new companies, Coca-Cola India, the corporate and marketing office, and Coca-Cola Beverages were the result of the merger. The merger brought with it over 10,000 employees to Coca-Cola, doubling the number of employees it had in 1998.

Coca-Cola had to go in for a massive restructuring exercise focusing on the company's human resources to ensure a smooth acceptance of the merger. The first task was to put in place a new organizational structure that vested profit and loss accounting at the area level, by renaming each plant-in-charge as a profit center head. The country was divided into six regions as against the initial three, based on consumer preferences. Each region had a separate head (Regional General Manager), who had the regional functional managers reporting to him. All the regional general managers reported to VP (Operations) Sanjiv Gupta, who reported directly to CEO Alexander Von Bohr (Bohr). The 37 bottling plants of Coca-Cola, on an average six in each region, had an Area General Manager as the head, vested with profit-center responsibility. All the functional heads reported to the area general manager. Coca-Cola also declared VRS at the bottling plants, which was used by about 1,100 employees.

The merger carried forward employees from different work cultures and work value systems. This move toward regionalization caused dilution of several central jobs, with as many as 1,500 employees retiring at the bottling plants. The new line of control strengthened entry- and middle-level jobs at the regions and downgraded many at the center. This led to unrest among the employees and about 40 junior- and middle-level managers and some senior personnel including Ravi Deoi, Head (Capability Services) and Sunil Sawhney, Head (Northern Operations), left the company.

As part of the restructuring plan, Coca-Cola made a strategy-level decision to turn itself into a people-driven company. The company introduced a detailed career planning system for over 530 managers in the new set-up. The system included talent development meetings at regional and functional levels, following which recommendations were made to the HR Council. The council then approved and implemented the process through a central HR team. Coca-Cola also decided that the regional general managers would meet the top management twice a year to identify fast-track people and train them for more responsible positions. Efficient management trainees were to be sent to the overseas office for a three-week internship. To inculcate a feeling of belonging, the company gave flowers and cards on the birthdays of the employees and major festivals.

Coca-Cola also undertook a cost-reduction drive on the human resources front. Many executives who were provided accommodation in farmhouses were asked to shift to less expensive apartments. The company also decided not to buy or hire new cars, as it felt that the existing fleet of cars was not being used efficiently. In the drive for "optimum utilization of existing resources," Coca-Cola decided against buying a Rs 50 crore property in Gurgaon and it also surrendered a substantial part of its rented office space in Gurgaon, near Delhi. Company officials felt that this was justified because a lot of officials had moved out of the Delhi headquarters due to the localization. Moreover, this was necessitated by the resignations and sackings. Salaries were also restructured as part of this cost-reduction drive. Coca-Cola began benchmarking itself with other major Indian companies, whereas it was offering pay packages in line with international standards. Coca-Cola also realigned some jobs based on the employee's talent and potential.

However, the company's problems were far from over. In March 2000, Coca-Cola received reports of wrongdoing in its North India operations. The company decided to take action after the summer season.[2] In July 2000, Coca-Cola appointed Arthur Andersen to inspect the accounts of the North India operations for a fee of Rs 1 crore. The team inspected all offices, godowns, bottling plants, and depots of Jammu, Kanpur, Najibabbad, Varanasi, and Jaipur. The findings revealed that the North Indian team had violated discounting terms and the credit policy, apart from being unfair in cash dealings. The team was giving discounts that were five times higher than those given in the other regions of the country. There were also unexplained cancellations and re-appointments of dealerships.

In light of the above findings by Arthur Andersen's team, Coca-Cola carried out a performance appraisal exercise for 560 managers. This led to resignations en masse. Around 40 managers resigned between July and November 2000. Coca-Cola also sacked some employees in its drive to overhaul the HR functioning. By January 2001, the company had shed 70 managers, accounting for 12 percent of the management. Bohr said, "I had to make some tough decisions because the buck stops here. We needed to weed out certain practices. That's an important message sent out—that we'll take action if we can't work on principles of integrity. The investigation was the right thing. The business is healthier now."

However, media reports revealed a different side of the picture altogether. The managers who had quit voiced their thoughts vociferously against Coca-Cola, claiming that the whole performance appraisal exercise was farcical and that the management had already decided on the people to get rid of. They termed the issue as Coca-Cola's "witch-hunt" in India. Reacting to the management's comments regarding discount norm violations, one former employee commented, "All discounts were cleared by the top management. They always pushed for higher volumes and said profitability is not your problem. So, we got volumes at whatever costs. Nobody told us this was an unacceptable practice." This seemed to be substantiated by the fact that in the Delhi region, which consumed only 6,000–8,000 cases per day, the sales team received a target of pushing 25,000 cases a day. It was commented that this was done so as to "make things look good" when the company sent its financials to the global headquarters. It was also reported that the performance appraisals and the subsequent dismissals were carried out in a very "inhuman" and "blunt" manner.

Worried by such adverse comments about the company, Alexander decided to take steps to ensure a smooth relationship with the new people in the company. He personally met the finance heads in every territory and made the company's credit policy clear to them. Coca-Cola also standardized the discounting limits and best practices irrespective of market compulsions. The company launched a major IT initiative as well, to make the functioning of the entire organization transparent at the touch of a button. Things seemed to have stabilized to some

extent after this. Justifying the decision to let go of certain personnel, Alexander said, "We don't mind those quitting who were just okay. We told them where they could hope to be, based on their performance. Some who have left may not have had a good career with Coke."

The Dabur Way

Dabur's restructuring efforts began in April 1997, when the company hired consultants McKinsey & Co., at a cost of Rs 80 million. McKinsey's threefold recommendations were: to concentrate on a few businesses; to improve the supply chain and procurement processes, and to reorganize the appraisal and compensation systems. Following these recommendations, many radical changes were introduced. The most important was the Burman's decision to take a back seat. The day-to-day management was handed over to a group of professional managers for the first time in Dabur's history, while the promoters confined themselves to strategic decision making.

Dabur decided to revamp the organizational structure and appoint a CEO to head the management. All business unit heads and functional heads were to report directly to the CEO.

In November 1998, Dabur appointed Ninu Khanna as the CEO. The appointment was the first incident of an outside professional being appointed after the restructuring was put in place. Ninu Khanna, who had previously worked with Proctor & Gamble and Colgate-

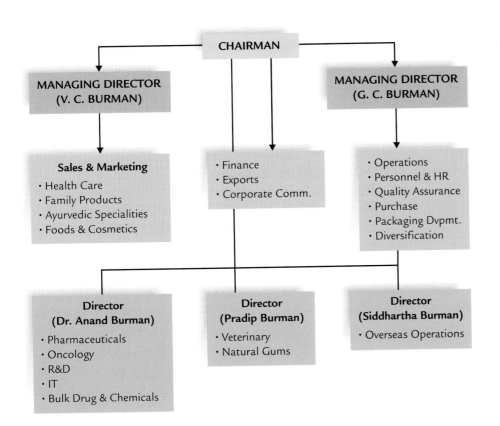

exhibit 1

Organizational Structure (Before Restructuring)

Source: Company Annual Report.

Palmolive, was roped in to give Dabur the much-needed FMCG focus. Dabur had also appointed Cadbury India's Deepak Sethi as Vice President–Sales and Marketing–Health Care Products division; Godrej Pilsbury's Ravi Sivaraman as Vice President–Finance, and ABB's Yogi Sriram as Vice President–HRD.

Dabur made performance appraisals more objective by including many more measureable criteria. Concepts such as customer satisfaction, increased sales and reduced costs, cycle-time efficiency, return on investment, and shareholder value were all introduced as yardsticks for performance appraisals. Harish Tandon, general manager, HR, Dabur, remarked, "Now Dabur is working toward making compensation more performance oriented, and the performance evaluation system is being worked on. Today, performance in terms of target achievement is the main factor followed by other criteria such as sincerity and longevity of service." The focus of appraisals thus shifted to what a person had achieved, as much as on what he or she was capable of.

Dabur's employee-friendly initiatives included annual sales conferences at places like Mauritius and Kathmandu. These conferences, attended by over 100 sales executives of the company, combined both "work-and-play" aspects for better employee morale and performance. Dabur also gave cash incentives to junior-level sales officers and representatives upon successful achievement of targets. Employees were also allowed to club their leaves and enjoy a vacation.

To increase employee satisfaction levels, Dabur identified certain key performance areas (KPAs) for each employee. Performance appraisal and compensation planning were now based on KPAs. Employee training was also given a renewed focus. To help employees communicate effectively with each other and for better dissemination of news and information, Dabur brought out a quarterly newsletter, "Contact." The interactive newsletter worked as a two-way communication channel between the employees. Dabur also commissioned consultants Nobel & Hewitt to formulate an Employee Stock Option Plan (ESOP). The scheme, effective from fiscal 2000, was initially reserved for very senior personnel. Dabur planned to extend the scheme throughout the organization in the future.

The After Effects

Both Coca-Cola and Dabur had to accept the fact that a major change on the human resources front was inevitable, although the changes in the two were necessitated by radically different circumstances. More importantly, the restructuring seemed to have been extremely beneficial for them. Besides improved moral and

exhibit 2

Organizational Structure (After Restructuring)

Source: Annual Report.

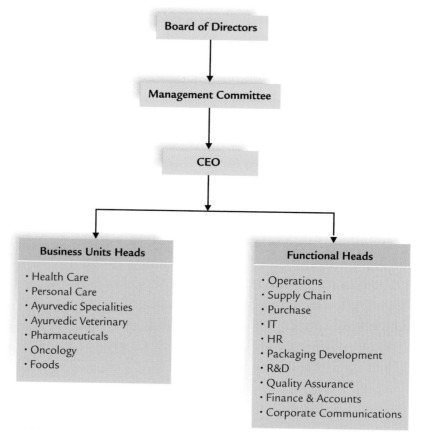

reduced employee turnover figures, the strategic, structural, and operational changes on the HR front led to an overall "feel-good" sentiment in the companies.

In 1999, Coca-Cola reported an increase in case-volume of 9 percent after restructuring. Volumes increased by 14 percent and market share increased by 1 percent after the regionalization drive. The company's improving prospects were further reflected with the 18 percent rise in sales in the second quarter of 2000. However, in spite of all the moves, Coca-Cola's workforce was still large. Given the scale of it investments, the future was far from "smooth sailing" for the company. With the newfound focus and a streamlined human resources front, Coca-Cola hoped to break even by the end of fiscal 2001.

At Dabur, with the restructuring moves in place by the late 1990s, the company's future business prospects were termed excellent by analysts. The new structure, the performance-oriented compensation, and the new performance appraisal system increased employee efficiency and morale. The annual sales conferences and cash incentives to junior-level sales officers helped in meeting higher sales targets. Dabur's sales increased to Rs 10.37 billion in 1990–2000 from Rs 9.14 billion in 1998–1999—an increase of 13.5 percent. Dabur's profits also increased by 53 percent from 501 million to Rs 770 million. The year was a milestone in Dabur's history as the company crossed the Rs 10 billion mark in sales turnover for the first time. Even in early 2001, Dabur's efforts toward emerging as a competitive and professionally managed company were yet to be completely reflected in its financials. Analysts commented that given its track record and the restructuring initiatives, Dabur was all set to reach its target of becoming an FMCG major.

references

CHAPTER 1

1. G. Davenport (trans. 1976). *Herakleitos and Diogenes.* Pt. 1, Fragment 23.

2. M.A. Hitt, R.D. Ireland, and R. E. Hoskisson, *Strategic Management: Competitiveness and Globalization* (Cincinnati, OH: Southwestern Publishing Co., 2003).

3. A. S. DeNisi, M.A. Hitt, and S. E. Jackson, "The Knowledge-Based Approach to Sustainable Competitive Advantage," in S. E. Jackson, M.A. Hitt, and A. S. DeNisi (eds.), *Managing Knowledge for Sustained Competitive Advantage* (San Francisco, CA: Jossey-Bass, 2003).

4. D.A. Sirmon, M.A. Hitt, and R. D. Ireland, "Managing the Firm's Resources in Order to Achieve and Maintain a Competitive Advantage." Paper presented at the Academy of Management Conference, August, 2003.

5. G. Edmondson, C. Palmeri, B. Grow, and C. Tierney, "BMW Will Panke's High-Speed Approach Hurt the Brand?" *BusinessWeek*, June 9, 2003, pp. 57-60.

6. D. Creighton and J. Annear, "Using Teamwork to Sell Employee-Benefit Plans," *American Agent & Broker* 73, no. 2, pp. 50-54.

7. P. Carlin, "Pure Profit," *Los Angeles Times Magazine*, February 15, 1995, pp. 12-15+.

8. R. E. Mueller, "The Inadvertent Entrepreneur: Accepting Change is a Shortcut to Success," February 15, 1995, *Success* 47, no. 11 (2000), p. 22.

9. K. Gilpin, "Home Depot Names Officer from GE as President," *New York Times*, December 6, 2000, p. C1.

10. S. Martin, "Thoughts on a Long Ride: An Interview with Ray Fowler," *Monitor on Psychology* 33, no. 11 (2002), p. 37.

11. K. Melymuka, "Internet Intuition," *Computerworld* 34, no. 2 (2000), pp. 48-51.

12. R. E. Silverman, "For Charlie Kim, Company of Friends Proves a Lonely Place," *Wall Street Journal*, February 1, 2001, p. A1.

13. www.mcdonalds.com/countries/index.html

14. W. Zellner, K.A. Schmidt, Ihlwan Moon, and H. Dawley, "How Well Does Wal-Mart Travel?" *BusinessWeek*, September 3, 2001, pp. 82-84.

15. M.A. Hitt, R. D. Ireland, S. M. Camp, and D. S. Sexton, *Strategic Entrepreneurship: Creating a New Mindset* (Oxford, UK: Blackwell Publishing, 2000).

16. R. McGrath and I. MacMillan, *The Entrepreneurial Mindset* (Boston: Harvard Business School Press, 2000).

17. R. D. Ireland, M.A. Hitt, and D. G. Sirmon, "A Model of Strategic Entrepreneurship: The Construct and Its Dimensions," *Journal of Management* 29: 963-89.

18. Ibid.

19. S. J. Carroll and D. J. Gillen, "Are Classical Management Functions Useful in Describing Managerial Jobs and Behavior" *Academy of Management Review* 12 (1987), pp. 39-51.

20. H. Mintzberg, "The Manager's Job: Folklore and Fact," *Harvard Business Review* 5, no. 4 (1975) pp. 49-61.

21. R. Stewart, "A Model for Understanding Managerial Jobs and Behavior," *Academy of Management Review* 7 (1982), pp. 7-13.

22. M.W. McCall and M. M. Lombardo, *Off the Track* (Greensboro, NC: Center for Creative Leadership, 1983).

23. L.W. Porter and L. E. McKibbin, *Management Education and Development: Drift or Thrust into the 21st Century?* (New York: McGraw-Hill, 1988).

CHAPTER 2

1. G. Hearn, "Managing Change is Managing Meaning," *Management Communication Quarterly* 16 (2003), pp. 440-446; T.A. Stewart, "Gray Flannel Suit? Moi?," *Fortune* 137(5) (1998), p. 76; F. M. van Ejnatten, "Chaos, Dialogue and the Dolphin's Strategy," *Journal of Organizational Change Management* 15 (2002), pp. 391+; Q. N. Huy, "Emotional Balancing of Organizational Continuity and Radical Change: The Contribution of Middle Managers," *Administrative Science Quarterly* 47. no. 1, (2002), pp. 31-69.

2. J. Kotter, *Leading Change* (Boston: Harvard Business Press, 1998); M. Beer and N. Nohria, "Cracking the Code of Change," *Harvard Business Review*, May-June 2000, pp. 133-41.

3. K. E. Weik, "Enacted Sensemaking in Crisis Situations," *Journal of Management Studies* 25, (1998), pp. 305-18.

4. S. D. Sidle, "Best Laid Plans: Establishing Fairness Early Can Help Smooth Organizational Change," *Academy of Management Executive* 17, no. 1, pp. 127-28.

5. C. M. Christensen and M. Overdorf, "Meeting the Challenge of Disruptive Change," *Harvard Business Review* 78, no. 2 (2000), pp. 67-77; L. D. Schaeffer, "The Leadership Journey," *Harvard Business Review* 80, no. 10, pp. 42-48 .

6. R. B. Reich, "Your Job Is Change," *Fast Company* 39, (2000), pp. 140-156; G. Hamel and L. Valikangas, "The Quest for Resilience," *Harvard Business Review* 81, no. 9 (2003), pp. 52-65.

7. M.W. McCall, *High Flyers: Developing the Next Generation of Leaders* (Boston: Harvard Business School Press, 1998); J. S. Black, A. J. Morrison, and H. B. Gregersen, *Global Explorers: The Next Generation of Leaders* (New York: Routledge, 1999).

8. J. S. Black, A. J. Morrison, and H. B. Gregersen, *Global Explorers: The Next Generation of Leaders* (New York: Routledge, 1999); M. L. McDonald and J. D. Westphal, "Getting By with the Advice of Friends: CEOs' Advice Networks and Firms' Strategic Responses to Poor Performance," *Administrative Science Quarterly* 48, no. 1, pp. 1-32.

9. N. Machiavelli, *The Prince* (trans. R. Prince) (New York: Cambridge University Press, 1988).

10. K. Lewin, "Frontiers in Group Dynamics," *Human Relations* 1, pp. 5-41.

11. M. L. Gick and K. J. Holyoak, "Analogical Problem Solving," *Cognitive Psychology* 12 (1980), pp. 306-55; M. L. Gick and K. J. Holyoak, "Schema Induction and Analogical Transfer," *Cognitive Psychology* 15 (1983), pp. 1-38; E. Laszlo, *Changing Visions: Human Cognitive Maps: Past, Present and Future* (Westport, CT: Praeger, 1996).

12. J.A. LePine, "Team Adaptation and Post-Change Performance: Effects of Team Composition in Terms of Members' Cognitive Ability and Personality," *Journal of Applied Psychology*, 88, no. 1 (2003), pp. 27-39.

13. D. M. Macri, "A Grounded Theory for Resistance to Change in Small Organizations," *Journal of Organizational Change Management* 15 (2002), pp. 292-309.

14. M. V. Makhija and A. C. Stewart, "The Effect of National Context on Perceptions of Risk: A Comparison of Planned Versus Free-Market Managers," *Journal of International Business Studies* 33, no. 4 (2002), pp. 737-56.

15. T. L. Saaty and L. G. Vargas, "Uncertainty and Rank Order in the Analytic Hierarchy Process," *European Journal of Operational Research* 32, no. 1 (1987), pp. 108-18.

16. Lewin, "Frontiers in Group Dynamics"; McDonald and Westphal, "Getting by with the Advice of Friends," pp. 1-32.

17. Lewin, "Frontiers in Group Dynamics."

18. J. S. Black and H. B. Gregersen, *Leading Strategic Change* (Upper Saddle River, NJ: Prentice Hall, 2002).

19. L. L. Paglis and S. G. Green, "Leadership Self-Efficacy and Managers' Motivation for Leading Change," *Journal of Organizational Behavior* 23 (2002), pp. 215-35.

20. Gick and Holyoak, "Analogical Problem Solving"; Glick and Holyoak, "Schema Induction and Analogical Transfer"; Warren Kim, "Exploring Competitive Futures Using Cognitive Mapping," *Long Range Planning* 29, no. 5 (1995), pp. 10-12.

21. F. Gavetti and D. Levinthal, "Looking Forward and Looking Backward: Cognitive and Experiential Search," *Administrative Science Quarterly* 45 (2000), pp. 113-37.

22. J. Brockner and E. T. Higgins, "Regulatory Focus Theory: Implications for the Study of Emotions at Work," *Organizational Behavior and Human Decision Processes* 86, no. 1 (2001), pp. 35-66.

23. M. J. Arean, "Changing the Way We Change," *Organization Development Journal* 20, no. 2 (2002), pp. 33-47; Macri, "A Grounded Theory for Resistance to Change in Small Organizations."

24. R. Cacioppe, "Using Team – Individual Reward and Recognition Strategies to Drive Organizational Success," *Leadership & Organization Development Journal* 20 (1999), pp. 322-31.

25. S. T. Fiske and S. E. Taylor, *Social Cognition* (2nd ed.) (Reading, MA: Addison-Wesley Publications, 1991).

26. N. Watson, "What's Wrong with This Printer?" *Fortune* 147, no. 3 (2003), pp. 120C-20H.

27. T. G. Donlan, "The 80-20 Rule," *Barron's* 83, no. 6 (2003), p. 39.

28. D. Blankenship, "Preparing Employees for Change," *Baylor Business Review* 13, no. 2 (1995), pp. 14+; M. Cortsjens and J. Merrihue, "Optimal Marketing," *Harvard Business Review* 81 no. 10 (2003), pp. 114-22.

29. J. Covington and M. L. Chase, "Eight Steps to Sustainable Change," *Industrial Management* 44, no. 6 (2002), pp. 8-11.

PART ONE INTEGRATIVE CASE

1. TIME Online Monday, August 9, 1999.

2. Vanessa Pawsey, "Rule Britannia," *European Legal Business* November/December 2002, p. 26.

CHAPTER 3

1. M. A. Hitt, M. T. Dacin, E. Levitas, J.-L. Arregle, and A. Borza, "Partner Selection in Emerging and Developed Market Contexts: Resource-based and Organizational Learning Perspectives," *Academy of Management Journal*, 43 (2000), pp. 449-67.

2. M. A. Hitt, D. Ahlstrom, M. T. Dacin, E. Levitas, and L. Svobodina, "The Institutional Effects on Strategic Alliance Partner Selection in Transition Economies: China Versus Russia," *Organization Science*, in press.

3. M. A. Hitt, R. D. Ireland, and R. E. Hoskisson, *Strategic Management: Competitiveness and Globalization* (Cincinnati, OH: South-Western Publishing Co., 2005).

4. www.cdc.gov, accessed on May 10, 2002; M. Moynihan, *Global Consumer Demographics* (New York: Business International, 1991).

5. S. Moffett, "For Ailing Japan, Longevity Takes Bite Out of Economy," *Wall Street Journal*, February 11, 2003, p. 1.

6. A. Sagie and Z. Aycan, "A Cross-cultural Analysis of Participative Decision-making in Organizations," *Human Relations* 56, no. 4 (2003), pp. 453-73.

7. S. P. Seithi and P. Steidlmeier, "The Evolution of Business' Role in Society," *Business and Society Review* 94 (Summer 1995), pp. 9-12; L. L. Martins, K. A. Eddleston, and J. F. Veiga, "Moderators of the Relationship Between Work–Family Conflict and Career Satisfaction," *Academy of Management Journal* 45, no. 2 (2002), pp. 399-409.

8. S. Gelsi, "Class for the Masses," *Brandweek* 38, no. 13 (1997), pp. 23-33.

9. J. Lawrence, "P&G Losing Ground in Product Innovation," *Advertising Age* 64, no. 48 (1993), p. 44; J. Lawrence, "It's Diaper D-Day with P&G Rollout," *Advertising Age* 64, no. 39 (1993), pp. 1, 60; J. Lawrence, "Kimberly, P&G Rev Up to Market Latest Twist in Disposable Diapers," *Advertising Age* 63, no. 26 (1992), pp. 3, 51.

10. B. Johnstone, "Rainbow Warriors," *Far Eastern Economic Review* 147, no. 7 (1999), p. 90.

11. A. Serwer, "The Next #1," Fortune.com, April 4, 2002; B. Caldwell, "Wal-Mart Ups the Pace," *Informationweek* 609 (1996), pp. 37-51.

12. Personal communication with Dofasco senior management, 2003.

13. "Glass Fibers Make Smokestacks Cleaner," *Machine Design* 67, no. 18 (1995), p. 123.

14. T. Mason and J. R. Norman, "Is It the Last Roundup for Texas Real Estate Tycoons?" *BusinessWeek* (Industrial/Technology Edition, 1986), pp. 86-88; J. R. Norman, J. E. Davis, M. Ivey, and T. Thompson, "Casualties Start to Pile Up in the Oil Patch," *BusinessWeek* (Industrial/Technology Edition, 1986), pp. 83-88.

15. C. Miller, "Contractors Fight for Share of Smaller Defense Market," *Marketing News* 24, no. 13 (1990), pp. 2, 17; S. N. Chakravarty, "36th Annual Report on American Industry: Aerospace and Defense," *Forbes* 113, no. 1 (1984), pp. 144-46.

16. A. K. Sundaram and J. S. Black, *The International Business Environment* (Upper Saddle River, NJ: Prentice Hall, 1995).

17. J. Muller, "Stolen Cars," *Forbes* 173, no. 3 (2004), p. 58; R. Meredith, "The China Connection," *Forbes Global* 7, no. 1 (2004); A. Taylor, "Finally GM Is Looking Good," *Fortune*, April 1, 2002; W. S. Hersch, "EDS Faces Simmering Challenges Despite Posting Strong 4Q Results," *Computer Reseller News* 776, no. 7 (1998), p. 16; "Face to Face: With Jack Smith, President of General Motors," *International Motor Business*, First Quarter 1995, pp. 6-20.

18. J. E. Oxley and B. Yeung, "E-Commerce Readiness: Institutional Environment and International Competitiveness," *Journal of International Business Studies* 32, no. 4 (2001), pp. 705-23.

19. C. M. Lau, D. K. Tse, and N. Zhou, "Institutional Forces and Organizational Culture in China: Effects on Change Schemas, Firm Commitment and Job Satisfaction," *Journal of International Business Studies* 33, no. 3 (2002), pp. 533-50.

20. M. Porter, *Competitive Strategy: Techniques for Analyzing Industries and Competitors* (New York: Free Press, 1980).

21. S. Slater and E. Olson. "A Fresh Look at Industry and Market Analysis," *Business Horizons* 45, no. 1 (2002), pp. 15-22.

22. "Retail Entrepreneurs of the Year: Harold Ruttenberg," *Chain Store Age* 72, no. 12 (1996), pp. 68-69.

23. M. Boyle, "The Shiniest Reputation in Tarnished Times," *Fortune,* March 4, 2002, D. Greising, "How High Can the Airlines Fly?" *Business Week* (1995), pp. 25-26.

24. N. Stein, "The DeBeers Story: A New Cut on an Old Monopoly," *Fortune*, February 19, 2001, pp. 186-206; "Glass with Attitude," *Economist* 345, no. 8048 (1997), pp. 113-15.

25. R. D. Ireland, M.A. Hitt, and D. Vaidyanath, "Alliance Management as a Source of Competitive Advantage," *Journal of Management* 28, no. 3 (2002), pp. 413–46; B. R. Koka & J. E. Prescott, "Strategic Alliances as Social Capital: A Multidimensional View," *Strategic Management Journal* 23, no. 9 (2002), pp. 795–816; D. Rigby and C. Zook, "Open-market Innovation," *Harvard Business Review* 80, no. 10 (2002), pp. 80–89.

26. D. Martin, "Gilded and Gelded: Hard-won Lessons from the PR Wars," *Harvard Business Review* 81, no. 10 (2003), pp. 44–54; P. Christmann and G. Taylor, "Globalization and the Environment: Strategies for International Voluntary Environmental Initiatives," *Academy of Management Executive* 16, no. 3 (2002), pp. 121–35.

27. www.sec.gov, accessed on February 22, 2003, Home page.

28. www.greenpeace.org, accessed on March 1, 2003, Home page.

29. www.usatoday.com, accessed February 19, 2003, Home page, lead story, "Microsoft Stock Split into 10 Billion Shares."

30. J. Barren, P. Newman, and P. Hotchner, "A Secret Recipe for Success," *Newsweek* 142, no. 18 (2004), pp. 48–49.

31. Sydney Finkelstein & A. C. Mooney, "Not the Usual Suspects: How to Use Board Process to Make Boards Better," *Academy of Management Executive* 17, no. 2 (2003), pp. 101–113; J. M. Ivancevich, T. N. Duening, J.A. Gilbert, and R. Konopaske, "Deterring White-collar Crime," *Academy of Management Executive* 17, no. 2 (2003), pp. 114–27.

CHAPTER 4

1. A. K. Gupta and V. G. Govindarajan, "Converting Global Presence into Global Competitive Advantage," *Academy of Management Executive* 15, no. 2 (2001), pp. 45–57.

2. M.A. Hitt, R. D. Ireland, and R. E. Hoskisson, *Strategic Management: Competitiveness and Globalization* (Cincinnati, OH: South-Western Publishing, 2005).

3. M. Koza and A. Lewin, "Managing Partnerships and Strategic Alliances: Raising the Odds of Success," *European Management Journal* 18, no. 2 (2000), pp. 146–51; M. Peng, "The Resource-Based View and International Business," *Journal of Management* 27 (2001), pp. 803–29.

4. E. Schein, "Coming to a New Awareness of Organizational Culture," *Sloan Management Review*, Winter (1984), pp. 3–16.

5. A. L. Kroeber and C. Kluckhohn, *Culture: A Critical Review of Concepts and Definitions* (Cambridge, MA: Harvard University Press, 1952).

6. E. Schein, "Coming to a New Awareness of Organizational Culture," pp. 3–16.

7. A. L. Wilkins and W. Ouchi, "Efficient Cultures: Exploring the Relationship between Culture and Organizational Effectiveness," *Administrative Science Quarterly* 28 (1983), pp. 468–81; K.A. Wade-Benzoni, T. Okumura, J. M. Brett, and D.A. Moore, "Cognitions and Behavior in Asymmetric Social Dilemmas: A Comparison of Two Cultures," *Journal of Applied Psychology* 87, no. 1 (2002), pp. 87–95; M. J. Gelfand, M. Higgins, L. H. Nishii, J. L. Raver, "Culture and Egocentric Perceptions of Fairness in Conflict and Negotiation," *Journal of Applied Psychology* 87, no. 5 (2002), pp. 833–45.

8. J. E. Dutton and S. Jackson, "Categorizing Strategic Issues: Links to Organizational Actions," *Academy of Management Review* 12 (1987), pp. 76–90; Gelfand et al., "Culture and Egocentric Perceptions of Fairness in Conflict and Negotiation," pp. 833–45.

9. R. G. Eord and R. J. Foti, "Schema Theories, Information Processing, and Organizational Behavior," ed. H. P. Simes and D.A. Gioia (San Francisco: Jossey-Bass, 1986); Wilkins and Ouchi, "Efficient Cultures"; Gelfand et al., "Culture and Egocentric Perceptions of Fairness in Conflict and Negotiation," pp. 833–45.

10. D. Druckman, "Nationalism, Patriotism, and Group Loyalty: A Social-Psychological Perspective," *Merson International Studies Review* (1994), pp. 43–68.

11. http://stats.bls.gov, accessed on June 3, 2002; H. Fullerton, "Labor Force Projections to 2008," *Monthly Labor Review*, November 1999, p. 20; *Statistical Yearbook of Immigration and Naturalization Service*, Fiscal Years 1820–2000.

12. Personal communication, 2001; R. Larsson, K. R. Brousseau, M. J. Driver, M. Homqvist, "International Growth Through Cooperation: Brand-driven Strategies, Leadership, and Career Development in Sweden," *Academy of Management Executive* 17, no. 1 (2003), pp. 7–21; W.A. Randolph and M. Sashkin, "Can Organizational Empowerment Work in Multinational Settings?" *Academy of Management Executive* 16, no. 1 (2002), pp. 102–15.

13. A. Zuckerman, "Strong Corporate Cultures and Firm Performance: Are There Tradeoffs?" *Academy of Management Executive* 16, no. 4 (2002), pp. 158–60; N. Nohria, W. Joyce, and B. Roberson, "What Really Works," *Harvard Business Review* 81, no. 7 (2003), pp. 42–52.

14. Schein, "Coming to a New Awareness of Culture."

15. Ibid.

16. J. H. Birnbaum, "How Microsoft Conquered Washington," *Fortune*, April 29, 2002, pp. 95–96; M. Roman, "Microsoft to Europe: Let's Talk," *BusinessWeek*, December 10, 2001, p. 42.

17. D. McGregor, *The Human Side of Enterprise* (New York: McGraw-Hill, 1960).

18. R. J. House, "Cultural Influences on Leaders and Organizations," in *Advances in Global Leadership*, vol. 1, pp. 171–233. (JAI Press, 1999); J. C. Kennedy, "Leadership in Malaysia: Traditional Values, International Outlook," *Academy of Management Executive* 16, no. 3 (2002), pp. 15–26.

19. J. Foley, "Hewlett-Packard Reaches a Cultural Crossroads," *Information Week*, July 23, 2001, p. 47.

20. G. Hofstede, *Culture's Consequences* (Beverly Hills, CA: Sage, 1980); G. Hofstede, "Dimensions Do Not Exist: A Reply to Brendan McSweeney," *Human Relations* 55, no. 11 (2002), pp. 1355–1631; A. Sagie and Z. Aycan, "A Cross-Cultural Analysis of Participative Decision-Making in Organizations," *Human Relations* 56, no. 4 (2003), pp. 453–73; D. Williamson, "Foreword from a Critique of Hofstede's Model of National Culture," *Human Relations* 55, no. 11 (2002), pp. 1373–95.

21. G. Colvin, "What's Love Got to Do with It?" *Fortune*, November 12, 2001, p. 60.

22. R. Suutari, "Memo to the CEO," *CMA Management* 74, no. 7 (2000), pp. 10–11.

23. B. McSweeney, "Hofstede's Model of National Cultural Differences and Their Consequences: A Triumph of Faith—A Failure of Analysis," *Human Relations* 55, no. 1 (2002), pp. 89–118.

24. J. Rokeach, *The Nature of Human Values* (New York: Free Press, 1973); T. Lenartowicz and J. P. Johnson, "A Cross-National Assessment of the Values of Latin American Managers: Contrasting Hues or Shades of Gray?" *Journal of International Business Studies* 34, no. 3 (2003), p. 266.

25. C. Hawkins and P. Oster, "After a U-turn, UPS Really Delivers," *BusinessWeek*, May 31, 1993, pp. 43–45.

26. Personal communication, 1998; "IBM Sports New Attitude," *Computerworld*, July 28, 1997, p. S5.

27. S. Black, H. Gregersen, M. Mendenhall, and L. Stroh, *Globalizing People through International Assignments* (Reading, MA: Addison-Wesley, 1999); S. M. Toh and A. S. Denisi, "Host Country National Reactions to Expatriate Pay Policies: A Model and Implications," *Academy of Management Review* 28, no. 4 (2003), pp. 606–21.

28. N. Adler, *International Dimensions of Organizational Behavior* (Boston, MA: Kent Publishing, 1994).

29. "Delphi Makes Another Investment in China," *Automotive News*, December 22, 2003, p. 25; M. Loden and J. Rosener, *Workforce America! Managing Employee Diversity as a Vital Resource* (New York: Irwin, 1991).

30. Adler, *International Dimensions of Organizational Behavior*.

31. M. K. Kozan, "Subcultures and Conflict Management Style," *Management International Review* 42, no. 1 (2002), pp. 89-105; C. M. Byles, "Brazil's Distinct Subcultures: Do They Matter to Business Performance?" *Academy of Management Executive* 16, no. 2 (2002), pp. 165-66.

32. S. Black and H. Gregersen, *Leading Strategic Change* (Upper Saddle River, N.J.: Prentice Hall, 2002); M. Cortsjens and J. Merrihue, "Optimal Marketing," *Harvard Business Review* 81, no. 10 (2003), pp. 114-22.

33. "James McNerney," *BusinessWeek*, January 12, 2004, p. 61; R. Mullin, "3M, or Tale of an Exiled Price," *Journal of Business Strategy* 22, no. 5 (2001), pp. 24-26.

34. V. Pothukuchi, F. Damanpour, J. Choi, C. Chen, C. Chao, and S. H. Park, "National and Organizational Culture Differences and International Joint Venture Performance," *Journal of International Business Studies* 33, no. 2 (2002), pp. 243-65; C. Fey and P. W. Beamish, "Organizational Climate Similarity and Performance: International Joint Ventures in Russia," *Organization Studies* 22, no. 5 (2001), pp. 853-82; W. M. Danis and A. Parkhe, "Hungarian-Western Partnerships: A Grounded Theoretical Model of Integration Processes and Outcomes," *Journal of International Business Studies* 33, no. 3 (2002), pp. 423-55.

35. Personal communication, 1998.

36. V. D. Miller and F. M. Jablin, "Information Seeking During Organizational Entry: Influences, Tactics, and a Model of the Process," *Academy of Management Review* 16 (1991), pp. 92-120; R. M. Kramer, "When Paranoia Makes Sense," *Harvard Business Review* 80, no. 7 (2002), pp. 62-69; R. Galford and A. S. Drapeau, "The Enemies of Trust," *Harvard Business Review* 81, no. 2 (2003), pp. 88-95.

37. E. Hall, *Beyond Culture* (Garden City, NY: Doubleday, 1976).

38. S. A. Zahra, R. D. Ireland, and M. A. Hitt, "International Expansion by New Venture Firms: International Diversity, Mode of Entry, Technological Learning and Performance," *Academy of Management Journal* 43 (2000), pp. 925-50.

39. S. Black, H. Gregersen, M. Mendenhall, and L. Stroh, *Globalizing People through International Assignments* (Reading, MA: Addison-Wesley, 1999); J. L. Graham and N. M. Lam, "The Chinese Negotiation," *Harvard Business Review* 81, no. 10 (2003), pp. 82-91.

40. M. Murphy and K. M. Davey, "Ambiguity, Ambivalence and Indifference in Organizational Values," *Human Resource Management Journal* 12, no. 1 (2002), pp. 17-32; Galford and Drapeau, "The Enemies of Trust," pp. 88-95.

41. S. Black et al., *Globalizing People through International Assignments*; Graham and Lam, "The Chinese Negotiation," pp. 82-91.

CHAPTER 5

1. M. A. Hitt, R. D. Ireland, and R. E. Hoskisson, *Strategic Management: Competitiveness and Globalization* (Cincinnati, OH: South-Western Publishing, 2005).

2. C. Loomis, "Inside Jay Walker's House of Cards," *Fortune* 142, no. 11 (2000), pp. 127-38.

3. D. Peterson, A. Rhoads, and B. C. Vaught, "Ethical Beliefs of Business Professionals: A Study of Gender, Age, and External Factors," *Journal of Business Ethics* 31, no. 3 (2001), pp. 225-32; E. Marnburg, "The Questionable Use of Moral Development Theory in Studies of Business Ethics: Discussion and Empirical Findings," *Journal of Business Ethics* 32, no. 4 (2001), pp. 275-83.

4. J. Tsalikis, B. Seaton, and P. Tomaras, "A New Perspective on Cross-Cultural Ethical Evaluations: The Use of Conjoint Analysis," *Journal of Business Ethics* 35, no. 4 (2002), pp. 281-92; L. Thorne and S. B. Saunders, "The Socio-Cultural Embeddedness of Individuals' Ethical Reasoning in Organizations (Cross-Cultural Ethics)," *Journal of Business Ethics* 35, no. 1 (2002), pp. 1-14; J. B. Hamilton III and S. B. Knouse, "Multinational Enterprise Decision Principles for Dealing with Cross Cultural Ethical Conflicts," *Journal of Business Ethics* 31, no. 1 (2001), pp. 77-94; C. J. Robertson and W. F. Crittenden, "Mapping Moral Philosophies: Strategic Implications For Multinational Firms," *Strategic Management Journal* 24, no. 4 (2003), pp. 385-92.

5. A. J. Dubinsky, M. A. Jolson, M. Kotabe, and C. U. Lim, "A Cross-National Investigation of Industrial Salespeople's Ethical Perceptions," *Journal of International Business Studies*, Fourth Quarter 1991, pp. 651-69; J. K. Giacobbe-Miller, D. J. Miller, W. Zhang, and V. I. Victorov, "Country and Organization-level Adaptation to Foreign Workplace Ideologies: A Comparative Study of Distributive Justice Values in China, Russia and the United States," *Journal of International Business Studies* 34, no. 4 (2003), pp. 389-406.

6. A. Kolk and R. Van Tulder, "Ethics in International Business," *Journal of World Business* February 2004, pp. 49-61; J. Tsui and C. Windsor, "Some Cross-Cultural Evidence of Ethical Reasoning," *Journal of Business Ethics* 31 (2001), pp. 143-50; C. J. Robertson and W. F. Crittenden, "Mapping Moral Philosophies: Strategic Implications for Multinational Firms," *Strategic Management Journal* 24, no. 4 (2003), pp. 385-92.

7. J. S. Black, H. B. Gregersen, and M. E. Mendenhall, *Global Assignments* (San Francisco, CA: Jossey-Bass, 1992).

8. C. Hess and K. Hey, "Good Doesn't Always Mean Right," *Across the Board* 38, no. 4 (2001), pp. 61-64; A. Chia and L. S. Mee, "The Effects of Issue Characteristics on the Recognition of Moral Issues," *Journal of Business Ethics* 27 (2000), pp. 255-69; A. Gaudine and L. Thorne, "Emotion and Ethical Decision Making in Organizations," *Journal of Business Ethics* 31, no. 2 (2001), pp. 175-87.

9. J. Rawls, *A Theory of Justice* (Cambridge, MA: Harvard University Press, 1971); J. Greenberg, "A Taxonomy of Organizational Justice Theories," *Academy of Management Review* 12 (1987), pp. 9-22; Giacobbe-Miller et al., "Country and Organization-level Adaptation to Foreign Workplace Ideologies," pp. 389-406.

10. T. Donaldson and T. W. Dunfee, "Toward a Unified Conception of Business Ethics," *Academy of Management Review* 19 (1994), pp. 252-84; J. A. Colquitt, R. A. Noe, and C. L. Jackson, "Justice in Teams: Antecedents and Consequences of Procedural Justice Climate," *Personnel Psychology* 55, no. 1 (2002), pp. 83-109.

11. R. Pillai, E. Williams, and J. J. Tan, "Are the Scales Tipped in Favor of Procedural or Distributive Justice? An Investigation of the U.S., India, Germany, and Hong Kong (China)," *International Journal of Conflict Management* 12, no. 4 (2001), pp. 312-32; D. Fields, M. Pang, and C. Chiu, "Distributive and Procedural Justice as Predictors of Employee Outcomes in Hong Kong," *Journal of Organizational Behavior* 21, no. 5 (2000), pp. 547-62; Y. Cohen-Charash and P. E. Spector, "The Role of Justice in Organizations: A Meta-analysis," *Organizational Behavior and Human Decision Processes* 86, no. 2 (2001), pp. 278-321; J. A. Colquitt, D. E. Conlon, M. J. Wesson, C. Porter, and Y. K. Ng, "Justice at the Millennium: A Meta-analytic Review of 25 Years of Organizational Justice Research," *Journal of Applied Psychology* 86, no. 3 (2001), pp. 424-45; S. L. Blader, C. C. Chang, and T. R. Tyler, "Procedural Justice and Retaliation in Organizations: Comparing Cross-nationally the Importance of Fair Group Processes," *International Journal of Conflict Management* 12, no. 4 (2001), pp. 295-311; J. Greenberg, "Who Stole

the Money, and When? Individual and Situational Determinants of Employee Theft," *Organizational Behavior and Human Decision Processes* 89, no. 1 (2002), pp. 985–1003; B. J. Tepper and E. C. Taylor, "Relationships Among Supervisors' and Subordinates' Procedural Justice Perceptions and Organizational Citizenship Behaviors," *Academy of Management Journal* 46, no. 1 (2003), pp. 97–105.

12. J. Dietz, S. L. Robinson, R. Folger, R. A. Baron, and M. Schultz, "The Impact of Community Violence and an Organization's Procedural Justice Climate on Workplace Aggression," *Academy of Management Journal* 46, no. 3 (2003), pp. 317–26.

13. J. M. Jones, "Ethical Decision Making by Individuals in Organizations: An Issue-Contingent Model," *Academy of Management Review* 16 (1991), pp. 366–95.

14. J. Paolillo and S. J. Vitell, "An Empirical Investigation of the Influence of Selected Personal, Organizational and Moral Intensity Factors on Ethical Decision Making," *Journal of Business Ethics* 35, no. 1 (2002), pp. 65–74.

15. Ibid.

16. Chia and Mee, "The Effects of Issue Characteristics on the Recognition of Moral Issues," pp. 255–69.

17. D. Carlson, K. M. Kacmar, and L. L. Wadsworth, "The Impact of Moral Intensity Dimensions on Ethical Decision Making: Assessing the Relevance of Orientation," *Journal of Managerial Issues* 14, no. 1 (2002), pp. 15–30; J. M. Dukerich, M. J. Waller, E. George, and G. P. Huber. "Moral Intensity and Managerial Problem Solving," *Journal of Business Ethics* 24, no. 1 (2000), pp. 29–38.

18. P. S. Ring and A. Van De Ven, "Developmental Process of Cooperative Interorganizational Relationships," *Academy of Management Review* 19 (1994), pp. 90–118.

19. D. Robin, M. Giallourakis, F. R. David, and T. Moritz, "A Different Look at Codes of Ethics," *Business Horizons*, January–February 1989, pp. 66–73.

20. C. C. Langlois and B. B. Schlegelmilch, "Do Corporate Codes of Ethics Reflect National Character? Evidence from Europe and the United States," *Journal of International Business Studies*, Fourth Quarter 1991, pp. 519–39.

21. G. Wood, "A Cross-Cultural Comparison of the Content of Codes of Ethics: USA, Canada, and Australia," *Journal of Business Ethics* 25, no. 4 (2000), pp. 281–98.

22. Robin et al., "A Different Look at Codes of Ethics."

23. Ibid.

24. B. Ettorre, "Ethics Inc.: The Buck Stops Here," *HR Focus*, June 1992, p. 11.

25. L. P. White and L. W. Lam, "A Proposed Infrastructural Model for the Establishment of Organizational Ethical Systems," *Journal of Business Ethics* 28, no. 1 (2000), pp. 35–42; S. A. DiPiazza, "Ethics in Action," *Executive Excellence* 19, no. 1 (2002), pp. 15–16.

26. C. Verschoor, "To Talk About Ethics, We Must Train on Ethics," *Strategic Finance* 81, no. 10 (2000), pp. 24, 26; T. Donaldson, "Editor's Comments: Taking Ethics Seriously—A Mission Now More Possible," *Academy of Management Review* 28, no. 3 (2003), pp. 363–366

27. "Stronger Than Ever," *LM Today*, January 2004, p. 8; K. Shelton, "The Dilbert Dilemma," *Executive Excellence* November 2003, p. 2; R. Carey, "The Ethics Challenge," *Successful Meetings* 47, no. 5 (1998), pp. 57–58.

28. M. McClearn, "A Snitch in Time," *Canadian Business*, June 18, 2004, pp. 60–67; M. P. Miceli and J. P. Near, *Blowing the Whistle* (Lexington, MA: Lexington Books, 1992).

29. Miceli and Near, *Blowing the Whistle*.

30. C. Daniels, "It's a Living Hell," *Fortune*, April 15, 2002, pp. 367–68.

31. M. P. Miceli and J. P. Near, "The Relationships among Beliefs, Organizational Position, and Whistle Blowing Status: A Discriminant Analysis," *Academy of Management Journal* 27 (1984), pp. 687–705.

32. M. P. Miceli and J. P. Near, "Whistle Blowing: Reaping the Benefits," *Academy of Management Executive* 8 (1994), pp. 65–71.

33. Miceli and Near, *Blowing the Whistle*.

34. R. Sims and J. Brinkmann, "Leaders as Moral Role Models: The Case of John Gutfreund at Salomon Brothers," *Journal of Business Ethics* 35, no. 4 (2002), pp. 327–39; R. Galford and A. S. Drapeau, "The Enemies of Trust," *Harvard Business Review* 81, no. 2 (2003), pp. 88–95; L. R. Offermann and A. B. Malamut, "When Leaders Harass: The Impact of Target Perceptions of Organizational Leadership and Climate on Harassment Reporting and Outcomes," *Journal of Applied Psychology* 87, no. 5 (2002), pp. 885–93.

35. *Columbia Journalism Review*, New York, November/December 2000, p. 13.

36. M. Zuckerman, "Policing the Corporate Suites," *U.S. News & World Report*, January 19, 2004, p. 72; *Modern Healthcare*, Chicago, April 20, 1998, 28(16), pp. 54–56.

37. M. Friedman, "The Social Responsibility of Business Is to Increase Its Profits," *New York Magazine*, September 13, 1970, pp. 32–33, 122, 126.

38. A. Smith, *An Inquiry into the Nature and Causes of the Wealth of Nations*, ed. R. H. Campbell and A. S. Skinner (Oxford, UK: Clarendon Press, 1976).

39. Friedman, "The Social Responsibility of Business Is to Increase Its Profits," p. 32; C. E. Bagley, "The Ethical Leader's Decision Tree," *Harvard Business Review* 81, no. 2 (2003), pp. 18–19.

40. M. Rothman, "Nightmare at Kaufman's," *Business Ethics*, November–December 1994, pp. 15–16.

41. J. Joha, L. Serbet, and A. Sundaram, "Cross-Border Liability of Multinational Enterprises: Border Taxes and Capital Structure," *Financial Management*, Winter 1991, pp. 54–67; C. Handy, "What's a Business For?" *Harvard Business Review* 80, no. 12 (2002), pp. 49–55.

42. Joha, Serbet, and Sundaram, "Cross-Border Liability of Multinational Enterprises: Border Taxes and Capital Structure," pp. 54–67.

43. B. Ruf, K. Muralidhar, R. Brown, J. Janney, and K. Paul, "An Empirical Investigation of the Relationship Between Change in Corporate Social Performance and Financial Performance: A Stakeholder Theory Perspective," *Journal of Business Ethics* 32, no. 2 (2001), pp. 143–56; C. Sanchez, "Value Shift: Why Companies Must Merge Social and Financial Imperatives to Achieve Superior Performance," *Academy of Management Executive* 17, no. 2 (2003), pp. 142–44.

44. ExxonMobil 2001, *Safety, Health and Environment Progress Report*; C. Watson, "Managing with Integrity: Social Responsibilities of Business as Seen by America's CEOs," *Business Horizons*, July/August 1991, pp. 99–109; Business Roundtable, *Statement on Corporate Responsibility* (New York: Business Roundtable, October 1981); T. J. Watson, "Ethical Choice in Managerial Work: The Scope for Moral Choices in an Ethically Irrational World," *Human Relations* 56, no. 2 (2003), pp. 167–85.

PART TWO INTEGRATIVE CASE

1. He was with sales and marketing at AT&T.

CHAPTER 6

1. M. A. Hitt, R. D. Ireland, and R. E. Hoskisson, *Strategic Management: Competitiveness and Globalization* (Cincinnati, OH: South-Western Publishing Company, 2005).

2. M. E. Porter, "Towards a Dynamic Theory of Strategy," *Strategic Management Journal* 12 (1991), pp. 95-117; R. Durand, "Competitive Advantages Exist: A Critique of Powell," *Strategic Management Journal* 23, no. 9 (2002), pp. 867-72; D. Miller, "An Asymmetry-based View of Advantage: Towards an Attainable Sustainability," *Strategic Management Journal* 24, no. 10 (2003), pp. 961-976; N. G. Carr, "IT Doesn't Matter," *Harvard Business Review* 81, no. 5 (2003), pp. 41-49; R. R. Wiggins and T. W. Ruefli, "Sustained Competitive Advantage: Temporal Dynamics and the Incidence and Persistence of Superior Economic Performance," *Organization Science* 13, no. 1 (2002), pp. 82-105.

3. B. Wernerfelt, "A Resource-Based View of the Firm," *Strategic Management Journal*, September-October 1984, p. 171; J. Barney, "Firm Resources and Sustained Competitive Advantage," *Journal of Management* 17, no. 1 (1991), pp. 99-120; R. Amit and P. J. H. Schoemaker, "Strategic Assets and Organizational Rent," *Strategic Management Journal*, January 1993, p. 3; K. R. Conner, "A Historical Comparison of Resource-Based Theory and Five Schools of Thought within Industrial Organization Economics: Do We Have a New Theory of the Firm?" *Journal of Management*, March 1991, p. 121; Porter, *Competitive Advantage* (New York: Free Press, 1986).

4. D. Bunch and R. Smiley, "Who Deters Entry?" *Review of Economics and Statistics* 74, no. 3 (1992), pp. 509-21; D. M. De Carolis, "Competencies and Imitability in the Pharmaceutical Industry: An Analysis of Their Relationship with Firm Performance," *Journal Of Management* 29, no. 1 (2003), pp. 27-78.

5. S. K. McEvily and B. Chakravarthy, "The Persistence of Knowledge-based Advantage: An Empirical Test for Product Performance and Technological Knowledge," *Strategic Management Journal* 23, no. 4 (2002), pp. 285-305; A. Andal and G. S. Yip, "Advantage Amnesia," *Business Strategy Review* 13, no. 1 (2002), pp. 1-11. A. Afuah, "Mapping Technological Capabilities into Product Markets and Competitive Advantage: The Case of Cholesterol Drugs," *Strategic Management Journal* 23, no. 2 (2002), pp. 171-81.

6. D. J. Collis and C. A Montgomery, "Competing on Resources: Strategy in the 1990s," *Harvard Business Review*, July-August 1995, pp. 119-28.

7. G. Hamel and C. K. Prahalad, *Competing for the Future* (Boston, MA: Harvard Business Press, 1994).

8. R. Emmerich, "What's in a Vision?" *CMA Management* 75, no. 8 (2001), p. 10.

9. O. Harari, "Three Vital Little Words," *Management Review* 84, no. 11 (1995), pp. 25-27; G. Hamel and C. K. Prahalad, "Strategy as Stretch and Leverage," *Harvard Business Review* 71, no. 2 (1993), pp. 75-84.

10. J. Collins and J. Porras, "Building Your Company's Vision," *Harvard Business Review* 74, no. 5 (1996), pp. 65-77; C. Rarick and J. Vitton, "Mission Statements Make Sense," *Journal of Business Strategy* 16, no. 1 (1995), pp. 11-12.

11. J. Younker, "Organization Direction-Setting," *Tapping the Network Journal* 2, no. 2 (1991), pp. 20-23; W. Schiemann, "Strategy, Culture, Communication: Three Keys to Success," *Executive Excellence* 6, no. 8 (1989), pp. 11-12.

12. Porter, *Competitive Advantage*; M. Partridge and L. Perren, "Developing Strategic Direction: Can Generic Strategies Help?" *Management Accounting-London* 72, no. 5 (1994), pp. 28-29.

13. K. Andrews, *The Concept of Corporate Strategy* (Homewood, IL: Richard Irwin, 1971); J. A. Aragon-Correa and S. Sharma, "A Contingent Resource-based View of Proactive Corporate Environmental Strategy," *Academy of Management Review* 28, no. 1 (2003), pp. 71-88; S. A. Zahra and A. P. Nielsen, "Sources of Capabilities, Integration and Technology Commercialization," *Strategic Management Journal* 23, no. 5 (2002), pp. 377-98; V. K. Garg, B. K. Walters, and R. L. Priem, "Chief Executive Scanning Emphases, Environmental Dynamism, and Manufacturing Firm Performance," *Strategic Management Journal* 24, no. 8 (2003), pp. 725-44.

14. E. Zajac, M. S. Kraatz, and R. Bresser, "Modeling the Dynamics of Strategic Fit: A Normative Approach to Strategic Change," *Strategic Management Journal* 21, no. 4 (2000), pp. 429-53.

15. M. E. Porter, *Competitive Advantage* (New York: Free Press, 1985).

16. R. W. Oliver, "Is It the Beginning, or Is It the End?" *Journal of Business Strategy* 22, no. 1 (2001), pp. 7-9.

17. M. E. Porter, *Competitive Advantage*.

18. D. Bovet and J. Martha, "From Supply Chain to Value Net," *Journal of Business Strategy* 21, no. 4 (2000), pp. 24-28; D. Bovet and J. Martha, "Value Nets: Reinventing the Rusty Supply Chain for Competitive Advantage," *Strategy and Leadership* 28, no. 4 (2000), pp. 21-26; A. Afuah, "How Much Do Your Competitors' Capabilities Matter in the Face of Technological Change?" *Strategic Management Journal* 21, no. 3 (2000), pp. 387-404.

19. A. Afuah, "How Much Do Your Competitors' Capabilities Matter in the Face of Technological Change?" pp. 387-404; J. Stock, T. Speh, and H. Shear, "Many Happy (Product) Returns," *Harvard Business Review* 80, no. 7 (2002), pp. 16-17; J. Hagel III, "Leveraged Growth: Expanding Sales Without Sacrificing Profits," *Harvard Business Review* 80, no. 10 (2002), pp. 68-77; V. Shankar and B. L. Bayus, "Network Effects and Competition: An Empirical Analysis of the Home Video Game Industry," *Strategic Management Journal* 24, no. 4 (2003), pp. 375-84.

20. J. Barney, "Looking Inside for Competitive Advantage," *Academy of Management Executive* 9, no. 4 (1995), pp. 49-61; W. Dyer and V. Sighn, "The Relational View: Cooperative Strategy and Sources of Interorganizational Competitive Advantage," *Academy of Management Review* 23, no. 4 (October 1998), pp. 660-79; B.-S. Teng and J. L. Cummings, "Trade-offs in Managing Resources and Capabilities," *Academy of Management Executive* 16, no. 2 (2002), pp. 81-91; M. A. Peteraf and M. E. Bergen, "Scanning Dynamic Competitive Landscapes: A Market-based and Resource-based Framework," *Strategic Management Journal* 24, no. 10 (2003), pp. 1027-41; A. M. Rugman and A. Verbeke, "Edith Penrose's Contribution to the Resource-based View of Strategic Management," *Strategic Management Journal* 23, no. 8 (2002), pp. 769-80; D. G. Hoopes, T. L. Madsen, and G. Walker, "Guest Editors' Introduction to the Special Issue: Why Is There a Resource-based View? Toward a Theory of Competitive Heterogeneity," *Strategic Management Journal* 24, no. 10 (2003), pp. 889-902.

21. K. Eisenhardt and J. Martin, "Dynamic Capabilities: What Are They?" *Strategic Management Journal* 21, nos. 10/11 (2000), pp. 1105-21; R. Adner and C. E. Helfat, "Corporate Effects and Dynamic Managerial Capabilities," *Strategic Management Journal* 24, no. 10 (2003), pp. 1011-25.

22. C. K. Prahalad and G. Hamel, "The Core Competence of the Corporation," *Harvard Business Review* 68, no. 3 (1990), pp. 79-91.

23. M. Gort and R. Wall, "The Evolution of Technologies and Investment in Innovation," *Economic Journal* 96, no. 383 (1986), pp. 741-57.

24. C. Anderson and C. Zeithaml, "Stage of the Product Life Cycle, Business Strategy, and Business Performance," *Academy of Management Journal* 27, no. 1 (1984), pp. 5-24; P. Ghemawat, "The Forgotten Strategy," *Harvard Business Review* 81, no. 11 (2003), pp. 76-84; M. Zeng and P. J. Williamson, "The Hidden Dragons," *Harvard Business Review* 81, no. 10 (2003), pp. 92-99; G. P. Cachon and P. T. Barker, "Competition and Outsourcing With Scale Economies," *Management Science* 48, no. 10 (2003), pp. 1314-33.

25. E. Comiskey and C. Mulford, "Anticipating Trends in Operating Profits and Cash Flow," *Commercial Lending Review* 8, no. 2 (1993), pp. 38-48.

26. J. Cantwell, "The Globalization of Technology: What Remains of the Product Life Cycle Model?" *Cambridge Journal of Eco-*

nomics 19, no. 1 (1995), pp. 155–74; T. Tyebjee, "Globalization Challenges Facing Fast Growing Companies," *Journal of Business and Industrial Marketing* 8, no. 3 (1993), pp. 58–64; D. Kelly, *Getting the Bugs Out* (New York: John Wiley & Sons, 2001).

27. J. Barney, "Looking Inside for Competitive Advantage," *Academy of Management Executive* 9, no. 4 (1995), pp. 49–61.

28. J. Kahn. "Wal-Mart Goes Shopping in Europe," *Fortune*, June 7, 1999, pp. 105–10; "How Well Does Wal-Mart Travel?" *BusinessWeek*, September 3, 2001, pp. 61–62.

29. B. Quinn, *Intelligent Enterprise* (New York: Free Press, 1992); C. B. Dobni and G. Luffman, "Determining the Scope and Impact of Market Orientation Profiles on Strategy Implementation and Performance," *Strategic Management Journal* 24, no. 6 (2003), pp. 577+; L. G. Love, R. L. Priem, and G. T. Lumpkin, "Explicitly Articulated Strategy and Firm Performance Under Alternative Levels of Centralization," *Journal of Management* 28, no. 5 (2002), pp. 611–27.

30. H. Mintzberg, "The Strategy Concept I: Five Ps for Strategy," *California Management Review*, Fall 1987, pp. 11–24.

31. F.A. Maljers, "Inside Unilever: The Evolving Transnational Company," *Harvard Business Review*, September–October 1992, p. 2.

32. G. Hamel, "Innovate Now!" *Fast Company*, December 2002, http://www.fastcompany.com.

33. M. A. Hitt, R. D. Ireland, S. M. Camp, and D. L. Sexton, *Strategic Entrepreneurship: Integrating a New Mindset* (Oxford, UK: Blackwell Publishing).

34. S. Black, A. Morrison, and H. Gregersen, *Global Explorers: The Next Generation of Leaders* (New York: Routledge, 1999); K. M. Sutcliffe and K. Weber, "The High Cost of Accurate Knowledge," *Harvard Business Review* 81, no. 5 (2003), pp. 74–82.

CHAPTER 7

1. C. W. L. Hill, M. A. Hitt, and R. E. Hoskisson, "Cooperative versus Competitive Structures in Related and Unrelated Diversified Firms," *Organization Science* 3 (1992), pp. 501–21.

2. B. W. Keats and M. A. Hitt, "A Causal Model of Linkages Among Environmental Dimensions, Macro Organizational Characteristics and Performance," *Academy of Management Journal* 31 (1988), pp. 570–98.

3. M. A. Hitt, R. D. Ireland, and R. E. Hoskisson, *Strategic Management: Competitiveness and Globalization* (Cincinnati, OH: South-Western Publishing Co., 2005).

4. H. Mintzberg, *The Structuring of Organizations* (Upper Saddle River, NJ: Prentice Hall, 1979).

5. P. Lawrence and J. Lorsch, *Organization and Environment* (Boston: Harvard University Press, 1967); J. Galbraith, *Designing Complex Organizations* (Reading, MA: Addison-Wesley, 1977).

6. Ibid.

7. D. Miller and C. Droge, "Psychological and Traditional Determinants of Structure," *Administrative Science Quarterly* 31 (1986), pp. 539–560; L. L. Levesque, J. Wilson, and R. Douglas, "Cognitive Divergence and Shared Mental Models in Software Development Project Teams," *Journal of Organizational Behavior*, March 2001, pp. 135–44.

8. Lawrence and Lorsch, *Organization and Environment*; Galbraith, *Designing Complex Organizations*; M.A. Schilling and H. K. Steensma, "The Use of Modular Organizational Forms: An Industry-level Analysis," *Academy of Management Journal* 44, no. 6 (2001), pp. 1149–68; O. Sorenson, "Interdependence and Adaptability: Organizational Learning and the Long-term Effect of Integration," *Management Science* 49, no. 4 (2003), pp. 446–63.

9. R. Steers and J. S. Black, *Organizational Behavior* (New York: HarperCollins, 1993); R. H. Hall, *Organizations: Structures, Process, and Outcomes*, 5th ed. (Upper Saddle River, NJ: Prentice Hall, 1991); Sorenson, "Interdependence and Adaptability," pp. 446–63.

10. R. Cyert and J. March, *The Behavioral Theory of the Firm* (Upper Saddle River, NJ: Prentice Hall, 1963); J. R. Galbraith, "Organization Design: An Information Processing View," *Interfaces* 4, no. 3 (1974), pp. 28–36; Hall, *Organizations*; J. Birkinshaw, R. Nobel, and J. Ridderstrale, "Knowledge as a Contingency Variable: Do the Characteristics of Knowledge Predict Organization Structure?" *Organization Science* 13, no. 3 (2002), pp. 274–89; R. J. Trent and R. M. Monczka, "Pursuing Competitive Advantage through Integrated Global Sourcing," *Academy of Management Executive* 16, no. 2 (2002), pp. 66–80.

11. E. E. Klein, "Using Information Technology to Eliminate Layers of Bureaucracy," *National Public Accountant*, June 2001, pp. 46–48.

12. D. Nadler and M. Tushman, *Competing by Design: The Power of Oganizational Architecture* (New York: Oxford University Press, 1997).

13. Y. Rhy-song and T. Sagafi-nejad, "Organizational Characteristics of American and Japanese Firms in Taiwan," *National Academy of Management Proceedings*, 1987, pp. 111–15.

14. C.A. Bartlett and S. Ghoshal, "Organizing for Worldwide Effectiveness: The Transnational Solution," *California Management Review*, Fall 1988, pp. 54–74; D. H. Doty, W. H. Glick, and G. P. Huber, "Fit, Effectiveness, and Equifinality: A Test of Two Configurational Theories," *Academy of Management Journal* 36 (1993), pp. 1196–1250.

15. J. R. Lincoln, M. Hanada, and K. McBride, "Organizational Structures in Japanese and U.S. Manufacturing," *Administrative Science Quarterly* 31 (1986), pp. 338–64.

16. J. Schachter, "When Hope Turns to Frustration: The Americanization of Mitsubishi Has Had Little Success," *Los Angeles Times*, July 10, 1988, p. 1.

17. E. Wang, "Linking Organizational Context with Structure," *Omega* 29 (2001), pp. 429–43.

18. "JCPenney 100th Anniversary: The Man in the Center," *Chain Store Age* 78, no. 6 (2002), pp. 56–60.

19. A. Coia, "Leaving Logistics in Capable Hands," *World Trade* 15, no. 7 (2002), p. 26.

20. R. Duncan, "What Is the Right Organizational Structure?" *Organizational Dynamics*, Winter 1979, pp. 59–79; Hall, *Organizations*; Y. Luo, "Market-seeking MNEs in an Emerging Market: How Parent–Subsidiary Links Shape Overseas Success," *Journal of International Business Studies* 34, no. 3 (2003), pp. 290+.

21. M. Badri, D. Davis, and D. Davis, "Operations Strategy, Environmental Uncertainty and Performance: A Path Analytic Model of Industries in Developing Countries," *Omega* 28, no. 2 (2000), pp. 155–73; M. Van Gelderen, M. Frese, and R. Thurik, "Strategies, Uncertainty and Performance of Small Business Startups," *Small Business Economics* 15, no. 3 (2000), pp. 165–81; V. K. Garg, B. A. Walters, and R. L. Priem, "Chief Executive Scanning Emphases, Environmental Dynamism, and Manufacturing Firm Performance," *Strategic Management Journal* 24, no. 8 (2003), pp. 725–44.

22. R. Engdahl, R. Keating, and K. Aupperle, "Strategy and Structure: Chicken or Egg? (Reconsideration of Chandler's Paradigm for Economic Success)," *Organization Development Journal* 18, no. 4 (2000), pp. 21–33; D. E. W. Marginson, "Management Control Systems and Their Effects on Strategy Formation at Middle-management Levels: Evidence from a U.K. Organization," *Strategic Management Journal* 23, no. 11 (2002), pp. 1019–31; J. Smith David, Y. Hwang, B. K. W. Pei, and J. H. Reneau, "The Performance Effects of Congruence Between Product

Competitive Strategies and Purchasing Management Design," *Management Science* 48, no. 7 (2002), pp. 866-85; M. Goold and A. Campbell, "Do You Have a Well-designed Organization?" *Harvard Business Review* 80, no. 3 (2002), pp. 117-24.

23. J. Stopford and L. Wells, *Managing the Multination Enterprise* (New York: Basic Books, 1972).

24. J. Daniels, R. Pitts, and M. Tretter, "Strategy and Structure of U.S. Multinationals: An Exploratory Study," *Academy of Management Journal* 27 (1984), pp. 292-307.

25. J. Wolf and W. Egelhoff, "Reexamination and Extension of International Strategy-Structure Theory," *Strategic Management Journal* 23 (2002), pp. 181-89.

26. Ibid.

27. C. Bartlett and S. Ghoshal, *Managing Across Borders* (Boston: Harvard Business School Press, 1989); P. Ghemawat, "The Forgotten Strategy," *Harvard Business Review* 81, no. 11 (2003), pp. 76-84.

28. M. Dell, "Collaboration Equals Innovation," *Informationweek*, January 27, 2003; pp. 24-26.

CHAPTER 8

1. M.A. Hitt, L. Bierman, K. Shimizu, and R. Kochhar, "Direct and Moderating Effects of Human Capital on Strategy and Performance in Human Service Firms: A Resource-based Perspective," *Academy of Management Journal* 44 (2001), pp. 13-28.

2. M.A. Hitt, R. D. Ireland, and R. E. Hoskisson, *Strategic Management: Competitiveness and Globalization* (Cincinnati, OH: South-Western Publishing Co., 2005).

3. J.A. Pearce, K. Robbins, and R. Robinson, "The Impact of Grand Planning Formality on Financial Performance," *Strategic Management Journal*, March–April 1987, pp. 125-34.

4. R. Van Wingerden, "Managing Change," *International Journal of Technology Management* 21, nos. 5, 6 (2001), pp. 487-95.

5. D. Rheault, "Freshening Up Strategic Planning: More than Fill-in the Blanks," *Journal of Business Strategy* 24, no. 6 (2003), pp. 33-38; B. Walters, I. Clarke, S. Henley, and M. Shandiz, "Strategic Decision-making among Top Executives in Acute-care Hospitals," *Health Marketing Quarterly* 19, no. 1 (2001), pp. 43-59.

6. J. Camillus, "Reinventing Strategic Planning," *Strategy and Leadership*, May–June 1996, pp. 6-12; L. Olson, "Strategic Lessons," *Association Management* 44, no. 6 (1992), pp. 35-39; J. J. Murphy, "Identifying Strategic Issues," *Long Range Planning* 22, no. 2 (1989), pp. 101-05.

7. "The Times that Try Men's Souls," *Journal of Business Strategy*, January/February 1999, p. 4.

8. C. Ngamkroeckjoti and L. Johri, "Management of Environmental Scanning Processes in Large Companies in Thailand," *Business Process Management Journal* 6, no. 4 (2000), p. 331; M.A. Peteraf and M. E. Bergen, "Scanning Dynamic Competitive Landscapes: A Market-based and Resource-based Framework," *Strategic Management Journal* 24, no. 10 (2003), pp. 1027-41; M. D. Watkins and M. H. Bazerman, "Predictable Surprises: The Disasters You Should Have Seen Coming," *Harvard Business Review* 81, no. 3 (2003), pp. 72-80.

9. C. Jain, "Forecasting Process at Wyeth Ayerst Global Pharmaceuticals," *Journal of Business Forecasting Methods & Systems*, Winter 2001/2002, pp. 3-6; E.A. Boyd and I. O. Bilegan, "Revenue Management and E-commerce," *Management Science* 49, no. 10 (2003), pp. 1363-1386; M. Spann and B. Skiera, "Internet-based Virtual Stock Markets for Business Forecasting," *Management Science* 49, no. 10 (2003), pp. 1310-26.

10. G. Vastag, S. Kerekes, and D. Rondinelli, "Evolution of Corporate Environmental Management Approaches: A Framework and Application," *International Journal of Production Economics* 43, nos. 2/3 (1996), pp. 193-211; B. Boyd and J. Faulk, "Executive Scanning and Perceived Uncertainty: A Multidimensional Model," *Journal of Management* 22, no. 1 (1996), pp. 1-21; D.

Lane and R. Maxfield, "Strategy Under Complexity: Fostering Generative Relationships," *Long Range Planning* 29, no. 2 (1996), pp. 215-31; Watkins and Bazerman, pp. 72-80.

11. Michael J. Hileman, "Future Operations Planning Will Measure Plan Achievability," *Oil and Gas Journal*, March 18, 2002, pp. 84-87; L. Rouleau and F. Segui, "Strategy and Organization Theories: Common Forms of Discourse," *Journal of Management Studies* 32, no. 1 (1995), pp. 101-17.

12. "Benchmarking Strategies," *Brand Strategy*, December/January 2004, p. 3; A. Kouzmin, E. Loffler, H. Klages, and N. Korac-Kakabadse, "Benchmarking and Performance Measurement in Public Sectors: Towards Learning for Agency Effectiveness," *International Journal of Public Sector Management* 12, no. 2 (1999), p. 121; R. Bergstrom, "Benchmarking," *Automotive Production* 108, no. 9 (1996), pp. 63-65; J. Vezmar, "Competitive Intelligence at Xerox," *Competitive Intelligence Review* 1, no. 3 (1996), pp. 15-19; David J. Smith, Y. Hwang, B. K. W. Pei, and J. H. Reneau, "The Performance Effects of Congruence between Product Competitive Strategies and Purchasing Management Design," *Management Science* 48, no. 7 (2002), pp. 866-85.

13. C. Barker, C. Thunhurst, and D. Ross, "An Approach to Setting Priorities in Health Planning," *Journal of Management in Medicine* 12, no. 2 (1998), p. 92; A. Bhid, "The Questions Every Entrepreneur Must Ask," *Harvard Business Review* 74, no. 6, pp. 120-30.

14. E.A. Locke and G. P. Latham, *A Theory of Goal Setting and Task Performance* (Upper Saddle River, NJ: Prentice Hall, 1990); A. Lederer and A. Mendelow, "Information Systems Planning and the Challenge of Shifting Priorities," *Information and Management* 24, no. 6 (1993), pp. 319-28.

15. D. Federa and T. Miller, "Capital Allocation Techniques," *Topics in Health Care Financing* 19, no. 1 (1992), pp. 68-78.

16. F. Sunderland and M. Kane, "Measuring Productivity on a Value Basis," *National Productivity Review* 15, no. 4 (1996), pp. 57-76; S. D. Pugh, J. Dietz, J. W. Wiley, and S. M. Brooks, "Driving Service Effectiveness through Employee-Customer Linkages," *Academy of Management Executive* 16, no. 4 (2002), pp. 73-84.

17. J. P. Morgan, "EVA Measures Competitiveness," *Purchasing*, September 4, 2003, pp. 16-18; K. Lehn and A. Makhiji, "EVA and MVA: As Performance Measures and Signals for Strategic Change," *Strategy and Leadership* 24, no. 3 (1996), pp. 34-38; R. Kaplan and D. Norton, "Strategic Learning and the Balanced Score Card," *Strategy and Leadership* 24, no. 5 (1996), pp. 18-24; I. Morgan and J. Rao, "Aligning Service Strategy through Super-Measure Management," *Academy of Management Executive* 16, no. 4 (2002), pp. 121-31; L. Aiman-Smith and S. G. Green, "Implementing New Manufacturing Technology: The Related Effects of Technology Characteristics and User Learning Activities," *Academy of Management Journal* 45, no. 2 (2002), pp. 421-30; L. G. Love, R. L. Priem, and G. T. Lumpkin, "Explicitly Articulated Strategy and Firm Performance under Alternative Levels of Centralization," *Journal of Management* 28, no. 5 (2002), pp. 611-27.

18. A. Bhid, "The Questions Every Entrepreneur Must Ask," *Harvard Business Review* 74, no. 6, pp. 120-30.

19. L. Rivenbark and M. Frost, "Strategic Planning for Success," *HR Magazine*, July 2003, pp. 120-21; L. Kempfer, "Planning for Success," *Computer-aided Engineering* 13, no. 4 (1994), pp. 18-22; P. Sweet, "A Planner's Best Friend?" *Accountancy* 113, no. 1206 (1994), pp. 56-58; J. Rakos, "The Virtues of the Timebar Chart," *Computing Canada* 18, no. 17 (1992), p. 32.

20. S. Mallya, S. Banerjee, and W. G. Bistline, "A Decision Support System for Production/Distribution Planning in Continuous Manufacturing," *Decision Sciences*, Summer 2001, pp. 545-56; P. Cowling and M. Johansson, "Using Real Time Information for Effective Dynamic Scheduling," *European Journal of Operational Research*, June 1, 2002, pp. 230-44; S. G. Taylor, "Finite Capacity Scheduling Alternatives," *Production and Inventory Management Journal*, Third Quarter 2001, pp. 70-74.

21. F. Harrison, "Strategic Control at the CEO Level," *Long Range Planning* 24, no. 6 (1991), pp. 78-87; A. Di Primo, "When Turnaround Management Works," *Journal of Business Strategy* 9, no. 1 (1988), pp. 61-64.

22. W. R. Guffey and B. J. Nienhaus, "Determinants of Employee Support for the Strategic Plan of a Business Unit," *S.A.M. Advanced Management Journal*, Spring 2002, pp. 23-30.

23. M. Ishman, "Commitment–Compliance: Counterforces in Implementing Production and Inventory Control Systems," *Production and Inventory Management Journal* 36, no. 1 (1995), pp. 33-37.

24. J. White, "Almost Nothing New under the Sun: Why the Work of Budgeting Remains Incremental," *Public Budgeting and Finance* 14, no. 1 (1994), pp. 113-34.

25. W. Llewellyn, "A Review of the Budgeting System," *Assessment* 1, no. 5 (1994), pp. 47-50.

26. H. Weihrich, *Management Excellence: Productivity through MBO* (New York: McGraw-Hill, 1985); H. Levinson, "Management by Whose Objectives?" *Harvard Business Review* 81, no. 1 (2003), pp. 107-16.

27. G. P. Latham and L. M. Saari, "The Effects of Holding Goal Difficulty Constant on Assigned and Participatively Set Goals," *Academy of Management Journal*, March 1979, pp. 163-68; A. Drach-Zahavy and M. Erez, "Challenge versus Threat Effects on the Goal-Performance Relationship," *Organizational Behavior and Human Decision Processes* 88, no. 2 (2002), pp. 667-82.

28. M. Erez, P. C. Earley, and C. L. Hulin, "The Impact of Participation on Goal Acceptance and Performance: A Two-step Model," *Academy of Management Journal*, March 1985, pp. 50-66.

29. Locke and Latham, *A Theory of Goal Setting and Task Performance*.

30. P. Mali, *MBO Update* (New York: Wiley, 1986); J. M. Jackman and M. H. Strober, "Fear of Feedback," *Harvard Business Review* 81, no. 4 (2003), pp. 101-107; R. E. Kaplan, "Know Your Strengths," *Harvard Business Review* 80, no. 3 (2002), pp. 20-21.

CHAPTER 9

1. G. R. Ungson and D. N. Braunstein, *Decision Making* (Boston: Kent, 1982).

2. D. Miller and M. Star, *The Structure of Human Decisions* (Upper Saddle River, N.J.: Prentice Hall, 1967).

3. J. E. Dutton and S. E. Jackson, "Categorizing Strategic Issues: Links to Organizational Action," *Academy of Management Review* 12 (1987), pp. 76-90; A. Drach-Zahavy and M. Erez, "Challenge Versus Threat Effects on the Goal-Performance Relationship," *Organizational Behavior and Human Decision Processes* 88, no. 2, (2002), pp. 667-82.

4. H. A. Simon, *The New Science of Management Decisions* (Upper Saddle River, NJ: Prentice Hall, 1977); J. Parking, "Organizational Decision Making and the Project Manager," *International Journal of Project Management* 14, no. 5 (1996), pp. 257-63.

5. H. A. Simon, *Administrative Behavior* (New York: The Free Press, 1957).

6. J. G. March and H. A. Simon, *Organizations* (New York: Wiley, 1958) pp. 140-41.

7. F. Phillips, "The Distortion of Criteria After Decision Making," *Organizational Behavior and Human Decision Processes* 88, no. 2 (2002), pp. 768-84.

8. P. Soelberg, "Unprogrammed Decision Making," *Industrial Management* (1967), pp. 19-29; D. Cray, G. H. Haines, and G. R. Mallory, "Programmed Strategic Decision Making," *British Journal of Management* 5, no. 3 (1994), pp. 191-204.

9. G. Loveman, "Diamonds in the Data Mine," *Harvard Business Review* 81, no. 5 (2003), pp. 109-113; E. Bonabeau, "Don't Trust Your Gut," *Harvard Business Review* 81, no. 5 (2003), pp. 116-23.

10. J. Johnson, et al. "Vigilant and Hypervigilant Decision Making," *Journal of Applied Psychology* 82, no. 4, pp. 614-22; E. Bonabeau, "Don't Trust Your Gut."

11. D. A. Rettinger and R. Hastie, "Content Effects on Decision Making," *Organizational Behavior and Human Decision Processes* 85, no. 2 (2001), pp. 336-59.

12. Simon, *The New Science of Management Decisions*.

13. T. R. Mitchell and J. R. Larson, *People in Organizations* (New York: McGraw-Hill, 1987).

14. E. Harrison, *The Managerial Decision Making Process* (Boston: Houghton Mifflin, 1975); J. R. Hough and M. A. White, "Environmental Dynamism and Strategic Decision-Making Rationality: An Examination at the Decision Level," *Strategic Management Journal* 24, no. 5, (2003), pp. 481-89.

15. R. Ebert and T. Mitchell, *Organizational Decision Processes Concepts and Analysis* (New York: Crane, Russak, 1975).

16. S. S. K. Lam, X. P. Chen, and J. Schaubroeck, "Participative Decision Making and Employee Performance in Different Cultures: The Moderating Effects of Allocentrism/Idiocentrism and Efficacy," *Academy of Management Journal* 45, no. 5 (2002), pp. 905-14.

17. N. Margulies and J. Stewart Black, "Perspectives on the Implementation of Participative Approaches," *Human Resource Management* 26, no. 3 (1987), pp. 385-412.

18. J. Stewart Black and Hal B. Gregersen, "Participative Decision Making: An Integration of Multiple Perspectives," *Human Relations* 50 (1997), pp. 859-78.

19. V. Vroom and P. Yetton, *Leadership and Decision Making* (Pittsburgh: University of Pittsburgh Press, 1973); V. Vroom and A. Jago, *The New Leadership: Managing Participation in Organizations* (Upper Saddle River, N.J.: Prentice Hall, 1988).

20. R. Hof, "Why Once-Ambitious Computer Firm Quit," *Peninsula Times Tribune*, September 29, 1984, p. B1.

21. K. Eisenhardt and L. J. Bourgeois, "Making Fast Strategic Decisions in High-Velocity Environments," *Academy of Management Journal* 32 (1989), pp. 543-76; Hough and White, "Environmental Dynamism and Strategic Decision-Making Rationality."

22. I. Janis, *Victims of Groupthink* (Boston: Houghton Mifflin, 1972); M. E. Turner and A. R. Pratkamis, "Twenty-Five Years of Groupthink Theory and Research: Lessons from the Evaluation of a Theory," *Organizational Behavior and Human Decision Processes* 73, nos. 2, 3 (1998), pp. 105-15; J. K. Esser, "Alive and Well After 25 Years: A Review of Groupthink Research," *Organizational Behavior and Human Decision Processes* 73, nos. 2, 3 (1998), pp. 116-41.

23. S. Schulz-Hardt, M. Jochims, and D. Frey, "Productive Conflict in Group Decision Making: Genuine and Contrived Dissent as Strategies to Counteract Biased Information Seeking," *Organizational Behavior and Human Decision Processes* 88, no. 2, (2002), pp. 563-86.

24. B. M. Staw, "The Escalation of Commitment to a Course of Action," *Academy of Management Review* 6 (1981), pp. 577-87; G. Whyte, A. M. Saks, and S. Hook, "When Success Breeds Failure," *Journal of Organizational Behavior* 18, no. 5 (1997), pp. 415-32; D. R. Bobocel and J. P. Meyer, "Escalating Commitment to a Failing Course of Action," *Journal of Applied Psychology* 79, no. 3 (1994), pp. 360-63; J. Ross and M. Straw, "Organizational Escalation and Exit: Lessons from the Shoreham Nuclear Power Plant," *Academy of Management Journal* 36, no. 4 (1993), pp. 701-32.

25. Staw, "The Escalation of Commitment to a Course of Action," p. 578.

26. G. McNamara, H. Moon, and P. Bromiley, "Banking on Commitment: Intended and Unintended Consequences of an Organiza-

tion's Attempt to Attenuate Escalation of Commitment," *Academy of Management Journal* 45, no. 2 (2002), pp. 443-52.

27. J. S. Black, H. B. Gregersen, and M. E. Mendenhall, *Global Assignments* (San Francisco: Jossey-Bass, 1992).

28. K. Y. Ng and L. Van Dyne, "Individualism-Collectivism as a Boundary Condition for Effectiveness of Minority Influence in Decision Making," *Organizational Behavior and Human Decision Processes* 84, no. 2 (2001), pp. 198-225.

29. C. Schwenk and H. Thomas, "Formulating the Mess: The Role of Decision Aids in Problem Formulation," *Omega* 11 (1983), pp. 239-52.

30. A. VanDeVen and A. Delbecq, "The Effectiveness of Nominal, Delphi, and Interacting Group Decision-Making Processes," *Academy of Management Journal* 17 (1974), pp. 607-26.

31. B. B. Baltes, M. W. Dickson, M. P. Sherman, C. C. Bauer, and J. S. LaGanke "Computer-Mediated Communication and Group Decision Making: A Meta-Analysis," *Organizational Behavior and Human Decision Processes* 87, no. 1 (2002), pp. 156-79; Bonabeau, "Don't Trust Your Gut."

32. J. Levere, "Low-Fare Airline Aims to Build on Attitude and Hostility," *New York Times*, December 1, 2000.

33. Baltes et al., "Computer-Mediated Communication and Group Decision Making: A Meta-Analysis."

PART THREE INTEGRATIVE CASE

1. NewTel Enterprises Limited 1996 Annual Report, supplemented as necessary by the reports for years 1994, 1995, 1997 and 1998.

2. Paragon Information Systems presentation to the Newfoundland and Labrador Employers' Council Fall Conference: November 13, 1997.

3. Paragon, op. cit.

CHAPTER 10

1. S. Finkelstein and D. C. Hambrick, *Strategic Leadership: Top Executives and Their Effects on Organizations* (St. Paul, MN: West Publishing Company, 1996).

2. R. D. Ireland and M. A. Hitt, "Achieving and Maintaining Strategic Competitiveness in the 21st Century: The Role of Strategic Leadership," *Academy of Management Executive* 13, no. 1 (1999), pp. 43-57.

3. M. A. Hitt and R. D. Ireland, "The Essence of Strategic Leadership: Managing Human and Social Capital," *Journal of Leadership and Organizational Studies* 9 (2002), pp. 3-14.

4. R. M. Stogdill, "Historical Trends in Leadership Theory and Research," *Journal of Contemporary Business*, no. 4 (1974), pp. 1-17 (p. 2)

5. R. Levering and M. Moskowitz, *The 100 Best Companies to Work for in America*, rev. ed. (New York: Plume, 1993); R. Galford and A. S. Drapeau, "The Enemies of Trust," *Harvard Business Review* 81, no. 2 (2003), pp. 88-95; A. C. Edmondson and S. E. Cha, "When Company Values Backfire," *Harvard Business Review* 80, no. 11 (2002), pp. 18-19; T. Simons, "The High Cost of Lost Trust," *Harvard Business Review* 80, no. 9 (2002), pp. 18-19.

6. D. Katz and R. L. Kahn, *The Social Psychology of Organizations*, 2nd ed. (New York: Wiley, 1978); S. D. Dionne, F. J. Yammarino, L. E. Atwater, and L. R. James, "Neutralizing Substitutes for Leadership Theory: Leadership Effects and Common-source Bias," *Journal of Applied Psychology* 87, no. 3 (2002), pp. 454-64.

7. G. Romano, "Never Walk Past a Mistake," *Association Management* 50, no. 10 (1998), pp. 42-48.

8. J. Pfeffer, *Managing with Power: Politics and Influence in Organizations* (Boston: Harvard Business School Press, 1992), p. 45.

9. D. A. Whetten and K. S. Cameron, *Developing Management Skills*, 4th ed. (Reading, MA: Addison-Wesley, 1998), p. 229.

10. G. E. G. Catlin, *Systematic Politics* (Toronto: University of Toronto Press, 1962), p. 71.

11. M. Davids, "Where Style Meets Substance," *Journal of Business Strategy* 16 (1995), pp. 48-52+.

12. Pfeffer, *Managing with Power*.

13. W. G. Bennis and B. Nanus, *The Strategies for Taking Charge*, (New York: Harper & Row, 1985), p. 6.

14. B. M. Bass, *Leadership, Psychology, and Organizational Behavior* (New York: Harper, 1960); A. Etzioni, *A Comparative Analysis of Complex Organizations: On Power, Involvement, and Their Correlates* (New York: Free Press of Glencoe, 1961); G. A. Yukl, *Leadership in Organizations,* 3rd ed. (Upper Saddle River, NJ: Prentice Hall, 1994).

15. J. R. P. French and B. Raven, *The Bases of Social Power*, in D. Cartwright (ed.), *Studies in Social Power* (Ann Arbor, MI: Institute for Social Research, 1959), pp. 150-67.

16. D. Mechanic, "Sources of Power of Lower Participants in Complex Organizations," *Administrative Science Quarterly* 7 (1962), pp. 349-64.

17. B. Breen, "Trickle-up Leadership," *Fast Company*, November (2001), pp. 52, 70.

18. Pfeffer, *Managing with Power*, p. 46; N. Nicholson, "How to Motivate Your Problem People," *Harvard Business Review* 81, no. 1 (2003), pp. 56-65; M. Mongeau, "Moving Mountains," *Harvard Business Review* 81, no. 1 (2003), pp. 41-47.

19. D. Kipnis, S. M. Schmidt, and I. Wilkinson, "Intra-organizational Influence Tactics: Explorations in Getting One's Way," *Journal of Applied Psychology* 65 (1980), pp. 440-52; L. W. Porter, R. W. Alien, and H. L. Angle, "The Politics of Upward Influence in Organizations," in L. L. Cummings and B. M. Staw (eds.), *Research in Organizational Behavior*, Vol. 3 (Greenwich, CT: JAI Press, 1981), pp. 109-39; G. Yukl and C. M. Falbe, "Influence Tactics and Objectives in Upward, Downward and Lateral Influence Attempts," *Journal of Applied Psychology* 75 (1990), pp. 132-40; G. Yukl, R. Lepsinger, and T. Lucia, "Preliminary Report on the Development and Validation of the Influence Behavior Questionnaire," in K. Clark and M. Clark (eds.), *The Impact of Leadership* (Greensboro, NC: Center for Creative Leadership, 1992); G. Yukl and J. B. Tracey, "Consequences of Influence Tactics Used with Subordinates, Peers, and the Boss," *Journal of Applied Psychology* 77 (1992), pp. 525-35; Mongeau, "Moving Mountains," pp. 41-47.

20. W. Bennis and B. Nanus, *Leaders*; R. M. Kanter, "Frontiers for Strategic Human Resource Planning and Management, *Human Resource Management* 1, no. 2 (1983), pp. 9-21; J. A. Conger, "Leadership: The Art of Empowering Others," *Academy of Management Executive* 3 (1989), pp. 17-24; J. A. Conger and R. N. Kanungo, "The Empowerment Process: Integrating Theory and Practice," *Academy of Management Review* 13 (1988), pp. 471-482; P. G. Foster-Fishman and C. B. Keys, "The Inverted Pyramid: How a Well Meaning Attempt to Initiate Employee Empowerment Ran Afoul of the Culture of a Public Bureaucracy," *Academy of Management Journal*, Best Papers Proceedings (1995), pp. 364-68; G. M. Spreitzer, "Psychological Empowerment in the Workplace: Dimensions, Measurement, and Validation," *Academy of Management Journal* 38 (1995), pp. 1442-65; G. M. Spreitzer, "Social Structural Characteristics of Psychological Empowerment," *Academy of Management Journal* 39 (1996), pp. 483-504; N. M. Tichy and M. A. Devanna, "The Transformational Leader," *Training and Development* 40, no. 1 (1986), pp. 27-32.

21. N. Moskowitz and R. Levering, "Great Companies in Europe: Novo Nordisk," *Fortune*, 145, no. 3 (2002), pp. 60-61.

22. Bennis and Nanus, *Leaders*; Kanter, "Frontiers for Strategic Human Resource Planning and Management," Conger and Kanungo, "The Empowerment Process"; Tichy and Devanna,

"The Transformational Leader"; R. Kark, B. Shamir, and G. Chen, "The Two Faces of Transformational Leadership: Empowerment and Dependency," *Journal of Applied Psychology* 88, no. 2 (2003), pp. 246–55; N. Turner, J. Barling, O. Epitropaki, V. Butcher, and C. Milner, "Transformational Leadership and Moral Reasoning," *Journal of Applied Psychology* 87, no. 2 (2002), pp. 304–11; T. Dvir, D. Eden, B. J. Avolio, and B. Shamir, "Impact of Transformational Leadership on Follower Development and Performance: A Field Experiment," *Academy of Management Journal* 45, no. 4 (2002), pp. 735–44.

23. R. M. Stogdill, "Personal Factors Associated with Leadership: A Survey of the Literature," *Journal of Psychology* 25 (1948), pp. 35–71.

24. R. G. Lord, C. L. De Vader, and G. M. Alliger, "A Meta-analysis of the Relation Between Personality Traits and Leadership Perceptions: An Application of Validity Generalization Procedures," *Journal of Applied Psychology* 71 (1986), pp. 402–41; S. A. Kirkpatrick and E. A. Locke, "Leadership: Do Traits Matter?" *Academy of Management Executive* 5, no. 2 (1991), pp. 48–60; Yukl, *Leadership in Organizations*; R. M. Kramer, "The Harder They Fall," *Harvard Business Review* 81, no. 10 (2003), pp. 58–66.

25. Kirkpatrick and Locke, "Leadership"; Yukl, *Leadership in Organizations*; D. V. Day, D. J. Schleicher, A. L. Unckless, and N. J. Hiller, "Research Reports—Self-monitoring Personality at Work: A Meta-analytic Investigation of Construct Validity," *Journal of Applied Psychology* 87, no. 2 (2002), pp. 390–401.

26. J. B. Miner, "Twenty Years of Research on Role-motivation Theory of Managerial Effectiveness," *Personnel Psychology* 31 (1978), pp. 739–60; F. E. Berman and J. B. Miner, "Motivation to Manage at the Top Executive Level: A Test of the Hierarchic Role-motivation Theory," *Personnel Psychology* 38 (1985), pp. 377–91.

27. Bennis and Nanus, *Leaders*; J. M. Kouzes and B. Z. Posner, *The Leadership Challenge: How to Get Extraordinary Things Done in Organizations* (San Francisco: Jossey-Bass, 1987).

28. A. Bandura, *Social Foundations of Thought and Action: A Social Cognitive Theory* (Upper Saddle River, NJ: Prentice Hall, 1986); B. M. Bass, *Handbook of Leadership: A Survey of Theory and Research* (New York: Free Press, 1990); D. C. McClelland and R. E. Boyatzis, "Leadership Motive Pattern and Long-term Success in Management," *Journal of Applied Psychology* 67 (1982), pp. 737–43; A. Howard and D. W. Bray, *Managerial Lives in Transition: Advancing Age and Changing Times* (New York: Guilford Press, 1988).

29. Kouzes and Posner, *The Leadership Challenge*.

30. J. R. O'Neil, *The Paradox of Success: When Winning at Work Means Losing at Life: A Book of Renewal for Leaders* (New York: G. P. Putnam & Sons, 1994); M. Maccoby, "Narcissistic Leaders: The Incredible Pros, the Inevitable Cons," *Harvard Business Review* 82, no. 1 (2004), pp. 92–100.

31. Bass, *Handbook of Leadership*; Bennis and Nanus, *Leaders*; Howard and Bray, *Managerial Lives in Transition*; C. D. McCauley and M. M. Lombardo, "Benchmarks: An Instrument for Diagnosing Managerial Strengths and Weaknesses," in K. E. Clark and M. B. Clark (eds.), *Measures of Leadership* (West Orange, NJ: Leadership Library of America, Inc., 1990), pp. 535–45; D. Goleman, R. Boyatzis, and A. McKee, *Primal Leadership: Realizing the Power of Emotional Intelligence* (Boston: Harvard Business School Press, 2002); D. L. Coutu, "Putting Leaders on the Couch: A Conversation with Manfred F. R. Kets de Vries," *Harvard Business Review* 82, no. 1 (2004), pp. 64–71.

32. R. I. Westwood and A. Chan, "Headship and Leadership," in R. I. Westwood (ed.), *Organizational Behavior: Southeast Asian Perspectives* (Hong Kong: Longman, 1992), pp. 118–43.

33. Goleman, Boyatzis, and McKee, *Primal Leadership;* D. Goleman, "What Makes a Leader?" *Harvard Business Review* 7, nos. 5, 6 (1998), pp. 92–103; J. D. Mayer and P. Salovey, "Emo-

tional Intelligence and the Construction and Regulation of Feelings," *Applied and Preventive Psychology* 4 (1995), pp. 197–208; J. D. Mayer, D. Goleman, C. Barren, S. Gutstein et al., "Leading by Feel," *Harvard Business Review* 82, no. 1 (2004), pp. 27–37; Goleman, "What Makes a Leader?" pp. 82–91; J. E. Dutton, P. J. Frost, M. C. Worline, J. M. Lilius, and J. M. Kanov, "Leading in Times of Trauma," *Harvard Business Review* 80, no. 1 (2002), pp. 54–61.

34. Goleman, "What Makes a Leader?"

35. D. Goleman, *Emotional Intelligence* (New York: Bantam Books, 1995).

36. Goleman, Boyatzis, and McKee, *Primal Leadership*.

37. J. Misumi and M. E. Peterson, "The Performance–Maintenance (PM) Theory of Leadership: Review of a Japanese Research Program," *Administrative Science Quarterly* 30 (1985), pp. 198–223; R. T. Lewis, "New York Times Company President and Chief Executive Officer Russell Lewis on 'The CEO's lot is not a happy one . . . ' (with apologies to Gilbert and Sullivan)," *Academy of Management Executive* 16, no. 4 (2002), pp. 37–42.

38. E. A. Eagly and B. T. Johnson, "Gender and Leadership Style: A Meta-analysis," *Psychological Bulletin* 108 (1990), pp. 235–56; J. B. Rosener, "Ways Women Lead," *Harvard Business Review* 68, no. 6 (1990), pp. 119–225; G. N. Powell, "One More Time: Do Female and Male Managers Differ?" *Academy of Management Executive* 4, no. 3 (1990), pp. 68–75; D. J. Campbell, W. Bommer, and E. Yeo, "Perceptions of Appropriate Leadership Style: Participation versus Consultation Across Two Cultures," *Asia Pacific Journal of Management* 10, no. 1 (1993), pp. 1–9; G. Morse, "The Emancipated Organization," *Harvard Business Review* 80 (9), (2002) 20–21.

39. E. P. Hollander, "The Essential Interdependence of Leadership and Followership," *Current Directions in Psychological Science* 1, no. 2 (1992), pp. 71–75; R. Stewart, *Choices for the Manager* (Upper Saddle River, NJ: Prentice Hall, 1992). Cited in: E. P. Hollander, "Leadership, Followership, Self and Others," *Leadership Quarterly* 3, no. 1 (1992), pp. 43–54; L. R. Offermann, "When Followers Become Toxic," *Harvard Business Review* 82, no. 1 (2004), pp. 54–60.

40. S. Motsch, "Think Gray," *Incentive* 169, no. 4 (1995), pp. 59–60; N. Shope Griffin, "Personalize Your Management Development," *Harvard Business Review* 81, no. 3 (2003), pp. 113–19.

41. R. E. Kelly, "In Praise of Followers," *Harvard Business Review* 66, no. 6 (1988), pp. 142–49.

42. Hollander, *The Essential Interdependence of Leadership and Followership*, p. 44.

43. R. G. Lord and K. H. Maher, "Alternative Information-processing Models and Their Implications for Theory, Research, and Practice," *Academy of Management Review* 15 (1990), pp. 9–28.

44. B. J. Calder, "An Attribution Theory of Leadership," in B. M. Staw and G. R. Salancik (eds.), *New Directions in Organizational Behavior* (Chicago: St. Clair, 1997); R. G. Lord, C. L. Devader, and G. M. Alliger, "A Meta-analysis of the Relation Between Personality Traits and Leadership Perceptions," *Journal of Applied Psychology*, 71 (1986), pp. 402–10; A. C. Edmondson and S. E. Cha, "When Company Values Backfire," *Harvard Business Review* 80, no. 11 (2002), pp. 18–19.

45. Calder, "An Attribution Theory of Leadership"; J. Pfeffer, "The Ambiguity of Leadership," *Academy of Management Review* 2 (1977), pp. 104–12.

46. G. B. Graen, R. C. Liden, and W. Hoel, "Role of Leadership in the Employee Withdrawal Process," *Journal of Applied Psychology* 67 (1982), pp. 868–72; G. B. Graen, T. A. Scandura, and M. R. Graen, "A Field Experimental Test of the Moderating Effects of Growth Need Strength on Productivity," *Journal of Applied Psychology* 5 (1986), pp. 484–91.

47. F. Dansereau, G. Graen, et al., "A Vertical Dyad Lineage Approach to Leadership within Formal Organizations," *Organizational*

Behavior and Human Performance 13, no. 1 (1975), pp. 46-78; G. Grae and J. F. Cashman, "A Role-making Model of Leadership in Formal Organizations—A Developmental Approach," *Organization and Administrative Sciences* 6, nos. 2, 3 (1975), pp. 143-65; J. F. Cashman, F. Dansereau, G. Graen, and W. J. Haga, "Organizational Understructure and Leadership: A Longitudinal Investigation of the Managerial Role-making Process," *Organizational Behavior and Human Performance* 15 (1976), pp. 278-96; G. B. Graen and M. Uhl-Bien, "Relationship-based Approach to Leadership: Development of Leader–Member Exchange (LMX) Theory of Leadership over 25 Years: Applying a Multi-Domain Perspective," *The Leadership Quarterly. Special Issue: Leadership* 6 (1995), pp. 219-47; M. Uhl-Bien and G. B. Graen, "Leadership Making in Self-managing Professional Work Teams: An Empirical Investigation," in K. E. Clark, M. B. Clark, and D. P. Campbell (eds.), *The Impact of Leadership* (West Orange, NJ: Leadership Library of America, 1993), pp. 379-87.

48. T. N. Bauer, and S. G. Green, "Development of Leader–Member Exchange: A Longitudinal Test," *Academy of Management Journal* 39 (1996), pp. 1538-67; C. R. Gerstner and D. V. Day, "Meta-analytic Review of Leader-Member Exchange Theory: Correlates and Construct Issues," *Journal of Applied Psychology* 82 (1997), pp. 827-44; Graen et al., "Role of Leadership in the Employee Withdrawal Process"; Graen, Scandura, and Graen, "A Field Experimental Test"; T. A. Scandura and G. B. Graen, "Moderating Effects of Initial Leader-Member Exchange Status on the Effects of a Leadership Intervention," *Journal of Applied Psychology* 69 (1984), pp. 428-36.

49. Bauer and Green, "Development of Leader–Member Exchange"; D. A. Hofmann, S. J. Gerras, and F. P. Morgeson, "Climate as a Moderator of the Relationship between Leader–Member Exchange and Content Specific Citizenship: Safety Climate as an Exemplar," *Journal of Applied Psychology* 88, no. 1 (2003), p. 170.

50. Graen and Uhl-Bien, "Relationship-based Approach to Leadership"; Uhl-Bien and Graen, "Leadership Making in Self-managing Professional Work Teams"; R. T. Sparrowe and C. R. Liden, "Process and Structure in Leader–Member Exchange," *Academy of Management Review* 22 (1997), pp. 522-52; W. C. H. Prentice, "Understanding Leadership," *Harvard Business Review* 82, no. 1 (2004), pp. 102-9; S. J. Wayne, L. M. Shore, W. H. Bommer, and L. E. Tetrick, "The Role of Fair Treatment and Rewards in Perceptions of Organizational Support and Leader–Member Exchange," *Journal of Applied Psychology* 87, no. 3 (2002), pp. 590-98.

51. A. N. Turner and P. R. Lawrence, *Industrial Jobs and the Worker: An Investigation of Response to Task Attributes* (Boston: Harvard University, Division of Research, Graduate School of Business Administration, 1965); R. W. Griffin, *Task Design: An Integrative Approach* (Glenview, IL: Scott, Foresman, 1982); J. R. Hackman and G. R. Oldham, *Work Redesign* (Reading, MA: Addison-Wesley, 1980).

52. R. D. Ireland, M. A. Hitt, and D. G. Sirmon, "A Model of Strategic Entrepreneurship: The Construct and Its Dimensions," *Journal of Management* 29 (2003), pp. 963-89.

CHAPTER 11

1. M. A. Hitt, R. D. Ireland, and G. W. Rowe, "Strategic Leadership: Strategy, Resources, Ethics and Succession," in J. Doh and S. Stumpf (eds.), *Handbook on Responsible Leadership and Governance in Global Business* (Cheltenham, UK: Edward Elgar Publishing, Ltd., in press).

2. M. A. Hitt, H. Lee, and E. Yucel, "The Importance of Social Capital to the Management of Multinational Enterprises: Relational Networks Among Asian and Western Firms," *Asia Pacific Journal of Management* 19 (2002), pp. 353-72.

3. J. R. Meindl, S. B. Ehrlixh, and J. M. Dukerich, "The Romance of Leadership," *Administrative Science Quarterly* 30 (1985), pp. 78-103.

4. R. R. Blake and J. S. Mouton, *The Management Grid* (Houston: Gulf Publishing, 1964).

5. P. Hersey, *Situational Selling* (Escondido, CA: Center for Leadership Studies, 1985); P. Hersey, K. H. Blanchard, and Dewey Johnson, *Management of Organizational Behavior: Leading Human Resources*, 8th ed. (Upper Saddle River, NJ: Prentice Hall, 2001).

6. L. R. Anderson and F. E. Fiedler, "The Effect of Participatory and Supervisory Leadership on Group Creativity," *Journal of Applied Psychology* 48 (1964), pp. 227-36; F. E. Fiedler, *A Theory of Leadership Effectiveness* (New York: McGraw-Hill, 1967); M. M. Chemers and F. E. Fiedler, "The Effectiveness of Leadership Training: A Reply to Argyris," *American Psychologist* 33 (1978), pp. 391-94.

7. M. J. Strube and J. E. Garcia, "A Meta-analytic Investigation of Fiedler's Contingency Model of Leadership Effectiveness," *Psychological Bulletin* 90 (1981), pp. 307-21; L. H. Peters, D. D. Hartke, and J. T. Pohlmann, "Fiedler's Contingency Theory of Leadership: An Application of the Meta-analysis Procedures of Schmidt and Hunter," *Psychological Bulletin* 7 (1985), pp. 274-85.

8. M. G. Evans, "The Effects of Supervisory Behavior on the Path-Goal Relationship," *Organizational Behavior and Human Performance* 5 (1970), pp. 277-98; R. J. House, "A Path-Goal Theory of Leader Effectiveness," *Administrative Science Quarterly* 16 (1971), pp. 321-29; R. J. House and G. Dessler, "The Path-Goal Theory of Leadership: Some Post Hoc and A Priori Tests," in J. Hunt and L. Larson (eds.), *Contingency Approaches to Leadership* (Carbondale, IL: Southern Illinois Press, 1974), pp. 81-87; R. J. House and T. R. Mitchell, "Path-Goal Theory of Leadership," *Journal of Contemporary Business* 3, no. 4 (1974), pp. 81-97.

9. House, *A Path-goal Theory of Leader Effectiveness*, p. 324.

10. V. H. Vroom and P. W. Yetton, *Leadership and Decision-Making* (Pittsburgh, PA: University of Pittsburgh Press, 1973); B. H. Vroom and A. G. Jago, *The New Leadership: Managing Participation in Organizations* (Upper Saddle River, NJ: Prentice Hall, 1988).

11. Vroom and Jago, *The New Leadership*.

12. S. Kerr and J. M. Jermier, "Substitutes for Leadership: Their Meaning and Measurement," *Organizational Behavior and Human Performance* 22 (1978), pp. 375-403; J. P. Howell, D. E. Bowen, P. W. Dorfman, S. Kerr, and P. M. Podsakoff, "Substitutes for Leadership: Effective Alternatives to Ineffective Leadership," *Organizational Dynamics* 19 (1990), pp. 20-38; J. P. Howell and P. W. Dorfmann, "Substitutes for Leadership: Test of a Construct," *Academy of Management Journal* 24 (1981), pp. 714-28; P. M. Podsakoff, S. B. MacKenzie, and W. H. Bommer, "Transformational Leader Behaviors and Substitutes for Leadership as Determinants of Employee Satisfaction, Commitment, Trust, and Organizational Citizenship Behaviors," *Journal of Management* 22 (1996), pp. 259-98; S. B. MacKenzie, P. M. Podsakoff, and R. Fetter, "The Impact of Organizational Citizenship Behavior on Evaluations of Salesperson Performance," *Journal of Marketing* 57 (1993), pp. 70-80; P. M. Podsakoff, B. P. Nichoff, S. B. MacKenzie, and M. L. Williams, "Do Substitutes for Leadership Really Substitute for Leadership? An Empirical Examination of Kerr and Jermier's Situational Leadership Model," *Organizational Behavior and Human Decision Processes* 54 (1993), pp. 1-44.

13. S. Finkelstein, "Seven Habits of Spectacularly Unsuccessful People," *Strategy Review* 14, no. 4 (2003), pp. 39-51; N. Nohria, W. Joyce, and B. Roberson, "What Really Works," *Harvard Business Review* 81, no. 7 (2003), pp. 42-52; W. G. Bennis and B. Nanus, *Leaders: Strategies for Taking Charge*, 2nd ed. (New York: Harper Business, 1997); J. P. Kotter, "What Leaders Really Do," *Harvard Business Review* 68, no. 3 (1990), pp. 103-211; A. Zaleznik, "Managers and Leaders: Are They Different?" *Harvard Business Review* 70, no. 2 (1992), pp. 126-35.

14. M. Weber, *The Theory of Social and Economic Organization*, A. M. Henderson and T. Parson, trans.; edited with an introduction by T. Parsons (New York: Free Press, 1948).

15. S. Callan, "Charismatic Leadership in Contemporary Management Debates," *Journal of General Management* 29(1), 1-14; M. Frese, S. Beimel, and S. Schoenborn, "Action Training for Charismatic Leadership: Two Evaluations of Studies of a Commercial Training Module on Inspirational Communication of a Vision," *Personnel Psychology* 56, no. 3 (2003), pp. 671-97; R. Khurana, "The Curse of the Superstar CEO," *Harvard Business Review* 80, no. 9 (2002), pp. 60-66; S. W. Tester, B. M. Meglino, and M. A. Korsgaard, "The Antecedents and Consequences of Group Potency: A Longitudinal Investigation of Newly Formed Work Groups," *Academy of Management Journal* 45, no. 2 (2002), pp. 352-68; D. De Cremer and D. van Knippenberg, "How Do Leaders Promote Cooperation? The Effects of Charisma and Procedural Fairness," *Journal of Applied Psychology* 87, no. 5 (2002), pp. 858+; J-C. Pastor, J. R. Meindl, and M. C. Mayo, "A Network Effects Model of Charisma Attributions," *Academy of Management Journal* 45, no. 2 (2002) pp. 410-20; O. Behling and J. M. McFillen, "A Syncretical Model of Charismatic/Transformation Leadership," *Group and Organizational Management* 21 (1996), pp. 163-91; J. A. Conger, "*The Charismatic Leader: Beyond the Mystique of Exceptional Leadership*" (San Francisco: Jossey-Bass, 1989); J. A. Conger, R. N. Kanungo, S. T. Menon, and P. Mathur, "Measuring Charisma: Dimensionality and Validity of the Conger-Kanungo Scale of Charismatic Leadership," *Canadian Journal of Administrative Sciences* 14 (1997), pp. 290-302; R. J. House, "A 1976 Theory of Charismatic Leadership," in J. G. Hunt (ed.), *Leadership: The Cutting Edge* (Carbondale, IL: Southern Illinois Press (1977); R. J. House, W. D. Spangler, and J. Woycke, "Personality and Charisma in the U.S. Presidency: A Psychological Theory of Leader Effectiveness," *Administrative Science Quarterly* 36 (1991), pp. 364-96.

16. House, "A 1976 Theory of Charismatic Leadership."

17. C. Macrae, I. Ryder, J. Yan, J. Caswell, T. Kitchin, T. Power, M. McQuarrie, and S. Anholt, "Can Brand Leadership Recover Local Trust and Global Responsibility?" *Journal of Brand Management* 10, nos. 4, 5 (2003), pp. 268-79; Robert L. Veniga, "Five Ways to Rebuild Trust," *Executive Excellence* 75, no. 10 (2001), pp. 13-14.

18. Conger, *Leadership*; Conger and Kanungo, "Toward a Behavioral Theory of Charismatic Leadership in Organizational Setting," *Academy of Management Review* 12 (1987), pp. 637-47.

19. C. G. Emrich, "Images in Words: Presidential Rhetoric, Charisma, and Greatness," *Administrative Science Quarterly* 46 (2001), pp. 527-61; J. A. Conger, R. N. Kanungo, and S. T. Menon, "Charismatic Leadership and Follower Effects," *Journal of Organizational Behavior* 21 (2000), pp. 747-67.

20. L. Lee, "Tricks of E*Trade: In His Drive to Create a Net Powerhouse, Christos Cotsakos Is Building a Culture That's Edgy, a Bit Bizarre—And Often Brilliant," *BusinessWeek*, p. EB18.

21. D. Tourish and A. Pinnington, "Transformational Leadership, Corporate Cultism, and the Spirituality Paradigm: An Unholy Trinity in the Workplace?" *Human Relations* 55, no. 2 (2002), pp. 147-72; R. Kark, B. Shamir, and G. Chen, "The Two Faces of Transformational Leadership: Empowerment and Dependency," *Journal of Applied Psychology* 88, no. 2 (2003), pp. 246-55; T. Dvir, D. Eden, B. J. Avolio, and B. Shamir, "Impact of Transformational Leadership on Follower Development and Performance: A Field Experiment," *Academy of Management Journal* 45, no. 4 (2002), pp. 735-44; J. Barling, C. Loughlin, and E. K. Kelloway, "Development and Test of a Model Linking Safety-specific Transformational Leadership and Occupational Safety," *Journal of Applied Psychology* 87, no. 3 (2002), pp. 488-96; B. M. Bass, D. I. Jung, B. J. Avolio, and Y. Berson, "Predicting Unit Performance by Assessing Transformational and Trans-

actional Leadership," *Journal of Applied Psychology* 88, no. 2 (2003), pp. 207-18; J. M. Burns, *Leadership* (New York: Harper & Row, 1978).

22. Burns, *Leadership*.

23. B. M. Bass, "Leadership: Good, Better, Best," *Organizational Dynamics* 13, no. 3 (1985), pp. 26-40; B. M. Bass and B. J. Avolio, "Developing Transformational Leadership: 1992 and Beyond," *Journal of European Industrial Training* 14, no. 5 (1992), pp. 21-27.

24. Bass, *Leadership*.

25. Bass, Jung, Avolio, and Berson, "Predicting Unit Performance," 207-18; B. J. Avolio, "Re-examining the Components of Transformational and Transactional Leadership Using the Multifactor Leadership Questionnaire," *Journal of Occupational and Organizational Psychology* 72 (1999), pp. 441-63.

26. C. L. Hoyt and J. Blascovich, "Transformational and Transactional Leadership in Virtual and Physical Environments," *Small Group Research* 34, no. 6 (2003), pp. 678-716; N. M. Tichy and M. A. Devanna, "The Transformational Leader," *Training and Development* 40, no. 7 (1986), pp. 27-32; G. A. Yukl, *Leadership in Organizations*, 3rd ed. (Upper Saddle River, NJ: Prentice Hall, 1994).

27. Bennis and Nanus, *Leaders*.

28. Yukl, *Leadership in Organizations*.

29. B. J. Avolio and S. S. Kahai, "Adding the 'E' to E-leadership: How It May Impact Your Leadership," *Organizational Dynamics* 31, no. 4 (2003), pp. 325-39; M. Raffoni, "E-Leadership, Take Two," *Harvard Business* Update; B. J. Avolio, S. Kahai, and G. E. Dodge, "E-leadership: Implications for Theory, Research, and Practice," *Leadership Quarterly* 77 (2001), pp. 615-68.

30. S. D. Friedman, "Leadership DNA: The Ford Motor Story," *Training and Development* 55, no. 3 (2001), pp. 22-31.

31. R. J. House, et al., "Cultural Influences on Leadership and Organizations: Project GLOBE," in W. Mobley (ed.), *Advances in Global Leadership*, vol. 1 (Stamford, CT: JAI Press, 1998).

32. R. I. Westwood and A. Chan, "Headship and Leadership," in R. I. Westwood (ed.), *Organizational Behavior: Southeast Asian Perspectives*, (Hong Kong: Longman, 1992).

33. S. Ronen, *Comparative and Multinational Management* (New York: Wiley, 1986).

34. Westwood and Chan, *Headship and Leadership*.

35. E. Ogliastri, C. McMillen, C. Altschul, M. E. Arias, C. Bustamante, C. Davila, P. Dorfman, M. Ferreira, C. Finmen, and S. Martinez, "Cultura y Liderazgo Organizacional en America Latina: El Estudio Globe" (Culture and Organizational Leadership in Latin America: The Globe Study), *Revista Latinoamericana de Administración*, 1999.

36. M. Dickson, D. N. Den Hartog, and J. K. Mitchelson, "Research on Leadership in a Cross-cultural Context: Making Progress, and Raising New Questions," *Leadership Quarterly* 14, no. 6 (2003), pp. 729-69; P. W. Dorfman and J. P. Howell, "Leadership in Western and Asian Countries: Commonalities and Differences in Effective Leadership Processes Across Cultures," *Leadership Quarterly* 8 (1997), pp. 233-74.

37. House, "Cultural Influences on Leadership and Organizations."

38. B. Powell, R. Tomlinson, E. Nee, J. Fox, et al., "25 Rising Stars," *Fortune*, 2001, pp. 140-64.

39. W. Bennis, "The End of Leadership: Exemplary Leadership Is Impossible without Full Inclusion, Initiatives, and Cooperation of Followers," *Organizational Dynamics* 25, no. 1 (1999), pp. 71-80.

40. M. A. Hitt, R. D. Ireland, and R. E. Hoskisson, *Strategic Management: Competitiveness and Globalization* (Cincinnati, OH: South-Western Publishing Co., 2005).

CHAPTER 12

1. G. Hofstede, "Culture and Organizations," *International Studies of Management and Organization* 70, no. 4 (1980), pp. 15–41; C. Sue-Chan and M. Ong, "Goal Assignment and Performance: Assessing the Mediating Roles of Goal Commitment and Self-efficacy and the Moderating Role of Power Distance," *Organizational Behavior and Human Decision Processes* 89, no. 2 (2002), pp. 1140–61; P. E. Spector, C. L. Cooper, J. I. Sanchez, M. O'Driscoll, and K. Sparks, "Locus of Control and Well-being at Work: How Generalizable are Western Findings," *Academy of Management Journal* 45, no. 2 (2002), pp. 453–66.

2. A. H. Maslow, *Motivation and Personality*, 2nd ed. (New York: Harper & Row, 1970).

3. R. Jacob, "Secure Jobs Trump Higher Pay," *Fortune*, 1995, p. 24.

4. K. Schoenberger, P. J. McDonnell, and S. Hubler, "Thais Found in Sweatshop Are Released," *Los Angeles Times*, August 21, 1995, pp. A1+.

5. Hofstede, *Culture and Organizations*, pp. 55–56 and Figure 7.

6. C. P. Alderfer, "An Empirical Test of a New Theory of Human Needs," *Organizational Behavior and Human Performance* 4 (1969), pp. 142–75; C. P. Alderfer, *Existence, Relatedness and Growth: Human Need in Organizational Settings* (New York: The Free Press, 1997); H. Levinson, "Management by Whose Objectives?" *Harvard Business Review* 81, no. 1 (2003), pp. 107–16.

7. F. Ferris, "Unlocking Employee Productivity," *American Printer* 2, no. 5 (1995), pp. 30–34.

8. D. C. McClelland, *Human Motivation* (Glenview, IL: Scott, Foresman, 1985); D. C. McClelland and R. E. Boyatzis, "Leadership Motive Pattern and Long-term Success in Management," *Journal of Applied Psychology* 67 (1982), pp. 734–43; D. C. McClelland and D. G. Winter, *Motivating Economic Achievement* (New York: The Free Press, 1969).

9. S. H. Schwartz and W. Blisky, "Toward a Universal Psychological Structure of Human Values," *Journal of Personality and Social Psychology* 53 (1987), pp. 550–62; S. H. Schwartz and W. T. Bilsky, "Toward a Theory of the Universal Content and Structure of Values: Extensions and Cross-cultural Replications," *Journal of Personality and Social Psychology* 58 (1990), pp. 878–81.

10. M. Erez and P. C. Earley, *Culture, Self-Identity, and Work* (New York: Oxford University Press, 1993), p. 102.

11. J. W. Connor and G. A. DeVos, "Cultural Influences on Achievement Motivation and Orientation: Towards Work in Japanese and American Youth," in D. Stern and D. Eichorn (eds.), *Influences of Social Structure, Labor Markets, and Culture* (Hillsdale, NJ: Lawrence Erlbaum Associates, 1989), pp. 291–326.

12. A. Sagie, D. Elizur, and H. Yamauchi, "The Structure and Strength of Achievement Motivation: A Cross-cultural Comparison," *Journal of Organizational Behavior* 17 (1996), pp. 431–44; K. P. Parboteeah and J. B. Cullen, "Social Institutions and Work Centrality: Explorations Beyond National Culture," *Organization Science* 14, no. 2 (2003), pp. 137–48; K. S. Law, D. K. Tse, and N. Zhou, "Does Human Resource Management Matter in a Transitional Economy? China as an Example," *Journal of International Business Studies* 34, no. 3 (2003), pp. 255–65.

13. F. Herzberg, *Work and the Nature of Man* (Cleveland, OH: Worth Publishing, 1966); F. Herzberg, "One More Time: How Do You Motivate Employees?" *Harvard Business Review* 46 (1968), pp. 54–62; F. Herzberg, B. Mausner, and B. B. Snyderman, *The Motivation to Work* (New York: Wiley, 1959).

14. M. Murray, "Giant Task: GE's Immelt Starts Renovations on the House that Jack Built—Under Intense Spotlight, CEO Focuses on Core Operations that Welch Had Trimmed, Opening the Books a Bit Wider," *Wall Street Journal*, February 6, 2003, p. A1.

15. R. W. Griffin, *Task Design: An Integrative Approach* (Glenview, IL: Scott, Foresman, 1982); J. L. Pierce and R. B. Dunham, "Task Design: A Literature Review," *Academy of Management Review* 1 (1976), pp. 83–97.

16. J. R. Hackman and G. R. Oldham, *Work Redesign* (Reading, MA: Addison-Wesley, 1980).

17. R. B. Tiegs, L. E. Tetrick, and Y. Fried, "Growth Need Strength and Context Satisfaction as Moderators of the Relations of the Job Characteristics Model," *Journal of Management* 18 (1992), pp. 575–93; X. Huang and E. Van De Viert, "Where Intrinsic Job Satisfaction Fails to Work: National Moderators on Intrinsic Motivation," *Journal of Organizational Behavior* 24, no. 2 (2003), pp. 159–80; S. Friday and E. Friday, "Racioethnic Perceptions of Job Characteristics and Job Satisfaction," *Journal of Management Development* 22, nos. 5, 6 (2003), pp. 426–42.

18. M. Attaran and T. T. Nguyen, "Creating the Right Structural Fit for Self-directed Teams," *Team Performance Management* 6, no. 12 (2000), pp. 25–33; W. A. Randolph and M. Sashkin, "Can Organizational Empowerment Work in Multinational Settings?" *Academy of Management Executive* 16, no. 1 (2002), pp. 102–15.

19. J. S. Adams, "Towards an Understanding of Inequity," *Journal of Abnormal and Social Psychology* 67 (1963), pp. 422–36; J. S. Adams, "Inequity in Social Exchange," in L. Berkowitz (ed.), *Advances in Experimental Social Psychology*, vol. 2 (New York: Academic Press, 1965), pp. 267–99; R. T. Mowday, "Equity Theory Predictions of Behavior in Organizations," in R. M. Steers, L. W. Porter, and G. A Bigley (eds.), *Motivation and Leadership at Work*, 6th ed. (New York: McGraw-Hill, 1996); J. D. Shaw, N. Gupta, and J. E. Delery, "Pay Dispersion and Workforce Performance: Moderating Effects of Incentives and Interdependence," *Strategic Management Journal* 23, no. 6 (2002), pp. 491–512; C. C. Chen, J. Choi, and S-C. Chi, "Making Justice Sense of Local-Expatriate Compensation Disparity: Mitigation by Local Referents, Ideological Explanations, and Interpersonal Sensitivity in China Foreign Joint Ventures," *Academy of Management Journal* 45, no. 5 (2003), pp. 807–17.

20. C. C. Pinder, *Work Motivation in Organizational Behavior* (Upper Saddle River, NJ: Prentice Hall, 1998), p. 287.

21. L. W. Porter, G. A. Bigley, and R. M. Steers, *Motivation and Work Behavior*, 7th ed. (New York: McGraw-Hill, 2003), p. 47; L. K. Scheer, N. Kumar, J-B. E. M. Steenkamp, "Reactions to Perceived Inequity in U.S. and Dutch Interorganizational Relationships," *Academy of Management Journal* 46, no. 3 (2003), pp. 303–16.

22. V. H. Vroom, *Work and Motivation* (New York: Wiley, 1964).

23. J. Caisson, "Jump Start Motivation," *Incentive* 775, no. 5 (2001), pp. 77, 88; A. Erez and M. A. Isen, "The Influence of Positive Affect on the Components of Expectancy Motivation," *Journal of Applied Psychology* 87, no. 6 (2002), pp. 1055–67.

24. A. D. Stajkovic and F. Luthans, "Social Cognitive Theory and Self-efficacy: Going Beyond Traditional Motivational and Behavioral Approaches," *Organizational Dynamics* 26, no. 4 (1998), pp. 62–74; T. A. Wright, "What Every Manager Should Know: Does Personality Help Drive Employee Motivation?" *Academy of Management Executive* 17, no. 2 (2003), pp. 131–33.

25. A. D. Stajkovic and F. Luthans, "Social Cognitive Theory and Self-efficacy: Implications for Motivation Theory and Practice," in L. W. Porter, G. A. Bigley, and R. M. Steers (eds.), *Motivation and Work Behavior*, 7th ed. (New York: McGraw-Hill, 2003); A. Bandura and E. A. Locke, "Negative Self-efficacy and Goal Effects Revisited," *Journal of Applied Psychology* 88, no. 1 (2003), pp. 87–99.

26. M. Erez, "Goal Setting," in N. Nicholson (ed.), *Blackwell Encyclopedic Dictionary of Organizational Behavior* (Cambridge, MA: Blackwell Business Publishing, 1995), pp. 193–94; E. A. Locke, "The Motivation Sequence, the Motivation Hub, and the Motivation Core," *Organizational Behavior and Human*

Decision Processes 50 (1991), pp. 288-99; E.A. Locke and G. P. Latham, *A Theory of Goal Setting and Task Performance* (Upper Saddle River, NJ: Prentice Hall, 1990); W. Q. Judge, G. E. Fryxell, and R. S. Dooley, "The New Task of R&D Management: Creating Goal-directed Communities for Innovation," *California Management Review* 39, no. 3 (1997), pp. 72-85; Wright, "What Every Manager Should Know," pp. 131-33.

27. E.A. Locke and G. P. Latham, "Goal Setting Theory: An Introduction," in R. M. Steers, L. W. Porter, and G.A. Bigley (eds.), *Motivation and Leadership at Work*, 6th ed. (New York: McGraw-Hill, 1996).

28. Erez, *Goal Setting*; A. Drach-Zachavy and M. Erez, "Challenge versus Threat Effects on the Goal-Performance Relationship," *Organizational Behavior and Human Decision Processes* 88, no. 2 (2002), pp. 667-82; T.W. Britt, "Black Hawk Down at Work," *Harvard Business Review* 81, no. 1 (2003), pp. 16+; N. Nicholson, "How to Motivate Your Problem People," *Harvard Business Review* 81, no. 1 (2003), pp. 56-58.

29. Ibid.

30. L. Helliker, "Pressure at Pier 1: Beating Sales Numbers of Year Earlier Is a Storewide Obsession," *Wall Street Journal,* December 7, 1995, p. B1.

31. M. Erez and P. C. Earley, "Comparative Analysis of Goal-setting Strategies Across Cultures," *Journal of Applied Psychology* 72 (1987), pp. 658-65; S. S. K. Lam, X.-P. Chen, and J. Schaunbroeck, "Participative Decision Making and Employee Performance in Different Cultures: The Moderating Effects of Allocentrism/Idiocentrism and Efficacy," *Academy of Management Journal* 45, no. 5 (2002), pp. 905-14.

32. Erez and Earley, *Culture, Self-Identity, and Work*, p. 107.

33. J. E. Komaki, T. Coombs, and S. Schepman, "Motivational Implications of Reinforcement Theory, " in R. M. Steers, L. W. Porter, and G.A. Bigley (eds.), *Motivation and Leadership at Work,* 6th ed. (New York: McGraw-Hill, 1996).

34. S. Kerr, "On the Folly of Rewarding A While Hoping for B," *Academy of Management Journal* 18 (1975), pp. 769-83.

35. S. Kerr, *Ultimate Rewards* (Boston: Harvard Business School Press, 1997).

36. Komaki, Coombs, and Schepman, *Motivational Implications of Reinforcement Theory.*

37. Ibid.

38. H. C. Triandis, "Collectivism vs. Individualism: A Reconceptualization of a Basic Concept in Cross-cultural Social Psychology," in G. K. Verma and Y. C. Bagley (eds.), *Cross-Cultural Studies of Personality, Attitudes, and Cognition* (London: Macmillan, 1988, pp. 60-95); Erez and Earley, *Culture, Self-Identity, and Work.*

39. S. E. Seashore, *Group Cohesiveness in the Industrial Work Group* (Ann Arbor, MI: Survey Research Center, Institute for Social Research, University of Michigan, 1954).

40. D. Krackhardt and L. W. Porter, "When Friends Leave: A Structural Analysis of the Relationship Between Turnover and Stayers' Attitudes," *Administrative Science Quarterly* 30 (1985), pp. 242-61.

41. L. Chang, "Amway, Once Barred in China, Now Finds Business Booming," *Wall Street Journal*, March 21, 2003, p. B1.

42. F. Dansereau, Jr., G. Graen, and W. J. Haga, "A Vertical Dyad Linkage Approach to Leadership within Formal Organizations: A Longitudinal Investigation of the Role Making Process," *Organizational Behavior and Human Performance* 13 (1975), pp. 46-78; G. B. Graen and J. F. Cashman, "A Role Making Model of Leadership in Formal Organizations: A Developmental Approach," in J. G. Hunt and L. L. Larson (eds.), *Leadership Frontiers* (Kent, OH: Kent State University Press, 1975), pp. 143-65; M. Mongeau, "Moving Mountains," *Harvard Business Review* 81, no. 1 (2003), pp. 41-47.

43. D. Mechanic, *Students Under Stress: A Study in the Social Psychology of Adaptation* (New York: Free Press, 1962).

44. C. O'Reilly, "Corporations, Culture, and Commitment: Motivation and Social Control in Organizations," *California Management Review* 31, no. 4 (1989), p. 12.

45. E. Schonfeld, "Have the Urge to Merge? You'd Better Think Twice," *Fortune* 135, 1997, pp. 114-16.

46. M. Rokeach, *The Nature of Human Values* (New York: Free Press, 1973).

47. Erez and Earley, *Culture, Self-Identity, and Work*; Eocke, *The Motivation Sequence, the Motivation Hub, and the Motivation Core.*

48. F. Elashmawi and R. R. Harris, *Multicultural Management: New Skills for Global Success* (Houston, TX: Gulf Publishing, 1993), table 6.2, p. 144; G. Morse, "Why We Misread Motives," *Harvard Business Review* 81, no. 1 (2003), p. 18.

49. H. C. Triandis, R. Brislin, and C. H. Hui, "Cross-cultural Training across the Individualism-Collectivism Divide," *International Journal of Intercultural Relations* 12 (1988), pp. 269-89.

50. K. Leung and M. H. Bond, "How Chinese and Americans Reward Task-related Contributions: A Preliminary Study," *Psychologia: An International Journal of Psychology in the Orient* 25, no. 1 (1982), pp. 32-39; M. H. Bond, K. Eeung, and K. C. Wan, "How Does Cultural Collectivism Operate? The Impact of Task and Maintenance Contributions on Reward Distribution," *Journal of Cross-Cultural Psychology* 47 (1982), pp. 793-804; K. Eeung and H. Park, "Effects of Interactional Goal on Choice of Allocation Rule: A Cross-national Study," *Organizational Behavior and Human Decision Processes* 37 (1986), pp. 111-20; K. I. Kim, H. Park, and N. Suzuki, "Reward Allocations in the United States, Japan, and Korea: A Comparison of Individualistic and Collectivistic Cultures," *Academy of Management Journal* 33 (1990), pp. 188-98; Chen, Choi, and Chi, "Making Justice Sense of Local-Expatriate Compensation Disparity," pp. 807-17.

51. M. Weber, *The Protestant Work Ethic and the Spirit of Capitalism* (T. Parsons, trans.) (New York: Scribner's, 1958); R. Wuthnow, "Religion and Economic Life," in N. J. Smelser and R. Swedbert (eds.), *The Handbook of Economic Sociology* (Princeton: Princeton University Press, 1994), pp. 620-46.

52. G. W. England and I. Harpaz, "Some Methodological and Analytic Considerations in Cross-national Comparative Research," *Journal of International Business Studies* 14, no. 2 (1983), pp. 49-59.

53. I. Harpaz and H. Fu, "Sork Centrality in Germany, Israel, Japan, and the United States," *Journal of Cross-Cultural Research* 31 (1997), pp. 171-200.

54. D. Finegold and S. Mohrman, "What Do Employees Really Want: The Perception vs. the Reality." Paper presented at the World Economics Forum Annual Meeting, Davos, Switzerland, 2001.

CHAPTER 13

1. J. Bunderson, "Team Member Functional Background and Involvement in Management Teams: Direct Effects and the Moderating Role of Power and Centralization," *Academy of Management Journal* 46 (2003), pp. 458-74; S. Finkelstein and D. Hambrick, *Strategic Leadership* (St. Paul, MN: West Publishing Company, 1996).

2. M.A. Hitt, R. D. Ireland, and R. E. Hoskisson, *Strategic Management: Competitiveness and Globalization* (Cincinnati, OH: South-Western Publishing, 2005).

3. S. Barsade, A. Ward, J. Turner, and J. Sonnenfeld, "To Your Heart's Content: A Model of Affective Diversity in Top Management Teams," *Administrative Science Quarterly* 45 (2000), pp. 802-36.

4. P. Sellers, "Get Over Yourself," *Fortune*, 2001, pp. 76-88.

5. H. J. Leavitt, "The Old Days, Hot Groups, and Managers' Lib," *Administrative Science Quarterly* 41 (1996), pp. 288-300; L. I. Glassop, "The Organizational Benefit of Teams," *Human Relations* 55, no. 2 (2002), pp. 225-49.

6. B. I. Kirkman and D. L. Shapiro, "The Impact of Cultural Values on Employee Resistance to Teams: Toward a Model of Globalized Self-managing Work Team Effectiveness," *Academy of Management Review* 22 (1997), pp. 730-57; S. S. K. Lam, X-P. Chen, and J. Schaubroeck, "Participative Decision Making and Employee Performance in Different Cultures: The Moderating Effects of Allocentrism/Idiocentrism and Efficacy," *Academy of Management Journal* 45, no. 5 (2002), pp. 905-14; D. C. Thomas and K. Au, "The Effect of Cultural Differences on Behavioral Responses to Low Job Satisfaction," *Journal of International Business Studies* 33, no. 2 (2002), pp. 309-26.

7. E. Sundstrom, K. P. de Meuse, and D. Futrell, "Work Teams: Applications and Effectiveness," *American Psychologist* 45, no. 2 (1990), pp. 120-33.

8. M. Cotrill, "Give Your Work Teams Time and Training," *Academy of Management Executive* 11, no. 3 (1997), pp. 87-89; R. D. Banker, J. M. Field, R. G. Schroeder, K. K. Y. Sinha, "Impact of Work Teams on Manufacturing Performance: A Longitudinal Field Study," *Academy of Management Journal* 39 (1996), pp. 867-90.

9. R. Peterson, "Ergonomics and an Office Renovation," *Editor and Publisher* 128, no. 44 (1995), pp. 14P-15P.

10. J. D. Zbar, "Hispanics Attract Publishers' Notice," *Advertising Age*, 1995, p. 12.

11. Anon, "Employee Empowerment Works for Revlon," *Quality* 34, no. 12 (1995), pp. 59-60.

12. E. Krapf, "Utility Player," *America's Network* 99, no. 11 (1995), p. 40.

13. K. A. Jehn and P. P. Shah, "Interpersonal Relationships and Task Performance: An Examination of Mediation Processes in Friendship and Acquaintance Groups," *Journal of Personality and Social Psychology* 71 (1997), pp. 775-90; Anon., "Friends Make Good Teammates," *Quality* 36, no. 1 (1997), p. 12; K. A. Mollica, B. Gray, and L. K. Trevino, "Racial Homophily and Its Persistence in Newcomers' Social Networks," *Organization Science* 14, no. 2 (2003), pp. 123-36.

14. Sundstrom et al., "Work Teams," p. 126; B. B. Baltes, M. W. Dickson, M. P. Sherman, C. C. Bauer, and J. S. LaGanke, "Computer-mediated Communication and Group Decision Making: A Meta-analysis," *Organizational Behavior and Human Decision Processes* 87, no. 1 (2002), pp. 156-79.

15. B. Mullen, C. Symons, L. Hu, and E. Salas, "Group Size, Leadership Behavior, and Subordinate Satisfaction," *Journal of General Psychology* 116, no. 2 (1989), pp. 155-70.

16. B. Mullen, D. A. Johnson, and S. D. Drake, "Organizational Productivity as a Function of Group Composition: A Self-attention Perspective," *Journal of Social Psychology* 127 (1987), pp. 143-50.

17. B. Latane, K. Williams, and S. Markings, "Social Loafing," *Psychology Today* 13, no. 5 (1979), pp. 104-10; P. C. Barley, "Social Loafing and Collectivism: A Comparison of the United States and the People's Republic of China," *Administrative Science Quarterly* 34 (1989), pp. 565-81; S. M. Murphy, S. J. Wayne, R. C. Liden, and B. Erdogan, "Understanding Social Loafing: The Role of Justice Perceptions and Exchange Relationships," *Human Relations* 56, no. 1 (2003), pp. 61-84; X-P. Chen and D. G. Bachrach, "Tolerance of Free-riding: The Effects of Defection Size, Defection Pattern, and Social Orientation in a Repeated Public Goods Dilemma," *Organizational Behavior and Human Decision Processes* 90, no. 1 (2003), pp. 139-47; H. Goren, R. Kurzban, and A. Rapoport, "Social Loafing vs. Social Enhancement: Public Goods Provisioning in Real-time with Irrevocable Commitments," *Organizational Behavior and Human Decision Processes* 90, no. 2 (2003), pp. 277-90.

18. K. L. Bettenhausen, "Five Years of Group Research: What We Have Learned and What Needs to Be Addressed," *Journal of Management* 17 (1991), pp. 345-81.

19. K. D. Williams, S. A. Nica, L. D. Baca, and B. Latane, "Social Loafing and Swimming: Effects of Identifiability on Individual and Relay Performance of Intercollegiate Swimmers, *Basic and Applied Social Psychology* 70 (1989), pp. 73-81.

20. W. K. Gabrenya, Y. Wang, and B. Latane, "Social Loafing on an Optimizing Task: Cross-cultural Differences among Chinese and Americans," *Journal of Cross-Cultural Psychology* 16 (1985), pp. 223-42.

21. M. E. Shaw, *Group Dynamics: The Psychology of Small Group Behavior*, 3rd ed. (New York: McGraw-Hill, 1981).

22. R. E. Silverman, "For Charlie Kim, Company of Friends Proves a Lonely Place," *Wall Street Journal*, pp. A1+.

23. L. H. Pelled, "Demographic Diversity, Conflict, and Work Group Outcomes: An Intervening Process Theory," *Administrative Science Quarterly* 7 (1996), pp. 615-31; L. H. Pelled, K. M. Eisenhardt, and K. R. Xin, "Exploring the Black Box: An Analysis of Work Group Diversity, Conflict, and Performance," *Administrative Science Quarterly* 44 (1999), pp. 1-28; K. Jehn, G. B. Northcraft, and M. A. Neale, "Why Differences Make a Difference: A Field Study of Diversity, Conflict, and Performance in Workgroups," *Administrative Science Quarterly* 44 (1999), pp. 741-63.

24. S. Caudron, "Keeping Team Conflict Alive," *Training and Development* 52, no. 9 (1998), pp. 48-52; G. S. Van der Vegt and O. Janssen, "Joint Impact of Interdependence and Group Diversity on Innovation," *Journal of Management* 29, no. 5 (2003), pp. 729-51.

25. S. G. Cohen, "What Makes Teams Work: Group Effectiveness Research from the Shop Floor to the Executive Suite," *Journal of Management* 23 (1997), pp. 239-90; J. T. Polzer, L. P. Milton, and W. B. Swann, Jr., "Capitalizing on Diversity: Interpersonal Congruence in Small Work Groups," *Administrative Science Quarterly* 47, no. 2 (2002), pp. 296-324; Van der Vegt and Janssen, "Joint Impact of Interdependence," pp. 729-51.

26. Pelled, "Demographic Diversity, Conflict, and Work Group Outcomes," Pelled et al., "Exploring the Black Box"; J. A. Chatman and F. J. Flynn, "The Influence of Demographic Heterogeneity on the Emergence and Consequences of Cooperative Norms in Work Teams," *Academy of Management Journal* 44 (2001), pp. 956-74; D. A. Harrison, K. H. Price, and M. P. Bell, "Beyond Relational Demography: Time and the Effects of Surface- and Deep-level Diversity on Work Group Cohesion," *Academy of Management Journal* 41 (1998), pp. 96-107; Jehn et al., "Why Differences Make a Difference"; J. S. Bunderson and K. M. Sutcliffe, "Comparing Alternative Conceptualizations of Functional Diversity in Management Teams: Process and Performance Effects," *Academy of Management Journal* 45, no. 5 (2002), pp. 875-93; Harrison, Price, Gavin, and Florey, "Time, Teams, and Task Performance," pp. 1029-45.

27. Chatman and Flynn, "The Influence of Demographic Heterogeneity."

28. Harrison et al., "Beyond Relational Demography."

29. J. Gordon, M. Hequet, C. Lee, M. Picard, et al., "Workplace Blues," *Training* 35, no. 2 (1996), p. 16.

30. M. S. Abramson, "First Teams," *Government Executive* 18, no. 5 (1996), pp. 53-58; L. F. Brajkovich, "Executive Commentary," *Academy of Management Executive* 17, no. 1 (2003), pp. 110-11; L. Thompson, "Improving the Creativity of Organizational Work Groups," *Academy of Management Executive* 17, no. 1 (2003), pp. 96-97; Van der Vegt and Janssen, "Joint Impact of Interdependence and Group Diversity," pp. 729-51; R. Sethi, D. C. Smith, and C. W. Park, "How to Kill a Team's Creativity," *Harvard Business Review* 80, no. 8 (2002), pp. 16-17.

31. C. C. Manz and H. P. Sims, Jr., "Leading Workers to Lead Themselves: The External Leadership of Self-managing Work Teams," *Administrative Science Quarterly* 32 (1987), pp. 106-29.

32. S. Caminiti, "What Team Leaders Need to Know," *Fortune*, 1995, pp. 93-100.

33. C. Fishman, "Creative Tension," *Fast Company*, November, 2000, pp. 359-66.

34. Shaw, *Group Dynamics*; M. C. Thomas-Hunt, T. Y. Ogden, and M. A. Neale, "Who's Really Sharing? Effects of Social and Expert Status on Knowledge Exchange within Groups," *Management Science* 49, no. 4 (2003), pp. 464-77; T. R. Tyler and S. L. Blader, "Autonomous vs. Comparative Status: Must We Be Better than Others to Feel Good About Ourselves?" *Organizational Behavior and Human Decision Processes* 89, no. 1 (2002), pp. 813-38; P. M. Valcour, "Managerial Behavior in a Multiplex Role System," *Human Relations* 55, no. 10 (2002), pp. 1163-88.

35. J. E. Driskell and E. Salas, "Group Decision Making Under Stress," *Journal of Applied Psychology* 76 (1991), pp. 473-78.

36. Shaw, *Group Dynamics*.

37. Ibid.

38. D. C. Feldman, "The Development and Enforcement of Group Norms," *Academy of Management Review* 9 (1984), pp. 47-53.

39. R. A. Proehl, "A Panacea or Just Another Headache?" *Supervision* 57, no. 1 (1996), pp. 6-8.

40. Shaw, *Group Dynamics*. See also N. Nicholson (ed.), *Encyclopedic Dictionary of Organizational Behavior* (Oxford, UK: Blackwell, 1995), p. 199.

41. Cohen, "What Makes Teams Work."

42. D. Druckman and J. A. Swets (eds.), *Enhancing Human Performance: Issues, Theories and Techniques.* National Research Council. (Washington, DC: National Academy Press, 1988).

43. Ibid.

44. Shaw, *Group Dynamics*; Sethi, Smith, and Park, "How to Kill a Team's Creativity," pp. 16-17.

45. Ibid., p. 218; Sethi, Smith, and Park, "How to Kill a Team's Creativity," pp. 16-17.

46. D. M. Landers, M. O. Wilkinson, B. D. Hatfield, and H. Barber, "Causality and the Cohesion–Performance Relationship," *Journal of Sport Psychology* 4, no. 2 (1982), pp. 170-83; J. A. LePine, J. R. Hollenbeck, D. R. Ilgen, J. A. Colquitt, and A. Ellis, "Gender Composition, Situational Strength, and Team Decision-making Accuracy: A Criterion Decomposition Approach," *Organizational Behavior and Human Decision Processes* 88, no. 1 (2002), pp. 445-75.

47. J. R. Hackman, "The Design of Work Teams," in J. W. Lorsch (ed.), *Handbook of Organizational Behavior* (Upper Saddle River, NJ: Prentice Hall, 1987), pp. 315-42.

48. Caminiti, "What Team Leaders Need to Know."

49. Banker et al., "Impact of the Work Teams on Manufacturing Performance."

50. C. D. Cramton, "The Mutual Knowledge Problem and Its Consequences for Dispersed Collaboration," *Organization Science* 12 (2001), pp. 346-67; C. D. Cramton, "Finding Common Ground in Dispersed Collaboration," *Organizational Dynamics* 4 (2002), pp. 356-71; M. K. Ahuja and J. A. Galvin, "Socialization in Virtual Groups," *Journal of Management* 29, no. 2 (2003), pp. 161-86.

51. Cramton, "Finding Common Ground in Dispersed Collaboration"; Ahuja and Galvin, "Socialization in Virtual Groups," pp. 161-86.

52. B. E. Ashforth and F. Mael, "Social Identity Theory and the Organization," *Academy of Management Review* 14 (1989), pp. 20-39; Bettenhausen, "Five Years of Group Research."

53. J. S. Heinem and E. Jacobsen, "A Model of Task Group Development in Complex Organizations and a Strategy of Implementation," *Academy of Management Review* 1, no. 4 (1976), pp. 98-111; B. W. Tuckman and M. A. Jensen, "Stages of Small-group Development Revisited," *Group and Organization Studies* 2 (1977), pp. 419-27; R. L. Moreland and J. N. Levine, "Group Dynamics Over Time: Development and Socialization in Small Groups," in J. M. McGrath (ed.), *The Social Psychology of Time: New Perspectives* (Sage Focus editions, vol. 19, pp. 151-81) (Newbury Park, CA: Sage, 1988); Sundstrom et al., "Work Teams"; Bettenhausen, "Five Years of Group Research"; A. Chang, P. Bordia, and J. Duck, "Punctuated Equilibrium and Linear Progression: Toward a New Understanding of Group Development," *Academy of Management Journal* 46, no. 1 (2003), pp. 106-17.

54. B. W. Tuckman, "Development Sequence in Small Groups," *Psychological Bulletin* 63 (1965), pp. 384-99; Tuckman and Jensen, "Stages of Small Group Development Revisited."

55. Sundstrom et al., "Work Teams," p. 127.

56. J. M. Perdue, "A Global Success Story," *Oil and Gas Investor. Supplement: ExxonMobil's Hoover/Diana—A deepwaterpioneer*, pp. 16-19.

57. A. De Marco, "Teamwork Pays Off for Ross and Sterling Winthrop," *Facilities Design and Management* 72, no. 12 (1993), pp. 38-41.

58. S. Convey. "Performance Measurement in Cross-functional Teams," *CMA Magazine* 68, no. 8 (1994), pp. 13-15.

59. M. H. Safizadeh, "The Case of Workgroups in Manufacturing Operations," *California Management Review* 35, no. 4 (1991), pp. 61-82; A. Erez, J. A. Lepine, and H. Elms, "Effects of Rotated Leadership and Peer Evaluation on the Functioning and Effectiveness of Self-managed Teams: A Quasi-experiment," *Personnel Psychology* 55, no. 4 (2002), pp. 929-48; L. I. Glassop, "The Organizational Benefit of Teams," *Human Relations* 55, no. 2 (2002), pp. 225-49.

60. J. Thompson, "Joe versus the Bureaucracy," *Government Executive* 27, no. 10 (1995), pp. 50-55.

61. Kirkman and Shapiro, "The Impact of Cultural Values on Employee Resistance to Teams."

62. P. Baker, "Open Sesame!" *Works Management* 54, no. 8 (2001), p. 35.

63. K. Lovelace, D. L. Shapiro, and L. R. Weingart, "Maximizing Cross-functional New Product Teams' Innovativeness and Constraint Adherence: A Conflict Communications Perspective," *Academy of Management Journal* 44 (2001), pp. 779-93.

64. A. R. Jassawalla, and H. C. Sashittal, "Building Collaborative Cross-functional New Product Teams," *Academy of Management Executive* 13, no. 3 (1999), pp. 50-63; Bunderson and Sutcliffe, "Comparing Alternative Conceptualizations of Functional Diversity in Management Teams," pp. 875-93; Sethi, Smith, and Park, "How to Kill a Team's Creativity," pp. 16-17.

65. J. M. Liedtka, "Collaborating Across Lines of Business for Competitive Advantage," *Academy of Management Executive* 10, no. 2 (1996), pp. 20-38; Sethi, Smith, and Park, "How to Kill a Team's Creativity," pp. 16-17.

66. J. J. Distefano and M. L. Maznevski, "Creating Value with Diverse Teams in Global Management," *Organizational Dynamics* 29 (2000), pp. 45-63.

67. S. Caspar, "Virtual Teams, Real Benefits," *Network World* 18, no. 39 (2001), p. 45.

68. J. A. Cannon-Bowers and E. Salas, "Teamwork Competencies: The Interaction of Team Member Knowledge, Skills, and Attitudes," in H. F. O'Neil Jr. (ed.), *Workforce Readiness: Competencies and Assessment* (Mahwah, NJ:. Lawrence Erlbaum Associates, 1997), pp. 151-74; J. A. Cannon-Bowers and E. Salas, "A Framework for Developing Team Performance Measures in Training," in M. T. Brannick, E. Salas, and C. Prince (eds.), *Team*

Performance Assessment and Measurement: Theory, Methods, and Applications (Mahwah, NJ: Lawrence Erlbaum Associates, 1997); J.A. Cannon-Bowers, S. I. Tannenbaum, E. Salas, and C. E. Volpe, "Defining Competencies and Establishing Team Training Requirements," in R.A. Guzzo, E. Salas and Associates (eds.), *Team Effectiveness and Decision Making in Organizations* (San Francisco: Jossey-Bass, 1995); E. Salas, T. L. Dickinson, S.A. Converse, and S. I. Tannenbaum, "Toward an Understanding of Team Performance and Training," in R. Swezey and E. Salas (eds.), *Teams: Their Training and Performance* (Norwood, NJ: Ablex, 1992), pp. 3–29; G.A. Okhuysen and K. M. Eisenhardt, "Integrating Knowledge in Groups: How Formal Interventions Enable Flexibility," *Organization Science* 13, no. 4 (2002), pp. 370–86.

69. Cannon-Bowers et al., "Defining Competencies and Establishing Team Training Requirements."

70. Cannon-Bowers and Salas, "Teamwork Competencies"; Cannon-Bowers and Salas, "A Framework for Developing Team Performance Measures in Training"; Cannon-Bowers et al., "Defining Competencies and Establishing Team Training Requirements"; Salas et al., "Toward an Understanding of Team Performance and Training."

71. S. Caudron, "Keeping Team Conflict Alive," pp. 48–52.

72. A. C. Amason, W.A. Hochwater, K. R. Thompson, and A. W. Harrison, "Conflict: An Important Dimension in Successful Management Teams," *Organizational Dynamics* 24, no. 2 (1995), pp. 20–35; S. Schulz-Hardt, M. Jochims, and D. Frey, "Productive Conflict in Group Decision Making: Genuine and Contrived Dissent as Strategies to Counteract Biased Information Seeking," *Organizational Behavior and Human Decision Processes* 88, no. 2 (2002), pp. 563–86.

73. K.A. Jehn, "A Multimethod Examination of the Benefits and Detriments of Intragroup Conflict," *Administrative Science Quarterly* 40 (1995), pp. 256–82; Schulz-Hardt, Jochims, and Frey, "Productive Conflict in Group Decision Making," pp. 563–86.

74. Amason et al., "Conflict"; K. M. Eisenhardt, J. L. Kahwajy, and L. J. Bourgeois, III, "Conflict and Strategic Choice: How Top Management Teams Disagree," *California Management Review* 39, no. 2 (1997), pp. 42–62; K.A. Jehn and E.A. Mannix, "The Dynamic Nature of Conflict: A Longitudinal Study of Intragroup Conflict and Group Performance," *Academy of Management Journal* 44 (2001), pp. 238–51; T. L. Simons and R. S. Peterson, "Task Conflict and Relationship Conflict in Top Management Teams: The Pivotal Role of Intragroup Trust," *Journal of Applied Psychology* 85 (2000), pp. 102–11; Pelled, Eisenhardt, and Xin, "Exploring the Black Box."

75. Jehn, "A Multimethod Examination of the Benefits and Detriments of Intragroup Conflict."

76. Amason et al., "Conflict."

77. Ibid.; Jehn, "A Multimethod Examination of the Benefits and Detriments of Intragroup Conflict."

78. Pelled, Eisenhardt, and Xin, "Exploring the Black Box."

79. Pelled, "Demographic Diversity, Conflict, and Work Group Outcomes."

80. Jehn, Gregory, and Neale, "Why Differences Make a Difference."

81. Amason et al., "Conflict."

82. Eisenhardt et al., "Conflict and Strategic Choice."

83. Jehn et al., "Why Differences Make a Difference."

84. Jenn and Mannix, "The Dynamic Nature of Conflict."

85. D. R. Forsyth, "An Introduction to Group Dynamics" (Monterey, CA: Brooks/Cole Publishing, 1983).

86. G.A. Neuman and J. Wright, "Team Effectiveness: Beyond Skills and Cognitive Ability," *Journal of Applied Psychology* 84 (1999), pp. 376–89; D. E. Hyatt and T. M. Ruddy, "An Examination of the Relationship Between Work Group Characteristics and Performance: Once More into the Breech," *Personnel Psychology* 50 (1997), pp. 553–85; M.A. Campion, E. M. Papper, and G. J. Medsker, "Relations Between Work Team Characteristics and Effectiveness: A Replication and Extension," *Personnel Psychology* 49 (1996), pp. 429–52; Cohen and Bailey, "What Makes Teams Work."

87. J. Fitz-Enz, "Measuring Team Effectiveness," *HR Focus* 74, no. 8 (1997), p. 3.

88. J. R. Hackman (ed.), *Groups That Work (and Those That Don't)*.

89. J. Huey, "Eisner Explains Everything," *Fortune* 1995, pp. 44–68.

90. Hackman, *Groups that Work*.

91. Campion et al., "Relations Between Work Team Characteristics and Effectiveness"; Hyatt and Ruddy, "An Examination of the Relationship Between Work Group Characteristics and Performance."

92. R. Wageman and G. Baker, "Incentives and Cooperation: The Joint Effects of Task and Reward Interdependence on Group Performance," *Journal of Organizational Behavior* 18, no. 2 (1997), pp. 139–58.

93. Banker et al., "Impact of Work Teams on Manufacturing Performance"; Cottrill, "Give Your Teams Time and Training."

94. Abramson, "First Teams."

95. Cohen and Bailey, "What Makes Teams Work."

96. G. L. Hallam, "Seven Common Beliefs About Teams: Are They True?" *Leadership in Action* 17, no. 3 (1997), pp. 1–4.

97. G. Ahuja and M. Lampert, "Entrepreneurship in the Large Corporation: A Longitudinal Study of How Established Firms Create Breakthrough Inventions," *Strategic Management Journal* 22 (Special Issue) (2001), pp. 521–43.

CHAPTER 14

1. S. Bing, "Business as a Second Language," *Fortune*, 1998, pp. 57–58.

2. K. Krone, F. M. Jablin, and L. L. Putnam, "Communication Theory and Organizational Communication: Multiple Perspectives," in F. M. Japlin, L. L. Putnam, K. H. Roberts, and L. W. Porter (eds.), *Handbook of Organizational Communication: An Interdisciplinary Perspective* (Newbury Park, CA: Sage Publications, 1987).

3. H. C. Triandis, *Culture and Social Behavior* (New York: McGraw-Hill, 1994); B.A. Bechky, "Sharing Meaning Across Occupational Communities: The Transformation of Understanding on a Production Floor," *Organization Science* 14, no. 3 (2003), p. 312; M. Becerra and A. K. Gupta, "Perceived Trustworthiness within the Organization: The Moderating Impact of Communication Frequency on Trustor and Trustee Effects," *Organization Science* 14, no. 1 (2003), pp. 32–44.

4. R. L. Daft and R. H. Lengel, "Information Richness: A New Approach to Managerial Behavior and Organization Design," in L. L. Cummings and B. Staw (eds.), *Research in Organizational Behavior*, vol. 6 (Greenwich, CT: JAI, 1984), pp. 191–223; R. L. Daft and R. H. Lengel, "Organizational Information Requirements, Media Richness and Structural Design," *Management Science* 32 (1986), pp. 554–72; K. Miller, *Organizational Communication: Approaches and Processes*, 2nd ed. (Belmont, CA: Wadsworth, 1999).

5. L. K. Trevino, R. L. Daft, and R. H. Lengel, "Understanding Managers Media Concerns," in J. Fulk and C. Steinfeile (eds.), *Organizations and Communication Technology* (Newbury Park, CA: Sage Publications, 1990); Anonymous, "How to Create Communications Materials Employees Will Actually Use," *Harvard Business Review* 80, no. 1 (1990), p. 102.

6. B. B. Baltes, M. W. Dickson, M. P. Sherman, C. C. Bauer, and J. S. LaGanke, "Computer-mediated Communication and Group Decision Making: A Meta-analysis," *Organizational Behavior and Human Decision Processes* 87, no. 1 (2002), pp. 156–79.

7. J. Yates and W. J. Orlikowski, "Genres of Organizational Communication: A Structural Approach to Studying Communication and Media," *Academy of Management Review* 17 (1992), pp. 299-326.

8. L. W. Porter, E. E. Lawler, III, and J. R. Hackman, *Behavior in Organizations* (New York: McGraw-Hill, 1975).

9. K. Davis, "The Care and Cultivation of the Corporate Grapevine," *Dun's Review* 102, no. 1 (1973), pp. 44-47.

10. C. Dellarocas, "The Digitization of Word of Mouth: Promise and Challenges of Online Feedback Mechanisms," *Management Science* 49, no. 10 (2003), pp. 1407-24.

11. Anon, "BASF Launches SM/PO Venture," *Chemical Market Reporter* 262, no. 11 (2002), p. 23.

12. "He Said, She Said," *Communications* 46, no. 9 (2003), p. 11; H. Ibarra, "Homophily and Differential Returns: Sex Differences in Network Structure and Access in an Advertising Firm," *Administrative Science Quarterly* 37 (1992), pp. 422-47; H. Ibarra, "Personal Networks of Women and Minorities in Management: A Conceptual Framework," *Academy of Management Review* 18 (1993), pp. 56-87; H. Ibarra, "Race, Opportunity, and Diversity of Social Circles in Managerial Networks," *Academy of Management Journal* 38 (1995), pp. 673-703; K. A. Mollica, B. Gray, and L. K. Trevino, "Racial Homophily and Its Persistence in Newcomers' Social Networks," *Organization Science* 14, no. 2 (2003), pp. 123-36.

13. J. M. Beyer, P. Cattopadhyay, E. George, W. H. Glick et al., "The Selective Perception of Managers Revisited," *Academy of Management Journal* 40 (1997), pp. 716-37.

14. A. Tversky and D. Kahneman, "Rational Choice and the Framing of Decisions," *Journal of Business* 59 (1986), pp. S251-78; I. Grugulis, "Nothing serious? Candidates' Use of Humour in Management Training," *Human Relations* 55, no. 4 (2002), pp. 387-406.

15. C. M. Jones, "Shifting Sands: Women, Men, and Communication," *Journal of Communication* 49 (1999), pp. 148-55.

16. C. R. Rogers and F. J. Roethlisberger, "Barriers and Gateways to Communication," *Harvard Business Review* 69, no. 6 (1991), pp. 105-11; L. Perlow and S. Williams, "Is Silence Killing Your Company?" *Harvard Business Review* 81, no. 5 (2003), pp. 52-58.

17. R. Wilkinson, "Do You Speak Obscuranta?" *Supervision* 49, no. 9 (1988), pp. 3-5; C. Argyris, "Four Steps to Chaos," *Harvard Business Review* 81, no. 10 (2003), p. 140.

18. R. Harrison, *Beyond Words: An Introduction to Nonverbal Communication* (Upper Saddle River, NJ: Prentice Hall, 1974); A. Kristof-Brown, M. R. Barrick, and M. Franke, "Applicant Impression Management: Dispositional Influences and Consequences for Recruiter Perceptions of Fit and Similarity," *Journal of Management* 28, no. 1 (2002), pp. 27-46; H. A. Elfenbein and N. Ambady, "Predicting Workplace Outcomes from the Ability to Eavesdrop on Feelings," *Journal of Applied Psychology* 87, no. 5 (2002), pp. 963-71.

19. J. A. Mausehund, S. A. Timm, and A. S. King, "Diversity Training: Effects of an Intervention Treatment on Nonverbal Awareness," *Business Communication Quarterly* 58, no. 1 (1995), pp. 27-30.

20. J. H. Robinson, "Professional Communication in Korea: Playing Things by Eye," *IEEE Transactions on Professional Communication* 39, no. 3 (1996), pp. 129-34; G. E. Kersten, S. T. Koeszegi, and R. Vetschera, "The Effects of Culture in Computer-mediated Negotiations," *Journal of Information Technology Theory and Application* 5, no. 2 (2003), pp. 1-28.

21. T. E. McNamara and K. Hayashi, "Culture and Management: Japan and the West Towards a Transnational Corporate Culture," *Management Japan* 27, no. 2 (1994), pp. 3-13.

22. S. Okazaki and J. Alonso, "Right Messages for the Right Site: Online Creative Strategies by Japanese Multinational Corporations," *Journal of Marketing Communications* 9, no. 4 (2002),

pp. 221-240; M. Rosch and K. G. Segler, "Communication with Japanese," *Management International Review* 27, no. 4 (1987), pp. 56-67.

23. C. Gouttefarde, "Host National Culture Shock: What Management Can Do," *European Business Review* 92, no. 4 (1992), pp. 1-3.

24. H. Triandis, "Cross-Cultural Contributions to Theory in Social Psychology," in W. B. Gudykunst and Y. Y. Kim (eds.), *Reading on Communication with Strangers* (p. 75) (New York: McGraw-Hill, 1992), p. 75; R. S. Marshall and D. M. Boush, "Dynamic Decision-making: A Cross-Cultural Comparison of U.S. and Peruvian Export Managers," *Journal of International Business Studies* 32, no. 4 (2001), pp. 873-93; T. R. Tyler and S. L. Blader, "Autonomous vs. Comparative Status: Must We Be Better Than Others to Feel Good About Ourselves?" *Organizational Behavior and Human Decision Processes* 89, no. 1 (2002), pp. 813-38; L. Huff and L. Kelley, "Levels of Organizational Trust in Individualist versus Collectivist Societies: A Seven-nation Study," *Organization Science* 14, no. 1 (2003), pp. 81-90; A. C. Lewis and S. J. Sherman, "Hiring You Makes Me Look Bad: Social-identity Based Reversal of the Ingroup Favoritism Effect," *Organizational Behavior and Human Decision Processes* 90, no. 2 (2003), pp. 262-76.

25. S. Carlson, "International Transmission of Information and the Business Firm," *Annals of the American Academy of Political and Social Science* 412 (1974), pp. 55-63; Marshall and Boush, "Dynamic Decision-making," pp. 873-93; Y. Luo, "Building Trust in Cross-cultural Collaborations: Toward a Contingency Perspective," *Journal of Management* 28, no. 5 (2002), pp. 669-94.

26. J. Main, "How 21 Men Got Global in 35 Days," *Fortune*, 1989, pp. 71-79.

27. C. Peter, P. Scott, and J. Calvert, "Chinese Business Face: Communication Behaviors and Teaching Approaches," *Business Communication Quarterly* 66, no. 4 (2003), pp. 19-23; R. S. Burnert, "Ni Zao: Good Morning, China," *Business Horizons* 33, no. 6 (1990), pp. 65-71.

28. R. Alsop, "Playing Well with Others," *Wall Street Journal*, September 9, 2002, p. R1-1; A. Kristof-Brown, M. R. Barrick, and M. Franke, "Applicant Impression Management: Dispositional Influences and Consequences for Recruiter Perceptions of Fit and Similarity," *Journal of Management* 28, no. 1 (2003), pp. 27-46.

29. T. D. Lewis and G. H. Graham, "Six Ways to Improve Your Communication Skills," *Internal Auditor* (1988), p. 25.

30. G. M. Barton, "Manage Words Effectively," *Personnel Journal* 69, no. 1 (1990), pp. 32-40.

31. L. W. Porter and L. E. McKibbin, *Management Education and Development: Drift or Thrust into the 21st Century* (New York: McGraw-Hill, 1988).

32. S. L. Silk, "Making Your Speech Memorable," *Association Management* 46, no. 1 (1994), pp. L59-L62.

33. A. DeMeyer, "Tech Talk: How Managers Are Stimulating Global R&D Communication," *Sloan Management Review* 32, no. 3 (1991), pp. 49-58.

34. R. Fisher and W. Ury, *Getting to Yes* (London: Simon & Schuster, 1987); K. A. Wade-Benzoni, A. J. Hoffman, L. L. Thompson, D. A. Moore et al., "Barriers to Resolution in Ideologically Based Negotiations: The Role of Values and Institutions," *Academy of Management Review* 27, no. 1 (2002), pp. 41-57.

35. Ibid.

36. Ibid., p. 54.

37. N. J. Adler, *International Dimensions of Organizational Behavior*, 2nd ed. (Boston: PWS-Kent, 1991), p. 185.

38. G. Fisher, *International Negotiations* (Chicago: Intercultural Press, 1980); J. L. Graham, "Brazilian, Japanese, and American Business Negotiations," *Journal of International Business*

Studies 14, no. 1 (1983), pp. 47-61; J. L. Graham and N. M. Lam, "The Chinese Negotiation," *Harvard Business Review* 81, no. 10 (2003), pp. 82-91; J. K. Sebenius, "The Hidden Challenge of Cross-border Negotiations," *Harvard Business Review* 80, no. 3 (2002), pp. 76-85; L. J. Kray, A. D. Galinsky, and L. Thompson, "Reversing the Gender Gap in Negotiations: An Exploration of Stereotype Regeneration," *Organizational Behavior and Human Decision Processes* 87, no. 2 (2002), pp. 386-409.

39. J. L. Graham and R. A. Herberger Jr., "Negotiators Abroad Don't Shoot from the Hip," *Harvard Business Review* 83, no. 4 (1983), pp. 160-68.

40. R. Fisher and W. Ury, *Getting to Yes*.

41. M. Lee, "10 Myths about Multicultural Customers," *Selling*, November 2003, pp. 10-12; K. Kumar, S. Noneth, and C. Yauger, "Cultural Approaches to the Process of Business Negotiation: Understanding Cross-Cultural Differences in Negotiating Behaviors," in C. L. Swanson (ed.), *International Research in the Business Disciplines* (Greenwich, CT: JAI Press, 1993), pp. 79-90; B. M. Hawrysh and J. L. Zaichkowsky, "Cultural Approaches to Negotiations: Understanding the Japanese," *International Marketing Review* 7, no. 2 (1990), pp. 28-42.

42. Kumar et al., "Cultural Approaches to the Process of Business Negotiations."

43. Graham and Herberger, "Negotiators Abroad Don't Shoot from the Hip."

44. Kumar et al., "Cultural Approaches to the Process of Business Negotiations."

45. N. Woliansky, "We Do (Do Not) Accept Your Offer," *Management Review* 75, no. 12 (1989), pp. 54-55; Kumar et al., "Cultural Approaches to the Process of Business Negotiations."

46. Kumar et al., "Cultural Approaches to the Process of Business Negotiations," p. 86.

47. Graham and Herberger, "Negotiators Abroad Don't Shoot from the Hip."

48. J. L. Graham and N. J. Adler, "Cross-cultural Interaction: The International Comparison Fallacy?" *Journal of International Business Studies* 20 (1989), pp. 515-37; C. Barnum and N. Wolniasky, "Why Americans Fail at Overseas Negotiations," *Management Review* 75, no. 10 (1989), pp. 55-57.

49. Kumar et al., "Cultural Approaches to the Process of Business Negotiations."

CHAPTER 15

1. S. A. Snell, M. A. Shadur, and P. M. Wright, "Human Resources Strategy: The Era of Our Ways," in M. A. Hitt, R. E. Freeman, and J. S. Harrison (eds.), *Handbook of Strategic Management* (Oxford, UK: Blackwell Publishing, 2001).

2. M. A. Hitt and R. D. Ireland, "The Essence of Strategic Leadership: Managing Human and Social Capital," *Journal of Leadership and Organization Studies* 9 (2002), pp. 3-14.

3. P. M. Wright, B. B. Dunford, and S. A. Snell, "Human Resources and the Resource-based View of the Firm," *Journal of Management* 27 (2001), pp. 701-21.

4. M. W. McCall and M. M. Lombardo, *Off the Track: Why and How Successful Executives Get Derailed* (Greensboro, N.C.: Center for Creative Leadership, 1983).

5. D. Ulrich, *Human Resource Champions* (Boston: Harvard Business School Press, 1997).

6. R. W. Rowden, "Potential Roles of the Human Resource Management Professional in the Strategic Planning Process," *S.A.M. Advanced Management Journal* 64, no. 3 (1999), pp. 22-27.

7. M. Huselid, S. Jackson, and R. Schuler, "Technical and Strategic Human Resource Management Effectiveness as Determinants of Firm Performance," *Academy of Management Journal* 40 (1997), pp. 171-88; K. S. Law, D. K. Tse, and N. Zhou, "Does

Human Resource Management Matter in a Transitional Economy? China As an Example," *Journal of International Business Studies* 34, no. 3 (2003), pp. 255-65; S. L. Rynes, K. G. Brown, and A. E. Colbert, "Seven Common Misconceptions About Human Resource Practices: Research Findings Versus Practitioner Beliefs," *Academy of Management Executive* 16, no. 3 (2002), pp. 92-102; R. Batt, "Managing Customer Services: Human Resource Practices, Quit Rates, and Sales Growth," *Academy of Management Journal* 45, no. 3 (2002), pp. 587-97.

8. J. Pfeffer, *Competitive Advantage through People: Unleashing the Power of the Workforce* (Boston: Harvard Business School Press, 1994).

9. S. Bates, "Growing Pains Are Cited in Study of HR Outsourcing," *HRMagazine* 47, no. 8 (2002), p. 10; D. P. Lepak and S. A. Snell, "Examining the Human Resource Architecture: The Relationships Among Human Capital, Employment, and Human Resource Configurations," *Journal of Management* 28, no. 4 (2002), pp. 517-43.

10. W. Wiggenhorn, "Motorola U: When Training Becomes an Education," *Harvard Business Review*, July-August 1990, pp. 71-83; Lepak and Snell, "Examining the Human Resource Architecture," pp. 517-43.

11. M. O'Daniel, "Online Assistance for Job Seekers," *New Strait Times*, November 11, 2003; L. Goff, "Job Surfing," *Computer-World* 30, no. 36 (1996), p. 81; M. K. McGee, "Job Hunting on the Internet," *Informationweek* 576 (1996), p. 98.

12. D. Terpstra, "The Search for Effective Methods," *HR Focus* 73, no. 5 (1996), pp. 16-17.

13. J. S. Black, H. B. Gregersen, M. E. Mendenhall, and L. Stroh, *Global People through International Assignments* (Reading, MA: Addison-Wesley, 1999).

14. J. Conway, R. Jako, and D. Goodman, "A Meta-Analysis of Inter-rater and Internal Consistency Reliability of Selection Interviews," *Journal of Applied Psychology* 80, no. 5 (1995), pp. 565-79; M. McDaniel, D. Whetzel, F. Schmidt, and S. Maurer, "The Validity of Employment Interviews: A Comprehensive Review and Meta-Analysis," *Journal of Applied Psychology* 79, no. 4 (1994), pp. 599-616.

15. G. Dessler, *Human Resource Management*, 8th ed. (Upper Saddle River, NJ: Prentice Hall, 2000), Chapter 6.

16. L. Rudner, "Pre-Employment Testing and Employee Productivity," *Public Management* 21, no. 2 (1992), pp. 133-50; P. Lowry, "The Assessment Center: Effects of Varying Consensus Procedures," *Public Personnel Management* 21, no. 2 (1992), pp. 171-83; T. Payne, N. Anderson, and T. Smith, "Assessment Centres: Selection Systems and Cost- Effectiveness," *Personnel Review* 21, no. 4 (1992), pp. 48-56; D. J. Schleicher, D. V. Day, B. Mayes, and R. E. Riggio, "A New Frame for Frame-of-Reference Training: Enhancing the Construct Validity of Assessment Centers," *Journal of Applied Psychology* 87, no. 4 (2002), pp. 735-46; F. Lievens, "Trying to Understand the Different Pieces of the Construct Validity Puzzle of Assessment Centers: An Examination of Assessor and Assessee Effects," *Journal of Applied Psychology* 87, no. 4 (2002), pp. 675-86; W. Arthur, Jr., E. A. Day, T. L. McNelly, and P. S. Edens, "A Meta-analysis of the Criterion-related Validity of Assessment Center Dimensions," *Personnel Psychology* 56, no. 1 (2003), pp. 125-54; D. J. Woehr and W. Arthur, Jr., "The Construct-related Validity of Assessment Center Ratings: A Review and Meta-analysis of the Role of Methodological Factors," *Journal of Management* 29, no. 2 (2003), p. 231; K. Dayan, R. Kasten, and S. Fox, "Entry-level Police Candidate Assessment Center: An Efficient Tool for a Hammer to Kill a Fly?" *Personnel Psychology* 55, no. 4 (2002), pp. 827-49.

17. R. Bentley, "Candidates Face Alternative Testing," *Computer Weekly*, November 18, 2003, p. 54; S. Adler, "Personality Tests for Salesforce Selection," *Review of Business* 16, no. 1 (1994), pp. 27-31.

18. M. McCullough, "Can Integrity Testing Improve Market Conduct?" *LIMRA's Marketfacts* 15, no. 2 (1996), pp. 15–16; H. J. Bernardin and D. Cooke, "Validity of an Honesty Test in Predicting Theft among Convenience Store Employees," *Academy of Management Journal* 36, no. 50 (1993), pp. 1097–108.

19. B. Murphy, W. Barlow, and D. Hatch, "Employer-Mandated Physicals for Over-70 Employees Violate the ADEA," *Personnel Journal* 72, no. 6 (1993), p. 24; R. Ledman and D. Brown, "The Americans with Disabilities Act," *SAM Advanced Management Journal* 58, no. 2 (1993), pp. 17–20.

20. C. Fisher, "Organizational Socialization: An Integrative Review," in K. Rowland and J. Ferris (eds.), *Research in Personnel and Human Resource Management* 4 (1986), pp. 101–45.

21. T. J. Fogarty, "Socialization and Organizational Outcomes in Large Public Accounting Firms," *Journal of Managerial Issues* 12, no. 1 (2000), pp. 13–33; M. K. Ahuja and J. E. Galvin, "Socialization in Virtual Groups," *Journal of Management* 29, no. 2 (2003), p. 161; E. W. Morrison, "Newcomers' Relationships: The Role of Social Network Ties During Socialization," *Academy of Management Journal* 45, no. 6 (2002), pp. 1149–60.

22. B. Jacobson and B. Kaye, "Service Means Success," *Training and Development* 45, no. 5 (1991), pp. 53–58; J. Brechlin and A. Rossett, "Orienting New Employees," *Training* 28, no. 4 (1991), pp. 45–51.

23. W. P. Anthony, P. L. Perrewé, and K. M. Kacmar, *Strategic Human Resource Management* (Fort Worth, TX: Harcourt Brace Jovanovich, 1993).

24. L. W. Porter and L. E. McKibbin, *Management Education and Development* (New York: McGraw-Hill, 1988); A. Kristof-Brown, M. R. Barrick, and M. Franke, "Applicant Impression Management: Dispositional Influences and Consequences for Recruiter Perceptions of Fit and Similarity," *Journal of Management* 28, no. 1 (2002), pp. 27–46.

25. J. De Kok, "The Impact of Firm-provided Training on Production," *International Small Business Journal* 20, no. 3 (2002), pp. 271–95.

26. J. K. Eskildsen and J. J. Dahlgaard, "A Causal Model for Employee Satisfaction," *Total Quality Management* 11, no. 8 (2000), pp. 1081–94.

27. M. Hammer and J. Champy, *Reengineering the Corporation* (New York: HarperCollins, 1993); D. A. Buchanan, "Demands, Instabilities, Manipulations, Careers: The Lived Experience of Driving Change," *Human Relations* 56, no. 6 (2003), p. 663.

28. T. Redman, E. Snape, and G. McElwee, "Appraising Employee Performance: A Vital Organizational Activity?" *Education and Training* 35, no. 2 (1993), pp. 3–10; R. Bretz, G. Milkovitch, and W. Read, "The Current State of Performance Appraisal Research and Practice," *Journal of Management* 18, no. 2 (1992), pp. 321–52.

29. R. Cardy and G. Dobbins, *Performance Appraisal* (Cincinnati, OH: South-Western Publishing, 1994).

30. L. Gomez-Mejia, "Evaluating Employee Performance: Does the Appraisal Instrument Make a Difference?" *Journal of Organizational Behavior Management* 9, no. 2 (1988), pp. 155–272.

31. C. Rarick and G. Baxter, "Behaviorally Anchored Rating Scales: An Effective Performance Appraisal Approach," *Advanced Management Journal* 51, no. 1 (1986), pp. 36–39; D. Naffziger, " BARS, RJPs, and Recruiting," *Personnel Administrator* 30, no. 8 (1985), pp. 85–96; M. Hosoda, E. F. Stone-Romero, and G. Coats, "The Effects of Physical Attractiveness on Job-related Outcomes: A Meta-analysis of Experimental Studies," *Personnel Psychology* 51, no. 2 (2003), p. 431; T. J. Watson, "Ethical Choice in Managerial Work: The Scope for Moral Choices in an Ethically Irrational World," *Human Relations* 56, no. 2 (2003), pp. 167–85.

32. K. Clark, "Judgment Day," *U.S. News & World Report* 134, no. 2 (2003), p. 31; D. Bohl, "Minisurvey: 360 Degree Appraisals Yield Superior Results," *Compensation and Benefits Review* 28, no. 5 (1996), pp. 16–19.

33. P. W. B. Atkins and R. E. Wood, "Self versus Others' Ratings as Predictors of Assessment Center Ratings: Validation Evidence for 360-degree Feedback Programs," *Personnel Psychology* 55, no. 4 (2002), pp. 871–904.

34. S. Brutus and M. Derayeh, "Multisource Assessment Programs in Organizations: An Insider's Perspective," *Human Resource Development Quarterly* 13, no. 2 (2002), pp. 187–202; M. Vinson, "The Pros and Cons of 360 Degree Feedback," *Training and Development* 50, no. 4 (1996), pp. 11–12.

35. J. Lawrie, "Steps Toward an Objective Appraisal," *Supervisory Management* 34, no. 5 (1989), pp. 17–24.

36. "Changing with the Times," *IRS Employment Review*, February 21, 2003, pp. 14–17; J. Kanin-Lovers and M. Cameron, "Broadbanding—A Step Forward or a Step Backward?" *Journal of Compensation and Benefits* 9, no. 5 (1994), pp. 39–42.

37. L. Stroh, J. Brett, J. Baumann, and A. Reilly, "Agency Theory and Variable Pay Compensation Strategies," *Academy of Management Journal* 39, no. 3 (1996), pp. 751–67.

38. J. Herman, "Beating the Midlife Career Crisis," *Fortune*, 1993, pp. 52–62.

39. Personal communication with vice president of human resources at Sony.

40. A. M. Chaker, "Luring Moms Back to Work," *Wall Street Journal*, December 30, 2003, pp. D1–2; A. Leibowitz and J. Merman, "Explaining Changes in Married Mothers' Employment Over Time," *Demography* 32, no. 3 (1995), pp. 365–78; S. Werner, "Recent Developments in International Management Research: A Review of 20 Top Management Journals," *Journal of Management* 28, no. 3 (2002), pp. 277–305.

41. J. S. Black and H. B. Gregersen, *So You're Going Overseas: A Handbook for Personal and Professional Success* (San Diego, CA: Global Business Publishers, 1999).

42. H. S. Farber and B. Western, "Accounting for the Decline of Unions in the Private Sector, 1973–1998," *Journal of Labor Research* 22, no. 3 (2001), pp. 459–85.

43. Personal communication with human resource executive at Delta Airlines.

44. P. Feltes, R. K. Robinson, and R. L. Fink, "American Female Expatriates and the Civil Rights Act of 1991: Balancing Legal and Business Interests," *Business Horizons*, March–April 1993, pp. 82–86.

45. N. Adler, "Expecting International Success: Female Managers Overseas," *Columbia Journal of World Business* 19 (1987), pp. 79–85.

46. E. P. Gray, "The National Origin of BFOQ Under Title VII," *Employee Relations Law Journal* 11, no. 2 (1985), pp. 311–21.

PART FOUR INTEGRATIVE CASE

Sources listed at the end of the case.

CHAPTER 16

1. R. E. Hoskisson and M. A. Hitt, *Downscoping: How to Tame the Diversified Firm* (New York: Oxford University Press, 1994).

2. G. Orwell, *1984: A Novel* (New York: New American Library, 1950); D. E. W. Marginson, "Management Control Systems and Their Effects on Strategy Formation at Middle-management Levels: Evidence from a U.K. Organization," *Strategic Management Journal* 23, no. 11 (2002), pp. 1019–31; M. Goold and A. Campbell, "Do You Have a Well-designed Organization?" *Harvard Business Review* 80, no. 3 (2002), pp. 117–24; W. Nasrallah, R. Levitt, and P. Glynn, "Interaction Value Analysis: When Structured Communication Benefits Organizations," *Organization Science* 14, no. 5 (2003), pp. 541–57.

3. A. S. Tannenbaum (ed.), *Control in Organizations* (New York: McGraw-Hill, 1968); Marginson, "Management Control Systems and Their Effects," pp. 1019–31; Goold and Campbell, "Do You

Have a Well-designed Organization?" pp. 117-24; Nasrallah, Levitt, and Glynn, "Interaction Value Analysis," pp. 541-57.

4. L. Seism, "Prudential's Auditor Gave Early Warning Signals about Sales Abuses," *Wall Street Journal*, August 7, 1997, pp. A1, A4.

5. http://www.dartadvantage.com/vision.html, accessed November 30, 2002.

6. V. Govindarajan, "Impact of Participation in the Budgetary Process on Managerial Attitudes and Performance: Universalistic and Contingency Perspectives," *Decision Sciences* 7 (1986), pp. 496-516.

7. D. Drickhamer, "Europe's Best Plants: Medical Marvel," *Industry Week* 257, no. 3 (2002), pp. 47-49.

8. E.A. Lock, "The Ubiquity of the Technique of Goal Setting in Theories of and Approaches to Employee Motivation," *Academy of Management Review* 3 (1978), pp. 594-601; A. Drach-Zachavy and M. Erez, "Challenge Versus Threat Effects on the Goal-Performance Relationship," *Organizational Behavior and Human Decision Processes* 88, no. 2 (2002), pp. 667-82.

9. R. N. Anthony and J. S. Reece, *Accounting Principles*, 7th ed. (Chicago: Richard D. Irwin, 1995).

10. Ibid.

11. J. Hope and R. Fraser, "Who Needs Budgets?" *Harvard Business Review* 81, no. 2 (2003), pp. 108-15.

12. G. Palmer, "Back on Top," *Banker* 144, no. 824 (1994), pp. 31-34.

13. Ibid., pp. 31-34; A.W. Clausen, "Strategic Issues in Managing Change: The Turnaround at BankAmerica Corporation," *California Management Review* 32, no. 2 (1990), pp. 98-105.

14. F. D. Buggie, "Set the 'Fuzzy Front End' in Concrete," *Research Technology Management* 45, no. 4 (2002), pp. 11-14.

15. Marginson, "Management Control Systems and Their Effects," pp. 1019-31; M. Goold and J. J. Quinn, "The Paradox of Strategic Controls," *Strategic Management Journal* 77 (1990), pp. 43-57.

16. J. Hogan and B. Holland, "Using Theory to Evaluate Personality and Job-Performance Relations: A Socioanalytic Perspective," *Journal of Applied Psychology* 88, no. 1 (2003), p. 100; P. Lorange and D. C. Murphy, "Strategy and Human Resources: Concepts and Practice," *Human Resource Management* 22, nos. 1/2 (1983), pp. 111-35; Hogan and Holland, "Using Theory to Evaluate Personality and Job-Performance Relations," p. 100.

17. J.A. Alexander, "Adaptive Change in Corporate Control Practices," *Academy of Management Journal* 34 (1991), pp. 162-93; V. Govindarajan and J. Fisher, "Strategy, Control Systems, and Resource Sharing: Effects on Business-unit Performance," *Academy of Management Journal* 33 (1990), pp. 259-85.

18. A. Zuber, "McD Restructs to Beef Up Performance," *Nation's Restaurant News* 35, no. 44 (2001), pp. 1, 6.

19. Alexander, "Adaptive Change in Corporate Control Practices," p. 181.

20. G. Hamel and L. Valikangas, "The Quest for Resilience," *Harvard Business Review* 81, no. 9 (2003), pp. 52-63; Goold and Quinn, "The Paradox of Strategic Controls."

21. Ibid., figure 2, p. 55.

22. L. Strauss, "Come Fly with Me," *Barron's* 52, no. 33 (2002), p. T8.

23. Goold and Quinn, "The Paradox of Strategic Controls."

24. N. C. Churchill, "Budget Choice: Planning vs. Control," *Harvard Business Review* 62, no. 4 (1984), pp. 150-64.

25. R. Whiting, "Crystal-ball Glance into Fiscal Future," *Information Week*, July 22, 2002, p. 37.

26. W.A. Van der Stede, "The Relationship Between Two Consequences of Budgetary Controls: Budgetary Slack Creation and Managerial Short-term Orientation," *Accounting, Organizations, and Society* 25 (2000), pp. 609-22.

27. M. Gallagher and V. S. Radcliffe, "Internal Controls in Nonprofit Organizations: The Case of the American Cancer Society, Ohio Division," *Nonprofit Management and Leadership* 12, no. 3 (2002), pp. 313-25.

28. D. Brown, "Using Competencies and Rewards to Enhance Business Performance and Customer Service at the Standard Life Assurance Company," *Compensation and Benefits Review* 33, no. 4 (2001), pp. 14-24.

29. J. R. Barker, "Tightening the Iron Cage: Concertive Control in Self-managing Teams," *Administrative Science Quarterly* 38 (1993), pp. 408-37; Goold and Quinn, "The Paradox of Strategic Controls"; W. G. Ouichi, "A Conceptual Framework for the Design of Organizational Control Mechanisms," *Management Science* 25 (1979), pp. 833-48; W. G. Ouichi, "Markets, Bureaucracies, and Clans," *Administrative Science Quarterly* 25 (1980), pp. 129-41; R. E. Walton, "From Control to Commitment in the Workplace," *Harvard Business Review* 63, no. 2 (1985), pp. 76-84.

30. Barker, "Tightening the Iron Cage."

31. W. H. Newman, *Constructive Control: Design and Use of Control Systems* (Upper Saddle River, NJ: Prentice Hall, 1975).

32. Anon., "How Conrail Is Building a 'Transparent' Physical Plant," *Railway Age* 795, no. 12 (1994), pp. 41-42.

33. P. Odell, "Wine.com Plans Big October E-mailing," *Direct* 14, no. 11 (2002), p. 11; E. Gunn, "A Good Year," SmartBusinessMag.com, pp. 40-42.

34. R. N. Anthony, J. Dearden, and V. Govindarajan, *Management Control Systems*, 8th ed. (Burr Ridge, IL: Richard D. Irwin, 1995).

35. R. S. Kaplan and D. P. Norton, "The Balanced Scorecard—Measures That Drive Performance," *Harvard Business Review* 70, no. 1 (1992), pp. 71-80; A. Neely and M. Bourne, "Why Measurement Initiatives Fail," *Quality Focus* 4, no. 4 (2000), pp. 3-6.

36. Kaplan and Norton, "The Balanced Scorecard."

37. Neely and Bourne, "Why Quality Initiatives Fail"; E. M. Olson and S. F. Slater, "The Balanced Scorecard, Competitive Strategy, and Performance," *Business Horizons* 45, no. 3 (2002), pp. 11-16.

38. Olson and Slater, "The Balanced Scorecard, Competitive Strategy, and Performance."

39. Neely and Bourne, "Why Quality Initiatives Fail."

40. G. F. Hanks, M.A. Freid, and J. Huber, "Shifting Gears at Borg-Warner Automotive," *Management Accounting* 75, no. 8 (1994), pp. 25-29.

41. G.A. Bigley and K. H. Roberts, "The Incident Command System: High-Reliability Organizing for Complex and Volatile Task Environments," *Academy of Management Journal* 44 (2001), pp. 1281-1299.

42. K. H. Roberts, "Managing High Reliability Organizations," *California Management Review* 34, no. 4 (1990), pp. 101-13.

43. D. M. Iadipaolo, "Monster or Monitor? Have Tracking Systems Gone Mad?" *Insurance and Technology* 17, no. 6 (1992), pp. 47-54.

44. M.A. Hitt, R. E. Hoskisson, R.A. Johnson, and D. D. Moesel, "The Market for Corporate Control and Firm Innovation," *Academy of Management Journal* 39 (1996), pp. 1084-1119.

CHAPTER 17

1. M.A. Hitt, R. D. Ireland, and R. E. Hoskisson, *Strategic Management: Competitiveness and Globalization* (Cincinnati, OH: South-Western Publishing Co., 2005).

2. A. Serwer, "The Hottest Thing in the Sky," *Fortune*, March 8, 2004, pp. 86-88, 101-2.

3. P. F. Drucker, "The New Society of Organizations," *Harvard Business Review* 70, no. 5 (1992), pp. 95-104; C. K. Wagner, "Managing Change in Business: Views from the Ancient Past,"

Business Horizons 38 (1995), p. 812; G. Hamel and L. Valikan-gas, "The Quest for Resilience," *Harvard Business Review* 81, no. 9 (2003), pp. 52-63; H. Tsoukas and R. Chia, "On Organiza-tional Becoming: Rethinking Organizational Change," *Organization Science* 13, no. 5 (2002), pp. 567-82.

4. Anon., "Business: Flying High; Lufthansa," *Economist* 365, no. 8298 (2002), p. 78; Anon., "Boeing Said It Will Cut Another 5,000 Jobs in 2003," *Aviation Week and Space Technology* 757, no. 22 (2002), p. 19.

5. E. Walzer, "Eye on Fiber: DuPont Trims Its Textile Subsidiary," *Sporting Goods Business* 35, no. 6 (2002), p. 56.

6. D. Machan, "Is the Hog Going Soft?" *Forbes*, 1997, pp. 114-19.

7. C. Covault, "Kennedy Cutbacks Could Risk Capability," *Aviation Week and Space Technology* 145, no. 10 (1996), pp. 53+.

8. A. Capon, "Peddling Mellon in Europe," *Institutional Investor-International Edition* 28, no. 11 (November 2003), p. 77; J. McTague, "New and Improving," *Barron's* 82, no. 14 (2002), pp. 19-20.

9. C. Fox, "Reducing Risk," *Business Mexico* 72, no. 11 (2002), pp. 38-41.

10. B. Breen, "Forced to Face the Web," *Fast Company* 43, no. 2 (2001), pp. 162-67.

11. Anon., "Workplace Smoking Ban Would Help Kick Habit," *Occupational Health* 54, no. 9 (2002), p. 7; L. Doss, "Operators Feel Del. Smoke Ban's Heat, Fear Law Will Filter Business," *Nation's Restaurant News* 36, no. 23 (2002), pp. 8, 12; P. Frumpkin, "N.Y. County's Smoke Ban Sparks Downstate Furor," *Nation's Restaurant News* 36, no. 42 (2002), pp. 4, 6.

12. U.S. Census Bureau, Population Projections Program, Popula-tion Division, Washington, DC 20233, (301) 763-2428.

13. J. Pfeffer, "Understanding Power in Organizations," *California Management Review* 34, no. 2 (1992), pp. 29-50.

14. E. J. Sobo and B. L. Sadler, "Improving Organizational Communi-cation and Cohesion in a Health Care Setting Through Employee-Leadership Exchange," *Human Organization* 61, no. 3 (2002), pp. 267-77.

15. E. Iritani and M. Dickerson, "Tallying Port Dispute's Costs," *Los Angeles Times*, November 25, 2002, p. B1.

16. N. Venkatraman, "IT-enabled Business Transformation: From Automation to Business Scope Redefinition," *Sloan Manage-ment Review* 35, no. 2 (1994), pp. 73-87.

17. P. Bradley, "Emerson Retools," *Logistics Management* 41, no. 41 (2002), pp. 22-24.

18. J. Evans, "Grand Cathay's Assets Take a Walk," *Asiamoney* 73, no. 9 (2002), p. 49.

19. J. Champy, "Reengineering Management: The Mandate for New Leadership" (New York: Harper Business, 1996).

20. A. D. Chandler, *Strategy and Structure: Chapters in the His-tory of the Industrial Enterprise* (Cambridge, MA: M.I.T. Press, 1962); T. L. Amburgey and T. Dacin, "As the Left Foot Follows the Right? The Dynamics of Strategic and Structural Change," *Academy of Management Journal* 37 (1994), pp. 1427-52; M. T. Hannan, L. Polos, and G. R. Carroll, "Cascading Organizational Change," *Organization Science* 14, no. 5 (2003), pp. 463-82.

21. D. A. Nadler and M. L. Tushman, "Beyond the Charismatic Leader: Leadership and Organizational Change," *California Management Review* 32, no. 2 (1990), pp. 77-97; Hannan, Polos, and Carroll, "Cascading Organizational Change," pp. 463-82.

22. M. Wall, "Manufacturing Flexibility," *Automotive Industries* 183, no. 10 (2003), pp. 44-46; T. Sonoda, "Honda: Global Manu-facturing and Competitiveness," *Competitiveness Review* 72, no. 1 (2002), pp. 7-13.

23. "Nokia Restructures for More 'Mobility,'" *Electronic News* (North America) 49, no. 39 (2003).

24. L. A. Armour, "Me and the Mayo," *Fortune*, 1997, pp. 86-89.

25. D. L. Madison, R. W. Alien, L. W. Porter, P. A. Renwick et al., "Orga-nizational Politics: An Exploration of Managers' Perceptions," *Human Relations* 33, no. 2 (1980), pp. 79-100; M. C. Kernan and P. J. Hanges, "Survivor Reactions to Reorganization: Antecedents and Consequences of Procedural, Interpersonal, and Informational Justice," *Journal of Applied Psychology* 87, no. 5 (2002), pp. 916-28.

26. D. Clark, "Inside Intel, It's All Copying," *Wall Street Journal*, October 28, 2002, p. B1.

27. A. Barrett and J. Carety, "Merck's New Alchemist," *BusinessWeek*, December 16, 2002, p. 40.

28. S. Ghoshal and C. A. Bartlett, "Rebuilding Behavioral Context: A Blueprint for Corporate Renewal," *Sloan Management Review* 37, no. 2 (1989), pp. 23-36.

29. W. Weitzel and E. Johnson, "Decline in Organizations: A Litera-ture Integration and Extension," *Administrative Science Quar-terly* 34 (1989), pp. 91-109.

30. B. Dumaine, "Times Are Good? Create a Crisis," *Fortune*, 1993, pp. 123-30.

31. S. Holmes, "Planet Starbucks," *BusinessWeek*, September 9, 2002, pp. 100-10.

32. M. L. Tushman, W. H. Newman, and E. Romanelli, "Convergence and Upheaval: Managing the Unsteady Pace of Organizational Evolution," *California Management Review* 29, no. 1 (1986), pp. 29-44.

33. C. Yang, "AOL: Anatomy of a Long-shot," *BusinessWeek*, Decem-ber 16, 2002, pp. 58-60; B. Steinberg, "You've Got a Makeover! This Is Time Warner's AOL," *Wall Street Journal*, December 3, 2002, p. A1.

34. C. Ponicki, "Case Study: Improving the Efficiency of Small Busi-ness Lending at First National Bank of Chicago," *Commercial Lending Review* 11, no. 2 (1996), pp. 51-60.

35. C. Piller, "So What if Amelio's File Is Closed? Apple Can Reboot," *Los Angeles Times*, July 10, 1997, pp. D1+; J. Carlton and L. Gomes, "Apple Computer Chief Amelio Is Ousted: Co-founder Jobs to Assume Broader Role as Search for a Successor Begins," *Wall Street Journal*, July 10, 1997, p. A3.

36. Anon, "Winning Team Plays: The Dream Team," *Supervisory Management* 40, no. 5 (1995), p. 10; Q. N. Huy, "Emotional Bal-ancing of Organizational Continuity and Radical Change: The Contribution of Middle Managers," *Administrative Science Quarterly* 47, no. 1 (2002), pp. 31-69.

37. J. Barbian, "Mark Spear," *Training* 38, no. 10 (2001), pp. 34-38.

38. M. MacCallan, "Re-engineering Treasury at Cookson Group," *TMA Journal* 16, no. 4 (1996), pp. 45-51.

39. F. Warner, "In a Word, Toyota Drives for Innovation," *Fast Com-pany*, August 2002, pp. 36-38.

40. K. Ballen, "Report Card on the Baby Bells," *Fortune*, 1988, pp. 87-96; P. Coy and M. Lewyn, "The Baby Bells Learn a Nasty New Word: Competition," *BusinessWeek*, 1991, pp. 96-101; N. Staudenmayer, M. Tyre, and L. Perlow, "Time to Change: Tempo-ral Shifts as Enablers of Organizational Change," *Organization Science* 13, no. 5 (2002), pp. 583-97.

41. L. Maneth, "A Hoosier in Budapest," *CFO: The Magazine for Senior Financial Executives* 77, no. 1 (1995), pp. 34-46.

42. T. A. Stewart, "3M Fights Back," *Fortune*, 1996, pp. 94-99.

43. C. R. Leana, "Stability and Change as Simultaneous Experiences in Organizational Life," *Academy of Management Review* 25 (2000), pp. 753-62; Q. N. Huy, "Emotional Balancing of Organi-zational Continuity and Radical Change: The Contribution of Middle Managers," *Administrative Science Quarterly* 47, no. 1 (2002), pp. 31-69.

44. V. Baxter and A. Margavio, "Assaultive Violence in the U.S. Post Office," *Work and Occupations* 23 (1996), pp. 277-96.

45. S. K. Piderit, "Rethinking Resistance and Recognizing Ambivalence: A Multidimensional View of Attitudes Toward an Organizational Change," *Academy of Management Review* 25 (2000), pp. 783-95; V. J. Mabin, "Harnessing Resistance: Using the Theory of Constraints to Assist Change Management," *Journal of European Industrial Training* 25, nos. 2/3/4 (2001), p. 168; M. S. Feldman and B. T. Pentland, "Reconceptualizing Organizational Routines as a Source of Flexibility and Change," *Administrative Science Quarterly* 48, no. 1 (2003), pp. 94-118; Huy, "Emotional Balancing of Organizational Continuity and Radical Change," pp. 31-69; R. Vince, "The Politics of Imagined Stability: A Psychodynamic Understanding of Change at Hyder plc.," *Human Relations* 55, no. 10 (2002), pp. 1189-1208.

46. Anon, "Shake-up or Cock-up?" *The Economist* 343, no. 8019 (1997), p. 67.

47. Piderit, "Rethinking Resistance and Recognizing Ambivalence"; Vince, "The Politics of Imagined Stability," pp. 1189-1208.

48. K. Lewin, *Field Theory in Social Science; Selected Theoretical Papers* (New York: Harper, 1951).

49. D. Wong-MingJi, "Dealing with the Dynamic Duo of Innovation and Inertia: The "in-"Theory of Organization Change," *Organization Development Journal* 20, no. 1 (2002), pp. 36-52.

50. B. K. Spiker and E. Lesser, "We Have Met the Enemy," *Journal of Business Strategy* 16, no. 2 (1995), pp. 17-21.

51. J. Kurtzman, "Is Your Company Off Course: Now You Can Find Out Why," *Fortune*, 135, 1997, pp. 58-60.

52. W. L. French, C. H. Bell Jr., and R. A. Zawicki, *Organizational Development and Transformation: Managing Effective Change*, 4th ed. (Burr Ridge, IL: Richard D. Irwin, 1994).

53. Ibid.

54. R. Beckhard, *Organization Development: Strategies and Models* (Reading, MA: Addison-Wesley, 1969); R. D. Smither, J. M. Houston, and S. D. McIntire, *Organization Development: Strategies for Changing Environments* (New York: HarperCollins, 1996); B. Pitman, "Leading for Value," *Harvard Business Review* 81, no. 4 (2003), pp. 41-46.

55. Smither et al., *Organization Development: Strategies for Changing Environments.*

56. Ibid.

57. K. Lewin, "Frontiers in Group Dynamics," *Human Relations* 1 (1947), pp. 5-41; A. Clardy, "Learning to Change: A Guide for Organization Change Agents," *Personnel Psychology* 56, no. 3 (2003), pp. 785-88.

58. Smither et al., *Organization Development: Strategies for Changing Environments*; N. J. Foss, "Selective Intervention and Internal Hybrids: Interpreting and Learning from the Rise and Decline of the Oticon Spaghetti Organization," *Organization Science* 14, no. 3 (2003), pp. 331+.

59. W. L. French and C. H. Bell, Jr., *Organization Development: Behavioral Science Interventions for Organizational Improvement*, 5th ed. (Upper Saddle River, NJ: Prentice Hall, 1995); M. J. Benner and M. E. Tushman, "Exploitation, Exploration, and Process Management: The Productivity Dilemma Revisited," *Academy of Management Review* 28, no. 2 (2003), pp. 238-56; M. J. Benner and M. Tushman, "Process Management and Technological Innovation: A Longitudinal Study of the Photography and Paint Industries," *Administrative Science Quarterly* 41, no. 4 (2002), pp. 676-706.

60. D. A. Garvin, "Leveraging Processes for Strategic Advantage," *Harvard Business Review* 73, no. 5 (1995), pp. 76-79; Hammer and Champy, "Reengineering the Corporation," pp. 65-69.

61. D. Rigby, "Management Tools and Techniques: A Survey," *California Management Review* 43, no. 2 (2001), pp. 139-61.

62. Ibid.

63. G. Hall, J. Rosenthal, and J. Wade, "How to Make Reengineering Really Work," *Harvard Business Review* 71, no. 6 (1993), pp. 119-31.

64. J. B. White, "Next Big Thing: Reengineering Gurus Take Steps to Remodel Their Stalling Vehicles," *Wall Street Journal*, November 26, 1996, pp. A1, A10; Rigby, "Management Tools and Techniques"; D. Elmuti and Y. Kathawala, "Business Reengineering: Revolutionary Management Tool, or Fading Fad?" *Business Forum* 25, nos. 1/2 (2000), pp. 29-36.

65. Hall and Rosenthal, "How to Make Reengineering Really Work"; Benner and Tushman, "Exploitation, Exploration, and Process Management," pp. 238-56.

66. Elmuti and Kathawala, "Business Reengineering"; M. C. Kernan and P. J. Hanges, "Survivor Reactions to Reorganization: Antecedents and Consequences of Procedural, Interpersonal, and Informational Justice," *Journal of Applied Psychology* 87, no. 5 (2002), pp. 916-28; D. A. Buchanan, "Demands, Instabilities, Manipulations, Careers: The Lived Experience of Driving Change," *Human Relations* 56, no. 6 (2003), pp. 663-84.

67. White, "Next Big Thing"; Benner and Tushman, "Process Management and Technological Innovation," pp. 676-706; Huy, "Emotional Balancing of Organizational Continuity and Radical Change," pp. 631-91; A. E. Akgun, G. S. Lynn, and J. C. Byrne, "Organizational Learning: A Socio-Cognitive Framework," *Human Relations* 56, no. 7 (2003), pp. 839-68.

68. D. M. Rousseau, "Organizational Behavior in the New Organizational Era," *Annual Review of Psychology* 48 (1997), pp. 515-46; C. Argyris and D. A. Schoen, *Organizational Learning II: Theory, Method, and Practice* (Reading, MA: Addison-Wesley, 1996); D. A. Garvin, "Building a Learning Organization," *Harvard Business Review* 71, no. 4 (1993), pp. 78-91; E. C. Nevis, A. J. DiBella, and J. A. Gould, "Understanding Organizations as Learning Systems," *Sloan Management Review* 36, no. 2 (1995), pp. 73-85; E. A. Schein, "How Can Organizations Learn Faster? The Challenge of Entering the Green Room," *Sloan Management Review* 34, no. 2 (1993), pp. 85-92; P. M. Senge, "The Leader's New Work: Building Learning Organizations," *Sloan Management Review* 32, no. 1 (1990), pp. 7-23; P. M. Senge, *The Fifth Discipline* (New York: Doubleday, 1990); S. F. Slater, "Learning to Change," *Business Horizons* 38, no. 6 (1996), pp. 13-20.

69. A. D. Ellinger, A. E. Ellinger, Y. Bayin, and S. W. Howton, "The Relationship Between the Learning Organization Concept and Firms' Financial Performance: An Empirical Assessment," *Human Resource Development Quarterly* 13, no. 1 (2002), pp. 5-21.

70. Garvin, "Building a Learning Organization," p. 80.

71. Nevis et al., "Understanding Organizations as Learning Systems."

72. Garvin, "Building a Learning Organization."

73. J. Levinson, "Benchmarking Compliance Performance," *Environmental Quality Management* 6, no. 4 (1997), pp. 49-60.

74. http://www.nummi.com/tours.html, accessed December 10, 2002.

PART FIVE INTEGRATIVE CASE

1. The P/E ratio is calculated by dividing the market price of a share by the earnings per share (EPS). In other words, if a company is reporting an EPS of Rs 2, and the stock is selling for Rs 20 per share, the P/E ratio is 10—because the buyer would be paying 10 times the earnings. [Rs 20 per share divided by Rs 2 per share earnings = 10 P/E].

2. Summer was the peak demand season for colas, hence Coca-Cola was hesitant to disrupt the operations in any way.

credits

glossary

acquired needs theory motivation theory that focuses on learned needs that become enduring predispositions for affiliation, power, and achievement

affirmative action programs hiring and training programs intended to correct past inequalities for certain categories of people based on gender, race and ethnicity, age, or religion

approved budget specifies what the manager is actually authorized to spend money on and how much

artifacts visible manifestations of a culture such as its art, clothing, food, architecture, and customs

assessment centers a work sampling technique in which candidates perform a number of exercises, each one designed to capture one or more key aspects of the job

assumptions beliefs about fundamental aspects of life

at-risk compensation pay that varies depending on specified conditions, including the profitability of the company; hitting particular budget, revenue, or cost savings targets for a unit; or meeting specified individual performance targets

balanced scorecard an integrated and "balanced" set of measures for four critical areas or perspectives: financial, customers, internal business, and innovation and learning

behavioral process orientation key distinguishing feature of the OD approach to organizational change that focuses on new forms of behavior and new relationships

behaviorally anchored rating scales (BARS) a performance appraisal system in which the rater places detailed employee characteristics on a rating scale

benchmarking the investigation of the best results among competitors and noncompetitors and the practices that lead to those results

benchmarking identification analysis and comparison of the best practices of competitors against an organization's own practices

bona fide occupational qualifications (BFOQ) qualifications that have a direct and material impact on job performance and outcomes

boundaryless organization barriers to effective integration are overcome by people empowered to work across boundaries

bounded rationality model (administrative man model) a model that assumes that people usually settle for acceptable rather than maximum options because the decisions they confront typically demand greater information-processing capabilities than they possess

brainstorming a process of generating many creative solutions without evaluating their merit

break-even point (B-E P) amount of a product that must be sold to cover a firm's fixed and variable costs

broadband systems pay structures in which the range of pay is large and covers a wide variety of jobs

budgetary control a type of tactical control based on responsibility for meeting financial targets and evaluating how well those targets have been met

budgetary slack basing bonuses on budgeting targets can be an incentive to budget game play with high cost and low revenue estimates

budgets used to quantify and allocate resources to specific activities

bureaucratic control an approach to tactical control that stresses adherence to rules and regulations and is imposed by others

cafeteria-style plans benefit plans in which employees have a set number of "benefit dollars" that they can use to purchase benefits that fit their particular needs

capital expenditure budget specifies the amount of money to be spent on specific items that have long-term use and require significant amounts

career paths sets and sequences of positions and experiences

cash cows products or SBUs that have relatively high market share in markets with unattractive futures

centralized organizations restrict decision making to fewer individuals, usually at the top of the organization

change agents individuals who are responsible for implementing change efforts; they can be either internal or external to the organization

charismatic leadership leadership by someone who has influence over others based on individual inspirational qualities rather than formal power

code of ethical conduct a formal settlement that outlines types of behavior that are and are not acceptable

coercive power a type of position power based on a person's authority to administer punishments, either by withholding something that is desired or by giving out something that is not desired

cognitive differentiation the extent to which people in different units within an organization think about different things or about similar things differently

cohesion the degree to which members are motivated to remain in the group

collaboration part of negotiation in which parties work together to attack and solve a problem

collectivism the extent to which identity is a function of the group to which an individual belongs

command (supervisory) group a group whose members consist of a supervisor or manager and all those who report to that person

commitment (clan) control an approach to tactical control that emphasizes consensus and shared responsibility for meeting goals

committee a group that is either permanent or temporary (ad hoc) whose members meet only occasionally and otherwise report to different permanent supervisors in an organization's structure

communication the process of transferring information, meaning, and understanding from sender to receiver

communication networks identifiable patterns of communication within

673

and between organizations, whether using formal or informal channels

compensatory justice if distributive and procedural justice fail, those hurt by the inequitable distribution of rewards are compensated

competitive advantage the ability of a firm to win consistently over the long term in a competitive situation

concentration of effect the extent to which consequences are focused on a few individuals or dispersed across many

concurrent control a type of operational control that evaluates the conversion of inputs to outputs while it is happening

conformity close adherence to the group's norms by the individual members

content theories motivation theories that focus on what needs a person is trying to satisfy and on what features of the work environment seem to satisfy those needs

context-driven competencies competencies that are specific to both the unique nature of the particular tasks and the particular composition of the team

contingency plans identify key factors that could affect the desired results and specify what actions will be taken if key events change

contrast a means by which people perceive differences

confrontation a means of helping people to perceive contrasts by providing an inescapable experience

control regulation of activities and behaviors within organizations; adjustment or conformity to specifications or objectives

controlling regulating the work of those for whom a manager is responsible

core competency focuses on an interrelated set of activities that can deliver competitive advantage in the short term and into the future

core value a value that is widely shared and deeply held

corporate social responsibility the obligations that corporations owe to their constituencies such as shareholders, employees, customers, and citizens at large

cost leadership striving to be the lowest-cost producer of a product or

provider of a service and yet charge only slightly less than industry average

critical incidents recording of specific incidents in which the employee's behavior and performance were above or below expectations

cross-functional job rotation opportunities for employees to work in different functional areas and gain additional expertise

cross-functional teams employees from different departments, such as finance, marketing, operations, and human resources, who work together in problem solving

cultural distance the overall difference between two cultures' basic characteristics such as language, level of economic development, and traditions and customs

culture a learned set of assumptions, values, and behaviors that have been accepted as successful enough to be passed on to newcomers

cultural context the degree to which a situation influences behavior or perception of appropriateness

customer segment a group of customers who have similar preferences or place similar value on product features

decentralized organizations tend to push decision-making authority down to the lowest level possible

decision making a process of specifying the nature of a particular problem or opportunity and selecting among available alternatives to solve a problem or capture an opportunity

decoding the act of interpreting a message

delphi technique a decision-making technique that never allows decision participants to meet face-to-face but identifies a problem and offers solutions using a questionnaire

demographics the descriptive elements of people in society, such as average age, level of education, financial status, and so on

devil's advocate a group member whose role is to challenge the majority position

dialectical inquiry a process to improve decision making by assigning a group member (or members) the role of questioning the underlying assumptions associated with the formulation of the problem

differentiation the extent to which tasks are divided into subtasks and performed by individuals with specialized skills

directing the process of attempting to influence other people to attain organizational objectives

distributive justice the equitable distribution of rewards and punishment, based on performance

dogs products or SBUs that have relatively low market share in unattractive markets

downward communication messages sent from higher organizational levels to lower levels

dual-career couples couples in which both partners work full-time in professional, managerial, or administrative jobs

early wins early and consistent positive reinforcement of desired change confrontation

effective leadership influence that assists a group or an organization to meet its goals and objectives and perform successfully

efficiency (activity) ratio of amount of sales to total cost of inventory

efficiency perspective the concept that a manager's responsibility is to maximize profits for the owners of the business

e-leadership involves heavy reliance on the use of information technology to supplement more traditional leadership methods

emotional intelligence involves an awareness of others' feelings; and a sensitivity to one's own emotions and the ability to control them

empathy the ability to put yourself in someone else's place and to understand his or her feelings, situation, and motives

empowerment sharing of power with others

encoding the act of constructing a message

entry barriers obstacles that make it difficult for firms to get into a business

equity theory motivation theory that focuses on individuals' comparisons of their circumstances with those of others and how such comparisons may motivate certain kinds of behavior

escalating commitment the tendency to exhibit greater levels of commitment to a decision as time passes and investments are made in the decision, even after significant evidence emerges indicating that the original decision was incorrect

ethical dilemmas having to make a choice between two competing but arguably valid options

ethical lapses decisions that are contrary to an individual's stated beliefs and policies of the company

ethnocentrism the belief in the superiority and importance of one's own group

expatriate employees employees sent overseas on temporary assignments of three to five years

expectancy theory motivation theory that focuses on the thought processes people use when they face particular choices among alternatives, especially alternative courses of action

expense budget includes all primary activities on which a unit or organization plans to spend money and the amount allocated for the upcoming year

expert power a type of personal power based on specialized knowledge not readily available to many people

external environment a set of forces and conditions outside the organization that can potentially influence its performance

externalities indirect or unintended consequences imposed on society that may not be understood or anticipated

extinction the absence of positive consequences for behavior, lessening the likelihood of that behavior in the future

feminine societies value activities focused on caring for others and enhancing the quality of life

flat organization structure has fewer layers in its hierarchy than a tall organization

focus groups small groups involved in intense discussions of the positive and negative features of products or services

force field analysis uses the concept of equilibrium, a condition that occurs when the forces for change, the "driving forces," are balanced by forces opposing change, the "restraining forces," and results in a relatively steady state

Foreign Corrupt Practices Act (FCPA) a law prohibiting employees of U.S. firms from corrupting the actions of foreign officials, politicians, or candidates for office

formal communication channels routes that are authorized, planned, and regulated by the organization and that are directly connected to its official structure

formal group a group that is designated, created, and sanctioned by the organization to carry out its basic work and to fulfill its overall mission

formalization the official and defined structures and systems in decision making, communication, and control in an organization

formulation a process involving identifying a problem or opportunity, acquiring information, developing desired performance expectations, and diagnosing the causes and relationships among factors affecting the problem or opportunity

frames of reference existing sets of attitudes that provide quick ways of interpreting complex messages

gatekeepers individuals who are at the communication interface between separate organizations or between different units within an organization

general environment forces that typically influence the organization's external task environment and thus the organization itself

glass ceiling an invisible barrier that prevents women from promotion to the highest executive ranks

globalization the tendency to integrate activities on a coordinated, worldwide basis

global team a highly diverse multinational team representing one or several function areas and various cultural backgrounds

goal-setting theory assumes that human action is directed by conscious goals and intentions

Gresham's law of planning the tendency for managers to let programmed activities overshadow nonprogrammed activities

gross domestic product the total dollar value of final goods and services produced within a nation's borders

group a set of people limited in number (usually from 3 to 20), who have some degree of mutual interaction and shared objectives

groupthink a mode of thinking in which pursuit of agreement among members becomes so dominant that it overrides a realistic appraisal of alternative courses of action

heuristic a rule that guides the search for alternatives into areas that have a high probability for yielding success

human resource policies and procedures a type of tactical control based on the organization's overall approach to utilizing its human resources

incentive plans systems that tie some compensation to performance

incremental budgeting approach where managers use the approved budget of the previous year and then present arguments for why the upcoming budget should be more or less

individualism the extent to which people base their identities on themselves and are expected to take care of themselves and their immediate families

influence tactics specific behaviors used to affect the behavior and attitudes of other people

informal communication channels routes that are not prespecified by the organization but that develop through typical and customary activities of people at work

informal group a group whose members interact voluntarily

informal organization the unofficial but influential means of communication, decision making, and control that are part of the habitual way things get done in an organization

in-group group to which a person belongs

integration the extent to which various parts of an organization cooperate and interact with each other

interdependence the degree to which one unit or one person depends on another to accomplish a task

intergroup conflict differences that occur between groups

internal environment key factors and forces inside the organization that affect how it operates

interventions sets of structured activities or action steps designed to improve organizations

intragroup conflict differences that occur within groups

intuitive decision making the primarily subconscious process of identifying a decision and selecting a preferred alternative

job analysis determination of the scope and depth of jobs and the requisite skills, abilities, and knowledge that people need to perform their jobs successfully.

job characteristics model approach that focuses on the motivational attributes of jobs through emphasizing three sets of variables: core job characteristics, critical psychological states, and outcomes

job design the structuring or restructuring of key job components

job enrichment increasing the complexity of a job to provide greater responsibility, accomplishment, and achievement

job posting an internal recruiting method whereby a job, its pay, level, description, and qualifications are posted or announced to all current employees.

job sharing situation in which two people share the same job by each working part-time

justice approach focuses on how equitably the costs and benefits of actions are distributed

lateral communication messages sent across essentially equivalent levels of an organization

leader–member exchange (LMX) theory a relationship-based approach to leadership that focuses on the importance of strong, mutually respectful, and satisfying relationships between leaders and followers

legitimate power (formal authority) a type of position power granted to a person by the organization

leverage ratio of total debt to total assets

liaisons individuals designated to act as a bridge or connection between different areas of a company

line of authority specifies who reports to whom

liquidity measure of how well a unit can meet its short-term cash requirements

localization the tendency to differentiate activities country by country

LPC (least preferred co-worker) theory a contingency theory of leadership that identifies the types of situations in which task-oriented or person-oriented leaders would be most effective

magnitude of the consequences the anticipated level of impact of the outcome of a given action

management the process of assembling and using sets of resources in a goal-directed manner to accomplish tasks in an organizational setting

managerial grid a method for measuring the degree to which managers are task oriented and people oriented

managerial ethics the study of morality and standards of business conduct

masculine societies value activities focused on success, money, and possessions

Maslow's need hierarchy theory that states people fulfill basic needs, such as physiological and safety needs, before making efforts to satisfy other needs, such as social and belongingness, esteem, and self-actualization

media richness different media are classified as rich or lean based on their capacity to facilitate shared meaning

medium the mode or form of transmission of a message

mental map habitual cognitive patterns

mission statement articulates the fundamental purpose of the organization and often contains several components

moral intensity the degree to which people see an issue as an ethical one

moral rights approach focuses on examination of the moral standing of actions independent of their consequences

motivation set of forces that energize, direct, and sustain behavior

movement changing perceptions based on the level of certainty or uncertainty associated with the change

multiple advocacy a process to improve decision making by assigning several group members to represent the opinions of various constituencies that might have an interest in the decision

negative reinforcements undesirable consequences that, by being removed or avoided, increase the likelihood of a behavior being repeated in the future

negotiation the process of conferring to arrive at an agreement between different parties, each with their own interests and preferences

negotiation "interests" a party's or parties' concerns and desires—in other words, what they want

negotiation "positions" a party's or parties' stance regarding their interests

networking a process of developing regular patterns of communication with particular individuals or groups to send and receive information

network structures formal or informal relationships among units or organizations (e.g., along the firm's value chain)

neutralizers of leadership aspects of the organization or work situation that can defeat the best efforts of leaders

niche strategy a limited scope or breadth of focus

noise potential interference with the transmission or decoding of a message

nominal group techniques a process of having group members record their proposed solutions, summarize all proposed solutions, and independently rank solutions until a clearly favored solution emerges

nonprogrammed decision a decision about a problem that is either poorly defined or novel

normative decision model a contingency model that prescribes standards to determine the extent to which subordinates should be allowed to participate in decision making

norms a group's shared standards that guide the behavior of its individual members

objectives the end states or targets that company managers aim for

operational control assessment and regulation of the specific activities and methods an organization uses to produce goods and services

operational plans translate tactical plans into specific goals and actions for small units of the organization and focus on the near term

opportunity a chance to achieve a more desirable state than the current one

organizational charts illustrate relationships among units and lines of authority among supervisors and subordinates

organizational design the process of assessing the organization's strategy and environmental demands and then determining the appropriate organizational structures

organizational development (OD) approach to organizational change that has a strong behavioral and people orientation, emphasizing planned, strategic, long-range efforts focusing on people and their interrelationships in organizations

organizational leadership an interpersonal process involving attempts to influence other people in attaining some goal

organizational learning exhibited by an organization that is skilled at creating, acquiring, and transferring knowledge, and at modifying its behavior to reflect new knowledge and insights

organizational renewal a concept of organizational change that proposes a goal of flexibility and capability for continual change

organizational structure the sum of the ways an organization divides its labor into distinct tasks and then coordinates them

organizations interconnected sets of individuals and groups who attempt to accomplish common goals through differentiated functions and intended coordination

organizing systematically putting resources together

outsourcing the practice of taking a significant activity within the organization and contracting it out to an independent party

paternalism where a leader is regarded as the provider "father" who will take care of the subordinate in return for responsible behavior and performance

path–goal theory of leadership a contingency theory of leadership that focuses on the leader's role in increasing subordinate satisfaction and effort by increasing personal payoffs for goal attainment and making the path to these payoffs easier

pay structure a range of pay for a particular position or classification of positions

people behaviors behaviors that focus on interaction, such as being friendly and supportive, showing trust and confidence, being concerned about others, and supplying recognition

perception a way one sees a situation based on experiences, personality, and current needs

perceptual distortion highlighting the positive features of the implicit favorite over the alternative

personal power power based on a person's individual characteristics

planning a decision-making process that focuses on the future of an organization and how it will achieve its goals

plans the means by which managers hope to hit the desired targets

portfolio analysis techniques designed to assist managers in assessing the attractiveness of a market

position power power based on an organizational structure

positive reinforcements desirable consequences that, by being given or applied, increase the likelihood of behavior being repeated in the future

postcontrol a type of operational control that checks quality after production of goods or services outputs

power the capacity or ability to influence

power distance the extent to which people accept power and authority differences among people

precontrol a type of operational control that focuses on the quality, quantity, and characteristics of the inputs into the production process

prices differentiation strategy for making a product or service different from those of competitors

primary activities activities that are directly involved in the creation of a product or service, getting it into the hands of the customer, and keeping it there

probability of effect the moral intensity of an issue rises and falls depending on how likely people think the consequences are

problem a gap between existing and desired performance

procedural justice ensuring that those affected by managerial decisions consent to the decision-making process and that the process is administered impartially

process costs increasing costs of coordination as group size increases

process redesign (reengineering) involves a fundamental redesign of business processes to achieve dramatic improvements

process technological changes alterations in how products are made or how enterprises are managed

process theories motivation theories that deal with the way different variables combine to influence the amount of effort people put forth

product technological changes changes that lead to new-product features and capabilities of existing products or to completely new products

profit center unit or product line in which the related expenses are deducted from the revenue generated

profitability ratio of cost to benefit

programmed decision a standard response to a simple or routine problem

project/task force a temporary group put together by an organization for a particular purpose

proposed budget provides a plan for how much money is needed, and is submitted to a superior or budget review committee

prospective rationality a belief that future courses of action are rational and correct

proximity the physical, psychological, and emotional closeness the decision maker feels to those affected by the decision

punishments undesirable consequences that are applied to decrease the likelihood of behavior being repeated in the future

question marks products or SBUs that have relatively low market share in attractive markets

rational model (classical model) a seven-step model of decision making that represents the earliest attempt to model decision processes

reengineering fundamental rethinking and radical redesign of business processes to achieve dramatic improvements in critical, contemporary measures of performance, such as cost, quality, service, or speed

referent power a type of personal power gained when people are attracted to, or identify with, that person; this power is gained because people "refer" to that person

refreezing the process of reinforcing change so that it becomes established

relationship (affective) conflict interpersonal differences among group members

retrospective decision model (implicit favorite model) a decision-making model that focuses on how decision makers attempt to rationalize their choices after they are made

reward power a type of position power based on a person's authority to give out rewards

rituals symbolic communication of an organization's culture

ROE (return on equity) alternative term for ROI

ROI (return on investment) measure of profitability obtained by dividing net income by the total amount of assets invested

role ambiguity a situation in which the expected behaviors for a group member are not clearly defined

role conflict a situation in which a member of a group faces two or more contrasting sets of expectations

satisficing the tendency for decision makers to accept the first alternative that meets their minimally acceptable requirements rather than pushing them further for an alternative that produces the best results

selective perception the process of screening out some parts of an intended message because they contradict our beliefs or desires

self-efficacy an individual's confidence about his or her abilities to mobilize motivation, cognitive resources, and courses of action needed to successfully execute a specific task within a given context

self-managing (autonomous) workgroup a group that has no formally appointed supervisor but is similar to command groups in that the members coordinate their organizational work as if they all reported to the same formally appointed supervisor; members usually appoint their own informal team leader

short-term or long-term orientation societies that focus on immediate results and those that focus on developing relationships without expecting immediate results

situational leadership model a model that states that different types of appropriate leadership are "contingent" on some other variable, in this case "the situation"

social cognitive theory (SCT) a theory that focuses on how individuals think about, or "cognitively process," information obtained from their social environment

social consensus the extent to which members of a society agree that an act is either good or bad

social intelligence the ability to "read" other people and their intentions and adjust one's own behavior in response

social loafing the phenomenon of reduced effort per person in large groups

societal values commonly shared desired end states

solution a process involving generating alternatives, selecting the preferred solution, and implementing the decided course of action

span of control the number of employees reporting to a given supervisor

stakeholders individuals or groups who have an interest in and are affected by the actions of an organization

standards targets of performance

standard operating procedure (SOP) established procedure for action used for programmed decisions that specifies exactly what should be done

stars products that have relatively high market share in markets with attractive futures

status the standing or prestige that a person has in a group, which can be based on a number of factors such as perceived leadership abilities, seniority, or special skills

stereotyping the tendency to oversimplify and generalize about groups of people

strategic control assessment and regulation of how the organization as a whole fits its external environment and meets its long-range objectives and goals

strategic intent pertains to what an organization ultimately wants to be and do

strategic objectives translate the strategic intent and mission of a firm into concrete and measurable goals

strategic partners organizations that work closely with a firm in the pursuit of mutually beneficial goals

strategic plans focus on the broad future of the organization and incorporate both external environmental demands and internal resources into managers' actions

strategic scope the scope of a firm's strategy or breadth of focus

strong versus weak cultural values the degree to which the cultural values are shared by organization members

structural changes changes that significantly affect the dynamics of economic activity

structured debate a process to improve problem formulation that includes the processes of devil's advocate, multiple advocacy, and dialectical inquiry

structured interview one in which interviewers ask a standard set of questions of all candidates about qualifications and capabilities related to job performance

subculture where values are deeply held but not widely shared

subjectively expected utility (SEU) model a model of decision making that asserts that managers choose the alternative that they subjectively believe maximizes the desired outcome

substitutes alternative products or services that can substitute for existing products or services

substitutes for leadership alternative approaches that can at least partially substitute for the need for leadership or can sometimes overcome poor leadership

substitution concerned with whether or not the customer's need that you fulfill can be met by alternative means

supernormal returns the profits that are above the average for a comparable set of firms

supervisory structure a type of tactical control based on reporting levels in an organization

support activities activities that facilitate the creation of a product or service and its transfer to the customer

switching costs the amount of difficulty and expense involved in customers' switching from one company to another

SWOT analysis requires managers to consider their firm's Strengths, Weaknesses, Opportunities, and Threats for its continued operation

tactical control assessment and regulation of the day-to-day functions of the organization and its major units in the implementation of its strategy

tactical plans translate strategic plans into specific goals for specific parts of the organization

tall organization structure one that has multiple layers or is high in terms of vertical differentiation

task (substantive) conflict conflict that focuses on differences in ideas and courses of action in addressing the issues facing a group

task behaviors behaviors that specify and identify the roles and tasks of leaders and their subordinates, such as planning, scheduling, setting standards, and devising procedures

task differentiation differentiation by what employees do

task environment forces that have a high potential for affecting the organization on an immediate basis

task-contingent competencies competencies that are needed in teams that perform a specific and recurring set of tasks but have varying sets of members

team a type of group that has additional characteristics: a high degree of interdependent, coordinated interaction and a strong sense of members' personal responsibility for achieving specified group outcomes

team-contingent competencies competencies that are specific to the particular team, but applicable to tasks that vary

temporal immediacy a function of the interval between the time the action occurs and the onset of its consequences

T-groups groups of individuals participating in organizational development sessions away from the workplace; also called basic skills training groups

Theory X managers assume the average human being has an inherent dislike for work and will avoid it if possible

Theory Y managers assume that work is as natural as play or rest

360-degree feedback performance appraisal system in which information is gathered from supervisors, coworkers, subordinates, and sometimes suppliers and customers

traits relatively enduring characteristics of a person

transactional leadership leadership that focuses on motivating followers' self-interests by exchanging rewards for their compliance; emphasis is on having subordinates implement procedures correctly and make needed, but relatively routine, changes

transformational leadership leadership that motivates followers to ignore self-interests and work for the larger good of the organization to achieve significant accomplishments; emphasis is on articulating a vision that will convince subordinates to make major changes

transportable competencies competencies that can be utilized in any situation

two-factor theory motivation theory that focuses on the presumed different effects of intrinsic job factors (motivation) and extrinsic situational factors (hygiene factors)

uncertainty avoidance the need for things to be clear rather than ambiguous

uncertainty the extent to which future input, throughput, and output factors cannot be forecast accurately

unfreezing undoing old patterns

unity of command the notion that an employee should have one and only one boss

universal approach choosing a course of action that you believe can apply to all people under all situations

unstructured interview one in which interviewers have a general idea of the questions they might ask but do not have a standard set

upward communication messages sent from lower organizational levels to higher levels

utilitarian approach focuses on the consequences of an action

valid selection technique a screening process that differentiates those who would be successful in a job from those who would not

values the enduring beliefs that specific conduct or end states are personally or socially preferred to others

value chain a set of key activities that directly produce or support the production of what a firm ultimately offers to customers

value proposition the ratio of what customers get from a firm to how much they pay relative to alternatives from competitors

virtual team a group composed of individuals who do not work together in close physical proximity

whistle-blower an employee who discloses illegal or unethical conduct on the part of others in the organization

work centrality the degree of general importance that working has in the life of an individual at a point in time

work simulation situations in which job candidates perform work they would do if hired or work that closely simulates the tasks they would perform

zero-based budgeting approach assumes that all allocations of funds must be justified from zero each year

name index

subject index

notes

notes

notes

notes